CHURCH DOGMATICS

KARL BARTH

VOLUME IV

THE DOCTRINE
OF RECONCILIATION

PART 1

TRANSLATOR
G. W. BROMILEY

EDITORS
G. W. BROMILEY
T. F. TORRANCE

T&T CLARK INTERNATIONAL
A Continuum imprint
LONDON • NEW YORK

T&T CLARK INTERNATIONAL
A Continuum imprint

The Tower Building
11 York Road
London SE1 7NX, UK

15 East 26th Street
New York 10010
USA

www.tandtclark.com

ISBN 0 567 09041 8 (hardback)
0 567 05129 3 (paperback)

British Library Cataloguing-in-Publication Data
A catalogue record for this book is available from the British Library

Printed and bound in the United States by the Data Reproductions Corporation

EDITORS' PREFACE

As mentioned in the Preface to I, 2, the publication of the more recent part-volume IV, 1 has been expedited in order that readers who so desire may keep in touch with the more recent development of the *Dogmatics*. The part-volume is of particular interest because it introduces us to the central doctrine of the Christian faith—the atonement. Barth's account of the doctrine entails three part-volumes devoted to the three forms of the doctrine corresponding to the threefold confession of Jesus Christ as very God, very Man and the God-Man. The first form—the theme of the present part-volume—starts with Christ as the God who humbled Himself as a servant to accomplish the work of reconciliation. The second is concerned with Christ as the royal man in whom man is exalted and adopted into the fellowship with God. And the third treats of Christ as the God-Man who is the Guarantor of atonement. The translation of the second part-volume will soon be in the printers' hands, but the third has yet to appear in German.

In addition to the general note on the structure and translation of the *Dogmatics* in the Preface to I, 2 (to which readers are referred), two particular observations may be made. The first concerns the word *Versöhnung*, which is given by Barth a rich content that includes both " atonement " and " reconciliation." Hence, while the latter term is preferred for the title, both are used in the body of the text according to the requirements of the context. The word " redemption," incidentally, is almost always used in connexion with the work of the Holy Spirit and with the eschatological perspective of God's saving work.

The second is in regard to the term *Stellvertretung*, which enshrines the notions both of representation and substitution, and never the one without the other. Representation by itself is particularly inadequate as a rendering, though this aspect is present, and the word is used more often perhaps than it ought to be in view of the prevailing prejudice against substitution. In most cases the latter is both fuller and truer, but, as the text discloses, it is given a sense more radical than is normally the case in English, because Barth envisages it as a total displacement of sinful man by the incarnate, crucified and risen Son ; and also more comprehensive, because it is related to the whole life and work of Jesus Christ, including His heavenly intercession. The objective reality, not only of Christ's historical birth, life, death and resurrection, but also of His once-for-all work of reconciliation on our behalf and in our place, is Barth's tacit but definitive answer to

vii

the " demythologisation " crusade of Bultmann, which involves the genuinely mythologising process of reinterpreting Christ's incarnation and reconciling work in terms of existentialist decision and timeless re-enactment. The point of this answer depends on the bold and thorough-going doctrine of *Stellvertretung*.

Our thanks are again due to the Assistant Editor, the Reverend Professor J. K. S. Reid, for his careful scrutiny of the proofs and many useful corrections and emendations ; and also to the publishers and printers for their unfailing patience, helpfulness and diligence.

EDINBURGH, *Michaelmas* 1956.

FOREWORD

Two more years have passed since the appearance of the last part-volume. For me they have been more than occupied by work on this first survey of the vast territory of the doctrine of reconciliation. I have been very conscious of the very special responsibility laid on the theologian at this centre of all Christian knowledge. To fail here is to fail everywhere. To be on the right track here makes it impossible to be completely mistaken in the whole. Week by week and even day by day I have had, and will have (in the continuation), to exercise constant vigilance to find that right track and not to lose it.

The necessary effort demands a corresponding concentration of time and energy. And it means that I must again excuse myself for refusing to perform many other tasks and legitimate claims and expectations. I am more with my contemporaries, and especially those who accompany this work, than I can make it appear to them directly. Every word or sign of sympathy expressed by them is a comfort and encouragement for which I am most grateful, even though I can say so only occasionally to a few. I must also excuse myself to those who think it necessary to attack me—either on account of the *Dogmatics* or of other actions or positions. I read their judicious (and often not so judicious) sayings and learn from them what I can : but the time when I had the liberty and desire to plunge into public or private disputations has completely passed. My " neighbours " are for the most part my students here in Basel, who in my lectures are always the first to hear the further instalments of the *Church Dogmatics*. Like their predecessors in Göttingen, Münster and Bonn, they see to it that I cannot become a " carefully preserved Jerome."

The present situation in theology and also the peculiar themes of this book mean that throughout I have found myself in an intensive, although for the most part quiet, debate with Rudolf Bultmann. His name is not mentioned often. But his subject is always present, even in those places where with his methods and results before me I have consciously ignored him. I respect the man, his mind and aim and achievements, and the zeal of his following. I only wish that I could do him greater justice. But if I have to choose between, on the one hand, accepting the rule which he has proclaimed and thus not being able to say certain things which I perceive and which I believe ought to be said, or having to say them very differently from how I perceive them, and on the other hand saying them quite freely, but making myself guilty of using what he regards as an " obscure conceptuality," then I have no option but to choose the second. His hermeneutical suggestions can become binding on me only when I am convinced that by following them I would say the same things better and more freely. For the time being, I am not so convinced.

Some casual readers may miss what I say about the division of the total material of this further main part of the whole work upon which I have now embarked, and of the reasons for it. They are now expressly reminded that what is offered in this first part-volume is only a first survey which has yet to be followed by two more (together with a chapter of ethics). Those who think that something important has been omitted must not judge before the time but wait to see if it will come up later.

I should like to take this opportunity to correct certain annoying errors committed in the earlier volumes. In III, 2, p. 338 I ascribed to Raphael a painting by Titian : how, I do not understand. In III, 4, p. 398 I translated Dr. Albert Schweitzer at a stroke from Ogowe in West Africa to the Zambesi in East Africa, a mistake I ought to have been able to spot even from my school days. A printer's error, for which I am also responsible, is that in III, 3, p. 417, l. 1, the sense was completely destroyed by the omission of a " not." Those who possess the volumes are requested to correct all this nonsense.

Students who deserve particular mention for help in the preparation of this volume are Friedrich Wilhelm Marquardt and Gerhard Bauer.

To conclude, I often think that there are few men who have cause to be so grateful to God and man as I have. I am still in good heart, and—without having to carry the dignity and responsibility of being head of a school—I can devote myself to this great task surrounded with as much consideration and loyalty. The result is that although the task is a heavy one I do not have to stagger under its weight, but year in year out it carries me along with it. I now turn to it again. The way is long. But " having still time on the earth . . ."

BASEL, *June* 1953.

CONTENTS

xi

THE SUBJECT - MATTER AND PROBLEMS OF THE DOCTRINE OF RECONCILIATION

THE SUBJECT-MATTER AND PROBLEMS OF THE DOCTRINE OF RECONCILIATION

§ 57

THE WORK OF GOD THE RECONCILER

The subject-matter, origin and content of the message received and proclaimed by the Christian community is at its heart the free act of the faithfulness of God in which He takes the lost cause of man, who has denied Him as Creator and in so doing ruined himself as creature, and makes it His own in Jesus Christ, carrying it through to its goal and in that way maintaining and manifesting His own glory in the world.

1. GOD WITH US

We enter that sphere of Christian knowledge in which we have to do with the heart of the message received by and laid upon the Christian community and therefore with the heart of the Church's dogmatics: that is to say, with the heart of its subject-matter, origin and content. It has a circumference, the doctrine of creation and the doctrine of the last things, the redemption and consummation. But the covenant fulfilled in the atonement is its centre. From this point we can and must see a circumference. But we can see it only from this point. A mistaken or deficient perception here would mean error or deficiency everywhere : the weakening or obscuring of the message, the confession and dogmatics as such. From this point either everything is clear and true and helpful, or it is not so anywhere. This involves a high responsibility in the task which now confronts us.

It would be possible and quite correct to describe the covenant fulfilled in the work of reconciliation as the heart of the subject-matter of Christian faith, of the origin of Christian love, of the content of Christian hope. But the faith and love and hope of the Christian community and the Christians assembled in it live by the message received by and laid upon them, not the reverse. And even if we tried to put them in the forefront, we should have to lay the emphasis upon their subject-matter, origin and content, which are not immanent to them, and which do not exhaust themselves in them. For Christian faith is faith *in*, Christian love is love *through*, and Christian hope is hope *in*

3

God the Father, Son and Holy Spirit. There is something prior, outside, different from them which encounters them. It is God whom
they encounter, from whom they have their being, whom they can
lay hold of but not apprehend or exhaust. Not even the message by
which faith and love and hope live, not even the confession with which
the community responds to the message, not even the dogmatics in
which it gives an account of the message and its own response, and
finally of its faith and love and hope as such, can take the place of
God. If we tried to start with faith and love and hope, we would
still have to go back to that free and higher other in which they have
their basis. And in the face of it we should have to say even of them
that at their heart they have to do with the covenant fulfilled in the
work of atonement, and that it is in their relation to this covenant
that they are secure or insecure, effective or impotent, genuine or false.

Our first task will be to describe this Christian centre in a first and
most general approximation. The title " God with Us " is meant as
a most general description of the whole complex of Christian understanding and doctrine which here confronts us.

At its heart the Christian message is a common statement on the
part of certain men, i.e., those who are assembled in the Christian
community. It includes a statement about themselves, about the
individual existence of these men in their own time and situation.
And it is essential to it that this should be so. But it only includes
it. For primarily it is a statement about God : · that it is He who is
with them as God. *Only* with those who dare to make this statement,
who as the recipients and bearers of the Christian message, as members
of the Christian community, must dare to make it ? With them, to
the extent that they know that it is actually the case : God with us.
They dare to make this statement because they were able to become
and can constantly become again the recipients of this message. God
with you, God with thee and thee, was its first form, and they are
what they are to the extent that they hear this again and again. But
as recipients they are also bearers of the message. And to this extent
it is not only to them. They dare to make the statement, that God
is the One who is with them as God, amongst men who do not yet
know this. And it is to such that they address the statement. They
do not specifically include them in that " us." Their aim is to show
them what they do not yet know but what they can and should know.
What ? About themselves, and their individual existence in their own
time and situation ? That is certainly included. Much depends upon
their coming to see that it applies to *them*. But everything depends
upon their coming to see that it all has to do with God ; that it is
God who is with them as God. For it is this that applies to them.
" God with us " as the core of the Christian message, the decisive
general statement of the Christian community, can indeed be interpreted as " God with us men," but with the clear distinction, with us

men who know it but are always learning it afresh—and as the word of our declaration to all others, and therefore with " us " other men who have always to learn it afresh because we do not yet know it, although we can know it. In this movement from a narrower to a wider usage the statement " God with us " is the centre of the Christian message—and always in such a way that it is primarily a statement about God and only then and for that reason a statement about us men.

That is the roughest outline of the matter. We must now look at this outline rather more closely in order that we may understand it correctly even in this basic form.

To this end it is perhaps instructive to recall that this " God with us " is the translation of the remarkable name Emmanuel which is mentioned three times in Is. 7^{14}, 8$^{8, 10}$, and according to Mt. 1$^{21f.}$ finds its fulfilment in the name of Jesus.

The three passages in Isaiah seem to belong to three independently transmitted oracles. In the redaction of the book of Isaiah they were all related to that remarkable period (cf. Martin Noth, *Geschichte Israels*, 1950, p. 218 f.) when Assyria began to emerge as a world-power and to encroach upon Syria and Palestine. This process was explained by the prophets, and primarily Isaiah, as something which ran quite contrary to the political and religious tradition of Israel, a change in the relationship between God and His people, not a breach between them, but the irruption of His judgment upon their unfaithfulness, the transition from the Yes of His grace to the No. The final form of that unfaithfulness is the refusal of Ahaz, King of Judah, to trust in Yahweh and therefore to be bold enough to offer resistance to the two kings Rezin of Damascus and Pekah of Samaria who, themselves a prey to illusions, try to force him into an alliance against Assyria. In face of this situation Isaiah announces (7$^{14f.}$) the divine sign which is at once a promise and a warning, a sign of grace and a sign of judgment : a child will now be conceived and born. The old controversy whether his mother is called a young wife or a virgin does not in any way affect the real sense. What is important in the text is that when the child is born, that is in less than a year, he will be given the name Emmanuel, because God will have saved His people from the threat of Rezin and Pekah and they will again be rejoicing in His goodness. That is the one side of the sign. But the other is that before the child can distinguish between good and evil, a few years later, he will have to eat milk and honey, the food of the nomad. The true evil, that of the Assyrians, will then have supervened. Emmanuel will be present, but only in the wilderness, under the wrath of God. We are told the same (according to this other aspect of the sign) in Is. 8^6 : " Forasmuch as this people refuseth the waters of Shiloah that go softly, and rejoice in Rezin and Remaliah's son, now therefore behold, the Lord bringeth upon them the waters of the river (Euphrates), strong and many, and he shall come up over all his channels, and go over all his banks : and he shall pass through Judah ; he shall overflow and go over, he shall reach even to the neck ; and the stretching out of his wings shall fill the breadth of thy land, O Emmanuel." In contrast, Is. 8$^{9f.}$ looks again in the opposite direction, evidently beyond the momentarily irresistibly triumphant Assyria (though this is not perhaps a compelling reason why we should not ascribe it to Isaiah) : " Rage furiously, ye people, and be afraid. Give ear, ye of far countries. Gird yourselves and be afraid, yes gird yourselves and be afraid. Take counsel together, and it shall come to nought. Resolve, and it shall not stand. For—Emmanuel."

Who is " Emmanuel ? " Hardly a historical figure of the period. Perhaps

a traditional name, or one selected by the prophet, to describe the expected
Redemptor-King of the last day, to whom a kind of pre-existence is here ascribed.
Perhaps the personification of what the remnant-Israel of Judah understood its
God to be, and therefore itself, or according to the prophets ought to have done
so. Perhaps both ? Certainly a special key to the continual mystery of the
history of this people in days of prosperity and in days of adversity, under the
hand of God in blessing and in cursing. " God with us " is true when the people
is at rest. It is also true when the enemy invades and devastates its land. It is
always true, in spite of and in the most irresistible movements of history. It is
so because and to the extent that in all these things there is revealed the gracious
action of God to His people. No matter who or what is concretely envisaged
in these passages, they obviously mean this : Emmanuel is the content of the
recognition in which the God of Israel reveals Himself in all His acts and dispositions ; He is the God who does not work and act without His people, but
who is with His people as their God and therefore as their hope.

We are reminded of this remarkable name in Mt. 1[21f.] The reference here is
to a single, final and exclusive act of the God of Israel as the goal and recapitula-
tion of all His acts. But this act, the birth and naming of Jesus, is similar to the
events in the days of King Ahaz in that once again we have come to a change in
the relationship between God and His people. As the Evangelist sees it, it is
this time the great change compared with which what took place before was only
from his point of view a prelude. And now it is the equally unexpected change
from perdition to salvation, from an age-long judgment to a new and final
blessing. And the Emmanuel-sign has it in common with the name of Jesus
that the latter, too, although this time in the reverse direction, is a sign for both :
a sign " for the fall and rising again of many in Israel" (Lk. 2[34]), a sign both of
the deepest extremity imposed by God (as in Is. 8[6f.]) and also of the uttermost
preservation and salvation ordained by God (as in Is.8[9f.]). Over and in both it
is Emmanuel, " God with us," and now therefore (ἵνα πληρωθῇ τὸ ῥηθὲν ὑπὸ κυρίου
διὰ τοῦ προφήτου λέγοντος) Jesus, Jehoshuah, " God helps."

1. Our starting-point is that this " God with us " at the heart of
the Christian message is the description of an act of God, or better,
of God Himself in this act of His. It is a report, not therefore a
statement of fact on the basis of general observation or consideration.
God with us, or what is meant by these three words, is not an object
of investigation or speculation. It is not a state, but an event. God
is, of course, and that in the strictest sense originally and properly,
so that everything else which is, in a way which cannot be compared
at all with His being, can be so only through Him, only in relation to
Him, only from Him and to Him. Now even when He is " with us,"
He is what He is, and in the way that He is ; and all the power and
truth of His being " with us " is the power and truth of His incomparable being which is proper to Him and to Him alone, His being as
God. He is both in His life in eternity in Himself, and also in His
life as Creator in the time of the world created by Him ; by and in
Himself, and also above and in this world, and therefore according to
the heart of the Christian message with us men. And He is who He
is, and lives as what He is, in that He does what He does. How
can we know God if His being is unknown or obscure or indifferent ?
But how can we know God if we do not find the truth and power of
His being in His life, and of His life in His act ? We know about God

only if we are witnesses—however distantly and modestly—of His act. And we speak about God only as we can do so—however deficiently—as those who proclaim His act. " God with us " as it occurs at the heart of the Christian message is the attestation and report of the life and act of God as the One who is.

But if it means that God is with us—and the message of the Christian community certainly implies that it does really apply to us men—then that presupposes that we men, in our own very different way, which cannot be compared with the being of God, but which on the basis of the divine being and life and act is a very real way, that we also *are*, and that we are in that we live in our time, and that we live in that we ourselves act in our own act. If the fact that God is with us is a report about the being and life and act of God, then from the very outset it stands in a relationship to our own being and life and acts. A report about ourselves is included in that report about God. We cannot therefore take cognisance of it, be more or less impressed by it, and then leave it as the report of something which has taken place in a quite different sphere in which we ourselves have no place. It tells us that we ourselves are in the sphere of God. It applies to us by telling us of a history which God wills to share with us and therefore of an invasion of our history—indeed, of the real truth about our history as a history which is by Him and from Him and to Him. The divine being and life and act takes place with ours, and it is only as the divine takes place that ours takes place. To put it in the simplest way, what unites God and us men is that He does not will to be God without us, that He creates us rather to share with us and therefore with our being and life and act His own incomparable being and life and act, that He does not allow His history to be His and ours ours, but causes them to take place as a common history. That is the special truth which the Christian message has to proclaim at its very heart.

2. We have just said, and this is what is meant in the Christian message, that we have to do with an event, with an act of God. The whole being and life of God is an activity, both in eternity and in worldly time, both in Himself as Father, Son and Holy Spirit, and in His relation to man and all creation. But what God does in Himself and as the Creator and Governor of man is all aimed at the particular act in which it has its centre and meaning. And everything that He wills has its ground and origin in what is revealed as His will in this one act. Thus it is not merely one amongst others of His works as Creator and Governor. Of course, it can and must be understood in this way, in accordance with the general will and work of God. But within this outer circle it forms an inner. The one God wills and works all things, but here He wills and works a particular thing : not one with others, but one for the sake of which He wills and works all others. As one with others this act is also the *telos* of all the acts

of God ; of the eternal activity in which He is both in Himself and in the history of His acts in the world created by Him. It is of this that the " God with us " speaks.

Therefore even from the standpoint of us men the " God with us " does not refer to the existence of man generally as the creaturely object of the will and work of His Lord. It does refer to it. It includes it. The being, life and act of man is always quite simply his history in relation to the being, life and act of his Creator. We can say the same of all creatures. But it is far more than this. For within and beyond this general activity, God Himself in His being, life and act as Creator wills and works a special act. All His activity has its heart and end in a single act. Within and out of the general history, which with all creatures man can have in common with God in His being, life and act, there arises this act of God and that which corresponds to it in the being, life and activity of man, as a qualified history, his true history. And if the " God with us " at the heart of the Christian message speaks of the unifying factor between God and man, it speaks of a specific conjoining of the two, not always and everywhere but in a single and particular event which has a definite importance for all time and space but which takes place once and for all in a definite *hic et nunc*.

3. From the standpoint of its meaning the particularity of this event consists in the fact that it has to do with the salvation of man, that in it the general history which is common to God and man, to God and all creation, becomes at its very heart and end a redemptive history. Salvation is more than being. Salvation is fulfilment, the supreme, sufficient, definitive and indestructible fulfilment of being. Salvation is the perfect being which is not proper to created being as such but is still future. Created being as such needs salvation, but does not have it : it can only look forward to it. To that extent salvation is its *eschaton*. Salvation, fulfilment, perfect being means —and this is what created being does not have in itself—being which has a part in the being of God, from which and to which it is : not a divinised being but a being which is hidden in God, and in that sense (distinct from God and secondary) eternal being. Since salvation is not proper to created being as such, it can only come to it, and since it consists in participation in the being of God it can come only from God. The coming of this salvation is the grace of God—using the word in its narrower and most proper sense. In the wider sense the creation, preservation and over-ruling of the world and man are already grace. For if this is not proper to created being as such, it can only come to it. Only from God as the One who is originally and properly can it come about that it also has being, that it is, and not that it is not. And by that very fact there is always held out to it the opportunity of salvation : the expectation of being in perfection in participation in the divine being. But the " God with us " at the heart of

the Christian message does not mean this general grace. It means the redemptive grace of God. It is this which constitutes, factually, the singularity of the event. It is this which marks out the event within the whole history of the togetherness of God and man. Not merely the creating, preserving and over-ruling of created being, not merely the creating of an opportunity for salvation, but the fact that it actually comes, that God gives it. God gives to created being what can only be given to it and what can be given only by Him. And He does really give it : Take what is mine—this final, supreme, insurpassable gift ; take it, it is meant for you. It is because it has to do with this that the activity of God indicated by the " God with us " is singular and unique. And so, too, is the invasion of the history of our own human being, life and activity described by this " God with us." And so, too, is the whole circle of God in which we find ourselves according to this centre of the Christian message. The general grace of God in creation, preservation and over-ruling still remains. That is already grace. We recognise it distinctly as such only when we see God and ourselves in the inner and special circle of His will and work, in the light of this one, particular, redemptive act of God. It is only from this standpoint that the general grace of being and the opportunity which it offers can and do become a subject for genuine gratitude and a source of serious dedication. For here it is provided that that opportunity is not offered in vain, that it is actually taken, taken by God Himself. What concerns us here is the redemptive grace of God, and to that extent something that is more and greater.

4. In the light of this we must now try to outline this particular event with rather greater precision. According to the Christian message " God with us " means God with the man for whom salvation is intended and ordained as such, as the one who is created, preserved and over-ruled by God as man. It is not as though the expectation belonged to his created being. It is not as though he had any kind of claim to it. God cannot be forced to give us a part in His divine being. The matter might have ended quite well with that general grace of being—which even in itself is great enough. But where God is not bound and man has no claim, even more compelling is the will and plan and promise of God. It goes beyond, or rather it precedes His will and work as Creator. Therefore it has to be distinguished from it, as something prior, which precedes it. The ordaining of salvation for man and of man for salvation is the original and basic will of God, the ground and purpose of His will as Creator. It is not that He first wills and works the being of the world and man, and then ordains it to salvation. But God creates, preserves and over-rules man for this prior end and with this prior purpose, that there may be a being distinct from Himself ordained for salvation, for perfect being, for participation in His own being, because as the One who loves in free-dom He has determined to exercise redemptive grace—and that there

may be an object of this His redemptive grace, a partner to receive it. A further point which we must now make in describing the event indicated by the " God with us " is this. The " God with us " has nothing to do with chance. As a redemptive happening it means the revelation and confirmation of the most primitive relationship between God and man, that which was freely determined in eternity by God Himself before there was any created being. In the very fact that man is, and that he is man, he is as such chosen by God for salvation ; that *eschaton* is given him by God. Not because God owes it to him. Not in virtue of any quality or capacity of his own being. Completely without claim. What takes place between God and man in that particular redemptive history is fulfilment to this extent too, that in it God—the eternal will of God with man—is justified, the eternal righteousness of His grace is active and revealed, in and with the divine right, and so too the right which He has freely given and ascribed to man by determining this concerning him. It belongs to the character of this event and its particularity that with the end it reveals the basis and beginning of all things—the glory of God, which is that of His free love, and with it—well below, but eternally grounded upon it—the dignity of man, that dignity with which He willed to invest man although it is not proper to him.

5. But again we must go further. " God with us " in the sense of the Christian message means God with us men who have forfeited the predetermined salvation, forfeited it with a supreme and final jeopardising even of our creaturely existence. As the way from that beginning in God to the end of man with God is revealed in this particular event, its line is not a straight one, but one which is radically and—if God Himself were not there as hope—hopelessly broken. The situation of man in this event is this. He occupies a position quite different from that which he ought to occupy according to the divine intention. He does not conduct himself as the partner God has given Himself to receive His redemptive grace. He has opposed his ordination to salvation. He has turned his back on the salvation which actually comes to him. He does not find the fulfilment of his being in participation in the being of God by the gift of God. Instead, he aims at another salvation which is to be found in the sphere of his creaturely being and attained by his own effort. His belief is that he can and should find self-fulfilment. He has himself become an *eschaton*. This is the man with whom God is dealing in this particular redemptive history : the man who has made himself quite impossible in relation to the redemptive grace of God ; and in so doing, the man who has made himself quite impossible in his created being as man, who has cut the ground from under his feet, who has lost his whole *raison d'être*. What place has he before God when he has shown himself to be so utterly unworthy of that for which he was created by God, so utterly inept, so utterly unsuitable ? when he has eliminated himself ? What

place is there for his being, his being as man, when he has denied his goal, and therefore his beginning and meaning, and when he confronts God in this negation ? Despising the dignity with which God invested him, he has obviously forfeited the right which God gave and ascribed to him as the creature of God. But it is with this lost son in a far country, with man as he has fallen and now exists in this sorry plight, that God has to do in this redeeming event. And this is what reveals the gulf. This is what shows us how it stands between God and man. This is where we see the inadequacy of the partner, the point where the relationship breaks down. At a pinch this can be overlooked if we do not think of the redeeming event as the heart and end of their interconnexion, if we conceive it abstractly as the interconnexion of Creator and creature. We may take this antithesis very seriously, but we shall always have good grounds to think of it as an antithesis which can be bridged. As such it does not contain any breach, any gulf, any enmity, either on the one side or on the other, any judgment and punishment on the part of God or suffering on the part of man. But this cannot possibly be overlooked in the redeeming event referred to in the " God with us." On the contrary, what constitutes the particularity of this event is that as a redeeming event, as the fulfil- ment of the gracious will of God, as the reaffirmation of His right and ours, it can be conceived only in the form of a Yet and a Never- theless, which means that it cannot be conceived at all. If man has forfeited his salvation, what do we have to grasp in this event but the inconceivable fact that all the same it is given to him ? If in so doing man has lost his creaturely being, what do we have to grasp but again the inconceivable fact that all the same he will not be lost ? Is it not the case that only here, in the light of the antithesis which is here revealed and overcome, is grace really known as grace, that is, as free grace, as mercy pure and simple, as *factum purum*, having its basis only in itself, in the fact that it is posited by God ? For who really knows what grace is until he has seen it at work here : as the grace which is *for* man when, because man is wholly and utterly a sinner before God, it can only be against him, and when in fact, even while it is for him, it is also a plaintiff and judge against him, showing him to be incapable of satisfying either God or himself ? And looking back once again, it is the grace of God as mercy pure and simple, as a sheer Yet and Nevertheless, which reveals, and by which we have to measure, how it stands with the man to whom it is granted. It is not independent reflection on the part of man, or an abstract law, but grace which shows incontrovertibly that man has forfeited his salvation and in so doing fatally jeopardised his creaturely being— which reveals his sin and the misery which is its consequence. From the redemption which takes place here we can gather from what it is that man is redeemed ; from the *factum purum* of the salvation which comes to man without and in spite of his own deserts we may know the *factum brutum* which he for his part dares to set against God. Because the " God with us " at the heart of the Christian message has to do with that *factum purum* of the divine mercy, we must not fail to recognise but acknowledge without reserve that we, and those for whom God is according to this message, are those who have nothing to bring Him but a confession of this *factum brutum* : " Father, I have sinned."

6. But if the Christian " God with us " does nevertheless speak, not of a renunciation, but of the fulfilment of the redemptive will of God in that event, then no matter how inconceivable may be that which we have to grasp in this connexion, it refers to something quite different from the blind paradox of an arbitrary act of the divine omnipotence of grace. We are confronted here by the determination of that event which reveals unequivocally its uniqueness amongst the acts of God, that it declares an absolutely unique being and attitude and activity on the part of God. " God with us " means more than God over or side by side with us, before or behind us. It means more than His divine being in even the most intimate active connexion with our human being otherwise peculiar to Him. At this point, at the heart of the Christian message and in relation to the event of which it speaks, it means that God has made Himself the One who fulfils His redemptive will. It means that He Himself in His own person—at His own cost but also on His own initiative — has become the inconceivable Yet and Nevertheless of this event, and so its clear and well-founded and legitimate, its true and holy and righteous Therefore. It means that God has become man in order as such, but in divine sovereignty, to take up our case. What takes place in this work of inconceivable mercy is, therefore, the free over-ruling of God, but it is not an arbitrary overlooking and ignoring, not an artificial bridging, covering-over or hiding, but a real closing of the breach, gulf and abyss between God and us for which we are responsible. At the very point where we refuse and fail, offending and provoking God, making ourselves impossible before Him and in that way missing our destiny, treading under foot our dignity, forfeiting our right, losing our salvation and hopelessly compromising our creaturely being—at that very point God Himself intervenes as man. Because He is God He is able not only to be God but also to be this man. Because He is God it is necessary that He should be man in quite a different way from all other men ; that He should do what we do not do and not do what we do. Because He is God He puts forth His omnipotence to be this other man, to be man quite differently, in our place and for our sake. Because He is God He has and exercises the power as this man to suffer for us the consequence of our transgression, the wrath and penalty which necessarily fall on us, and in that way to satisfy Himself in our regard. And again because He is God, He has and exercises the power as this man to be His own partner in our place, the One who in free

obedience accepts the ordination of man to salvation which we resist, and in that way satisfies us, i.e., achieves that which can positively satisfy us. That is the absolutely unique being, attitude and activity of God to which the " God with us " at the heart of the Christian message refers. It speaks of the peace which God Himself in this man has made between Himself and us.

We see the seriousness and force of the divine redemptive will in the fact that it is not too little and not too much for Him to make peace between Himself and us. To that end He gives Himself. He, the Creator, does not scorn to become a creature, a man like us, in order that as such He may bear and do what must be borne and done for our salvation. On the contrary, He finds and defends and vindicates His glory in doing it. Again, we see our own perversion and corruption, we see what is our offence and plight, in the fact that God (who never does anything unnecessary) can obviously be satisfied only by this supreme act, that only His own coming as man is sufficient to make good the evil which has been done. So dark is our situation that God Himself must enter and occupy it in order that it may be light. We cannot fully understand the Christian " God with us " without the greatest astonishment at the glory of the divine grace and the greatest horror at our own plight.

But even when we understand the entry of God for us in becoming man as the making of peace between Himself and us, we have still not said the decisive thing about this action. What He effects and does and reveals by becoming man—for us—is much more than the restoration of the *status quo ante*—the obviating of the loss caused by our own transgression and our restoration to the place of promise and expectation of the salvation ordained for us. God makes Himself the means of His own redemptive will, but He is obviously more than this means. And in making peace by Himself He obviously gives us more than this peace, i.e., more than a *restitutio ad integrum*, more than the preserving and assuring to us of our creaturely being and this as our opportunity for salvation. For when God makes Himself the means of His redemptive will to us, this will and we ourselves attain our goal. What is at first only God's gracious answer to our failure, God's gracious help in our plight, and even as such great and wonderful enough, is—when God Himself is the help and answer—His participation in our being, life and activity and therefore obviously our participation in His; and therefore it is nothing more nor less than the coming of salvation itself, the presence of the *eschaton* in all its fulness. The man in whom God Himself intervenes for us, suffers and acts for us, closes the gap between Himself and us as our representative, in our name and on our behalf, this man is not merely the confirmation and guarantee of our salvation, but because He is God He is salvation, our salvation. He is not merely the redeemer of our being but as such the giver and Himself the gift of its fulfilment

and therefore the goal and end of the way of God—and all that as
the peacemaker and saviour. It is when this great thing takes place
that there takes place the even greater. This great thing is included
in the " God with us " of the Christian message in so far as this speaks
of God's intervening and becoming man, but in this great thing there
is also included the even greater, indeed the greatest of all.

7. From all this it is surely obvious that the " God with us "
carries with it in all seriousness a " We with God " : the fact that we
ourselves are there in our being, life and activity.

This does not seem to be apparent at a first glance. For who
are we ? We have seen already that we are (1) those whose history
is absorbed into the history of the acts of God, and (2) made to participate in that event which is the centre and end of all the divine acts,
and (3) given a share in the grace with which God actually brings
salvation to man, and (4) that we are such as those whom God has
thereto ordained from all eternity, but unfortunately (5) we are those
who have refused His salvation and in that way denied their own
destiny and perverted and wasted and hopelessly compromised their
own being, life and activity, who inevitably therefore find themselves
disqualified and set aside as participants in that event, and cannot
be considered in relation to it. Yet beyond that and in a sense conclusively (6) we are those whose place has been taken by another,
who lives and suffers and acts for them, who for them makes good
that which they have spoiled, who—for them, but also without them
and even against them—is their salvation. That is what we are.
And what is left to us ? What place is there for us when we are like
that ? In what sense is the history of the acts of God at this centre
and end our history ? Are we not without history ? Have we not
become mere objects ? Have we not lost all responsibility ? Are we
not reduced to mere spectators ? Is not our being deprived of all life
or activity ? Or does it not lack all significance as our life and activity ?
" God with us "—that is something which we can easily understand
even in these circumstances. But how is it to include within it a
" We with God " ? And if it does not, how can it really be understood as a " God with us " ?

The answer is that we ourselves are directly summoned, that we
are lifted up, that we are awakened to our own truest being as life
and act, that we are set in motion by the fact that in that one man
God has made Himself our peacemaker and the giver and gift of our
salvation. By it we are made free for Him. By it we are put in the
place which comes to us where our salvation (really ours) can come to
us from Him (really from Him). This actualisation of His redemptive
will by Himself opens up to us the one true possibility of our own
being. Indeed, what remains to us of life and activity in the face of
this actualisation of His redemptive will by Himself can only be one
thing. This one thing does not mean the extinguishing of our humanity,

but its establishment. It is not a small thing, but the greatest of all. It is not for us a passive presence as spectators, but our true and highest activation—the magnifying of His grace which has its highest and most profound greatness in the fact that God has made Himself man with us, to make our cause His own, and as His own to save it from disaster and to carry it through to success. The genuine being of man as life and activity, the " We with God," is to affirm this, to admit that God is right, to be thankful for it, to accept the promise and the command which it contains, to exist as the community, and responsibly in the community, of those who know that this is all that remains to us, but that it does remain to us and that for all men everything depends upon its coming to pass. And it is this "We with God" that is meant by the Christian message in its central "God with us," when it proclaims that God Himself has taken our place, that He Himself has made peace between Himself and us, that by Himself He has accomplished our salvation, i.e., our participation in His being.

This " We with God " enclosed in the " God with us " is Christian faith, Christian love and Christian hope. These are the magnifying of the grace of God which still remain to us—and remain to us as something specifically human, as the greatest thing of all, as action in the truest sense of the word. We do not forget that it is a matter of magnifying God out of the deeps, *e profundis*. Our magnifying of God can only be that of the transgressors and rebels that we are, those who have missed their destiny, and perverted and wasted their being, life and activity. Therefore our magnifying of God cannot seek and find and have its truth and power in itself, but only in God, and therefore in that one Man in whom God is for us, who is our peace and salvation. Our faith, therefore, can only be faith in Him, and cannot live except from Him as its object. Our love can only be by Him, and can only be strong from Him as its basis. Our hope can only be hope directed upon Him, and can only be certain hope in Him as its content. Our faith, love and hope and we ourselves—however strong may be our faith, love and hope—live only by that which we cannot create, posit, awaken or deserve. And although our believing, loving and hoping themselves and as such are in us, they are not of us, but of their object, basis and content, of God, who in that one man not only answers for us with Him but answers for Himself with us, who gives it to us in freedom that we may believe, love and hope : open eyes, ears and hearts for Himself and His work, knowledge to the foolish, obedience to the wayward, freedom to the bound, life to the victims of death ; and all in such a way that the glory of our own being, life and activity is still His, and can be valued, and exalted and respected by us only as His ; but all in such a way that in and with His glory we too are really exalted, because in the depths where we can only give Him the glory, we find our true and proper place. It is in this way and in this sense that the Christian community proclaims " We with God " when it proclaims " God with us."

In these seven points we have said in rough outline—many things need to be amplified, explained and made more precise—almost everything that has to be said about the " God with us " as the covenant between God and us men fulfilled in the work of atonement. But we have not yet said it with the concreteness with which it is said at the heart of the Christian message, or at the heart (in the second article) of the Creed, and with which it must also be said at the heart of dogmatics, even in the briefest survey, if we are not to speak mistakenly or falsely.

For where does the community which has to deliver the message learn to know and say this " God with us " ? And to what does it point those to whom the message is addressed ? How far can and must this " God with us," the report of the event which constitutes its meaning and content, be declared and received in truth ? How can men come to stand where they obviously have to stand—in that inner circle of the relationship between God and man—to dare to make this report as a declaration of reality ? And how do other men come to hear this report in such a way that it is to them a report of reality, and they find themselves challenged and empowered to pass it on to others still ? How do they come to stand in the same place as the first men, as the Christian community ? In other words : How does it come about amongst men that there is a communication of this " God with us," of this report, or rather, of that which is reported ? That is the question which we can answer only as we say everything once again in the concrete way in which it is said at the heart of the Christian message. Everything depends upon its concrete expression : the whole truth and reality of the report, and the whole secret of the communication of the matter.

We must realise that the Christian message does not at its heart express a concept or an idea, nor does it recount an anonymous history to be taken as truth and reality only in concepts and ideas. Certainly the history is inclusive, i.e., it is one which includes in itself the whole event of the " God with us " and to that extent the history of all those to whom the " God with us " applies. But it recounts this history and speaks of its inclusive power and significance in such a way that it declares a name, binding the history strictly and indissolubly to this name and presenting it as the story of the bearer of this name. This means that all the concepts and ideas used in this report (God, man, world, eternity, time, even salvation, grace, transgression, atonement and any others) can derive their significance only from the bearer of this name and from His history, and not the reverse. They cannot have any independent importance or role based on a quite different prior interpretation. They cannot say what has to be said with some meaning of their own or in some context of their own abstracted from this name. They can serve only to describe this name—the name of Jesus Christ.

This name is the answer to our earlier question. In the Christian "God with us" there is no question of any other source and object than that indicated by this name. Other than in this name—as on the basis of the necessity and power of its conceptual context—it cannot be truth, either on the lips of those who speak it or in the ears and hearts of those who receive it. Without this name it is left insecure and unprotected. It is exposed to the suspicion that it might be only a postulate, a pure speculation, a myth. It is truth as it derives from this name and as it points to it, and only so. Where is it that the men stand who declare this message ? The answer is that they stand in the sphere of the lordship of the One who bears this name, in the light and under the impelling power of His Spirit, in the community assembled and maintained and over-ruled by Him. They have not placed themselves there but He has placed them there, and it is as they stand there by Him that their report is a report of actuality. Again, where will those others stand to whom they address their report and witness, who both receive it and then, on their own responsibility, spread it further ? The answer is that they too stand in the sphere of the lordship, which has now claimed them, of the One who bears this name, of His Spirit, of the call to His community which has now come to them. They too have not placed themselves there. And those who said to them "God with us" have not brought it about. But, again, it is He Himself who bears this name that has called and led and drawn them, and it is as that happens that it is given to them, too, to pass on to others their report of actuality as such. Therefore the One who shows and persuades and convinces and reveals and communicates from man to man that it is so, "God with us," is the One who bears this name, Jesus Christ, no other, and nothing else. That is what the message of the Christian community intends when at its heart it declares this name. If it were a principle and not a name indicating a person, we should have to describe it as the epistemological principle of the message. Where between man and man there is real communication of the report of what took place in Him and through Him, He Himself is there and at work, He Himself makes Himself to be recognised and acknowledged. The Christian message about Him—and without this it is not the Christian message —is established on the certainty that He is responsible for it, that He as the truth speaks through it and is received in it, that as it serves Him He Himself is present as actuality, as His own witness. He Himself by His Spirit is its guarantor. He Himself is the one who establishes and maintains and directs the community which has received it and upon which it is laid. He Himself is the strength of its defence and its offensive. He Himself is the hope of freedom and enlightenment for the many who have not yet received and accepted it. He Himself above all is the comfort, and the restlessness, and yet also the uplifting power in the weakness of its service. In a word, the Christian message lives as such by and to the One who at its heart bears the name of Jesus Christ. It becomes weak and obscure to the extent that it thinks it ought to live on other resources. And it becomes strong and clear when it is established solely in confidence in His controlling work exercised by His Spirit ; to the extent that it abandons every other conceivable support or impulse, and is content to rest on His command and commission as its strength and pledge. He, Jesus Christ, is Emmanuel, " God with us." How else can He be proclaimed except as the One who proclaims Himself ? And how else can human activity and speech and hearing be effective in His service except in the prayer and expectation that He will constantly do it ?

The name of Jesus Christ covers the whole power of the Christian message because it indicates the whole of its content, because at its heart, which is normative for the whole, it is a message about Him, and therefore a message about the event of that " God with us."

It means Jesus Christ when (1) with this " God with us " it describes an act of God, or rather the being of God in His life and activity. If as a statement about God it is the report of an event (not a statement of fact), the report of a history in which we have a part with our being, life and activity, which God has in common with us, which inaugurated by Him is our own history, then it is so because and in so far as it is a report about Jesus Christ as the One who actually unites the divine being, life and activity with ours.

It means Jesus Christ again when (2) it describes the " God with us " as an act of God, a particular, once and for all and unique event in the midst of events in general. It is a report of this one event and of this event alone, of its meaning and importance for all of us, for men of all times and places, because and to the extent that it is a report about Him as the person who in His existence and work is absolutely unique and therefore universal in effectiveness and significance. It means the event which unites God and man and which has been accomplished in Him and in Him alone, the event of which He alone is the subject and in which we can have a part only by Him.

It means Jesus Christ again when it describes the event of " God with us " (3) as a redemptive event ; as the fulfilment of man's being by participation in the divine being which comes to him by the grace of God. It is a message of redemption, and therefore a message of the last and greatest and unsurpassable thing which man can experience from God and has in fact experienced, of the gift of eternal life which has been made to him, because and in so far as it is the message of Jesus Christ—that He is the One who, Himself God, is also man, that He therefore was and is and will be the salvation of God for us other

men, that in one person He is the God who gives salvation and the
man to whom it is given and who allows it to be given by Him, that
as such He is the power and witness of the *eschaton* in the human
present—a human present which is itself in the *eschaton*.

But the Christian message again means Jesus Christ when (4) it
looks through the redemptive event of the " God with us " as through
glass to the basis and beginning of all things, of the world and of man,
in God, to the original ordination of man to salvation and of salvation
for man as the meaning and basis even of the divine creative will.
It has the particular emphasis and the specific weight of an original
Word which underlies and embraces all other words so that no other
word has any independent significance, as one historical report with
others, it has none of the contingence of the record of one historical
fact with many others, because and in so far as it is a message about
Jesus Christ : that He is the One who according to the free and gracious
will of God is Himself eternal salvation, the last and also the
first ; our eternal yesterday in God who is the same to-day and for
ever.

But it means Jesus Christ again when (5) it sees and presupposes
that we men with whom God is are those who have forfeited the
salvation destined for us from all eternity, letting slip the opportunity
for it, and in that way fatally jeopardising their creaturely being and
indeed perishing were it not that God is God and therefore their hope.
It is not out of mere pessimism that it sees and understands man in
this way. As a message about Jesus Christ it cannot do otherwise.
This name is the real Emmanuel-sign and therefore—although in the
reverse direction from Is. 7[14]—the twofold sign which speaks of both
the judgment of God and the grace of God in His dealings with His
people. Also and first of all the sign of judgment. The well-deserved
and incontestable sentence on man, His wrath and punishment, is
first introduced and revealed in Jesus Christ. And it is the utterly free
and unmerited nature of the grace of God introduced by Him as *factum
purum* which first reveals the true relationship with God of the man
to whom it is granted in Him, the *factum brutum* with which we have
to do on the part of man.

And now it is absolutely clear that the Christian message means Jesus
Christ, and has to name His name and does not know of any other,
when (6) it says that God has made Himself the One who fulfils His
redemptive will, that He has become man for us, that in the power of
His Godhead He might take up our cause in our place. Jesus Christ
is the man in whom God satisfies Himself in face of our transgression
and us in face of our plight. It says Jesus Christ when it speaks of
this absolutely unique being, attitude and activity of God, of the peace
which has been made by Him between Himself and us. And it does
so because in speaking of this peace made in this way by God as a
man amongst men, in speaking of this great thing, it at once goes on

to speak of a greater and of the greatest thing of all, of salvation itself, which has already come to us in and with the opportunity for salvation restored in Jesus Christ, which has already been given to us, which has already become our salvation.

To conclude : How can (7) the reverse side be possible or legitimate, how can a " We with God " be really included and enclosed in the " God with us," how can it be true or actual, if it does not have reference to Jesus Christ ? It is with reference to Him that in spite of all appearances to the contrary the Christian message dares to address man too as an active subject in the event of redemption, and to its content there belong the praise which we offer to the grace of God *e profundis*, man's own faith and love and hope. We have already seen in what sense this by no means self-evident fact is true, to what extent we others who are not that One belong to the redemptive act, that is, to the extent that our human being, life and activity, in the form of the praise of God, of faith and love and hope, live by their object, basis and content, to the extent that it is given to us in that way to be able to praise and believe and love and hope. But in that way means in Jesus Christ, in the fellowship between Him and us created by His Spirit, in virtue of our being, life and activity in His, and His in ours. We other men are Christians—or prospective Christians—and therefore partakers of His being, life and activity, in so far as Jesus Christ makes us such and wills to maintain and rule us as such. There is a Christian community with its special distinction and service to the extent that Jesus Christ assembles it and is present with it by His Spirit. Therefore this final part of the content of the Christian message stands or falls with Him—its characterisation and description with the naming of His name.

A note by way of final delimitation and confirmation. Our formulation is again and again that the Christian message (in all its content) means Jesus Christ. In the declaration and development of its whole content it always has reference to Him. His name, therefore, is not incidental to it. It is not a name which has to be pronounced for the sake of completeness or adornment. It is there at the very heart of it as the central and decisive Word, the Word which is always present with every other word and to which it must always return. For in uttering His name it says that it refers to Him, and therefore to its true object. It is not trying to say something in general, a mere this or that, but it is trying to speak of Him, to show Him, to proclaim Him, to teach Him. To do this it can and must say many things. But these many things are all His things. They can be rightly said only as they look back or look away to Him. As they are said they can only be referred to Him. The Christian message is service, and the one whom it serves is at all points Jesus Christ Himself. What it says at its heart as the doctrine of the atonement is that He Himself is and lives and rules and acts, very God and very man, and that He is peace and salvation. He Himself is the whole. And in every individual part He is the One of whom it speaks, the truth of all that it attests and proclaims as true, the actuality of all that it attests and proclaims as actual. It cannot be silent when it remembers His name and utters it. It can and must at once declare it. In and with His name it can and must at once declare His cause, but only in and

with His name and therefore only as His cause. This cause of His has no existence or life or validity of its own apart from or side by side with Him. It cannot be distinguished, let alone separated from Him. Everything that is said
about it is measured by whether it faithfully reflects Him, whether indirectly
but distinctly it refers to Him, declares Him, portrays Him, magnifies and exalts
Him. It is not, therefore, the case that properly and basically the Christian
message is concerned about is own affair and introduces His name only as the
One who is responsible for it. To avoid this impression we have chosen the way
of climax, showing the concrete form of the Christian " God with us " to be the
message of Jesus Christ, not at the outset, but at the very end. Everything moves
towards and everything stands and falls by the fact that it is the message about
Jesus Christ.

It is no mere battle of words whether we understand it merely as the Gospel
of Jesus Christ or also—and as such—the Gospel about Jesus Christ. Obviously
it is the Gospel of Jesus Christ. We have laid on this every possible emphasis.
He Himself is the " epistemological principle." But we must be careful not to
understand Him only in this way, for, if we do, the Christian message will at
once degenerate into the self-declaration of an ecclesiastical form of redemption
instituted indeed by Him but now self-resting and self-motivated, or into a
devotional and ethical system taught indeed by Him but self-justified and self-
sufficient, or into an illumination of existence strikingly fulfilled by Him in
history but living by its own light. And when this happens, the Christian
message as such will no longer have anything individual or new or substantial
to say to man. What it will have to say to him will not be worth saying because
in the last resort and basically he can say the same thing to himself. In one form
or another it has simply become the recitation of a myth. But the Christian
message does say something individual, new and substantial because it speaks
concretely, not mythically, because it does not know and proclaim anything side
by side with or apart from Jesus Christ, because it knows and proclaims all
things only as His things. It does not know and proclaim Him, therefore, merely
as the representative and exponent of something other. For it, there is no something other side by side with or apart from Him. For it, there is nothing worthy
of mention that is not such His. Everything that it knows and proclaims as
worthy of mention, it does so as His.

It is not, therefore, doing Him a mere courtesy when it names the name of
Jesus Christ. It does not use this name as a symbol or sign which has a certain
necessity on historical grounds, and a certain purpose on psychological and pedagogic grounds, to which that which it really means and has to say may be attached,
which it is desirable to expound for the sake of clarity. For it, this name is not
merely a cipher, under which that which it really means and has to say leads its
own life and has its own truth and actuality and would be worth proclaiming
for its own sake, a cipher which can at any time be omitted without affecting
that which is really meant and said, or which in other ages or climes or circumstances can be replaced by some other cipher. When it speaks concretely, when
it names the name of Jesus Christ, the Christian message is not referring simply
to the specific form of something general, a form which as such is interchange-
able : in the phrase of Lessing, a " contingent fact of history " which is the
" vehicle " of an " eternal truth of reason." The peace between God and man
and the salvation which comes to us men is not something general, but the
specific thing itself : that concrete thing which is indicated by the name of
Jesus Christ and not by any other name. For He who bears this name is Himself
the peace and salvation. The peace and salvation can be known, therefore, only
in Him, and proclaimed only in His name.

So much concerning the " God with us " as the most general
description of our theme.

2. THE COVENANT AS THE PRESUPPOSITION OF RECONCILIATION

Jesus Christ is God, God as man, and therefore " God with us " men, God in the work of reconciliation. But reconciliation is the fulfilment of the covenant between God and man.

" Reconciliation " is the restitution, the resumption of a fellowship which once existed but was then threatened by dissolution. It is the maintaining, restoring and upholding of that fellowship in face of an element which disturbs and disrupts and breaks it. It is the realisation of the original purpose which underlay and controlled it in defiance and by the removal of this obstruction. The fellowship which originally existed between God and man, which was then disturbed and jeopardised, the purpose of which is now fulfilled in Jesus Christ and in the work of reconciliation, we describe as the covenant.

Covenant, *berith*, διαθήκη, is the Old Testament term for the basic relationship between the God of Israel and His people. The etymology of the word (cf. W. Eichrodt, *Theologie des Alten Testaments*, Vol. I, 1933, p. 7, n. 5 ; G. Quell, *Theologisches Wörterbuch zum Neuen Test.* II, p. 106 f.) seems to be uncertain. Does it mean " circumcision " as a sacrificial ceremony, or " binding " as a binding of the will of the covenant-partner, or a " meal " as the ratification of the ceremony ? Or does it come from the same root as *barah* and mean " choice ? " Either way it denotes an element in a legal ritual in which two partners together accept a mutual obligation. We refer at this point to the historical reality with which the Old Testament is concerned whether it actually uses the word or not : " I will be your God, and ye shall be my people " (Jer. 7[23], 11[4], 30[22], 31[33], 32[38] ; Ezek. 36[28]).

" Your God " is the almighty and gracious and holy One who reveals Himself under the name of Yahweh. He is the One according to whose will and commandment and with whose powerful assistance a group of blood-related nomadic tribes of Semitic descent consciously set out to capture and did indeed capture the land of Canaan against the unforgettable background of an act of deliverance on the border of Egypt. He is the One in whose worship they found themselves united in that land, and to whose sole recognition as God and to the honouring of whose decrees they knew themselves to be pledged.

" My people " (the people " Israel ") is not simply the concept of those tribes in their interconnexion as a nation, let alone the state or one of the states in which this nation took on an external political form. It is rather the sacral federation (the Amphiktyonic league) of those tribes (only indirectly identical with the nation or state of Israel) gathered together as the twelve ; the Israelitish congregation or community of tribes which as such recognised in that God their unseen founder, overlord, protector and law-giver, and which had their visible cultic centre in the ark, which perhaps represented the empty throne of Yahweh and which was preserved first in Shechem, then in Bethel, then in Shiloh, being finally brought to Jerusalem in the time of David (cf. M. Noth, *Das Gesetz im Pentateuch*, 1940, p. 63 f., 70 f. ; *Geschichte Israels*, 1950, p. 74 f.). According to the formulation of G. Quell (*op. cit.* p. 111) the " covenant " between the two is the answer to that problem of man before God which is presupposed by Old Testament religion in all its forms and at all its stages. It is the relationship with God as such which is everywhere presumed in the Old Testament cultus, in the law-giving, the prophecy, the historical and poetical writings. It is ˙ ' a kind of common denominator " of Israelitish religion. There is relatively little direct mention of it. It is an " eternal covenant." It embraces everything that takes place between the two partners. The basic fact indicated by the word *berith* is presupposed even where on the ground and in the sphere of the covenant there are serious, even the most serious crises : movement of disloyalty, disobedience and apostasy on the part of portions or even the whole of that " community of tribes ; " and to meet them divine threatenings which seem ultimately to compromise the whole status of Israel, and indeed the almost (but not more than almost) unceasing execution of these threatenings. We can hardly agree with W. Eichrodt (*op. cit.* p. 11) that the covenant may be dissolved, that at its climax the judgment which breaks on Israel means the " setting aside " of the covenant (p. 250 f.). Does it not belong to the very nature of a *berith* even between man and man that it is " unalterable, lasting and inviolable " (G. Quell, *op. cit.*, p. 116) ? Can this be less, is it not much more, the case with the *berith* between God and man ? Does not the saying of Deutero-Isaiah about the covenant of peace which will not be removed (Is. 54[10]) stand over everything that takes place in the relations between Yahweh and Israel ?

What is true at all events is that the Old Testament covenant is a covenant of grace. It is instituted by God Himself in the fulness of sovereignty and in the freest determination and decree. And then and for that reason it is a matter of free choice and decision on the part of " Israel." God chooses for Himself this His people : this people, the community of tribes, chooses for itself this their God. This mutual choice, which takes place in this order and sequence, we have described as the basic fact, the presupposition of Old Testament religion, the standing of man before God which is always found in it. But the Old Testament understanding and the Old Testament representation of the early history of Israel make it clear that we can speak of a fact only with the greatest caution, for what is meant shows itself to be the occurrence of a basic act, something which happened there and then, and which as such can be placed alongside earlier—and also later—events. Obviously as an act which took place it cannot lose its actuality, but bears the character of an in itself inexhaustible occurrence. The Old Testament covenant, against the background and on the presupposition of which the events between God and Israel endorsed in the Old Testament take place, is not therefore a truth which is, as it were, inherent to this God or to the existence of this people or to their relationship one with another from a certain period in time, from an event which took place there and then. It is not a truth which as such has ceased to be event, the act of God and of Israel. It can, of course, be thought of as a historical fact. And it can be represented and worked out in institutions. But it is not itself an institution. It does not cease to be actual. It cannot be something given apart from the act of God and man. When the *berith* came to be understood as a given fact and an institution, in connexion with the ultimate location of a central worship in Jerusalem, but obviously even with the earlier cultus, especially in Shiloh, then at once it came under the fire of the severest prophetic criticism. The covenant remains—and it is in this way and only in this way that it does remain—the event of a divine and human choice, just as God Himself *exists* to the very depths of His being, and is therefore a (personally) living, active, acting and speaking God, and just as His human partner, His Israel, is actual only in its history, in the doing of its good and evil deeds, in the acting and suffering of the men who compose it.

For this reason there is no single and definitive narration of the original conclusion of this covenant—as there would have to be on that other view. According to the opinion advanced by many to-day, it is in the account in Josh. 24 of the action taken by Joshua in Shechem on the completion of the conquest that we have a representation which approximates most closely to an event of this kind. The conclusion of the covenant is portrayed in a very striking and solemn manner in this passage, so that if we did not know to the contrary, we might conclude that it was necessarily the only occurrence of this nature. But according to Deut. 26–30, already at the end of Moses' life and under his leadership—not this time in Canaan but in the land of Moab—it had been preceded by a conclusion of the covenant which is described as equally unique and definitive. And both these accounts stand under the shadow of the account in Ex. 24 of a covenant mediated by the same Moses at Sinai, which became so important in tradition right up to the time of the Christian Church. And even the priority of this covenant is apparently shaken by the covenant between God and Abraham which is narrated in two versions in Gen. 15 and 17, and later recalled with particular emphasis. But according to 2 K. 13[23] this could be understood as a covenant " with Abraham, Isaac and Jacob," and in any case it was preceded by the covenant with Noah in Gen. 8 and 9. And in Neh. 8–9, at the opposite end of the historical period covered by the Old Testament narratives, we have a description of the action taken in Jerusalem under Ezra after the return from exile, which can hardly be otherwise understood than as a further conclusion of the covenant, under whose strong impress—it might be supposed—the earlier narratives could easily have lost their force for that generation. And in the light of 2 Sam. 7[5-29] are we not forced to speak of a particular covenant with David, which also represents the whole ? And we ought at least to ask whether there are not many conversations reported in the Old Testament between God and various individuals who in their different ways represent the whole community of Israel, in which the word *berith* is not actually used as a description, but which in substance do belong to the same series : especially the calling and commissioning of the prophets, but also of Moses, Aaron, the Judges, Saul and David ? In these encounters between God and those who had special gifts in Israel, is it not possible that we have to do with the original view of the covenant between God and His people as such ? And when on festivals (like that of the enthronement) the people remembered the conclusion of the covenant, it was surely not understood as a " jubilee " of that event, but realistically as a contemporary happening. Certainly the conception of the covenant in the Old Testament represents a series of many such events, and we should not be thinking in Old Testament categories if we tried to understand one of them as the original, i.e., as the basic form of all the others which is simply repeated, renewed and varied in the others, and therefore as the basic act which constitutes Old Testament history and religion. The autonomy and importance which the Old Testament literature gives to each of these many events, quite irrespective of their mutual relationship, seems to make it impossible to try to find some pragmatic, historical connexion. We have to hold together Deut. 5[2] : " The Lord our God made a covenant with us in Horeb . . . not with our fathers, but with us, even us, who are all of us here alive this day "—and Deut. 29[14] : " Neither with you only do I make this covenant and this oath, but with him that standeth here with us this day before the Lord our God, and also with him that is not here with us this day." It is enough that all the accounts are at one in this, and that even in their puzzling variety they make it clear, that the presupposition of all the Old Testament happenings has itself always to be understood as an event, the event of the mutual electing of the God of Israel and His people.

But the concept of mutuality must now be elucidated. The saying of Jeremiah : " I will be your God and you will be my people " certainly speaks of a mutuality. But it also speaks (even in those passages in which the order of the two parts of the saying is reversed) of a willing on the part of God and of a subordinate obligation, or becoming and being on the part of Israel. And it is uttered as a statement made by God and not by a human writer. We have here a negation of " the compulsory union of God with His people " (W. Eichrodt, *op. cit.* p. 11) which is found in the other religious systems of the ancient east. Further, we have a decisive proof that in this context the word " covenant " does not denote a two-sided contract between two equal partners, but a more or less one-sided decree (M. Noth, *Geschichte Israels*, p. 111, n. 1). The covenant can (and must) be thought of as a " dictation on the part of an active to a passive person " (G. Quell, *op. cit.*, p. 120). In the words of Jacques Ellul (*Die theologische Begründung des Rechts*, 1948, p. 37 f.) it is a contract of adherence (*contract d'adhésion*), i.e., a contract in which one of the parties makes the arrangements and the other simply agrees. The sense in which the LXX and the New Testament speak about the διαθήκη brings out exactly the meaning of the Old Testament *berith*. It is " in every respect the arrangement of God, the mighty declaration of the sovereign will of God in history, by which He creates the relationship between Himself and the human race in accordance with His redemptive purpose, the authoritative ordinance (institution) which brings about the order of things " (J. Behm, *Theol. Wörterbuch zum N. Test.* II, p. 137). For that reason it was rightly described by the Reformed federal theologians of the 17th century as a *foedus μονόπλευρον*. This is clear in contexts like Deut. 27¹⁶⁻¹⁹, where the conclusion of the covenant is represented as an act of law, in which both partners clarify their position and engage in a mutual contract. Certainly Yahweh, too, accepts an obligation. But He does so on His own free initiative. He does not have to make a contract with Israel. And the obligation which He accepts consists only in the fact that He wills to be who He is as the God of Israel : " salvation " (*Yahweh shalom*, Jud. 6²⁴) and therefore—as " our " God—" our righteousness " (*Yahweh zidqenu*, Jer. 23⁶, 33¹⁶). Yahweh does not stand above the covenant, but in it, yet He is also not under it. It is always " my covenant." Certainly there is a parallel obligation on the part of Israel. Certainly Israel declares that it will be Yahweh's " peculiar people " (*am segullah*) and that as such it will keep His commandments. But it does not do so on its own judgment, but because it has been told by God that it is so. And its keeping of the commandments consists only in the fulfilment of its being as the people which God has made it (Ps. 100³). Certainly between the two obligations there is a correspondence which is brought out particularly by Deuteronomy. That Yahweh is the salvation and righteousness of Israel is something which is known and experienced by His people only when as such it keeps His commandments. Conversely, when this does take place on the part of Israel, it cannot fail to enjoy this knowledge and experience. But if it does not happen, if there is done in Israel what ought not to be done (Gen. 34⁷ ; 2 Sam. 13¹²), then the salvation of its God necessarily becomes loss and His righteousness judgment. But this correspondence, too, rests on the free ordering of God, and its fulfilment is on both sides a matter of His righteousness, judgment and control. He alone is King and Judge. The correspondence, therefore, is in no sense a relationship of *do ut des* between two equal partners, a limitation which can be imposed on the activity of God by the attitude of Israel, and the acceptance of such a condition by God. The obligation which rests on God is always one which He wills to lay upon Himself. If ever Israel takes up the attitude to God that its relationship with Him is one of *do ut des*, if ever it thinks that it can control God in the light of its own attitude, if ever it tries to assert a claim in relation to God, then it is unfaithful to its own election as His peculiar people and to its own electing of God. It has already fallen away to the worship of false gods and the transgression of all His commandments. It has already rushed headlong into the judgment of God and its own destruction. And when Israel does keep the commandments of its God, when it is faithful to His election and to its own electing of Him, it will necessarily appreciate that the knowledge and experience that He is its salvation and righteousness, and the blessing in which it stands, are God's free grace, the fulfilment of an obligation which God does not owe, but which He has Himself taken upon Himself, making the execution of it His own affair.

Now in the Old Testament the whole occurrence in and with and concerning the community of tribes which is " Israel," from its formation in the earliest period to the return of the captives from exile, is regarded as the fulfilment of this covenant, as the series of positive, critical and negative deductions which God draws from it and which this community comes to know and experience in the covenant in which it exists. Of these we cannot speak in the present context. They are the great example, the great commentary on the fulfilment of that covenant which now concerns us. But necessarily we shall be reminded of this example and commentary in our whole consideration of the doctrine of the atonement.

What we have still to consider is whether the Old Testament gives us any right or title to take over that concept of the covenant which is there shown to be the presupposition of the history of Israel and to use it as a description of the presupposition of the relationship and occurrence between God and all men— " the Jew first, but also the Greek " (Rom. 1[16])—of that free connexion between God and man, based on the free grace of God, which we always have before us when we consider the universal atonement which is an event in Jesus Christ. Does the Old Testament allow or does it even perhaps command us to give to the concept of covenant the wider sense which obviously it will have to have in this context ? So far there are three aspects of the meaning of the covenant in the Old Testament which we have not brought into consideration.

1. The (first) is at least touched on in the mention of the Noachic covenant. The detailed account offered in Gen. 9[1-17] belongs to the priestly writing. But this is making use of an older tradition, as is proved from the immediately preceding J passage in Gen. 8[20-22]. For although this does not mention the word covenant, and is only a soliloquy of Yahweh as He smells the sweet savour of the sacrifice offered up by Noah, there is in content a decisive connexion between what Yahweh says to Himself in this passage and what He says to " Noah and his sons " in Gen. 9[1, 8]. Both passages speak of an obligation which God imposes upon Himself. In both passages we can see a corresponding obligation on the part of man. But " man " here is not the community of tribes which is Israel but the whole of humanity after Noah. If, then, as accounts of a covenant —which they are—they stand in the same series as all the other accounts from Sinai to the covenant under Ezra, they differ from all the others in that they speak of a covenant of God with the whole of humanity before and outside Abraham, and indeed, in 9[10, 12, 15f.], with all the living creatures which with Noah escaped the Flood. If we compare this with Gen. 12 f. we find that in relation to the " covenant " there are indeed (cf. W. Eichrodt, *op. cit.*, p. 19) " two concentric circles " (Proksch) in which the relationship of God to man is actualised : in the Noachic covenant it is with the human race as a whole, in the covenant with Abraham only with Israel. But in its own way, according to the tradition enshrined in the texts in Gen. 8 and 9, the covenant in the outer circle is no less real and unforgettable than the other. There, too, in the general occurrence in the relationship " between me and all flesh " (Gen. 9[17]) we not only have to reckon with a living and active relation between the ruling and providing Creator and His creature, but we have also a covenant : a particular act of God in which He for His part pledges Himself to the man who is under pledge to Him. Nowadays the Noachic covenant is often referred to as a covenant of preservation in contrast to the covenant with Abraham as a covenant of grace and salvation. Certainly the Noachic covenant has to do with the " preservation " of the race. But we must not forget that even in the later covenant or covenants with Israel it is still a question of preservation. And again, in Gen. 8 and 9 it is not simply and abstractly a matter of " preservation," of the continuance of this relation between the Creator and the creature. What is attested here is not simply what we call the general control of divine providence. The very fact that the reference is only to man and to creatures subordinate to him ought in itself to warn us. What the texts say is not simply that the relation will in fact continue, but—and this is not quite so self-evident—that it will continue in face and in spite of the apostasy of man. " I will not again curse

the ground any more for man's sake ; for the imagination of man's heart is evil from his youth ; neither will I again smite any more every living thing, as I have done "—is what Yahweh says in Gen. 8²¹. And " neither shall all flesh be cut off any more by the waters of a flood ; neither shall there any more be a flood to destroy the earth " is what He pledges to Noah and his sons in 9¹¹. He has once carried out the threat of destruction evoked by the sin of man, in the Flood, although even then a remnant was preserved. But He will not do it again : " He lets go displeasure, and he does not ask concerning our guilt." Certainly it means preservation when He says : " While the earth remaineth, seedtime and harvest, and cold and heat, and summer and winter, and day and night shall not cease " (8²²). And for that reason : " Be ye fruitful and multiply ; bring forth abundantly in the earth, and multiply therein " (9⁷). But in view of the wickedness of the heart of man even after the Flood, which God knows well enough, this preservation of the race is by a special activity of God, that is to say, by the exercise of His longsuffering, in which He wills that men as they are—having been shown once and for all under what threat they stand—should go forward to meet One who (as yet completely unseen) has still to come, and therefore that they should not be allowed to perish, but preserved. Therefore the Noachic covenant—in a way which remarkably is much more perceptible than in the case of the covenant or covenants with Israel—is already a covenant of grace in the twofold sense of the concept grace : the free and utterly unmerited self-obligation of God to the human race which had completely fallen away from Him, but which as such is still pledged to Him (as is shown by the sacrifice of Noah in Gen. 8²⁰ and the divine direction in Gen. 9¹ᶠ·) ; and as the sign of the longsuffering of God obviously also the promise of the future divine coming which will far transcend the mere preserving of the race.

It is astonishing and yet it is a fact that the Old Testament should have considered the race prior to and outside Abraham in this way, on the presupposition not merely of the general relation of Creator and creature, but of a concrete activity of God in relation to it, which is not positively His redemptive activity—the same can be said of the covenant concluded with Israel—but an activity on the basis of which the nations preserved by God cannot be excluded from His redemptive work. In this sense the race, as a whole, is in covenant. It is the outer circle of which the inner is revealed from Gen. 12 onwards as Israel. It is in covenant, not by nature, not as humanity, to whom the Creator as such is obliged to show longsuffering, but on the basis of the free divine initiative and act. And genuinely so on this basis. In the light of Israel elected and called out from them, the nations can and must be regarded under this sign : under this correspondence to the sign under which Israel itself found itself placed, and therefore as itself to some extent a great community of tribes. From this point we can well understand how the Old Testament necessarily dared to present the history of creation—without using the word *berith* in the text, but factually—in an indissoluble relation to the divine covenant. The history of creation is a great cosmic prelude and example of that history of Israel which is the proper theme of the Old Testament. Creation is the outward basis of the covenant (Gen. 1) and the covenant the inward basis of creation (Gen. 2). Cf. *C D* III 1, § 41. Finally, the story of the Fall and its consequences (Gen. 3) is a happening which, for all its fearfulness, like the later resistance of Israel and the divine judgments which came upon it in consequence, does not take place outside but within a special relationship of the affirmation of man by God, of God's faithfulness to man, which is self-evidently presupposed to be unshakable. We can also understand how it is that, for all the exclusiveness with which the Old Testament speaks of the election and call of Israel, it never has any hesitation in allowing figures from outside, from the nations, time and again and sometimes with the very highest authority and function to enter the inner circle : Melchizedek, King of Salem, who in Gen. 14¹⁸ is called " a priest of the Most

High God," Jethro the Midianite, the father-in-law of Moses (Ex. 18$^{1f.}$), Balaam, the prophet of Moab (Num. 22–24) who is forced to bless Israel against his will, the harlot Rahab of Canaan (Josh. 2) who saves the spies, Ruth the Moabitess who is the ancestress of David, the Philistine Ittai (2 Sam. 15^{19}) who is one of the loyal few who pass over Kedron with David, the Syrian general Naaman (2 K. 5$^{1f.}$), to mention only a few out of a list which is remarkably continued in the New Testament. We can also understand the respect, the sympathy, even the granting of equality, which is so often enjoined upon Israel in the Law in relation to the " stranger," and the petition in which the stranger is expressly accepted in Solomon's prayer of dedication in 1 K. 8$^{41f.}$ (seeing that strangers could sometimes be found in the temple at Jerusalem). Those who come from outside do not come from a vacuum, but from the sphere of a relationship of God to man which is also in its own way effective—not generally and naturally, but historically, in virtue of a particular divine act.

2. A second important qualification of the Old Testament concept of the covenant arises from the conception of the final mission of Israel to the nations which we find particularly in the latter part but also in the earlier portions of the book of Isaiah. Why did God separate and take to Himself and address this people ? In the older tradition this question was left unanswered. But now in the light of the future an answer is given. It is given in the form of a prophecy which arises out of the situation of Israel at the end of its historical independence, but which absolutely transcends every historical consideration, possibility or probability. In the last days it will be wonderfully shown that the covenant of Yahweh with Israel was not an end in itself, but that it had a provisional and a provisionally representative significance. Israel had and has a mission—that is the meaning of the covenant with it. In Israel—this is what will be revealed in the last days—there is to be set up a sign and a witness to all peoples. The redemptive will of God is to be declared to all humanity. That is what we are told in the particularly important saying to the Ebed Yahweh in Is. 49^6 : " It is a light thing that thou shouldest be my servant to raise up the tribes of Jacob, and to restore the preserved of Israel : I will also give thee for a light to the Gentiles, that thou mayest be my salvation unto the end of the earth." The prophetic portrayal of this future event is not unitary. In Is. 2$^{2-4}$—which is ascribed to Isaiah, the son of Amoz, although it is found word for word in Mic. 4$^{1-4}$—we are told : " And it shall come to pass in the last days, that the mountain of the Lord's house shall be established in the top of the mountains, and shall be exalted above the hills ; and all nations shall flow unto it. And many people shall go and say, Come ye, and let us go up to the mountain of the Lord, to the house of the God of Jacob ; and he will teach us of his ways, and we will walk in his paths for out of Zion shall go forth the law, and the word of the Lord from Jerusalem. And he shall judge among the nations, and shall rebuke many people : and they shall beat their swords into ploughshares, and their spears into pruninghooks : nation shall not lift up sword against nation, neither shall they learn war any more." Zion is also referred to in Is. 25$^{6-8}$, but this time in relation to a redemptive happening of universal significance which does not go and, as it were, spread out from it, but which takes place within it : " And in this mountain shall the Lord of hosts make unto all people a feast of fat things, a feast of wines on the lees, of fat things full of marrow, of wines on the lees well refined. And he will destroy in this mountain the face of the covering cast over all people, and the vail that is spread over all nations. He will swallow up death in victory ; and the Lord God will wipe away tears from off all faces ; and the rebuke of his people shall be taken away from off all the earth : for the Lord hath spoken it." Different again is the picture unfolded in Is. 19$^{18-25}$. In the most concrete possible way the presentation of a historical situation—which seems to be very like that of the time of Isaiah himself—is merged into a vision of events in the last days: " In that day shall

five cities in the land of Egypt speak the language of Canaan and swear to the Lord of hosts. . . . In that day there shall be an altar to the Lord in the midst of the land of Egypt, and a pillar at the border thereof to the Lord. And it shall be for a sign and for a witness to the Lord of hosts in the land of Egypt. . . . And the Lord shall be known to Egypt, and the Egyptians shall know the Lord in that day, and shall do sacrifice and oblation ; yea, they shall vow a vow unto the Lord, and perform it. . . . In that day shall there be a highway out of Egypt to Assyria, and the Assyrian shall come into Egypt, and the Egyptian into Assyria, and the Egyptians shall serve with the Assyrians. In that day shall Israel be the third with Egypt and with Assyria, even a blessing in the midst of the land : whom the Lord of hosts shall bless, saying, Blessed be Egypt my people, and Assyria the work of my hands, and Israel mine inheritance."

In the texts so far quoted we may wonder whether the eschatological event described is not conceived too much as the onesided arrangement and miraculous operation of Yahweh. But in the Ebed-Yahweh songs of Deutero-Isaiah the emphasis is unmistakably on the active co-operation of the human partner of Yahweh. The question whether this partner, the servant of the Lord, is meant as collective Israel or as a single person—and if so, which ? a historical ? or an eschatological ?—can never be settled, because probably it does not have to be answered either the one way or the other. This figure may well be both an individual and also the people, and both of them in a historical and also an eschatological form. What is certain is that in and with this servant of the Lord Israel as such is at any rate introduced also as the partner of Yahweh. And in a whole series of passages it is introduced as the partner of Yahweh in an eschatological encounter with the nations, the powerful witness of Yahweh in the midst of the heathen. It is, therefore, in the light of a service which Israel has to perform that the actualisation of the prophecy of salvation is now understood. Is. 42$^{1-4}$: " Behold my servant, whom I uphold ; mine elect, in whom my soul delighteth ; I have put my spirit upon him ; he shall bring forth judgment (*mishpat*) to the Gentiles. He shall not cry, nor lift up, nor cause his voice to be heard in the street. A bruised reed shall he not break, and the smoking flax shall he not quench : he shall bring forth judgment unto truth. He shall not fail nor be discouraged, till he have set judgment in the earth ; and the isles shall wait for his law." And Is. 42$^{5-8}$: " Thus saith God the Lord, he that created the heavens, and stretched them out ; he that spread forth the earth, and that which cometh out of it ; he that giveth breath unto the people upon it, and spirit to them that walk therein : I the Lord have called thee in righteousness (*b'zedeq*), and will hold thine hand, and will keep thee, and give thee for a *berith am* (this remarkable expression recurs in Is. 49^8 : the Zurich Bible paraphrases : " a mediator of the covenant on behalf of the race "), for a light of the Gentiles ; to open the blind eyes, to bring out the prisoners from the prison, and them that sit in darkness out of the prisonhouse. I am the Lord, that is my name : and my glory will I not give to another, neither my praise to graven images."

The saying in Is. 49^6 has already been mentioned. But above all there is what is rightly the best known of all the Servant Songs, Is. 52^{13}–53^{12}, which, however we understand the one of whom it speaks, definitely belongs to this context. It is now the nations themselves—once again we have the eschatological event—who acknowledge that they have at last understood the meaning of the existence of Israel amongst them—its historical role as a mediator and the message which it has addressed to them : " Behold, my servant shall prosper, he shall be exalted and extolled, and be very high. As many were astonied at thee ; his visage was so marred more than any man, and his form more than the sons of men : So shall he astonish many nations ; the kings shall shut their mouths at him : for that which had not been told them shall they see ; and that which they had not heard shall they consider " (Is. 52$^{13-15}$). The historical background and outlook of the song is a time and situation of the last and deepest and most hopeless abasement of the people of the covenant, or of its (kingly? or prophetic?) representative. But according to this song, in the last days the nations will recognise and acknowledge that his mission, and the universally valid word and universally effective work of God, is present even in this utter hiddenness of the historical form of His witness: "Who hath believed our report? and to whom is the arm of the Lord revealed? For he shall grow up before him as a tender plant, and as a root out of a dry ground: he hath no form nor comeliness; and when we shall see him, there is no beauty that we should desire him. He is despised and rejected of men; a man of sorrows, and acquainted with grief: and we hid, as it were, our faces from him; he was despised, and we esteemed him not" (53^{1-3}). "He was cut off out of the land of the living" (v. 8). "He made his grave with the wicked, and with the rich in his death" (v. 9). "Who shall declare his generation?" (v. 8). And then the great confession of the nations at the end of the age, which does not deny but confirms and even lights up this appearance: "Surely he hath borne our griefs, and carried our sorrows" (v. 4). "But he was wounded for our transgressions, he was bruised for our iniquities: the chastisement of our peace was upon him; and with his stripes we are healed. All we like sheep have gone astray; we have turned every one to his own way; and the Lord hath laid on him the iniquity of us all" (vv. 5–6). And all this means: "He shall see his seed, he shall prolong his days, and the cause of the Lord shall prosper in his hand," because he made himself "an offering for sin" (v. 10). Just as the passage begins with a soliloquy of Yahweh, so it also ends, accepting and confirming this confession of the Gentiles: "He shall see of the travail of his soul, and shall be satisfied: by his knowledge shall my righteous servant justify many; for he shall bear their iniquities. Therefore will I divide him a portion with the great, and he shall divide the spoil with the strong; because he hath poured out his soul unto death: and he was numbered with the transgressors; and he bare the sin of many, and made intercession for the transgressors" (vv. 11–12).

Seen and understood eschatologically, this is the meaning and function of the particular covenant of God with Israel. The word *berith* occurs only once in the passages quoted, in the obscure *berith am* of Is. 42^8. But, in fact, it forces itself upon us, for it is the covenant people which lives and cries and suffers here, which is hemmed in and oppressed and threatened, which is more than threatened, actually overthrown and given up to destruction (and all according to the will and disposing of its God). The relatively short time of its modest existence in the sphere of world-history or of contemporary middle-eastern politics draws quickly to its close—in pain and grief and shame. What is it that the covenant-God is saying in all this? What is it that He wills by this work of His—He who has from the first and again and again shown and attested Himself as the One who is in covenant with His people? The prophets evidently associated the happenings primarily with the message that Israel had to see in it that judgment for its unfaithfulness to the Lord of the covenant which had been held before it from the very first. When that judgment began to fall—first on Samaria, then on Jerusalem—at every stage they warned and admonished and pleaded and threatened, like swimmers struggling against the twofold stream of human disobedience and the consequent wrath of God, which they tried to arrest with their call to repentance, but which by reason of its ineffectiveness they could not arrest, and therefore did not try to do so any longer but could only affirm it to be holy and just and necessary. But quite apart from the vain and empty confidence held out by the false prophets, even the true and authentic spokesmen for the covenant-God spoke always of His unchangeable faithfulness in contrast to the unfaithfulness of Israel, of the inflexibility of His purpose for His people, and therefore of the positive meaning of its history including its end. It is in this context that there arises the prophecy of the redemptive future of Israel in the last days. It presupposes the dark state of things at the present. It views it with pitiless clarity. And it does not overlay this view with the mere promise of better times to come. It does not offer by way of comfort the prospect of later historical developments. Its nerve and centre is the reference to an event which will terminate all history and all times, a history of the end. It is in this—and from this point of view the necessary destruction of Israel is only " a moment of wrath " (Is. 54⁷ᶠ·; Ps. 30⁵)—that the Yes which Yahweh has spoken to His people in and with the conclusion of the covenant will be revealed and expressed as a Yes. The last time, the day of Yahweh, will indeed be the day of final judgment—the prophets of a false confidence must make no mistake about that. But as such it will also be the day of Israel's redemption—the day when the covenant which Yahweh has made with it finds its positive fulfilment.

And it is particularly the teaching of the book of Isaiah which makes it clear that as such the last day which is the day of redemption for Israel will also be the day of redemption for the nations—the day of judgment, too, but, as the day of the last judgment, the day of redemption. It will then be revealed to the nations that it is not in vain and not for its own sake that Israel was and is, that its divine election and calling and all the history which followed in its brighter or darker aspects was no mere episode but an epoch, was not accidental but necessary, that its purpose was not a particular one, but the universal purpose of its mission, that its existence was the existence of a light for all men, a light which was once overlooked, but which then shone out unmistakably in the gross darkness which covered the earth (Is. 60¹ᶠ·—we may also recall the four rivers of Paradise in Gen. 2¹⁰ᶠ·, and the river which flows out of the temple in Ezek. 47¹⁻¹²). It will then be the case actually and visibly that " salvation is of the Jews " (Jn. 4²²). All the texts quoted speak of this in their varied eschatological imagery. They make it plain that the race as a whole is not forgotten in the importance of those shattering events between Yahweh and Israel which are the main subject of the Old Testament testimony. They do not speak only of the judgments which necessarily fall on the nations in relation to that which overtakes Israel. They also connect the salvation which is the final goal of the history of Israel with the salvation of the Assyrians and the Egyptians and all nations, and in such a way that the special existence of Israel is an instrument by which God finally manifests and accomplishes salvation for the nations. They speak, in fact, of a concrete presupposition which underlies the dealings of God as Lord of the world and the nations, and which for all its dissimilarity is similar to that of the history of Israel, and indeed identical with it, in that it has as its aim the grace which is to come upon them. The line which reveals this eschatological aspect of the Old Testament is not a broad one. It is only a kind of border to the true narrative and message of the Old Testament. But it belongs to it quite unmistakably. It is like the reference to that corresponding event in the earlier history, the covenant of God with the human race before Abraham, which is also a narrow line marking the earlier border of the true narrative and message of the Old Testament. But that narrative and message do have their beginning at the one point and their end at the other, the one in primal history, and the other in the corresponding eschatological history. They have this aspect even as the narrative and message of the happenings which take place on the basis of the covenant. And how could they be understood as a unity unless they had this aspect ? By these strangely complementary aspects on the borders of the Old Testament we are not merely enabled but summoned to take even the most exclusive thing of which it speaks, the covenant relationship between Yahweh and Israel, which is the presupposition of everything that takes place in the relations between these two partners, and, without denying its exclusiveness, to understand it inclusively, as that which points to a covenant which was there at the beginning and which will be there at the end, the covenant of God with all men.

3. We come finally to a third strand which we cannot overlook in an intensive amplification of the Old Testament covenant concept. Even in itself and as such the covenant with Israel is capable of a radical change in structure which it will actually undergo in the last days, as we learn from Jer. 31[31f.] and 32[38f.]. "Behold, the days come, saith the Lord, that I will make a new covenant with the house of Israel, and with the house of Judah" (31[31]). "I will make an ever-lasting covenant with them" (32[40]). The elements are exactly the same as in that covenant with Abraham, Moses and Joshua which is normative for the Old Testament as a whole. The formula "I will be your God, and ye shall be my people" is emphatically endorsed in both these passages and in the parallel passage in Ezek. 11[20]. We cannot therefore speak of a "replacement" of the first covenant by this "new" and "eternal" covenant of the last days except in a positive sense. Even in the verses Jer. 31[35-37] which immediately follow the main passage 31[31-34], there is a most definite stress on the imperishable nature of the covenant with Israel: neither here nor elsewhere can there be any question of its interruption or cessation. What happens to this covenant with the conclusion of a new and eternal covenant is rather—and the wider context of the passage points generally in this direction—that it is upheld, that is, lifted up to its true level, that it is given its proper form, and that far from being destroyed it is maintained and confirmed. There is no question of a dissolution but rather of a revelation of the real purpose and nature of that first covenant. The relationship of God with Israel, which is the substance of the covenant, is not held up,[1] that is to say, arrested, and set aside and destroyed, even on the New Testament understanding of the passage. What is done away (Calvin) is only its "economy," the form in which it is revealed and active in the events of the Old Testament this side the last days. In accordance with the completely changed conditions of the last time this form will certainly be altered, and so radically that it will no longer be recognisable in that form, and to that extent a new covenant will actually have been concluded. The form in which it was revealed and active in all the events from the exodus from Egypt to the destruction of Israel and Judah was such that in it the faithfulness and power of Yahweh seemed always to be matched and limited by the perpetually virulent and active disobedience and apostasy of the covenanted people. The prophecy says that this will end in the last days. The new and eternal covenant will not be "according to the covenant that I made with their fathers in the day that I took them by the hand to bring them out of the land of Egypt; which my covenant they brake, although I was a Lord unto them" (31[32]). It is this that God will no longer tolerate in the last days, but will repeal and remove: "But this shall be the covenant that I shall make with the house of Israel; After those days, saith the Lord, I will put my law in their inward parts, and write it in their hearts; and will be their God, and they shall be my people" (31[33]). "And I will give them one heart, and one way, that they may fear me for ever, for the good of them, and of their children after them" (32[39f.]). Ezek. 11[19f.] (cf. 36[26f.]) is even clearer: "And I will . . . put a new spirit within you; and I will take the stony heart out of their flesh, and will give them an heart of flesh; that they may walk in my statutes, and keep mine ordinances, and do them: and they shall be my people, and I will be their God." Similarly in Deut. 30[6] we are told about a circumcision of the heart of the people which God Himself will accomplish: "to love the Lord thy God with all thine heart, and with all thy soul, that thou mayest live." All this clearly means that the circle of the covenant which in its earlier form is open on man's side will in its new form be closed: not because men will be better, but because God will deal with the same men in a completely different

---

[1] Note: There is a play here on the German word *aufheben*, which positively means to "raise up," but negatively means to "repeal" or "set aside."—Trans.

way, laying His hand, as it were, upon them from behind, because He Himself will turn them to Himself. To His faithfulness—He himself will see to it—there will then correspond the complementary faithfulness of His people. The covenant —God Himself will make it so—will then be one which is mutually kept, and to that extent a *foedus δίπλευρον*.

The strange but necessary consequence will then be : " And they shall teach no more every man his neighbour, and every man his brother, saying, Know the Lord : for they shall all know me, from the least of them unto the greatest of them, saith the Lord " (31³⁴). But if the new and eternal form of the covenant means the ending of the fatal controversy between God and man it also means the ending of the corresponding necessity (the redemptive necessity) for that human antithesis or opposition between wise and foolish, prophets and people, teachers and scholars, the *ecclesia docens* and the *ecclesia audiens*, which even at its very best indicates a lack and encloses a judgment. It is at this point that Paul comes in (2 Cor. 3⁶ᶠ·) with his doctrine of the old and the new διαθήκη, the one of the prescriptive letter, the other of the liberating spirit which leads to obedience. In the light of this he expounds the covering on the face of Moses (Ex. 34³⁵ᶠ·) as that of the temporal nature of his ministry, and he finds the same covering on the hearts of the Jews who hear Moses read without perceiving that his ministry (i.e., the ministry of the prescriptive letter) does in fact belong to the past (2 Cor. 3¹⁵ᶠ·). He then goes on to proclaim : " Now the Lord is that Spirit : and where the Spirit of the Lord is, there is liberty " (2 Cor. 3¹⁷). He then contrasts the Jew who is one only outwardly with the Jew who is one inwardly and in truth : " by the circumcision that is of the heart, in the spirit, and not in the letter " (Rom. 2²⁹)—that is to say, the Gentiles who have come to faith in Jesus Christ, who apart from the Law do by nature the works of the Law, who are a law to themselves in that they reveal that the Law is written in their hearts (Rom. 2¹⁴ᶠ·). He then can and must say with reference to the Christian community (cf. also Rom. 15¹⁴ ; Phil. 1⁹ᶠ·) that although prophecy, tongues and knowledge will fade away, love can never fail (1 Cor. 13⁸).

And now we come to the most remarkable thing of all : What is the basis and possibility of this complete change in the form of the covenant which is to take place in the last days and therefore beyond the history of Israel considered in the Old Testament ? A conclusive answer is given in Jer. 31³⁴ᵇ : " For I will forgive their iniquity, and I will remember their sin no more." I would not say with G. Quell (*op. cit.*, p. 126) that a covenant which has this basis is obviously no longer a covenant. I would say rather that in this way and on this basis it becomes a perfect covenant. For in this way and on this basis God will break the opposition of His people, creating and giving a new heart to the men of His people, putting His Spirit in their inward parts, making the observance of His commandments self-evident to them (Paul in Rom. 2¹⁴ uses the word φύσις in relation to Gentile Christians), and in that way completing the circle of the covenant. In this way and on this basis the Israelitish history in the old form of the covenant—in so far as it stood under the sign of the sin of Israel and the divine reaction against it—will come to an end, together with that earlier form, to give way to the new and proper form. This ending and new beginning will be posited in the fact that God not only exercises patience as in the Noachic covenant, but that He remits guilt, that He does not remember sin, and that in this way and on this basis He not only allows an unmerited continuation of life, again as in the Noachic covenant, but reduces to order, and in a sense compulsorily places in the freedom of obedience which we owe Him as His covenant partners. This sovereign act of God which fulfils His will and plan and in which He vindicates at one and the same time His own right and that of man, is the subject of the prophecy in Jeremiah : the new basis of the new covenant. This covenant will be the covenant of the free but effective grace of God.

We must remember, however, that this conclusion of the covenant in the last days, like the Noachic covenant of the first days, is in the same series as those which were made first with Abraham and finally with Ezra. As we have seen, the prophecy of it does not mean to discredit or invalidate these others, or the covenant with Israel as such. It denies what had so far taken place on the basis of the presupposition to which those conclusions of the covenant point : the breaking of the covenant on the part of the people, and ensuing judgments on the part of God. But it does not deny the presupposition as such. It negates— or rather according to this prophecy God Himself negates—the unfaithfulness of Israel, but not the faithfulness of God Himself, nor His covenant will in relation to His people. What God will do in accordance with this prophecy will be a revelation and confirmation of what He had always willed and indeed done in the covenant with Israel. And for all the antithesis between the faithfulness of God and unfaithfulness of man, and the divine judgments which follow this antithesis, in everything that takes place in the Old Testament do we not find something of the forgiveness of the guilt and the gracious forgetting of the sin of His people, which belong to the last days, and which in fact obviously answer to the deepest being of the covenant, however out of place they may seem to be outwardly ? And on this basis were there not always in this people new and fleshly and circumcised hearts, and the Spirit and freedom, and even a simple and genuine keeping of the commandments ? How could there ever have been prophets, how could there have been that remnant in Israel, how could there have been penitence and prayer and also the bright and joyful worship of God in the Psalms, if not on the basis which Jer. 31 describes as the new basis of the new covenant ? This basis was not simply absent in the " old " covenant— or in the one covenant in its old form (as though this had had some other basis !). It was only hidden : hidden under the form of a relationship in which, viewed as a whole, the human lack of grace was bound to be revealed side by side with the divine grace, in which therefore even grace itself, viewed as a whole, was bound to have the form of judgment. Jer. 31 is the final word in matters of the divine covenant with Israel. In the light of the last days it describes it as the covenant of the free but effective grace of God. But at the same time it is also the first word in these matters. And this description is an indication of what the divine covenant with Israel had been in substance from the very first.

What, then, we gather from the Noachic covenant, and everything that belongs to this strand, is that according to the Old Testament conception itself the special divine covenant made with Israel does not exclude the human race as a whole from the gracious will of God towards it. What we find in Isaiah's view of the status of Israel as a representative and messenger to the nations is that the covenant made with Israel has a meaning and purpose which reaches out beyond the existence of Israel. And now, from the prophecy in Jeremiah of a new covenant of forgiveness and of the Spirit and of free obedience on the part of man, we learn that the Old Testament looks beyond the past and present to a form of the relationship between God and Israel in which the covenant broken by Israel will again be set up, that the Israelite, for whom ultimately God has nothing but forgiveness, but does have it actually and effectively, must now take his place directly alongside his Gentile fellows, and that if at all he can hope for the grace and salvation of God only on this presupposition. In the light of this passage in Jer. 31 we are indeed enabled and summoned to give to the concept of the covenant the universal meaning which it acquired in the form which it manifestly assumed in Jesus Christ.

Jesus Christ is the atonement. But that means that He is the maintaining and accomplishing and fulfilling of the divine covenant as executed by God Himself. He is the eschatological realisation of the will of God for Israel and therefore for the whole race. And as such He is also the revelation of this divine will and therefore of the covenant. He is the One for whose sake and towards whom all men from the very beginning are preserved from their youth up by the longsuffering of God, notwithstanding their evil heart. And in this capacity He reveals that the particular covenant with Israel was concluded for their sake too, that in that wider circle it also encloses them. He is the servant of God who stands before God as the representative of all nations and stands amongst the nations as the representative of God, bearing the judgments of God, living and testifying by the grace of God—Himself the Israel elected and called to the covenant and to be the mediator of the covenant. And in that capacity He reveals that this covenant with Israel is made and avails for the whole race. In His own person He is the eschatological sovereign act of God who renews men and summons them to obedience by forgiving their sins. And in that capacity He reveals that the meaning and power of the covenant with Israel for the whole race is that it is a covenant of free and therefore effective grace.

The work of God in Jesus Christ is also the (Word of God)—the Word in which He makes known His will even as it is done to those who can hear it. And this will of God which is done begins with the institution and establishment of His covenant with man. It is done in acts of grace and mercy, of judgment and punishment, and in His Word as Gospel and Law, as comfort, admonishment and counsel. It is done primarily and basically as His will to be the God of man, to let man be His man. The whole actualisation of the will of God has its source there, in the " kindness of God toward man " (Tit. 3⁴). This is the presupposition of all the works and words of God. The whole plan and law and meaning of them derives from this source, that God the Creator wanted to make and did in fact make Himself the covenant partner of man and man the covenant partner of God. The whole doing of the will of God is the doing of His covenant will. As this covenant will it strives and conquers against the sin of man and its consequences in the atonement accomplished in Jesus Christ. But primarily, in face of the sin of man, and God's striving with it and conquering of it and of its consequences, it is His covenant will. It remains His covenant will in this antithesis, conflict and victory. It is through these that it finds its fulfilment. And the (antithesis) conflict and fulfilment reveal it for what it is. They also show its origin—that it was first of all His covenant will.

It is in Jesus Christ that that (antithesis) is met and overcome. It is Jesus Christ who accomplishes and fulfils the will of God in face of human sin and its consequences. It is not something provisional but final that takes place in the atonement accomplished by Him. In Him God Himself enters in, and becomes man, a man amongst men, in order that He Himself in this man may carry out His will. God Himself lives and acts and speaks and suffers and triumphs for all men as this one man. When this takes place, atonement takes place. But the final thing which takes place here—just as it cannot be something provisional—cannot be a second or later thing. It can only reveal the first thing. What takes place here is the accomplishment and therefore the revelation of the original and basic will of God, as a result of which all the other works and words of God take place. What breaks out at this point is the source of all that God wills and does.

This, then, is the actualisation of the will of God in this matter, in the overcoming of this antithesis. The will of God is done in Jesus Christ, in God's own being and acting and speaking as man. But if this is so, then this actualisation, the overcoming of this antithesis, is characterised as an act of faithfulness, of constancy, of self-affirmation on the part of God, as the consequence of a presupposition already laid down by Him, as the fulfilment of a decision which underlies and therefore precedes that actualisation, an " earlier " divine decision, as the successful continuation of an act which God had already begun, from the very beginning. He becomes and is man in Jesus Christ, and as such He acts and speaks to reconcile the world to Himself, because He has bound Himself to man by the creation of heaven and earth and all things, because He cannot tolerate that this covenant should be broken, because He wills to uphold and fulfil it even though it is broken. The work of atonement in Jesus Christ is the fulfilment of the communion of Himself with man and of man with Himself which He willed and created at the very first. Even in face of man's transgression He cannot allow it to be destroyed. He does not permit that that which He willed as Creator—the inner meaning and purpose and basis of the creation—should be perverted or arrested by the transgression of man. He honours it and finally fulfils it in this conflict with the transgression and overcoming of it. The transgression can and must be understood as an episode and its overcoming in Jesus Christ as the contingent reaction of God in face of this episode. But the reaction as such takes place along the line of that action determined from the very first in the will of God and already initiated. It is only the particular form of that action in face of this episode. And in this particular form, in the fact that God becomes man for our sake, to set aside our sin and its consequences, we see both the fact and also the manner in which it is determined from the very first and already initiated. It is not only a reaction, but a work of the faithfulness of God. And the faithfulness of God has reference to the covenant between Himself and men. Even in this particular form it is the accomplishment of His covenant will. Even more, it is the affirmation and consummation of the institution of the covenant between Himself and man which took place in and with the creation. It is this covenant will which is carried out in Jesus Christ. It is this institution of the covenant which is fulfilled in Him. He does it in face of human sin, as the One who overcomes it, as the Mediator between God and man. He does it, therefore, in fulfilment of the divine reaction in face of that episode. But primarily it is the action of God, disturbed but not broken by that episode, which is now consummated. He therefore fulfils and reveals the original and basic will of God, the first act of God, His original covenant with man. It is of this, the presupposition of the atonement, that we must first speak.

(What is revealed) in the work of atonement in Jesus Christ, as its presupposition, is that God does not at first occupy a position of neutrality in relation to man. He is not simply distant from him and high above him. He is not merely God in His own divine sphere allowing man to be man in his sphere. He does not merely know about him and view him as a spectator. This is excluded from the outset by the fact that He is the living Creator and Lord of man, and therefore the One who actively guarantees and accompanies and controls his existence. This might, of course, imply a certain neutrality, for He is the Creator and Lord of heaven and earth and all creatures, the living One who preserves and accompanies and controls them all, so that He is for man only what He is for all other things. But in becoming man for the sake of man in the work of atonement, He reveals an attitude and purpose in respect of man which goes beyond His attitude and purpose as Creator and Lord in respect of all things. He is disposed towards man in a special way which could not be said of any other creature, and which is not only that of the Creator and Lord of man. He remains his Creator and Lord. With all other creatures, and in a special way amongst other creatures, He lavishes upon him all the riches of His goodness as Creator—why should we not say, of His grace as Creator ? He gives and preserves to this human creature his human life in all the plenitude and with all the limitations of its particular possibilities. He is to him a faithful and watchful Father. He does not leave him without counsel and commandment. But that is not all. And all that, His general acting and working and speaking as Creator, has in relation to man a particular meaning and purpose : not only because it has to do with the particular creature which is man, but because from the very first His relationship with this creature is of itself a particular one and has a particular goal. The fatherly faithfulness and provision shown to him by God has a different meaning and purpose from that which is undoubtedly exercised in respect of other creatures. And so, too, the counsels and commandments which are given him by the Creator have a different meaning and purpose from the ordinances under which all other creatures undoubtedly have their being according to His will.

What God does to man and for man even as Creator has its origin in the fact that among all the creatures He has linked and bound and pledged Himself originally to man, choosing and determining and making Himself the God of man. The distinguishing mark of Israel is the fact that there is said to Israel and heard by Israel that which at the end of the history of Israel becomes an event in Jesus Christ : " I will be your God and ye shall be my people." And this is a revelation of the divine choice and decision, the divine word and the divine act, in which, in and with creation, it became truth and actuality that God made Himself the God of man : that in willing man God willed to be God for him, with him, in relation to him, acting for him, concerned with him, for his sake. God : and therefore nothing other than what He was and is and always will be in Himself as Father, Son and Holy Spirit ; and all that, not for Himself alone, but for ' man, in his favour, in a true and actual interest in his existence, with a view to what he is to become, and therefore in a participation in what he is and lives and does and experiences ; just that, nothing more but also nothing less, in fellowship with man. " I will be your God " : that is the original emergence of God from any neutrality, but also His emergence from what is certainly a gracious being and working as Creator and Lord in relation to man. That is more than the creation, more than the preservation, accompaniment and overruling of His creatures. That is the covenant of God with man, from which He has bound and pledged Himself always to begin, and in virtue of which He has constituted Himself his God.

And that is the presupposition of the atonement as revealed in its actualisation in Jesus Christ : the presupposition whose consequences are deduced in the atonement ; the presupposition which in the atonement is fulfilled in spite of the opposition of man. We do not postulate it. We do not grope for it in the void. We find it in that which has actually taken place in Jesus Christ. But we cannot refuse to find it in that which has actually taken place in Jesus Christ. If the final thing is true, that in Him God has become man for us men, then we cannot escape the first thing, that it is the original will of God active already in and with creation that He should be God for us men. If for us men God Himself has become man, we can, we must look into the heart of God—He Himself has opened His heart to us—to accept His saying as a first as well as a final saying : " I will be your God." We cannot, therefore, think of Him except as the One who has concluded and set up this covenant with us. We would be mistaking Him, we would obviously be making ourselves guilty of transgression, of sin, if we were to try to think of Him otherwise, if we were to try to reckon with another God, if we were to try to know and fear and love any other God but Him—the One who from the very first, from the creation of heaven and earth, has made Himself the covenant God of man, our covenant God. For according to the Word which He Himself has spoken in His supreme and final work, there is no other God. All other gods, all gods which are hostile to man, are false gods. Even though we bring the deepest reverence or the highest love, even though we bring the greatest zeal or sincerity, if they are offered to other gods.

to gods that are hostile to man, we are simply beating the air, where there is no God, where God is not God. " I will be your God " : not only for Israel, but, according to the revelation accomplished in Jesus Christ at the end of the history of Israel, for all men of all times and places, this was and is the critical point of all faith in God and knowledge of God and service of God. This God, or none at all. Faith in this God, the knowledge and service of this God, or godlessness. He Himself has decided this in revealing Himself as the One who was and is and is to come—God for us, our God, the God who has concluded and set up the covenant.

It is simply a matter of analysis when we go on to say that the covenant is a covenant of grace. This concept implies three things.

The first is the freedom in which it is determined and established by God, and therefore the undeservedness with which man can receive and respond to the fact that God has chosen and determined and made Himself his God. In the atonement in which the presupposition is revealed, " I will be your God," this is clear beyond any possible doubt. By his transgression man has prevented God from affirming it and holding any further fellowship with him. Man is not in a position to atone for his transgression, to reconcile himself with God. Man cannot bring forward a Jesus Christ in which his atonement with God can take place. If it is to take place, it must be from God, in the freedom of God and not of man, in the freedom of the grace of God, to which we have no claim, which would necessarily judge and condemn us, because we have sinned against it and always will sin against it, because we have shown ourselves unworthy of it. Atonement is free grace. Even the fact that God wills to be our God and to act and speak with us as such is free grace on God's side and something entirely undeserved on ours. We have only to think—God for us men, God in His majesty, God the Father, Son and Holy Spirit, God in all the fulness of His divine being, God in His holiness, power, wisdom, eternity and glory, God, who is completely self-sufficient, who does not need a fellow in order to be love, or a companion in order to be complete : God for us men. If that is what He is, if that is what He is as the true and real and living and only God—as the One who Himself willed to become man, and in so doing proved and revealed that He cares for man, and that He does so originally and properly and intensely, if He is this God, the *Deus pro nobis*, the covenant-God, then He is so, not as limited and conditioned by our freedom, but in the exalted freedom of His grace. That is what free grace, the overflowing of His love, was and is, that He willed to ' be our Creator and Lord, and how much more the One who says : " I will be your God." Why among all creatures does He will to be our God ? Why the God of man ? Because of the peculiarities and qualities of human creatureliness ? But other creatures have theirs too, and how are we to say that those of men are greater ? And even if they were, it would by no means follow that man would have a claim that God must be God for man, that He should enter into covenant with us, that there should be this divine Yes originally addressed only to us. The covenant of God with man is a fact which, since it is a fact according to His revelation in Jesus Christ, we cannot deny as such. But according to the prophetic warnings God entered into covenant with other peoples as well as Israel. Why then (if He willed to contract such a relationship with creatures at all) should He not also have done so with some quite different creature as well ? Why not to His greater honour with some creature which is supposed to be or actually is lower or more lowly ? The fact of the covenant of God with man is obviously a fact of His free choice, the choice of His grace. There is no complementary claim of man to such a distinction. We can only accept and affirm this choice as true and actual. We can only cling to it as a fact which He has chosen and posited. We can only recognise and honour it as completely undeserved. That is the first sense in which we have to say that the covenant as the presupposition of all God does and says in relation to us men is a covenant of grace.

The second thing implied in the concept is the beneficent character proper to this presupposition of the atonement. Positively, grace means the giving of something good and redemptive and helpful. Grace is a powerful Yes spoken to the one to whom it is addressed. This, too, can be perceived at once in the atonement in which it is revealed. Atonement means the redemption of man, the fact that he is prevented from falling into the abyss into which he ought to fall as a transgressor, as the one who has interrupted the divine purpose, as the enemy of grace. And consisting as it does in the fellowship of temporal man with Jesus Christ and therefore with God, it means further that he is placed in the certain expectation of eternal salvation, which has become a temporal present and a living promise in Jesus Christ. But in this sense, too, it is simply a matter of grace to grace. For the divine benefit is simply the first thing in consequence of which the second took place. We think again—God for us men. God who in His triune being, in the fulness of His Godhead, is Himself the essence of all favour, the source and stream and sea of everything that is good, of all light and life and joy. To say God is to say eternal benefit. Now the work of His creation, and His control as the One who preserves and accompanies and rules the creature and therefore man, is certainly a favour out of His fulness. But in the covenant with man, as his God, He does not merel· give out of His fulness. In His fulness He gives Himself to be with man and for man. As the benefit which He is in Himself, He makes Himself the companion of man. He does not merely give him something, however great. He gives Himself, and in so doing gives him all things. It is only of God that what man comes to experience in covenant with Him is favour. It is not always so, not by a long way in all the supposed or actual experience of man. Even in his experience of what comes to him from God, man can be blind or half-blind, and can therefore make mistakes, and can find terror and destruction in what God has allotted and given as a supreme benefit. And necessarily the benefit offered him by God can in fact and objectively become terror and destruction if he flees from God and opposes Him. Even the divine favour will then take on the aspect of wrath. God's Yes will then become a No and His grace judgment. The light itself will blind him and plunge him in darkness. Life will be to him death. But this does not mean that God will not keep His covenant, or that this will cease to be the covenant of grace, or that its meaning and purpose will cease to be the favour shown to man. How can Yahweh cease to be salvation ? What it does mean is that in certain situations of its execution and history the true character must be hidden under another form—which may later be put off and (whether it is recognised by man or not, or properly recognised or not) give place again to its true form. In this form, in itself, by virtue of its meaning and purpose, and just as surely as that God is always sovereign in it, the covenant is always a relationship in which there is the conferring and receiving of a benefit, not the opposite, not a relationship of wrath and perdition, not even when it does (necessarily) appear to men like that (as it did to Job), not even when the merciful but just and holy God Himself can and will maintain and execute it in that other form (as He did so often in the history of Israel). In this positive sense, too, in its proper form and by virtue of its origin it is always the covenant of grace.

The third thing which we maintain when we describe the covenant as the covenant of grace is that the covenant engages man as the partner of God only, but actually and necessarily, to gratitude. On the side of God it is only a matter of free grace and this in the form of benefit. For the other partner in the covenant to whom God turns in this grace, the only proper thing, but the thing which is unconditionally and inescapably demanded, is that he should be thankful. How can anything more or different be asked of man ? The only answer to χάρις is εὐχαριστία. But how can it be doubted for a moment that this is in fact asked of him ? χάρις always demands the answer of εὐχαριστία. Grace and gratitude belong together like heaven and earth. Grace evokes gratitude like the voice an echo. Gratitude follows grace like thunder lightning. Not by virtue of any necessity of the concepts as such. But we are speaking of the grace of the God who is God for man, and of the gratitude of man as his response to this grace. Here, at any rate, the two belong together, so that only gratitude can correspond to grace, and this correspondence cannot fail. Its failure, ingratitude, is sin, transgression. Radically and basically all sin is simply ingratitude — man's refusal of the one but necessary thing which is proper to and is required of him with whom God has graciously entered into covenant. As far as man is concerned there can be no question of anything but gratitude ; but gratitude is the complement which man must necessarily fulfil.

This leads us to a further point which is revealed in the atoning work accomplished in Jesus Christ, and as the presupposition of that work, that man cannot first be neutral towards God. Man is not simply distant from God and far beneath Him. He cannot let Him be God in His sphere in order in his own sphere to try to be man *in abstracto* and on his own account. He cannot simply know about God, or believe " in a God." We may say that such neutrality is excluded already by the fact that man is the living creature of God, and that as such in all his movements—whether he knows it or not— he is thrown back entirely upon God, he is dependent upon Him and bound up with Him. But there is more to it than that, for he is bound to all other creatures in that way, and all other creatures are similarly bound. When God Himself becomes man for men in the work of atonement, then quite apart from the general and in a sense external being of men under and with God this means that as creatures preserved, accompanied and over-ruled by God men have a character, we can call it a *character indelibilis*, which transcends their creatureliness as such. When God reveals in Jesus Christ that from the very first He willed to be God for man, the God of man, He also reveals that from the very first man is His man, man belongs to Him, is bound and pledged to Him. The man for whose sake God Himself became man cannot be basically neutral. He can only be a partner in His activity. For as in Jesus Christ there breaks out as truth the original thing about God : " I will be your God," so in Jesus Christ there breaks out as truth the original thing about man, " Ye shall be my people." That was and is the distinctive mark of Israel, which at the end of the history of Israel became event in Jesus Christ and in that event is revelation, the divine revelation of the destiny of man, of all men, as their determination for Him. According to this revelation, from the very first God was and is God for man, inclined to him, caring for him, his God. But so, too, according to this revelation of God from the very first man was and is man for God, subordinated and referred to Him. " Ye shall be my people " means that it is proper to you and required of you in your being, life and activity to correspond to the fact that in My being, life and activity for you I am your God.

And if the essence of God as the God of man is His grace, then the essence of men as His people, that which is proper to and demanded of them in covenant with God, is simply their thanks. But this is actually and necessarily proper to and demanded of them. Thanks is the one all-embracing, but as such valid and inescapable, content of the law of the covenant imposed upon man. It is the one and necessary thing which has to take place on the part of man. All the laws of

Israel and all the concrete demands addressed by God to individual men in Israel are simply developments and specific forms of this one law, demands not to withhold from the God of the covenant the thanks which is His due, but to render it with a whole heart. The grace of God calls for this modest but active return. It is for this reason and on this basis that in the Old Testament even the detailed commands are always urged so forcefully and earnestly and emphatically, that which God wills of man being unconditionally pressed irrespective of the apparent greatness or littleness of the thing which is demanded. What is divinely required in the Old Testament has this irresistible force, the force of an either-or, which is a matter of life and death, because the thanks is demanded which cannot possibly fail to follow grace. Obedience to the commands of other gods, false gods, is usually a matter of the free inclination and judgment of man. But where the One who commands is the *Deus pro nobis*, obedience is not something which is in our hands, but the self-evident human complement and response. It is only here in the existence of man in the covenant which as such is the covenant of grace that we see the true horror of disobedience, of sin. That he should be thankful is the righteousness which is demanded of him before God. And if he is not thankful, that is his unrighteousness.

This is the basic determination of the relationship between God and man which is revealed as applicable to all men from the very first in the atonement which took place in Jesus Christ and in which the history of Israel attained its goal. This is the last thing which is revealed as the first thing for man too. When (in Jesus Christ) we look into the heart of God—for in Him He has revealed to us: " I will be your God "—we are permitted, indeed we are constrained, to look at ourselves, that what is proper to and is required of us is : " Ye shall be my people." As God is gracious to us, we may—and this " may " is the seriousness and force of every " ought "—on that account be thankful. By deciding for us God has decided concerning us. We are therefore prevented from thinking otherwise about ourselves, from seeing or understanding or explaining man in any other way, than as the being engaged and covenanted to God, and therefore simply but strictly engaged and covenanted to thanks. Just as there is no God but the God of the covenant, there is no man but the man of the covenant : the man who as such is destined and called to give thanks. And it is again transgression, sin, if even for a moment we ignore this man who is true man, trying to imagine and construct a man in himself, and to regard his destiny to give thanks to God as something which is in his own power, a matter of his own freedom of choice. The real freedom of man is decided by the fact that God is his God. In freedom he can only choose to be the man of God, i.e., to be thankful to God. With any other choice he would simply be groping in the void, betraying and destroying his true humanity.

Instead of choosing in freedom, he would be choosing enslavement. By revealing Himself in Jesus Christ as from the very first the gracious God, God has decided that man can only be grateful man, the man who takes up and maintains his place in the covenant with Him, the gracious God.

It can only be by way of analysis and emphasis that we maintain that grace is not only the basis and essence, the ontological substance of the original relationship between God and man which we have described as the covenant between them willed and instituted and controlled by God. The recognition of this original covenant is also grace and therefore a free divine favour. We have described the covenant as from every point of view the presupposition of the atonement which is revealed and therefore can be recognised only in the atonement. We now need to emphasise : only in the atonement, and therefore only in Jesus Christ. Concerning the covenant fulfilled as God became man in Jesus Christ, concerning the covenant will of God executed and accomplished in Jesus Christ, concerning God's institution of the covenant as the first and basic divine act continued and completed in the action fulfilled in Jesus Christ— concerning all these things we have no other source of knowledge than through the One who is the one Word of God "whom we must hear, and trust and obey in life and in death." In all that we have said about the original place and status of God and man in their relationship one with another, we have tried never to look past Jesus Christ, but always to consider it as seen through Him and with a steadfast regard fixed on Him, " as it was in the beginning."

We have tried to make the movement to which we are summoned by the fact that in the New Testament we are told both directly (e.g., Jn. 1[8, 10] ; Col. 1[16] ; Heb. 1[3]) and also indirectly that the creation of God took place in Him, i.e., that it was willed and planned and completed with a view to Him as the *telos* of all things and all events, and that He is " the first-born of all creation " (Col. 1[15]). We have tried to paraphrase and give the sense of Eph. 1[4-6] : " According as he hath chosen us in him before the foundation of the world ($\pi\rho\grave{o}$ $\kappa\alpha\tau\alpha\beta o\lambda\hat{\eta}\varsigma$ $\kappa\acute{o}\sigma\mu o\upsilon$), that we should be holy and without blame before him in love : having predestinated us ($\pi\rho oo\rho\acute{\iota}\sigma\alpha\varsigma$ $\mathring{\eta}\mu\hat{\alpha}\varsigma$) unto the adoption of children by Jesus Christ to himself, according to the good pleasure of his will, to the praise of the glory of his grace." We have understood the atonement as " predestinated according to the purpose ($\kappa\alpha\tau\grave{\alpha}$ $\pi\rho\acute{o}\theta\epsilon\sigma\iota\nu$) of him who worketh all things according to the counsel of his own will " (Eph. 1[11]), as accomplished " according to the eternal purpose ($\kappa\alpha\tau\grave{\alpha}$ $\pi\rho\acute{o}\theta\epsilon\sigma\iota\nu$ $\tau\hat{\omega}\nu$ $\alpha\mathring{\iota}\acute{\omega}\nu\omega\nu$) which he purposed (or : already fulfilled as such ? $\mathring{\eta}\nu$ $\mathring{\epsilon}\pi o\acute{\iota}\eta\sigma\epsilon\nu$) in Christ Jesus our Lord " (Eph. 3[11]).

From that which in Jesus Christ took place in time according to the will of God we have tried to gather what was and is and will be the will of God at the beginning of all time, and in relation to the whole content of time. By the perception of grace at the end of the ways of God we have been led to the perception of grace at their beginning, as the presupposition of all His ways. We are certainly not in any position, nor are we constrained, to recognise this pre-supposition of all the ways of God, and finally of the atonement accom-plished in Jesus Christ, as the covenant of grace, if we look to any other source, if we follow any other supposed Word of God than that which is spoken in Jesus Christ and in His work. When we spoke of the original and basic will of God, of His " first act " fulfilled in and with creation but transcending creation, we did not speak of an " original revelation " which we must differentiate from Jesus Christ because it is in fact different from Him. We did not speak in the light of the results of any self-knowledge or self-estimate of human reason or existence. We did not speak with reference to any observa-tions and conclusions in respect of the laws and ordinances which rule in nature and human history. We certainly did not speak in relation to any religious disposition which is supposed to be or actually is proper to man. There is only one revelation. That revelation is the revelation of the covenant, of the original and basic will of God. How else could this be revealed to us ? The concept of an " original revelation " which must be differentiated from the revelation in Jesus Christ because it is actually different from it is a purely empty concept, or one that can be filled only by illusions.

In a word, the covenant of grace which is from the beginning, the presupposition of the atonement, is not a discovery and conclusion of " natural theology." Apart from and without Jesus Christ we can say nothing at all about God and man and their relationship one with another. Least of all can we say that their relationship can be pre-supposed as that of a covenant of grace. Just because it is a covenant of grace, it cannot be discovered by man, nor can it be demonstrated by man. As the covenant of grace it is not amenable to any kind of human reflection or to any questions asked by man concerning the meaning and basis of the cosmos or history. Grace is inaccessible to us : how else can it be grace ? Grace can only make itself accessible. Grace can never be recalled. To remember grace is itself the work of grace. The perception of grace is itself grace. Therefore if the covenant of grace is the first thing which we have to recognise and say about God and man in their relationship one with another, it is something which we can see only as it makes itself to be seen, only as it fulfils itself—which is what happened in Jesus Christ—and therefore reveals itself as true and actual. From all eternity God elected and deter-mined that He Himself would become man for us men. From all eternity He determined that men would be those for whom He is God : His fellow-men. In willing this, in willing Jesus Christ, He wills to be our God and He wills that we should be His people. Ontologically, therefore, the covenant of grace is already included and grounded in Jesus Christ, in the human form and human content which God willed to give His Word from all eternity. The order of cognition cannot be disobedient to, but must follow, the actual order of things. If we are to know God and man and their basic and unalterable relationship one with the other, we have to hear the Word of God only in the form and with the content which God Himself has given to it, and by which He willed to lay down His own place and status, and ours, from the very first. It is only by this Word, which is Jesus Christ, and which is itself in this form and with this content the basis and meaning of the covenant, that we can learn about the covenant. This Word is not only the basis and meaning of the covenant. As a revealed Word it is also the instruction concerning it which we have to receive.

What is involved in this knowledge of the covenant, the covenant of grace which is the presupposition of the atonement fulfilled and revealed in the atonement ? It is important that we should be clear about this point. For we are not in fact dealing with a theologumenon which is no doubt permissible and may be introduced in passing, but which is in any event dispensable and may in the last resort be regarded as superfluous.

In this knowledge or recognition we make the right distinction between the atonement accomplished in Jesus Christ, which is the centre and the proper subject of the Christian message and the Christian faith, and all events which are purely contingent, which have only a relative significance, which concern certain men but not all men, which may not even be necessary *rebus aliter stantibus*. Or, to put it positively, in this recognition we make a proper acknowledgment of the unconditional, eternal and divine validity and scope of the atonement accomplished in Jesus Christ, of the general and inescapable and definitive claim of that which took place in it. It is in this recognition that we are committed to a genuine regard for this centre of the Christian message and the Christian faith. Without it we cannot attain to the joy or certainty or freedom to which we are summoned by this event.

The atonement accomplished in Jesus Christ is God's retort to the sin of man and its consequences. And the sin of man is an episode. It is the original of all episodes, the essence of everything that is unnecessary, disorderly, contrary to plan and purpose. It has not escaped the knowledge and control of God. But it is not a work of His creation and not a disposition of His providence. It really comes about and is only as that which God did not will and does not will and never will will. It has its being only in the fact that it is non-being, that which from the point of view of God is unintelligible and intolerable. It takes place only as the powerful but, of course, before God absolutely powerless irruption of that which is not into the fulfilment of His will. It takes place, therefore, only under the original, radical, definitive and therefore finally triumphant No of God. It is not a limitation of His positive will. Rather it exists as it is completely conditioned by His non-will. It is alive and active in all its fearfulness only on the left hand of God.

But the atonement accomplished in Jesus Christ, like creation and the providential rule of God, is a work on the right hand of God, a work of His positive will. It is so in the highest possible sense, in a way which gives it priority and precedence over creation and providence. In Jesus Christ God comes to grips with that episode. Jesus Christ is in fact God's retort to the sin of man. This does not mean even remotely that it, too, is only an episode. Even from the point of view of God's antithesis to the sin of man, what took place in it is rather the execution, that is, the sealing and revelation, the original fact of the positive will of God in His relationship with man, and therefore of His whole will in creation and preservation. It is not simply to combat the interruption of that will, it is not merely to assert and purify polemically and yet also irenically His relationship with man, and therefore with the whole world as it was created by Him, in face of the breaking out and in of human sin, that God willed to become man and did in fact do so. He willed to do it and did it first and foremost for this positive end, to give concrete reality and actuality to the promise " I will be your God " and the command " Ye shall be my people " within the human race which could not say this of itself, but was to hear it as His Word and to live by this Word to His glory. He willed to do it and did it in order to fulfil both the promise and the command in divine truth and power, in order not only to make it possible for us men to receive them, but actually to make them heard by us (in an act which is at once one of utter condescension and supreme majesty), in order to set them amongst us and therefore to make them effective for us. What takes place in Jesus Christ, in the historical event of the atonement accomplished by Him in time, is not simply one history amongst others and not simply the reaction of God against human sin. It stands at the heart of the Christian message and the Christian faith because here God maintains and fulfils His Word as it was spoken at the very first. He affirms to us and sets among us His original promise and His original command in the concrete reality and actuality of His own being as man. He maintains and fulfils it in His conflict with our sin, vindicating His own glory and accomplishing our salvation. But He maintains and fulfils it first and foremost in affirmation and execution of the original purpose of His relationship with us men : *propter nos homines* and therefore *propter nostram salutem* (*Nic. Const.*). The atonement in Jesus Christ takes place as a wrestling with and an overcoming of human sin. But at the same time and primarily it is the great act of God's faithfulness to Himself and therefore to us—His faithfulness in the execution of the plan and purpose which He had from the very first as the Creator of all things and the Lord of all events, and which He wills to accomplish in all circumstances. For this reason in Jesus Christ we are not merely dealing with one of many beings in the sphere of the created world and the world of men. He is this, too. Because He is this, because He is a being like us and with us, He enables us actually to hear the Word of God and the promise and commandment of God, and the execution of the divine purpose is fulfilled for us and as such revealed to us. As such He is born in time, at His own time. But in Jesus Christ we are not merely dealing with the author of our justification and sanctification as the sinners that we are. We are not merely dealing with the One who has saved us from death, with the Lord and Head of His Church. As such, as the One who fulfils this divine work in the world, which would be lost without Him, He is born in time, at His own time. But at the same time and beyond all that—and the power of His saving work as the Mediator is rooted and grounded in this—He is " the first-born of all creation " (Col. 1^{16})—the first and eternal Word of God delivered and fulfilled in time. As very God and very man He is the concrete reality and actuality of the divine command and the divine promise, the content of the will of God which exists prior to its fulfilment, the basis of the whole project and actualisation of creation and the whole process of divine providence from which all created being and becoming derives. Certainly the sin of man contradicts this first and eternal Word of God. But in the first and eternal Word of God the sin of man is already met, refuted and removed from all eternity. And in delivering and fulfilling this first and eternal Word in spite of human sin and its consequences, as He would in fact have delivered and fulfilled it quite apart from human sin, sin is also met, refuted and removed in time.

In this sense the atonement accomplished in Jesus Christ is a necessary happening. This is its unconditional validity and scope and binding force. This is why it commands the reverence due to it as the heart of the Christian message (a reverence which is the basis of all the joy and certainty and freedom of faith). For in Jesus Christ we do not have to do with a second, and subsequent, but with the first and original content of the will of God, before and above which there is no other will—either hidden or revealed in some other way—in the light of which we might have to understand and fear and love God and interpret man very differently from how they are both represented in Jesus Christ. We do not need to look beyond Jesus Christ. We do not need to consider whether it may be obligatory or legitimate to look beyond Him. When we look at Him we have all conceivable clarity and certainty. We only need to look at Him. We only need to hear the word of His historical existence and we shall hear the Word of God and look into the basis and essence of God and man and all things. The covenant between God and man, the promise and command of God, which Jesus Christ announces to us as their unity, is therefore the final thing to which we can and should and must cling, because Jesus Christ as their unity is also the first thing, because the covenant is by promise and commandment eternally grounded in Him, in the unity of God and man accomplished in Him. The recognition

that this covenant is the presupposition of the atonement is therefore
nothing more or less than a recognition of the sure basis of the Christian
message and the Christian faith. Quite apart from the fact that it is
true and necessary in itself, it would be quite out of place to ignore it.

In this recognition it is a matter of the basis of a right distinction,
a right acknowledgment and a right regard for the act of atonement.
Therefore once again—and from two angles—we must be quite clear
with what we have to do in the presupposition which it confirms and
reveals. It consists in this, that Jesus Christ, very God and very
man, born and living and acting and suffering and conquering in
time, is as such the one eternal Word of God at the beginning of all
things.

This means at once that as the beginning of all things the presupposition of the atonement is a single, self-sufficient, independent
free work of God in itself, which is not identical with the divine work
in creation or with the divine creative will realised in this work. The
achievement of atonement and therefore the historical actuality of
Jesus Christ is not the highest evolutionary continuation, the crown
and completion of the positing which God has willed and accomplished
of a reality of the world and man which is distinct from Himself. It
is not the immanent *telos* of such a reality.

Here again we part company with Schleiermacher. To do him justice, he
was in his own way concerned about the eternal basis and necessity of the appearance of Jesus Christ and therefore of the atonement as the overcoming of human
sin. But this was how he conceived of the connexion and made the required
reference and regress to the beginning of all things. The fulfilling of time in
Jesus Christ meant for him that at the end of their historical development man,
and in man finite being as such, attained in Jesus Christ that form to which they
had always been potentially inclined and endowed in the relationship of complete
dependence on God as infinite being. God's eternal will is done in Jesus Christ
in such a way that in Him—in the undisturbed unity of His man-consciousness
with His God-consciousness—man attains to the perfection ordained and necessary to him as man.

In this conception (as so often in Schleiermacher) there is a strange mixture
of truth and error. (Truth,) because the New Testament itself indicates quite
clearly, in the light of what is revealed in Jesus Christ, that we cannot understand too intimately or emphasise too strongly the relationship of the being of
man and the world in their creatureliness with the being of Jesus Christ. (Error)
because everything is plainly topsy-turvy if we picture this relationship in such
a way that the being of Jesus Christ is deduced and interpreted from the being
of man and the world instead of the other way round, if we derive the atonement
from creation instead of creation from the atonement, if we describe as the first
and eternal Word of God that which we think we can recognise, i.e., postulate
and maintain as the final word on the evolutionary process of finite being and
development. No ideas or pronouncements on a supposedly attainable or attained
telos of the immanent development of creaturely being can do justice to the
telos, and therefore the beginning, revealed in Jesus Christ. We cannot overlook
the fact that in relation to Jesus Christ the New Testament speaks of a new
creation (Gal. 6[15]; 2 Cor. 5[17]), of a new man created by God (Eph. 4[24]), not of
a continuation of man but of a " new birth " (Jn. 3[3]), and indeed of a new heaven
and a new earth (Rev. 21[1]; 2 Pet. 3[13]). And Jesus Christ is not regarded as

the fulfilment and highest form of the first Adam, but in sharp antithesis He is described as the last Adam (" The first man is of the earth, earthy, the second man is the Lord from heaven," I Cor. 15⁴⁴ᶠ·).

The right distinction of the atonement from every purely contingent event, the right acknowledgment of its validity and scope, the right regard for that which God has said and done in it, and therefore the right recognition of the covenant which is its presupposition and which is revealed in it, the right recognition, then, of the sure basis of the Christian message and Christian faith—all these things depend on the insight that in Jesus Christ we really have to do with the first and eternal Word of God at the beginning of all things. With the beginning of all things in God, in His will and purpose and resolve, which does not follow or derive from but underlies and precedes all that reality which is distinct from Himself, the existence and history of the world and man, and therefore creation. Jesus Christ is in truth the first, i.e., the content and subject of that first divine will and purpose and resolve which underlies the beginning of the creaturely world and is therefore superior to it. This is what makes Him so new in relation to all that precedes Him in the creaturely world. He is the other, the second and last Adam as opposed to the first, just because He was before him. This is what marks Him out and distinguishes Him from Adam and from everything else that is, happens, becomes, comes and goes before and after and beside Him. He cannot, therefore, be deduced from that which is other than Himself, from that which was before Him. He is not a product—not even the most perfect —of the created world as such. He is in it. He belongs to it. He exists and works and reveals Himself in its history. But He does not derive from it : it derives from Him. He is in it but He is also quite different from it. He stands over against it as the One who was from the beginning—its beginning—with God. He is the content and form of the divine thought of grace, will of grace and decree of grace in relation to the created world, before the created world was. He is the One for whose sake God willed it and created it. He is the meaning and purpose which it has because God willed to give it to it and did in fact give it to it. The creation, too, and the preservation and direction of the world and man, must be described as pure acts of divine grace. But even here we must think strictly of Jesus Christ in whom these acts had and have their meaning and purpose. The existence and work of Jesus Christ do not follow from the gracious act of creation or the gracious act of divine providence. It is for the sake of Jesus Christ that creation takes place and God rules as the preserver and controller of world-events. These things are all acts of divine grace only because they take place for His sake.

For in Jesus Christ we have to do with something that is new and special in relation to creation as such—the fact that God has elected and determined Himself as the fellow and friend of man, and elected and determined man as His own friend and fellow. This is the divine thought of grace and will of grace and decree of grace in relation to the world before the world was. This is the meaning and purpose which He had in creating it. How can this derive from the world itself? How can it be its product or *telos*? How can it be deduced from it or explained by it? Man has his real being in the fact that his existence was willed and is actual in this meaning and purpose. Man is—and he is what he is as the creature of God and by divine providence—only as and because, before he himself was, there was in the will and purpose and decree of God this grace towards him. He is in virtue of this eternal Word of God, which is free in relation to himself and the whole world, which has already made disposition concerning himself and the whole world. He is in virtue of the covenant already concluded with God. This is the presupposition of the atonement revealed in it and fulfilled in history by the fact that God became man. But this covenant of God with man is grace. It is not given in and with the nature of the creature. It is not the product or goal of that nature, although that nature itself is from God. God did not and does not owe it to the creature, not even to man, to elect and determine Himself for him, and him for Himself, to will and posit his existence and essence according to this meaning and purpose. Man has no right or claim as man—because he is created man for this purpose—to stand in covenant with God. The fact that he is created for it is something beyond the grace of his created nature. It is the free covenant grace of God which is especially for him. He can perceive and accept it only in the first eternal Word of God as spoken to him in the atonement accomplished in time, in Jesus Christ. It is not in an act of spontaneous self-knowledge, but in the hearing of this first and eternal Word of God, that he can know that he does actually stand on this ground, that he is actually placed in this sphere and atmosphere, in the sphere of the covenant as the being with whom God has associated Himself and whom God has associated with Himself. But that this grace is truth, the first and final truth behind which there is concealed no other or different truth, that he can be and live absolutely by this truth, is something which he can and must perceive and accept in the first and eternal Word of God as it is spoken to him in time. This is the presupposition of the atonement revealed in the atonement. And in the recognition of this presupposition he comes to a right distinction, acknowledgment and regard.

But we must now add, or emphasise and underline a second point. The first and eternal Word of God, which underlies and precedes the creative will and work as the beginning of all things in God, means in fact Jesus Christ. It is identical with the One who, very God and very man, born and living and acting and suffering and conquering in time, accomplishes the atonement. It is He alone who is the content and form of the gracious thought and will and resolve of God in relation to the world and man before ever these were and as God willed and created them.

ἄσαρκος

In this context we must not refer to the second " person " of the Trinity as such, to the eternal Son or the eternal Word of God *in abstracto*, and therefore to the so-called λόγος ἄσαρκος. What is the point of a regress to Him as the supposed basis of the being and knowledge of all things ? In any case, how can we make such a regress ? The second " person " of the Godhead in Himself and as such is not God the Reconciler. In Himself and as such He is not revealed to us. In Himself and as such He is not *Deus pro nobis*, either ontologically or epistemologically. He is the content of a necessary and important concept in trinitarian doctrine when we have to understand the revelation and dealings of God in the light of their free basis in the inner being and essence of God. But since we are now concerned with the revelation and dealings of God, and particularly with the atonement, with the person and work of the Mediator, it is pointless, as it is impermissible, to return to the inner being and essence of God and especially to the second person of the Trinity as such, in such a way that we ascribe to this person another form than that which God Himself has given in willing to reveal Himself and to act outwards. If it is true that God became man, then in this we have to recognise and respect His eternal will and purpose and resolve—His free and gracious will which He did not owe it either to Himself or to the world to have, by which He did not need to come to the decision to which He has in fact come, and behind which, in these circumstances, we cannot go, behind which we do not have to reckon with any Son of God in Himself, with any λόγος ἄσαρκος, with any other Word of God than that which was made flesh. According to the free and gracious will of God the eternal Son of God is Jesus Christ as He lived and died and rose again in time, and none other. He is the decision of God in time, and yet according to what took place in time the decision which was made from all eternity. This decision was made freely and graciously and undeservedly in an overflowing of the divine goodness. Yet—for us to whom it refers and for whose sake it was taken—it was also made bindingly, inescapably and irrevocably. We cannot, therefore, go back on it. We must not ignore it and imagine a " Logos in itself " which does not have this content and form, which is the eternal Word of God without this form and content. We could only imagine such a Logos. Like Godhead abstracted from its revelation and acts, it would necessarily be an empty concept which we would then, of course, feel obliged to fill with all kinds of contents of our own arbitrary invention. Under the title of a λόγος ἄσαρκος we pay homage to a *Deus absconditus* and therefore to some image of God which we have made for ourselves. And if we were to deal with a figure of this kind, we should be dangerously susceptible to the temptation, indeed we could hardly escape it, of asking whether the revelation and activity of this " Logos in itself " can altogether and always be confined to this phenomenon, the incarnation in Jesus Christ. If this is not as such the content of the eternal will of God, if Jesus Christ is not the one Word of God from all eternity, why are we not free, or even perhaps obliged, to reckon with other manifestations of the eternal Word of God, and to look at Him in the light of such manifestations ? But how can we really, as it were, bracket that which God has actually done and therefore willed in Jesus Christ, not taking it seriously as His eternal will, not holding to it as the beginning of all things which in His free grace God willed to posit and has in fact posited, to which therefore we must hold ? How can we look away past and beyond Him ? Is it real faith and obedience which concerns itself with this regress to a pre-temporal being of the Word of God which is not His incarnate being, the being of the *Deus pro nobis* ? Is it real faith and obedience which tries to set itself on the throne of God and there to construct the content and form of His will and Word which He Himself has not chosen, although He might perhaps have chosen it ?

We are told that it is inconceivable that all men, " even those who lived thousands of years before Jesus," should have their being in the history of Jesus, that the history of human existence should derive from that of the man Jesus (Brunner, *ZThK* 1951, p. 98). But is it so inconceivable, does it need such a great imagination to realise, is it not the simplest thing in the world, that if the history of Jesus is the event of atonement, if the atonement is real and effective because God Himself became man to be the subject of this event, if this is not concealed but revealed, if it is the factor which calls us irresistibly to faith and obedience, then how can it be otherwise than that in this factor, and therefore in the history of Jesus, we have to do with the reality which underlies and precedes all other reality as the first and eternal Word of God, that in this history we have actually to do with the ground and sphere, the atmosphere of the being of every man, whether they lived thousands of years before or after Jesus ? Does not this question, this protest against the incarnate Word as the content of the eternal will of God, involve a retrogression even behind Schleiermacher, who with his doctrine of the fulfilment of creation accomplished in Jesus Christ could at least in his own way do justice to the necessary connexion between the totality of the human race and the particular history of Jesus ? What is there to protest against if we simply accept that act of the greatest divine condescension and supreme divine majesty, the incarnation of His Word in Jesus Christ in the work of atonement, thus taking it in all earnest and not merely half in earnest.

But if Jesus Christ is the content and form of the first and eternal Word of God, then that means further that the beginning of all things, of the being of all men and of the whole world, even the divine willing of creation, is preceded by God's covenant with man as its basis and purpose : His promise, in which He binds and pledges Himself to man, and His command by which He pledges and binds man to Himself. At the beginning of all things in God there is the Gospel and the Law, the gracious address of God and the gracious claim of God, both directed to man, both the one Word of the *Deus pro nobis* who is the one God and beside whom there is no other. For Jesus Christ—not an empty *Logos*, but Jesus Christ the incarnate Word, the baby born in Bethlehem, the man put to death at Golgotha and raised again in the garden of Joseph of Arimathea, the man whose history this is— is the unity of the two. He is both at one and the same time. He is the promise and the command, the Gospel and the Law, the address of God to man and the claim of God upon man. That He is both as the Word of God spoken in His work, as the Word of God which has become work, is something which belongs to Himself as the eternal Son of God for Himself and prior to us. In this He is the pre-existent *Deus pro nobis*. He alone is at once and altogether very God and very man. To that extent He alone is there at the beginning of all things. As the basis and purpose of the covenant He and He alone is the content of the eternal will of God which precedes the whole being of man and of the world. But that which He is for Himself and prior to us. He is with a view to us. He is, therefore, the concrete reality and actuality of the promise and command of God, the fulfilment of both, very God and very man, in one person amongst us, as a fellow-man. This first and eternal Word of God is not spoken in the void, but addressed to us. Therefore the event of the atonement is clearly His being for our sake, for our salvation, for the restoration of our relationship with God interrupted by sin. It is, therefore, this relationship with God, grounded on God's relationship with us, which in His person, that is so different and yet directed to us and in its humanity so near to us because perfectly identical with us, is revealed as the basis of the atonement and made effective for us—the pre-existent *Deus pro nobis*.

He and He alone is very God and very man in a temporal fulfilment of God's eternal will to be the true God of man and to let the man who belongs to Him become and be true man. Ultimately, therefore, Jesus Christ alone is the content of the eternal will of God, the eternal covenant between God and man. He is this as the Word of God to us and the work of God for us, and therefore in a way quite different from and not to be compared with anything we may become as hearers of this Word and those for whose sake this work is done. Yet in this difference, in the majesty with which He confronts us, but does confront us, He is the Word and work of the eternal covenant. In the truth and power of this eternal Word and work He speaks the Word and accomplishes the work of atonement in its temporal occurrence. And as we look at this Word and work, and trust in it and build upon it, we can be assured of the atonement which in it has been made in time. And since Jesus Christ is not only the subject but also the eternal and primary basis of this act of atonement, this act is definitively distinguished from all others. It demands our unconditional recognition. It lays claim to our regard. And we can have the certainty and the joy and the freedom of the faith that in spite of our sin and to take away our sin and all its consequences it has taken place once and for all. All this depends on a right recognition of the presupposition of the atonement in the counsel of God, and especially on the fact that we perceive and maintain the content and form of the eternal divine counsel exactly as it is fulfilled and revealed in time.

It is now time, and it will serve as an illustration of what we have just said, to consider a development in the history of theology to which we have so far only alluded. In the older Reformed Church there was a theology in which the concept of the covenant played so decisive a role that it came to be known as the Federal theology. It is usually connected with the name of John Coccejus (1603–1669, and Prof. in Bremen, Franeker and Leiden) in whose *Summa doctrinae de foedere et testamento Dei* (1648) it did indeed find classical and systematic form. But even before Coccejus the concept *foedus* had with varying emphasis been given prominence in a variety of conceptions, expositions and applications by quite a number of writers of whom only the best-known will be mentioned. The immediate predecessors of Coccejus were his own teachers, the theologians of the Herborn school (with whom we must also reckon the then Count John the Elder of Nassau-Dillenburg): Matthias Martini, Ludwig Crocius, W. Amesius, J. Cloppenburg. But these in turn were preceded by the Basel writers Polanus and Wolleb and the Dutch Gomarus, and we can then work back to Z. Ursinus (who was not uninfluenced by Melanchthon) and K. Olevian in Heidelberg,

Andreas Hyperius in Marburg, Wolfgang Musculus in Berne, P. Boquin in France, Stephan Szegedin in Hungary, and ultimately the Reformers themselves, Zwingli, Bullinger and Calvin. And the Federal Theology continued to develop even after Coccejus, making headway in spite of the opposition of the older aristotelian-scholastic schools. In Holland it made alliance with Cartesian philosophy and found well-equipped and independent champions in Abraham Heidan and Franz Burmann, also Heinrich Heidegger in Zurich. We can say indeed that in the second half of the 17th century it was the ruling orthodoxy of the Reformed Church. Certainly what H. Heppe in the 19th century represented as the theology of the Reformed Evangelical Church corresponds to it. It even had an influence on political and juridical theory in the person of J. Althusius, a jurist of the Herborn school which preceded Coccejus. The Bremen theologian, F. A. Lampe, then secured its acceptance amongst the Pietists, who developed and applied it in many different ways. At the beginning of the 18th century it also had an occasional influence amongst Lutherans, and if the Lutheran historian G. Schrenk is right (*Gottesreich und Bund im älteren Protestantismus*, 1923) the earlier form of the " redemption-history " school of Erlangen and especially J. C. K. von Hofmann would have been quite unthinkable without it, and indirectly it had a certain exemplary significance for the philosophy of history of German Idealism, and in this way even for the Marxist view of history. This is not the place for a historical or systematic exposition and estimate of a development which was certainly remarkable in its own way. But from the standpoint which we have ourselves reached we must make certain distinctions in relation to what was and was not said in the course of this doctrinal tradition of the older Reformed Church.

1. The Federal theology was an advance on mediæval scholasticism, and the Protestant scholasticism which preceded and surrounded it, in that (true to the century of the *baroque*) it tried to understand the work and Word of God attested in Holy Scripture dynamically and not statically, as an event and not as a system of objective and self-contained truths. When we read Coccejus—even as compared with Polan, Wolleb and the Leidner Synopsis—we cannot escape the impression that the traditional dogmatics had started to move like a frozen stream of lava. The " Loci " are no longer " Loci," common places, to which this and that must be related either not at all or on the basis of a presupposed concept, as abstract doctrine and truth revealed in and for itself. They are now different stages in a series of events, the individual moments in a movement. This movement is now understood as such to be Christian truth, and Christian doctrine is the description of this movement. This theology is concerned with the bold review of a history of God and man which unfolds itself from creation to the day of judgment. In relation to the two partners it is concerned with the history of the covenant (a history which is naturally initiated and controlled and guided to its proper end by God)—or what in the 19th century came to be called the history of redemption. We find something of the living dynamic of this history in the famous chapters in which Calvin himself (*Instit.* II, 9–11) had tried to apprehend the relationship between the Old and the New Testament under the concept of the one covenant.

But the more embracing and central and exact this apprehension becomes in the main period of the Federal theology, the more insistently the question imposes itself from what standpoint this occurrence is really regarded and represented as such. What happens when the work, the Word of God, is first isolated and then reconnected, according to the teaching of pragmatic theology, with a whole series of events which are purposefully strung out but which belong together ? Does this really correspond to the state of affairs as it is prescribed for theology in Scripture ? Can we historicise the activity and revelation of God ? The Federal theologians were the first really to try to do this in principle, just as they were the first to read the Bible as a divinely inspired source-book by the study of which the attentive and faithful reader can gain an insight and perspective into the whole drama of the relationship between God and man, act by act, as by the help of some other source-book he might do in any other historical field. They saw excellently that the Bible tells us about an event. But they did not see that in all its forms this narrative has the character of testimony, proclamation, evangel, and that it has as its content and subject only a single event, which in every form of the attestation, although they all relate to a whole, is the single and complete decision on the part of God which as such calls for a single and complete decision on the part of man. They overlooked the fact that in all the forms of its attestation this single and complete event is a special event which has to be understood in a special way. Because of the difference of the attestation it cannot be broken up into a series of different covenant acts, or acts of redemption, which follow one another step by step, and then reassembled into a single whole. The Federal theologians did not notice that for all the exclusiveness with which they read the Scriptures, in this analysis and synthesis of the occurrence between God and man they were going beyond Scripture and missing its real content. If we think that we can handle the work and Word of God in this manner, then in our dynamic way we go beyond or fall short of Scripture and its content no less than did the older orthodoxy with its predominantly static terminology. As becomes increasingly plain in the sketches of the Federal theologians, the atonement accomplished in Jesus Christ ceases to be the history of the covenant, to which (in all the different forms of expectation and recollection) the whole Bible bears witness and in face of which theology must take up and maintain its standpoint, and it becomes a biblical history, a stage in the greater context of world-history, before which, and after which, there are other similar stages. In the case of the Federal theologians the standpoint directly in face of the witness to this one event changed its character and became a higher vantage-point from which they could see it together with all the other stages, from which they thought that they could and should make it their business to portray these stages in their variety and inter-relationship. They brought the whole under the concept of the covenant, but they did not read the concept out of this one event. Instead, they imported the concept into this one event like all the others, as the supposed essence of the varied occurrence at every stage. The Federal theology was a theological historicism to the extent that it did not allow itself to be bound to Scripture and confined to the event attested in Scripture in accordance with its reformation inheritance. And with its analysis and synthesis was it not more autonomous in relation to Scripture than it would admit to itself and gave impression to others—for it was here that what is still called " biblicism " had its origin ? Could it be long before there would be a necessary demand for a wider outlook from that vantage-point, and a transition to a philosophy of general religious history, the perception and portrayal of a gradual " education of the human race " ? It is clear that we cannot follow this theology even in its first and formal statement.

2. We will now look in a different direction. There was a very remarkable reason for the first introduction of the covenant concept by Zwingli (cf. G. Schrenk, *op. cit.* p. 36 f.). He used it purely and simply for the defence of infant baptism. The Anabaptists in Switzerland and elsewhere liked to describe themselves as " covenant-members," and their believers' baptism as a covenant, the sign of the true covenant, the covenant of grace, in contrast to the Abrahamic covenant of circumcision—the covenant which in a wild misunderstanding of the name Pontius [1] in the Apostles' Creed they described as the covenant of Pilate under which Christ suffered. In his writings *De peccato originali* (1526) and *In catabaptistarum strophas elenchus* (1527)—his practical concern was to defend the national Church—Zwingli used against them the following argument.

---

[1] The misunderstanding derives from the superficial resemblance between the Swiss-German " *puntnus* " (covenant) and Pontius.—Trans.

God first made a covenant with Adam, then with Noah, for the whole human race. He then made a covenant with Abraham for the people of Israel. But it was always the one covenant valid from the foundation of the world to its end, providing for human sin with the determination of Jesus as Mediator and Redeemer. Therefore we heathen who believe in Jesus are one in faith with Abraham, and therefore one people, one Church, with the people of Israel, heirs of the one testament, the only difference being that now that Christ has appeared in accordance with the original determination it is proclaimed and delivered to all nations, the ceremonies of the covenant with Israel are done away, and the light which lightened the fathers has shone out all the more brightly on us. (The drift of the argument is this.) If the children of Israel were as such, before they believed, included in the Abrahamic covenant, why should the same not be true of our children ? If they received the covenant sign of circumcision, are ours not placed at an intolerable disadvantage if they do not receive baptism ? But—apart from the christological content—the real point of interest in Zwingli's conception is the universal meaning and purpose which he tried to give to the covenant concept, his insistence on the covenant with Noah and even a covenant with Adam, in relation to which, and in the light of its limitations done away at the appearance of Christ, the Abrahamic covenant would almost appear to be an episode were it not that by virtue of its aiming at Christ it is already so complete that everything *post Christum natum* is seen to be only the carrying out of it and is measured by it as its standard. For Bullinger, too—who had the same practical concern about infant baptism—the new covenant is the fulfilment of the covenant with Abraham, and as such it is also the ratification of the *fœdus Dei æternum* with the whole human race, which did not cease to be a covenant of grace, or to apply to all men, because of the intervention of the law of the covenant with Israel. If it can be said that these two Zurich reformers already had a Federal theology, this universalism is its most remarkable feature. As they see it, the covenant consists in the primitive institution and revelation of a promise and of the command of faith in that promise, and of the corresponding obedience. The people or Church of the covenant is not identical with the whole race. But from the very first the covenant is open to the whole race. It is not a private concern either of Israel or of pious Christians. If the covenant is understood as the presupposition of the atonement accomplished in Jesus Christ as it is revealed in that event, then necessarily the concept does have this universal orientation : not in the sense that all men are members as such and without further ado—if that were the case it would no longer be a covenant of the free grace of God—but in the sense that as the promise and command of God it does seriously apply to all men and is made for all men, that it is the destiny of all men to become and to be members of this covenant. In this way it is the living work and Word of God in contrast to a truth concerning the being of all men as such, a metaphysical concept necessarily implicated in the being of man—or in contrast to a truth concerning the being of some men but not of others. The scheme was not altogether satisfactory as a basis for infant baptism, but in its actual content it stood for something which cannot be surrendered, the character of the covenant as the true light which lighteth every man (Jn. 1⁹) and for which, therefore, every man is claimed.

Unfortunately in the later development of the (Federal theology) this universalism in the thought of the covenant was quickly obscured if not obliterated, as we can see from its classical form in Coccejus. The reason was that these " modern " theologians, and it is remarkable that it was the " moderns," tried to maintain the grim doctrine (which does logically follow from Calvin's conception of predestination) that Christ did not die for all men but only for the elect. It was deduced that the covenant, at any rate the covenant of grace (beside which they now believed they could discern another covenant) is from all eternity and in its temporal fulfilment a kind of separate arrangement between

God and these particular men, the *electi*, which means in practice the true adherents of the true Israelitish-Christian religion. A theology of biblical history was now replaced by a theology of biblical histories. In the recognition of the covenant the atonement made in Jesus Christ was no longer accepted as the revelation of it. Scripture was not understood as the witness to this one event. It was not read as a witness at all, but as a historical record of a pragmatico-theological character. In these circumstances the outcome was inevitable. The most significant thing in these histories and the *telos* of all of them was that they offered examples in which certain men as distinct from others emerged as genuine hearers of the Word of God and partners in His work. They, and others like them, must obviously be regarded as the covenant-partners of God, and only they. In this way the conception of the covenant led into a blind alley in which it could not embrace and apply to all but only to some : those who could be regarded as the elect in virtue of their personal relationship with God as determined one way or another — as though this is not necessarily contradicted by the calling and attitude of all genuine hearers of the Word of God and partners in His work ; as though in relation to the God active and revealed in Jesus Christ we cannot, and must not, see that all other men are under the sign of the covenant set up by Him, so that far from any particularism we have to look on them with hope. But if we do not look exclusively to Jesus Christ and therefore to God we lose the capacity on this basis to think inclusively. Historicism in theology always involves psychologism, and with those who try to be serious Christians in spite of their historicism it will be of a gloomy and pessimistic and unfriendly type ; although at any moment, and this is what happened in the 18th century, it can transform itself without difficulty into its very opposite, a cheap universalism. Clearly we cannot follow the Federal theology when it takes this path, in opposition to its own earlier, from a historical standpoint, very remarkable form.

3. What is the meaning and character of the covenant according to this theology ? We have seen that Zwingli and Bullinger regarded it quite unequivocally as a covenant of grace. So, too, does Calvin in those two chapters of the *Institutes*, II, 9–11, which the shadow of his doctrine of an eternal double predestination has hardly touched. As he sees it, the covenant made with the fathers was already the *foedus evangelii*, of which Christ was not only the fulfilment but the eternal basis. The distinctions between the fathers and us do not any of them relate to the substance of the covenant, which was and is the same, but only to the *modus administrationis*. It is only its *accidentia, annexa accessoria*, which have been abrogated and made obsolete by the appearance of Christ. We live with them, and they lived with us, by the same promises, under the same command, by the same grace. The only difference is that for us they are incomparably more sure and certain, and that whereas for them the covenant meant servitude for us it means freedom. Similarly—and here Calvin was writing against the Anabaptists and in favour of the national Church—the sacraments of the Old Testament have changed only in form, but in substance they are identical with those of the New. In Calvin there can be no question of the Law destroying the character of the covenant as a covenant of grace, nor can we find any combination of the covenant concept with a primitive *lex naturae*. This idea came in as a result of the influence which Melanchthon came to exercise on Reformed theology—in his old age he for his part was accused of a leaning to Calvinism. In this respect we first find it in W. Musculus and S. Szegedin. Here, in contrast to Zwingli, Bullinger and Calvin, the concept of the *foedus* is suddenly divided into that of a *foedus generale*, the temporal covenant of God with the universe, the earth and man as part of creation, and the eternal *foedus speciale*, which embraces all the elect from the beginning of the world as the true seed of Abraham, and which is split up into three periods, *ante legem, sub lege, post legem*. Notice the part allotted already to the Law as a principle of order.

Notice, too, that here the *foedus speciale* is the eternal covenant while the *foedus generale* is only a temporal. The introduction of what later became the dominant twofold concept must be attributed to Ursinus (*S. Theol*, 1584, *qu.* 36, cf. 10 and 30 f.). There is a *foedus naturae* which was contracted with man at creation and is therefore known to man by nature. It promises eternal life to those who obey, but threatens eternal punishment to those who disobey. In contrast there is a *foedus gratiae* which is not known to man by nature. This is the fulfilling of the Law accomplished by Christ, our restoration by His Spirit, the free promise of the gift of eternal life to those who believe in Him. Nature and grace are both on the same historical level, and confront one another as the principles of individual covenants. We hear the voice of Calvin again and find traces of a different spirit in Olevian's work, *De substantia foederis gratuiti* (1585), in which, following Jer. 31, the covenant is again described uniformly, unequivocally and exclusively as the covenant of grace. But although Coccejus thought of Olevian with particular gratitude as his predecessor, in this important respect the later development followed the lead of Ursinus. In Franz Gomarus (*Oratio de foedere Dei*, 1594), who was clearly inclined to a certain unity of outlook—he was a strict Supralapsarian—we find the peculiar doctrine of two covenants which are founded at the same time and run concurrently and everywhere merge into each other. The first is a *foedus naturale*, which demands perfect obedience, concluded with the first parents and in them with the whole of the human race after creation, and repeated by Moses the Lawgiver. The second is a *foedus supernaturale*, in which Christ is made over to those who believe in Him and repent, not by the power of nature, but by grace. But the rivalry of the two principles cannot be overcome. Polan (in whom the covenant played only an incidental role) seems to have rendered the doubtful service of replacing the concept *foedus naturale* by what was regarded as a better description *foedus operum*, and occasionally at any rate Wolleb followed his example.

We can ignore the variations of the Herborn school in their presentation of what had now become an established dualism (given confessional status for the first time in Art. 7 of the *Westminster Confession*). Instead we will turn at once to Coccejus himself. He begins with the covenant of works, which is for him the ruling principle. This covenant is based on the Law with its promise and threats. The Law was written on the heart of Adam and is still attested by conscience. It was pronounced as the Word of God in the prohibition concerning the tree of knowledge of good and evil in Paradise, and in content it agrees with the Mosaic decalogue. The tree of life is the symbol and sacrament of the eternal life promised to the perfectly obedient man and accruing to him as a reward. The divine likeness of Adam, which is taken to mean the wisdom of his understanding, the right disposition of his will and the innocence of his spirit and affections, meant that he was fully equipped (and with him the human race covenanted with God in his person) to keep the command and therefore to participate in the promise. But his will was not unalterable and it had not yet become established in obedience. According to Coccejus everything else follows as a series of abrogations (*abrogationes, antiquationes*) of this covenant of works.

The first abrogation is by sin. Consciously and voluntarily, and with God's permission, Adam does that which is forbidden. In so doing, he and all his descendants forfeit their friendship with God, their divine likeness and the status of promise, falling under the divine curse and judgment.

The second is related to the first and consists in the institution of the covenant of grace. Man as mercifully preserved by God is bound to Him by the law of nature and the mercy of God, but He is incapable of fulfilling his obligation. Therefore God creates an effective instrument to restore man, an instrument which answers at once both to His goodness and also to His righteousness. He adopts man into a new agreement by which He wills to give man a Mediator and therefore in this just person new fellowship and peace with Himself and the promised eternal life—not now as a reward which has been earned but as a free gift. The only response demanded of sinful man is that of faith. This third step, and therefore the second abrogation of the covenant of works—we will return to this later—is understood by Coccejus as the unfolding of a pre-temporal occurrence, an eternal and free contract (*pactum*) made between God the Father and God the Son, in which the Father represents the righteousness and the Son the mercy of God, the latter adopting the function of a Mediator and pledge in the place of men.

In the third abrogation of the covenant of works as Coccejus sees it, we return to the earth and history. It is the announcing of the covenant of grace in the economy of the Old Testament prefigured in the proto-Gospel of Gen. 3¹⁵ᶠ·. This is a form of the relationship between God and man which has the covenant of grace as its hidden basis, but a basis which is occasionally revealed. In this form as we are told in Rom. 3, there is a πάρεσις, an overlooking and ignoring of human sin, but not its ἄφεσις, its real forgiveness, and therefore the justification of sinners. It is all still a matter of type and instruction. The righteous are still intermingled with the wicked. Bondage still rules, and with it the fear of death. But all the same the Law, with its demand for righteousness and its types and shadows, is a witness to the promise. Circumcision and the passover already point to the atoning death of Christ. Everything is still a matter of expectation. It is only the Old Testament. But it is a sure expectation of the covenant of grace and therefore of the New Testament. And to that extent it is an abrogation of the first, of the covenant of works. This is revealed in the benefits of the New Testament: in the demonstration of our perfect righteousness in the obedience of the Son of God fulfilling the whole Law; in the revelation of the name of God; in the writing of the Law on our human hearts by the Spirit; in the freeing of consciences by that ἄφεσις τῶν ἁμαρτιῶν which now replaces the mere πάρεσις; in the liberation from the fear of death and the planting of the Church among the Gentiles.

The fourth abrogation of the covenant of works Coccejus calls the death of the body, i.e., the sanctification which in the work of Christ goes hand in hand with justification, sanctification as purification, as the destruction of the works of the devil and the darkness of the intellect and the badness of the human will. The Law is now a weapon in the warfare of the spirit against the flesh. The tribulations which still remain, including death, are instruments for the testing of faith and the taming of sin, opportunities for the exercise of love. That this conflict takes place distinguishes the regenerate from the unregenerate. The regenerate will not commit wilful sin, and from those that remain he will always seek refuge in the grace of God, earnest self-examination, and prayer for a pure heart.

The fifth and final abrogation of the covenant of works is what Coccejus calls the reawakening of the body. He is thinking here of the eschatological redemption and consummation. With this the validity of the covenant of works ceases altogether—that is, for the righteous. Nothing remains but the operation of the mediatorship of the guarantor of the covenant of grace and its obedience, and this operation is eternal life and salvation by the resurrection from the dead in virtue of His merit, in which the souls of the pious participate directly at death.

We relate our question concerning the essence and character of the covenant to this sketch of Coccejus because for all his individuality in relation to his predecessors and successors Coccejus represents the Federal theology in a form which is not only the most perfect, but also the ripest and strongest and most impressive.

There was one point in which the successors of Coccejus at once departed from his scheme, and it has been the subject of most of the objections against him right up to the presentations given in the dogmatic history of our own day. This is his at first sight exclusively negative estimate and presentation of the whole history of the covenant in relation to its beginning, as a gradual abrogation of the covenant of works. And in this respect two discordant features have to be noted. (First,) the second and obviously decisive abrogation as distinct from all the others is not a temporal event, but—like a scene in heaven in the religious plays of the Middle Ages—an eternal happening between the Father and the Son. And (second,) the New Testament economy has no autonomous place among these temporal events, but is mentioned only in contrast with that of the Old. In my estimation the main strength of the thinking of Coccejus is at the very point where formally the main objection is made against him, and at the point where these two discordant features are to be found within the order selected by him. Certainly, he took over from his predecessors that idea of a covenant of nature or works which was alien to the Reformers. But—and it was because of this that he felt so strong an affinity with Olevian—he had such a strong sense of the uniqueness of the divine covenant as a covenant of grace that, although he could begin his narration with the covenant of works, he could understand everything that followed only in antithesis to it, as its increasing abrogation. The doctrine of the covenant of grace was developed in relation, but only in this negative relation, to a covenant of works. The fact that he did try to bring the two together, but could do so only in the antithetical form of the abrogation of the one by the other, was obviously even to himself a disquieting reminder that his attitude to the second—if it really was the second—would have to be quite different from his attitude to the first. That is how we have to judge the scene in heaven which so singularly interrupts the series of temporal events to form the second stage. Coccejus could find no similar eternal pact between God the Father and God the Son to correspond to the covenant of nature or works. In presenting the institution of the covenant of grace in this way, did he not contradict his own historicism and say that in this covenant we have to do with a *Prius* and not a *Posterius* in relation to that which he and his predecessors had sought to characterise and describe as a special and supposedly first *foedus naturale* or *legale* or *operum* ? In spite of the inconsistency in his own scheme, was he not faithful here to what he saw very well to be the real logic of the matter ? And is not the same true of his other architectonic failure—that he did not try to understand and explain the particular subject of the New Testament witness, the historical incarnation of the Son of God, and the atonement made in Him, as a particular stage in this series of events, but " only " as the fulfilling or replacing of the Old Testament economy ? How is it that he could and necessarily did look at it in that way ? For one thing, because obviously—and this must be said in his favour—he did not want to give to the historical difference between the two economies, which he perceived and emphasised very strongly (much more strongly than Calvin), the character of a theological antithesis, but aimed rather to present the Old Testament as the witness to the promise of Jesus Christ and the New as the witness to its fulfilment. And then most of all because everything that can be said of the New Testament economy as such is already included and stated in and with what has been said in relation to that abrogation of the covenant of works which has already taken place in the bosom of the Godhead. For him the new thing in the New Testament is the oldest thing of all, that which goes back to the very beginning. And this original thing he found revealed and active as the first thing (not as a second economy following that of the Old Testament) in the New Testament economy which dissolved that of the Old Testament.

The questions which we can answer only·with difficulty if at all in respect of Coccejus do not begin until we have done him justice in these matters. The meaning and character of the covenant as a covenant of grace impressed itself upon him forcefully in this way. And in his outline (even in the very things which might formally be objected against him) he has emphasised this in a remarkable manner. How was it, then, that he came to put first the covenant of nature or works or Law, negatively at least taking his direction from it, as though the covenant of grace were a covenant of grace only in antithesis to it, and ultimately therefore only in its fulfilment and confirmation ? The same question may be asked of his predecessors from Ursinus onwards. Granted that we can seriously speak of a *lex naturae*, how does it come to be connected with the divine likeness of man, his status before the Fall, the Word of God to Adam, the tree of life in Paradise, and the decalogue ? And in this connexion, within the series of main theological concepts, how does it attain to the dignity of a first and special divine covenant, which then becomes the schema within which (antithetically in Coccejus) the covenant of grace is set up and its history gradually fulfilled ? The more so as men who knew the Scripture as Coccejus and his fellows undoubtedly did could never speak of any institution of this second covenant in God Himself (as Coccejus did in relation to the covenant of grace) ! But it is still this covenant which becomes the first and is as such the framework and standard of reference for the covenant of grace. There is only one historical explanation for this innovation, the introduction of this first stage in the history for which the Federal theology thought that it had biblical reference. This is that biblical exegesis had been invaded by a mode of thought in which this history, however extraordinary the course it took, could only unfold itself and therefore only begin as the history of man and his works, man who is good by nature and who is therefore in covenant with God—a God who is pledged to him by virtue of his goodness. To this mode of thinking it became more and more foreign to think of the history as conversely the history of God and His works, the God who originally turns to man in grace, and therefore as from the very first the history of the covenant of grace. We have seen that Coccejus did try (with Calvin and Olevian and all the older tradition) to think this second thought which was becoming so foreign to his generation. But in face of the increasing pressure to a mode of thought which started exclusively with man (for his contemporaries had come to terms with the Cartesians), he no longer had. sufficient freedom to make the leap which he really ought to have made in accordance with the biblical control of his thinking. Formally, at any rate, the thought which was becoming so foreign to the new thinking of his generation, but to which he wanted to do justice, and in his own way did do justice, could have only a secondary authority even in his writings. The first place is taken by the strange spectacle of man in Paradise to whom eternal life is promised as a reward which he has earned, whose works can perfectly fulfil the command of God (even if his obedience is not yet secure), to whom God is just as much bound by this fulfilment as he is to God, between whom and God the relationship is clearly that of a *do ut des*. And this relationship is supposed to be the original form of the covenant. In this original form it breaks down in that series of abrogations. And it does not break down first by reason of the divine covenant of grace, but by reason of human sin. Characteristically, and necessarily in view of that pressure, the second most pressing problem is not that of God's grace but that of man's sin. Through all the abrogations of the covenant of nature and works, what sin is—even as it will finally disappear—is measured by the Law of this first covenant. And it will be the decisive gift of the covenant of grace, and the function of the Mediator as the second Adam, to fulfil in our place the Law of the covenant of nature and works which was transgressed by Adam and all of us, and in that way to become our guarantor with God. And far from the first covenant being really superseded by the intervention of the Mediator, the gifted righteousness of Law (which is promised and certain to faith in Him) is necessarily followed by that further abrogation of the Law, distinguished under the concept of sanctification, which Coccejus calls the " death of the body," the battle of spirit against the flesh in the regenerate, in which the decisive weapon is once again the Law, while grace is the place to which the regenerate must always flee in view of the imperfection of his fulfilment of the Law. The first covenant and its Law loses its relevance only in that *eschaton* which is the fifth and final stage of the whole development. In spite of all assurances to the contrary, this side of the *eschaton*, in time, there is no effective abrogation of the covenant of nature and works, either in the Old Testament economy or consequently in the New. For the New Testament freedom is only freedom from the Law of the Old Testament—impressively maintained by Coccejus, e.g., in relation to the Sabbath—but the validity of the Law of that first covenant is the guiding thread which runs through the whole development, indeed it controls that development. Grace itself, whether as justification or sanctification, is always the fulfilling of that Law (perfect in Christ, imperfect in us). There is no escape from the relationship of *do ut des*, no liberation from the insecurity of the whole connexion between man and God, the fear of punishment and the expectation of reward, no radical cessation of the unfortunate preoccupation of man with himself and his works and of the even more unfortunate control of God to which this inevitably gives rise. This is impossible even in the covenant of grace connected with the covenant of works and orientated by it. This covenant of grace could not be clearly and convincingly portrayed as such. Where it was portrayed as such in the proclamation of the older Reformed Church, this was not because but in spite of its starting-point, in virtue of those elements which were foreign and ran contrary to it, and made it innocuous. Unfortunately they did not always make it innocuous.

4. We have seen that Coccejus solemnly distinguished the covenant of grace, his second abrogation of the covenant of works, by describing it as a pretemporal and intertrinitarian happening, a pact between God the Father and God the Son. It is grounded, not in the proclamation of the proto-Gospel, or in the Noachic or Abrahamic covenants, not between God and man at all, but in eternity before all worlds, in the bosom of the Godhead itself. We can ignore the rather difficult juristic details of the conception in Coccejus and his predecessors and successors. What is essential is that: God forgives sinful man and gives him a new righteousness on the one condition of faith and repentance. Ultimately this rests on the free disposing of God the Father, by virtue of which He has once and for all ascribed to a chosen portion of sinful humanity righteousness and eternal life in His Son. There is a corresponding disposing of the Son of God in virtue of which He for His part has undertaken once and for all the cause of those sinful men who are elected to sonship. The two together result in the covenant : the *pactum mutuum inter Patrem et Filium, quo Pater Filium dat ut λυτρώτην et caput populi praecogniti et Filius vicissim se sistit ad ἀπολύτρωσιν hanc peragendam* (F. Burmann, *Syn. Theol.*, 1671, II, 15, 2). The whole christologico-soteriological happening of the atonement is simply the historical execution of the engagements freely accepted by, but strictly binding on, the two divine partners, i.e., God with God. The older Reformed theology had spoken more simply of an eternal divine " decree," as an *opus Dei internum ad extra*, and its temporal fulfilment. And in content this decree could only be the eternal divine election of grace. Coccejus and those who shared his view could also understand that which they described as the *testamentum aeternum* or the *sponsio aeterna* between the Father and the Son as an aspect of the decree of predestination (in so far as this has positive reference to election to salvation in Christ). We will have to return to this in a fifth and final point. The question we must now ask as it arises from the third point is as follows. When this supreme basis was ascribed to the covenant of grace, how was it thought possible that another covenant, the *foedus naturae* or *operum*, could be placed alongside it and even given precedence over it ?—a covenant which had already been superseded and rendered superfluous by this eternal basis of the covenant of grace ? which could at once be broken by the sin of man ? which could then be destroyed and abrogated

and made obsolete by the historical promise and fulfilment of the covenant
of grace ? which would completely disappear in the *eschaton* ? but which, as
we have seen, still constitutes the guiding thread which actually runs through
the whole occurrence of salvation and by which it is measured right up to the
very end ? Although this covenant and its Law are plainly opposed to the covenant
of grace ! Although it is not possible to try to explain it by a divine decree, an
eternal and intertrinitarian decision and agreement ! If the covenant of grace
alone was seen to be grounded in God, did not this mean that any dualism in
the concept of the covenant was at once negated ? Even where it was thought
necessary to speak of a first covenant of nature or works, was it really possible
to see anything but the one covenant of grace, which had been instituted in
eternity, which had come into force, therefore, in and with the beginning of human
history, which at once embraced man and claimed him, which man had, of
course, broken, but which God in faithfulness to Himself and His partner had
not abrogated but maintained and ratified ? Why was it thought necessary to
see man in any other light than that of the pledge which God Himself had made
for him in His Son even before he ever existed ? Why was it thought necessary
to see him in any other way than the one who in the eternal will of God was
predestinated to be the brother of this Son and therefore to divine sonship ?
Why is there ascribed to him a status in which he did not need the Mediator and
which, if it had lasted, would have made superfluous the appearance of the
Mediator and therefore the fulfilment of the eternal (!) covenant of grace ? Why
was sin robbed of its true and frightful seriousness as a transgression of the law
given to man as the predestinated brother of the Son and child of the Father,
as a falling away from the special grace which the Creator had shown him from
all eternity ? Why instead was the grace of God made a second or a third thing,
a wretched expedient of God in face of the obvious failure of a plan in relation
to man which had originally had quite a different intention and form ? Why,
again, was it not possible completely to banish all thought of this other plan in
relation to the historical promise and fulfilment, the Old and New Testament
economy ? Why had the history of the covenant of grace to be presented as
though it had to do only with the execution of that original plan ?—of that plan
concerning whose divine meaning and basis there was nothing that could be
said because nothing was or could be known of it from the Gospel they were
trying to expound ? Why on this side of the *eschaton* is everything always
measured by a form of the relationship between God and man which had been
maintained as the beginning of all things only with a *sic volo sic iubeo* ? How
was that even possible ? How was it possible to know of the eternal basis of the
covenant of grace and then not to think exclusively in the light of it, to understand and present it as the one covenant of God, as though there were some
other eternity in God or elsewhere, an eternity of human nature and its connexion
with God and its law and the works of this law ?

5. The riddle posed by the older Federal theology at this its strongest point
appears to be insoluble. But perhaps we shall find the solution if we examine
rather more closely how it understood that eternal basis of the covenant of
grace. As we have seen, it was taken to consist in an intertrinitarian
decision, in a freely accepted but legally binding mutual obligation between
God the Father and God the Son. Now there are three doubtful features in this
conception.

For God to be gracious to sinful man, was there any need of a special decree
to establish the unity of the righteousness and mercy of God in relation to man,
of a special intertrinitarian arrangement and contract which can be distinguished
from the being of God ? If there was need of such a decree, then the question
arises at once of a form of the will of God in which this arrangement has not
yet been made and is not yet valid. We have to reckon with the existence of a
God who is righteous *in abstracto* and not free to be gracious from the very first,

who has to bind to the fulfilment of His promise the fulfilment of certain conditions by man, and punish their non-fulfilment. It is only with the conclusion of this contract with Himself that He ceases to be a righteous God *in abstracto* and becomes the God who in His righteousness is also merciful and therefore able to exercise grace. In this case it is not impossible or illegitimate to believe that properly, in some inner depth of His being behind the covenant of grace, He might not be able to do this. It is only on the historical level that the theologumenon of the *foedus naturae* or *operum* can be explained by the compact of the Federal theology with contemporary humanism. In fact it derives from anxiety lest there might be an essence in God in which, in spite of that contract, His righteousness and His mercy are secretly and at bottom two separate things. And this anxiety derives from the fact that the thought of that inter-trinitarian contract obviously cannot have any binding and therefore consoling and assuring force. This anxiety and therefore this proposition of a covenant of works could obviously never have arisen if there had been a loyal hearing of the Gospel and a strict looking to Jesus Christ as the full and final revelation of the being of God. In the eternal decree of God revealed in Jesus Christ the being of God would have been seen as righteous mercy and merciful righteousness from the very first. It would have been quite impossible therefore to conceive of any special plan of a God who is righteous *in abstracto*, and the whole idea of an original covenant of works would have fallen to the ground.

The conception of this inter-trinitarian pact as a contract between the persons of the Father and the Son is also open to criticism. Can we really think of the first and second persons of the triune Godhead as two divine subjects and therefore as two legal subjects who can have dealings and enter into obligations one with another ? This is mythology, for which there is no place in a right understanding of the doctrine of the Trinity as the doctrine of the three modes of being of the one God, which is how it was understood and presented in Reformed orthodoxy itself. God is one God. If He is thought of as the supreme and finally the only subject, He is the one subject. And if, in relation to that which He obviously does amongst us, we speak of His eternal resolves or decrees, even if we describe them as a contract, then we do not regard the divine persons of the Father and the Son as partners in this contract, but the one God—Father, Son and Holy Spirit—as the one partner, and the reality of man as distinct from God as the other. When the covenant of grace was based on a pact between two divine persons, a wider dualism was introduced into the Godhead—again in defiance of the Gospel as the revelation of the Father by the Son and of the Son by the Father, which took place in Jesus Christ. The result was an uncertainty which necessarily relativised the unconditional validity of the covenant of grace, making it doubtful whether in the revelation of this covenant we really had to do with the one will of the one God. If in God there are not merely different and fundamentally contradictory qualities, but also different subjects, who are indeed united in this matter, but had first of all to come to an agreement, how can the will of God seen in the history of the covenant of grace be known to be binding and unequivocal, the first and final Word of God ? The way is then opened up on this side too for considering the possibility of some other form of His will. The question is necessarily and seriously raised of a will of God the Father which originally and basically is different from the will of God the Son. And this naturally carried with it the hypothesis of a covenant of quite a different structure and purpose preceding and underlying the covenant of grace, the hypothesis of a law in the relationship of God to man which is not the Law of His grace and which in default of a special revelation of the Father can be pictured at once according to the analogy of human ordinances. And how is the will of the eternal Son or Word of God in Himself and as such, in His pure Godhead, to become so clear and certain that we can and must cling to it alone as the revealed eternal and therefore unequivocal and binding will of God as the basis of the covenant of grace ? Even the thought of the eternal divine Logos is not in itself and as such necessarily a defence against the thought of a law which is different from the Law of grace.

And this leads us to the third and decisive point. The thought of a purely inter-trinitarian decision as the eternal basis of the covenant of grace may be found both sublime and uplifting. But it is definitely much too uplifting and sublime to be a Christian thought. What we have to do with it is not a relationship of God with Himself but the basis of a relationship between God and man. How can even the most perfect decision in the bosom of the Godhead, if the Godhead remains alone, be the origin of the covenant, if it is made in the absence of the one who must be present as the second partner at the institution of the covenant to make it a real covenant, that is, man ? To unite God in His attitude to man —whether in respect of His properties, or as Father, Son and Holy Spirit—there is no need of any particular pact or decree. God would not be God if He were not God in this unity. And a covenant with man is not grounded merely in this unity of God in and with Himself. It is not self-evident but a new thing that in His unity with Himself from all eternity God wills to be the God of man and to make and have man as His man. This is the content of a particular act of will which has its basis neither in the essence of God nor in that of man, and which God does not owe either to Himself or to any other being, and least of all to man. This is what we can call a decree, an *opus Dei internum ad extra*, and therefore a pact : God's free election of grace, in which even in His eternity before all time and the foundation of the world, He is no longer alone by Himself, He does not rest content with Himself, He will not restrict Himself to the wealth of His perfections and His own inner life as Father, Son and Holy Spirit. In this free act of the election of grace there is already present, and presumed, and assumed into unity with His own existence as God, the existence of the man whom He intends and loves from the very first and in whom He intends and loves all other men, of the man in whom He wills to bind Himself with all other men and all other man with Himself. In this free act of the election of grace the Son of the Father is no longer just the eternal Logos, but as such, as very God from all eternity He is also the very God and very man He will become in time. In the divine act of predestination there pre-exists the Jesus Christ who as the Son of the eternal Father and the child of the Virgin Mary will become and be the Mediator of the covenant between God and man, the One who accomplishes the act of atonement. He in whom the covenant of grace is fulfilled and revealed in history is also its eternal basis. He who in Scripture is attested to be very God and very man is also the eternal *testamentum*, the eternal *sponsio*, the eternal *pactum*, between God and man. This is the point which Coccejus and the Federal theology before and after Coccejus missed. Their doctrine of a purely inter-trinitarian pact did not enable them to give an unequivocal or binding answer to the question of the form of the eternal divine decree as the beginning of all things. The result was that for all their loyalty to Scripture they inherited the notion that the covenant of grace fulfilled and revealed in history in Jesus Christ was perhaps only a secondary and subsequent divine arrangement (the foundation and history of a religion ?) and not the beginning of all the ways of God. Their view of the covenant became dualistic. The idea of a basic and always determinative and concurrent covenant of nature or works was superimposed on their conception of the covenant of grace. Yet this could have been avoided —even though as children of their time they were exposed to the temptation of humanism—if they could have determined to know the eternal and therefore the only basis of the divine work in the work itself, in its temporal occurrence, to know the eternal divine Logos in His incarnation. And on this basis they might well have overcome the other weaknesses in their doctrine : the abandonment of an original universalism in the conception of the covenant ; and finally the radical historicism of their understanding of Scripture.

3. THE FULFILMENT OF THE BROKEN COVENANT

From the concept of the covenant as the presupposition of the reconciliation which took place in Jesus Christ we will now turn to the reconciliation itself and therefore to the fulfilment of the covenant. It consists in the fact that God realises His eternal will with man, that He makes the covenant true and actual within human history. It consists in the historical proclamation attested in the Old Testament, and the historical existence attested in the New, of the Mediator, that is, of the eternal Word of God and therefore of God Himself in His historical identity with the man Jesus of Nazareth: in the coming of His kingdom on earth, that is, in the coming and being and living and speaking and acting of this man, in the establishing and maintaining and revealing in Him of the sole supremacy of His grace in the world of men, and of the subordination of that world to this supremacy. It consists in the fact that He causes the promise and command of the covenant: "I will be your God and ye shall be my people," to become historical event in the person of Jesus Christ. It consists, therefore, in the fact that God keeps faith in time with Himself and with man, with all men in this one man.

But this fulfilment of the covenant has the character of atonement. The concept speaks of the confirmation or restoration of a fellowship which did exist but had been threatened with disruption and dissolution. Atonement does have its eternal and unshakable basis in the covenant between God and man which God willed and set up before the foundation of the world. But the covenant is successfully fulfilled by the overcoming of an obstruction which if the basis had not been unshakable would inevitably have made that fulfilment doubtful or impossible. In face of that obstruction the fulfilment can be regarded only as a divine protest effectively and redemptively made with the power of that eternal basis. And in relation to man it can be regarded only as an inconceivable overflowing of the grace of God to him.

This history of man from the very first—and the same is true of the history of every individual man—consisted, not in the keeping but the breaking of the covenant, not in the receiving but the rejecting of the promise, not in the fulfilling but the transgressing of the command, not in the gratitude which corresponds to the grace of God but in a senseless and purposeless rebellion against it, a rebellion which at bottom is quite negative, but terribly real even in this negativity. It was revealed from the very first, and it is revealed daily in small things as well as big, in the disposition as well as the acts of man, that the eternal grace of God is not merely undeserved by man, but was and is given to him as one who does not deserve it. He does not

recognise it. He does not want it. At bottom he hates it. He does
not see that this and this alone is life in freedom. He chafes for another
freedom which can only be bondage. He does not accept the fact
that he can be a member of the people of God. Therefore he does not
accept the fact that God is the Lord of His people. He finds and
chooses other lords and gods, and lives as though he belonged to their
people. And so the grace of God to him seems to be in the void.
The man to whom it comes fails to receive it. As far as he is concerned
he is without grace, and therefore he fails even as a creature. Therefore it seems that although God elected man to a covenant with Himself, and created heaven and earth and man himself for the sake of
this covenant, He will finally be left by Himself : God above, but not
God—which is surely impossible—in these dark depths ; God in heaven,
but not God on an earth which is the scene of this nonsensical history ;
God in His own inner glory, but without that attestation of the creature
for which He designed and made it and which is not merely the capacity
but the destiny of its nature as He made it ; God with His covenant
will, but without the execution of that will, the execution of it hindered
by the one whom He honoured and singled out and exalted in this
will from all eternity.

This is the enormous incident of sin which openly opposes the fulfilment of the covenant and in face of which that fulfilment, if it is to
come about at all, can have only the character of an atonement. And
this atonement can come only from God. In face of human ingratitude, it can consist only in an overflowing of His grace and therefore
in the overcoming and removing of that obstruction. There is nothing
that man can contribute to it as the one who has denied his relationship
with God and failed as God's partner. He cannot accomplish or expect
or explain and comprehend it for himself. If it takes place, he can
only accept it as a fact, whose validity and effectiveness, as the enemy
of God that he is and must recognise and acknowledge himself to
be, he can believe only because God does in fact show Himself and
make Himself known as the one who is the master of man and his
sin.

God's faithfulness cannot be mistaken, nor can it be mocked. What
is the unfaithfulness of man in relation to it, and what can it accomplish ? The grace of God triumphs over man and his sin—that is the
fulfilment of the covenant which takes place in Jesus Christ. But it
assumes and has the character of a " Yet " and a " Notwithstanding." It
triumphs now—in face of human opposition—miraculously, unilaterally
and autocratically—to its own self-glory.

Can we say : all the more gloriously ? Is it only now that it acts
and reveals itself as free grace ? Is it only now that there is disclosed
and operative the sovereign divine resolve which is its basis ? We
can and must say : " Where sin abounded, grace did much more
abound " (Rom. 5[20]). It is true that the nature and power of the grace

of God is finally and unmistakably revealed only where it shows itself and acts as His free grace to the undeserving, as grace for lost sinners.

But, all the same, when the Early Church dared to sing : *O felix culpa quae tantum et talem meruit habere salvatorem*, it went too far with the *meruit habere*. For there can be no more question of man " deserving " and achieving and winning that overflowing of the grace of God by his sin than there can in any other way. It can only be recognised and acknowledged and reverenced as a fact that this depth of the love of God is revealed and active in relation to human sin in a way which is so inconceivably profound, in all the power and mystery of eternity. How can we ever ascribe this fact to ourselves ? The recognition of this fact carries within it the deepest and most comforting but also the most terrifying abasement of man : that as the transgressor he is he can live only by that which he does not do himself, which it is impossible even to ask of him, which, in fact, he denies and resists ; by the atonement which God has made— and all because the grace of God makes against him and the opposition he has stirred up that triumphant, effective and redemptive protest. Even the association of the words *felix* and *culpa* cannot really stand. This divine protest is effective and redemptive, but it is in bitter earnest. The grace of God does not abandon us, but only because it makes good what we have spoiled, and therefore only in that humiliation of us which brings us help and comfort, but which is inescapable in this wealth of help and comfort. Therefore—unless we do not recognise and accept this humiliation as such—we cannot possibly speak of a " happy fault." To be at fault before God is unhappiness even where the grace of God overflows in answer to and in favour of the guilty, even where the faithfulness of God is first active and revealed as such in face of man's unfaithfulness. If we cannot boast of any happy sufficiency of our being and work, we certainly cannot do so of our " happy fault," which is far more than an insufficiency, which stands indeed in opposition to and conflict with the gracious will of God.

No praise can be too high for the mighty and triumphant grace of God in the atonement as the fulfilment of the covenant. But this praise must not be spoiled by any undertone which directly or indirectly minimises or even approves the incident in virtue of which the fulfilment of the covenant necessarily has the character of an atonement. It must not be made misleading or harmful to those who hear it, or unacceptable to God. The wisdom of God which allows this episode in order to make, not the episode itself, but the overcoming of it an occasion to magnify His grace and to reveal and actualise it— we have to say for the first time—as free grace in it, in accordance with His eternal will and purpose : that wisdom is one thing. But quite a different thing is the human pseudo-wisdom which tries to pretend that this episode is in some sense necessary, and in that way to excuse or exculpate the man who is responsible for it, or even to hide from him the full danger and fatality of his action. The sin which abounds is indeed sin. As the opposition of man to the God who is in covenant with Him it is inexcusable. As the self-opposition of the man who is in covenant with God it is fatal. And the fact that grace much more abounds does not alter or limit or weaken this fact. It is a fact which must be included in our praise of the grace of God. Our praise cannot be genuine except as the praise of faith. But faith flees and clings and reclines and trusts on the God who in His free grace leads us to judgment. Faith finds its comfort and praise in His grace. But it knows that this grace is " dear " and not " cheap " (Dietrich Bonhoeffer). Therefore it does not lessen our accusation and sentence. If we live, we do not live because the confession of our sin and guilt laid on our hearts and lips by the grace of God has been weakened or embellished, but because the forgiveness of our sin has been accomplished by God in the event of the atonement. Therefore the praise of faith cannot be a denial of the truth but rather a confirmation of it : first and primarily in respect of the inconceivable glory of that which is said and given to man; but then and consequently in respect of the unutterable unworthiness of man as the recipient. Where this is not clear, with all that it entails, there is no faith. What are thought to be believing thought and speech do not revolve around the more abundant free grace of God present in the atonement made in Jesus Christ. They are in fact speculation about a myth current under the name of Jesus Christ. There is no knowledge and proclamation of what has actually been done by God under this name. We must pay attention to the warning which there is here. There is no doctrine more dangerous than the Christian doctrine of the atonement, it does indeed make " wild and careless folk " (*Heid. Cat., qu.* 64), if we do not consider it with this warning in view. The fact that it speaks of God making good what we have spoiled does not mean that we can call evil good (unless we would also call good evil). All our thinking and all that we say on this matter must be disciplined by an observance of this limit, and a refusal to transgress it in any circumstances, sense or direction.

We will now give a very general outline of what is meant by reconciliation as the fulfilment of the covenant. For this purpose we will take and expound two of the New Testament sayings which in a classic way encompass the whole of this field.

Precedence must be given to Jn. 3[16] : " For God so loved the world, that he gave his only begotten Son, that whosoever believeth on him should not perish, but have everlasting life."

ἠγάπησεν tells a definite story, gives news of a unique event : the event of God's loving. This event did not take place in heaven but on earth. It did not take place in secret, but it can be known (i.e., not as a purely spiritual process, but as something which, according to 1 Jn. 1[1], can be heard and seen with our eyes and touched, yes, handled with our hands). This being the case, it became, it made itself the content of the message proclaimed by the Christian community. Now the object of the divine loving was the κόσμος, which means (for what follows, cf. R. Bultmann, *Das Evangelium Johannes*, 1950) the human world as a single subject in hostile antithesis to God. Not from the very first. Not because it is bad in itself. For the world was made by God (Jn. 1[10]). Not because it is posited against God in itself. Not because it is authorised or empowered to stand in this position of hostility to God. It is His possession (Jn. 1[11]). Not because God has left it to itself. Not because He has given it cause for this hostility. The true light, the light of the covenant promising life, was and is present : and bright enough for every man (Jn. 1[9]). But the world knew it not (Jn. 1[10]).

In contrast to it the world is σκοτία, darkness (Jn. 1⁵). It does not understand God—either in itself as His creature or as illuminated by that light. But with all these characteristics it is the object of the divine loving. For with all these characteristics it is the cosmos. Created by God and illuminated by Him from the beginning, not recognising Him and therefore dark, it is still the object of His loving. This event takes place absolutely. It has this in common with the creation of the world, and the illumination which comes to it from God by creation (the covenant with God from which man always derives as from his creation), that God does not owe it to the world to love it. The world is not, as Philo and others imagined, the son of God. It is not begotten by Him. It does not share His nature, so that He is bound to it by nature, essentially. It is the free will and the free act of God that He willed to be the basis of its existence and its light. The meaning of this event is from the very first a free loving. And in its relation to that loving and in every other respect the cosmos is darkness. It has disqualified itself. Even as the world created and illuminated by Him it has ceased to be worthy of His love. But God did not in fact cease to love it. Only now did He begin genuinely and supremely to love it. Only now did this event take place and irresistibly as the event of His own pure free love, a love grounded in Himself and not in the object, a love turned toward the object only for His own sake. There can be no question of any claim of the cosmos to be loved, or consequently of any mitigation of its character as darkness, which is only revealed in all its impossibility in this event, and for which it will now be plainly accused and judged and sentenced. But this does not take place because God rejects it, but because He loves it. And His love is not merely a disposition but an act, an active measure in relation to it. Jn. 3¹⁶ describes the fulfilment and scope of this measure.

The οὕτως in relation with the later ὥστε means more than "in such a way," *hoc modo*. It does not refer only to the divine *procedere* as such, although I have often expounded it in this narrower sense in the *C.D.* It implies this *hoc modo*, but it has the force of "so much." It indicates (as Luther intended when he translated it *also*) the extraordinary nature of this loving. It is not self-evident that there should be a divine loving of the cosmos in any case. It is even less so that the divine act of love should take this form. God loves the cosmos so much, with such inconceivable strength and depth, "that (ὥστε) He gave his only begotten son." God has a Son. This Son is not the cosmos but the One whom He gave in loving the cosmos. Can we interpret the "Son" here as the "Revealer"? He is that (although not only that) when God gives Him. The fact that He is—that He declares the grace and truth of God which no man has seen (Jn. 1¹⁸)—presupposes that He was πρὸς τὸν θεόν and that He Himself was θεός (Jn. 1¹), that He was "in the bosom of the Father" (Jn. 1¹⁸), the beloved Other in relation to whom God is called and is love in Himself, in His inward life (1 Jn. 4⁸), the One who knows God as Himself and Himself as God, who does the will of God as His own will and His own will as the will of God, the One without whom—and we cannot say this of the cosmos—God would not only not be revealed but would not be God, whose existence πρὸς τὸν θεόν and as θεός is a constituent part of the existence of God. Therefore, υἱὸς μονογενής, the only one of His kind? or the only-begotten, and therefore the One beside whom God has no other son, no one who is His equal, or who corresponds to Him, no other who is in Himself the object of His love, a constituent part of His divine being? In both senses: as this eternally Other in God Himself the only One who as such is able to fulfil all that God wills and does.

But it is not self-evident that in loving the world God should "give" this one. ἔδωκεν in the first instance means "gifted" Him. He did not merely gift a highest and best, a power of life and light which would help the cosmos, perhaps an endowment of the creation, perhaps a strengthening of the light of His covenant. No: He gifted to the cosmos His only Son and therefore nothing more or less than Himself. And in this context ἔδωκεν has the same force as παρέδωκεν : He surrendered Him, He gave Him up, He offered Him. He sends Him into the cosmos which is actually darkness as the light (Jn. 1⁵) which is to shine in the darkness but which will not be apprehended or grasped, which cannot be apprehended or grasped by the darkness. In giving Him—and giving Himself—He exposes Himself—and Himself—to the greatest danger. He sets at stake His own existence as God. " He came unto His own, and His own (that is, those who are His possession) received him not " (Jn. 1¹¹). He did it. But what result is possible when in relation to Him the world is irremediable darkness ? What will it mean for God ? Well, in this act God loved the world so much, so profoundly, that it did in fact consist in the venture of His own self-offering, in this hazarding of His own existence as God. It is His self-revelation and self-realisation (in and for the world) as a gift, and *rebus sic stantibus* that can mean only as the offering of that without which He cannot be God, and therefore of the greatest possible danger for Himself. " God so loved the world." The Christian message is the message of this act of God, of the atonement which was made in this way, of God's pledging of Himself for His creature, for His partner in the covenant, for the man who has opposed Him as an enemy. It consists in the fact that God has given Himself up into the hands of this enemy. It is in this radical sense that according to the Christian message God has loved first (πρῶτος, 1 Jn. 4¹⁹), not merely before we loved Him, but while we were yet sinners, while we were yet enemies (Rom. 5⁸, ¹⁰).

And now the clause introduced by ἵνα (an ἵνα which is both *finale* and *consecutivum*) speaks of the effect, the result of this offering of the Son and self-offering of God, and therefore of the purpose and the actual scope of this so perfect act of love. Those who believe in Him will not perish but have everlasting life. To understand this we do well to remember the opening and controlling part of the sentence : " For God so loved the world." What happens to those who believe on the Son is the effect of the love with which in that event God has loved not only them but the world. In the person of believers, therefore, it happens indirectly, with a view, and as a witness, to the world. We also do well to follow the hint in the commentary of E. Hoskyns (*The Fourth Gospel*, 1947, p. 218), and especially to notice what it is that is here described as happening to believers : " the divine purpose in the sending of Jesus Christ is redemption and not judgment, eternal life and not destruction and perdition." It is a matter primarily of salvation from perishing. This is the reverse side of the darkness in which the world opposes God, ranging itself against God, contradicting and withstanding Him. It has fallen a victim to destruction and perdition. In so doing it has forfeited its right to exist as the creature of God. It cannot continue but can only be delivered up to the nothingness to which it has itself turned. The divine loving in the form of the sending of the Son is the will of God not to allow the destruction and perdition of the world. This will is His redemptive will in relation to the creature—His will not to let it perish, to maintain His creation and not to cause it to perish, not even because of the opposition of the creature, especially not because of it. But that is not all. Eternal life as the continuance of man in fellowship with God Himself, in the *consortium divinitatis*, is not in any way assured to man simply because he is the creature of God. It is rather the particular promise of that light which lighteth every man from the beginning, the light of the covenant which God has made with man. When he denies this light, when he is therefore darkness, when he does not know God, he excludes himself from the sphere of this promise. When he is lost as a creature, how can he participate in eternal life ? If he breaks the covenant, he is lost as a creature, and if he is lost as a creature, the promise of the covenant cannot hold good for him. But the divine loving in the form of the sending of the Son is the confirmation of the will of God not to acquiesce in this but to cause man to have the eternal life which he has forfeited with his right to exist as a creature.

It is His will not merely to rescue, but to save. He not only wills the creature to continue, but to continue in eternal fellowship with Himself. And He does not allow Himself to be foiled even in this far-reaching purpose for man by the opposition of man.

This loving Yet and Notwithstanding of God (proclaimed in the sending and therefore in the offering of the Son, in the divine self-offering) is what actually happens within this world to those who believe on the Son. Those who believe on the Son are the members of the cosmos who, while they necessarily participate as such in its opposition, and are therefore subject to perishing and have forfeited eternal life, in the sending of the Son and therefore in the self-offering of God can and must recognise God as God, and His will as a will of love, a will to rescue and to save, being ready to accept its validity and application against themselves and therefore for themselves. Those who believe on the Son are those in the cosmos who in face of the work and revelation of God, because in the giving of the Son it includes within itself God's own presence, are free but also constrained to justify God (even against themselves as members of the cosmos, and therefore against the whole cosmos). They are those who without being in any way different from others are under the forceful permission and command to affirm God and the will of God as it has been revealed to them. This is not because, as distinct from others, they are disposed and able of themselves, but because God is too strong for them. Their freedom and constraint cannot be explained by the men themselves. It can be explained only by the presence of God, His glory in the flesh (Jn. 1^{14}). Only then is it genuine and strong and lasting. That is why the New Testament describes it as discipleship, the result of an act of majesty on the part of Jesus. And it is this that constitutes faith. And just as the Son on whom they believe is not of this world (ἐκ τοῦ κόσμου), so it is with believers (Jn. 17$^{14, 16}$), although they are undoubtedly in the world (Jn. 17^{11}). They are not of the world, or, to put it positively—in believing in the Son, in seeing His glory in the flesh—they are " born from above " (Jn. 3^{3}). It is in this way that there takes place in them what is the purpose of the divine loving of the cosmos and therefore of the giving of the Son. As those who believe on the Son they do not perish with the world but they are rescued ; they do not lose eternal life but have it. That this is the case with believers is the scope of that event and its promise for the whole world. What happens to them, and as such is only theirs, applies to the whole world, as we see from the verse which immediately follows, and is connected to v. 16 by a γάρ : " For God sent not his Son into the world to condemn the world, but that the world through him might be saved " (v. 17). Within the world, and therefore as a witness directed and appointed to it, there are men who belong to it, yet who do not perish but have everlasting life. In the setting up of this witness within the world the atonement is shown to be an atonement which is made for the world.

We will now turn to the parallel saying of Paul in 2 Cor. 5^{19} : " God was in Christ reconciling the world unto himself, not imputing their trespasses unto them ; and hath committed unto us the word of reconciliation."

We are taking this sentence out of its context, and even out of its (in any case loose) syntactical connexion with the preceding verse. It is the main verse in the passage, enclosing and bringing together in a pregnant way all the decisive elements in the surrounding verses. It, too, speaks of that fulfilling of the covenant which is our concern here—its execution and its scope—and in doing so it makes express use of the concept of atonement (cf. for what follows the article καταλλάσσειν, etc., by F. Büchsel, in THWB 3.N.T., I, p. 254 f.).

Again in the main part of the sentence a story is recounted. And it is obviously the same as that which we found in Jn. 3^{16}. θεός is again the acting subject and κόσμος the object of His activity. The narrative serves as a basis for the preceding verse where Paul had said that his being as καινὴ κτίσις, a man for whom old things have passed away and all things have become new (v. 17), is the work of God (ἐκ τοῦ θεοῦ) who has reconciled him to Himself in Christ and committed to him the ministry of reconciliation. In verse 19 this is repeated with a wider reference, the particular being made universal and basic. Instead of the apostle being reconciled by God to Himself in Christ, it is now the world which is reconciled by God to Himself in Christ. The apostolic ἡμεῖς in v. 18 and the κόσμος in v. 19 are not contrasted, but in a remarkable way the apostolic " we " is a kind of particle of the world (almost the world *in nuce*, a microcosm) and the " world " is only the supreme form, the widest reference of the apostolic " we." In this way the saying about God's reconciling of the world can in fact be the basis of the preceding saying about His reconciling of the apostle. Naturally, this does not exclude the fact that for the apostle the knowledge of the reconciling of the world is grounded in the knowledge of his own reconciliation. The context makes it quite certain that the two cannot be separated.

We must insist at once that the initiative and the decisive action in the happening described as atonement are both with God (as in Jn. 3¹⁶). This is not to say that man's part is only passive ; we will see later that there is a proper place for his activity, and what this activity is. But atonement is not " mutual " in the sense of both parties becoming friends instead of enemies. Rather, in every respect the transcendence of God over man is safeguarded in the atonement " (Büchsel). We must put this even more strongly. Atonement is altogether the work of God and not of man ; καταλλάσσειν is said only of God, and καταλλαγῆναι only of man. Compared with Jn. 3¹⁶, the statement of this divine reconciling is striking in its compactness. It does not say that God loved the world in what He did, but it simply describes the act itself. And nothing is said about the " giving of the Son " or the sending of Christ. All the more impressive, therefore, is the way in which the decisive point of Jn. 3¹⁶ is made in the participle construction, " God was in Christ reconciling . . ." : it is God Himself who intervened to act and work and reveal. The apostle and the world came to have dealings with God Himself. In Paul the concept '"world " is not so all-embracing but in most passages it has the same negative force as in John, and certainly in this context. Atonement takes place only where there has been strife. According to Rom. 5⁶ᶠ·, those who are reconciled with God are such as were formerly weak and godless, sinners and enemies. That is how Paul judged his own case, and it is in the light of this that he usually understands and uses the concept κόσμος. Neither here nor in Rom. 5 does he speak of an enmity of God against man which is removed by the atonement. According to Rom. 5¹, the peace established by the atonement is our peace, πρὸς τὸν θεόν, not the reverse. And his subject here is the reconciling of Paul and the world made by God with Himself, not the reconciling of God with Paul and the world. The hurt which has to be made good is on our side. Notice that in Rom 1¹⁸ the presentation of the ὀργὴ θεοῦ consists solely in a description of the corruption of man to which God has given him up. God does not need reconciliation with men, but men need reconciliation with Him, and this verse tells us that God has made this reconciliation, and how He has made it. We are clearly taught the aim of His reconciling activity in Rom. 5⁵ : " The love of God is shed abroad in our hearts by the Holy Ghost which is given unto us." It is remarkable enough that if that is the goal there has to be a reconciling of the world, and this has already taken place. But that there is a reconciling activity of God in relation to the world may be read in Rom. 11¹⁵ and Col. 1²⁰. And the goal is undoubtedly this complete conversion of the world to Him. That is how Paul had clearly experienced and known it as God's activity in his own life. But he sees this activity in his own life in the context of God's activity in the world—according to the common denominator of the event of God's intervening in Christ to reconcile the world, and His actual reconciling of the world to Himself. We cannot overlook the scope of this thought in this verse any more (and even less) than we can in Jn. 3¹⁶.

But what does " reconciling " mean ? How does God accomplish this conversion of the world to Himself ? Here Paul agrees with John : By His own active presence in Jesus Christ, by His special presence and activity under this name and in this form, as distinct from His being in Himself as God and within His activity as Creator and Lord of the world. With his ἦν καταλλάσσων he, too, recounts the concrete and unique story of Christ. What took place in this story ? I do not see how in this context we can avoid going back to the basic meaning of καταλλάσσειν. The conversion of the world to Himself took place in the form of an exchange, a substitution, which God has proposed between the world and Himself present and active in the person of Jesus Christ. That is what is expressly stated in the verse (21) with which the passage closes.

On the one side, the exchange : " He hath made him to be sin for us (in our place and for our sake), who knew no sin (God Himself being present and active in Him)." Here we have it in the simplest possible form. He has set Him there and revealed Him and caused Him to act and Himself acted as one who was weak and godless, a sinner and an enemy like ourselves. Here we see what is involved in that sending, that offering of the Son, that self-offering and self-hazarding of God for the sake of the world, of which we read in Jn. 3¹⁶. It means that in being present and active in the world in Christ, God takes part in its history. He does not affirm or participate in its culpable nature, its enmity against Himself, but He does take it upon Himself, making His own the situation into which it has fallen. Present and active in Christ, He enters into it. Indeed, it is His divine will—naturally without sinning Himself—to accept a complete solidarity with sinners, to be one with us.

And on the other side, the exchange : He does it, He takes our place in Christ, " that we (again in the simplest possible form) might be made the righteousness of God (δικαιοσύνη θεοῦ) in Him." It does not say simply that He was made sin and we the righteousness of God. The first is obviously the means or the way to the second. But here, too, the ἵνα is both final and consecutive. God willed the second with the first, and brought it about by means of it. There is an exchange on this side, too. In Christ we are made the righteousness of God as Christ was made sin for us. To be made the righteousness of God means (as the positive complement to Christ's being made sin) being put in a place or status in which we are right with God, in which we are pleasing and acceptable to Him, in which we have already been received by Him, in which we are no more and no less right than God Himself is right. And all this in utter contrast to our place and status as the enemies of God, in which we cannot possibly be right with Him, in which we break His covenant with us as far as in us lies. To be made the righteousness of God means to become covenant-partners with God who keep the covenant just as faithfully as He Himself does. To make us that, God made Christ sin. And because He made Christ sin, we have in fact become that. For because He in whom God was present and active, He who knew no sin took our place and status, caused our situation to be His, accepted solidarity with us sinners, in so doing He made our place and status as sinners quite impossible. For in so doing He has finally judged sin in our place and status (ἐν σαρκί, Rom. 8³), i.e., He has done away with it as our human possibility. Where are we as sinners when our sin has been done away in Him ? Where can we stand when our former place and status has been made impossible as such ? There is obviously no other place or status than that of the One who expatriated us by becoming ours : the place and status of the faithful covenant-partner who is pleasing and acceptable to God and who has been accepted by Him ; the place and status of Christ Himself, yes, of the God present and active in Him. In that He took our place, and was made sin for us, we are made the righteousness of God in Him, because we are put in His place.

This exchange is what happened in Christ, according to v. 21. And of the happening in Christ understood in this way Paul says in v. 19 that it is the

atonement, or reconciliation—we can now return to the more obvious meaning
of the concept—of the world with God which has taken place in Him. The
conversion of the world to God has therefore taken place in Christ with the
making of this exchange. There, then, in Christ, the weakness and godlessness
and sin and enmity of the world are shown to be a lie and objectively removed
once and for all. And there, too, in Christ, the peace of the world with God,
the turning of man to Him, his friendship with Him, is shown to be the truth and
objectively confirmed once and for all. That is the history which Paul has to
narrate. As such it is the history of God with Himself, as he has already said in
v. 18. But now it is also the history of God with the world, as we are told in
v. 19. And notice that in this respect too (and the two cannot be separated)
it has taken place once and for all, the history of a decision which has been
taken and which cannot be reversed or superseded. That is how He was in
Christ—we might say with Jn. 3[16] that is how He loved the world—and it is
so, it is in force, and must and will be, whether there are few or many who know
the fact, and whatever attitude the world may take to it. The world is God's.
Whatever else we may have to say about it (e.g., that it perishes) we must also
remember that it is God's—not merely because it is His creature, not merely
because God has sworn to be faithful to man, but because God has kept His
oath, because He has taken the world from a false position in relation to Himself, because He has put it in that place which belongs to it in relationship with
Himself. The reconciliation of the world with God has taken place in Christ.
And because it has taken place, and taken place in Christ, we cannot go back
on it. The sphere behind it has, in a sense, become hollow and empty, a sphere
which we cannot enter. The old has passed away, everything has become new.
The new is conversion to God. In v. 18 Paul said that this had happened to
him personally in Christ. In v. 19, and as the basis of the former verse, he says
that it has happened to the world in Christ. It was a definitive and self-contained
event.

Against this understanding of the statement we cannot appeal to v. 20 of
the same passage, in which Paul singles out as the content of his activity in the
" ministry of reconciliation " the entreaty : " Be ye reconciled to God." This
does not refer to an extension of the atonement in the form of something which
man himself can decide. We recall that in Jn. 3[16] there is a corresponding
mention of faith in the Son gifted, or offered up by God. The Pauline concept
of faith is perhaps too narrow to permit us to equate the " Be ye reconciled to
God " with a call for faith. But it does point in this direction. We can put it
generally in this way. It is a request for the openness, the attention and the
obedience which are needed to acknowledge that what has happened in Christ
has really happened, to enter the only sphere which is now left to man, that of
the new, that of the conversion to God which has taken place in Christ. The
ministry of reconciliation which consists in this entreaty is not of itself self-
contained, but it begins only with this self-contained and completed event. This
ministry is its first concrete result. The world (the Jew first but also the Gentile)
needs this ministry. The community in the world also needs it in order to
be and to remain and continually to become a community. But reconciliation
in itself and as such is not a process which has to be kept in motion towards
some goal which is still far distant. It does not need to be repeated or extended
or perfected. It is a unique history, but as such—because God in Christ was its
subject—it is present in all its fulness in every age. It is also the immediate
future in every age. And finally, it is the future which brings every age to an
end. It rules and controls all the dimensions of time in whose limits the world
and the human race exist. It is that turning from the lie to the truth, i.e., from
the unfaithfulness of man to his faithfulness, and therefore from death to life,
which is the basis of all world occurrence, and in a hidden but supremely true
sense the purpose and measure of all contemporary occurrence, and also its goal,

enclosing it on every side in order to direct it and set it right. As this completed and perfectly completed turning, reconciliation makes necessary the ministry of reconciliation, giving to it a weight and a power to arouse and edify which no other ministry and indeed no other human activity can ever emulate.

The second participle-clause in v. 19 is as follows : " not imputing their trespasses unto them " (i.e., to men in the world). It indicates the presupposition of this ministry. God took the trespasses of men quite seriously. But He did it, as we are told in v. 21, by accepting solidarity, oneness, with those who committed them. And by taking them seriously in this way, He did something total and definitive against human trespasses. He took them out of the world by removing in that exchange their very root, the man who commits them. They cannot continue, just as a plant or tree cannot live on without its root. They can still be committed, but they can no longer count, they can no longer be entered up—like items in a well-kept statement or account. What counts now, what is reckoned to men, is the righteousness of God which they are made in Jesus Christ. That and that alone is their true yesterday and to-day and to-morrow. It is on this basis that Paul takes himself and the world seriously. And it is on this basis that the world must take itself seriously, not on the basis of its trespasses which are written off in Jesus Christ, but on the basis of the righteousness of God which is reckoned to it in Jesus Christ. To call the world to the very different accounting which is only possible in Jesus Christ, that is the task and goal of the ministry of reconciliation, in which Paul finds himself placed as one who has experienced and known it.

This is what we are told in the third participle-clause in v. 19 : " and hath committed unto us (the person of the apostle) the word of reconciliation." Between the apostle and the rest of the world there is the decisive difference that he has eyes and ears for the atonement which has been made, and therefore for the conversion of the world to God, for the new thing which has come and therefore for the passing away of the old, whereas the world is still blind and deaf to it. The world still lives as though the old had not yet passed away and the new come. Not recognising the truth, it still regards the lie as the truth. It still believes that it can and must maintain itself in that sphere which is hollow and empty and in which we cannot live. It is still self-deceived. And Paul sees it dreadfully held by this deception and doomed to its consequences. But it is not this difference, and the tension of it, and the dynamic of this tension, which makes him an apostle. What moves him in this difference, what prevents him from evading the tension as a kind of private person reconciled with God, what forces him to make it his own, to bear it in his own person, is the fact that what has come about for him in Christ as his reconciliation with God has come about for him for the sake of the world. His conversion as such was his calling to be an apostle, his placing in this ministry of reconciliation, or, as it is expressed here, the committing of the " word of reconciliation " to the existence of his person. The " word of reconciliation " is the indicating and making known of reconciliation in the world to which it is still unknown and which is still in the grip of the most profound and tragic self-deception. As Paul is given by Christ eyes and ears for Christ, as the atonement made in Christ becomes his, the God to whom he owes this makes him a mouthpiece to speak of this atonement to those who are still blind and deaf, who are not yet aware of the valid and effective atonement which has been made for them, who therefore lived in opposition to this fact as those who are still unreconciled, as strangers to Christ and therefore to God, and for that reason in the most painful sense of the word, strangers also to the world and to themselves. As one who has been made to see and hear, Paul cannot be silent. Called to this office by God, he has to be the mouthpiece of reconciliation. And that is what makes him an apostle. That is what constrains him. And it is the concrete reach of the turning made in Christ that where it is experienced and known it evokes this movement, underlying the community and its ministry of attestation in the world and against the world and yet also for the world.

We concluded our consideration of Jn. 3[16] with a reference to the ministry of those who, believing on the Son of God, do not perish but have everlasting life. It is not there explicitly in the text. We can only say that the verse can be logically understood only when we find in it this reference. But in 2 Cor. 5[19] both the context and the wording make it the point of the whole verse. Where the atonement made in Jesus Christ is experienced and known, it necessarily evokes this witness. In this case, therefore, we have even better justification for concluding with the judgment that reconciliation manifests itself in the establishment and the actual bearing of a witness to it as the reconciliation of the world.

THE DOCTRINE OF RECONCILIATION (SURVEY)

The content of the doctrine of reconciliation is the knowledge of Jesus Christ who is (1) very God, that is, the God who humbles Himself, and therefore the reconciling God, (2) very man, that is, man exalted and therefore reconciled by God, and (3) in the unity of the two the guarantor and witness of our atonement.

This threefold knowledge of Jesus Christ includes the knowledge of the sin of man : (1) his pride, (2) his sloth and (3) his falsehood—the knowledge of the event in which reconciliation is made : (1) his justification, (2) his sanctification and (3) his calling —and the knowledge of the work of the Holy Spirit in (1) the gathering, (2) the upbuilding and (3) the sending of the community, and of the being of Christians in Jesus Christ (1) in faith, (2) in love and (3) in hope.

1. THE GRACE OF GOD IN JESUS CHRIST

In order to be able to survey the whole, we will first select from the many things that we have to consider and explain in greater detail one primary thing, that in reconciliation as the fulfilment of the covenant of grace, as in the covenant of grace itself, we have to do with a free act of the grace of God. God re-establishes the covenant, or, rather, He maintains and continues it, in order to lead to his goal the man whom He has brought into covenant with Him. Whatever connexions there may be before or behind, they do not alter the fact that in so doing God makes a completely new start as the freest possible subject. No one who really knows Him in this activity will ever be able to think of Him as bound by these connexions or committed to this activity.

He acts to maintain and defend His own glory. But no one and nothing outside Himself could ordain for Him that this should be a matter of His glory. He acts with a view to the goal to which He wills to bring man, but there is not really any necessity which constrains Him to do this. He acts as a Creator to a creature, but sin is the self-surrender of the creature to nothingness. If this is what man wanted, God might easily have allowed man to fall and perish. He had and has plenty of other creatures in whose presence man would not necessarily be missed. He acts with the faithfulness of a covenant-Lord, but He would not have been unfaithful to Himself if He had regarded the covenant which man had broken as invalidated and destroyed. He loved the world of men, but He did not need to continue to love the sinful world of men. We can only say that He has actually done so, and that this decision and act invalidate all questions whether He might not have acted otherwise. He did make it His glory not to allow this creature to perish, not to punish the covenant-breaker by abolishing the covenant, to love sinful man in spite of and even by reason of his sin, to bring him to his goal and not to set any limits to His own faithfulness. He chose this for Himself in spite of everything. And since this was and is His choice and decision and act, those who recognise and value them as His sovereign act will not regard them as fortuitous but will find in the temporal happening of atonement God's eternal covenant with man, His eternal choice of this creature, His eternal faithfulness to Himself and to it. They will see the connexions and in them they will find the constancy of God, the divine will which is preconceived and unalterable and which is therefore necessary and triumphant in this happening. But in the light of this fulfilment of His will they will see that its eternity and inflexibility are those of His free grace, and that the glory which He willed to maintain and defend is that of His mercy—His covenant a covenant of grace and His election an election of grace ; so that conversely the atonement made in Jesus Christ will be seen to be wholly an act of the grace of God and therefore an act of sovereignty which cannot be understood in all its profundity except from the fact that God is this God and a God of this kind.

The Christian dialectic of covenant, sin and reconciliation cannot therefore be subjugated at any point to the Hegelian dialectic of thesis, antithesis and synthesis. To understand it according to this formula is utterly to misunderstand it. Sin does not follow from creation and the covenant. It is already negated and excluded by the will of God active in creation. The covenant established by the free will of God is for the very purpose of safeguarding man against it. Again, sin itself is far from having reconciliation as its necessary consequence. The only necessary consequence of sin is that man should be damned and lost. Again, reconciliation is anything but a synthesis of creation and the covenant on the one hand and sin on the other. Between these there is no higher third thing in which they can be peacefully united. And reconciliation is not a higher unity, but in it God contends one-sidedly for His work in creation and the covenant and therefore one-sidedly against sin. In it the antithesis of sin is, for the first time, sharp and clear-cut. It also differs from the Hegelian synthesis in the fact that as the definitive and self-contained work of God it points beyond itself, not, of course, to a new decline into thesis and antithesis, but forward to the *eschaton* of the resurrection and eternal life, in which it has its goal and every antithesis fades. Speculators of every kind are therefore warned. But it is only the knowledge of the God who speaks and acts in the whole process in free grace which makes all speculation radically impossible.

If the atonement is an act of divine sovereignty, we are forbidden to try to deduce it from anything else or to deduce anything else from it. But, above all, we are commanded to accept and acknowledge it in all its inconceivability as something that has happened, taking it strictly as it is without thinking round it or over it. This is the place and the only place from which as Christians we can think forwards and backwards, from which a Christian knowledge of both God and man is possible. And this is the only place from which we can see and judge from the Christian standpoint what sin is. It is here that Christian preaching and instruction and pastoral care and dogmatics and ethics can begin with their own Yes and No, their *pro* and *contra*. We cannot come to them by any other way or from any higher vantage point. It is here that all natural theology perishes even before it has drawn its first breath. Why ? Because this is the Word in which God Himself has set the beginning of knowledge in the vacuum where there is no beginning for man as estranged from God and himself. It is the possibility of life in general. It is also the possibility of knowledge. And beside it there is no other. This means that basically our knowledge can never get beyond it. As a knowledge of God as well as man, as a looking back to God's election, creation and covenant, and a looking forward to His coming eternal kingdom, it converges upon it from every side. Only here and not elsewhere can it try to see and clarify its presuppositions and deductions. It is therefore true that Christ is the mystery of God, that all the treasures of wisdom and knowledge are hidden in Him and not elsewhere, and that they are to be acquired in Him and not elsewhere (Col. 2³). Why ? Because He who has been appointed by God the beginning of all knowledge is also the One who decides its total compass. It is, therefore, only at the risk of immediate and total blindness that we separate ourselves from it, trying to escape by discovering other depths and heights in other spheres.

Yet it is not the prohibitions that are decisive, but the command— to realise fearlessly and indefatigably in all its aspects the possibility of life and knowledge given us with the atonement made in Jesus Christ. From this source we draw our knowledge of God and man and of eternity behind and above and before us. For individuals, for the whole Church and for each succeeding generation in the Church it is an inexhaustible source. And the knowledge we draw from it is always sure and useful and necessary. It does not need to fear the suspicion that it is perhaps only an uncertain and unpractical and idle play of human thought. On the contrary, it is something which has to be brought out and thought and expressed. Why ? Because God has not posited that beginning of all knowledge in vain, but as the light which does indeed lighten our way and which we have to follow confidently and obediently, with steps which may be great or small but will in any case be unfaltering. In the atonement we are dealing with a sovereign act of God. Therefore we are faced with a command which must direct all our knowing and be fulfilled in our knowing.

This sovereign act is the act of God's grace. The grace of God in the atonement is God's triumph in the antithesis, in the opposition of man to Himself. It is the lordship of His goodness *in medio inimicorum* —original, unilateral, glorious and truly divine—in which He acts quite alone, doing miracle after miracle, in which, therefore, He alone is worthy of honour and praise and glory and worship and thanksgiving. In this activity He cannot be understood except as the One who constantly surpasses Himself in His constancy and faithfulness, and yet who never compromises Himself, who does a new thing and yet does everything in order, who could not be more powerfully holy and righteous than when by His Word and in His Son He calls us who are His enemies His children, when He causes us to be His children, because in His freedom to do that He is truly the Lord. Reconciliation is God's crossing the frontier to man : supremely legitimate and yet supremely inconceivable—or conceivable only in the fact of His act of power and love.

We are reminded of the remarkable verbs used by Paul to indicate the reality of grace when he came to speak of it *expressis verbis* : πλεονάζειν (to grow, to increase, Rom. 6[1, 2], 2 Cor. 4[15]), ὑπερπλεονάζειν (to be present in fulness, 1 Tim. 1[14]), ὑπερβάλλειν (to surpass, to exceed, to excel, 2 Cor. 9[14]), ὑπερπερισσεύειν (to overflow, to superabound, Rom. 5[20]). We find a kind of boundless astonishment on the part of the apostle at the divine intervention acknowledged in the concept grace (or love).

The frontier is a real one. On the one side there is God in His glory as Creator and Lord, and also in the majesty of His holiness and righteousness. And on the other side there is man, not merely the creature, but the sinner, the one who exists in the flesh and who in the flesh is in opposition to Him. It is not merely a frontier, but a yawning abyss. Yet this abyss is crossed, not by man, not by both God and man, but only by God. It happens that God the Creator and the Lord, the Holy and the Righteous, the One who can only hide His face from what man is and does, emerges from the impenetrable mystery of His Godhead, which has become so dreadful to the sin of man, and gives Himself to man and to be known by man, to the one who has the faculties to receive and know Him, but has no will or capacity to use these faculties. He gives Himself to him as his God, as the One who did not and will not cease to be his God, the God of sinful and wholly carnal man. This man does not even know how it comes about or happens to him (" Depart from me, for I am a sinful man, O Lord," Lk. 5[8]). Even afterwards he cannot explain what has happened by any point of contact which God has found in him. But it does in fact happen that by God's intervention this man finds himself accused and humbled and judged by his God, but also and primarily received by Him and reclaimed as His possession and hidden in Him and sustained by Him and addressed and treated as His friend and indeed His child.

So, then, man can have " peace with God " (Rom. 5^1). But how and on what basis ? We can only answer : by the Word of God, in Jesus Christ, by faith in Him, by the Holy Spirit who awakens faith. But all that (and especially the naming of the name of Jesus Christ) simply points us to a riddle which confronts every human How ? or On what basis ?, because it is the grace of God, the coming of God to man which is grounded only in itself and can be known only by itself, the taking place of the atonement willed and accomplished by Him, the sovereign act which God did not owe to Himself or the world or any man, on which no one could bank, yet which has in fact taken place and been made manifest. It is only as willed and accomplished by God that it can be true and known to be true that that peace is given to man, that he can have it, because the covenant broken by us has been kept and fulfilled by God and is therefore in being, that in spite of ourselves, and therefore in a way which at bottom is inconceivable to us, we who are gainsayers and rebels are genuinely converted to God and are His people in the same sense that He is our God. That is the insoluble mystery of the grace of God enclosed in the name of Jesus Christ before which we stand at this point.

As His act, it is the most actual thing in heaven or earth. Effective by Him, it is effective as nothing else is effective. Revealed in Him, as His revelation it is brighter and clearer and more certain than the light of the sun or the light of any other knowledge. Already in this preliminary survey we can and must state that the righteousness with which man finds himself in some sense clothed is His righteousness and therefore new and strange, the holiness is His holiness and therefore new and strange, the truth His truth and therefore new and strange : " crowned with mercy and lovingkindness " (Ps. 103^4, cf. Ps. 5^{12}). Because of this everything depends absolutely on His blessing, everything on His Word which is itself the reconciling act, everything on God Himself in the uniqueness of His action in Jesus Christ for each and every man, which as such is also the mystery of the present and future of each and every man. Everything depends on Him who is above, and therefore on what comes to man from Him and therefore from above. It does not depend at all on what man had or has or will have to contribute from below. When man is asked concerning his righteousness or holiness or truth, he can only point to his utter lack of all these things and then at once point away from himself to his clothing or crowning with all these things, that is, to Jesus Christ. The event of atonement and the actuality of man reconciled with God can be described by those who know it only in the words of Lk. 15^2 : " This man receiveth sinners, and eateth with them." It is the Holy Spirit who lays this self-knowledge upon their hearts and this confession upon their lips. It is faith and love and hope which know and speak in this way. Christian obedience consists in this, and its joy and certainty rest and renew themselves on this : that by the grace of God this is the relationship of God with man. For what the Christian community can have specially as knowledge and experience of the atonement made in Jesus Christ, for the power, therefore, of its witness to the world, everything depends on the simplicity of heart which is ready to let the grace of God be exclusively His grace, His sovereign act, His free turning to man as new and strange every morning, so that it does not know anything higher or better or more intimate or real than the fact that quite apart from anything that he can contribute to God or become and be in contrast to Him, unreservedly therefore and undeservedly, man can hold fast to God and live by and in this holding fast to Him.

In this introductory survey we must also state that unfortunately the paths of Evangelical and Roman Catholic understanding have diverged widely at this point. In the light of the latest doctrine in relation to the Virgin Mary (1950), the proclamation of which has shed a new and garish light on the situation, we can only say that, humanly speaking, they have diverged hopelessly. The heart and guiding principle of the Romanist doctrine of grace is the negation of the unity of grace as always God's grace to man, as His sovereign act which is everywhere new and strange and free. It is the negation of the unity of grace as His grace in Jesus Christ. It is the division of grace by which it is first of all His, but then—and this is where the emphasis falls—effected and empowered by His grace, it is also our grace. Against this view we must at once and quite definitely set our face (for what follows, cf. the survey given in B. Bartmann, *Dogm. Handb.* vol. 2, 1929, 113).

In the Romanist teaching a distinction is made between *gratia increata*, which is God Himself, who is the divine will of love and therefore the ground of all grace, and *gratia creata*, which is the " finite product " of the former, " but which is essentially different from God Himself, a created good." We ask : What is this created good when it is a matter of peace between man and the Creator who has been offended by him ? How and in what sense can he rely on this " finite product " ? How can it be essentially different from God and yet be His grace which reconciles us with Himself ?

In the Romanist teaching there is a *gratia externa* which works on us only from without in the form of teaching and example. " We have to do here with the life and death of Christ, His Gospel, His miracles, providence, personal experiences, the effectiveness of the Church, the exemplary conversation of the saints. This influence is moral." For the most part it is, of course, connected with the *gratia interna*. It aims ultimately at inward effects. But it does not produce them of itself. It simply prepares the way. It makes the soul receptive. In contrast, the inward grace " effects the soul and its basic faculties, raising it to a new order of being. Its influence is physical." It adheres to the soul as a new form. We ask : How can the life and death of Christ and the Gospel (mentioned in the same breath as the effectiveness of the Church and the exemplary conversation of the saints and other good things) be described as " only " an external grace and as such obviously impotent and defective ? What is this " physical " influence compared with which that of the Gospel is " only " moral ? —as though the outward moral grace were not the most inward and physical. And what is this form of the soul in a higher order of being in which we are not referred absolutely and exclusively to that *gratia externa* which has only moral significance but can find comfort and be reconciled with God physically, in and by ourselves ?

Within the decisive *gratia interna* there is a personal grace of sanctification (*gratia gratiam faciens*) and a grace of office (*gratia gratis data*), the charismatic endowment " which is for the most part firmly linked with the priestly *ordo* " and which reveals itself in the official power of the priesthood. We ask : Is there a personal sanctification, or a charismatic, or shall we say a priestly endowment which can be wrested even for a moment from the hand of the God who shows His grace to sinful man, and made a possession of the man who receives it, so that it does not have to be sought and received every morning afresh from God ? If either the one or the other or both are really effective, how can they be so except from the very first in the event of their giving and receiving ?

A further distinction is then made between *gratia actualis* and *gratia habitualis*. Both of these are subdivisions of the grace of sanctification. The first is a *motio divina* " which is given only for a time to do one or more acts." It serves to prepare the way for the reception of habitual grace, and to maintain it when it has been received, increasing it and enabling it to bring forth fruit. Habitual grace itself is constant, creating in man a kind of state of grace. We ask : Can a *motio divina* really be only a preparation for something higher and better, a means only to maintain and prosper it ? Not an awakening of faith and obedience, but the *conditio sine qua non* of a real grace which consists in a human competence ? And what kind of a competence is this ? And what place is there for it in face of the actuality—not of human acts, but of the being and action of the gracious God ? Is there a human *habitus* which deserves to be called a *habitus* of grace in itself, and as such is opposed to the actual grace of God ?

There is a further distinction between *gratia medicinalis* and *gratia elevans*. Once again, the first is simply a preparation for the second, the capacitating of men for acts of the supernatural life, by the healing of his nature from the wounds of original sin and the removal of human ignorance and concupiscence. As against this, *gratia elevans*, which is the substance of *gratia interna*, as its very name indicates, accomplishes the lifting up of the faculties of the soul to another order of being, making men capable of purely supernatural activities. We ask : Is then the work of Christ as a Healer only preparatory ? Does He not in this way lift us up to the supernatural life ? Does He only prepare us in this way for a true being in grace, in which we will no longer need Him as a Healer, in which we are no longer the sick folk that He came to heal ?

Again, there is a distinction between *gratia praeveniens* and *gratia concomitans*. The first precedes our free decision, stirring up the will to do good. The other accompanies and supports and gives stability to the activity of man as he is already free. We ask : In relation to the free will of sinful man, is grace only a stirring up of that will to do good, and then the accompanying and supporting and continual strengthening of its activity ? Is there then no new creation ? No awakening from the dead ? Of what two partners are we really speaking then ? If we are speaking of the gracious God and sinful man, how can we ever cease at any point to understand the grace which comes from God to man wholly and utterly and exclusively as *gratia praeveniens* ? Can it really be understood, will it be understood, except as the grace which heals us and for that very reason lifts us up ?

A further distinction is made between *gratia operans* and *gratia cooperans*. The first is active in us alone and without any co-operation on our part (*in nobis sine nobis*). Again, this is thought of as only preparatory to our own good actions : " It sets in motion those pious thoughts and stimulations of the will which always precede the free decision." As against that, *gratia cooperans* always works together with the free will (*in nobis cum nobis*). We ask : On what basis is there ever a *cooperari* in the relationship between the gracious God and sinful man which is not also and as such a pure *operari* ? How do the work of God and the work of man ever come to stand on the same level, so that they can mutually limit and condition each other ? How can the " above " of God which renews, and the " below " of man which stands in need of renewal, ever be placed side by side ? How can the " below " of man, even when it has in fact been renewed, ever come to imagine that its renewal is a result of co-operation between the renewing " above " of God and itself ?

Again, there is a distinction between *gratia sufficiens* and *gratia efficax*. The one is a grace which merely reaches out and is sufficient, but is not in itself and as such accompanied by any result. It is a grace which has to be completed by the free decision of the human will or by *gratia efficax* (a grace maintained by the Thomists in their controversy with the Molinists). This latter grace is added to the former and lends it the necessary force. We ask : Is grace as such ever *sufficiens* without being *efficax*? Is it ever effective objectively without being effective subjectively ? Is grace ever a pre-condition for something else, a pre-condition which can come into force only by the free will of man or the addition of a further grace ? Does the fact that man believes he can evade or resist it mean that we can speak of a grace which is not effective ? Is not the really dreadful thing about human resistance to it the fact that in itself and as such, as an act of divine sovereignty, it is not merely a condition proposed to man but the absolutely binding and effective determination of his existence, which he contradicts by his resistance ?

Finally, there is a distinction (the most remarkable of all) between *gratia Christi* and *gratia Dei*, or *gratia supernaturalis* and *gratia naturalis*. Since all the graces so far mentioned are extended in virtue of the merits of Christ, " they are all called the grace of Christ." Over against, or rather preceding them, there is a special " grace of God," *gratia sanitatis*, granted to man in Paradise when he was at any rate not positively unworthy of it. This grace became his own, and it is evident that it was not simply removed even from sinful man, but still remains as *gratia naturalis*. We ask : Is the concept "grace of Christ " only a kind of generic name for all the other graces ? Are they merely called the grace of Christ, or are they all really His one grace ? And if they are called this because they really are, is it enough to say that they are because the merits of Christ constitute the possibility and condition of their distribution ? Does not this mean that at bottom the grace of Christ is restricted to those graces which are distinguished by the special concepts of *gratia externa, praeveniens, operans, sufficiens*, whereas the true graces, *gratia interna, habitualis, cooperans, efficax*, being only prepared and made possible by it, will necessarily bear another name because they derive from another source ? Can we say " the grace of Christ " and mean less than the whole reality of the grace of God, the grace which cannot be exceeded by any other or higher grace, which cannot precede a true grace because it is itself the only true grace and all that grace ? " The Catholic conception understands the essence of grace to be that which mediates between the will of God and the will of man " (Bartmann, p. 17). If we accept this as our " conception," how then in this mediatorial capacity can it be anything other than the grace of Christ and therefore the one grace of God—as though there were other mediators or mediations which we have to distinguish from the one Mediator ? But if it is the one grace of God, how does it come about that before or alongside it there is a special *gratia Dei*, a *gratia sanitatis* or *naturalis* extended to our first parents or to man in his creaturely nature ? At what point in his history or in what depth of his creaturely nature can the grace of God come to man except as the grace of Christ ? Is it that we are dealing with another God than the One who is Father, Son and Holy Spirit, and who has elected from all eternity to be the God of man in Jesus Christ—so that naturally we are dealing with the other grace of this other God ? But what other God can be the God of man, and what other grace can there be as a *gratia sanitatis* ? But again, if the grace of Christ is the one grace of God, what place is there for these distinctions, which all have the one result, of distinguishing and indeed separating a grace in itself from a grace for us, a grace which is objectively indispensable from a grace which is subjectively effective, a grace which is merely stimulative and preparatory from a grace which co-operates with us, e.g., a *gratia operans* which, as a pure act of God, is enclosed in itself as in a glass-case from a *gratia co-operans* which lays claim upon us, or a grace which merely cleanses us from a grace which lifts us up, in short a grace which is manifestly incomplete from a grace which is perfect and complete ? How dare we split up the grace of Christ and the grace of God in this way ? Is it not the case that as outward grace, for example (that which is described as the grace of the life and death of Christ, of the Gospel, etc.), it is wholly inward and proper to man, and conversely, that as inward grace which is proper to us it is altogether outward, the grace of the life and death of Christ and the grace of the Gospel ? Similarly, is it not the case that actual grace is habitual, and habitual actual ? That *gratia praeveniens* is *concomitans*, and *sufficiens efficax*, and *vice versa* ? How can that which is described as the second and perfect be perfect except in the power of the first, which is regarded as so meagre and impotent as a purely enabling and preparatory grace ? How can the first not have already in itself the perfection of the second ? If there is one God, and one Mediator between God and man, and therefore one grace— what place is there for all these abstractions ? These are the questions which crowd in upon us as we face the final Roman Catholic distinction.

But the Romanist doctrine of grace insists on these abstractions. Naturally it also maintains—rather more emphatically on the Thomist side and rather less emphatically on the Jesuit—that in the last resort there is only one grace. But it merely says this : it does not make any use of it. It simply commemorates the fact. It says it as a precaution, e.g., to ward off the kind of questions that we have been putting. When left to itself and following its own inclination it says something very different ; it talks about the division of grace. It says the first thing as a bracket in which to say the second : but it does not abolish the parenthesis in order to say it.

For, if it did, the fact would be revealed which is plainly enough proclaimed by all these characterisations and emphases, that it is definitely much more interested in the *gratia interna* than the *gratia externa*, in habitual grace than actual, in the grace which uplifts than the grace which heals, in *gratia cooperans* than *gratia operans*, in other words in the state and life and activity of grace in man than in Christ as the One who accomplishes the sovereign act of God and what man is in and by Him, in Mary than the Son of Mary, in the sacraments as the supposed means of grace than the Word and Spirit of God who reveals and attests and in that way really mediates it, in the Church as the form of grace, in the priesthood and its authority than the Lord of the community which lives by the Word and Spirit of God and therefore in His service. This is the system of fatal preferences which would be revealed if the theology of Rome were to speak of the unity of grace instead of its division, and it is to be feared that the unity which it would choose would necessarily be that of man in grace, of Mary, of the sacraments, of the Church ruled and directed by the priesthood.

Alternatively, the revelation of this strange preference might cause it to take fright and to abandon it. It would then have to decide to become a real doctrine of the grace of Christ. It would have to notice that the subjective side to which it has everywhere addressed itself in the sphere of those twofold concepts is utterly dependent upon and can be known and determined only by the objective, which it has commemorated but then abandoned it as though it were only a *conditio sine qua non*. It would have to learn to trust that the genuinely subjective is already included in the true objective, and will be found in it and not elsewhere. But in this case the Romanist theology would have to become Evangelical. And in view of its authoritative pronouncements it seems less likely to happen to-day than at any time.

What is certain is that we have to take warning at this point. If it is a matter of the grace of the one God and the one Christ, there can be only one grace. We cannot, therefore, split it up into an objective grace which is not as such strong and effective for man but simply comes before him as a possibility, and a subjective grace which, occasioned and prepared by the former, is the corresponding reality as it actually comes to man. But the grace of the one God and the one Christ, and therefore the objective grace which never comes to man except from God, must always be understood as the one complete grace, which is subjectively strong and effective in its divine objectivity, the grace which does actually reconcile man with God. And the test of this understanding of grace must be that the state of man in relation to it—apart from what we can positively say concerning him in the light of it—is clearly and unequivocally described as one of absolute need : a state in which—with all that this involves—he is and remains always a recipient, a state in which he not only does not cease but can never do more than begin (and he will always be a beginner) to beg and to reach out for it in his poverty, in order that in that poverty he may be rich. The Romanist doctrine of grace cannot survive this test. It ascribes to man in grace an *exousia* in which he can look back to the grace of Christ as such as to an indispensable but preliminary stage which he has already passed. It furnishes him with a wealth in which he is no longer poor and needy and hungry and sick, in which, therefore, he cannot be the recipient of the one complete grace of God and of Christ. At the point where its true interest emerges, it definitely does not describe him as the being which has known and experienced and acknowledged the atonement as the sovereign act of God. As reflected in its description of man in grace, God has ceased to be the free subject of the atonement, the grace of the atonement has ceased to be His grace. And since this is so, there can be no peace between this and the Evangelical doctrine of grace.

But we must not omit an irenical and ecumenical word at the conclusion of this confessional polemic. There is a very deep peace (beyond any understanding) between us Evangelical Christians and our Catholic fellow-Christians who are badly instructed in this doctrine. We cannot believe that they do in fact live by the grace which is so dreadfully divided in their dogmatics. Rather, we have to believe, and it is comforting to believe, that they as well as we—if only we did it better—do live by the one undivided grace of Jesus Christ. We have badly misunderstood what we have had to say in clear opposition to their teaching if we do not believe and therefore confess this. We wish that they would abandon both their teaching and many—very many—things in their practice which correspond so closely to it. We wish that they would give God the glory which their dogmatics (and not only their dogmatics) obviously does not give, so that we could then stand with them in a genuine *communio in sacris*. But we trust in that *communio in sacris* which—not made with hands—has already been achieved by the sovereign act of the God who reconciles us men with Himself and therefore with one another : on the far side of the Church's doctrine and practice, which even at its best (whether Evangelical or Catholic) can only be a witness made with the best of human understanding and conscience to the God who is greater than us all.

It is fitting that at this point we ourselves should now look very carefully in this other direction—at the man to whom this sovereign act applies, the man who is reconciled with God on the basis of this sovereign act. God has acted in His grace (which is always His). He has acted, therefore, without us and against us and for us, as a free subject in Jesus Christ. He has by Himself posited a new beginning. But He has really acted. What He has done is not just something which applies to us and is intended for us, a proffered opportunity and possibility. In it He has actually taken us, embraced us, as it were surrounded us, seized us from behind and turned us back again to Himself. We are dealing with the fulfilment of the covenant. God has always kept it but man has broken it. It is this breach which is healed in the sovereign act of reconciliation. God was not ready to acquiesce in the fact that while He was for us we were against Him. That had to be altered, and in Jesus Christ it has in fact been altered once and for all. That is the original and unilateral and sovereign triumph of God. That is the meaning of the crossing of the frontier or abyss from God's side as it took place in the existence of the man Jesus. The offence offered to God by the unfaithfulness of His covenant-partner, and the misery of that partner, are both removed in Him. In Him man keeps and maintains the same faithfulness to God that God had never ceased to maintain and keep to him. God keeps and maintains His faithfulness by looking and going away past the transgression of man and Himself entering in and providing for the faithfulness of man and therefore for the fulfilment of the covenant, even on the side of man. In this way God takes care for His own glory. And He does it by bringing man to glory. That is His sovereign act in the atonement. That is the grace of Jesus Christ.

It is apparent at once that the formula " God everything and man nothing " as a description of grace is not merely a " shocking simplification " but complete nonsense. Man is nothing, i.e., he has fallen a prey to nothingness, without the grace of God, as the transgressor who has delivered himself up to death, as the covenant breaker he has shown himself to be in relation to God. In the giving of His Son, however, in reconciling the world to Himself in Christ, God is indeed everything but only in order that man may not be nothing, in order that he may be His man, in order that as such he, too, may be everything in his own place, on his own level and within his own limits. The meaning and purpose of the atonement made in Jesus Christ is that man should not cease to be a subject in relation to God but that he should be maintained as such, or rather—seeing that he has himself surrendered himself as such—that he should be newly created and grounded as such, from above. This creating and grounding of a human subject which is new in relation to God and therefore in itself is, in fact, the event of the atonement made in Jesus Christ. This is what was altered in Him. This is what was accomplished by the grace of God effective and revealed in Him. In Him a new human subject was introduced, the true man beside and outside whom God does not know any other, beside and outside whom there is no other, beside and outside whom the other being of man, that old being which still continues to break the covenant, can only be a lie, an absurd self-deception, a shadow moving on the wall—the being of that man who has been long since superseded and replaced and who can only imagine that he is man, while in reality he is absolutely nothing. Yes, the atonement is the filling of this abyss of nothing, of human perdition. And it is by the abyss of the divine mercy that that other abyss is filled. It is this pure divine mercy which fills the abyss, the mercy which we have to recognise and adore in this act of God, the mercy which we have to seek afresh every morning, the mercy for which we can only ask and reach out as beggars, the mercy in relation to which we can only be recipients. By the grace of God, therefore, man is not nothing. He is God's man. He is accepted by God. He is recognised as himself a free subject, a subject who has been made free once and for all by his restoration as the faithful covenant partner of God. This is something which we must not conceal. It is something which we must definitely proclaim in our Evangelical understanding of grace. We cannot say and demand and expect too much or too great things of man when we see him as He really is in virtue of the giving of the Son of God, of the fact that God has reconciled the world to Himself in Christ.

We underline the fact that it is a matter of a being of man. We can and must experience and know this—that is what makes a Christian a Christian. But first of all, and in itself, and as the object of this experience and knowledge it is a being. Being reconciled is not a matter of the mere hoping or thinking or feeling or experience or even conviction of man. It cannot in any sense be interpreted as a matter of hypothesis (with all the " uncertainty " to which this necessarily gives rise). Its force does not depend upon the intensity with which it is hazarded, while all the time its truth is in the last resort a matter for doubt. No, the old has indeed passed away, all things are become new, God was in Christ reconciling the world to Himself, and those who believe in Him do not perish but have everlasting life. The new man who keeps the covenant has been born and is alive and revealed. Therefore we have peace with God—without any uncertainty. This alteration in the human situation has already taken place. This being is self-contained. It does not have to be reached or created. It has already come and cannot be removed. It is indestructible, it can never be superseded, it is in force, it is directly present. This is the mystery of the man reconciled to God in Jesus Christ. This is what is experienced and known in Christian knowledge and experience. And if in describing this knowledge and experience as such we have to mention all kinds of human hopes and thoughts and feelings and experiences and convictions and hypotheses and " uncertainties "—and why should not this be the case, why is it not necessarily the case in this connexion ?—it is always clear that if we are really dealing with Christian knowledge and experience all these things are only comparable with the foam of a waterfall plunging down from the highest mountain tops. They derive necessarily from that being. Any truth and power that they have can come only from that in itself enduring being. Human experience and knowledge cannot of themselves attain to the being of reconciled man. They have no power to rise from appearance to being. The being is there first, and in the power of it it is then followed by everything which may happen as a more or less clear and certain acknowledgment on the part of man. Notice that we are not talking *in abstracto* of the being of God or the reality and power of the divine act of sovereignty. We are now looking at man. We are speaking of the being of man reconciled to God in Jesus Christ For it is the meaning and reach of the atonement made in Jesus Christ, the power of the divine act of sovereignty in grace, that God willed not to keep to Himself His own true being, but to make it as such our human being and in that way to turn us back to Himself, to create the new man, to provide for the keeping of the covenant by us, to give us peace with Himself. In the atonement it is a matter of God and His being and activity for us and to us. And that means an alteration of the human situation, the result of which is an altered being of man, a being of man divinely altered. It is on this basis that as Christians we cannot think or demand or expect too much or too high things of man. He is reconciled to God in Jesus Christ. If he is to be understood aright, he can and should be understood in the light of this fact. This is the denominator by which we have to view everything that he is and does and everything that we can think and say concerning him. He can still rebel and lie and fear, but only in conflict, in impotent conflict, with his own most proper being. He can and necessarily will be judged, but his own most proper being will be his judge. All his mistakes and confusions and sins are only like waves beating against the immovable rock of his own most proper being and to his sorrow necessarily breaking and dashing themselves to pieces against this rock. But human obedience, too, human constancy and virtue, useful human knowledge, human faith and love and hope, all these are only a standing and walking on the rock which bears him up, the rock of the new being given to him as his own. An Evangelical doctrine of the grace of God—if it is not to give offence and to lay itself open to the objections of its Romanist opponents—will not be guilty of a nominalism which compromises or even negates this being of the man reconciled to God in Jesus Christ. This being is the first and basic thing which we must seriously and definitively ascribe to the man reconciled to God in Jesus Christ. It is something that we have to expound and understand. We cannot go back a single step behind this being of the reconciled man. Whatever we have to think and say of man, and not only of the Christian but of man in general, at every point we have to think and say it of his being as man reconciled in Jesus Christ.

We speak of man reconciled in Jesus Christ and therefore of the being which is that of man in Him. In so doing we will characterise and describe it in its concrete reality, its individuality and power. The grace of God in which it comes and is made over to us is the grace of Jesus Christ, that is, the grace in which God from all eternity has chosen man (all men) in this One, in which He has bound Himself to man—before man even existed—in this One. He, Jesus Christ, is the

One who accomplishes the sovereign act in which God has made true and actual in time the decree of His election by making atonement, in which He has introduced the new being of all men. Notice that it is those that know this new being as their own who can openly and confidently and joyfully hail it as such. It is Christians therefore who, when they have spoken of it relevantly, seriously and authoritatively, have always characterised and described it as the being which has met them as their own in Jesus Christ, which they sought and found, and found again in Him, on which they cannot pride themselves, and by which they can live only because they found it exclusively in Him.

Those who believe in Jesus Christ will never forget for a single moment that the true and actual being of reconciled man has its place in that Other who is strange and different from them, and that that is why they can participate in it with a fulness and clarity the knowledge of which would only be broken if they were to look aside to any other place. They will know that they can speak about the being of the new man only in the light of this One, and that they can never speak about it definitely enough in the light of this One. It is the being of the new man reconciled with God which in Him has truly and actually been appropriated to them and to all men.

2. THE BEING OF MAN IN JESUS CHRIST

We cannot speak of the being of man except from the standpoint of the Christian and in the light of the particular being of man in Jesus Christ. To the Christian it is a matter of experience and knowledge. He knows about Jesus Christ, and the reconciliation of the world to God made in Him, and therefore the new being of man in Him. He can give an account and testify to himself and others how this new being originates. God has given it to all men in Jesus Christ. But we cannot expect that all men will be in a position to know and to give an account of Him and therefore of their true and actual being as it is hidden and enclosed and laid up for them in Him. Yet we must remember that what we can say primarily only of the Christian has a general application in the sense that we could at once say it of all men if they came to know of Jesus Christ and of what they are in Him. Christians exist in Him. In practice this is the only thing that we can call their peculiar being. But they do so only as examples, as the representatives and predecessors of all other men, of whom so long as their ears and eyes and hearts are not opened we can only say definitely that the same being in Jesus Christ is granted to them and belongs to them in Him. But Christians know and can declare what it is that belongs to them and all other men in Jesus Christ. And by the existence of the Christian we can make this clear. The being of man reconciled with God in Jesus Christ is reflected in the existence of the Christian. That is something we cannot say of others. It is not that they lack Jesus Christ and in Him the being of man reconciled to God. What they lack is obedience to His Holy Spirit, eyes and ears and hearts which are open to Him, experience and knowledge of the conversion of man to God which took place in Him, the new direction which must correspond to the new being given to them in Him, life in and with His community, a part in its ministry, the confession of Him and witness to Him as its Lord and as the Head of all men. For that reason the being of man reconciled to God in Jesus Christ is not—yet—reflected in them. To understand and describe it, therefore, we must confine ourselves to Christians and the Christian community. The being of man reconciled to God in Jesus Christ has three aspects which are clearly different. We will first of all describe these under the three concepts of faith and love and hope. We will then see how the being of the new man described in this way has its root and basis in Jesus Christ Himself, His person and mission and work, how it is in fact hidden and enclosed and laid up in Him. But in the faith and love and hope of the Christian that which is hidden in Jesus Christ is known, that which is enclosed is opened, that which is laid up is distributed and shared. Yet they know, and they keep to this strictly, that it is known to them only as that which is hidden in Him, it is opened only as that which is enclosed in Him, it is shared only as that which is laid up in Him. They are put in this relationship to Him by the presence and operation of the Holy Spirit. It is this relationship which is described by the concepts of faith and love and hope. We will now try to follow the lines indicated by these three concepts.

The conversion of man to God in Jesus Christ takes place (1) in the fulfilment and revelation of a verdict of God on man. The being of the new man in the form of faith is man's recognition, acknowledgment and acceptance of this verdict, the making of his own subjection to this verdict. That man does accept and bow to this verdict is the work of the Holy Spirit which makes him a Christian. The verdict of God to which faith subjects itself is two-sided. It has both a negative and also a positive meaning and content.

On the one side it is a verdict which disowns and renounces. With all the truth and validity and force of a sentence which has not only been pronounced but executed, and therefore pronounced once and for all, it declares that man is no longer the transgressor, the sinner, the covenant-breaker that God has found him and he must confess himself to be, that as such he has died and perished from the earth, that he cannot be dealt with as such, that as such he has no future. Jesus Christ has taken his place as a malefactor. In his place Jesus Christ has suffered the death of a malefactor. The sentence on him as a sinner has been carried out. It cannot be reversed. It does not need to be repeated. It has fallen instead on Jesus Christ. In and with the man who was taken down dead on Golgotha man the

covenant-breaker is buried and destroyed. He has ceased to be. The
wrath of God which is the fire of His love has taken him away and all his
transgressions and offences and errors and follies and lies and faults
and crimes against God and his fellowmen and himself, just as a whole
burnt offering is consumed on the altar with the flesh and skin and
bones and hoofs and horns, rising up as fire to heaven and disappearing. That is how God has dealt with the man who broke covenant
with Himself. God has vindicated Himself in relation to this man, as
He did as Creator in relation to chaos. He could not, and would not,
use this man. He could not, and would not, tolerate and have him
any longer. He could and would only do away with him. He could
and would only disown and renounce his existence. And that is what
He has done, not merely in the form of a protest and contradiction,
which would clarify but not alter the situation between them, but in
the form of his destruction. This event is the divine verdict, the
Word in which Christian faith believes. In virtue of this Word, i.e.,
in the power of this event, the existence of man as a sinner and all
his transgressions are now behind him. Whatever else he may be, he
will no longer be this man, the transgressor. Most definitely not, as
the man who is placed under this Word. The word " forgiveness "
speaks of a judicial act in which God has maintained His glory in
relation to man. But it does not speak of a new purpose or disposition
or attitude on the part of God. And least of all does it speak of any
mitigation of the severity with which sinful man is rejected by God.
Rather it speaks of the fulfilment of that rejection. The being of the
new man reconciled with God in Jesus Christ is one in which man has
no more future as sinful man. And in the form of Christian faith it is
a being in subjection to this verdict, and in that way and to that
extent a being in " the forgiveness of sins."

But the verdict of God on man in which the conversion of man to
God is fulfilled has also a positive meaning and content. It is a verdict
which recognises and accepts. With all the truth and validity and
force of a sentence which has not only been pronounced but executed
and therefore pronounced once and for all, it declares that God receives
man, and that man in accordance with his election and institution as a
covenant-partner—can confess himself a faithful servant of God, His
recognised friend and well-loved child. In that event and verdict and
Word God willed to snuff out and kill and destroy. He has done so.
But He did it to secure freedom for the man in whom He delights,
the man who is not merely innocent but positively righteous, the man
who fulfils His will. This man alone is man's future. For it was as
such that Jesus Christ took his place. And in his place Jesus Christ
rendered that obedience which is required of the covenant partner of
God, and in that way found His good pleasure. He did it by taking
to Himself the sins of all men, by suffering as His death the death to
which they had fallen a prey, by freely offering Himself as the sacrifice

which had to be made when God vindicated Himself in relation to man, by choosing to suffer the wrath of God in His own body and the fire of His love in His own soul. It was in that way that He was obedient. It was in that way that He was the righteous One. It was in that way that He was recognised by God—and since He took the place of all, all men in Him. Even on this side, as the positive justification of man, the judgment of God was executed, and can never be reversed and does not need to be repeated. The resurrection of Jesus Christ from the dead is at once the fulfilment and the proclamation of this positive sentence of God. Man is a suitable human partner for the divine partner. He is the one in whom God delights. He is a faithful servant and a friend and a dear child of God. This man was brought in with the resurrection of Jesus Christ from the grave, and with just the same energy with which the old man of contradiction and opposition was done away in the death of Jesus Christ. With the creation of the new man God has vindicated Himself to us, pronouncing His verdict upon us. He willed this man. And what He willed took place. This man came, the man who is righteous for us all, who is our righteousness before God. There is no room for any fears that in the justification of man we are dealing only with a verbal action, with a kind of bracketed " as if," as though what is pronounced were not the whole truth about man. Certainly we have to do with a declaring righteous, but it is a declaration about man which is fulfilled and therefore effective in this event, which corresponds to actuality because it creates and therefore reveals the actuality. It is a declaring righteous which without any reserve can be called a making righteous. Christian faith does not believe in a sentence which is ineffective, or only partly effective. As faith in Jesus Christ who is risen from the dead it believes in a sentence which is absolutely effective, so that man is not merely called righteous before God, but is righteous before God. He believes that God has vindicated Himself in relation to man, not partly but wholly, not negatively only but positively, replacing the old man by a new and obedient man. He believes that by calling that One His own dear Son in whom He is well pleased, God has set up not a provisional but a definitive order in the relationship between Himself and man. He believes in the freedom of the children of God which is not merely demonstrated but given and made over in the resurrection of Jesus Christ from the dead. He believes in the fulfilment of the divine election actualised in this event, and therefore in the revelation and demonstration of it given in this event. As faith it lives by the divine Word of power spoken in this event. The being of the new man reconciled with God in Jesus Christ is one in which man has a future only as the righteous one that he is before God in Jesus Christ. In Christian faith man subjects himself to the judgment by which eternal life is already—effectively—ascribed and promised to him, a judgment beside which he is not able to see before him any other.

We have been speaking of what is usually comprised under the concept of justification. Justification definitely means the sentence executed and revealed in Jesus Christ and His death and resurrection, the No and the Yes with which God vindicates Himself in relation to covenant-breaking man, with which He converts him to Himself and therefore reconciles him with Himself. He does it by the destruction of the old and the creation of a new man.

But we can understand the concept justification (the justification of the sinner) in all its truth and individual force only when we see that basically and inclusively it stands for God's acting and speaking in His own cause, in fulfilment of His eternal will with man. Only then and on that basis does it stand for the grace and goodness and mercy of God as they come to man. These inconceivable benefits do, of course, come to man. It is the eternal will of God to let them do so. But Christian faith finds all its comfort and joy in the fact, and it clings to it, that this gracious and good and merciful judgment of God on man is primarily God's own cause, that in this judgment the cause of man is safeguarded—and with a sovereign assurance—by the fact that God has made it His own cause, and that as such, quite apart from anything that we can do about it, He carried it through to a successful conclusion. In the light of this Christian faith itself, as man's subjection to this verdict, can be understood as a form of the being of the new man. It is in faith that man can find and know that he is justified with an ultimate confidence and assurance. For His own honour and glory, acting solely in His own cause, God has denied and renounced his being in unrighteousness. That is the force of this verdict on the negative side. That is the meaning of it in all circumstances. That is why the believer will not perish. That is why his sins are forgiven. Again, for His own honour and glory, acting solely in His own cause, God has recognised and accepted a being in righteousness. That is the force of the verdict on the positive side. And in all circumstances man can and should hold to the fact that this verdict is in force and that he is the servant and friend and child of God. In virtue of this verdict he has eternal life. The truth and power of faith depend on the fact that it is not a work of human arbitrariness, not even the arbitrariness of a supreme need and longing for redemption, but man's subjection to the divine verdict in which it is a matter of God's own honour and glory—and as such a subjection an act of pure obedience. As this act of obedience faith is a work of the Holy Spirit, and as true faith, and only as such, it is justifying faith.

Why is it so necessary to be clear about this? There are other forms of the new man besides faith and therefore subjection to God's sentence of negative and positive pardon. But in the conversion of man to God we have to do with this basic thing. The being of the new man is a being in the truth and force of this twofold pardon. To that extent faith is the only form of this new being. Before God, i.e., in relationship to God, we are not unrighteous and rejected but righteous and accepted only by faith, not by love and hope. And we are this by faith in so far as faith is that act of obedience, that subjection to the will of God acting and speaking in His own cause and therefore in sovereign power, that acknowledgment of the honour and glory of God in relation to man. It cannot, therefore, be an arbitrary human act. Even if it is a knowledge and acceptance of what has taken place negatively and positively for all men in Jesus Christ, it is not enough—if it is really to be justifying faith and the form of the new being of man—that it should simply know this and accept it. Even if it is the heart's confidence of this or that man that what took place for all men in Jesus Christ took place and is true and actual and applies in his case, too, it is still not enough—however great may be the depth and sincerity of this confidence—if faith is to justify him and in faith he is to be a new man. It is not enough because that twofold divine pardon was pronounced in Jesus Christ, that destruction of the unrighteous and creation of the righteous being took place—and this is why it is true and actual—in Him. It was for man, but it was for man in Him, in the One who is another, a stranger, confronting even man with his sincere acceptance and heart's confidence, in the One to whom man can only cling as to the high-priest who officiates and speaks and acts for him, that is to say, in faith in Him. Not in faith in himself.

To put it even more clearly and pointedly—only with a lack of faith in himself. The great gulf between the believer and the One in whom he believes carries with it the fact that he cannot receive that pardon and experience his liberation from unrighteousness and to righteousness without having to become aware and recognise and confess that in himself he is altogether unworthy of it, that although he is liberated in very truth by Jesus Christ, yet in himself, in his daily and even hourly thoughts and words and works, he is not liberated at all. His own being contradicts his being in Jesus Christ. Confronted with that being, in the clear light of that being, he finds that in his own being the old man is not yet dead or the new created. In his own being—contrary to the divine judgment—he will again and again find that he is a covenant-breaker, a sinner, a transgressor. In his own being—contrary to the divine verdict—he will never find the faithful servant and friend and dear child of God. In his own being he will never with his own eyes see himself as in any respect justified, but always in supreme need of justification by God. And all this in faith itself and as such. How then is he going to find himself sinless, and even positively righteous? Certainly not by the sincerity and depth of his faith, or the fineness of it as a theological virtue. For where would be the virtue of this faith if as a believer he saw himself in the light and under the judgment of the One in whom he believes? As a being and work liberated from the unrighteousness of the old man and

D.R.—4

filled with the righteousness of the new he cannot plead before Him
his faith—let alone anything else. And remarkably enough, the more
sincere and deep our faith actually is, the less we will find in our faith
as in all our other being and activity, the more strange and impossible
will be the thought that we can please God with this one work of
faith, the more we will try to cling to the fact that we have died as
the old man in Jesus Christ, and that we are created and alive as a
new man in Jesus Christ, and that we have not to produce our own
confirmation of this righteousness before God in our life and being,
not our own Christian righteousness, not our own righteousness of
faith as a product and achievement and state of our own heart and
mind in which we can lay hold of the truth and power of the divine
verdict. In faith the Christian will find himself justified because
believing in this divine sentence fulfilled and revealed in Jesus Christ
he dashes himself against the rock of that work of God which God has
willed and done, certainly on behalf of man, but primarily for His own
sake, to assert His honour and to maintain His glory against him.
Believing in Jesus Christ he will encounter the divine decision which is
basically the self-affirmation of God against the creature and therefore
the decision of grace in his favour, thus making quite impossible and
irrelevant any counter-question concerning that which might correspond to it in the way of human work or life or faith. Because seriously
and ultimately the justifying sentence of God is the self-affirmation
of God worked out and revealed in this way, it will have incontrovertible truth and an unconditional force against everything that man
either is of himself or does of himself, the truth and force of the divinity
with which God intervened against man and therefore for him, and
which cannot be limited by anything that may or may not correspond
on the part of man. Christian faith will cling to and find its confidence
and support in this divinity of the justifying sentence, without concerning itself about anything—indeed in face and spite of anything—
that the believer may find and will necessarily bewail as his own being
and essence. This divine judgment will demand a subjection and sheer
obedience (and find them in faith) in which man must resolutely turn
his back on his own being, in which he finds the old man still there
and the new man not yet present, and sets his face equally resolutely
to his being in Jesus Christ in which the former is dead and the latter
lives. In faith there will be no place for looking back to our own
righteousness or unrighteousness; for conclusions as to the freedom
reached or not reached by us, for reflections concerning the worthiness
or unworthiness of our response to the divine verdict. Faith can and
must be faith only in the truth and actuality of the work of God done
and revealed in Jesus Christ, faith in the transcendent and victorious
nature of this work, based upon the honour and glory of God which
are so clearly asserted in face of all human opposition that however
dark and malicious this may be it can never be more than a shadow

dispersing before the light, and can be regarded and treated only as such. Both before and behind man will dare to live only by his faith. When faith is like this, it is the faith which justifies a man in spite of his sin. For then it is his genuine conversion from himself as a covenant-breaker and transgressor to the gracious and mighty God— a conversion in which he ceases to be unrighteous and begins to be the righteous man he is, pleasing to God and God's dear child. Faith of this kind is the work of the Holy Spirit which makes man a Christian.

But this is not the only form of the conversion of man to God accomplished in Jesus Christ. It is the first form : negative and positive justification by the true and mighty sentence of God, and therefore the form of faith. But there is also another form, (2) the placing of man under the divine direction. We might also speak of the law, commandment, ordinance, demand or claim of God. The being of man in the form of Christian love consists in the fact that he accepts the divine direction. That he does this is another form of the work of the Holy Spirit which makes him a Christian.

God's justifying sentence is His all-powerful decision what man really is and is not. In Jesus Christ he is not a rebel but a servant, not an enemy but a friend, not lost to God but a child in the Father's house. God's direction is also an all-powerful decision, His own divine act of lordship. By this means, too, God vindicates His honour and maintains His glory. By this means, too, He exercises authority. But in God's direction it is plain how He exercises authority, how His divine authority is constituted as opposed to all other authorities, what it means radically and finally to stand under the divine lordship. God's direction is the directing of man into the freedom of His children. It is this which has taken place in Jesus Christ no less uniquely than the once-for-all fulfilment of the divine sentence on man. In suffering in our stead the death of the old man, and bringing in by His resurrection the life of the new, He has made room for the being of all men at peace with God. On the basis of what man is and is not by virtue of the divine sentence passed and revealed in Jesus Christ, in face of that twofold pardon, he has no other place but this—the kingdom in which God can be at peace with him and he at peace with God. Jesus Christ —and this is the second element in His work and ministry as the Reconciler between God and us—is the all-powerful direction of God to us to occupy this place, to live in this kingdom. If we are told in Him who we are and are not, we are also told in Him where we belong, where we have to be and live. Only told ? Only directed ? Only informed ? Is it only an invitation or a demand to enter ? All that and more. Jesus Christ is God's mighty command to open our eyes and to realise that this place is all around us, that we are already in this kingdom, that we have no alternative but to adjust ourselves to it, that we have our being and continuance here and nowhere else. In Him we are already there, we already belong to it. To enter at

His command is to realise that in Him we are already inside. To follow His invitation and demand is to find ourselves in the situation already created in Him and in Him already our own situation. That is man's reconciliation with God in the form of the issuing and receiving of the divine direction.

Words like law, commandment, ordinance, etc., although they are quite possible and relevant, do not quite suffice to indicate what is meant, because they so easily give the impression of something which has not been already done, which has still to be done by the decision and act which are demanded of man himself. The decision and act of man are, of course, required by the direction given and revealed in Jesus Christ. But the requirement of the divine direction is based on the fact that in Jesus Christ man has already been put in the place and kingdom of peace with God. His decision and act, therefore, can consist only in obedience to the fact that he begins and does not cease to breathe in this place and kingdom, that he follows the decision already made and the act already accomplished by God, confirming them in his own human decision and act ; that he, for his part, chooses what has already been chosen and actualised for him. That is why we use the word direction—we might almost say the advice or hint. It is not a loud and stern and foreign thing, but the quiet and gentle and intimate awakening of children in the Father's house to life in that house. That is how God exercises authority. All divine authority has ultimately and basically this character. At its heart all God's ruling and ordering and demanding is like this. But it is in the direction given and revealed in Jesus Christ that the character of divine authority and lordship is unmistakably perceived.

What is it, then, that we are dealing with ? What is this place and kingdom in which God's direction summons man to awaken and remain and act ? We have already mentioned the decisive concept : it is a matter of man's direction into the freedom for which he is made free in Jesus Christ (in that twofold pardon), in peace with God. It is the place and kingdom which already surrounds him, in which he is already placed, in which he has only to find himself. God's direction is the direction to do this, to make use of his freedom. He has not won his freedom himself. He has not come to this place in his own power or worth, by reason of his own virtue or skill. He does not control it. The kingdom of freedom is not one in which he can act as lord. It is not for him to try to act in it according to his own judgment. If he did, he would certainly not be free, he would secretly have left that place. It is the house of his Father, and he needs the Father's guidance to act in it and therefore to be free. But he receives and has this. And it is the essence of the freedom for which he is freed in Jesus Christ that he is not alone, that he is not left to himself, that he is not directed to his own judgment, that he must not be his own lord and master, or exist in himself imprisoned in his own arbitrariness and self-sufficiency. In every form this would be bondage—the unfreedom of the lost rebel and enemy from which he has been loosed. Freedom means being in a spontaneous and therefore willing agreement with the sovereign freedom of God. This freedom is the being of man, not in himself but in Jesus Christ, in the place and kingdom which have been opened up to us in Him and which already surround us in Him. Because it is not in ourselves but in Jesus Christ that we are free, that we are the covenant-partners and children of God, we need His direction and lordship and therefore the direction and lordship that come to us in Him. And because it is in Him that we are really free, He is Himself our direction, our guiding into freedom, our awakening to life in that freedom, our guidance to make use of it, our Lord and King, and therefore in this sense too our reconciliation with God, the One who fulfils our conversion to Him.

As distinct from justification, and as its necessary consequence, this subjection of man to the divine direction is usually called sanctification. It is nothing other than the basic presupposition of all Christian ethics. Sanctification is the claiming of all human life and being and activity by the will of God for the active fulfilment of that will.

We must note first that this subjection of man under God's direction and therefore his sanctification is a form of the atonement, of the conversion of man to God accomplished and revealed in Jesus Christ. It is an element in His activity as man's reconciliation with God. Sanctification cannot then be separated from justification, as though it has to do with man's contribution to his reconciliation with God. Sanctification does not mean our self-sanctifying as the filling out of the justification which comes to man by God. It is sanctification by and in Jesus Christ, who, according to I Cor. 1[30], is made unto us both justification and sanctification. Certainly we have to do with the work of man, what he does and what he leaves undone. But it is his work in a peace with God which he himself has not made, and in which he cannot of himself take a single step that is a work in which he really shows himself a faithful and adequate covenant-partner of God and God's dear child. The fact that he does take these steps, that he does good works, is something which takes place only in the truth and power of the divine direction. It is just as much a matter of God's free grace as is the decision who and what he is and is not before God. In Christian ethics, therefore, the atonement made in Jesus Christ cannot simply be a presupposition which has been left far behind. Ethics, too, must testify directly to the atonement which man himself does not make, but which God has made in him as His own work, by giving him direction in Jesus Christ.

And equally clearly we must then say that sanctification consists in the fact that in and through Jesus Christ man is called by God into freedom ; summoned to use the freedom in which he has already been put in Jesus Christ. God's direction and man's subjection to it has no other meaning and purpose than this. Everything that it means concretely, all the individual directions which have to be unfolded in Christian ethics, can only be concretions of the one necessary direction to the freedom given to man. The placing of man under this direction must not be understood as his subjection to any other law. On the contrary, all the legislation and commanding of God that we meet with in the Old and New Testaments has to be understood as a call to the awakening to that freedom, as a direction to make use of that freedom which is given us once and for all in Jesus Christ, and which we can never abandon on any pretext if our action is obedience. It is a matter of learning to breathe and to live in that freedom, of taking it with all seriousness.

As Christian faith is the human response to God's justifying sentence, so Christian love is the human response to His direction. The reconciliation of the world with God, i.e., man's conversion to God in Jesus Christ, his being as liberated both negatively and positively— this is something which is experienced and known and acknowledged in Him. And when this is the case, then in the truth and power of the one Holy Spirit God's direction or guidance or hint is also received : in Jesus Christ man is directed by God to awakening and life in the freedom for which He has made him free. If it is given to us to know Jesus Christ as the priestly Representative of all men, that is, as the One in whom in the name of all, and therefore for us, the human covenant-breaker was put to death and the faithful servant and intimate friend and dear child of God is brought into being, then it is ordained and given that we should accept Him as the King and Lord of all men and therefore as our Lord. The obedience of faith is followed by the obedience of love—in practice, of course, it may sometimes precede, but it always accompanies it as a second form of the particular being of the Christian in Jesus Christ, which cannot be separated from the first but is quite distinct from it. Sanctification is the second aspect of the reconciliation of man with God willed and accomplished and revealed by God. It comes after and together with the redemption of man from the power of darkness. It consists in his placing into " the kingdom of the son of his love " (Col. 1[13]). God Himself is love and revealed Himself as such by sending His only Son into the world in order that we might live through Him (1 Jn. 4[8f.]). In Jesus Christ God has created a final and indestructible fellowship between Himself and all men, between all men and Himself, a fellowship which is final and indestructible because it is based upon His own interposition and guaranteed by it. That is the actualisation and revelation of His love which is as such the direction to which man is subjected and the Christian love which receives it responds. It consists simply in the affirmation of the existence of this fellowship as such, just as faith consists in the affirmation of its foundation. In Jesus Christ God has demonstrated, He has made it visible and audible and perceptible, that He loved the world, that He did not will to be God without it, without all men, without each individual man in particular. And in the same Jesus Christ He has demonstrated, He has made it visible and audible and perceptible, that the world and all men and each individual man in particular cannot be without Him. The demonstration that He belongs to the world and the world to Him is the choice and work of His love in Jesus Christ, "the kingdom of the son of his love." In general terms Christian love is the active human recognition of this proof of the love of God. It recognises it by following it, imitating it, modelling itself upon it. It is the attitude in which man gives himself to reflect the divine attitude. That he can do this, that he can love, is his sanctification, his breathing and living in the place and atmosphere of freedom, his keeping of the covenant as a faithful partner. That he can love is the work of the Holy Spirit which makes man a Christian. And now we must distinguish two separate elements, or, better, dimensions, in Christian love.

The love of God in Jesus Christ is decisively, fundamentally and comprehensively His coming together with all men and their coming together with Him. This coming together is not deserved by man, but forfeited. Yet it has been accomplished by God in His free grace, defying and overcoming the sin of man. As this coming together the love of God active and revealed in Jesus Christ is the fulfilling of the covenant by Him. It embraces *realiter* both the world and the community, non-Christians and Christians. But the knowledge and proclamation of it is a matter only for the Christian community. Those who know it are marked off from all other men as Christians. But this coming together of God and man cannot be known to be fulfilled except as it is actively worked out. God has conjoined Himself with man, existing in his own activity, and He has conjoined man existing in his own activity with Himself. God is not idle but active. For good or evil, therefore, man must be active too. Therefore the recognition of this coming together as such is not merely a conscious but an active being of man in God. And this active being consists in the fact that man for his part in answer to that divine activity not merely knows himself to be brought together but does actively come together with God in thought and word and work : within the limits, of course, of his human capacity, and humbly seeking the One who has already found him in His own free grace, but within those limits with all his heart and soul and mind and strength (Mk. 12$^{29f.}$). This active coming together of man with God will be the realising of all the possibilities of his active being beside which, in the knowledge of the communion achieved by God and therefore of the love of God, he cannot see any other possibilities. In this way it will be an activity which is at bottom voluntary, which excludes the fear of any other forces but God, which claims him wholly and utterly. It will be accomplished as an act of pure gratitude, which does not make any claim and which is therefore complete. And in all this it will be a kind of silhouette of the elective, free and total activity of God Himself to whom he makes a human response. To that extent it will be a following and imitation of that activity, the love to God which is the response to the love of God. In accordance with what He did and revealed in Jesus Christ, God willed from all eternity not to be without man. And now, recognising this will of God, man wills not to be without God. His activity is therefore characterised by the will to seek God and to find Him, that is, to enquire concerning His commandment, to be guided by His decisions and attitudes, and to follow His direction. Existence without love has now been left behind as an error and a lie. Therefore he no longer needs to have any fear. He no longer takes pleasure in being self-sufficient and self-responsible, his own lord and master because his own owner. That is the delusion which he has left behind in the knowledge of his coming together with God as God willed and accomplished it. He cannot live in it any longer. He still knows it. It still presses in upon him. But because of that knowledge it has no more power over him. He now lives by suppressing it wherever it arises. He now lives as one who seeks God in his activity. Poetically and rhetorically we might describe the Christian life in much stronger terms. But we will be careful to remember that the substance of anything we might say will always be this, that we are dealing with a fact which is not at all self-evident—that man for his part will seek the God who in Jesus Christ has already sought and found him that was lost, corresponding to the divine action, realising on his side the fellowship which has been set up by God. And above all we will be careful not to separate the concept of this love for God and therefore of this seeking of God from the human activity conditioned by it. We need not be fanatically anti-mystical. As one element in the activity which puts the love to God into effect, there may be a place for a feeling of enjoyable contemplation of God. But it cannot take the place of that activity. Man's being reconciled with God, his conversion to God, is from this second standpoint of sanctification his active being. It is in this being as such that God is either loved or not loved.

But this carries with it the fact that there can be no question of a justification of man by his love to God—perhaps as a continuation or actualisation of his justification by faith. Certainly the divine direction, the direction into love to God, can never be lacking in the man who has subjected himself to the divine sentence in the knowledge of it. But it is the pardoning sentence of God alone which is the basis of fellowship between God and man, and which therefore justifies man. And the fact that he is justified is something which he finds to be true and actual only in faith. That he can love, i.e., seek God is his freedom to live in that fellowship on the basis which has been laid down by God and God alone. But because we are here dealing with human activity, with the sum of the Christian *ethos* and its always doubtful fulfilment, it can as little contribute to the setting up of that fellowship and therefore to justification as can faith itself as the human recognition that it has been set up.

It amounts to this, that in love man is occupied with something else, and he ought always to be so. It would completely destroy the essential character of Christian love as the freedom given to man and to be kept by man if we tried to burden it with the, in itself, impossible and superfluous task of accomplishing or actualising or even completing the justification of man. No one can and will love God who does not believe. No one can and will love God except in the grounding of his being in the fellowship with God realised in that divine judgment. If we are to be justified by faith, in faith we will not look either at our works or our sins. Similarly in love—in the works of our love to God —we will not consider the possibility of trying subsequently to fulfil or to complete of ourselves that grounding of our being. Christian love does not will anything from God. It starts from the point that there is nothing to will which has not already been given. It does not will anything from the One who is everything to it. It wills only God Himself because He is God, because He is this God. It wills simply to love Him, as the man who is reconciled with Him on the basis of His sentence fulfilled and revealed in Jesus Christ can love Him immediately and unquestioningly and unreservedly, but as also he must love Him. The love in which man thinks that he can justify himself before God is not as such a love which derives from faith. It is not a free and pure love which loves God for His own sake, because He is God. It is rather a work of the old mercenary spirit, of the man who at bottom hates the grace of God instead of praising and honouring it. It is therefore a return to the state of sin, of covenant-breaking. Christian love to God is a free and pure love which honours and praises unreservedly the grace of God. For Christian ethics everything depends on the fact that it should be understood as an independent form of the conversion of man to God (and therefore of His reconciliation with Him) and not otherwise. The erroneous teaching of the Council of Trent involves a false understanding both of justification by faith and also of sanctification in love.

But Christian love has a second dimension inseparably connected with the first. The love of God in Jesus Christ brings together Himself with all men and all men with Himself. But at the same time it is obviously the coming together of all men one with another. And as that communion is known it is at once and necessarily evident that there is a solidarity of all men in the fellowship with God in which they have all been placed in Jesus Christ, and a special solidarity of those who are aware of the fact, the fellowship of those who believe in Him, the Christian community. In this horizontal dimension Christian love is love to the neighbour or the brother. This must be distinguished

from love to God which is Christian love in the vertical dimension
It will not take place without love to God. And there would be no
love to God if it did not take place. But while it can only follow,
and must follow, this prior love, it is an autonomous loving, for God
in heaven and the neighbour on earth are two and not one. Love to
others cannot exhaust itself in love to God, nor can love to God exhaust
itself in love to others. The one cannot be replaced and made unnecessary by the other. But love to God—to the God who reconciles
the world to Himself in Jesus Christ—evokes love to the neighbour
and the brother. And love to the man who is made a neighbour and
a brother in Jesus Christ follows love to God. The following of the
divine loving in Christian love would be incomplete, indeed it would
fail altogether—and we must remember the very sharp warnings on
this point in the first Epistle of John—if it did not take this twofold
form, the one having priority as the great commandment of Mk. 12²⁹ᶠ·
and the other being subordinate to it as the second commandment.
Within the great reflection of the love of God in Christian love as such
and generally, love to the neighbour and the brother must again reflect
the Christian love to God. Jesus Christ alone is made unto us sanctification. He is the King who is appointed the ruler and lawgiver and
judge of every man. But with His known people this King has also
a much larger unknown people, which, according to Heb. 2¹¹, He, the
only Son of the Father, is not ashamed to call His brethren even down
to the most lowly members. And according to Mt. 25³¹ᶠ· the criterion
at His judgment will be the question what we have done or not done
to Him in the person of the least of His brethren. They are not
identical with Him, but they are witnesses which we must not overlook or ignore, witnesses of the poverty which He accepted to establish
that fellowship between God and man which is given to the world and
gives light to the Christian community, witnesses of the wealth which
in Him is given secretly to the world and openly to the Christian community in that fellowship. In their person they represent Him as the
neighbour, as the one who fell among thieves, and as the Good Sam-
aritan who took him and poured oil into his wounds and brought him
to the inn at his own expense. They are not identical with Him. But
He cannot be had without them. And that means that God cannot
be had without them, nor can reconciliation with Him nor conversion
to Him. He cannot be had without gratitude for their witness and a
willingness to be witnesses to them, without love to them, without
their indispensability to each one whom God loves, without that one
seriously setting out and never ceasing to seek and to find them, both
in the community and therefore in the world as well, Christian and
also non-Christian neighbours. Christian love is at one and the same
time love to God and love to the neighbour—and it is love to the
neighbour because it is love to God. This is the test whether it is the
response to God's own love, whether it is the work of the Holy Spirit.

If it stands this test, then *mutatis mutandis* but substantially everything that can be said of love to God can be said of love to the neighbour. It is a coming together on the horizontal level, of man and man. As such it is not merely conscious, but ready and indeed voluntary. It is a total coming together which excludes all other possible relationships to the neighbour and claims a man wholly and utterly. To that extent it is a perfect counterpart to the vertical coming together of man with God. And it cannot be exhausted by mere feelings, or a mere outlook, let alone mere words. It is an active being.

But it does not on that account contribute anything at all to the justification of man. And it is the glory of it that it cannot even think of trying to do so, because it derives from the justification of man, from the divine sentence of pardon, and therefore it lives by the faith in which we cannot look away to anything else—either our good works or bad—but must be content to be what we are by God's sentence fulfilled and revealed in Jesus Christ without any co-operation on our part. Even neighbourly love cannot look away to anything that might be won or attained from God by means of it. Just as love to God can envisage and seek and love only God, and for His own sake, so love to the neighbour can envisage and seek and love only the neighbour, and for his own sake. As in the vertical, so in the horizontal dimension, it is free and pure love. There is no question of any gain accruing to the one who loves, either in time or in eternity. There is no ulterior thought of another end, even if this were the highest and most necessary end for man. The neighbour will notice the fact, and he will not find himself loved even in the most fervent and zealous works of Christian charity, if this love is one which looks away, and not a pure act of obedience—as faith also is in its own way. Christian love as the complement of love to God is real neighbourly and brotherly love to the extent that it is exercised without any ulterior thought or question, being shown freely and purely to the neighbour as a neighbour and the brother as a brother, being shown only because in his Christian and also in his non-Christian form he is a member of the people of which Jesus Christ is the King, because this King wills that those who recognise Him should recognise Him again in the members of His people in the narrower and wider sense, because the coming together of God and man accomplished in Him carries with it unconditionally and without reserve and therefore with genuine force the work of bringing together man and man.

Where love exists in both dimensions without any ulterior motive, where it is grounded in itself and does not try to be anything but a necessary response to the love of God, it is that " fulfilling of the law " of which we read in Mk. 12$^{29f.}$ and Rom. 13^{10}. It is obedience to God's direction, the keeping of covenant faithfulness by man, the meaning of the whole *ethos* of the man reconciled and converted to God in Jesus Christ.

The conversion of man to God which took place in Jesus Christ has another form as well as these two, and it will now be our task to characterise and briefly to describe this final form. It consists (3) in the positing and equipping of man as the bearer of the divine promise. In the fact that he participates in this promise and lives in the light of it the being of man consists in Christian hope. And in this third form the work of the Holy Spirit which makes man a Christian is that man—for this is hope—is obedient to the promise as Abraham was, that he is ready to participate in it and to live in the light of it.

God's judgment and direction, and therefore man's justification and sanctification, and therefore faith and love do not embrace the whole of that act of atonement accomplished and revealed in Jesus Christ which reconstitutes the being of man, and therefore they do not embrace the whole of the specifically Christian being established and formed by the knowledge of Jesus Christ. In our presentation so far there is lacking any consideration of what we might call the teleological determination of the being of man and of the Christian in Jesus Christ.

In that section of dogmatics which is specifically known as soteriology, i.e., the doctrine of the salvation which comes to man in Jesus Christ, it has been customary since the Reformation to think in the main only in the two categories so far mentioned. The doctrine of Luther centred upon the contrast and complementarity of faith and works, that is, love, or, conversely, the Law and the Gospel. And Calvin returned constantly to the dialectic of justification and sanctification. These were the two concepts which dominated the Reformed theology which succeeded Calvin. But they are also the iron basis and core of what the Lutheran orthodox thought it possible to describe as the *ordo salutis*. And in line with the general Protestant tradition Schleiermacher in this context treated first of regeneration (conversion and justification) and then of sanctification. Our consideration of the two spheres described in this or some similar way has certainly convinced us of the correctness and importance—an importance which cannot be over-estimated—of these two aspects, and their indispensability as the basic description of the man reconciled in Jesus Christ and especially of the Christian who knows Jesus Christ. The Reformers did well to concentrate on them as they wrestled with the problems of their own day. In the controversy with Roman Catholicism their exact treatment will always play a decisive part. Even in relation to the subject-matter as presented for our consideration by the biblical witness, there can be no question that here in justification and sanctification, or faith and love, or at an even higher level God's verdict and direction, we find ourselves at what is from this standpoint, the being of man reconciled to God in Jesus Christ, the very heart and centre of the Christian message. There can be no escaping the questions : How can I lay hold of a gracious God ? and, How can I live in accordance with the fact that I have a gracious God ? And these questions must always be rightly answered with all the actuality which they can never lose. But we must not overlook the fact that as we take note of the witness of the New Testament at this very heart and centre of the matter there is a third moment which we have to treat independently and as true in and for itself. It is of this that we must now speak, the moment of the promise given to man in Jesus Christ, and therefore Christian hope, and therefore the calling of man side by side with his justification and sanctification.

It was not enough—that is, it did not correspond to the fulness of the New Testament witness and a comprehensive investigation of the point at issue—when under the title *De vocatione* the Protestant tradition tried to speak only in an introductory and comprehensive way about the subjective *applicatio salutis*, i.e., man's entry into the sphere of justification and sanctification, of faith and love, his regeneration and conversion as his entry into a state of grace, the basic activity of the Holy Spirit in general and the rise of faith in particular. In a treatment of this kind it necessarily seems that the sphere of justification and sanctification, of faith and love, is marked off from behind as that which is properly sacred— although not without some reference to its limitation by what has to be said separately in the doctrine of the last things. We must admit that Calvin did see very clearly the problem of the teleological determination and direction of the whole being and status of man as changed in Christ and shaped for conversion to God. He felt the problem, and he treated it in a lasting and impressive way in his conception of the *promissio* as the basis of faith and his presentation of the *vita christiana* as directed to the *vita futura*. But for him the *spes* seems to be only an essential and indeed the properly compulsive element in *fides*. It is this in the New Testament. But in the New Testament it is more than this. And in the New Testament the calling of God is never simply as it was described in Protestant orthodoxy, the basis of the entry into the specific state of grace, or Christianity. This state never has the character of a being which is included and exhausted in the form of faith and love, a being which will then be super-seded by and merged into the, as it were, quite different being in eternal glory to which it moves. In the New Testament the being of man in Jesus Christ is rather a being under and with the promise, as it is also a being under the verdict and direction, of God. It is a being which in its totality is teleologically directed, an eschatological being. Calling speaks of more than calling into a state of justification and sanctification. As such and with independent truth and power calling is man's forward direction to God as his future, his new creation as a being which not only derives from the sentence of God in faith and is placed under His present direction in love but beyond that receives and embraces His promise in hope, looking forward therefore and moving forward to Him. The Protestant tradition was, of course, helped and corrected by the fact that it never neglected to consider the last things. Inevitably, too, something of this had to be brought out indirectly in the discussion of justification and sanctification, of faith and love. But it is still only too true that in that tradition the being of man in Jesus Christ has as such a very this-worldly, immanentist, even middle-class appearance. The older Protestant soteriology with its classical and in its way magnificent pre-occupation with the two first points did not make it sufficiently clear that this being as such is a being under the promise, that the reality of the salvation given to man is as such the gift of this promise, that the Christian affirmation and appropriation of the divine gift is as such hope based upon and directed to this promise. In Evangelical dogmatics we must not neglect the two first points. But we must bring out no less emphatically the prophetic element of the being of man reconciled with God in Jesus Christ.

The restoration, renewal and fulfilment of the covenant between God and man in the atonement made and revealed in Jesus Christ is complete as man's justification as a covenant-partner and his sanctifi-cation to be a covenant-partner, as the establishment and formation of the fellowship between himself and God, just as God's creation was perfect as the beginning of all His ways with the created order. But, like creation, it is not an end but a beginning—complete in itself and as such, but still a beginning. It is not, therefore, an end in itself. Nor is it simply conditioned by what might happen further between God and man on quite different presuppositions, just as the (in itself) perfect creation of God was not simply conditioned by the subsequent history of the covenant, but took place for the sake of the covenant and to that extent was itself the beginning of the covenant. So, too, reconciliation, the being of man converted to God in Jesus Christ, is as such a beginning. It is not merely a *restitutio ad integrum*. It is not merely the creation of a final and stable relationship in which the disturbance of the balance between God and the world has been corrected, and, with the re-establishment of the normal order of superiority demanded by their conjunction, God and the world can co-exist quietly and contentedly : God having pronounced His verdict and giving His direction, man in faith in Him and in love to Him and his neighbour. It is not the restoration of a parallelism and equipoise in which God and the world, God and man, will now continue to live together happily. This is—slightly caricatured—the this-worldly, immanentist and middle-class understanding of the being in Jesus Christ given by God to the world and known and experienced by Christians. In contrast to all such ideas, this being in all its completeness is only a beginning—a being in which man looks eagerly forward to the activity of God and his own fellowship with Him, just as in faith he looks back to it and in love he sees it as present. It is a being which is still open for God, open for that which has not yet happened in the restoration of the covenant as such, for that which has yet to happen on the basis of that restoration. It is not only under the verdict and direction of God but also under the promise of God, in which we have to do with this future event, with this still expected being of God for man, with yet another form of the fellowship between God and man. The justification and sanctification of man have a purpose and goal.

It is not self-evident that they should have, that apart from what he may be under God's verdict and direction man as reconciled with God should also be given by this same God a future, a *telos*. Those limited ideas might well correspond to the reality. For what man may be under God's verdict and direction, in faith and love, is certainly complete enough in itself. But, in fact, they do not correspond to the reality. In fact the perfection of the being in Jesus Christ (without anything lacking in the first two forms) has a further extension. The justification and sanctification of man do in fact include a purpose and goal. This is not self-evident. It is only as a further proof of the overflowing goodness of God that it is in fact the case that the being of man in Jesus Christ is a being not merely in possession and action but also in expectation. And for this reason the calling of man is obviously a thing apart and additional to his justification and sanctification, as is also Christian hope in relation to Christian faith and Christian love. For it is a thing apart, it is the grace of God in a new and particular form, that He not only wills to make man His servant and friend and child, His faithful covenant-partner, to have him as such and to cause him to walk before Him as such, but also that beyond and in all this (as is shown in a type in the figure of Abraham) He wills to make something of him, He has for him a purpose, an end. According to the promise given him in Jesus Christ, God has in fact a purpose for man in all this. And in the knowledge of the promise given in Jesus Christ man is, in fact, called to give to God not merely the response of the obedience of faith and the obedience of love, but also the response of the obedience of hope. We must therefore regard the calling of man as the third aspect of the reconciliation of man with God which God Himself has willed and accomplished and revealed.

What does the promise of God mean ? It means that the being of man acquires a direction, because it acquires a destiny and a perspective. This is something which the verdict and direction of God do not mean taken and understood by themselves, even though they are as such the perfect Word of God. The end of man's justified and sanctified being, of Christian faith and Christian love, belongs to the conversion of man to God. Man cannot take this to himself. But God gives it to him in reconciling him to Himself in Jesus Christ. He gives him His pledge—already redeemed and operative in Jesus Christ —that is the strong sense of the word promise. And now he can and must live as the one who has this pledge, and therefore with the forward direction and destiny given by it and perspective opened up by it : forward to what he will be according to this pledge. In the fulfilment of the covenant he receives this pledge and accepts this call to advance.

But to what does it point him ? In a very general way, to the actualisation and preservation of the fellowship between God and himself established in the fulfilment of the covenant. God's promise shows him that this fellowship is not simply a—two-dimensional—connexion, not simply a relationship, but that it has a depth in which at first it is alien and unknown to man, yet in which it is to be confided and made known to him, that there is something common to both God and man upon which man cannot lay his hand but which God promises to lay in his hand.

For a proper understanding everything depends upon our giving the right name to what is shown and pledged to man by the divine promise. In the New Testament it is briefly and very well described as " eternal life " (cf. Jn. 3¹⁶). This brings out with a clarity which can hardly be excelled the fact that it is a being in a depth of fellowship with God which has yet to be disclosed. Only God lives an " eternal life." If man is to have it, it can only be on the ground that God wills to live in fellowship with him. But if God wills that, it can be said and promised by Him to man living in his present only as a thing which is new to him in his present. It is, then, to his actual future with God that he moves forward in the possession of this promise. But what is meant by " eternal life " if it is promised to man as his future with God, if, therefore, in eternal life he is not to cease to be a man, a creature and as such identical with himself, the one he now is ? if in that depth of fellowship with God he is not to be merged into God or changed into some quite different being ?—which would necessarily mean that it was not really a matter of his future, that the promise did not concern and apply to him, man, as such, that it had nothing whatever to do with his present.

How can eternal life be promised to him, man ? How can it be his future with God in this present ? In this connexion we usually speak of man's future resting in God or his future supreme bliss before God, or of a contemplation and adoration of God which in its permanence constitutes his future beatitude. And, rightly understood, all this must not be rejected. But if we describe the content of the promise in this way, we must be careful not to form pagan conceptions of God and the eternal life that He lives and the eternal life that He promises to man, as though at bottom God was a supreme being with neither life, nor activity, nor history, in a neutrality which can never be moved or affected by anything, a being with which man can ultimately be united only in rest or in some kind of passive enjoyment or adoring contemplation. The God who is Father, Son and Holy Spirit, active and revealed to us as the eternally living God in Jesus Christ, is not in any sense this supposedly " supreme " being. And unless we say something very much more, rest and enjoyment and contemplation are not the right words to describe a being in the depth of fellowship with Him. According to the witness of Holy Scripture— in correspondence with His triune being, and as indicated by the biblical concept of eternity—God is historical even in Himself, and much more so in His relationship to the reality which is distinct from Himself. He is the Lord of His kingdom, deciding, acting, ruling, doing good, creating peace, judging, giving joy, living in His will and acts. And that kingdom is not merely a kingdom which He possesses in the cosmos created by Him. It is the kingdom which He sets up in the course of a historical movement which has a beginning, a middle and an end. It is the kingdom which comes from heaven to earth. And that is how He encounters us and reveals Himself to us in Jesus Christ, for He is still the active ruler when He combats the sin and misery of the world, when in the work of atonement He converts it to Himself in this One. If it is the case that man is given a promise for his own future in this as yet unrevealed depth of fellowship with God, it cannot be otherwise than that the content of the promise should correspond to the being of God. The fellowship of man with God is completed and completes itself as it enters this depth. And this complete fellowship, the " eternal " life of man, must consist in a future being of man with God as this active ruler. And it is hard to see how we can better describe it in summary form than by calling it a being which is in the words of Lk. 20[36] like that of the angels in that it is a being in the service of God. Luther showed a perception amounting to genius—for in some way he transcended himself—when in his exposition of the second article in the *Shorter Catechism* he described the end of the redemption of man accomplished in Jesus Christ in the following way : " in order that I may be His, and live under Him in His kingdom, and serve Him in eternal righteousness and virtue and blessedness, as He is risen from the dead and lives and reigns in eternity." To live under Him in His kingdom and to serve Him : it is here that all rest and joy and contemplation and adoration in the eternal life promised to man have their meaning and basis. It is the calling to this which is the *telos* of justification and sanctification. The future of man in covenant with God (in the position and function which he will have in relation to that of God) is to be the partner of God and to live as such. We are, in fact, dealing with what synergism of every age and type has tried to ascribe to man at a place where it does not—yet—belong to him, and has confused and falsified everything by trying to ascribe it to him at that place, that is, in his status under the verdict and direction of God. The fact that he is subjected to the divine verdict and can believe in the knowledge of it, the fact that he is placed under the divine direction and can love in the knowledge of it, does not in any sense include within itself a co-operation of man with God, but in faith and love man responds, he corresponds, to what is simply the work of God for him and to him, the Word of God spoken to him and concerning him. Of course, the same is true in hope. As a recipient and bearer of the divine promise he stands in relation to God as one who can only respond or correspond.

But here we are speaking of the content of the promise, not of his status in hope, but of what he hopes for as he receives the promise and knows it as such. And of this, of the future of man as indicated and pledged in the divine promise, we have to say that it is a being in a co-operation of service with God. This being is in His kingdom, and therefore under Him. But its form now is not simply one of response and correspondence. It is not simply in the distinctness and antithesis which even in the status of hope must be our attitude. To be sure, the creatureliness and identity of man will certainly not be destroyed. Therefore the distinctness and antithesis in relation to God will also remain. But this being will be a being by the side of God, the participation of man in the being and life of God, a willing of what He wills and a doing of what He does. It will be a being not only as object, but as an active subject in the fellowship of God with the created world and man, a being in a partnership with God which is actively undertaken and maintained, a being in man's own free responsibility with God for the cause of God. That is the inconceivable height which is promised to man when he is reconciled with God, converted to God, justified and sanctified. That is the honour, the dignity, the glory of eternal life which God has pledged. That is how man will come to eternal rest and enter into eternal joy and really contemplate God and adore Him. He will serve God, for that is what God has ordained for him and for the race, that is what He has appointed ultimately for the whole non-human cosmos. God does not regard man as too lowly or incapable or unworthy to consider him for this or to promise that this is what he will be. And He does not regard Himself as too exalted to will to set him beside Him and to make use of his service like that of the angels. It is obviously because everything depends on man being set there and used in that way, on his being called to service at His side, it is obviously for that reason—and we can only wonder afresh when we consider the fact—that He let it cost Him the offering of His Son and therefore His own interposition to convert man to Himself.

And the men of the Christian community are those who hear the promise given to the world of men, just as they are those who hear the verdict pronounced on it and the direction given to it. They are those who see the light as it shines before man, as it has already shone most definitely into and for the present being of man. They are those who can therefore walk with open eyes in this light given to the world. They are those who know that everything and all things—including themselves, and they are the ones who grasp it—are appointed and set up for this purpose. They are those who have the perspective that they will " live under Him in His kingdom, and serve Him." Christians, therefore, are those who are able not only to believe and love but also to hope—to hope for the future of the world with God and therefore for their own future with Him. Christians are those who are able to accept and consciously to apprehend not only the justification and sanctification of man, but also his calling in Jesus Christ to eternal life.

This calling took place in what was done for man and the world in the atonement made in Jesus Christ. The atonement accomplished in Him is not only the fulfilment of the sentence and the disclosure of the direction but also the effective proclamation of the promise or pledge of God. It is the divine call to advance under which man is placed by the fulfilment of the covenant and his conversion to God. It alone! We have to do here again only with the grace of God. How can man—even the man who believes and loves—ever come to the point of calling himself to advance, of promising himself the inconceivable height of eternal life with God in His service ? As the content of his hope he could perhaps imagine either " immortality " in another life decked out with various characteristics, or all kinds of significant possibilities in this life. Let him beware lest he be deluded and disillusioned in the one respect no less than the other. But no man can imagine of himself his future with God, his service of God as his future being (in this life as in that which is to come). No man can take and ascribe it to himself, anticipating it as his eternal or even his temporal future, that he will render to God a service which he himself offers and God accepts, a service which is complete and real both objectively and subjectively. Not even the pious Christian can do this, any more than he can take and ascribe to himself his justification and sanctification. He can and should live under the promise. He is so placed and equipped that he can have this future and move towards it in the present. But only because the promise and the pledge of it are given him by God, just as he can only accept the verdict and direction of God and therefore his justification and sanctification. The more clearly we see that in the content of this pledge we have to do with nothing less than the acceptance of what synergism falsely believes can be ascribed to man, the more clearly we will see that the pledge that he will serve God can only be given to man and can never be the arrogant postulate of man. Here, as everywhere in the event of atonement, such a postulate is quite superfluous. For in Jesus Christ the promise or pledge of God—which cannot be compared with anything we might promise ourselves—is already given to us. It is actually made to the world. So then (without having to create illusions about itself) the world is no longer a world without hope. As it stands under the verdict and direction of God, so too it stands under the promise of God. It is the world set in the light of its future with God. Hence man is the being which exists in this direction, under this determination, with this perspective. And the Christian is the man who for himself and others can know this and therefore hope. His hope derives from Jesus Christ, for Jesus Christ is Himself the divine pledge as such. And He hopes in Jesus Christ, for Jesus Christ is also the content of the divine pledge. That is what we have now briefly to explain.

Jesus Christ is the divine pledge as such—its effective and authentic proclamation. In Him that to which it refers has already taken place. It is already present. He is the man who lives not only under the verdict and direction of God but also in the truth of His promise. He is not merely righteous and well-pleasing to God and the object of His love, but beyond that He is taken and used by Him, standing in His service and at His side, working with Him, living eternal life, clothed with His honour and dignity and glory. He Himself as the eternally living God is also the eternally living man. The world is reconciled and converted to God in Him in the fact that He is this man, not merely in distinctness and antithesis in relation to God, but also in participation in His being and work, not merely in responsibility to Him, but with a responsibility for His cause, not merely as His servant and friend and child, but as a ruler in His kingdom. No one beside Him is man in this way, just as no one beside Him is as man the same divine Son of the Father. For that reason He (alone) is for all of us (only) the pledge of what we ourselves will be, we who are and will be only men and not God. For that reason in His present (alone) we have to do (only) with our future with God. For that reason the **future allotted to us in Him** cannot be that of rulers, but only of

servants of the one God who alone is King. Our present emphasis, however, must not be upon the qualifications but upon the positive truth
that the reconciliation of the world with God consists in the fact that
a promise is given it by God Himself and therefore absolutely, that in
Him its own future is already present, that in Him even in its present
life it is already seized and determined by its future being. Because
God has made Himself one with it in Jesus Christ, because He Himself
was and is present in it, it has the divine pledge of its future life.
Therefore whether it knows it or not, it is not a world without hope,
just as on the same ground it cannot be simply a lost world or a completely loveless and unsanctified world. In Him it has become a
world in which the divine call to advance has been heard once and
for all and is now regulative. In Him it has been constituted in the
fact and appointed to it, it exists in the perspective, that it belongs to
God, and that while it will not be divinised in some way and made
identical with Him, it will find the essence of all creaturely glory in
serving Him, actively siding with Him and helping Him and in this
way—for all its unlikeness like Jesus Christ—being clothed with all
the honour and also with all the joy and peace of eternal life. When
the Christian knows Jesus Christ as the One in whom this has taken
place for the world, he not only believes and loves, but also hopes.
And his hope derives from Jesus Christ, i.e., as he hears and understands the pledge which God has given in Him, making it his own,
letting his life be shaped by this promise and opened up for the future.

But Jesus Christ is also the content of the divine pledge, the One
in whom the Christian is summoned to hope. It is a terrible thing if
at this point, at the last moment, we ignore Him as though He were
only a means or instrument or channel, and look to something different
from Him, some general gift mediated by Him, regarding this as the
object of Christian hope, the future posited for the world and man.
The question of the future of the being of man and its direction to
that future is such an important and burning question that everything
hinges upon whether we answer it rightly or wrongly. If we look
aside here, trying to understand the awaited and expected being of
man and all creation in the service of God only as the manifestation
of a general idea of man or of being, we shall betray the fact that for
all our recalling and appealing to the name of Jesus Christ earlier—
indeed from the very first in our discussion of the being of reconciled
man—we have not really been thinking or answering in relation to
Him, but have been developing an anthropological concept which we
have found elsewhere and to which we have simply given a christological superscription. In its own way this might or might not have
value. But it does not belong to the Christian message or to the
heart of that message. The great truth which is proper to what we
have to see at this point does not shine out from a concept like that,
nor can we expect from it that comfort in living and dying which we

need to find at this point. This can be expected, and the divine promise can be understood in its kerygmatic and pneumatic force, only when it is continually seen and understood that, like the divine verdict and the divine direction, the divine promise of the future of the being of man is not only revealed but is actual, an event, only in Jesus Christ, that it is therefore in every way, not only noetically but ontically, enclosed in Him and indeed identical with Him. If we abide by the witness of the New Testament, it will keep us at this point from the mistake of separating the promise itself from that which is promised, and therefore from a new uncertainty. By that witness we are compellingly summoned to regard Jesus Christ not only as the revelation and form of the divine promise but also as its fulfilment and content. The future promised to the world and man, and awaited by the uplifted head of the Christian, is in the New Testament concentrated and comprehended in the one event of the coming of Jesus Christ Himself. He is the eternally living man who as such is the future of the world and of every man, and the hope of the Christian. By His coming to His disciples after His resurrection in the revelation of the forty days He pointed to Himself as their hope and future. In so doing He showed them and the whole community that their own hope and future and that of the world are to be found in His own coming as revealed in a way which none will fail to see and recognise. His own coming is the end to which in its supreme consummation, in its form as God's promise, the covenant fulfilled by Him, the reconciliation of the world with God accomplished by Him, can only move and point as to something beyond itself. As He is the meaning and basis of creation, so He is the bearer and substance of the redemption and consummation which closes the time of the creature, human time. Therefore the calling to expect and hasten towards this end and goal and new beginning, the divine call to advance which opens up the way for man, is the summons to look and to move forward to the One who not only was—before all time and in His own time—who not only is, as the centre of all time, but who also comes as the end of all time, as the Judge of all things which have lived and will live at any time, and therefore as the beginning of the being of the world and man the beginning of their eternal being on the right hand or the left. The calling of man is related to Him no less totally than his justification and sanctification. In hope no less than faith and love we have to do with Him, with the revelation and operation of the grace of God shown to the world and man in Him. And according to what we have already said, this means that in Him man is taken up into that dimension of depth of his being in fellowship with God which is still concealed, which is still only indicated to him. The fact that man can serve God, like the fact that he is justified and sanctified before God, is His affair. It is true for us in Him. The eternal life of man will be found in Him. In Him it will be true, and it will remain true and always be true afresh in eternity as the time of God, that man " may live under Him in His kingdom, and serve Him." In Him he will show himself accepted by God, worthy and capable and usable, able to be with Him to will what He wills, to do what He does, to support His cause. In Him all this will be his rest and joy in God, his eternal contemplation and adoration of God. In Him he will be clothed with the glory of his own eternal life with God. In eternal life, in the glory of the service of God promised to man, it is not a question of a future which is peculiar to man as such and in general. It is a question of His future, the future of Jesus Christ, and of the future of humanity and each individual man in Him.

In Him alone ! The exclusiveness of the promise as of the sentence and direction of God, of the calling as of the justification and sanctification of man—the fact that everything is enclosed in Jesus Christ alone —inevitably carries with it the judgment of the world to which each individual moves. For if everything is in Him alone, there is nothing outside of Him. Who does not have to fear this " outside of Him," since none of us can take and ascribe it to himself that he will be found in Him and that he will therefore live under Him and serve Him in His kingdom ? But how can our fear be anxious, how can it be anything but a joyful awe even in respect of all men, when the exclusiveness of this future is known as His, when He is known as the Judge who will come to judge the quick and the dead ? And when He is not known ? Then He must be believed and loved and hoped for as the eternally living One, and the future of the whole world, by those who do know Him. The last word in the matter, both in theory and in practice, is that it is their concern, their task, their responsibility to shine as light in the darkness, to proclaim Him to others as the eternally living One, even to those who do not seem to know Him as such. It is one thing to be unreservedly in earnest to-day about the possibility of eternal damnation for some, and to rejoice equally unreservedly to-morrow at that of eternal reconciliation for all. But it is quite another (and this is the task of the Christian community) to know that one is responsible for attesting with the Christian word and the Christian existence (and the existence no less clearly than the word) Jesus Christ not only as the Lord but also as the Saviour of the world and therefore its future. Christians will never find that they are called to anything other than hope—for themselves and the world. If they were, they would find that they were called to look and to move forward to someone or something other than their Saviour. But then *eo ipso* they would no longer be Christians.

We have still to say a few words about the hope of Christians as such. Let us say first that in their own case they hope for the eternal life in the service of God which comes to them in Jesus Christ. The fact that they can be obedient to the divine calling, recognising and understanding the divine promise as such, includes the fact that as these men amongst others they are themselves reached and approached by that promise, that they can relate themselves to it in person. Jesus Christ and their future in Him is their own personal hope, the hope of their own personal redemption and consummation. They await their own personal being at the end to which they are pointed by the covenant fulfilled in Jesus Christ. But if this is their affair it is not their private affair. Called by God, they are called with their hope of their own future, without asking what will be the outcome, to be the first representatives of all those who so far do not have this hope either for themselves or at all, just as faith and love are so far alien to them, because Jesus Christ Himself is not known to them, because they do not yet know of the atonement made in Him. The relation of Christians to others is that they can hope for them. The one thing is the measure of the other. The more earnestly they hope for themselves, the more earnestly they will do so as (scattered and isolated) witnesses to the promise given to the whole world in their by no means easy status as representatives of others. And the more serious they are in their hoping for others—however isolated and scattered—the more seriously they will be able to hope for themselves, the more compellingly they will have to ask themselves whether they really do hope for themselves.

But what does it mean to hope ? We have said concerning the divine promise that, like the divine verdict and the divine direction in the atonement made in Jesus Christ, it has come down, as it were, from above, from God into the world of men loved by God, that it has in a sense been incorporated or implanted into their status and being and non-being, so that objectively they cannot be without it, objectively they have their goal and future in Jesus Christ and therefore in the service of God. In the light of this we can and must understand Christian hope as the coming alive of the promise incorporated in the world of men, or as the taking root of the promise implanted in it. From this standpoint the coming alive or taking root of the promise in the world of men is the work of the Holy Spirit which makes man a Christian. And that means that in the act of Christian hope the objective becomes subjective. It is affirmed. In the person of the Christian the world of men strives after and seizes the goal and future given to it in Jesus Christ. It waits for it, it hastens towards it, it reaches out for it. In the act of Christian hope that which is promised (as promised and therefore future) is already present. Jesus Christ as the (promised and coming) eternally living One is already present. Not merely virtually and effectively, but actually and actively in the person of the Christian. In the act of Christian hope man lives not merely in the factuality of the decision made by God concerning his whole being, but also in the factuality of his own corresponding thoughts and words and works in relation to the service of God, conditioned for and directed towards that service, and in the perspective

of that goal. This particular factuality constitutes the particularity
of Christian being in hope which is revealed only in the particularity
of Christian perception. Christians do not merely see things differently
from others. From God's point of view they are different from others,
just as they are different from others in relation to the divine verdict
and direction when the Holy Spirit awakens them to faith and love.
They do not merely live under the promise, which could be said of all
men. They live in and with and by the promise. They seize it. They
apprehend it. They conform themselves to it. And therefore in their
present life they live as those who belong to the future. That which
is promised and He who is promised are seen and heard by them in
all their futurity. Here and now in their hearts and minds and senses
He unsettles and consoles them, moves and compels them, carries and
upholds them (judging and establishing and directing). Within their
present life and that of the world they are arrested by this future One
and pledged and committed to Him. This particularity of their present
being distinguishes Christians from other men, and it is in this very
particularity that they are the representatives of other men. And to
hope means to be different from other men and to act for them in this
particularity.

But at this point we must take note of an important distinction.
Christian hope is a present being in and with and by the promise of
the future. But in the one hope there will always be inseparably the
great hope and also a small hope. All through temporal life there
will be the expectation of eternal life. But there will also be its
expectation in this temporal life. There will be confidence in the One
who comes as the end and new beginning of all things. There will
also be confidence in His appearing within the ordinary course of things
as they still move towards that end and new beginning. There is a
joy in anticipation of the perfect service of God which awaits man
when God is all in all. But in this joy there is also a joy and zest for
the service which to-day or to-morrow can be our transitory future.
The promise and therefore our calling are in two dimensions. They
refer to the last and ultimate things, but also to the penultimate and
provisional. They refer to the whole, but also concretely to the
details, to the one in all, but also to the all in one. The promised
future is not only that of the day of the Lord at the end of all days,
but because it is the end and goal of all days it is also to-day and
to-morrow. In Christian hope there is no division in this respect, but
again the one is the measure of the other.

Hope seizes, or rather is seized by, the promise of the future. To
that extent it is the great hope, the expectation of the eternal life
which has still to be manifested and given to us, confidence in the
coming Jesus Christ as the end and new beginning of all things, the
joy in anticipation of the perfect being of man and all creatures in
the service of God which is pledged because it is already actualised in

Him. As it seizes the promise of the future it is in every respect—not only hope which derives from Him but also hope in Him as the eternally living One. He, the content of the promise and the object of hope, cannot be replaced by any other. If there is also a small hope for to-day and to-morrow, if there are also temporal, penultimate, provisional and detailed hopes for the immediate future, it is only because He is the future One who shows Himself in every future; it is only in the framework and setting, in the power and the patience of the great and comprehensive hope which is present to man in Him. It is He alone in His futurity, and to that extent as the One who is beyond, who gives hope to the present, the life of man in this world, where otherwise there is no hope. The small hopes are only for the sake of the great hope from which they derive. The provisional promise is only in the light and power of the final promise. If the latter is weak, the former cannot possibly be strong. If the latter perishes, the former will perish with it. If man does not seriously wait for Jesus Christ, at bottom he will not wait for anything else. Daily hope can persist only where in basis and essence it is itself eternal hope.

But the converse must also be perceived and stated. Christian hope is a present being in and with and by the promise of the future, a being which is seized by the promise of God and called. If a man does not seize this hope, apprehend it, conform himself to it here and now as a man who belongs to the future, he is not one who has Christian hope. Rather, it will be revealed that he does not genuinely hope for the perfection and wholeness of His being in the service of God, for eternal life in its futurity, that he does not wait for Jesus Christ as the coming One. If he waits for Him here and now, then the here and now cease to be futureless. He looks for Him, the coming One, to-day and to-morrow, that is, in the decisions in which he has to live to-day and to-morrow as long as time and space are given him. He does not make them without direction or into a future which is empty, but in obedience to his calling, towards that future promised him by God by which the future of to-day and to-morrow is surrounded and lit up, in the light of which every temporal, provisional, penultimate, detailed future necessarily becomes a sign and summons, a detailed and therefore a concrete call to advance which he can only observe and obey. Where there is the great hope, necessarily there are small hopes for the immediate future. These hopes have their basis and strength only in the great hope. They are small, relative and conditioned. In their detailed content they may be mistaken and open to correction. But within these limits they are genuine hopes. And it is certainly in these many little hopes that the Christian lives from day to day if he really lives in the great hope. And perhaps he is most clearly distinguished from the non-Christian by the fact that, directed to the great hope, and without any illusions, he does not fail and is

never weary to live daily in these little hopes. But this necessarily
means that he is daily willing and ready for the small and provisional
and imperfect service of God which the immediate future will demand
of him because a great and final and perfect being in the service of
God is the future of the world and all men, and therefore his future also.

3. JESUS CHRIST THE MEDIATOR

To get a complete view of the event of the reconciliation of man
with God as the fulfilment of the covenant we have so far looked in
two directions : first upwards, to God who loves the world, and then
downwards, to the world which is loved by God ; first to the divine
and sovereign act of reconciling grace, then to the being of man reconciled with God in this act. We must now look at a third aspect,
between the reconciling God above and reconciled man below. Even
when we looked in those two first directions we had continually to
bear in mind that there is a middle point between them. And more
than a middle point, there is one thing which both differentiates and
comprehends the reconciling God above and reconciled man below,
one thing in which there is actualised and revealed both in themselves
and in their inseparable connexion, indeed identity, the reconciling
God as such in the sovereign act of His grace, and reconciled man as
such in his being grounded in that divine act, the turning of God to
man, and based upon it the conversion of man to God. The atonement
as the fulfilment of the covenant is neither grace in itself as the being
of the gracious God, nor is it the work of grace in itself and as such,
the being of the man to whom God is gracious. Nor is it the sum of
the two nor their mutual relationship. It is rather the middle point,
the one thing from which neither the God who turns to man nor man
converted to God can be abstracted, in which and by which both are
what they are, in which and to which they stand in that mutual
relationship. It is only from this middle point that we have been able
to look upwards and downwards, and as we tried always to find and
name something concrete we had all the more necessarily to come
back to it again and again. But that one thing in the middle is one
person, Jesus Christ. He is the atonemen as the fulfilment of the
covenant. In Him that turning of God to man and conversion of
man to God is actuality in the appointed order of the mutual inter-
relationship, and therefore in such a way that the former aims at the
latter and the latter is grounded in the former. In Him both are in
this order the one whole of the event of reconciliation. Our third task
—in our present order of thinking—is obviously to understand Him
as this one whole.

We have already been on our guard against the possibility of regarding and treating the name of Jesus Christ in a purely " nominalistic "

way, as a formal historical or symbolical sign of the event of atonement. This event is not merely outward but inward. It corresponds not only to cognition but to being. It is not in any sense accidentally but necessarily enclosed in Him, as it also took place in Him. It looks both to the reconciling God and reconciled man, and it is found in its unity and completeness in His existence. For that reason He who bears this name, and His existence, must really be regarded as the middle point which embraces the whole and includes it within itself, the middle point in which the sovereign act of the reconciling God and the being of reconciled man are one.

We spoke about a third task, but this third task is simply to show the basis and aim of the answers we gave to the first two, to name and describe the truth in all answers to the question of the gracious God and the man who participates in His grace. Jesus Christ cannot be a third theme which we can separate from the two first. He is the one theme expounded in the two first. If we could speak of the reconciling God and reconciled man only by looking upwards and downwards from Jesus Christ, and constantly looking back to Him, we can speak of Jesus Christ only as we consistently keep before us the one whole of the covenant between God and man fulfilled by Him, and therefore of both the above and the below. He exists as the Mediator between God and man in the sense that in Him God's reconciling of man and man's reconciliation with God are event. He exists in the sense that in this event God encounters and is revealed to all men as the gracious God and in this event again all men are placed under the consequence and outworking of this encounter and revelation. He exists in this action of God for and with all men and in that which happens to all men in the course of it. He exists in the totality of his being and work as the Mediator—He alone as the Mediator, but living and active in His mediatorial office. When we come to speak of Jesus Christ, therefore, it is necessary that what we have to say about Him particularly should for all its particularity be shown to be that which gathers together all that we said in relation to both the above and the below.

But at this point we have to make an important decision in relation to the form and method of the Christian doctrine of the atonement.

It was and is customary to have a single complete and self-contained chapter on Jesus Christ, the so-called " Christology," as the climax in the whole presentation. This includes (1) a special doctrine of the " person " of Christ, i.e., the incarnation of the Word of God, and also His Godhead and manhood in their relationship the one to the other, (2) a special doctrine of His work (following the *munus triplex* arrangement of the Reformation period), and usually (3) a special doctrine of the two " states " of Christ, His humiliation and exaltation. It is then customary to leave the Christology and to develop a special doctrine of the subjective application and appropriation of the salvation objectively accomplished by Jesus Christ, and finally a doctrine of the Church and the means of grace as the mediation between Christ and the Christian. It is also part of the traditional form of the doctrine, just to mention it in passing, that this whole complex is preceded by a doctrine of sin as its negative presupposition and the *terminus a quo* for the whole.

For the moment our question is simply this, whether it is actually the case that what we have to say concerning Jesus Christ can be gathered together in the one section on Christology, over against which there is a completely different section which includes what we have to say concerning man and the Church. This schematism seems logically very illuminating, and didactically useful. At a first glance it may even seem unavoidable from this standpoint. Yet it is not really calculated to enable us to expound the actual subject-matter. In the New Testament there are many christological statements both direct and indirect. But where do we find a special Christology ?—a Christ in Himself, abstracted from what He is amongst the men of Israel and His disciples and the world, from what He is on their behalf ? Does He ever exist except in this relationship ? Certainly He is the absolutely dominating figure, the absolutely unique One in this environment. Certainly He is the determinative and creative subject of everything that takes place in it. But how and in what sense can He be separated from it and considered apart ? Where and how else can He be seen and heard and grasped except as their revelation and grace and judgment and liberation and calling and promise, as the One who is absolutely with and for these men ? And at what point do the New Testament writers leave their Christology behind ? At what point does it not constantly advance in the form of new insights concerning both God and man ?

We have said that Jesus Christ exists in the totality of His work as the Mediator. He alone is the One who fulfils it, but He does completely fulfil it, so that in and with what we have to say about Him in particular we necessarily speak about that comprehensive whole which constitutes its particularity.

But we shall do this either obscurely or not at all if we think that we can crystallise the necessary statements concerning Jesus Christ Himself and as such into a self-contained Christology, in which what He is and means and does and accomplishes for man is not yet revealed or revealed only in the far distance, which must be completed by a special presentation of the relevance of His existence for us, by a related but relatively autonomous soteriology and ecclesiology. The necessary result which this separation has always had is twofold. On the one hand Christology takes on the appearance of an ontology and dramatics arbitrarily constructed from Scripture and tradition. The bearing of it may or may not be seen, but in any case it can never emerge from the half-light of the contingency or non-necessity of a purely historical record or even the recitation of a myth. On the other hand, soteriology and ecclesiology either as a doctrine of the grace and justification and sanctification which comes to us or simply as a doctrine of Christian piety can never escape the tendency to commend itself in relation to Christology, and ultimately to free itself from it, as that which is true and essential, as that which is of practical importance and necessity, as that which is " existentially relevant." And at a pinch can we not omit and dispense with Christology altogether as a doctrine of the being and work of Christ as such ? In the last resort, even if we do away with the christological preliminaries, can we not still succeed in working out either a doctrine of grace, of sanctification or justification, or a practical individual or congregational life as such—especially in relation to the non-Christian world ? Is not the Christology ultimately only so much ballast which can be jettisoned without loss ?—especially when this appears to be desirable on historico-critical and philosophical grounds ? On two sides the traditional order has given too much occasion for this kind of division and abstraction for us not to have to ask seriously whether we ought still to follow it. What is said about Jesus Christ Himself, the christological propositions as such, are constitutive, essential, necessary and central in the Christian doctrine of reconciliation. In them we have to do with that one whole. They cannot, therefore, bear that respectful isolation with which they have been and are so often treated. They cannot and will not stand alone and be true alone, with all the other statements about God and man and sin and grace and justification and the Church true alongside them. Rather they must be represented and thought of as the statement from which all truth derives, which control the whole nexus, which themselves constitute and reveal this nexus. Self-evidently they have to be made, they cannot simply disappear, their own content must not be dissolved, they cannot be transposed into purely interpretative subordinate statements descriptive of the grace actual and active in Jesus Christ. Otherwise we would be well on the way to asserting the autonomy of the event of atonement in relation to the One who must be regarded and under-stood as the subject, executor and Lord.

To all appearances Franz Hermann Reinhold Frank has not escaped this tendency, although of all modern dogmaticians he is of special interest in that he felt strongly, as I see it, the problematical nature of the traditional order and made the most determined efforts to overcome it. The whole doctrine of the atonement (which he calls "regeneration") is brought by him (*Syst. der Chr. Wahrheit*, 2, 2, 1886) under the one concept of the "evolving humanity of God with its centre in the divine-human redeemer." He then describes how this "humanity of God" evolved in fallen humanity and especially in Israel for the sake of the God-man, how it was posited in the person of the God-man in order to grow out of the God-man: objectively by the Holy Spirit and the means of grace in word and sacrament; subjectively in the *ordo salutis* of justifying and renewing faith; objectively-subjectively in the existence of the Church. Here we have a powerful concern—in its own way it amounts to what we can only call a genius—to see together what traditional dogmatics had always separated, the God-man and the humanity of God. And in its own way it is very impressive. But we have to ask whether in spite of his fine "for the sake of" and "in" and "out of" Frank has not (in an excess of good intention) slipped speculatively into a view which alters ever so slightly the Christian message. His main theme is the regenerate "humanity of God." The God-man is rightly described as the centre, but He is pictured only in this function, being made subservient to the evolving and positing and growing of the humanity of God. But while it is true that He does serve this end, does this exhaust what He is for it and in relation to it? Ontologically is it not a matter of Him first, and only then and in Him of the "humanity of God"?

On the one side, then, our task is so to present the doctrine of reconciliation that it is always clear that it has to do wholly and utterly with Jesus Christ, that He is the active subject (and not simply a means or predicate of its happening). This means that we have to develop and present the doctrine of reconciliation in the light of definite christological perceptions and propositions, focussing attention upon Jesus Christ as the beginning and the middle and the end. And it is clear that to do this we must introduce what we have to say particularly about Jesus Christ in all its particularity into the basis of every individual thought-sequence. For in its particularity it includes within itself the whole. But, on the other hand, it is our task not to separate what we have to say particularly about Jesus Christ but to bring it into immediate connexion with what He is not for Himself but for us, what He is as the One who makes reconciliation, as the One who fulfils the covenant, as the One in whom the world and man have been and are converted to God. This means that we have to indicate the fact and the extent to which He does in fact establish and control this happening, to which He is its beginning and middle and end. It is clear, then, that what we have to say particularly about Jesus Christ can only be the culminating sentence in every thought-sequence, the sentence which controls the whole, and in the light of which we can apply ourselves seriously to the problems of soteriology and ecclesiology, of the application and appropriation of the salvation which appeared in Him and was given to man, the problem, therefore, of the existence of the community.

But who is He, the One who is the middle point, the Mediator between the reconciling action of God and the reconciled being of man, in whom both at once are actual and revealed ? If we have rightly grasped and described the event of reconciliation in these two main points, then we shall not be mistaken if in relation to the Mediator Jesus Christ we start with the fact that in Him—we will make a general statement and then explain it later—we have to do wholly with God and wholly with man, and with both in their complete and utter unity. Not with any god, but with the God who in all the divine freedom of His love, in all His omnipotence and holiness and eternity, is gracious and merciful and long-suffering, who is this not as the One who is self-existent, self-reposing and self-motivated, but in His movement to man. And not with any man, but with the man who in all his creaturely and earthly humanity is converted to God and willing and ready in relation to Him, who is only as he is thankful and therefore obedient. And not with any relationship between them, not with a mere encounter and mutual correspondence, not with a mere being together, but with their unity, with the being of God in and with the human being of man, with the being of man in and with the divine being of God. This is Jesus Christ. We cannot avoid the old formula : very God, very man, very God-man. It is as this One that He is the middle point, and the being of God in His sovereign action of grace and the being of reconciled man are both in Him and are both one in Him. As this One He is the subject of the act of reconciliation between God and all men. As this One He is known in the Christian community : its Lord, the Messiah of Israel, the Saviour of the world, the object of its faith, the basis of its love, the content of its hope.

We hasten to explain that the being of Jesus Christ, the unity of being of the living God and this living man, takes place in the event of the concrete existence of this man. It is a being, but a being in a history. The gracious God is in this history, so is reconciled man, so are both in their unity. And what takes place in this history, and therefore in the being of Jesus Christ as such, is atonement. Jesus Christ is not what He is—very God, very man, very God-man—in order as such to mean and do and accomplish something else which is atonement. But His being as God and man and God-man consists in the completed act of the reconciliation of man with God.

We are again faced with a critical decision in relation to the form of the doctrine of reconciliation.

We have seen that a distinction was and is made between a doctrine of the " person " and a doctrine of the " work " of Christ : *De persona Christi θεαν-θρώπου* and *De officio Christi mediatorio*. Of the conceptual perspicacity of the two titles and the convenience of the division there can be no question. But, again, we have to consider whether it corresponds to the facts, i.e., whether Jesus Christ is rightly seen if first of all (to follow especially the thinking of the Eastern Church) He is seen in a being which does, of course, rest on an act, the incarnation, but which—introduced and established in this way—is as a *unio* of the person of the Logos and therefore of the divine nature with the human only a static and idle being, not an act or a work—and only then (here we come to the special interest of the Western Church) seen in a work, which does, of course, have its presupposition in that being, but only a formal presupposition, not being identical with it. We have to ask again whether there is in the New Testament any precedent for this division of approach and concept. In the Fourth Gospel does the Son of God exist in any other way than in the doing of the work given Him by the Father ? Does the Jesus of the Synoptics exist in any other way than in His addresses and conversations and miracles, and finally His going up to Jerusalem ? Does the Christ of Paul exist in any other way than as the Crucified and Risen ? Does the New Testament *kyrios* generally ever exist except in the accomplishment and revelation of His ministry and lordship as such ? Certainly it is always a matter of His divine and human being and of both in their unity, not yet described in the formulæ of the 4th and 5th centuries, but with no other meaning and intention in relation to the presupposed content. The only thing is that we have to seek the presupposition, the answer to the question " Whom say men that I am ? " (Mk. 8²⁷), not behind but directly within the speech and action and living and suffering and dying (Mt. 11⁴ᶠ·) of the New Testament Jesus or Christ or Jesus Christ. The consequences of abstraction at this point can never be good. We must not forget that if in the doctrinal decisions of Nicaea and Constantinople and Ephesus and Chalcedon it was a matter of the being of Jesus Christ as such, these decisions had a polemical and critical character, their purpose being to delimit and clarify at a specific point. They are to be regarded as guiding lines for an understanding of His existence and action, not to be used, as they have been used, as stones for the construction of an abstract doctrine of His " person." In Himself and as such the Christ of Nicaea and Chalcedon naturally was and is a being which even if we could consistently and helpfully explain His unique structure conceptually could not possibly be proclaimed and believed as One who acts historically because of the timelessness and historical remoteness of the concepts (person, nature, Godhead, manhood, etc.). He could not possibly be proclaimed and believed as the One whom in actual fact the Christian Church has always and everywhere proclaimed and believed under the name of Jesus Christ. An abstract doctrine of the person of Christ may have its own apparent importance, but it is always an empty form, in which what we have to say concerning Jesus Christ can never be said. Again, it is almost inevitable that a doctrine of the work of Christ separated from that of His person will sooner or later give rise to the question, and perhaps even impose it, whether this work cannot be understood as that of someone other than that divine-human person. Can we not make use of the concept of a created *tertium quid* (as in certain gnostic speculations concerning angels), or more simply of a man specially endowed with divine grace, to help us to understand the subject of this action ? Is not such a concept more serviceable than the *vere Deus vere homo* of a doctrine of the person which is merely presupposed ? If this is the way of it, an abstract doctrine of the work of Christ will always tend secretly in a direction where some kind of Arianism or Pelagianism lies in wait. What is needed in this matter is nothing more or less than the removal of the distinction between the two basic sections of classical Christology, or positively, the restoration of the hyphen which always connects them and makes them one in the New Testament. Not to the detriment of either the one or the other. Not to sacrifice the Eastern interest to the Western. Not to cause the doctrine of the person of Christ to be absorbed and dissolved in that of His work, or *vice versa*. But to give a proper place to them both, and to establish them both securely in that place.

It is in the particular fact and the particular way that Jesus Christ is very God, very man, and very God-man that He works, and He works in the fact and only in the fact that He is this One and not another. His being as this One is His history, and His history is this His being. This is the truth which must light up the doctrine of reconciliation as Christology. When this is done, it will naturally follow that, as a whole, as a doctrine of the justifying and sanctifying and calling grace of God, as a doctrine of thankfulness, of faith and love and hope, as a doctrine of the community, its human and divine reality, its existence and task, it will be completely dominated and determined by Christ-ology. It will also follow that Christology will not be idle or come under the suspicion that it may be dispensed with. It will take its place without diminution or alteration as the necessary beginning. And it will work itself out in the whole.

4. THE THREE FORMS OF THE DOCTRINE OF RECONCILIATION

If in this sense and with this understanding we return to the being of Jesus Christ as we have briefly defined it, we find at once that there are three " christological " aspects in the narrower sense—aspects of His active person or His personal work which as such broaden into three perspectives for an understanding of the whole event of the atonement.

The first is that in Jesus Christ we have to do with very God. The reconciliation of man with God takes place as God Himself actively intervenes, Himself taking in hand His cause with and against and for man, the cause of the covenant, and in such a way (this is what distinguishes the event of reconciliation from the general sway of the providence and universal rule of God) that He Himself becomes man. God became man. That is what is, i.e., what has taken place, in Jesus Christ. He is very God acting for us men, God Himself become man. He is the authentic Revealer of God as Himself God. Again, He is the effective proof of the power of God as Himself God. Yet again,

He is the fulfiller of the covenant as Himself God. He is nothing less or other than God Himself, but God as man. When we say God we say honour and glory and eternity and power, in short, a regnant freedom as it is proper to Him who is distinct from and superior to everything else that is. When we say God we say the Creator and Lord of all things. And we can say all that without reservation or diminution of Jesus Christ—but in a way in which it can be said in relation to Him, i.e., in which it corresponds to the Godhead of God active and revealed in Him. No general idea of " Godhead " developed abstractly from such concepts must be allowed to intrude at this point. How the freedom of God is constituted, in what character He is the Creator and Lord of all things, distinct from and superior to them, in short, what is to be understood by " Godhead," is something which—watchful against all imported ideas, ready to correct them and perhaps to let them be reversed and renewed in the most astonishing way—we must always learn from Jesus Christ. He defines those concepts : they do not define Him. When we start with the fact that He is very God we are forced to keep strictly to Him in relation to what we mean by true " Godhead."

This means primarily that it is a matter of the Godhead, the honour and glory and eternity and omnipotence and freedom, the being as Creator and Lord, of the Father, Son and Holy Spirit. Jesus Christ is Himself God as the Son of God the Father and with God the Father the source of the Holy Spirit, united in one essence with the Father by the Holy Spirit. That is how He is God. He is God as He takes part in the event which constitutes the divine being.

We must add at once that as this One who takes part in the divine being and event He became and is man. This means that we have to understand the very Godhead, that divine being and event and therefore Himself as the One who takes part in it, in the light of the fact that it pleased God—and this is what corresponds outwardly to and reveals the inward divine being and event—Himself to become man. In this way, in this condescension, He is the eternal Son of the eternal Father. This is the will of this Father, of this Son, and of the Holy Spirit who is the Spirit of the Father and the Son. This is how God is God, this is His freedom, this is His distinctness from and superiority to all other reality. It is with this meaning and purpose that He is the Creator and Lord of all things. It is as the eternal and almighty love, which He is actually and visibly in this action of condescension. This One, the One who loves in this way, is the true God. But this means that He is the One who as the Creator and Lord of all things is able and willing to make Himself equal with the creature, Himself to become a creature ; the One whose eternity does not prevent but rather permits and commands Him to be in time and Himself to be temporal, whose omnipotence is so great that He can be weak and indeed impotent, as a man is weak and impotent. He is the One who

in His freedom can and does in fact bind Himself, in the same way as
we all are bound. And we must go further : He, the true God, is the
One whose Godhead is demonstrated and plainly consists in essence
in the fact that, seeing He is free in His love, He is capable of and
wills this condescension for the very reason that in man of all His
creatures He has to do with the one that has fallen away from Him,
that has been unfaithful and hostile and antagonistic to Him. He is
God in that He takes this creature to Himself, and that in such a way
that He sets Himself alongside this creature, making His own its
penalty and loss and condemnation to nothingness. He is God in
the fact that He can give Himself up and does give Himself up not
merely to the creaturely limitation but to the suffering of the human
creature, becoming one of these men, Himself bearing the judgment
under which they stand, willing to die and, in fact, dying the death
which they have deserved. That is the nature and essence of the
true God as He has intervened actively and manifestly in Jesus Christ.
When we speak of Jesus Christ we mean the true God—He who seeks
His divine glory and finds that glory, He whose glory obviously consists, in the fact that because He is free in His love He can be and
actually is lowly as well as exalted ; He, the Lord, who is for us a
servant, the servant of all servants. It is in the light of the fact of His
humiliation that on this first aspect all the predicates of His Godhead,
which is the true Godhead, must be filled out and interpreted. Their
positive meaning is lit up only by this determination and limitation,
only by the fact that in this act He is this God and therefore the true
God, distinguished from all false gods by the fact that they are not
capable of this act, that they have not in fact accomplished it, that
their supposed glory and honour and eternity and omnipotence not
only do not include but exclude their self-humiliation. False gods
are all reflections of a false and all too human self-exaltation. They
are all lords who cannot and will not be servants, who are therefore
no true lords, whose being is not a truly divine being.

The second christological aspect is that in Jesus Christ we have
to do with a true man. The reconciliation of the world with God takes
place in the person of a man in whom, because He is also true God,
the conversion of all men to God is an actual event. It is the person
of a true man, like all other men in every respect, subjected without
exception to all the limitations of the human situation. The conditions
in which other men exist and their suffering are also His conditions
and His suffering. That He is very God does not mean that He is
partly God and only partly man. He is altogether man just as He is
altogether God—altogether man in virtue of His true Godhead whose
glory consists in His humiliation. That is how He is the reconciler
between God and man. That is how God accomplishes in Him the
conversion of all men to Himself. He is true man, and altogether
man, for in Him we have to do with the manifestation of the glory of

the One who is true God and altogether God, and with the conversion to God of the One who is true man and altogether man. Here, too, there is no reservation and no diminution, which would be an immediate denial of the act of atonement made in Him. Jesus Christ is man in a different way from what we are. That is why He is our Mediator with God. But He is so in a complete equality of His manhood with ours. To say man is to say creature and sin, and this means limitation and suffering. Both these have to be said of Jesus Christ. Not, however, according to the standard of general concepts, but only with reference to Him, only in correspondence with His true manhood. As in relation to His Godhead, so also in relation to His manhood, we must not allow any necessary idea of the human situation and its need to intervene. What His manhood is, and therefore true manhood, we cannot read into Him from elsewhere, but must be told by Him. But then we find that it is a matter of the manhood of the eternal Son of God. It is a matter of the real limitation and suffering of the man with whom the high God has ordained and elected and determined to be one, and has therefore humbled Himself. In His limitation and suffering, this is the true man. And that means at once that He is the man exalted by God, lifted above His need and limitation and suffering in and out of His need and limitation and suffering. In virtue of the fact that He is one with God He is free man. He is a creature, but superior to His creatureliness. He is bound by sin, but quite free in relation to it because He is not bound to commit it. He is mortal, and has actually died as we must all die. But in dying He is superior to death, and at once and altogether rescued from it, so that (even as a man like us) He is triumphant and finally alive. As the true God, i.e., the God who humbles Himself, Jesus Christ is this true man, i.e., the man who in all His creatureliness is exalted above His creatureliness. In this He is also exalted above us, because He is different from us, and is given the precedence in the ranks of our common humanity. But He does precede us. As God He was humbled to take our place, and as man He is exalted on our behalf. He is set at the side of God in the humanity which is ours. He is above us and opposed to us, but He is also for us. What has happened in Him as the one true man is the conversion of all of us to God, the realisation of true humanity. It is anticipated in Him, but it is in fact accomplished and revealed. As in Him God became like man, so too in Him man has become like God. As in Him God was bound, so too in Him man is made free. As in Him the Lord became a servant, so too in Him the servant has become a Lord. That is the atonement made in Jesus Christ in its second aspect. In Him humanity is exalted humanity, just as Godhead is humiliated Godhead. And humanity is exalted in Him by the humiliation of Godhead. We cannot regard the human being of Jesus Christ, we cannot—without denying or weakening them—interpret His predicates of liability to sin and suffering and death, in any other way than in the light of the liberation and exaltation accomplished in His unity with God. It is in its impotence that His being as man is omnipotent, in its temporality that it is eternal, in its shame that it is glorious, in its corruptibility that it is incorruptible, in its servitude that it is that of the Lord. In this way, therefore, it is His true being as man—true humanity.

The Evangelists clung to this in their representation of the human being of Jesus Christ. They left no doubt that it was a human being like others, but even less so that as such it was the human being of the true God, and therefore in spite of its likeness to all others distinguished from all others in its freedom in face of limitation and suffering. From the very first they describe it in the light and clear reference of the final thing they have to report concerning Him : His resurrection from the dead as the event in which His exaltation cannot merely be discerned but is openly manifested—lighting up both that which precedes and that which follows. Therefore they describe the man Jesus as the One who, being tempted and suffering and dying as King, overcomes as King, and therefore passes through the midst of all others as King. That is how we m ust see Him.

In so far as He was and is and will be very man, the conversion of man to God took place in Him, the turning and therefore the reconciliation of all men, the fulfilment of the covenant. And in the light of Jesus Christ the man who is still not free in relation to limitation and suffering, who is still not exalted, who is still lowly (lowly, as it were, *in abstracto*), can be understood only as false man—just as in the light of Jesus Christ the empty loveless gods which are incapable of condescension and self-humiliation can be understood only as false gods.

Before we pass on to the third christological aspect, we may at this point interpose another discussion concerning the method of treating the doctrine of reconciliation. In considering the first two aspects we brought together in rather an unusual way two elements in traditional Christology : the doctrine of the two " natures " of Christ, His deity and humanity, and the doctrine of the two " states " of Christ, His humiliation (*status exinanitionis*) and His exaltation (*status exaltationis*). We must now consider to what extent this presentation involves a change in traditional Christology and soteriology, and how far that change is right and necessary.

In comparison with older dogmatics, our presentation has undoubtedly the advantage that it does far greater justice to the particular doctrine of the two states.

In the older Lutherans this doctrine forms a great excursus in the doctrine of the human nature of Christ, which as they understood it was not merely exalted in the incarnation but actually divinised, i.e., according to their particular doctrine of the communication of the attributes furnished with all the attributes of Godhead. For them the only significance of the doctrine of the two states was that it answered what was for them the very difficult question how far Jesus Christ could have lived and suffered and died as a real man in time and space and under all the other restrictions of human life. For them *exinanitio* meant that for a time, for the period of His life up to and including death, the God-man denies Himself that divinisation of His humanity (either by concealment or by genuine renunciation), but then reassumes it with the *exaltatio* which begins with His triumphant descent into hell.

The older Reformed writers described the two states rather obscurely as the humiliation and exaltation of the divine Logos, and with them the doctrine is simply left in the air, following that of the work of Christ but not organically related to it. It was brought in for the sake of completeness, but on their presuppositions it had only an incidental application. If our presentation is right, then at least the doctrine of the humiliation and exaltation of Christ does acquire a place and function in line with its scriptural and factual importance. But this necessitates certain decisive innovations in relation to the older dogmatics which we must openly admit and for which we must give our reasons.

Now (1) we have not spoken of two " states " (*status*) of Jesus Christ which succeed one another, but of two sides or directions or forms of that which took place in Jesus Christ for the reconciliation of man with God. We used the concepts humiliation and exaltation, and we thought of Jesus Christ as the servant who became Lord and the Lord who became servant. But in so doing we were not describing a being in the particular form of a state, but the twofold action of Jesus Christ, the actuality of His work : His one work, which cannot be divided into different stages or periods of His existence, but which fills out and constitutes His existence in this twofold form. Our question is whether this does not better correspond to the witness of the New Testament concerning Jesus Christ. Where and when is He not both humiliated and exalted, already exalted in His humiliation, and humiliated in His exaltation ? Where in Paul, for example, is He the Crucified who has not yet risen, or the Risen who has not been crucified ? Would He be the One whom the New Testament attests as the Mediator between God and man if He were only the one and not the other ? And if He is the Mediator, which of the two can He be alone and without the other ? Both aspects force themselves upon us. We have to do with the being of the one and entire Jesus Christ whose humiliation detracts nothing and whose exaltation adds nothing. And in this His being we have to do with His action, the work and event of atonement. That is the first reason for this alteration of the traditional dogmatic form.

But even more penetrating (2) is the fact that understanding the doctrine of the two states in this way we have tried to interpret it in the light of the doctrine of the two natures, and *vice versa*.

Notice that there can be no question of abandoning the *vere Deus vere homo*. If it is a matter of the reconciliation of man with God in Jesus Christ, i.e., the reconciliation of man with God and by God, then obviously we have to do truly and wholly with God and truly and wholly with man. And the more exact determination of the relationship between God and man in the famous Chalcedonian definition, which has become normative for all subsequent development in this dogma and dogmatics, is one which in our understanding has shown itself to be factually right and necessary. But according to our understanding there can be no question of a doctrine of the two natures which is autonomous, a doctrine of Jesus Christ as God and man which is no longer or not yet related to the divine action which has taken place in Him, which does not have this action and man as its subject matter. There is no such doctrine in the New Testament, although we cannot say that the New Testament envisages the being and relationship of God and man in Jesus Christ in any other way than it became conceptually fixed in the doctrine of the two natures.

Similarly, there can be no autonomous doctrine of the humiliation and exaltation which took place in Jesus Christ, especially without a reference to what took place in Jesus Christ between God as God and man as man. There is a humiliation and exaltation—it hardly needs to be demonstrated that in Phil. 2⁶ᶠ· and indeed all the New Testament Jesus Christ is regarded in the light of these two aspects and concepts. But if there is, it is not something incidental to His being. It is the actuality of the being of Jesus Christ as very God and very man. We cannot, therefore, ascribe to Jesus Christ two natures and then quite independently two states. But we have to explain in mutual relationship to one another what Jesus Christ is as very God and very man and what takes place as the divine work of atonement in His humiliation and exaltation.

But this brings us (3) to what is perhaps the greatest objection which might be brought against our presentation from the standpoint of the older dogmatics. To explain in the light of each other the deity and humanity of Jesus Christ on the one hand and His humiliation and exaltation on the other means that in Jesus Christ God—we do not say casts off His Godhead but (as the One who loves in His sovereign freedom) activates and proves it by the fact that He gives Himself to the limitation and suffering of the human creature, that He, the Lord, becomes a servant, that as distinct from all false gods He humbles Himself —and again, that in Jesus Christ man, without any forfeiture or restriction of His humanity, in the power of His deity and therefore in the power of and thanks to the humiliation of God, is the man who is freed from His limitation and suffering, not divinised man, but man sovereign and set at the side of God, in short, man exalted by God. The humiliation, therefore, is the humiliation of God, the exaltation the exaltation of man : the humiliation of God to supreme glory, as the activation and demonstration of His divine being ; and the exaltation of man as the work of God's grace which consists in the restoration of his true humanity. Can we really put it in this way ? We have to put it in this way if we are really speaking of the deity and humanity of Jesus Christ, of *His* humiliation and exaltation, of *His* being and *His* work.

For who is the God who is present and active in Him ? He is the One who, concretely in His being as man, activates and reveals Himself as divinely free, as the One who loves in His freedom, as the One who is capable of and willing for this inconceivable condescension, and the One who can be and wills to be true God not only in the height but also in the depth—in the depth of human creatureliness, sinfulness and mortality.

And who is the man Jesus Christ ? He is the One in whom God is man, who is completely bound by the human situation, but who is not crushed by it, who since it is His situation is free in relation to it, who overcomes it, who is its Lord and not its servant.

Conversely, what is the humiliation of Jesus Christ ? To say that He is lowly as a man is tautology which does not help us in the least to explain His humiliation. It merely contains the general truth that He exists as a man in the bondage and suffering of the human situation, and is to that extent actually lowly—a general truth which is in fact very forcibly called in question by the humanity of Jesus Christ. But the peculiar thing about the humiliation of Jesus Christ, the significant thing, the effective thing, the redemptive thing, is that it is the work of atonement in its first form. In Him it took place that while maintaining His true deity God became man, in Him to make His own the cause of man. In Him God Himself humiliated Himself—not in any disloyalty but in a supreme loyalty to His divine being (revealing it in a way which marks it off from all other gods). That is the secret of Christmas and Good Friday and the way which leads from the one to the other. Jesus Christ is the Reconciler of all men of all times and places by the fact that in Him God is active and re-vealed as the One who in His freedom, in His divine majesty, so loves that in Him the Lord became a servant, a servant like all of us, but more than that, the servant of us all, the man who did for us what we ourselves would not and could not do.

Again, what is the exaltation of Jesus Christ ? To say that as God He is transcendent, free, sovereign, above the world, and therefore above the limita-tion and suffering of the human situation is again tautology which does not help us to understand His exaltation. God is always free in His love, transcendent God. He does not cease to be God transcendent when He makes it His glory to be in the depths, in order to make peace on earth to the men of His goodwill.

In His Godhead, as the eternal Son of the Father, as the eternal Word, Jesus Christ never ceased to be transcendent, free, and sovereign. He did not stand in need of exaltation, nor was He capable of it. But He did as man—it is here again that we come up against that which is not self-evident in Jesus Christ. The special thing, the new thing about the exaltation of Jesus Christ is that One who is bound as we are is free, who is tempted as we are is without sin, who is a sufferer as we are is able to minister to Himself and others, who is a victim to death is alive even though He was dead, who is a servant (the servant of all servants) is the Lord. This is the secret of His humanity which is revealed in His resurrection and ascension and therefore shown retrospectively by the Evangelists to be the secret of His whole life and death. It is not simply that He is the Son of God at the right hand of the Father, the *Kyrios*, the Lord of His community and the Lord of the cosmos, the bearer and executor of divine authority in the Church and the world, but that He is all this as a man—as a man like we are, but a man exalted in the power of His deity. This is what makes Him the Mediator between God and man, and the One who fulfils the covenant.

If we have correctly related these four considerations concerning the deity, the humanity, the humiliation and the exaltation of Jesus Christ, we not only can but must speak as we have done on this matter. The doctrine of reconciliation in its first two forms will then necessarily begin with a discussion of the God who humbles Himself in Jesus Christ and of the man who in Jesus Christ is exalted.

In the light of this we shall have to consider the whole event of atonement twice over, examining it in detail. The correct titles for these first two sections will be " Jesus Christ, the Lord as Servant " and " Jesus Christ, the Servant as Lord." We shall still follow the traditional path to the extent that in content and meaning this division corresponds exactly to what earlier dogmatics worked out as the doctrine of the high-priestly and kingly office of Christ (in the framework of that doctrine of the threefold office of Christ in which they used to picture His work). I prefer the first two titles as more precise and also more comprehensive (since they also include the earlier doctrine of the person of Christ).

The third christological aspect to which we must now turn is at once the simplest and the highest. It is the source of the two first, and it comprehends them both. As the God who humbles Himself and therefore reconciles man with Himself, and as the man exalted by God and therefore reconciled with Him, as the One who is very God and very man in this concrete sense, Jesus Christ Himself is one. He is the " God-man," that is, the Son of God who as such is this man, this man who as such is the Son of God.

The New Testament obviously speaks of Jesus Christ in both these ways : the one looking and moving, as it were, from above downwards, the other from below upwards. It would be idle to try to conclude which of the two is the more original, authentic and important. Both are necessary. Neither can stand or be understood without the other. A Christ who did not come in the flesh, who was not identical with the Jesus of Nazareth who suffered and died under Pontius Pilate, would not be the Christ Jesus—and a Jesus who was not the eternal Word of God, and who as man was not raised again from the dead, would not be the Jesus Christ—of the New Testament. The New Testament, it is true, knows nothing of the formulæ of later ecclesiastical Christology, which tried to formulate the two aspects with conceptual strictness. But it knows even less of the docetic and ebionite abstractions, the attempts to make absolute either the Godhead or the manhood, which it was the concern of the later Christology to rebut. In fact the one aspect is given the greater prominence at this point., the other at that. But it knows only the one person, Jesus Christ Himself, who without division or distinction is both God and man. We remember : both, not in a general and arbitrarily determined sense of the concepts, but in that sense which has been specifically filled out and made concrete. We must never lose sight of Him in the (often very abstract) content given to the concepts in the fathers and later development. The One who is both in this concrete sense is the Jesus Christ of the New Testament. To understand, we must emphasise the phrase : the One who is both—both, and not a third between God and man or a mixture of the two. The Judaic and Hellenistic environment of the New Testament did know such mixtures. The New Testament speaks the language of this environment, but it does not speak of this kind of third. The concrete views of God and man which it has before it in Jesus Christ cannot be mixed but can only be seen together as the forms of a history : the reconciling God and the man reconciled by Him. In face of the history which took place in Jesus Christ the New Testament says that these two elements of the one grace, the divine and the human, are one in Him, not in one form but in two. For that reason its statements concerning Him always move in either the one direction or the other, from above downwards or from below upwards. The only statement in the New Testament which brings together both in one is properly the name of Jesus Christ, which forbids and makes quite impossible any separation of the one from the other or any fusion of both in a third. When, therefore, the later Christology safeguarded against any confusion or transmutation of the two natures the one into the other and therefore into a third, the innovation was not one of substance but only of theology, and one which the substance itself demanded.

There can be no question of our trying to see a third thing in what we have called the third christological aspect. Everything that can be said materially concerning Jesus Christ and the atonement made in Him has been said exhaustively in the twofold fact—which cannot be further reduced conceptually but only brought together historically— that He is very God and very man, i.e., the Lord who became a servant and the servant who became Lord, the reconciling God and reconciled man. The third aspect can be only the viewing of this history in its unity and completeness, the viewing of Jesus Christ Himself, in whom the two lines cross—in the sense that He Himself is the subject of what takes place on these two lines. To that extent the reconciliation of the world with God and the conversion of the world to God took place in Him. To that extent He Himself, His existence, is this reconciliation. He Himself is the Mediator and pledge of the covenant. He is the Mediator of it in that He fulfils it—from God to man and from man to God. He is the pledge of it in that in His existence He confirms and maintains and reveals it as an authentic witness—attesting Himself, in that its fulfilment is present and shines out and avails and is effective in Him. This is the new thing in the third christological aspect. Jesus Christ is the actuality of the atonement, and as such the truth of it which speaks for itself. If we hear Jesus Christ, then whether we realise it or not we hear this truth. If we say Jesus Christ, then whether we realise it or not we express and repeat this truth : the truth of the grace in which God has turned to the world in Him and which has come to the world in Him ; the truth of the living brackets which bring and hold together heaven and earth, God and all men, in Him ; the truth that God has bound Himself to man and that man is bound to God. The One who bears this name is Himself this truth in that He is Himself this actuality. He attests what He is. He alone is the pledge of it because He alone is the Mediator of it. He alone is the truth of it. But He is that truth, and therefore it speaks for itself in Him. It is not in us. We cannot produce it of ourselves. We cannot of ourselves attest it to ourselves or to others. But it encounters us majestically in Him—the promise of the truth which avails for us as the atonement—of which it is the truth—took place for us and as ours, the truth which for that reason can and should be heard and accepted and appropriated by us, which we can and should accept as the truth which applies to us. It encounters us in Him as the promise of our own future. It is He, and therefore the actuality of our atonement, who stands before us. It is to Him, and therefore to the revelation of this actuality, that we move. He is the Word of God to men which speaks of God and man and therefore expresses and discloses and reveals God and ourselves—God in His actual relationship to us and us in our actual relationship to God. He is the Word of God by which He calls us in this relationship and therefore calls us to Him and therefore calls us also to ourselves. He was and is the will of God to speak this Word—this Word of His act. And it is our destiny to hear this Word, to live under and with and by this Word. That is the third christological aspect.

Of the doctrine of reconciliation as such we must now say that in the light of this aspect a third and concluding section will be necessary in our presentation : concluding, but at the same time opening up and forming a transition to the doctrine of the redemption or consummation, the " eschatology " in which all dogmatics culminate. It is easy to find a title for this third section : " Jesus Christ the Guarantor." " Jesus Christ the Witness " would also be possible and impressive, but it might be understood too formally, whereas the neutral concept " guarantor " expresses more clearly what we are trying to say—that He who is Himself the material content of the atonement, the Mediator of it, stands security with man as well as God that it is our atonement— He Himself being the form of it as well as the content.

In this section we shall be dealing substantially with what the older dog-matics used to present as the doctrine of the " prophetic " office of Christ. We can only say that as compared with the doctrines of the *munus sacerdotale* and the *munus regium*—which it normally preceded as a kind of unaccented syllable —this doctrine played a rather difficult part and one which did not seem to shed any very great light of its own. It was hardly related, if at all, to the first two offices, and for that reason it had a largely formal character and could be left out altogether by some of the later writers. And it was because its proper role could not be found in the orthodox period that at the time of the *Aufklärung* it emerged from its decline in a form which was fatal. For it now pushed to the forefront as the supposed truth behind all Christology, but in the form of the representation of Jesus as the supreme teacher and example of perfect divine and human love—a representation which has practically nothing in common with the biblical concept of prophecy. The result was that the doctrines of the priestly and kingly office of Christ were now pushed back into the same obscurity of the less important in which this doctrine itself had laboured for so long. The atonement as a work of divine grace for man and to man, which means, the whole actuality of Jesus Christ, was necessarily concealed apart from a few confused and tedious and not very profitable relics. That this may not happen again, we must give due weight to the *munus propheticum* in its proper content and its peculiar significance.

It is not a matter of the content of truth but of the character of truth, of the identity of the divine work of grace with the divine Word of grace, of Jesus Christ who not only is what He is and does what He does but in so doing encounters us, testifying to us, addressing us, promising to us, pledging Himself to us, in all His majesty summoning us—in the right sense as a teacher and example—to come to Him, and in that way His own prophet, the prophet of His future as ours and ours as His.

We have to develop the whole doctrine of reconciliation in accordance with our Christology and the three basic christological aspects. We shall do so in three sections which correspond to the three aspects. The Christology is the key to the whole. From each of the three aspects suggested it will be our starting point and will necessarily control all the detailed developments. But in the light of the Christology there have to be these developments : the three great expositions of the fact and the extent to which the reconciliation of the world with God is actual in Him—in His servitude for us, in the humiliation of God for man which took place in Him, in His lordship over us, in the exaltation of man to God's glory which took place in Him, and all this as truth which He Himself has guaranteed and pledged.

But the christological bases of the doctrine of reconciliation bring us face to face at once and directly with a problem which has met us everywhere in this survey. This problem seems to form, as it were, a second and obscure centre side by side with Jesus Christ. The whole event of atonement seems to be strangely related to it on its negative side just as on its positive side it is grounded and enclosed in Jesus Christ. But so far we have not given it any independent consideration. It is the problem of the sin which has come into the world, or of man as the responsible author but also the poor victim of sin, the one who is blinded by it and closed to the truth. Atonement is the fulfilment by God of the covenant broken by man. Because he sins, and because the world is the world of sin and its consequences, man has need of conversion to God if he is not to perish. And it is in face of this, striving against and overcoming the sin of man, that God in His mercy does what He does, and there happens to man what does happen to him in the divine mercy when Jesus Christ intervenes as the Mediator of the covenant. It is clear that at this heart of its message Christian proclamation must speak very definitely of this hostile element, that therefore there has to be a very clear doctrine of sin in the Church's dogmatics.

But it must not be a doctrine of sin which is autonomous, which considers the matter and investigates and presents it in a vacuum, and therefore again abstractly.

That is what we find in the older theology and, of course, in most modern theology as well. Between the doctrine of creation and that of the atonement it was and is customary (and logically it is very instructive and didactically most illuminating) to interpose a special section *De peccato* : a doctrine of the fall, of original sin and its consequences, of the state and constitution of sinful man, of individual or actual sins.

It cannot be disputed that this whole sphere—this dark prelude or counterpart to the divine covenant and work of grace—has to be taken very seriously. If there is to be any understanding of the Christian message, we have to investigate it closely and take it into account. There is in fact no page in the Bible in which it does not figure, and many pages in which it seems to do so almost alone. But all the same, we cannot with a good conscience follow the procedure which would give it a treatment which is independent, self-originating and self-contained.

For what is the ontological place of sin in the Bible ? Surely not in a realm of its own where it has its own being and can exist in and for itself ? In the sphere of Christian thinking at any rate, we cannot seriously and responsibly maintain that it was created by God and belongs, therefore, to the constitution of the world as He willed it. There is no support for any such view in what the Bible itself says. In the Bible sin in all its fearful reality is at a disadvantage compared with even the most modest creature in that it has only " entered into " the world, as we are told in Rom. 5[12]. It does not belong to the creation of God. It can be present and active within it only as an alien. It has no appointed place, no place which belongs to it. If it has its place, it is that of an usurpation against the creative will of God, the place of an interloper. It is there where it has no business at all to be as that which God has not willed. It is there where it has nothing either to seek or to tell. And only there can it be sought out and found. And even there, in its nothingness, it does not exist in any way on the basis of its own independent right, or even in its dreadful reality by its own independent power. How could it ever have any such right or power ? It has its right, but it is the stolen right of wrong. It has its power, but it is the stealthy power of impotence. It exists and is only in opposition to the will of God and therefore in opposition to the being and destiny of His creature. It can only say No where God says Yes, and where in its own very different fashion the creature

of God can also say Yes. When and where has the word and work of
sin ever been a solemn Yes ? It can only negate, deny, destroy, break
down, dissolve. Even where God uses it in His service—and there is
no doubt that it is under His lordship and must serve Him, as the
Bible makes perfectly plain—it can serve only to fulfil His judgment,
which is to shame and oppose and punish itself, or contrary to its own
nature to accomplish some positive good in unwilling subservience to
His higher control. It is neither a creature nor itself a creator. It is
not only incapable of creation, but, being without root or soil in the
creaturely world into which it has pushed its alien being, it is quite
unproductive. In all its forms it exists and is only as that which
negates and therefore as that which is itself negated, on the left hand
of God, where God in saying Yes has already said No, where in electing
He has rejected, where in willing He has not willed.

But the divine Yes which sin negates and by which it is negated is
the Yes of God's covenant with man which is the mystery of creation—
the covenant of grace concluded in Jesus Christ from all eternity and
fulfilled and revealed in time. What God has determined and done as
the Lord of this covenant is His will. The sin of man, being his doing
and accomplishing of what God does not will, negates and withstands
and rejects it. Sin is therefore not merely an evil, but a breach of
the covenant which as such contradicts God and stands under His
contradiction. Sin is man's denial of himself in face of the grace of
His Creator. It is not directed against a so-called law of nature. There
is no law of nature which is both recognisable as such and yet also
has divine character and authority. There is no law and commandment of God inherent in the creatureliness of man as such, or written
and revealed in the stars as a law of the cosmos, so that the transgression of it makes man a sinner. It is characteristic of the sin of
man—and one of its results—that man should think he can know such
a law of nature and direct and measure himself and others in accordance with it. But in his creatureliness, in his nature—which is the
sum of his possibilities and destiny and nothing more—man is called
to hold to the grace of His Creator, to be thankful for it, to bow to
it and adapt himself to it, to honour it as the truth. And the essence
of sin is that he does not do this. He denies and despises and hates
grace and breaks its commandment, the law of the covenant. It is
in this opposition that sin takes place, that it has its place and reality :
as man's turning aside from God, and therefore as the perversion of
his own nature ; as the abuse and disturbance and destruction of the
possibilities of his creaturely being and the radical compromising of
his destiny.

This being the case, sin cannot be recognised and understood and
defined and judged as sin in accordance with any general idea of man,
or any law which is different from the grace of God and its commandment, the law of the covenant. If it takes place as a breach of the

covenant, and not in any other way, it can be known only in the light of the covenant. But since man has broken the covenant, that can mean only in the light of the covenant fulfilled and restored in Jesus Christ and therefore in the light of the atonement made in Him. The Old Testament dispensation with its Law consists in the proclamation of it. But what in the Old Testament Law was meant to be the Law of the covenant of grace moving to its fulfilment has now been revealed by the actual fulfilment of the covenant, by the accomplishment in Jesus Christ of that which was proclaimed in the covenant of God with Israel. God wills what He has done in Jesus Christ. And in so doing He has brought in the Law given to man, the Law against which man as a covenant-breaker has sinned from the very first, the Law in whose transgression all human sin has consisted and does consist and will consist. In the light of Jesus Christ the darkness is revealed as such. It is made plain that man is a sinner. It is shown in what his sin consists. It is that being and acting and thinking and speaking and bearing of man which in Jesus Christ God has met, which in Him He has opposed and overcome and judged, which in Him He has passed over, in spite of which He has converted man to Himself in Him. God is the Lord of the covenant of grace and none else. As such He is revealed in the fulfilment of it and therefore in Jesus Christ, and not otherwise. What He has done in Him is His will with man and therefore that and nothing else is His commandment. But if this is the case, sin is simply that in which man contradicts this will of God, and because of which he for his part is decisively contradicted and opposed by this will of God. The knowledge of sin can relate only to what we are told concerning our being and activity by Jesus Christ as the Mediator and Guarantor of the atonement, to what we have to say after Him, if that knowledge is to be serious. And the confession of sin (" Against thee only have I sinned," Ps. 51[6]) can be accomplished only in the turning to Him and therefore in the knowledge of the conversion of man to God which has taken place in Him. Only in this way is it an actual confessing of real sin as opposed to outbreaks of remorse or depression or bemoaning or despair.

But this means that there can be no place in dogmatics for an autonomous section *De peccato* constructed in a vacuum between the doctrine of creation and that of reconciliation. Who can summon us to keep a law of God which is supposed to be known to man by nature ? Who can try to measure the sin of man by such a law ? To do that—even in the form of a " doctrine of sin "—is surely to do precisely what we are forbidden to do by the real Law of God revealed by God Himself. To do that is surely to pass by the grace of God, to evolve our own thoughts in relation to the will of God instead of those which He Himself has given us in the commandment held out before us in His grace. And is not this necessarily to sin again— theologically ! Or, again, who can summon us in this matter of sin to follow the abstractly considered Law of the covenant of the Old Testament dispensation which is only moving to its fulfilment ?—as though we had not yet heard or taken to heart the warnings of Paul against the *nomos* abstractly understood in this way ; as though there were even one unconverted Jew who had come to a knowledge of his real sin by following this law ; as though it were a good thing to advise Christians first to become such unconverted Jews and to follow this law, in order to push them forward from that point to what will certainly never be a knowledge of their real sin.

If we are not to be guilty of these two errors, we have no option but to consider and answer the question of sin in the light of the Gospel and therefore within the doctrine of reconciliation, to take it up into that doctrine instead of giving it precedence over it as though it were an autonomous question.   In this context we shall find the natural place for it immediately after the Christology.   It is in the knowledge of Jesus Christ as the revelation of the grace of God that we shall necessarily perceive step by step both the fact that man is a transgressor, and the nature of the transgression in which he contradicts the grace of God and for the sake of which he is decisively contradicted by that grace.   Step by step, for if the content of the doctrine of sin— man's active opposition to the God who actively encounters him—is really to be brought out, the complex of the doctrine, like that of the Christology, demands a definite structure in which we will be safest to follow that of the Christology.   Necessarily, therefore, it will appear not simply at one point, but at three points corresponding to the three christological bases of the three main sections of the doctrine of reconciliation, and at every point in a corresponding form.

Sin is obviously (1) the negation, the opposite of what God does for us in Jesus Christ in condescending to us, in humbling Himself, in becoming a servant to take to Himself and away from us our guilt and sickness.   This is the grace of God in its first form : God gives Himself to us, He makes Himself responsible for our cause, He takes it into His own hand.   And the commandment is clear—it is necessarily a matter of our basing our being and activity on the fact that God is ours, that we are the recipients of this gift which is so inconceivably great.   Sin in its first form is pride.   When God condescends to man, when He makes Himself one with Him in order to be truly his God, man cannot fall way from the work of this mercy of God to him.   But what Adam did, what Israel did at all stages in its history, what the world does so long as it does not see itself as the world reconciled in Jesus Christ, what even the Christian does when he forgets that he is a Christian, is the very thing which is forbidden by this first form of grace, the very thing which is made impossible, which is excluded, which is negated because it is itself a negation.   It is the fall in the form of presumption, acting as though God had not humbled Himself to man, as though He had not encountered man as the unfathomably merciful One, as though He had not taken to Himself the cause of man. Sin is man's act of defiance. In this first part of the doctrine of reconciliation the doctrine of sin will have to be described and portrayed in the closest connexion with the consideration of Jesus Christ as the Lord who became an obedient servant for us (and therefor with His high-priestly office). It will be characterised, therefore, as the act of pride.

But further, sin is (2) the negation, the opposite of what God did in Jesus Christ, the servant who became Lord, to exalt man—not to deity but to His own right hand in a fellowship of life with Himself. This is the grace of God in its second form : He wills and seeks us as we are, in our creatureliness, as men, that we may be raised to the status of children. That is why He humbled Himself. That is the meaning and force of His mercy. And again the commandment is clear—it is a matter of our being and activity as men in accordance with the exaltation which has come to us. As against that, sin in its second form is sloth. God Himself has not merely shown man the way, but made it for him. God Himself has already exalted him. Therefore man must not wilfully fall. He must not set against the grace of God which is addressed to him, and leads him, and orders his going, his own dark ways of frivolity or melancholy or despair which he seeks and chooses and follows. Adam at the very first fell into this sin too. Israel did it again and again. The world lives and thinks and speaks and seeks and finds on this downward way. Even forgetful Christians are on this way. This is man's disorder—corresponding to the order established by the grace of God. The doctrine of sin will have to treat of this sloth of man in the second part of the doctrine of reconciliation, and therefore in connexion with the consideration of Jesus Christ as the servant who became Lord (the doctrine of His kingly office).

Finally, sin is (3) the negation, the opposite of the fact that God in Jesus Christ has made Himself the Guarantor of the reality of that which has been done by Him as servant and Lord in that movement from above downwards and below upwards, of the fact that in Jesus Christ God has made Himself the witness of the truth of the atonement. This is the grace of God in its third form : God does not act above our heads, He does not ignore us, but He addresses us and calls us. He tells us what He does and He tells us as He does it. His action for us and with us is itself and as such His Word to us. Again the commandment of His grace is clear—it is a matter of hearing and obeying the truth which is told us, a matter of active joy in it. We have to see that that which is told us is true for us : that Jesus Christ is the Lord who became a servant for us, and the servant who became Lord for us, our Lord. As against this, sin in its third form is falsehood. When God Himself is the pledge that He has done all this, man cannot pretend that he knows better. When the truth speaks for

itself, man's knowing better is only falsehood, a lie. And, again, this
is the sin of Adam, and repeated in many forms it is the sin of Israel,
and of the world and of all forgetful Christians. We are all at times,
incorrigibly, those who know better—and, therefore, because grace is
the truth revealed and known to us, we are all incorrigible liars. The
consequences follow. Falsehood is self-destruction. Because man and
the world live under the dominion of sin, lying to God and deceiving
themselves, they live in self-destruction. At this point it is plain that
sin cannot say Yes but only No, that it cannot build up but only pull
down, that it can create only suffering and death. Sinful man is as
such man without hope. This conflict of sin against the promise and hope
given to man in the Word of God will have to be presented in the third
part of the doctrine of reconciliation in connexion with the consideration of Jesus Christ as the Guarantor, the doctrine of His prophetic office.

And now we must try to go further. Sin is a reality—as the antithesis to God it is so almost as God Himself is, *sui generis*. But it is
not an autonomous reality. As the No which opposes the divine Yes,
it is only a reality related to and contradicting that Yes. Therefore it
can be known—and all the horror of it can be known—only in the
light of that Yes. In all its reality and horror it can never be a first
word, nor can it ever be a final word. The atonement made in Jesus
Christ teaches us (as nothing else can) to know it and to take it seriously, but we also have to perceive and state that the gracious will
and act of God in Jesus Christ are superior to it and overcome it.
We ourselves do not look down on it or master it or conquer it or set
it aside. We ourselves are not superior to it. But Jesus Christ, against
whom sin properly and finally rears itself, is superior to it. In all the
forms of the grace of God revealed and active in Him He is superior
to sin in all its forms. He looks back on it. He looks down on it.
And when we look at Him, for good or evil we, too, can and must look
back on it and down on it. He has already effectively contradicted
its contradicting. He has already banished the alien and defeated
the usurper. In Him, in opposition to this enemy, the kingdom of
God has already been victoriously inaugurated, and is present and
revealed in power. We should be questioning everything that He is
and has done, we should be making ourselves guilty of sin in its last
mentioned form of falsehood (and therefore in its other forms as ingratitude and disorder), if we were to try to have it otherwise, if we
were to try to think and speak less confidently in relation to Him,
with reservations and limitations, and probably at bottom with doubts
and denials. The reality of sin cannot be known or described except
in relation to the One who has vanquished it. In His light it is darkness, but a darkness which yields. That He is the victor is therefore
a Christian axiom which is not only not shaken but actually confirmed
by sin. It is He who has the final word.

The fact that He does have the final word, and the extent to which

He does, is something which we will have to show in the further development of the doctrine of reconciliation. It will be a matter of perceiving that the atonement made in Him is God's triumphant and effective decision in relation to sin as the great episode. And it will be a matter of understanding this decision concretely and in its context, which is obviously in the light of the Christology and the three christological bases. Therefore we shall have to adduce three propositions, all of which have the same content—that the sinful No of man has been matched and opposed and destroyed by the divine Yes spoken by Jesus Christ even in the sphere of man and the world which we have just considered in the doctrine of sin. Or positively, we shall have to show what is the divine Yes spoken by God in answer to the human No, in what form it is maintained and fulfilled in the sphere of sinful man and the sinful world, how it is vindicated as the first and final word.

To explain at this point the one and threefold being and work of Jesus Christ in its relevance for the world we shall have to speak first of the three forms of the grace of God which comes to man in Him. We are here dealing with the objective material presented in older dogmatics under the title *De applicatione salutis* (soteriology). On the basis of our presuppositions this complex will work out as follows.

1. In relation to the doctrine of God's self-humiliation for us men accomplished in Jesus Christ, and in direct answer to the doctrine of sin as the human act of pride, the first part of the doctrine of reconciliation will necessarily continue with the doctrine of the divine verdict in Jesus Christ by which man is justified. This justifying sentence of God is His decision in which man's being as the subject of that act is repudiated, his responsibility for that act, his guilt, is pardoned, cancelled and removed, and there is ascribed to him instead a being as the subject of pure acts of thankfulness for this liberation. At this point we have to make it plain that the Gospel is an effective because a well-founded word of consolation resting on the righteousness of God. This is the positive content of the Reformation insight into salvation in the form particularly affected by Luther. And we must weigh it in relation to the Roman (Tridentine) doctrine and also mark it off and confirm it against Protestant misunderstandings and misrepresentations. But all this must be done with the reservation that in spite of the great importance of this insight we are dealing here with only one form of the grace of Jesus Christ. Only Jesus Christ Himself can be the principle of the doctrine of reconciliation, not justification or any other of the true but secondary forms of His grace.

2. In relation to the doctrine of the exaltation of man by God in Jesus Christ, and in direct answer to the doctrine of sin as the sloth of man, the second part of the doctrine of reconciliation will necessarily emphasise the direction given in Jesus Christ in which the sanctification of man is accomplished. This sanctifying direction of man is His decision by which sinful man is addressed and treated as a new

subject, so that instead of causing himself to fall he can stand and proceed along the way which God has appointed for him as the way of true freedom, in this way rendering obedience. At this point we have to make it plain that the Gospel is a saving committal and an uplifting obligation, the Reformation insight into salvation as particularly understood and represented by Calvin. We must do this primarily in its positive content, but also in antithesis especially to the Roman conception of the Christian life and to every form of secular humanism. In some respects we will have to set it even against Lutheranism, marking it off from all kinds of false developments both internal and external, old and new. But, of course, in spite of the rightness and importance of the matter, we shall never do so as though sanctification could or should replace Jesus Christ as the principle, the One and All, of the doctrine of reconciliation.

3. In relation to the doctrine of the unity of God and man introduced in Jesus Christ, and in direct answer to the doctrine of sin as the falsehood of man, the third part of the doctrine of reconciliation will have to set out the promise of God proclaimed in and with His verdict and direction, in which the calling of man takes place. This promise of God, which as the truth overcomes the lie, is God's decision in which He has given to man, quite contrary to the destruction of his existence, an eternal future in fellowship with Himself, that is, in His service, and therefore a teleological direction of his life in time, so that even this life in time acquires a perspective and therefore (small, relative and provisional) ends. In this respect we have to speak of the Gospel as a clarifying directive. And it is here that historically we have to look beyond the circle of vision of the 16th century Reformation, or, rather, to bring to light certain insights into Christian salvation which were then dismissed too summarily or suppressed altogether : life in the present, in expectation of the kingdom of God, in the rest and unrest which this causes, in the discipleship of Jesus Christ, in its eschatological orientation, in its dynamic in this-worldly criticism and construction. In short, this is the place where on the one hand we must find a place for what, since the Reformation, we have surely added to our understanding of the New Testament in respect of its teleological elements, and where, on the other, we may seek agreement between what to-day is felt to be and is, in fact, an antithesis between continental Protestantism and Anglo-Saxon, which was more influenced by the humanistic and enthusiastic movements of the Reformation period. In the light of the particular christological starting-point— and here the doctrine of the prophetic office of Christ will be normative —it will now be a question of bringing together the first two soteriological aspects. All the more carefully, then, we must avoid all appearance of claiming that from this standpoint of calling we are dealing with more than a part of what is the One and All in this matter. It is clear that this, too, can only be one form of the grace of Jesus Christ.

In all three developments we must ensure that Jesus Christ is constantly known and revealed as the One and All that is expounded. He is the One who justifies, sanctifies and calls. He is the High-Priest, King and Prophet. In the measure that He is shown to be the subject of the whole occurrence, the *autor* and *applicator salutis*, the doctrine of His grace, of the mercy of God directed in Him to man, will not in any way obscure by the necessary systematising and sub-dividing of its presentation the unity in which that grace is His grace.

In the whole event of atonement, justification, sanctification and calling, as grounded in the divine verdict, direction and promise, have as it were a central function. In them, in the understanding of grace under these concepts, it is still a matter of expounding the being and work of Jesus Christ as the Reconciler of the sinful world and therefore of sinful man with God. It is still a matter, then, of what took place in Him for the conversion of the world to God. That is how it must be to the very end. When we say justification, sanctification and calling, on the one side we are already expounding the relevance of what was done in Jesus Christ, but, on the other, we are expounding only the objective relevance of it and not its subjective apprehension and acceptance in the world and by us men. We might say, we are dealing with the ascription but not the appropriation of the grace of Jesus Christ, or with what has taken place in Him for the world as such but not for the Christian in particular. In the Christian there is an appropriation of the grace of God ascribed to all men in Jesus Christ, a subjective apprehension of what has been done for the whole world in the happening of atonement. It is absolutely and exclusively in the being and work of Jesus Christ Himself and not in men that this specific form of grace has its basis and power, that it is true and actual that there are amongst other men those who are reconciled with God in Jesus Christ, who recognise and affirm their being as such, who can confess from the heart, with word and deed, that God makes Himself known to the world in the work of atonement, that He faithfully maintains and fulfils His covenant with man in opposition to the fall and sin of man, that He activates and reveals Himself in Jesus Christ as the God of man, that in so doing He has claimed man in all His omnipotence as His man. The doctrine of justification, sanctification and calling must obviously be followed by a discussion of this particular form of grace.

In this connexion the specific point that we have to make is that the being and work of Jesus Christ—for even here we cannot abandon the christological basis—must now be understood as the being and work of His Holy Spirit, or His own spiritual being and work. The appropriation of the grace of Jesus Christ ascribed to us, the subjective apprehension of the reconciliation of the world with God made in Him, the existence of Christians, presupposes and includes within itself the presence, the gift and the reception, the work and accomplishment of

His Holy Spirit. The Holy Spirit is the one eternal God in His particular power and will so to be present to the creature in His being and activity, so to give Himself to it, that it can recognise and embrace and experience Himself and His work and therefore the actuality and truth of its own situation, that its eyes and ears and senses and reason and heart are open to Him and willing and ready for Him. The particular existence of the Son of God as man, and again the particular existence of this man as the Son of God, the existence of Jesus Christ as the Lord who becomes a servant and the servant who becomes Lord, His existence as the Guarantor of truth is itself ultimately grounded in the being and work of the Holy Spirit. He is *conceptus de Spiritu sancto.* And this is the distinctive mark of the existence of the men who perceive and accept and receive Him as the Reconciler of the world and therefore as their Reconciler, who—vicariously for the whole world reconciled by Him—discover that they are His because He is theirs, who on the basis of this discovery and therefore in this special sense exist " in Him," who can be with Him and for Him as He is with them and for them (with and for the whole world). It is the Holy Spirit, the being and work of the one eternal God in this special form, that is still lacking in the world at large. That God did not owe His Son, and in that Son Himself, to the world, is revealed by the fact that He gives His Spirit to whom He will. The hand of God the Reconciler is over all men. Jesus Christ was born and died and rose again for all. The work of atonement, the conversion of man to God, was done for all. The Word of God is spoken to all. God's verdict and direction and promise have been pronounced ov er all. To that extent, objectively, all are justified, sanctified and cal led. But the hand of God has not touched all in such a way that they can see and hear, perceive and accept and receive all that God is for all and therefore for them, how therefore they can exist and think and live. To those who have not been touched in this way by the hand of God the axiom that Jesus Christ is the Victor is as such unknown. It is a Christian and not a general axiom ; valid generally, but not generally observed and acknowledged. Similarly, they do not know their sin or even what sin is, since it can be known only in the light of that axiom. And naturally they do not know their justification, sanctification and calling as they have already taken place in Jesus Christ. But the hand of God has touched and seized Christians in this way— which means the presence and activity of the Holy Spirit. In this special sense Christians and only Christians are converted to Him. This is without any merit or co-operation on their part, just as the reconciliation of the whole world in Jesus Christ is without its merit or co-operation. But they are really converted to God in this special sense. The free grace of the sovereign God has in relation to them the special form that they themselves can reach after it. They can understand it as the grace directed to the world and therefore to them.

They can live in the light and power of it—under its judgment, but all in all, under the Word, and readily and willingly under the Word, under the divine sentence and direction and promise. Therefore the being and work of Jesus Christ, the One and All of His achievement and the relevance of it has also this—shall we call it for the sake of clarity subjective?—dimension, in which the same One and All is now in the eyes and ears and hearts, in the existence of these men, Christians, who are specially taken and determined by His Holy Spirit. They have over the rest of the world the one inestimable advantage that God the Reconciler and the event of reconciliation can be to them a matter of recognition and confession, until the day when He and it will be the subject of His revelation to all eyes and ears and hearts, and therefore of the recognition and confession of all men. The being and work of Jesus Christ in the form of the being and work of His Holy Spirit is therefore the original and prefigurative existence of Christianity and Christians.

It is of this that we shall have to speak in the two concluding sections of all the three parts of the doctrine of reconciliation. And two things will have to be borne in mind. It is a matter of Christendom and of Christians, of the community (" Church ") of Jesus Christ and of its members (individual Christians in their personal relationship to Jesus Christ). There cannot be the one without the other. The Holy Spirit is not a private spirit, but the power by which the Son of God (*Heid. Cat. Qu.* 54) " has from the beginning of the world to the end assembled out of the whole race of man, and preserves and maintains, an elect congregation." But He assembles and preserves and maintains it, not as a pile of grains of sand or as an aggregate of cells, but as a community of those of whom each one can individually recognise and confess by His power " that I am a living member of the same, and will be so for ever." Within this particular group of problems it is clearly a matter of a correspondence, a reflection and a repetition of the relationship between the objective ascription and the subjective appropriation of salvation. Salvation is ascribed to the individual in the existence of the community, and it is appropriated by the community in the existence of the individuals of which it is composed.

In the light of this correspondence it is more fitting to take the question of Christendom before that of the individual Christian.

Traditional dogmatics went to work differently. Logically, and again most instructively from the didactic standpoint, it proceeded at once from the objective demonstration of divine grace to its subjective apprehension in the life of man, i.e., the individual Christian. Or it treated both in the one context, speaking of personal Christian faith, for example, in the same breath as justification, and personal Christian obedience in the same breath as sanctification. We, too, must speak of them in the same breath, so that it is clear that the work of the Holy Spirit is in fact only a particular form of the being and work of Jesus Christ Himself. But we should be making it private in a way which is quite illegitimate if we were to relate it directly to the personal appropriation of salvation by the individual Christian. It was an intolerable truncation of the Christian message when the older Protestantism steered the whole doctrine of the atonement—and with it, ultimately, the whole of theology—into the *cul de sac* of the question of the individual experience of grace, which is always an anxious one when taken in isolation, the question of individual conversion by it and to it, and of its presuppositions and consequences. The almost inevitable result was that the great concepts of justification and sanctification came more and more to be understood and filled out psychologically and biographically, and the doctrine of the Church seemed to be of value only as a description of the means of salvation and grace indispensable to this individual and personal process of salvation. We will only ask in passing whether and to what extent Luther's well-known question in the cloister—which was and will always be useful at its own time and place—contributed if only by way of temptation to this truncation, or whether it is simply an aberration first of orthodoxy and then of the Pietism which began in it and followed it. What is more to the point is to remember (and this, too, is something we can only mention) that we will do well not to allow ourselves to be crowded again into the same *cul de sac* on the detour via Kierkegaard.

Certainly the question of the subjective apprehension of atonement by the individual man is absolutely indispensable. And it belongs properly to the concluding section of the doctrine of reconciliation—yet not in the first place, but in the second, and therefore at the close of this concluding section.

Our theme is the reconciliation of the world with God in Jesus Christ, and only in this greater context the reconciliation of the individual man. This is what was completely overlooked in that truncation. And if it is to be brought to light again, the prior place which the Christian individual has for so long— we might almost say unashamedly—claimed for himself in the dogmatics of the Christian community must be vacated again. We must not cease to stress the individual. We must not throw doubt on the importance of his problem. But !

Only in the proper place. The " pillar and ground of truth " (1 Tim. 3^15), the salt of the earth, the light of the world, the city set on a hill, is the community of God and not the individual Christian as such, although the latter has within it his assured place, his indispensable function, and his unshakable personal promise. It is not he but the *ecclesia una sancta catholica et apostolica* that stands (in close connexion with the Holy Spirit) in the third article of the Creed. It is the Church which with its perception and experience of the grace of God stands vicariously for the rest of the world which has not yet partaken of the witness of the Holy Spirit. It is the Church which in this particularity is ordained to the ministry of reconciliation and the witness of the grace of God in relation to the rest of the world. It is in its existence, therefore—and only in the sphere of its existence in that of individual Christians—that the salvation ascribed to the world is appropriated by man. It is primarily in it that there is fulfilled in the sphere of sinful man and his world, as the work of the Holy Spirit of Jesus Christ, the subjective apprehension of the atonement objectively made in Him. It is of the Church, then, that in the light of the three christological origins we shall have to speak first in all three parts of the doctrine of reconciliation.

1. The Holy Spirit as the Spirit of Jesus Christ is the awakening power of the Word spoken by the Lord who became a servant and therefore of the divine sentence which judges and justifies sinful man. The work of the Holy Spirit as this awakening power is the historical reality of the community. When that verdict—that verdict of God which, we recall, repudiates and accepts, kills and makes alive—is heard by men, there is in their inner fellowship and there arises in their outward assembly a new humanity within the old. A new history begins within world-history. A new form of fellowship is quietly founded amongst other sociological forms : the apostolate, the disciples, the community, the Church. Its members are those who can believe and understand that sentence, and therefore regard as accomplished the justification of man in Jesus Christ. It is not the faith and understanding of its members which constitute the community, but the Word and verdict of God believed and understood, Jesus Christ Himself in whose death on the cross that verdict is pronounced. It is not that they know God, but that they are known of God. But these men can know and believe and understand God in that verdict. In the midst of others they are one and conjoined by the fact that they must accept His saying. It is only by that, but actually, visibly and perceptibly by that—and irrevocably—that they are constituted the community. At this point we shall have to speak of the origin and being of the Church in its humanity—of that being which since it is always conditioned by the Holy Spirit as the awakening power of that divine verdict must again and again be an insignificant origin : a continual awaiting of the Holy Spirit as pictured in its constant gatherings, its ever renewed proclamation of the Word, its repeated prayer, its celebration of baptism ; but an awaiting in the certainty of receiving, and therefore of its own life in His presence. The community exists in this fruitful expectation which can never cease and never be unrealised. In its humanity it is one historically feeble organism with others, but it is the redeemed community justified by the divine sentence and honoured with the knowledge of the justification of the world.

2. The Holy Spirit of Jesus Christ is the life-giving power of the Word spoken by the servant who became Lord, and therefore of the divine direction which sanctifies sinful man. The work of the Holy Spirit as this life-giving power is the inner upbuilding of the community. When that direction is heard by men, these men are united in a common action, in a common action orientated by a commonly imposed obedience, and, we can and must also say, by a commonly given freedom. The community grows in rendering this obedience, or in this freedom. In it it gains consistency, it acquires order and form, it becomes capable of action. Its members are men who not only regard that direction

as given and normative, but who love it for the sake of the One who
has given it, who accept it because they see in it the love in which
God loved the world and themselves in this special way. The direction of God willingly followed in the power of the Holy Spirit is the
life-principle of the Christian Church. Again, it is not by the obedience,
the freedom, or even the love of these men that the Church is built up
and lives. It lives wholly in the power of its Lord and His Spirit.
In His power : the power of its Lord exalted as man to the right hand
of God, who summons and draws it onwards and upwards as the
community of His brethren, who transforms it into His image (2 Cor.
3^{18}), by whom it is given to it to seek and to find that which is above,
in whom it has already here and now a part in His resurrection and
therefore in the future life of eternity. Because and to the extent
that He is mighty in the community by His Spirit, that which it does
can and must be done with joy ; its worship, its order, the fellowship
of Christians, its mutual service, the celebration of the Lord's Supper,
even its teaching and theology can and must take on the character
of a festival ; and in it all God can and must be thanked and worshipped.
What we have to show is the fact and way in which the Church has
never to look after itself, to build up itself, to rule and maintain and
defend itself, but simply to live according to the direction of its Lord
and His Spirit and in that way to be vigorous and active and truly
alive.

3. The Holy Spirit as the Spirit of Jesus Christ is the enlightening
power of Him who as very God and very man is the Guarantor of the
truth of the atonement made in Him—and therefore the summoning
power of the promise given in Him to sinful man. When the promise
is heard by men, inwardly and outwardly these men are together
ordained to be the community sent out as a witness in the world and
to the world. The historical reality and inward upbuilding of this
community are not ends in themselves. It is now actually the case
that in its particular existence it stands vicariously for the whole
world. The Holy Spirit is the enlightening, and as the enlightening
the summoning power of the divine promise, which points the community beyond itself, which calls it to transcend itself and in that
way to be in truth the community of God—in truth, i.e., as it bears
witness to the truth known within it, as it knows itself to be charged
with this witness and sent out to establish it. Its members are men
who can hope on the basis of the promise. But if they hope seriously,
they hope in God, and in God for the world—for themselves, too, but
for themselves as those who belong to the world which God has reconciled with Himself in Jesus Christ. They hope to see this the case,
i.e., to see the world—and themselves with it—fulfilling its being in
the service of God. But, again, it is not the sincerity or drive of this
Christian hope which constitutes the light of the community sent out
to witness. Only the Holy Spirit of Jesus Christ active within it is

this light. But He is the light of the Christian community which shines here in the darkness on earth and in time. And since He is this light, and the community lives by God's promise, necessarily the community itself is bright in the world : a community which proclaims the coming kingdom of God as the substance of the whole future of man ; but for that reason a missionary community ; a community which is responsible and looks and points forward in face of every development in state or society ; an element of prophecy in relation to the world, of greater and smaller rest and unrest, of soberness and daring confidence in relation to the ultimate, and also and for that reason to penultimate horizons. It is of the community in this ministry of witness that we must speak in the third ecclesiological section of the doctrine of reconciliation.

And then, to conclude, we have to speak in all three parts of the life of individual Christians as such, of their being in Jesus Christ, of their personal knowledge and experience of the atonement, i.e., of the work and witness of the Holy Spirit, by whom in the community, by the service and for the service of the community, but as individuals, they are (1) awakened to faith, (2) quickened in love and (3) enlightened in hope.

It is not necessary to develop this here, since it has already been anticipated under the second heading of this section. We will simply make a general observation on this final theme. In the theology of Schleiermacher and his more or less loyal and consistent followers, this last theme was the first, and it also became the last because on their presupposition there could not be any other. Theology in general and with it the doctrine of the atonement could only be the self-interpretation of the pious Christian self-consciousness as such, of the *homo religiosus incurvatus in se*. In this way Schleiermacher's genius was to bring to its logical conclusion the truncating tendency in the older Protestantism to which we have already alluded. From the very first the present sketch of the doctrine of reconciliation has stood implicitly in the most decided opposition to this conception. We do not intend to avoid the problem of the *homo religiosus* or *christianus*. In the final development of the doctrine of reconciliation we shall have to treat very seriously of this special question of the *homo christianus*, of the Christian and what makes him a Christian, of his understanding of himself. It is, in fact, " self-understood " that he must occupy a special place in dogmatics, and undoubtedly in the analysis of the concepts faith, love and hope we have to do with a *conditio sine qua non* of the whole. Apart from the faith and love and hope of the individual Christian and his understanding of himself as such we cannot see the Christian community, nor can we see the justifying verdict, the sanctifying direction and the summoning promise of God. But faith and love and hope are relative concepts. The being of the Christian indicated by them is a being in relation. Faith lives by its

object, love by its basis, hope by its surety.   Jesus Christ by the Holy
Spirit is this object and basis and surety.   And faith and love and
hope in this relation to Jesus Christ are all primarily His work, and
His work first in the community of God, and only then His work in
individual Christians.   We must not confuse the *conditio sine qua non*
of the knowledge of the atonement with its *ratio essendi*.   The doctrine
of reconciliation must end where it began.   We shall speak correctly
of the faith and love and hope of the individual Christian only when it
remains clear and constantly becomes clear that, although we are dealing
with our existence, we are dealing with our existence in Jesus Christ
as our true existence, that we are therefore dealing with Him and not
with us, and with us only in so far as absolutely and exclusively with
Him.

CHAPTER XIV

JESUS CHRIST, THE LORD AS SERVANT

CHAPTER XIV

JESUS CHRIST, THE LORD AS SERVANT

§ 59

THE OBEDIENCE OF THE SON OF GOD

That Jesus Christ is very God is shown in His way into the far country in which He the Lord became a servant. For in the majesty of the true God it happened that the eternal Son of the eternal Father became obedient by offering and humbling Himself to be the brother of man, to take His place with the transgressor, to judge him by judging Himself and dying in his place. But God the Father raised Him from the dead, and in so doing recognised and gave effect to His death and passion as a satisfaction made for us, as our conversion to God, and therefore as our redemption from death to life.

1. THE WAY OF THE SON OF GOD INTO THE FAR COUNTRY

The atonement is history. To know it, we must know it as such. To think of it, we must think of it as such. To speak of it, we must tell it as history. To try to grasp it as supra-historical or non-historical truth is not to grasp it at all. It is indeed truth, but truth actualised in a history and revealed in this history as such—revealed, therefore, as history.

But the atonement is the very special history of God with man, the very special history of man with God. As such it has a particular character and demands particular attention. As such it underlies and includes, not only in principle and virtually but also actually, the most basic history of every man. It is the first and most inward presupposition of his existence, and it reveals itself as such. (First of all,) there took place and does take place the history of God with man and man with God, and then and for that reason and definitely on that basis man exists, and he can be called to knowledge and his own fully responsible decision and in that way have an actual part in that happening. The atonement takes precedence of all other history. It proves itself in fully responsible attitudes. It cannot be revealed and grasped and known without this proof. But when it is revealed and grasped and known, it is so in its priority, its precedence, its superiority to all other histories, to the existence of all the men who take part in it. In this sense everyone who knows it as truth knows in it the truth of his own existence.

The atonement is, noetically, the history about Jesus Christ, and ontically, Jesus Christ's own history. To say atonement is to say Jesus Christ. To speak of it is to speak of His history. If we do not simply speak of it, but know it as we speak of it, if we take part in it as we know it, if we decide with full responsibility as a result of it, we decide in relation to Jesus Christ. For He is the history of God with man and the history of man with God. What takes place in this history—the accusation and conviction of man as a lost sinner, his restoration, the founding and maintaining and sending of the community of God in the world, the new obedience of man—is all decided and ordained by Him as the One who primarily acts and speaks in it. It is His work which is done. He Himself accomplishes and guarantees it, for in Him it comes to pass that God is the reconciling God and man is reconciled man. He is Himself this God and this man, and therefore the presupposition, the author, in whom all human existence has its first and basic truth in relation to that of God. It is in His self-offering to death that God has again found man and man God. It is in His resurrection from the dead that this twofold rediscovery is applied and proclaimed to us. It is in His Holy Spirit that it is present and an event for us. In all its different aspects the doctrine of reconciliation must always begin by looking at Him, not in order to leave Him behind in its later developments, but to fix the point from which there can and must be these later developments.

The (first aspect) under which we shall try to consider the doctrine of reconciliation in this chapter is that of the condescension active and known in it, that condescension in which God interests Himself in man in Jesus Christ. We might put it in this way : the aspect of the grace of God in Jesus Christ in which it comes to man as the (sinful) creature of God freely, without any merit or deserving, and therefore from outside, from above—which is to say, from God's standpoint, the aspect of His grace in which He does something unnecessary and extravagant, binding and limiting and compromising and offering Himself in relation to man by having dealings with him and making Himself his God. In the fact that God is gracious to man, all the limitations of man are God's limitations, all his weaknesses, and more, all his perversities are His. In being gracious to man in Jesus Christ, God acknowledges man; He accepts responsibility for his being and nature. He remains Himself. He does not cease to be God. But He does not hold aloof. In being gracious to man in Jesus Christ, He also goes into the far country, into the evil society of this being which is not God and against God. He does not shrink from him. He does not pass him by as did the priest and the Levite the man who had fallen among thieves. He does not leave him to his own devices. He makes his situation His own. He does not forfeit anything by doing this. In being neighbour to man, in order to deal with him and act towards him as such, He does not need to fear for His Godhead. On the contrary. We will mention at once the thought which will be decisive and basic in this section, that God shows Himself to be the great and true God in the fact that He can and will let His grace bear this cost, that He is capable and willing and ready for this condescension, this act of extravagance, this far journey. What marks out God above all false gods is that they are not capable and ready for this. In their otherworldliness and supernaturalness and otherness, etc., the gods are a reflection of the human pride which will not unbend, which will not stoop to that which is beneath it. God is not proud. In His high majesty He is humble. It is in this high humility that He speaks and acts as the God who reconciles the world to Himself. It is under this aspect first that we must consider the history of the atonement.

That is why the title of this chapter is " Jesus Christ, the Lord as Servant." At every point we shall be dealing with the action and work of the Lord God. This is true in relation to the eternal decree, and the execution of the atonement once and for all. It is also true of the fruit of it brought forth by the Holy Spirit, and the existence of the Christian community and the human decision of faith. But because we are dealing with the true Lord God, because it is a matter of the atonement which was made and is made in His action and work, we have to do with Him in that form of a servant which as the true Lord He was capable and willing and ready to assume in order to exist in it, and in which He is the true Lord God and as such the true Reconciler of man with God.

That is why the title of our first section is " The Obedience of the Son of God." Our theme in it is Christology in the narrower sense of the word, a first aspect of the person of Jesus Christ acting for the world and us and of the work of Jesus Christ done for the world and us : how He was and is and will be very God in the fact that as the Son He willed to be obedient to the Father, and to become the servant of all and therefore man and therefore the One who fulfilled in His death the reconciling will of God ; and how in the power of His resurrection He is all this for us by the Holy Spirit. In relation neither to His person nor to His work can we under this aspect say everything that has to be said about Him, or everything that makes the history of the atonement this particular history. It is a matter of the whole Christ and the whole atonement from this one standpoint. And obviously here—in dealing with the person and work of the true Son of the true God—we have to do with the indispensable basis and substance of all that follows.

To come to the point. The New Testament tradition—in this respect most clearly documented in the so-called synoptic Gospels—is self-consistent in one great truth. There can be no doubt about the full and genuine and individual humanity of the man Jesus of Nazareth, but in that man there has entered in and there must be recognised and respected One who is qualitatively different from all other men. He is not simply a better man, a more gifted, a more wise or noble or pious, in short a greater man. But as against all other men and their differences we have in the person of this man One who is their Lord and Lawgiver and Judge. He has full power to condemn them or to pardon. He has full power to call them and bind them to Himself. He has full power, as against their cosmic limitation, to pronounce in His existence a final Word concerning them and all human history. He is the Saviour before whom there was none other, neither shall be after. This is the " act of God," the " eschatological event of salvation," to use our modern jargon. In attestation of this understanding of the man Jesus the New Testament tradition calls Him the Messiah of Israel, the *Kyrios*, the second Adam come down from heaven, and, in a final approximation to what is meant by all this, the Son or the Word of God. It lifts Him right out of the list of other men, and as against this list (including Moses and the prophets, not to mention all the rest) it places Him at the side of God.

The New Testament community does not merely think, but lives and acts in the knowledge and on the presupposition that in this man " dwells all the fulness of the Godhead bodily " (Col. 2⁹). In seeing Him, it sees the Father (Jn. 14⁹). In honouring Him, it honours the Father (Jn. 5²³). It calls on His name (1 Cor. 1², Rom. 10¹², Ac. 9¹⁴, ²¹, 22¹⁶), and in so doing, according to Jn. 20²⁸, it addresses Him : " My Lord and my God." Stephen prays to Him (Ac. 7⁵⁹), as does also Paul (2 Cor. 12⁸), and the whole community expects that requests made to God in His name will be heard (Jn. 14¹³ᶠ·).

The post-apostolic community was based on this knowledge of Jesus Christ and the corresponding confession.

In this respect we have to note what is said and expounded with great · theological naivete but for that reason all the more clearly in the first Christian sermon known to us, the so-called 2 Clement : " Brethren, we must think of Jesus Christ as of God (ὡς περὶ θεοῦ), as of the judge of the quick and the dead. For we ought not to think meanly of our redemption. If we think meanly of Him (περὶ αὐτοῦ), that means that we expect only mean things . . . that we do not know whence and by whom and to whom we are called." And although the accounts are uncertain and primitive, it is noteworthy that what the governor Pliny had heard from lapsed Christians and reported to the emperor Trajan about 113 was this : They had confessed that the sum (*summa*) of their error or fault was that they used to meet before sunrise *carmenque Christo quasi Deo dicere secum in vicem*, and to pledge themselves—not to break the law, but to refrain from theft, murder and adultery, and not to break faith or loyalty, etc. It may be that these songs were like those which have come down to us in Phil. 2⁵ᶠ·, Rev. 5⁹ᶠ· or 1 Tim. 3¹⁶. Pliny seems to have in mind this peculiar practice and theory in relation to Christ when he summed up his own judgment of the matter in the view that they were dealing with a *superstitio prava, immodica*. On his orders the lapsed had to show their true repentance by paying respect to images of the emperor and the gods and cursing Christ. In the same connexion we might mention the caricature found in the Palatine at Rome, although it belongs to a later date. It depicts an ass fastened to a cross, and the form of a man worshipping it, with the inscription : " Alexamenos (obviously a Christian who is meant to be ridiculed) honours God (σέβεται θεόν)." It is quite clear from the impressions and reactions of these outsiders in what category the primitive Christians placed Christ, quite apart from more exact doctrinal definitions.

The dogma of the 4th and 5th centuries tried to formulate this same insight in the face of several obscurities and ambiguities which still obtained in the first centuries and also in face of the conceptual denials which constantly arose. The primitive insight presupposed and confirmed in the dogma—not the dogma itself—was the decisive point at which the different spirits in the Church (or rather that which was the Church and not the Church) always divided. And to this day there is hardly a point of Christian knowledge and confession which is not positively or negatively, directly or indirectly, related to this one point, to this primitive Christian insight.

It has been described as a " religious valuation " (F. Loofs) or estimation or judgment added later to the man Jesus by the disciples or the early Palestinian or especially the Hellenistic Church. This valuation rests, we are told, on the impression which the Christians had of the person and word and work of Jesus, and it was filled out intellectually in the form offered by the ideology of the later Jewish and Hellenistic world in which they lived. It is obviously true that in Jesus the disciples and the first communities were confronted with a riddle which they had to solve, a question which they had to answer on the basis of what they had seen and heard, a phenomenon which they had to estimate at its meaning and judge accordingly. It is also true that they gave their judgment in the language of the intellectual world to which they belonged. It is from them that there derive the titles of value " attached " to the man Jesus in the New Testament. But the following considerations have to be kept clearly in mind.

There is no discernible stratum of the New Testament in which—always presupposing His genuine humanity—Jesus is in practice seen in any other way or—whatever terms may be used—judged in any other way than as the One who is qualitatively different and stands in an indissoluble antithesis to His disciples and all other men, indeed to the whole cosmos. There is no discernible stratum which does not in some way witness that it was felt that there should be given to this man, not merely a human confidence, but that trust, that respect, that obedience, that faith which can properly be offered only to God. Allowing for every difference in viewpoint and concept, the heavenly Father, His kingdom which has come on earth, and the person of Jesus of Nazareth are not quantities which can be placed side by side, or which cut across each other, or which can be opposed to each other, but they are practically and in effect identical. This would still be true even if it could be proved and not merely suspected that Jesus

Himself did not expressly speak of His majesty, His Messiahship, His
divine Sonship. In the context of what we know of the disciples and
the community in the New Testament there is no ground for even
suspecting the existence of disciples or a community which could be
practically related to Him except on the presupposition of His majesty.

So, then, we can speak of this and that title being " conferred " on
Jesus only with the reservation that this conferring is not represented
as something arbitrary which we might omit or handle otherwise.
This conferring, and the valuation and estimation and judgment which
underlies it, has nothing whatever to do with the free apotheosis of a
man. In spite of all the mitigations of later Judaism this would have
been an unprecedented thing in the original Palestinian community,
in the direct sphere of the Old Testament concept of God. And since
there has never been a Christian community without the Old Testament, it could not possibly have been carried through in Hellenistic
Christianity (or only *per nefas*). The exaltation of a man as a cult-god,
or his investiture with the dignity of a gnostic hypostasis, was not at all
easy on this presupposition. We do not understand either the practical
attitude to Jesus discernible on all levels of the New Testament tradition, or the titles of majesty conferred upon Him, if we do not at least
hazard the hypothesis that the peculiar place and function of the man
Jesus for New Testament Christians was not a hypothesis, that the
practice and theory of their relationship to Him was not a religious
experiment—however earnest and sincere—against the background of
an " as though " which secretly left the question open. Their estimation and judgment of Jesus is as such something secondary, a necessary consequence. It is not itself their theme, the subject-matter of
their preaching. They are occupied with Jesus Himself. They aim
to be His witnesses. They answer His question. They give an account
of His existence. He has placed them in this attitude. He has put
these titles of majesty on their lips. They do not try to crown Him
in this way, but they recognise Him as the One who is already crowned,
to whom these titles belong.

And so they do not try to win others for their own sure christological conviction, but they aim to " bring into captivity every thought to the obedience
of Christ " (2 Cor. 10⁵). If possible, this fact is brought out even more clearly
if we are ready to accept that when they spoke about Christ they often used
directly or indirectly sayings of Jesus about Himself, repeating them as coming
from His mouth. It is not they who represented Him, but He who represented
Himself to them, in this majesty.

He is to them the Christ, the *Kyrios*, the Son of Man and the Son
of God, the One who is absolutely different and exalted, even before
they describe Him in this way. And when they do describe Him in
this way, they appeal in some sense to Himself—that He Himself
continually attests Himself as such. And in relation to others they
count on it happening that they too may accept—not their own

representation and appraisal of a man honoured by them—but the Word of Jesus, His self-attestation of His majesty, of His unity with God.

It is clear that we can reject this New Testament witness concerning the man Jesus. It has been rejected again and again—even within the community. But there can be no disputing the fact that, in the sense of those who gave it, this witness is to the simple effect that, prior to any attitudes of others to Him or statements of others about Him, the man Jesus did in fact occupy this place and function, that, prior to any knowledge of His being or temporally conditioned confession of it, He actually was and is and will be what He is represented in the reflection of this witness, the Son of the Heavenly Father, the King of His kingdom, and therefore " by nature God." We have to let go the whole New Testament witness step by step and turn it into its opposite if we read it as a documentation of " religious valuations," if we do not see and admit that step by step it relates to the being and revelation of this man in the unprecedented and quite unique determination of His existence. It is not a Christian conception of Him, and to that extent not the Christian *kerygma*, but He Himself in His revelation and being, who according to the New Testament builds His community and calls the world to decision: He Himself in the power of His resurrection, the Lord who is the Spirit. Only when this is seen and admitted do we know what we are doing when we either accept or reject the New Testament witness.

But now we must be more precise. Assuming that the witness of the New Testament is true because it is grounded in its object and corresponds to it and is confirmed by it, it is to the man Jesus that according to the New Testament this majesty belongs. It is as this man that He is the Messiah, the *Kyrios*, or—in a final approximation to the mystery of His existence—the Son, or as the prologue to the Gospel of St. John has it, the Word of God. But the fact that He is this has to be called the mystery of His existence—on this point the New Testament is quite clear. The fact that He is this can be known only as He Himself reveals it, only by His Holy Spirit. When the New Testament attests Him to be such, it speaks of His resurrection from the dead. Only secondarily, and in this way, does it speak of the records of it. And in relation to others His witnesses expect that the same Holy Spirit who has revealed this to them will not be silent to others. The witness concerns the self-revelation of the Son of God who is identical with this man, not an existing acquaintance with His being and work as such. All such acquaintance with Jesus the Son of God is repudiated. His form as a man is regarded and described rather as the concealing of His true being, and therefore this true being as the Son or Word of God is a hidden being.

The New Testament does not speak of the One whom it calls " Lord " in the way we might expect, as a human lord furnished with sovereignty and authority and the plenitude of power, maintaining and executing his own will. According to this presentation what distinguishes the man Jesus as the Son of God is that which apparently stands in the greatest possible contradiction to the being of God: the fact that in relation to God—and therefore to the world as well—this man wills only to be obedient—obedient to the will of the Father, which is to be done on earth for the redemption of man as it is done in heaven.

At the river Jordan (Mk. 1¹¹) the voice of God proclaims this man the beloved Son at the very time when He allows Himself to be baptised by John, thus sub-jecting Himself to God with the same publicity and obligation as those who were baptised with Him. He shows that He is the Son of God (Mt. 4¹ᶠ·) by resisting the temptation—expressly described as the temptation of the devil—to prove it in the way that a human lord endowed with divinity would have had to do, as the wonder-workers of the time, who also called themselves " sons of God ", tried to do. In direct distinction from and opposition to this, His prayer in Gethsemane (Mt. 26³⁹) was : " Not as I will, but as thou wilt." Because He is the servant of God, He is the servant of all men, of the whole world, not come to be ministered unto but to minister (Mk. 10⁴⁵). He is the man in the parable who when invited to a wedding did not take the chief place but the lower (Lk. 14¹⁰), or even more pointedly (Lk. 22²⁷) the One who serves His disciples as they sit at meat, or even more pointedly (Jn. 13¹⁻¹¹) the One who washes their feet before they sit down to meat. This is obviously the concrete will of God to which He is obedient. Nowhere is the recognition of the divine Sonship more explicit than in the Gospel of John, yet it is this Gospel which causes Jesus to say expressly : " The Father is greater than I " (Jn. 14²⁸). And in line with this it is this Gospel which cannot emphasise too much that Jesus does not seek His own glory (8⁵⁰), that He does only that which He has been commissioned to do by the Father (14³¹, cf. 10¹⁸), that He keeps His Father's commandments (15¹⁰, cf. 8²⁹), that it is His meat to do the will of Him that sent Him and to finish His work (4³⁴, cf. 5³⁶, 17⁴).

The true God—if the man Jesus is the true God—is obedient. We have to keep before us the difficulty of this equation if we are to be clear what we have to understand and to accept or reject as the content of the New Testament witness to Christ. Obedience—even obedience which serves—does not of itself exclude a way of outstanding human greatness and power and glory, a being as man which is fulfilled in the best sense, and effective and successful in the world, and in its own way satisfying and triumphant. But according to the New Testament it is not the being of the man Jesus which has this character. On the contrary, the New Testament describes the Son of God as the servant, indeed as the suffering servant of God. Not accidentally and inci-dentally. Not merely to prove and show His mind and disposition. Not merely to win through by conflict to a concrete goal. Not merely as a foil to emphasise His glory. But necessarily and, as it were, essentially, and so far as can be seen without meaning or purpose. He is a suffering servant who wills this profoundly unsatisfactory being, who cannot will anything other in the obedience in which He shows Himself the Son of God.

In this respect the decisive expressions are in what is now accepted as a hymn quoted by Paul in Phil. 2 from some earlier source. They are as follows :

" He emptied (ἐκένωσεν) Himself (that is, of His divine form : He renounced it) and took the form of a servant " (v. 7) ; and again, " He humbled (ἐταπείνωσεν) Himself, and became obedient unto death, even the death of the cross " (v. 8). In the words of Paul Himself : " He who was rich became poor " (2 Cor. 8⁹). In Heb. 5⁸ : " He who is the Son learned obedience in what He had to suffer." The Lucan narrative of the childhood of Jesus mentions no less than three times that the first resting place of Jesus was a crib, because His parents could find no room in the inn (2⁷). The narrative in Matthew tells of the shadow of death which immediately fell on Him : of Herod, who sought His life; of the flight into Egypt and the slaughter of the innocents in Bethlehem (Mt. 2¹³f.). The later saying fits in with this : " The foxes have holes, and the birds of the air have nests, but the Son of man hath not where to lay his head " (Lk. 9⁵⁸). In Jn. 17⁵ we also hear of a glory which the Son had with the Father before the world was, but which He prays that He may be clothed with again, which He has therefore obviously renounced. He has taken " flesh and blood " (Heb. 2¹⁴). He has suffered and been tempted (2¹⁸), being made like His brethren in everything (2¹⁷), " feeling for our infirmities " and " in all points like as we are " (κατὰ πάντα καθ' ὁμοιότητα, 4¹⁵). The community confesses (1 Jn. 4²f·, 2 Jn. 7) that Jesus Christ " is come in the flesh." " God sent his Son in the likeness of sinful flesh to condemn sin in the flesh " (Rom. 8³). In the pregnant words of Jn. 1¹⁴, the Word became flesh. " Flesh " in the language of the New (and earlier the Old) Testament means man standing under the divine verdict and judgment, man who is a sinner and whose existence therefore must perish before God, whose existence has already become nothing, and hastens to nothingness and is a victim to death. " Flesh " is the concrete form of human nature and the being of man in his world under the sign of the fall of Adam—the being of man as corrupted and therefore destroyed, as unreconciled with God and therefore lost. In 2 Cor. 5²¹ we have it in a way which is almost unbearably severe : " He (God) hath made him to be sin who knew no sin ". He has caused Him to be regarded and treated as a sinner. He has Himself regarded Him and treated Him as a sinner. He was made a curse for us, as Paul unhesitatingly concluded from Deut. 21²³ (Gal. 3¹³). What this means is reflected in all the dreadful things which the Evangelists report were said of Jesus : " He is beside Himself " (Mk. 3²¹), " He hath Beelzebub " (Mk. 3²²), He is a " gluttonous man and a wine-bibber, a friend of publicans and sinners " (Mt. 11¹⁹), " He deceiveth the people " (Jn. 7¹²), " He blasphemeth God " (Mt. 9³, 26⁶⁵). There is unmistakable reference to the suspicion which surrounded His birth (Mt. 1¹⁹). His first public appearance is that of a penitent in unreserved solidarity with other penitents who confess themselves to be such in the baptism of John, and can look only for the remission of their sins in the coming judgment (Mt. 3¹⁵)—a clear anticipation of the story of the passion, towards which the narrative in all the Evangelists hastens with a momentum recognisable from the very first, and at the climax of which Jesus is crucified between two thieves (Mt. 27³⁸). The prophecy which occurs three times in all the Synoptics, that the Son of Man must and will be delivered up to men, to the high-priests and the scribes, and finally the Gentiles, explicitly reveals the character of the whole story of the man Jesus as a story of suffering—whatever we may think of the place of these passages in the history of the tradition. To the same context belongs also the fact, which is constantly emphasised, that among the twelve—that is to say, in the original form of the new people of God of the last days—and himself a disciple and apostle, there is the " traitor " Judas. In short, according to the New Testament the *Heidelberg Catechism* is quite right when in *Qu.* 37 it says that " during the whole time of His life on earth Jesus . . . bore the wrath of God against the sin of the whole human race." And in the same sense the ancient creeds were also right when under the concepts *passus, crucifixus, mortuus, sepultus*, they believed that they were saying everything that is decisive about the man Jesus. In the dreadfully paradoxical language of Jn. 3[14], 8[28], 12[32], this humiliation, this raising up as the One nailed to the cross, is His " lifting up from the earth " (His ὑψοθῆναι). And this humiliation, this human existence of Jesus in the flesh and therefore under the wrath and judgment of God, is not an accident or fate, but His own free and in that way genuinely obedient will. The story of Gethsemane (like the story of the temptation at the beginning of the Gospels) shows two things : first, that we have to do with His genuine human decision ; and second, that it is a decision of obedience. He chooses, but He chooses that apart from which, being who He is, He could not choose anything else. As the Lamb whose blood is shed He " is foreordained before the foundation of the world " (1 Pet. 1[19f.]). God did not spare Him, but delivered Him up (Rom. 8[32]). It is written of the Son of Man that " He will suffer many things and be set at nought " (Mk. 9[12]). And in accordance with the divine determination He emptied Himself, He humbled Himself (Phil. 2[7f., 8]), He gave Himself up (Gal. 2[20], Eph. 5[2]) even before Judas did. He came in order to give His life. " No man taketh it from me, but I lay it down of myself. I have power to lay it down, and I have power to take it again. This commandment have I received of my Father " (Jn. 10[18]). Peter with his " Be it far from thee " does not think in divine terms but human, and he has to be resisted as a satanic tempter (Mt. 16[22f.]). Jesus would not be Jesus if His way could be different or bear a different character.

Exegetes old and new have been right in their references and comments when they have seen all this and tried to consider the deity of Jesus Christ in the light of it. On the other hand, it has always led and always does lead to confusion where this more precise understanding of the human being of God and the divine being of the man Jesus is disregarded or weakened or not taken as the starting-point for all further discussion.

But there is one thing which we must emphasise especially. It is often overlooked in this context. It is not taken seriously or seriously enough. Yet from this one thing everything else, and particularly what we have just stressed, acquires its contour and colour, its definiteness and necessity. The Word did not simply become any " flesh," any man humbled and suffering. It became Jewish flesh. The Church's whole doctrine of the incarnation and the atonement becomes abstract and valueless and meaningless to the extent that this comes to be regarded as something accidental and incidental. The New Testament witness to Jesus the Christ, the Son of God, stands on the soil of the Old Testament and cannot be separated from it. The pronouncements of New Testament Christology may have been shaped by a very non-Jewish environment. But they relate always to a man who is seen to be not a man in general, a neutral man, but the conclusion and sum of the history of God with the people of Israel, the One who fulfils the covenant made by God with this people. And it is as such that He is the obedient Son and servant of God, and therefore the One who essentially and necessarily suffers.

It may be maintained, and it may actually be the case, that the philosophical and conceptual world of the New Testament was influenced by Gnosticism and the mystery religions. But this does not alter in the least the fact that the New Testament message as such does not find its subject-matter, which is also its origin, in the empty sphere of abstract principles and relations, or in the sphere of myth. On the contrary, in its decisive factual statement concerning what took place between God and man it definitely resists translation into a statement about an event which did not take place at a specific time and place, and therefore takes place at all times and in all places. Nor does it accidentally concern a man of a particular type and descent which might just as well have been different. Necessarily and emphatically it concerns an event which was prophesied in the testimonies of the dealings of God with the people Israel and fulfilled within the sphere of this people. It concerns, therefore, the existence of a man of Israel, an Israelite. The Christian message is at its heart a message about Jesus the Son of God. But when it is addressed to men and groups of men who are of non-Israelitish type and descent, it not only presupposes this original connexion, but it has always to be accepted and understood with this original connexion. The Christian *kerygma* as it is addressed to the world has this statement about an Israelite at its very heart. This means nothing more or less than the bringing of the world into the sphere of the divine dealings with the people Israel. It does not speak generally of the existence of a Son of Man who became man for many (with many in view), but of the fact that the Jesus who has come as the Messiah of Israel has come into the world as the Saviour of the world. It relates to Jesus as such. It describes Him as the One who proclaims Himself in the history of Israel, as the aim and end of that history. It describes Him as the One who has in that very way appeared to all peoples. His universality is revealed in this particularity, which is plain even in a writing so obviously directed to the Gentiles as the Gospel of Luke. It was so plain that at first it could appear to the Gentile world to be simply a particular form or corruption of Jewish propaganda—rather strangely repudiated by official Judaism. It was only in the 2nd century (and, theoretically, first of all in the well-meant efforts of the so-called Apologists) that Christian universalism began to lose its particularist character, to the great detriment of the understanding of this very heart of the Christian message. It was Marcion who tried to do away with it in principle, taking the Old Testament to be the document which attests the work and revelation of another and evil god, the demiurge, from whose lordship we have been freed by Christ. Marcion wanted to see the Old Testament completely eliminated as the source and norm of Christian proclamation. The Church was now preponderately a Gentile Church, but it instinctively kept itself from this dangerous temptation. It did the same later in relation to the Socinians, to Schleiermacher and to Harnack. In spite of all the allegorising and generalising interpretation which it has not escaped to soften the offence, the Old Testament still remains from generation to generation to ensure that the particularist aspect of the Christian message directed to the world, the simple truth that Jesus Christ was a born Jew, is never lost sight of, but constantly survives the irruption of all too generalised views of the man Jesus.

This is the meaning and purpose of the complete linking of the New Testament witness with that of the Old which the New Testament itself never overlooks. It prevents the rounding off of the picture of Jesus into a kind of ideal-picture of human existence, which would necessarily degenerate into a free sketch of the man who was and is the Son of God, i.e., a sketch which is quite independent of the Israelitish components of the New Testament. It keeps before the attention of the reader and hearer the fact that the end and point of the Gospel of Jesus Christ, His self-proclamation documented in the Gospel, the nerve of the history between God and man which took place in it, the history of redemption, is essentially the history of the passion. The fact that it is this essentially and necessarily, the fact that it is a history of victory only with this orientation, is something which we always miss, in plain contradiction to the New Testament itself, if we are not ready to listen to the Old Testament as an authentic commentary whenever we listen to the New.

In its bracketing with the Old Testament the New closes the door against every kind of Docetism, however crude or subtle, by positing the man who was and is the Son of God in His singularity and at the same time in the relevance of His existence for every man of every place, by setting the happening of the redemption history between God and man in world history, at a cosmic place, a place on earth. Docetism is the old enemy, an enemy which is constantly reappearing, of the concrete truth of the history of redemption as the history of the passion. When Docetism threatens, this truth is threatened. And when the authenticity of the Old Testament is disputed in its unity with the New, Docetism threatens. When it names Israel as that place, the New Testament says that it is a definite and limited place, this place and no other. When it recognises and addresses and proclaims Israel as the people of God from which the man who was and is the Son of God came forth at the time appointed by God, when it refers back to the covenant made between God and Israel, when it describes this man as the Christ promised to this people, or as the Son of Man from heaven whose future (according to Dan. 7) will destroy and overcome the beast-kingdoms of the great world-powers, when it lets Him be born in Bethlehem as the Son of Mary and therefore as the Son of David, it says that this place is not such by chance, but is elected and ordained by God from the very first, indeed from all eternity. " The Word was made flesh " means that the Son of God does not take any place as man, but this place. As God's Son in His unity with the Father He stands necessarily—with a divine necessity—at this place. The act of God which takes place in this man for us takes place contingently on earth and in time, as the creeds have emphasised with their mention of Mary and Pilate. The particularity of the man Jesus in proceeding from the one elect people of Israel, as the confirmation of its election, means decisively that the reconciliation of sinful and lost man has, above all, the character of a divine condescension, that it takes place as God goes into the far country. The Father who is one with the man Jesus His Son (Jn. 10[30]) is the God who years before was not too good, and did not count it too small a thing, to bind and engage Himself to Abraham and his seed, and to be God in this particularity and limitation—" I will be your God." From the horizontal point of view, and in terms of human history, He attested and revealed Himself as a national numen like so many others, to be precise, the common numen of that coalition of tribes in which the people of Israel emerged as a unit. He is the one true God who is respected and worshipped as the only God by this people, and neither theoretically nor practically will He be compared or exchanged with other gods. He is the same high God who in supreme humility elected Himself the God of this one small people.

Under the name of Son of God Jesus took the very place which in the Old Testament had often enough been allotted to the " children " of Israel in their relation with God. According to Ex. 4^{22} it is the task of Moses to tell Pharaoh : " Israel is my firstborn, and I command thee : Let my son go, that he may serve me." Similarly in Hosea (11^1) God says : " Out of Egypt have I called my son." And Jeremiah (31^{20}) : " Is Ephraim my dear son ? Is he a pleasant child ? for since I spake against him, I do earnestly remember him still : therefore my bowels are troubled for him ; I will surely have mercy upon him." This is affirmed by the voice of God Himself at the time of the exile : " Bring my sons from far, and my daughters from the ends of the earth ; even every one that is called by my name, for I have created him for my glory, I have formed him " (Is. $43^{6f.}$). The same answer is given in the last book of the Old Testament : " I will spare them, as a man spareth his own son that serveth him " (Mal. 3^{17}). And in the same way a later prophet cries in the name of the people to their God : " Doubtless thou art our father, though Abraham be ignorant of us, and Israel acknowledge us not : thou, O Lord, art our father. . . . Why hast thou made us to err from thy ways, and hardened our heart from thy fear ? " (Is. 63^{16}). Yahweh can be called the Father of Israel and Israel His son because He has created and made and prepared this people as such (Deut. 32^6), and that to His own glory (Is. 43^7) ; because it is the " work of his hand " (Is. 45^{11}). Because the Israelites are His sons in this sense, He does not allow Himself to be questioned or commanded by anyone concerning them, but it is also presupposed that they for their part are bound to obey and serve Him, as is specifically emphasised in Ex. 4^{23} and Mal. 3^{18}. The most direct saying in this respect is in Deut. 14^1: " Ye are the children of the Lord your God," and its purpose is simply to initiate a series of particular prohibitions in relation to participation in heathen mourning customs and the eating of unclean foods. We will see later how important it is to emphasise this ethical moment in the concept.

Mal. 1^6 perhaps presupposes that occasionally the priests were also called " sons of God " : " A son honoureth his father, and a servant his master : if then I be a father, where is mine honour ? and if I be a master, where is my fear ? saith the Lord of hosts unto you, O priests, that despise my name." There is no doubt—and here the connexion with general eastern mythology and phraseology can hardly be questioned—that although the Old Testament monarchy is a rather problematic institution the king is also given this name on occasion. " I will be to him a father, and he shall be to me a son " is promised to David (2 Sam. 7^{14}) in relation to his son and successor. The verse continues : " If he commit iniquity, I will chasten him with the rod of men, and with the stripes of the children of men, But my mercy shall not depart away from him." And in Ps. 89 (which is closely related with the whole context of 2 Sam. 7) we are told in v. 26 f. : " He shall cry unto me, Thou art my father, my God, and the rock of my salvation. Also I will make him my first-born, higher than the kings of the earth." Here again, in v. 30 f., there is not lacking a warning of divine punishment in case the king's descendants forsake the Law of God. But here again it is, of course, capped by the promise that the grace of God will not depart from them. Finally there is the well-known passage in Ps. 2^7, where the king himself declares : " I will declare the decree : the Lord hath said unto me, Thou art my Son ; this day have I begotten thee." If in spite of the extra-biblical analogies these verses are not to be torn completely out of the setting of Old Testament thought, we must accept the fact that in them the king is envisaged as the *membrum praecipuum* of the people elected to divine sonship, and that he is so in the form of the eschatological future. And there can be little doubt that all these statements—and in the last resort the saying about the priests in

Malachi—do conform in sense with what must be said about the people as the son of God. It is God who creates the king and priests as such, making and preparing them for their office. By the grace of God they stand under the promise of His faithfulness, but also under the obligation to be obedient to Him. They are what they are as a particular form of that which makes Israel as such the chosen people of God. It is to be noted that in the Old Testament this father-son relationship is undoubtedly only the relationship between God and Israel, this people, and in particular its king and priests. In the Old Testament God has defined and limited it in that way from the very first. It is in that way, therefore, that He has condescended in His grace. It was and is electing grace, but the grace which elects Israel.

But where in the Old Testament we find Israel, or the king of Israel, in the New Testament we find the one Israelite Jesus. He is the object of the same electing will of the Creator, the same merciful divine faithfulness. He is bound to the same obedience and service of God. He is the Son of the Father with the same singularity and exclusiveness. Of course, what is and takes place between Him and the Father is relatively much greater, and as the self-humiliation of God much more singular, than anything indicated by the father-son relationships of the Old Testament. For this one man—it is as if the framework is now filled out and burst through—is the Son of God who is one with God the Father and is Himself God. God is now not only the electing Creator, but the elect creature. He is not only the giver, but also the recipient of grace. He is not only the One who commands, but the One who is called and pledged to obedience. He does not merely go into lowliness, into the far country, to be Himself there, as He did in His turning to Israel. But now He Himself becomes lowly. He Himself is the man who is His Son. He Himself has become a stranger in Him. And Israel and its kings and priests were only the provisional representatives of this incomparable Son. The mystery of Israel was merely the proclamation, which had still to be unriddled, of the real mystery which unriddles itself from within. In the Old Testament we cannot find anything more than these representatives. But we must not overlook these representatives. The Old Testament, and also the New Testament in its constant implicit and explicit connexion with the Old, makes it quite clear that for all its originality and uniqueness what took place in Christ is not an accident, not a historical *novum*, not the arbitrary action of a *Deus ex machina*, but that it was and is the fulfilment—the superabundant fulfilment—of the will revealed in the Old Testament of the God who even there was the One who manifested Himself in this one man Jesus of Nazareth—the gracious God who as such is able and willing and ready to condescend to the lowly and to undertake their case at His own cost.

But we must go further. The grace and work and revelation of God has the particular character of election. To that extent it includes a self-limitation and a self-humiliation on the part of God. But that is only the general fact which makes the Old Testament a provisional witness to Christ and distinguishes the New as its fulfilment. The next thing that we are unequivocally and indispensably told by the Old Testament is the particular fact that the man elected by God, the object of the divine grace, is not in any way worthy of it. From what we hear of the people of Israel and its kings, he shows by his action that he is a transgressor of the commandment imposed on him with his election, an enemy of the will of God directed and revealed to him. The God of the Old Testament rules amongst His enemies. He is already on the way into the far country to the extent that it is an unfaithful people to whom He gives and maintains His faithfulness.

We have seen that according to the Old Testament Israel is the son who is pledged to obedience and service to God as its Father and Creator, and that according to the New Jesus accepted this obligation in its place. But what is the normal answer of Israel to the question put to it in its election ? The information given by the Old Testament in connexion with the thought of Israel's sonship is unequivocal : The " children " of Israel are " corrupted children ; they have forsaken the Lord, they have provoked the Holy One of Israel unto anger, they are gone away backward " (Is. 1⁴). " I have nourished and brought up children, and they have rebelled against me " (Is. 1²). They are " rebellious children, that take counsel but not of me " (Is. 30¹). They are " lying children, children that will not hear the law of the Lord " (Is. 30⁹). They are " backsliding children " who have " perverted their way, and forgotten the Lord their God " (Jer 3²¹ᶠ·). In the verse that tells us of the Son called out of Egypt, the continuation is : " The more I called them, the more they went from me " (Hos. 11²). We have seen that in Mal. 1⁶ the same complaint was lodged against the priests as the sons of God. And we hardly need to develop in detail the way in which the history of the kings in Samaria and Jerusalem—who are the special bearers of this title—is, as a whole—there are exceptions which only confirm the rule— a history of defiance of the promises of 2 Sam. 7 and Ps. 89—bringing out the gracious character of these promises. It is a history of the most outrageous and fatal insubordination to Yahweh as the " Father " of these kings. The place taken by the one Israelite Jesus according to the New Testament is, according to the Old Testament, the place of this disobedient son, this faithless people and its faithless priests and kings.

This involves an obvious sharpening of the idea and concept of the humiliation of the Son of God, of the alien life in which He identifies Himself with the man Jesus, of the revelation of the grace in which God compromises Himself. " The Word was made flesh." The Old Testament testifies pitilessly what is meant by " flesh." The Old Testament was needed to testify this because the Old Testament alone attests the election of God, and it is only in the light of God's election that we see who and what is man—his unfaithfulness, his disobedience, his fall, his sin, his enmity against God. Without anything to excuse or cover it, without any appearance of the accidental or merely external, the being and nature of man are radically and fundamentally revealed in the human people of Israel as chosen and loved by God, in the history of that people, in Jewish flesh. From the negative standpoint that is the mystery of the Jews and their representative existence. That is what anti-Semitism old and new has constantly thundered, but without understanding that we have here a mirror held up to the men of all peoples. The Son of God in His unity with the Israelite Jesus exists in direct and unlimited solidarity with the representatively and manifestly sinful humanity of Israel. Everything which can be said against it, everything which is said against it, not by men, but by God speaking through His prophets—He allows to be said against Him. He accepts personal responsibility for all the unfaithfulness, the deceit, the rebellion of this people and its priests and kings. And that is infinitely more than when Israel itself (and in Israel more or less expressly every individual Israelite) comes under this accusation. It is infinitely more than could and did take place when the perception and confession of communal sin and guilt came together in an individual Israelite in such a way that, among others incapable of this perception and unprepared for this confession, they became to him a question of personal life in relation to God. Naturally, Moses, David, Jeremiah, the authors of many of the Psalms, and, above all, the significant figure of the Servant of the Lord in Isa. 53, do seem, as it were, to be projected shadows of the one Lamb of God which taketh away the sin of the world. And naturally they are that. But there takes place here infinitely more than can be shadowed in the figures of these men who representatively perceive and confess the sin of the whole people ; and infinitely more, of course, than could be represented by the institution of sacrificial worship, in which an innocent beast was regarded and dealt with as the object of the accusation made by God against the people, against man. Infinitely more—for in the one Israelite Jesus it was God Himself who as the Son of the Father made Himself the object of this accusation and willed to confess Himself a sinner, and to be regarded and dealt with as such. What is all our human repentance either in our own name or in that of others compared with this perfect repentance ? In this respect, too, we cannot expect to find in the Old Testament more than a prophecy which is supremely inadequate in relation to this fulfilment. The radical and fundamental admission of human incapacity, unwillingness and unworthiness manifest in the human people of Israel as chosen and loved by God is not their own work. Or rather, it takes place as their own work only in the person of the one Israelite in whom God Himself has come amongst sinners in the form of a sinner. It is He who reveals how it is with man in his relation to God. But, again, He does not do it abruptly, abstractly, as a *Deus ex machina*, but in continuity with His grace as already demonstrated and revealed. It was always grace for sinners—grace shown to His enemies—grace in the light of which man can only stand and acknowledge himself a transgressor, and therefore unworthy of it. The Son of Man from heaven had to be the friend of publicans and sinners, and die between two thieves. He had to, because God was already the God who loved His enemies, who " endured such contradiction of sinners against himself " (Heb. 12³).

For a knowledge of this continuity of the being and activity of God, of His condescension, the Old Testament is indispensable as the presupposition of the New.

And now we must make a final step, in which we are directed no less decisively to the Old Testament. Because he negates God, the man elected by God, the object of the divine grace, is himself necessarily, and logically, and with all that it involves, the man negated by God. It is also true that God has sworn to be, and actually is, faithful, that God's grace does not fail but persists towards him. But within these limits it is unconditionally the case that as a sinner he is rejected by God, that he not only stands under the wrath and accusation of God, but because this wrath is well-founded and this accusation is true, he stands under His sentence and judgment. The grace of God is concealed under His sentence and judgment, His Yes under His No. The man elected by God is the man who with his contradiction is broken and destroyed by the greater contradiction of God. He cannot stand before Him, and therefore he cannot stand at all. He chooses a freedom which is no freedom. He is therefore a prisoner of the world-process, of chance, of all-powerful natural and historical forces, above all of himself. He tries to be his own master, and to control his relations with God and the world and his fellow-men. And as he does so, the onslaught of nothingness prevails against him, controlling him in death in an irresistible and senseless way and to his own loss. This is the *circulus vitiosus* of the human plight presupposed and revealed in and with the grace of God. And there is no man who, whether he experiences it or not, is not in this plight. But the man elected by God not only suffers and experiences it. He knows it. He knows that he must perish. He considers that he must die. The connexion between his guilt and the righteous judgment of God is constantly before him. Occasionally and for the moment he may forget it, he may deceive himself about it, he may fall asleep to it. But he would not be the elect of God if the dreadful fact did not awaken him again, and pursue him even in his dreams, that everything is as it is and will come to pass as it will come to pass, that there is no escape from it. He is not merely in the jaws of death, but out of the depth of his election, from God whose elect he is, he must constantly hear the voice which tells him and charges him and forces him to live in the knowledge that he is in the jaws of death, that he is lost. " It is a fearful thing to fall into the hands of the living God " (Heb. 10^{31}).

This is the situation of Old Testament man. He may, of course, eat and drink and sleep in this plight. He may distract himself in his care and sorrow. He may console himself like others with all kinds of illusions of self-help. But— because Israel is the chosen people of God—the voice of the prophets brings before him again and again the sentence and judgment under which he lives, writing it in the heart where he cannot escape it, in spite of all his pride or levity or complacency. He does not merely perish, but he must constantly be told, and tell himself that he has to perish. The writings of the prophets and the

Psalms are full of passages which confirm this. Of several individual texts, I will quote only from one, the so-called Song of Moses in Deut. 32, in which the thought of sonship again plays a particular part : " For the Lord's portion is his people ; Jacob is the lot of his inheritance. He found him in a desert land, and in the waste howling wilderness ; he led him about, he instructed him, he kept him as the apple of his eye. As an eagle stirreth up her nest, fluttereth over her young, spreadeth abroad her wings, taketh them, beareth them on her wings ; so the Lord alone did lead him, and there was no strange god with him. He made him ride on the high places of the earth, that he might eat the increase of the fields " (v. 9 f.). But what happened ? " They have corrupted themselves, they are not his children, that is their blot : they are a perverse and crooked generation. Do ye thus requite the Lord, O foolish people and unwise ? is not he thy father that hath bought thee ? hath he not made thee and established thee ? " (v. 5 f.). " But Jacob ate and was satisfied ; Jeshurun waxed fat, and kicked ; thou art waxen fat, thou art grown thick . . then he forsook God which made him, and lightly esteemed the rock of his salvation. . . . Of the rock that begat thee thou art unmindful, and hast forgotten God that formed thee " (v. 15 f.). And then the answer : " The Lord saw it, and he abhorred them, because of the provoking of his sons, and of his daughters " (v. 19). " For a fire is kindled in mine anger, and shall burn unto the lowest hell, and shall consume the earth with her increase, and set on fire the foundations of the mountains. I will heap mischiefs upon them ; I will spend mine arrows upon them. They shall be burnt with hunger, and devoured with burning heat, and with bitter destruction : I will also send the teeth of beasts upon them, with the poison of serpents of the dust. The sword without, and terror within, shall destroy both the young man and the virgin, the suckling also with the man of gray hairs " (v. 22 f.). " How should one chase a thousand, and two put ten thousand to flight, except their Rock had sold them, and the Lord had shut them up ? " (v. 30 f.). The clear commentary on this and many similar passages is the history of Israel in its broad outlines and in its outcome and result. In the light of its great beginning and of the opportunities and assistances and redemptions and hopes continually given to this people that history is the history of a great humiliation and disillusionment, a history of suffering. Necessarily it evoked again and again the question : " Where is now thy God ? ", the desire to reckon with God, to complain about His hiddenness, to remind Him of His covenant and promises. But it had to be a history of suffering and it had to be fulfilled as such—not in spite of the fact but because of the fact that it was the history of the chosen people of God, because it was inevitable that there should be revealed in the people chosen and loved and blessed by God not only the fall and disobedience of man, but the scorching fire of the love of God, and the breaking and destruction of man on God. Hence the necessary silence of man suffering before Him, not able to plead any right, not able to confront Him with any well-grounded " Why ? ", able only as Job finally did to submit under His mighty hand—because as the God who has turned in grace to a sinful and therefore a lost people He is always in the right. In the sphere of the Old Testament there is no legitimate human complaint against God—not even in face of the most bitter thing which man might experience at His hand. Man knows that it comes to him in a righteousness which is supremely necessary and therefore in confirmation of the faithfulness and grace of God. He knows that his history is necessarily what the history of Job was, a history of suffering.

We now have a complete outline of what it means that according to the New Testament the Word, or Son of God, was made flesh. To be flesh means to exist with the " children " of Israel under the wrath and judgment of the electing and loving God. To be flesh is to be in a state of perishing before this God. This is what the Old Testament says, and we can hardly maintain that the mythologies and tragedies and philosophies of the rest of antiquity have said the same thing in different words. The Old Testament says this of man. But the New Testament says that the Son of God was a man, and therefore it says it of Him, too. *He* stands under the wrath and judgment of God, *He* is broken and destroyed on God. It cannot be otherwise. It has to be like this. His history must be a history of suffering. For God is in the right against Him. He concedes that the Father is right in the will and action which leads Him to the cross. At this point we can and must think of the history of the Jews right up to our own day. Whether the Jews and those around them understand it or not, it has been a part of the living Old Testament that in its great outlines this history, too, is an individual history of humiliations and dis-illusionments, a history of suffering. If the Old Testament history was the type, this history has been an additional attestation of its fulfil-ment in the one Israelite Jesus. The Son of God in His unity with this man exists in solidarity with the humanity of Israel suffering under the mighty hand of God. He exists as one of these Old Testament men. He does not suffer any suffering, but their suffering ; the suffer-ing of children chastised by their Father. He does not suffer any death, but the death to which the history of Israel moves relentlessly forward. He is silent where Job too had to be silent before God. But, again, there takes place here something quite different from what took place there. In Him God has entered in, breaking into that *circulus vitiosus* of the human plight, making His own not only the guilt of man but also his rejection and condemnation, giving Himself to bear the divinely righteous consequences of human sin, not merely affirming the divine sentence on man, but allowing it to be fulfilled on Himself. He, the electing eternal God, willed Himself to be rejected and therefore perishing man. That is something which never happened in all the dreadful things attested in the Old Testament concerning the wrath of God and the plight of man. In the Old Testament there is always the antithesis between the righteous God and the bitter things which man has to accept from Him without murmuring. In the passion story of the New Testament this antithesis is done away. It is God Himself who takes the place of the former sufferers and allows the bitterness of their suffering to fall upon Himself. In this respect, too, the prophecy is quite inadequate in relation to the fulfil-ment. There is suffering and death in the Old Testament, but it is only in the New that we see what suffering and death really means, as it becomes the work of God Himself, as God gives Himself to this most dreadful of all foreign spheres. But, again, it is the indispensable function of the Old Testament to show that the grace of God in the form of His judgment on man and man's perishing before Him in suffering and death is an element in the previously existing order.

What took place on the cross of Golgotha is the last word of an old history and the first word of a new. God was always the One whose condescension showed itself to be unlimited in the suffering and death of the man Jesus. He is the same God who was truly gracious to Israel in the hiddenness of His love in the form of His righteous wrath.

According to the unanimous testimony of the New Testament, in the man Jesus of Nazareth described by those titles of majesty we have to do with the One who is qualitatively different, transcendent and uplifted in relation to all other men and the whole cosmos. His friends and enemies, and those to whom He means nothing, and all men of all times and countries have to do in Him with God. And again according to the unanimous testimony of the New Testament, this is the mystery of His existence. In other words, it is true, but in hiddenness, in a way which is unexpected, which is new in relation to all general concepts of God and those concretely delivered in other places, in a way which contradicts them, and to that extent in a way which is not perceived or known. The Almighty exists and acts and speaks here in the form of One who is weak and impotent, the eternal as One who is temporal and perishing, the Most High in the deepest humility. The Holy One stands in the place and under the accusation of a sinner with other sinners. The glorious One is covered with shame. The One who lives for ever has fallen a prey to death. The Creator is subjected to and overcome by the onslaught of that which is not. In short, the Lord is a servant, a slave. And it is not accidental. It could not be otherwise. For on the presupposition of the Old Testament witness and in the closest connexion with it, the New Testament tells us that it is essential and necessary for the one true God whom it finds in the man Jesus to act and to reveal Himself in this way, to take this form in the coming of His kingdom and the accomplishment of the reconciliation of the world with Himself, in this way to be in the world and for the world the Almighty, the Eternal, the Most High, the Holy One, the Living One, the Creator, the Lord. Prophecy shows (and in this respect it is indissolubly connected with its fulfilment) that God was always the One who worked and was indirectly revealed as He now reveals Himself directly in the secret of the existence of the man Jesus of Nazareth, having set Himself as a man among men for men.

The secret of God's making Himself present in this way was already known to Christian theology even in the 2nd century—especially that which derived from the tradition of Asia Minor. In Ignatius of Antioch (*ad Eph.* 19³) Jesus Christ is called θεὸς ἀνθρωπίνως φανερούμενος, or, in clear reminiscence of the passages adduced from John, ἐν σαρκὶ γενόμενος θεός (*ad Eph.* 7²), or simply ὁ θεὸς ἡμῶν (*ad Rom. prooem.*), so that in relation to Him He could speak of an αἷμα θεοῦ (*ad Eph.* 1¹) and a πάθος θεοῦ (*ad Rom.* 6³). Similarly in Irenaeus (*C.o.h.* III, 16, 6) we read : *Invisibilis visibilis factus et incomprehensibilis comprehensibilis et impassibilis passibilis.* And in Melito of Sardis (*fragm.* 13) : *Horruit creatura stupescens ac dicens : quidnam est hoc novum mysterium ? iudex iudicatur et quietus est; invisibilis videtur neque erubescit, incomprehensibilis prehenditur neque indignatur; incommensurabilis mensuratur neque repugnat; impassibilis patitur neque ulciscitur; immortalis moritur neque respondet verbum.*

That God as God is able and willing and ready to condescend, to humble Himself in this way is the mystery of the " deity of Christ " —although frequently it is not recognised in this concreteness. This deity is not the deity of a divine being furnished with all kinds of supreme attributes. The understanding of this decisive christological statement has been made unnecessarily difficult (or easy), and the statement itself ineffective, by overlooking its concrete definition, by omitting to fill out the New Testament concept " deity " in definite connexion with the Old Testament, i.e., in relation to Jesus Christ Himself. The meaning of His deity—the only true deity in the New Testament sense—cannot be gathered from any notion of supreme, absolute, non-worldly being. It can be learned only from what took place in Christ. Otherwise its mystery would be an arbitrary mystery of our own imagining, a false mystery. It would not be the mystery given by the Word and revelation of God in its biblical attestation, the mystery which is alone relevant in Church dogmatics. Who the one true God is, and what He is, i.e., what is His being as God, and therefore His deity, His " divine nature," which is also the divine nature of Jesus Christ if He is very God—all this we have to discover from the fact that as such He is very man and a partaker of human nature, from His becoming man, from His incarnation and from what He has done and suffered in the flesh. For—to put it more pointedly, the mirror in which it can be known (and is known) that He is God, and of the divine nature, is His becoming flesh and His existence in the flesh.

We have seen that this includes in itself His obedience of suffering, i.e., (1) the obedience of the Son to the Father, shown (2) in His self-humiliation, His way into the far country, fulfilled in His death on the cross. It is in these two moments, and their combination, that there is enclosed the mystery that He is very God and of the divine nature. It is a mystery because true being as God and in the divine nature is His alone of all men and all creatures. It is enclosed and can be found only in Him. It is therefore completely and necessarily closed to any consideration or reflection which does not look at Him. It is a genuine mystery because it is disclosed, if at all, from within, as it is spoken as the Word of God and received by His Holy Spirit. From the point of view of the obedience of Jesus Christ as such, fulfilled in that astonishing form, it is a matter of the mystery of the inner being of God as the being of the Son in relation to the Father. From the point of view of that form, of the character of that obedience as an obedience of suffering, of the self-humiliation of Jesus Christ, of the way of the Son into the far country, it is a matter of the mystery of His deity in His work *ad extra*, in His presence in the world.

To light up these two moments and their relationship to one another it will be helpful to look at the remarkable sayings in Mt. 11²⁵⁻³⁰, and their parallels in Lk. 10²¹⁻²⁴.

The passage speaks of a " time "—Matthew connects it with the sayings about the Baptist and the woes on Chorazin and Bethsaida, Luke with the sending out of the disciples—when Jesus addressed to the Father a joyful Yes (ἐξομολογοῦμαί σοι, πάτερ, κύριε τοῦ οὐρανοῦ καὶ τῆς γῆς)—Luke indeed says that He " rejoiced in the Holy Spirit " (ἠγαλλιάσατο τῷ πνεύματι τῷ ἁγίῳ). Why ? In the first instance, strangely enough, because of an obvious defeat, a failure : " that thou hast hid these things from the wise and prudent ". But then there follows, " and hast revealed them unto babes." The former were obviously those who had succeeded in this world, the far-sighted and clear-sighted spiritual leaders of the people of whom it might be hoped and expected that they would welcome the proclamation of the kingdom and recognise the Son of God. They have not done so. The Father has hidden it (ταῦτα) from them. The others (νήπιοι) are the innocent and naive and unimportant disciples of Jesus. They have followed Him. The Father, the Lord of heaven and earth has—strangely and disappointingly—revealed it (the kingdom which has come, the presence of the Son) to them. The continuation shows that the sequence is not accidental. It is for this puzzling and scandalising distribution of the divine hiding and revealing that Jesus as Son gives thanks to the Father. A. Schlatter (*Der Evangelist Matthäus*, 1929, p. 382) says quite rightly that " this saying makes a passion of the work of Jesus." " Even so, Father, for so it seemed good in thy sight," i.e., in this course of events, which is humanly and externally a failure, in which the first are last and the last first, in which the work of Jesus becomes a passion, in which His cross is plainly foreshadowed, the will of God is done to which He says Yes, to which He subjects Himself, willingly and with joy. There can be no doubt that Jesus is the unconditionally omnipotent executor of God upon earth.

" All things are delivered unto me of my Father." Again in accordance with the sense Schlatter underlines the fact " that πάντα does not carry any limitations . . . there are no limits for the giver and therefore no limits for the recipient " (p. 384). Therefore the saying implies the deity of Jesus. But it is in complete hiddenness that He is who and what He is. " No man knoweth the Son, but the Father ; neither knoweth any man the Father, save the Son, and he to whomsoever the Son will reveal him." But that means that who and what He is as the human bearer of that unlimited omnipotence, and who and what is the One who has given it to Him, what there is of divine majesty in the giving and receiving of it—this and the revelation of it is not something which can be laid down and judged and evaluated from without. It does not shine out clear and bright and sparkling in the world. It does not appear to men as such. Its form does not correspond to it but contradicts it, so that—although it is its form— it cannot be deduced from it, it is more likely not to be recognised in this form, and in the ordinary course of things it will not be recognised. This door to the majesty of Jesus can open only from within. And when it does open it is this door—the poor humanity of the divine being and activity, the strange form of the divine majesty, the humility in which God is God and the Son the Son, and to that extent the Father the Father, the alien life in which He is manifest only to Himself alone.

Both Evangelists now add other sayings which they obviously regard as characteristic forms of that revelation, as descriptions of the opening of that door from within. In Luke (10²³ᶠ·) there follows the blessing of the few and the lowly, the disciples, to whom at the coming of the last time it is given to see and to hear what many (here equivalent to all) prophets and kings desired to see and to hear but did not in fact see and hear. This revelation has therefore the character of a breaking out from the general and profoundest hiddenness, which indirectly is simply confirmed by it (as the darkness is when a light is kindled). As Ignatius of Antioch later wrote (*ad Magn.* 8, 2), it has the character of a breaking of the great silence in which God had previously and still for the most part conceals Himself.

Matthew (11²⁸ᶠ·) inserts at this point the so-called " call of the Saviour." To whom does it apply ? To whom, therefore, does the self-revelation of the Son apply ? Whom does He call to Himself ? Not those who are religiously, morally, politically and socially vital and exalted and triumphant in this world, but the " weary and heavy-laden," those who are retiring in their relation to God and men, those who are at an end of their own resources in both respects, those who are at their wits' end in both respects. The affinity of Jesus is not with the former class, but the latter. Not the former but the latter are His people, in whom He can see Himself again and to whom He for His part can give Himself to be known as Saviour and prove Himself as such. It is to these that He promises rest, a fulfilment which the others can never enjoy, because they do not know of it, because it cannot mean anything to them, His own rest, the rest of His own being in the unity of the obedient Son with the will of the Father and with the Father Himself. It is these that He summons to come to Himself, to be with Him in this rest, to take His yoke upon them. His rest consists in the fact that He carries the yoke and burden of the obedience of the Son to the Father—an easy yoke, a light burden, as whose bearer He is really at rest, and can promise rest (ἀνάπαυσιν) to those whom He calls, as Joshua (1¹³) promised possession of the land to the Israelites, and a dwelling in their former and latter homeland. Freely and willingly and in complete agreement with His commission He bears what He has to bear. But He does bear a yoke and a burden. He is at rest, but He is poor not rich, weak not strong, One who is subject not One who triumphs, like the weary and the heavy-laden, the man who finally will bear a cross and die on the cross. As this man He is the Saviour for those who are willing to be and are weary and heavy-laden with Him. He is πραΰς and ταπεινός, and that not by any chance or fate but " from the heart," not made from without but appointed from within, not forced by that which is inevitable, but of His own choice, in free obedience a bearer of the yoke and burden, and therefore at rest, and able to promise the same rest to others, that is, to call them to take His yoke upon them and to learn of Him, to follow Him, to be His disciples. That is the self-revelation of Jesus in His call as Saviour.

We will begin our attempt to understand this with a consideration of the second of those two moments of the mystery of the deity of Christ, and therefore with a consideration of the mystery of His being and work in the world, of the becoming man, the incarnation of the Son of God with all that it involved, of His way as a way into the far country.

The Christian theological tradition has always been in agreement that the statement " The Word was made flesh " is not to be thought of as describing an event which overtook Him, and therefore overtook God Himself, but rather a free divine activity, a sovereign act of divine lordship, an act of mercy which was necessary only by virtue of the will of God Himself. The statement cannot be reversed as though it indicated an appropriation and overpowering of the eternal Word by the flesh. God is always God even in His humiliation. The divine being does not suffer any change, any diminution, any transformation into something else, any admixture with something else, let alone any cessation. The deity of Christ is the one unaltered because unalterable deity of God. Any subtraction or weakening of it would at once throw doubt upon the atonement made in Him. He humbled Himself, but He did not do it by ceasing to be who He is. He went into a strange land, but even there, and especially there, He never became a stranger to Himself.

The word ἐκένωσεν in Phil. 2⁷ certainly does not mean this. It says that "being in the form of God," enjoying it, freely disposing of it (ἐν μορφῇ θεοῦ ὑπάρχων) He carried through a self-emptying, that is, He took the form of a servant (μορφὴν δούλου). The κένωσις consists in a renunciation of His being in the form of God alone. The decisive commentary is given by the text itself. He did not treat His form in the likeness of God (τὸ εἶναι ἴσα θεῷ) as a robber does his booty. He was not bound by it like someone bound by his possessions, a servant of unrighteous mammon. He did not treat it as His one and only and exclusive possibility, as though He stood or fell by it. It was not to Him an inalienable necessity to exist only in that form of God, only to be God, and therefore only to be different from the creature, from man, as the reality which is distinct from God, only to be the eternal Word and not flesh. He was not committed to any such "only." In addition to His form in the likeness of God He could also—and this involves at once a making poor, a humiliation, a condescension, and to that extent a κένωσις—take the form of a servant. He could be like men. He could be found in fashion as a man. As God, therefore, (without ceasing to be God) He could be known only to Himself, but unknown as such in the world and for the world. His divine majesty could be in this alien form. It could be a hidden majesty. He could, therefore, humble Himself in this form. He could be obedient in the determination corresponding to the being of this form, although contradicting point blank the actualisation of this form by other men. He could be obedient even to death, even to the death of the cross. He had this other possibility : the possibility of divine self-giving to the being and fate of man. He had the freedom for this condescension, for this concealment of His Godhead. He had it and He made use of it in the power and not with any loss, not with any diminution or alteration of His Godhead. That is His self-emptying. It does not consist in ceasing to be Himself as man, but in taking it upon Himself to be Himself in a way quite other than that which corresponds and belongs to His form as God, His being equal with God. He can also go into the far country and be there, with all that that involves. And so He does go into the far country, and is there. According to Phil. 2 this means His becoming man, the incarnation.

At the most decisive point, this was the exposition of Augustine : *Sic se inanivit : formam servi accipiens, non formam Dei amittens ; forma servi accessit, non forma Dei discessit* (*Sermo*, 183, 4 f.). *Occultavit quod erat* (*Sermo*, 187, 4). Origen (*De princ. praef.* 4) thought that it is self-evidently established as a rule of faith that the Logos *homo factus mansit, quod erat*. It was only to men, says Gregory of Nyssa (*or. cat.* 26), that the humanity of Christ concealed the glory of the Logos ; the Godhead is in Christ ὑπὸ τῆς ἀνθρωπίνης φύσεως κεκαλυμμένη.

It was the same basic thought which many years later Calvin was trying to express in his well-known statement : *Etsi in unam personam coaluit immensa Verbi essentia cum natura hominis, nullam tamen inclusionem fingimus.* An absolute *inclusio* of the Logos in the creature, the man Jesus, would mean a subordination of the Word to the flesh, a limitation and therefore an alteration of His divine nature, and therefore of God Himself. For that reason, according to Calvin, we ought to say side by side or rather together : *Mirabiliter de caelo descendit Filius Dei, ut caelum tamen non relinqueret. Mirabiliter in utero virginis gestari, in terris versari et in cruce pendere voluit, ut semper mundum impleret sicut ab initio* (*Instit.* II, 13. 4). This is what was known as the *Extra Calvinisticum* of Lutheran polemics. The Lutherans rejected it because they thought they could see in it a " Nestorian " separation of the divine and human natures, because on their doctrine of the communication of the attributes the fact that He " filled the whole world " had also to be said of the man Jesus as such on the basis of His union with the Logos. We may concede that there is something unsatisfactory about the theory, in that right up to our own day it has led to fatal speculation about the being and work of the λόγος ἄσαρκος, or a God whom we think we can know elsewhere, and whose divine being we can define from elsewhere than in and from the contemplation of His presence and activity as the Word made flesh. And it cannot be denied that Calvin himself (and with particularly serious consequences in his doctrine of predestination) does go a good way towards trying to reckon with this " other " god. It may also be noted, however, that the theory was not an innovation on the part of Calvin, nor was it a revival of the teaching condemned under the name of Nestorius. For in this matter Athanasius, Cyril of Alexandria and Hilary of Poitiers had all thought and taught as he did, as had indeed the whole early and mediæval Church, so that it was the abstract Lutheran denial of a being of the Logos *extra carnem* which was the real innovation (cf. F. Loofs, Art. *Kenosis P.R.E.*[3] 10, 246 f.). Nor for his part did Calvin any more than his predecessors try to maintain an abstract *Extra*, thus separating again, at any rate in part, the Son of God and the man Jesus. On the contrary, it was his aim in that theory to hold to the fact that the Son of God who is wholly this man (*totus intra carnem* as it was formulated by a later Calvinist) is also wholly God and therefore omnipotent and omnipresent (and to that extent *extra carnem*, not bound or altered by its limitations). He is the Lord and Creator who because He becomes a creature and exists in that *forma servi* does not cease to be Lord and Creator and therefore to exist in the *forma Dei*.

We can only mention in passing the great controversy about the *kenosis* which broke out at the beginning of the 17th century between the Lutheran theologians of Giessen and those of Tübingen. It was not a matter of the intactness of the Godhead of Christ in the state of His humiliation. Both parties were agreed in giving a positive answer to this question in line with earlier tradition. It was a problem which arose only on the specifically Lutheran presupposition of the divinisation of the man Jesus as such, but on this presupposition it was almost necessarily an acute problem : Whether the man Jesus exalted to unity with the Son of God and therefore divinised—according to the logic of the Lutherans—was even in the state of His humiliation secretly present to all His creatures, and ruled the world ? The Giessen party denied this, the Tübingen group affirmed it. In what did the *kenosis* consist ? Both sides agreed that it does not consist in the surrender or diminution of the possession (κτῆσις) of the divine glory imparted to the man Jesus. But adopting a statement of Martin Chemnitz the Giessen party taught a genuine κένωσις χρήσεως, an at any rate partial abstention by the man Jesus, in the *exinanitio*, from the use of the majesty imparted to Him. Jesus Christ *regnavit mundum*, but *non mediante carne*, only *qua* Logos, only in the power of His deity. But in Tübingen, following J. Brenz, there was taught a far more subtle κρύψις χρήσεως, an abstention by the man Jesus in the *exinanitio* only from the visible use, a *retractatio* and *occultatio* of the revelation of His power, or positively, a majesty of the Son of God which is, in fact, exercised and operative and actual, but concealed.. When the Saxon theologians were called in to decide the matter (*Decisio saxonica*, 1624), in the main issue they found in favour of Giessen. And in this they were followed by later Lutheran orthodoxy. That is surprising and noteworthy. The thesis of Giessen derived from a concern at the threatened Docetism of the Tübingen antithesis. But on Lutheran soil this concern had come too late. Already in the 16th century it had been expressed by the Reformed theologians against the Lutheran doctrine of the communication of the attributes, by Zwingli against

Luther. It is a fact that a bold Lutheran theologian does not need to fear the menace of Docetism unduly, but must accept the risk and suspicion involved. The intention of the basic view common to all Lutherans, that the man Jesus as such shares the totality of the divine attributes, undoubtedly points in the direction taken in Würtemberg with the mere κρύψις χρήσεως. Ready to follow through their logic, they challenged their opponents on their own theory (and not unjustly from the Lutheran standpoint) : *Hic Rhodus ! Hoc est illud ipsum Extra Calvinisticum, cui se hactenus nostri opposuerunt.* Granted the κένωσις χρήσεως maintained by them, there would be a time at least, the time of Christ's state in humility, *quo λόγος sic est in carne, ut etiam sit extra carnem.* Among the Lutheran theologians of the period the great J. Gerhard expressly repudiated the *Decisio saxonica* which approved this. And on the specifically Lutheran presupposition we are forced to ask whether the Giessen idea of a merely potential and facultative divine majesty and glory only partly used and actualised is not logically and theologically an impossible one, an inner contradiction ? That is how it was unashamedly described by a 19th century Lutheran, G. Thomasius (*Christi Person und Werk* [3], vol. I, 1886—in which there is a detailed discussion of the whole controversy).

The victory of the impossible theory of Giessen anticipated a step which in the 19th century was taken first of all by Ernst Sartorius (*Lehre von der heiligen Liebe*, 1844), then by G. Thomasius, then by the more extreme W. F. Gess (*Das Dogma von Christi Person und Werk*, 1887) and others. Ostensibly (and in one respect perhaps not only so) this step was taken in fulfilment of the original Lutheran intention. But clearly it was not uninfluenced by the modern "historical" problem of the "life of Jesus." And it meant an open breach with the whole tradition of the Church. Alongside the theses of Giessen and Tübingen (and avoiding the threatened "Nestorianism" or Calvinism of the former and the even more dreaded Docetism of the latter), there was a third alternative rejected in the earlier controversy, but already visible from afar along the line of the Giessen teaching. This was the alternative of a partial or complete abstention not only on the part of the man Jesus as such but on the part of the Son of God, the Logos Himself, from the possession and therefore the power to dispose of His divine glory and majesty, a κένωσις κτήσεως. This was the possibility seized by the so-called modern "kenotics" under the mounting modern pressure of the need to find a place for the historical form of Jesus in its human limitation—the idea of a self-limitation of God in the incarnation (or, to put it in the categories of the so-called doctrine of the attributes, the possibility of a *genus tapeinoticum*). "The Son of God closes His all-embracing eye on earth, and gives Himself to human darkness, and then opens His eye again as the rising light of the world, until He causes it to shine in full glory at the right hand of the Father" (E. Sartorius, p. 21 f.). Or, according to the teaching of Thomasius, the *kenosis* consisted in the fact that in the incarnation the divine Logos renounced the attributes of majesty in relation to the world (omnipotence, omnipresence, etc.), in order that in the man Jesus, until His exaltation, He might be God only in His immanent qualities, His holiness and love and truth. In Gess (who used the rash heading, "The Degradation of the Logos," *op. cit.* p. 344) we are told that "a change took place in the Son of God." In the incarnation He ceased to be actually God, in order to become conscious of Himself as God with the developing self-consciousness of Jesus, undergoing an "evolution" (p. 366 f.) in His identity with the man Jesus, and finally (p. 400 f.) being clothed again with the glory which He had had before in His exaltation. A. E. Biedermann called this doctrine "the complete *kenosis* of reason." But that is not its worst feature. The knot which the earlier Lutheran Christology had arbitrarily tied rather too tightly was certainly loosed. But it was loosed at too great a cost when it meant the open abandonment of the presupposition common to all earlier theology, including Calvinists and Lutherans, Giessen and

Tübingen, that the Godhead of the man Jesus remains intact and unaltered. It was this surrender which even among the Liberals of the 19th century and in the school of Ritschl earned for " modern kenotics " only the taunt that in trying to improve and complete orthodox Christology they had simply reduced it to absurdity. Their intention was good. They wanted to clear away the difficulties of the traditional teaching and make possible a " historical " consideration of the life of Jesus. But they succeeded only in calling in question the " God was in Christ " and in that way damaging the nerve of a Christology orientated by the Old and the New Testaments. There are many things we can try to say in understanding the christological mystery. But we cannot possibly understand or estimate it if we try to explain it by a self-limitation or de-divinisation of God in the uniting of the Son of God with the man Jesus. If in Christ—even in the humiliated Christ born in a manger at Bethlehem and crucified on the cross of Golgotha—God is not unchanged and wholly God, then everything that we may say about the reconciliation of the world made by God in this humiliated One is left hanging in the air.

But it is not enough simply to follow the great line of theological tradition and to reject all thought of an alterability or alteration of God in His presence and action in the man Jesus. What depends on this rejection is clear. If God is not truly and altogether in Christ, what sense can there be in talking about the reconciliation of the world with God in Him ? But it is something very bold and profoundly astonishing to presume to say without reservation or subtraction that God was truly and altogether in Christ, to speak of His identity with this true man, which means this man who was born like all of us in time, who lived and thought and spoke, who could be tempted and suffer and die and who was in fact tempted, and suffered and died. The statement of this identity cannot be merely a postulate. If with the witnesses of the New Testament we derive it from what took place in this man, if it only confirms that the reconciliation of the world with God has actually taken place in the existence of this man, if it can only indicate the mystery and the miracle of this event, we must still know what we are presuming to say in this statement. It aims very high. In calling this man the Son or the eternal Word of God, in ascribing to this man in His unity with God a divine being and nature, it is not speaking only or even primarily of Him but of God. It tells us that God for His part is God in His unity with this creature, this man, in His human and creaturely nature—and this without ceasing to be God, without any alteration or diminution of His divine nature. But this statement concerning God is so bold that we dare not make it unless we consider seriously in what sense we can do so. It must not contain any blasphemy, however involuntary or well-meant, or however pious. That it does do this is to this very day the complaint of Judaism and Islam against the Christian confession of the deity of Christ. It cannot be taken lightly. It cannot be secured by a mere repetition of this confession. We must be able to answer for this confession and its statement about God with a good conscience and with good reason. We must be able to show that God is honoured and not dishonoured by this confession. And at this point the traditional theology of the Church gives rise to an ambiguity. One service which we cannot deny to earlier and more recent discussions of the *kenosis* is that they drew attention to this ambiguity. The ambiguity is one which needs to be removed.

Cur Deus homo? is the question we shall have to deal with in the second part of this section—the question concerning the necessity of the incarnation of the Word. But it presupposes that we have already answered the question concerning its possibility from the standpoint of God: *Quo iure Deus homo?* And we must pause to consider this for a moment. At this point the following alternatives suggest themselves.

The incarnation of the Word, the human being of God, His condescension, His way into the far country, His existence in the *forma servi*, is something which we can understand—this is (or appears to be) the first alternative—by supposing that in it we have to do with a *novum mysterium* (in the strict and literal sense of the expression of Melito of Sardis), with what is noetically and logically an absolute paradox, with what is ontically the fact of a cleft or rift or gulf in God Himself, between His being and essence in Himself and His activity and work as the Reconciler of the world created by Him. It therefore pleased Him in this latter, for the redemption of the world, not to alter Himself, but to deny the immutability of His being, His divine nature, to be in discontinuity with Himself, to be against Himself, to set Himself in self-contradiction. In Himself He was still the omnipresent, almighty, eternal and glorious One, the All-Holy and All-Righteous who could not be tempted. But at the same time among us and for us He was quite different, not omnipresent and eternal but limited in time and space, not almighty but impotent, not glorious but lowly, and open to radical and total attack in respect of His righteousness and holiness. His identity with Himself consisted strictly in His determination to be God, our God, the Reconciler of the world, in this inner and outer antithesis to Himself. The *quo iure*, the possibility of the incarnation, of His becoming man, consisted in this determination of God to be " God against God," in His free will to be this, in His fathomless mercy as the meaning and purpose of that will. On this view God in His incarnation would not merely give Himself, but give Himself away, give up being God. And if that was His will, who can question His right to make possible this impossibility? Is He not supremely right to exercise His mercy in this way?

Of course this view is seldom or never expressly stated in this pointed way. But it can and must be said that when there is no mention of the second alternative (as is usually the case in traditional theology) the matter has to be more or less clearly stated as though this first alternative has been chosen, as though this " God against God " has to be accepted as the presupposition of the incarnation, of the existence of God in humility. Even the modern kenotics did not go so far as to express themselves in this way. And although in the *Christologie* of Heinrich Vogel (Vol. I, 1949) we may at first get the impression of a tendency in this direction, there are constant warnings against this deduction, and even some clear and positive statements which point in a completely different direction (cf. especially the twenty theses on the unity of the truth in the reconciliation of the contradiction, p. 192–218). But what we need to show and to say clearly at this point is that we do not choose this alternative and why we do not choose it. We also need clearly to set against it its opposite as the only possible alternative.

We must not deceive ourselves. The incarnation, the taking of the *forma servi*, means not only God's becoming a creature, becoming a man—and how this is possible to God without an alteration of His being is not self-evident—but it means His giving Himself up to the contradiction of man against Him, His placing Himself under the judgment under which man has fallen in this contradiction, under the curse of death which rests upon Him. The meaning of the incarnation is plainly revealed in the question of Jesus on the cross : " My God, my God, why hast thou forsaken me ? " (Mk. 15³⁴). The more seriously we take this, the stronger becomes the temptation to approximate to the view of a contradiction and conflict in God Himself. Have we not to accept this view if we are to do justice to what God did for man and what He took upon Himself when He was in Christ, if we are to bring out the mystery of His mercy in all its depth and greatness ?

But at this point what is meant to be supreme praise of God can in fact become supreme blasphemy. God gives Himself, but He does not give Himself away. He does not give up being God in becoming a creature, in becoming man. He does not cease to be God. He does not come into conflict with Himself. He does not sin when in unity with the man Jesus He mingles with sinners and takes their place. And when He dies in His unity with this man, death does not gain any power over Him. He exists as God in the righteousness and the life, the obedience and the resurrection of this man. He makes His own the being of man in contradiction against Him, but He does not make common cause with it. He also makes His own the being of man under the curse of this contradiction, but in order to do away with it as He suffers it. He acts as Lord over this contradiction even as He subjects Himself to it. He frees the creature in becoming a creature. He overcomes the flesh in becoming flesh. He reconciles the world with Himself as He is in Christ. He is not untrue to Himself but true to Himself in this condescension, in this way into the far country. If it were otherwise, if in it He set Himself in contradiction with Himself, how could He reconcile the world with Himself ? Of what value would His deity be to us if—instead of crossing in that deity the very real gulf between Himself and us—He left that deity behind Him in His coming to us, if it came to be outside of Him as He became ours ? What would be the value to us of His way into the far country if in the course of it He lost Himself ? In the folly of such a contradicton to Himself He could obviously only confirm and strengthen us in the antithesis to Him in which we find ourselves. A God who found Himself in this contradiction can obviously only be the image of our own unreconciled humanity projected into deity. We cannot, therefore, choose this alternative in understanding the possibility of His becoming flesh. Nor can we leave it open as a possibility with which we can seriously reckon and sometimes toy. We have to reject it. But it can be positively rejected only as it is firmly replaced by the other alternative (which is not really another, but the only possible one).

We begin with the insight that God is " not a God of confusion, but of peace " (1 Cor. 14[33]). In Him there is no paradox, no antinomy, no division, no inconsistency, not even the possibility of it. He is the Father of lights with whom there is no variableness nor interplay of light and darkness (Jas. 1[17]). What He is and does He is and does in full unity with Himself. It is in full unity with Himself that He is also—and especially and above all—in Christ, that He becomes a creature, man, flesh, that He enters into our being in contradiction, that He takes upon Himself its consequences. If we think that this is impossible it is because our concept of God is too narrow, too arbitrary, too human—far too human. Who God is and what it is to be divine is something we have to learn where God has revealed Himself and His nature, the essence of the divine. And if He has revealed Himself in Jesus Christ as the God who does this, it is not for us to be wiser than He and to say that it is in contradiction with the divine essence. We have to be ready to be taught by Him that we have been too small and perverted in our thinking about Him within the framework of a false idea of God. It is not for us to speak of a contradiction and rift in the being of God, but to learn to correct our notions of the being of God, to reconstitute them in the light of the fact that He does this. We may believe that God can and must only be absolute in contrast to all that is relative, exalted in contrast to all that is lowly, active in contrast to all suffering, inviolable in contrast to all temptation, transcendent in contrast to all immanence, and therefore divine in contrast to everything human, in short that He can and must be only the " Wholly Other." But such beliefs are shown to be quite untenable, and corrupt and pagan, by the fact that God does in fact be and do this in Jesus Christ. We cannot make them the standard by which to measure what God can or cannot do, or the basis of the judgment that in doing this He brings Himself into self-contradiction. By doing this God proves to us that He can do it, that to do it is within His nature. And He shows Himself to be more great and rich and sovereign than we had ever imagined. And our ideas of His nature must be guided by this, and not *vice versa*.

We have to think something after the following fashion. As God was in Christ, far from being against Himself, or at disunity with Himself,

He has put into effect the freedom of His divine love, the love in which He is divinely free. He has therefore done and revealed that which corresponds to His divine nature. His immutability does not stand in the way of this. It must not be denied, but this possibility is included in His unalterable being. He is absolute, infinite, exalted, active, impassible, transcendent, but in all this He is the One who loves in freedom, the One who is free in His love, and therefore not His own prisoner. He is all this as the Lord, and in such a way that He embraces the opposites of these concepts even while He is superior to them. He is all this as the Creator, who has created the world as the reality distinct from Himself but willed and affirmed by Him and therefore as His world, as the world which belongs to Him, in relation to which He can be God and act as God in an absolute way and also a relative, in an infinite and also a finite, in an exalted and also a lowly, in an active and also a passive, in a transcendent and also an immanent, and finally, in a divine and also a human—indeed, in relation to which He Himself can become worldly, making His own both its form, the *forma servi*, and also its cause; and all without giving up His own form, the *forma Dei*, and His own glory, but adopting the form and cause of man into the most perfect communion with His own, accepting solidarity with the world. God can do this. And no limit is set to His ability to do it by the contradiction of the creature against Him. It does not escape Him by turning to that which is not and losing itself in it, for, although He is not the Creator of that which is not, He is its sovereign Lord. It corresponds to and is grounded in His divine nature that in free grace He should be faithful to the unfaithful creature who has not deserved it and who would inevitably perish without it, that in relation to it He should establish that communion between His own form and cause and that of the creature, that He should make His own its being in contradiction and under the consequences of that contradiction, that He should maintain His covenant in relation to sinful man (not surrendering His deity, for how could that help? but giving up and sacrificing Himself), and in that way supremely asserting Himself and His deity. His particular, and highly particularised, presence in grace, in which the eternal Word descended to the lowest parts of the earth (Eph. 4⁹) and tabernacled in the man Jesus (Jn. 1¹⁴), dwelling in this one man in the fulness of His Godhead (Col. 2⁹), is itself the demonstration and exercise of His omnipresence, i.e., of the perfection in which He has His own place which is superior to all the places created by Him, not excluding but including all other places. His omnipotence is that of a divine plenitude of power in the fact that (as opposed to any abstract omnipotence) it can assume the form of weakness and impotence and do so as omnipotence, triumphing in this form. The eternity in which He Himself is true time and the Creator of all time is revealed in the fact that, although our time is that of sin and death, He can enter it and Himself be temporal in it, yet without ceasing to be eternal, able rather to be the Eternal in time. His wisdom does not deny itself, but proclaims itself in what necessarily appears folly to the world ; His righteousness in ranging Himself with the unrighteous as One who is accused with them, as the first, and properly the only One to come under accusation ; His Holiness in having mercy on man, in taking his misery to heart, in willing to share it with him in order to take it away from him. God does not have to dishonour Himself when He goes into the far country, and conceals His glory. For He is truly honoured in this concealment. This concealment, and therefore His condescension as such, is the image and reflection in which we see Him as He is. His glory is the freedom of the love which He exercises and reveals in all this. In this respect it differs from the unfree and loveless glory of all the gods imagined by man. Everything depends on our seeing it, and in it the true and majestic nature of God : not trying to construct it arbitrarily ; but deducing it from its revelation in the divine nature of Jesus Christ. From this we learn that the *forma Dei* consists in the grace in which God Himself assumes and makes His own the *forma servi*. We have to hold fast to this without being disturbed or confused by any pictures of false gods. It is this that we have to see and honour and worship as the mystery of the deity of Christ—not an ontic and inward divine paradox, the postulate of which has its basis only in our own very real contradiction against God and the false ideas of God which correspond to it.

To establish this point from Scripture we must turn again to Phil. 2. We have already drawn attention to the twofold ἑαυτόν used in relation to the emptying and humbling of the One who exists in the divine form of the divine likeness. Whatever He Himself does, even this, takes place in His freedom, and therefore in unity and not in contradiction with Himself, as a self-giving but not as a giving up, not at the cost of Himself, not as an entering into conflict with Himself. And having pictured this self-giving the passage continues : " Wherefore (not ' Nevertheless ') God also hath highly exalted him, and given him a name which is above every name "—the name *Kyrios* given (to the glory of God the Father) to the One who emptied and humbled Himself. And that means that not in spite of the fact that He emptied and humbled Himself, but because of it, because of the fact that in Him that self-giving and concealment of God (in and under the form of a servant) actually took place, there belongs to Him the name as the bearer of which He exercises the function in which He glorifies God with all creatures in heaven and earth and under the earth, in which He is the One in acknowledging whom all creation must give God the glory. We are again reminded of the call of the Saviour in Mt. 11²⁸ᶠ·, the imperative of which : Come unto me, Take my yoke upon you, Learn of me, has such an astonishing basis : For I am meek and lowly in heart. This basis is meaningful if the One who speaks the imperative is the Lord and has authority and can give a binding command for the very reason that He is meek and lowly in heart. But at this point we have to do with a far-reaching consideration in New Testament ethics.

The hymn on the humiliated and therefore the exalted Jesus Christ quoted by Paul in Phil. 2⁶ᶠ· is obviously set in the context of an exhortation to concord, in which the final lesson is that in lowliness of mind (τῇ ταπεινοφροσύνῃ) the readers should each esteem other better than themselves, not looking every man on his own things, but every man also on things of others. They are to have the mind (τοῦτο φρονεῖτε) in them (ἐν ὑμῖν) which was also in Christ Jesus (ἐν Χριστῷ Ἰησοῦ), who having the form of God. . . . As we have seen, the law of ταπεινοφροσύνη applies in the first instance to Christ Jesus. He entered under this law, and because He went His way under it He was exalted to be the Lord. They are to model themselves on His bowing beneath this law. In this way they are to live with one another and to be at peace. We have to do with the one binding law for both the Head and the members, for Jesus and His people, and because for Jesus therefore also for His people. Why is it this law ? Why is it in ταπεινοφροσύνη that Christians are to unite themselves with Christ ?

The same thought occurs elsewhere in Paul. With a remarkable similarity to this passage in Phil. 2 he says in 2 Cor. 11⁷ : " I abase myself that ye might be exalted." According to 2 Cor. 10¹ he had been κατὰ πρόσωπον base among the Corinthians. According to 2 Cor. 7⁶ His God is the God " that comforteth them that are cast down." In Phil. 4¹² Paul boasts that he knows how to abase and how to abound. The exhortation in Rom. 12¹⁶ is to the same purport : " Mind not ὑψηλά but condescend to that which is lowly." Hence the summons in Gal. 6² to bear one another's burdens and so fulfil the law of Christ. Hence ὑποταγή as the basic concept in the Christian attitude to the civil powers (Rom. 13¹ᶠ·), but also in the attitude of wives to their husbands (Col. 3¹⁸), and also according to Eph. 5²⁰ in the attitude of all Christians one toward another. Hence the ὑπακοή of children to their parents (Col. 3²⁰) and servants to their masters (Col. 3²²). Hence the τιμή, the respect in which, according to Rom. 12¹⁰, all Christians are to prefer one another, and which, according to 1 Pet. 2¹⁷, they all owe one another. Hence the description of ταπεινοφροσύνη in 1 Pet. 5⁵ as the " girdle " with which all Christians are to be girdled in their relationship one to another, setting themselves in the appropriate place. And to the same category there obviously belongs 1 Cor. 1²⁶ᶠ·, the well-known passage on the external aspect of the Christian community : " For ye see your calling, brethren, how that not many wise men after the flesh, not many mighty, not many noble are called ; but God hath chosen the foolish things of the world to confound the wise ; and God hath chosen the weak things of the world to confound the things which are mighty ; and base things of the world, and things which are despised, hath God chosen, yea, and things which are not, to bring to nought things that are : that no flesh should glory in his presence." Why is this necessarily the case ? Why is there this radical downward trend ? Why do the authors of the First Epistle to Peter (5⁵) and the Epistle of James (4⁶) love that saying from the Proverbs (3³⁴) : " God resisteth the proud, but giveth grace to the humble " ? Why can Paul (necessarily) write in 1 Cor. 15³¹ : " I die daily," and in 2 Cor. 12⁹ᶠ· : " Most gladly therefore will I rather glory in my weakness, that the power of Christ may rest upon me," and : " I take pleasure (εὐδοκῶ) in infirmities, in reproaches, in necessities (ἐν ἀνάγκαις), in persecutions, in distresses for Christ's sake : for when I am weak, then am I strong " ? And what is the Word of the Lord addressed to him and heard by him : " My grace is sufficient for thee : for my strength is made perfect (τελεῖται) in weakness " ? We see that it is a matter of fellowship with Christ, with His life and finally with His suffering : " Always bearing about in the body the dying (in Gal. 6¹⁷ the marks, στίγματα) of the Lord Jesus . . . always in our mortal flesh delivered unto death for Jesus' sake " (2 Cor. 4¹⁰ᶠ·). The necessity to follow in His steps rests on a looking to Christ and His way as an example (ὑπογραμμός), just as in the First Epistle of Peter (2²¹ and *passim*) we are in the same context compellingly summoned to patience in suffering. Even in 1 Cor. 1²⁶ᶠ· it is a matter of the connexion of the communion of the lowly with the crucified Jesus. But what is the authority and force of the law that necessarily leads into this community with Christ ?

At this point we are taken beyond the indications which point in this direction in the New Testament Epistles to the (if possible) even more radical and comprehensive sayings of the Gospels. The kind of thing that we already find in Lk. 1[51] in the Song of Mary even before the birth of Christ : " He hath put down the mighty from their seats, and exalted them of low degree." Why does it say this ? Or the saying that we must humble ourselves like a child placed in the midst of adults if we are to be the greatest in the kingdom of heaven (Mt. 18[4]). Or the saying in Lk. 14[11] : " For whosoever exalteth himself shall be abased, and (the second part is remarkably like Phil. 2) he that humbleth himself shall be exalted." Or the similar inversion in Mk. 10[31] : " But many that are first shall be last and the last first." Or even more sharply in Mk. 8[35], the saying about trying to save one's life and losing it, and saving it in losing it for the sake of Jesus and the Gospel. Or in Mk. 8[34] the saying about the necessity to deny one's self and take up one's cross. Or at the beginning of the Sermon on the Mount (Mt. 5[3f.]) the blessing of the poor in spirit—taken simply as praise of the poor in Luke's Gospel and the Epistle of James—of those that mourn, of the meek, of those that hunger and thirst after righteousness, of the merciful, of those who are persecuted and reviled and slandered for righteousness' sake. Or (in Mt. 5[39f.]) the command not to resist evil, to allow oneself to be smitten on both cheeks, to give one's coat and one's cloak also, and above all, in Mt. 5[43f.], the injunction to love one's enemies and to pray for one's persecutors. Why is it that here too—and especially here—this is the tenor of New Testament exhortation ?

The very strange and yet in some way remarkably illuminating content and the unconditional form of these demands have often been rather idly admired and valued as exemplary, while their manifest impracticability has been indolently affirmed and deplored. As against that, men like Francis of Assissi and Tolstoy and others have called us to take it all quite literally and to put it into practice, and that was obviously the original idea of monasticism in a Church which was being rapidly secularised. Again, it was this which so dreadfully affected the nerves of Nietzsche as the perverse philosophy of the small man triumphing at the time of the decadence of antiquity. Our simple question is : What underlies this conception of human life ? What is it that gives to New Testament ethics this direction, this tendency, this dynamic, this pull which in experience has again and again been found to be dominant and exclusive and irresistible, setting aside all pretexts and excuses, the pull from the heights to the depths, from riches to poverty, from victory to defeat, from triumph to suffering, from life to death ? This pull is obviously connected with the way and example of Jesus Christ. It is nothing other than the call accepted by the New Testament witnesses, the compulsion which they felt, to enter into and to remain in fellowship with the Crucified. This is clearly enough emphasised in many passages in the New Testament. Col. 1[24] is a culminating statement with a genuine Pauline flavour. Here the apostle describes his sufferings as a filling up in the place of Christ, an ἀνταναπληροῦν τὰ ὑστερήματα, " of the afflictions of Christ for his body's sake, which is the church." To understand this properly, we must disperse any remaining appearance of chance or arbitrariness with which the whole phenomenon might be enshrouded.

As we have seen, in its ethics the New Testament is speaking in terms of necessity, not of chance or arbitrariness, if in all these sayings—as in those concerning the lowly existence of the man Jesus as the Son of God—we have to do with a reflection of the New Testament concept of God. If in fellowship with Christ Christians have to be μιμηταὶ θεοῦ (Eph. 5[1]), if the τελειότης, the fulfilment of the being and essence, of their heavenly Father is the measure and norm of their own τελειότης (Mt. 5[48]), then in its original and final authority and compulsion the demand addressed to them is necessarily this and no other. The περισσόν, the special thing which is commanded of and has to be done by them as distinct from the publicans and Gentiles, is that which marks them out as the children of the Father in heaven, the περισσόν of God Himself which cannot be lacking in His children. God does not love only those who love Him, or greet only His brethren : " He maketh his sun to rise on the evil and on the good, and sendeth rain on the just and on the unjust " (Mt. 5⁴⁵). He obviously does not have to be exalted ; He can also be lowly. He does not have to be alone or among friends ; He can also be abroad among enemies. He does not have to judge only ; He can also forgive. And in being lowly He is exalted. Among His enemies as their God He is supremely exalted. In forgiving He judges in righteousness. As this God, in this divine nature, as the " Father of mercies " (2 Cor. 1³), as the " God that comforteth those that are cast down " (2 Cor. 7⁶), He is the Father of Jesus Christ, the One who in Him reconciles the world to Himself. And as this God He is the Law-giver and Himself the law for those who know Him in Jesus Christ, who can rejoice in their own atonement made in Jesus Christ : those who can recognise themselves as the children of God in Jesus Christ (exalted in Him and by Him). From this point their way leads into the depths, and ταπεινο-φροσύνη is not to them something strange or remarkable, an ideal which is quite impracticable in its strict sense. It is necessarily that which is natural to them. From this point they cannot choose whether they will exalt or abase themselves, whether they will save their life or lose it and in that way save it, whether they will leave or take up their cross, whether they will be offended by the beatitudes or put themselves under the light of them, whether they will hate their enemies or love them, whether they will accept or not accept the exhortation to ὑποταγή, to ὑπακοή, to τιμή, to the bearing of the burdens of others, to suffering in the discipleship of Christ. This could and would be a matter of choice, and the choice would not be in accordance with the directions of the New Testament, if the God in whose name and authority it is demanded were like the scribes and Pharisees of whom it is said in Mt. 23⁴ : " For they bind heavy burdens grievous to be borne, and lay them on men's shoulders ; but they themselves will not move them with one of their fingers," or if He were like the doctors who take good care not to take the medicine they prescribe for others, if He had no part in the ταπεινοφροσύνη He demands of others, if He were the wholly other God, absolute, high and exalted, far removed from any lowliness and quite alien to it. To achieve the obedience demanded in the New Testament no less than every-thing depends upon the fact that He is not this God. If He were, then that strange basic feature in New Testament ethics might be regarded as accidental and arbitrary, as facultative and non-obligatory. There would then be good reason to turn this ethics into a moral system, with high praise for its idealism or impatience at its unworldliness and unpractical nature, or perhaps in the form of doubtful experiments, filling it out from the goodly store of practical wisdom and so reducing it *ad absurdum*. According to the New Testament this obviously cannot happen because God does not stand in the far distance high above this ethics, but it is His divine nature to exist in the sense of this ethics, this ethics being only the reflection of His own being. It does not call man under a yoke that He must bear in the name of God because God wills it. It calls him into the freedom of the children of God, into a following of the freedom and the work in which God Himself is God.

Although it has seldom been appealed to in this way, New Testament ethics is an indirect and additional attestation of the true Godhead of Christ. True Godhead in the New Testament is being in the absolute freedom of love, and therefore the being of the Most High who is high and almighty and eternal and righteous and glorious not also but precisely in His lowliness. The direct New Testament attestation of this Godhead of Christ is the attestation of the man Jesus Himself as the Son of God become flesh and suffering and crucified and dying for us, the message of Christ crucified (1 Cor. 1²³, 2²). It is clear that in the sense of the New Testament this and this alone is decisive and basic. There is no lowliness which is divine in itself and as such. There is therefore no general principle of the cross in which we have to do with God (in principle). The cross in the New Testament is not a kind of symbol of an outlook which is negatively orientated, which speculates *à la baisse*. The limits of humanity are one thing, but God's visitation of us in the limits of humanity, in our creatureliness, in our humanness, in our sinfulness and mortality, in the incarnation of His Word and the crucifixion of His Son, that is quite another. Salvation is not in those limits, but in the concrete event of this visitation, in what took place in the man Jesus. And the Godhead revealed and active in this event is His Godhead. But the Godhead which the New Testament attests directly as His alone it attests indirectly in the form of the commandment under which it sees His people placed with Him, which it applies to the men of this people. The existential factor in the Christian claim which calls men from the heights to the depths, and therefore to suffering and dying with Christ, is not the first thing in the New Testament but the second, not the *a priori* of the *kerygma* but the *a posteriori*. The content of the New Testament *kerygma* is in substance the way of Jesus Christ and only in accident the way of the believer in Him. The second stands or falls with the first. First of all Jesus Christ is the Son of God and as such, in conformity with the divine nature, the Most High who humbles Himself and in that way is exalted and very high. Only then are Christians " in Christ," delivered by God " from the power of darkness, and translated into the kingdom of the Son of his love " (Col. 1¹³). It is only because He is the Son of God in this sense that they are called and empowered in fellowship with Him to choose the ταπεινοφροσύνη which is natural to the children of God. Always this second and existential aspect follows and confirms the first. That it should follow and confirm it is necessary, just as it is necessary that there should be this fellowship of man with the God who is in being and essence this God, just as it is necessary that this fellowship should be a fellowship with Christ in whom He has made His being and essence open and accessible to men, just as it is necessary that this fellowship grounded in Him should be lived out by men and put into effect in their existence. The true deity of Christ is to be known and understood and believed and confessed in both the first and the second, the direct and the indirect form, but in this irreversible order and sequence. It is the deity of the true God revealed in the humility of Christ which as such can and must find its confirmation in our own humiliation. But the confirmation is of something which so far as I know Gregory of Nyssa (*Or. Cat.* 24) was the only one of the Church fathers expressly to mention : that the descent to humility which took place in the incarnation of the Word is not only not excluded by the divine nature but signifies its greatest glory : περιουσία τίς ἐστιν τῆς δυνάμεως.

The way of the Son of God into the far country is the way of obedience. This is (*in re*) the first and inner moment of the mystery of the deity of Christ. Now that we have dealt with the second and outer moment, it is to this that we must turn.

We have seen already that if in faith in Jesus Christ we are ready to learn, to be told, what Godhead, or the divine nature, is, we are confronted with the revelation of what is and always will be to all other ways of looking and thinking a mystery, and indeed a mystery which offends. The mystery reveals to us that for God it is just as natural to be lowly as it is to be high, to be near as it is to be far, to be little as it is to be great, to be abroad as to be at home. Thus that when in the presence and action of Jesus Christ in the world created by Him and characterised *in malam partem* by the sin of man He chooses to go into the far country, to conceal His form of lordship in the form of this world and therefore in the form of a servant, He is not untrue to Himself but genuinely true to Himself, to the freedom which is that of His love. He does not have to choose and do this. He is free in relation to it. We are therefore dealing with the genuine article when He does choose and do this. Even in the form of a servant, which is the form of His presence and action in Jesus Christ, we have to do with God Himself in His true deity. The humility in which He dwells and acts in Jesus Christ is not alien to Him, but proper to Him. His humility is a *novum mysterium* for us in whose favour He executes it when He makes use of His freedom for it, when He shows His love even to His enemies and His life even in death, thus revealing them in a way which is quite contrary to all our false ideas of God. But for Him this humility is no *novum mysterium*. It is His sovereign grace that He wills to be and is amongst us in humility, our God, God for us. But He shows us this grace, He is amongst us in humility, our God, God for us, as that which He is in Himself, in the most inward depth of His Godhead. He does not become another God. In the condescension in which He gives Himself to us in Jesus Christ He exists and speaks and acts as the One He was from all eternity and will be to all eternity. The truth and actuality of our atonement depends on this being the case. The One who reconciles the world with God is necessarily the one God Himself in His true Godhead. Otherwise the world would not be reconciled with God. Otherwise it is still the world which is not reconciled with God.

But we must dig deeper if we are to understand the free love of God established in the event of atonement. If the humility of Christ is not simply an attitude of the man Jesus of Nazareth, if it is the attitude of this man because, according to what takes place in the atonement made in this man (according to the revelation of God in Him), there is a humility grounded in the being of God, then something else is grounded in the being of God Himself. For, according to the New Testament, it is the case that the humility of this man is an act of obedience, not a capricious choice of lowliness, suffering and dying, not an autonomous decision this way, not an accidental swing of the pendulum in this direction, but a free choice made in recognition of an appointed order, in execution of a will which imposed itself authoritatively upon Him, which was intended to be obeyed. If, then, God is in Christ, if what the man Jesus does is God's own work, this aspect of the self-emptying and self-humbling of Jesus Christ as an act of obedience cannot be alien to God. But in this case we have to see here the other and inner side of the mystery of the divine nature of Christ and therefore of the nature of the one true God—that He Himself is also able and free to render obedience.

We remember again the prayer in Gethsemane, and also the fact that in Phil. 2⁸ His ταπεινοφροσύνη is explained in terms of a becoming obedient, and in Heb. 5⁸ His suffering in terms of a learning of obedience. In Heb. 12² the fact

D.R.—7

that He suffered on the cross and despised the shame is described as a ὑπομένειν and in Heb. 2[18] as endurance in temptation. Rom. 5[19] tells us unmistakably that through the obedience of one many shall be made righteous, and in 2 Cor. 10[5] Paul shows us that it is his aim to bring every thought captive to the ὑπακοὴ τοῦ Χριστοῦ, an expression which surely has to be understood as a *Gen. sub.* as well as a *Gen. obj.* To the same context belongs the fact that there is at least one stratum in the tradition, still maintained in the 2nd century, in which Jesus Christ (Mt. 12[18] ; Ac. 3[13, 26] ; 4[27, 30]) is not called υἱός, or rather this concept is given a particular nuance in reminiscence of David and the Servant of the Lord (Is. 53) and He is called the holy παῖς θεοῦ. We also remember the pitiless δεῖ of the Synoptic prophecies of the passion. And it should again be emphasised that the same Gospel of John which leaves no possible doubt about the deity of Christ in His unity with the Father no less plainly—and with particular reference to His way of suffering and death—represents Him as the One who is sent, who has a commission and who has to execute it as such, as the Son who lives to do His Father's will, to speak His words, to accomplish His work and to seek His glory.

Why is it so important to see that when we say all these things about the man Jesus we say them about God ? Obviously because the being of Jesus Christ in humility, His suffering and dying, and therefore the act of atonement made in Him, are marked off by their characterisation as an act of obedience from the accidental events of nature or destiny. Jesus cannot go any other way than this way into the depths, into the far country. And if it is the case that as the Son of God He is not alone on this way, if the Father is on this way with Him (Jn. 16[32]), if therefore in going this way He acts in the freedom of God, making use of a possibility grounded in the being of God, then the fact that He does so in obedience makes it plain that there is no question of God Himself being controlled by caprice or chance. The freedom in which God can be lowly as well as exalted, abroad as well as at home, our God in the hidden form of One who is accused and judged as well as in Himself (and known only to Himself) the Lord of glory—this freedom of which God makes use in His action as the Reconciler of the world is not simply an arbitrary ability. It is not a mere capacity to be now in this way and now in some other way, now above and now below. It is not a disorderliness and carelessness in God. But if " the Father's Son, by nature God, A guest this world of ours He trod " (Luther), if God made use of His freedom in this sense, then the fact that the use of this freedom is an act of obedience characterises it as a holy and righteous freedom, in which God is not a victim driven to and fro by the dialectic of His divine nature, but is always His own master. He does not make just any use of the possibilities of His divine nature, but He makes one definite use which is necessary on the basis and in fulfilment of His own decision. If this really happens, if God (in virtue of the richness of His divine being) does make it a fact in our history, in the created world and as a temporal event, that He " dwells in the high and holy place, with him also that is of a contrite and humble spirit," if in virtue of His true divine nature it is His own good pleasure actually in this condescension "to revive the spirit of the humble, and to revive the heart of the contrite ones " (Is. 57[15]), then this is quite in order, since it is His own will which is done, His own plan and decision which is executed. In this happening we have to do with a divine commission and its divine execution, with a divine order and divine obedience. What takes place is the divine fulfilment of a divine decree. It takes place in the freedom of God, but in the inner necessity of the freedom of God and not in the play of a sovereign *liberum arbitrium*. There is no possibility of something quite different happening. When we are confronted with this event as the saving event which took place for us, which redeems us, which calls us to faith and penitence, we do not have to do with one of the throws in a game of chance which takes place in the divine being, but with the foundation-rock of a divine decision which is as we find it divinely fulfilled in this saving event and not otherwise. It is therefore worthy of unlimited confidence and only in unlimited confidence can it be appreciated. It can demand obedience because it is not itself an arbitrary decision but a decision of obedience. That is why it is so important to see that this is the character of the self-humiliation of God in Jesus Christ as the presupposition of our reconciliation.

But it is clear that once again, and this time in all seriousness, we are confronted with the mystery of the deity of Christ. Let us grant that this insight is right, that what the New Testament says about the obedience of Christ, on His way as a way of suffering, has its basis, even as a statement about the man Jesus, in His divine nature and therefore in God Himself. Does this make the mystery of His deity even more difficult and perhaps impenetrable ? Or do we have in this insight the real key to an understanding of it, to the knowledge of it as an open secret ?

We cannot conceal the fact that it is a difficult and even an elusive thing to speak of obedience which takes place in God Himself. Obedience implies an above and a below, a *prius* and a *posterius*, a superior and a junior and subordinate. Obedience as a possibility and actuality in God Himself seems at once to compromise the unity and then logically the equality of the divine being. Can the one God command and obey ? Can the one God be above and below, the superior and the subordinate ? If we speak of an obedience which takes place in God, do we not have to speak necessarily of two divine beings, and then of two beings who are not equally divine, the first and commanding properly divine, the second and obeying only divine in an improper sense ? But what is divinity in an improper sense ? Even if this second being which is divine in an improper sense is supremely distinguished by the true and proper God both in quality and in orientation to Him, is he not still on the side of the world created by Him and therefore of the reality which is distinct from Him, and therefore not qualified to be the subject of the reconciliation of the world with God ?

Subordinationism of every age and type has committed itself to this questionable path. It has solved the mystery of the deity of Christ by dissolving it, by taking the statement about the deity of Christ only in an improper sense, by trying to understand it as the designation of a second divine being of lesser divinity—which, if we follow it through logically, necessarily means the hyperbolic description of a heavenly or earthly creature standing in supreme fellowship with God and to that extent itself supremely qualified. In favour of those who support this view we have to admit that they were obviously impressed by, and tried to take with full seriousness, the witness of the New Testament to the humiliation of Christ and therefore to His lowliness and obedience. But they regarded it as quite impossible to harmonise the assertion of His true deity with this witness. Obstinately preferring this witness, and in order to maintain it, they interpreted the assertion in such a way that its content was explained away and lost. They did not see that in doing this they destroyed the meaning and weight of the witness to the humiliation and the lowliness and the obedience of Christ. If the deity of Christ is interpreted in that way, this obedience acquires the character of an event in this world. But it was and is impossible to see how many can be made righteous by the obedience of a being which is not properly God, of a supremely qualified creature (Rom. 5[19]). It was and is impossible to see what value or justification there can be for trying to bring every thought captive to the obedience of such a being.

A second alternative which presents itself is as follows. We must certainly accept and take seriously the whole sphere in which we have to speak of a divine obedience, in which, therefore, we have to reckon with an above and a below, a *prius* and a *posterius*, a superiority and a subordination in God. We must regard it as a definite sphere of God's revelation, of His speaking and activity and operation. But we must isolate this whole sphere by stating that in it we have to do only with a kind of forecourt of the divine being, with a divine dispensation (economy) in favour of, and with respect to, the particular nature of the world, not therefore with the true and proper and non-worldly being of God. There is, then, a commanding and an obeying divine being, but in a true equality, only as worldly forms or appearances of true Godhead, and therefore only in the sphere of the improper being of Godhead. But that is the weakness of this explanation. For obviously we have to ask what is this worldly, and purely economic, and therefore improper being of the true God. If His economy of revelation and salvation is distinguished from His proper being as worldly, does it bring us into touch with God Himself or not? Has He Himself really taken up the cause of the world or not? Has He really made Himself worldly for the world's sake or not? Obviously, according to this theory, He has not done so. In fact He has only acted as though He had done so. But if He has not, how can there be on this theory any reconciliation of the world with God?

We are referring to a solution—the direct opposite of Subordinationism—which has been attempted both in ancient and more modern times along the lines of Modalism. The main point of Modalism is to try to keep the true deity of the humiliated and lowly and obedient Christ, but to interpret the being of this Christk as a mere mode of appearance or revelation or activity of the one true Godhead, beside which there are the other modes of the ruling Father and also of the Holy Spirit. Sometimes, indeed, it is preferred, as it was originally, to identify God the Father with the true Godhead which does not appear in this world. On this view Christ is not deprived of true deity, but of any true and proper being. The drift is obvious. We must maintain the true deity of Christ as identical with the Godhead of the Father, but only in such a way that no hurt is done to His deity by His humiliation, lowliness and obedience. Hence the distinction between a proper and an improper being of God, an immanent and a purely economic. Hence the true deity of Christ only in this second sense, only in the forecourt of the divine being, only as a mode of appearance of the true Godhead which is untouched by this dualism of above and below. Unfortunately it was not noticed that in this way the meaning and relevance of the statement maintained against the Subordinationists were compromised, and it was no less emptied of force than on the opposite side where it was explained and ultimately explained away. For if in His proper being as God God can only be unworldly, if He can be the humiliated and lowly and obedient One only in a mode of appearance and not in His proper being, what is the value of the true deity of Christ, what is its value for us ? It is as the humiliated and lowly and obedient One that He is the Reconciler. But can He reconcile if He has no proper being as the Reconciler, but only that of a form of appearance of the one true God, who has no part in the atonement ?

These two attempts at a solution were often made in the 2nd and 3rd centuries in relatively harmless, because inconsistent and ambiguous, forms. We find both of them in acknowledged teachers of the Church : a kind of Subordination-ism in Tertullian, for example, and a kind of Modalism in Irenaeus. Both were finally rejected as unsatisfactory by the Early Church. In their developed form (in the doctrine of Paul of Samosata, on the one hand, and that of Sabellius on the other) they were recognised to be heretical, being condemned as errors in which we cannot do justice to the mystery of the deity of Christ.

The questions raised by these two solutions are questions which we cannot evade. It will be wiser, then, not to try to circumvent the difficulty as these two solutions did, but to engage it in frontal assault.

Let us first review the three presuppositions which, at all costs, we must accept and affirm.

It is a matter (1) of determining the acting subject of the reconciliation of the world with God. According to the witness of the New Testament, when we have to do with Jesus Christ we are dealing with the author and finisher of this work, with the Mediator between God and man, with the One who makes peace between the two, with no other and no less than the One who has taken upon Himself and away from the world the enmity of the world against God and the curse which rests upon it, with the One who (we shall treat of this in the second part of the section) accomplishes the ineluctable judgment of the world in such a way that He Himself bears it in order to bear it away. We have to do with the One who has the competence and power for this work. In relation to the fact that He is the One who does this, the New Testament witness to His deity has to be under-stood and taken seriously as expressed in the different titles under which it speaks of Him. Everything depends upon our seeing and understanding as the New Testament does that He is the acting subject in this work. If we grant that we are at one with the New Testament in this, we must also follow it in seeing the true God at work in Him. In matters of the atonement of the world with God the world itself cannot act—for it is the world which is at enmity with God, which stands in need of reconciliation with Him. It cannot act even in the form of a supreme and best being produced by it and belonging to it. Anyone other or less than the true God is not a legitimate subject competent to act in this matter. At this point the subordinationist interpretation is evasive. And it has to be rejected as unsatisfactory. When we have to do with Jesus Christ we have to do with God. What He does is a work which can only be God's own work, and not the work of another.

But (2) it is a matter of the subject of the atonement as an event which takes place not only to the world but in the world, which not only touches the world from without but affects it from within to convert it to God, which is itself an event in the world. According to the witness of the New Testament, the world is not abandoned and left to its own devices. God takes it to Himself, entering into the sphere of it as the true God, causing His kingdom to come on earth as in heaven, becoming Himself truly ours, man, flesh, in order to overcome sin where it has its dominion, in the flesh, to take away in His own person the ensuing curse where it is operative, in the creaturely world, in the reality which is distinct from Himself. It is in relation to the fact that what He does in the atonement He does in this way, in the power of His own presence and action, that we have to take seriously the New Testament witness to the being of the one true God in Jesus Christ ; the realistic and not the nominalistic sense in which it accords these titles to Jesus Christ, whatever they are and however their formulation may be taken. Again everything depends on our accepting and following out in all its realism the New Testament presupposition " God was in Christ." If we grant this—as the *credo* of Christian confession assumes—we have to follow the New Testament in understanding the presence and action of God in Jesus Christ as the most proper and direct and immediate presence and action of the one true God in the sphere of human and world history. If this is not so, then as the subject of the act of atonement He can only touch the world from without, not affect it from within, not truly convert it to Himself. It would not, therefore, be a real reconciliation of the world with Him. At this point the modalistic interpretation of the deity of Christ is evasive. And for that reason it must be regarded as unsatisfactory and rejected. When we have to do with Jesus Christ we do have to do with an " economy " but not with the kind of economy in which His true and proper being remains behind an improper being, a being " as if." We have to do with an economy in which God is truly Himself and Himself acts and intervenes in the world. Otherwise the atonement made in this economy is not a true atonement.)

It is a matter (3)—and this is the connecting point—of the one true God being Himself the subject of the act of atonement in such a way that His presence and action as the Reconciler of the world coincide and are indeed identical with the existence of the humiliated and lowly and obedient man Jesus of Nazareth. He acts as the Reconciler in that—as the true God identical with this man—He humbles Himself and becomes lowly and obedient. He becomes and is this without being in contradiction to His divine nature (He is not therefore exposed to the postulate that He can become and be this only as a creature), but in contradiction to all human ideas about the divine nature. He becomes and is this without encroaching on Himself (He is not subject to the postulate that He can become and be this only improperly, in an appearance which is alien to His own being), but as a saving approach to us, an encroachment upon us which is authoritative and demands our conversion. According to the New Testament witness we have the presence and action not only of the man Jesus, but in the existence of that man the action and presence which is supremely proper to God Himself as the Reconciler of the world. God chooses condescension. He chooses humiliation, lowliness and obedience. In this way He illuminates the darkness, opening up that which is closed. In this way He brings help where there is no other help. In this way He accepts solidarity with the creature, with man, in order to reconcile man and the world with Himself, in order to convert man and the world to Himself. The God of the New Testament witness is the God who makes this choice, who in agreement with Himself and His divine nature, but in what is for us the revelation of a *novum mysterium*, humbles Himself and is lowly and obedient amongst us. In this respect, too, the New Testament witness has to be taken seriously. Everything depends on our accepting this presupposition, on our seeing and understanding what the New Testament witnesses obviously saw and understood, the proper being of the one true God in Jesus Christ the Crucified. Granted that we do see and understand this, we cannot refuse to accept the humiliation and lowliness and supremely the obedience of Christ as the dominating moment in our conception of God. Therefore we must determine to seek and find the key to the whole difficult and heavily freighted concept of the " divine nature " at the point where it appears to be quite impossible—except for those whose thinking is orientated on Him in this matter—the fact that Jesus Christ was obedient unto death, even the death of the cross. It is from this point, and this point alone, that the concept is legitimately possible.

We can now see the error which is common to the subordinationist and the modalist presentation and solution of the problem. Both suffer from the fact that they try to evade the cross of Jesus Christ, i.e., the truth of the humiliation, the lowliness and the obedience of the one true God Himself as it became an event amongst us in Jesus

Christ as the subject of the reconciliation of the world with God. They evade it because they start from the assumption that it cannot be accepted as true. And they then err in their different ways as they try to escape the dilemma which they themselves have created, interpreting the obedient Christ either as some heavenly or earthly being distinct from God, or as a mere mode of appearance of the one true God. Both damage and indeed destroy the nerve of the New Testament knowledge of Christ. Both solve the christological mystery by juggling it away, and for that reason both show themselves to be quite useless.

They were both rightly rejected by the Early Church. We can add that in the first instance they could both be undertaken in good faith, because even serious and perspicacious theologians of both schools did not at first see that they were in fact taking offence where no offence must be taken, and that by trying to remove the offence they were compromising the very centre of all Christian knowledge. We can also add that the attempts had to be made because only then could their unsatisfactory character be exposed. If they had not been made, the possibility of evasion in one or other of these directions would have worked like an arrested fever in the thought of the Church. In the history of theology and dogma there have been many such blind alleys which had to be followed to the point where they proved to be such in order that they should no longer be confused with the right way, and in order to make necessary and to stir up a search for the right way. This is the relative necessity more than once ascribed to heresy by the fathers. In fact, Athanasius and Nicaea would not have been possible without the obscurities and errors of the 2nd and 3rd centuries.

It is another question to maintain, and to make again as we ought, the distinction between the right and the wrong path as it was made by Athanasius and at Nicaea. The blind alleys are always there, and have proved attractive again and again as they still do to-day. The warning signs set up at the entrance to them can easily be overlooked, and have often been overlooked. The right way found at that time can still be lost again, and has from time to time been lost. Subordinationism and Modalism, the teachings of Paul of Samosata and Sabellius, are not dead, and by nature we all of us incline to one or the other or perhaps both in some form. We have continually to seek afresh for the right way in thankfulness for what has been known and stated. That is what we have tried to do here. We shall not serve the cause of the recognition which is necessary in the Church to-day simply by retreating or paraphrasing or commentating on the decision which brought the controversy to the 2nd and 3rd centuries to a victorious end. We are reminded by Nicaea in which direction we have to look. Our own conclusions, which are formally independent of the dogma proclaimed there, have inclined us to look in the same direction. We will now try to go further in this direction, not losing contact with the dogma but again following our own path.

Is it a fact that in relation to Jesus Christ we can speak of an obedience of the one true God Himself in His proper being ? From the three inalienable presuppositions just expounded it is plain that we not only can do so but have to do so, that we cannot avoid doing so either on the one side or on the other. We have not only not to deny but actually to affirm and understand as essential to the being of God the offensive fact that there is in God Himself an above and a below, a *prius* and a *posterius*, a superiority and a subordination. And our present concern is with what is apparently the most offensive fact of all, that there is a below, a *posterius*, a subordination, that it belongs to the inner life of God that there should take place within it obedience.

We have to reckon with such an event even in the being and life of God Himself. It cannot be explained away either as an event in some higher or supreme creaturely sphere or as a mere appearance of God. Therefore we have to state firmly that, far from preventing this possibility, His divine unity consists in the fact that in Himself He is both One who is obeyed and Another who obeys.

There is another thing outside of God, the world created by Him as the totality of the reality willed and posited by Him and distinct from Him. In this totality as His elect creature there is another person, His worldly counterpart κατ᾽ ἐξοχήν man, who, according to Gen. 1²⁷, is in his twofoldness as man and woman the image of God, the image primarily of His co-existence as Creator with the creature, His will not to be alone as God, but to be together with His creature, the God of His creature—yet not merely the image of this relationship *ad extra*. God did not need this otherness of the world and man. In order not to be alone, single, enclosed within Himself, God did not need co-existence with the creature. He does not will and posit the creature necessarily, but in freedom, as the basic act of His grace. His whole relationship to what is outside Himself—its basis and history from first to last—rests on this fact. For everything that the creature seems to offer Him—its otherness, its being in antithesis to Himself and therefore His own existence in co-existence—He has also in Himself as God, as the original and essential determination of His being and life as God. Without the creature He has all this originally in Himself, and it is His free grace, and not an urgent necessity to stand in a relationship of reciprocity to something other outside Himself, if He allows the creature to participate in it, if, as it were, in superfluity He allows its existence as another, as a counterpart to Himself, and His own co-existence with it. In superfluity—we have to say this because we are in fact dealing with an overflowing, not with a filling up of the perfection of God which needs no filling.

Primarily and originally and properly it is not the cosmos or man which is the other, the counterpart of God, that which co-exists with God. Primarily and originally and properly God is all this in Himself. He does not need on this account to divide into two gods of unequal divinity. That is how myth would have it, confusing the world and man with God, and carrying its own inner differentiation into the Godhead, speaking of the co-existence and reciprocity of a superior god in heaven and a subordinate goddess of earth. No, not in unequal but equal, not in divided but in the one deity, God is both One and also Another, His own counterpart, co-existent with Himself. We can say quite calmly : He exists as a first and as a second, above and below *a priori* and *a posteriori*. To grasp this we have to free ourselves from two unfortunate and very arbitrary ways of thinking.

The first consists quite naturally in the idea that unity is necessarily equivalent with being in and for oneself, with being enclosed and imprisoned in one's own being, with singleness and solitariness. But the unity of God is not like this. It is, of course, exclusively His unity. No other being, no created being, is one with itself as God is. But what distinguishes His peculiar unity with Himself from all other unities or from what we think we know of such unities is the fact that —in a particularity which is exemplary and instructive for an understanding of these others—it is a unity which is open and free and active in itself—a unity in more than one mode of being, a unity of the One with Another, of a first with a second, an above with a below, an origin and its consequences. It is a dynamic and living unity, not a dead and static. Once we have seen this, we will be careful not to regard that mean and unprofitable concept of unity as the last word of wisdom and the measure of all things. And its application to God will be ruled out once and for all.

The second idea we have to abandon is that—even supposing we have corrected that unsatisfactory conception of unity—there is necessarily something unworthy of God and incompatible with His being as God in supposing that there is in God a first and a second, an above and a below, since this includes a gradation, a degradation and an inferiority in God, which if conceded excludes the *homoousia* of the different modes of divine being. That all sounds very illuminating. But is it not an all too human—and therefore not a genuinely human—way of thinking ? For what is the measure by which it measures and judges ? Has there really to be something mean in God for Him to be the second, below ? Does subordination in God necessarily involve an inferiority, and therefore a deprivation, a lack ? Why not rather a particular being in the glory of the one equal Godhead, in whose inner order there is also, in fact, this dimension, the direction downwards, which has its own dignity ? Why should not our way of finding a lesser dignity and significance in what takes the second and subordinate place (the wife to her husband) need to be corrected in the light of the *homoousia* of the modes of divine being ?

As we look at Jesus Christ we cannot avoid the astounding conclusion of a divine obedience. Therefore we have to draw the no less astounding deduction that in equal Godhead the one God is, in fact, the One and also Another, that He is indeed a First and a Second, One who rules and commands in majesty and One who obeys in humility. The one God is both the one and the other. And, we continue, He is the one and the other without any cleft or differentiation but in perfect unity and equality because in the same perfect unity and equality He is also a Third, the One who affirms the one and equal Godhead through and by and in the two modes of being, the One who makes possible and maintains His fellowship with Himself as the one and the other. In virtue of this third mode of being He is in the other two without division or contradiction, the whole God in each. But again in virtue of this third mode of being He is in neither for itself and apart from the other, but in each in its relationship to the other, and therefore, in fact, in the totality, the connexion, the interplay, the history of these relationships. And because all division and contradiction is excluded, there is also excluded any striving to identify the two modes of being, or any possibility of the one being absorbed by the other, or both in their common deity. God is God in these two modes of being which cannot be separated, which cannot be autonomous, but which cannot cease to be different. He is God in their concrete relationships the one to the other, in the history which takes place between them. He is God only in these relationships and therefore not in a Godhead which does not take part in this history, in the relationships of its modes of being, which is neutral towards them. This neutral Godhead, this pure and empty Godhead, and its claim to be true divinity, is the illusion of an abstract " monotheism " which usually fools men most successfully at the high-water mark of the development of heathen religions and mythologies and philosophies. The true and living God is the One whose Godhead consists in this history, who is in these three modes of being the One God, the Eternal, the Almighty, the Holy, the Merciful, the One who loves in His freedom and is free in His love.

And His speaking and activity and work *ad extra* consist in the fact that He gives to the world created by Him, to man, a part in the history in which He is God, that there is primarily in the work of creation a reflection, in the antithesis of Creator and creature an image and likeness, and in the twofoldness of the existence of man a reflection of this likeness of the inner life of God Himself. And then supremely and finally (at the goal and end of His whole activity as established at its beginning) they consist in the fact that God Himself becomes a man amongst men in His mode of being as the One who is obedient in humility. In the work of the reconciliation of the world with God the inward divine relationship between the One who rules and commands in majesty and the One who obeys in humility is identical with the very different relationship between God and one of His creatures, a man. God goes into the far country for this to happen. He becomes what He had not previously been. He takes into unity with His divine being a quite different, a creaturely and indeed a sinful being. To do this He empties Himself, He humbles Himself. But, as in His action as Creator, He does not do it apart from its basis in His own being, in His own inner life. He does not do it without any correspondence to, but as the strangely logical final continuation of, the history in which He is God. He does not need to deny, let alone abandon and leave behind or even diminish His Godhead to do this. He does not need to leave the work of the Reconciler in the doubtful hands of a creature. He can enter in Himself, seeing He is in Himself not only the One who rules and commands in majesty, but also in His own divine person, although in a different mode of being, the One who is obedient in humility. It is the free grace of the atonement that He now not only reflects His inner being as God as He did in creation, that He not only represents it in a likeness as He did in the relationship of Creator and creature, but that He causes it to take outward form in itself and as such. In His mode of being as the One who is obedient in humility He wills to be not only the one God but this man, and this man as the one God. He does not owe this to the creaturely world. He does not owe it even to Himself. He owes it just as little and even less than He did the creation. Neither in the one case nor in the other —and even less in this case—can there be any question of the necessary working of an inward divine mechanism, or a mechanism which controls the relationship of God and the world. God gives Himself to the world in coming to the world as its Reconciler. But He can give Himself to it. He is His own master in such a way that He can go into the far country to do it. He does not need to cease to be radically and totally above, the first, in order to become radically and totally below, the second. Even below, as this second, He is one with Himself, equal with Himself as God. He does not change in giving Himself. He simply activates and reveals Himself *ad extra*, in the world. He is in and for the world what He is in and for Himself. He is in time what He is in eternity (and what He can be also in time because of His eternal being). He is in our lowliness what He is in His majesty (and what He can be also in our lowliness because His majesty is also lowliness). He is as man, as the man who is obedient in humility, Jesus of Nazareth, what He is as God (and what He can be also as man because He is it as God in this mode of divine being). That is the true deity of Jesus Christ, obedient in humility, in its unity and equality, its *homoousia*, with the deity of the One who sent Him and to whom He is obedient.

Up to this point we have refrained from using the concepts which dominate the New Testament and ecclesiastical dogma. Our first task has been to show what is their place and purpose in our present context. We can now introduce them. Jesus Christ is the Son of God who became man, who as such is One with God the Father, equal to Him in deity, by the Holy Spirit, in whom the Father affirms and loves Him and He the Father, in a mutual fellowship.

For the basis and development and explanation of the doctrine of the Trinity in its own context and in all its details, and for an understanding of its exegetical and historical implications, we must refer back to *C.D.* I, 1 § 8–12. We have here approached this first and final Christian truth from a special standpoint, and in this context we can speak of it only briefly, selectively, and in a limited way.

By Father, Son and Spirit we do not mean what is commonly suggested to us by the word " persons." This designation was accepted

—not without opposition—on linguistic presuppositions which no longer obtain to-day. It was never intended to imply—at any rate in the main stream of theological tradition—that there are in God three different personalities, three self-existent individuals with their own special self-consciousness, cognition, volition, activity, effects, revelation and name. The one name of the one God is the threefold name of Father, Son and Holy Spirit. The one " personality " of God, the one active and speaking divine Ego, is Father, Son and Holy Spirit. Otherwise we should obviously have to speak of three gods. And this is what the Early Church not only would not do, but in the conception of the doctrine of the Trinity which ultimately prevailed tried expressly to exclude, just as it did any idea of a division or inequality between Father, Son and Holy Spirit. Christian faith and the Christian confession has one Subject, not three. But He is the one God in self-repetition, in the repetition of His own and equal divine being, and therefore in three different modes of being—which the term " person " was always explained to mean. He does not exist as such outside or behind or above these modes of being. He does not exist otherwise than as Father, Son and Holy Spirit. He exists in their mutual interconnexion and relationship. He exists in their difference, not in their identity : the Father in His mode as the Father of the Son ; the Son in His as the Son of the Father ; the Spirit in His as the Spirit of the Father and the Son. He is not threefold, but trine, triune, i.e., in three different modes the one personal God, the one Lord, the one Creator, the one Reconciler, the one Perfecter and Redeemer. He is all this as He is Father, Son and Holy Spirit. He is it in the relationships to Himself thereby posited. His being as God is His being in His own history.

The terms for these modes of being in which God is God are human terms, the best possible, but inadequate approximations, attempts to describe what since the New Testament has always been found in God on the basis of the revelation which takes place in His action, which we cannot therefore pass over in silence, let alone deny, but are forced to confess. The Church has always known and constantly stated that it cannot in these terms reach or comprehend or exhaust the sense of what it knows in faith. It has always confessed the incomprehensibility of God. And it has always made this clear in its understanding of the triune being of God and especially of His three modes of being. It has been well aware that in these terms it can only aim at the real thing which is in question.

This is also true of that description of Jesus Christ as the Son of God which particularly concerns us. There can be no doubt that linguistically the New Testament took over this term from the Old, although there was, of course, a certain co-operation and stimulation from the Hellenistic environment, and some regard for the concepts more or less current within it. And it is no accident that of all the titles used of Jesus Christ in the New Testament sphere it was that of Son which came to the forefront when it was desired to refer to His being as revealed in His activity from the standpoint of its origin ; when it was intended to describe Him as the One who in a particular and unique way had come from God, who was revealing God, who belonged wholly and directly to God, who was united with God ; when it was purposed to refer to the deity of the subject by which we are here confronted. Even in the Creeds it is this title which takes precedence in the second article : Jesus Christ is the Son of God, and as such He is the Lord (as we are told in the enlarged and completed Creed of 381). He is " of one substance with the Father, by Whom all things were made, who for us men and for our salvation came down from heaven, and was made man "—*et incarnatus est*—who as such is the subject of all the events that follow, who as such is *conceptus de Spiritu Sancto, natus ex Maria virgine*, who as such is crucified, risen and seated at the right hand of the Father, who as such will come again to judge the quick and the dead. He is all this, and He does all this divine work, because He is the Son of God, the only Son, the only begotten Son of God, *Filius Dei unicus*, as was added from the very first (cf. Jn. 1[14-18]) in order to distinguish Him from others who were given this title, in order to distinguish Him even from Christians who are called by this name as they are exalted to be His brethren, in order to bring out the singularity and the uniqueness of this subject and therefore of His work.

But what does it mean : the Son of God ? We do not ask what the strange conjunction of these two words may or can mean in any reference, but what they do mean in reference to Jesus Christ, as a description of what He was and is and will be. What does the New Testament mean, and what did the Early Church mean, when in an emphatic way and at a decisive point—as though it were the key to the whole—it gave Him this title ? What can we try to mean and say when we accept the confession : Amen, yes, Jesus Christ is the only Son of God ?

It certainly will not serve any useful purpose to burden the New Testament, or the Church which followed it, or ourselves, with the idea that Jesus Christ as the Son of God is begotten in time, in an event in which God does that which makes a man a father, and that He was born in consequence of this event as such. When we are dealing with Jesus Christ there is no question of a temporal event in which He began to be the Son of God, of an action on the part of God like that of a human father in which He began to be the Father of this Son, and therefore of a so-called " physical divine Sonship " of Jesus Christ in the fairly well-known sense of so many mythologies. The New Testament and the Church never understood His Sonship in this way. Even in the light of the Old Testament it was impossible to think along these lines. And what confronted the New Testament witnesses and through them the Church, what laid the term " Son of God " on their lips as they looked at Jesus Christ, compelled them to exclude this idea and to think on quite different lines. There is therefore no reason to pursue this thought.

It would have to be imported into the passages in Mt. 1[18-25] and Lk. 1[26-38] and the credal statement about the Virgin Birth in the creeds founded on these passages (cf. for what follows C.D., I, 2 § 15, 2). And careful exegesis and dogmatics have always safeguarded them against this importation. In the Creeds the assertion of the Virgin Birth is plainly enough characterised as a first statement about the One who was and is and will be the Son of God. It is not a statement about how He became this, a statement concerning the basis and condition of His divine Sonship. It is a description of the way in which the Son of God became man. The New Testament and the Early Church never understood the relationship between the Holy Spirit and the Virgin Mary in mythical fashion as a ἱερὸς γάμος. The Holy Spirit has never been regarded or described by any serious Christian theologian as the divine Father even of the man Jesus. In the exposition of this dogma—and thoroughly in the sense of its New Testament presuppositions—it has been frequently and energetically explained that it might have pleased God to let His Son become man in some quite different way than in the event of the miracle attested as the Virgin Birth. It did in fact please Him to let Him become man in this way, but this event is not the basis of the fact that the One who there became man was the Son of God. It is the sign which accompanies and indicates the mystery of the incarnation of the Son, marking it off as a mystery from all the beginnings of other human existences. It consists in a creative act of divine omnipotence, in which the will and work of man in the form of a human father is completely excluded from the basis and beginning of the human existence of the Son of God, being replaced by a divine act which is supremely unlike any human action which might arise in that connexion, and in that way characterised as an inconceivable act of grace. " Conceived by the Holy Ghost " does not, therefore, mean " begotten by the Holy Ghost." It means that God Himself—acting directly in His own and not in human fashion—stands at the beginning of this human existence and is its direct author. It is He who gives to man in the person of Mary the capacity which man does not have of himself, which she does not have and which no man could give her. It is He who sanctifies and ordains her the human mother of His Son. It is He who makes His Son hers, and in that way shares with humanity in her person nothing less than His own existence. He gives to her what she could not procure for herself and no other creature could procure for her. This is the miracle of the Virgin Birth as it indicates the mystery of the incarnation, the first attestation of the divine Sonship of the man Jesus of Nazareth, comparable with the miracle of the empty tomb at His exodus from temporal existence. The question is pertinent whether His divine Sonship and the mystery of His incarnation are known in any real seriousness and depth when these attestations of it are unrecognised or overlooked or denied or explained away. But in any case these attestations are based on His divine Sonship, not His divine Sonship on these attestations. They have a great deal to do with it noetically, but nothing at all ontically.

To answer our question concerning the sense in which Jesus Christ is called and is the Son of God, we have to look in another direction altogether. And why not in the direction in which we have constantly looked from the very first ? So far we have tried to understand Jesus Christ as the One who humbles Himself, as the One who is obedient in humility, and therefore as the fulfilment of the Old Testament concept of a Son. In His being and activity, in His suffering and dying as this obedient One, He is quite different from all other men. He is a man, but quite unlike all other men. He is among men, yet in contrast to all other men He is at the side of God. In His human person He is the kingdom of God come down from heaven to earth. This kingdom (the power of God exercised by Him as Lord, His glory as King) is incorporated and truly present and active in Him. It has truly and actually become flesh in Him. And it has done so because He is simply but totally its first and proper subject, because He realises perfectly the ὑπακοή and ὑποταγή and τιμή which correspond to the perfect lordship of God as its necessary complement. He sets up the lordship of God and reveals it in the quite free but quite necessary decision, in the determination which is native to Him and therefore utterly natural, to go the way of the servant of God, the way downwards, to lowliness and finally to the cross. He activates and reveals the unconditional royal power of God by living it out unconditionally as man ; in its likeness, in its correspondence, as it must be lived out on earth and among us men if there is to be a reconciliation of the world with God. The image, the correspondence in which He has set it up and revealed it among us, for our salvation, for the reconciliation of the world with man, is, however, His obedience in humility. What the whole world lacks, what it cannot produce of itself—as a creature and especially as a sinful creature—is this complement, this obedience which corresponds to the lordship of God and reflects it. Jesus Christ achieves it. He does so self-evidently, naturally, in His own freedom, and therefore perfectly. He knows and goes this way alone. He enters and treads it without ever missing the way, without ever making any mistakes, pursuing it to the very end. It is His whole being to be this obedient One. This is what distinguishes Him from all creatures either in heaven or earth. This is what proves Him to be the Mediator between God and man. This is what proves Him to be the Son of God. It is as the One who proves Himself to be the Son of God by entering this way that He is attested by the miracle of the Virgin Birth ; and by the miracle of the empty tomb He is attested as the One who has pursued this way to the bitter end.

But in this way He does show Himself to be the Son of God. In this way He is the Son of God made flesh. The fact that He shows Himself to be the Son of God in this way does not mean that He becomes the Son of God thereby, let alone by the miracle which attests Him as such. He shows Himself the One He is by the obedience which He renders as man. And His unconditional, self-evident, natural and wholly spontaneous being in obedience is just as little the affair of a man, or of a creature generally, as the unconditional lordship to which this being corresponds, and which He reflects in it, can ever be the affair of a man or of any creature. In rendering obedience as He does, He does something which, as in the case of that lordship, only

God can do. The One who in this obedience is the perfect image of the ruling God is Himself—as distinct from every human and creaturely kind—God by nature, God in His relationship to Himself, i.e., God in His mode of being as the Son in relation to God in His mode of being as the Father, One with the Father and of one essence. In His mode of being as the Son He fulfils the divine subordination, just as the Father in His mode of being as the Father fulfils the divine superiority. In humility as the Son who complies, He is the same as is the Father in majesty as the Father who disposes. He is the same in consequence (and obedience) as the Son as is the Father in origin. He is the same as the Son, i.e., as the self-posited God (the eternally begotten of the Father as the dogma has it) as is the Father as the self-positing God (the Father who eternally begets). Moreover in His humility and compliance as the Son He has a supreme part in the majesty and disposing of the Father. The Father as the origin is never apart from Him as the consequence, the obedient One. The self-positing God is never apart from Him as the One who is posited as God by God. The One who eternally begets is never apart from the One who is eternally begotten. Nor is the latter apart from the former. The Father is not the Father and the Son is not the Son without a mutual affirmation and love in the Holy Spirit. The Son is therefore the One who in His obedience, as a divine and not a human work, shows and affirms and activates and reveals Himself—shows Himself to be the One He is—not another, a second God, but the Son of God, the one God in His mode of being as the Son.

It is clear that this brings us to the final meaning and limit of the term " Son of God " as used in relation to Jesus Christ.

What we call " Son " points in the right direction, but does not reach the fulness of what is here in question and what the term is meant to convey here. What the term can convey is the natural determination of a son to subjection to a father, the self-evident presupposition that a son owes obedience to a father, the mutual relationship revealed in what a father can expect and demand of a son and also in the way in which a son has to respect the will of his father. And the unity of the will and aims of a father and a son rests on the fact that there is a close relationship between them, that the one cannot be the father without his son, nor the other the son without his father.

But the term cannot bring out the ontological necessity in which this Father has this Son, and this Son this Father, the perfection in which this Father and this Son are one, i.e., are the different modes of being of one and the same personal God, the eternity of the fatherly begetting and of the being begotten of the Son, which is the basis of their relationship, their free but also necessary fellowship and love in the activity of the Holy Spirit as the third divine mode of being of the same kind, the self-evident fulfilment of that determination of a son to his father, the actual rendering of a perfect obedience, the ceaseless unity of the One who disposes and the One who complies, the actual oneness and agreement of that which they will and do. The history in which God is the living God in Himself can only be indicated but not conceived by our terms son and father and spirit.

The sense in which the New Testament speaks of men as the " children of the kingdom " (Mt. 8^{12}), the " children of the resurrection " (Lk. 20^{36}), the " children of promise " (Gal. 4^{28}), the " children of light " (Jn. 12^{36} ; Eph. 5^9), or the " children of the day " (1 Thess. 5^5), or on the other side as the " children of unbelief " or the " children of wrath " (Eph. 2$^{2f.}$), or even the " children of the devil " (1 Jn. 3^{10}), does, of course, include within it something of the relationship, the dependence, the subordination, the good or evil love, the good or evil obedience, in which these men may find themselves to forces of a *quasi* fatherly character. But even formally it does not attain to what the New Testament means when it calls Jesus Christ the Son of God. Therefore it can be used as an analogy only with the greatest caution. The same is true of the description of Christians as the " children of your Father in heaven " (Mt. 5^{45}) or the " children of God," which presupposes the incomparable and in the last resort inconceivable divine sonship of the one Jesus Christ. We are called the sons of God, and in our own way are the sons of God, only because in His own way, for which there are ultimately no analogies, Jesus Christ is the Son of God.

As applied to Jesus Christ we can legitimately call the term " Son of God " a true but inadequate and an inadequate but true insight and statement. This means that on the one side we can be sure that the term as applied in this way does correspond to its object, that it does express it, that it is therefore true, that it tells us what Jesus Christ in fact is. We have no better term, and this one forces itself necessarily upon us. From the standpoint from which we have tried to understand Jesus Christ it is very suitable and indeed indispensable if we are to say what has to be said concerning His deity. It is quite right that it should have acquired its very particular importance and role in the New Testament and in the language of the later Church. It confesses the final thing that we have to confess of Him, and therefore necessarily it takes the first place. But it confesses it in the way that we men can confess the mystery to which it points. As a true description of Jesus Christ it goes far beyond anything that it can say in any other application. As applied to this " Son " it is in a certain sense burst wide open, and can be thought through to the end only as we bring into it meanings which it cannot have in any other use which we can make of it. As applied in this way it deserves our every confidence because it is true, but it must be used with great reserve because of its inadequacy. And is it not fitting that the true deity of the One who is obedient in humility, of the Son who is in this way the only begotten Son of the Father, wills to be known and can be known only in this way—with every confidence but also with great modesty ? For in this matter, as others, what can all our Christian statements be but a serious pointing away to the One who will Himself tell those who have ears to hear who He is ?

2. THE JUDGE JUDGED IN OUR PLACE

When I formulated this title I first thought of *Qu.* 52 of the *Heidelberg Cate-chism*, in which the returning Christ is called the judge who " has represented me before the judgment of God, and has taken away all cursing from me," whom the Christian can therefore await " with uplifted head in every affliction and persecution." From the passage in Melito of Sardis (*fragm.* 13), which I quoted in another connexion (p. 167), and which sets at the head of a whole string of paradoxes the statement : *judex judicatur et quietus est*, I realised that we are dealing with a thought which was not unknown to the Early Church. A well-versed patristic scholar who heard my lecture on this theme has pointed out to me that at the head of a similar string Eusebius of Emesa (ed. E. M. Buytaert, 1949, p. 72) also wrote : *judex noster judicatus est, vita morti tradita est, cibans universum fuit in fame*, and also that Athanasius (presupposing the genuineness of the tractate on " The Cunning of the Devil," edited by R. P. Casey, 1935) found the deepest point in the grace shown by God to man in the fact : ὁ τῶν ὅλων κοιτὴς ἐκοίθη διά σε, ἵνα σὺ ὑψωθῆς (*op. cit.* p. 81 f.). I cannot vouch for the detailed thinking of the fathers in this connexion—if what they say is more than rhetorical, as it certainly seems to be in the passage from Athanasius.

The way of the Son of God into the far country, i.e., into the lowliness of creaturely being, of being as man, into unity and solidarity with sinful and therefore perishing humanity, the way of His incarnation is as such the activation, the demonstration, the revelation of His deity, His divine Sonship. That is the conclusion of our first section.

But now we enter a whole sphere of new considerations. For this way has an end, a scope, a meaning. It does not contradict His deity, His divine Sonship. It conforms supremely to it. By going this way Jesus Christ represents and discloses to us the mystery of the riches, the height and the depth of His deity which is the one true deity, and the particular mystery of His divine Sonship, Himself as the image of the ruling and commanding Father in the humility of His obedience, and therefore as the Son who is one with Him and equal with Him. That is the one side. And we had to begin with this side—the doctrine of the " person of Christ "—because it is the presupposition of everything that follows : not merely of the further development which is now necessary of the christological basis of this first part of the doctrine of reconciliation, but of all that we can think and say within this first part, under the first controlling aspect, in our attempt to understand the whole reconciliation of the world with God. We had to know who the servant is who is here actively at work as subject. We had to know that He is the Lord, the Lord of all lords, the one true God, the Son of God, to whom in Mt. 11²⁷ and 28¹⁸ everything, all power in heaven and in earth is given. That is one thing. Quite another is the answer to the question : Why did He become a servant ? why did the Son of God concretely render obedience in this way, concretely manifesting and disclosing Himself in this way as the One He is ? why did He go this way in divinely free compliance with the freely

disposing will of the Father ?   In other words :   *Cur Deus homo ?*
With what purpose and to what end does God will this and do this ?

Certainly we shall not be answering incorrectly, but indicating the
background against which we have to understand everything else, if
we begin by simply repeating that He wills this and does this in an
outward activation and revelation of the whole inward riches of His
deity in all its height and depth, that He wills it and does it especially
that the world created by Him might have and see within it, in the
Son as the image of the Father, its own original, that He wills it and
does it for the sake of His own glory in the world, to confirm and
proclaim His will not to be without the world, not to be God in isolation.

We must not be put off from thinking in this direction by the charge that it
is mere speculation and far too good to be true.   If we will not accept the fact
that God is also and primarily *pro se*, we shall find it hard to understand what
it means that in being *pro se* He is also *pro nobis*, and therefore *pro me*.   It is
no accident that in the song of the Christmas angels (Lk. 2¹⁴) the " Glory to
God in the Highest " comes first, and the " Peace on earth to the men of the
(divine) good pleasure " only second.   And a similar consideration seems to
have guided the New Testament writer when (in Lk. 19³⁸) the words ἐν οὐρανῷ
εἰρήνη καὶ δόξα ἐν ὑψίστοις are added to the ὡσαννὰ ἐν ὑψίστοις of Matthew and
Mark in the disciples' song of praise on the entry into Jerusalem, thus giving
to the event a clear significance for God Himself.   Preceding everything that
the event can mean for men, there is obviously something prior and higher at
which we have to rejoice.   And it seems to be not only good but true that quite
apart from anything else, and before anything else, the act of atonement, and
therefore the incarnation of the Word, includes within itself the fact that by His
presence, action and self-proclamation in the world, as the King of Glory who
comes in through its doors and gates (Ps. 24⁷ᶠ·), God vindicates Himself, and is
therefore Himself the meaning and basis and end.   Whatever else may be called
the meaning and basis and end of the divine being and action in Jesus Christ
can best be understood, can it not, if we understand this divine work as above
all else purposeful in itself, and everything else within the realisation of this
divine self-purpose ?

But this answer is obviously not enough unless it is given with the
more precise and concrete definition which the situation demands—
that God reveals and increases His own glory in the world by this
event, by hastening to the help of the world as its loyal Creator, by
taking up its cause.   In doing what He does for His own sake, He
does it, in fact, *propter nos homines et propter nostram salutem.*   For
Himself He did not need that He and His glory should be revealed
and confessed in the world and by us.   He might have been content
with His own knowledge of Himself, just as He might have been content earlier with His being as God in glory, not needing the being of
the creature and its co-existence with Him, not being under any
necessity to be its Creator.   But the world had radical need of His
work as Creator, to which it owes no less than its very being.   And,
again, it has radical need that He should take up its cause in the work
of atonement.   Not by divine creation, but by the sin of man, it is
the world which is thrown back on the faithfulness of God, a world

which is lost apart from the fact that He Himself hastens to its help and takes up its cause. It has perverted the being which He lent it. It has fallen, i.e., it is rushing headlong into nothingness, into eternal death. Of itself it is not capable of any counter-movement to arrest this fall. In itself it has no power, no effective will, no sufficient basis, for any such counter-movement. On the contrary, of its own will and ability it makes only such movements as serve to repeat the origin of its fall, which is sin, and to accelerate its headlong course to the abyss. But God reveals and increases His own glory in the world in the incarnation of His Son by taking to Himself the radical neediness of the world, i.e., by undertaking to do Himself what the world cannot do, arresting and reversing its course to the abyss. He owes this neither to the world nor to Himself. Not to the world, because the sin of man as the origin of its fatal movement to eternal death is directed against Himself, is always presented and characterised as enmity against Himself. Not to the world because the world has no claim that He should exercise in its favour the omnipotence of His free love, and in the perfect form of Himself accepting unity and solidarity with sinful man. And not to Himself, because nothing would be lacking in His inward being as God in glory, as the Father, Son and Holy Spirit, as the One who loves in freedom, if He did not show Himself to the world, if He allowed it to complete its course to nothingness : just as nothing would be lacking to His glory if He had refrained from giving it being when He created it out of nothingness. That He does, in fact, will to reconcile it with Himself, and to save it, and therefore to magnify His glory in it and to it, is from every standpoint the sovereign will of His mercy. We cannot deduce it or count on it from any side. We cannot establish in principle from any side that it must be so, that God had to link the revelation and increase of His glory with the maintaining and carrying through to victory of our cause, that He had to cause it to take place as an event in which salvation is given to us. How can it be necessary in principle that He should take to Himself—and conjoin and unite with what He does to His own glory—the cause which we had so hopelessly lost, turning it in His own person to good, to the best of all ? If we can speak of a necessity of any kind here, it can only be the necessity of the decision which God did in fact make and execute, the necessity of the fact that the being of God, the omnipotence of His free love, has this concrete determination and is effective and revealed in this determination and no other, that God wills to magnify and does in fact magnify His own glory in this way and not in any other, and therefore to the inclusion of the redemption and salvation of the world. This fact we have to recognise to be divinely necessary because it derives from and is posited by God. This fact we have to perceive and reverence and receive and glorify as the mystery of the atonement, the incarnation of the eternal Word. And we have to do it with a thankfulness which cannot be limited by any supposed necessity of this free gift. *Cur Deus homo?* Because the salvation of the world and of men, we ourselves and our salvation, are in fact included in the self-purposiveness of this divine action. Because the great and self-sufficient God wills to be also the Saviour of the world. Because what He does for Himself takes place with the intention and is complete in the fact that in its purpose and result we will not perish but have everlasting life. This, then, is why the Lord became a servant. This is why concretely the Son of God rendered that obedience, the obedience of self-humiliation. This is why in free compliance with the freely disposing will of the Father He entered on the strange way into the far country and followed it to the bitter end.

Here, then, we have our general answer to the question confronting us. We cannot deduce it from any principle, from any idea of God or of man and the world. We can read it only from the fact in which the omnipotent mercy of God is exercised and effective and revealed, in which His own glory and our salvation meet, in which that which God does for Himself is also done for us. Our answer can only be a repetition of the answer which God Himself has given in this fact, in which He Himself has pronounced concerning the end and scope and meaning of His activity. *Deus pro nobis* is something which He did not have to be or become, but which, according to this fact, He was and is and will be—the God who acts as our God, who did not regard it as too mean a thing, but gave Himself fully and seriously to self-determination as the God of the needy and rebellious people of Israel, to be born a son of this people, to let its wickedness fall on Him, to be rejected by it, but in its place and for the forgiveness of its sins to let Himself be put to death by the Gentiles—and by virtue of the decisive co-operation of the Gentiles in His rejection and humiliation to let Himself be put to death in their place, too, and for the forgiveness of their sins. The end and scope and meaning of this downward way, the reconciliation of the world with Himself, is God Himself as the God of this mean and wicked people for the men of this people, and at the end of its history God Himself in the midst of this people and all peoples for the men of this people and all peoples, God in this direct relationship to men and man, God the one man for many. In all that follows we can only hear and intelligently repeat the answer which God Himself has already given to our question.

But we must now state rather more precisely the general meaning of this *Deus pro nobis*. How is God for us? How has He taken up the cause of the world in revealing and magnifying His own glory? How has He met its radical need? How has He arrested and reversed its course to the abyss? How especially has He met the fact that the cause of its impending destruction is the sin of man, his enmity against God? How has He shown Himself to be its Saviour in face and in spite of this cause of its impending destruction?

In giving Himself in the Son to this alien life, in becoming concretely the God of Israel and an individual man of this people and as such a man amongst all men, He obviously did it first of all simply by taking upon Himself to share with it its place and status, its situation, by making it His own situation. The way of His humiliation is simply the way which leads Him to us, the way on which He draws near to us and becomes one of us. And this means first that the mortal peril in which man stands becomes and is His peril, the need of man His need. The Son of God exists with man and as man in this fallen and perishing state. We should be explaining the incarnation docetically and therefore explaining it away if we did not put it like this, if we tried to limit in any way the solidarity with the cosmos which God accepted in Jesus Christ. We have already said that in this event God allows the world and humanity to take part in the history of the inner life of His Godhead, in the movement in which from and to all eternity He is Father, Son and Holy Spirit, and therefore the one true God. But this participation of the world in the being of God implies necessarily His participating in the being of the world, and therefore that His being, His history, is played out as world-history and therefore under the affliction and peril of all world-history. The self-humiliation of God in His Son would not really lead Him to us, the activity in which we see His true deity and the divine Sonship of Jesus Christ would not be genuine and actual, the humble obedience of Jesus Christ would not be rendered or the will of the Father fulfilled, the way into the far country would not be followed, if there were any reservation in respect of His solidarity with us, of His entry into world-history. But the self-humiliation of God in His Son is genuine and actual, and therefore there is no reservation in respect of His solidarity with us. He did become—and this is the presupposition of all that follows—the brother of man, threatened with man, harassed and assaulted with him, with him in the stream which hurries downwards to the abyss, hastening with him to death, to the cessation of being and nothingness. With him He cries—knowing far better than any other how much reason there is to cry: " My God, my God, why hast thou forsaken me ? " (Mk. 15³⁴). (*Deus pro nobis*) means simply that God has not abandoned the world and man in the unlimited need of his situation, but that He willed to bear this need as His own, that He took it upon Himself, and that He cries with man in this need.

But on the same lines we have to go further and say that in giving Himself up to this alien life in His Son God did not evade the cause of man's fall and destruction, but exposed Himself to and withstood the temptation which man suffers and in which he becomes a sinner and the enemy of God. We should again be explaining the incarnation docetically and therefore explaining it away, we should be closing our eyes to the plainest possible statements of the New Testament, concealing the central point which we have to grasp and consider, if we had any reservations in this respect. That the Word became

" flesh " means that the Son of God made His own the situation of man in the sense that with him He faced the impossible in all its power, that He faced the dreadful possibility of ingratitude, disobedience, unfaithfulness, pride, cowardice and deceit, that He knew it as well as He did Himself, that He came to closer grips with it than any other man. He had to achieve His freedom and obedience as a link in the chain of an enslaved and disobedient humanity, the new thing in a strict and, for Him and Him alone, hampering connexion with the old. He had to wrestle with that which assaulted Him as one man with others, which for the first time brought all its force to bear against Him as the Son of God in the flesh. He was not immune from sin. He did not commit it, but He was not immune from it. In this respect, too, He became the brother of man. He did not float over the human situation like a being of a completely different kind. He entered into it as a man with men. In this second and more incisive sense *Deus pro nobis* means that God in Jesus Christ has taken our place when we become sinners, when we become His enemies, when we stand as such under His accusation and curse, and bring upon ourselves our own destruction.

But now we have to face the question in all seriousness : Why did He come amongst us, why did He enter our situation, as our brother ? What is it that takes place when the Son of God becomes flesh of our flesh ?

We are not only at liberty, but it is right and relevant, to give first of all the great positive answer as we have it·in a verse like 1 Jn. 4[14] : " The Father sent the Son to be the Saviour of the world." Therefore our salvation, the salvation of men and the world, takes place in Him, in His being and activity as one with us. " God became man on thy behalf, O man." He humbles Himself to our status in order to be our companion in that status, in order to share with us the assault and temptation, in order to be with us in the misery of that status with all the omnipotence of His divine mercy, in order to change that status from within, in order to turn it for good, for the very best, in order to take away the curse which rests upon us, in order to obviate the impending destruction. He comes, therefore, as a helper, as a redeemer, as the one who brings another and proper order, a life which is life indeed. He comes as the kingdom of God in person. He comes to reconcile the world with God, i.e., to convert it to God.

But we cannot pass on at once to the development of this positive answer. It is the answer of the grace of God and we must hear and understand it as such. But the grace of God is not a cheap grace. It cost God dear enough to give this answer, to send His Son as the Saviour of the world. Therefore if our answer is to correspond to His, if it is to have weight and meaning, it cannot be a cheap or over-hasty answer. We must pause for a moment to consider a statement which plays no little part in the New Testament, that the coming into the world of the Son of God includes within itself the appearance and work of the Judge of the world and of every man. If He were not the Judge, He would not be the Saviour. He is the Saviour of the world in so far as in a very definite (and most astonishing) way He is also its Judge.

And it is to the point if we remember that the Judge is not simply or even primarily the One who pardons some (perhaps a few or perhaps none at all) and condemns the rest (perhaps many and perhaps all)—whose judgment therefore all have to fear. Basically and decisively—and this is something we must never forget when we speak of the divine Judge—He is the One whose concern is for order and peace, who must uphold the right and prevent the wrong, so that His existence and coming and work is not in itself and as such a matter for fear, but something which indicates a favour, the existence of One who brings salvation.

The so-called " Judges " of the Old Testament in the early period of the occupation of Canaan are described as men awakened by God and their main office is to be helpers and saviours in the recurrent sufferings of the people at the hand of neighbouring tribes. It was only in addition to this activity in " foreign affairs " that they engaged in judging in the narrower sense of the term. Similarly in the New Testament—a fact which was later forgotten—the coming of the Judge means basically the coming of the Redeemer and Saviour.

But, of course, this involves judging in the more obvious sense of the word, and therefore pardoning and sentencing. Thus the solemn question arises : Who will stand when the Son of God—to create order and peace, but by setting some on His right hand and others on His left—comes into the world, when He calls the world and therefore all men (and every individual man) to render an account and to make answer for its condition ? *Quid sum miser tunc dicturus, quem patronum rogaturus, cum vix justus sit securus ?* All other men will be measured by the One who is man as they are under the same presuppositions and conditions. In His light, into which they are *nolentes volentes* betrayed by His being as a fellow-man, they will be shown for what they are and what they are not. With His existence there will fall upon them in all its concreteness the decision, the divine and ultimate decision. What will become of them ? How shall they stand ?

In this respect we must not overlook especially the message of John the Baptist. According to the Synoptic narrative he stands in the closest relationship with the appearance and work of Jesus. And he gives to it a character which, as we read on, we may easily overlook and forget because of its strangeness, but which we ought not to forget or overlook. In one place (Lk. 3¹⁸) the function of the Baptist is itself called an εὐαγγελίζεσθαι. And at the end of the quotation from Is. 40 (about the voice crying in the wilderness to prepare the way of the Lord), which the same Evangelist uses to show that the coming of the Baptist has to be understood as a fulfilment of Scripture, there stands the saying : " And all flesh shall see the salvation of God " (Lk. 3⁵). But what we are told of his proclamation of the near coming of the kingdom (Mt. 3²) has at first quite a different ring. According to Mt. 3⁷ the scribes and Pharisees who came to him by Jordan (and in Lk. 3⁷ the ὅχλοι) are welcomed with the words : "Ye generation of vipers, who hath warned you to flee from the wrath to come (μέλλουσα ὀργή) ? The axe is already laid at the root of the tree, and every tree that bringeth forth not good fruit will be hewn down and cast into the fire (Mt. 3¹⁰). This is what happens when the kingdom of God comes. And in express reference to the greater one who will then come after the Baptist : "He shall baptise you with the Holy Ghost, and with fire : Whose fan is in his hand, and he will throughly purge his floor, and gather his wheat into the garner ; but he will burn up the chaff with unquenchable fire" (Mt. 3¹²). No appeal : "We have Abraham to our father," will then be of any help (Mt. 3⁹). No, to obtain forgiveness of sins and to escape the coming wrath on the day when this One comes, repentance is necessary to-day (Mk. 1⁴), the confession of sins (Mk. 1⁵), and fruits meet for repentance (Mt. 3⁸). What this means is shown by some examples in Lk. 3¹⁰ᶠ· The baptism of John is therefore the sign of penitent expectation of the Judge and His *dies irae*. And it is to this baptism that Jesus of Nazareth submits, having come to Jordan from Galilee and accepting it with all the people. He does so as the Judge who has been proclaimed. This is surprising enough to the Baptist himself, who had need to be baptised of Him (Mt. 3¹⁴) ; but he had to suffer it to be so, for "thus it becometh us to fulfil all righteousness" (Mt. 3¹⁵). Here we see the limit of this strand.

But it is rewarding to note that the same strand appears again and again in the New Testament. Whether one has built on the rock or on the sand is determined by whether one does or does not do the words of Jesus (Mt. 7²⁴ᶠ·). "Why call ye me, Lord, Lord, and do not the things which I say ?" (Lk. 6⁴⁶). Those who confess Him before men, He will also confess, but those who deny Him before men He will also deny before His Father in heaven (Mt. 10³²ᶠ·). He is not come to bring peace on the earth but a sword (Mt. 10³⁴), or, according to Lk. 12⁴⁹, "to send fire on the earth." Those who will not take up their cross and follow Him are not worthy of Him (Mt. 10³⁸). Only those who will lose their lives for His sake will find them (Mt. 10³⁹). The Saviour of the Evangelists is also the One who pronounces those woes on Chorazin, Bethsaida and Capernaum because they have seen His mighty works and not repented (Mt. 11²⁰ᶠ·). He is also the One who pronounced that almost intolerably severe woe on the scribes and Pharisees which our clever modern exegetes have mildly reproved (Mt. 23¹³⁻³⁶). He always proclaims His last and manifest appearance to the whole world as the event when He will make a distinction between those who have watched and those who have fallen asleep, between those who have been found ready and loyal, and those who have not been found ready and loyal, between those who have seen and supported Him in suffering brethren and those who have failed to do so, between those who are merely called and those who are chosen.

We find the same teaching again and again in the Gospel of St. John. Here the concept of judgment is explicitly used, and there is a distinctive correlation of the judicial decision which has yet to be revealed with the decision which is in fact already being made : "He that believeth not the Son shall not see life ; but the wrath of God abideth on him" (Jn. 3³⁶). "He that rejecteth me, and receiveth not my words, hath one that judgeth him : the word that I have spoken, the same shall judge him in the last day" (Jn. 12⁴⁸). Conversely, "He that heareth my word, and believeth on him that sent me, hath everlasting life, and shall not come into condemnation ; but is passed from death unto life" (5²⁴). For to Him, the Son, the Father "hath committed all judgment" "because he is the Son of man" (5²², ²⁷). He judges, and His judgment is just because He hears Him that sent Him and seeks His will (5³⁰). His judgment is true, because He does not execute it alone, but in fellowship with Him that sent Him (8¹⁶). And according to the remarkable sayings in 9⁴¹ and 15²²ᶠ· it is only in confrontation with Him that there is any real sin : "If I had not done among them the works which none other man did, they had not had sin : but now have they both seen and hated both me and my Father " (15²⁴).

The Paul of Acts seems to see things in a similar light : " And the times of this ignorance God winked at ; but now commandeth all men every where to repent : Because he hath appointed a day, in which he will judge the world in righteousness by that man whom he hath ordained " (Ac. 17³⁰ᶠ·). And 2 Cor. 5¹⁰ maintains : " We must all appear before the judgment seat of Christ ; that every one may receive the things done in his body, according to that he hath done, whether it be good or bad." Again, in Ac. 10⁴² and 2 Tim. 4¹ Jesus is called the One who will judge the quick and the dead. In Rev. 1¹⁶, too, He is described as the One out of whose mouth there issues a sharp, two-edged sword. And in Heb. 12²⁹ the exhortation to thankfulness for the received " kingdom which cannot be moved " is based on the statement that " our God is a consuming fire."

The *locus classicus* for this significance and function of Jesus Christ as the Judge, and therefore for the judicial work of the Gospel concerning Him, is the whole sequence from Rom. 1¹⁸–3²⁰. In the following sections, in which—in the light of Christology—we shall be dealing for the first time with the doctrine of sin, we shall have to return expressly to this context. The passages already adduced, which are not by any means complete, are sufficient to bear out what we wished to maintain—that the " Saviour of the world " has also this character and commission and aspect. We cannot, therefore, overlook this fact or dismiss it from our mind. What follows can be understood only if we see that He has this aspect. He would not be who He is, nor would He do what, as the Son of God who has come to us, He does do for us, if He were not this Judge who pronounces against us.

Even more incisively, it is not just any judgment which He exercises and executes, but the judgment of God. And as we have already said, it is for this reason the ultimate judgment. It is the judgment against which there can be no appeal to a higher court. Nor is this merely because the world is in the power of this Judge and has no means to refuse or escape Him. It is decisively because this Judge is the measure of all righteousness, because any right which man might seek apart from Him or set up and assert side by side with Him could only be wrong, because conversely any right being or action on the part of man can consist only in His bowing before the judgment of this Judge and recognising and accepting His sentence as just whatever it may be.

This fact that God has here come amongst us in the person of His Son, and that as a man with us He exercises judgment, reveals the full seriousness of the human situation. In this judgment God obviously has something to say to man which apart from this direct confrontation with God he is unwilling to say to himself, and caught in this unwillingness he cannot say to himself. Man has obviously given himself quite a different account of himself than that which he is now given by God. It obviously was and is something strange to him that he, for his part, can be in the right and do right only in subjection to the judgment of God. Obviously the righteousness of God is something strange to him as the measure of all righteousness, and therefore God Himself is a stranger. Obviously he for his part is estranged from God ; although as the creature, the human creature of God, he is appointed to know God, although he is as near, no, nearer to God, than he is to himself, and therefore can and must be truly acquainted with Him. Obviously he does that which in the knowledge of God he could never do : he sets up his own right against God ; he measures himself by this right ; he thinks that measuring himself by this right he can pronounce himself free and righteous. He wants to be his own judge, and he makes himself his own judge. All sin has its being and origin in the fact that man wants to be his own judge. And in wanting to be that, and thinking and acting accordingly, he and his whole world is in conflict with God. It is an unreconciled world, and therefore a suffering world, a world given up to destruction.

It is for this reason—the fault and evil are evidently great and deep enough to make it necessary—it is for this reason that God Himself encounters man in the flesh and therefore face to face in the person of His Son, in order that He may pass on the one who feels and accepts himself as his own judge the real judgment which he has merited. This judgment sets him in the wrong as the one who maintains his own right against God instead of bowing to God's right. We will have to explain this when we come to speak of sin as such. For the moment it is enough to maintain that because it is a matter of the appearance and work of the true Judge amongst those who think they can and should judge and therefore exalt themselves, therefore the abasement of the Son to our status, the obedience which He rendered in humility as our brother, is the divine accusation against every man and the divine condemnation of every man. The whole world finds its supreme unity and determination against God in looking for justification from itself and not from God. And as a world hostile to God it is distinguished by the fact that in this way it repeats the very sin of which it acquits itself. In this way that which is flesh is flesh. And for this reason the incarnation of the Word means the judgment, the judgment of rejection and condemnation, which is passed on all flesh. Not all men commit all sins, but all men commit this sin which is the essence and root of all other sins. There is not one who can boast that he does not commit it. And this is what is revealed and rejected and condemned as an act of wrong-doing by the coming of the Son of God. This is what makes His coming a coming to judgment, and His office as Saviour His office as our Judge.

But those who are judged and rejected and condemned by God as wrong-doers are lost and condemned to perish, indeed they are already perishing. They stand on the left hand of God, under the divine No, in the sphere of that which God does not will, but rejects, and therefore in the sphere of that which is not, in the darkness in which there is no light, in the affliction in which there is no help, in the need from which there is no redemption. The power of God still rules over them, but as the power which holds and imprisons them, the power of His condemnation. The love of God burns where they are, but as the fire of His wrath which consumes and destroys them. God lives for them, but the life of God can only mean death for those who are His enemies. That is how the men exist who will be their own judges, who will acquit themselves, who in so doing commit all sins *in nuce*, and who are therefore judged and rejected and condemned by God as wrong-doers. And because all men are determinedly against God in this, this is how every man necessarily exists—in a lost state as one who is lost. God would not be God if there could be any altering the universality and logic and completeness of what is necessarily done here, if there could be any escaping this sequence of sin and destruction. It means eternal perdition to have God against us. But if we will what God does not will, we do have God against us, and therefore we hurry and run and stumble and fall into eternal perdition.

But again God would not be God if His reaction to wrong-doers could be compared to a mechanism which functions, as it were, independently of His free ruling and disposing. That is not how it is on His right hand, where He says Yes to the creature, where He frees his powers and blesses his love and gives him life which is life indeed. God is the Lord in all His rule, even in that of His wrath and the destruction and perdition which it brings. He Himself determines the course and direction and meaning of it : not some necessity immanent to its occurrence ; not a force to which man when he sins against God becomes subject absolutely, i.e., otherwise than in conformity to the sovereign will and disposing of God which obtains even in His rule on the left hand. How God will fulfil the sentence to which man has fallen inescapably victim is a matter for Him to decide. He can fulfil it—in all its strictness—in such a way that in fulfilling it there is attained that which man in his perversity tried and never could secure for himself—his pardon. Without relaxing or mitigating the sentence, let alone as a judge who is unjust by reason of his laxity, He can exercise grace even with His judgment and in execution of it. He can be so much in earnest against sinful man that He is for him. He can bring on him all that must come on him as a wrong-doer at the left hand of God and under His No, in order to set him at His right hand, in order finally to say Yes to him, in order to address and treat him as one who does right and not wrong. God is free to judge in this way. He is not obliged to do so. There is no inner compulsion forcing Him to exercise this strange judgment. Even less is there any right or claim on the part of man on the ground of which he can expect this strange judgment. Everything is against any such judgment being even conceivable : a serious judgment of God's enemies the result of which is grace, liberation, redemption proceeding out of captivity, love out of wrath, life out of death ; a judgment which in the event makes the enemies of God His friends ; a judgment in which this does not happen arbitrarily but in a fixed order, not in a wild divine inconsequence but with a clear purpose and according to a firm plan ; and therefore a judgment beside and after and beyond which there need be no further fear of judgment ; a judgment which concludes once and for all with the redemption and salvation of the man who had been rightly accused and condemned and had fallen a helpless victim to destruction. Everything is against the possibility of a judgment like that. But we cannot encroach on the freedom of God. We cannot, therefore, say that it could not please God in His grace, out of sheer faithfulness and mercy to us men, to be our Judge in this strange fashion.

But in the last resort there is only one thing which tells us that this is in fact possible—that in Jesus Christ His Son our Lord He has acted in this and no other way as our Judge and the Judge of all men. We now return to our question : Why did the Son of God become man, one of us, our brother, our fellow in the human situation ? The answer is : In order to judge the world. But in the light of what God has actually done we must add at once : In order to judge it in the exercise of His kingly freedom to show His grace in the execution of His judgment, to pronounce us free in passing sentence, to free us by imprisoning us, to ground our life on our death, to redeem and save us by our destruction. That is how God has actually judged in Jesus Christ. And that is why He humbled Himself. That is why He went into the far country as the obedient Son of the Father. That is why He did not abandon us, but came amongst us as our brother. That is why the Father sent Him. That was the eternal will of God and its fulfilment in time—the execution of this strange judgment. If this strange judgment had not taken place, there would be only a lost world and lost men. Since it has taken place, we can only recognise and believe and proclaim to the whole world and all men : Not lost. And since it did take place, what does it matter what may be said against the possibility of it ?

But what did take place ? At this point we can and must make the decisive statement : What took place is that the Son of God fulfilled the righteous judgment on us men by Himself taking our place as man and in our place undergoing the judgment under which we had passed. That is why He came and was amongst us. In this way, in this " for us," He was our Judge against us. That is what happened when the divine accusation was, as it were, embodied in His presence in the flesh. That is what happened when the divine condemnation had, as it were, visibly to fall on this our fellow-man. And that is what happened when by reason of our accusation and condemnation it had to come to the point of our perishing, our destruction, our fall into nothingness, our death. Everything happened to us exactly as it had to happen, but because God willed to execute His judgment on us in His Son it all happened in His person, as His accusation and condemnation and destruction. He judged, and it was the Judge who was judged, who let Himself be judged. Because

He was a man like us, He was able to be judged like us. Because He was the Son of God and Himself God, He had the competence and power to allow this to happen to Him. Because He was the divine Judge come amongst us, He had the authority in this way—by this giving up of Himself to judgment in our place—to exercise the divine justice of grace, to pronounce us righteous on the ground of what happened to Him, to free us therefore from the accusation and condemnation and punishment, to save us from the impending loss and destruction. And because in divine freedom He was on the way of obedience, He did not refuse to accept the will of the Father as His will in this self-giving. In His doing this for us, in His taking to Himself—to fulfil all righteousness—our accusation and condemnation and punishment, in His suffering in our place and for us, there came to pass our reconciliation with God. *Cur Deus homo ?* In order that God as man might do and accomplish and achieve and complete all this for us wrong-doers, in order that in this way there might be brought about by Him our reconciliation with Him and conversion to Him.

It came to pass, we have just said ; as we do when we tell the story of something that happened in the world at a definite place and a definite point of time. To think the matter out further and to understand it in detail, all that remains actually for us to do is simply to recount it in the manner of a story which has come to pass (which it is), to bring it before ourselves as something which has objectively happened. There and then, in the existence of the man Jesus of Nazareth, who was the Son of God, this event came to pass in the kingly freedom of the God who is holy and righteous in His faithfulness and mercy. There and then there took place the strange judgment which meant the pardon and redemption of man the wrong-doer, the making possible of that which seemed to be contrary to every possibility. It was made possible as it was done. And it was done as God became man in Jesus Christ, in order to do that in our place and for us. It took place in Him, in the one man, and therefore there and then, *illic et tunc,* and in significance *hic et nunc,* for us in our modern here and now. To be known and explained and proclaimed with this significance it cannot and must not be ignored or dissolved in favour of its significance, so that it disappears in it. Before there is any consideration of its significance, it can and must be taken as that which is significant in its significance, and therefore in and for itself as the history of Jesus Christ as it took place there and then, and as it can be and is recounted : That is how it happened for us. For upon the fact that it happened for us there depends the further fact that it has a significance for us as something which happened for us. Upon the fact that it confronts us as something that happened there depends the further fact that it can be seen by us to have this significance. Where there is nothing significant, and seen to be significant, there can be no significance or recognition of it. But the significant thing is what happened in Him, in Jesus Christ, in this one man. It is His history as such. It alone is the basis of faith. Its proclamation alone is the summons to faith—faith in this strange judgment, and the invitation and constraint to submit to it. Jesus Christ for us as a supremely objective happening is the word of reconciliation on the basis of which there is a ministry of reconciliation.

The New Testament distinguishes this happening in relation to its significance by an ἅπαξ or ἐφάπαξ. This marks it off as an event which has to be considered in its uniqueness and particularity, which cannot be dissolved, or merely commemorated *sotto voce* for the sake of completeness. Jesus Christ died for sin once, is the highly compressed form in which it is stated in Rom. 6¹⁰. And it is from this that in v. 11 there is derived the necessity to reckon ourselves dead indeed unto sin. According to Rom. 5⁶ᶠ· it happened at a particular time (κατὰ καιρόν). It was indeed when we were still without strength, sinners (v. 8), even enemies (v. 10), that He died for us (ὑπὲρ ἡμῶν, v. 8), that we were reconciled to God by the death of His Son (v. 10). Christ died once for our sins, the just for the unjust, to bring us to God (1 Pet. 3¹⁸). And especially in the Epistle to the Hebrews : Not with a daily repetition like the High Priests of the Old Testament, but once only did Christ offer sacrifice with the offering of Himself (7²⁷). Again in contradistinction to the sacrificial ministry of the Old Testament, He entered once into the holy place by His own blood and made (in that way) an eternal redemption (αἰωνία λύτρωσις) for us. Just as man dies once, so He is once revealed at the end of the age to take away sin by His sacrifice (9²⁶ᶠ·). And all that has still to be done, according to this passage, is that He should finally appear in correspondence to the judgment which awaits man after death. In that He fulfilled the will of God we are sanctified once and for all by the sacrificial offering of His body (10¹⁰, ¹⁴), again in contradistinction to the Old Testament order, within which there can be no question of a cleansing of man once and for all (10²).

In order to see and grasp this event as such, and therefore in its uniqueness and distinction in relation to its significance, we must try to find some way of making the accustomed unaccustomed again, the well-known unknown and the old new : that is, the outline of the evangelical history with which we are so familiar and the stimulating singularity of which we may so easily overlook, especially in the form in which it is presented in the synoptic Gospels. It is obvious that in these Gospels there is relatively little express mention of the significance of the Christ event which took place then and there. For that reason, up to our own day they have often been estimated less highly (even by Luther) in comparison with Paul and John as mere " history," although, of course, on the other hand, they have sometimes been given a no less dubious preference. But now let us consider this history carefully once more : how radically puzzling and therefore significant it is just as it stands, factually and without any great attempt to draw attention to it, in its simple character as history. What do we find in this history ?

In a first and larger part we have a picture of the sayings and acts of Jesus Christ in His entry into and life in Galilee within the wider and narrower circle of His disciples, the multitudes, and the spiritual and (on the margin) the political leaders of the people. Jesus over against and in the midst of His disciples stands out in marked contrast to this whole world of men. He belongs to it, and He intensively addresses Himself to it, but He is a stranger within it. His indications of the kingdom of God coming on earth, both spoken and confirmed in signs and wonders ; the imperatives spoken by Him as a summons to recognise and acknowledge this kingdom : all these are seen again and again to be in practical and theoretical antithesis to the whole being and thinking and willing of these men. He brings, and in His whole existence He is, the evangel, good news for all of them. But what comes of it ? What can and will the crowds finally make of it ? What comes of it in the ears and hearts of the scribes and Pharisees ? What does it mean for a Herod ? We hear of the poor and sick and publicans and sinners who seem to receive it gladly and willingly, as Jesus believes they can and will. But where are they at the last ? What has become of them and the Gospel they heard ? When Jesus goes to Jerusalem, they remain anonymously in Galilee, and none of the Evangelists thinks it worth while even to mention them again. We hear of the disciples and women who followed Him, and that Jesus counted those blessed who did so. Among them is Peter, who is honoured (Mt. 16¹⁶ᶠ·) with that revelation of the Father concerning the Son, who became the first confessor and who was described by Jesus as the rock on which He would build His Church. But immediately after Peter is rebuked as Satan because he will not and cannot think as God but only as man. And later Peter will deny Him thrice. Among them, too, is Judas, who will betray Him. And finally all the disciples will forsake Him and flee, just flee. What has really happened ? According to this presentation there has passed through the midst of all these men One who is absolutely superior to them, exalted above them, and fearfully alone. And He has finally gone from them after confirming and for the first time revealing their corruption, after showing and revealing them to be, in His light and confronted by Him, blind and deaf and lame, driven and controlled by all kinds of demons, even dead. The Lord has been among them. And in the course, and as the result of His being among them, in fulfilment of His proclamation and work, and as its consequence, the Lord has shown Himself their Judge, the One for whom not one of them was a match, on whom they were all broken to pieces, in face of whom they all showed themselves once more and this time finally to be sinful and lost Israel, sinful and lost humanity and—we have to see and say it—an inadequate and also a sinful and lost band of disciples.

Certainly from the very first the Evangelists do indicate one or two strands which point in another direction, which soften this hard picture of the contrast, the picture of the judgment that falls on all flesh with the coming of the kingdom, which plainly give us to understand that in this picture we have the first, but not the final, word. But these are either obvious reminiscences of sayings and acts which the disciples did not then understand on that first stage of the way of Jesus, prophecies the meaning of which they only perceived and introduced into their accounts in the light of their fulfilment—or else (and there are passages in which this is palpable) *vaticinia ex eventu*, an expression of the instruction which the community itself had later to undergo in face of the event in which that strange progress of the Lord through their midst came to its inconceivable climax. It is often difficult to decide whether we are dealing with the one group or the other when we come across these strands. But the main strand gives us the picture offered by the first main section of the evangelical records, and, impartially considered and estimated, it undoubtedly confirms the hard picture which John the Baptist had and drew of the One who was to come : the picture of the man with the fan in His hand, of the judgment of God which would fall in His existence, of the One at whose coming the Baptist saw the axe laid at the root of the trees. It has to be added that we go far beyond this picture, for at the end of this first part of the evangelical record there are no good trees left to stand. The formulation in which Paul gathered together the results of the first part of the Epistle to Romans is not too stringent to fit here : that every mouth will be stopped, and the whole world guilty before God. By the works of the Law—even the Gospel Law as proclaimed by Jesus of Nazareth— no flesh will be pronounced righteous before God (Rom. 3¹⁹ᶠ·).

But now there comes the great surprise of the second part of the history.

In the Synoptic tradition it overlaps a good deal with the first. The sections from the record of the entry into Jerusalem up to and including the last supper can be regarded as belonging to the first or the second part, or as the transition from the one to the other. But from the description of the scene in Gethsemane at any rate the second part forms a self-contained whole. It is essentially shorter than the first, but it obviously presents the—strange—end towards which the earlier narratives hasten. Yet it cannot fail to be noticed formally by the unity of its subject-matter, and by the unbroken sequence of the events reported in it (which are substantially the same in all the Evangelists). And in substance it stands out by reason of the fact that we have now very few sayings of Jesus and no actions at all, although more than once there seems to have been a temptation to act (the twelve legions of angels in Mt. 26⁵³, and that He should " come down from the cross " in Mt. 27⁴²). Jesus no longer seems to be the subject but the object of what happens. His speech is almost exclusively that of silence and His work that of suffering.

What these chapters bring before us is an arrest, a hearing and prosecution in various courts, a torturing, and then an execution and burial. They are, of course, a logical consequence of the first part as seen in the light of the result of what it has to tell us and of the initial preaching of John the Baptist. It is only to be expected that Jesus of Nazareth will try the world which has so shamefully rejected Him, will try Israel and even the band of disciples. It is not difficult to postulate that there will now take place the destruction of Jerusalem and the temple, and that the presentation of it will form the continuation and a suitable complement to the first part. In the last larger collection of sayings before the transition to the second part, the Synoptic apocalypse, this later event already emerges in its main outlines. And Jesus has a saying about His destruction and re-erection of the temple which, whether it was understood or misunderstood, played a particular role in the hearing before the high priests in Mk. 14⁵⁸, and then again in the taunting of the Crucified in Mk. 15²⁹. To the same context belongs quite naturally the saying to the daughters of Jerusalem in Lk. 23²⁸, when He tells them not to weep for Him but for themselves and their children. But all that is still future. And—however obvious—it is not in the events of A.D. 70 that the Gospels and the rest of the New Testament find the decisive divine answer to Israel's rejection of its Christ. Even in the Synoptic apocalypse this forms only, as it were, the next horizon of the final events there depicted, with no autonomous significance in relation to the true centre. And although in the real second part of the Gospels we have the description of a judgment which falls on Israel, the surprising thing is that it is not a judgment which falls directly on the guilty—as formerly on Samaria and Jerusalem. The One who is prosecuted according to this story, the One whose passion is enacted in all its stages, is the only innocent One, the One who has indeed divine authority to accuse in the midst of sinful Israel, the " King of the Jews." There is, in fact, a complete reversal, an exchange of roles. Those who are to be judged are given space and freedom and power to judge. The Judge allows Himself to be judged. That is why He came to Jerusalem, entering it as a King. He is, in fact, judged. The content of the second part of the Gospel story gives us, therefore, a second and a difficult picture : difficult because of the oppression, anguish and execution of the one man who stands silent and suffering in the midst ; difficult because the accusation, condemnation and punishment to which it refers all fall on the very One on whom they ought to fall least of all, and not at all on those on whom they ought to fall. The most forceful expression of this scandalous contrast is the Barabbas episode (Mk. 15⁶⁻¹⁵) in which a murderer is in every respect acquitted instead of Jesus, and Jesus is condemned to be crucified in his place. It is only under compulsion that Simon of Cyrene (Lk. 23²⁶) carries His cross after Him. And those who are—unwillingly—crucified with Him are both robbers (Mk. 15²⁷ᶠ·) whose fellowship with Him shows that He is not dying a hero's death, but the death of a criminal—" He was numbered with the transgressors " (Is. 53¹²), He, the King and the Judge of Israel. Those who taunted Him on the cross (Mk. 15²⁹) were quite right: instead of the destruction of the temple—this! the man who had seemed to threaten it hanging in shame and agony and helplessness on a Roman gallows. That is what we are told in the second part of the Gospel story.

It is content simply to tell the story—this is how it was, this is how it happened. There is interpretation only in the lightest and sometimes rather alien strokes, of which we have to say much the same as we did of what we called the softenings occasionally found in the first part. The real commentary on this first part and the whole is, of course, the Easter story, which we can describe as the third and shortest part of the Gospel history. This tells us that God acknowledged this Jesus of Nazareth, the strange Judge who allowed Himself to be judged, by raising Him from the dead. It tells us of the forty days in which this same One—whose history this was and had to be—was again in the midst of His disciples, differently, but still actually in time and space, talking with them, eating and drinking with them, beginning with them a new Gospel history, the time of His community, the time of the Gospel as the good news about the Judge who allowed Himself to be judged, the time of the proclamation of this event. He Himself was and is this event, the origin, the authority, the power, the object of the proclamation laid on the community. He Himself, He alone : He who was alone and superior and majestic in Galilee ; He who was again alone but beaten and humiliated in Jerusalem, in the very midst of Israel. He, the Judge who allowed Himself to be judged, lives and rules and speaks and works. He is Himself the word which is to be proclaimed to all creatures as the Word of God. That is what the Easter narrative tells us. It gathers together the sum of all that has been told before. Or, rather, it tells us how the sum which God Himself had already gathered together in all that had gone before was revealed as such to the disciples—again by Jesus Himself. The Easter story is the Gospel story in its unity and completeness as the revealed story of redemption. The Easter story is the record of how it became what it was (in all its curious structure a history of redemption) for the disciples—not by their own discovery but by the act of God in the word and work of Jesus Himself. It tells us, therefore, that this history, Jesus Christ Himself as He exists in this history, is significant in and by itself. It tells us that all the significance which Jesus Christ as the subject and subject-matter of this history can acquire for individual men by means and as a result of proclamation (which has Him as its origin and object), has its basis and truth and practical and theoretical power in the fact that He is significant in and by Himself—even as He exists in this history. What is significant in itself has the power to become significant and will in fact become significant. But only that can become significant which is already significant, and in such a way that this being is the power of the corresponding becoming.

The Gospel story in its unity and completeness, Jesus Christ Himself who was the Judge and who allowed Himself to be judged in execution of His judgment, is the being which is the power of the corresponding becoming, the significant thing which can and will acquire significance for many individual men. It is of Him that we can and must speak, His story that we must recount, in Him as the One who existed in this story that we can and must believe. That this should happen is the meaning and purpose of the time of the community which begins with the Easter story. But He does not need first to be spoken of. Existing in that history, living and ruling and speaking and working as the One who exists in that history, He speaks for Himself whenever He is spoken of and His story is told and heard. It is not He that needs proclamation but proclamation that needs Him. He demands it. He makes it possible. He makes Himself its origin and object. He is its basis and truth and power. Our need of proclamation is another matter, but we need the proclamation which has its centre not in itself but outside itself in Him, in His history. Again, He does not need our faith, but our faith needs Him. He awakens and nourishes and maintains it by making Himself its origin and object, by allowing man to believe in Him. It is, of course, true that we need faith, but only the faith in which we look beyond ourselves, not to something that cannot be passed on to us, but to Him, considering and apprehending Him in the history in which He has His existence. Again, He does not need a fulfilment in our life, the life of believers. But if there is to be a fulfilment, if faith is not to be a mere acceptance of the truth of an old story, but the determination of our actual life in time, there is again a need of Him, of the fact that in virtue of the Easter story by which it happened, in the power of the sum which God has gathered in it, His history is itself not an old and past history, but a history which is the new history for every man, the presence and action of Jesus Christ Himself, true in the sense of being actuality for us, to be accepted as true because it proves itself to be actuality by its own power. We need this proof, this fulfilment in life—but only the proof and fulfilment which He gives, the actuality which does not need first to be brought about in us, but which is proper to Him, to His history and the telling of His history in itself, so that from Him and by Him it can become actuality for us. Jesus Christ as He exists in this history cannot, therefore, be merged into all the significances which do, in fact, come to Him, or disappear in them. He cannot, therefore, be identified with them or forgotten by reason of them or shamefacedly relegated to the sphere of a purely historical beginning and cause of the thing which really matters, proclamation, faith, fulfilment (and, if possible, the Church and sacraments). He Himself is the thing which really matters. He is always the Lord over and in everything that has its beginning and cause in Him. It all comes from Him, or better : He comes when it comes. It all lives by Him. It cannot be without Him. It looks back to Him. It also looks forward to the future as His future. It has to be guided by Him. It has to be interpreted by Him, and not *vice versa*. He Himself and His history as it took place then and there is identical with the Word of God, not with that which may result from the Word of God in the way of proclamation and faith and fulfilment in and through and from us men who hear it. The relationship between the significant thing which He is in Himself and the significances which He may acquire for us is an irreversible relationship.

On this basis and in this sense we say and must say, as when we tell a story : It came to pass that Jesus Christ, the Son of God, as man, took our place in order to judge us in this place by allowing Himself to be judged for us. In saying this, and saying it in this way, we keep to the Easter story as the commentary on the Gospel story in the unity and completeness of its first two parts : to the affirmation made in the event of Easter that in and for itself, in and through the existence of the One who acts and suffers in it, and therefore objectively for us, this Gospel story is the story of redemption.

We now turn to the question of a right understanding of the decisive words " for us " in this formula of the Judge judged for us.

We must begin by making a basic delimitation. In this context " for us " cannot have merely the general and formal meaning that what took place in Jesus Christ stands in relation to us to the extent that it applies to us, that our own existence is intended and envisaged and affected in this happening, in the existence of Jesus Christ. This is true, of course, but it needs to be defined much more precisely.

We could say the same of the creation of God both as a whole and in detail. What creature of God is there in which we do not to some extent find ourselves and our existence intended and envisaged and affected, so that in our own existence we have to come to some sort of reckoning with it ? Jesus Christ is, of course, a fellow-creature, and only as He is with us as such can He be " for us." But He is not " for us " merely in the sense that He is with us in this sense. Every fellow-man impinges on us as such in a most penetrating way, so that we could not fulfil our own human existence if we refused to fulfil it as a fellow human existence in relation to, and in encounter with, those who are near to us and implicitly those who are far away from us. But it is only in a very remote sense that we can say of the men that are with us that because by the very nature of things they are with us they are also " for us." Even the strongest " with us " is not enough to describe what Jesus Christ is in relation to us. No one and nothing in the order of creation can be " for us " in the strict sense, in the way in which Jesus Christ is " for us " in the order of reconciliation.

But we must be careful that the strict " for us " that we have to do with here does not become a " with us " which unites our existence with that of Jesus Christ, in which He is simply the author and initiator of what has to be fulfilled in and through us on the same level, in His discipleship and in fellowship with Him, as though the redemptive happening which has to be proclaimed and believed under His name were something which embraces both Him and us. It is true that Jesus Christ is the fellow-man who goes before us as an example and shows us the way. It is true that there is a discipleship, a fellowship with Him, and therefore an existence of Christians. It is true that what took place in Him, the redemptive happening which has to be proclaimed and believed under His name, does embrace Christian exist-ence and in a certain sense all human existence. But if we are to look and think and speak more precisely it is not a redemptive happening which embraces both Him and us, but the redemptive happening which embraces us in His existence, which takes us up into itself. He is the fellow-man who goes before us as an example and shows us the way because and in the power of the fact that He is " for us " : in a " for us " which cannot be equated with any " with us," by which every con-ceivable " with us " is established—as it were from without, from which all discipleship must derive its meaning and its power. Discipleship, the being of the Christian with Him, rests on the presupposition and can be carried through only on the presupposition that Jesus Christ is in Himself " for us "—without our being with Him, without any fulfilment of our being either with or after Him—on the contrary (Rom. 5 [6f.]), even when we were without strength, godless, and enemies. He does not become " for us " when there is some self-fulfilment either with or after Him, but He is for us in Himself, quite independ-ently of how we answer the question which is put to us of our fulfil-ment with or after Him. The event of redemption took place then and there in Him, and therefore " for us." In Him, as that which took place then and there, it embraces us, it becomes the basis of fellowship, it calls us to discipleship, but not in such a way that it becomes an event of redemption only through our obedience to this call, or is not an event of redemption through our disobedience, but in such a way that as the event of redemption which took place for us in Him it always comes before the question of our obedience or disobedience, it is always in itself the event of redemption which took place for us, whatever may be our answer to that question.

" Jesus Christ for us " means that as this one true man Jesus Christ has taken the place of us men, of many, in all the authority and omnipotence and competence of the one true God, in order to act in our name and therefore validly and effectively for us in all matters of reconciliation with God and therefore of our redemption and salvation, representing us without any co-operation on our part. In the event of His, the Gospel history, there took place that which permits and commands us to understand our history as a history of redemption and not of perdition. It has happened fully and exclusively in Him, excluding any need for completion. Whatever may happen in consequence of the fact that Jesus Christ is for us cannot add to it. It can only be the consequence of that which has taken place fully in Him and needs no completion. We can speak of it only as we look back to the fact that this One has acted as very man and very Son of God, that He has acted as our Representative and in our name, that His incarnation, His way of obedience has had and has fulfilled as its ultimate meaning and purpose the fact that He willed to do this and has done it : His activity as our Representative and Substitute.

In the New Testament the words ἀντί, ὑπέρ and περί are used to bring out the meaning of this activity of Jesus Christ. They cannot be understood if—quite apart from the particular view of the atonement made in Him which dominates these passages—we do not see that in general these prepositions speak of a place which ought to have been ours, that we ought to have taken this place, that we have been taken from it, that it is occupied by another, that this other acts in this place as only He can, in our cause and interest, that we cannot add to anything that He does there because the place where we might do so is occupied by Him, that anything further which might happen can result only from what is done by Him in our place and in our cause. If someone gives his life a λύτρον ἀντὶ πολλῶν (Mk. 10⁴⁵), then he necessarily acts in the place and as the representative of πολλοί,.paying on their account but without their co-operation what they cannot pay for themselves. If he sheds his blood περὶ πολλῶν (Mt. 26²⁸), that again is an act which is to the advantage of πολλοί, but it is his blood which is shed and not a drop of theirs. Whoever it is, Peter who fled or one of the Roman soldiers, they none of them have a part in this blood-shedding. The Jesus who was condemned to be crucified in the place of Barabbas (Mk. 15⁶⁻¹⁵) stands on the one side, and Barabbas who was pardoned at the expense of Jesus stands on the other ; for he was not crucified, nor did he really contribute to his own liberation which came about when sentence was pronounced on that other. The Lamb of God which takes away the sin of the world (Jn. 1²⁹) stands on the one side in this supremely active relationship to the world, and the world for which it is done stands on the other side, with nothing to add to this relationship. If the good shepherd of Jn. 10$^{11, 15, 17}$ gives His life ὑπὲρ τῶν προβάτων, He does so to save the life of the sheep, but without any co-operation on their part. If, according to the saying of the High Priest in Jn. 11^{50}, it was expedient that one man should die ὑπὲρ τοῦ λαοῦ, this expressly involves that the people should not die, but that he should die in place of the people to save the people. The same contrast is very clearly developed in the passage in Rom. 5$^{6f.}$ to which we have frequently alluded. Jesus Christ " maketh intercession for us " (ἐντυγχάνει ὑπὲρ ἡμῶν), we are told in Rom. 8^{34} in a passage which shows the significance for believers to-day of an event of redemption which took place once and for all. And according to the Pauline eucharistic formula what Christians continually receive at the Lord's Table is τὸ σῶμά μου τὸ ὑπὲρ ὑμῶν (1 Cor. 11^{24}). He obviously pursues our interest in our place by " giving Himself for our sins, that he might deliver us from the present evil world " (Gal. 1^4). But, again, there is no suggestion of our participating in this action. He is made a curse for us (Gal. 3^{13}) to free us from the curse : for us, but without us—everything depends on this— without our having any longer to bear or partially to bear the curse. We are simply those who have been redeemed from the curse by Him. And when we consider the many New Testament passages which point to the meaning and purpose of the existence of Jesus Christ " for us," whether or not they use these prepositions, can we understand any one of them except in the light of this unbridgeable antithesis ? Can they point us to any other activity than that which involves this consistent exchange ? It is true that certain imperatives result from this exchange. But where is the meaning and purpose of the event made dependent on what we have to do or not to do on the basis of this event ? Where especially is the decisive demand of faith as it is addressed to us related to anything but this in itself meaningful event, to the " for us " there and then accomplished in Jesus Christ once and for all, and therefore valid before ever we even heard the demand of faith, let alone fulfilled it ?

We will now try to expound and understand in detail the " for us " interpreted in this strict sense. In so doing it will be our concern (in contrast to certain one-sided elements in earlier dogmatic conceptions) to keep in view as far as possible the whole of the New Testament witness to this event, and especially, of course, the whole of the event itself.

1. Jesus Christ was and is " for us " in that He took our place as our Judge. We have seen that in its root and origin sin is the arrogance in which man wants to be his own and his neighbour's judge. According to Gen. 3^5 the temptation which involves man's disobedience to God's commandment is the evil desire to know what is good and evil. He ought to leave this knowledge to God, to see his freedom in his ability to adhere to God's decisions in his own decisions. He becomes a sinner in trying to be as God : himself a judge. To be a man—in the world which is hostile to God and unreconciled with Him—is to be the pseudo-sovereign creature which finds its dignity and pride in regarding it as its highest good and most sacred duty to have knowledge of good and evil and to inform itself about it (in relation to itself and others). To be a man means in practice to want to be a judge, to want to be able and competent to pronounce ourselves free and righteous and others more or less guilty. We enjoy ourselves in this

craft and dignity. We find our consolation and refuge and strength in exercising it. In our supposed right to do this we all have our safe stronghold, a trusty shield and weapon in relation to ourselves, our neighbours and God. The event of redemption in Jesus Christ not only compromises this position, not only attacks this safe stronghold, but destroys it. It is not merely a moral accusation against the pride of man. It is not merely an intellectual exposure of the error which has led him into it. It is the fact by which the position of man is taken away, by which it is made impossible and untenable, by which the safe stronghold is breached. Jesus Christ as very man and very God has taken the place of every man. He has penetrated to that place where every man is in his inner being supremely by and for himself. This sanctuary belongs to Him and not to man. He has to do what has to be done there. What is man in relation to Him? One who is dispossessed, expelled, a displaced person. He has no more say even in this home of his, this place where the flesh is most intensively and happily and seriously flesh. His knowledge of good and evil is no longer of any value. He is no longer judge. Jesus Christ is Judge. He is not only over us—a final court which we must finally remember and respect. He is radically and totally for us, in our place. He knows and judges and decides at the very point where we regard it as our business to do this. To do this is really His affair, not ours, and He sees to it. Certainly this knowing and judging and deciding, this judgment has necessarily to do with us. To be a man means to exist under the occurrence of this judgment. Yet not— this is the error of man reversed in Jesus Christ—in the occurrence of the judgment in which man himself is the judge, but in the occurrence of the judgment in which this function is that of God Himself. It is this function of God as Judge which has been re-established once and for all in Jesus Christ. What we want to do for ourselves has been taken out of our hands in Him. Not by a prohibition, the renewal of the command not to eat of the tree of knowledge. We have transgressed this command, and how would its repetition help us? The fruit of this tree which was eaten with such relish is still rumbling in all of us. It is by an action that we are removed from the judge's seat, by the fact that Jesus Christ did for us what we wanted to do for ourselves. However radically we are transgressors of that command, however much that fruit may rumble in us, we are not what we wanted to be because He is for us, He—the man who knows and judges and decides for us. In His hand there lies this solemn and powerful and redemptive instrument. In ours there is only a copy, a foolish and dangerous but ultimately ineffective toy. That is how things are between Him and us.

The fact that Jesus Christ judges in our place can and must be understood from two different standpoints. It certainly means the

abasement and jeopardising of every man. This happening puts an
end to his supposed greatness, his dream of divine likeness. At the
very place where he finds his own glory he must see another dispose
and rule. Another man ? It is not merely a matter of some harmless
idea of God, the comfortable transcendence which we can know and
which makes us exalt ourselves all the more self-consciously. No, it
is a matter of the concrete form of a fellow-man occupying that place
which we all think it our sacred right to occupy. It is a matter of
the very man Jesus of Nazareth in whom God has crossed our path
and by whom we find ourselves deposed. Abasement by an abstract
" god " is a safe enough matter which we can turn to our own glory.
But abasement by God in the flesh, in the person of this fellow-man, is
a dangerous matter. It is a real and concrete abasement. If this
man is my divine Judge, I myself cannot be judge any longer. I have
forfeited the claim to be it and the enjoyment of being it. In the
history of this man it came to pass that I was relegated from the
sphere in which I wished to judge and placed in the sphere in which
I can only see and hear and learn what the judgment really is by which
I have to judge myself. And that means that I am jeopardised. For
where does our own judgment always lead ? To the place where we
pronounce ourselves innocent, and where, on account of their venial
or mortal sins, and with more or less indulgence and understanding or
severity and inflexibility, we pronounce others guilty. That is how we
live. And that is how we can no longer live in the humiliating power
of what took place in Jesus Christ. We are threatened by it because
there is a complete turning of the tables. He who has acted there as
Judge will also judge me, and He and not I will judge others. What
then ? Do I not gather from His coming in my place and my deposition
that I have been a bad judge, that all my judgments are annulled, and
that my turn will now come in a way in which it could not do before ?
Before this Judge I obviously cannot stand, because all my previous
being and activity was based on and determined by the fact that I
wanted to be my own judge and acted as such. And will not others
be justified, at least—and to my shame—in relation to the fine way
in which I judged them, which was in fact so bad and incompetent a
way ? That is the one aspect.

The other is that the fact that Jesus Christ judges in our place
means an immeasurable liberation and hope. The loss which we always
bewail and which we seem to suffer means in reality that a heavy and
indeed oppressive burden is lifted from us when Jesus Christ becomes
our Judge. It is a nuisance, and at bottom an intolerable nuisance, to
have to be the man who gives sentence. It is a constraint always to
have to be convincing ourselves that we are innocent, we are in the
right. It is similarly an affliction always to have to make it clear to
ourselves so that we can cling to it that others are in one way or
another in the wrong, and to have to rack our brains how we can

make it clear to them, and either bring them to an amendment of their ways or give them up as hopeless, withdrawing from them or fighting against them as the enemies of all that is good and true and beautiful. It is a terrible thing to know good and evil if only in this ostensible and ineffective way, and to have to live with this doubtful knowledge. It agrees quite simply with what is written in Gen. 2^{17}, that if we eat of this tree we must die. We are all in process of dying from this office of judge which we have arrogated to ourselves. It is, therefore, a liberation that it has come to pass in Jesus Christ that we are deposed and dismissed from this office because He has come to exercise it in our place. What does that mean but that at one stroke the whole of the evil responsibility which man has arrogantly taken to himself is taken from him ? It is no longer necessary that I should pronounce myself free and righteous. It is no longer necessary that even if only in my heart I should pronounce others guilty. Neither will help either me or them in the very least. Whatever may be the answer to the question of their life and mine, at any rate it no longer needs to be given by me. To find it and to pronounce it is no longer my office or in any way my concern. I am not the Judge. Jesus Christ is Judge. The matter is taken out of my hands. And that means liberation. A great anxiety is lifted, the greatest of all. I can turn to other more important and more happy and more fruitful activities. I have space and freedom for them in view of what has happened in Jesus Christ. And that also means hope. I have good cause to fear before the true Judge, who is not I. When I think of Him I may have fears for others. But not in the obscure or reluctant fear I might have before any judge and his rule if they are outside my control. In fear before the Son of God who became man for me, whose coming in my place as Judge—for all the hardship it involves for me—is a benefit, being made as part of God's turning to man and therefore to me, for the reconciliation of the world with God and therefore for my reconciliation with God. That means, therefore, in fear before the Judge on whose good and redemptive will I can already count, whose decision I can look forward to with trust whatever it may be, in whose hands I can know that my own case and that of others is at least safe. In a fear, therefore, which at bottom is hope. He who knows about myself and others as I never could or should do, will judge concerning me and them in a way which is again infinitely more just than I could ever do—and judge and decide in such a way that it will be well done. Indeed, in such a way that it *is* well done, this real Judge having already decided at the point when the Word became and was flesh. And whatever the decision may be, I have reason to look forward to its disclosure with terror, but with a terror-stricken joy.

This is the first concrete sense in which we have to see and understand the fact that Jesus Christ was and is for us.

That He is the Judge, and that He makes judgment impossible for us and takes it away from us, is the explanation of the terrible address to the scribes and Pharisees who let themselves be called rabbis, fathers and teachers (Mt. 23$^{1f.}$). It is the indicative which stands behind the evangelical command not to take the top seats but the lower (Lk. 14^8), not to exalt but to abase ourselves (Mt. 23^{12}), and especially : " Judge not, that ye be not judged. For with what judgment ye judge, ye shall be judged ; and with what measure ye mete, it shall be measured to you again " (Mt. 7$^{1f.}$). The One who forbids men to judge, who restrains and dispenses them from it, is the One who has come as the real Judge. He makes clear what is true and actual in His existence among men as such : that the one who exalts himself as judge will be abased, that he can only fall into the judgment which will come upon himself. The evangelical prohibition frees us from the necessity of this movement in a vicious circle. Freed in this sense, Paul writes in triumph : " But with me it is a very small thing that I should be judged of you, or of man's judgment : yea, I judge not mine own self . . . he that judgeth me is the Lord " (1 Cor. 4$^{3f.}$). And even more strongly in Rom. 8^{34} : " Who is he that condemneth ? It is Christ that died, yea rather, that is risen again, who is even at the right hand of God." Hence the admonition that the brethren must not judge one another, for we must all appear before the judgment seat of God (the βῆμα τοῦ Χριστοῦ in 2 Cor. 5^{10}). " As I live, saith the Lord, every knee shall bow to me, and every tongue shall confess to God " (Rom. 14$^{11f.}$). No man can judge another man's servant (Rom. 14^4). This is the reflection of the first sense of the " for us " in the mirror of Christian ethics.

It is the basic sense for all that follows. We should have to suppress or obviously misinterpret the first great section of the Gospel story—Jesus in Galilee —if we tried to ignore the fact that as He judges for us it is decided who it is that lets Himself be judged for us in order to pronounce that divine word of power by which we are pardoned : the One who is justified and who overcomes for us. He is the subject and not the object of what happens—the subject even when He is object. He is the Lord as He fulfils the work which He has under-taken for us, the work of His own deepest humiliation. He has the omnipotence in the power of this work to bear our sins, to bear them away from us, to suffer the consequences of our sins, to be the just One for us sinners, to forgive us our sins. He has this because primarily He Himself is the Judge who overlooks and eliminates our liability to be judged. It is in this omnipotence that He confronts Israel, goes to Jerusalem, enters the city of the kings as-a King, shows and promises and gives His body and blood to His disciples with the bread and wine of the Lord's Supper, allows Himself to be kissed by Judas and delivers Himself up into the hands of the soldiers. This is all a sovereign action. It is completed and its meaning is revealed in the passion of Christ, on the cross. Even on the cross it is a divine act. Rightly to understand the passion and cross of Christ, we must not abstract it from the sequence in which this is clear. We must understand the first part of the story as a commentary on the second, and *vice versa*. His passion and the cross are therefore to be understood as His action. It is as the One who carries His cross to Golgotha that He comes to judge the quick and the dead.

2. Jesus Christ was and is for us in that He took the place of us sinners. That sounds hard, and naturally it needs to be explained. But the fact itself is a hard one however we explain it. From what we have just said it is not for us to judge. It is our basic sin to take the place of the judge, to try to judge ourselves and others. All our other sins, both small and great, derive ultimately from this source.

But if this is so, how can the Son of God take our place, which means in this context the strange place where we make the illegitimate and impossible attempt to leave the place which belongs to us and to occupy that which does not ? How does He come to the place where we are caught in this sin and therefore in the outbreak of every sin ; our place as wicked disputants and therefore evil-doers ; our place as enemies against God ?

We must say at once that He does not come to this place to do there what we ourselves do. In taking our place as Judge He takes the place which belongs to Him, which is His own from all eternity. He does not, therefore, do anything illegitimate. And it is not like ours an unrighteous but a righteous judgment which He exercises in this place. He does in this place the very opposite of what we usually do. In this place He is pure and spotless and sinless. From the fact that He takes it there do not follow any of the transgressions which in our case follow from that first transgression.

But the great and inconceivable thing is that He acts as Judge in our place by taking upon Himself, by accepting responsibility for that which we do in this place. He " who knew no sin " (2 Cor. 5^{21})— who knew nothing of that illegitimate and impossible attempt and all the transgression that it inevitably brought with it, nothing of our disputing and evil-doing and enmity against God—gives Himself (like a *rara avis*) to the fellowship of those who are guilty of all these things, and not only that, but He makes their evil case His own. He is above this fellowship and confronts it and judges it and condemns it in that He takes it upon Himself to be the bearer and Representative, to be responsible for this case, to expose Himself to the accusation and sentence which must inevitably come upon us in this case. He as One can represent all and make Himself responsible for the sins of all because He is very man, in our midst, one of us, but as one of us He is also very God and therefore He exercises and reveals amongst us the almighty righteousness of God. He can conduct the case of God against us in such a way that He takes from us our own evil case, taking our place and compromising and burdening Himself with it.

And as He does that, it ceases to be our sin. It is no longer our affair to prosecute and represent this case. The right and possibility of doing so has been denied and taken away from us. What He in divine omnipotence did amongst us as one of us prevents us from being our own judges, from even wanting to be, from making that senseless attempt on the divine prerogative, from sinning in that way and making ourselves guilty. In that He was and is for us that end is closed, and so is the evil way to that end. He is the man who entered that evil way, with the result that we are forced from it ; it can be ours no longer.

But that means that it became His way : His the sin which we commit on it; His the accusation, the judgment and the curse which necessarily fall on us there. He is the unrighteous amongst those who can no longer be so because He was and is for them. He is the burdened amongst those who have been freed from their burden by Him. He is the condemned amongst those who are pardoned because the sentence which destroys them is directed against Him. He who is in the one person the electing God and the one elect man is as the rejecting God, the God who judges sin in the flesh, in His own person the one rejected man, the Lamb which bears the sin of the world that the world should no longer have to bear it or be able to bear it, that it should be radically and totally taken away from it.

This is undoubtedly the mystery of the divine mercy. God acted in this way because He grieved over His people, because He did not will to abandon the world in its unreconciled state and therefore on the way which leads to destruction, because He willed to show to it an unmerited faithfulness as the Creator, because in His own inconceivable way He loved it. But in this respect it is as well to be clear that the mystery of His mercy is also the mystery of His righteousness. He did not take the unreconciled state of the world lightly, but in all seriousness. He did not will to overcome and remove it from without, but from within. It was His concern to create order, to convert the world to Himself, and therefore genuinely to reconcile it. He did not, therefore, commit an act of arbitrary kindness—which would have been no help to the world. He did what we might call a neat and tidy job. He accepted the world in the state in which He found it, in its alienation from Himself, in the state of sinful men. To bring about this conversion He really took the place of this man. And He did not take the place of this man merely as God but as man : " to fulfil all righteousness," to do right at the very place where man had done wrong, and in that way to make peace with man, to the triumph of His faithfulness, to His own magnifying in creation and by the creature. The Word became flesh that there might be the judgment of sin in the flesh and the resurrection of the flesh.

We must be careful not to describe this event, the coming of Jesus Christ in place of us sinners, this exchange between the divine and our false human position, as an exchange only in appearance, as a kind of dressing up or masquerade, in view of the sinlessness of Jesus Christ. If anything is in bitter earnest it is the fact that God Himself in His eternal purity and holiness has in the sinless man Jesus Christ taken up our evil case in such a way that He willed to make it, and has in fact made it, His own. He did not, in fact, spare His only Son but delivered Him up for us all (Rom. 8³²). And the sinlessness, the obedience of this one man (we shall have to speak of it later), is that He did not refuse to be delivered up and therefore to take the place of us sinners.

As such He is quite alone amongst us, the only One who is judged and condemned and rejected, just as He is the only One who has come and acts amongst us as the Judge. He is quite alone as disputatious man, the transgressor, the enemy against God, which each of us must recognise in ourselves, but because He is there and we can look at Him, we no longer have to recognise in ourselves, being freed from the intolerable responsibility of it—not because it is no longer a fact, but because He has made it His own for us. It can only be the pride which will not bow to Him as the Judge acting in our place which in face of the fact that He has made Himself a sinner for us still clings to it as man's own case, still tries to ascribe it to man that he will and can and must answer for his own sin before God. Our sin is no longer our own. It is His sin, the sin of Jesus Christ. God— He Himself as the obedient Son of the Father—has made it His own. And in that way He has judged it and judged us as those who committed it.

Luther was not exaggerating when he put the alternative : *Oportet peccatum nostrum fieri Christi proprium peccatum, aut in aeternum peribimus* (*On Gal.* 3[13], 1535, *W.A.* 40[1], 435, 17). When in fulfilment of the divine judgment it took place that He willed to make our sin His own, and did in fact make it His own, it was decided that in no other way could it cease to be our sin which as such would inevitably bring us to eternal perdition. And in substance Luther's drastic commentary on this exchange is quite right, that God the Father said to God the Son : *Tu sis Petrus ille negator, Paulus ille persecutor, blasphemus et violentus, David ille adulter, peccator ille qui comedit pomum in Paradiso, latro ille in cruce, in summa : Tu sis omnium hominum persona, qui feceris omnium hominum peccata, tu ergo cogita, ut solvas, et pro eis satisfacias* (*ib.* 437, 23). And so Christ must and is willing to stand as *omnium maximus latro, homicida, adulter, fur, sacrilegus, blasphemus, etc., quo nullus maior unquam in mundo fuerit* (*ib.* 433, 26). And it is the secret of what took place in Jesus Christ that in Him there met and clashed, *summum, maximum et solum peccatum* and *summa, maxima et sola iustitia*, but in such a way that there could be no doubt as to the outcome : *In Christo vincitur, occiditur et sepelitur universum peccatum et manet victrix et regnatrix iustitia in aeternum* (*ib.* 439, 13).

To verify this, to see the truth of it, we have only to look at the Gospel passion-narrative and especially the role of Jesus in it. We have already said that the divine subject of the judgment on man as which Jesus appears in the first part of the evangelical record becomes the object of this judgment from the time of the episode in Gethsemane onwards. If this judgment is fulfilled at all—and that is what the Evangelists seem to be trying to say in the second part of their account—then it is with this reversal. Jesus represents men at the place which is theirs according to the divine judgment, by putting Himself in the place which is theirs on the basis of and in accordance with their human unrighteousness. Jesus maintains the right by electing to let Himself be put in the wrong. He speaks for Himself by being silent. He conquers by suffering. Without ceasing to be action, as action in the strongest sense of the word, as the work of God on earth attaining its goal, His action becomes passion.

The Gospel records betray something of the great and well-grounded astonishment at the unheard of nature of this happening, this transition, this reversing of roles. The shrinking of Jesus in the prayer in Gethsemane is a strong trace of it. According to this record it is not self-evident that He should be given this cup to drink and that He should take it upon Himself to drink it (Mk. 14[36]). This prayer is, as it were, a remarkable historical complement to the eternal decision taken in God Himself, one which was not taken easily but with great difficulty, one to which He won through, which He won from Himself. And, of course, the question of the Crucified : Had God forsaken Him ? (Mk. 15^{34}), points even more strongly in the same direction. On a very different level we can think of the shrinking of the unrighteous judge Pilate as he made the human decision : its unusual and scandalous nature is not concealed from him. Similarly we may think of the darkness which we are told later came down at the hour of Jesus' death (Mk. 15^{33}), the rending of the veil of the temple (Mk. 15^{37}), the earthquake which shook the rocks and opened the graves (Mt. 27^{51}), as though—in anticipation of its own end—the cosmos had to register the strangeness of this event : the transformation of the accuser into the accused and the judge into the judged, the naming and handling of the Holy God as one who is godless. But it could not be prevented. It had to take place, and it did in fact take place. Not by the reign of chance, nor in consequence of a human nexus of guilt and destiny. The historical pragmatics which is necessary to bind together the two parts of the Gospel story, to explain the transition from action to passion, is as obscure as it possibly could be in the Gospels. In what happens to Jesus, the participants, both Jews and Gentiles, are described in the factual commentary of Acts (2^{23}, 4^{28}) as—for all the obvious and supreme guilt and reprehensibility of their action—only instruments in the hand of God, agents and executors of " the determinate counsel and foreknowledge of God." It does not excuse them—but it was necessary that Christ should " suffer these things " (Lk. 24^{26}). No, His God had not really forsaken Him. In that strange and scandalous reversal we have a necessary fulfilment of the divine purpose which the Son accepts in fear and trembling as the will of His Father, and which the participants in what is done to Jesus must serve *nolentes volentes.* They thought to do Him evil, as once the brethren of Joseph had done (Gen. 50^{20}) : " But God meant it unto good, to bring to pass, as it is this day, to save much people alive." Yet the divine benefit consists with merciless clarity in the hard thing that Jesus must and will allow Himself to be the one great sinner among all other men : *quo nullus maior unquam in mundo fuerit*—to be declared to be such by the mouth of every man, and treated as such at the hand of every man, yet not apart from the will of God, not in abrogation of it, but according to its eternal and wise and righteous direction, in fulfilment of the divine judgment on all men. Jesus must and will allow Himself to take the place which is presumably not His but theirs for the sake of righteousness in the supreme sense. This allowing was determined and effected in divine necessity and freedom. It took place when Jesus was sought out and arrested as a malefactor, when He was accused as a blasphemer before the Sanhedrin and as an agitator against Cæsar before Pilate, in both cases being prosecuted and found guilty. It took place when He refrained from saving Himself, from proving His innocence, from defending and justifying Himself, from making even the slightest move to evade this prosecution and verdict. It took place when by means of His great silence He confessed eloquently enough that this had to happen, that He must and will allow it to do so. We might ask why—even if His life was forfeit—He set so little store by His honour as the One sent by God ? We can explain this only if He saw the triumph of His honour as the One sent by God in what happened to Him, in what He had to suffer when He was set in antithesis to all other men as the one great sinner, because He fulfilled the will of God in so doing, because He did what had to be done for them and the world, taking upon Him their sin and in that way taking it away from them. If this action is the meaning of His passion, then it is meaningful as such. The Gospel story says this factually. It does not offer any theological explanation. It says hardly anything about the significance of the event. But in telling us what it has to tell, and in the way it does, it testifies that we are dealing with the event which at bottom cannot bear any other theological explanation than that which we have here tried to give it in actual agreement with every Church which is worthy of the name of Christian.

We now turn to a short discussion of the scope of this event. In view of the fact that Jesus Christ took the place of us sinners there are three directions at least in which we have to look.

If it is the case that Jesus Christ made His own our evil case, our sin, then in Him we obviously have to do with the reflection, the supremely objective source of knowledge of that case. That we are sinners, and what our sin is, is something we can never know by reflection about ourselves in the light of a standard of good and evil which we have freely chosen or discovered. This is made impossible by the fact that with His coming we are displaced from the office of judging. We cannot tell ourselves that we are accused, and what the accusation is against us. We have to be told it by that in which we fail. We have to learn it where God Himself has told it to us by taking so seriously the accusation against us and our corruption that He took it upon Himself in His Son, that He willed to encounter us as the man corrupted and accused. For what do we know of ourselves, so long as He does not tell us, so long as He does not tell us in such a way that in His own person He holds out to us and shows us what we are ? He knows, and He gives us authentic information about ourselves, about our way as the disputants and wrong-doers and enemies of God that we are. He does it by coming amongst us in the character and form and role of a man like that, and therefore showing us by example what the being of every man is in His eyes and therefore in truth : How He knows us, and what we are before Him. In that He takes our place it is decided what our place is. In that He allows Himself to be sentenced as man, sentence is pronounced on us. The wrath of God against all ungodliness and unrighteousness of men, who hold the truth in unrighteousness, is revealed, and revealed concretely and finally from heaven (Rom. 1[18]), in the fact that God gives Himself not only to encounter the man against whom He must and does turn His wrath but to take His place. In Jesus Christ we see who we are by being seen as those we are—being seen as God in Him acknowledges what we are, accepting solidarity with our state and being, making Himself responsible for our sin. In respect of the knowledge of our evil way there is in face of Jesus Christ no escape. There are no excuses or explanations. There is no possibility of understanding evil in the light of some higher necessity. There can be no diminution of its essence as that which is against God, or of our responsibility for it. In face of Jesus Christ we are forced to a simple recognition of the nature of evil as that which is against God, and of the fact that we do it. For in Him God has sought us out in our own state and being, accepting solidarity with us. He does not lie. In that God acknowledges us as sinners in Jesus Christ, His truth is the guarantee that we are such : that we are doers of that which is against Him. We would have to deny Him instead of acknowledging Him if we tried to deny that we are such, if we tried to deny that we are those in whose place Jesus Christ came to convert us to Himself. A confession of faith which in, with and under the confession of faith was not ready to be a confession of sin would not be a confession of faith.

From the same point we look at another dimension. If it is the case that Jesus Christ has made our sin His own, then He stands in our place as the Representative of our evil case and it is He who answers for it (as ours). It is then (as ours) the sin which is forgiven us in Him. If we are not to say something which is merely cheap and frivolous at this point we have to say most emphatically : as ours. The knowledge of what we are which is based on His coming for us must not be forgotten or obliterated in the other things this coming means for us. As the One who bears our sin, as the One who answers for it while it is taken away from us and forgiven, He does not stand in some far-off neutral state. He is not for us in such a way that we hardly see Him, that we can let His work be done for us as spectators of an alien work which is indeed done in our favour but which hardly affects us because it is done for us, that we do not have to let it take place to us in the true sense. It is true that we are crowded out of our own place by Him in that He made our sin His own. It is true that we can dwell only beside His being for us—His being as th∙ One who has made Himself responsible for our evil being. It is true that we can look on His work only as in fact an alien work. It is true that we cannot contribute anything at all to this His being and work for us. But it is also true that the place from which we find ourselves crowded out is always our place. It is also true—and if our consideration is not to be an idle and unprofitable gaping, if it is to be the active and fruitful contemplation of the redemption which has taken place for us in Him, the looking of faith, this is something we must remember as the old Passion-songs always do remember so impressively : *tua res agitur* ; it is our sin which He has made His own and which now rests on Him. Made sin for us, He stands in our place. He represents us in that which we truly are. That He represents us in it does not mean that we are not it, but that what we truly are, our being in sin, is taken over by Him, that He is responsible for it in divine power, that it is taken from us with divine authority, and forgiven. But although He takes it over, and is responsible for it and it is forgiven us, it is still our being in sin. To look in faith on the One who took our place means always to see ourselves in Him as the men we are, to recognise ourselves in Him as the men for whom He has taken responsibility, who are forgiven. It is on the fact that this first aspect remains and does not disappear, that in Him we again find ourselves and indeed for the first time see ourselves as we really are, that there rests the meaning and power of the further fact, that we know that He has taken over from us that which we are, that we are no longer responsible for it, that as our own sin it is forgiven us in Him. It is a matter of this liberation. Because our evil case otherwise meant our inevitable destruction, God willed to, make it His own in Jesus Christ. What we are He Himself willed to become, in order to take and transform it from within, to make of it something new, the being of man reconciled with Himself. Our being in sin is now in His hands : as such in all its reality it is no longer in our own hands. It is no longer the object of our care and anxiety before Him as our Judge. But no more is it the object of all kinds of artifices by which we try to justify ourselves, to save ourselves from what we are. As such we can only effect and confirm once again what we really are, those who die at the judgment throne of God, and therefore sinners. If our being in sin in all its reality is now in the hands of God (and in Jesus Christ it has happened that God has put it in His hands), then as such it is, of course, the object of our knowledge—not of our knowledge of ourselves, but of our knowledge of God. But if it is the object of our knowledge of God, then in Jesus Christ we find that as our being in sin it has been taken over by God. He took it upon Himself as a matter of the care and anxiety and shame and anguish which He accepted in His Son when the Son took to Himself the accusation which was against us. Therefore it cannot be any more a matter of our care and anxiety and shame and anguish. In Him, not in ourselves but in Him, we see its removal, its taking away, its destruction as an object of our responsibility. We are now summoned—not in ourselves but in Him—to see and acknowledge that we are liberated, and that—again not in ourselves but in Him, by His coming for us, by His taking our place—our sin is cancelled and forgiven. We are summoned to accept our life on this presupposition, as those who are liberated, whose sin is cancelled and forgiven in Him : in the genuine confidence that our being in sin (as our own) belongs to God and not to us, that the responsibility which we owe Him in this matter has been borne by Him. We do not believe in Jesus Christ if this is not our fully assured confidence. The Son of God has sought and found His glory in accepting the dishonour of our state. We therefore do Him despite if we try to shake the fact that He has done it truly and effectively, so that the wrestling with our dishonour, our thought and imagination, has been taken once and for all out of our own hands.

This forces us to look in yet another direction. If Jesus Christ came and took our place as the Representative of our evil case, then there is nothing more that we can seek and do there even as evildoers. Even at the place where we had and exercised our supposed glorious liberty to justify ourselves, to prove ourselves in the right, to make a sin of our freedom, He Himself now stands, accused and condemned and rejected for us, but in all His divine majesty. The way back is therefore cut off and barred to us. To look at Jesus Christ who is for us means to look at ourselves as those who are utterly guilty of sin but who are no longer pledged and committed to it, who have no other ground to do evil now that the ground has been cut from under our feet. It is only if we look past Jesus Christ, not in faith but in unbelief, that we can still think that we have that freedom. We will have something even more strong and radical to say about this later. For the moment it is enough to state that if we find in Jesus Christ the One who stands in our place as the one great sinner, if we find ourselves again in Jesus Christ, ourselves as sinners represented by this One, then we can never again ascribe to ourselves this freedom, nor can we see any further future for us in our sin, as we confess ourselves guilty of it. In the reflection of the existence of Jesus Christ who took our place, who made His own the disputing of which He Himself knew nothing, we find ourselves utterly accused and condemned and rejected for what we are, but in Him who took our place. The only possibility which is still open to us as we look at Him and at ourselves in Him is that of repentance, of turning away from the being and activity, from all that we have to see and acknowledge as guilty in Him, of readiness for this, of turning to what can be made of our evil case now that it is the case of Jesus Christ, now that He has undertaken to be responsible for it and to wrestle with it. As we look at Jesus Christ we can no more will and affirm and accept it than the responsibility of it can cause us care and anxiety. The two belong directly together : If we want to be careful and anxious about it, we are back again on the crooked way of inquiring concerning our own self-justification and therefore on the way of sin ; and if we take this way again, our sin will inevitably cause us fresh care and anxiety. As we look at Jesus Christ and ourselves in Him, we are prevented from doing either and both. There is no " way back."

As we look back on the whole of our second point we are reminded that it has a clear complement in New Testament ethics.

Why is it so forcefully impressed upon the heart of a Christian that he must not only not regard persecution as a " strange thing " (1 Pet. 4[12]), or fear it (Mt. 10[26], 1 Pet. 2[14]), but that he must think of being persecuted and despised and slandered for righteousness sake as joy (Mt. 5[12], 1 Pet. 4[13]), and blessedness (Mt. 5[10f.], 1 Pet. 3[14]) and acceptable with God (1 Pet. 2[20]) ? What is the meaning of this self-sacrifice ? Might it not be perhaps a kind of masochism, and therefore an introverted sadism, which can sometimes revert to its real self ? Why are Christians not to avenge themselves (Rom. 12[19]), not to resist evil (Mt. 5[39]), not to give evil for evil or reviling for reviling (Rom. 12[17], 1 Pet. 3[9]) ? Why not ? Does not this give an opening for all kinds of unrighteousness and folly and wickedness amongst men ? How can this defencelessness not be dishonourable ? Why are Christians even to love their enemies (Mt. 5[43f.]), to give them food and drink (Rom. 12[20]), to pray for them (Mt. 5[44]), as Stephen actually did (like Jesus Himself in Lk. 23[34]), when in his final words he said : " Lord, lay not this sin to their charge " (Ac. 7[60]) ? Is not this command of an exaggerated enthusiasm of love binding only on a few, without our being able to say in what way it can be binding even on them ? And if not, in what sense and on what ground is it a clear commandment of God ?

It would be difficult if not impossible to answer these questions if we had not to take account of the fact that when we look at the Lord by whose work and word the New Testament community was assembled and ordered we are looking at the One who did not come to call the righteous but sinners (Mt. 9¹³), who from the very first (Lk. 15²) received sinners and ate with them and therefore held the most concrete fellowship with them, and in the end took the place of all other sinners as the one great sinner. If the disciples are persecuted and despised and slandered, then their existence is a faint but not obscure reflection of His. " The disciple is not above his master, nor the servant above his lord. It is enough for the disciple that he be as his master, and the servant as his lord. If they have called the master of the house Beelzebub, how much more shall they call them of his household ? " (Mt. 10²⁴ᶠ·). For that reason—we have here a participation in the passion of Christ (1 Pet. 4¹³)—it is all joy and blessedness and grace to be persecuted, not something strange or to be feared. " For even hereunto were ye called : because Christ also suffered for us, leaving us an example, that ye should follow his steps " (1 Pet. 2²¹). For that reason, under the compelling power of our consideration of the One who was and acted for us as One accused and condemned and rejected, we are given the admonition : " Who, when he was reviled, reviled not again ; when he suffered, he threatened not ; but committed himself to him that judgeth righteously ; who his own self bare our sins in his own body on the tree, that we being dead to sins should live unto righteousness " (1 Pet. 2²²ᶠ·). From this we learn that we are not to oppose evil, as we are tempted, by repaying it with evil. Christians who know that He did this for them belong to Him. In their opposition to evil and evil men they have to comport themselves as these words demand. From this there follows quite naturally the supreme command to love our enemies. Jesus Christ fought His enemies, the enemies of God—as we all are (Rom. 5¹⁰, Col. 1²¹)—no, He loved His enemies, by identifying Himself with them. Compared with that what is the bit of forbearance or patience or humour or readiness to help or even intercession that we are willing and ready to bring and offer in the way of loving our enemies ? But obviously when we look at what Jesus Christ became and was for us, we cannot leave out some little love for our enemies as a sign of our recognition and understanding that this is how He treated us His enemies. It is indeed a very clear commandment of God which points us in this direction from the cross of shame.

3. Jesus Christ was and is for us in that He suffered and was crucified and died. Along the line that we are following, the witness to Christ in the New Testament moves towards this statement (in the Gospels) in order to proceed from it (in the Acts and Epistles). The work of the Lord who became a servant, the way of the Son of God into the far country, His appearance in the flesh, His humiliation, all aims at that of which this statement speaks. The work of His obedience rendered in humility is when it is completed in this happening. The Judge who judges Israel and the world by letting Himself be judged fulfils this strange judgment as the man who suffered under Pontius Pilate, was crucified, dead and buried. It is clear that we must give to this statement our very special attention.

On the basis of the presuppositions indicated in the two preceding discussions we now have to do with the true fulfilment of what God had to do for us in Jesus Christ—the passion of Jesus Christ. We must first emphasise generally that (1) in it as a passion we have to do with an action. That in it the subject of the Gospel story became an object does not alter this fact. For this took place in the freedom of this subject. According to the common consent of the Gospels Jesus Christ not only knew but willed that this should happen. This distinguishes His passion from the series of other passions in world history (which we might describe and understand as one long passion in view of the flood of blood and tears which it seems always to be). But it also makes it very puzzling. An offering which offers itself— and that without any obvious meaning or end! But it is with a free self-offering of this kind and therefore with an act and not a fate that we have to do in this passion. In explanation we must add (2) that we are dealing with an act which took place on earth, in time and space, and which is indissolubly linked with the name of a certain man. The history of religious and cultic speculation knows of other suffering and dying gods, and the similarity with these pictures forces itself upon our attention. But the Gospels do not speak of a passion which might just as well have been suffered in one place as another, at one time as another, or in a heavenly or some purely imaginary space and time. They indicate a very definite point in world history which cannot be exchanged for any other. They point to its earthly theatre. They do not speak of a passing moment in the occurrence of a myth which is cyclic and timeless and therefore of all times. They speak of a unique occurrence for which there is no precedent and which cannot be repeated. They speak of it (3) as an act of God which is coincident with the free action and suffering of a man, but in such a way that this human action and suffering has to be represented and understood as the action and, therefore, the passion of God Himself, which in its historical singularity not only has a general significance for the men of all times and places, but by which their situation has objectively been decisively changed, whether they are aware of it or not. It is, of course, necessarily the case that the knowledge of it as the act of God and the knowledge of the change in the world situation brought about by it can come about individually only in the decision of faith, in which this act becomes to the individual a word, the Word of God accepted in obedience, in which the passion of Jesus Christ is attested as having happened for him, and therefore in very truth for the world.

Let us now try to understand it in general terms.

It cannot be ignored that many men have suffered grievously, most grievously, in the course of world history. It might even be suggested that many men have perhaps suffered more grievously and longer and more bitterly than did this man in the limited events of a single day. Many who have suffered at the hands of men have been treated no less and perhaps more unjustly than this man. Many have been willing as He was to suffer in this way. Many in so doing have done something which, according to their intention and it may be in fact, was significant for others, perhaps many others, making a redemptive change in their life. And in face of any human suffering do we not have to think ultimately of the obscure but gracious control of divine providence and therefore of the goodwill of God which becomes act and event in it ? The suffering of man may be deserved or undeserved, voluntary or involuntary, heroic or not heroic, important for others or not important for others. But even if it is only the whimper of a sick child it has in it as such something which in its own way is infinitely outstanding and moving and in its human form and its more or less recognisable or even its hidden divine basis something which we can even describe as shattering. This is true of the passion of Jesus of Nazareth, but in so far as it is a human passion it is not true in a way which is basically different from that of any other human passion. If this is the scope of the Gospel story and the starting point of Gospel proclamation, it was not the intention of the New Testament, nor was it seriously the intention of the Church as it understood itself in the light of the New Testament, that the fundamentally unique occurrence should be found in the human passion as such. If we single out this human passion above others, we may be able to see and to say something which is noteworthy as such, but we shall not be helped forward a single step towards an understanding of what this occurrence is all about. For this reason we have already had to look beyond the human story at every point.

The mystery of this passion, of the torture, crucifixion and death of this one Jew which took place at that place and time at the hands of the Romans, is to be found in the person and mission of the One who suffered there and was crucified and died. (His person :) it is the eternal God Himself who has given Himself in His Son to be man, and as man to take upon Himself this human passion. (His mission :) it is the Judge who in this passion takes the place of those who ought to be judged, who in this passion allows Himself to be judged in their place. It is not, therefore, merely that God rules in and over this human occurrence simply as Creator and Lord. He does this, but He does more. He gives Himself to be the humanly acting and suffering person in this occurrence. He Himself is the subject who in His own freedom becomes in this event the object acting or acted upon in it. It is not simply the humiliation and dishonouring of a creature, of a noble and relatively innocent man that we find here. The problem posed is not that of a theodicy : How can God will this or permit this in the world which He has created good ? It is a matter of the humiliation and dishonouring of God Himself, of the question which makes any question of a theodicy a complete anticlimax ; the question whether in willing to let this happen to Him He has not renounced and lost Himself as God, whether in capitulating to the folly and wickedness of His creature He has not abdicated from His deity (as did the Japanese Emperor in 1945), whether He can really die and be dead ? And it is a matter of the answer to this question : that in this humiliation

God is supremely God, that in this death He is supremely alive, that He has maintained and revealed His deity in the passion of this man as His eternal Son. Moreover, this human passion does not have just a significance and effect in its historical situation within humanity and the world. On the contrary, there is fulfilled in it the mission, the task, and the work of the Son of God : the reconciliation of the world with God. There takes place here the redemptive judgment of God on all men. To fulfil this judgment He took the place of all men, He took their place as sinners. In this passion there is legally re-established the covenant between God and man, broken by man but kept by God. On that one day of suffering of that One there took place the comprehensive turning in the history of all creation—with all that this involves.

Because it is a matter of this person and His mission, the suffering, crucifixion and death of this one man is a unique occurrence. His passion has a real dimension of depth which it alone can have in the whole series of human passions. In it—from God's standpoint as well as man's—we have to do not merely with something but with every-thing : not merely with one of the many hidden but gracious over-rulings of God, but in the fulness of its hiddenness with an action in which it is a matter of His own being or not being, and therefore of His own honour or dishonour in relation to His creation. We are not dealing merely with any suffering, but with the suffering of God and this man in face of the destruction which threatens all creation and every individual, thus compromising God as the Creator. We are dealing with the painful confrontation of God and this man not merely with any evil, not merely with death, but with eternal death, with the power of that which is not. Therefore we are not dealing merely with any sin, or with many sins, which might wound God again and again, and only especially perhaps at this point, and the consequences of which this man had only to suffer in part and freely willed to do so. We are dealing with sin itself and as such : the preoccupation, the orientation, the determination of man as he has left his place as a creature and broken his covenant with God ; the corruption which God has made His own, for which He willed to take responsibility in this one man. Here in the passion in which as Judge He lets Himself be judged God has fulfilled this responsibility. In the place of all men He has Himself wrestled with that which separates them from Him. He has Himself borne the consequence of this separation to bear it away.

The New Testament has this in mind when in the Gospels it looks forward to the passion story of Jesus Christ and in the Epistles it looks forward from it to the future of the community and therefore to the future of the world and of every man. It is a matter of history. Everything depends upon the fact that this turning as it comes from God for us men is not simply imagined and presented as a true teaching of pious and thoughtful people, but that it happened in this way, in the space and time which are those of all men. But it is a matter of this history. That it took place once at this time and place as this history is what distinguishes the passion, crucifixion and death of this one Jew from all the other occurrences in time and space with which the passion of Jesus Christ is otherwise similar in every respect. Distinguished in this way, it is the subject of Christian faith and proclamation.

But what do we have to believe? and proclaim? It is true enough to say that in this one passion at this time and place, the passion of this one man, we have to do with God's act for us. But the question of content still remains. And we must not turn it into a question concerning the significance of this act, i.e., the determination of the being of man which takes place when the passion is proclaimed to a man and believed by him. This question, too, is legitimate and necessary. But to answer it presupposes a definite message concerning the passion itself and as such. New Testament faith and proclamation do in fact imply a definite experience by the being of the man who accepts in faith the proclamation concerning Jesus Christ. They imply the imperatives which come to him in this acceptance, the questions before which and the decision in which he is posited. But they do not exhaust themselves in these implicates. New Testament faith does not curve in upon itself or centre on itself as *fides qua creditur*. The content of New Testament proclamation does not consist only of the description and reception of this *fides qua creditur*. Rather they relate to and are based upon a primary message concerning Jesus Christ Himself, to which New Testament faith is open and has constantly to open itself, which must always be the first word of New Testament proclamation not only because in this message we have its historical starting-point, but because in it we have its origin and primary theme, because without it there cannot be those implicates, because this message is the thing which implies, without which anything we might say here about the being of man would be left hanging in the air, like a subsidiary clause which has no principal clause. Our present question is primarily a question concerning this principal clause, the message about the passion of Jesus Christ itself and as such. To answer it we must keep to the original form of the question and not evade it.

If we are to keep to it, if we are not to turn the " What " into something else, but answer it with a plain " This," then we must not be afraid to take the true statement that in the passion of Jesus Christ we have to do with God's act for us, and to put it in a slightly different form, that it is in the passion of Jesus Christ that we have to do with the act of God for us. It then tells us—further elucidation is, of course, necessary—something definite about this act of God for us, something which has real content, something which is independent of the particular experience of being envisaged and implied in faith in it and its proclamation. It speaks to us of that which is the basis of this experience, of the source of the imperatives which come to the men who receive the proclamation in faith, of the source of the questions before which, and of the decision in which, they are posited. As an answer to this question of the " What," it will then run as follows : Allowing for all the explanations, and for the legitimate and necessary implications of this occurrence, it is the passion of Jesus Christ itself and as such which has to be believed and proclaimed as the act of God for us.

In the reversal of this declaration, in the question of the source, the independent basis of the Christian experience of being, we are not dealing with a question of idly speculative interest, and certainly not with an attempt to back up the certainty of faith and proclamation. On the contrary, it is a question of simple truth, or rather of a recognition of the answer to the question of truth which is given and included in the act of God for us. Truth is the disclosure and recognition of that which *is* as it appears to man. It is, therefore, the disclosure and recognition of that without which man cannot live unless he consoles himself with a mere and probably deceptive appearance, but which he cannot tell to himself because by its very nature it is accessible only in appearance and not in essence, which he can only allow himself to be told and told concretely, which he has always concretely to learn afresh. When this happens in the encounter with that which is, we attain to truth, to that disclosure and recognition. To be of the truth is to " hear his voice " (Jn. 18³⁷). The act of God for us fulfils and includes the answering of the question of its own truth—and the same is true of faith in it and its proclamation—for in it we have to accept His voice as the voice which speaks of Him as that which is and which appears as such. Christian experience, as the manifestation of that which is, i.e., of Him who is, can be true and of the truth. But it is not so *in abstracto*, in itself and as such. It is true to the extent that it proceeds from the truth, and therefore from that disclosure and recognition. It is true to the extent that it rests on something that is said concretely to man about Him and learned concretely about Him, to the extent that it lives entirely by Him and cannot curve in upon itself in self-sufficiency. It is true in and by its source, in and by Jesus Christ as its basis, upon which it is dependent but which is not dependent upon it. It is true in its openness to this location and source of its truth. For that reason we cannot be content to define the passion of Jesus Christ as the act of God for us, however true that may be, but we must go on to define the act of God for us as the passion of Jesus Christ. In this, and this alone, is it the act of God for us. With this there stands or falls the truth of Christian experience.

The most simple, and in its simplicity the most impressive, explanation of this definition has always consisted in its mere repetition. As, for instance, in the action and words at the giving of the bread in the Lord's Supper : This is my body (which is given for you). Its strength lies in the fact that it simply points to the event itself. It presupposes that the event speaks for itself, is self-explanatory. It only needs to be indicated. And faith only needs to confess that it has happened. It happened for us, but it happened without us, without our co-operating or contributing. Even the intellectual activity of our understanding and explaining cannot add to what happened and is and is effective.

It cannot add to its authenticity, or to its open validity, or even to the physical force of its fulfilment. It does not receive all this from our insight into its inner coherence. It has this inner coherence, and we can and should perceive it. But its authenticity, its validity and its force are in itself. The *theologia crucis* can and should point to them, but all theology lives by the fact that the cross of Jesus Christ is itself the work and therefore the wholly sufficient Word of God : not a Word which is empty, but one which is filled and which can be heard in its fulness, God's own Word. Simply to co-relate without commentary *crux* and *unica spes* cannot and must not be the totality of what we have to say on this matter. But in its simplicity it is a basic and indispensable reminder who is at work and who is speaking.

There are many New Testament passages from which we may gather that in the most primitive communities there was no need to do more than mention the death of Jesus Christ as God's accomplished act of redemption, because those who read or heard already knew of whom or what they were reminded by it, because everything that was decisive was included in it. The event itself, testified as such by the apostles—" set forth before your eyes," as Paul says in Gal. 3[1]—was through the thin veil of this human mediation its own proclamation awakening and sustaining faith. It could be and had to be explained what " the word of the cross " was (1 Cor. 1[18]), that it was to preach Christ crucified (1 Cor. 1[23]) or to " shew the Lord's death " (1 Cor. 11[26]), but it was already perceived and known even before it was explained. God gave His Son " for us all " (Rom. 8[32]). He gave Himself " for me " (Gal. 2[20]). He " suffered for you " (1 Pet. 2[21]). He died for us (1 Thess. 5[9]). By the grace of God " he tasted death for every man " (Heb. 2[9]). He gave His life " for his friends " (Jn. 15[13]). As the Good Shepherd, He gave His life for the sheep (Jn. 10[11]). In our brother we have to see the one " for whom Christ died " (Rom. 14[15]). All these and similar sayings are expressions to indicate the passion of Christ, expressions which certainly could be and needed to be interpreted in the ears of New Testament Christians, but which certainly did not sound empty or obscure, but filled out and very clear ; not by virtue of faith as the existential reaction of these men, but by virtue of the event itself as it happened in space and time and as it is simply indicated in these expressions.

We may well ask whether the preaching of Good Friday would not in many cases be better if it took the form, not of all kinds of inadequate theology, but of a simple repetition—*Spiritu sancto adiuvante*—of the evangelical passion-narrative ; whether it would not be a more " existential " address as such.

All the same, the event and the recollection do call for further explanation, not to add to this event, but for joy at that which has happened in it, in consideration of it and thankfulness for it. Its very content demands an explanation in this sense, the *intellectus fidei*.

What actually took place in this suffering and dying ? We are still speaking in more general terms when in relation to the statements of the New Testament and our own previous considerations we reply : In this suffering and dying of God Himself in His Son, there took place the reconciliation with God, the conversion to Him, of the world which is out of harmony with Him, contradicting and opposing Him. The world is not itself capable of this reconciliation. Man cannot convert Himself. He cannot make himself the friend of God instead of the enemy of God. He cannot save himself from the destruction which must inevitably follow His enmity against God. He cannot do anything to escape the wrath of God which threatens him in the position in which he has placed himself. He cannot alter the fact that this position is a place of shadows, and that from this place he enters irresistibly on a slope which leads to outer darkness.

It is not a pessimistic anthropology or an exaggerated doctrine of sin which makes us say this but the fact that, according to the decision of God made and revealed in power, it needed nothing less than God Himself to remedy the corruption of our being and ourselves, to restore order between Himself as Creator and the world as His creation, to set up and maintain again the covenant broken by man, to carry it through against man for the sake of man, and in that way to save man from destruction. Where the intervention of God in person is needed, everything is obviously lost without that intervention, and man can do nothing to help himself. That God has intervened in person is the good news of Good Friday. For in the suffering and dying of Jesus Christ He has done this in the event in which He, the Judge, delivers Himself up to be judged. He could do this only against us, opposing to our contradiction His own superior contradiction, to our opposition His own superior opposition. We are all on the other side. In ourselves, we are always on the other side. Therefore what He has done He has done without us, without the world, without the counsel or help of that which is flesh and lives in the flesh—except only for the flesh of Jesus Christ. He has done it entirely in this His Word which became flesh. Reconciliation is a comprehensive occurrence, embracing many in the One in whom it was made, and through the many embracing all. But it is not a repeated, let alone a general occurrence. There is no other reconciliation of the world with God for any other man than that which took place in this One, that which comes to the world and directly or indirectly to every man in Him. In Him the world is converted to God. In Him man is the friend of God and not His enemy. In Him the covenant which God has faithfully kept and man has broken is renewed and restored. Representing all others in Himself, He is the human partner of God in this new covenant—He in the authenticity, validity and force of His suffering and dying.

But He is this for us. In Him—as He fulfils His judgment on us all, but fulfils it in this way—God Himself is for us. In this divine judgment the atonement made in the passion of this One is ours. This is the origin and primary theme of faith and proclamation. And from this it follows that in faith we believe primarily in Jesus Christ, and in proclamation we primarily proclaim Jesus Christ: Him in whom God will freely give us all things (Rom. 8³²). All things! But the relation between Him and the all things which He will give us cannot be reversed if we are not to come into conflict with the question of truth, or rather with the answering of the question of truth as we have it in God's act fulfilled in Him for us. He is the truth. He is the disclosure and knowledge of that which is. For He is. To be of the truth means to hear His voice in encounter and confrontation with Him: not to hear first the voice of that which God will give us in Him but to hear His voice. To be of the truth means first to believe in Him. And to proclaim the truth means first to proclaim Him, to proclaim this principal clause and only then the subsidiary clauses which derive from it.

In the accounts of the Last Supper in 1 Cor. 11²⁵ and Lk. 22²⁰ that which is actuality and truth in Jesus Christ, that which takes place in Him as event and revelation, is called "the new covenant in my blood," while in Mk. (14²⁴) and Mt. 26²⁸ it is described conversely and more simply as "my blood of the covenant." In both cases the unity of outlook and concept is evident. In the shedding of Christ's blood, i.e., in the offering of His life to the powers of death we have the constancy, the maintenance or the restitution of the covenant between God and man. "We have peace with God" and προσαγωγὴν εἰς τὴν χάριν is how it is put in Rom. 5¹ꜝ·, and in Rom. 5¹⁰ "we are reconciled by the death of his Son"—both agreeing with the chief passage in 2 Cor. 5¹⁸ꜝ·. The message of Col. 1²⁰ is obviously the same: God determined "by him to reconcile all things to himself, making peace διὰ τοῦ αἵματος τοῦ σταυροῦ αὐτοῦ, or as we have it in Col. 1²² "in the body of his flesh through death." He Himself is "our peace" is what we are told in Eph. 2¹⁴, He who in His own flesh removed the enmity between Jew and Gentile and their common enmity against God to reconcile both (2¹⁶) in one body (His own) with God by the cross, having ἐν αὐτῷ (in or by Himself) slain the enmity thereby. In substance 1 Pet. 3¹⁸ says exactly the same: "He died, the just for the unjust, to bring us to God. And in Heb. 10¹⁹ꜝ· we are told that in the blood of Jesus Christ we have τὴν εἴσοδον τῶν ἀγίων "by a new and living way which he hath consecrated for us, through the veil, that is to say, his flesh." Therefore if this covenant, this peace, this reconciliation with Him, this access to Him is the meaning and purpose of the act which He has accomplished for us, then it is the unanimous witness of these passages that this act took place in the blood, in the cross, in the death of Jesus Christ and not in any other place, at any other time or in any other way.

Our final question is why and in what sense it is in the suffering and dying of Jesus Christ that we have to do with the act of God which has taken place for us? In our answer (in which again we have regard to the very express statements of the New Testament and the course we have so far followed), we must pay particular attention to the concept and reality of human sin, to its relation to the reality of the atonement on the one side and to that of death on the other.

The sin and sins of man form the disruptive factor within creation which makes necessary the atonement, the new peace with God, the restoration of the covenant with a view to the glory of God and the redemption and salvation of man as the work of God's free mercy. Sin, therefore, is the obstacle which has to be removed and overcome in the reconciliation of the world with God as its conversion to Him. But it is also the source, which has to be blocked in the atonement, of the destruction which threatens man, which already engulfs him and drags him down. Its wages is death (Rom. 6²³). It is the sting of death (1 Cor. 15⁵⁶). By it death came into the world (Rom. 5¹²). And the concept death in the New Testament means not only the dying of man but the destruction which qualifies or rather disqualifies it, eternal death, death as the invincibly threatening force of dissolution. It is to this place that man moves as a sinner.

The very heart of the atonement is the overcoming of sin : sin in its character as the rebellion of man against God, and in its character as the ground of man's hopeless destiny in death. It was to fulfil this judgment on sin that the Son of God as man took our place as sinners. He fulfils it—as man in our place—by completing our work in the omnipotence of the divine Son, by treading the way of sinners to its bitter end in death, in destruction, in the limitless anguish of separation from God, by delivering up sinful man and sin in His own person to the non-being which is properly theirs, the non-being, the nothingness to which man has fallen victim as a sinner and towards which he relentlessly hastens. We can say indeed that He fulfils this judgment by suffering the punishment which we have all brought on ourselves.

The concept of punishment has come into the answer given by Christian theology to this question from Is. 53. In the New Testament it does not occur in this connexion. But it cannot be completely rejected or evaded on this account. My turning from God is followed by God's annihilating turning from me. When it is resisted His love works itself out as death-dealing wrath. If Jesus Christ has followed our way as sinners to the end to which it leads, in outer darkness, then we can say with that passage from the Old Testament that He has suffered this punishment of ours. But we must not make this a main concept as in some of the older presentations of the doctrine of the atonement (especially those which follow Anselm of Canterbury), either in the sense that by His suffering our punishment we are spared from suffering it ourselves, or that in so doing He " satisfied " or offered satisfaction to the wrath of God. The latter thought is quite foreign to the New Testament. And of the possible idea that we are spared punishment by what Jesus Christ has done for us we have to notice that the main drift of the New Testament statements concerning the passion and death of Jesus Christ is not at all or only indirectly in this direction.

The decisive thing is not that He has suffered what we ought to have suffered so that we do not have to suffer it, the destruction to which we have fallen victim by our guilt, and therefore the punishment which we deserve. This is true, of course. But it is true only as it derives from the decisive thing that in the suffering and death of Jesus Christ it has come to pass that in His own person He has made an end of us as sinners and therefore of sin itself by going to death as the One who took our place as sinners. In His person He has delivered up us sinners and sin itself to destruction. He has removed us sinners and sin, negated us, cancelled us out : ourselves, our sin, and the accusation, condemnation and perdition which had overtaken us. That is what we cannot do and are not willing to do. How can we be able and willing to remove ourselves as those who commit sin and therefore sin itself ? That is what He could and willed to do and actually did for us in His right and authority and power as the Son of God when He took our place as man. The man of sin, the first Adam, the cosmos alienated from God, the " present evil world " (Gal. 1⁴), was taken and killed and buried in and with Him on the cross. On the one side, therefore, He has turned over a new leaf in the history of the covenant of God with man, making atonement, giving man a new peace with God, reopening the blocked road of man to God. That is what happened when Jesus Christ, who willed to make Himself the bearer and Representative of sin, caused sin to be taken and killed on the cross in His own person (as that of the one great sinner). And in that way, not by suffering our punishment as such, but in the deliverance of sinful man and sin itself to destruction, which He accomplished when He suffered our punishment, He has on the other side blocked the source of our destruction ; He has seen to it that we do not have to suffer what we ought to suffer ; He has removed the accusation and condemnation and perdition which had passed upon us ; He has cancelled their relevance to us ; He has saved us from destruction and rescued us from eternal death.

The passion of Jesus Christ is the judgment of God in which the Judge Himself was the judged. And as such it is at its heart and centre the victory which has been won for us, in our place, in the battle against sin. By this time it should be clear why it is so important to understand this passion as from the very first the divine action. As the passion of the Son of God who became man for us it is the radical divine action which attacks and destroys at its very root the primary evil in the world ; the activity of the second Adam who took the place of the first, who reversed and overthrew the activity of the first in this place, and in so doing brought in a new man, founded a new world and inaugurated a new æon—and all this in His passion. It is only as His passion that it can be this action ; only as sin is, as it were, taken in the rear, only as it is destroyed by the destruction and eternal death which threatens the world, only as this worst becomes an instrument in the hand of the merciful and omnipotent God for the creation of the best. For the sake of this best, the worst had to happen to sinful man : not out of any desire for vengeance and retribution on the part of God, but because of the radical nature of the divine love, which could " satisfy " itself only in the outworking of its wrath against the man of sin, only by killing him, extinguishing him, removing him. Here is the place for the doubtful concept that in the passion of Jesus Christ, in the giving up of His Son to death, God has done that which is " satisfactory " or sufficient in the victorious fighting of sin to make this victory radical and total. He has done that which is sufficient to take away sin, to restore order between Himself as the Creator and His creation, to bring in the new man reconciled and therefore at peace with Him, to redeem man from death. God has done this in the passion of Jesus Christ. For this reason the divine judgment in which the Judge was judged, and therefore the passion of Jesus Christ, is as such the divine action of atonement which has taken place for us.

From this we may readily understand that in the overwhelming majority of passages in the New Testament which touch on it directly or indirectly the death of Jesus Christ is explicitly set in some relationship to sin. The positive side is always in the background, as in Jn. 6⁵¹ : " The bread that I will give is my flesh, which I will give for the life of the world," or Rom. 5⁹ : " Being now justified by his blood," or 2 Cor. 5¹⁵ : " He died for all, that they which live should not henceforth live unto themselves, but unto him which died for them, and rose again," and in this sense, Ac. 20²⁸ : " He has purchased the church with his own blood." But the direct end of the passion is a negative one—the overcoming of the rift which has come between God and man, of the enmity of man against God. Jesus Christ was delivered " for our offences " (Rom. 4²⁵), or " for our sins " (Gal. 1⁴). He died " once for sins " (1 Pet. 3¹⁸), or " for our sins according to the Scriptures " (1 Cor. 15³) is how we have it in more general expressions which only indicate the problem. More concretely He is the " Lamb of God which (bears is not strong enough for αἴρων) removes, takes away, overcomes the sin of the world " (Jn. 1²⁹, cf. 1 Jn. 3⁵). Again, in Heb. 9²⁸ : " He was once offered to bear the sins of many," or 1 Pet. 2²⁴ : " Who his own self bare our sins in his own body on the tree that we should be dead to sins." In substance again : " The blood of Jesus Christ his Son cleanseth us from all sin " (1 Jn. 1⁷) ; " Offering himself, he purges our conscience from dead works " (Heb. 9¹⁴) ; " He purifies unto himself a peculiar people " (Tit. 2¹⁴). By His blood, the blood of the Lamb, the clothes of His own people are washed and made white (Rev. 7¹⁴). Even more pointedly : " God sent his own sin in the likeness of sinful flesh, and for sin, and condemned sin in the flesh " (Rom. 8³). And very much to the point : " Through death he destroyed him that had the power of death, that is, the devil " (Heb. 2¹⁴) ; " He slew the enmity in himself " (Eph. 2¹⁶) ; " He died unto sin once " in such a way that Christians can and should reckon themselves dead unto sin (Rom. 6¹⁰ᶠ·). It is the case that " if one died for all, then were all dead " (2 Cor. 5¹⁴). And because all this took place (in Him for us), according to the remarkable verses in Col. 2¹⁴ᶠ·, God has blotted out the handwriting of ordinances that was against us, He has taken it out of the way, nailed it to His cross, spoiled principalities and powers, made a show of them openly (as prisoners), and triumphed over them—and all this in Him, in the circumcision of Christ, in which there has taken place already that of His people, in His putting off of the body of the flesh, in which they too have put it off (Col. 2¹¹).

It is in this sense that we have to understand the saying at the giving of the cup at the Last Supper as recorded by Matthew (26²⁸), which speaks of the " blood of the covenant " which is shed for many " for the forgiveness of sins." Elsewhere in the New Testament the latter concept is brought into surprisingly little direct relation to the death of Jesus Christ. The Word of the crucified Himself : " Father, forgive them ; for they know not what they do " (Lk. 23³⁴), can, of course, be mentioned in this connexion. In Eph. 1⁷ the ἀπολύτρωσις which has taken place in His blood is obviously equated with the " forgiveness of sins." And in Col. 1¹⁴ we find the same equivalent in plain juxtaposition with a mention of our redemption from the powers of darkness accomplished in Jesus Christ. Again in close proximity to a mention of the event of the cross, it is said of God in Col. 2¹³ : χαρισάμενος ἡμῖν πάντα τὰ παραπτώματα. And when we are told in Heb. 9²² that "without the shedding of blood there is no remission," this obviously does not refer only to the Old Testament rites then under discussion. Have we to assume that the direct relating of the concept of the forgiveness of sins, which is from the very first so important in the Gospels, with the death of Jesus Christ is relatively so infrequent for the very reason that for those who heard and read the New Testament writings it was self-evident that it could be meaningful only in this relationship ?   From what is said about the removing, the taking away, the judging, the destroying of sin which takes place in the death of Christ, the purging of it accomplished in the blood of Christ, it is clear that the forgiveness of sins, whether mentioned in connexion with this death or otherwise, cannot mean anything less radical than that. ἄφεσις, ἀφιέναι, χαρίζεσθαι is a releasing of man from a legal relationship fatal to him, from an intolerable commitment which he has accepted, from an imprisonment in which he finds himself.   And it is not something which comes accidentally or arbitrarily but in the strictest necessity, not partially but totally, not conditionally but unconditionally, not provisionally but definitively.   As the subject of sin, sins and transgressions man finds himself in this fatal relationship, under this intolerable commitment, in this imprisonment.   He cannot release himself from it.   But at one stroke he is wholly and finally released from it when Jesus Christ takes his place, takes from him his sin, sins and transgressions, deals with them Himself, removes them, takes them away, judges and destroys them in His death, purges him from them.   That is how his reconciliation with God is effected and he himself is saved from destruction.   Because Jesus Christ is the power of this decisive happening of the forgiveness of sins, the sin forgiven is now the old thing—the essence of all that is old, something which is past and done with, which is only the past, which is not the present and has no future : παρῆλθεν (2 Cor. 5¹⁷).   To that extent the forgiveness of sins is the central meaning of the divine action in the passion of Jesus Christ, and because it concerns the forgiveness of sins, this action must consist in a passion.

4. Jesus Christ was and is for us in that He has done this before God and has therefore done right.   We must now return for a moment to the first three aspects.   We have spoken of the Judge, the judged and the judgment, and in each of these we have spoken of Jesus Christ who took our place and acted for us.   What we have still to do is to say that this aspect of the atonement made for us in Him only *seems* to be purely negative.   In fact—to take up again our earlier concept —in the disclosure and knowledge of that which truly is as it takes place in this act of God, it is the case that this action which is negative in form is the great positive act of God within and against the world which is hostile to Him, which does not do Him honour and which therefore destroys itself.   The Judge, the judged, the judgment—the one Jesus Christ who is all these things and in and by Himself does all these things—is the justice or righteousness of God in the biblical sense of the term : the omnipotence of God creating order, which is " now " (νυνὶ δέ Rom. 3²¹) revealed and effective as a turning from this present evil æon (Gal. 1⁴) to the new one of a world reconciled with God in Him, this One.   This righteousness cannot come from the world, from us.   It cannot be done by us, fulfilled by us, or in any way completed or improved or maintained by us.   It is the righteousness of God.   And because *rebus sic stantibus* this " without us "

necessarily means " against us " the action has to take this negative
form; Jesus Christ has to be the Judge, the judged and in His own
person the fulfilment of the judgment; His decisive work and word
has to be His suffering and dying. But that is only the negative form
of the fulness of a positive divine righteousness, which itself and as
such is identical with the free love of God effectively interposing
between our enmity and Himself, the work and word of His grace.
The suffering and death of Jesus Christ are the No of God in and with
which He again takes up and asserts in man's space and time the
Yes to man which He has determined and pronounced in eternity.
Because Jesus Christ is the Yes of God spoken in world-history and
itself become a part of world-history, therefore and to that extent
God is in Jesus Christ *pro nobis. Cur Deus homo ?* Because God, who
became man in His Son, willed in this His Yes to do this work of His,
but His human work, and therefore this work for the reconciliation
of the world which is effective for us men.

Our task now is to understand the fact and extent to which this
did take place for us in Jesus Christ in this negative form. And first
of all we have to say comprehensively that in this action Jesus Christ
was amongst us and lived and acted for us as the just or righteous
man : " the just for the unjust " (1 Pet. 3¹⁸). The omnipotence of
God in the world, without and against the world, and therefore creating
order for the world, is concretely identical with this righteous man,
this second Adam who took the place of the first and put right what
he had perverted. As the Judge, as the judged, as the One who in
His own person has accomplished the judgment, He is the end of the
old æon and the beginning of the new. He is the righteousness which
dwells in the new heaven and the new earth (2 Pet. 3¹³). We wait
for Him when, placed in Him and with Him at this turning-point of
the times, we wait for this new heaven and new earth. He sits on
the throne and says : " Behold, I make all things new," and more
than that : " It is done. I am Alpha and Omega, the beginning and
the end " (Rev. 21⁵ᶠ·)—He, this righteous man.

But He is the righteous man in that—and here we take up again
the title of this whole section—as the Son of God obedient to the
Father in fulfilment of this action of God He lived and acted as the
one man obedient to God. For the righteousness which is upon earth,
the righteousness of man, in and against and for world-history, is the
obedience of the creature—just as sin is unrighteousness (1 Jn. 3⁴)
because it is the disobedience of the creature (Rom. 5¹⁹). In obedience
man lives and acts in freedom. He is true to his own nature as the
creature of God, the creature which is appointed in its own decisions
to follow and correspond to the decisions of God, to follow and correspond to the decisions of God in its decisions which are its own. In
sin, and therefore in disobedience, man forfeits this freedom. He is
therefore untrue not only to God but also to his own nature as the

D.R.—9

creature of God. This is his unrighteousness, the unrighteousness of the first Adam, of this present evil æon. Every man shares this unrighteousness and is therefore in the wrong before God. The atonement is therefore positively the removal of this unrighteousness by the existence of the one obedient and therefore free man. He is " the new man." And in fulfilment of the divine action and therefore in His passion Jesus Christ has acted for us as this new and obedient and therefore free man. As the Son obedient to the Father—and therefore in the freedom which, like the freedom of God Himself, has the character of obedience—He has brought in the man who is the child of this God, this new and obedient and free man. As this man He has revealed and made operative the righteousness of God on earth.

But the righteousness of Jesus of Nazareth for us as the obedient Son of God consists simply in His complete affirmation of this reversal, this execution of judgment in the judging of the Judge. It consists in the fact that He delivered Himself up to this. Our second point is decisive for a true understanding : Jesus Christ was obedient in that He willed to take our place as sinners and did, in fact, take our place. When we speak of the sinlessness of Jesus we must always think concretely of this. It did not consist in an abstract and absolute purity, goodness and virtue. It consisted in His actual freedom from sin itself, from the basis of all sins. That is why He was not a transgressor and committed no sins. That is why He could take on Himself and deliver up to death the sins of all other men. That is why He could forgive sins and transgressions. He came and occupied, as it were, an archimedian point from which He could move, and did in fact move, the earth. He did it by willing to take our place as sinners, and thus putting God in the right against Him. From the time of Adam it had been man's sin to want to become and be his own judge in place of God. The fall of man is that he would not keep to the limits appointed for him in relation to God as a human creature. And man's being in sin is that he will not accept that he is the rebel against God that he is, that he will not see and acknowledge his usurpation for what it is, that he will not confess it and therefore his own fall, that he wants to explain and excuse and justify himself, to be in the right against God. If he ceased to do this, He would acknowledge that God is in the right against him, thus returning to the place which is proper to him as a creature in relation to God, and reversing the fall which consists in his usurpation. His unwillingness to repent is the constant renewal of his sin. The sinlessness of Jesus Christ consists in the fact that He does not take part in this game. He was a man as we are. His condition was no different from ours. He took our flesh, the nature of man as he comes from the fall. In this nature He is exposed every moment to the temptation to a renewal of sin—the temptation of impenitent being and thinking and speaking and action. His sinlessness was not therefore His condition. It was the act of His being in which He defeated temptation in His condition which is ours, in the flesh. Note that He who as the Son of God was like God did not count it His " prey " (a prize to be held fast) to be like God, to be God, but He emptied Himself, becoming as we are—and in so doing demonstrating and confirming the true deity of God—placing Himself in the series of men who rebelled against God in their delusion that they would be as God, not in order to try to refuse or conceal or deny this, but in the place of all other men—who refuse to do so—to confess it, to take upon Himself this guilt of all human beings in order in the name of all to put God in the right against Him. In so doing He acted justly in the place of all and for the sake of all. In their place and for their sake, instead of committing fresh sin, He returned to the place from which they had fallen into sin, the place which belongs to the creature in relation to God. In so doing, in His own person, He reversed the fall in their place and for their sake. He acted justly in that He did not refuse to do what they would not do. The one great sinner, with all the consequences that this involves, penitently acknowledges that He is the one lost sheep, the one lost coin, the lost son (Lk.15$^{3f.}$), and therefore that as the Judge He is the One who is judged. In this way He was obedient to God. For this reason He, Jesus of Nazareth—among the many who in Jordan received the baptism of John for the future forgiveness of sins—was the One in whom God was well pleased as His beloved Son, the One upon whom John saw the Spirit descend from heaven, Himself the One who, proclaimed by John, was to come as the bringer of forgiveness. In this way, in the free penitence of Jesus of Nazareth which began in Jordan when He entered on His way as Judge and was completed on the cross of Golgotha when He was judged—there took place the positive act concealed in His passion as the negative form of the divine action of reconciliation. In this penitence of His He " fulfilled all righteousness " (Mt. 3^{15}). It made His day—the day of the divine judgment— the great day of atonement, the day of the dawn of a new heaven and a new earth, the birthday of a new man.

That Jesus could be tempted—like all other men—is something upon which the Epistle to the Hebrews lays particular emphasis. Because " he that sanctifieth and they that are sanctified are all of one (Abraham ? Adam ?) he is not ashamed to call them brethren " (2^{11}). " Forasmuch then as the children are partakers of flesh and blood, he also himself likewise (παραπλησίως) took part of the same " (2^{14}). " Wherefore it behoved him in all things (κατὰ πάντα) to be made like unto his brethren, that he might be to them (in his likeness with them) a merciful and faithful high priest in things pertaining to God " (2^{17}). Like them, therefore, in being able to be tempted and in the fight against temptation. How else could He represent them except in a serious entering into their whole situation ? Therefore : " In that he himself hath suffered being tempted, he is able (δύναται) to succour them that are tempted " (2^{18}). And again in 4^{15} : " For we have not an high priest which cannot be touched with the feeling of our infirmities (συμπαθῆσαι ταῖς ἀσθενείαις ἡμῶν—" sympathise " with them is too weak a rendering and one that evokes false associations), but one that was in all points tempted like as we are, yet without sin." In His likeness He was also unlike in that He did not yield to temptation. That He learned obedience by the things which he suffered (5⁸) means that He maintained it in freedom in a way which was not by any means self-evident. In His acts He was without sin. He was perfectly obedient. In the τελειότης of His decision, although His condition was like that of all other men, He broke the common rule of all their decisions. In this way He surpassed this likeness, and became " the author of eternal salvation unto all them that obey him " (5⁹).

To what is this Epistle referring ? Obviously in 5⁷ᶠ· to the conflict of Jesus in Gethsemane as reported in the Synoptics (but not in John). But to understand this we must return to the story of His temptation in the wilderness, which again is not mentioned in John, is referred to only briefly by Mark, but is developed in threefold form in Mt. 4¹ᶠ· and Lk. 4¹ᶠ·.

In Matthew and Mark it is significantly placed immediately after His baptism, and in Luke it is separated from it only by the genealogy. With the baptism it forms the supreme dialectical *anacrusis* to the first main part of the Gospel story. From it we can see in what way the Judge who has just come will finally fulfil the divine judgment. All three Evangelists agree that it was not chance or caprice but the Spirit—the same Spirit that the Baptist had seen descending on Him in Jordan—who led and indeed drove Jesus into the wilderness (Mk. 1¹² ἐκβάλλει).

Why ? According to Matthew and Luke for a forty-day fast. To these forty days—and nights as stressed in Mt. 4²; it was a total fast—at the beginning of the whole Gospel story there correspond the forty days after Easter at the end (Ac. 1³). The fasting until He was an hungred, which forms the content of this period in contrast to the later one, points back to the penitence of Jesus and His fulfilling of all righteousness in the baptism of John, and it is obviously a continuation and emphasising of the same strand. Fasting expresses man's knowledge of his unworthiness to live, his readiness to· suffer the death which he has merited for his sins, and therefore the radical nature of his repentance. There is no question of any glory in this achievement of Jesus as such.

The Spirit does not drive Him into the wilderness—as many commentators have suggested with a view to edification—because of the stillness and solitude of the wilderness and the opportunity which it offers for concentration, contemplation and prayer. In another sense J. A. Bengel was quite right when he said : *in his diebus, in hoc secessu maximae res intercesserunt inter Deum et Mediatorem.* But Mt. 4¹ tells us expressly : Jesus was brought here to be tempted (πειρασθῆναι). On the old view the wilderness was a place which, like the sea, had a close affinity with the underworld, a place which belonged in a particular sense to demons. It was to encounter these that He was led there and kept His fast there. For Him as the Son, the One in whom God was well-pleased, this had to be the case. He will frequently encounter demons again. His way will never be at a safe distance from the kingdom of darkness but will always be along its frontier and finally within that kingdom. But already at the outset it brings Him into confrontation and encounter with it. Bengel is again right when he says that the story of the temptation to which particular prominence is here given is a *specimen totius exinanitionis Christi, omniumque tentationum . . . epitome, quas machinatus est diabolus ab initio.* The Pharisees themselves tempted Him later (Mk. 8¹¹ᶠ·) when they asked of Him a sign from heaven. Their question about the tribute money (Mk. 12¹³ᶠ·) was recognised and rejected as a temptation. And Jesus is not simply proof against the temptation of this kingdom. He is a man, flesh and blood, as we are. He is the Son of God who has come into the far country, who has come to us and become one of us. He is therefore able to be tempted. But—and in this His way diverges from all other human ways—He is also willing to expose Himself to temptation. All other men can and ought and must refrain from seeking out temptation.

But He cannot. He has to suffer it on the offensive and not on the defensive, just as later He goes with open eyes to the death of the cross, to Jerusalem. It is to this offensive that the Spirit drives Him.

And now temptation does in fact break over Him—the temptation which, as the Evangelists imply, has never broken over man before or since, the temptation with which He alone could be assailed. The great and definitive decision does not figure here, but it is authentically prefigured by what takes place here. Satan, the πειραζόμενος, the διάβολος, comes to Him (προσελθών, Mt. 4³) ; he speaks with Him ; he takes Him with him (παραλαμβάνει, Mt. 4⁵, ⁸), he takes Him up into an high mountain (ἀναγαγών, Lk. 4⁵). In view of the One with whom the temptation has to do, this power—which is almost like that of the Spirit—is quite astonishing. But the Evangelists state that it has this power over Jesus. What was it all about ? Mark does not say. But Matthew and Luke have given us a threefold exposition of the πειράζεσθαι of Satan and the πειρασθῆναι of Jesus. Are these three little stories the original sequence of the story in which they now appear (in a slightly different order) in these two accounts ? They are a little disjointed and may go back to three sources which were originally different. But there is a thread which runs through them all and confirms their identity in substance. In none of the three temptations is there brought before us a devil who is obviously godless, or dangerous or even stupid. And in none of them is the temptation a temptation to what we might call a breaking or failure to keep the Law on the moral or judicial plane. In all three we have to do " only " with the counsel, the suggestion, that He should not be true to the way on which He entered in Jordan, that of a great sinner repenting ; that He should take from now on a direction which will not need to have the cross as its end and goal. But if Jesus had done this He would have done something far worse than any breaking or failure to keep the Law. He would have done that which is the essence of everything bad. For it would have meant that without His obedience the enmity of the world against God would have persisted, without His penitence the destruction of the cosmos could not have been arrested, and man would inevitably have perished. All the three stories assembled by Matthew and Luke speak in different ways of this temptation. The order and climax are different in the two Evangelists. At a first glance those of Matthew seem to be logically and pragmatically the more illuminating. But here we will follow that of Luke, for on a closer inspection it is the more instructive.

In both Evangelists the first satanic suggestion is that after the forty days of hunger He should change the stones of the wilderness into bread in the power of His divine Sonship by His Word. What would it have meant if Jesus had yielded ? He would have used the power of God which He undoubtedly had like a technical instrument placed at His disposal to save and maintain His own life. He would then have stepped out of the series of sinners in which He placed Himself in His baptism in Jordan. Of His own will He would have abandoned the role of the One who fasts and repents for sinners. He would have broken off His fasting and repentance in the fulness of divine power and with the help of God, but without consulting the will and commandment of God, because in the last resort His primary will was to live. He would have refused to give Himself unreservedly to be the one great sinner who allows that God is in the right, to set His hopes for the redemption and maintenance of His life only on the Word of God, in the establishment of which He was engaged in this self-offering. He would have refused to be willing to live only by this Word and promise of God, and therefore to continue to hunger. In so doing He would, of course, only have done what in His place and with His powers all other men would certainly have done. From the standpoint of all other men He would only have acted reasonably and rightly. " Rabbi, eat " is what His disciples later said to Him (Jn. 4³¹) quite reasonably and in all innocence. But then He would not have made it His meat " to do the will of him that sent him, and to finish his work " (Jn. 4³⁴). Instead of acting for all other men and in their place, He would have left them in the lurch at the very moment when He had made their cause His own. Jesus withstood this temptation. He persisted in obedience, in penitence, in fasting. He hungered in confidence in the promise of manna with which the same God had once fed the fathers in the wilderness after He had allowed them to hunger (Deut. 8³). He willed to live only by that which the Word of God creates, and therefore as one of the sinners who have no hope apart from God, as the Head and King of this people. His decision was, therefore, a different one from that which all other men would have taken in His place, and in that way it was the righteousness which He achieved in their stead.

According to Luke, the second satanic suggestion is that Satan, to whom the world belongs, should give him lordship over it, at the price of His falling down and worshipping him. What would it have meant if Jesus had done this ? Obviously He would have shown that He repented having received the baptism of John and that He did not intend to complete the penitence which He had begun. He would have ceased to recognise and confess the sin of the world as sin, to take it upon Himself as such, and in His own person to bring to an issue the conflict with it (as with man's contradiction against God and himself). He would have won through and been converted to a simpler and more practical and more realistic approach and way. He would have determined to drop the question of the overcoming and removing of evil, to accept the undeniable fact of the overlordship of evil in the world, and to do good, even the best, on this indisputable presupposition, on the ground and in the sphere of this overlord-ship. Why not set up a real kingdom of God on earth ? an international order modelled on the insights of Christian humanitarianism, in which, of course, a liberal-orthodox, ecumenical, confessional Church might also find an appropriate place ? Note that to do this He was not asked to renounce God or to go over to atheism. He had only to lift His hat to the usurper. He had only to bow the knee discreetly and privately to the devil. He had only to make the quiet but solid and irreversible acknowledgment that in that world of splendour the devil should have the first and final word, that at bottom everything should remain as it had been. On this condition we can all succeed in the world, and Jesus most of all. In the divine and human kingdom set up on this condition there would have been no place for the cross. Or rather, in this world ostensibly ruled by Jesus but secretly by Satan, the cross would have been harmlessly turned into a fine and profound symbol : an ornament in the official philosophy and outlook ; but also an adornment (e.g., an episcopal adornment) in the more usual sense of the word ; a suitable recollection of that which Jesus avoided and which is not therefore necessary for anyone else. What other man in Jesus' place would not have been clever enough to close with this offer ? But what He had to do and willed to do in place of all would not then have been done. He would again have left them in the lurch and betrayed them, in spite of all the fine and good things that the world-kingdom of Satan and Jesus might have meant for them. For of what advantage is even the greatest glory to a world which is still defini-tively unreconciled with God ? Of what gain to man are all the conceivable advantages and advances of such a kingdom ? But Jesus resisted this temptation too. He refused to be won over to this attractive realism. As the one great sinner in the name and place of all others, without any prospect of this glory, quite unsuccessfully, indeed with the certainty of failure, He willed to continue worshipping and serving God alone. He willed to persist in repentance and obedience. This was the righteousness which He achieved for us.

The third temptation, according to Luke's account, is the most astonishing of all. The dignity of the setting, the temple of God in the holy city of Jeru-salem, is obviously incomparably greater than the still secular dignity of that high mountain from which Jesus was shown and offered all the kingdoms of the world. It is of a piece that Satan now appears as an obviously pious man who can even quote the Psalms of David, and he gains in the seriousness and weight of his approach. Above all, his suggestion—we can hardly describe it by the horrible word temptation—is quite different from everything that has preceded it. It now consists in the demand to commit an act of supreme, unconditional, blind, absolute, total confidence in God—as was obviously supremely fitting for the Son of God. We might almost say, an act in the sense of and in line with the answers which Jesus Himself had given to the first two temptations, to live only by the Word of God, to serve and worship Him alone. In the last decades we have become accustomed to think of the seeking and attaining of totalitarian dominion as the worst of all evils, as that which is specifically demonic. But if the climax in Luke is right, there is something even worse and just as demonic. It is not just a matter of a miraculous display to reveal the Messiahship of Jesus. It is often interpreted in this way, but by a reading into the text rather than out of it. The text itself makes no mention whatever of spectators. It is rather a question of the testing and proving, of the final assuring of His relationship to God *in foro conscientiae*, in the solitariness of man with God. Jesus is to risk this headlong plunge with the certainty, and to confirm the certainty, that God and His angels are with Him and will keep Him. Schlatter has rather mischievously said that what we have here is what is so glibly described "in contemporary theological literature" as the "leap" of faith. It certainly does seem to be something very like "existence in transcendence," or "the leap into the unknown," or in Reformation language "justification by faith alone," justification in the sense that (in face of death and the last judgment, and in the hope that in trust in God these can be overcome) man presumes to take it into his own hands, to carry it through as the work of his own robust faith, and in that way to have a part in it and to be certain of it; just as Empedocles (we do not know exactly why, but seriously and with courage) finally flung himself into the smoking crater of Etna, which is supposed to have thrown out again only his sandals; just as on this very same rock of the temple, when it was stormed by the Romans in A.D. 70, the last of the high priests put themselves to death with their own hands, possibly in despair, possibly in the hope that there would be a supreme miracle at that last hour. What would it have meant if Jesus had taken this leap? Note the remarkable closeness of the temptation to the way which Jesus did in fact tread. In this respect the Lucan order, in which this is the last and supreme temptation, is most edifying. He will "dare the leap into the abyss, the way to the cross, when the will of God leads Him to it" (Schlatter). But what would have led Him to it here would have been His own will to make use of God in His own favour. He would have experimented with God for His own supreme pleasure and satisfaction instead of taking the purpose of God seriously and subjecting Himself to His good pleasure and command. He would have tried triumphantly to maintain His rightness with God instead of persisting in penitence, instead of allowing God to be in the right against Him. In an act of supreme piety, in the work of a mystical enthusiasm, He would have betrayed the cause of God by making it His own cause, by using it to fulfil His own self-justification before God. If He had given way to this last and supreme temptation He would have committed the supreme sin of tempting God Himself, i.e., under the appearance of this most robust faith in Him demanding that He should accept this Jesus who believes so robustly instead of sinful man by Him and in His person. He would have demanded that He should be the most false of all false gods, the god of the religious man. And in so doing He would Himself have withdrawn from the society of sinful men as whose Representative and Head He was ordained to live and act. He would have left in the lurch the world unreconciled with God. "Farewell, O world, for I am weary of thee." But again we may ask, what other man, all things considered, would not actually have done this in His place? For Adamic man reaches his supreme form in religious self-sacrifice as the most perfect kind of self-glorification, in which God is in fact most completely impressed into the service of man, in which He is most completely denied under cover of the most complete acknowledgment of God and one's fellows. Jesus did not do this. He rejected the supreme ecstasy and satisfaction of religion as the supreme form of sin. And in so doing He remained faithful to the baptism of John. He remained the One in whom God is well-pleased. He remained sinless. He remained in obedience. In our place He achieved the righteousness which had to be achieved in His person for the justification of us all and for the reconciliation of the world with God, the only righteousness that was necessary.

We cannot ignore the negative form in which the righteousness of God appears in the event handed down in these passages. This is unavoidable, because we have to do with it in the wilderness, in the kingdom of demons, in the world unreconciled with God, and in conflict with that world. It is unavoidable because what we have here is a prefiguring of the passion. But in the passion, and in this prefiguring of it, the No of God is only the hard shell of the divine Yes, which in both cases is spoken in the righteous act of this one man. That this is the case is revealed at the conclusion of the accounts in Mark and Matthew by the mention of the angels who, when Satan had left Him, came and ministered unto Him. The great and glorious complement to this at the conclusion of the passion is the story of the resurrection.

In Luke (4¹³) the story of the temptation concludes with the statement of the narrator : " And when the devil had (unsuccessfully) ended all the temptation, he departed from him until the decisive moment " (ἄχρι καιροῦ). The last phrase cannot refer to any specific incident in the activity of Jesus in Galilee or to this activity as a whole. Jesus has to do constantly with the kingdom of darkness in this activity, and in many different forms. But neither in Luke nor in any of the other Gospels (apart from the saying to Peter in Mt. 16²²) do we hear explicitly of any special encounter with the διάβολος or of a renewal of the temptation in all its forms. If this reference to a coming καιρός is not an empty one, then obviously it must mean the night and day of the passion (as in Mt. 26¹⁸ and Jn. 7⁶, ⁸). We obviously have to think of His cry of dereliction on the cross (although this is not reported by Luke, cf. Mk. 15³⁴). We obviously have to think of all the events of Good Friday. We obviously have to think especially of the story of Gethsemane. In this story there is already compressed the whole happening of Good Friday to the extent that it already speaks of a passion of Jesus, but of a passion which has to do strictly with the establishment of His definitive willingness for the real passion which comes upon Him immediately after. In this respect the story forms the turning-point between the two parts of the whole Gospel record. It is now shown where the victory which Jesus won in the temptation in the wilderness leads, that the end will involve the death of the victor. The penitence and the fulfilment of righteousness which Jesus has undertaken is now approaching its climax. The reversal in which the Judge becomes the judged is now about to take place. The story closes with the present : " The hour is come ; behold, the Son of man is betrayed (παραδίδοται) into the hands of sinners."

But it brings out once again the whole absolutely inconceivable difficulty of the matter : the Son of man come down from heaven, the King and Judge sent by God, in the hands of sinners, betrayed, delivered up, surrendered to them. " The hour is come," and in a moment there will appear, and with him the first of those ἁμαρτωλοί, the little παραδιδούς Judas, a chosen apostle, who with his kiss sets the whole event in train. Does all this have to happen ? In this solemn moment, quite naturally but unexpectedly and disruptively in view of all that has gone before, there is a pause. Jesus Himself—in prayer to God—raises the whole question afresh. He prays that " if it were possible, the hour might pass from him " (Mk. 14³⁵). This is repeated in direct speech : " Abba, Father, all things are possible unto thee ; take away this cup from me " (Mk. 14³⁶).

But had not His whole way from Jordan been a single march—which Satan could not arrest, not even in the form of Peter (Mt. 16²³)—to this very hour, a single and determined grasping of this cup of the divine wrath (Is. 51¹⁷) ? But now there is a stumbling, although only for a—repeated—moment : a moment in which there is a pause and trembling not only on earth and in time, not only in the soul of Jesus which is " sorrowful even unto death " (Mt. 26³⁸), but in a sense in heaven, in the bosom of God Himself, in the relationship between the Father and the Son ; a moment in which the question is raised of another possibility than that which will in fact be realised relentlessly and by divine necessity in view of all that has gone before. We may well be surprised that the Synoptics regarded it not only as not repellent but as important and right to record this moment, to incorporate this story so directly and emphatically into their witness to Jesus and His way. We are told of an ἐκθαμβεῖσθαι of Jesus (Mk. 14³³) ; of a horror which gripped Him in face of the frightful event which confronted Him ; of an ἀδημονεῖν ; of a foreboding from which there was no escape, in which He could find no help or comfort, which was only foreboding ; of an ἀγωνία (Lk. 22⁴⁴) in which His sweat fell to the earth like drops of blood ; of a λυπεῖσθαι, a sorrow, a heaviness, an oppression which was " even unto death " (Mt. 26³⁸)— *talis tristitia communem hominem potuisset ad sui necem adigere* is the comment of Bengel. The words of Heb. 5⁷ are also relevant : " Who in the days of his flesh, when he had offered up prayers and supplications with strong crying and tears unto him that was able to save him from death." And the Gospel of John, if it is not more explicit, does not conceal His situation immediately before the actual onset of His passion : " Now is my soul troubled (τετάραχται) ; and what shall I say ? Father, save me from this hour " (Jn. 12²⁷). The question arises whether He has not taken up once again the suggestion of Peter (Mt. 16²²ᶠ·) which He had rejected as all too human and even satanic : " Be it far from thee, Lord ; this shall not be unto thee." Schlatter has rightly pointed out that there is completely lacking here that defiance with which we see the martyr receiving joyfully and boldly the baptism of blood, not to speak of the glad resignation with which Socrates is supposed to have drunk his cup.

There is a striking difference between the story of Gethsemane and that of the temptation in the wilderness. In the latter there is not even the remotest glimpse of any hesitation or questioning on the part of Jesus Himself. Self-evidently and with the greatest precision the tempter is at once resisted. But then it was only a matter of continuing without deviation on the way He had entered at Jordan. Now He had to face the reckoning. Now He was confronted with the final fruit and consequence of what He had begun. Why is His attitude so different ? Especially, why is it so different from that displayed by many a Christian martyr, by a Socrates, by many Communists—as we can see from their letters—who were under sentence of death in the time of Hitler, even by the German general Jodl, executed as a war-criminal in Nuremberg ? It is obviously not simply a matter of suffering and dying in itself and as such. But what then ? What is the frightful thing which, according to these passages, He foresaw in His suffering and dying, which now forces Him to this terrified and shaken halt, to this question whether it really has to be, as had not been the case in the wilderness ? We shall find the answer in a further comparison with that first and very different form of His conflict.

There is no mention now of suggestions on the part of Satan, or even of his presence. If this hour, as we must gather from Luke, is the second and final καιρός of Satan, if he is in some way present and at work in this event as the other Evangelists seem to presuppose—if he will now (and obviously finally) be " rejected " according to Jn. 12³¹, and " judged " according to Jn. 16¹¹—then he is present in quite a different way and quite a different form from that of the earlier occasion. Jesus is quite ready to deal with him as a counsellor, to deal with the temptation that he should leave the way of penitence and obedience which He had entered at Jordan, that he should be forced away from His mission as " the friend of publicans and sinners." Indeed, in spite of the seriousness of the temptation it is almost child's play for Him to deal with it. Perhaps the saying in Lk. 10[18] has something to say to us in this connexion: " I beheld Satan as lightning fall from heaven." But Satan has not yet done with Him. He has more than one form. He can do more than speak and entice. He can do more than " tempt " in the simple or rational or religious form. He can just act and work. His equipment includes not only " much cunning " but also in the last resort " great power." When He is resisted as the tempter he can return all the more powerfully as the avenger of this defeat. In place of other things he can speak for himself in the simple language of facts. It is of something like this that he boasts in Lk. 4[6] : that the power and glory of the kingdoms of this world belong to him. To the extent that the world is the world which is at enmity and unreconciled with God, this is so in the old æon. *Per definitionem* it is his sphere of influence, the world in which apart from the counter-operation of God it is his will which is not only revealed but everywhere done. As we are so clearly told in Eph. 2[2], he is the prince of the power (ὁ ἄρχων τῆς ἐξουσίας) of the air, of the atmosphere, of the conditions of life in this æon, or, to put it plainly : " the spirit that now worketh in the children of disobedience," the motor which drives them, the driver who without their knowing it determines and directs their activity. And because in this æon all men are as such " children of disobedience," because they are ἁμαρτωλοί, sinners, those who fall into the hands of men fall into the hands of this prince, of this spirit, and therefore of Satan, who acquires his power—whether he knows it or not—under the pseudonym of human will and action, who acquires it as the highest secular power to fbeseen. So Jesus falls into the hands of men, of sinners. Note, into the hands io those in line with whom He had placed Himself and willed to be and to remain n His utter obedience. It now came to Him what that·involved and carried with it, to what He had given Himself, the power of the unbreakable law to which these men are subject in their willing and doing, to which the world itself is subject, the overwhelming retribution which must come upon Him at the hand of these men because He has undertaken and dared to be unique amongst them, to resist temptation, to achieve righteousness in their place. He saw that in so doing He would not only be alone but would necessarily have them all against Him : those who had not resisted temptation, but constantly gave way to it ; who all existed and acted as more or less useful instruments of the power of temptation and the tempter ; who could act in relation to Jesus only in the service of the will and dominion of Satan. This was the world which in His own person He was to reconcile and willed to reconcile with God. He saw this world as it was. He saw what it was that dominated it and was fulfilled in it. He saw and felt the " great burden of the world." He saw what even the greatest of Christian and other martyrs did not see : that this burden is overwhelming, that in the last resort it can only overwhelm and crush Himself and other men. He saw this because He had contradicted and withstood the tempter, because He had chosen and done that which is right. But it was one thing to enter and continue on this way, it was another to tread it to the end, and in this world its necessarily bitter end. It was one thing to contradict and withstand the tempter, it was another to see him actually triumphant as he necessarily would be in this world, in the humanity ruled by him, to be refuted by him in the hard language of facts. From this we may gather something at least of the convulsion of that hour.

But the real meaning of the hour in Gethsemane was not this vision of the world and of that which rules in it. In the texts there is no mention at all of any coming of Satan. And the men who serve him appear and act only when the hour is over. It is not a matter of the riddle of the world and the riddle of evil as such. Nor can we really say that in the problem of the world and evil as

forcefully presented in this way it was a question of God, or the problem of a
theodicy, or reflection where God is in this triumph of humanity and the world
as ruled by Satan, whether He is forced to retreat or to abdicate or to die in
face of it. Considerations like this are quite foreign to the New Testament
context. If we find them there they will have had to be imported. There is
no question of considerations at all, whether about Satan and the world or
about God. Above and in and through the event which is now disclosed and
works itself out, God rules and does His work, the work which Jesus has to finish
and is determined to finish. He is the living Lord even of the world which is
in conflict with Him. As such He can never be idle, He can never grow weary,
He can never resign. In this world Satan can have only the power which is
given and allowed him as he is powerfully upheld by the left hand of God. This
is the self-evident presupposition of everything that happens. Jesus does not
think about this God, but speaks to Him. And we have to seek the problem
of Gethsemane (1) in the content of what He says, (2) in the fact that He is
quite alone in what He says, without companion or helper, and (3) in the fact
that the answer of God will be given only in the language of facts.

We will take the second point first. It is emphasised in the texts in a way
that we cannot overlook. They tell us plainly that Jesus wished to pray this
prayer a little ahead of His disciples but in their presence and with their participation. To do this He withdraws only a little (Mk. 14³⁵), only " about a stone's
cast " from them (Lk. 22⁴¹). That His soul is sorrowful even unto death is
something which He does not tell to God but to them (Mk. 14³⁴), and He asks
that they should watch with Him (Mt. 26³⁸), and later expressly that they should
pray with Him (Mk. 14³⁸) ; that is, that they should see what He sees, world-
occurrence as it is, and God ruling over and in and through it, and that they
should do what He does, call upon this God. It is not self-evident that He
should be alone in this matter. He had called the disciples to be His apostles,
the foundation of His community in the world. He had made His cause theirs.
He had promised that where two or three of them were gathered in His name
He Himself would be there in the midst (Mt. 18²⁰). It could and indeed necessarily was the case that where He was at any rate two or three of them would
be gathered. And Jesus knew—here we see directly the connexion between
Gethsemane and the temptation in the wilderness—that what was about to
happen would again mean temptation, πειρασμός, that with the event which was
about to break in all its malice there might come the suggestion of an easier way
for Himself and His disciples than that which He had entered. That is why
He Himself watches and prays in this hour. That is why He calls to His disciples :
" Watch and pray, lest ye enter into temptation." He knows that man is lost
unless he is in some sense aware of it. He knows that for Himself and His
disciples calling on God is the only way to meet and defeat it. For the spirit is
willing, but the flesh is weak (Mk. 14³⁸). The flight of the disciples at the crucial
moment (Mk. 14⁵⁰) and the denial of Peter (Mk. 14⁶⁶f.) will show how weak the
flesh is, how quickly they will find and take the easier way, how necessary it
was for them to obey His call to watch and pray. For His sake and for their
own they ought not to have left Him alone when He went forward to pray.
But they did leave Him quite alone. " Couldest not thou watch one hour ? "
He asks Peter (Mk. 14³⁷). No, he could not, and neither could the others. Again
and again He was to find them sleeping : " For their eyes were heavy, and they
wist not what to answer him " (Mk. 14⁴⁰). In other words, the apostolate, the
community, Christendom, the Church (far from existing eschatologically) sleeps.
It is present, but it has no part at all in that prayer to God. Jesus makes it
alone. There is no one to bear the burden with Him. There is none to help.
No Christian individual had the insight, and no Christian group put it into effect,
that this was a matter for Christians and Christianity itself, that for their own
sake Christians and Christianity had good reason to have a part in this prayer,

to join with Jesus in crying to God. In doing this for Himself Jesus does it for them, and " for them " in the strictest sense, in their place. It is now true : " Simon, Simon, Satan hath desired to have you (as once he desired to have Job), that he may sift you as wheat ; But I have prayed for thee, that thy faith fail not " (Lk. 22³¹ᶠ·). If Jesus had not prayed in their place (and in the same way acted in their place in His passion) the apostolate and the community would have fallen victim to the satanic determination of world occurrence like its other agents. The Fourth Evangelist regarded this aspect of the matter, this meaning of the final hour, as so decisively important that at the very place where we miss the report of Gethsemane (Jn. 17) he has reported the " high-priestly " prayer of Jesus which anticipates so remarkably the whole event of the passion : " And now I am no more in the world, but these are in the world " (v. 11). " I pray not that thou shouldest take them out of the world, but that thou shouldest keep them from the evil " (v. 15). " And for their sakes I sanctify myself, that they also might be sanctified through the truth " (v. 19). " Father, I will that they also, whom thou hast given me, be with me where I am " (v. 24), " that the love wherewith thou hast loved me may be in them and I in them " (v. 26). We must have this glorified picture before us to understand the account of the Synoptics. But properly to estimate Jn. 17 we must also have before us the hard picture of the Synoptics : the complete denial of Christ-ianity and the Church in relation to Jesus ; their notorious non-participation in His decisive action ; the frightful loneliness in which they left Him, and in which quite alone—not with them but without them and therefore for them—He had to do and did what had to be done. If there is anything which brings out clearly this simple " for us " as the content of the Gospel, then it is this aspect of the event in Gethsemane, in which the act of God in Jesus Christ had absolutely nothing to correspond to it in the existence of those who believe in Him. They could not watch with Him even one hour. He alone watched and prayed in their place.

We must now take up the third point we mentioned. It is only with reserva-tions that we can call the prayer in Gethsemane a " conversation " with God. In the texts there is no mention of any answer corresponding to and accepting the address of Jesus. We might think of the appearance of the angel to strengthen Him mentioned in Luke (22⁴³). And this naturally recalls the angels who, according to Mark and Matthew, came and ministered to Him in the wilderness. But this ἐνισχύων αὐτόν in the Lucan account does not form a conclusion, but is, as it were, refreshment by the way. It is only after the strengthening which comes to Jesus that we hear of His ἀγωνία (v. 44), of the sweat which fell to the earth like great drops of blood. It is not an ending of the necessary conflict brought about from heaven, but, according to the presentation in Luke, the battle in which He is engaged only becomes severe after this strengthening. Jesus does not, in fact, receive any answer, any sign from God. Or, rather, He has " the sign of the prophet Jonah " (Mt. 12³⁹ᶠ·) who was three days and three nights in the whale's belly. For Him, as for all this evil and adulterous genera-tion, the only sign will be the actual event of His death : " So shall the Son of man be three days and three nights in the heart of the earth." God will give His answer to the prayer only in this inconceivable, this frightful event, and not otherwise. For the event of His resurrection lies beyond the answer. It is the disclosure of its meaning. The answer which Jesus receives is in itself this and no other, this answer which was no answer, to which His prayer itself alluded. Note that it came in the same language in which Satan now spoke with Him as the prince of this æon, triumphantly avenging His contradiction and opposition in the wilderness. The will of God was done as the will of Satan was done. The answer of God was identical with the action of Satan. That was the frightful thing. The coincidence of the divine and the satanic will and work and word was the problem of this hour, the darkness in which Jesus addressed God in Gethsemane.

This brings us to the main question of the content and meaning of this address. For a moment it holds out before the reader another possible form of the coming event : not in any clear outline, only vaguely—for Jesus is not proposing to God any alternative plan—defined only in a negative way ; not this event, the frightful event which now impends. Jesus prays that this hour, this cup of wrath might pass from Him, might be spared Him. He prays, therefore, that the good will and the sacred work and the true word of God should not coincide with the evil will and the corrupt work and the deceitful word of the tempter and of the world controlled by him, the ἁμαρτωλοί. He prays that God should not give Him up to the power the temptation of which He had resisted and willed to resist in all circumstances. He prays that God will so order things that the triumph of evil will be prevented, that the claim of Satan to world dominion will not be affirmed but given the lie, that a limit will be set to him, and with him to the evil course of the world and the evil movement of men. He prays that, directed by God's providence, the facts might speak a different language from that which they are about to speak, that in their end and consequence they should not be against Him, just as He had decided for God and not against Him in the wilderness. He prays that for the sake of God's own cause and glory the evil determination of world-occurrence should not finally rage against Himself, the sent One of God and the divine Son. Surely this is something which God cannot will and allow. Such is the prayer of Jesus as prayed once in Luke, twice in Mark and as many as three times in Matthew.

In the continuation of the prayer He set this content in opposition to the real will of God as His own will, which He was determined to surrender to the former. We must be careful to explain that the content of this petition, the passing of the cup, would have been the will of Jesus if it had corresponded to the real will of God. But it is not. Jesus clearly wished that it might have been so. But the texts do not tell us that He set His will in this direction, first resisting what was revealed to be the real will of God, and then abandoning it in favour of this will. They tell us that He would have set His will in this way, and quite legitimately, if it had corresponded to the real will of God. At the very beginning of the prayer there is interposed the proviso : " Abba, Father, all things are possible to thee " (Mk. 14³⁶), " if it be possible " (Mt. 26³⁹), or even more simply and clearly " if thou be willing " (Lk. 22⁴²), then let it be done otherwise. The prayer and the expressed wish of Jesus stand from the very first under this pre-condition. He did not think out and choose some other possibility. He did not reject the impending reality. He did not establish some other direction of His own will. He did not refuse that which forced itself upon Him in view of what lay ahead. He made His request to God only with a view to some other possibility which might be God's own will, and not with any particular bias in this or that direction.

This does not affect the urgency of His request, to which the texts refer in such a drastic way. Nor does it affect the extremity in which He prays. Nor does it affect the full seriousness with which He gives to His prayer this content. The riddle confronts Him with all the horror that it evokes : that of the impending unity between the will of God on the one hand, that will which He had hitherto obeyed, and which He willed to obey in all circumstances and whatever it was, that will which He was quite ready should be done—and, on the other hand, the power of evil which He had withstood, and which He willed to withstand in all circumstances and in whatever form He might encounter it, which He could not allow to be done. What shook Him was the coming concealment of the lordship of God under the lordship of evil and evil men. This was the terrible thing which He saw breaking on Himself and His disciples and all men, on His work as the Reconciler between God and man, and therefore on God's own work, destroying everything, mortally imperilling the fulfilment of His just and redemptive judgment. This was what He saw, and which His disciples, not to speak of other men, did not see. It was to avoid this dreadful thing that He prayed, He alone, while His disciples did not pray. It was to prevent this event that He cried alone to God—that some other possibility should be put into effect, that this future should not become the present.

But He only prays. He does not demand. He does not advance any claims. He does not lay upon God any conditions. He does not reserve His future obedience. He does not abandon His status as a penitent. He does not cease to allow that God is in the right, even against Himself. He does not try to anticipate His justification by Him in any form, or to determine it Himself. He does not think of trying to be judge in His own cause and in God's cause. He prays only as a child to the Father, knowing that He can and should pray, that His need is known to the Father, is on the heart of the Father, but knowing also that the Father disposes what is possible and will therefore be, and that what He allows to be will be the only thing that is possible and right.

If we understand the beginning of Jesus' prayer to God in this way—and how else can we understand it in view of what the texts say and in the context of the Gospels ?—then the meaning of what follows is clear : " But ($\dot{a}\lambda\lambda\dot{a}$), or nevertheless ($\pi\lambda\dot{\eta}\nu$), not what ($\tau\dot{\iota}$, or as, $\dot{\omega}s$) I will, but what (as) thou wilt " (Mk. 14[36], Mt. 26[39]). Or more explicitly : " Nevertheless, not my will, but thine, be done " (Lk. 22[42]). Or even more explicitly : " O my Father, if this cup may not pass away from me except I drink it, thy will be done " (Mt. 26[42]). If our previous interpretation is correct, this is not a kind of return of willingness to obey, which was finally forced upon Jesus and fulfilled by Him in the last hour ; it is rather a readiness for the act of obedience which He had never compromised in His prayer. The proviso " if it be possible " which was an integral part of the prayer now comes into force. The prayer reckoned on the possibility of quite a different answer. This is what had made it a genuine prayer to God. But now this possibility fades from view. Jesus does not change His mind when He says, " Thy will be done." After pausing with very good reason, He now proceeds all the more determinedly along the way which He had never left. But we must be careful how we praise the humility which Jesus displayed in the second form of His prayer. Naturally, it is the prayer of humility of the Son of God made man. But we must also see that in the " Thy will be done " He emerges from the serious and inevitable astonishment and oppression in which He had prayed that the cup should pass from Him. He stands upright in what we might almost call a supreme pride. He faces the reality the avoidance of which He had so earnestly desired. Because it is the reality of the will of God He grasps it as that which is better, which alone is good. He does not do so in sad resignation, therefore, but because He will and can affirm this reality and this alone. In the last analysis, therefore, we can describe what Jesus does as renunciation only if we explain it more closely. He does renounce the content of that wish which He had spread before God, and therefore the prospect of a different future from that which actually came to Him, and therefore the fixing of a different will to correspond to this different future. But what Jesus did is ill adapted to be used, as we love to use it, as an example of that renunciation of all kinds of hopes and fears which is demanded of man. For, according to the sense of the texts, we cannot speak of any intention which was opposed to that of God and which He then renounced. Above all, the emphasis of the prayer is not at all upon that which might not happen, as in all kinds of mysticism both new and old, both higher and lower. It is upon that which might happen. It is a positive prayer and not a negative. The statement—and in this it goes far beyond the answers of Jesus to the tempter in the wilderness—is at its open core a radiant Yes to the actual will of God. It is radiant because the decision which it expresses and fulfils ceases to regard any other divine possibilities which there might be and fixes itself on the one actual will of God—" what thou wilt "—and unreservedly accepts it. This is not a withdrawal on the part of Jesus, but a great and irresistible advance. It is not a resignation before God. It is an expression of the supreme and only praise which God expects of man and which is rendered to Him only by this One man in place of all, the praise which comes from the knowledge that He does not make any mistakes, that His way, the way which He whose thoughts are higher than our thoughts actually treads Himself, is holy and just and gracious. But in all this we do not forget what it was all about, what Jesus was affirming and accepting and taking on Himself, with this " Thy will be done." It was not simply that He had to suffer and die, and that in contrast to others who have gone a similar way He accepted it rather painfully and tardily, as the moralists have easily been able to hold against Him. It was not a matter of His suffering and dying in itself and as such, but of the dreadful thing that He saw coming upon Him in and with His suffering and dying. He saw it clearly and correctly. It was the coming of the night " in which no man can work " (Jn. 9⁴), in which the good will of God will be indistinguishably one with the evil will of men and the world and Satan. It was a matter of the triumph of God being concealed under that of His adversary, of that which is not, of that which supremely is not. It was a matter of God Himself obviously making a tryst with death and about to keep it. It was a matter of the divine judgment being taken out of the hands of Jesus and placed in those of His supremely unrighteous judges and executed by them upon Him. It was a matter of the enemy who had been repulsed as the tempter having and exercising by divine permission and appointment the right, the irresistible right of might. It was a matter of the obedience and penitence in which Jesus had persisted coming to fruition in His own rejection and condemnation—not by chance, but according to the plan of God Himself, not superficially, but in serious earnest. That was what came upon Him in His suffering and dying, as God's answer to His appeal. Jesus saw this cup. He tasted its bitterness. He had not made any mistake. He had not been needlessly afraid. There was every reason to ask that it might pass from Him.

" Thy will be done " means that Jesus, like all this " evil and adulterous generation," is to receive only the sign of the prophet Jonah, but that as the one man, the only One in this generation, He willed on behalf of this generation to see in it the true sign of God. " Thy will be done " means that He put this cup to His lips, that He accepted this answer of God as true and holy and just and gracious, that He went forward to what was about to come, thus enabling it to happen. " Thy will be done " means not only that Jesus accepted as God's sentence this language of facts, this concealment of the lordship of God by the lordship of evil, this turning and decision against Him according to the determined counsel of providence, but that He was ready to pronounce this sentence Himself and therefore on Himself; indeed, He was ready to fulfil the sentence by accepting His suffering and dying at the hands of ἁμαρτωλοί. That is what He did in His prayer when there was none to stand by Him, when there was none who could or would help Him, when He was not surrounded or sustained by any intercession, when He could only intercede for others, when He prayed for His disciples and therefore for the world that most necessary, most urgent and most decisive prayer, the high-priestly prayer.

But what happened when Jesus prayed in this way in Gethsemane ? How was this prayer heard, which no other ever could pray or ever has prayed before or since, but which was in fact heard as no other prayer was heard when it received the answer which it requested ?

One thing is clear. In the power of this prayer Jesus received, i.e., He renewed, confirmed and put into effect, His freedom to finish His work, to execute the divine judgment by undergoing it Himself, to punish the sin of the world by bearing it Himself, by taking it away from the world in His own person, in His death. The sin of the world was now laid upon Him. It was now true that in the series of many sinners He was the only One singled out by God to be its bearer and Representative, the only One that it could really touch and oppress and terrify. That the deceiver of men is their destroyer, that his power is that of death, is something that had to be proved true in the One who was not deceived, in order that it might not be true for all those who were deceived, that their enmity against God might be taken away from them, that their curse might not rest upon them. This was the will of God in the dreadful thing which Jesus saw approaching—in that conjunction of the will and work and word of God with those of evil. The power of evil had to break on Jesus, its work of death had to be done on Him, so that being done on Him it might be done once and for all, for all men, for the liberation of all men. This is what happened when Jesus took the cup and drank it to the last bitter drops. " For this cause came I unto this hour " is what He says in Jn. 12²⁷ when He had just prayed on this occasion too : " Father, save me from this hour." If the Father was the Father of Jesus, and Jesus His Son, He could not save Him from this hour. That would have been not to hear His prayer. For Jesus had come to this hour in order that the will of God should be done in this hour as it actually was done.

And Satan, the evil one, and the world ruled by him, and the ἁμαρτωλοί as his agents and instruments ? Is it not clear that in the prayer prayed by Jesus in this hour the " prince of this world " is judged (Jn. 16¹¹), " cast out " (Jn. 12³¹) ? " He hath nothing in me." He does Him every possible injury, but He cannot injure that which He does when He allows this to happen. In relation to Him he makes his supreme and final effort. He has his supreme καιρός. For the world must " know that I love the Father, and as the Father gave me commandment, even so I do" (Jn. 14³¹). He uses his power to overwhelm Jesus, and he succeeds, but his power loses its subjects, for the world and men escape him once and for all, and it ceases to be power over them, an impassable gulf being opened between him and the world ruled by him, between him and the ἁμαρτωλοί deceived by him. He Himself is impressed into the service of the will of God as fulfilled in the suffering and death of Jesus. · His act of violence on this one man can achieve only what God has determined to His own glory and the salvation of all. A limit is therefore set to his lordship and its end is already in sight. That is what happened to him when Jesus prayed that not His will but God's will should be done.

Moreover in this prayer it also takes place that the world, even the sinful men at whose hands Jesus will suffer and die—all of them from Judas to Pilate —will all actively take part in the event of His self-giving to death which takes place for the reconciliation of the world with God. Note that they will do so as His enemies, not in the decision of faith but in the decision of a supreme unbelief. But even as His enemies, His accusers, His judges and His executioners they will actively take part in it. They are no longer merely wicked men, but in their very wickedness they are involuntary instruments of God. In all their speaking and tumult, in all the evil and foolish activity with which they bring about Good Friday, they necessarily testify to themselves and to all men of all ages how much this happening affects them, and that it is their own cause which is prosecuted in it.

One last thing : in this prayer of Jesus there took place quite simply the completion of the penitence and obedience which He had begun to render at Jordan and which He had maintained in the wilderness. Had not His whole resistance in that temptation, the No which He had victoriously opposed to it, aimed at the different but no less victorious Yes which He said to the will of God in this hour ? Was He not even then representing God and therefore the world and sinful men ? In the light of it, what else does His " Thy will be done " mean but that this first word of His was and remained His final word ? So, then, in this prayer we can see the essence of the positive content of the suffering and dying of Jesus—the act of righteousness (δικαίωμα) and obedience (ὑποταγή) of the one man, in the power of which the vindication of all men was accomplished as the promise of life (δικαίωσις εἰς ζωήν), in which in the last judgment many will be presented righteous (δίκαιον) in the sight of God and His angels and the whole world (Rom. 5¹⁸ᶠ·).

We are now at the end of the important section dealing with the general question (closely linked with that of the previous section) which was asked by Anselm : *Cur Deus homo ?* and with the particular question what Jesus Christ was and did *pro nobis*, for us and for the world. To this question we have given four related answers. He took our place as Judge. He took our place as the judged. He was judged in our place. And He acted justly in our place. It is important to see that we cannot add anything to this—unless it is an Amen to indicate that what we say further has this fourfold but single answer as a pre-supposition. Whatever we say further depends upon the fact that in the sense we have noted He was the Judge judged in our place. All theology, both that which follows and indeed that which precedes the doctrine of reconciliation, depends upon this *theologia crucis*. And it depends upon it under the particular aspect under which we have had to develop it in this first part of the doctrine of reconciliation as the doctrine of substitution. Everything depends upon the fact that the Lord who became a servant, the Son of God who went into the far country, and came to us, was and did all this for us ; that He fulfilled, and fulfilled in this way, the divine judgment laid upon Him. There is no avoiding this strait gate. There is no other way but this narrow way. If the nail of this fourfold " for us " does not hold, everything else will be left hanging in the void as an anthropological or psychological or sociological myth, and sooner or later it will break and fall to the ground. If it is to be meaningful and true, and with it all those doctrines of man's plight and redemption, of his death and life, of his perdition and salvation, which seem to be so sure in themselves, then it must first be demythologised in the light of this " for us." For that reason this is the place for a full-stop. Many further statements may follow, but the stop indicates that this first statement is complete in itself, that it comprehends all that follows, and that it can stand alone.

To make this point, we will not proceed any further for the moment, but test the statement by asking whether it still holds good even in the variations forced upon us by the different ways in which the New Testament speaks of this *pro nobis* and in which the Church too will always speak of it. If we fail to notice these variations, there will be a formal if not a substantial lacuna in our presentation, and we shall also miss certain definite insights. A long, retrospective note is therefore required.

When we spoke of Jesus Christ as Judge and judged, and of His judgment and justice, we were adopting a definite standpoint and terminology as the framework in which to present our view of the *pro nobis*. In order to speak with dogmatic clarity and distinctness we had to decide on a framework of this kind. And the actual importance of this way of thinking and its particularly good basis in the Bible were a sufficient reason for choosing this one. But exegesis reminds us that in the New Testament there are other standpoints and terminologies which might equally be considered as guiding principles for dogmatics

The fact that in the New Testament more than one starting-point is proposed for our systematic reflection on the *pro nobis* ought to be a salutary reminder that in dogmatics we cannot speak down from heaven in the language of God but only on earth as strictly and exactly as we can in a human language, as the New Testament writers themselves did—the variety of the standpoints and concepts which they adopted being the attestation. In all its contexts theology can speak only approximately. It is a matter of finding and keeping to those lines of approximation which are relatively the best, which correspond best to what we want to express. That is what we have tried to do in this matter of the *pro nobis* with the selection and exposition of four concepts taken from the sphere of law. But we have to recognise that in the New Testament there are other similar spheres, and therefore that other lines of approximation are possible in principle.

For example, in addition to the forensic imagery which we have chosen there is also, strangely enough, a financial in which the being and activity and even the self-offering of Jesus Christ for us and in our place are described as the payment of a ransom (λύτρον, Mk. 10⁴⁵), and therefore as a λυτροῦν (1 Pet. 1¹⁸, Tit. 2¹⁴), an ἀπολύτρωσις (Rom. 3²⁴), an ἐξαγοράζειν (Gal. 3¹³, 4⁵). In the majority of these passages, although not all, the important concept ἀπολύτρωσις does, of course, speak of an event which will take place only in and with the appearance of Jesus Christ. This strand is relatively slender. Not infrequently (as in Rom. 3²⁴) it crosses the one of which we have been particularly thinking. And it would be difficult and not very profitable to try to think out the whole event within the framework of this imagery. Fundamentally, no doubt, that is possible. But it is surely enough if we are ready to use the particular force of these categories in an occasional and subsidiary manner to clarify the matter to ourselves and others.

There is perhaps also a military view of the work of Jesus Christ behind passages like Mk. 3²⁷ (the invasion of the house of the strong man and his binding), or Col. 1¹³ (our snatching away from the power of darkness and removal to the kingdom of God's Son), or even the πανοπλία θεοῦ of Eph. 6¹¹ᶠ. The Eastern Church especially, but also Luther, loved to regard and describe this work as a victorious overcoming of the devil and death which took place on our behalf. But it may again be asked whether it is advisable to try to work out systematically our thinking in this direction. What is clear is that a place should be found for this group of images and the particular truth which it presents.

There is, however, one group of New Testament views and concepts and terms which stands apart both from those we have just mentioned, and from the forensic group we have preferred, with sufficient distinctness and importance to merit a special appraisal. We can give it the general title of cultic. One important New Testament writing, the Epistle to the Hebrews, is almost completely dominated by it. But it is obviously presupposed and expressly used in Paul and the Johannine writings. May it not be that the most primitive Christianity, because of its great nearness to the Old Testament, partly in agreement with it and partly in opposition to it, did in fact think and speak far more in the images and categories of this group than we can detect from the New Testament ? It occurs again and again in unmistakable allusions. For example, the Jesus Christ who gives Himself for us is called the " Lamb of God," and the giving of His life is referred to as " His blood." When this happens, we are clearly using cultic language. Of course in the New Testament the different groups of terms cut across each other very frequently. It is therefore inevitable that we should have occasionally met expressions from this group in our previous discussion. And of itself it would be quite possible to put our whole presentation within the framework of this standpoint. The older Protestant dogmatics did in fact give to the doctrine of the work of Jesus Christ the title *munus Christi sacerdotale* when they treated it under the aspect of the *pro nobis* as we have done in this section. The only trouble was that their expositions under this title did at their heart slip into forensic notions (which were more or less foreign, or were applied in a way that was more or less foreign to the Bible itself). At any rate, they did not bring out the specific features in the cultic standpoint and terminology. If we ourselves have refrained from presenting the whole in this framework it is for two reasons. First, and quite simply, material which is already difficult would have been made even more difficult by trying to understand it in a form which is now rather remote from us. Second, and above all, we are able to see the matter better and more distinctly and more comprehensively under the four selected concepts taken from the forensic area of biblical thinking than would have been possible even at the very best if we had committed ourselves radically to a cultic view. But this need not prevent us from now trying briefly to see and test from this different standpoint, which is so very important in New Testament thinking, the knowledge which we have gained in the framework of this other outlook. In this respect we may remember Zinzendorf, whose theology of blood I have not really been trying to avoid. What we have tried to say in another way, if it is said correctly, cannot be anything other than that which could and can be said in the images and categories of cultic language. It would therefore bode ill for our results if we could not recognise them in the mirror of this other language in which it was so important to the men of the New Testament to think and speak. For the moment, then, we will not continue our thinking, but re-state and verify it in another direction.

1. Jesus Christ took our place as Judge. We can say the same thing in this way. He is the Priest who represented us. He represented a people oppressed by its sins, threatened because of them, and in need of propitiation, a people from which the will of Yahweh is concealed, which will not be instructed properly concerning His rights and law, which cannot really sacrifice or pray for itself. The priest is the mediator and representative who by virtue of his office (originally, perhaps, understood in charismatic terms) actually makes possible the access of the people to its god. We must not be vexed when we see that the close parallel between this image and the work of Jesus lies in the very characteristics of the concept of priest which make it quite impossible for us to use the term to describe any order of men in the Church. According to the definition of Thomas Aquinas (*S. th.* III, 22, 1) a priest is a *mediator inter Deum et populum in quantum scilicet divina populo tradit, unde dicitur sacerdos, quasi sacra dans*. In relation to the work of Jesus Christ for us this is not only not too strong, but not strong enough. The exclusiveness with which the priest acts alone, not only in His function of imparting the *divina* or *sacra* to the people, but also in that of representing the people before God, is, of course, the *tertium comparationis*. Jesus Christ is *the* Priest, between God and man, the one μεσίτης (1 Tim. 2⁵). The image indicates the fact. But the fact is greater and more powerful than the image. It necessarily transcends it.

The exclusiveness of all other priests is limited by the fact that all other priests, even the high priests of the Old Testament in their representative capacity, need to do for themselves what they do for others. " He shall make atonement for himself, and for his household, and for all the congregation of Israel " (Lev. 16⁶, Heb. 9⁷). This reservation makes his position and function understandable and tolerable from the human standpoint but it also compromises it. He acts as a *primus inter pares*. But only symbolically, or representatively, is he a *sacra dans*. He himself must receive the *sacra* no less than others. There is no such reservation in the case of Jesus Christ. As the Son of God He acts exclusively on behalf of the people and not for Himself.

For this reason He is the true, and essential and original Priest, the " great high-priest " (Heb. 4¹⁴), " not after the law of a carnal commandment, but after the power of an endless life " (Heb. 7¹⁶), not " after the order of Aaron, for even as man He did not belong to the tribe of Levi, but to that of Judah " (Heb. 7¹¹ᶠ·), but as Hebrews constantly repeats from Ps. 110[4] " after the order of Melchisedec, King of Salem " (Gen. 14[18f.]), who met Abraham and blessed him, to whom Abraham (and in his loins Levi) paid tithes and therefore recognised his precedence, who was a king of righteousness and peace, " without father, without mother, without descent, having neither beginning of days, nor end of life ; but made like unto the Son of God " (Heb. 7[1f.]). What the priest after the order of Aaron does must be authorised by the Law, which is before him and after him and therefore over him and those like him. And the dignity and force of his offering consists in the fact that it is brought according to this Law, that the bringing of it is a single case under this Law. That is why it has to be repeated. That is why—and this is the great limitation of all other priestly work—it is not the thing itself, the reconciliation of man with God, but only the " type and shadow " of it (Heb. 8[5]), an indication only, a powerful symbolising and attesting of the atonement which will be made by God Himself. If in Jesus Christ we had to do with a high-priest of this kind, with another symbolical representation of the atonement, then we have to ask under what law He stands, what He represents, what general necessity there is for the " satisfaction " He makes, what higher truth is revealed in the reality of His cross. There is always a strong temptation to look for Him on this level and therefore to put questions like this. But He is a Priest after the order of Melchisedec. That is, He is an instance of priestly action for which there is no parallel, which cannot be deduced from anything else, which stands under no law but that established and revealed in the fact that there was this instance. And this is the instance of effectively priestly action because in it the action is complete. It is not the symbol for a general truth which lies above it. It is the instance in which satisfaction—that which suffices for the reconciliation of the world with God—has been made (*satis fecit*) and can be grasped only as something which has in fact happened, and not as something which had to happen by reason of some upper half of the event ; not, then, in any theory of satisfaction, but only as we see and grasp the *satis-facere* which has, in fact, been achieved.

From this it follows that in His ministry, unlike other priests and high priests, He cannot and need not be replaced by any other priestly person. He does not have and exercise this office within the framework of an institution, as one of its many representatives, but on the basis of an oath which God swore by Himself, and therefore as a Priest for ever (Heb. 7[20-24]), not with daily or annual repetitions, but ἐφάπαξ (Heb. 7[27], 9[12, 26], 10[10]), in a single action accomplished and effective once and for all, by a θυσία, by a προσφορά (Heb. 10[12, 14]) accomplished, not in the forecourt or the outer court, but with His entry into the innermost tabernacle, the Holiest of Holies of God Himself (Heb. 9[1f.]). In this way the work of Jesus Christ is at once the essence and fulfilment of all other priestly work but also that which replaces it and makes it superfluous. At the point to which the existence of the Old Testament priest, the human priest called by God, points and can only point, there now stands and acts Jesus Christ in a way which is different from that of every other human priest, even the priest and high priest of the Old Testament. And from this point He has now crowded out and replaced from the very outset every other human priest. He is the Mediator, the Representative of His people before God. He is that which every other priest can only signify in his work—and signifying it in this way can only do that which—as the Epistle to the Hebrews emphasises again and again—is completely insufficient : insufficient to create a genuine correspondence of man to God in the divine covenant ; insufficient to make man capable of acting in relation to God ; insufficient for the reconciliation of the world with God. In the work of Jesus Christ and in that work alone there takes place the real and sufficient priestly work, the *sacra dare*. In Him we have the One we need as a Priest to act for us (Heb. 4[14], 8[1], 10[21]) : ἔχομεν. And by Him we obviously have that which we also have as those justified by Him as Judge (to revert to our earlier terminology), that is, peace with God, access to Him, and hope in Him (cf. Heb. 10[19f.] with Rom. 5[1f.]).

In fact we can equally well describe the work of Jesus Christ as His high-priestly work as His judicial work, and we shall mean and say exactly the same thing. In both cases He takes the place of man, and takes from man an office which has to be filled but which man himself cannot fill. In both cases a new order comes into force to establish a new covenant, which is really the genuine fulfilment of the old. It does so in this very different man who in both cases as the Son of God made man takes the matter into His own hands to execute it according to its true meaning and purpose. In both cases this involves the deposing and therefore the serious discrediting and humiliating of man. And in both cases this and this alone means the liberation and hope of man.

2. We will combine the second and third points of our main discussion. Jesus Christ is the One who was accused, condemned and judged in the place of us sinners. But we can say the same thing in this way: He gave Himself to be offered up as a sacrifice to take away our sins. It is perfectly plain that whichever view we take or expression we use it is with reference to the same thing, the passion of Jesus Christ. We have not yet mentioned that which according to the Epistle to the Hebrews constitutes the decisive difference between Himself and all other priests and high priests. The supreme and distinctive function of the priest is to offer sacrifice. But this Priest—and here the image breaks down completely and the parallel with Melchisedec is abandoned—is not only the One who offers sacrifice but also the sacrifice which is offered ; just as He is also the Judge and the judged. He does not offer anything else—not even the greatest thing—He simply offers Himself. He does not pour out the blood of others, of bulls and calves, to go into the Holiest with this offering (Heb. 9[12, 25]). It is a matter of His own blood, of the giving of His own life to death. " Through the eternal Spirit He offered himself without spot to God " (Heb. 9[14, 23, 26] ; cf. 7[27], 10[12, 14])—Himself as προσφορὰ καὶ θυσία Eph. 5[2]). He Himself is the Lamb of God which taketh away the sin of the world (Jn. 1[29])—a lamb without spot or blemish, i.e., the lamb most suitable for this offering, as is emphasised in 1 Pet. 1[19]. He Himself was offered as our Passover (1 Cor. 5[7]). Similarly the expression " my blood of the covenant " in the saying at the giving of the cup at the Last Supper (Mk. 14[24]) undoubtedly involves a similar comparison of His own self-giving with the blood of sacrifice which, according to Ex. 24[8], was sprinkled over the people on the conclusion of the covenant at Sinai. Or, again, His blood is for those who believe in Him that which the *kapporeth* sprinkled with the blood of the animal sacrifice, the ἱλαστήριον of the covenant, could only signify for the people of the old covenant : the demonstration, the revelation, the event, the ἔνδειξις τῆς δικαιοσύνης θεοῦ on earth (Rom. 3[25]). Because it is this Priest, the Son of God, who makes this offering, which is Himself, therefore in contrast to all others His sacrifice is effective and complete, making an " eternal " redemption (Heb. 9[12]). It is the one true sacrifice, just as He who makes it is the one true Priest : the fulfilment of what is meant by all sacrifices, and at the same time the end of all sacrifices, just as He who makes it fulfils the concept priest and at the same time makes the existence of any further priests superfluous and impossible.

For what does the term sacrifice mean ? There is no doubt that like the term priest it stands in relation to that of sin, to that of the discord in which man finds himself with God and himself. Sacrifice is an attempt to deal with this discord. This is something which can perhaps be shown even from most or perhaps all the views of sacrifice that we find in non-biblical religions. But there is no doubt that in the system of sacrifice which was normative for the New Testament, that of the covenant with Israel in its completed form, its purpose is to order the encounter of a sinful people with God in the way which God Himself has instituted. It is the possibility and actuality of a communication and communion of Israel and the individual Israelite with God which, if they do not do away with that gulf, do at least temporarily bridge it. The member of the covenant people still belongs to Yahweh even though he has a part in the rebellion and transgression in which this people is caught up. He cannot forget Him. He cannot escape his guilt and responsibility in relation to Him, his commitment to Him. He can and must make an offering (this is where the mediatorial ministry of the priest is so important). Offerings are substitutes for what he really ought to render to God, but never does do, and never will. They are gifts from the sphere of his most cherished possessions which represent or express his will to obey, which symbolise the life which has not in fact been offered to God. He can bring these gifts. He ought to do so. He acknowledges Yahweh and the fact that he belongs to Him by bringing them. He recognises his guilt and obligation. He confesses that he is a member of the people which, in spite of everything, is His elect people. It is not, therefore, a fact that in his sacrifices the man of the Old Testament merely gave proof of a longing for reconciliation, that he only expressed and tried to mitigate the unrest which filled him by reason of his situation in conflict with God and himself. The sacrifices of the Old Testament do belong to the human history of religion, but there is more to them than that. They are also a provisional and relative fulfilment of the will and commandment of God. They are a genuine element in the history of the covenant and the history of redemption. In sacrifice Israel —fallible, sinful and unfaithful Israel—is summoned to bow beneath the divine judgment, but also to hold fast to the divine grace. Of course, this living meaning of sacrifice can sometimes fade. It may become a mere religious observance. It may be understood as a *do ut des*. It may become an attempt on the part of the people to acquire power over God, to assure oneself before Him, to hide one's sin instead of acknowledging it. Instead of a terror-stricken flight to God it may become a sinful flight from Him to a sacred work. When this happens, but only when this happens and as an attack upon it, the prophets (Amos 5²¹ᶠ·, Is. 1¹⁰ᶠ·, Jer. 7²¹ᶠ·) and many of the Psalms (like 40⁷ᶠ·, 50¹³ᶠ·, 51¹⁸ᶠ·) take up their well-known inflexible attitude against it.

The real problem of sacrifice is not the imminent misuse to which like any cult it can be put, but the fact that in face of the sin of man, while it can mean an impressive summons to repent and convert, a cheerful encouragement to do the best we can, and even a serious encouragement, and while its fulfilment does call us to remember the presence and will and commandment of the holy and merciful God, it does not in any way alter either sin itself or the situation of conflict and contradiction brought about by sin. As Paul has put it in Rom. 3²⁵, we have to do with a πάρεσις τῶν προγεγονότων ἁμαρτημάτων ἐν τῇ ἀνοχῇ τοῦ θεοῦ which has to be sought and attained again and again. Sacrifice in the Old Testament cannot bring to an end the state of things between God and His people, replacing it by a new state. It can only restore a temporary order (so far as this is possible without more savage penalties). It can only leave open and in the air the disturbed and broken relationship between the two, making a common existence at least bearable and possible. But the alteration which it brings about is only temporary and incidental. Things are made easier and better until the next time. There is promise, but no fulfilment. There is truth, but no actuality. That is why in the bitter terms of Heb. 10³ it is ultimately only an ἀνάμνησις ἁμαρτιῶν. It does shed a certain light, but in so doing it can only make man all the more bitterly conscious of the dark background to his existence, which is still unchanged. It aims at atonement, but it only represents it; it only symbolises it, it does not make it. It is permitted. It is commanded. At its best, it is offered with obedience and thankfulness and a readiness to serve. But it is still only a substitute for what has to happen, for an offering which is made to God in true faithfulness. It is only a substitute for what has to happen when the people and individuals who are disobedient to God are set aside, in order to make way for the new individual and the new people. Sacrifice does not do this. An animal is brought and slain, and its blood is shed. But this animal is not the old man which has to be made to disappear. And the showing of it is not that ἔνδειξις τῆς δικαιοσύνης θεοῦ (Rom. 3²⁵, ²⁶). It is not the establishment of that radical and effective and definitive new order in which a man who is righteous before God can encounter the righteous God. It does not accomplish any τελειῶσαι of those who bring the animal. The offering of it is only a " shadow of things to come " (Heb. 10¹). *Significat ?* Yes. *Est ?* No. That is the limitation and problem of sacrifice in the Old Testament.

Of course alongside this we can and must set the fact that the history of Israel attested in the Old Testament is one great series of dark and heavy judgments on the part of God, and that Israel is a people which is constantly judged by God in the severity of His faithfulness. The forbearance of God revealed in His institution and acceptance of sacrifices is not without its limits. There are some sins of individuals which cannot be atoned by any sacrifices but when they are committed can be met only by the extirpation of the guilty from the community. Similarly, sacrifices do not exclude the punishments of God for the inconstancy and obstinacy of the people as a whole. The history of the dealings of God in and with this people is one which gives many proofs of His goodness and help, but it is also a history of the great and greatest retributions and excisions which come upon it. These, too, are full of the secret grace of God. They are signs of the election of this people. They are never without promise. But nowhere is it apparent that any one of them (not even the destruction of Jerusalem and the temple) could really or basically alter the perverted situation between God and this people, the disharmony in its existence as the unfaithful people of its faithful God. At his own time and place and in his own way, does not each of the prophets who have to announce these judgments have to begin at the beginning like his predecessors, as though nothing had happened ? They all attest the judgment, the day of the Lord, which will be accompanied and followed by salvation. But the day itself remains obstinately on the horizon of the history of Israel. It is not any of the days in that history. None of the events in that history is this judgment. None of them brings in an Israel which has been really and finally judged by its God, that is, put finally in the right, effectively and definitively subjected to His will and therefore well-pleasing to Him. It is judged again and again, just as it must offer sacrifice again and again. But in all the frightful events of this history there is as little of the ἔνδειξις τῆς δικαιοσύνης θεοῦ as in the offerings of its sacrifices. This people is always the same and fundamentally untrustworthy partner in relation to God. On its side the covenant of God with it is always the covenant which has not been kept but broken. The punishments which come upon it from God, like the sacrifices which are commanded by God and made according to His institution, can be described only as " shadows of things to come." Israel signifies man judged by God and judged therefore to his salvation, man brought to actual conversion by the judgment of God, man passing through death to life. But Israel is not that man.

This is where the one sacrifice of Jesus Christ intervenes : the real sacrifice for sin, the sacrifice which sets it aside, which effects and proclaims its effective and complete forgiveness, which brings before God the just man which Israel could signify in its sacrifices as well as in the judgments it had to undergo, but which it could only signify, which it could introduce only in substitute, in a kind of *Quidproquo.* The sacrifice of Jesus Christ, the offering of which is taken out of the hands of all priests, is entirely His own affair, and it is no longer a shadow and figure, but a fulfilment of the reconciliation of man with God. That ἔνδειξις of the righteousness of God is no longer an episode on the way, but the goal of the history of the covenant and redemption determined by God from all eternity and initiated with the election of Israel. To what extent ? To the extent that in it we no longer have to do with a human and therefore a merely human, an improper and provisional fulfilment of the divine will. It is, of course, a human action—but in and with the human action it is also a divine action, in which there takes place that which all human offerings can only attest, in which the reservation under which all human offering takes place, and its character as merely representative, symbolical and significative are done away, in which the concept of sacrifice is fulfilled and the true and effective sacrifice is made. Our whole understanding depends upon our recognising that God's own activity and being, His presence and activity in the One who is His own Son, very and eternal God with the Father and the Holy Spirit, is the truth and power of that which takes place here as a history of human sacrificing and sacrifice.

God wills and demands—what? Further substitutes in a further ἀνοχή for the purpose of further πάρεσις? Further attestations of the covenant which He has established between Himself and man? Further temporary communications and communions of man with Himself? The further and more serious and perfect offerings of all kinds of *Quidproquo*? A further and perhaps final history of priests and sacrifices? No: all the things which are temporary and on this level are done away and superseded. God Himself has intervened in His own person. His great day has come. He now wills and demands the fulfilment of the covenant, the new man who not only knows and recognises and actively gives it to be understood, but lives wholly and utterly by the fact that He belongs to God, that He is His man. He wills and demands not merely the bridging and lessening of the conflict between Himself and us, but its removal, not only light in darkness, but as on the first day of creation the dispersal of darkness by light. He wills and demands the sacrifice of the old man (who can never be this man, who can only die). He wills and demands the setting aside of this man, his giving up to death, which is not fulfilled merely by giving up this or that, even the best he has. God wills and demands the man himself, to make an end of him, so that the new man may have air and space for a new life. He wills and demands that he should go through death to life. He wills and demands that as the man of sin he should abandon his life, that his blood as this man should finally be shed and fall to the ground and be lost, that as this man he should go up in flames and smoke. That is the meaning and end of sacrifice. And that is the judgment which is not fulfilled in any other sacrifices. It is fulfilled in the sacrifice of Jesus Christ, in the shedding of His " precious blood " (1 Pet. 1[19]). It has the power of a real offering and taking away of the sinful man, the power to bring about his end and death as such, and therefore to create a new situation in which God no longer has to do with this man, in which His own faithfulness will meet a faithful people and a faithful man. In the sacrifice of Jesus Christ the will of God is fulfilled in this turning, in this radical conversion of man to Himself which posits an end and therefore a new beginning.

But it is fulfilled in this sacrifice because now it is God Himself who not only demands but makes the offering. He makes it in that He the Lord willed to become a servant, in that His Son willed to go into the far country, to become one with us and to take our place as sinners, to die for us the death of the old man which was necessary for the doing of the will of God, to shed our wicked blood in His own precious blood, to kill our sin in His own death. In Israel's sacrifices in obedience to the command of God this could only be intended and willed and attested and represented—because they were made within and under the presupposition of a constant rebellion against God, and in the sign of the constant provocation of His wrath. But now it has actually taken place—taken place because and to the extent that in Jesus Christ God Himself has acted in place of the human race, Himself making the real sacrifice which radically alters the situation between Himself and man. In Him God not only demands but He gives what He demands. In Him He does that which has to take place to set aside sin and remove the conflict. He shows Himself to be pure and holy and sinless by not refusing in Him to become the greatest of all sinners, achieving the penitence and conversion which is demanded of sinners, undertaking the bitter reality of being the accused and condemned and judged and executed man of sin, in order that when He Himself has been this man no other man can or need be, in order that in place of this man another man who is pleasing to God, the man of obedience, may have space and air and be able to live. He who gives Himself up to this is the same eternal God who wills and demands it. Christ *certo respectu sibi ipsi satisfecit* (Hollaz, Ex. *Theol. acroam.*, 1707, III, 3, *qu.* 77). Both the demanding and the giving are a single related decision in God Himself. For that reason real satisfaction has been done, i.e., that which suffices has been done, that setting aside and repudiation has been utterly and basically accomplished.

3. We have seen that Jesus Christ was just in our place. In cultic terms this is equivalent to saying that in our place He has made a perfect sacrifice. He who as the perfect Priest took the place of all human priests, by offering Himself, has substituted a perfect sacrifice for all the sacrifices offered by men.

That He has made a perfect sacrifice means primarily and comprehensively and decisively that He has fulfilled the will of God the doing of which the action of all human priests and all the sacrifices made by men could only proclaim and attest. With His sacrifice He has left the sphere of that which is improper and provisional and done that which is proper and definitive. His offering was that which God affirmed, which was acceptable and pleasing to Him, which He accepted. His sacrifice meant the closing of the time of the divine ἀνοχή, the time of the mere πάρεσις of human sins endlessly repeating themselves, the time of the alternation of divine grace and divine judgment, in which human priests had their function and the offerings made by men had a meaning. His sacrifice means that the time of being has dawned in place of that of signifying—of the being of man as a faithful partner in covenant with God, and therefore of his being at peace with God and therefore of the being of the man reconciled with Him and converted to Him. We are told in Jn. 19²⁸ concerning the crucified Jesus that He knew ὅτι ἤδη πάντα τετέλεσται. And His last word when He died was τετέλεσται (Jn. 19³⁰). Jesus knew what God knew in the taking place of His sacrifice. And Jesus said what God said : that what took place was not something provisional, but that which suffices to fulfil the divine will, that which is entire and perfect, that which cannot and need not be continued or repeated or added to or superseded, the new thing which was the end of the old but which will itself never become old, which can only be there and continue and shine out and have force and power as that which is new and eternal. Notice the exposition of Ps. 40⁷ in Heb. 10⁸ᶠ· : " Above when he said, Sacrifice and offering and burnt offerings and offering for sin thou wouldest not, neither hadst pleasure therein ; which are offered by the law ; Then said he, Lo, I come to do thy will, O God. He taketh away the first, that he may establish the second. By the which will we are sanctified through the offering of the body of Christ once for all." In this respect we can and must think of the positive intention and meaning of the Old Testament opposition to the sacrifices which Israel misused and therefore God rejected, and even to the institution of sacrifice itself. For in and with this one perfect sacrifice it comes about that " judgment runs down as waters, and righteousness as a mighty stream " (Amos 5²⁴). The evil deeds of men are removed from the sight of God. The doing of evil ceases. It is now learned how to do good. Regard is now had for right. The violent are now restrained, the orphans are helped to their right and the cause of the widow is taken up (Is. 1¹⁶ᶠ·). Thanks is brought to God, and in this way vows are paid to the Most High. In the day of need He is now called upon, that He may redeem man and that man may praise Him (Ps. 50¹⁴ᶠ·). There is now offered to God the sacrifice which pleases Him and which He will not despise, that of a broken spirit and a contrite heart (Ps. 51¹⁹). Ears are open to Him ; there is a desire to do

His will ; His Law is in the hearts of men (Ps. 40⁷ᶠ·). All these things have now taken place : " by the which will (the taking place of the sacrificial action of Jesus Christ) we are sanctified." There has been brought about that radically altered human situation to which all human priests and all the offerings brought by men could only look forward, the reconciliation which lit up their whole activity only as a promise on the horizon, warning and comforting, but only as an indication, not as presence and actuality. Now that Jesus Christ has done sacrifice as a priest and sacrificed Himself, all these things have come, for in Him that which God demanded has taken place ; it has been given and accomplished by God Himself. In the person of His Son there has taken place the event towards which the history of the old covenant was only moving, which it only indicated from afar—the rendering of obedience, humility and penitence, and in this way the conversion of man to God, and in this conversion the setting aside, the death, of the old rebellious man and the birth of a new man whose will is one with His. In Jesus Christ there has come the Priest who feels with the ignorant and errant, who is Himself compassed with infirmity (Heb. 5²), who as a Son " learned obedience by the things which he suffered " (Heb. 5⁸), and in this way proved Himself to be " holy, harmless, undefiled, separate from sinners " (Heb. 7²⁶), " in all points tempted like as we are, yet without sin " (Heb. 4¹⁵)—in fact, the only Priest who is qualified to act. And in that He has offered Himself there has been done by this Priest the acceptable work, indeed the work which was already accepted and approved by God even as it was performed, the work which was necessary on man's side for the making of atonement. In His sacrifice God has affirmed Himself and the man Jesus as His Son. This is, therefore, the true and perfect sacrifice.

We do not add to the completeness of this exposition, but simply describe it once more, when we say that this perfect sacrifice which fulfils the will of God took place in our stead and for us. For what other reason was there ? God did not need to act as a priest and to suffer as a sacrifice in the person of His Son. But we need this Mediator and His mediation. The will of God towards us is the purpose of this sacrifice, and His good pleasure towards us is its end. In Him there takes place that which we need but which we cannot do or bring about for ourselves. It is a matter of our reconciliation, our peace with God, our access to Him, our freedom for Him, and therefore the basic alteration of our human situation, the taking away of that which separates us from Him and involves His separation from us, our death as sinful men and our living as obedient men. The perfection of the sacrifice of Jesus Christ, the whole divine height and depth of the turning made in Him, is therefore the perfection of the love with which God has loved us. In the making of this sacrifice He loved us in perfect love ; He Himself and by Himself doing and bringing about all that is necessary for us ; without any merit of ours, indeed against all our merits ; without any assistance from us, indeed in face of our resistance. As we close it is as well to look at this perfection again in contrast with us whom it favours. There can be no question of a love with which we loved Him in the fact that this happened, that He sent His Son as ἱλασμός for our sins (1 Jn. 4¹⁰ ; cf. 2²). For who are we ? We are defiant sinners, the obstinately godless, the open enemies of God, who cannot contribute anything to this happening, who if it were in our power would only interrupt and prevent it. The only good thing that can be reported of us is that this perfect sacrifice was made in our place and for us—a superior act of divine defiance meeting our defiance ; that it is the perfect action of God in this turning to us (which we cannot interrupt or prevent). All that can be said of us is that without this perfect action of God we would be lost ; that apart from it we can have no refuge or counsel or consolation or help. But of God we have to say that this perfect action which He Himself did not need has in His merciful good pleasure taken place for us ; that He willed to make it and did make it a need of His, a matter of His own glory, to do this for us, that is, to accept the perfect sacrifice, the righteousness of Jesus Christ as our righteousness, our sacrifice, and therefore as the finished work of our reconciliation. Not only as though we had brought this sacrifice, but as the sacrifice which we have brought. Not only as though the righteousness of Jesus Christ were ours, but as the righteousness which we have achieved. Not only as though the work of reconciliation finished in Him were our work, but really as the work which we have done. We remember that in the sacrifice of Jesus Christ we no longer have a substitute for that which we cannot do. It is no longer a question of a *Quidproquo*, an " as if," beyond which we still need something more perfect, a real reconciliation which has still to come. In the doctrine of the justification of man, of the reach of that which has taken place in Jesus Christ, we have to see that we are saying far too little when we use a favourite expression of the Reformers and call it an imputation of the alien righteousness of Jesus Christ. It cannot in any sense be an improper justification of man which has its basis in this happening. Otherwise how could it be a perfect happening, and how could the love of God for man realised in it be a perfect love ? Rather, the alien righteousness which has been effected not in and by us but in the sacrifice of Jesus Christ does become and is always ours, so that in Him we are no longer unrighteous but righteous before God, we are the children of God, we have the forgiveness of our sins, peace with God, access to Him and freedom for Him. That this is the case is the righteousness which Jesus Christ has accomplished for us, the perfection of His sacrifice which cannot be added to by anyone or anything. He has sacrificed in our name with a validity which cannot be limited and a force which cannot be diminished. What He has done He has done in order that being done by Him it may be done by us ; not only acceptable to God, but already accepted ; our work which is pleasing to Him ; our own being as those who are dead to sin and can live to righteousness. He alone has done this, but because He has done it, in a decision which cannot be reversed, with a truth which is absolute, He has done it for us.

3. THE VERDICT OF THE FATHER

In the first part of this section we dealt with the way of the Son of God into the far country—a part of what the older dogmatics used to call the doctrine of the person of Christ and especially the doctrine of His true deity. Then in the second we dealt with the Judge judged in our place—a part of the old doctrine of the work of Christ and especially His " high-priestly " work. We will have to proceed to an understanding of the sin of man (in this instance, pride) from the particular standpoint of this first part of the doctrine of reconciliation and in the light of the humiliation of the Lord as servant which has taken place in Jesus Christ. It will also be our task to understand the justification of man as the immediate consequence of that divine human action, the existence of the Christian community in its human and historical form as that which provisionally corresponds to it, and faith as that which grasps and apprehends it all. At every point we can only proceed along the way the beginning of which we have already learned to know. We can only build on the christological basis which has been exposed. We shall proceed and build in our own anthropological sphere. For it is in this sphere that the atonement made in Jesus Christ has taken place. It is here in the context of human history, at a certain point in this sphere, that it took place that this sphere was entered by God Himself in the person of His Son, that He, the Judge, was judged in our place and favour. It was this sphere which needed atonement with God, and it has a part in it. To what extent ? With what effects and consequences ? This is what we shall have to show under the concepts sin, justification, community and faith (which all belong to the anthropological sphere) and in the light of that event, in demonstration of the reach of that event.

But before we enter on this series of further problems, and in order to do so with good protection and clear conscience, in the third part of this section we must engage in a kind of transitional discussion between the problems and answers we have just given and the further questions we will now have to add to them. What is the connexion between these new problems and our previous questions and answers ? How are we going to proceed and build on this christological basis ? Why do we think that this is even possible, that our anthropological sphere will prove to be one which is co-ordinated with and subordinated to the christological, which both needs that which has taken place in Jesus Christ and also has a part in it ? Or, conversely, why do we think that there can be any demonstration of the relevance of that one event in and for this whole sphere ? With what right can we speak of our sin, of our justification, of ourselves as a community and of our faith, in the light of what Jesus Christ is and has done for us ? How does He come to us or we to Him ?

It is true that He has already come to us and we are already with Him. For what is the meaning of the incarnation and the τετέλεσται of the Crucified if it does not tell us of His being with us and our being with Him ? From the very first we have not thought of His being abstractly, but *per definitionem* as belonging to us and us to it. Again, from the very first we have thought of His activity *per definitionem* as His activity for us, *pro nobis*. In the great turn which will now have to be executed by us it can only be a matter of explaining what we have to say *per definitionem* of His being and activity, His person and work, of explaining the form of His being and activity which is from the very first concrete and comprehensive. His being as it belongs to us (and ours as it belongs to Him), His activity *pro nobis*, does not need any amplification. When we work out the bearing of the one event of His being and activity, the basis and climax will always have to be in specific statements about Himself and His person and work. And the basic transitional discussion on which we must now engage, the question of the legitimacy of the turn which we will have to execute as we work it out, does not in any way compromise but can only confirm the fact that it is He Himself in whom this turn has already been executed and is a fact.

It is a fact. I emphasise this in opposition to the conception represented by G. Thomasius in *Christi Person und Werk*, Vol. 3, 2, 1888, p. 206. Thomasius makes a distinction between the restoration of fellowship between God and man accomplished once and for all in Jesus Christ, and the " continual " mediation of it. He introduces his presentation of the latter with the words : " It is only with the objective reconciliation by which humanity has become the object of the grace of God that the actual possibility, i.e., the right and power to be reconciled with God, is won for the individual members of the race. But this possibility has to become actuality. That which Christ has worked out once and for all for the whole race, that which is available for everyone in Him, now has to come to every individual, so that there is a real fellowship of men with God. This is the purpose of the whole objective mediation of salvation, and with it it reaches its goal." A doubtful feature in this presentation is the distinction between an objective atonement and a subjective which is obviously quite different from it. So, too, is the distinction between that which has been worked out and is available in Christ and that which has still to come to me. So, too, and above all, is the description of the antithesis in categories of possibility and actuality, which later becomes the differentiation of a purpose which is only present in Jesus Christ and which attains its goal only in some other occurrence. To express ourselves in the language of Thomasius we should have to attempt the paradoxes of trying to understand the once and for all as that which is also continual and comes, the objective side as the essence of the required subjective, the so-called possibility as the true reality, the purpose achieved in Jesus Christ as the goal of all goals. There is no room for a cramping " only " in relation to the atonement made in Jesus Christ, unless we are going to open wide the door to historicisation, i.e., mythologising, and in this way to make the knowledge of its relevance ineffective from the very first. It is a remarkable fact in theological history that a very " positive " theologian like Thomasius could, and in fact did, do this in so unsuspecting a way. And what do we find in R. Bultmann in our own day (*Theol of the N.T.*, E.T., 1952, I, p. 252) ? " By Christ there has been created nothing more than the possibility of ζωή, which does, of course, become an assured actuality in those that believe." This is the very thing which will not do.

This does not make our question superfluous. In our christological basis, in Jesus Christ Himself, everything that can be said of the relevance of His being and activity in our sphere is already included and anticipated. That is one thing, the thing to which all our knowledge of this relevance must constantly be referred back. But there is another thing which is not so self-evident. This is that we are not merely in a position to hear and accept as an assertion (possibly in something like the form we have tried to give it in our own more detailed commentary) the *pro nobis* of the being and activity of Jesus Christ, and because *per definitionem* His being and activity is *pro nobis*, the being and activity itself. We can also believe and accept it as true in the sense that we truly believe ourselves to be those for whom He is and has acted. Our christological basis includes within itself the fact (and with it quite simply ourselves, our participation in that event), that the turn from Jesus Christ to us has already been executed and is a fact in Him, that in and with Him we, too, are there as those for whom He is and has acted. This fact is the subject of a specific second step as we try to follow out the truth of it. Naturally the first step must precede. Jesus Christ must have come to us in that existence of His which embraces ours but is also proper

Jesus comes to us from above

We are the pro nobis

to Himself and superior to ours. He must have met us in that Word of His which is a new word and strange to us. He must have encountered us from afar, from outside. It has to be like this. We have to be told and have to let ourselves be told by Him that He is for us and has acted for us. But when we have made the first step we then have to make a specific second step when we realise, that is, when we can and will say to ourselves, that we are those to whom His *pro nobis* refers. This seems to follow very simply from the first one, with the simplicity with which in logic a minor and conclusion can be deduced from a given major. It is simple, so long as we hold fast by the major as such, the being and action of Jesus Christ for us. Why should we not be ready to hear this and to accept its relevance to ourselves ? But this being and action takes place in our sphere. This major is spoken in all its completeness in our sphere. Our sphere is not as such qualified for this novelty. It is the sphere of the unreconciled world, of man contradicting and opposing God. There is a great gulf between " Jesus Christ for us " and ourselves as those who in this supremely perfect word are summoned to regard ourselves as those for whom He is and acts. How do we come to find ourselves in these, or these in us, as is really and actually the case in virtue of this major, in Jesus Christ ? By what right or power dare I make the corresponding minor, or draw the simple conclusion, that I myself am one of those for whom Jesus Christ is and acts ? thus recognising and confessing that He is for me : " I know that my Redeemer liveth " ? By what right do we follow the invitation and summons of that major, applying that which He is and does to us who are not He ? How can we dare to extend His being and activity so that we count it our own, speaking of our own sin (this, too, is a new thing that we cannot know of ourselves), of our own justification, of ourselves as His community, and of our own faith, in relation to Him ? Who calls and authorises us to set up these standards in our own sphere ? in short, to execute the turn which, according to the Word and message of Jesus Christ, has already been executed and completed in Him ? How can that which is proper to Him be recognised as proper to us ? No, this thing which is apparently simple, and which is in fact simple in Jesus Christ, cannot be simple for us, as we work it out for ourselves. Yet on every presupposition, even on the best conceivable, we do need to recognise its real simplicity. That is the transitional problem which must concern us in this section.

But before we can say anything positive about it we must try to define the problem rather more precisely. Why and to what extent is it not self-evident that we can proceed and build on Jesus Christ in our own sphere ? Why is it that the turn which has been executed in the person and work of Jesus Christ, in a perfect way which needs no amplification, why is it that the " Jesus Christ for us," still needs this more detailed explanation ?

According to the (most recent view) our problem is at bottom only a particular form of the problem of time. How can that which has happened once, even if it did happen for us, be recognised to-day as having happened for us, seeing it does not happen to-day? Or, to put it in another way, how can that which happened once have happened for us when we who live to-day were not there and could not experience it ourselves? Or, to put it in yet another way, how can we to-day exist as those for whom it happened when it happened once and not to-day? The only answer which it seems we can give is the profoundly ambiguous and unsettling one that it can do so only as we accept it from others, from the tradition of the Church and ultimately from the biblical witnesses; that it is, in fact, the case that " Jesus Christ for us " is valid to-day, and is relevant to us, only as we accept what is told to us as true in this sense. But how can we hold to be true what we have not seen and cannot attest to be true? especially a truth which is so decisive for ourselves as that of the then being and activity of Jesus Christ for us to-day and in our place?

Put in this way, the problem is identical with one which was widely treated in the first decade of this century—the problem of faith and history. It was posed with particular acuteness in the theology of W. Herrmann. In our own day the discussion has been renewed by R. Bultmann in the form of the problem of the relationship between the act of God which took place once and for all historically in Jesus of Nazareth and the existential actuality of the Christian faith referred to and based upon it. In substance it is identical with Lessing's question concerning the relationship between the contingent truths of history and the necessary truths of reason (*Der Beweis des Geistes und der Kraft*, 1777). " This, this is the gaping and wide chasm which I cannot cross, however often and seriously I have attempted the leap. If anyone can help me over, let him do so; I implore and entreat him. He deserves from me a divine reward."

It should be noted that for an older type of Christian thinking—and especially for Christian mysticism in every age—the problem was not so much one of time as of space, not that of the relationship of the then and now but of the there and here. That is how it was represented, e.g., by Calvin, who attacked strongly the idea of a *Christus otiosus* existing *frigide extra nos, procul a nobis*, apparently separated from us and we from Him *eminus nobis*—an idea which he described as an *obliquum cuniculum* of Satan designed to undermine our assurance of salvation. As the basis of his whole exposition *De modo percipiendae Christi gratiae* he opposed to it his peculiar doctrine of the *societas, coniunctio, communio* created by the Holy Spirit between Christ and us, of a *coniugium* between Him and us, of our *insitio in Christum* (*Instit.* III, 1, 3 and 2, 24). And in a way which is more direct and less guarded theologically, but obviously in answer to the same question, in face of the same gaping and wide chasm, and in an attempt to leap it, Angelius Silesius (in the first book of his *Cherubinischer Wandersmann*, 61–63) wrote :

> Were Christ a thousand times to Bethlehem come,
> And yet not born in thee, 'twould spell thy doom.
> Golgotha's cross, it cannot save from sin,
> Except for thee that cross be raised within.
> I say, it helps thee not that Christ is risen,
> If thou thyself art still in death's dark prison.

The problem has indeed this temporal and spatial aspect. It has the form of the problem of the historical distance between the being and activity of Jesus Christ in its own place and our being and activity in a different place. That there is this distance cannot be denied. " Jesus Christ for us," the incarnation and the crucifixion, do not exist or take place in an abstract always and everywhere in which our here and now are included, but in a concrete and singular then and there which cannot be taken away or exchanged—outside our here and now and opposed to it. In this respect the greatness of the historical remove does not greatly matter. It may exceed 1900 years or it may not. It is enough that it is there. It is enough that the connexion between the here and there, the now and then, can apparently take only the form of recollection, that it can apparently be only indirect or historical, mediated by the report and tradition and proclamation of others, bound up with their truthfulness and credibility, with whether we are able to trust them, to accept the truth of what they say, to make the connexion in this roundabout way as recollection. And if everything does finally hang by this thread, it is obviously a very disturbing fact. We can accept many things on the word of others and with full confidence in them, but can we accept the being and activity of Jesus Christ for us and in our place ? Can a second-hand report of this—even one which is most certain and stimulates the greatest confidence—really serve as a basis for our faith in it ? Can the connexion of which the message speaks really be a matter of mere recollection ? If it is really to be received, can it come to us or be received by us in any but a direct way, removing the distance altogether, establishing between the one remembered and our recollection a contemporaneity which has to be explained but which is real, enabling that distant event to become and to be true to us directly and therefore incontrovertibly ? But what is the mediation in which recollection becomes presence, indirect speech direct, history present-day event, the *Christus pro nobis tunc* the *Christus pro nobis nunc*, the Christ who meets us, the Christ who is our Saviour not only as He is known and remembered historically, but as He Himself saves us to-day ? The genuineness of this question cannot be disputed. The problem has this aspect, and has to be considered from this standpoint.

But we ought not to stand, as it were, rooted to this one spot, trying to find and remove the difficulty only in this spot. The well-known offence in the fact of atonement does not exhaust itself in this problem of distance. We ought to be warned against too great or exclusive a preoccupation with this aspect by the fact that this problem which has become so acute within more recent Protestantism has, all things considered, more the character of a technical difficulty in thinking than that of a spiritual or a genuine theological problem. In it it is only formally and not in substance, only incidentally and secondarily and not primarily and centrally, that the question concerns God and ourselves, Jesus Christ and His cross and our reconciliation. It is a methodological question. There must have been innumerable serious-minded Christians—even theologians and even in the modern period—who have been disturbed and very radically disturbed by the point which is really and basically at issue, and yet who have not been touched at all, or only very slightly, by the concern which occupies us to-day.

For example, when Paul (in 1 Cor. 1[23]) writes that the crucified Christ is to the Jews a stumbling-block and to the Greeks foolishness, he can hardly have been thinking of the paradox of the relationship between faith and history, or of the relationship between the historical singularity of His existence and cross and our contemporaneity with Him, or of the relationship between indirect and direct news concerning Him. And Calvin in the passage we have mentioned may perhaps have given us a faint outline of the problem of Lessing, but, according to the context and tenor of his remarks, he certainly did not have only this problem before him, nor was it of primary importance. He was dealing rather with its deeper presuppositions.

This does not prevent us from taking the problem of distance with the seriousness proper to it. What it does prevent us from doing is stopping at this discussion, as though it was there that we had to, and could, come to the decision which is necessary. What it does enjoin upon us is that we should consider the deeper presuppositions which we have to treat if we are to handle it rightly. When we solve this problem, our real difficulties are only just beginning. For is there really no difficulty more serious than that of the formal anti-thesis of the then and the now, the there and the here, with all the questions involved in this antithesis? Is there not a difficulty of which this antithesis is only representative and indicative? May it not be that the real scandal is grounded in the fact, in the Christ-occurrence, in the event of the atonement itself? May it not be that it consists simply in the strangeness and remoteness of this event as it has taken place in our anthropological sphere? Is it not the case that it is not primarily its historical distance and singularity but its own nature which makes this event a riddle, a kind of erratic block in our sphere and time and space? How can the Son of God be ours who as such went into the far country? How can this our Judge be judged for us? How can He be anything to us but a stranger, and His activity a new and peculiar activity to which access is not open but closed? Not in spite of the fact but just because it concerns us so much! What can His being and activity mean in our sphere? We have to remember the immeasurable alteration in our situation, in our whole existence, which has taken place in Him, which His being and activity inexorably brings with it. What are we going to make of that, or, rather, what are we going to make of ourselves in relation to it? How are we going to deal with that? How are we going to apprehend Jesus Christ, or, rather, how are we going to apprehend

D.R.—10

ourselves in relation to Him, ourselves as those for whom that has taken place which has taken place in Him ? What does it mean to live as His fellow ? What does it mean to live as a man, as one for whom this took place in Him, as one whose conversion to God took place in His death ?

The whole difficulty which really faces us here is gathered up in the saying of Peter in Lk. 5[8] : "Depart from me, for I am a sinful man, O Lord." Does not this mean : How is it that You have come into my presence, and what will become of me in Yours ? How can You and I be together in the same time and space ? But we can also think of the saying of Isaiah (6[5]), who, seeing Yahweh sitting on the throne high and lifted up, and His train filling the temple, and hearing the threefold *Sanctus* of the seraphim, cries out : "Woe is me ! for I am undone ; because I am a man of unclean lips, and I dwell in the midst of a people of unclean lips." These are the sayings of men who saw and heard, for whom there was no problem of distance in the form in which it occupies us, to whom the question of the possibility of accepting the testimony of others or of their credibility could not present any difficulty. Their difficulty was a problem of distance of quite another kind. We can and should think of the description of the attitude of the women when they were confronted by the empty tomb, at the end of the genuine St. Mark : "And they went out quickly, and fled from the sepulchre ; for they trembled and were amazed : neither said they anything to any man, for they were afraid." And do we not read something similar in Lk 2[9] concerning the shepherds of Bethlehem who were the first and direct hearers of the Christmas message ? The directness of the encounter with the Lord, the absence of Lessing's "gaping and wide chasm," contemporaneity with the historical act of God, does not mean any easing of the relationship to that act, any lessening of the tension, but at the very point where there seems to be no room for it it attains its maximum, and the difficulty of the encounter with the God acting and speaking in history seems to become intolerable. "But who may abide the day of his coming ? and who shall stand when he appeareth ? (Mal. 3[2]). "Thou canst not see my face : for there shall no man see me, and live " (Ex. 33[20]).

This is obviously the underlying form of our problem—the real distance in which the God appearing in the human sphere, and acting and speaking for us in this sphere, confronts us to whom He turns and for whom He acts. Note that on the one hand it is God for man, on the other man against God. There are two orders (or, rather, order and disorder), two opposite world-structures, two worlds opposing and apparently excluding one another. Note that it is He and we—and He and we in a direct encounter, we before Him—how can we live before Him and with Him ?—we with the God who by Himself reconciles us with Himself, we in His presence, in the sequence of His work and Word. On the side of man the only possible word seems to be a deep-seated No, the No of the one who when God comes and acts for Him and tells him that He is doing so is forced to see that his day is over and that he can only perish.

And now we have to ask whether our whole concern about our temporal distance from Jesus Christ, our indirect relationship to Him, is not a genuine problem only in the sense that it represents a genuine movement of flight from this encounter. Are we not putting up a technical difficulty, knowing all the time that it is not this difficulty which oppresses us, but rather the concern that this difficulty is not so great that it cannot be removed, that it has in fact been removed?

Supposing our contemporaneity with the Word of God made flesh, with the Judge judged in our place, is already an event? Supposing the *Christus pro nobis nunc* is already *Christus pro nobis praesens nunc*, here and now, present with us? Supposing it is in fact incontrovertible, the most certain of all things, that He is present here and now for us in the full efficacy of what, according to the Gospel, He was and did then and there? Supposing that by Him and in Him our judgment has been accomplished? that in consequence we now and here are those for whom He went to His death? that in and with Him we are crucified and dead as the sinners that we are? that we can therefore have the space to live which is granted to us after this event (and to that extent *post Christum*)? that we can exist only as those who have no more freedom to sin? Supposing this is so? Supposing we have to recognise that it is so? that this is the situation in which we find ourselves? Does not this mean that we have to see that it is all up with us, that our case has been taken out of our hands as an evil case, and ended and removed and done away? but that since we have no other case, our existence has lost its point, and we, too, are removed and done away and without any future? It is obvious that we do not want this, that we do not want to accept the fact that our evil case is done away and ourselves with it, that we do not therefore want to accept the coming of the Son of God in our place, His being and activity in contemporaneity with us, and our being in contemporaneity with Him. The assault this makes on us is too violent and incisive. If all this is true and actual, it is clear that we have good reason to close our eyes to it, to keep as far from us as we can the knowledge of this truth and actuality.

And if there is a technical difficulty in the matter—the difficulty of making the contemporaneity of Jesus Christ with us and of us with Him conceptually intelligible and perspicuous—do we not have good reason to occupy ourselves with it as much as possible, not to minimise but to magnify it as much as possible, to see to it that its force remains? As long as we are occupied with this difficulty, we do not really need to worry about what has taken place and been done to us with the incarnation of the Son of God, in His appearance in our place, in His effective action for us now as well as then and here as well as there. As long as we can question and discuss the presence of that once and for all event, as long as we can make it the most serious question how we can honestly accept as true to-day that which comes to us as the truth and actuality of something which happened then and which is maintained by others—so long we are obviously protected against the catastrophe which the knowledge of the content, the knowledge of the

Christus pro nobis praesens, would mean for us. We do not then have to notice that we are in exactly the same position as Peter in the boat and the women at the empty tomb and the shepherds of Bethlehem, that we can only tremble as on the day of the Lord which has dawned for us, that we can only be afraid and terrified. We find ourselves in a relatively sheltered corner where we can dream that we are still in some way existing *ante Christum* since He is not there for us, where we can imagine that it is not yet all up with us ; and all because we think that we are excused and safeguarded by the gaping and wide chasm of temporal distance ; all because of the existence of Lessing's question. It is understandable that we have a supreme interest in trying to make out that our relationship to Jesus Christ is purely historical and therefore mediated and indirect, that it is a relationship of mere recollection. We need to be able to question and discuss this relationship. We need the consciousness of historical distance, the neutralising historical consideration, the remembrance of the 1900 years, the thought of the message and tradition and proclamation of others which binds but also separates the there and here, the question of authenticity and credibility, the feeling of the uncertainty of the mediation, the unsettlement which it involves for us. We need all this because it seems to create a delay. The genuineness of Lessing's question cannot be disputed in that it springs from a very genuine need : the need to hide ourselves (like Adam and Eve in the garden of Eden) from Jesus Christ as He makes Himself present and mediates Himself to us ; the need to keep our eyes closed to that about which we ask with such solemn concern, taking ourselves and our " honesty " with such frightful seriousness ; the need to safeguard ourselves as far as this movement of flight allows against the directness in which He does in fact confront us, against His presence, and the consequences which it threatens.

In any other sense than this the question of Lessing, the question of historical distance, is not a genuine problem. In a singular way it derives and has its real weight from the very fact that it is soluble and has actually been solved. Its seriousness is the seriousness of human concern that Jesus Christ is in fact yesterday and to-day. It is the product of this concern, and therefore of fear of the truth. This fear is well-founded. The being and activity of Jesus Christ for us bring us face to face with a vacuum, a place where we apparently have no place or future. What is to become of the sinner when his being as such is taken away from him and made over to death, when he cannot therefore be any more ? What then ? What can he be when he cannot be a sinner any longer, because God in Jesus Christ has put behind Him his being as a sinner, making it a thing only of the past, but when he cannot of himself be anything but a sinner ? Here we come to the spiritual and the theologically relevant difficulty of the relationship between Jesus Christ and us. And before this

(margin, top left, rotated) we read the distance to hide behind

(margin, bottom left, rotated) Fear : JC takes + removes our identity as sinner — what else do we know how to be?

difficulty we have to pause. Put in this way its character is not simply technical or logical or methodological. To be or not to be is the question now, the question, be it noted, posed in acute and unavoidable form by the grace of God. Our task is to answer this question. It is in answering it that we make the decision we have to make in this context whether it is legitimate and practicable that Christology should break through and go forward in the anthropological sphere which is our sphere. In the answer we shall give it will become clear that, however great the difficulty is, it has been overcome. The fear of the truth which is well-founded when this difficulty is perceived is not ultimately well-founded. From the point of view of the whole truth it has no final validity and can therefore be dissipated. We ought not to fear, and we do not need to fear. The movement of flight into Lessing's problem is unnecessary. In and with the overcoming of the real and spiritual problem of the relationship between Jesus Christ and us, the technical problem of the relationship between the then and there and the now and here is also soluble and has in fact been solved.

(To sum up:) Granted the possibility of an actual contemporaneity ~SUM~ of Jesus Christ with us, and therefore of the directness of our encounter and presence with Him, and of the overcoming of the temporal barrier between Him and us, we are forced to put the question with a final and true seriousness : how will it stand with us when we are alongside Jesus Christ and follow Him, when we are in His environment and time and space ? can the reconciliation of the world with God accomplished in Him consist in anything but the dissolution of the world ? can the transition from the christological to the anthropological sphere consist in anything but an assertion that the latter has been displaced altogether by the former ? is it not impossible to proceed from Christ and to build on Him in this sphere because of the very perfection of that which Jesus Christ has done for us ? Is this so ? Or is this an imperfect understanding of the perfection of what has taken place in Christ ? Has theology to content and limit itself, perhaps, to be nothing more than Christology ? Or would this mean that in this totality and exclusiveness we neither do justice to the problem of Christology, nor are in actual agreement with the full witness to Christ in the New Testament ? However that may be, it is here that we come face to face with the real problem of decision. It is here that we come to our point of departure, to the turning to us which has, as we have stated, actually taken place in Jesus Christ for us, to the question of what this turning to us as it has actually taken place in Jesus Christ can in fact mean for us. It is here that we have to do with the thing itself, not with its outward aspect as in the problem of time. That we have made this provisional presupposition in respect of the problem of time means simply that we have accepted the call back to Jesus Christ and the thing itself. In a new and full discussion of it, in which we take into account the whole of the New Testament

witness, it will necessarily be seen whether we can or cannot proceed
any further from the understanding which we have gained so far.
And in this new discussion it will be occasionally revealed what we
have and have not to teach concerning the problem of its outward
aspect, the temporal distance between Jesus Christ and us.

Undoubtedly the proper starting-point for a positive answer to
the question as put in this way is that it is not at all self-evident that
it should not be answered in the negative. There is indeed every
reason to fear that the being and activity of Jesus Christ for us can
be understood only as the ending of all other human being, the reconciliation of the world with God accomplished in Him only as the
reversal of its creation, only as its end. In this case the question of a
point of departure and a transition is a completely empty one, seeing
that we do not exist at all, or that we do so only in the nothingness
to which we are delivered by that which Jesus Christ has done in our
place. We must not too easily dismiss such a possibility as absurd.
It might have pleased God to execute His good and holy will with the
world in this way. This did not have to include either the continuance
of the world or a further being of man. His grace might have consisted
in the fulfilment of a final judgment. The way of the Son of God into
the far country might have been for the purpose of setting a term to
this foreign being by simply removing its existence. The judgment
executed on Him in the place of all might have meant the end of all
things. We would do well to keep before us this possibility and the
negative answer to our question which corresponds to it. For one
thing, the reality of our atonement, which God has actually elected,
is in direct contrast to this possibility. The positive answer to the
question does confront this negative answer. There can thus be no
understanding or appraisal of it without an honest consideration of
this negative alternative. Again, although this negative alternative
has been forcefully surpassed by what God has actually willed and
done in Jesus Christ, it has not simply been excluded but maintained
by it, so that it cannot be ignored in the positive answer which we have
to give but must be seriously considered. If God in Jesus Christ has
reconciled the world with Himself this also means that in Him He
has made an end, a radical end, of the world which contradicts and
opposes Him, that an old æon, our world-time (the one we know and
have of ourselves) with all that counts and is great in it, has been
brought to an end. The humility in which God willed to make Himself like us, the obedience of Jesus Christ in which this self-humiliation
of God and in it the demonstration of His divine majesty became a
temporal event, does mean, in fact, that our hour has struck, our time
has run its course, and it is all up with us. For the fact that God
has given Himself in His Son to suffer the divine judgment on us men
does not mean that it is not executed on us but that it is executed on
us in full earnest and in all its reality—really and definitively because

He Himself took our place in it. That Jesus Christ died for us does not mean, therefore, that we do not have to die, but that we have died in and with Him, that as the people we were we have been done away and destroyed, that we are no longer there and have no more future.

"Old things are passed away" (2 Cor. 5¹⁷). How? "Ye are dead" (Col. 3³), for "if one died for all, then were all dead" (2 Cor. 5¹⁴). "I am crucified with Christ, I live no more" (Gal. 2²⁰). "We are (Rom. 6⁸), ye are (Col. 2²⁰) dead with Christ." σύμφυτοι γεγόναμεν τῷ ὁμοιώματι τοῦ θανάτου αὐτοῦ (Rom. 6⁵), which is then explained as follows : " Our old man is crucified with him, that the body of sin (our person as the victim of sin) might be destroyed " (Rom. 6⁶). " In whom also ye are circumcised with the circumcision made without hands, in putting off the body of the sins of the flesh by the circumcision of Christ " (Col. 2¹¹). By the cross of our Lord Jesus Christ " the world is crucified unto me, and I unto the world " (Gal. 6¹⁴). That is what took place unequivocally and definitively when " God commended his love toward us, in that, while we were yet sinners, Christ died for the ungodly " (Rom. 5⁸). It took place once and for all on Golgotha. We were there, for there took place there the dying of the Son of God for us. It was, therefore, His dying for our sins (1 Cor. 15³). In His death the wages of our sins were paid in our place (Rom. 6²³). In Him we are dead to sin (Rom. 6²). For then and there, in the person of Christ taking our place, we were present, being crucified and dying with Him. We died. This has to be understood quite concretely and literally. In His dying, the dying which awaits us in the near or distant future was already comprehended and completed, so that we can no longer die to ourselves (Rom. 14²ᶠ·), in our own strength and at our own risk, but only in Him, enclosed in His death. We died : the totality of all sinful men, those living, those long dead, and those still to be born, Christians who necessarily know and proclaim it, but also Jews and heathen, whether they hear and receive the news or whether they tried and still try to escape it. His death was the death of all : quite independently of their attitude or response to this event, not only when the proclamation of it comes to them and is received and accepted by them, not only in virtue of the effect of certain ecclesiastical institutions and activities, not only in the dark process of their taking up the cross, certainly not only in certain sacramental or mystical or even existential repetitions or reflections or applications of the event of the cross, not only by the various channels through whose mediation it does finally become actual and significant for them. Not, then, as though on Golgotha it was simply a matter of the creation of a possibility, the setting up of a model and example, an extraordinary offer of dying, or quite simply the institution of a law : " Die and become," the reality of which will come only when it is followed. That is how Angelus Silesius viewed the matter, with many others, in the verses quoted above. But the New Testament views it quite differently. Certainly there are exhortations and imperatives which stand in very clear connexion to the happening at Golgotha : to " mortify the deeds of the body" (Rom. 8¹³); to " put off the old man " (Col. 3⁹) ; to " crucify the flesh with its affections and lusts " (Gal. 5²⁴). These are consequences of the dying of man which has already taken place. They are commands to attest this event which can be characterised only indicatively, in the form of a narrative, because it can be grasped only as we look back to Golgotha. These attestations of the affirmation and acknowledgment of what took place there are still lacking ; they must be filled up, as we are told in the much quoted text, Col. 1²⁴, which does not really say anything about a perfection or completeness or efficacy lacking in the event itself. Similarly, in the demand for the " reasonable service " (Rom. 12¹) which must be offered with the self-offering of the Christian there can be no question of any repetition or representation of that event, or even of an actualisation which has still to be effected. It needs no completion or re-presentation. It would encroach on its perfection and glory if we were to place alongside it events which complete or represent or actualise it. The confession of Christians, their suffering, their repentance, their prayer, their humility, their works, baptism, too, and the Lord's Supper can and should attest this event but only attest it. The event itself, the event of the death of man, is that of the death of Jesus Christ on Golgotha : no other event, no earlier and no later, no event which simply prepares the way for it, no event which has to give to it the character of an actual event. This is the one *mysterium*, the one sacrament, and the one existential fact before and beside and after which there is no room for any other of the same rank.

And we must be clear that this event as such has the character of a catastrophe breaking on man, and that the grace of God effective and revealed in it has indeed the form of a judgment executed on man. Jesus Christ dies because of trespasses, but for man, for the man who is " dead in trespasses and sins " (Col. 2¹³ ; Eph. 2¹), who has fallen a victim to death because of His transgressions. In His death He dies the death of man. Order is created, then, not by any setting aside of sins, but by that of the sinner himself, of the σῶμα τῆς ἁμαρτίας (Rom. 6⁶), of the σῶμα τῆς σαρκός (Col. 2¹¹), of the subject of sin. Can we avoid the comparison that it is not by the giving of medicine, or by an operation, but by the killing of the patient that help is brought ? No word of separating him from his sin, or his sin from him. He stands or falls with it. If it disappears, he disappears. And that is what happened on Golgotha. The dying took place in the death of Jesus Christ for him, intervening powerfully and effectively for him and taking up his case. In His own person, in His giving up to death, He actually took away sinful man, causing him to disappear. This man as he was was of no use to the kingdom of God and as the covenant-partner of God. He could not be helped except by his extinction. If the faithfulness of God and the love of God towards him in Jesus Christ was to attain its goal, it had in fact to have the form of the consuming fire of His wrath, burning down to the very foundation, consuming and totally destroying the man himself who had become the enemy of God.

God sent His Son into the world in order that this might happen to it in His person. The reconciliation with Him which has taken place in Jesus Christ has also the aspect that it is the end of the world. The " for us " of His death on the cross includes and encloses this terrible " against us." Without this terrible " against us " it would not be the divine and holy and redemptive and effectively helpful " for us " in which the conversion of man and the world to God has become an event. This is something we have also to take into account. It is the decision and act of God which has taken place actually, irrevocably, and with sovereign power. It is a completed fact, to which nothing can be added by us in time or in eternity, and from which nothing can be taken away by us in time and in eternity. It is something that we have to see and read like an opened page which we have no power to turn, like a word which we cannot go beyond dialectically, making it equal with some other word, and thus depriving it of all its force. Judgment is judgment. Death is death. End is end. In the fulfilment of the self-humiliation of God, in the obedience of the Son, Jesus Christ has suffered judgment, death and end in our place, the Judge who Himself was judged, and who thereby has also judged. In His person, with Him, judgment, death and end have come to us ourselves once and for all. Is there something beyond

For + against

this coming to us, and above it ? Is there a sure place and basis from which the judgment which has fallen upon us, the end in which we are posited, and the death which has overtaken us in that Jesus Christ died for us, can be seen in all their frightful seriousness and yet not accepted as final and absolute, but only in a certain relationship and connexion and subordination ? Is there a point from which a positive aspect of the event of atonement is disclosed, and disclosed as the decisive and controlling aspect, the one which originally and exclusively determines the particularity of the event ?

To be clear about this matter we must not weaken what we have just said, or take away anything from it. There can be no question of avoiding or overlooking what happens. And we must understand that this beyond cannot be a matter of a human postulate, or the content of a human assertion, or the result of a dialectical operation of the human mind, if it is to be a genuine beyond, if in it we are to find a sure place and basis in face of this catastrophic event. It cannot be had cheaply, but this is too dear a price. It will not be by such violent and serious exertion, in any supreme height or depth of our consideration and comprehension, that we shall be able to attain this beyond, and that it will be possible and legitimate for us to think in the light of it. What has come to us in the crucifixion of Jesus Christ would not be our judgment, end and death if we could (even theoretically) transcend it, if we could even hypothetically place ourselves on an upper level of this event, and view and penetrate and understand and interpret it from this level. If we have to do with such a beyond, then in no case or form can it be on the basis of an independent human judgment or an invention or intuition reached in this way.

If there is to be a genuine beyond of this kind, then it must positively fulfil at least five conditions.

1. It must be the beyond of an equally effective and sovereign and irrevocable act of the same God who judged man in Jesus Christ, and brought him to his end and delivered him up to death. Our recognition of this beyond must rest on, and refer to, the fact that the same God has turned another page after the first one, has spoken a new word after the first one. An act of the same one true God will necessarily enable and permit us to count on the actuality of this beyond. As His act this beyond will be actual and revealed (together with what has come to us in the crucifixion of Jesus Christ).

2. This beyond must be actual and revealed in a new act of God which is clearly marked off from the first. To be above the first, to stand to it in a definite relationship in which the first is co-ordinated with and subordinated to it, it must be in distinctive contrast to the first. It cannot simply be a predicate, or adjunct, or closer definition of the first. It cannot be a second event which simply consists in an extending or deepening or manifesting of the first : just as it cannot cancel or encroach upon the first, degrading it to the level of a mere appearance

3. This beyond must stand to that first event in a relationship which is meaningful in substance. It must correspond to it in all its distinctiveness. It must have in it its presupposition, and it must affirm it. It must be a beginning where the first is an end, an answer and solution where the first is a riddle. In the sequence of these two acts of God—for all the autonomy, the utter freedom with which the second follows the first—there must actually be, and be revealed, the identity of the acting divine Subject, the unity of His will and way. Both events must be independent and complete, but both must stand to one another in a relationship which is concealed but which is none the less real and unbreakable.

4. The beyond of that first event (if it is to be no less actual and revealed and to be taken no less seriously as the act of God) must have no less than the first the character of an event which has taken place in human history, in the time and space of man ; of an event which is perhaps peculiar and even unique ontically as well as noetically ; but of a definite event, of a concrete, specific, once and for all, contingent fact of history, and not merely of a horizon which embraces all occurrence yesterday, to-day and to-morrow, here, there and everywhere, and which itself can be equally well apprehended always and anywhere and nowhere and never, a horizon of the kind of transcendence which *per definitionem* is immanent to human existence. This event must stand in a sequence of time and space. However different it may be in other respects, as history it must be like all other history in regard to its historicity.

5. The beyond which is this new historical act of God must above all form a unity with the event which precedes and is opposed to it by being together with the first an event in the existence of the same historical Subject, a moment in the history of Jesus Christ and therefore in the history of all other men. The actuality and revelation of this event cannot, therefore, be a matter of another divine intervention which is foreign to the divine action in Jesus Christ and in competition with it. There is, of course, a general activity and operation of God in the course of the over-ruling of His providence and world-government. But even this is not independent of His work as Lord of the covenant, as the Reconciler of the world and the human race as they have fallen away from Him (cf. *C.D.*, III, 3, § 49, 3). And in the course of this general divine over-ruling there is no Word or work of God which does not directly or indirectly have its subject and object in His Son. The new act of God in which He introduced the genuine beyond of the judgment, end and death which comes on man in Jesus Christ must, like this event, be an event which takes place by and in and to Jesus Christ.

We have not spun these five conditions out of the void. We do not need merely to postulate or to affirm in this matter. No dialectical skill is required to demonstrate this beyond. The New Testament witness to Christ knows and names an event which corresponds to and satisfies all the five conditions of the actuality of such a beyond. We have, in fact, taken the conditions from the event. We have to speak of this event if we are to see the positive aspect of the reconciliation of the world with God which took place in Jesus Christ, and in that way to give a positive answer to the transitional question of this third section. This event is the awakening or resurrection from the dead of the crucified and dead Jesus Christ (the Jesus Christ who was really and truly dead according to the emphasised fact of His burial). The beyond which, according to the New Testament witness, is introduced in this event is really above. In this event there is taken a decision on the whole meaning and character of the whole Christ-occurrence attested by it. This event is undoubtedly the sure ground and basis from which the New Testament witnesses could look back to the crucifixion and death of Jesus Christ, but also to the way which led and had to lead to this goal, to what this way and goal implied for themselves and all men, to the happening which broke catastrophically upon us all in and with Jesus Christ. We can say confidently, and we have to say, that the whole New Testament thinks and speaks in the light of this event, and to understand it we must be prepared to think with it in the light of this event.

The New Testament proclaims the death of the Lord (1 Cor. 11²⁶), the crucified Christ (1 Cor. 1²³), the One who is dead ἀποθανών—μᾶλλον δὲ ἐγερθείς (Rom. 8³⁴). But it proclaims this One who is crucified and dead (in and with whom the death of Christians and all men has taken place) as the One whom God has raised from the dead, as the One who is alive, as πάντοτε ζῶν εἰς τὸ ἐντυγχάνειν ὑπὲρ αὐτῶν (Heb. 7²⁵). It proclaims His death (and in and with it the death of Christians and of all men, the judgment, the end of the world which has come upon us), but as the death of the One who has been called ἐκ τῶν νεκρῶν, from the ranks of the dead, the first of the dead to escape death (1 Cor. 15²⁰, Col. 1¹⁸), the raising of whom is to the men of the New Testament the guarantee of their own future resurrection and that of all men, in whose resurrection they have the basis of a life in this world which is assured of a future resurrection, which hastens towards it, which anticipates in hope their own future life out of death. It is to Him, the Resurrected, that their μνημονεύειν (2 Tim. 2⁸) and witness (Ac. 1²², 4³³) refer. Their proclamation and the faith which it evokes are not "empty" or "vain" (κενὸν τὸ κήρυγμα ἡμῶν, κενὴ—ματαία—ἡ πίστις ὑμῶν) ; they are not still in their sins ; those who have fallen asleep in and with Him are not lost, because the One who died on the cross has been raised again from the dead (1 Cor. 15¹⁴, ¹⁷f·). To know Him is identical with knowing the power of His resurrection (Phil. 3¹⁰). The confession that He is the Lord is based on the faith that God has raised Him from the dead (Rom. 10⁹). Even the Christian's faith in God is itself and as such faith in the One who raised Him from the dead (1 Pet. 1²¹). It is because according to the Scriptures this took place on the "third day" that we can and must positively and thankfully confess what took place on the "first" day, the day of His cross : He died for our sins "according to the scriptures" (1 Cor. 15³f·). He, the risen One, opened up the Scriptures to them and opened their eyes to the Scriptures (Lk. 24²⁵f·).

For a more precise understanding it will be best, for the sake of comprehensiveness, to follow the way which we have already indicated.

We begin therefore (1) by stating basically that the raising of Jesus Christ (with all that it implies for us and for all men) is in the New Testament comprehended and understood as an act of God with the same seriousness as the preceding event of the cross with its implication for us and for all men. The judgment of the grace of God fulfilled there was the work of God which could be fulfilled and was fulfilled only by Him. So, too, it is with the emergence here of the grace of this judgment, the grace which as such does not cancel or encroach upon this judgment but leaves it behind as its presupposition, its first work.

With the same seriousness, but in a way which is characteristically marked off and distinguished from the first, it can be fulfilled and was, in fact, fulfilled by God alone. The death of Jesus Christ was, of course, wholly and altogether the work of God to the extent that it is the judgment of death fulfilled on the Representative of all other men appointed by God. The way to the cross and death in which this judgment took place is indeed the work of the Son of God obedient in humility. But it is also as such the work of the obedient man Jesus of Nazareth in His identity with the Son of God, just as His condemnation and execution, although it was determined and willed by God, was also the work of the sinful men who put into effect the decision and will of God, the Jews and Gentiles into whose hands Jesus was delivered, or delivered Himself. As the judgment of God, the event of Golgotha is exclusively the work of God. Its fulfilment is ordained by God even in detail. But all the same it has a component of human action—both obedient and good on the one hand and disobedient and evil on the other. In the light of this part we can say of the event of the cross that it has a " historical " character, that it can be understood and interpreted in the pragmatic context of human decisions and actions, although, of course, in this case it will be misinterpreted and misunderstood, and its real meaning will not be perceived.

The happening on the third day which followed that of Golgotha is the act of God with the same seriousness, but it is unequivocally marked off from the first happening by the fact that it does not have in the very least this component of human willing and activity. Not merely in purpose and ordination, but in its fulfilment, too, it is exclusively the act of God. It takes place quite outside the pragmatic context of human decisions and actions. It takes place in such a way that it cannot possibly be understood and interpreted, i.e., misinterpreted and misunderstood, in the light of this context. It takes place, but it obviously does so without our being able to see it in this context, to ascribe to it a " historical " character in this sense. Like creation, it takes place as a sovereign act of God, and only in this way.

We do not come to this conclusion merely because of its specific content, the coming to life of a man who was actually and in truth dead and buried.

It is, of course, true that even in this respect it breaks through this context ; it is not the kind of event which can be the result of human will and activity or can be made clear or intelligible as such. An event which continues the being of man after death cannot be the result of the will and activity either of the man himself or of other men. To be dead means not to be. Those who are not, cannot will and do, nor can they possibly be objects of the willing and doing of others. ἀνάστασις ἐκ νεκρῶν is not one possibility of this kind with others. Where it takes place, God and God alone is at work. To raise (ἐγείρειν) the dead, to give life (ζωοποιεῖν) to the dead, is, like the creative summoning into being of non-being, a matter wholly and exclusively for God alone, quite outside the sphere of any possible co-operating factors (Heb. 11¹⁹ ; 2 Cor. 1⁹ ; Rom. 4¹⁷). And this is primarily and particularly the case in the resurrection of Jesus Christ.

The coming alive and living of a dead man would be a *contradictio in adiecto* as a human work. This consideration is a true one. Yet when we say that the raising of Jesus Christ, His coming alive and living after death, his resurrection from the tomb, is God's act, and as opposed to His death on the cross only God's act, we are not saying something which can be arrived at only by way of this consideration— for to talk of that which is impossible to man is not by a long way to speak of God—but something which can be taken only from the divine revelation which has taken place in this event. What it was for the New Testament witnesses of this event was not a miracle accrediting Jesus Christ, but the revelation of God in Him. It was not, therefore, something merely formal and noetic. It was also the true, original, typical form of the revelation of God in Him and therefore of revelation generally, the revelation which lights up for the first time all God's revealing and being revealed (in Him and generally). For the first community founded by this event, the event of Easter Day and the resurrection appearances during the forty days were the mediation, the infallible mediation as unequivocally disclosed in a new act of God, of the perception that God was in Christ (2 Cor. 5¹⁹), that is, that in the man Jesus, God Himself was at work, speaking and acting and suffering and going to His death, and that He acted as, and proved Himself, the one high and true God, not in spite of this end, but on this very way into the far country which He went to the bitter end, in this His most profound humiliation, at the place where an utter end was made of this man.

To the community this event was the mediation of a perception hitherto closed and inaccessible to them. It had not been given them by the fact that the Son of God was amongst them as man, in the flesh and to that extent to be known by them after the flesh (2 Cor. 5¹⁶). It had not been given them by the fact that the whole occurrence of the living, speaking, acting, suffering and dying of Jesus had been played out before their very eyes and ears. An anticipatory exception like the confession of Peter at Cæsarea Philippi can in this respect only prove the general rule. In a strange way this perception was unattainable by the disciples as long as they had the opportunity for it, as long as it seemed to be attainable, as long as the happening still had that component of human willing and action, and could to that extent be accepted and understood by them. In this form the character of the happening as the act of God was not revealed to them. In other words, it was not revealed to them at the very point where we might have thought that it could and should be revealed to them. They were in fact witnesses of this act of God. It took place before their very eyes and ears—but before eyes that were blind and ears that were deaf. According to Lk. 24²⁵, in spite of the witness of Moses and the prophets speaking to them, they were, like the rest of Israel, " fools and slow of heart " in relation to it. The perception was mediated, their eyes and ears and hearts were opened, not in and with this event, but in the event which presupposed the closing of this event. The glory of the Word made flesh (Jn. 1¹⁴), the kingdom of God which had drawn near to them in bodily form, the obedience of the Son of God, His death in our place and for our redemption, for the restoration of our peace with God—all this as the mystery of the way of the man Jesus, and of the end of that way on the cross of Golgotha, was first revealed to them and perceived by them when the event was already past, when the man Jesus was dead and buried and had been taken from them and was no longer there, when all the bridges between Himself and them which had previously been available and possible had been broken.

The perception was mediated to them when on the third day, Easter Day, He came amongst them again in such a way that His presence as the man He had been (had been !) was and could be exclusively and therefore unequivocally the act of God without any component of human will and action ; that it was and could be understood by them only and exclusively as such, exclusively and therefore unequivocally as the self-attestation of God in this man without any co-operation of a human attestation serving it. The perception was therefore mediated. God in Christ became conceivable to them in the inconceivable form of the unmediated presence and action of its origin and subject-matter without any other mediation at all—in such a self-attestation of the Lord that in face of it the disciple can only fall at His feet as dead, until He lays His right hand upon Him and allows and commands him not to fear : " I was dead, and behold, I am alive for evermore " (Rev. 1¹⁸ᶠ·). This was the formal side of the resurrection of Christ which made it the true and original and typical form of the revelation of God made in Him. This was what gave it as an act of God its special and distinctive character for the first community, deciding and underlying their whole knowledge of Jesus Christ. This was what gave it its peculiarly indisputable certainty. This was what made the forty days for them the sure and higher place from which they looked back to the life and death of Jesus Christ with an enlightened perception of the act of God which took place in this life and death, and from which they then looked forward to the determination of their own existence, and that of the whole world, given by this life and death.

This is underlined in Gal. 1¹ and Rom. 6⁴ by the fact that the Subject of the resurrection is not simply θεός, according to the regular usage, but θεός πατήρ. Obviously there can be no question of any co-operation of God with the man Jesus, or even with the will and activity of other men (for He is now dead and buried). And we must also be careful how we handle the thought (which is correct not merely in the sense of later trinitarian theology) that Jesus Christ as the Son of God was associated with the Father as the Subject of His own resurrection. The New Testament does not put it in this way. The saying " I am the resurrection and the life " (Jn. 11²⁵) could, of course, be turned in this direction, but on the analogy of similar Johannine statements it means only that in and with me that becomes event and actuality which even outside the Christian community is proclaimed as ἀνάστασις and ζωή. The one whom Jesus Christ, very man and very God, was dead and buried. It is true that as such He had the power to give His life and to take it again (Jn. 10¹⁸) : that is, as the Son of the Father to receive and take again what the Father willed to give back to Him. The passage tells us that as opposed to all other creatures the dead and buried Jesus Christ as the Word made flesh is worthy of this (in the sense of the doxology of Rev. 5¹²). We have to compare it with Jn. 5²⁶, where we are told that the Father has given it to the Son to have life in Himself even as He, the Father, has life in Himself ; and with Rom. 1⁴, where we are told that in His resurrection from the dead by the power of the Holy Spirit He was characterised, designated, declared to be the Son of God (as opposed to all others who are dead and buried) : ὁρισθείς—not that He made and proved Himself to be such. Above all, we have to note Phil. 2. In v. 7 we are, of course, told that " He emptied himself, and took the form of a servant," and in v. 8 that " he humbled himself, even unto death." But in v. 9 it says : " Wherefore God also hath highly exalted him, and given (ἐχαρίσατο) him a name which is above every name." It is one thing that He " rises again " and shows Himself (ἐφανερώθη) to His disciples as the One raised again from the dead (Jn. 21¹⁴). Quite another thing is the act of this resurrection. He shows Himself alive to His disciples (Ac. 1³), but He lives, after He (ἐξ ἀσθενείας) was crucified, ἐκ δυνάμεως θεοῦ (2 Cor. 13⁴). " The God of peace has brought him again from the dead " (Heb. 13²⁰). The resurrection, the being alive of One who was dead and buried, His new presence and action, are not simple equivalents for His raising from the dead, with He Himself the acting Subject in the one case and God (the Father) in the other. This is how the matter has recently been stated by H. Vogel (*Gott in Christo*, 1951, p. 739 f.). But we have to remember that on this view we are enmeshed in the particular difficulty of having to speak of a mere " impotence " of the One dead and buried from which He recovered on His own initiative and in His own strength. If this does not amount to the theory of a mere appearance of death once put forward by Schleiermacher and others, it approximates to a suspiciously docetic view of what is meant by death. But the facts themselves tell us decisively that the event of Easter has to be understood primarily as the raising which happens to Jesus Christ, and only secondarily and (actively) on that basis as His resurrection. For in the New Testament it is everywhere described as an act of divine grace which follows the crucifixion but which is quite free. Phil. 2⁹ tells us expressly that the name which is above every name is given to Him, and Heb. 5¹⁰ that He is greeted and addressed (προσαγορευθείς) by God as a High Priest " after the order of Melchisedec." Certainly it is said of His raising by

God no less than of His putting to death by men that it had to happen (ἔδει, Lk. 24²⁶, Acts 17³; δεῖ, Jn. 20⁹), that it was "according to the scriptures" (1 Cor. 15⁴), that is, according to the continuity of the divine will and plan as especially attested in the transition in Is. 53⁹⁻¹⁰f. or in Ps. 16⁸⁻¹¹ as quoted in Ac. 2²⁵f.. But this "had to" does not mean that in this event God was acting any the less freely than in the giving of His Son or in the divine act of the obedience of the Son even to the death of the cross. His resurrection did not follow from His death, but sovereignly on His death. It was not the result of His death. Its only logical connexion with it was that of the sovereign and unmerited faithfulness, the sovereign and free and constantly renewed mercy of God. Certainly in the resurrection of Jesus Christ we have to do with a movement and action which took place not merely in human history but first and foremost in God Himself, a movement and action in which Jesus Christ as the Son of God had no less part than in His humiliation to the death of the cross, yet only as a pure object and recipient of the grace of God. We must not be afraid of the apparently difficult thought that as in God Himself (as we have seen), in the relationship of the Son to the Father (the model of all that is demanded from man by God), there is a pure obedience, subordination and subjection, so too in the relationship of the Father to the Son (the model of all that is given to man by God) there is a free and pure grace which as such can only be received, and the historical fulfilment of which is the resurrection of Jesus Christ. We obscure and weaken the character of the resurrection as a free pure act of divine grace (in contrast to the character of His death on the cross suffered in obedience), if appealing to His divine sonship we describe it as His own action and work. No, not simply as man, but even as the Son of God Jesus Christ is here simply the One who takes and receives, the recipient of a gift, just as in His death on the cross it is not only as man but as the Son of God that He is wholly and only the obedient servant. The fact that as very God and very man He is worthy of the divine gift of new life from the dead does not alter in the slightest the fact that He did not take this new life but that it was given to Him. We may also ask, and must ask, why Jesus Christ can be called the "first-begotten from the dead" (Col. 1¹⁸) if the case is otherwise, if His resurrection is also something that the resurrection of others can never be—His own work. In what sense can it then be—as we shall see it is—the pledge and indeed the actual beginning of the resurrection of us all ? The comprehensive relevance of the resurrection, its redemptive significance for us, depends upon its being what it is described in the New Testament, God's free act of grace.

2. We have to emphasise that in relation to the happening of the cross it is an autonomous, new act of God. It is not, therefore, the noetic converse of it ; nor is it merely the revelation and declaration of its positive significance and relevance. It is this, as we have seen. And obviously it is in fact related to that first event. But in spite of this it is distinguished from it as an event of a particular character. It is not enclosed in it, but follows on it as a different happening. On the other hand, it is not a light which makes that first happening a meaningless shadow. The *theologia resurrectionis* does not absorb the *theologia crucis*, nor *vice versa*. The event of Easter in its indissoluble connexion with the event of the cross is an event which has its own content and form. We have already said one important thing in relation to this statement when we have laid down that the event of Easter must be understood as the true and original and typical act of revelation, and therefore as an act of God *sui generis*—a free act of

grace, free even in its innermost divine basis, according to the New Testament evidence. But we now have to add the fresh consideration that as the act of God's grace the resurrection of Jesus Christ from the dead confronted His being in death, that is, His non-being as the One who was crucified, dead, buried, and destroyed, as the One who had been and had ceased to be. It was to His being in death that He had gone as the end of His way into the far country, in fulfilment of His obedience in our place, in His self-offering as the Judge who is judged and as the Priest who is sacrificed. He was " delivered up for our trespasses " (Rom. 4²⁵). He had delivered Himself up (Gal. 2²⁰). His resurrection from the dead did not cancel this. It had its unaltered *terminus a quo* in His death in our place. The One who was raised was the One who was crucified, dead and, to prove it, buried. The One who was exalted was the One who was abased.

The Gospel of St. John (20²⁵ᶠ·) thought it worth reporting that the risen Christ bore the wounds of the Crucified. Life was given to the One who had been slain. The One who belonged hopelessly to the past was present. The Humiliated was exalted, being given the name of *Kyrios* (Phil. 2⁹), being declared the Son of God (Rom. 1⁴)—to be seen and heard and handled (1 Jn. 1¹) as such by His disciples for forty days, to eat and drink with them as such (Ac. 10⁴¹), and as such to die no more (Rom. 6⁹).

His raising, His resurrection, His new life, confirmed His death. It was God's answer to it, and to that extent its revelation and declaration. But as God's answer to it, it was distinct from it. It was God's acknowledgment of Jesus Christ, of His life and death. As a free act of divine grace, it had formally the character of an act of justice on the part of God the Father in His relation to Jesus Christ as His Son, just as the obedience of the Son even to the death of the cross, as a free act of love, had formally the character of an act of justice of the Son in His relation to God the Father. It came in the midst of His real death and delivered Him from death. To that extent it was the expression and fulfilment of the sentence of the Father on the way which He had gone—His judicial sentence that the action and passion of Jesus Christ were not apart from or against Him, but according to His good and holy will, and especially that His dying in our place was not futile but effective, that it was not to our destruction but to our salvation. It was a second act of justice after the first to the extent that it was the divine approval and acknowledgment of the obedience given by Jesus Christ, the acceptance of His sacrifice, the proclamation and bringing into force of the consequences, the saving consequences, of His action and passion in our place.

In the concepts answer, confession and sentence, we gather together the distinctive thing which the New Testament sees in the resurrection of Jesus Christ as opposed to the event of His death. It is all summarised in the remarkable phrase used to describe the resurrection in the hymn quoted in 1 Tim. 3¹⁶ : ἐδικαιώθη ἐν πνεύματι. He Himself, Jesus Christ, the Son of God made man, was justified by God in His resurrection from the dead. He was justified as man, and in Him as the Representative of all men all were justified. Hence the continuation of the statement in Rom. 4²⁵: ἠγέρθη διὰ τὴν δικαίωσιν ἡμῶν.

But what gives to the justification which took place there its true and decisive power is that in the unity of God with this man (and in and with Him in His fellowship with us all), in the resurrection of Jesus Christ, God Himself, His will and act in the death of Jesus Christ, was justified by God, by Himself and therefore definitively. Was this necessary? Certainly not in the sense that at Golgotha everything had not taken place which had to take place for the reconciliation of the world with God, that the representation and sacrifice of Jesus Christ in His death were not wholly sufficient, that they were therefore referred back to some completion and continuation. Anything pointing in this direction, any limitations of the τετέλεσται are quite alien to the New Testament. But the direct continuation of the τετέλεσται in Jn. 19³⁰ is: καὶ κλίνας τὴν κεφαλὴν παρέδωκεν τὸ πνεῦμα. And the occurrence of Golgotha which is complete in itself consists ultimately in the fact that Jesus " bowed his head." What does this mean? In obedience to the will of God? Before God as Father? His obedience consists in the fact that He commends or offers up His spirit, that is, Himself—He delivers up Himself. To whom? To God His Father, to His decree and disposing? Naturally, and this is emphasised in the saying handed down in Lk. 23⁴⁶: " Father, into thy hands I commend my spirit," myself. But there, too, there is the continuation: τοῦτο δὲ εἰπὼν ἐξέπνευσεν. It is therefore to death that He bows His head and commits Himself. In and with the fulfilment there of the will of God it is nothingness which can triumph over Him—and in and with Him over the whole of the human race represented by Him. According to the disposition and in the service of God death and nothingness are brought in and used for the reconciliation of the world with God, as instruments in His conflict with the corruption of the world and the sin of man—but death and nothingness in all their evil and destructive power. It is also to the wrath of God which permits this force and judges evil by evil that Jesus commits Himself and in and with Himself the world and the individual sinner. The reconciliation of the world with God which took place in Jesus Christ had therefore the meaning that a radical end was made of Him and therefore of the world.

And that might have exhausted its meaning. The saying: " My God, my God, why hast thou forsaken me? " (Mk. 15³⁴) shows how close was this frightful possibility. It might have been that God turned away His face finally from us. It might have been that by the same eternal Word by which as Creator He gave being to man and the world He now willed to take away that being from them, to let them perish with all their corruption and sin. The relationship between Himself and His creation might have been regularised by depriving it of its perverted actuality. He might have repented of having created it (Gen. 6⁷), and carried this repentance to its logical conclusion. Ruling as the Judge, He might have given death and nothingness the last word in relation to the creature. He would still have been in the right.

But He would have been in the right only in complete concealment, within Himself, and only by granting to death and nothingness as the instruments of His judgment a final right in relation to the creature. He would then have surrendered to them His own right in relation to the creature. He would then have renounced His own right, His own creature. And in so doing He would have recognised the power of death and nothingness over the creature, *de facto* if not *de iure*. He would not have confirmed His original choice between heaven and earth on the one hand and chaos on the other, His decision for light and His rejection of darkness (Gen. 1³), Himself therefore as the Creator of the world and humanity which He made and found to be good. In short, He would not have justified Himself. But this is to say that He would have been in the right only in and for Himself. In His wrath He would have been content to maintain His right against the world, in its destruction. He would not have sustained or demonstrated or revealed His right to the world and in the world.

Did He need to do this? Certainly not. On what ground can we postulate that He had to do it? What reason is there to blame Him if He willed not to do so? He did not owe it to anyone to justify Himself. It could only be His grace which bade Him do it. But in His grace He was, in fact, free to do it; and therefore not to go back on His choice between chaos and the world which He created good, even in view of its corruption and in His righteous anger; not to resign as Creator and Lord of the creature, but to act and confirm Himself as such; to call in and use death and nothingness in His service, to fulfil His judgment on sinful man and a perverted world, but in grace not to surrender His own right, and His creature; and therefore to be in the right without giving chaos the last word and supreme power over the creature; to throw aside and trample underfoot these instruments when they have served their purpose; to act and demonstrate and reveal Himself as God and Lord of the world after the fulfilment of His judgment on the world; in relation to it not to be in the right in and for Himself in His wrath, but beyond that to maintain His right to it in an inconceivable love, which is again, to justify Himself; and in so doing, when judgment has taken its course, when that which is worthy of death and nothingness has fallen a prey to death and nothingness, when that which is dust has returned to dust, to justify the creature, to justify man, to acknowledge Himself the Creator once again and this time in fulness, to create him afresh with a new: " Let there be light," to beget him and to cause him to be born again from the dead, freed from his sin and guilt, freed from the claim and power which death and nothingness and chaos necessarily had over him in his former corrupted state, freed for life for Him and with Him, and therefore for life everlasting. God was free to do this. He did not have to do it, but He was free to do it.

And this is what in His grace He actually has done in raising Jesus Christ from the dead when He had been delivered up to death for our trespasses, as our Representative, in fulfilment of the judgment which ought to have fallen on us. In so doing He answered the question which in Mark and Matthew forms the last words of the Crucified. But we can and must say that in so doing He has shown that as recorded in St. Luke's account Jesus commended His spirit into His hands, and that only in so doing did He subject Himself to death, that He bowed His head before Him, and only because He bowed before Him did He also bow before the claim and power of nothingness, that He was obedient even unto death only in this way and in this order (and to that extent as already the secret Lord of the death to which He subjected Himself). God abandoned Him to chaos, as had to happen because of our transgressions, only in order to save Him from it—the One whom chaos could only serve, in order to do despite to it and to make a show of it: " Death is swallowed up in victory. O death, where is thy victory? O death, where is thy sting " (1 Cor. 15⁵⁴ᶠ·). He made Him the victor over death by letting death conquer Him, as He had to do in fulfilment of the judgment laid upon Him. He recognised and proclaimed not merely the innocence but the supreme righteousness and holiness, the incomparable and unsurpassable goodness, of the work of Him who gave Himself up to death in pure obedience—who was not a sinner in the very fact that He took upon Himself the sin of the world. According to the rendering of Ps. 16¹⁰ in Ac. 2²⁷, He did not suffer His Holy One to see corruption. And in that He did not suffer it, in that He reopened the doors of death which had necessarily closed behind Him, in that He caused Him to rise from the grave to life unto Himself (Rom. 6¹⁰), and therefore to eternal life, He confirmed the verdict which, according to Mk. 1¹¹, He had already pronounced at Jordan when He entered on the way which led Him to Golgotha: " Thou art my beloved Son, in whom I am well pleased." In raising Him from the dead, He justified Him (1 Tim. 3¹⁶).

And in and with Him He justified us (Rom. 4²⁵)—we shall be returning to this. But primarily He justified Himself. He did this first in the revelation of His faithfulness as the Creator and Lord of heaven and earth and all men, to whom in the person of this their Representative, after their destruction in their old and corrupted form of life, He has spoken a second Yes which creates and gives them new life : a Yes which He did not owe them, but which He willed to speak, and which was the gracious confirmation of His own original will to create and His act of creation. But then, and at an even higher level, He did it in the revelation of His faithfulness as the Father of this Son, in the revelation of the love with which He loved Him from all eternity and all along His way into the far country, at Jordan and in the wilderness and in Gethsemane, and never more than when the Son asked Him on the cross (Mk. 15³⁴) whether He had forsaken Him, and when He then cried with a loud voice and gave up the ghost. His whole eternal love would still have been His even if He had acquiesced in His death as the Judge who was judged, if His mission had concluded at that ninth hour of Good Friday, if it had been completed with His fulfilling and suffering in His own person the No of the divine wrath on the world. But then, like His right as Creator and Lord of the world, it would have been, and remained, a completely hidden love : without witnesses, without participants, because without proclamation, without outward confirmation and form, concealed in the mystery of the inner life and being of the Godhead. It pleased God, however, to justify Himself, that is, to reveal and give force and effect to His faithfulness and love in this supreme sense, by an ὁρίζειν (Rom. 1⁴) of His Son which the disciples of Jesus could see and hear and grasp, and which was ordained to be publicly proclaimed. He willed to give to His eternity with Him and therefore to Himself an earthly form. He willed to give to the inner and secret radiance of His glory an outward radiance in the sphere of creation and its history. He willed to give to His eternal life space and time. And that is what He did when He called Jesus Christ to life from the dead.

This helps us to understand an important characteristic in the New Testament view of the resurrection of Jesus Christ, that as a free work demonstrating and revealing the grace of the Father it took place by the Holy Spirit : ἐδικαιώθη ἐν πνεύματι is how we have it in 1 Tim. 3¹⁶, and in Rom. 1⁴ : ἐν δυνάμει κατὰ πνεῦμα ἁγιωσύνης. Similarly in 1 Pet. 3¹⁸ : ζωοποιηθεὶς πνεύματι. And surely this is the sense of Rom. 6⁴ : ἠγέρθη . . . διὰ τῆς δόξης τοῦ πατρός, of 2 Cor. 13⁴ : ζῇ ἐκ δυνάμεως θεοῦ, and Col. 2¹² : διὰ τῆς πίστεως τῆς ἐνεργείας τοῦ θεοῦ, as it clearly is of Rom. 8¹¹, which speaks of the Spirit indwelling the Christian as Him who raised Christ Jesus from the dead.

The Holy Spirit—who is also the κύριος according to 2 Cor. 3¹⁷—is within the Trinity : God Himself maintaining His unity as Father and Son, God in the love which unites Him as Father with the Son, and as Son with the Father ; and outside the Trinity, in His work as Creator and Reconciler of the world : God Himself as the One who creates life in freedom, who gives life from the dead, thus making His glory active in the world : τὸ πνεῦμά ἐστιν τὸ ζωοποιοῦν, according to the definition of Jn. 6⁶³ ; τὸ πνεῦμα ζωοποιεῖ (2 Cor. 3⁶)—and revealing it in this its characteristic activity : as πνεῦμα τῆς ἀληθείας (Jn. 14¹⁷, 15²⁶, 16¹³ ; 1 Jn. 4⁶), as the Spirit by whom God discloses Himself to man in all His profundity (1 Cor. 2¹⁰, Eph. 3⁵), who helps our infirmities (Rom. 8²⁶), who bears witness with our spirit with a divine incontrovertibility (Rom. 8¹⁶), by whom the love of God is shed abroad in our hearts (Rom. 5⁵).

In this context it is important that at least one group in the New Testament tradition understood the human existence of the Son of God, that is, the justification and sanctification of human nature in the person of the Virgin Mary which was indispensable to union with the Son of God, as the work of the Holy Spirit (Mt. 1¹⁸, ²⁰, Lk. 1³⁵). It is also important that another series of passages—not 2 Cor. 3¹⁷, but 1 Cor. 15⁴⁵ (" the second Adam was made a πνεῦμα ζωοποιοῦν "), Jn. 3⁶ (" That which is born of the Spirit, is spirit ") and especially the accounts of His baptism in Jordan—understands His whole being as πνεῦμα, that is, as filled and controlled by the Spirit, so that in Heb. 9¹⁴ it can already be said of His way to death that διὰ πνεύματος αἰωνίου He offered Himself without spot to God. If we were to try to speak of a necessity of His resurrection, then it is along these lines that we could and would have to do so, applying the question of Gal. 3³ whether that which has begun and is continued in the Spirit can be made perfect in the flesh—which is here the destruction of the flesh. But it is better not to follow this track, remembering Jn. 3⁸ : " The Spirit bloweth where it listeth, and thou hearest the sound thereof, but canst not tell whence it cometh, or whither it goeth," and also 2 Cor. 3¹⁷ : " Where the Spirit of the Lord is, there is liberty ; " remembering, therefore, that when we speak of the Spirit, *per definitionem* we do not speak of a necessary but of a free being and activity of God. The fact that Jesus Christ was raised from the dead by the Holy Spirit and therefore justified confirms that it has pleased God to reveal and express Himself to the crucified and dead and buried Jesus Christ in the unity of the Father with the Son and therefore in the glory of the free love which is His essence : a revelation and expression which as such—and where the Spirit of God blows, where the Holy Spirit is at work, this does take place necessarily— must consist in the merciful work of creating the καινότης ζωῆς (Rom. 6⁴) of this One who is dead, in His presentation and exhibition as the One who is alive for evermore.

To sum up, the resurrection of Jesus Christ is the great verdict of God, the fulfilment and proclamation of God's decision concerning the event of the cross. It is its acceptance as the act of the Son of God appointed our Representative, an act which fulfilled the divine wrath but did so in the service of the divine grace. It is its acceptance as the act of His obedience which judges the world, but judges it with the aim of saving it. It is its acceptance as the act of His Son whom He has always loved (and us in Him), whom of His sheer goodness He has not rejected but drawn to Himself (and us in Him) (Jer. 31³). In this the resurrection is the justification of God Himself, of God the Father, Creator of heaven and earth, who has willed and planned and ordered this event. It is the justification of Jesus Christ, His Son, who willed to suffer this event, and suffered it to the very last. And in His person it is the justification of all sinful men, whose death was decided in this event, for whose life there is therefore no more place. In the resurrection of Jesus Christ His life and with it their life has in fact become an event beyond death : " Because I live, ye shall live also " (Jn. 14¹⁹).

We come to the point which is decisive for our investigation when we ask (3) what is the positive connexion between the death of Jesus Christ and His resurrection. The comprehensive answer to this question with which the whole investigation must terminate can only be this. They belong together in that in these two events of God with and after one another there is effective and expressed the Yes of the reconciling will of God—the Yes fulfilled and proclaimed by the one Jesus Christ, first in His act of obedience in our place, then—again in our place—as the first recipient of the grace of God the Father. But before we come to this final answer we have to say concerning the question of this relationship that which is implied in it, that the positive connexion between the death and resurrection of Jesus Christ consists in the fact that these two acts of God with and after one another are the two basic events of the one history of God with a sinful and corrupt world, His history with us as perverted and lost creatures. The one concerns our trespasses, the other our justification (Rom. 4^{25}). In a comprehensive sense Jesus Christ " died and rose again for us " (2 Cor. 5^{15}). It is our case which is undertaken, our conversion to God which is brought about, both in the one and in the other, on the way from the one to the other, in the sequence and correspondence of the two. The relationship of the two events is that of the alteration in our situation and status and being which took place in them. To the making of this alteration and therefore to the reconciliation of the world with God there belong both the free obedience of the Son in His death and also the grace of God the Father in His resurrection : the event of Golgotha and the event in the garden of Joseph of Arimathea.

The fact that the alteration of our situation is made in both events does not mean that their sequence and correspondence is that of repetition, or that their relationship is that of the unity of two equal factors, of which either the one or the other might appear to be superfluous or simply a closer definition. On the contrary, it is a genuine sequence and correspondence in a differentiated relationship in which both factors have their proper form and function. In all this alteration we have to do with the conversion of man to God and therefore with his reconciliation and that of the world with God. It is, therefore, clear that we have to distinguish a *terminus a quo* and a *terminus ad quem* : first, a negative event (with a positive intention), a turning away (for the purpose of turning to), a removing (in the sense of a positing), a putting off (with a view to a putting on, 2 Cor. 5^2, Eph. 4^{22-24}), a freeing from something (with a view to freeing for something else) ; then a positive event (with a negative presupposition), a turning to (made possible by a definite turning from), a putting on (after a previous putting off), a freeing for something (based upon a freeing from something else). According to the resurrection the death of Jesus Christ as the negative act of God took place with a positive intention. It had as its aim the turning of man to Himself, his positing afresh, his putting on of a new life, his freeing for the future. And, according to the prior death of Jesus Christ, the resurrection has this negative presupposition in a radical turning of man from his old existence, in a total removing of man in his earlier form, in his absolute putting off, in his complete freeing from the past. It is in this correspondence that we see their difference but also their relationship—which is, of course, necessarily a differentiated relationship.

We will try to put it in another way, reversing the sequence. The justification which took place in the resurrection of Jesus Christ confirmed and revealed in what sense God was in the right in His death—

not surrendering but asserting His right against sinful men who, as such, were judged in the death of their Representative, being destroyed and necessarily crucified and dying with Him ; but also not surrendering His right over these men as His creatures, and therefore not surrendering the right of these creatures of His, but with a view to re-establishing and maintaining it. The death of Jesus Christ preceded His resurrection. God established and maintained His own right against man and over man, and the right of man Himself. This makes it clear in what sense in the resurrection of Jesus Christ He willed to justify both Jesus and Himself, and has in fact done so, proclaiming His own twofold right and the right of man as His creature as they were there established and maintained to be the basis and the beginning of a new world, putting them into force and effect, making it plain that the history of the humiliation of His Son, the history of His way into the far country, is redemption history within universal history ; against man, and therefore for him.

This is the sequence and correspondence of the death of Jesus Christ and His resurrection. This is how they are with and after one another the basic events of the alteration of the human situation in which there took place the reconciliation of the world with God. This, then, is the differentiated relationship between the two events.

We read of this whole alteration in the remarkably central verse 2 Cor. 5[17] : " If any man be in Christ, he is a new creation : old things are passed away ; behold, all things are become new." Alongside this we have to place Rom. 8[10] : " And if Christ be in you, the body (you yourself in virtue of what has taken place for you in the death of Jesus Christ) is dead because of sin (judged there in His body as your Representative) ; but the Spirit (you yourself in virtue of what is promised and has already taken place for you in the resurrection of this your Representative) is life because of righteousness (proclaimed and put into effect there)." Alongside it, too, we must put Rev. 21[4f.] : " And God shall wipe away all tears from their eyes ; and there shall be no more death, neither sorrow, nor crying, neither shall there be any more pain : for the former things are passed away. And he that sat upon the throne said, Behold, I make all things new." All these can and should be read (according to the meaning of the New Testament writers) as a commentary on Is. 43[18f.] : " Remember ye not the former things, neither consider the things of old. Behold, I will do a new thing ; shall ye not know it ? I will even make a way in the wilderness, and rivers in the desert." Or on Is. 65[17f.] : " For, behold, I create new heavens, and a new earth : and the former shall not be remembered, nor come into mind. But be ye glad and rejoice for ever in that which I create : for, behold, I create Jerusalem a rejoicing, and her people a joy." The New Testament community knows what is meant by this. It stands at the heart of the event which is proclaimed here, face to face with the Jerusalem which comes. Again, the prophetic word is for it a commentary on that which confronts it as its basic text. It is the witness of it. The old, the former thing, has passed away : the new has come, has grown, has been created. It is " in Christ "—the Crucified and Risen —and Christ is in it. In His death its own death and that of the world is, in fact, already past, and in His life its own life and that of the future world is before it. It has turned away from the one, it has turned to the other. It has put off the one, it has put on the other. Its existence looks back to the Crucified and forward to the Risen. It is an existence in the presence of the One who was and will be.

He is its *terminus a quo* and its *terminus ad quem*. It is an existence in that alteration, that is, in that differentiated relationship between the death and the resurrection of Christ. When a man is in Christ, there is a new creation. The old has passed, everything has become new. This means that the event of the end of the world which took place once and for all in Jesus Christ is the pre-supposition of an old man, and the event of the beginning of the new world which took place once and for all in Jesus Christ is the goal of a new man, and because the goal, therefore the truth and power of the sequence of human existence as it moves towards this goal. The world and every man exist in this alteration.

Note that it is not dependent upon whether it is proclaimed well or badly or even at all. It is not dependent upon the way in which it is regarded, upon whether it is realised and fulfilled in faith or unbelief. The coming of the kingdom of God has its truth in itself, not in that which does or does not correspond to it on earth.

By way of illustration, let us suppose that the kingdom of heaven is like a king whom it has pleased to confer on someone an order. Now normally the man will be in the happy position of being able to receive the distinction. But there may be the abnormal case when because of pressing or tragic circumstances, or because he is hindered by outside forces, he is not in a position to do this. Is it not clear that in both cases the will and act of the king form a complete action, and all is well and good for the recipient even in the second and abnormal case ? Has he failed to receive the order because he could not do so in person ?

The men of the New Testament are the normal case, those who not only receive that which has taken place in Jesus Christ, but do so in person, those who with open eyes and ears and hearts, in faith and in the knowledge of faith, hold to the fact that they can and must, not only exist, but walk ($\pi\epsilon\rho\iota\pi\alpha\tau\epsilon\hat{\iota}\nu$, $\sigma\tau o\iota\chi\epsilon\hat{\iota}\nu$, $\pi o\lambda\iota\tau\epsilon\acute{\upsilon}\epsilon\sigma\theta\alpha\iota$) from this presupposition to this goal and in this sequence, who are therefore summoned and empowered and enabled to proclaim this alteration and therefore the death and resurrection of Jesus Christ, or rather the crucified and risen Jesus Christ Himself. The divine verdict pronounced in the resurrection of Jesus Christ has been heard by them. The " blowing " (Jn. 3[8]) of the Holy Spirit which creates life and leads into all truth is received by them. They are " baptised " (Mk. 1[8]) by Jesus Christ Himself, or they have " drunk " of Him (1 Cor. 12[13]). As they pray for Him, He is to them the One who is " given " by their Father in heaven (Lk. 11[13]). He " dwells " in them (Rom. 8[11]). They are " led " by Him (Gal. 4[6], 5[18] ; Rom. 8[14]). They walk in conformity with Him ($\kappa\alpha\tau\grave{\alpha}$ $\pi\nu\epsilon\hat{\upsilon}\mu\alpha$, Rom. 8[4]) or in Him ($\pi\nu\epsilon\acute{\upsilon}\mu\alpha\tau\iota$, Gal. 5[16], 2 Cor. 12[18]), not as blind and deaf participants in this alteration of the human situation, but as those who see and hear.

But what is said in the New Testament concerning the alteration of the human situation which has its basis in the death and resurrection of Jesus Christ compels us to make a further distinction in our understanding of this relationship. It is a matter of the character of the two events which underlie this alteration as temporal events, their relation as they are with and after one another in time. In respect of their distinctness in this regard the third of the points in our investigation which now occupy us is the decisive one—decisive, that is, in the answering of our main question whether and to what extent we can and must proceed from the obedience which Jesus Christ rendered for us to the thought of its relevance for us. We have seen that the resurrection of Jesus Christ from the dead, as a second and new divine act, was the revelation of the meaning and purpose of the obedience demanded from and achieved by Jesus Christ, and therefore of His death, the answer of the grace of God the Father to the self-humiliation of the Son, His confession of Him, the validation of His act as the establishment and maintaining of His right against and for us, the justification of God Himself as the Father and our Creator, and therefore the justification of Jesus Christ and our justification as His creatures, the verdict of God. So far we have tried to understand these two acts of God, these two basic events in the alteration of the human situation, as they took place through and to Jesus Christ, in their differentiated togetherness in content.

To appreciate the matter further, we must now start from the fact that there is also a togetherness in time.

The resurrection of Jesus Christ tells us—and it is decided in this second divine act, the act of God fulfilled in His verdict—that as the Crucified " He lives and reigns to all eternity " (Luther), that as the One who was, having been buried, He is not of the past, He did not continue to be enclosed in the limits of the time between His birth and death, but as the One who was in this time He became and is the Lord of all time, eternal as God Himself is eternal, and therefore present in all time. But the fact that He is risen to die no more, to be taken from the dominion of death (Rom. 6[9]), carries with it the fact that His then living and speaking and acting, His being on the way from Jordan to Golgotha, His being as the One who suffered and died, became and is as such His eternal being and therefore His present-day being every day of our time. That which took place on the third day after His death lifted up the whole of what took place before in all its particularity (not in spite of but because of its particularity) into something that took place once and for all. It is in the power of the event of the third day that the event of the first day—as something that happened there and then—is not something which belongs to the past, which can be present only by recollection, tradition and proclamation, but is as such a present event, the event which fills and determines the whole present.

In virtue of His resurrection from the dead Jesus Christ—" the man Christ Jesus, who gave himself a ransom for all "—is (in the same way as the One God) the one Mediator between God and man (1 Tim. 2[5]). He was this in the event of Good Friday to be it for ever—this is what the event of Easter Day revealed and confirmed and brought into effect. He not only did represent us, He does represent us. He not only did bear the sin of the world, He does bear it. He not only has reconciled the world with God, but as the One who has done this, He is its eternal Reconciler, active and at work once and for all. He not only went the way from Jordan to Golgotha, but He still goes it, again and again. His history did not become dead history. It was history in His time to become as such eternal history—the history of God with the men of all times, and therefore taking place here and now as it did then. He is the living Saviour. This would be a fantastic and not very helpful statement if it simply meant that He is something like this for certain men of His own age, and that He can be something of the same for certain men of other ages by their recollection of Him, by the tradition and proclamation concerning Him, by a sympathetic experience of His person, or by some form of imitation of His work. He would then be alive only in virtue of the life breathed into Him as a historical and therefore a dead figure by the men of other ages. But the fact that He is the living Saviour is true and helpful because He is risen from the dead and therefore—the Father of whom the same can be said has given it to Him—He has life in Himself (Jn. 5²⁶), and in His own omnipotence, on His own initiative, and by His own act, He is the same here and now as He was there and then : the Mediator between God and us men.

Therefore He not only did but does stand before God for us—not in a different form but in exactly the same form as He stood before Him for us " in the days of His flesh " as the Judge judged and the priest sacrificed. Ἐντυγχάνει ὑπὲρ ἡμῶν : He who died, yea rather, who is risen, is at the right hand of God. Therefore, on this basis and in relation to this fact, it can and must be asked triumphantly : " Who will condemn ? ", and further : " Who will separate us from the love of Christ ? " (Rom. 8³⁴ᶠ·). Similarly in 1 Jn. 2¹ᶠ· : " If any man sin, we have an advocate (παράκλητον) with the Father, Jesus Christ the righteous : and he is the propitiation for our sins : and not for ours only, but also for the sins of the whole world." Similarly in Heb. 7²⁵ : " He is the One that ever (πάντοτε) liveth to make intercession for us." His sacrifice has power for ever (εἰς τὸ διηνεκές, Heb. 10¹⁴). By His blood He has entered in once into the Holiest of Holies, gaining an eternal redemption (Heb. 9¹²). He is a " high-priest for ever " (Heb. 5⁶, 6²⁰, 7¹⁷). His is an unchangeable priesthood (Heb. 7²⁴). He appears now for us in the presence of God (Heb. 9²⁴). It is not that we had but have Him as a High Priest (Heb. 4¹⁴ᶠ·, 8¹, 10¹⁹). He is " the same yesterday, today, and for ever " (Heb. 13⁸). It is no accident that the Epistle to the Hebrews which emphasises this so strongly brings out the To-day so sharply in the call to faith, repentance and obedience (3⁷, ¹⁵, 4⁷). These are just a few of the explicit statements of the New Testament about the eternal unity, or the temporal togetherness, of the humiliated and the exalted, the crucified and the risen Jesus Christ, the obedience of the Son and the grace of the Father. It might also be shown that quite a number of verses in the so-called " high-priestly " prayer (Jn. 17) ought to be regarded even in the sense of the Evangelist himself as prayers of the exalted Christ for His own and for His work in the world. This unity and togetherness are—if we look back to the event of Easter—among the self-evident presuppositions of the whole of the New Testament.

It was in this connexion that in the doctrine of the *munus sacerdotale* the older dogmatics had a second section on the *intercessio Christi* side by side with the idea of the *satisfactio vicaria : victimae Christi in terra oblatae et mactatae in coelo repraesentatio et nova velut oblatio* (J. H. Heidegger, *Med. Theol. chr.*, 1696, XIX, 59). In fact it had to do with the same problem as now concerns us—that of the transition from the understanding of the person and work of Christ to soteriology proper, to the question of the *applicatio salutis* : How does the atonement made then and there come to us and become our atonement ? And at this supreme point the question is answered by the recognition that Jesus Christ as the Son who was once obedient to the Father and offered Himself and reconciled the world and us with God is in eternity and therefore to-day now, at this very hour, our active and effective Representative and Advocate before God, and therefore the real basis of our justification and hope. If only this recognition had been maintained, then for all its apparent inflexibility the alternative of contingent facts of history and necessary truths of reason would necessarily have been thought through in the 18th century and rejected and overcome. The moment of this particular " contingent fact of history " was the moment of all moments. There is no moment in which Jesus Christ is not Judge and High Priest and accomplishes all these things. There is no moment in which this perfect tense is not a present. There is no moment in which He does not stand before God as our Representative who there suffered and died for us and therefore speaks for us. There is no moment in which we are viewed and treated by God except in the light of this *repraesentatio* and *oblatio* of His Son. All honour to the human and historical pragmatism of recollection, tradition and proclamation. But in relation to the divine history of this *repraesentatio* and *oblatio* it can be considered only as an epiphenomenon, with a significance which is only secondary, and indirect, that of an instrument and witness. The eternal action of Jesus Christ grounded in His resurrection is itself the true and direct bridge from once to always, from Himself in His time to us in our time. Because as crucified and dead He is risen and lives, the fact of His death on the cross can never be past, it can never cease to be His action, the decision which God makes *hic et nunc* to His own glory and in our favour, summoning us on our part to responsibility, as is brought out so impressively and in a way to stir the conscience in Heb. 10[19-29]. " Let us draw near with a true heart in full assurance of faith, having our hearts sprinkled from an evil conscience, and our bodies washed with pure water. Let us hold fast the profession of our hope without wavering, for he is faithful that promised " (Heb. 10[22-23]). Jesus Christ Himself lives, His obedience pleading for our disobedience. His blood shed in obedience speaks against us and for us to-day as it did on the day of Golgotha. He receives for us to-day as on Easter Day the grace of God which we have not deserved. For this reason the judgment fulfilled by Him, the sacrifice offered by Him, is effective for us. Not therefore in some answer of ours to our questions : What are we going to make of it ? How can we bring home this matter to ourselves and other men ? Or how can we bring ourselves and other men to this matter ? Where and how do we experience and prove its efficacy ? There is a relative place for these questions and answers, but only in the light and in strict explanation of the one question and answer which God Himself has put and given in Jesus Christ, which indeed He does put in eternity and therefore to-day, and which He answers in the antithesis of the obedient Son and the gracious Father. Our answer and our question have to be sought (Col. 3[1]) " above, where Christ is seated at the right hand of God." But this means in prayer, prayer in the name of Jesus, prayer which we expect to be heard only—but without doubt or hesitation—because God has loved and loves and will love the one who offers it as a lost sinner in Jesus Christ, because, therefore, Jesus Christ has come between this one and God, and is there between to-day and every day.

To this we have to add that this living being of Jesus Christ the Mediator is the immovable barrier opposed to all who have tried to make to themselves another saviour than the Saviour of sinners crucified between and with the thieves ; to all who are too proud to pray with the publican : " God be merciful, to me a sinner ; " to all who try to believe that they can treat and act on their own account in relation to God. They must be clear that even in Christian history and the Christian Church, in spite of the *kerygma*, with or without the sacraments, in spite of their faith and discipleship, they would necessarily be lost and damned were it not that as their Representative between themselves and His and their Father there stands " above " the crucified Son of God, the Saviour of sinners who was crucified between and with the thieves as the One who gave Himself up for our trespasses. " If we say that we have no sin, we deceive ourselves, and the truth is not in us. If we confess our sins, he is faithful and just to forgive us our sins, and to cleanse us from all unrighteousness " (1 Jn. 1⁸ᶠ·). In this sense the *intercessio Christi* is not simply the origin and the lasting basis of our righteousness and hope, but its continual turning point, the way which is always open to God and the sharp corner around which it leads us. And in this twofold sense it is the eternal act of the crucified and risen One for us, the one truly contemporaneous divine act to us, the To-day, To-day ! of atonement against which we must not harden our hearts.

He who was crucified is risen, and as such He lives unto God (Rom. 6¹⁰). He is the same yesterday, to-day and for ever. This temporal togetherness of the Jesus Christ of Good Friday and the Jesus Christ of Easter Day as created by the divine verdict is the basis of life for men of all ages. And as such it is the basis of the alteration of their situation. The event of Easter Day is the removing of the barrier between His life in His time and their life in their times, the initiation of His lordship as the Lord of all time. What He has done in His time He has done as the Representative of all other men, as the elect man, for them. In His resurrection it is fixed that what He did in His time He did in their time for and to them. The fact that in His death God maintained and asserted His right against and to them and therefore their right as His creatures is their justification. And God's verdict when he raised Him to life beyond death was His verdict on them. This answer of grace to His obedience was the answer to the question of their being in disobedience, the revelation of the judgment which came on them in Jesus Christ, of the death which they died in Him, of the end to which they were brought in Him. God's gracious answer in the resurrection of Jesus Christ from the dead was this. In their quite different time with its quite different content (in and with what Jesus Christ was and did in His time, in and with this Son who became man and died as man and was raised again as man), as those who are elected with Him, as the brothers of this His Son, He has called them His children and received them as such. This was said to them, no, is said to them, by the Word of God made flesh, in the glory in which it was spoken and heard on Easter Day, and in which from that day it will be spoken and can be heard as the living Word, as the redemptive history which takes place to-day within universal history.

Thus the death and resurrection of Jesus Christ are together—His death in the power and effectiveness and truth and lasting newness given to it by His resurrection—the basis of the alteration of the situation of the men of all times. In virtue of the divine right established in the death of Jesus Christ, in virtue of the justification which has come to them in His resurrection, they are no longer what they were but they are already what they are to be. They are no longer the enemies of God but His friends, His children. They are no longer turned away from Him, but away from their own being in the past, and turned to Him. They are no longer sinners, but righteous. They are no longer lost, but saved. And all this as He belongs to them and they to Him, He who was in His time to them in their time, and they in their time to Him in His time. All this as He is and does the same for them to-day as He was and did yesterday, the Lord of every time and its content. The resurrection of Jesus Christ affirms that which is actual in His death, the conversion of all men to God which has taken place in Him. For it is the pure and acceptable word which is spoken in every age, that all men are in Him the One, and that He the One is in them, He the One in the midst of them.

Not all hear this word. Not all are obedient to Him. But it comes to all, it is relevant to all, it is said for all and to all, it is said clearly and acceptably enough for all. And the situation of all is the situation which is altered by this word. It is not one which is first altered in and by them. They can and must recognise and acknowledge that they are altered in and by it, drawing out the consequences of this alteration, bowing before the divine verdict, repenting in face of the judgment of God which has come upon them and does come upon them. They can and must believe only the justification which has come and still comes to them, accepting that they are the children of God, accepting that which is old as old, and that which is new as new. What makes the community the community and Christians Christians is that the alteration of the human situation is manifest to them (and not in vain), that they cannot therefore evade or arrest the consequences of it, that they can make use of the freedom which is granted to them by it, that they cannot refrain from attesting it to others in the world as it has been attested to them. But this alteration is not made and being made by them, or in the consequences which they can and must deduce from it. This word does not become pure and acceptable only as they hear it with their ears and believe it in their hearts and confess it with their mouths. Rather they hear and believe and confess it as a word which, whether they hear and believe and confess it or not, is clear and acceptable in and for itself, as the word of the crucified and risen Lord, speaking in truth about reality, and significant and right for their own as for every age, for themselves and for all men. In Jesus Christ the alteration of the human situation did take place, and does take place to-day, the situation of Christians and of all men, the reconciliation of the world with God in Him who is the living Mediator between God and man in the power of His resurrection. What remains for them is high and appropriate and joyful and stringent enough—to welcome the divine verdict, to take it seriously with full responsibility, not to keep their knowledge of it to themselves, but by the witness of· their existence and proclamation to make known to the world which is still blind and deaf to this verdict the alteration which has in fact taken place by it. Their existence in the world depends upon the fact that this alone is their particular gift and task. They have not to assist or add to the being and work of their living Saviour who is the Lord of the world, let alone to replace it by their own work. The community is not a prolongation of His incarnation, His death and resurrection, the acts of God and their revelation. It has not to do these things. It has to witness to them. It is its consolation that it can do this. Its marching-orders are to do it.

But we must now turn our attention to another aspect or form of the relationship between the two events. According to the report and message of the New Testament they are separated by the gulf between the first and the third days. They stand to one another, therefore, in a relationship of temporal sequence. On the one side there is the time of the way of Jesus Christ moving towards and fulfilling itself in His death. On the other there is that of His new life limited in the first instance to the forty days. He is the living Saviour in these two times, the one after the other, on the two sides of His death, now humiliated, now exalted, the One who lives and rules eternally, in all ages, as the Lord of time. But the fact that the two times followed one another means that the forty days too, being a temporal event, have their beginning and end like the first form of the life of Jesus. What took place in these days was the divine acceptance, putting into effect, and revelation of what had taken place before, something complete in itself, sufficiently clear as a living word for the men of all times, sufficiently true as the divine verdict on the whole world, sufficiently high and deep to alter its situation, a sufficient missionary impulse for the disciples and basis of the community which receives and proclaims that verdict. The resurrection of Jesus Christ, His living presence, His *parousia* in the direct form of the events of Easter was, however, a happening in time with a definite beginning and end like other happenings. Its end was marked by the ascension as a sign of His exaltation to the right hand of God, to eternal life and rule; of His transition to a presence which is eternal and therefore embraces all times. But it did end with the ascension, just as it had begun with the sign of the empty tomb. With the end of the time of this particular event there began the time of another form of His *parousia*, His living present—no less complete and sufficient in itself, but quite different. There began a time in which He was no longer, or not yet again, directly revealed and visible and audible and perceptible (as He had been) either to the disciples, the community, or the world: directly, of course, in the divine verdict pronounced in that event and received by them, but not without the mediation of recollection, tradition and proclamation; the living Word of God, but not without the ministry of the attesting word of man which is proclaimed and heard. There began a time in which He was and continues to be and ever again will be directly present and revealed and active in the community by His Spirit, the power of His accomplished resurrection (although not, of course, without that mediating ministry); but in which the alteration of the human situation which has taken place in Him can be, and apart from the community is in fact, hidden from the world. There began a time in which the community, Christians, are aware, and will and must always be aware, that they themselves, the hearers of the Word, those who are justified by it, the children of God, believers, the witnesses to the Crucified and Risen, are still in the world, and are still like it in the sphere of human perception, so that to themselves and one another they are not visible or audible or perceptible as those who are dead and resurrected to new life, they cannot be known outwardly or inwardly as such, they are still hidden, they can recognize in themselves as in others an altered world only in relation to Jesus Christ, only according to the verdict of the Holy Spirit, only by faith and not by sight. There began a time in which the light of the One who in His own time was crucified and raised again did in fact give light to all that were in the house, but to them all—believers and unbelievers—only as the isolated light of the event of that time, of the resurrection. This light is shed abroad, of course, over the events of all times, and to that extent it is the indication of the comprehensive alteration of the human situation which has already taken place. It is not yet, however, the light of the altered world itself which we can expect on the ground of this alteration. It is not yet the revelation of the altered creation, of the children of God as they are transformed by what has taken place for them and to them in Jesus Christ. It is not yet the time of the resurrection of all the dead. Obviously, therefore, it is not yet the time of the fulfilment of the resurrection which has come to them in Jesus Christ. To that extent it is not yet the fulfilment of His *parousia* and presence and salvation in the world reconciled by Him.

This time, which begins with the end of the forty days and therefore with the resurrection of Jesus Christ, is the time of the community in the world, its grounding on the foundation of the apostles and prophets (Eph. 2[20]), its appearance and tribulation and activity in the world, its internal and external history right up to the present day. The development of the New Testament belongs to this time. And everywhere it has its characteristics. It looks back both to the life and death of Jesus and also to the happening of the forty days. It looks forward in the light of the consequences of these two related events, first to its own time and then to all the times that follow. It understands and attests the life and death of Jesus Christ in the light of His presence and revelation in the forty days. It understands and attests the Crucified, therefore, as the Resurrected, the One who for us took His place for ever at the right hand of the Father, who therefore lives and reigns in every age, who from there speaks and acts and works on earth, in human history, by His Spirit, in the power of His resurrection as it is disclosed and given to His disciples and enlightens and guides them. It understands and reveals Him, therefore, on the clear presupposition that He is no longer present and revealed to its own time as He once was in the forty days, but in a way which does not correspond to that type and form and appearance. We have to say at once, therefore, that the New Testament not only relates its own time and the ensuing time of the community in the world to the time of the new present of the Crucified, but also clearly differentiates them from it.

It does relate them to it to the extent that it sees them in the light of the time which began on Easter morning and ended with the ascension, to the extent, therefore, that it looks and holds to the fact that Jesus Christ risen and alive, as He appeared to and encountered His disciples, is the Lord of all times and that (even here and now, in its own time, the time of the community in the world) He lives and reigns and acts and is at work in the power of His resurrection, the force and authority of the verdict of the Holy Spirit.

The Early Church knew what it was doing when it remembered the accounts of His sayings and acts before His death, collecting them, finally putting them together in different ways—although always under the name and title of εὐαγγέλιον—and repeating and hearing and reading them, and all this with an understanding of what had not previously been understood, and not merely for the sake of writing and maintaining and repeating the history of it or occupying themselves with it as such. The much quoted verse in 2 Cor. 5^{16} is relevant here: " Though we have known Χριστὸς κατὰ σάρκα, yet now henceforth know we him no more." There is no question of appealing to His remembered form as it had necessarily appeared to His disciples before the verdict of the Holy Spirit was pronounced on His life and death, abstracted from the verdict of the Holy Spirit. In the editing and composition of the Evangelical narratives the interest and art and rules of the historian do not matter. What matters is His living existence in the community and therefore in the world. What matters is His history as it had indeed happened but as it is present and not past. What matters is His speaking and acting and suffering and dying to-day as well as yesterday. What matters is the " good news " of His history as it speaks and rings out *hic et nunc*. It is not a question of digging out and preserving Himself and His history in order to have them before us and study them. It is a matter of living with Him the living One, and therefore of participating in His history as the history of the salvation of the world and our own salvation, to hear Himself speak to the men of our own age in the *logia* which have been handed down, to see Him act among the men of our own day in the records of His miracles, in the story of His passion to stand to-day before the fact that in His death everything —the gracious judgment, the redemptive sacrifice for the sins of all men—is accomplished, the old has passed away, and all things have become new ; in the astonishing accounts of His resurrection on the third day to see here and now, with those who were the witnesses of His appearing, that He lives, He who there and then went that way, He who there and then was crucified and died for us. It is a matter of discovering and receiving as the life of all men and our own life, and of letting it take root and grow, that life of His which is the life of the Son of God in the place of all men and as the Mediator between all men and God. It is quite right that the voice and form of Jesus cannot in practice be distinguished with any finality in the Gospels from the community founded by Him and sharing His life. The historian may find this disconcerting and suspicious (or even provocatively interesting). It is further evidence of that submission to the divine verdict without which the Gospels could never have taken shape as Gospels.

In the New Testament this relating of the time of the community to the time of the living and dying of Jesus in the light of His presence and revelation in the forty days corresponds to a very definite view of the alteration of the human situation which took place in the first time and determines the second as a living event. In other words, from this standpoint the men of this second time are to address themselves not merely to the redemptive judgment, death and end which came to them with the death of their Representative Jesus Christ, not merely to the right established and asserted against them and for them in the happening of Golgotha, but to its validity and proclamation for them as it took place in the resurrection of this Representative, to the fulfilment of their own justification, to the beginning of their own new life in and with Jesus Christ. The saying about the καινὴ κτίσις (2 Cor. 5¹⁷, cf. Gal. 6¹⁵) which there is when any man is in Christ must surely be taken to mean that this man is a new creature already. " Reckon ye also yourselves to be dead indeed unto sin, but alive unto God through Jesus Christ our Lord " (Rom. 6¹¹). " Whether we live, we live unto the Lord " (Rom. 14⁸). " For to this end Christ both died, and rose, and revived, that he might be Lord both of the dead and the living " (Rom. 14⁹). " I live, yet not I, but Christ liveth in me " (Gal. 2²⁰). To Paul, to live is Christ (Phil. 1²¹). " For we are his workmanship, created (κτισθέντες) in Christ Jesus unto good works " (Eph. 2¹⁰). " He hath delivered us from the power of darkness, and hath translated us into the kingdom of his dear Son " (Col. 1¹³). Which means, " ye are risen with him " (συνηγέρθητε, Col. 2¹², cf. 3¹). God has made us who were dead alive (συνεζωοποίησεν) in Christ. He has raised us up (συνήγειρεν) with Him. Indeed, in and with Him He has already set us (συνεκάθισεν, Eph. 2⁶ᶠ·) in the heavenly world. We can, of course, say that these latter formulations are peculiar to Ephesians and Colossians, but we cannot deny that they are the necessary consequence or rather presupposition of the earlier formulations. How can there be ascribed to them a life from the dead here and now in their own time, which is the time after the forty days, if the meaning is not the same as in the case of their death after the death of Christ on Golgotha, that as their own death took place there, so in the resurrection of Jesus Christ their own raising from the dead has already been initiated ?—so that it can be said to them personally : " Ye have put on Christ " (Gal. 3²⁷) ; " Ye are washed, ye are sanctified, ye are justified in the name of the Lord Jesus and by the Spirit of our God " (1 Cor. 6¹¹) ; " Ye are all the children of God by faith in Christ Jesus " (Gal. 3²⁶) ; or : " The Spirit beareth witness . . . that we are the children of God " (Rom. 8¹⁶) ; we " are called " and are the children of God (1 Jn. 3¹). These are the indicatives which describe the human situation as altered by that first time present in the second.

But the imperatives, too, derive from the human situation as it is altered in this dimension : " Walk worthy of the gospel of Christ" (Phil. 1²⁷) ; " Awake, thou that sleepest, and arise from the dead " (Eph. 5¹⁴) ; " Like as Christ was raised up from the dead by the glory of the Father, even so we also should walk in newness of life " (Rom. 6⁴). As the living people they are, Christians should offer to God themselves and their members as " instruments " in the service of the justification which has come to them in and with Jesus Christ (Rom. 6¹³, ¹⁹). They are dead to the Law in the death of Christ in order to live to another, Him who has been raised from the dead, and to bring forth fruit unto God (Rom. 7⁴). " If we live in the Spirit, let us also walk in the Spirit " (Gal. 5²⁵). " If ye then be risen with Christ, seek those things which are above " (Col. 3¹). It is a matter of putting on the new man, which " after God is created in righteousness and true holiness " (Eph. 4²⁴). " Ye are all children of light, and the children of the day : we are not of the night, nor of darkness. Therefore let us not sleep, as do others, but let us watch and be sober. For they that sleep sleep in the night ; and they that be drunken are drunken in the night. But let us, who are of the day, be sober, putting on the breastplate of faith and love ; and for an helmet the hope of salvation. For God hath not appointed us to wrath, but to obtain salvation by our Lord Jesus Christ, who died for us, that, whether we wake or sleep, we should live together with him " (1 Thess. 5[5f.]). It is clear that these are not demands to give ourselves a new life and resurrection and glory by the fulfilment of a new law. Those who are dead in Christ (Col. 2[20]) and therefore liberated (Gal. 5[1]), are expressly warned against such dangerous and futile undertakings. It is equally clear that these are consequences which we have necessarily to draw from the alteration of our situation. If we come from this point and stand in this place, this is again the acknowledgment and affirmation which has become inevitable, the grateful praise of God for what He has done for us and to us. Walking worthy of the Gospel does not work the work of God. God Himself does that and only God, the God who calls Himself our Father and us His children in Jesus Christ. Nor does our walk guarantee the work of God. The Holy Spirit alone does that, dwelling in us and constraining us as such. But where the work of the Father who alone can do it is done, where it is guaranteed by the only One who can guarantee it, His Holy Spirit, it is inevitable that it should be honoured and attested by the walk of Christians. This is the intention and the demand of the imperatives addressed to them.

That is one side of the matter. But the other is equally and even more insistent, that the New Testament clearly differentiates its own time, the time of the community in the world, from the time of the new present of the Crucified and Risen, not merely looking back to His appearance and action to understand it again and again as a present event, yet looking forward to it, knowing and presupposing that He has come, but awaiting and expecting the coming of the Lord in His new Easter form, understanding Him in that way too as the One who is already present, who knocks at the door to-day and here.

The differentiation of the times does not, of course, affect as such the action and revelation of the Crucified as He was made eternal and therefore always present in His resurrection and for every age from the days of His resurrection. It does not, therefore, alter the fact of the relation of the time of the community in the world with that time, the reality of the life from the dead which is here and now an event in the community and therefore in the world in virtue of that time, the actuality of the alteration of the human situation which has taken place in the death of Jesus Christ in virtue of His resurrection from the dead. It does not in any way limit this or call it in question. In the New Testament there is no minimising of what it clearly says along these lines, of what it had to say in view of the actual death and resurrection of Jesus Christ from which it derived and to which it bore witness, of what it had to say in view of the fact that His death was absolutely present in the power of the verdict of the Holy Spirit spoken in the resurrection of the Crucified.

But the differentiation of the times does affect the manner of the making present of the Crucified and His living word and effective action, the form of the relation of His time with that of the community in the world which followed it, the form of its life out of and with the life of the Resurrected, the appearance of the alteration of the human situation as it took place there and then. The New Testament understands the being of Jesus Christ as the One who rose from the dead not only as the being of the One who was and is as such, but of the One who comes and is as such. Therefore it understands its own time, in the present of the One who was there and then, as the time of the expectation of, and hope in, the One who is also future as the One that He was and is.

The men of the New Testament, therefore, have not ceased to look forward to Him with the men of the Old. On the contrary, those to whom He has come, those who could know Him as the One who has come, who did not do so, but then did do so in truth, were the first to learn to read and understand the Old Testament as the book of those who looked forward to Him, the record of prophecy. They were the first to know that their Old Testament predecessors could and had to look forward to Him, and the reason why they could and had to do so. Knowing the event for which these others had looked, and as it had now taken place and was present, knowing the present of that event, they are the first to know what is meant by future and expectation and hope.

From the present of the Crucified in which they stand, trusting and obeying the divine verdict, they reach forward to a new and different and complete and definitive form of His presence. From the relation of His time with theirs they stretch out to a new form of this relation. From their life from and with the life of the Resurrected they stretch out to a new form of life with Him. From the alteration of the human situation which He has brought about and in which they stand, they stretch out to its definitive manifestation.

As they do this, they no longer see the two times together (that of Jesus Christ and their own), but they come to distinguish them. The time of Jesus Christ is marked off from their own as not merely present but future, the time which has still to come but is expected and hoped for. And their own time (in and with its retrospective unity with the time of Jesus Christ) becomes to them a time between the times. It is the time between the times of the crucified and risen Jesus Christ, between a first and present form of His presence and a form which is still to come but will come, between the present form of life with Him and a future form, between the present manifestation of the alteration of the human situation and a future manifestation.

Strangely enough the position of the men of the New Testament has on this so-called eschatological aspect an unmistakable similarity with the being of Jesus Christ Himself between His death and resurrection, with His being in the tomb, where the rendering of the obedience demanded of Him as the Son, in the fulfilment and suffering of the divine judgment, of the offering of the sacrifice which redeems the world, is already as completely behind Him as the grace of God the Father in His reawakening is before Him. The time of the community and the world after the first time of Jesus, and before the second time which has now come into view, has a similarity with the three days which in the New Testament record and testimony form a puzzling interval between the two great acts of God by and in Jesus Christ.

In this respect we have to note that Christians recognise and confess their position between the times. They are those who believe in the Jesus Christ crucified for them and hope in the Jesus Christ raised again for them. Paul describes them in fact as those who—in their baptism—are buried with Christ : συνετάφημεν αὐτῷ (Rom. 6⁴), συνταφέντες αὐτῷ (Col. 2¹²). And we have to ask very seriously what it means for the Pauline understanding of baptism, and the understanding of baptism generally, that Christians are called, not those who are dead or raised again with Christ in their baptism, but those who in it are buried with Him.

We must now try to give some account of the basis, the meaning, the *ratio*, of this differentiation of the times. How is it that the risen One is future, that we look, therefore, for a new and different form of His *parousia*, His living presence ? We must be careful not to formulate the answer in a way which would give to this final coming and consummation any other necessity than that of the free grace of God. The New Testament does not do this. It confesses the One who was and is as the One who comes, who will come at the end of this time and all times, at the last day. But it does not deduce this statement from any general insight or truth. The resurrection of Jesus Christ gives us the insight that He is the Lord of time. And from this we might argue that He who was and is cannot be without being the One who comes. But the well-known text in Revelation which describes Him in this threefold way is a threefold witness to Him as the Lord of time, not an analysis of the concept of time. As the One who lives eternally He does in fact demand this threefold witness. The verdict of God pronounced in His resurrection tells us that He not only was and is but also will be, not only at the end of time, but as Himself the end of time. He is not, therefore, just one future of men and the world behind and after which there might be others. He is the absolute and final future. The verdict of God forbids the men of the New Testament to be satisfied with Jesus Christ as the One who was, as the One who is in the time of the community in the world which follows, as the One who will continue to be in that time. It forbids them to " hope in Christ only in this life " (1 Cor. 15¹⁹), that is, to hope only for continuations of His present in the mode in which He now is the One He was. The verdict of God commands that they should look afresh to Himself beyond the whole future of their present being in and with Him, beyond the whole present manifestation of the alteration of the human situation as accomplished in and by Him, beyond all the deduction which they themselves can now draw from it. It commands that they should look afresh to Himself as the final future of the world and man, their own ultimate and definitive future. The verdict of God wills this from them. Jesus Christ Himself,

empowered by the Father and operative by His Holy Spirit, attests and
proves Himself to them not only as the First but also as the Last
(Rev. 1^{17}, 2^8), and therefore as the One who comes (Rev. $1^{4, 8}$). By
the free grace of God He is this Last, the One who comes. That
and that alone is the necessity of expectation, and therefore of the
differentiation of the times attested in the New Testament.

We have to emphasise this strongly because there is a temptation
to base and deduce the New Testament hope of the final presence of
Jesus Christ not from Himself but pragmatically from a state of things
in the time after the end of the forty days, the time of the community
in this world, a state which points forward to and demands a consummation. There is a temptation to deduce it from the imperfection
of the form of present of the Crucified in this our own time, from the
incompleteness of the form of its relation with the time of Jesus Christ,
from a deficiency in the present form of life by and with the life of
the Resurrected, from the insufficiency of the present manifestation
of the alteration of the human situation which has come about with
His death, in short, from a limitation of the presence and action and
revelation of the living Jesus Christ as we have it in this our time.

That in this our time of the community in the world there is this
limitation of His being with us and ours with Him cannot be denied.
We have already mentioned some of the aspects in which it may be
stated. There is the indispensability of an indirect and historical
connexion with Him in the service or as a garment of the true and
direct connexion which He Himself institutes and continues between
Himself and us from the right hand of the Father. Again, there is the
isolation of the community which confesses Him in faith and serves
Him in love in a world in which He appears to be and to remain a
stranger. Again, there is the hiddenness of the calling and sanctification and justification and divine sonship even of Christians. Again,
there is the focussing of the light of His resurrection on a sphere which,
apart from the forty days, seems afterwards as well as before to be
very like that of the dead bones of Ezekiel. All these things speak
plainly of the existence of this limitation. And we might go on to
ask : Where is the alteration of the human situation, the peace and
joy of man converted to God ? Where are the tears wiped away, and
no more death, the pain removed, the sorrow stilled, the hurt healed,
not to speak of the silencing of the groaning of non-human creation ?
Where is then the new heaven and the new earth, the old passed
away and all things become new ? In a word, where is the kingdom
of Jesus Christ as it has come on earth in virtue of His resurrection ?
Again, where is the right there established ? Where is life in the
power of the justification there accomplished ? At bottom, and in the
last resort, it may not be wise to ask these questions in this time of
ours. But we certainly *can* ask them in this time of ours. And who
can dispute that the presence and action and revelation of the living

Lord in this our time, the time of the community in the world, have in fact this limitation ?

And now the temptation arises to find the basis for His eternal future and the Christian hope directed towards it simply in these statements and questions, to regard it as the answer which we necessarily have to give to these questions, the necessary making good of these very obvious deficiencies, the necessary removing of this undeniable limitation. But it cannot be grounded in this way, and it ought not to be regarded in this way.

The New Testament was well enough aware of the limitation of its own time and all that is in it. There are no illusions about the presence or actuality of this limitation. It does not describe the world or the community or even the existence of individual Christians in optimistic terms, but very soberly, with an awareness of the presence of this limitation, and therefore with an incisiveness of judgment on the actual state of affairs which has always been to the detriment of an optimistic outlook, and which has prevented quite a number from thinking that they can accept the good news which it nevertheless proclaims.

But it was definitely not with the presence of this limitation that the men of the New Testament began when they hoped for the coming of the Lord and prayed : " Even so, come, Lord Jesus." In the last resort they did not simply cry to heaven out of the depth of human imperfection, corruption and need, out of the depth of the visible and palpable contradiction of the world, out of the depth of the sorrow of creation also crying to heaven. They did not attempt a rash assault on heaven : " O Saviour, rend the heavens in twain, And from the heavens descend again." They did not picture and in some sense posit a God who would reveal Himself and help them, or Jesus Christ as such, as some kind of *Deus ex machina*, eagerly and with expectation hoping for Him and looking to Him. They certainly expected the removal of that limitation at His return. But they did not postulate and prove His return because they wanted that limitation removed, because their confinement by it seemed intolerable. They lived with a burning longing for the sight denied them in this time, for the liberation and redemption which are still to come, for an immediacy of contact with the Lord without the help or the distraction of mediation, for the breaking down of the wall of partition between the Christian community and a world which is a-Christian or non-Christian or anti-Christian, for the manifestation of the Judge, for the revelation of their own divine sonship, for the general resurrection of the dead. But they had this burning longing because they looked for Jesus Christ Himself. And they looked for Him because He Himself in His present as the Crucified and Resurrected as He encountered them in this time showed Himself to them as the One He once was, as the One who was with them and indeed in them, but also as the One who stood before them as eternally future. They looked for Him because as they came from Him, as He went with them and they had to go with Him, they were necessarily aware that He comes to us and we must go forward to Him. He " encloses us before and behind " (Ps 139⁵), and therefore altogether and in eternity. That we are in Him is true unreservedly and without any loophole for escape.

They knew only too well their human and Christian poverty and need, as we see from the apostle Paul (Rom. 7). But it was not this which compelled them to look in this dimension, to look forward to a final and eternal future quite different from any temporal future. It was the fulness of Jesus Christ Himself, " the breadth and the length and the height and the depth " (Eph. 3¹⁸), the fulness of the love and power of God active in Him and speaking through Him, the fulness of the revelation and knowledge given to them in His present in spite of and in that limitation, which invited and indeed summoned them to this forward looking. It was not, therefore, that Jesus Christ was too small for them within this limitation, that the salvation and life given them in Him were too little and mean and deficient. Even within this limitation they knew and believed and loved Him as the One who lives eternally, and they found that they themselves, and indirectly the whole world which God loved in Him, were granted eternal life and true and heavenly benefits. Was there not present in Him everything that was still lacking even to the new heaven and the new earth ? The triumph-songs into which Paul burst at the end of 1 Cor. 15 and Rom. 8, the majestic assurances in the introduction to Ephesians, the well-known words in John about the eternal life which those who believe already have, all refer to that being of man accepted by Christians now, on this side of the coming of Jesus Christ envisaged in the New Testament, on this side of all that is hoped from and with that coming. And when we read passages like this we might well ask where is the deficiency or limitation—what is still lacking—in His present action and revelation.

Indeed, His final coming is not something which is still lacking in His present action and revelation, but positively, the finality proper to it which opens up to Christians as it takes place in the mode of their present time. The eschatological perspective in which Christians see the Crucified and Resurrected and the alteration of their own situation in Him is not the minus-sign of an anxious " Not yet," which has to be removed, but the plus-sign of an " Already," in virtue of which the living Christ becomes greater to them and altogether great, in virtue of which they here and now recognise in Him who is the first word the final word, in Him who is the subject and object of the basic act of God the subject and object of the consummating act of God which reveals that basis, so that believing in Him and loving Him they can also hope in Him ; in Him—and because in Him in the removal of that limitation in which He is now present and revealed and within which they here and now find themselves with Him ; in Him, and because in Him the setting aside of that fatal " still " which also characterises their Here and Now. That in this their time, the time of the community in the world, they can only look forward to the removal of the barrier, does not mean that their present being in and with Him is in any way minimised, but that it is augmented, that it is immeasurably deepened and enriched in its extent. For all that it is provisional, this time between is made for them a time of joy, in which every moment and every hour means not simply the continuation of that which has been received, not simply an advance in the consequences which can be drawn from it, but also the approach of the making absolute of that which has been received, of its new and definitive form : not in virtue of their human faithfulness and effort, but in virtue of the new and conclusive act of the Giver Himself proclaimed to them (in and with what they have received), in virtue of His grace and the fact that He is alive for evermore. Between the New Testament relating of the times, to which we referred earlier, and the differentiating, between the fact that the men of the New Testament come from the Crucified and Resurrected and the fact that they move towards Him, there is therefore no contradiction. How could they come from Him if they did not move towards Him ? How could He Himself have come, how could He have been truly delivered up for our offences and raised again for our justification, if He were not also the One who comes as the eternal future of man and the world ? Conversely, how could He come as such if He had not already come, if He had not done all that had to be done for the reconciliation of the world with God, for its conversion to Him, if He had not done all that was necessary in the way of additional revelation for its consummation ?

It is, therefore, clear that between that view of the human situation which comes from a relating and that which comes from a differentiating of the times there cannot be more than a formal antithesis. From both standpoints it is the situation which has been radically and irrevocably altered in the crucifixion of Jesus Christ. It is only the manifestation of the alteration that is different in the time which moves from the sign of the ascension to its end. It is only a provisional manifestation which will yield to the final in the time of that coming and revelation of the Resurrected which we still await. The one crucified and risen Jesus Christ is the object of New Testament faith and the content of New Testament hope. There can, therefore, be no question of understanding the alteration as more real and complete in its final form and less real and complete in its provisional. As we are told in 2 Cor. 3[18], in His image we are " changed from glory to glory " (" from one distinctness to another " : Luther). Yet it is also the case that the great alteration in the provisional form in which we know it in this interim is directed and looks forward to its final manifestation. It is directed and looks forward to it. We know it now in its first and earthly and temporal manifestation, not in its second and heavenly and eternal. In the New Testament as such there can be no disputing that the alteration of the human situation has taken place, just as there can be no disputing that the death and resurrection of Jesus Christ have taken place. In the power of the divine verdict they are a present event in this time between. But with a frequency which borders on regularity a distinction is made—corresponding to that between the first and the second times of Jesus Christ Himself—between the form and manifestation of the alteration which is known to us and the future and definitive manifestation which is not yet known to us but has still to come.

For reasons which we can well understand this distinction is very prominent in the New Testament. We cannot do more than indicate it by recalling the various passages. In formal contradistinction to the statements concerning our resurrection as it has already taken place in Jesus Christ, we know " that he which raised up the Lord Jesus shall raise up us also with Jesus " (2 Cor. 4¹⁴, cf. 1 Cor. 6¹⁴). " As in Adam all died, even so in Christ shall all be made alive " (1 Cor. 15²²). " If we be dead with Christ, we believe that we shall also live with him " (Rom. 6⁸). " He that raised up Christ from the dead shall also quicken your mortal bodies by his Spirit that dwelleth in you " (Rom. 8¹¹). " He that soweth to the Spirit shall of the spirit reap life everlasting " (Gal. 6⁸). Our Lord Jesus Christ died for us, that " we should live with him " (1 Thess. 5¹⁰). " We always bear about in our body the dying of the Lord Jesus, that the life also of Jesus might be manifest in our body. For we which live are always delivered unto death for Jesus' sake, that the life also of Jesus might be made manifest in our mortal flesh " (2 Cor. 4¹⁰ᶠ·). To the same category there belongs perhaps the saying in 2 Cor. 1¹⁰ about the God " who delivered us from so great a death, and doth deliver : in whom we trust that he will yet deliver us."· If these are all statements which also describe the event which has already taken place and the standing of Christians as determined by it, and if for the most part they also bring out the ethical imperative, it is unmistakable that in the second instance they have to be understood temporally, speaking of something future which is the goal and purpose of that which has already happened and is now happening. To look in this dimension too belongs inseparably to the glory of the present standing of man as grounded in the death and resurrection of Jesus Christ. It is impossible to hope in Christ only in this life (1 Cor. 15¹⁹). The doctrine of a certain Hymenæus and Philetus that the resurrection (i.e., the general resurrection of the dead) is already past (ἤδη γεγονέναι)—something similar seems to have been taught by those who denied the resurrection in 1 Cor. 15—is for that reason sharply rejected in 2 Tim. 2¹⁸ as a deviation from the truth. Being made conformable (συμμορφιζόμενος) to the death of Christ, that event being already behind him, or present in the power of His resurrection, Paul is only pressing on to his resurrection from the dead : " Not as though I had already attained, either were already perfect : but I follow after, if that I may apprehend that for which I am apprehended of Christ Jesus . . . forgetting those things which are behind, I reach forth unto those things which are before, and press toward the mark for the prize of the high calling of God in Christ Jesus" (Phil. 3¹⁰ᶠ·). And in Col. 3³ᶠ·, " Ye are dead, and your life is hid with Christ in God (κέκρυπται : we can hardly help thinking here of an *analogatum* of the great *analogans* of the being of Christ in the tomb, on which there is in fact a play some verses later). When Christ, who is our life, shall appear, then shall ye also appear with him in glory." " We through the Spirit wait for the (fulfilment of the) hope of righteousness by faith "

(Gal. 5⁵). " We wait for the adoption " (υἱοθεσία) in so far as this is " the re-demption of our body " (Rom. 8²³). " Now are we the sons of God, and it doth not yet appear what we shall be : but we know that, when he shall appear, we shall be like him, for we shall see him as he is " (1 Jn. 3²). " Blessed be the God and Father of our Lord Jesus Christ, which according to his abundant mercy hath begotten us again unto a lively hope by the resurrection of Jesus Christ from the dead "—the hope of " an inheritance incorruptible, and undefiled, and that fadeth not away, reserved in heaven for you, who are kept by the power of God through faith unto salvation ready to be revealed in the last time " (1 Pet. 1³ᶠ·). If by the resurrection of Jesus Christ from the dead we have been born again to a life which we now live in hope, then already we are the children of God, already *per definitionem* we have been rightly instituted as heirs (Gal. 4⁷, Rom. 8¹⁷)—joint-heirs with Christ, those who await that inheritance, those who have the certain promise of it (Gal. 3²⁹, Heb. 9¹⁵). The kingdom of God in its final and definitive form is the inheritance promised to His children (Gal. 5²¹). Already, in Jesus Christ, as brothers of the Son of God, we have a legal right to this inheritance. But, of course, we have not yet entered into it. It has not yet been divided and handed over. We still wait and hope for it in this time between. This will be the revelation of our hidden sonship. Already in what we are and have here and now, in the being and work of the Spirit in us, we have an instalment (ἀρραβών, 2 Cor. 1²², 5⁵ ; Eph. 1¹⁴) of this future possession, or a first-fruits, or a gift from the income (ἀπαρχή, Rom. 8²³) on the capital of this future inheritance as it is laid up for us and appointed and assured to us as the brothers of Jesus Christ and the children of God. We possess it in a way which corresponds to the manner of this possession, eternal life. We possess it as the gift of God's grace of which we ourselves cannot dispose (Rom. 8²³). We do possess it as such. Our hands are not altogether empty. But we only have an instalment, a first-fruits, not the capital, not the kingdom of God which is promised. Even in this possession we cannot cease to pray : " Thy kingdom come."

It is all provisional : not our new creation and regeneration as accomplished in the cross and resurrection of Jesus Christ, but its present manifestation ; not our justification, but its present form ; not the being of Jesus Christ in us and our being in Him, but the form in which we are now with Him, raised and quick-ened and resurrected with Him. This is the reference of the New Testament differentiation of the times and the corresponding depiction of the situation. According to 2 Cor. 5¹ᶠ· we now live in a tent which has to be dissolved, knowing that " we have a building of God, an house not made with hands, eternal in the heavens." Therefore we sigh and groan, not to be unclothed and found naked, but to be clothed upon with this eternal οἰκητήριον, or negatively, for mortality to be swallowed up by life, according to 1 Cor. 15⁵⁴, and death in victory. Accord-ing to 1 Cor. 15⁴²ᶠ·, it will be sown in corruption, raised in incorruption, sown in dishonour, raised in glory, sown in weakness, raised in power, sown a natural body and raised a spiritual body. According to 1 Cor. 15⁵³, this " corruptible must put on incorruption, and this mortal must put on immortality." Even in the sowing, the passing, the dying and the burying of our temporal life we are a new creation, born again, the children of God, justified, partakers of the Holy Spirit. But this whole reality of our being in and with Christ is not visible in this sowing. What is visible is the temporal, the sowing as such, but the eternal which is to be raised up is invisible (2 Cor. 4¹⁸). What is visible is the destruc-tion of the outward man which perishes day by day, but the renewal of the inward man which forbids us to be discouraged is invisible (2 Cor. 4¹⁶). What is visible is the present θλίψις which causes us to sigh, but that this will quickly pass and is light, that " it worketh for us a far more exceeding and eternal weight of glory " (2 Cor. 4¹⁷), that the sufferings of this present time are not worthy to be compared with the glory which shall be revealed in us " (Rom. 8¹⁸), that the earnest expectation of the rest of creation does not wait in vain for the revelation of us the children of God (Rom. 8¹⁹ᶠ·), that love will not perish when prophecy and tongues and knowledge are done away with every else that is transitory (1 Cor. 13⁸ᶠ·) : all this is invisible. It is something which can be seen when we look not at that which is seen but at that which is not seen (2 Cor. 4¹⁷). σκοπεῖν τὰ μὴ βλεπόμενα : according to the explanation in Rom. 8²⁴ᶠ·, which almost amounts to a definition, it is the nature of hope to wait patiently (δι' ὑπομονῆς ἀπεκδέχεσθαι) for the coming, at that day, of the revelation of this invisible.

Hence the antithesis in 1 Cor. 13¹² : " For now we see through a glass darkly ; but then face to face : now I know in part ; but then shall I know even as also I am known." And the even simpler antithesis in 2 Cor. 5⁷ : " We walk διὰ πίστεως and not διὰ εἴδους. The two manifestations or forms of the alteration of the human situation, which has taken place in Jesus Christ and is now in train, differ comprehensively in this way : in the one it is invisible, or only indirectly visible, in the other it is visible in the true and direct sense ; in the one it is hidden, in the other it is revealed. The faith of the community in the world is, therefore, essentially bound up with hope, with the confidence that the reality which is now believed will be seen. ἐσώθημεν is the in itself complete and unassailable statement of New Testament faith as far as concerns the human situation, but τῇ ἐλπίδι ἐσώθημεν (Rom. 8²⁴), in a state of hope in a revelation of this redemption which has still to come—for hope which is seen is not hope—which is still awaited with the new and definitive coming of the crucified and risen Jesus Christ.

Perhaps the strongest New Testament account of this New Testament faith, which is not only bound up with hope but ultimately identical with it, is the eleventh chapter of the Epistle to the Hebrews. It is not for nothing that this is the New Testament passage in which the human situation *post Christum natum* is most strongly related to the Advent situation of the men of the Old Testament (or *vice versa*). It begins with that statement which has the force of a definition : " Faith is an assurance of things hoped for, a conviction of things not seen (ἐλπιζομένων ὑπόστασις ἔλεγχος οὐ βλεπομένων—it may be asked seriously whether the Vulgate for all its obscurity : *sperandarum substantia rerum, argumentum non apparentium*, does not come closer to what is meant than the customary modern translation in German, French and English). The statement is then made in v. 2 that in the faith which they had in God as defined in this way the elders (πρεσβύτεροι) obtained confirmatory witness. This is illustrated with variations by the examples of Abel, Enoch, Noah, Abraham, Isaac, Jacob, Moses, and the harlot Rahab, with references to the Judges Gideon, Barak, Samson and Jephtha, to David and Samuel, and to the prophets. Yet in their day they were never granted to see that which was promised (v. 39), the πράγματα ἐλπιζόμενα, the οὐ βλεπόμενα. They will not therefore (v. 40) be made perfect without us, but with us, for whom God has laid up a new and better promise. And in the continuation in Heb. 12¹ᶠ· this is shown to mean that formally we have the same faith as this " cloud of witnesses." On a better presupposition we, too, are in Advent. We look forward in hope. We are on the way to the fulfilment, τελείωσις. In v. 8 it is said of Abraham that " by faith, when he was called to go out into a place which he should after receive for an inheritance, he obeyed ; and he went out, not knowing whither he went " ; and again, that dwelling in tents— we are irresistibly reminded of 2 Cor. 5¹ᶠ·—" he looked for a city which hath foundations, whose builder and maker is God." Similarly it is said of Moses in v. 27 : " By faith, he endured, as seeing him who is invisible." And of all those so far mentioned it is said in vv. 13–16 : " These all died in faith, not having received the promises, but having seen them afar off, and were persuaded of them and embraced them, and confessed that they were strangers and pilgrims on earth. For they that say such things declare plainly that they seek a country. And truly, if they had been mindful of that country from whence they came out, they might have had opportunity to have returned. But now they desire a better country, that is, an heavenly : wherefore God is not ashamed to be called their God : for he hath prepared for them a city."

It is relevant to recall at this point what Calvin said concerning the relationship of *fides* and *spes* at the end of the great chapter *Inst.* III, 2 and with reference to Heb. 11. Like the other Reformers, he was not always at his best when dealing with eschatology. But this exposition can claim to be a genuine interpretation of the twofold view of things that we find in the New Testament. Preferring the Vulgate rendering, Calvin paraphrases (*ad loc.* 41) the definition of Heb. 11¹ in this way : that the *substantia*, the object and content of the promise, is the true basis of faith, the *fulcrum, cui pia mens innititur et incumbit.* On this basis faith, as a grasping of the content and object of the promise, is a *certa quaedam et secura possessio eorum quae nobis a Deo promissa sunt.* But we must be clear that until the last day, when (according to Dan. 7¹⁰) the books will be opened, this that is promised us by God is too high to be apprehended by our reason or seen with our eyes or grasped by our hands. We have to remember that we cannot possess it except as we go beyond all the capacities of our own spirit, looking beyond everything that is in the world, in a *superar* (transcending) of ourselves. To help us to do this Heb. 11¹ adds that in this *securitas possidendi* we have to do with things that stand in hope and are therefore invisible. The expression ἔλεγχος οὐ βλεπομένων (which Calvin renders *index non apparentium*) gives us the unavoidable paradox that faith is the *evidentia non apparentium rerum*, the *visio eorum, quae non videntur*, the *perspicuitas obscurarum*, the *praesentia absentium*, the *demonstratio occultarum*, in short, the seeing and apprehending of that mystery of God, which in itself cannot be seen or apprehended, by the Word of God which speaks for itself and is in itself certain. Where there is a living faith in the Word of God, Calvin continues (*ad loc.* 42), it cannot be otherwise than that that faith should have hope as its inseparable companion, or rather, that it should beget and create it. If we have no hope, we can be sure that we have no faith. Those who believe, those who apprehend the truth of God with the certainty which corresponds to it, which is demanded and imparted by it, expect that God will fulfil the promises which He has spoken in truth. At bottom hope is simply the expectation of what faith believes as that which God has truly promised. *Ita fides Deum veracem credit : spes expectat, ut in temporis occasione veritatem suam exhibeat ; fides credit, nobis esse patrem : spes expectat, ut se talem erga nos semper gerat ; fides datam nobis vitam aeternam credit : spes expectat, ut aliquando reveletur ; fides fundamentum est, cui spes incumbit : spes fidem alit ac sustinet.* Waiting quietly for the Lord, hope restrains faith, preventing it from rushing forward in too great a hurry. It confirms it so that it does not waver in its trust in God's promises or begin to doubt. It revives it so that it does not grow weary. It keeps it fixed on its final goal so that it does not give up half-way or when it is in captivity. It continually renews and re-establishes it, thus seeing to it that it continually rises up in more vital forms and perseveres to the end.

We have now made three statements with regard to the resurrection of the crucified Lord Jesus Christ. The first was that it has to be understood wholly and exclusively as an act of God. The second was that in relation to the crucifixion it is a new and independent act of God in which the former is acknowledged and proclaimed as the act of obedience of the Son of God which has taken place for the redemption and salvation of all men. The third was the decisive one which we have just considered and to which we had to give the greatest attention, that the resurrection of Jesus Christ is connected with His death in two ways : in the first *parousia* of the risen Crucified which began on Easter Day, and in virtue of which He is the same then and now, yesterday and to-day, the One who lives, who has come, who is present ; and in His final *parousia*, in which (as the risen Crucified who lives and is present then and now, yesterday and to-day) He is the One who will be revealed and come at the end and as the end of all time and history. Here in particular there is disclosed the possibility and necessity of understanding the death of Jesus Christ, not as a conclusion, but as a beginning, and therefore of considering the existence of man in the light of the decisive word of Christology, of turning to the problem of the sin and justification of man, the problem of the community and the faith of the community. This possibility is disclosed, this necessity created, by the resurrection of Jesus Christ, or more exactly, by the being of the crucified Jesus Christ raised from the dead in His twofold form as the One who has come and is present and the One who is present and has still to come, by the verdict of the Father which has been passed and which is in force in this being of the Resurrected. The interval between the first and the final *parousia* of Jesus Christ is that of the existence of man, and therefore of the secondary problems of the doctrine of reconciliation. But before we come to this conclusion and therefore to the answer to the question raised in this third part of the section, we must make two shorter and concluding statements in relation to the resurrection of Jesus Christ itself. On the resurrection of Jesus Christ there depends the permission and command to proceed from Him, from His person and from the work which He completed in His death. Does it give us this permission, this command ? Is it, as we said at the outset, the other side of the end which came upon man and the world in His death ? Can we, must we think forward past this happening, this end, because by it—revealed and demonstrated in the being of Jesus Christ as the Resurrected—man and the world are again disclosed, or rather disclosed for the first time in their true reality ? What we have said in our first three statements about the resurrection of Jesus Christ still needs formal but important amplification in two ways.

4. The resurrection of Jesus Christ from the dead, with which His first *parousia* begins to be completed in the second, has in fact happened. It has happened in the same sense as His crucifixion and His death, in the human sphere and human time, as an actual event within the world with an objective content. The same will be true of His return to the extent that as the last moment of time and history it will still belong to time and history. But we need not deal with this question here, because we are not looking backward from His return but forward from His resurrection. To do this as the New Testament does, it is possible and necessary only because it happened in time, as a particular history in history generally, with a concrete factuality. In the course of this particular history Jesus Christ appears to His

disciples, revealing Himself to them as the One who has risen again from the dead, who is no longer under the threat of death, but under God (Rom. 6[10]), and therefore as the One who lives to-day as yesterday. That He appeared to them, with all that this implies, that this history took place, is the content of the apostolic *kerygma*, the theme of the faith of the community which it awakened (1 Cor. 15[14]). The *kerygma* tells us, and faith lives by the fact, that God has ratified and proclaimed that which took place for us, for redemption, for our salvation, for the alteration of the whole human situation, as it will finally be directly and everywhere revealed. That this history has happened crowns and reveals the obedience rendered by the Son, and the grace and mercy of the Father shown with Him and in Him to all men. That it has happened is our justification as it follows the divine and human right established and maintained there. It is itself the verdict of God radically altering the human situation. It is the indication and the actual initiation of the direct and definitive revelation of this justification and alteration as it will be consummated in the second coming of Jesus Christ. In the light of it the community understands itself and its time in the world, and looks forward to its end and goal in the second coming of Jesus Christ. Because the resurrection has taken place just as surely as the crucifixion, the cross of Jesus Christ is to us light and not darkness, and it does not have to be changed from a " bare cross " into something better by the fact that we take up our cross.

We must not miss the differences between the two events. They differ in substance as God's right and God's justification, as end and new beginning, as work and revelation. They also differ as the act of the obedient Son and the act of the gracious Father. They also differ formally in the way in which they take place in the human sphere and human time, and therefore in the way in which they have to be understood as history.

We cannot read the Gospels without getting the strong impression that as we pass from the story of the passion to the story of Easter we are led into a historical sphere of a different kind. It is striking that, as at the beginning of the evangelical narratives, mention is made of the appearance and words of angels. Again there is a full account of how Jesus suffered and was crucified and died, but there is no real account of His resurrection. It is simply indicated by a reference to the sign of the empty tomb. Then it is quietly presupposed in the form of attestations of appearances of the Resurrected. This is all the more striking because the Gospels did fully narrate and describe other resurrections, that of Jairus' daughter (Mt. 9[18-25]), that of the young man at Nain (Lk. 7[11-16]), and that of Lazarus (Jn. 11)—the latter in a direct and almost plastic way. But here it is not possible to speak of someone superior to Jesus Christ who took Him by the hand and by his word called Him to life from the dead. Here we can think only of the act of God which cannot be described and therefore cannot be narrated, and then of the actual fact that Jesus Himself stood in the midst (Lk. 24[36]). Whether we take the accounts of the resurrection appearances in detail or put them together, they do not give us a concrete and coherent picture.

a history of the forty days. Rather we are confronted by obscurities and irre-
concilable contradictions, so that we are surprised that in the formation of the
canon no one seems to have taken offence at them or tried to assimilate the
various accounts of this happening which is so basically important for the New
Testament message.   There is the further difficulty that Paul not only presupposes and gives in 1 Cor. 15[4-7] another account of what happened, which is
different again from the Gospels, but that in 1 Cor. 15[8] (cf. Gal. 1[16]) he connects
the appearance to himself (obviously the Damascus experience as presented
several times in Acts) with the events of those days, although it took place long
after the forty days, and the *schema* of the forty days is thus strangely broken.
From this side, too, there is the final point that the reported appearances according to all the New Testament accounts came only to those who by them were
quickened to faith in the crucified Jesus Christ.   The appearances cannot, in
fact, be separated from the formation and development of the community (or
of the original form of the community as the narrower and wider circle of the
apostles).   It was in them that this formation and development took place.
None of them is represented as having occurred outside this context.

It is beyond question that the New Testament itself did not know
how to conceal, and obviously did not wish to conceal, the peculiar
character of this history, which bursts through all general ideas of
history as it takes place and as it may be said to take place in space
and time.   There is no proof, and there obviously cannot and ought
not to be any proof, for the fact that this history did take place (proof,
that is, according to the terminology of modern historical scholarship).

Even 1 Cor. 15[4-8] cannot be claimed as an attempt at such a proof, and
therefore as an attempt at an external objective assurance that the history did,
in fact, take place.   For the witnesses to whom Paul appeals with such solemnity
are not the outside impartial witnesses which such an attempt would demand.
They are the tradition which underlies the community, which calls for a decision
of faith, not for the acceptance of a well-attested historical report.   They are
those who have themselves made this decision of faith, Cephas, the Twelve,
five hundred brethren, James, then all the apostles, then finally, and in the
same breath, Paul himself.   In these well-known verses there is an appeal to
faith, not on the basis of Paul's knowledge, but in recollection of the faith which
constitutes the community.

No such proof is adduced or even intended in the New Testament.
Therefore we ought not to try to deduce such a proof from it.   If in
modern scholarship " historical ground " means the outline of an
event as it can be seen in its " How " independently of the standpoint
of the onlooker, as it can be presented in this way, as it can be proved
in itself and in its general and more specific context and in relation
to the analogies of other events, as it can be established as having
certainly taken place, then the New Testament itself does not enable
us to state that we are on " historical ground " in relation to the event
here recorded.   There is no reason to deplore this.   After all that we
have seen of the nature and character and function of the resurrection
of Jesus Christ as the basis, and in the context, of the New Testament
message, it is inevitable that this should not be the place for the
" historicist " concept of history.   There is also no reason to protest

if in common with the creation story and many others, indeed the decisive elements in biblical history, the history of the resurrection has to be regarded and described—in the thought-forms and terminology of modern scholarship—as " saga " or " legend." The death of Jesus Christ can certainly be thought of as history in the modern sense, but not the resurrection.

On the other hand, we should be guilty of a fundamental misunderstanding of the whole New Testament message if, because the history of the resurrection is not history in this sense, we tried to interpret it as though it had never happened at all, or not happened in time and space in the same way as the death of Jesus Christ, or finally had happened only in faith or in the form of the formation and development of faith. Even the use of the terms " saga " and " legend " does not force us to interpret it in this way. If we want to understand what the New Testament says, we must not allow ourselves to be forced into it by the use of these terms—perhaps through confusing them with the term " myth " which does not apply in this context. Even accounts which by the standards of modern scholarship have to be accounted saga or legend and not history—because their content cannot be grasped historically—may still speak of a happening which, though it cannot be grasped historically, is still actual and objective in time and space. When we have to do with the kind of event presented in such accounts, the event which has actually happened although it cannot be grasped historically, it would be better to speak of a " pre-historical " happening. But whatever terms we select to describe the New Testament records of the resurrection and their content, it is quite certain that we do not interpret them, i.e., we do not let them say what they are trying to say, if we explain away the history which they recount, a history which did take place in time and space, and that not merely in the development of a conception of the disciples, but in the objective event which underlay the development.

The problem narrows itself down to this final point. It is certainly a unique thing which the New Testament records in so singular a manner at this decisive point in its message. But that it has necessarily to do with an event is something which cannot be disputed on any exegesis which is in any way sound or permissible. And we can widen the circumference of agreement which can be presupposed : the New Testament is speaking of an event in time and space. It must not be overlooked that in this event we have to do on the one hand with the *telos*, the culminating point of the previously recorded concrete history of the life and suffering and death of Jesus Christ which attained its end with His resurrection, and on the other hand with the beginning of the equally concrete history of faith in Him, of the existence of the community which receives and proclaims His Word, Himself as the living Word of God. Since the presupposition and the consequence of the Easter message of the New Testament are of this nature, it would be senseless to deny that this message (between the two) does at least treat of an event in time and space. It would be senseless to suppose that it is really trying to speak of the non-spatial and timeless being of certain general truths, orders and relationships, clothing what it really wanted to say in the poetical form of a narrative.

If the latter is the case, what is really intended and expressed in these texts is a veiled cosmology, anthropology, theology or mysticism—a partial consideration of the system of that which is always and everywhere, but which has never taken place as such and never can or will take place. The veil, the poetic form, of the accounts is then this consideration in the form of the report of something that has happened in time and space, a report given with a twitching of the eyelids *ad usum* of the esoterics. In these Easter narratives we are dealing with a myth only if we ascribe to their authors, i.e., the original community which formed and handed down the accounts, the intention to speak at this point— and because at this decisive point at many other points as well—of a non-spatial and timeless being (the being of God or the world or man or the religious man) instead of an event which took place in time and space. We are dealing with a myth only if we are challenged by the accounts to separate their true content from their poetic form as narratives, bringing out that content by an idealised, symbolical and allegorical interpretation of the form. Among Christian gnostics and mystics both ancient and modern there have never been lacking exegetes who have been bold to see here the true intention of the New Testament passages and the hermeneutical key to their exposition.

A. E. Biedermann seems to come near to this view of the relationship of content and form in these passages when in his *Dogmatik* (1869) he gives classical form to the distinction between the Christian as the supreme religious " principle " on the one hand, and on the other the personality of Jesus as presented in the Bible and ecclesiastical doctrine and mythologically identified with this principle. He sums up his discussion of the resurrection of Jesus Christ in the words that " when we get back to the real factuality of the story, it was an actualisation in the symbolical form of world history of that truth which is the heart of the dogma, that to the absolute spirit even the natural finitude of the human spirit necessarily serves as a medium for historical revelation and self-demonstration " (§ 828). But he only appears to be of this view, for he can still speak of the factuality of a story, of the actualisation of that truth in the symbolical form of world history. He can still describe the resurrection as " a real event in the history of Jesus " which, as such, formed " the foundation of apostolic preaching." The heart of the dogma of the resurrection of Christ is still the impressing into service of the finite spirit of man to reveal the absolute. As he sees it, dogma and history come together in " one point " in the " historical fact " of the resurrection of Christ. The dogma can be deduced from the history because in the latter there has taken place that revelation of the absolute spirit in the finite and human as its " positive medium." " The point of departure of the dogma is an historical event " (§ 588).

We therefore presuppose agreement that a sound exegesis cannot idealise, symbolise or allegorise, but has to reckon with the fact that the New Testament was here speaking of an event which really happened, as it did when it spoke earlier of the life and death of Jesus Christ which preceded it and later of the formation of the community which followed it. And in relation to modern discussion we can extend the scope of this agreement. Agreement also extends to the fact that we can do justice to the Easter narratives of the New Testament only if we accept their presupposition that in the story which they recount we have to do with an " act of God," the act of God in which it was revealed to the disciples that the happening of the cross was the redemptive happening promised to them, on which therefore the community and its message were founded.

But now we come to our first real decision. In what did this story consist ? What was it that God did in this happening ?

We might start by saying that the result of it was the awakening and establishing of the faith of the disciples in the living presence and action of Jesus Christ, and by the creation of this Easter faith the laying of the foundation of the community, " the foundation of the apostolic message."

But this statement needs closer definition. According to the New Testament account, it was not in the events of the forty days directly and as such that there took place the beginning of the existence of the community and the going out of the apostles to the people of Jerusalem, let alone to the nations. In the events of the forty days the disciples were ordained and commissioned for this task. But in the strict sense these events are only the presupposition of this happening which began with the story of Pentecost. It is only in and with the outpouring of the Holy Spirit that the faith of the disciples is revealed as such and becomes a historical factor. It is only there that they become what they are here ordained and commissioned to be—those who bear the *kerygma*. It is only there that the community develops from its original form as the company of disciples believing in the living Jesus Christ into the Church which grows and expands in the world. It is only there that there is laid the indispensable foundation for this building which does inevitably follow the Easter happening. We can say that this foundation was the faith of the disciples in the living Jesus Christ, and therefore that what took place in the forty days was the laying of this foundation. We have to distinguish between the act of laying a foundation, the creation of a presupposition, and the result of this act or action. In the strict sense the Easter narratives do not speak so much of the result as of the act as such. It may be asked whether an exegesis of the passages will suffice which simply equates the happening described in them and attested as the act of God with the awakening and development of the faith of the disciples, treating everything that does not seem to merge into this— rather after the manner of the exposition which scraps the history altogether—merely as a narrative and mythologising form, which is in the last resort irrelevant for an understanding of the texts and has therefore to be isolated. But the texts are relatively very scanty, or, at any rate, very reserved in the information which, according to this exegesis, is their essential and ultimately their only affirmation, the Easter faith of the disciples.

In this respect ought we not to take warning from the lexicographical observation that the word πίστις does not occur at all in the Easter narratives and the word πιστεύειν only in Jn. 20 ?

What interests these narratives is who and what brought and impelled and drove the disciples to this faith, but not, or not primarily the fact and the manner of their coming to it, of its development in them. They do not tell us anything at all about a tangible form of this faith, unless we are to describe as the form which their faith took at this stage of its formation that confusion and astonishment in face of an incontrovertible fact which is described as the attitude of the disciples. The decisive element in the texts is surely that the disciples did find themselves faced with an incontrovertible fact, a fact which led to the awakening and development of their faith. Are we really giving a true interpretation if we take an aspect which at very best forms only the content of a secondary affirmation and describe it as the true and primary message, that which the texts regarded as the act of God ?

Let us accept—as indeed we must—that they were really speaking of the laying of this foundation, the creation of the presupposition of the whole history which followed. Do we explain their particular account of the history which lays this foundation by simply repeating that the real subject of this history is the formation of the faith of the disciples, that this, and at bottom only this, was the real Easter happening ? We have seen what this happening is supposed to be. The Easter happening now described in this way is understood as a special act of God. It is certainly understood as a special act of God in the texts. But if it is restricted to the development of the faith of the disciples, what can this mean ? A kind of parthenogenesis of faith without any external cause ; without any cause in an external event which begets it ? A faith which is in the true and proper sense otherworldly ? A Nevertheless which reached out defiantly, Prometheus-like, into the void and posits and maintains itself there ? A faith which of itself—without any given reason—can explain the figure of the Crucified and recognise in the Crucified the living Lord ? A faith which of itself (before the outpouring of the Holy Spirit) is able to reveal and make effective the happening of the cross as a redemptive happening ? Is not this a concept of faith of which only God Himself could really be the Subject ? Well, nothing is impossible with God. Even according to the texts it was God, and God alone, who created the faith of the disciples—or the original form of faith which is here in question. And certainly God might have created this faith in the form of a *creatio ex nihilo*. But then we should have to reckon with the fact that, under the name of faith in the resurrection of Jesus

Christ and in Jesus Christ as the Resurrected, the Church and the New Testament were really believing in the development of this Easter faith of the disciples as a *creatio ex nihilo*. And we should then have to admit that the riddle which replaces the riddle posed in the texts as they are is not an easier but a much more difficult one. This interpretation will no doubt please those who think that the truth is most likely to be found where the paradox is most severe. If only we had one example in the Bible of God creating a faith out of nothing in this way! If only the texts gave us some slight indication that in the happening reported by them they were at bottom treating of such a *creatio ex nihilo*! If only they demanded that we should look in this direction! But most definitely they do not demand it. Like the rest of the Bible, they speak of a foundation of faith which comes to those who have it, of a faith which is described in terms of its object. And it is this foundation, an act of God fashioned as this object, a series of appearances and sayings of Jesus Christ risen from the dead and raised from the tomb, which is plainly the theme of their affirmation and the content of their narrative. That they speak of this (and only in the light of it of the rise of that original form of the faith of the disciples) is the presupposition of the rest of the New Testament. Whatever attitude we take up, an exegesis of these texts has to grapple with the fact that this is the theme of their affirmation and the content of their narrative.

We have to ask seriously whether the older criticism of the Easter narratives (in the 18th and 19th centuries) was not in advance of more recent criticism in that it did face squarely and try to do justice to the problem of the objective foundation of the Easter faith as it is posed by the meaning and wording of the texts.

Certainly the older criticism took some strange paths. It even supposed—the great Schleiermacher took this view—that Jesus may have come round from an apparent death. There were rationalists who did not shrink from explaining the empty tomb by a return to the hypothesis suggested in Mt. 27⁶²ᶠ·, that the disciples fraudulently removed the body. It is astonishing that even in our own day no less a figure than R. Seeberg (*Chr. Dog.*, 1925, II, p. 205) expresses the view that the removal of the body of Jesus might be explained by its being covered over, and the rolling away of the stone at the entrance to the tomb by tremors caused by an earthquake. Above all, to explain the appearances of Jesus recourse has been had to the term " vision." Some have tried to think of them only in terms of the purely subjective visions of the disciples. Others have had to correct them and go further, speaking of objective visions, visions which have an objective basis in the corresponding activity of God or in the continuing power of the personality of Jesus. A. E. Biedermann, for example, was thinking of this kind of objective vision when (§ 588) he spoke of the resurrection of Jesus as an " historical event." To-day we rightly turn up our nose at this, because (quite apart from the many inconsistencies in detail) it all smacks too strongly of an apologetic to explain away the mystery and miracle attested in the texts. And this is something that cannot be said of the identification of the Easter event with the rise of the Easter faith, which does not seem to make the paradox any less but greater. But in favour of these explanations which have now gone out of currency we can at least say this, that they did in different ways try to stick to the question of the concrete derivation of the Easter faith. They did at least keep closer to the texts by not only maintaining but trying to show that the disciples did not come to this faith of themselves, but were brought to it by some factor concretely at work in the world—however perversely this factor might be represented.

This is where the decision must be made. The texts do not speak primarily of the formation of the Easter faith as such but of its foundation by Jesus Christ Himself, who met and talked with His disciples after His death as One who is alive (not outside the world but within it), who by this act of life convinced them incontrovertibly of the fact that He is alive and therefore of the fact that His death was the redemptive happening willed by God. According to the texts, this event of the forty days, and the act of God in this event, was the concrete factor—the concrete factor in its externality, its objectivity, not taking place in their faith but in conflict with their lack of faith, overcoming and removing their lack of faith and creating their faith.

The " legend " of the finding of the empty tomb is not of itself and as such the attestation of Jesus Christ as He showed Himself alive after His death. It is ancillary to this attestation. The one can be as little verified " historically " as the other. Certainly the empty tomb cannot serve as an " historical " proof. It cannot be proclaimed and believed for itself but only in the context of the attestation. But it is, in fact, an indispensable accompaniment of the attestation. It safeguards its content from misunderstanding in terms of a being of the Resurrected which is purely beyond or inward. It distinguishes the confession that Jesus Christ lives from a mere manner of speaking on the part of believers. It is the negative presupposition of the concrete objectivity of His being. Let those who would reject it be careful—as in the case of the Virgin Birth—that they do not fall into Docetism. The older criticism of the Gospels already referred to did at least take it seriously—however well or badly it understood and treated it. We would do well to-day not to rush too hastily past it.

According to the texts, and in spite of the obscurities and contradictions with which they speak of it, in spite of their legendary, their non-historical or pre-historical manner of statement, the Easter event is quite plainly one of an encounter, an encounter with God, an act of God to the disciples in which, as before and for the first time, truly—revealed to them and recognised by them as such—God Himself confronted them and spoke with them in the person of Jesus Christ. They beheld the glory of the Word made flesh (Jn. 1¹⁴) ; they heard and handled it (1 Jn. 1¹). In this seeing and hearing and handling, in this encounter, they were brought to faith and they for their part came to faith. We are not required to try to know and to be able to say more of this encounter, of the How of it, than the accounts themselves tell us. We are not required to translate into express terms the inexpressible thing which they attest (as was earlier attempted with theories about the new corporeality of the One who met them or the way in which He was seen and heard and handled). Any such translation can only obscure and efface the decisive thing which is told us. What we are required to do is to let ourselves be told what the texts do tell us, and whatever our attitude may be—affirmation, rejection or doubt—to stick to that which is told us, not trying to replace it by something that is not told us on the pretext that it needs to be interpreted. And what is told us is that Jesus Christ risen from the dead appeared to His disciples prior to their faith in Him, that He existed as the living One in clear distinction from their own existence as determined not by faith in Him but by lack of faith. What is told us is His action and Word as the object which underlies their faith. They tell us that this happened to the disciples after His death and prior to their faith, and that on this presupposition, taught by this event, knowing Jesus Christ as He gave Himself to be known by them, they later received from Him the Holy Spirit. They did not have Him themselves. They were able only to receive Him from Jesus Christ, in that confrontation in which He had disclosed Himself to them in the Easter period. In this sense the rest of the New Testament looked back to that which is attested in the Easter texts as the beginning of the *parousia* of the Lord in glory, the history which underlies and impels and legitimatises and authorises the *kerygma*, the history which follows the history of the life and death of Jesus Christ and precedes that of the community in the world, itself a real history within the history of the world.

5. The second amplification that we have to make is again with reference to the connexion between the death and resurrection of Jesus Christ, meaning by His resurrection (as we worked it out under 3.) the whole of His *parousia* as it began with the Easter events and will be completed as the end of all time, but equally His living present in which in the time between the Once and the One Day He is now concealed in God for us, being present and active in the work of the Holy Spirit, but also on earth, in history, in our very midst.

We have so far spoken of two different acts of God and therefore only of the " relationship " between them. But the time has now come when we must use a stronger term. For these are not two acts of God, but one. The two have to be considered not merely in their relationship but in their unity. It is the one God who is at work on the basis of His one election and decision by and to the one Jesus Christ with the one goal of the reconciliation of the world with Himself, the conversion of men to Him.

We have thought of the resurrection as the other side of His death, of the judgment which fell upon Him as our Representative, which therefore passed conclusively and irrevocably upon all men and every individual man in Him. But it is wholly and utterly the other side of " this side." It is the justification of Jesus Christ and our justification and therefore God's own justification in virtue of which life has actually come from this death—the life of Jesus Christ, and our life in Him. We have thought of the resurrection of Jesus Christ as the work of grace of God the Father. But this work of grace is wholly and utterly the answer to the work of obedience of the Son fulfilled in His self-offering to death. This work of grace and this work of obedience as the act of God the Father, Son and Holy Spirit are one work. We have thought of the resurrection of Jesus Christ as God's proclamation and revelation. But what can it proclaim and reveal, what can it disclose, but the act of reconciliation and redemption once and for all accomplished in His death, in the judgment fulfilled in Him and suffered by Him, the divine Yes already concealed under the No? It brings to light the grace, it puts into effect the mercy, which was God's purpose and goal in the dark event of Golgotha. And if the death of Jesus Christ on the cross is confronted by His life as the Resurrected in all its fulness—in the Easter period, at the right hand of the Father, and among us by the Holy Spirit, until He comes again in glory—yet in all the forms of His life this living One is none other than the One who once was crucified at Golgotha, who there took our place, who in His person allowed our judgment to be visited on Himself, who in that way accomplished our reconciliation with God, our conversion to Him. He lives as the One who has done this for us, and in Him as such we have the promise of our life ; in Him our life has already begun. In this unity the death and resurrection of Jesus Christ are together the history of Jesus Christ, and as such the redemptive history to which everything earlier that we might call redemptive history in the wider sense moved and pointed, and from which everything later that we might call redemptive history in the wider sense derives and witnesses. Here in the unity of this death and this resurrection from death that history takes place *in nuce*. It is an inseparable unity. We can and must explain each of these two moments by the other. We do not speak rightly of the death of Jesus Christ unless we have clearly and plainly before us His resurrection, His being as the Resurrected. We also do not speak rightly of His resurrection and His being as the Resurrected if we conceal and efface the fact that this living One was crucified and died for us.

But there is something else we have to say concerning this unity. It is the unity of a sequence. It is rather like a one-way street. It cannot be reversed. The crucifixion and death of Jesus Christ took place once. As this happening once it stands eternally before God and it is the basis and truth of the alteration of the human situation willed and brought about by God : from sin to righteousness, from captivity to freedom, from lying to truth, from death to life, our conversion to Him. For that reason the crucifixion and death of Jesus Christ does not ever take place again. But the life of the Resurrected as the life of the Crucified, as it began in that Easter period, and needs no new beginning, is an eternal life, a life which is also continuous in time. And that means that God, and we too, have to do with the Crucified only as the Resurrected, with the one event of His death only as it has the continuing form of His life. There is no Crucified *in abstracto*. There is no preaching of the cross or faith in the cross *in abstracto*. For that reason there are serious objections to all representations of the crucified Christ as such. There is no going back behind Easter morning. To the extent that they may contain or express such a going back, all theologies or pieties or exercises or æsthetics which centre on the cross—however grimly in earnest they may be—must be repudiated at once. " He is not here. He is risen." We must understand clearly what such a going back involves. It involves going back to the night of Golgotha as not yet lit up by the light of Easter Day. It involves going back and into the event of judgment not yet proclaimed and revealed as that of salvation. It involves going back into the sphere where the divine Yes to man which He Himself alone can reveal is still inaccessibly concealed under His No. It involves going back into the death in which all flesh is hopelessly put to death in and with the Son of God. As though we could find Jesus Christ in any other place, as though we could expect to be with Him in any other way, than in the wholeness of His history as it took place according to the witness of the New Testament! As though we had to begin again at the place where He made an end for us and of us! As though He had not done this once and for all for us all! As though—irrespective of the fact that we are not allowed to do this—there were still some place from which we ourselves have to take just one further step! As though it were something other than an act of desperation, or a radically culpable toying, to try to repeat for ourselves that which cannot be repeated because it has been accomplished by God! As though it were something other than the setting up of a new and most frightful law, or an idle fancy, where there is a practical or a theoretical or a cultic attempt to go back in this way, where we have not yet escaped from it and cannot escape from it ! The community is not called upon to repeat this act of God, let alone to expect and demand that the world should be ready to do so. In every age, *post Christum* means *post Christum crucifixum et resuscitatum*. The two are one. The first is included in the second, the death of Jesus Christ in His life, the judgment of God in the grace of God. " Death is swallowed up in victory " (1 Cor. 15[54]). The relationship can never be reversed. The second is no longer closed up and concealed and kept from us in the first, the life of Jesus Christ in His death, the grace of God in His judgment, His Yes in His No. Things can appear in this light only to unbelief, ingratitude, disobedience, and the uncertainty which results from it. It is only where these are present that a blind effort is made to begin with the first, the " bare cross," judgment, the divine No, the Law fulfilled for us in Jesus Christ, the wrath of God which He has suffered once and for all for us. The One who has done this, who in and with Himself has delivered us up to death, reigns and lives to all eternity and dies no more. And in and with Him we have life before us and not death. The way of God the Father, Son and Holy Spirit, the way of the true God, is not a cycle, a way of eternal recurrence, in which the end is a constant beginning. It is the way of myth which is cyclic, an eternal recurrence, summoning man to endless repetitions, to that eternal oscillation between Yes and No, grace and judgment, life and death. We must not mythologise the Gospel of the way of the true God (not even in the name of Kierkegaard or Luther himself). We must not interpret it in terms of a cycle. We must not make the Christian life and theological thinking and the Church's preaching and instruction and pastoral care like the ox which is bound to a stake and, driven by the owner's whip, has to trot round and round turning the wheel. We must not violently make of Christianity a movement of reaction and think that we can force it on the world in this form. God has rejected from all eternity. He has condemned and judged and put to death in time. He has put all to death in a Son who obediently willed to suffer death in the place of all. And He never comes back to this point. He never begins here. And in faith, in gratitude, in obedience, in the knowledge of His way, we ourselves can only be prevented from beginning here. Rather we are invited, indeed required, to accept this as something that has happened for us and to us, in order that we may go forward with this decision already behind us. God in His own action has Himself gone further along this road, and He summons us to go further. It was for the sake of His electing that from all eternity He rejected. It was in His love that in time He was wroth and condemned. It was to save that He judged. It was to make alive that He put to death. And now He has indeed elected and loved and saved and made alive. And the *telos* of the way which He has gone in the person and work, in the history of Jesus Christ, is our beginning—His electing, therefore, His love, His saving, His making alive.

Jesus lives—as the One who was crucified for us, as the One who has made an end for us and of us, as the One who once and for all in His resurrection—preventing any going back or looking back—has made a new beginning with us. Jesus lives—as the Lord, not as an indolent, easy-going Lord who invites us to be easy-going, but as a stern Lord. But He is stern in that He prevents us from going back or looking back, demanding that we should take up our little cross— our cross, not His—and follow Him, but follow Him where He Himself has long since carried His own, by way of Golgotha to the throne of God, to lay it down there with all the sin and guilt of the whole world, with our death, and to receive in our name as the obedient Son of the Father the grace of everlasting life. Jesus lives—relieved of the anguish and pain and distress of what He did for us as the Judge judged and the priest sacrificed for us. What we have to do is simply to take this consequence as our starting-point, to enjoy this Sabbath rest with Him as those who hear the message of Easter Day and are obedient to the verdict of the Holy Spirit pronounced there, praying that it may daily be disclosed afresh to us, looking forward in hope to the consummation of His *parousia* and therefore to our redemption, which is grounded in our reconciliation with God as it has already taken place on His cross, which has already begun in His resurrection, in which the disciples beheld His glory.

This is the unity of the act of God in the death and resurrection of Jesus Christ, or, rather, the unity of the act of God in the person and work of His Son, who was put to death for our transgressions, but who now lives for our justification as the guarantor and giver of our life, having been raised from the dead in our mortal flesh. It is a unity which is securely grounded. It is the unity of an irreversible sequence. It is a unity which is established teleologically. Jesus Christ as attested in Holy Scripture is the One who exists in this unity.

In conclusion, we may add that as the One who exists in this unity He is the one Word of God that we must hear, that we must trust and obey, both in life and in death. If the crucified Jesus Christ is alive, if His community is the company of those among whom this is seen and taken seriously, as the axiom of all axioms, then the community cannot take account of any other word that God might have spoken before or after or side by side with or outside this word, and that He willed to have proclaimed by it. It accepts and proclaims this one Jesus Christ as the one Word, the first and final Word, of the true God. In it it hears the Word of all God's comfort, commandment and power. It is altogether bound to this Word, and in it it is altogether free. It interprets creation and the course of the world and the nature of man, his greatness and his plight, wholly in the light of this Word and not *vice versa*. It does not need to accept as normative any other voice than this voice, for the authority of any other voice depends upon the extent to which it is or is not an echo of this voice. As it seeks to know this voice, it is certainly allowed and commanded to hear other voices freely and without anxiety: as an echo of this voice they may share its authority. But it will always come back to the point of wanting to hear first and chiefly this true and original voice, and wanting to give itself to the service of this voice. And because He lives it will always be able to hear this voice which is His voice, and to give itself effectively to the service of this voice. In this respect we can say with Zwingli (and against any supposedly " natural " theology) : " The holy Christian Church, whose one Head is Jesus Christ, is born of the word of God. It remains in the same, and it hears not the voice of a stranger."

The living Jesus Christ, who is this one Word of God, is the Crucified, the One who was delivered up to death, and who in His death delivered up to death the world of sin and the flesh and death. But because He is risen and lives we have to add at once : the One who was crucified for us, for the sake of the burning fire of the love of God, for our redemption ; who in His death delivered up the world to death in order that reconciled with God it might be a new world ; not therefore for the death of the sinner, but that he should be converted and live ; not therefore to his destruction but to his salvation. In this light, as the Word of the cross understood in the light of the resurrection of the Crucified, the one Word of God is certainly the word of judgment on all the arrogant pretension with which man would judge and justify himself. It is the disclosing and punishing of the sin which at its root consists in this obstinate ignoring of the truth that we do not need to help ourselves because God is for us and our cause is His cause. The community which hears the one Word of God in virtue of the life of the crucified Jesus Christ is that place in the world where man subjects Himself to this judgment, where he is willing to let it come upon him and to accept its consequences. And the community will not be afraid of the offence and hostility and hatred which come in the world when it proclaims the message of this judgment which has been passed on all men. It can spare neither itself nor the world in its witness to that which has taken place for its salvation.

But because the risen and living Jesus Christ is the one Word of God, this Word—as the community hears and proclaims it—is the one Word of the divine will and act of reconciliation. It is God's Yes to man and the world, even in the No of the cross which it includes. God says No in order to say Yes. His Word is the Word of that teleologically established unity of the death and resurrection of Christ. It is the Word of the cross as the promise of life, not as the threat of death ; as the Gospel, not as the Law ; or as the Law only as it judges and directs as Gospel, demanding unconditional trust and total obedience. That is how the community hears this one Word. And it serves it as this one Word. It does not come before the world, therefore, as an accuser, as a prosecutor, as a judge, as an executioner. It comes before it as the herald of this Yes which God has spoken to it. It will be careful not to present God as a jealous competitor, a malevolent opponent or a dangerous enemy. It will not try to conceal the fact that as the Creator God has loved it from all eternity, and that He has put this love into action in the death of Jesus Christ. The community lives by the fact that the first and final Word of God is this Yes. It lives by the freedom in which when it hears this Word it is pledged in advance of the world but also to the world. It lives by the fact that Jesus lives, and therefore for the task of telling this good news to all people, to a people which is troubled because it has not yet been told to it, or not told in such a way that it has brought about its liberation.

We are now in a position to take up again the question we put at

the beginning of the sectio , and therefore to conclude the great
transitional discussion which was necessary at this point.

The question was as follows : How can we arrive at the perception
(grounded in the being of Jesus Christ as the Lord who became a
servant, and in His action as the Judge judged for us) that Jesus
Christ belongs to us and we belong to Him, that His cause is our cause
and our cause is His ?   How can there be a doctrine of the atonement
in a form which is not exclusively christological, a doctrine of the
atonement which is a doctrine of the determinations of our own human
destiny on a christological basis ?   We have already seen how this
question arises and why it is so acute.   Not in the fact of a temporal
gulf between Jesus Christ and us, and the need to bridge it.   This is
one aspect of it, the aspect in Lessing's question.   But on this aspect
the difficulty is purely conceptual and can be overcome.   We have
seen that a concern for this difficulty is a movement of flight in an
attempt to evade the real kernel of the question which arises in this
context.   The kernel of the question is simply the incompatibility of
the existence of Jesus Christ with us and us with Him, the impossibility of the co-existence of His divine-human actuality and action
and our sinfully human being and activity, the direct collision between
supreme order and supreme disorder which we perceive when we start
with the fact that our contemporaneity with Him has been made
possible in the most radical form—and not merely by the device of a
concept of time which enables us to accept it.   For what will become
of us if the real presence of Jesus Christ is going to be a fact in our
time and therefore in the sphere of our existence ?   In face of this
contrast and antithesis between Him and us—a contrast which is
weighted absolutely in His favour as the Son of God—how can we
ever arrive at the perception which is so well grounded in His person
and work that He does belong to us and we to Him ?   How are we to
understand that we are His fellows, i.e., those who are represented
before God in Him ?   How dare we ever count on the fact that we
are His, and therefore move on from Christology to an anthropology
which is embraced by Christology, and in which we have to understand
ourselves, us men, as His ?   In His work, His death on the cross, as
the death of our Representative and substitute, it came to pass that,
as the sinners and enemies of God we are, we were delivered up to
death, and an end was made of us, and we came to an end with this
whole world of sin and the flesh and death.   Where are we then ?
And what is there to say of us ?   Is there something beyond this
death, this conclusion, this end of man, in the light of which we can
look back on all this and forward from it, to the men we are as those
who have a place with Jesus Christ, who do in fact belong to Him
because He belongs to them, who are not only there, but as the men
they are can be there as His, concerning whose being as His there is
therefore something that we dare to say ?   Is there something beyond

this death, this conclusion, this end, in the light of which Christology is not exclusive but inclusive, in the light of which it is false if it is exclusive, in the light of which it can and must comprehend within itself as yet another element in the doctrine of reconciliation a perception of our sin first, but then of our justification, of the community as the people of justified sinners, of what makes men members of this community, our faith ? Is there something beyond in the light of which we can look forward in this way ?

This was the question, and we have seen what the answer is as it is given by the same New Testament witness which forced us to put the question in this way. The answer is the resurrection of Jesus Christ from the dead, His life as the Resurrected from the dead, the verdict of God the Father on the obedience of His Son as it was pronounced in this event and as it is in force in His being from this event. We must now explain to what extent this event and this being are the answer to our question.

We will develop the answer by running through once more the results or the main points we have just reached under our five heads, but this time in the reverse order, placing them alongside our original question in the expectation that in them—both in detail and as a whole—we shall find that something beyond for which we have been asking.

We begin at once with the result of our fifth and final insight, that the crucified but also the risen and living Jesus Christ is God's Yes to man, which includes God's No, but in such a way that it is a mistake to try to hear the No independently, as a final word, with a validity which is absolute. " Death is swallowed up in victory."

It is death—how can we know what death is if it is not present and revealed to us in the death of Jesus Christ ? According to the witness of Scripture our dying took place in the person of the Son of God who died in our flesh as the bearer of our sin and of that of the whole world. Here there came upon us that which had to come upon us as sinners and enemies of God. Here judgment fell upon the world as the only possible form in which God could and would reconcile it with Himself, convert it to Himself. Here—in exact correspondence with what He did as Creator when He separated light from darkness and elected the creature to being and rejected the possibility of chaos as nothingness—He pronounced His relentless and irrevocable No to disordered man. Here, in and with this No, He made an end of that man once and for all. That is why the Lord became a servant, why the Son of God went into the far country in obedience to the Father. That is why He took His way among us as the Judge judged and the Priest sacrificed. As the One who went this way He will be the end of all time. As the world in which and for which He went this way He will in His own person lay it at the feet of the Father (1 Cor. 15^{28}). The judgment on us fulfilled in Him will then be revealed as such.

But if it is true that this Jesus Christ who was crucified and delivered up to death for us is risen and alive, then it is also true that we who are crucified and dead in Him have a future and hope in the light of the judgment and end which has come upon us in Him. For all the strictness of its force, the negative aspect of that " for us," the No which fell upon us in the death of Jesus Christ, has no autonomous. or definitive or absolute significance. With His death our death, the death which every man must some day suffer, the death of all flesh, is in fact " swallowed up in victory." But this means that it is revealed and put into effect that the judgment which came on the whole world, on all flesh, in Jesus Christ, is for all its strictness the form in which God willed, and in this judgment effected, the reconciliation of the world with Himself, converting it to Himself, not in its destruction but to its salvation. The No pronounced in the cross of Jesus Christ can and should be heard and accepted only as the necessary and in the true sense redemptive form of His Yes. The subjection of man to this No, to which he is relentlessly compelled, is then revealed as the exaltation which has already come to him by the Yes which is the purpose of the No, under which he is placed, under which he will be placed again and again by Jesus Christ risen again from the dead. It is not that he has first to acknowledge himself rejected by God, then to break through if possible to a discovery and appropriation of his election, calling and redemption. He is rejected, not in his own person, but in that of the one beloved and obedient Son of God. His suffering is only a pale reflection of the great and only true suffering of this One. And if this One who alone is truly rejected, and truly suffers, is revealed in His resurrection from the dead as the One He is, revealed and confirmed as the beloved and obedient Son of God and therefore as His Elect from all eternity, then in the true rejection and suffering which He has borne as our substitute and Representative we stand before our own election, calling and redemption. That which came upon Him—and in His person us—in His death, under the relentless and irrevocable No of God, is our reconciliation with God as it took place not at our charge but at His, not to our disadvantage but to our advantage. It is, then, our conversion to Him, which cannot be understood only, or even at all in its end and consequence, as an abdication, a surrender, a destruction, but has to be understood positively as our setting in fellowship and peace with God, as our adoption as His children and to the inheritance of His children, and therefore as men who have a future and hope. We are not oppressed and extinguished in the death of Jesus Christ, but liberated and refashioned. In virtue of the death of Jesus Christ we are allowed to be. Christology cannot, therefore, be exclusive but inclusive. We cannot and we must not be afraid of Jesus Christ, or ask Him to depart from us as Peter did because we are sinful men. We are this. But as the Son of the Father He posited Himself for us—really for us and for our salvation—to suffer in our place the divine rejection, the divine No, the divine judgment, and faithful to His election to fulfil the divine Yes, the divine grace. As the One who has done this He was raised again from the dead by the life-giving Spirit. As the One who has done this He lives as the first-begotten from the dead, and therefore as the word of the divine assent, as God's permission and command that as the sinners we are we should be there with Him. " I shall not die, but live ; and declare the works of the Lord " (Ps. 118¹⁷). Because Jesus Christ the Crucified is risen again and lives there is room for us and therefore—this is what we wanted to know—for the problems of the doctrine of reconciliation in our own anthropological sphere. This is what we gather from our fifth and final consideration.

Our fourth consideration concerned the historical character of the content of the Easter stories. Why was it so important to emphasise and underline the concrete objectivity of the history there attested as against their evaporation into a history of the development of the Easter faith of the disciples ? Certainly not in order to explain the resurrection of Jesus Christ as a historically indisputable fact. Certainly not to create for faith in the Resurrected a ground in terms of this world which we can demonstrate and therefore control. Certainly not to destroy its character as faith, to transform it into an optional knowledge, which is not moved by any astonishment, which does not demand any contradiction, which does not require any hazard of trust and obedience. This is opposed, as we have seen, by the decisive content and therefore by the form of the stories. But the concrete objectivity of the Easter event cannot be interpreted out of the Easter stories. And on the objectivity of that event as the beginning of the *parousia* of the living Jesus Christ there depends the otherness of His existence, His concrete otherness, the unequivocal way in which we are placed over against Him, to hear in Him the Yes which has been spoken in and with and under the No of His death and ours, to find ourselves addressed in Him as those who are liberated from judgment and death, as those who are set in fellowship and peace with God, as those who are adopted as the children of God. This address, He Himself as the One who addresses us in this way, is the basis of our faith. We do not, therefore, only believe that we are called and are the children—on the basis of a parthenogenesis or *creatio ex nihilo* of our faith regarded as an act of God. We are the children of God because we who could not say this of ourselves, however strong our faith, are addressed as such by the Son of God who was made flesh and raised again in the flesh—we who in the death of Jesus Christ as it happened concretely and objectively (according to the narratives which precede the Easter story) are judged and put to death and brought hopelessly to our end. If Jesus Christ is not risen—bodily, visibly, audibly, perceptibly, in the same concrete sense in which He died, as the texts themselves have it—if He is not also risen, then our preaching and our faith are vain and futile; we are still in our sins. And the apostles are found " false witnesses," because they have " testified of God that he raised up Christ, whom he raised not up " (1 Cor. 15$^{14f.}$). If they were true witnesses of His resurrection, they were witnesses of an event which was like that of the cross in its concrete objectivity. The message that Jesus the Crucified lives, and that in Him there is given us a future and hope and room to be, has force and weight, the force and weight to summon to faith and to awaken faith, only in view of this content of their witness, and most definitely not in view of the fact that in the form of this mythological content they attested only the evocation and development of their own faith. The apostles witnessed that Jesus Christ risen from the dead had encountered them, not in the way in which we might say this (metaphorically) of a supposed or actual immanence of the existence, presence and action of the transcendent God, not in an abstract but in a concrete otherness, in the mystery and glory of the Son of God in the flesh. He encountered them formally (eating and drinking with them) in the same way as He had encountered them before, and as they for their part encountered Him, as living men in the flesh (eating and drinking with Him)—in a real encounter, themselves on the one side, alive but moving forward to death, and He on the other, alive from the dead, alive no more to die, alive eternally even now in time. We can therefore say quite calmly—for this is the truth of the matter—that they attested the fact that He made known to them this side of His (and their) death wholly in the light of the other side, and therefore that He made known to them the other side, His (and their) life beyond, wholly in terms of this side, even as spoken in His resurrection from the dead, as the Yes of God to Him (and therefore to them and to all men) concealed first under the No of His (and their) death. As the One who really encountered them in this sense He constituted Himself the basis of their faith and the theme and content of their witness. And in the faith which had this basis they made their witness, as filled out in this way, the witness of His self-attestation as the living One : confident that the power and truth of the same divine verdict in the power of which He encountered them as the living One would prove effective to those to whom they made this witness, and confident that this witness would summon them to faith and awaken faith ; confident that the self-attestation of Jesus Christ as the living One would repeat itself in the making of their human witness to it. He Himself as the One raised from the dead is the other side which has invaded this side, and by which life is promised and given as life in and with Him to those who are put to death in and with Him. The possibility of witness to Him as this other side, and the possibility of faith in Him as the One who is this other side, are, as human actions, possibilities within this world and on this side (even though their theme and basis is the other side). As such they depend on the fact that Jesus Christ has attested and still attests Himself as the other side within this world and therefore on this side (and, because on this side, in a real confrontation of all other men). They depend upon the objectivity with which He has done this according to the Easter narratives (taken in their true sense). Because He has done this, it can be proclaimed and believed by men, it can be recognised by men, that with and after His death (and that of all men) there 'is freedom for human life (participant in His life), and a place for the problems of it (as they are posed and as they will be solved by Him). This is what we gather from our fourth consideration in answer to our question.

The third consideration, which was also the longest, culminated in the question of the meaning of the interval in the *parousia* of Jesus Christ as it began in the event of Easter and will be completed in His final revelation. We found its meaning in the existence of the community as the reality of the people of God in world history, the company of those who are not only His but can know and confess themselves as His, and therefore Him as theirs, their Head. Where this community lives by the Holy Spirit, Jesus Christ Himself lives on earth, in the world and in history. It is immediately apparent that here we have the most tangible answer to our question. In the existence of the community in the world we have immediately before our eyes the fact that even after the event of the cross revealed in that of Easter, God still allowed and had time and space for human existence and history and problems. Man can and must come into view in all seriousness as such even *post Christum crucifixum et resuscitatum*—not as perfect man as He will be presented in and with the final revelation of Jesus Christ, to live as such eternally with God, having passed through judgment, and not as perverted and sinful and lost man, but as man who in his perversion, sin and lostness has been visited by the reconciliation of the world with God as accomplished in Jesus Christ, and altered at the very root of his being. He is the man who, whether he knows it or not—the community knows it—stands in the light of the resurrection of Jesus Christ. He is the man who, whether he fulfils it or not—the community is what it is by fulfilling it—stands under the determination to give the answer of his little human Yes, his modest praise of God and his actions, to the great Yes which God has spoken to him. God is not too great to expect this Yes from man and to accept it. God gives him the opportunity and summons him to utter it. That is the meaning and purpose of the interval between the first *parousia* of Jesus Christ and the second. And in the answer to this particular question we obviously have the direct answer to our main question of the legitimacy and possibility of dealing not only with Jesus Christ Himself but, because with Him, therefore also with us as those who are visited by the reconciliation of the world with God accomplished in His death. In virtue of the resurrection of Jesus Christ, and with the same historical actuality within the world with which this took place, there now exists the community of Jesus Christ in the world, as the first-begotten of all God's creatures, as a lasting and living and concrete indication of the fact that all creation stands in this light, that the condescension of God is so great that He expects praise from all men and every man, that every man finds himself in the circle of which Jesus Christ is the centre. We should have to overlook this special dimension of the condescension of God revealed in the existence of the community if we tried to ignore the fact that our question is in fact answered by the resurrection of Jesus Christ from the dead, that the will of God, as it is in force and revealed in the calling and existence of the community, has decided that Christ would not be Christ without His own people (in the narrower and wider senses of the term), that there cannot, therefore, be an exclusive but only an inclusive Christology which embraces the existence of men both negatively and positively, that the doctrine of reconciliation cannot stop at that of the person and work of Jesus Christ. So much for the result of our third consideration.

Our second inquiry culminated in the term which we have adopted as a title for the whole of this transitional discussion. The resurrection is marked off from the death of Jesus Christ as a new and specific act of God by the fact that in it there is pronounced the verdict of God the Father on the obedience of the Son : His gracious and almighty approval of the Son's representing of the human race ; His acceptance of His suffering and death as it took place for the race ; the justification of the will of the Father who sent the Son into the world for this purpose, of the Son who willed to submit to this will, and of the totality of sinful men as brought to an end in the death of this their Representative. We can now say that as this creative and revelatory divine verdict, as this divinely effective approval, acceptance and justification, the resurrection of Jesus Christ from the dead is the answer to our question concerning the participation of the whole race in the person and work of the one man Jesus Christ as the Son of God, our question concerning the significance of His being and activity as it embraces us, as it embraces the anthropological sphere. In so far as this divine verdict has been passed and is in force in the resurrection of Jesus Christ, Jesus Christ lives and acts and speaks for all ages and in eternity, and in such a way that we are promised a future and hope, a being before God in reality and in truth. In this connexion we remember once more the words of Jn. 14[19] : " I live and ye shall live also." This is the comprehensive form of the divine verdict pronounced in the resurrection of Jesus Christ from the dead. But where in faith in the raised and living Jesus Christ this verdict is heard and accepted and understood as already passed and effective, there is a recognition of the divinely active approval, acceptance and justification, and therefore a recognition of the being which God has promised us in reality and in truth. This verdict is therefore both the ontic and also the noetic—first the ontic and then the noetic—basis of our being—not outside but in Jesus Christ as the elected Head of the whole race—but of our own being and to that extent of our being with Him and side by side with Him. In this verdict God willed to justify Himself and His Son after the death of His Son on the cross and in relation to it. But we all fell victim to death in that death, and therefore in relation to it He has also justified us ; He has declared and addressed and accepted us as the brothers of the Son who was justified there, and children of the Father who was justified there. We have, therefore, the right and we are directed to understand the reconciliation which took place in the death of Jesus Christ as signifying for us not only an end but also a beginning, as giving to us something beyond this death. We are summoned by that verdict of God which has been passed and is in force to take seriously ourselves and the problems of our situation as it has been altered by His death. The hearing and receiving and understanding of this verdict, faith in the risen and living Jesus Christ, is the presupposition that we do this, that we make this recognition of our being in Him. Over this presupposition we have no power. Being as it is a matter of the Holy Spirit, of the faith which leads into all the truth in the power and enlightenment of the Holy Spirit, it is only given and will continually be given to us. Without prayer for it this presupposition cannot be had ; we cannot possibly count on it or on its consequences ; the recognition that we are and have a place in Jesus Christ, and therefore together with and side by side with Him, cannot be anything but imaginary and illusory ; thought about our being can only be irrelevant and our speaking about it mere talk. This is something we must continually keep before us in our whole development of the doctrine of reconciliation. But in real prayer for it, the prayer which is confident that it will be heard, this presupposition, the hearing and receiving and understanding of the verdict pronounced by God, is quite possible, for as His verdict it has already been passed and is valid and divinely effective. Calling on the fact that Jesus lives—for this is the real prayer which is confident from the very first that it will be answered—can never be in vain. It lays hold of the promise : Ye shall live, and therefore the answer to the question which here concerns us. So much we learn from our second discussion.

We now go back to the beginning, and recall the result of our first consideration. We started by understanding the resurrection as an act of God. We had to be more precise : in its character as an event which is objective in this world, it was exclusively an act of God, without any components of human will and activity. In this it differed from the suffering and death of Jesus Christ   It was a concrete revelation of God, and pure in its concreteness. It was God's self-attestation (the attestation of His glory in the flesh of His Word) without any co-operation on the part of a human witness serving it. As we say, it was the very model of a gracious act of God, the Son of God as such being active only as the recipient, God the Father alone being the One who acts, and God the Holy Spirit alone the One who mediates His action and revelation. This made the resurrection of Jesus Christ from the very first the sure and unequivocally transcendent place, the true other side here on this side, from which we can look back with enlightened and indisputable assurance on the first act of God which took place in His death, and forward to the determination which is there newly given to the being of man.

From the place which we describe in this way we had and have to look forward to the being of humanity as it has come to its end in the death of Jesus Christ, but also to its salvation, with the disclosure of a future and hope, with the promise of life which has there been newly attained for it. The resurrection of Jesus Christ from the dead was the exclusive act of God, a pure divine revelation, a free act of divine grace. It is of this that we speak when we say : " Jesus lives," and when we deduce and continue : " and I with Him." The statement has this deduction and continuation. For Jesus lives as the One who was put to death for me, as the One in whom I am put to death, so that necessarily His life is the promise of my life. But with His life, my life too, the life of man who is not himself Jesus Christ but only His younger brother, is an exclusive act of God, a pure divine revelation, a free act of divine grace. Let us leave it now to emphasise that as such it is " hid with Christ in God " (Col. 3³) in a way that we cannot comprehend or control. We were recalling the same thing when we understood it as the work of the divine verdict which is valid in Jesus Christ. More important for us is the positive side that as such, as that which is created and revealed in that divine act of sovereignty, our life, the life of man in and with Jesus Christ, is promised from the place whose sureness and unequivocal transcendence gives to the promise a clarity and certainty which are beyond comparison or compromise. It is a matter only of the act of God, the self-revelation of God, the free grace of God. The free act and self-revelation of God cannot be called in question. They are there. And that gives an unsurpassable clarity and an axiomatic certainty. The Yes of God, which cannot be disputed by any conceivable No, has been pronounced and has to be received. It was and is His Yes to the Son whom He elected and loved from all eternity. It was and is the Yes of His faithfulness to Himself. But as such it was and is His Yes to the human people whom from all eternity He has also elected and loved in His Son. He has spoken and speaks and will speak it in His Son ; and on earth with the same sovereignty in which He is God in heaven. To that extent it is also spoken to us, without involving or leaving the way open for any possible objections or doubts or questions. " Peace on earth to men of good-will." In the Word of God spoken with this sovereignty we are the men of this good-will. We do not simply think or believe that we are. We believe that we are because we are. That is why we can go on to think of the existence of man as determined by the saving event of the death of Jesus Christ.

60

THE PRIDE AND FALL OF MAN

The verdict of God pronounced in the resurrection of Jesus Christ crucified for us discloses who it was that was set aside in His death, the man who willed to be as God, himself lord, the judge of good and evil, his own helper, thus withstanding the lordship of the grace of God and making himself irreparably, radically and totally guilty before Him both individually and corporately.

1. THE MAN OF SIN IN THE LIGHT OF THE OBEDIENCE OF THE SON OF GOD

We now turn to questions of the perception of the human situation in the light of the event in which for our sake the Lord became a servant, the Son was obedient to the Father, the Word became flesh of our flesh, the Judge was Himself judged on the cross of Golgotha. In the verdict of God it is decided that this took place once and for all for us. It is also decided what it incontrovertibly means for the human situation. This verdict has been revealed in the resurrection of Jesus Christ from the dead, in the first instance to those to whom it is proclaimed and who can confess it in faith, but to these in anticipation of the final revelation in which (as it concerns all men) it will be revealed to all men.

The determination of the human situation which we have to consider at this point is the sin of man, or rather the man of sin, man as he wills and does sin, man as he is controlled and burdened by sin; and we have to consider this man in the particular form in which he is revealed under the aspect of the divine act of reconciliation which concerns us in this context. It is to this man that there relates the justification which we shall have to portray as we turn to the positive content of the divine verdict. From the standpoint which is here regulative for us it is the light of the resurrection of the crucified servant of God. But this light arises from a shadow, and it can be seen as light only in relation to this shadow. It is the solution of the riddle posed by the existence of man. It is the radically new determination of the human situation which as such causes an existing situation to vanish. It is the *iustificatio impii*. To understand it we have to know this shadow, this riddle, this existing situation, the *impius*, the man of sin.

In this section we are apparently going back a step behind the knowledge that we have already won of the salvation which has come to man in the self-sacrifice and death of the Son of God in our flesh and which is revealed in His resurrection. We are apparently concerned with the negative presupposition of this event, the disruption of the relationship between God and man which made this event necessary and which was overcome by this event. In our discussion so far we have always assumed this disruption. We have dealt with the way of the Son of God into the far country, with His self-humiliation to solidarity with sinful men, with His suffering and death in their place, with the judgment fulfilled on them in His person. But we have not so far looked specifically at the contrary element which forms the occasion for this divine action. We have treated its presence and nature and significance as something that we already know. We must now return to it because its clarification is essential to all that follows.

But the question immediately poses itself : Why is it only now that we have come to speak of this matter ? Why have we not followed the example of the dogmatics of all ages, Churches and movements and begun with a doctrine of sin, first stating the problem, then giving the decisive answer to it in the doctrine of the incarnation and atoning death of Jesus Christ, then continuing along the same direct line and developing it in the doctrine of justification, of the Church and of faith ? Why have we begun with Christology, thus making it necessary to go back to an understanding of its negative presupposition ? Or is it the case that the going back is only in appearance ? Had we not to speak first of the incarnation and atoning death of Jesus Christ because the man of sin, his existence and situation and nature, is revealed and can be known only in the light of it ? Are we not really going straight forward when we turn our attention to it now, only now, in this light, and directed to it from this point ? This is the question to which we must give a radical answer in the first part of this section.

Let us suppose that the traditional and current view of the knowledge of sin is right. The knowledge of it precedes that of Jesus Christ, and in some way it has a basis which is autonomous in relation to it. The knowledge of Jesus Christ must look back to it. If this is the case, then it is too late for us to turn our attention to it at this point. At that earlier point or even now, our first task should be to state from where we think we have this knowledge if Jesus Christ is not the basis of it.

But in the knowledge of sin we have to do basically and in general with a specific variation of the knowledge of God, of God as He has mediated Himself to man, and therefore of the knowledge of revelation and faith. This we can presuppose as something which is acknowledged and maintained by all serious Christian theology. That man is evil, that he is at odds with God and his neighbour, and therefore with himself, is something which he cannot know of himself, by communing with himself, or by conversation with his fellow-men, any more than he can know in this way that he is justified and comforted by God. Anything that he accepts in this matter which is not from God, but from communing with himself and his fellows, from his own understanding and consciousness of himself, may well be the inner tension between a relative Yes and a relative No, between becoming and perishing, between strength and weakness, between the great and the small, between achievement and will : the dialectic in which human existence has a part in the antithesis or dualism of light and darkness which runs through the whole of creation. But this tension has nothing whatever to do with man's being in sin as such. It may be a sphere for his good nature and actions as well as his bad. There may be an analogy to evil in it. But it is not as such the evil which makes man the enemy of God and his neighbour and himself, and puts him in need of atonement, of conversion to God. In itself and as such it belongs rather to the nature of man as God created it good. An understanding and consciousness of himself which man can attain of himself may also embrace the fact that he does not merely suffer but creates this inward tension, that he continually produces this dialectic. He may understand and recognise that he is limited, deficient and imperfect. He may be aware of the problematic nature of his existence as man. But this does not mean even remotely that he is aware of his being as the man of sin, at odds with God and his neighbour and himself. The imperfection and the problematical nature of his existence is not as such his sin. Not by a long way. It is only his limit. Within the sphere of self-understanding how can he ever come to accuse himself of this contradiction, to regard himself not as imperfect but as evil, to confess that he is finally and totally guilty in relation to God and his neighbour and himself ? Certainly in the sphere of his self-understanding he can understand that he is limited. But does there not always remain the possibility of turning this limitation to his own advantage as a mitigating circumstance ? He may accept that his being in tension is his own work. He may not be a complete stranger to something like remorse. But can he not still give to this remorse the form of self-pity, and because of the very sincerity of this pity think that he is excused, or even justified, and therefore at bottom good ? Within its limit the nature created by God is indeed good and not bad. Within the sphere of the self-knowledge not enlightened and instructed by the Word of God there is no place for anything worthy of the name of a " knowledge of sin." There is not revealed that which, if man is not to remain a sinner and perish, can be removed and made good only by the death of Jesus Christ on the cross. Men preoccupied with themselves have no eyes to see this or categories to grasp it. They do not have these because they lack the will to see it and to grasp it. Access to the knowledge that he is a sinner is lacking to man because he is a sinner. We are presupposing agreement on this point. All serious theology has tried to win its knowledge of sin from the Word of God and to base it on that Word.

If there is agreement on this point, it is better not to consider the insight into the problematical nature of his existence which man can reach of himself apart from the Word of God even as a preparation or a kind of initial understanding in relation to the knowledge of sin. It is true, of course, that in and with the knowledge of actual sin we do win through to a very useful insight into the problematical nature of human existence. It is true that while this is not identical with man's disharmony with God and his neighbour and himself, with the real breach in his existence, it can be an analogy to it which may help to make his guilt and need all the more plain. But it is not true that his inner conflict as such, and the remorse and pity with which he experiences it, have for him even such an anagogical significance that they can bring him in any way closer to a knowledge of his guilt and need, and therefore of the breach in which he does actually live. On the contrary, it is also unfortunately true that the real evil in which man enmeshes himself and is enmeshed is only too active in the way in which he experiences and understands the inner conflict of his existence. Even in the knowledge of sin which he has in the sphere of self-understanding without listening to the Word of God, he is the man of sin and therefore one who has no knowledge, who is completely closed to this negative determination. This is revealed in the fact that he does not see beyond the natural inward contradiction of his existence, in face of which he is capable of remorse and pity and melancholy, or even rueful irony, but not of genuine terror, in face of which he can always quieten and excuse himself, remaining obstinately blind and deaf to the contradiction which is his guilt and the breach which is his need. He sees and thinks and knows crookedly even in relation to his crookedness. And this being the case, how can he be even on the way to seeing and grasping that which he needs to see and grasp enlightened and instructed by the Word of God ? Crooked even in the knowledge of his crookedness, he can only oppose the Word of God which enlightens and instructs him concerning his crookedness.

In this connexion we may recall what Paul wrote in 2 Cor. 7⁸⁻¹¹ concerning the twofold possibility of λύπη (concern or sorrow). There is a λύπη κατὰ θεόν. This is a self-concern, a concern about the corruption revealed by God (as had happened to the Corinthians as a result of Paul's letter), which comes from God Himself and therefore corresponds to the will of God. It leads to an attitudè which, although it has the character of λύπη, no one will ever regret accepting : μετάνοιαν εἰς σωτηρίαν ἀμεταμέλητον ἐργάζεται (the repentance in which man is already on the way to salvation, in which he cannot give way to self-pity even though it does cause him this "concern," from which he cannot even wish to escape). Because Paul thinks he can assume that the letter which disturbed the Corinthians has put them on the way to this repentance—the signs or fruits of which he describes as σπουδή (carefulness), ἀπολογία (clearing of themselves, in the sense of *deprecatio*), ἀγανάκτησις (indignation), φόβος (fear), ἐπιπόθησις (longing) and ἐκδίκησις (zeal)—he himself does not repent but rejoices that they had been given a concern—κατὰ θεόν—by His apostolic word. But in v. 10 he contrasts this concern with quite another, the λύπη τοῦ κόσμου which works death. Was he afraid for a moment that he had plunged the Corinthians into this concern ? If so, he would have repented it, for they would not have understood and accepted his word as apostolic, as the Word of God, and they, for their part, would have taken a way which they also would repent. They would have been given the kind of concern which is all that the world, all that autonomous and self-sufficient man, is either capable of or wills, disturbed, unsettled, alarmed, working it out in one of the movements of human dialectic, but not finally frightened or perplexed, not stirred up to a horror of his own existence and the desire for a different existence, ready to come to terms with himself at a level which is deep, but not too deep. This kind of concern would not have led them to repentance and its works, but from one obstinacy to another, from an optimistic to a pessimistic, and then perhaps back again to the reverse. Not σωτηρία but θάνατος would then have been the final end and goal of their way. It is quite clear that Paul could not regard this λύπη as a kind of preparation for the first. In it man is looking in quite a different, indeed the opposite direction. He must live in either the one or the other. But as he cannot go back from the first to the second, he cannot move forward from the second to the first. Obviously, therefore, he cannot regard his self-understanding in the second λύπη as an initial understanding of the first.

But quite apart from this special question we cannot say that we are altogether satisfied with the basic and general agreement that the knowledge of sin is possible and can be actual only as the knowledge of God and therefore as the knowledge of revelation and of faith. For in the *locus de peccato* which precedes the doctrine of reconciliation the agreement of older and more recent theology consists concretely in the view that by the knowledge of God, which makes possible and actual the knowledge of sin, we mean the knowledge of God in His basic relationship with man—as distinct from His presence, action and revelation in Jesus Christ : that is, the knowledge of God in His majesty and holiness as Creator and Ruler of the world, in the demand with which He confronts man or encounters him in history. But, concretely, this means the knowledge of God by the law which is revealed to man by nature and generally (through the mediation of conscience), or the knowledge of God which is specially revealed in history, especially in a particular part of the biblical message which is distinct from the Gospel. In this knowledge of God, which is before and outwith Jesus Christ, and in the law of it as understood in the broader or narrower sense, we are thus dealing with that Word of God which has the special function of teaching man that he is a sinner and showing him in what his sin consists. Man finds himself confronted by God in the sublimity of His pure Godhead. He sees himself unmasked and has to recognise and confess himself as disobedient to God, as the one who is at odds with Him and with his neighbour and himself, as the man of sin. The existence, revelation and claim of this God are the judgment in which the divine sentence is proclaimed to him, in which he finds himself reached and scorched by the fire of the divine wrath, by which he is plunged into the divine sorrow by which he is led to repentance—perhaps when he hears the same Word of God as the Word of Jesus Christ and therefore as the Gospel. Against this presentation of the matter serious objection must be taken.

In the first place, it presupposes a division of the knowledge and Word of God. In this context we can only indicate our objection to this presupposition. We have developed it at length and given our reasons for it in earlier chapters of the *Church Dogmatics*, especially in the doctrine of God and creation. The notion of an abstract existence of God in His pure Godhead as Creator and Ruler of the world, the notion of an abstract authority of His claim as such, are elements which are alien to the biblical knowledge of God and cannot, therefore, be put to any Christian use. According to the biblical knowledge of God, God, the Father, Son and Holy Spirit, is concretely one both in His inner being and in His presence, action and revelation in the world and for us. Similarly His eternal election and will, and His action as it is the basis and fulfilment of time, are one. And whether this is known to the men of different times and places or not, this one God and His one work and Word is Jesus Christ. He, the Son of the Father (in the unity of the Holy Spirit), is the face of God, the name of God, the form of God, outside which God is not God. He is the beginning and end of all the ways of God, even in His control and activity as Creator and Ruler of the world, and in His authority and claim in relation to man. In this basic relationship especially God is this God and no other. A division of God into a god in Christ and a god outside Christ is quite impossible. We cannot start from such a division even in our question concerning the basis of the knowledge of human sin.

In general terms it is true enough that the knowledge of God alone includes within itself the knowledge of sin, and that this knowledge arises only in the confrontation of man by the majesty and holiness of God.

Obviously we cannot contradict Luther when in a sermon (dated 1532 according to *E.A.* 6, 49) he declared : " Theology teaches us to compare man with God and say : God is eternal, righteous, true and *in summa* everything good. As against that, man is mortal, unrighteous, deceitful, full of vice, sin and blasphemy. God means everything that is good, man means death and the devil and hell-fire. God is from eternity and to eternity. Man is set in sins, and in the midst of life he is constantly in death. God is full of grace. Man is without grace and under the wrath of God. Such is man compared with God."

But to be true, this general statement needs to be filled out concretely. It does not involve the confrontation of man by the abstract law of an abstract god, because according to the biblical testimony such a god and his law are a product of the free speculation of the human reason and of arbitrary human imagining, and therefore an unreal quantity. If we compare man with this god we can only expect that the resultant knowledge of human sin will correspond to what man himself understands by it and not what Holy Scripture itself understands by it. If this god—the abstract god of an abstract law— cannot justify man (and even those who maintain this opinion do not believe that he can), then how can he really and truly and validly accuse and condemn him ?

It can be shown that he cannot and does not do so. Let us suppose for a moment that this division of the concepts God and law is legitimate. Outside God in Jesus Christ we still have to do with the same God—distinct from this form—in the quite different form of ·the Creator and Ruler of the world. We still have to do with His law, revealed to us in our individual or collective conscience, or in a native law of nature, or in a concrete manifestation of His will and commandment (as in the Decalogue or the Sermon on the Mount). Such a confrontation may serve and be quite useful to stir up a sense of, and to measure intellectually, the infinitely qualitative difference between God and man. But can it also awaken the knowledge that man finds himself in contradiction against God (and therefore against his neighbour and himself) ?—a contradiction which he brings about himself, for which he therefore knows himself to be responsible, so that he must acknowledge that he is guilty. This divine being and his law obviously confront man with demands. But in what sense can and will their demands be binding on man—binding in such a way that he is unsettled by his failure to meet them, binding in such a way that he regards himself as responsible for not meeting them, and knows that because of them he is accused and sentenced and condemned ? Will the self-knowledge necessarily induced by this confrontation lead him in fact any further than the point which he can and usually will reach by mere self-communing and without this confrontation the knowledge of his imperfection ? Can he not easily retreat to the statement that his failure to measure up to God and his deviation from His law is laid upon him by nature in view of the difference between himself and the being that commands—for what is the creature in relation to the Creator ?—that it is therefore necessary and insuperable, that it cannot, therefore, be understood as in any true sense wilful disobedience ? Are we not excused and indeed justified from the very outset in the position in which we find ourselves when confronted in this way ? For in what position do we find ourselves but that of our natural limitation ? Is there a single man who has seen himself to be evil, the man of sin, in this confrontation ? And in the obvious ineffectiveness of this supposed confrontation, of this imaginary god and his claim, is it not shown that he is simply a supposed and imaginary god, an arbitrary invention, the positing of which is simply another act of self-understanding ? Is not this god simply a reflection of our own existence, the essence of our own " existence in transcendence," in relation to which we have merely sublimated and dramatised and mythologised our own self-communing ? Is it not pure imagination that in respect of it we have received a word addressed to us from outside and by someone else ? Is it not the case that we have really been soliloquising ?

Concerning this god and his law and how these fictions arise and what is their significance for the life of man, we shall have more to say when we come to speak of sin itself. This god and his law are not by any means harmless fictions, for in them the real God is dishonoured and His real Law is emptied of content. The man of sin has every reason to divide the living God in His living Word, regarding Him as God, and His Word as the Law which is given to him, only in the form of this abstraction. But God is not mocked, and He will not allow this division to go unpunished. There can be no question, however, that there is no knowledge of sin when the god and his law to whose revelations man listens are in fact this idol and his imaginary claim.

Nor is it clear how it can be otherwise than that a doctrine of sin which precedes Christology and is independent of it should consciously or unconsciously, directly or indirectly, move in the direction of this idol and his claim. To affirm evil as such it is forced to have a standard of good and to apply that standard. But independently of Christology what standard can there be other than a normative concept constructed either from philosophical or biblical materials or a combination of the two ?—a concept of righteousness and holiness, or of a supreme good, or of pure spirit, or of supreme personality, concerning the content of which we can boldly accept and maintain that it is the nature or will or law of God, the authority which demands from man faith and obedience or humility or even love and sacrifice, and that the rejection of it, the infraction, transgression and negation of its demands, is human sin, to forgive and to remove which Jesus Christ came into the world and died for men. As was said in Ex. 32⁴ when the molten calf was set up : " Behold thy gods, O Israel."

It is not inevitable that the concept used in this process should be this idol and his claim. And from this process there can, in fact, arise a fairly—and in some respects supremely—relevant knowledge of sin. This happy situation arises when the concept is constructed, not out of philosophical, but wholly or mainly out of biblical materials, as was done with very great care in Reformation theology especially. If in setting up this standard and determining the nature and will and law of God we keep directly or indirectly to the texts of Holy Scripture, if we allow them forcefully to interrupt us—as did Augustine—correcting the concept which we have originally formed from some very different source, then the worst dangers of this method will not be quite so acute. There cannot lack at least the severity of the judgment that man is a sinner before God, and guilty before Him. For the texts of the Bible are all in some way or other orientated and determined and characterised by the substance of the Bible, in the Old Testament by God's covenant of grace with His people, and in the New by the appearance and person and work of Jesus Christ Himself as the fulfilment of the covenant proclaimed there. Because of that they have a weight which, if we let them speak for themselves, will necessarily lead to the greatest severity in the judgment of man. Where they are accepted and used as the source of knowledge, and in proportion as they are the only source, this will be seen even where—as was unfortunately the case with all the Reformers—we do not allow ourselves to be guided in the establishment of this norm by the substance and centre of the Bible, but only by individual pronouncements and passages determined by that centre and substance.

That this was the case in Reformation theology is one (and not the only) result of the lack of attention which was then paid to Christology. In this respect the doctrine of the early creeds was subscribed as self-evident. It formed the presupposition without which the Reformation doctrine of justification and faith is unintelligible. Because of the rift in the question of the Lord's Supper there were, too, certain interesting differences of emphasis in Christology in Luther, Zwingli and Calvin. But no independent attention was paid to this central theme. Interest in Christ was mainly within the framework of the *beneficia Christi*. It was, of course, said that Holy Scripture is the Word of God to the extent that it presents Christ. But the programme of Reformation theology did not allow for any radical consideration of the meaning, importance and function of Christology in relation to all Christian knowledge. For that reason this theology was in many spheres—with illuminating exceptions—able to think and argue from Christology only very indirectly and implicitly, or not at all. This was the case in the doctrine of sin, and the question of the standard by which we know good from evil.

The inevitable result of this omission was that no very certain or illuminating and relevant answer could be given to the question of the judgment, and the content of the judgment, which has to be pronounced on man in accordance with this standard. Of course, under the guidance of the Scripture principle what was said concerning this judgment was quite true in spite of the omission, thanks to the force of the texts as seen directly or indirectly in relation to the centre of the Bible. Indeed many true and important things were brought to light. It was certainly not by that idol and his claim that man was measured and his state as the man of sin was seen and understood. Although from a distance and with a certain indistinctness, it was by the true and living God and His Law.

To refer to Calvin, we can see this clearly from *Instit.* 1, 1, 2–3, where he emphasises that man can have a true self-knowledge (*pura sui notitia*) only when he looks at God and from that comes down to consider himself. Why then and only then ? Because of ourselves and without a clear proof to the contrary we always regard ourselves as upright, wise and holy. But we can never find this clear proof to the contrary so long as we look at ourselves and not at the Lord.

By nature we are inclined to hypocrisy. We are satisfied with an empty show of righteousness, as though that were true righteousness. We regard as pure that which in a mass of impurity is a little less impure. We regard as light a mere glimmer in the darkness. Because our perceptivity is sufficient for things around and beneath us we think that it cannot be surpassed, not pausing to consider what becomes of it when we lift up our eyes to the sun. Hence our satisfaction with our own goodness within the limit of our humanity. But this falls to pieces when we lift our eyes to God and His perfection by which we are really measured. Where then is our righteousness, wisdom, virtue and purity ? Our wickedness and folly and impotence are mercilessly exposed. Hence the terror ascribed by Scripture even to holy men in the presence of God. Obviously it is only in this encounter, but then truly and radically, that they experience this terror at their own state, the *cognitio humilitatis*, the *consternatio*, which involves a *horror mortis*. " We shall surely die, because we have seen God " (Jud. 13²²). This was the experience of Job, and Abraham, and Elijah and Isaiah. *Sola est lux Domini, quae potest oculos nostros aperire, ut perspicere queant latentem in carne nostra foeditatem,* while in the darkness of our sin in blind self-love we are not able to estimate the nature and extent of the filth (*sordes*) heaped up in us (*Comm. on Rom.* 6²¹, *C.R.* 49, 117).

It is noteworthy that Calvin plainly regarded the Old Testament as supremely instructive in this respect. It never seems to have struck him that this *lux Domini* has truly and decisively shone upon us and exposed us in man's confrontation by God in the crucified and risen Jesus Christ, not even when he came to discuss this part of the New Testament. There is simply a general antithesis : God on the one hand and man on the other. It is simply maintained that this antithesis breaks through man's self-deception and gives a genuine self-knowledge. (It seems doubtful to me whether we can agree with T. F. Torrance in his fine book, *Calvin's Doctrine of Man*, 1949, p. 83 f.—and we would be only too ready to do so if it were a fact—that with Calvin the doctrine of the corruption of man is a corollary of the doctrine of grace.) In the introduction to the *Institutio*—at the beginning of the book *De cognitione Dei creatoris*—he seems to have regarded it as self-evident that for the moment we cannot and ought not to speak of man in his confrontation with Jesus Christ. For this reason his account of the encounter with God and its effect is not altogether dissimilar to that given by R. Otto (in his book *Das Heilige*) of what he calls the experience of man—even non-Christian man—in relation to the *fascinosum* of the Wholly Other. The consequence is that for all the impressiveness of the statement the description of the effect on man cannot (1) offer any real explanation of what occurs or (2) describe it in other than strong but very general terms (that man is shown in all his unrighteousness, folly, impurity, depravity, etc.). When Calvin wrote he had constantly before him the examples of Job, Abraham, Elijah and Isaiah. Thus we are always in the sphere of the biblical concept of God, even though we are not at the centre. The presentation does not leave anything to be desired in clarity. It is God alone who convinces man of his corruption, and when God does it He does it radically, and there is no possibility of any softening of the verdict that man is corrupt. We find the same methodical weakness but unmistakable practical strength of presentation in Luther, Zwingli, the younger Melanchthon, and to a large extent the older Protestant orthodoxy. When in the application of the method the thinking and teaching are biblicist if not biblical, by a happy inconsistency they could and can produce serious results.

But this caveat is not in itself a justification of the method. If we are determined not to keep to the biblical centre and substance and therefore to Jesus Christ in this matter of the fall of man, if, therefore, we are forced to construct our own normative concept as a standard by which to measure man, then it is hard to see what will prevent us from taking supplementary (and sometimes basic) material from some very different source—from philosophy, combining the Scripture principle with one form or other of that of reason.

We must not forget that the transition from biblical to biblicist thought does involve the transition to a rationalism—supranaturalistic though it is in content. Therefore the relationship of theology to the truths of revelation which it has taken from the Bible is no longer the relationship to an authority which is superior to man. It has fundamentally the same assurance and control with regard to them as man as a rational creature has in regard to himself, his experience, his thinking and therefore his world, believing that he is the master of himself as subject and therefore of his objects, or of his own relation to them.

As is well known, the supreme achievement of the older Protestant orthodoxy was the doctrine of the verbal inspiration of Holy Scripture as developed in the later 17th century and given confessional status in the Helvetic *Formula of Concord* in 1675. There can be no doubt, however, that this was not merely worked out as a bulwark against a growing rationalism, but that it was itself, not an expression of an over-developed faith of revelation, but a product of typical rationalistic thinking—the attempt to replace faith and indirect knowledge by direct knowledge, to assure oneself of revelation in such a way that it was divorced from the living Word of the living God as attested in Scripture, pin-pointing it, making it readily apprehensible as though it were an object of secular experience, and therefore divesting it in fact of its character as revelation.

The irremediable danger of consulting Holy Scripture apart from the centre, and in such a way that the question of Jesus Christ ceases to be the controlling and comprehensive question and simply becomes one amongst others, consists primarily in the fact that (even pre-supposing a strict and exclusive Scripture principle) Scripture is thought of and used as though the message of revelation and the Word of God could be extracted from it in the same way as the message of other truth or reality can be extracted from other sources of knowledge, at any rate where it is not presumably speaking of Jesus Christ. But if Scripture is read in this way, the Scripture principle will not stand very long. Secretly the book of revelation is being treated and read like other books ; and the question cannot long be denied whether the message we gather from it cannot be gathered from other books either by way of addition or even basically ; whether the truths of revelation in the Bible are not of a series with all kinds of other truths ; whether in them we do not simply have concretions of what is revealed concerning God and His will to all other men as such and by nature, of themselves, by the dictate of their reason ? If Jesus Christ is seen to be the whole of Scripture, the one truth of revelation, this question cannot even be put, let alone given a positive answer. There is no other book which witnesses to Jesus Christ apart from Holy Scripture.

This decides the fact that only in Holy Scripture do we have to do with the one and the whole Word and revelation of God. But if we do not see this, it is inevitable that the question of other sources of revelation should be put, and that sooner or later it should be given a positive answer.

The rise of this danger can be illustrated by examples from 17th century Reformed theology.

It is clear that when it first threatened plainly it was seen or felt, and could be avoided. J. Piscator, in his *Aphorismi Doctrinae christianae* of 1589, gives us a short summary of Calvin's *Institutio*, in which on the very first pages he gives excerpts from Calvin and an interpretation which makes Calvin say something which in *Instit.* 1, 1–5 he did not really say at all. According to Piscator, there is a twofold knowledge of God : *una naturalis, altera acquisita.* The natural knowledge of God is impressed on the natural instincts of all rational adults (*sana mente praeditis*) as is plain from the religions, or the religious awe of the heathen. The *cognitio Dei acquisita* is based on instruction, either by human philosophy or by Holy Scripture. The natural knowledge, and that which is attained by the instruction of human philosophy, is what Calvin called the *semen religionis.* But, of course—and here we have a powerful safeguard—this is corrupted by human folly and wickedness, and in practice can lead only to false religions. Even the knowledge of God from His own Word—the general knowledge which is gained *affectu pietatis*—can serve only to make man inexcusable before God. There can be a true and saving knowledge of God from His Word only where He is known with a heart's trust not only as Creator but as Redeemer. Piscator had neither the capacity nor the desire to develop systematically his doctrine of a twofold knowledge any more than Calvin. Even in his doctrine of the Law and sin we seek in vain for any outworking of this doctrine. The Law is given by God through the ministry of angels and Moses. Sin is the transgression of the positive commandment which was given to our first parents. That is all. But with the further development of Reformed theology both Law and sin came gradually but irresistibly to be spoken of in quite different terms.

Already W. Bucanus (*Instit. theol.*, 1605, XIX, 3) was defining the law as the *doctrina hominum mentibus a Deo indita et postea a Mose repetita.* According to the well-known misunderstanding of Rom. 2¹⁴ᶠ·, the Law was thought of as the law of nature written on the heart of man, which Moses merely repeated, expressly proclaiming and interpreting it (11). We seem to be listening again to Luther who, in his work *Wider die himmlischen Propheten*, 1525 (*W.A.* 18, 81, 18) had written : " Why do we keep and teach the ten commandments ? Because nowhere are the natural laws so finely and orderly stated as in Moses." But Bucan seems to have meant seriously his reference to the obscuring of this natural law which made necessary its fresh promulgation. And it is remarkable that in his presentation of the fall of Adam he only hints at this thought : the fall consisted in the *voluntaria transgressio* of the first positive divine commandment and the *ordo divinus* (XV, 13), by which is meant this primitive form.

Polanus, too (*Synt. Theol. chr.*, 1609), as was now the general custom in Protestantism (VI, 9), allowed quite definitely and eloquently for a twofold *patefactio : tum naturalis, tum supernaturalis.* In the first of these all men have a share *qua homines.* Apart from the *liber naturae*, i.e., the visible external works of God in creation, it includes the *liber conscientiae* or the *lex naturae*, i.e., the *naturalis notitia in prima creatione cordibus hominum impressa, tradens discrimen honestorum et turpium.* Polan accepts this *lex naturalis*, which being identical with the *vera philosophia* cannot contradict the Word of God. But against it, and he obviously means this seriously, he sets the statement that the unregenerate man (by reason of his native blindness and corruption) can deduce from this natural revelation only false ideas of God. What is left is a warm defence of the legitimacy of a formal use of the *recta ratio*. But materially theology must keep strictly to Scripture. In the chapter on the Law (VI, 10) Polan does not actually mention the *lex naturae* again, let alone allow the concept to be palpably determined by it. The same is true of his doctrine of sin (VI, 3). Here, indeed—one of the happy inconsistencies—we find the definition that sin is the evil which arises in the will of man and which deserves and will necessarily bring death apart from forgiveness for the sake of Christ the Mediator.

But with J. Wolleb (*Chr. Theol. comp.*, 1626, I, 9, 1) the case is different. The definition of 1 Jn. 3⁴ is now made a consistent formula : sin is ἀνομία. What Bucan had only hinted is now stated expressly. By the law which our first parents transgressed we have to understand *tum praecepta et interdicta homini primitus proposita, tum lex naturae cordi eius insculpta*. Even more plainly (I, 9, 2, *can.* 6) sin is transgression of the whole *lex naturalis*, which does not differ in content, but only in the form of revelation, from that impartation of the will and commandment of God (in the Decalogue, etc.) which was revealed by Moses and later purged by Christ from its Pharisaic corruptions (I, 13, *can.* 1 and 7).

Meanwhile a further step had obviously been taken in Reformed Holland. The *Leidener Synopsis* appeared for the first time in 1624. In the opening section (*Disp.* 1, 9) we read that the theology presented is to be based on the " supernatural " revelation mediated by God through the Holy Spirit. But in the doctrine of the Law (*Disp.* 18, 13 f.) we learn that there is a *lex naturalis* identical with the *lumen et dictamen rectae rationis in intellectu, hominem* κοιναῖς ἐννοίαις *seu communibus notionibus ad iusti et iniusti, honesti ac turpis discretionem informans, ut quid faciendum sit vel fugiendum, intelligat*. These *notiones communes* have indeed been obscured and almost extinguished, at any rate as practical principles of the human spirit, but as *scintillae* of the fall of man they still remain in such strength—as outwardly attested by the laws of the heathen and inwardly by conscience—that they are sufficient to accuse and condemn sin. According to this presentation the moral law transgressed by our first parents (*Disp.* 14, 7) is simply the ὑποτύπωσις of this natural law.

From the second half of the 17th century we will consult the *Synopsis Theologiae* (first published in 1671) of that great systematiser of Federal theology, F. Burmann of Utrecht. The introduction of the term covenant which underlies the whole is promising. But almost from the very first in this school the covenant between God and man in its original form is, unfortunately, not a covenant of grace, but of nature, law and works. The way was thus opened for an even more zealous preoccupation with the conviction of a moral law of nature normative in this original covenant. According to Burmann (IV, 3, 2), the *lex moralis* is *in sese eadem*, and therefore identical with the *lex naturalis* written on the heart of man, of which there remain even in sinful man certain *reliquiae et rudera*, certain *principia et ideae* in respect of right and wrong, and the universal validity of which is proclaimed in the law-codes of all nations— with certain vacillations in understanding, and the less clearly the more the conclusions deduced have departed from it. It is claimed of the *lex naturalis* that in its original form it proceeds from the nature of God Himself. As such, therefore, it is necessary and inescapable, and it is called the *lex aeterna* (3). Its form in connexion with the created order is, within limits, unalterable and indispensable, in contrast to its form in the positive divine commandment which is clearly alterable (4). But as the *lex aeterna* it is the *expressissima sanctitatis divinae imago, plenissima officiorum omnium norma : cum erga Deum, tum erga homines, denique hominis erga seipsum* (7), the sacred guarantee (*sanctimonia*) of all human laws (11). It is, therefore, very much the same as what we have called the normative concept of good by which we can measure evil. That this is Burmann's meaning is no mere conjecture ; he says it himself quite expressly in his depiction of the covenant of nature broken by Adam (II, 2, 18) : *lex ipsi lata proprie lex fuerit naturae et conscientiae dictatus ac lux.* What was really demanded of Adam was obedience to this law, the concrete commandment of God being only a *praeceptum symbolicum* to give him the test which he failed. Returning to Reformed Switzerland, we find the same view expressed, if anything even more clearly, in J. H. Heidegger's *Medulla Theol. christ.*, 1696. Heidegger, too, was a Federal theologian. And he, too, based the original covenant between God and man on a law of nature given by God and to be kept by man. But he says directly what his predecessors, and even Burmann, had never stated, although it was in keeping with their thought : that this law is called the *lex naturae* because in it nature as the principle of all human activity not only had, but has, its norm and canon (*habuit et habet*). In the person of Adam, God implanted the *notitia honesti et turpis* in the rational nature common to all men (IX, 11). The statements which describe Adam historically are all formulated in the present. The reason given to all men knows the existence of God, the strict demand for obedience, the necessity for ordered human society. Heidegger can make the noteworthy statement that the way in which the divine law is imparted has nothing whatever to do with its nature (content, authority and function) : *neque enim modus legem promulgandi ad essentiam eius pertinet* (IX, 12). It is of no importance whether the promulgation of the divine law takes place in such a way that God speaks with man in the revelation of His will as the Lord of the covenant or whether the law revealed by God resides in the heart of man and he speaks with himself. Moreover, although there is still a caveat in view of the obscuring of this knowledge by sin, its importance is only theoretical. In practice there is no hesitation in giving the first and decisive word to the law inwardly revealed and therefore to the man who interprets it. It is in that which agrees with the *recta ratio*, with the principles of every rational being, with the social character of all human life as obviously striven after by all men and affirmed by all civilised peoples, that we have to see the dictate of this natural law, which cannot have any other source, which has therefore supreme authority (13). The Decalogue is an instrument to facilitate a recognition of this law, and it emphasises that the obedience we must give it should be primarily inward (14–15). The binding force and authority of the positive and concrete commandments of God derives from the commandment of the *lex naturae*, which cannot be altered even by God Himself, and which summons us to obedience towards Him as our legitimate Master (16–17). In this connexion Heidegger can make the further pregnant statement that God allows us to judge even Himself by the standard of the natural law, and he thinks that there is a biblical foundation for this statement, e.g., in Is. 5[3] : " And now, O inhabitants of Jerusalem, and men of Judah, judge, I pray you, betwixt me and my vineyard," or Gen. 18[25] (cf. Rom. 3[6]) : " Shall not the judge of all the earth do right ? " In the original covenant of law and works one of the positive commandments of God (given for the purpose only of testing man, according to Heidegger) was the prohibiting of the first man from eating of the tree of knowledge (18). If therefore—as is laid down generally in the doctrine of sin—the obligation to obey God does not rest only on this or that concrete expression of the will of God (a *lex Dei libera et arbitraria*), but on the law of nature—for otherwise Heidegger fears that man's obedience might acquire the character of an act which is correspondingly free—then sin is not evil merely as a failure to keep this or that *lex libera* of God but primarily and decisively as a failure to keep the natural law written on the heart (X, 2–3).

It must be noted that the voice which we have heard is not that of 18th century rationalism but 17th century orthodoxy. This theology had not been taught by the Reformers themselves to learn from Jesus Christ as the substance and centre of Scripture what is the will and Law of God and therefore what the sin of man is. And the theology itself obviously had no power of itself to rectify the omission. For this reason it could and indeed had to think with a growing intensity and speak with an increasing clarity along the lines discussed. At this critical point in its exposition of revelation—hesitantly at first, but then more confidently—it could and had to go beyond the Scripture principle which it proclaimed so loudly to another principle, that of reason. The transition to the Enlightenment and all that that involved was not the terrible innovation that it has often been called. In many respects, and in this respect also, orthodoxy itself was engaged in a wholehearted transition to the Enlightenment—a further proof that the slogan " Back to Orthodoxy," and even the slogan " Back to the Reformers," cannot promise us the help that we need to-day. " Back to . . ." is never a good slogan.

Why and to what extent is it dangerous to try to learn what the Law is and what sin is from another source—and perhaps radically and decisively from another source—than from Scripture, from the concrete expression of the will of God and the concrete proclamation of the judgment of God as attested in Scripture ? There is no doubt that in the measure that we think we know what the Law and sin are " by nature " and therefore (because the Law of God is written on the heart) of ourselves, to that extent our knowledge will not in fact be the knowledge of faith. It will not be the knowledge which is mediated by the Word and Spirit of God, but the knowledge which we suppose to be immediate, which we have won from our self-communing. But what if the knowledge of faith from Holy Scripture and knowledge in the form of immediate self-knowledge do not compete with one another ? What if the true and basic form of all man's knowledge of the Law and sin is immediate self-knowledge ? What if the concrete expression of the will of God degenerates into a *praeceptum symbolicum* to make clear that which man can learn from himself by this immediate self-knowledge ? What if the concrete proclamation of the divine judgment is only an underlining of the verdict that man can and must pronounce upon himself ? What if in this matter man is at bottom only engaged in a soliloquy which he has dramatised and mythologised with the help of biblical reminiscences—a discussion in which he not only presents both sides of the case but is also the chairman who can terminate it with a casting vote ? Well, we can only repeat our question whether in this case there will be, or can be, any knowledge of the real demand of God and the real sin of man. We have seen—and Reformation theology proves this—that this is possible so long as an equilibrium is maintained between the two factors ; so long as the supposed law of nature in the heart of man does not become the over-riding norm, the decisive canon of human self-knowledge ; so long as the concrete expression of the divine will and proclamation of the divine judgment as attested in Holy Scripture can in its own power compete with and control and correct the voice of that supposed natural law. Even then the situation is dangerous. And if the reversal takes place, then all the biblicist dramatising and mythologising of that self-communing cannot prevent man from sooner or later forming notions of God and His Law on the one hand, and His own guilt and need on the other, which deviate considerably from the witness of Scripture and the truth, which are very acceptable to himself but most inappropriate because they are harmless and conciliatory and compromising.

They are notions which will quickly invade and colour his conception of justification and then his understanding of the atonement. He may not at first be moved away from the statements of Scripture and dogma—although that will not be for long. But soon, in all probability he will no longer understand that there can be for him and for the race no atonement, no hope or peace, apart from the forgiveness and righteousness purchased for them by Jesus Christ in His death on the cross. He will then be easily satisfied with the hope and peace which we can have and know without the resurrection of Jesus Christ and the verdict of the Holy Spirit, except perhaps in a symbolical and illustrative form. He will then very quickly find himself in the sphere of a general philosophy of religion or life or existence. Once we begin to toy with the *lex naturae* as the inner *lex aeterna* we are well on the way to this. And once the reversal has taken place— as it did in Protestant theology at the turn of the 17th century—there can be no stopping on this way. It is not our present task, however, to follow the matter to its final end, in which God Himself is ultimately reduced to a mere symbol or cipher.

What concerns us now is the form of the danger as it arises at the beginning of the way. It consists in this, that sin takes on the appearance of something which is quite comfortable. The biblical statements concerning it are still repeated with a certain uneasiness, but at bottom they cannot be made with conviction. The contours in which they describe it are too sharp. The contrast between God and man as sketched in the light of it is too deep. The assertion of the irremediable nature of human guilt and need is carried too far. Syntheses are sought and found. The relationship between grace and sin must not be exclusive. It must be one of continuity and compensation. The conflict in which man finds himself must be passed over and man understood in his unavoidable limitation and relativity. God and the world which is so very different from Him, God and man in his distance from and antithesis to Him, must be seen, not in a history, in the fulfilment of a decision, but as substances which are formally of the same character. The grace of God and the sin of man must be approached as states on the one level, in a relationship which—if it has been disturbed—cannot be really jeopardised or broken, and therefore at bottom does not have to be renewed. Sin must be seen as a possible element in this relationship, not altogether unprofitable, indeed in its way indispensable. It is the middle act in a drama, preceded by others and followed by others, and in the strict sense necessary by reason of that which precedes and follows. Taking everything into account, the moment man acknowledges that he is a sinner he is already comforted (because he has never really been discomfited); he is already definitively and totally at peace, because he has never been anything other than at peace with God and his neighbour and himself. At bottom, man is quite able to cope with himself even as the man of sin. He always was. And the supposed *lex naturae* in his own heart certainly will not prevent him but invite and demand that he should see it in this way. In so far as this law is in our own hearts it gives us the competence, in so far as it is eternal it gives us the authority, and in so far as we ourselves are the men of sin we have the need and the desire and the self-confidence, to arrange and deal with ourselves as the men we are in this very comfortable way.

There is nothing of all this in the Bible. And we will soon tire of using it symbolically and by way of illustration because quotations from other good books are better adapted for the purpose. The Bible itself insists on saying something quite different concerning Law and sin from what man says about or to himself—whether or not he uses the texts of the Bible, whether or not—directly or indirectly, mildly or more severely—he criticises that which it says.

We will illustrate this unavoidable consequence of the process under discussion by some examples from later theological history, from the newer Protestantism as it came to its full form from the beginning of the 19th century onwards after the transitional period of the 18th century. We are not now asking how men came to think and speak in the way that we shall see, but simply what was in fact the concept of human sin at the end of the way, the beginning of which we have illustrated from the orthodox Reformed of the 17th century.

As is proper, we will mention first two representatives of the " rationalistic " school of the first half of the 19th century (using the term " rationalistic " in the narrower sense). The first of these is J. A. L. Wegscheider in his *Institutiones Theol. chr. dogm.*, 1815. According to Wegscheider, the case with sin is as follows. It is only with great effort and continual application that man can raise himself to the dignity and divine likeness marked out for him. For together with the desire for this and the consciousness of what is right, there is also a *propensio quaedam et proclivitas ad peccandum*, an inclination to listen more to the enticement of the senses than to the voice of reason and the known standard of good. This is explained by the fact that the majority of men lack the necessary culture and education. But every man is in danger of sinning as long as he is on the earth (§ 113). He may actually be made to do so by the inheriting of fatal qualities, errors of perception and experience, an undeveloped reason, immediate or more distant social environment and its influences. But we cannot speak of an incapacity of man for the good. On the contrary, the Romanist catechism is right when it says that indwelling concupiscence has nothing to do with sin so long as it is not voluntarily approved (§ 117). God could not prevent the first man actually sinning without encroaching on his freedom. The only presupposition of individual sinful action is an *infirmitas quaedam moralis* which he can fight and overcome and thus rise gradually to true virtue. He can and should do this. What is necessary is that he should be made conscious, not of his sinfulness, but of this capacity, and that he should be invited to make use of it (§ 118).

The second is K. G. Bretschneider in his *Handbuch d. Dogm. der ev.-luth. Kirche*, 1838, Vol. 1, p. 718 f. As he sees it, sin is only a subjective and relative evil, existing only in the relationship of our activity to our consciousness of the divine law and our duty. It cannot exist, for example, in the child, arising only " when virtue (conscious obedience to the law) begins, which, like anything formative, is at first imperfect." It therefore denotes the " rise of moral development and it is the point at which virtue breaks through, disappearing as the development moves to its goal. It is not something which remains, but something which passes and disappears, a means to an end." It is the will of God that we should go through this process of development. And it has for us the advantage " that we have a share in the attaining of moral freedom," that we have the possibility of being " fellow-creators of ourselves (as free beings), that in this way alone there is given us the possibility of joy in moral good as our own work—a joy which in our feeling is a great blessedness for finite spirits." There are, of course, individuals in whom this process of development does not succeed, who therefore die as sinners. But death is not the end of all moral being and all development, but the transition to its continuation beyond. Between the virtuous man and the sinner, there is the difference—but only the difference—that the one " attains the goal of freedom along the way of inner peace and happiness," the other " of inner unhappiness and external misery " ; the one with the lofty feeling of having advanced by his own effort along the way of divine likeness, the other with the depressing consciousness of having done little to prosper and much to retard it. " Objectively, therefore, in relation to the development ordained by God, sin is not an evil, but, like obedience, it is a way to freedom, the difference being that it attains the goal by a way of thorns, obedience by a way of roses."

We will now rise to a higher level and consult the great Hegel. In 1821 he gave some lectures on the philosophy of religion under the title *Die absolute Religion*. In the third part of these he developed his Christian dogmatics grouped under the headings : The Kingdom of the Father, of the Son, and of the Spirit. Under the title " The Kingdom of the Son ", he treated first of creation, man and sin, then of the God-man and the atonement. It looks as though we ought to pay attention when we find sin dealt with in the Kingdom of the Son. But we are quickly disillusioned. With Hegel, too, the doctrine of sin precedes that of the God-man and the atonement, and is not, therefore, derived from it. For Hegel, God is identical with absolute concept, absolute spirit, absolute truth, the dialectical movement of which takes place in human thought as the finite form of the one absolute spirit. The Father, then, is eternal, comprehensive and total generality. The Son is the eternal particularity of phenomenon. The Spirit is individuality as such, with which the circle of thought begins again from the beginning. Or, again, the Father is the movement of thought from immediacy to objectivity. The Son is its transition to the mediacy of reflection and presentation. The Spirit is its return to itself, to pure knowledge as the unity of antitheses. In exactly the same way creation, sin and atonement are only the three necessary moments in the circular history of finite spirit, which is itself the central moment in the process of absolute spirit, in which " the divine attains to its supreme being outside itself, finding there its turning point " (ed. Lasson, p. 95). Spirit as finite spirit is in the first instance natural spirit. In its highly problematical innocence as such it is " essentially that which it cannot continue to be " (p. 96). It is good in itself, but only in name and not in reality (p. 114). But it is also free spirit, raising itself from mere willing to thinking, conscious in its being in and for itself of that antithesis as an infinite contradiction in which it is evil (p. 112). In that it posits itself as evil, regarding itself as that which it ought not to be (p. 106), " the removal of evil begins, the eternal return of spirit to itself, its reconciliation with itself." The same point is therefore the source of evil, " the poison-cup from which man drinks death and destruction," and also the source of reconciliation and health (p. 96). It is one and the same knowledge which " causes the wound and heals it," so that the wound, or evil itself (self-seeking, as Hegel sees it), has to be thought of—and the description proves to be unavoidable—as a " necessary momentary or longer point of transition " (p. 105). In short, there is an unbroken continuity between creation and sin, and sin and atonement. And since the finite spirit in whose existence this process takes place is itself only a moment in the life of the movement of absolute spirit, absolute concept and absolute truth, of God Himself, this continuity, this point of transition is sanctioned and guaranteed by the existence and life of God Himself.

We must also consider briefly the teaching of Schleiermacher on this point (*The Christian Faith*, § 65–85, and cf. *C.D.*, III, 3, § 50, 3 for a detailed presentation and criticism). We have here what is technically the most complete and, in substance, the most promising achievement of the new Protestantism. It therefore makes the limitation of the solutions possible on this basis all the more palpable. According to Schleiermacher, sin is the qualification of our self-consciousness by our God-consciousness, which makes us aware of the relative impotence or constriction of our God-consciousness as disinclination. There is no consciousness of sin without that of God, and in the soul of the Christian without that of the power of redemption. Again, there is no consciousness of God or redemption without that of sin. Again, there is no sinfulness later coming to consciousness before the awakening of God-consciousness without the presupposition of an original perfection which has not been overthrown. Conversely, there is no Christian consciousness of God (in the knowledge of the sinlessness and spiritual effectiveness of the Redeemer) without the certainty of a future human perfection free from sin as the goal of our own development. Sin, therefore, is the opposition of which man becomes guilty in his dependence on the form given to life by preceding generations and as his own act. From two standpoints the teaching of Schleiermacher is both significant and suspect. First, he aims to understand sin as that which in our consciousness is negated by the grace of God. In so far as man is conscious of it, God makes the being and activity of man sin in order to keep him for and in redemption, in order to awaken and continually to renew in him the need for it. It is in virtue of this divine negation (which is positive in intention) that sin has its being and existence. What a prospect would be opened up if Schleiermacher were thinking of the negation which comes to man in his confrontation by Jesus Christ, understanding sin as that which is excluded and condemned in Him, and therefore by the grace of God ; as that which in its own dark way is real in its negative relation to Him ! But as he sees it, the negation in which sin has its reality takes place only in our consciousness of God, not in an encounter and history of man with God. For Schleiermacher there is no such thing as a Christian in whom this encounter and history take place, who is therefore anything more than the embodied idea of an undisturbed and powerful God-consciousness fulfilling and controlling our consciousness of the world. The result is that God Himself has no direct or personal part in the negation which takes place in the human consciousness. He is neither affronted nor does He suffer. He is not wrathful at sin nor merciful to the sinner. He merely sees to it from without that there arises in us a consciousness of this negation. But how can man take his sin seriously as sin if in it he does not have to do with God, if God Himself has no part at all in his consciousness of sin ? How can he take it so seriously that in relation to it he has to recognise that he needs redemption ? Second, Schleiermacher will not admit any being of sin except in relation to redemption. It is as we have a consciousness of our redemption—and in it a consciousness of the original unity of our existence and of a future overcoming of the discord—that we are aware of the discord as such, of our sinfulness and guilt. Hence the definition of sin as the ineffectiveness, the constriction, the limitation, the shrinking of our God-consciousness. This " disinclination " of our consciousness of sin is a failure of our God-consciousness, its rejection in favour of the consciousness of the world which it ought to penetrate and sanctify. As that which is negated by our God-consciousness, sin is only actual as that consciousness is aware of its limitation. Evil is only present with good, the good of redemption. Once again a real prospect opens up. This might mean the non-absoluteness, the relativity in which sin can alone be actual as man's contradiction of the grace of God present to him in Jesus Christ—a frightful actuality in relation to it, but an actuality which is negative and empty. But not being warned, let alone prevented by his Christology, Schleiermacher thought that he could reverse the statement. Good is only present with evil. Our consciousness of God, as a consciousness of grace and redemption, is only present with that of our incapacity for the good and our sin which yields before grace. To that extent sin is, in a sense, necessary in human development if that development is to take place at all, for otherwise man would not be a free being ; he would not be man. With Schleiermacher the correct relativising of sin in relation to grace becomes its co-ordination with grace, its appraisal and justification and even its defence as the complement of grace. As in Bretschneider and Hegel, although in another context, its necessity is established. For all the emphasis on its negative character sin is thought of positively. But is it real sin ? Can we say of real sin, as Schleiermacher says, that this thing which has no place belongs to a definite stage in the existence of man, and that in relation to this stage it was willed and posited by God ? Conversely, can a grace which lives by its opposition to sin, which is referred and related to it, be real grace ? Can a good which is only present with evil be a divine good ? Are we speaking of real sin and real grace where there can be no mention of a real history, a real collision and conflict, a decision between the two ? There is no place for either real sin or real grace in the sphere of Christian consciousness which Schleiermacher selected and posited absolutely as the source of all theological knowledge, sealing it off both from without and from above. For that reason the two items in his doctrine of sin, the significance of which we cannot over-estimate, can only lead us to these very doubtful conclusions.

Within the modernised determinism of one definite trend in the older Reformed theology, Schleiermacher's most faithful disciple, Alexander Schweizer, came to the very same conclusions, although his thinking is less subtle and it does not open up the same prospects as that of Schleiermacher. As he sees it, the central Christian dogma and therefore the controlling principle of his *Christliche Glaubenslehre* (2nd edit., 1877) is the doctrine of the providence and world-governance of God, or subjectively, the doctrine of the religion of the feeling of absolute dependence, which in its supreme form as the Christian faith, i.e., the religion of redemption, contains within itself the religions of nature and law as transitional stages—again this distinctive notion. The necessary transitional stage of the religion of law is characterised by the antithesis of law and sin. Without this antithesis, without permitting sin, God could not have willed the humanity which develops to the good, to the religion of redemption (Vol. I, p. 372). " There can be no development of good without that of evil also " (pp. 319, 372). " Without the evil which is disapproved, in a world which morally is only good, we could not know the holiness of God " (pp. 319, 340). " With the development of good, God must will the possibility and the actuality of that of evil in the world " (p. 319), if only as " the limit, the reverse side and the antithesis of good, so that it has no real being but is there only as a deficiency of being " (p. 340). Or subjectively, the knowledge of our incapacity to be justified by the religion of law and attain our destiny is always the decisive presupposition of the rise of Christian piety (p. 372 f.). This incapacity, and, therefore, the real possibility of evil, is a state in which we always find ourselves as we become transgressors and have to accuse ourselves. It " inheres to the infirm nature of man " as such (p. 375). Schweizer's definition is much more primitive than that of Schleiermacher. It is the " hindering of the undeveloped determinative power of the spirit by the autonomy of the sensual functions "

(p. 378). This hindering has for us the appearance of sinfulness, but it cannot be called our " express sin " in the same way as our transgressions, only the lack of power or capacity which is presupposed in it (p. 376). What else can Schweizer mean but the *infirmitas quaedam moralis* of Wegscheider ? But now we see the bearing of the central dogma, for this weakness has its basis in the divine order of things : " It is God who causes our spiritual life to develop as placed and buried in the natural organism, so that when the developed life of the spirit remains buried in mere naturalness, sin arises "—although God Himself does not bring this about and is not responsible for it (p. 378). The man who does bring it about, its subject, is the " carnal or psychic man, sometimes simply called the flesh," in whom " there necessarily arises the awareness that this state is incompatible with the being of the spirit, but in so far as it wills to maintain itself in opposition to the developing spirit, sin arises " (p. 379). There can be no question of a complete incapacity for good, which would exclude all possibility of redemption, but only of an incapacity to satisfy the religion of law. The reality and knowledge of this incapacity is the indispensable condition for the transition to the religion of redemption (p. 381).

A. E. Biedermann described himself in his *Christl. Dogmatik* (1st ed., 1869) as in substance a disciple of Hegel. In its way his work is one of the most outstanding in modern theology. Our best starting-point is his insistence on the creatureliness of man as finite spirit. This implies his finitude—the finitude of his external being but also of his spiritual life, which is mediated and conditioned by the sensual basis of his nature—the process of spiritual development which is bound up with the possibility of self-contradiction (in error and sin) (§ 745 f.). As a finite spirit he is the creaturely image of God (the absolute spirit). God has placed within him the potency and determination to actualise a life of the spirit which corresponds to His own being in the spirit, which has its root substantially in that being, but which is also outside it in its own finite existence (§ 752). Thus the natural Ego is actually flesh, the pure antithesis of the state of the fulfilment of its determination, but potentially it is spirit, and by virtue of this immanent potency, i.e., by the revelation of God in the impulse of reason it enters the process of the becoming of spirit. From the religious standpoint this takes place as the moral world-order which is immanent in him as the substance of his being in the spirit comes successively into his consciousness by the commandments or prohibitions of the revelation of God in conscience (§ 764). But the flesh, the natural determination, always constitutes the life-content of the Ego which is immediate and subjective. Therefore in the freedom in which the Ego is distinct from that content it is never without the inclination to sin (§ 766), to that self-determination of the finite spirit which is contrary to God in its carnal self-seeking. In content, sin is the self-willing of the finite Ego in its finitude as such, therefore in its natural determination as directly or indirectly sensual, in opposition to its conscious determination for spiritual lordship over natural being as rooted in absolute spirit (§ 767). The fact that man is sinful by nature, " that with the development of the subjective life of the spirit there arose that inclination to sin," has as its material cause his being as finite spirit, and especially the fact that the life-impulses which determine his will are not yet in agreement as such in inward rational purpose and among themselves (§ 769)— a deficiency which is increased by the fact that the natural basis of every individual is more or less affected by the evil influence of alien factors which precede his self-determination (§ 771). The formal basis of sinfulness is in the determination for freedom, and therefore for self-determination, which is natural to the spirit, but which, as long as man lives in that distinction of the Ego from its true being as spirit, manifests itself as a tendency to self-will, which increases the natural (and ethically indifferent) craving for sinful lusts (§ 777). But neither extensively nor intensively is the natural sinfulness an absolute determination of the natural Ego. For it does not arise *eo ipso* in every moment of man's ethical self-determination (his natural determination of will can of itself agree with the objective demand of the moral world-order). And even where it is active, the inclination to sin does not *eo ipso* determine the will itself to sin (the natural Ego *qua* spirit maintains a formal freedom, and its living expression *qua* nature need not be sin, § 772). There is no absolute necessity that man should go through sin itself, only through the alternative of sin and obedience, through inward temptation, for although that which is sinful in an ethical act passes under his self-determination, what passes before it is not sin, only the tendency to sin, which has its basis in the being of finite spirit (§ 773). Wegscheider would have called it the *propensio et proclivitas ad peccandum* which is inseparably bound up with the inclination to good and the divine likeness. Of Biedermann we can only say that of all its exponents he was the one who was able to bring out most purely and sharply and fully the characteristic features of the Neo-Protestant doctrine of sin.

It was within the limits already known to us, in spite of variations in detail, that the doctrine of R. A. Lipsius moved as represented in the main statements of his *Lehrb. der ev.-prot. Dogmatik* (2nd ed., 1879). At the supreme point it did take a surprising turn, but instead of following this through radically it came back again to the old direction, saying as a whole only what it is inevitable should be said on this basis. I will summarise quite briefly his main points, which he holds in common with the others. " The actualisation of man's spiritual determination to real divine likeness and fellowship with God takes place, in accordance with the definition of man, as a gradual spiritual development from a finite determination of nature, as a progressive rise from it to freedom over the world or to an actual self-conscious and self-desired unity of life and love with God " (§ 467). It is within this framework that Lipsius, too, comes to deal with the problem of sin. Beginning with an immediate naturalness in which flesh and spirit are not yet known as antitheses, man becomes conscious of his spiritual life subjectively as freedom and objectively as law (§ 468 f.). The original incompatibility of his natural determination in relation to his spiritual being now comes before him as actual sinfulness, as real evil, to the extent that he experiences the antithesis as something which he himself has willed (§ 471). It is a " personal self-determination against God," personal guilt (§ 474). He does, of course, reflect that the sinful determination of his will " is well-grounded in the original preponderance of flesh over spirit, or of his sensuous natural determination over his developing spiritual freedom, which means that the growth of the spiritual life involves necessarily an inclination to sin " (§ 476). In the nature of finite spirit lies the basis both of the consciousness of sin as guilt and therefore of its avoidability, and also the thought of its unavoidability in view of this inclination (§ 477). This inclination has to be described as the " disorderly rule of individual natural impulses as grounded in the sensual nature of man . . . impulses which are not yet integrated into the unitary life-purpose of man," and which therefore necessarily hinder spiritual development to free self-determination (§ 479). But this nature is in some way posited with the growth of moral freedom in man as the power to act (§ 483). And for their part the natural impulses of human action are not sinful in themselves (§ 484). We may say that the natural inclination to evil never determines the will absolutely : at every point in human development it is confronted by a possibility of spiritual self-determination in contrast to its finite natural determination (§ 485). At no stage of his development is man absolutely corrupt, i.e., absolutely incapable of good. In so far as the consciousness of his life's determination and his commitment determines his will, it is morally free (§ 486). For this reason Lipsius believes that in relation to moral life in society he must not only guard against the insistence on the total corruption of the race, but that he can maintain that in history " we cannot fail to see a steady progress in the moral development of the race," the moral development of the heathen world *ante Christum natum* being regarded as a " positive preparation for Christianity " in spite of Rom. 1[1st.] (§ 487). It is here, of course, that there comes the remarkable turn in which for a time—as though he had noted and wished to take up the tendencies in this direction in Schleiermacher—Lipsius seems to raise himself above his contemporaries in time and spirit. For we are told fairly directly in §§ 490–491 that we can win through to the full concept of man and the full knowledge of sin only in the light of the redemptive order revealed in Christianity. In the light of this the failure to reach the Christian (which is the perfect) religious relationship is shown to be sin, the positive opposition of the creature's own end against the divine work of salvation, on the one hand as Jewish self-righteousness and on the other as heathen idolatry. From the standpoint of the Christian faith the real subject of sin is revealed as the common life of the race, and individual life only in its self-excused involvement in this sinful life of the whole. It may be imagined what would have happened if Lipsius had carried through this thought which had obviously not been reached with a closed Bible but with a Bible opened at any rate in passing. It may be imagined what would have happened if—provisionally bracketing his previous discussions—he had begun again from the very first with this consideration, and tried to think through everything again from this standpoint. He did not do so. Indeed, he could not do so, for (as in the case of the tendencies in Schleiermacher) it would have made necessary a revision of his whole theology. He sees clearly that what was demanded from this standpoint was " true humility, true faith, true love for God," and that the sinner is the unregenerate man, the one who is not willing or able to fulfil this demand, the man who stands in contradiction to this demand and rebellion against it. But he does not dare use the word rebellion in this context except in inverted commas. And from this point he simply weakens and obscures the insight. This rebellion must not be equated with the definitive decision of the will against the good offered in the divine order of redemption, a decision which inevitably involves judgment. Even this (the rejection of the Gospel) is only " a specific form of the contradiction of the spirit by the flesh, which does not fill up the whole of human life in its concrete actuality and which for that reason still includes the possibility of redemption." In this connexion humanity outside the sphere of redemption is not described as sinful in and for itself, but only in so far as it rejects the grace of redemption. How can " a spiritual unreadiness for the religion of redemption be sin in and for itself " ? And so on. The good thought has been discarded without being thought through. By the grace and religion and sphere of redemption, and the order of salvation, Lipsius, like the others, could not mean anything but the perfect " religious relationship " achieved in Christianity as the climax of historico-religious development. No wonder that he could not bring himself to take this element seriously as a standard in the question of good and evil and to apply it accordingly. The one swallow could not make a summer.

The older 19th century Liberalism we have been following had only one more noteworthy representative. This was H. Lüdemann, whose *Christliche Dogmatik* still deserves respect because of its consistent and determined position. It was published too late (1926), however, to be either impressive or instructive in a theological and general spiritual situation which had altered so much since the days of Schweizer, Biedermann and Lipsius. Lüdemann, like Lipsius, followed Schleiermacher rather than Hegel in his philosophy of religion, Kant in his epistemology and ethics, and Leibnitz in his metaphysics. He did not attain to any insights about sin which differed decisively in content from the statements we have already considered. According to him, sin is man's " consciously willed tarrying in a stage of development which is recognised as one that has to be left behind " (Vol. 2, p. 402). Its nature is grounded in the natural prominence of the motives which impel each given individuality to assert itself—a prominence which continues even in face of the developing consciousness of a moral standard, i.e., the divine law, producing the different forms of tarrying in a lower stage of development which are contrary to our duty and determination (p. 397). Lüdemann went to great pains on the one hand to show that this tarrying is a refusal to obey and therefore an obstacle for which we ourselves are responsible, and on the other to bring out our absolute need of redemption. But he could not break through the basic view which he shared with the whole Neo-Protestant school. Sin is only an " obstacle," and this obstacle is posited with the nature of man as finite spirit (p. 370). Redemption consists in the forward movement from an immature to a mature self-will (pp. 347, 374, 399). The impulse of self-assertion which flows from the nature of individuality—being morally indifferent—does not, therefore, constitute sin (pp. 345, 399). Even in the state of disobedience there is no absolute darkening of the moral consciousness. " Obstinacy " can be regarded only as the symptom of a psychosis. To accept an obliteration of the Ego's capacity for redemption would be to accept its destructibility, which " cannot possibly be allowed for as an element in the world " (here we see the influence of Lüdemann's metaphysics, p. 403). And in a larger setting the rise of human guilt has to be regarded as a necessary stage in the development of finite spirit (p. 341), a defect which is compensated in the overall course of the divinely directed development of the world (p. 342). " If the nature of the morality which we will and attain for ourselves is worthy to be willed by God—and there is no doubt about that— then sin, or our willing of that which ought not to be, must also be divinely willed as the ineluctable presupposition, as the lower stage of immaturity of moral self-will which has to be passed through first . . . as the obstacle which is appointed to be surmounted by the developing moral self-will " (p. 347). Moreover, in virtue of his religious consciousness the Christian " understands as a sign of divine leading already begun that rise of the sinful will " which precedes the rise of his Christian life of faith (p. 408). In Lüdemann there is no trace whatever of a movement in the direction we noted in Schleiermacher and Lipsius. Probably in the context of his final basis in Leibniz, Lüdemann was able to give to the common conception a shape which approximates closely to what was reached in Biedermann and Hegel.

We now go back a step, and half a step outside the general line so far followed, to survey the teaching of Albrecht Ritschl. Ritschl's theology was anti-metaphysical, anti-speculative, anti-mystical and anti-pietistic. In positive terms it can best be described as ethical. It was a bold return to Kant on the one side and Luther on the other. And if, in the last resort, it did not mark a new era it was certainly a distinctive variation in the course of Neo-Protestant thinking. This is true of his specific doctrine of sin (*Die chr. Lehre von der Rechtfertigung und Versöhnung*, 4th ed., 1895, Vol. 3, Ch. 5, cf. *Unterricht in der chr. Rel.*, 1875, 6th ed., 1903, § 34–42). At a first glance it seems to meet the postulate stated in our discussion of the doctrine of Lipsius. It begins at once with the thesis that the basis of the knowledge of human sinfulness is " the Gospel of the forgiveness of sins " (*Recht. u. Vers.*[4], p. 310). It must be formed from the New Testament as a " deduction from the valuation of Christian salvation " (p. 311). It is the result of " a comparison with the picture of life given us in Christ," " with His indication of the righteousness of the kingdom of God " (p. 313). What is meant by this ? Unfortunately all that is meant—for this is how Ritschl understood the New Testament—is the Christian ideal of life actualised in Christ (p. 315), the problem of the kingdom of God perfectly solved in Christ's conduct of life (p. 312). And this does not teach us the fact and interpretation of sin itself—which can be known apart from Christianity—but only (as Lipsius said) a right estimate of its extent and worthlessness (p. 311). Is the Gospel of the forgiveness of sins, is Christ Himself, really essential to Ritschl's definition of sin, that it consists in deeds in the active direction of enmity against God (p. 310), which are characterised by an essential lack of respect and trust, by indifference and lack of trust in relation to God (p. 316) ? Which of the older Liberals could not have said the same on his own presupposition ? Was the presupposition of Ritschl basically very different ? For this pre-supposition did not, and as he understood it, could not yield the deduction that the actuality of sin is a truth of faith, and that we have a knowledge of it not so much as we compare ourselves with Christ but as He Himself compares us with Himself before his judgment-throne. Sin for Ritschl is the contradiction of man against the " common good " " which, according to the Christian standard, ought to be reached by general co-operation." It is therefore opposition to the kingdom of God understood as " the unbroken reciprocal action of acts which are motivated by love, in which there is made that connexion of all with each man who bears the marks of a neighbour, that connexion of men in which all goods are appropriated in their subordination to the supreme good " (p. 317). If it is surprising that Ritschl thought he could find such an account of the kingdom of God in the New Testament, it is not surprising that from it he attained to the view that the subject of sin (we are again reminded of Lipsius) is the race as the sum of individuals, seeing that the self-seeking activity of the indi-vidual which disturbs the relation of good to the good, " setting the individual in an incalculable reciprocal action with all others, is directed in some measure to the opposite of good, and brings about the connexion of individuals in a common evil " (p. 317 f.). This is the kingdom of sin in opposition to the kingdom of God (p. 320), and it can also be called the world (p. 332). In Ritschl this concept the kingdom of sin is not so much an interpretation of original sin. It crowds it out and replaces it (p. 326). According to Ritschl there are only active or concrete sins. There is no being of man in sin, in enmity against God. He can speak of the development of an evil character in man, but the idea to which his contemporaries made so great appeal (in interpretation of the term original sin), that of an evil inclination which precedes the evil act, is resolutely set aside, as is also the radical evil of Kant and, of course, the doctrine of " innate " sin. For if this were true, there could be no responsibility or education or acceptance of different gradations of evil in individuals (p. 319 f.). And it was always on the basis of the Gospel of the forgiveness of sins, of Christ, that Ritschl thought that he could and indeed had to pontificate and argue in this way ! How strange that from this point (far from leaving the general line which led to Pelagius) he thought it necessary to make an even more determined advance along it ! And from this point, too, he came to his further assertions. Historical and natural evils in the world and death itself are the punishment of sin only by the mediation of the feeling of guilt (p. 335 f.), the punishment consisting properly in the " diminu-tion of the right of divine sonship " and ultimately, therefore, only in the un-resolved feeling of guilt itself, and only in that way in the lack of freedom in relation to the world which it involves (p. 345). It does not seem to have dawned on Ritschl from his study of the New Testament that evil and death and sin might have, and be, an actuality which is first and foremost alien and hostile to God. For that reason he thought that he could deduce from it that sin cannot be regarded as " infinite," " for the acts of the creature cannot as such be infinite " (p. 349). Again, the concept sin can be referred only " in a modified way " to the elect and the redeemed—how mistaken Paul and the Psalmists must have been ! (p. 351). Again, the worth, or worthlessness, of sin is graded. There is (" as we learn from the experience of children ") the pardonable sin of ignorance, in contrast to that which has the form of a final decision against Christian redemption, or incorrigible self-seeking. Not every sin is an actual-isation of the extreme of opposition to the good. Not every sin is conscious general wickedness. Again, we cannot dispute either *a priori* or *a posteriori* that there may be a sinless development (p. 357 f.). Again, if God loves sinful man, this means that to the extent that it does not exclude redemption He adjudges his particular sin as an attribute which does not destroy or finally determine the value of sinful man for Him. It is different " when sin as enmity against God has reached the stage that the will purposely seeks evil. Where it is suspected that this is the case, we cannot regard even the love of God as possible. This love can be thought of only in relation to the sins which do not reach the grade of sin which excludes a conversion of the will " (p. 360 f.). Ritschl's chapter on sin closes with this remarkable distinction. It is a matter for astonishment that in all this (and the doctrine of justification which he drew up in the light of it) he believed that he was a particularly loyal disciple of Luther and the great renewer of his insights and teaching. We must not overlook the fact that his anti-speculative position did prevent him from accepting a view on which sin can be regarded as an operation of God and a purposeful link in His ordering of the world (p. 360). We do not find in him this element in the general view of things within the framework of which his thought so evidently moves. But for the rest it is certain that on this parallel to the main road of Neo-Protestantism—and for a time it seemed as though it might become the main road—we do not find any improvement on the knowledge of sin to which the great Liberal theologians were impelled by their general presupposition. Indeed, we might almost say that matters are made worse, or more banal. There is a lowering of the level that we find in Wegscheider and Bretschneider—and this in spite of the protestation (it was no more) that the doctrine would be orientated in accordance with quite a different basis of knowledge. We do not need a great deal of perspicacity to see that what Ritschl called the Gospel of the forgiveness of sins was, in fact, only another term for the *lex aeterna* supposedly written on the heart of man and used by all his predecessors in their thinking on this subject.

We will bring this series of studies to a close with a glance at the *Glaubenslehre* of Ernst Troeltsch, 1925, which was posthumously published on the basis of the dictated statements and notes of his Heidelberg lectures of 1911–12. This, too, has had no lasting influence in theological discussion. Troeltsch distinguished four stages of development in Christian history, the primitive, the Catholic, the older Protestant and the Neo-Protestant. He claimed expressly to be the theologian of the latter, in the " conviction " that in it there lay the " structure of the Christian world which corresponds to the present-day spiritual and social basis " (p. 3). It was he who coined the term " Neo-Protestantism " and introduced it into discussion as at once a historical category and a normative theological concept. Indeed, we find this conception of a " stage of development " everywhere in Troeltsch (including his doctrine of sin). He was its last great systematic exponent. And we must not fail to note that it was with him that a crisis came on Neo-Protestantism as a whole. We can see this at once in the very relativistic way in which for all its self-consciousness he formulates this " conviction " : its content is a historical statement. The doctrine of Troeltsch depends on the fact that he is conscious of corresponding to the present-day structure of the Christian world. Its understanding of itself is historicist. Schleiermacher had seen the task of dogmatics in the same light. It belongs to historical theology. It has to develop the doctrine which is current in the Church and which corresponds to the principle of the period. This was one of the elements in Schleiermacher's teaching which had been passed over and forgotten. In actual fact neither Schweizer nor Biedermann, neither Lipsius, Lüdemann nor Ritschl saw the task in the same light. They believed in Neo-Protestantism as such. They regarded its decisive conceptions and their own presentations of it as timelessly true. Naturally Troeltsch, too, believed that what he said was true. But only in so far as he thought that he had to say it in the light of " present-day Christian life " (the period immediately before the first world war). And he was conscious of this limitation, much more conscious than Schleiermacher had been. And to that extent he could keep to the general line of Neo-Protestantism, often formulating it in a much more sharp and provocative way than his predecessors, only by raising all kinds of problems and questions and attitudes which he then either left or tried to master with all kinds of wild speculations, which he accepted only as hypotheses. The new thing that he says is the old said by his predecessors, but the old in a state of flux, of self-dissolution, just as two hundred years before the old of older Protestant theology had been the old in a state of flux and self-dissolution in its representatives in the so-called " rational " orthodoxy. Thus in his doctrine of sin Troeltsch simply returns to what had been so often said during the last hundred years, presenting it for the most part with his customary lack of precision. Sin is the " dark and secret, the mysterious side of the thought of the divine likeness " (p. 308). Not all opposition to the ideal determination of the being of man is, of course, sin. We have only to think of the " actual and natural relationships and constrictions and frictions, of the weakness and the complicated and unpredictable nature of the moral powers and ends of men." But beyond all that there is a conscious opposition—ignoring and contesting that which is divine (p. 300 f.). From the standpoint of the spirit it has the form of a " self-affirmation in opposition to God." The thought of God demands a disposition of faith and trust. Sin is the rejection of this disposition, and a consequent hardening in the force and interests of the finite self (p. 303). But this derives from the " freedom and developing character " of the spirit. It is posited with individual being and its determination as such as an evil which has to be overcome, inasmuch as the impulse of self-seeking of the developing (*sic*) spirit, the impulse which constitutes natural being, reveals itself to be the principle of all possible evil and of the evil which has actually been committed. General sinfulness has its basis, therefore, " in the metaphysical construction of man." As such it is sinfulness only in an improper sense, and it has only a qualified guilt. Every individual must pass afresh through the sin and guilt of this animal and sensual self-affirmation (p. 306). In the light of this, Troeltsch can say quite freely : " God has ordained for man the possibility and therewith the probability of sin. He has placed him in the midst of conflict and toil and temptation. His aim is to thrust him outside the limits of a complacent worldliness, and to teach him the limitations of his own strength." Again : " God can forgive the sin which He Himself has forced upon man." Again : " The possibility of sin is itself the means to lead man to the true good." It is not, therefore, unjust to say that in these circumstances it is obvious why no place can be found for a " doctrine of satisfaction " which rests on a view of God in terms of law and retribution and which, in any case, " cannot be harmonised with the modern picture of the historical Christ " (p. 340). Of course, in so far as man maintains himself in a direction against the spirit, resisting the spirit, there is a genuine sinfulness, and there is also a feeling of guilt as an experience of the reaction of the divine will provoked by it. But there is no objective guilt. There is no infringement of the divine order which needs to be made good. The repudiation of the substitutionary suffering of Christ rests on this doctrine (p. 317). There is only a subjective feeling in which the recognition of a sinful disturbance of the relationship with God finds expression (p. 306 f.). This had all been said by the older Liberals, and by Ritschl too, and with much greater precision. Troeltsch has been able to say it again only in a halting way and with a remarkable diffuseness of outward presentation — diffuseness because although the main strand is unmistakable it is crossed at all points by the assertion of quite heterogeneous views. It does not fit very well with what he has been saying when—sawing off the branch on which he is sitting—he suddenly declares to be " quite false the ecclesiastical doctrine (he means that doctrine which has become the common heritage of the Church), which is bound up with the distinction between a natural and a supernatural revelation, that the feeling of sin necessarily arises out of the pre-Christian knowledge of God of which it is the fruit." As against this he claims that " this feeling arises only in the context of the Christian thought of God " (p. 302 f.). Sin (as opposition to and rejection of God) consists " wholly and utterly in opposition to the grace which draws us to itself " (p. 309). Is this any more seriously meant than the corresponding statements in Schleiermacher, Lipsius and Ritschl ? Perhaps, but most likely not. But Troeltsch goes further. He accuses the older dogmatics of nothing more nor less than separating " between God as the bearer of the law and God as the bearer of grace." Psychologically this distinction has often been useful. But it involves a division in the Christian thought of God. It is disruptive, crude, inwardly inept, artificial and violent (p. 312). Troeltsch knows and says that the knowledge of sin becomes " truly shattering " only when confronted with the thought of " holy love " (p. 303). Is it from this " shattering "—and if not, from where ?—that there springs his championing of Kant's concept of radical evil, a concept which was so offensive to the 19th century and had never been satisfactorily explained in relation to Kant's thinking as a whole ? Is it in the light of this that he speaks of a " general and essential sinfulness," and protests against the optimistic monism which would ignore evil or interpret it only negatively as good which is not yet present ? And how does this view, this protest, agree with what he said earlier (p. 301) ? How does it agree with the main strand of his own and all Neo-Protestant thinking when he declares that sin is " a mistake in principle and totality, which results in a destruction of the good even though the will for good is present with it " (p. 303), when he accepts " two principles, each of which desires the whole man," when he maintains that " there is a totality in every act," and that to " infringe the law of God at one point is to infringe it at every point " (p. 313) ? In the light of this, what becomes of his distinction between proper and improper sinfulness ? And how can sinfulness—however it is described—inhere in the " metaphysical construction of man " ? How can it be posited by God, ordained by God, imposed upon man, made a means of raising man to genuine good ? Conversely, if the statements which define sin quantitatively are true, how can the statements also be true in which they seem to be so severely qualified ? None of the older Neo-Protestants would have contradicted himself in this way. Which of the two sequences of thought is the one that we ought to take seriously and that Troeltsch himself meant to be taken seriously ? Perhaps neither of them, but only that which—in an obvious attempt to bring them together—he calls the " religious conception of history." According to this view the story of humanity is that of the indecisive conflict of a good and evil principle, the battle between flesh and spirit which is posited with the very nature of man. Is it to remain indecisive ? No, we seem to be told first. Prophetic monotheism, " the proclamation by Jesus of the kingdom of God " and the Church's doctrine of salvation history are all attestations of the view that the conflict will have a positive outcome—but " to-day, of course, only as a mythical and symbolical expression for faith in a divine education and elevation of humanity " (p. 317 f.). And a religious faith in history of this kind must not lose contact with " empirical history "— with the result that the latter again tells us in general that the " conflict of ethically religious forces against a purely natural determination is the main theme of history." Not the end, not even the only theme, but the main theme of history. Or does it tell us something more ? On the next page (p. 320) Troeltsch actually says that our most immediate historical knowledge does " support " the idea of " a continual and comprehensive progress," so that the " spread of European culture and Christianity " seems to be " quite conceivable " : rather like the fulfilment of the kingdom of God on earth as it " hovered " before the prophets and Jesus, and the apostolic faith and as it has been taken up again by the Christian Socialists. But obviously Troeltsch has no real confidence either in his " quite conceivable " or in what " hovered " before Jesus and the rest. For how much he sees against this view : the fact that " the totality of European culture dominated by Christianity is only a small part of history as a whole ; " " the weariness and exhaustion which can overtake whole spheres of culture;" the prospect of ever greater difficulties in the external maintenance of human life, and even of an ultimate geological calcination of the earth. And note that even " from the standpoint of pure faith " this continuity cannot be maintained consistently, for the prospect is not of an earthly goal, but of " further development beyond "—where now is the religious conception of history ? and how do we know of this *Deus ex machina* who suddenly appears ? What awaits us in these circumstances is " hardly " that progress, but a battle which is continually renewed on different fronts, in which the Christian faith—and in virtue of its divine certainty it has the power to do this—guarantees the possibility that " at every point we can break into eternity " and " ethicise the battle of life to the extent that this is always possible where there is a will most capable of sacrifice " (p. 321). Are we just to Troeltsch if we tie him down to a historical picture in which sin appears again only as " flesh," as the natural determination of man, and therefore as one of the two participants in this conscious battle ? Was this (really) gnostic and mythological dualism his final word ? It can only be mentioned here that he did, in fact, have a final word *in petto*, and that in Heidelberg he gave it responsible utterance in the form of directives (p. 217 f.) : " This dualism ('twofold constituent') " of history " must be followed right back into the divine being itself," " in which we have to accept a conflict between the aims of holy love and actual nature, between the aims of the spiritual world and the aberrations of the spirit." " This thesis cannot be avoided " (p. 237). Creation, then, is the " divine education in the ensuing sufferings of the motley factuality of nature and in spiritual and moral errors " (p. 218). " God educates Himself to be the helper of finite spirits by whom the world is ethicised and spiritualised " (p. 237). And in the last analysis redemption is the " self-redemption of God, the return of God to Himself," which shows why the essence of religion consists in redemption, and perfect religion is necessarily perfect moral and spiritual redemption (p. 218). Between creation and redemption, however, we can speak of a self-amelioration, self-multiplication and self-enrichment of God through the finite processes of life, interrupted by our opposition (pp. 220, 237), and completed in the return of finite spirits to the essence of God, with perhaps a dissolution of their individual existence, an end in which the moments of truth in theism and pantheism converge (p. 238). Does this mean that we are back at Jacob Boehme and Master Eckhard ? " Troeltsch hears the rustling of the divine mantle in history. He sees the divine omnipotence and the infinite fulness of the divine life . . . whirling and raging and boiling. God is a rolling wheel . . . ever onward, ever onward " : this is how Walter Köhler put it in his eulogy of the *Glaubenslehre* (*Ernst Troeltsch*, 1941, p. 191). Was this, then, the final word of Neo-Protestantism, or, at any rate, of Troeltsch himself ? But we should be doing him an injustice if we tried to tie him down to this view. For at the very last moment he made a disclaimer, stating (pp. 219 f., 238 f.) that the fusion of these two moments of truth is quite impracticable, that although the premises for this concept of God are true enough, our whole comprehension breaks down when it comes to God. He bewails the fact that in this respect the Bible " naturally leaves us without an answer," and concludes with the statement that we are thrown back from all these " speculations " on " our points of departure in the Bible and history and inner experience." And it was inevitable that right at the end we should hear those lines of K. F. Meyer, which all the more recent Neo-Protestants love to quote :

> " What God is, no man will ever know,
> But from His covenant He will never go."

He comments that " we find this covenant at the point where the thought of God raises man from the level of the beasts " (p. 239). Here we can break off. Troeltsch was a gifted and, in his own way, a pious man. The same may be said of many of his great predecessors. But it was obvious that with him the doctrine of faith was on the point of dissolution into endless and useless talk, and that for all the high self-consciousness of its conduct Neo-Protestantism in general had been betrayed on to the rocks, or the quicksands. It was because we could no longer take part in this that about the end of the second decade of this century we left the ship. For some it was to Catholicism, e.g., Gertrud von le Fort, to whom we owe the posthumous editing and publication of this book and who did, in fact, become a Roman Catholic immediately after she had completed the work. For others it meant a fresh beginning of serious theological study on a quite different basis.

We return to the point from which we started. This was the hypothesis that in the knowledge of sin we have to do with an autonomous knowledge which precedes the knowledge of Jesus Christ. What kind of a knowledge will this be ? What will be its basis ? From what source will it draw its sustenance ? What will be its content ? We have laid it down as fundamental and accepted it as a presupposition that in some way it will have to be a knowledge which proceeds from God, a knowledge of revelation and faith (and not the self-knowledge of man left to himself). And we have had to bear in mind that by a knowledge which proceeds from God, a knowledge of revelation and faith, we can, and in this case we will have to, understand the knowledge of God and man in an abstractly constructed basic relationship between God the Creator and man His creature, the knowledge of a law which supposedly derives from this abstractly constructed relationship, which God has set up and man has to fulfil, and therefore the knowledge of the sin of man as the transgression of this law. We have seen the danger which threatened from the very first, that the knowledge of human sin against the background of this arbitrary construction will finally prove to be only a dramatised form of the self-knowledge of man left to himself, and that in this confrontation there can be no knowledge of the real sin by which man is accused by God and of which he is guilty before Him. Of course, in relation to Reformation theology, which took this path, we have had to admit that the threatened danger of serious error was averted so long as active measures were taken to leave a place for the consultation of the Bible in the presentation of the decisive concept of law and norm. But we ourselves cannot be satisfied with this safeguard. Is it not the case that this whole construction of a basic relationship, and of a normative concept deducible from it, is an arbitrary act which does not promise well, even though the statements of the Bible are ever so carefully noted and quoted and the Bible is not prevented from exercising its wholesome influence ? When this arbitrary act is accomplished, is it not inevitable, and does not its very character as an arbitrary act make it so, that sooner or later the use of the Bible will prove to be optional and then dispensable to the man who works out for himself this normative concept ? Once this path is entered, what is there to prevent man remembering the source of knowledge which is close at hand in his own nature and reason, first dividing his attention between the two sources of revelation, but finally reversing the relationship and replacing the teaching of the Bible by that which he can give himself as he seeks a norm by means of the supposed divine knowledge, the knowledge of revelation and faith, the source of which is his own heart and conscience ? (In our first historical excursus we have seen in relation to the history of orthodox-Reformed theology in the 17th century how this transition from a strictly formal fidelity to the Bible to pure rationalism did take place and can obviously do so at any time.) But if this takes place, then the safeguard which the Bible can always give falls away. And if the character of an arbitrary act which lay over the construction from the very first is revealed in its pure form, if the knowledge of the law is still only the result of the self-communing of man as left to himself, then what becomes of the knowledge of sin ? Is it not inevitable that in the judgment of man judging himself sin will be regarded as something innocuous, something that we can survey and master in the form of all kinds of distinctions and syntheses, an element in the view of things, in anthropology, which can be arranged because at bottom it has been arranged already, an element in relation to which man is finally free, however seriously he may regard its peculiar nature and significance ? In this case, will it not be the experience of man that although he is not perfect, he is merely imperfect ; that although he has knowledge of a fall from God, he has no knowledge of an infinite fall, of a breach, but only the reassuring knowledge of a continuity of relationship between Himself and God which is still unbroken ; that although he has a feeling of guilt, he has no objective guilt and is not therefore affected by the wrath of God or thrown back on the mercy of God ; that although there is a conflict between spirit and flesh, by spirit is meant the spiritual nature of man and by flesh his sensual nature ; that although he is in need of redemption he is also capable of redemption ; that although he disapproves and bewails his sinful actions, he sees to it carefully that he is not himself regarded as a sinner, the man of sin ? Will he not finally be able to reassure and console himself with the thought that secretly and at bottom his evil is a good, or the transition to it, that his sinning is imposed and posited and ordained by God, until at last he suspects that it may have something corresponding to it in the essence and life of God Himself ? (In our second excursus a survey of 19th century Neo-Protestant theology has shown clearly how this development did take place, and can take place at any time, when the *lex biblica* is first rivalled and then replaced by the *lex aeterna* in the heart and conscience of man.) But this conception of sin, which is so acceptable in its basic perversion, is the fatal fruit of that arbitrary act as such in which man himself undertakes to set up a criterion for the knowledge of sin, in which this knowledge is simply a matter of self-communing, and man becomes his own law-giver and accuser and judge. Is it not inevitable that the man who has arbitrarily attained to these offices will be able, and will certainly be ready, to acquit himself, to pronounce himself, if not holy, at any rate relatively just ? And the self-enthronement which produces this result is always an arbitrary act, even when it is done with an appeal to and the help of the Bible, even when care is taken to arrest the process and not to allow its final consequences to be at once or perhaps for a long time apparent. But if we do not want the consequences we must not want the presupposition. We must not allow the example of Reformation theology (which was graciously preserved from the consequences) to mislead us into tempting God and committing ourselves to the slope of which we have been made aware. The incline obviously begins at the point where we think we have to create the message of sin from some other source than that of the message of Jesus Christ. This forces us to ask for an independent normative concept, and to move forward to the construction of it, and we fall at once into the whole arbitrary process. The root of the arbitrariness is the belief that we can and should try to escape the one true word of God in this matter. And why should we not avoid the mistake at the point where it begins ? What reason is there for that first belief that the doctrine of sin must precede Christology and therefore be worked out independently of it ?

The belief is a traditional one which has seldom been questioned but has usually been treated as more or less self-evident. In opposition to it we maintain the simple thesis that only when we know Jesus Christ do we really know that man is the man of sin, and what sin is, and what it means for man.

It is a matter of the divine knowledge of revelation and faith. This is the basic and general proposition on which we are agreed. But we have to understand this concretely and not in an abstraction of our own choosing. It is a matter of the knowledge of the one God who in His Word became flesh for us, and therefore of the knowledge of His truth in this one revelation, and therefore of the one indivisible knowledge of the Christian faith, the basis and subject of which is God in His atoning work and therefore God in Jesus Christ. The knowledge of human sin is enclosed in this knowledge. The knowledge of human sin is acquired in and with the acquiring of this knowledge : not anywhere else, not as separated from it in any respect or to any degree, but strictly and accurately and fully in it. God Himself has spoken and speaks. It is irrelevant and superfluous to seek for a normative concept by which to measure sin, to construct such a concept from biblical or extra-biblical materials, to learn about it either openly or secretly in our own self-communing. More than that, it is misleading and futile to do so. It is indeed a form of sin (perhaps the main form). Why ? Not because we can find and produce another and better method, the christological, but because Jesus Christ

Himself is present, living and speaking and attesting and convincing; because in this matter we need not and cannot and should not speak to ourselves ; because the man of sin and his existence and nature, his why and whence and whither, are all set before us in Jesus Christ, are all spoken to us directly and clearly and incontrovertibly : Thou art the man ! This is what thou doest ! This is what thou art ! This is the result ! We hear Him and we hear this verdict. We see Him, and in this mirror we see ourselves, ourselves as those who commit sin and are sinners. We are here inescapably accused and irrevocably condemned. There is nothing that we can bring in our favour. We have to acknowledge that we are wholly unrighteous. We have to see that we not only do unrighteously and are in unrighteousness, but that we are unrighteous. We find our competence to work out the standard by which to measure ourselves denied. We are no longer permitted to parley and come to terms with ourselves about ourselves. We have simply no room or breath for fine distinctions between evil deed and evil being, proper and improper sinfulness, the feeling of guilt and all the rest, let alone for the even finer syntheses between creatureliness and sin on the one side and sin and redemption on the other. We are arrested, marched away and locked up. There can be no pardon attained by our own devices, no explanation and interpretation of sin and the man of sin, when we are confronted by Jesus Christ and hear the Word spoken in His existence. We are simply there as this man. If in this judgment there is no grace, or more exactly no mercy, no free grace, then we have no refuge ; we have no claim to such free grace (otherwise how could it be free ? how could it be mercy ?) ; we have no means of attaining it ; we have no light even to know it. We are in darkness before a wall which can be pierced only from the other side. There can be no question of any thought of redemption which we can manipulate, any capacity for redemption which we can put into effect. There is no stay or comfort in the idea of a freedom and capacity (which are finally and effectively ours) to look at ourselves as the man of sin from without, to take ourselves by the hand and to re-interpret and change ourselves. Knowledge of sin at this point consists in the knowledge : I am this man. To this extent it is the knowledge of real sin.

But this knowledge of real sin takes place in the knowledge of Jesus Christ. Why in this knowledge ? We will first give the comprehensive answer : Because the God against whom the man of sin contends has judged this man, and therefore myself as this man, in the self-offering and death of Jesus Christ His own Son, putting him to death, and destroying him ; and because He has revealed and continually reveals him as this one who is judged and put to death and destroyed in the resurrection of Jesus Christ from the dead and His being and living and speaking and witness for all ages. Because the verdict passed in His resurrection from the dead unmasks this old man, showing what every man is before God, and therefore what I myself am before Him, the man who is judged and put to death and destroyed. All this came upon Jesus Christ for every one of us and therefore for me, in our place and therefore in my place. We are all those and that of which God Himself made an end in Jesus Christ, which was transferred to the past in Jesus Christ. We are all wearers of the old garment which was there taken off and destroyed. Indeed, we are all the old man himself who there in Jesus Christ was overtaken by the wrath of God and condemned and executed. Jesus Christ suffered and died in our place, in solidarity with this old man and therefore with us, without any clever reservation in respect of a secret innocence or freedom or capacity for redemption which might be maintained and ascribed to this man and therefore to us; without any contradiction or protest as though what was happening to this old man and therefore to us in this judgment was unjust; without any control over the grace of God, which surely could not be too severe; without reckoning on any sudden turn in His favour, simply in hope in God, but in that hope only in the form of the obedience in which Jesus Christ allowed that God was in the right and He Himself—and therefore the old man and ourselves whose place He had taken—in the wrong, taking it upon Himself to be one with us, and as such to suffer what our acts and we ourselves had deserved before God. Because He is the One who has done this for us, the verdict of God passed in His resurrection and revealed in His being and living and speaking and witness is relevant to all men and therefore to ourselves as we have described it in a first approximation. As the verdict of God it has this complete and comprehensive content, including ourselves and our activity and being, and excluding any conceivable possibility of self-excuse and self-justification. And as the verdict of God it has the authority of His own direct and personal self-knowledge as the basis of what is now our true self-knowledge — true because in the self-knowledge which has this basis we cannot turn to any other revelation of God, to any God in a more original form, to any faith in such a form of God, attaining there to what is supposed to be a better knowledge of ourselves. In this verdict we learn what God knows about us, and therefore how it really is with us. For this reason its content is valid. For this reason, when we hear it, we have no option but to receive it and accept its validity.

In the thesis of the knowledge of sin in the knowledge of Jesus Christ we follow the remarkable hints found in our survey of Neo-Protestant theology first in Schleiermacher, then in Lipsius, in Ritschl as a definite programme, and finally in Troeltsch. The fact that man is a sinner, and what his sin is, is something that in the last resort we can measure properly and fully only by that which on the New Testament understanding is man's salvation, the redemptive grace which comes from God to man. M. Kähler (*Die Wissenschaft d. chr. Lehre*, 1893, p. 270) stated this more clearly than any of the others mentioned. In what is at times an almost word for word agreement with the delimitation that we have made, he tells us that the key which unlocks the secret of the basis of salvation " must not be sought in the anxious self-judgment of man left to himself, as though this could measure the need for salvation and settle in advance the corresponding reassurance. For only the revelation of salvation čan throw light on the state of alienation. It is at the cross of Christ that the justified man measures the significance of human sin."

There are several texts and passages of the New Testament which point expressly in this direction. The prodigal son in Lk. 15¹¹ᶠ· comes to the decision to return to his father and confess himself a sinner against heaven and before him, when, in his misery, he remembers the superfluity in his father's house, and it is as he carries out this decision that his father sees him and has compassion on him and runs to meet him and falls on his neck and kisses him. Again, in Lk. 5⁸ᶠ·, it is the divine favour in the unexpected success of the draught ordered by Jesus which brings terror to Peter and all those who are with him, forcing him to his knees and causing him to cry out : " Depart from me," on the ground : " I am an ἀνὴρ ἁμαρτωλός." Again, it was when the Lord looked on him in the court of the high-priest after he had denied Him that Peter went out and wept bitterly (Lk. 22⁶¹ᶠ·). Similarly in Jn. 15²², Jesus says of the sin of the world : " If I had not come and spoken unto them, they had not had sin : but now they have no cloke for their sin." And in v. 24 : " If I had not done among them the works that none other man did, they had not had sin : but now they have both seen and hated both me and my Father." Again in relation to the witness to Him in Jn. 16⁸ : " And when he (the Comforter, the Spirit of truth whom He will send) is come, he will reprove the world of sin, and of righteousness, and of judgment." According to the hymn quoted in Eph. 5¹²ᶠ·, it is when Christ rises on men as light, and only then, that their secret shame is disclosed and punished and made manifest, i.e., brought to light. And it is not a new revelation of the Torah, let alone a revelation of conscience or the like, but a revelation of the living Jesus Christ which, according to the account in Ac. 9³ᶠ·, struck down and blinded Saul on the road to Damascus, revealing him as the' man who in his raging against His community was really persecuting Him, according to His own teaching in Mt. 25³¹ᶠ·, that He will separate the good from the bad by what they have or have not done to Him in the person of the least of His brethren. What is said generally and formally in Rom. 14²³ : " Everything which is not of faith is sin," acquires concreteness and content in the well-known and specifically Johannine conception that the sin of which the Spirit of truth will convince the world is, in the words of Jn. 16⁹, that of " not believing on me." Similarly in Jn. 3¹⁸ : " He that believeth not (on Him) is condemned already, because he hath not believed on the name of the only begotten Son of God." And, again, in Jn. 8²⁴ : " If ye believe not that I am he, ye shall die in your sins." And, again, in Jn. 12⁴⁸ : " He that rejecteth me, and receiveth not my words, hath one that judgeth him : the word that I have spoken, the same shall judge him in the last day." The remarkable words with which Simeon blessed the parents of Jesus in the temple (Lk. 2³⁴) obviously have the same import : " This child is set for the fall and rising again of many in Israel." So, too, has the saying which Rom. 9³³ quotes from Is. 8¹⁴ about the " stone of stumbling and rock of offence " which God has laid, a stone which 1 Pet. 2⁸ equates with that stone which the builders rejected but which became the head of the corner (Ps. 118²²).

Above all, it is impossible to understand the important passage Rom. 1¹⁸–3²⁰ unless we see that it belongs to this same series. It is not a digression. It is the first and basic statement about the Gospel which Paul has made it his business to expound in this his (only) teaching letter. This first statement is as follows. The Gospel is God's condemnation of man, of all men and every man. In Rom. 1¹⁶ he had called it the δύναμις θεοῦ—the almighty power of God which is effective in the salvation which reaches its goal in all believers. Because it is this divine omnipotent work of redemption, the way of which begins with the Jews and then leads from the Jews to the Gentiles, Paul is not ashamed of it amongst either the one or the other. He explains in v. 17 what takes place in this work of redemption and therefore in the Gospel : the revelation of the righteousness, the legal and judicial decision of God upon the world of men. The Redeemer of men who acts and speaks in divine power in the Gospel—Jesus Christ—is therefore the Judge. The Gospel itself is the revelation of this Judge, the event in which He comes forth and pronounces His sentence as God's judicial sentence against which there can be no appeal. And redemption consists in the fact that this takes place. The one who is justified by faith, who receives the sentence of this Judge, trusting that it is valid and right, who subjects himself to it in obedience, will live, will partake of redemption. And Paul is not thinking of a second or prior revelation, but of the same revelation of the judging Redeemer in the Gospel, and of His sentence as it calls men to faith, when in v. 18 he speaks of a revelation of the wrath of God which is from heaven on all the unrighteousness and wickedness of men. There can be no doubt that v. 17 and v. 18 are complementary and are linked together. And in the preface to the letter Paul had introduced himself so solemnly as the apostle of Jesus Christ to both Jew and Gentile, and in vv. 16–17 he had stated the actual purpose of his letter so clearly, that it seems absurd to suppose that he abandoned this role and digressed from his real theme in the first part of the letter. The judgment revealed in the Gospel, which aims at the salvation of men, is also the judgment of wrath. In this connexion we should note the threefold γάρ in vv. 16, 17, 18. These statements all explain why Paul is not ashamed of the Gospel : it is the power of God unto salvation (v. 16) ; this work consists in the definitive decision of the divine Judge (v. 17) ; and in this decision there is expressed the divine contradiction of the opposition of all men, Jews and Gentiles, to God. The preacher has no need to be ashamed of the Gospel, but only of himself and all men. The judicial sentence of God includes within it His No to the man who opposes Him. In face of this opposition the redemption at which it aims, His love and faithfulness, is revealed as burning and consuming wrath. This opposition must be made to disappear. Where this wrath of God is revealed from heaven on earth, how this fire which consumes man's opposition will work itself out, burning it to the ground, how it causes it to become transitory, his readers will learn in the part of the letter which follows, in which Paul will speak of the way in which man is justified and set at peace and sanctified and liberated in the death of Jesus Christ. It is in the light of this that he knows and begins by saying that the redemptive judgment of God has this other aspect, recognising the sovereign contradiction of God which humbles and threatens us. It is in the light of this that man, all men, would have fallen victim to the wrath of God if He had spared His only Son (8³²), if He had not fulfilled His judicial decision in such a way that He set forth His Son as ἱλαστήριον, sacrificing Him for all (3²⁵). It is in the light of this that he knows that the man who does not recognise and accept and obey this decision, who does not believe, cannot count on anything but the wrath of God, and even now that the clear day has broken, can exist only in darkness and corruption. It is in the light of this that in the first part of his letter Paul brings us into the darkness in order to bring Jew and Gentile out of the darkness. It is in the light of this that his criticism of man is so outrageously cutting and radical and comprehensive. It is in the light of this that he says conclusively in 3⁹ : " We have before proved both Jews and Gentiles, that they are all under sin " ; and again in 3¹⁹ : " That every mouth may be stopped, and that all the world may become guilty before God " ; and again at the beginning of the second part in 3²³ : " For there is no difference, for we have all sinned, and come short of the glory of God " ; and again (and to be noted particularly) in 3²⁷ : " Where is boasting then ? It is excluded. By what law ? of works ? Nay : but by the law of faith." It is from the validity of this Law of faith which he has not yet depicted or explained but which he presupposes as self-evident, and therefore as an apostle of Jesus Christ, that in these chapters he disputes with Jews and Gentiles and all men as such. In this context we cannot give a detailed exegesis but simply establish the general line—that the accusation summarily raised against the nations and with a double emphasis against the elect people of God is valid only on one presupposition. This is that in virtue of His revelation made and proclaimed in the Gospel God is one, that He was one from all eternity, that He has spoken and acted as one in Israel. And this one God is the One who has made the salvation of men and the order of their relationship to Him His own affair, who has not left it to their own wisdom and will and work, who relentlessly demands of them only that they should look away from themselves to Him, that renouncing their own arbitrary thinking and willing and capacity they should trust in Him, that in this trust—in faith—they should be righteous before Him. It is on this presupposition that Jews and Gentiles are measured. And measured on this presupposition—by the perfect goodness of God to them and the gratitude demanded of them—they are all rebels and their apostasy is revealed. For they all resist this presupposition, and in so doing they would all fall victim to the wrath of God and their own corruption and perish if it were not that God had asserted this presupposition against them once and for all, conclusively, incontrovertibly and irresistibly, by actualising His will with man in the offering up of His Son. Against the background of this assertion Paul will later explain what this actualisation involves, and seeing that with it the last hour has struck he will call to faith, " the obedience of faith " (1⁵). But in the first part of his letter he simply makes the statement that human sin is the disobedience which has to be overcome in the obedience of faith, the unrighteousness whose place must be taken by the righteousness of faith we now have to proclaim and apprehend. For this reason the " law of faith " and that alone is the mirror in which the disobedience, the unrighteousness, the sin of man is revealed and known. This Law is the truth which all men " hold in unrighteousness " (1¹⁸). This Law as now proclaimed is the truth which was objectively present to all nations from the creation of the world, standing before them in nature and history and speaking of the One from whom it came. In face of it, measured by it, the world neither was nor is innocent but guilty, progressively guilty (1¹⁹⁻²⁰). It is so in that it denies to this truth and therefore to God Himself the glory which belongs to Him, and refuses to be thankful for His goodness. It is so concretely in that it has created and posited and formed all kinds of exalted and beneficent deities according to its own wisdom and invention and artistic power, furnishing them with every form of immanence and transcendence, and worshipping them both cultically and, above all, practically (1²¹⁻²³). And in doing this, in its arbitrary piety, in the very highest and best it believed it should think and do apart from the grace of God and its own salvation, in its religious arrogance, it fell victim to the disintegration to which its whole life bears witness. It is not that the heathen sinned or sin against an ideal in which God was revealed to them. The sin of the heathen was against the living God who from the beginning had been their helper, from whom they had been permitted and commanded from the very beginning to expect all good. And it was the sin of setting up these ideals and living by them. This is their sin, which underlies and includes all their other sins and the wrath of God which inevitably comes upon them. This is what is revealed by the light of the Gospel falling on their darkness (1²⁴⁻³²). But fundamentally this same " holding of the truth " was the sin and guilt of the Jews, the members of the elect people of God. Of this Paul speaks in 2¹⁻³, ²⁰. It is a sin and guilt which is better concealed because in this case we cannot speak of a fabrication of false gods and a related ethical collapse. This people is marked off from the heathen by the fact that it has, and knows, and believes that it keeps the Law revealed by God (the Law of the covenant of His grace). " Unto them were committed the oracles of God " (3², cf. 9⁴⁻⁵). They are therefore in a position to judge the heathen, to see and condemn their mistakes and folly and wickedness. Paul takes seriously both this distinctive mark and the Law of Israel. The Jews not only start like all the heathen with the presence and revelation of the gracious God which is objectively real from the very first. They are also specially called by God. They have heard His concrete promise and commandment. The existence of the Jews as such is ordained by God. But just because of this the Jew, before everyone else—not after—and more than everyone else—not less—is the man accused and condemned by God, the man who provokes His wrath. He is told at once in 2¹ that he does the very thing which he judges : in this judgment he judges himself. The judgment of God is without respect of persons (2¹¹), κατὰ ἀλήθειαν (2²)—the truth which is the same for all men. It demands obedience from him, and he, too (he more than anyone), is disobedient. Note that here Paul says expressly what he means by the truth according to which God judges : it is (v. 1) " my gospel by Jesus Christ," which in substance is identical with the Law of the covenant of grace as established in Israel. The Jew especially should not despise " the goodness and forbearance and long-suffering " of God, but he is the very one who does so. The goodness of God ought to lead him to repentance, but he denies this (v. 4). And for this reason he treasures up the wrath of God to himself (v. 5). Why the Jew ? Because he has and knows and believes that he keeps the Law, the Law of the covenant of grace. He does indeed have it, but he does not know and does not keep it : the Law which as the Law of God aims at the hallowing of the covenant in all that it demands, the Law which is the Law of faith, which calls him to the one good work that the one God concretely and directly expects and demands of the Israelite ; the Law in virtue of which the believer is the one who is righteous to God and righteous before God, which therefore forbids every attempt of man to justify himself. The Jew is the flagrant transgressor of this Law and prohibition, and as such he is accused and condemned by the very thing by which he (rightly) sees that he is marked off. The definite form of obedience and right is concretely and explicitly demanded from him, beside which there is no other. And he sidesteps this one and only form of obedience and right. He does not do what he ought to do as a member of the people elected by the free grace of God, what he is summoned to do by the Law of God concretely and directly given to him. And to his shame his attention has to be drawn to the fact that outside the old circle of the divine election, among the ἔθνη, where the Law revealed to men in this circle cannot be known, there are men in an obviously new and wider circle of election who, having the Law of God written on their hearts, being circumcised in heart—in fulfilment of the promise given to Israel—do actually do that which is demanded from him. They believe, and in so doing they do the thing by which man is righteous before God. They fulfil the Law. They are therefore the true Israel, although this is hidden from the eyes of men and known only to God (2¹⁴⁻¹⁶, ²⁶⁻²⁹). But the Jew—even though he may belong as such to this true and obedient Israel—is judged by the God of whom he boasts and the Law in which he trusts (2¹²). He is repaid according to his works (2⁶). What the Law says it says to those who are under it, within its range (3¹⁹). It tells him, therefore, that he is a transgressor, a typical transgressor who has fallen under judgment. By the Law, because he has the Law and knows it and tries to justify himself by fulfilling the works demanded by it, there arises the disclosure, the knowledge, the perception of his sin (3²⁰). We wrest this statement from its context and misunderstand it if we take it to mean, as some did, that there is a Law which is different from the Gospel, a Law by which we are confronted and have to be confronted if we are to come to a knowledge of sin and to be led to repentance and to become receptive and ready for the Gospel. The Law of which Paul speaks in Rom. 2–3 is the Law of God, which, as the Law of His covenant of grace, calls man away from any attainment of his own righteousness to repentance and obedience in the form of trust in God's goodness. It is the Law which Paul does not interpret apart from the Gospel, but in the Gospel and therefore authentically, as opposed to the Jewish abstraction which tries to see in it and to use it as a direction for the achievement of self-righteousness. It is by this Law that there comes the knowledge of sin. It does not come by any abstract law, by a conception which is itself a work of sin. That can lead only to man's setting out, as the Jew does, to order and shape for himself his relationship with God. It can lead only to the self-boasting of the Jew that he is the one who has and knows and fulfils the Law. It can lead only to his doing exactly the same as the heathen does—although without the idolatry and debauchery of the heathen. The Jew tries to be in the right with God and he puts himself in the wrong. In this way he moves from one sin to another. There is no question of his being led to repentance and becoming receptive and ready for the Gospel. Rather he has to hear the Gospel and learn to know the true Law of God in order that he may be told by it that in trying to be in the right with God he puts himself most terribly in the wrong, by boasting of his possession and knowledge of the Law and his efforts to keep it. With him as with the heathen (2^{17-24}), all sins flow from the one sin. For this reason the Jews as well as the Gentiles, as Paul tells us in 11^{32}, are "concluded by God in disobedience." The Law of faith, the Gospel, is the norm according to which they, as well as the Gentiles, are measured, and in the light of which he has to say to them that, although their unfaithfulness will not destroy the faithfulness of God, every man—and the Jew first of all—is shown to be a liar when God reveals His truth ($3^{3f.}$).

It is surprising but true, and we must not conceal the fact, that even Luther could sometimes express himself very forcibly as though he found the basis of the knowledge of sin in the Gospel as the Law of faith. " We do not count sin as anything very great, but toss it to the wind as though it were a little thing which is nothing. And even if it comes about that sin bites into our conscience, we think that it is not so very great but we can wipe it out with a little work or merit. But if we see the greatness of the precious and priceless treasure which is given for it, we are then made aware that sin is a great and mighty thing, that we can never wipe it out with our own works or powers, but that the Son of God had to be offered up to do this. If we take this to heart and consider it well, we will understand what the word sin includes, the wrath of God as well as the whole kingdom of Satan, and that sin is not such a small and light thing as the complacent world dreams and thinks " (*W.A. Tischr.* 6, 103, 1). " No one belongs to the kingdom but the Gospel shows him his sin. . . . The Gospel proclaims that everything that is in us is sin " (*Pred. üb. Matth.* 9$^{1f.}$, 1524 ; *W.A.* 15, 702, 35). *Unicum verbum indicat nos non servasse* 10 *praecepta, nempe Remissio peccatorum (Kat. Pred.,* 1528, *W.A.* 30^{I} 1, 26, 1). " Not only I but none of the apostles could think or believe that there is such great wickedness in the world if the Gospel had not come and revealed this and brought it to light. For before the Gospel came there were many excellent and pious people who lived virtuously and honestly. There were many wiser and more prudent folk than we could swear to. The world outside the Gospel was at its very brightest in art and wisdom and virtue and honesty. And it has an even brighter aspect in the air of spirituality which the spiritual orders have invented and made, as we have learned to know from the Papacy, of which all who saw it have to say that it was a holy and blessed thing. That is how the world is when the Gospel is not there : we find in it wise and prudent and honest and humble and holy folk. And reason is caught, for both worldly virtues and the spiritual estate if they are maintained lead them to the devil with their show of being pious and wise and holy and humble. But when the Gospel comes, that the child Jesus is to be preached, it belongs to it that we must understand that the holy are the greatest sinners, the wise the greatest fools, and the quiet and upright in heart the most bloodthirsty murderers. And certainly the Gospel has no more bitter enemies than high and prudent and wise and virtuous and holy folk. The more advanced they are in such virtues, the more bitter they are against the Gospel, as we see " (*Pred. üb. Luk.* 2³³ᵗ·, 1544, *W.A.* 52, 70, 26). And in a sermon on Jesus in Gethsemane : " For if you look rightly in this mirror and keep your eye fixed on it, you will see such a heap of sins as will terrify you. For look earnestly on this person. He is the Son of God who is eternal righteousness. And although he has taken our flesh and blood it is a flesh and blood without any sin. And yet because he takes to himself the sin of others, to pay for them, this alien sin comes upon him in such a way that it makes him heavy and sad, it terrifies him to such an extent that he begins to tremble and shake, and he says freely that his anguish is so great that he is half dead with it. If, then, the sin of others terrifies this pious and innocent heart to such an extent, how do you think it will be with us if our own sin comes upon us to be judged, and our hearts are still sinful and corrupt and inclined to despair ? " (1545, *W.A.* 52, 736, 17). It is an open question whether or to what extent these utterances enable us to pin Luther down. In the 1544 sermon it is obvious that by the Gospel he meant the doctrine proclaimed by him in his own century, and when he spoke of the disclosing of human corruption by the Gospel he had in mind his own opponents, so that he was speaking more *historice* than *theologice*. It is also noteworthy that we find only isolated passages which point in this direction. As a rule, his thinking and utterance were undoubtedly along other lines.

The same is true of Melanchthon. In his apology for the *C.A.* (IV, 61)— perhaps in reminiscence of similar sayings in Luther—he could write : *Evangelium arguit omnes homines, quod sint sub peccato, quod omnes sint aeternae irae ac mortis (et offert propter Christum remissionem peccatorum . . .).* And again (XII, 29) : *Haec est summa praedicationis evangelii : arguere peccata (et offerre remissionem peccatorum . . .).* Even in the later editions of the *Loci* (V), with reference to Jn. 16⁸ᶠ·, he made a remarkable move in this direction. All peoples do see and know the frightful confusion and lawlessness and corruption of human things. *Tamen sola ecclesia Dei docet, et unde sit et quid sit peccatum et audit verbum Dei de ira divina et de poenis praesentibus et aeternis.* For all its moral earnestness human wisdom does not see *hoc quod est proprium in peccati ratione,* its character as indebtedness to God. And it can see only the outward actions of men. But the Church knows the root of sin and therefore its fruit—the inner abyss in man, his doubting of the will of God, the turning aside of his own will from it, his failure to know and esteem the Son of God, his despising of the Gospel and the *beneficia Christi*. But Melanchthon did not develop his doctrine of sin from this point any more than Luther. And, in any case, statements of this kind are just as little characteristic and influential in relation to the main body of Lutheran teaching as in relation to that of the Reformed. All the same, it is a remarkable fact that they were spoken and written in this sphere.

We will now try to show that we are, in fact, forced to think along these lines : carefully, because we are on a way which has hardly been trodden before ; but resolutely, because from what we have seen there is no other way open, and all things considered, this is the most obvious and the one that promises to be the most rewarding. In this section we will deal with the basic question, to what extent we really have in the obedience of the Son of God and therefore in Jesus Christ the mirror in which we can see the man of sin as such. In this respect four decisive points have to be noted.

1. The existence of Jesus Christ is the place where we have to do with human sin in its absolutely pure and developed and unequivocal form.

It consists always and everywhere in trespass against God and fratricide. Always and everywhere man has to recognise and confess (as in *Qu.* 5 of the *Heidelberg Cat.*) : " I am inclined by nature to hate God and my neighbour." And it is always and everywhere true that in so doing he becomes guilty of self-destruction, of treachery against his own nature as given by God and created good.

But how do we come to the point of knowing this so definitely that we can think and say it with certainty, without the uncertainty that after all it may be a morosely pessimistic exaggeration ; in such a way, therefore, that our own inward opposition to this harsh judgment is beaten down once and for all ; in such a way that we simply have to accept it and make it the starting point for all further reflection on ourselves and every man ? Where do we meet with this dark determination of man in another form than that of mere suspicion and assertion, or of a merely human judgment—very occasionally on ourselves but in the majority of cases on others—but in either case a merely human judgment which, for all the force it may have, can still be qualified or set aside ? Where do we meet it as a plain and undeniable and unforgettable fact ? It belongs to the very nature of evil that it is equivocal in its appearance. Where, then, do we see it otherwise than—if not in the lustrous garment of the good (as may happen)—at any rate with an admixture of the good, to some extent covered over and adorned and excused by all kinds of historical circumstances which have to be taken into account, by the praiseworthy aims and intentions of the human misdoer, or by the happy accompaniments or its indisputable appearances to the contrary or its undeniably positive results ? Such a good case can be made out for the theory that evil is always in and for the good. And where then is the stringency and certainty of the judgment ? Where, especially, do we see the three moments of evil, rebellion against God, enmity with one's neighbour and sin against oneself, so equally balanced that there can be no doubt about the genuineness of the phenomenon, about the reality of evil which consists in the conjunction of these three moments, that man cannot seem to be excused because one or other of these moments appears to be absent ? Not every man who denies God openly hates his fellow, nor does every one who hates his fellow openly deny God, nor is it necessarily apparent that either the one or the other is engaged in self-destruction ; and there are many who are obviously destroying themselves without appearing either to deny God or to hate their fellows, let alone both. Where is the man who is the man of sin in this one and threefold and therefore genuine form ? And who is there that we would not at least try to restrain if he maintained that he found this form of the man of sin in others ?

But the uncertainty disappears, the equivocal nature of the appearance of sin is removed, when we consider the being and attitude of man to Jesus Christ as attested in the New Testament, the being and attitude of those who as our fellows are no better or worse than we are, but who could not do anything better with Jesus Christ than what they did do when He took our place according to the gracious will of God : the religious leaders of Israel in their fanatical blindness ; the people in their stupidity and vacillation ; the statesman and judge with his unrighteous judgment ; the women with their useless tears ; the disciples with their flight ; Peter with his denial ; and the man who set it all in train, Judas with his treachery. Here in the light of the One to whom all this was done, who had to suffer all this, we see plainly the man of sin. Here we have the actuality and the totality of evil. And it is obvious that this is no product öf an excited and unbalanced and unjust phantasy but a fact. It is obvious that this is not for the good but against the good, and that it is at one and the same time a denial of God, a hatred of one's fellow and self-destruction. Of course, it is shown to be limited here—not limited in itself, as the being and activity of man (as such it seems to have no limit and man himself to be an abyss), but limited by God whose gracious will is supremely served by this evil instrument. What a contrast between that which God wills for man and does, not without him, but using him as an instrument, and what man wills and does, opposing his will but sub-servient and usable even in this opposition ! The contrast of the role which man has to play in the work of his atonement with God is itself the revelation of the offence of which he makes himself guilty and because of which he stands in need of atonement, an atonement which he does not deserve and cannot expect on the ground of any capacity of his own. In this role and function he is in every respect opposed to the will of God. He denies God, because Jesus Christ against whom he offends is God meeting him in the flesh in eternal love and for his salvation. He murders his brother because Jesus Christ is the fellow-man in whose image God has made every man, in whom as the Head of the human race every man is either honoured or despised, and is now actually despised and denied and rejected and put to death. He destroys himself because Jesus Christ is the eternal Word of God by whom all things are made, and by the suppression of this Word man causes himself to fall and delivers himself up to judgment—as we see from the example of Judas. This is man, the being whose heart, whose inmost and most proper nature, is disclosed in his attitude to Jesus Christ, in his encounter with the goodness of God, in the supreme fulfilment of the merciful will of God, in what he thinks and does in this situation. And this time there can be no talk or excuse or relative right or good reasons. As it touches Jesus Christ, sin is divested of that ambiguity in appearance which is not the least part of its strength. But if it is revealed here in its nakedness, from this point we can see the reality of it always and everywhere. In the light of this we cannot ignore the fact that man exists in this antithesis and contradiction.

2. The same Jesus Christ who " has endured such contradiction

of sinners against himself " (Heb. 12³) and revealed the reality of human sin in this His suffering is also the Judge who discloses its sinfulness.

What is the evil of evil ? Enmity against God, fratricide, self-destruction : why are they all classed as unconditionally negative ? Who has the authority and competence to say that the direction of human being and thought and activity as it is revealed plainly here, less plainly there, and quite unequivocally in relation to Jesus Christ, is forbidden and wrong ? The voice of individual conscience ? Or the voice of a *lex aeterna* in the general reason of man ? Or the voice of standards respected among all peoples and handed down from generation to generation ? Let us grant that these voices do tell man more or less definitely that he has, in fact, taken this direction, and make him aware of it. How can we say that this is a wrong direction ? Who is to tell him that he ought never to act or think in this way, and especially that he ought not to be the man who goes in this direction, that the man who does so is the man of sin ? It is not merely conceivable but it has in fact happened theoretically that the accusation of these voices has been opposed. And consciously or unconsciously, are we not able to oppose it in practice too, doing what we ought not to do, but refusing to admit that it ought not to be done, that it is forbidden, bad, evil, sinful, and that we ourselves are in the wrong ? What we are and do even consciously in this direction— shall we say in impiety or brutal egoism or wanton lust—may it not be something neutral, one expression of life with others, one of the possibilities of our own nature and human nature generally which we can take without having to be accused of being bad ? And perhaps it is not merely neutral, but the genuine good. This is the ground on which men have given themselves absolute licence. To weak consciences the idea is, of course, startling. It is inconceivable to general reason, which is not in any sense authoritative. It is contrary to the customs of society and proscribed by its traditions. But on that account it is all the more certain for the free and the bold. Evil is the defiance of Prometheus, the scorn of the *condottieri* and the violent, the self-consuming flame of the super-man, and, best of all, all these combined in one person. Although we call things good and evil, others in other times and places have thought differently or with less assurance and sometimes the very opposite. What is the basis of the accusation which gives evil its name and calls the man evil who takes this direction ? Who is the judge in this matter ?

The question is so serious that our statement that Jesus Christ is this Judge cannot survive a moment as a mere assertion, as a confession of faith apart from the knowledge of faith. It is, of course, a statement of the Christian confession of faith. But what is the content of it ? What does it mean when, in Mt. 3¹², the Baptist says that Jesus is the man whose fan is in his hand and he will throughly purge his floor, gathering the wheat into his barn, but burning up the chaff with unquenchable fire ? What does it mean when, in Mt. 4^{17}, Jesus begins His own preaching with the words : " Repent, for the kingdom of heaven is at hand " ? What sort of a kingdom is it, and what sort of a king whose presence involves the obviously radical crisis of baptism " with the Holy Ghost and with fire " (Mt. 3^{11}) : which means the necessity of repentance, a total conversion, and, above all, the disclosure of the utter perversion of all that man has previously been and done ? This is what the New Testament says. And it does not mean that the either-or, the differentiation of good and evil, the setting on the right hand and the left which now takes place, is merely one among several possibilities, in which an individual or a group has again dared to call one thing good and another bad, saying something which is relatively correct and makes a certain impression, but not escaping the question on what ground they base their differentiation and characterisation ; whether things may not really be slightly different ; whether the man or men who dare to make the distinction have not put themselves in the wrong as incompetents with their bold separating and qualifying and disqualifying. The New Testament does not betray any uncertainty in its witness to this Judge. It regards and describes Him as infallible. It witnesses to Him as the Judge of the last time which has already dawned and at the end of which the righteousness and force and validity of His judgment will be universally manifest. Why this Judge and His judgment ?

It witnesses to this Judge because He calls men to conversion, and in so doing charges them with the corruption, from a place which His sentence makes incontrovertible to everyone—the place to which they all come, where they all belong and are at home, no matter what ways or directions they take, so that His call can never be alien to them, so that it always refers to them whether they receive it or not, so that their fate is decided in His judgment, so that His verdict does not do them any injustice but justice in the deepest and final sense. What place is this ? There are two things that we have to see and say concerning it.

The first is this. The kingdom of heaven which He proclaimed and which came to earth in His person is no world of ideas to which man may be open or closed, to which he may know that he is committed or from which he may keep aloof. And the Father who is the King of this kingdom, in whose name and as whose Son or Word Jesus confronts man, every man, is not one of many lords to whom man may subject himself to-day, and to-morrow turn his back on them and defy them, playing with them like a ball or puppet, as though they were the creations of his own caprice and phantasy. This God— who is not made by man but has made man—is His God, His Lord, the gracious Lord who has turned to him in friendliness and covenanted with him, who, before he was, opened His heart to him and gave

Himself to him and willed and recognised him as His, and ordained him for fellowship with Him, for being in covenant with Himself. Man is by the grace of God, the grace which appeared in Jesus Christ, so that there is no place where he can be neutral to God, or act as his own master or an interpretation of his existence which is opposed to Him. God Himself comes in the coming of His kingdom, in the revelation and presence of His Son in His possession (Jn. 1[11]), so that man can just as little doubt or waver concerning what he learns from Him about himself as he can concerning himself. What this Judge calls unrighteous is unrighteous. The man He calls bad is bad, no matter how he may try to stop his ears to the description.

The second thing is this, and in substance it is the same as the first. This Jesus, with whom no man can range or compare himself, without being disqualified and accused as a transgressor, is not our fellowman in the sense that we can separate ourselves from His standpoint and opinion and judgment, considering and examining Him historically and psychologically and in that way freeing ourselves from Him, withdrawing philosophically into ourselves, asserting ourselves, sitting loose to the truth of His word, trying to understand ourselves independently of Him. We can take up this attitude to all other men, great or small, near or distant, competent or less competent. At a pinch we can even take up this attitude to the apostles and prophets, overlooking the fact that in their witness we have to do with His Word. But we cannot take up this attitude to Him. He is the neighbour whom we cannot avoid or resist, with whom we are in fact ranged and compared before we can do this ourselves. For God has made the nature of man with a view to Him. From all eternity He has appointed Him the Head of the human race. He is therefore the eternal brother and archetype of every man, the true and living *lex aeterna* which is not enclosed in our hearts and consciences but closes in on us, which does not acquire validity in our expositions but as a *iudex aeternus*—it is a person and not an idea—expounds itself and creates its own validity. We cannot relativise Him or dispute with Him. He speaks the truth from which human discussion can only derive and in which alone it can end if it is to the point. The disqualification of the man who from the very first is ranged and compared with Him is therefore well-founded, indisputable and irrevocable.

Because—from two standpoints—He judges from this place, He judges rightly. And because He alone judges from this place, He is the only One who knows what is in man (Jn. 2[25]), to whom it is given to distinguish between good and evil, right and wrong, to set on the right hand and the left. But this *is* given to Him, and He does it. From Him we learn that the direction which man has taken is clearly the wrong direction, and in such a way that it is impossible *a limine* to transpose this wrongness into something neutral or even right and good, because there is no standpoint from which we can try to do this.

His existence sees to it that there can be none of that (only too) human evasion which prefers to regard sin as something other than sin, an evasion which is always possible in all other courts. To believe and know and confess and proclaim His judgment, Himself as Judge, is to come into the light of genuine decision : known to be genuine by the very fact that the one who believes and knows and confesses and proclaims Him as Judge is necessarily the first to find himself affected by this decision, and in such a way that he cannot resist it or reinterpret it, but only stand firm by it as the one who is most affected by it. In the light of it every attempt to measure by other standards or to judge in any other way concerning oneself or others is shown to be an inept and futile undertaking : inept, because it has no commission, competence or authority ; futile, because man is only supposed to be judged, and there are all kinds of loopholes by which he can escape.

3. It is again Jesus Christ in whose existence sin is revealed, not only in its actuality and sinfulness, but as the truth of all human being and activity.

Evil in all its forms, even when it is unmistakably and incontrovertibly evil, might still be regarded as an accidental and external and improper and transitory determination of the being and activity of man. For it is quite true that it appears only in certain attitudes and actions. It is not always or in all men equally blatant or widespread or dangerous. It does not always appear in the attitudes and actions in which man is conscious of wickedness or for which others might regard him as unconditionally responsible. It is also true that even as a conscious sinner, known to himself and others as such, he does not cease to be the good creature of God. Again, it is true that sin is a determination in which man is estranged from himself, by which he is betrayed to a foreign sphere and foreign power. All this is true, and we will have to return to it. But here, as elsewhere, it is behind the great truths that man usually conceals the truth, or rather conceals himself from the truth. The truth is this. Sin does appear in all kinds of achievements and attitudes and acts, which are very different from one another, and which do not alter the fact that the man who commits them is still the good creature of God and selfestranged. But even so, sin does not exist except as his sin, and therefore he himself does not exist except as the one who commits them, the sinner, the man of sin. And this is what we will not have, and in such a way that we make those truths a pretext to separate between us and our sins, between what we are and what we do, just as we do between a subject and its predicate or a substance and its accidents. This separation has several implications. Above all, it involves the idea of a neutral Ego which is different from its evil actions and hardly affected by them, or not at all. To this Ego its actions may be more or less sincerely regrettable, but it has no reason to be horrified at itself, because it thinks that it knows and maintains itself aloof from them. On occasion, it is ready to confess its sins, but it is not inclined or ready to confess that it is itself the origin and base of those sins, the man of sin. This leads inevitably to the idea that its evil thoughts and words and works are external, accidental and isolated. They thus acquire the character of working accidents which we have to regret and repent and confess, and as far as possible make good, but which must appear to those to whom they come as limited in themselves, since they themselves have little or nothing to do with them, and think that they can stand firm and in the last resort not be shaken by them. This again leads to the idea of a difference between flagrant sins and those which are less obvious, between those which are conscious and those which are unconscious, between those which are serious and those which can be more easily explained and finally excused. Such an idea will almost at once arise where there is the objectivisation of evil, in which a phenomenon which can be weighed and measured occupies the centre of the picture. In the same connexion there then arises the idea of a gradation in which different men are sinners and participate in the worthlessness and sinfulness of sin at different levels, thus giving us the common picture of greater or lesser sinners, of sinners who are more responsible and guilty and those who are less, and therefore of the existence of better men and worse. And because the actions of others are plain to see in all their doubtful quality, whereas we never have the opportunity to weigh our own words and deeds and attitudes from without, the final result is the obvious belief and practice of finding disproportionately more evil in others than ourselves and of reckoning ourselves amongst those who are at least better—and this easily enough even when we do not consider ourselves to be faultless, because from the very first we have quietly separated and divorced ourselves from what we do—which may, of course, be mistaken. Once this first separation has been made, the rest follows necessarily. What a fine tissue, and how well it conceals at every point the real truth of sin!

Jesus Christ tore up this tissue once and for all and disclosed the real truth of sin by confessing Himself one with sinners, by making their situation His own, by declaring and creating His own solidarity with them, by undertaking to represent their case before God—the case of sinners, not of the righteous nor of the better among the unrighteous in preference to the worse. This tears away the last shreds of the tissue. For if we count ourselves among the better sinners, we are in greatest danger of compromising our part in Him. If we have a part in Him, we have no advantage over others of which to boast. We take our place with the publican in the temple, for it is there and there alone that Jesus Christ is to be found and God is gracious to us. The better can have a part in Him only in the most loyal solidarity with the worse, not in contrast and contradistinction to them. Jesus Christ acknowledged all men as sinners, every man as the particular sinner that he is, but not some men less because they are greater sinners and some more because they are less. The truth of sin revealed here is this, that we all do it, that we are all in equal need of His acknowledgment and representation of us. Again, when Jesus Christ enters in, there is still a difference in sins, and in the possibility and necessity of estimating and assessing them differently, but it is no longer possible to grade their sinfulness and danger according to this difference, to regard oneself and others as less or more seriously responsible in the light of it. " All sin hast thou borne." All sin, great or small, flagrant or less obvious, needed and needs to have been and to be borne by Him. When He bears it, even the greatest of sins cannot damn a man. If it were not that He bears it, even the smallest would be enough to damn him utterly. How do I know whether the grace in which He declares His solidarity with me is not most indispensable in relation to what I consider my smallest sin ? The truth of sin revealed in His light is that it is one in all its forms and that as such it must be rejected. Moreover, and we are now approaching the decisive point, it is the situation of sinful man in its totality which Jesus Christ has made His own, and for which He has accepted responsibility before God. It is for the whole man, man in his unity of being and activity, for whom He has died—in the ordered integrated unity in which he does what he is and is what he does. This disposes of the idea that actions are merely external and accidental and isolated. They are not, as it were, derailments. A man is what he does. Their wickedness and folly counts. They are his wicked works and by them he is judged. As the one who does them, who produces these wicked thoughts and words and works, he is the man of sin who would perish if Jesus Christ had not taken his place. Nothing that he does or leaves undone is neutral or indifferent or irresponsible or outside the sphere of his accountability. He is inwardly the one who expresses himself in this way outwardly. And this disposes again of the idea of an Ego which is untouched by the evil character of its actions, an Ego in which a man can remain neutral because he, too, is not touched or touched only remotely by the evil character of his actions. He has every reason not merely to be occasionally terrified at the way in which he works outwardly, at what he does by his attitude and activity, but to be terrified at himself as the one who does work in this way and do these things. His inward being is the source of his outward actions. He is what he does. For Jesus Christ takes his place. He himself would be lost if Jesus Christ did not do this, if he were left to plead his own case before God. This is the truth of the man of sin. This is what is revealed when Jesus Christ takes up his case. And now we come to the heart of the matter. In the light of the reconciliation of man with God made in Jesus Christ the distinction is removed which is the source and coherence of this whole tissue of lies : the distinction between a sinner and his sins as between a subject and predicate, a substance and accidents. It is true that the being and activity of man as a sinner involves self-estrangement. He sins against himself. When he wills and does that which is evil he makes himself a stranger to himself ; he loses himself (the basic meaning of ἁμαρτία and *peccatum* and even of the word " sin " seems to be that of a " missing "—of the right way). It is also true that that from which man estranges himself as a sinner is the nature which God gave him and which God created good, his determination for being in covenant with God, his humanity, and in that humanity his divine likeness, his ordered life as the soul of a body, his being in the span of time allotted to him with its beginning and its end. It is true that in relation to all these elements of his nature the man of sin becomes someone other than himself, that his nature is altered in all its elements when he commits sin. It is also true that his nature, he himself, is not destroyed and does not disappear when he becomes someone other than himself and his nature is altered. It is also true that the man of sin is not stronger than his Creator, that he cannot create another nature than that which God gave him and become a different being because of his sin. Even when he does evil, he is still himself, the good creature of God. And it is to him as the creature made good by God's grace that God maintains and proves His faithfulness in Jesus Christ by bringing him back out of the alienation and failure and aberration of which he has made himself guilty in his folly and wickedness, by converting him to Himself and therefore to his own good being as given to him as a creature and denied by him. We can indeed say that God hates sin but does not cease to love the sinner. But it is only as we see God in Jesus Christ that we can really say this. The faithfulness of God alone is the guarantee that in spite of that alienation and failure and aberration, man does not perish and is not destroyed. The grace of God alone is the power which can bring him back out of that alienation and aberration and failure. What man himself does is totally and exclusively a contradiction of the faithfulness and grace of God. This is the truth of sin which we cannot compass in its frightfulness. Man is the good creature of God, and nothing can change the fact that he is this and that God is faithful and gracious to him as such. But he has made himself this alien and stranger, he himself, within the limits set for him, who is not a second god, by the faithfulness and grace of God. So, then, there is no place for any distinction between himself as the neutral doer of sin, and sin as his evil deed. It was for him that Jesus Christ entered the lists, for him as the creature that God had not forgotten or abandoned or given up or lost, but for him himself who in sin as his own deed and therefore as the doer of it does everything to bring about his own destruction. He came to take up that case which without Him, without the faithfulness and grace of God,

would be lost, to liberate the one who is altogether guilty before God
from his guilt and its consequences, to maintain God's right against
the one who is wholly in the wrong and in so doing to restore the
human right which he had forfeited. Man himself is "in his sins."
What help to him is their forgiveness if he himself is not helped?
He himself needs renewal. He himself—this is how he is helped—is
the new man who has appeared in the obedience of Jesus Christ.
But for this very reason he himself is also the old man who has been
judged and put to death and removed, who has disappeared in the
death of Jesus Christ; he himself is the one who contradicts and
opposes God; he himself is the one who thinks and speaks and acts
against his Creator and therefore his own creatureliness; he himself
is the one who by himself has estranged himself from himself. This
is the truth of sin. It does not consist only in the accusation: Thou
hast done this, but in the disclosure which comes to every man and
points to the most inward and proper being of every man: Thou art
the man. We can, of course, evade the accusation. The tissue of
lies which enables us to do so can be sustained. And where man is
measured, or measures himself, by some other law, then even in the
best of cases the only result will be the accusation which he can and
certainly will evade. But this disclosure is something that we cannot
evade. Now that Jesus Christ has come, to represent the person of
man in His own person, to restore and renew the person of man and
therefore man himself in His own person, we are all of us disclosed as
the man who in his own person is the man of sin.

4. The knowledge of Jesus Christ is finally the knowledge of the
significance and extent of sin, or in the words of Anselm: *quanti
ponderis sit peccatum.*

Granted that we have before us the reality of sin, its negative
character, its truth as the determination of every man and the whole
man, of man himself, we still have to ask what it means that from all
these different standpoints man is the man of sin. May it not be that
even on all these presuppositions his existence can be comprehended
and expounded as a phenomenon which is purely relative, which can
be estimated, its irregularity being finally explained and its part in
the great nexus of God and the world and man understood?

Is it not conceivable that, although we have to correct all the individual
errors and weaknesses in the modern Protestant view of sin as we have seen
it, yet when we survey the whole we are brought back to the grandiose teaching
of Leibniz which underlies it? Wrong is simply the negation of good, that which
(like evil and death) is not willed and caused by God, but which since the possibility of it was necessary to man as a free rational creature He had to permit
for the sake of the relative imperfection and therefore the perfection of the world
distinct from Himself. In its own way, therefore, it is a necessary and in its own
place a positively ordered and effective element in the harmony of all existence
and therefore of the existence of man. Can we not finally hazard the construction that man can and does sin on the basis of his metaphysical imperfection

which is inalienable to him as man and the complement of his relative perfection, but that in so doing as an " asymptote of the Godhead " he is engaged in a constant approximation to its removal ? Of course, the creature is not God, so that this can only be an approximation, a relative and not an absolute perfection. But as an approximation it does represent the attainment of his relative perfection. Why should not the presuppositions to which we have just come enable us to think and say this or something similar ?

If we try to approach this aspect of the problem only in the light of Jesus Christ, we shall be well advised to start from the moment in which we see the element of truth in every form of optimism. From the act of atonement which has taken place in Jesus Christ it is clear that in evil we do not have to do with a reality and power which have escaped the will and work of God, let alone with something that is sovereign and superior in relation to it. Whatever evil is, God is its Lord. We must not push our attempt to take evil seriously to the point of ever coming to think of it as an original and indeed creative counter-deity which posits autonomous and independent facts, competing seriously with the one living God and striving with Him for the mastery. Evil is a form of that nothingness which as such is absolutely subject to God. We cannot legitimately deduce this from a mere contrasting of the idea of evil with the idea of good. But we can say it in the light of the fact that in Jesus Christ, in His death (the meaning of which is shown in His resurrection to be His victory and the liberation of man), we see evil overcome and indeed shattered and destroyed by the omnipotence of the love and wrath of God— and this in such a way that in its supreme aggression, in its most blatant manifestation, it was impressed into the service of God and contrary to its own nature became necessarily an instrument of the divine triumph. Whatever else we may say of its origin and nature, however seriously we have to take it in its significance for ourselves, it is certain that we have no reason to fear that in it we are dealing with a factor which is the complement of God and confronts Him on the same level. Its claim to be this was given the lie once and for all on the cross of Golgotha. But if in relation to God its impotence has been unmasked, then in relation to man and his world as the creation of God it may cause serious concern, but it cannot and must not give rise to any final doubt, to any unrestrained anxiety, to any pessimism, defeatism, hopelessness or despair. Certainly we can say this only with reference to God as the Lord and Creator of His creation and the covenant partner of man. Certainly we can say this only with reference to His grace, whose superiority over sin has been unequivocally demonstrated in Jesus Christ. But in the light of God and His grace which alone is sovereign there can be no absolute fear of evil, as though evil itself were an absolute. What we cannot do, the forgiveness of sins, the separating of man from his sin in the killing of the old and the raising up of a new man, God Himself has done and revealed. And in faith in Him and therefore in the knowledge of faith and therefore in what we have to think of ourselves and others, we cannot go back on that. We would be ignoring or denying what God has done for us in Jesus Christ if we did not hold steadfastly to the fact that the door has been closed on all dualistic views of evil by the eternal resolve of God which became a historical event on Golgotha, and that not even momentarily can it be opened again. There can be no question of our needing such views the better to understand the atonement and the justification of man which is grounded in it. On the contrary, such ideas are pagan and mythical, and they can only lead us into error. God has broken evil in Jesus Christ. And since He has done this, it is settled once and for all that it can exist only within limits which were fixed beforehand and beyond which it cannot go. This is the element of truth—it has, of course, become almost unrecognisable in the optimistic construction— in the assertion that the function and significance of sin are limited because from the very first they are subordinate. In so far as that assertion carries any other meaning, we can only oppose it, and on the very same ground as that on which we have accepted it in this— and only in this—sense.

If we understand the superiority of God over evil (and therefore the limitation of the threat of evil to man) in relation to Jesus Christ, then there can be no question of any harmony enfolding God and sin and man, of any order in which the three belong together. We are not placed before a living picture in which the details belong together and can be seen together. We are placed in the midst of a drama, a drama which concerns ourselves. The superiority with which God confronts sin in Jesus Christ is that of His unconditional No to this element and to us as its representatives. It is a No in which there is no hidden Yes, no secret approval, no original or ultimate agreement. It is the No of the implacable wrath of God. Sin is the enemy of God, and God is the enemy of sin. Sin has no positive basis in God, no place in His being, no positive part in His life, and therefore no positive part in His will and work. It is not a creature of God. It arises only as the exponent, and in the creaturely world the most characteristic exponent, of what God has not willed and does not will and will not will, of that which absolutely is not, or is only as God does not will it, of that which lives only as that which God has rejected and con- demned and excluded. When man sins, he does that which God has forbidden and does not will. The possibility of doing this is not some- thing which he has from God. That he can put this possibility into effect does not belong, as is often said, to his freedom as a rational creature. What kind of a reason is it which includes this possibility ! What kind of a freedom which on the one hand is a freedom for God and obedience to Him, and on the other a freedom for nothingness and disobedience to God ! Turn it how we will, if we regard this as a possibility of the creaturely nature of man, we shall always find it

excusable because it is grounded in man as such. But in the final
meaning of the term it is inexcusable. It has no basis. It has, therefore, no possibility—we cannot escape this difficult formula—except
that of the absolutely impossible. How else can we describe that
which is intrinsically absurd but by a formula which is logically
absurd ? Sin is that which is absurd, man's absurd choice and decision
for that which is not, described in the Genesis story as his hearkening
to the voice of the serpent, the beast of chaos. Sin exists only in this
absurd event. We say too much even if we say that this event may
take place according to the divine will and appointment. We must
not go beyond the negative statement, that since man is not God he
can be tempted along these lines and therefore it was not, and is not,
excluded that this event will take place. But this event was and is
actual only in its absurdity. There is no inner or outer necessity,
and therefore there is no inner or outer possibility. Its actuality is
the man who sins, who can recognise and confess but not explain and
understand himself as such, who certainly cannot interpret himself
as an " asymptote of the Godhead." The possibility in question can
be described only as that which God has denied and rejected and forbidden, as that which is nothing in itself, as that which is as such
impossible, which exists only on the left hand of God. How do we
know this ? A priori speculation has always thought that it knew
otherwise. We know it, we have to know it, from the fact that sin
has been treated in this way by God Himself in Jesus Christ, with an
opposition which excludes any compact with it, any explanation or
exculpation of the fact that it has taken place, with an uncompromising
No. If we see it in this light, in the light of what happened to it there,
we lose all our desire to bring it into a final harmony with God and
man. In all its forms—as enmity against God, as fratricide and as
self-destruction—it is then seen as that which is out of place and
will never be in place. Even the humblest being in the most obscure
part of the created world fits in somewhere and has some potentiality
and a God-given right of actualisation. But sin does not fit in anywhere and has no genuine potentiality and no right of actualisation.
Sin is transgression (1 Jn. 3⁴). In this respect the Old Testament is
the best commentary on the New, and in the Old Testament where
is sin anything else but transgression ? Where is it judged in the light
of a secret explicability and exculpability, of an ultimate compatibility
with the will and work of God ? And as transgression *sans phrase*
it is not tolerated let alone accepted in the death of Jesus Christ. It
is not even merely condemned, but broken and rejected. It can only
be covered by God. It can only be forgiven to man. Man can only
be separated from it. He can only be snatched, like a brand from the
burning, from the abyss into which he had plunged himself as the
doer of it. He can be affirmed as the creature of God only when sin
and he himself as the man of sin are utterly negated—with the No of

the supremely real wrath of God. And this is what took place in the death of Jesus Christ at Golgotha. We cannot, therefore, go back again behind the antithesis which was resolved there between God and man on the one side and evil on the other. And we ought not to try.

However serious this antithesis, however intolerable the actuality of sin, it can be measured only by the fact that in the existence of Jesus Christ God took to Himself the fulfilment of His judgment of wrath upon it. It was not necessary that God should become man and that the Son of God should die on the cross simply to deal with an interruption in the course of the world, simply to mitigate the relative imperfection of the human situation, or to strengthen and increase its relative perfection. The exponents of the Neo-Protestant doctrine of sin saw and said this quite rightly. But the fact remains that God did become man and that the Son of God did die on the cross. In view of this, we cannot deny that in sin we have to do with something more than an interruption or relative imperfection. In the event in which man becomes the man of sin there obviously takes place a menacing of the whole work of God, the whole world as created by Him, a menacing which in its impotence is quite intolerable to God Himself. It is now clear that the contradiction and opposition of man, his godlessness and inhumanity, his sin against himself, are not a little absurdity but one which is incommensurably great, provoking God Himself to direct action. God Himself in His high majesty as Creator and Lord—the very opposite of what Schleiermacher maintained—allows Himself to be affected and concerned and offended by this absurdity. It cannot encroach upon Him—Schleiermacher was right in this—because He is the high and majestic God even in His mercy ; but all the same He takes it to heart. He does not will to be God, high and majestic, without us who have fallen victim to it. And it is now before Him—in His judgment, and His judgment never fails— as an act which is so pregnant and menacing that there can be no question merely of an adjustment or correction in the course of the general over-ruling of His providence and control (with the proper use of the mediatorial services of all kinds of creatures, angels and prophets, and finally with the co-operation of sinful man himself). What is made clear in the incarnation of the Word of God and the offering up to death of the Son of God is that evil is not an element in the orderly course of the world, but an element, indeed *the* element, which absolutely threatens and obscures it—the sowing of the enemy in the good field, the invasion of chaos, the nihilist revolution which can result only in the annihilation of all creatures. But how is man to see this, to take sin as seriously as this—his own sin and that of others, however plain ? Are we not continually surprised by the insignificance of that act in which the first man—and with him every other man—became a sinner according to the story in Genesis ? And do we not take a restricted view of the guilt and sinfulness of evil in

all the measures that we believe we can and should take against its
origins and effects (our pedagogic and political and moral enterprises) ?
How small the harm appears when we think we can botch it up in
this way ! The truth is that Anselm's question : *quanti ponderis sit
peccatum ?* is given an answer either from the cross of Christ or not
at all. It is given an answer from the cross of Christ. The serious
and terrible nature of human corruption, the depth of the abyss into
which man is about to fall as the author of it, can be measured by the
fact that the love of God could react and reply to this event only by
His giving, His giving up, of Jesus Christ Himself to overcome and
remove it and in that way to redeem man, fulfilling the judgment
upon it in such a way that the Judge allowed Himself to be judged
and caused the man of sin to be put to death in His own person. It
is only when it is seen that this was the cost to God—in the person of
His Son—of our reconciliation with Him, that the frivolously complacent
assumption is destroyed that our evil is always limited by our good
(our good nature and our good actions), and that it is excused and
mitigated by this compensation. Our evil is indeed limited and compensated and more than counterbalanced, but not by our good, only
by the goodness of God. And because this is the only possible limitation and compensation we cannot think too stringently or soberly
about the seriousness of the human situation.

A final point : What Jesus Christ has done, He has done, and
God in Him, only for us and in our place. For us—which means not
simply without us but against us ; without any co-operation on our
part but that which we see in the works of the human figures who
surrounded Jesus Christ on Good Friday and who were only too truly
our representatives. Those who believe in Him, who see in Him their
Saviour and the Saviour of the world, will recognise themselves in
these figures rather than in the innocence and patience, the obedience
of Jesus Christ. It was not for men like Him and acting like Him,
but for these men, and for us as such men, that, suffering death, and
the one man obedient in that suffering, He came before God, He
reconciled us and the world with God. He has done all this alone.
All discipleship, all fellowship of our being and activity with His,
rests upon the fact that this is so, and that it is recognised to be so.
It can and will happen only in faith in Him. It follows, therefore,
that the man of sin has no possibility of overcoming himself as such,
no freedom to change himself from the old man that he is to the new
man that he ought to be, to die as the one and to live as the other.
It is only by the grace of God that he is in course of transition from
sinner to saint, that this change comes upon him, that he is redeemed.
But " by the grace of God " means that it comes upon him as God in
Jesus Christ represents him, acts in his place. It is in Him that this
change, this redemption is actuality. Therefore he can believe, if at
all, only in Him and not in himself : not in the good nature which

does in fact remain to him ; not in the success of his efforts to overcome evil ; not in his freedom to plead his own case with God, or to co-operate with, and contribute to, that which Jesus Christ does for him. His contribution in itself and as such can only be the work of those men who contradicted and opposed Jesus Christ on Good Friday. He can only believe that all that took place there took place for him. To combat the illusion of *liberum arbitrium* and man's co-operation to the glory of God and his own salvation it is not enough merely to reflect generally on the folly and wickedness of man, which can induce a certain pessimism, but which will not prevent a little optimism being introduced quite rightly to limit it. Nor is it enough merely to reflect on the incapacity and impotence of man. This will inevitably give rise to some form of determinism, which in turn will give new life and force to the counter-arguments of indeterminism. If there is to be a knowledge of the *servum arbitrium* and therefore of the incapacity of the man of sin to justify God and in that way to be justified, if this knowledge is to be infallible and of such a kind as to bring all discussion to an end, it will arise only where there can be a knowledge of the free grace of God in all its bitterness but also in all its sweetness. And this takes place in faith, in grasping the good news of the One who willed to take our place, to re-establish in our place the broken rights of God and man, to restore our shattered peace, to suffer our death and be the basis of our life, to convert us in Himself to God. The fact that He did all this proves that we ourselves are not capable of doing it either as a whole or in part. The man who is saved in the person of another, and can be saved only in that way, is obviously in himself a lost man. We can never have the negative knowledge except in this positive faith. But where there is this faith it is impossible that we should not have it at once and irresistibly : the self-knowledge of the man of sin. The mirror of the obedience of the Son of God is the compulsion—or rather the liberation—to this self-knowledge.

2. THE PRIDE OF MAN

We have now described the place from which the man of sin must be seen and understood and judged. But what is sin as seen from this place ? What is it that man does as the old man set aside in the death of Jesus Christ, in the man of sin as revealed in the resurrection of Jesus Christ and the divine verdict pronounced upon him in the resurrection ? From the particular christological standpoint which is our present norm, the answer is that the sin of man is the pride of man. This definition is not exhaustive. In the later chapters on reconciliation it will be supplemented from other christological standpoints. But even so, it denotes more than just a part of the content. Sin in its unity and totality is always pride ; just as in the later

sections on the reconciling grace of God—again with the proviso that
the definition is not exhaustive—we shall have to say that in its unity
and totality it is always the justification of man. Sin, therefore, in
its totality is pride. Why pride ?

The pride of man is a concrete form of what a more general definition rightly calls the disobedience of man and Christianity rightly and
more precisely calls the unbelief of man.

> *Initium ruinae apparet fuisse inobedientiam. . . .* But *infidelitas radix defec-
> tionis fuit. . . . Nunquam enim repugnare Dei imperio ausus fuisset Adam, nisi
> ejus verbo incredulus* (Calvin, *Instit.* II, 1, 3).

We are not going to contradict the more general definition, but
we shall not press it. It is only too true that sin is the breaking of
the divine command. According to the Johannine definition it is the
transgression of the law, and therefore the entry into a state of lawlessness. In sin, man does that which God does not will, which, seeing
that God is over him and he is the creature and covenant-partner of
God, he ought not to do. Sin is the act of man in which he ignores
and offends the divine majesty. Sin is, therefore, disobedience. And
this disobedience rests on man's self-alienation from the particular
character of the majesty of God, which does not consist in the empty
transcendence of a quite different being which is absolutely superior
to man and raises an absolute claim on him, but which is rather the
majesty and sovereignty and omnipotence and freedom of His love
and goodness. Man sins in that he ignores and despises the redemptive
significance of the divine command, and the promise which he has to
lay hold of in obedience. He sins in that he rejects the confidence
that God is the source of all goodness and good to man, that the right
which God demands from him is that which alone is right for himself,
for the maintenance of his life and the fulfilment of his destiny, and
that it is the good pleasure of God to demand this right from him. Sin
is therefore unbelief—man's most inward apostasy from that which is
most inward and proper to the being and existence and all the works
of God. It is apostasy from God's free grace. Of course man could
obey God and would have to obey God if he believed, if he laid hold
of His free grace, if he gave Him His due, if he willed to live by His
grace. But if he does not believe, how can he obey God and do His
will ? Disobedience springs up necessarily and irresistibly from the
bitter root of unbelief. It is true enough that unbelief is *the* sin, the
original form and source of all sins, and in the last analysis the only
sin, because it is the sin which produces and embraces all other sins.
In all sins it is unbelief which transgresses God's command, which
makes man lawless, which ignores and offends the divine majesty.

But this central and universal definition needs concretion. We
return to the basic fact gathered from the last section. What sin is,
what the unbelief is which gives rise to disobedience, is revealed in

man's relationship, his confrontation with Jesus Christ. Man's sin is unbelief in the God who was " in Christ reconciling the world to himself," who in Him elected and loved man from all eternity, who in Him created him, whose word to man from and to all eternity was and will be Jesus Christ. In Him there is revealed that which is most inward and proper to the being and existence and all the works of God, His free grace and therefore His majesty which demands faith and the obedience of faith. In Him God Himself is revealed as the One who commands in goodness, the One that He always was and will be, the One in whom—He was never any other—He confronted and will confront the men of every age. The disobedience and therefore the sin of man was revealed at Golgotha as unbelief in this God—but only revealed, for in fact (in Israel or among the nations) it was never anything else but unbelief in this God, and whenever and wherever there may be men it will never be anything else but unbelief in the Word, the Son, in whom God made them His and Himself theirs, unbelief in Jesus Christ. The man of sin does not have the concrete form which corresponds to this concrete form of the omnipotent grace of God. What God wills is revealed in what He has done in Jesus Christ. What He wills of man is that which corresponds in its human way to His own divine action in Jesus Christ. The sin of man is the human action which does not correspond to the divine action in Jesus Christ but contradicts it. To that extent it is the action of unbelief and therefore of disobedience.

That unbelief, and particularly unbelief in Jesus Christ is *the* sin, is in the New Testament a specific feature of the Johannine witness : " He that rejecteth me, and receiveth not my words, hath one that judgeth him " (Jn. 12[48]). " He that believeth not is condemned already, because he hath not believed in the name of the only begotten Son of God " (3[18]). " He that honoureth not the Son honoureth not the Father which hath sent him " (5[23]). " He that believeth not the Son shall not see life ; but the wrath of God abideth on him " (3[36]). " He that believeth not God hath made him a liar ; because he believeth not the record that God gave of his Son " (1 Jn. 5[10]). And the Holy Spirit will convict the world " of sin, because they believe not on me " (Jn. 16[9]).
Perhaps in reminiscence of these texts Augustine could incidentally say : *In his, quos damnat, infidelitas et impietas inchoat poenae meritum, ut per ipsam poenam etiam male operentur* (*De praed.* 3, 7). But primarily it was an insight of Luther, often expressed by him, especially when preaching on texts from John. He could formulate it in general terms as follows : " The result of unbelief is that we do not know God and therefore fear him, and when we fear him we hate him, and blaspheme him, and commit all kinds of sin . . . and do not keep any of his commandments " (*Pred. üb. Joh.* 3, 16, 1522, *W.A.* 10[III], 166, 5). " We cannot do any greater despite to our Lord God than by unbelief, for by it we make God a devil. Again, we cannot do him any greater honour than by faith, when we regard him as a Saviour. Therefore he cannot abide a doubting heart, like the Turk who doubts, or the monk who in despair runs to a monastery and says : O how hot is hell, I will therefore do good works to placate God. But by good works we do not become a Christian but remain a heathen " (*Pred. üb. Joh.* 4[47-54], 1534, *E.A.* 5, 229 f.). Usually, however, Luther expressed the insight more pointedly and concretely : " Unbelief is the chief sin, and the

source of all other sins. For where there is unbelief in the heart, so that we do not believe in Christ, the first result is that we do not receive his word, but either despise it or regard it as heresy and falsehood, persecuting it as though it had been spoken by the devil. A greater mischief then results, for we become disobedient to our fathers and mothers and the powers that be, not diligently pursuing our own office and calling, but living in all kinds of indiscipline and licence, except as restrained by fear and shame. These are the leaves and the whole tree which springs up and blooms from this root, as the Holy Spirit convicts the world of it, and cannot be resisted. For if we do not believe in Christ, we do not have the Holy Spirit and cannot have any good thoughts. And although we may do things which are good and not bad in themselves, we do them as servants out of fear and not out of a true and hearty obedience. The mind of the world is that of the devil which cannot purpose to speak or to do anything that is good. And the cause : the fount and source of all evil is unbelief. . . . For what is sin ? Is it not theft and murder and adultery and the like ? Yes, these are sins, but they are not the chief sin. The chief sin of which the Holy Ghost tells us is one of which the whole world is guilty, or he could not convict the world of it. And this sin is not to believe in Jesus Christ. The world knows nothing of this sin : it has to be taught it by the Holy Ghost. The world accepts as sin only that which is forbidden in the second table of Moses. It knows nothing of Christ, much less that it is sin not to believe in him. And why speak of the world ? Even in the schools and among learned Christians unbelief is not regarded as sin let alone as the root of sin. For no one but the Holy Ghost can proclaim unbelief a sin. And with this preaching he makes all men sinners, where otherwise they might adorn themselves with outward works and pass for righteous. The preaching of the Holy Ghost is that without exception all men are sinners, and for this reason, that they do not believe in Christ " (*Pred. üb. Joh.* 16$^{5f.}$, 1544, *W.A.*, 52, 292, 1 f., 291, 3 f.). God binds us all " without distinction and without exception to the man called Christ Jesus, His only Son. We often find this saying in John as though the Holy Ghost could preach only the one Son of God and Mary, and poor thing, had nothing else to preach. This is ridiculous to the wise and understanding of this world. As the poet says, *Ridetur chorda, qui semper oberrat eadem*, we laugh if a lutist plays only one little tune. Thus the world laughs at the Holy Ghost as a lutist that can play only on one string. These high and mighty masters who can teach the Holy Ghost how he ought to speak can rule themselves but not God and the Holy Ghost. For there it stands. If we believe in God, we have everlasting life. Others may do as they please, it is still the case that they are lost " (*Pred. üb. Joh.* 3$^{16-21}$, 1532, *E.A.* 4, 126). " The world will not be judged because it has not kept what God commanded by Moses, but the judgment is that it will not have the Son, but persecutes the Son and tries to destroy him. Fie on the Jews that they would not have the Son. For that reason they are destroyed and rejected. That is how those who despise and persecute the only begotten Son are always humbled. Fie on us Gentiles that we are so graceless and do not believe these high and excellent words. For it is often said that there is no greater sin in the world than unbelief. Other sins are only trivial offences that we can laugh at as though they were well done, as when my little Hans and Lena are dirty in a corner. For faith makes our stink not to rise up to God. *Summa summarum*, not to believe in the only-begotten Son is the only sin in the world by which the world will be judged " (*ib.* 131). " What sin is still left in the world ? Only that we will not receive this Saviour or have the one who takes away sin. For if he were there, there would be no sin, for as I have said he brings the Holy Ghost, who quickens the heart and gives it a desire to do good. The world is not, therefore, punished or condemned for other sins, because Christ has put them all away. The only sin remaining in the New Testament is not to know and receive him " (*Pred. üb. Joh.* 16$^{5f.}$, 1523, *W.A.* 12, 545, 7).

But when we call sin unbelief, unbelief in the God who comes to man in Jesus Christ, it is not a remote but a very obvious question whether in the light of this encounter there is not something more concrete that we can say about it. And is it not in the character of pride that sin appears as unbelief, as the unbelief which rejects Jesus Christ, and therefore as disobedience ?

To substantiate this statement we must return to the particular christological basis which controls this whole section (§ 59, 1). What is it that God does in Jesus Christ ? We have seen that He maintains and exercises and demonstrates His Godhead in the obedience of the eternal Son to the eternal Father, the obedience in which He gives Himself and humbles Himself to go into the far country, as very God to become and to be something other and infinitely less than God, that is, man, flesh of our flesh, to take to Himself human existence not only in its creaturely limitation but in its sinful contradiction and misery, to become and to be altogether what we are. The existence of Jesus Christ is the event of this divine obedience and humility. The truth of the one God—as opposed to all the divinities invented by men—is seen in Jesus Christ in the fact that He is free not only to be exalted but also to be lowly, not only to be remote but also to be near, not only to be God in Himself in His majesty but also to be God outside Himself as this One who is infinitely less than God, yet in this One who is infinitely less than God to be God Himself in His majesty, as the One who is near to be remote, in His lowliness to be truly exalted. The true Godhead present and revealed in Jesus Christ exists in this generous freedom. It is supreme freedom, and as such the freedom of love. God receives man to Himself, His kingdom comes on earth, His lordship is established among us, the reconciliation of the world with Himself takes place in that He can do this, He is free to do it and He actually does it. The Lord becomes a servant but does not cease to be the Lord. On the contrary, as a servant He is truly the Lord in His very Godhead. He is the omnipresent, the eternal, the almighty, the only wise and righteous and holy. He is not, therefore, untrue to Himself but true. He does not give Himself away or give Himself up, but offers Himself in His divine lordship, and as such maintains Himself. This is what God does in Jesus Christ. And He does not do it in the chance of a caprice or variation of His divine being, or under the compulsion of any inward or outward necessity, but in the determination of His free love on the basis of His eternal election, in fulfilment of the eternal decree of His mercy. The God who is great enough to be obedient and humble and small, and therefore truly great, wills to be and is this. This is what He does in Jesus Christ. And He does it for our sake, for us, to take us to Himself, to reconcile us with Him, to convert us to Him, to save us, to restore His covenant with us, to be our God, that we may live under and with Him in His kingdom. God elected us when in His Son He elected to offer Himself, to

D.R.—14

condescend, to humble Himself, to set up His lordship in that divine obedience and therefore in that humility. We are His intention and goal. It is for our sake (*pro nobis*) that God determined and came to this action which cuts right across all human belief and surmise and thought about God, this action in which His Word becomes flesh. And if it is not in vain that He does what He does, then it is right and proper that we should turn from His action to ours, that we should ask concerning the correspondence of our actions to His action, concerning our own form as reflected in what God does, and does for us. And we describe this reflection exactly when we say that it is the picture of human pride as the sin in which we do despite to Him, thus making ourselves impossible and plunging into the abyss of our corruption. It is in view of our pride and to overcome it that God wills to be our God, our Helper and Redeemer, as He is in Jesus Christ.

We will now try to consider from four different standpoints the human disorder which is the antithesis of the divine order of grace. At every point we shall be confronted by what is now a terrible paradox, that man is the being whose attitude not only does not correspond to the attitude of God as revealed and active in Jesus Christ, but contradicts it and actively opposes it, that the two attitudes move in a diametrically opposite direction, and that no other view seems to be possible than that they never seem to coincide. At every point it will be seen that the meaning and character of the human attitude, which is so supremely unlike the divine and indeed opposed to it, the meaning and character, therefore, of sin, is in fact the pride of man in contrast to what in the light of the being and activity of Jesus Christ we can only call the humility of God.

1. We will begin with the simplest and most comprehensive point. The Word became flesh. He did not cease to be the eternal Word of the eternal Father, Himself the one true God. But as this one true God He became flesh without reservation or diminution. He became man, true and actual man, man as he may be tempted and is tempted, man as he is subject to death and does actually die, man not only in his limitation but in the misery which is the consequence of his sin, man like us. This is how God is God—as the One who is free to do this and does it for His own sake, to put into effect His own almighty mercy, and therefore for our sake, who are in need of His mercy. The divine mercy, and in proof of it the inconceivably high and wonderful act of God, is that He becomes and is as we are. But we for whom God is God in this way, on whose behalf this act of God takes place—we want to be as God is, we want to be God.

We can state at once the impotence of this enterprise and therefore its inward futility. God becomes and is man. His condescension to us, His being as we are, is an event. It is actuality. It is the act of the One who is free and able to do this. It is the powerful execution of His eternal resolve. It is a triumphant and indisputable and irrevocable fact. But man, on the other hand, only wants to exalt himself and to be as God. He can never do it. He does not have the freedom or power. He may determine on it for long enough, but nothing will ever come of it. He will always fall back on himself and still be man. It is not paradoxical or absurd that God becomes and is man. It does not contradict the concept of God. It fulfils it. It reveals the glory of God. But it is certainly paradoxical and absurd that man wants to be as God. It contradicts the concept of man. It destroys it. Man ceases to be a man when he wants this. It does not involve any alteration in God for Him to become a creature. Even as such He is still the Creator. But it does require an alteration in man—and one that is not given to him—to become God. He cannot hope and he need not concern himself that this will finally be attained. For his own good it is provided that he cannot pass his own limits, try how he will. The only result of his attempts is the revelation of his impotence to do so, and, because he ought not to do so, the revelation of his shame.

But the impotence of the enterprise does not alter the fact that for all its perversion it does take place. Man does want to pass his limits, to be as God. His thoughts and attitudes and actions are the results of this desire, which is opposed to the will and work of God. He places himself in a self-contradiction which can result only in his destruction. He loves and chooses the inner nothingness which can only reveal itself to his shame in the impotence of his action. To this extent he does do something actual. It has only a negative character. It lacks both necessity and possibility. It has no basis. It cannot be deduced or explained or justified. It is simply a fact. But it is a fact. In his responsibility for it man cannot boast that he is the good creature of God. He cannot do anything. In this loving and choosing he does something which the good creature of God cannot do, and has no freedom to do. He simply makes himself impossible. But he does do it. In this act of his loving and choosing he is the good creature of God who does that which is bad. This contradiction of his being is the fact for which he is responsible, responsible in his will to be as God, in his contradiction and opposition to the God who becomes and is as he is. There is no explanation of this human will to be as God. We can only state it as a fact that it is our desire. We have to state it because obviously it is this fact which God confronts with His own superior opposition and contradiction when He becomes and is as we are. In taking pity on us and condescending to us God accuses us of being those who want to exalt themselves. The omnipotent act of His humility exposes us as proud men. We are summoned to see and confess ourselves as such. To deny it is to make God a liar. But we cannot explain how and why we are proud. The absurd act that we commit is as such inexplicable. We can only try to describe it.

In the first instance it is concealed from man that he wants to be as God. For this reason it can be said to him only by the Word of God. For this reason again it needs faith to let it be said. It is concealed from him by the fact that he simply wants to be himself, man, in a particular way : not responsible to any other, not disturbed by any address or claim, not subject to any disposition but his own, controlling himself, sufficient to himself, the first and the last in his being for himself, in an individual or collective—the distinction is not important—but at all events his human being for himself. The pride and sin of this desire are not obvious. Might it not be supreme humility that man wants to be only man and to win and enjoy aseity as such, to live of himself—not necessarily egotistically, but at the very worst in a healthy balance of egotism and altruism in which altruism is found to be the true egotism, to live of himself as man, to be his own norm and law, his own beginning and end, his own height and depth ? This does not appear to be any attempt to pass his limits, but an assured self-containment, an unconfused movement on his own way, an infallible return to himself, a steadfast repudiation of that which is mysterious and unreliable and inimical as something alien to the self, an unshakable satisfaction with his own being in himself. There is no need to deny God in all this. May it not be that God Himself has created and ordained man to be in himself, to control himself, to be sufficient to himself ? When man desires the enjoyment and use of his freedom, is he desiring anything more or other than the most obvious and natural thing in the world ? And in what does his freedom consist if not first and last in the capacity and the right to choose himself ? Where is the wrong in this ? That is the concealment of man's enterprise. It does not look as though man is wanting to be as God, to be God, and in that way becoming a sinner. It looks rather as though man is modestly doing that which is obvious and right, fulfilling his true humanity and in that way the will of God as rightly understood.

In this connexion we may recall the first of Melanchthon's B.A. theses in Wittenberg in 1519 : *Natura humana diligit sese propter seipsam maxime.* At the time it was, of course, a monstrous innovation that this should be advanced as a definition of sin. In the later mediæval scholasticism it had long since been understood, and comfort had been found in the fact, that a proper self-love not only does not exclude but in the right sense necessarily includes a love for God.

The speech of the famous serpent in Gen. 3[1f.], like all bad theology—of which this speech is the original—is itself only an interpretation of human existence which does not explicitly express but only implies a call to disobedience. And not merely the taking and eating of the fruit of the tree, but the entry into discussion with the serpent and the discovery that the tree was " pleasant to the eyes, and a tree to be desired " (v. 6), did not take place at all at the behest of the serpent—who only supplied the necessary myth—but in the free (or supposedly free) decision and act of man. The serpent's speech simply showed the existence of man to be formally autonomous, self-governing and self-sufficient.

It simply laid down the possibility that man might see his own needs and satisfy those needs by his own efforts. It simply safeguarded human autonomy. The autonomous belief and will and activity of man were not those of the beast, or caused by the beast—how could they be ?—but his own : he saw and took and ate, in the conviction that by taking up his own attitude to the commandment of God he was understanding God better than God understood Himself, in the intoxicating certainty that by asserting his autonomy he was seeing and doing the real will of God. This was the great and epoch-making thing which took place there. But, unfortunately, it was the groundless and inexplicable irruption of chaos into the good creation of God as the work of man, himself supremely the good creature of God.

The concealment is powerful, but it does not conceal what takes place not only under but in and with the concealment.

(1) The error of man concerning himself, his self-alienation, is that he thinks he can love and choose and will and assert and maintain and exalt himself—*sese propter seipsum*—in his being in himself, his self-hood, and that in so doing he will be truly man. Whether this takes place more in pride or in modesty, either way man misses his true being. For neither as an individual nor in society was he created to be placed alone, to be self-controlling and self-sufficient, to be self-centred, to rotate around himself. Like every other creature he was created for the glory of God and only in that way for his own salvation. And as man in particular he was created with a determination for being in covenant with God and therefore for life by His grace and in responsibility to Him. He is a man, himself, as he comes from God and moves towards God. He is a man as he is open to God, or not at all. If he chooses himself in any other way, *incurvatus in se*, in self-containment, then he misses the very thing that he seeks. He loses what he wills to save (Mk. 8³⁵). In this loving and choosing and willing, and in the activity determined by it, he becomes something which is not human but supremely non-human. He need not be surprised that the revelation of this loving and choosing and willing— even when it takes place in its purest and noblest and perhaps its most pious and philanthropic forms—is ultimately a revelation of the non-human.

(2) The mad desire to be as God is not an obvious delusion and titanism—although it may take this form. It consists in the fact that caught in this error about himself man thinks he can be his own source and standard, the first and the last, the object of a *diligere propter seipsum*. What does it matter if in so doing he does not deny God, but accepts Him as in His own way a good man, perhaps thinking that·he seriously believes in Him, or even imagining if possible that he is rightly promoting His true and supreme glory by this self-affirmation (and the more so the more consistent and joyful it is) ? A man's god is that which is supreme for him. If he himself is supreme, then he is his own god. The aseity which he ascribes to himself is proper only to God. It can belong only to Him to be loved for His own sake. And

so it comes to pass that self-centred man rotating about himself robs God of that which is only His, taking that which belongs only to God. Why ? To deck himself out with it, to be as God is, to be God. The mad exchange takes place. It does so, as we have seen, without any prospect that he will really succeed in being as God. He can only want this. He can only think and speak and act as the one who would have it, and as though it were possible for him to have it. All that he does when he arrogantly assaults the limits marked out for him is to attain a pseudo-divinity. He does do that. And as a pseudo-divinity he secretly worships himself, appearing as such even outside and deceiving others as he has first deceived himself. Even if man is quite powerless to become anything more than himself, his attempt to do so is real. And it takes place in and with the concealment under which it takes place.

(3) The error of man concerning God is that the God he wants to be like is obviously only a self-sufficient, self-affirming, self-desiring supreme being, self-centred and rotating about himself. Such a being is not God. God is for Himself, but He is not only for Himself. He is in a supreme self-hood, but not a self-contained self-hood, not in a mere divinity which is obviously presented to man in the mere humanity intended for man. God is *a se* and *per se*, but as the love which is grounded in itself from all eternity. Because He is the triune God, who from the first has loved us as the Father in the Son and turned to us by the Holy Spirit, He is God *pro nobis*. When man tries to make this mad exchange his first and supreme error is in relation to God. It is not only that he cannot succeed in worshipping the true Deity in himself, but that in positing himself as absolute what he thinks to see and honour and worship in himself is already the image of a false deity, the original of all false gods Ignoring the grace of God and renouncing his responsibility to Him, man chooses himself, and in so doing even in this—decisive—respect he chooses that which is not. As Luther rightly saw and said, he makes God the devil. For if (as the origin and object of a most extreme and terrifying limiting concept) there " is " a devil, he is identical with a supreme being which posits and wills itself, which exists in a solitary glory and is therefore " absolute." The devil is that being which we can define only as independent non-being. Of course, when man sets himself up in the image of this non-being, he cannot make himself a devil ; he cannot change his nature into that of this non-being ; he cannot make for himself this awful independence ; he can deny but he cannot dissolve his nature as proceeding from God and open to God. But it is not man himself who prevents it. And it cannot be denied that when he chooses to set himself up in this way he sells himself and " goes to the devil."

It should be noted that the *Eritis sicut Deus* (Gen. 3⁵) is an element in the explanation of existence given by the serpent. We have to do here with a thought of chaos, the thought of chaos which can as such be very powerful but can never be anything other than false and destructive. Powerful, because it makes so plain the true and final purpose, almost the promise, of the aseity and independence indicated, and so very attractive the movement into the swamps of this aseity and independence. False, because it is contrary to the whole Old Testament concept of God, because the God that man resembles when he desires this independence can only be a false god. Destructive because the corresponding decision of man can, in fact, only lead him into a marsh in which he will sink hopelessly unless he is rescued from it.

This is what our first glance tells us of the man whom God has reconciled and converted to himself in Jesus Christ when we view him as unreconciled, in his alienation from God, in his pride. Can we put the matter in any other way? In Jesus Christ God has condescended to this man who exalts himself in this way and falls so low. God knew him. God knew what he was doing. The remedy was exactly suited to the disease. To that attempt of man to become as God, an attempt which is so alien and dangerous in its futility, God has made answer with the gracious and triumphant act that He Himself became as man : '' The Word was made flesh.''

In biblical history the great concretion of this contrast in its first form is to be found in the story which comes between the divine concluding of the covenant and giving of the Law on the one hand and its renewal on the other. This story tells us of the breaking of the covenant by Israel at the foot of Mount Sinai (Ex. 32$^{1-6}$). We need not enter here into the complicated literary and historical questions in relation to this account and its context. The matter had come to be viewed in this way, as part of this sequence, as an " incident " (W. Vischer, *Das Christuszeugnis des A.T.*, Vol. 1, 1934, p. 251), at any rate by the time of the final redaction of the Pentateuch and probably at a much earlier period which we cannot fix with certainty. And it was in this way that the story passed into the definitive form of Old Testament tradition, just as the Paradise story was preceded and followed by pictures of the setting up of the divine order of grace, and stands out in terrible contrast to them. We can say conversely that the tradition which was normative for the definitive form of the Pentateuch viewed and understood the action of Yahweh in the establishment and maintenance and renewal of the covenant of grace with Israel as an action which could in some inconceivable way be interrupted but could not be arrested by the event of the fall, the covenant itself being at once and flagrantly and apparently hopelessly broken by Israel. What the people did on this occasion, led by Aaron, the priest who had himself been seduced, was a kind of typical happening for later Israel as it went through the period of the prophets and the judgment which they proclaimed—typical in the context in which it was placed in the Book of Exodus, just as the context itself was obviously typical in its significance for later Israel, the covenant willingness and faithfulness of Israel preceding and following the apostasy of Israel.

We will begin by a consideration of this context ; and first of that which precedes. According to Ex. 19$^{3f.}$, the real presupposition to which both the record of the covenant and that of the breach of the covenant look back is the divine act of revelation which underlies the historical existence of Israel : " Ye have seen what I did unto the Egyptians, and how I bare you on eagles' wings, and brought you unto myself " (19^4). Therefore the election of Israel and its existence as the people of Yahweh was a visible and tangible historical event. The covenant of Yahweh with Israel was concluded without Israel being asked, but simply as this liberation and its results came actually but miraculously on Israel. The grace of God had the first word absolutely, and it was this word which was spoken in the act or the sequence of acts recorded in the whole of the first part of the Book of Exodus. All that Israel is asked is to keep the covenant, consisting in its further hearing of the Word of Yahweh in accordance with the determination given to it with its whole existence. But it is seriously asked to do this : " Now therefore, if we will obey my voice indeed, and keep my covenant, then ye shall be a peculiar treasure unto me above all people : for all the earth is mine : and ye shall be unto me a kingdom of priests, and an holy nation " (19⁵ᶠ·). Therefore its election has a purpose and scope. Its determination as the covenant people of Yahweh is that among all the peoples of the earth who all belong to Yahweh it should fulfil a mediatorial ministry, and exercise a royal lordship in this ministry—not in any other way, not in seeking and attaining any other form of greatness, not in competition with the peoples—proving itself to be the possession (the royal domain) of King Yahweh in this way, to be His holy people, separated from the peoples for the peoples. In this way and in this sense God has turned to this people. The form of this turning, the direction to keep the covenant, is the Law which the Book of Exodus now records (20-31) in the form of the Ten Commandments, the so-called Book of the Covenant and some additions. " I am Yahweh thy God " (20²) is the indicative on which the imperatives rest, both great and small, both legal and cultic. When, or even before, Yahweh elected Israel to be His people, He elected Himself—we are already confronted by the phenomenon of the humility of God—to be the God of Israel. Without forfeiting anything of His holiness or majesty or even terribleness : on the contrary, thunder and lightning and the sound of the trumpet and smoke and clouds and an earthquake surround His condescension, proclaiming His " descent " (19²⁰) to Mount Sinai at the foot of which the people is encamped. It was in an act of liberation that the high God made Himself the God of this people. And it is liberation that He wills from this people in His commandments : " Thou shalt have no other gods before me." " Thou shalt not make unto thee any likeness or idol." " Thou shalt not bow down thyself to them or serve them." " Remember the sabbath day, to keep it holy." " Thou shalt not take the name of the Lord thy God in vain," i.e., empty His self-revelation by religious self-will. All this, and all the commandments of the second table, and all the intricate prescripts of the Book of the Covenant, which are again and again shot through by rays of clear light, are a message of salvation, a direction to freedom on the basis of this act of liberation, an introduction to the ministry to which He who elected this people has ordained it, an indirect exercise in the necessary attitudes, a warning against what has to be left, the commandment of this benevolent and beneficent God who is well-disposed to His people. It is not primarily because Israel belongs to Him but because He belongs to Israel and has covenanted with it that He is such a jealous God, the God who is so interested in every detail of its life, who demands of it so scrupulous an obedience. His concerns are the concerns of this people. The divine promise does not cease in the divine commanding recalled here. It ceases so little that we have to hear and understand the commanding itself as a promise. The Law is a Yes of this God to this people (as the representative of all peoples). This is true even of the directions concerning sacrifice, the priesthood of Aaron and his family, and the tabernacle " where I will meet you, to speak there unto thee. And there I will meet with the children of Israel, and the tabernacle shall be sanctified by my glory. And I will dwell among the children of Israel, and will be their God. And they shall know that I am the Lord their God, that brought them forth out of the land of Egypt, that I may dwell among them : I, Yahweh, thy God " (Ex. 29⁷ᶠ·). This, then, was His covenant and Law. And ᶠsrael ? It had already been said of Israel (19⁸) that all the people answered together : " All that the Lord hath spoken we will do," and (24⁸) that " Moses took the blood, and sprinkled it on the people, and said, Behold, the blood of the covenant, which the Lord hath made with you concerning all these words." We now come to that which follows in Ex. 32$^{7f.}$ and the rest of the Book. The " incident " has already taken place, and has not passed without leaving a trace. What has happened has brought everything into question—the election, the grace, the covenant of God, the separation and divine mission and therefore the existence of Israel. It seems as though the dissolution of the covenant must at once follow its institution, the end of the history of Israel its beginning : " I have seen this people, and, behold, it is a stiff-necked people. Now therefore let me alone, that my wrath may wax hot against them, and that I may consume them. And I will make of thee a great nation " (Ex. 32$^{9f.}$). So greatly, so radically, so profoundly did that which Israel willed and did—its sin—run counter to that which God willed and did, that it seemed as though God could only renounce Israel in His anger and break off the connexion which He had made. But now Moses came forward and into the centre, the one with whom God had spoken as with His messenger to the people on Sinai, the one to whom He had addressed this threatening word. And there is now ascribed to him a different function from that so far allotted to him in this Book. He is no longer merely the messenger of God and the prophetic and charismatic leader. Of course, he does still appear and act (Ex. 32$^{15-29}$) in accordance with this mission. We might say that he is the one who fulfils this wrathful saying of God. He throws down and smashes the tables given to him for this people and written with the finger of God. He burns the image of the calf and grinds it to powder. He makes the people drink of it. He orders a partial mass-execution which brings out clearly the terrible nature of the presence of the One who had elected Himself the God of Israel. But surprisingly, the picture of Moses in accordance with his mission is itself only an " incident " in relation to the singular overall picture given in the Book. It is framed by the accounts of the conversations which he had with God Himself (32$^{7-14}$ and 32^{30}–34^{10}), in which the same man plays quite a different part and one which is quite unique in the Old Testament. Anticipating the place of Israel among the nations (and in face of the now evident and unforgivable sin of Israel), it is the role of a mediator between this people and its God. He is the man who speaks with God face to face as a man with his friends (33^{11}), who not only has to listen to God in order to repeat what He has said to the people (as he had done), but who can also say things to God to which God will listen and which will be decisively regulative for His future attitude to the people (as is notably the case in the present instance immediately after the great " incident "). There is no talk now of receiving the Word of God : " Thy people, which thou broughtest out of the land of Egypt, have corrupted themselves " (32^7). It is not his people, but the people of Yahweh, and not he but Yahweh brought them out of the land of Egypt. There is no talk of him entertaining even for a moment the proposition held out to him (" I will make of thee a great nation," 32^{10}). On the contrary : " Yet now, if thou wilt forgive their sin— ; and if not, blot me, I pray thee, out of the book which thou hast written " (32^{32}). That is how, at a later date, Paul, too, was to speak with God : " I could wish that myself were accursed (ἀνάθεμα) from Christ for my brethren " (Rom. 9^3). There is no talk of him accepting the breach of the covenant which was first stated and described in all its radicalness not by himself but by God. On the contrary, this man dares to remind God of His own promise, to appeal to His faithfulness, beseeching Him, but also very definitely remonstrating with Him : " Lord, why doth thy wrath wax hot against thy people, which thou has brought forth out of the land of Egypt with great power, and with a mighty hand ? Wherefore should the Egyptians speak, and say, For mischief did he bring them out, to slay them in the mountains, and to consume them from the face of the earth ? Turn from thy fierce wrath, and repent of this evil against thy people. Remember Abraham, Isaac, and Israel, to whom thou swearest by thine own self, and saidst unto them, I will multiply your seed as the stars of heaven . . ." (32[11f.]). Is not this to flee from God to God, to appeal from God to God ? And is it not the case that in this flight, this appeal of Moses, God finds Himself supremely and most profoundly understood and affirmed, that in a sense Moses has prayed, or rather demanded, from the very heart of God Himself ? He hears and answers this prayer which is so defiant and dogmatic. He does, of course, plague the people because they worshipped the calf which Aaron made (32[35]). But he repents " of the evil which he thought to do unto this people " (32[14]). His destruction is well-merited and it seemed inevitable, but it does not take place. His covenant is not taken away. The history of this people, and its entry into the land of its fathers, is to proceed. But that is not all. For what the man Moses thinks he can ask or even demand of Yahweh is not less but more than what preceded the " incident." Relying on the promise, relying on the fact that Yahweh knows him by name and that he has found grace in His sight, in execution of his mediatorial function he asks : " See, thou sayest unto me, bring up this people : and thou hast not let me know whom thou wilt send with me " (33[12]). As though he had not been told : " Mine angel shall go before thee " (23[20], 32[34], 33[2]) ! A great promise, but one which is not enough, which does not seem to be enough in view of what has taken place. In it there is still a reservation, a refusal : " I will not go up in the midst of thee ; for thou art a stiff-necked people : lest I consume thee in the way." The actualisation of the direct presence of God would always be dangerous for a people which was constantly on the point of doing again what it had done at the foot of Mount Sinai when the covenant was being proclaimed. Was it not to spare that God made this reservation, that He refused to come too close to His people ? But Moses is bold not to accept it. He would rather see the people brought into danger than acquiesce in this refusal. The people does not need to be spared. It needs something greater which may involve danger. And so Moses dares to ask again, to demand, that which has been refused : " If thy presence go not with me, carry us not up hence. For wherein shall it be known here that I and thy people have found grace in thy sight ? is it not that thou goest with us ? so shall we be separated, I and thy people, from all the people that are upon the face of the earth " (33[15f.]). And again : " O Lord, let my Lord, I pray thee, go among us ; for it is a stiff-necked people ; and pardon our iniquity, and our sin, and take us for thine inheritance " (34[9]). And again God hears and answers. Obviously with this demand He sees that He has been genuinely understood and affirmed as from His own most proper essence and will. Anything less than His own accompanying and presence obviously does not suffice—especially in view of this typical breach of the covenant—to make possible the further existence of Israel, the fulfilment of the promise which He has given Israel, the carrying out of its mission among all peoples. And this indispensable thing—Himself, with all the risk that it involves—God will not deny His people (Moses had prayed rightly and therefore he is justified) : " I will do this thing that thou hast spoken : for thou hast found grace in my sight, and I know thee by name " (33[17]). Yahweh will do it. He will Himself actually dwell and act in the midst of His people : " Behold, I make a covenant : before all thy people I will do marvels, such as have not been done in all the earth, or in any nation : and all the people among which thou art shall see the work of the Lord : for it is a terrible thing that I will do with thee " (34[10]). He will do it, but—and here we reach the limits of the answer to the prayer of the man Moses ; here we reach the answer which can never really take place within the sphere of Old Testament promise and history—He Himself, His *kabod*, will not be seen but will remain hidden in His action. It is in another book that the words will be written : " We beheld his glory " (Jn. 1[14]). Here it is : " My face shall not be seen " (33[23]), not even by Moses, who does speak with God face to face, but who only speaks, who can only look after Him, who can only have a part in the proclaiming of His name. But he can and does have that part. And this is His name, His promise to this stiff-necked people (and remember that it is said after that fall of Israel and with reference to it) : " I will be gracious to whom I will be gracious, and will shew mercy on whom I will shew mercy " (33[19]). And again more expressly : " The Lord, the Lord God, merciful and gracious, longsuffering, and abundant in goodness and truth, keeping mercy for thousands, forgiving iniquity and transgression and sin, and that will by no means clear the guilty ; visiting the iniquity of the fathers upon the children, and upon the childrens' children, unto the third and the fourth generation " (34[6f.]). And in confirmation the record of chapters 34–40—not as though " nothing has happened," but after that has happened which has happened—closes with an account of the setting up of the " tent of meeting." Such is the later context in which we have to consider and estimate the " incident " which is our present concern.

And now—in the light of this—we turn to the breach of the covenant itself in Ex. 32[1-6]. In the preceding narrative there is nothing to prepare us for what is recorded in these verses. In the light of it, it is simply a senseless and causeless act of apostasy. And if the act is presupposed in all its seriousness in the texts which follow, when we have regard to their culmination in the illuminating revelation of the name of God, it seems if anything all the more inconceivable— a refusal in face of these pre-conditions, an unfaithfulness in face of this faithfulness of Yahweh, a withdrawal of Israel from the covenant which He has so securely grounded. The contrast is, if anything, even more clamant than that of the story of the fall. It is quite understandable that the tradition which viewed the beginning of the history of Israel in this way—as indelibly blotted in this way —should only be able to view the beginning of the whole race, of history, as it is, in fact, viewed in Gen. 3. Here in Ex. 32 the tradition of Israel speaks from direct knowledge. Here is the setting of the view of man in relation to God which is attested in Gen. 3, being there projected backwards and referred to the beginning of all peoples. Here we have a typical picture—a kind of crosssection—for it is against Ex. 32 that we obviously have to see texts like 1 K. 12[28f.] (the sin of Jeroboam) and corresponding passages in the prophets—of what always takes place in the history of Israel as the counterpart to the faithfulness and grace and mercy of God, the painful contradiction of its whole existence. No wonder that the contours and colours of Gen. 3 seem to be mild compared with what we find here. Here it comes home with a vengeance. It is not a matter now of Adam in a distant paradise in the distant past. It is the Israelite himself now, liberated out of Egypt, brought into the wilderness, sustained in it, brought back into the land of his fathers, a member of the covenant people elected and called and infinitely preferred and therefore infinitely responsible and committed before all other peoples. And this Israelite has to see that he is the Adam who sins so inconceivably, and to confess his own part in the transgression. He now knows to be true of himself what he has to attest in Gen. 3 concerning all men.

We will now turn to the decisive statement concerning the setting up and worshipping of the golden calf. Its description as a calf is a derogatory judgment on the part of the narrator, not merely in relation to the form of presentation of that which is meant, but in relation to the thing itself : a stupid and helpless and ridiculous calf is set up and worshipped as god : a *vitulum, in quo nihil consentaneum vel affine erat Dei gloriae* (Calvin). The matter is treated lightly, but what is meant—whether on the model of Egyptian or Canaanitish religion or not is a question we need not decide—is the bull as a symbol of virility and fertility, signifying the essence of the people's power as a people, of the mystery of its existence and continuance, of the demonstration of its being as deriving from the tribes themselves, of joy in its own present and of the ideal of its future. The bull is for Israel " a god who understands it and in whom it understands itself " (W. Vischer). Israel itself was this bull, defiantly standing on its short thick thighs and feet, tossing its horns and threshing its tail. But Israel in a divine eschatological form as felt and experienced and seen by itself. Israel transcending and hypostasising itself, and therefore its god. And Israel, too, in the divine form constructed and manufactured by itself—not without the joyful sacrificial offering of golden ear-rings. The god, therefore, which is its possession, which lives by its own imagination and art, by its riches, by the generous offering of its goods ; the god which belongs to it and is pledged to it, as it is brought forth by it. *Volunt esse Dei creatores* (Calvin). Creators of a new and alien god ? Not by a long way, however much the ideas of other peoples may have been imitated : " These be thy gods, O Israel, which brought thee up out of the land of Egypt " (v. 4). It is not a matter *novo et insolito ritu quidquam redemptori suo detrahere, sed potius hoc modo amplificari eius honorem* (Calvin). With the invention and construction and manufacture of the bull they think they can see and understand in themselves, in the mystery of the power of their own existence, their *redemptor*, Yahweh the Liberator, Helper and Lord, and the hope of their future. They do not plan and purpose any apostasy from their relationship with Him, but the deepest and most faithful and fitting interpretation of it, its actualisation in all its particularity. It is not to an idol that the altar to the bull is set up and offerings are brought, burnt offerings as the representation of unconditional worship, of complete and undivided sacrifice, and peace offerings as a witness to the freedom and joy of the sacrifice, culminating in a communion feast in which those who sacrifice enter into enjoyment of that which is sacrificed. What is described is not, therefore, an idol-feast : " And the people sat down to eat and drink, and rose up to play." No : what Aaron called them to, and what, as we learn later (v. 17), was celebrated with a noisy song like a noise of war, was a " feast to the Lord," as Aaron put it in his proclamation, a feast to Yahweh as now at last he was known and made present and existentially perceptible in his true form, to Yahweh as the champion and work and possession of Israel, to Yahweh the bull, and therefore in this image of the bull. This was the breach of the covenant, and Israel regarded it as the supreme fulfilment of the covenant, an act of concrete religion.

The role of Aaron in all this is worth noting. According to Ex. 6[20], he was the elder brother of Moses. According to 4[16] he was to speak for him to the people (and, according to 7[1], to Pharaoh), Moses himself being to him in the place of God. According to 17[10] he was one of the two who held up the arms of Moses in prayer during the battle with the Amalekites. According to 19[24] he went with Moses to the mount when the Ten Commandments were received. According to 24[9f.] he was at the head of the seventy elders who saw God, or, at any rate, the clear work under His feet. Are we to understand from chapters 28–29 that his investiture as high-priest had already taken place ? What is quite clear is that this elder brother is not, like Moses, a prophet. He is called a prophet in 7[1], but only as the one who speaks for Moses. He is not a charismatic, but the type of the institutional priesthood, the keeper of the tent of meeting and its possessions, the supreme official in the ministry of sacrifice. In his own way he is an indispensable figure. Yet he does not stand with Moses but with the people, mediating between him and the people (and to that extent between God and the people), over against Moses and under Moses, without any independent relationship with God and therefore without any independent mission to the people. The one who receives and mediates the divine revelation, the friend who speaks with God as an equal, is Moses himself. Aaron and all the others are only witnesses. For Aaron, too, Moses stands " in the place of God." " *L'institution et l'évenement* " (J. L. Leuba, 1950) are not two factors of equal but of different rank, the one being subordinate to the other. What this means from the point of view of the institutional priesthood and its activity is something which was revealed by Old Testament prophecy from the days of Amos onwards, and it is brought out very plainly in Ex. 32. Aaron the priest as such had not risen above the development and power of the sin of the people. On the contrary, he both takes part in it and he is the exponent of it. He is the man of the national Church, the established Church. He listens to the voice of the soul of the people and obeys it. He is the direct executor of its wishes and demands. He shows the people how to proceed and he takes the initiative. He orders the offering of the golden rings and he himself receives them. He pours the gold into a mould. He himself " fashions " the bull before which they see themselves and cry : " These be thy gods, O Israel." His later excuses are not without a certain humour. The people gave him their gold, he cast it into the fire, and there came out a calf (Luther : it became a calf)—entirely of its own accord, or by means of a little miracle. If the institution does not achieve the event of revelation and faith, it does not prevent the very different event of sin. The institution can always support and execute it. At any moment the calf can self-evidently proceed from it. Priestly wisdom as such can be effective in the form of supreme priestly folly. The priestly art as such—building altars and celebrating liturgies and ordering and executing sacrifices and proclaiming feasts of the Lord—is a neutral activity which can turn into the very opposite of all that is intended by it. The priest as such can always be a deluded and deluding pope. This is the role assigned to Aaron in the breach of the covenant—in this respect it is unmistakably influenced by prophecy. He is not above but under and actively in the activity of which Israel is guilty. There is no support in the text for a sharp personal judgment, such as we often find in commentaries and sermons. The rebuke which Moses addresses to him in v. 21 is remarkably gentle : " What did this people unto thee, that thou hast brought so great sin upon them ? " The people are called stiff-necked and indisciplined, but not Aaron, of whom the narrator simply says (v. 25) that " he had made them naked unto their shame among their enemies." As far as he is concerned the only offence is that of connivance. For that reason, although he might appear to be the chief offender before God, he is not one of the victims of the mass-execution carried out by the Levites (his own men). And there is no question of any personal punishment or expiation being laid upon him. His office does not seem to be compromised by what he has done. He has simply accepted the *vox populi* as the *vox Dei* and acted accordingly. According to the text the guilty party is the people and only the people. Aaron himself belongs neither to the side of light nor to that of darkness in this story. He is in the shadows, significant and great neither for good nor evil. What appears from his role is that he is not Moses, not a prophet, but only Aaron, only a priest, a man of religion, and that as such he cannot arrest but only acquiesce in the fall of Israel, which is itself a great religious occasion.

The key to the story is to be found in what is, if we come to it from chapter 31, its very surprising beginning. How does the people suddenly come to the point of gathering together unto Aaron and asking him to " make " a god to go before it ? The text points to a concealed development of which this is the culmination. The long delay of Moses has given rise to considerations which have led to this appeal to Aaron. The breach of the covenant, of the relationship between the people and Yahweh, arose out of the relationship of the people to Moses, or concretely out of the breach of that relationship.

We have to remember that Moses was what Aaron was not. He was the prophet, the charismatic leader of Israel. God spoke to him, calling him by his name. He was the man who heard and mediated the Word of God, advising and leading and, in fact, ruling the people, not in his own power, but in that of the Word of God which he heard and mediated. And we know, too, that he was the man who prayed for Israel in his solitariness with God, in a sense forcing himself upon God, keeping Him to His promises and earlier work as the covenant Lord of Israel, and being approved and heard by God. He was the man who anticipated in his relationship to Israel the mission ordained for it in its relationship with the nations as the meaning and scope of the covenant which God had concluded with it. He steadfastly represented the people before God even at the risk of his own person and his own relationship with Yahweh. In the Old Testament (with Jeremiah and the Servant of the Lord in Is. 53) he was the most concrete type of the One who represented all men before God and therefore God before all men. Because of this he was the prophet and leader and regent and ruler of the people. The mystery of the grace of God is the mystery of this man, and of the connexion between him and that One. The elevation of Israel stands or falls with his election. This mystery lies behind the claim with which he came to give direction and instruction to the people. By the word and act of this man Yahweh had led the people out of Egypt and brought them to the land of their fathers, showing them by him that the deliverance from Egypt which had come to it was the work of His electing goodness, proclaiming by him the covenant and the Law of the covenant. To look to God meant to Israel to look to this man, to hear God to hear the word of this man, to obey God to follow his direction, to trust God to trust his insight.

And now this man had disappeared and for a long time they had not been able to see and hear him. Had they really known him as the one that he was among them and for them ? Had they known themselves in him ? That is to say, had they known Yahweh as present in their midst, represented by him as His witness and servant : His grace, His holiness, His commandment, and therefore their own election, their own existence as the people of the covenant, their own responsibility before Him, their own mission, their own way with Him from the past to the future ? If they had known Moses, and by him God and themselves, the God who had condescended and given Himself to be their God, and themselves as the people sanctified by His grace, then even if they had not been able to see and hear Moses (for a long or short time) they would have had no option but to abide by what they had received from him ; to live just as though they could still see and hear him ; to be of themselves what they ought to be according to his witness and ministry, this people of their God ; to think and act of themselves in the freedom of the obedience and trust in which they had been placed by his witness and ministry ; in fact, to be those who were called by him—to a thankful actualisation of their election, i.e., to faith—just as though he were still in their midst.

But because—for a while—he was no longer in their midst, it was revealed that they were not, in fact, those who were called to faith, that they had received but not accepted his witness and ministry. They had understood him and allowed him to take control. They had respected him. They had even believed in him as the strong and clever and pious man who had, as they could see, brought them out of Egypt and led them thus far. On his authority they had even said a fairly convincing Yes to the God whom he had proclaimed to them as their God. They had rejoiced in His works and given their approval to His will and commandments. But on Moses' authority. They themselves, their hearts, were quite obviously not in it. They had made reservations in respect of the God proclaimed by Moses, and therefore in respect of Moses as His witness and servant. This was revealed when they could no longer see and hear Moses. All that remained now was they themselves, with the reservation which they had had for a long time in respect of Moses and His God ; they themselves as a race of men, including Aaron the priest and his priestly wisdom and craft, listening and looking in the void with empty ears and empty eyes ; they themselves with their historical existence, their past and their future, their needs and necessities and hopes, the greatness and the problematical nature of their being. Nothing more.

Is it not obvious that in these empty hearts, in the place which was left empty and was now shown to be empty, there had to rise up this snorting and stamping and tail-threshing bull, the picture of their own vital and creative power as a people when left to themselves and controlling their own life ? Those who at very best had listened to and trusted Moses and not God, who had subjected themselves to the authority of Moses and not to that of God, had of necessity, if their further life was to be possible at all now that Moses was no longer accessible, to fall back on something of their own which they had always reserved to themselves, on the confidence which they had obviously never given up but stored away under the impress of the authority of Moses : " God helps those who help themselves." What of it if this confidence had only the name Yahweh in common with the God whom Moses proclaimed, and His grace and covenant and will and commandment ? Why should they not know the true Yahweh in this confidence, in the idea, the symbol, the image of the bull created out of their own hearts ? Now that Moses had gone, why should they not trust in this Yahweh and therefore in themselves and their divinity ? Why should they not believe in themselves and therefore in the true God ? Why should they not satisfy themselves and therefore the true divine will ? Why not ? " Up, make us gods, which shall go before us ; for as for this Moses, the man that brought us up out of the land of Egypt, we wot not what is become of him." Aaron is there, and as a priest he is on their side, he is one of them, he is pledged *ex officio* to listen to their request. No opposition is to be feared from him. On the contrary, his priestly wisdom will find the correct theological interpretation of their request, the right symbol for the true Yahweh who has only just been discovered. And his priestly craft will not hesitate to show them how this can be achieved technically and cultically.

We must not misunderstand this appeal to Aaron. There is in it nothing of resignation. The zero hour of abandonment and doubt and uncertainty—if there ever was one—has already passed when the appeal is made. Nor is it in any sense the expression of a demand to hear further what the Word of God is. They know what they want. And what they want is not what they could have expected of Moses. The *horror vacui* has already had its effect. The void into which they may have looked for a moment has already been filled. The appeal is full of reforming zeal. The true Yahweh who has been discovered is already at work. He needs only revelation and a cultus. Therefore the sad reflection on the fate of Moses is equivocal. There is in it an admixture of genuine human regret at his probable and tragic death and at the, in its way, great period which Israel had experienced under his leadership—which involved, of course, his peculiar proclamation of Yahweh. He would certainly not have been denied a state burial. But there is obviously no desire to have him back. He and his authority are no longer indispensable. The bull-god and therefore Israel's own knowledge and power will now continue and improve what he has done. Above all, his proclamation of Yahweh, his exposition of the grace and holiness and covenant and commandments of God, the whole mystery about His person are no longer indispensable, indeed they have become antiquated and redundant and even destructive. It was now necessary that the whole mystery about His person should be explained clearly and simply as the mystery of the Israelite himself, that the consciousness of God should become a healthy self-consciousness, that the expectation of help from God should be transformed into a resolution boldly to help oneself, that the holiness of God should be understood as the dignity of Israel's humanity, the grace of God as the joy of thinking and acting in its own fulness of power, the covenant of God as its own understanding of its historical destiny, of its national nature and mission and the future development of it, the commandment of God as the cheerful will to live out its singular life. The time had come to move over from mediacy, and the regime of mediation in the form of a charismatic praying alone and hearing and authoritatively proclaiming only the Word of God, to the immediacy of the people as such, and man as such, to God, the regime of their own mediation and therefore of their own divinity. The time had come to take seriously the immanence of God, a concession being made to His undeniable transcendence by the setting up of an image which would inspire confidence from the very first because it was its own creation, the reflection of Israel and the Israelite. Moses with his Yahweh who stood so high above Israel and stooped down to it did not need to return, and would be better not to return. Moses was *passé*. The age of the bull, a new epoch in the religious and political history of Israel, had now dawned, and for this epoch Moses had no message. The true Yahweh, understood by and enlightening all, palpably glorious and serviceable, had both the word and the power to bring everything to a successful issue, and would increasingly do so. It was only right and proper to celebrate a feast to Him, to bring burnt offerings and peace offerings, to keep communion, to eat and drink before Him with joy, to make the greatest possible noise and to seek the greatest possible enjoyment. And no thought that perhaps the replaced Moses . . . and perhaps with him the replaced Yahweh . . . ? When things have gone so far men do not think of this perhaps, or of the absurdity of that which they think is their true god—the calf which is themselves—or of the danger into which they plunge themselves with this game.

Such was the breach of the covenant in Ex. 32—man as the *creator Dei*, self-controlling and self-sufficient and self-deifying man, the man of sin in this first form of his pride, and as exposed by the revelation of the God whose name is unchangeable : " I will be gracious to whom I will be gracious, and I will have mercy on whom I will have mercy."

2. We now return to the being and activity of Jesus Christ, and recall our main christological definition that the Lord became a servant. His rule consists in the fact that He became a subject. His power works itself out in His own obligation and binding—the obligation of the Son to the Father, and His binding to us men. He becomes the servant of all servants. This is the humility of the act of God which took place for us in Jesus Christ. But the man for whom God is God in this way in Jesus Christ is the very opposite—the servant who wants to be lord.

The futility of this undertaking is again plain to see. The true Lord not only wills to be a servant but becomes a servant : without reserve. Neither in heaven nor on earth is there any more real self-subjection, self-obligation and self-binding than that accomplished in Jesus Christ. Wherever else we see anything of this kind there is always a certain reservation and counter-movement which compromises its reality and totality. But the Lord Jesus Christ does what He does in royal omnipotence. What He wills takes place ; He becomes a servant. The man for whom He does this only wants to be lord. The power which he brings to the necessary thoughts and acts and attitudes is sneaked and stolen and therefore it is not genuine. In accordance with his creaturely nature, and his being in covenant with God, he might well have the power, when he is at peace with God as his Lord, to be strong as the friend of God, and to rule with Him even as a servant. But when he alienates himself from God in self-reliance, he forfeits this power. He thinks and acts only as a shadow of himself, as though he had it. Like the sergeant-major in Schiller's *Wallenstein*, he can only act as though he were a field-marshal.

He can only play the lord. There can never be any question of his becoming and being it in his movement away from God. In this way he can never attain the very thing that he wants and seeks. We have only to think of the monstrous caricatures produced by world history : Nero, Caligula, Napoleon, Nietzsche, Mussolini and Hitler. All that they do is to show us how impossible and grotesque is the human enterprise. Even the hollowness of the claims of the Papacy simply reveals at bottom the hollowness of the man, every man, who as such wills that which is against Christ, which is therefore impossible to him, which is beyond his capacity.

But he wants it all the same. He plays the role of a being which is superior to the world and his fellows, to himself and his destiny, even to his relationship with God, so that he can survey and penetrate and master and control all these things ; the role of the central monad before which all the others are destined to do obeisance (like the sheaves in Joseph's dream in Gen. 37^7). Even if he only plays this role, everything is quite different from what he sees it, since it is not really forced to circle round him and do obeisance. He does not really accomplish what from this height he thinks he can accomplish. The more he wants to compel and control, the more he is himself compelled and controlled. That is how it is with him in this role. The claim and arrogance and illusion in which he is cradled in this role, and which he spreads out to others, are a fact. So, too, is the character which he assumes more and more as he plays it. So, too, are the movements which he makes in it and the consequences which it involves for himself and for those around him. It is all empty, of course. In the last resort it is all ineffective. But it is still the real man in his perversion. This is how he dares to present himself before God. This is how he stands before God, although God knows him quite differently. This is how he will and must have it with himself, the lord who ought strictly to be the active servant under orders, who in his folly will not be this, but gives himself out and tries to be the master. He cannot do it. He cannot achieve anything but reveal his character as a servant or maid, and in so doing—that which he despises now becomes his shame—show that he is not a true servant or a true maid, and therefore and for that reason not a true lord or lady. Such is man, an inexplicable but actual absurdity. And he is revealed to be this man, and accused as such, by what God is and does for him. There is no question of any necessity. There is no question of any rational ground for it. He simply is this, on grounds or lack of grounds which are quite irrational. Even from this point of view we can only describe him.

Here, too, we have to note that he is it in concealment. For who is willing or able to confess to this purpose, that he wants to rule, or to what he is in this purpose ? In this respect, too, the pride and sin of human will and achievement are not plain to see. What is seen is a supremely legitimate use of the power given to man, of his knowledge and judgment and will and capacity, and therefore of the putting into effect of his human existence as such in which he encounters himself and the world around him with a certain aloofness and even superiority as master. It is true that this can also be the action of humility, the service of the true servant without the pretension or the self-lordship of the rebel, a well considered obedience to the Lord of men, the execution of his true commission, fulfilled in an enlightened fear of God and not in a denial of God. Evil always takes good care not to show itself as such. It always cloaks itself, hiding under the garment not only of innocence but of an exalted virtue. The Word of God is always needed to bring evil to the light. The emancipation of man, his exaltation from servant to lord, seems to be nothing other than his inevitable and ordained coming of age, and to that extent again the legitimate fulfilment of his true human development.

In this respect the speech of the serpent in Gen. 3 smacks throughout of true human development. It circles around the theme of the necessity open to and indeed laid upon man to judge and then to act in respect of that which is worthy of him and proper to him. First of all there is the general question which obviously creates the atmosphere with its tone of sincere sympathy (and it is worth noting that as opening the way to autonomous action it is addressed to the wife) : whether God has really said that they are not to eat of any of the trees of the garden ? (v. 1) whether poor man has actually to be content to live in paradise and to be deprived of its fruits ? No, is the correct and orthodox answer of the one addressed. God has not said that. It is not so bad as that. " We may eat of the fruit of the trees of the garden : But of the fruit of the tree which is in the midst of the garden, God hath said, Ye shall not eat of it, neither shall ye touch it, lest ye die " (v. 2 f.). A right understanding of the text shows that the very beginning of the conversation was the decisive point. The serpentine possibility of the thought had emerged that God had perhaps commanded something which was not worthy of man, or not proper, or, at any rate, less proper to him, with the result that man would have to take matters into his own hand in relation to God. He knows and confesses that the one is not true and the other not necessary. But the limit which God has set him (in respect of the fruit of one of the trees in the garden) has been brought to consciousness and under the scrutiny of the question whether God is not perhaps in some way a hard and unkind Lord in view of this limit, whether His grace is quite enough, whether this prohibition, even if he has nothing else to complain of, does not mean that man is being deprived of something very precious, the most precious thing of all ? The reflection whether it is not perhaps advisable to test his subordination to the will of God has already been introduced in spite of, and, we might say, in, with and under the orthodox answer. It would have been better not to give the serpent an orthodox answer. For in conversation with the serpent no orthodox answer is so sure that it cannot be demolished by the serpent. Was not this beast of chaos not only more subtle than any beast of the field that the Lord God had made (v. 1), but far cleverer than the man created by God—dangerously so from the moment that man allowed himself to converse with and answer it ? There are some men that we ought not even to greet (2 Jn. 10 f.), for " he that biddeth him God speed is partaker of his evil deeds." The serpent in paradise is the essence of all those that we ought not to greet. But the greeting took place, and it was followed at once by the demolition of man's orthodox answer. In effect the good lady comes to know that behind this limit which is set to man there lies the most precious thing of all, which man cannot do without but must have whatever else he may lack : " Ye shall not surely die : For God doth know that in the day ye eat thereof, then your eyes shall be opened, and ye shall be as gods " (v. 4). Therefore the grace of God does suffice up to a point, but it is not enough. God is in some sense a hard and unkind Lord. He will grant man all kinds of things, but not the best of all. He has led him by the nose in relation to this supreme good. He has indeed directed him falsely, pronouncing a threat where a supreme promise awaited him. In effect, this state of affairs cannot go on. In effect—the serpent does not need to say it but man can and will deduce it for himself—it is time for man to be enlightened and to come of age. It is time for him to appeal from a *Deus male informatus* to a *Deus melius informandus*, to do a little demythologising, to pass from the decision of obedience to God to that of his own choice, from service in the garden to rule. And what if his own perception supports and confirms the exegesis of the serpent ? what if the woman sees that the supposed tree of death is, in fact, " pleasant to the eyes and a tree to be desired " ? Then it follows at once : " She took of the fruit thereof, and did eat, and gave also unto her husband with her ; and he did eat " (v. 6). Man makes himself lord, or acts as such. And what is the evil ? Is it not a legitimate development, a necessary movement from dependence to independence, from heteronomy to autonomy, a required progress from childhood to maturity ? Is it not man's true development : " the education of the human race " ? Why should not the woman speak with the serpent and learn how unsatisfying is the orthodox answer and be convinced of the correctness of the serpent's teaching and with the man act accordingly ? Why not ? Of course, when we ask this, we have to ignore the fact that the serpent is the beast of chaos. But we can do this. Or we can interpret chaos in such a way that it is only in encounter and conversation and agreement and covenant with it that we attain our true manhood.

Again, the concealment is powerful. Evil would not be evil if in this respect, too, it did not know how to conduct its affairs in the form of light.

But again it is the case that, wanting to be lord instead of servant, man (1) finds himself in the severest error concerning himself, and in the process of a most serious self-alienation and self-destruction. In actual fact, he is below where God is above, the second where God is the first, dependent where God is sovereign, obliged to note the call of God and to obey His command, and in such a way that in the sphere and under the determination of this order—as servant where God is Lord—there comes to him the free and unreserved and perfect grace of God, in such a way therefore that he can be free in this order, realising his true being in true glory. *Adhaerere Deo* is the good thing beyond and beside which there is no better, and no greater glory and dignity. As the servant of God he can be essentially and perfectly man according to the purpose of his creaturely nature, participating in the lordship of God as he fulfils his determination as a partner in covenant with God. What a fool he is, fighting against himself, when he refuses and tries to escape from this order ! What he regards as infinitely more is infinitely less. Where he thinks to cover himself with glory he covers himself with shame. Where he thinks to exalt himself he falls. For his being and capacity and activity and development and freedom are limited, but also preserved and guaranteed, by this order. If he despises and denies it, it can be only to his destruction. In the very act of revolt the servant becomes a slave. In his pride he makes himself despicable. In the Lord whom he has cast off he does in fact acquire—for he no longer sees Him as He is—an incomprehensible and a hard Lord.

And (2) all the explaining of his enterprise does not avail against the sober truth that it is rebellion. But rebellion is disorder and disorder chaos. Man may call the thing his true development. He may think the foolish thought that it will lead to this. But it still disrupts and deforms the relationship which—apart from the relationship of Father, Son and Holy Spirit—we have to describe as the basic relationship of all created being: the relationship of Creator and creature, and of God and man in particular. It reverses the relationship in an undignified farce (and therefore impotently), but in a way which is very real within the framework of this farce. In the sphere of created being which rests upon it it causes the greatest conceivable confusion. It creates a world of phantasy in which the below appears to be above and the great first an insignificant second, in which every standard is false, in which every thought and word becomes self-contradiction and every act and attitude perverted. And at once the created world in which this takes place, and within it the relationship of man and man in particular, is forced to suffer with it. It cannot be otherwise. Wanting to act the lord in relation to God, man will desire and grasp at lordship over other men, and on the same presupposition other men will meet him with the same desiring and grasping. The struggle for power—the power of the sexes (did not this begin with the prominence of the woman in Gen. $3^{2f.}$?), the power of individuals, nations, classes and ranks—is bound to follow, and it will be accompanied by the execution of a mutual judgment which is a judgment without grace, for where is the grace to come from? And however necessary and fine and logical the enterprise may appear, this involves the irruption of chaos into the sphere of creation, the establishment of the counter-regime of that which is not, of that which God has denied and rejected, radical evil, that which is opposed to God and His work. It means the arrogant beginning of a false being which, if it continues and gains the upper hand, will mean the end of all true being. The concealment in which this takes place may be very effective but it is bound to fall. Indeed, since God has forbidden it by the act of His Word, it has already fallen. In this enterprise of man we have to do with something which is incorrigibly evil, with a being which can only be denied as such.

Again (3) behind what man sets out to do there is destructive error in which he is engulfed in relation to God. It is not true that God is a Lord whom there is any sense in repudiating or trying to replace. It is not true that it can even remotely be a burden to man to be the servant of God. From the very first God is to him genuinely and totally a gracious Lord, who not only does not withhold from him that which is good, but gives and imparts it superabundantly, who if He denies him anything does so to keep him from self-destruction. He does not demand any other obedience than that of a free and glad, because a natural, gratitude. Moreover, He wills that as servant he should participate in His own lordship. Moreover, He is not only the Lord, but in the majesty and fulness of His work and revelation He Himself becomes a creature, and therefore man, and therefore—in typical form—a servant, taking His place at our side and submitting to what He demands of us. Does this not show us how tolerable and indeed good it is ? how foolish it is for man to storm past God and into the void in an envious attempt to usurp His lordship ! If he only knew God—the way in which God is the one true " Grand-seigneur "—how could he ever play with Him the insolent democrat, trying to push himself, the little man, into His place, as though the exercise of his lordship could ever be anything but the most ridiculous failure, the most frightful blundering of a self-seeker, a usurper, a parvenu, a vain and evil and snobbish *nouveau riche* ? Again this third point is naturally the one which decides, which involves all the rest—the complete misunderstanding of God which is at the bottom of the human enterprise in this form too. Here again, then—from this second standpoint—we have the man whom God reconciled and converted to Himself in Jesus Christ—the self-seeker, the usurper, the parvenu. It is natural to think that the modern western world, especially of the 19th century, has given us many excellent examples of this man. But do we not find him, too, in all the men of all ages and places ? Do we not find him especially in ourselves, once we disperse the smoke-screen of respectability with which we all surround ourselves in this matter—when we see ourselves as we are. Pride is a very feeble word to describe this. The correct word is perhaps megalomania. But at any rate it is to this man that God has condescended. He has answered his enterprise with the corresponding counter-measure. He humbled Himself and became obedient.

We will now try to understand this second form of the matter in the light of an example from the sphere of the Old Testament witness. We might think of the story of Gideon's son Abimelech (Jud. 9), or of David's son Absalom (2 Sam. 15 f.), or of Adonijah (1 K. 1) with his arrogant proclamation, " I will be king " (v. 5). But the classical Old Testament illustration of all that we have tried to say is the story of Saul, the first king of Israel, with the questions which sur-rounded him at the outset, in the greatness to which he raised himself, in his failure and fall and final catastrophe. All that we can do here is to recall the main outlines of the story as it is told in 1 Sam. 8–31, in a sequence of various traditions, and in intimate connexion with the story of the rise of David. M. Noth (*Gesch. Israels*, 1950, p. 142) has described the kingship of Saul as no more than an episode with a final result (p. 155) which is " as tragic as it possibly could be." But the kingship of Saul has a peculiar significance at the head of all the stories of the kings first of united and then of divided Israel. The story as a whole also turns out to be an episode with a tragic end. At bottom, the only clear exception is the story of David, which is therefore an antithesis to that of Saul. Even the glory of Solomon is described in such glowing colours only because he is the promised son and successor of David. And because it was only for a time and not unequivocal, the fulfilment itself quickly became a promise and could pass into the tradition only with certain eschatological emphases. Later in David's dynasty there was, of course, a series of more or less " good " kings, but this, and the fact that there is not a single one in the northern kingdom, only serves to light up the shadow which was falling deeper and deeper over the whole institution, until it finally disappeared as it had come. The shadow had already given plain warning of its approach when the institution was set up with the kingship of Saul.

According to the tradition the beginning of the whole episode and of Saul's kingship in particular was permitted and authorised by a concession made to the no less fatal than noisy demand of the people by the seer and prophet Samuel, the last in the line of Judges. It was, therefore, allowed by an act of condescension on the part of God Himself. According to the account in 1 Sam. 8⁵ the elders of Israel assemble in Ramah and say to Samuel : " Make us a king to judge us like all the nations." Samuel is displeased. He prays to the Lord. The Lord is displeased also. That is why Samuel is. But He tells Samuel to grant their request : " For they have not rejected thee, but they have rejected me, that I should not reign over them " (v. 7). An obstacle is placed in the way. Samuel is told to warn them of the dangerous rights of a king. But it is all in vain. The elders answer : " Nay, but we will have a king over us " (v. 19 f.). Yahweh then decides : " Hearken unto their voice, and make them a king " (v. 22). Samuel then sends them home to await further developments. The matter is taken not merely out of their hands but his. It rests with God who has come to this decision.

From 1 Sam. 8 we see clearly that the existence and function of a human king in Israel are alien and indeed contrary to the original conception of the covenant (of Yahweh with the tribes and of the tribes among themselves). " The essence of the covenant consists in the fact that Yahweh rules Israel in person and that the Israelites are subject wholly to Him and to Him alone " (W. Vischer, *op. cit.*, II, 1942, p. 115). The Judges of an earlier period, of whom Samuel was the last, were called to their work directly by God and as the need arose. It was their duty to maintain the covenant both inwardly and outwardly. They were not monarchs, but freely appointed liberators in individual emergencies. Gideon was offered a hereditary rule after the battle with the Mideonites, but he gave the characteristic answer : " I will not rule over you, neither shall my son rule over you : the Lord shall rule over you " (Jud. 8²³). That and the similar attitude of Samuel are not a later construction. The idea of a king was not traditional in Israel and was contrary to its basic thinking (M. Noth, p. 146). Note that in the saying of Gideon and in the Book of Judges generally Yahweh himself is not actually called a " king." The word *melek* had for a long time the suggestion of something which did not belong, something profane in respect of Yahweh's relation with Israel and the mutual inter-relationship of Israel. In Ps. 2⁴ it is said of the kings and princes of the earth and their counsellors : " He that sitteth in the heavens shall laugh : the Lord shall have them in derision." Yahweh leads and rules and commands and controls with unlimited authority and power, not as *melek*, but as the great and primary liberator, *moshi'a*. This is also the character of the secondary authority and power of the charismatic heroes and leaders called and sent by Him from time to time. This lordship of the liberating God and of the liberating human leaders appointed by Him is something which, according to 1 Sam. 8, the Israelites have come to regret—it did not seem to be any adequate safeguard for their existence at the zenith of Philistine domination. They expect security by setting up the kind of authority and power that they saw exercised among other peoples, and especially their eastern neighbours, by the representative of an institutional and hereditary monarchy, the *melek*, who was furnished with definite rights and claims and fulfilled certain circumscribed expectations. It is clear that, represented and secured by the existence of such a figure, they want to become a political factor in their political environment. In all their littleness they want to be qualitatively great in the same way as others. They want it even if it means the jeopardising of their inner freedom which is the inevitable consequence of setting up such a figure, even if the desire necessarily involves a lack of confidence in their divine liberator, and in Samuel, the last of the human liberators appointed by Him. Note the speech in excuse : " Behold, thou art old, and thy sons walk not in thy ways " (v. 5)—we have here a misunderstanding of the strictly personal meaning of Samuel's mission. The word of Yahweh to Samuel brings the novelty they desire into line with Israel's worst fault : " According to all the works which they have done since the day that I brought them up out of Egypt, even unto this day, wherewith they have forsaken me, and served other gods, so do they also unto thee " (v. 8). The matter is abnormal from the very outset. The *melek*-ship now being set up in Israel is " a doubtful quantity " (M. Noth, p. 149), a *contradictio in adiecto*. Even when Saul has entered into his kingship and successfully proved himself the representative of it, it is expressly testified to the people by Samuel, and confirmed by a miracle : " Ye have done great wickedness in the sight of the Lord, in asking you a king " (1 Sam. 12[17]).

And now we come to the remarkable fact that in solidarity with the last of the Judges and liberators granted to Israel God satisfies the demand of the people. And He orders this His human representative in solidarity with Him to satisfy the demand. Indeed, Yahweh Himself undertakes the election and appointment of a king for Israel, and Samuel, for his part, can only be the instrument of this election and appointment which obviously contradict everything that has gone before and the Law which Israel has followed. What is the meaning of this astonishing development ? It is quite certain that God has not begun to doubt His purpose or to alter the commission of the prophet whom He has empowered or to dislocate the inner structure of the covenant. The word of Samuel at the dark crisis in the story of Saul is one which might equally well apply to the beginning and indeed to the whole context in which the story is set : " And also the strength of Israel will not lie, nor repent : for he is not a man, that he should repent " (1 Sam. 15[29f.], cf. Num. 23[19]). According to 1 Sam. 8[18] even God's connivance and condescension to the people in this matter are simply an act of judgment : " And ye shall cry out in that day because of your king which ye have chosen you ; and the Lord will not hear you in that day." God gave them up (Rom. 1[24, 26, 28]) to their own hearts' desire, to their perverted judgment. He punished their sin by their sin, simply letting it take its course. But that is not all, and it is not the decisive point. The grace of God is not extinguished or withdrawn in this His apparent concession. He knows very well what He is willing and doing when He accedes to the perverted judgment of Israel its place and possibility. Even in accepting Israel's plan He can master it. Undoubtedly the perversion of Israel consists in the fact that it wants to see at its head, instead of an obedient and therefore liberated and liberating servant, like Samuel, a sovereign lord who in his irresponsibility is neither liberated nor liberating. The presupposition of all that follows is that God gives it such a lord with the purpose and intention that, contrary to all that he is supposed to be by human standards, he will still be His own obedient and therefore liberated and liberating servant—a *melek* like that of other peoples, but even in the function of the *melek*, like the Judges, the one who is elected and called and empowered by God, the executor of His will, the liberator of Israel under His authority and in the ministry and power of His might. Israel was not merely to be punished but genuinely helped by that in which it sinned. In spite of all the folly and wickedness, the lack of confidence and pride, the self-confidence, expressed in that demand (and in spite of what it meant in other nations), the kingship was to express the monarchy and the sole lordship of the grace of God. This was the purpose of the divine concession to Israel's sinful and perverted demand. It is a concession in which Yahweh not only maintains His control but exercises it in a new way. He does not give up His will and plan. He carries it through in the face of and in opposition to Israel's sin. And this will and plan dominate the event by which Israel acquires its first king in the person of Saul, and in which the kingship of Saul is exercised even to its " tragic " end. For even in the apparent concession the divine intention is always the fixed standard by which Saul is measured, and David is measured, and the successors of David from the very ʾfirst to the very last, and to their condemnation the kings of Samaria— the standard by which they are all measured and either stand or fall. They are kings by the grace of God. As lords appointed by Him they are either faithful servants (types of the humility and obedience of the king Jesus Christ) or they are nothing. Certainly they are not relatively powerful and successful kings like those of other nations, nor are they even a partial fulfilment of the expectation which the people placed on the introduction of this institution. They stand or fall with the determination which is given to them—not as any kings, but as kings of the people of God and therefore as the servants of this God. And the first of them, Saul, is ruined because he does not conform to this determination.

To see and to understand this, note the peculiar dialectic of the event of Saul's elevation. In many respects the traditions in the first Book of Samuel are not uniform, but they do agree in this, that, while the elevation corresponds to the sinful desire and demand of the people, it also stands in very marked contradiction to it. Everything that took place has a double aspect, the form of discord and harmony between a human and a divine will and activity : Israel demands and God gives. Israel itself wills to elect and call (and lots are actually cast at Mizpah, 1 Sam. 10$^{17f.}$), but God Himself has already marked out the man and decided long ago for him. Israel rejoices when it has its wish (1 Sam. 10^{24}), crying, " God save the king," but this can only be its acclamation of the choice and decision already made by God. In the person of its king it establishes and proclaims its own sovereignty, but in so doing it affirms only that the chosen ervant of God is made its lord. In the person of Saul it rejoices in the guarantee of its power and efficacy amongst the nations, but in this person—whether recognised or not—it has before it quite unpolitically, or as the revelation of the only true politics, the power and efficacy of the lordship of its God and His grace.

Note (1 Sam. 9$^{1f.}$) that contrary to all political rules God chooses a man, not from one of the great tribes, but from Benjamin the smallest of all the tribes of Israel—the tribe, indeed, which, according to the final chapters of the Book of Judges, had become the enemy of the whole/confederation, being attacked and almost completely exterminated by it (Jud. 19–21). There is an echo of this strange choice in Ps. 68^{27} : " There is little Benjamin," and only then " the princes of Judah with their company, the princes of Zebulon and the princes of Naphthali." But they are all in the triumphant march of the God of Israel and it is there that this politically inconceivable order is valid. And not only that, but according to the saying put in the mouth of Saul himself (9^{21}) his family " is the least of all the families of the tribe of Benjamin." Gideon in Jud. 6^{15} had said the same to the angel of the Lord : " My family is poor in Manasseh.', Again, it is not at all that Samuel sought out the king which, according to the commandment of God, he was to " give " to the people, finding the one who was the best according to his own judgment. Saul is led to him apparently by accident, and it is made known by a special revelation of God that he is the right man. In his own part in the business Samuel, too, has to bow before a given fact. Saul himself had never even dreamed of the dignity and function allotted to him, let alone sought after it. He made his journey with the supremely banal purpose of seeking and returning his father's lost asses. And it is to try to find news concerning the whereabouts of these animals—not following his own idea but that of his servant—that coming into the land of Zuph he turns to the man of God, Samuel, who sees further than most people. And at first he does not note or understand what is meant by the solemn greeting and reception which he is accorded. And again he is not asked for his opinion, nor does anyone else even know about it, when the following morning (1 Sam. 10¹ᶠ·) Samuel anoints him with oil—an act of state which, strangely enough, is witnessed by only four eyes. Note, too, the formula used by Samuel : " Hath not the Lord anointed thee prince over his people Israel ? " He is already the anointed of the Lord : what Samuel does is only a subsequent confirmation of the fact. Anointed to what ? The term *melek* is obviously carefully avoided in the text. The people will hail him as " king " according to their demand. But God has anointed and called and appointed him *nagid*, the one whom He has ordained and therefore manifested to deliver His people from the hands of their enemies round about. This is what God intends where Israel intends a *melek*. And it is highly characteristic that of the three signs promised to Saul to confirm His anointing the text emphasises the third as clearly the most decisive : he will be met by a group of " prophets " making music and in a state of ecstasy. " And the Spirit of the Lord will come upon thee, and thou shalt prophesy with them, and shalt be turned into another man " (v. 6). And strangely enough—obviously there can be no question of collusion on the part of the prophets—the fulfilment comes in the reverse order : " And it was so, that when he had turned his back to go from Samuel, God gave him another heart : and all those signs came to pass that day " (v. 9)—including his encounter with the prophets and his transposition into a state of ecstasy, in view of which it was asked : " What is this that is come unto the son of Kish ? Is Saul also among the prophets ? " (v. 11). What the text wishes to convey by this episode is plain to see. Saul is more than a prophet and different, but he still belongs to the prophets ; his commission and office have to be seen and understood in this sequence. Finally, there is the gathering of the people of God at Mizpeh. Once again there is laid expressly before it the discontinuity of its will with the will of God : " And ye have rejected this day your God, who himself saved you out of all your adversities and your tribulations, and ye have said unto him, Nay, but set a king over us " (v. 19). But the continuity of the will of God is not broken by their opposition to it : the very ones who oppose it will make it plain by casting their lot. It falls on Saul. And now we come to the last of the many peculiarities of the process of his elevation : " And when they sought him, he could not be found." Yahweh Himself has to tell them that he is present and where he is to be found. Only then can they run and fetch him, the one who " when he stood among the people, was higher than any of the people from his shoulders and upward " (v. 21 f.). The acclamation and proclamation of his sovereignty follow. There is, of course, no question of any coronation or enthronement or similar ceremony. Samuel continues to advise as though nothing had happened and no king was present. He " sent all the people away, every man to his house. And Saul also went home to Gibeah ; and there went with him a band of men, whose hearts God had touched " (v. 25 f.), a minority which (not of themselves but by divine enlightenment) had seen and understood the meaning of all that had been done. It is hard to say what we are to make of the last verse (v. 27) : " But the children of Belial said, How shall this man save us ? And they despised him, and brought him no presents." We are perhaps to think of a minority which had noted the process—the unpolitical nature of it—and because of its problematical character opposed the king who had appeared in this way. The great majority obviously does not either affirm or deny in any particular way that which has taken place. It rejoices that it has what it wanted, and it is ready to wait to see whether and how the expectation with which its will has been executed will be fulfilled. And king Saul himself ? He is the final puzzle in the whole story of his elevation. He simply follows the advice of Samuel and returns to his home and his daily work in the fields. When he is called for the first time to take action as king, because the Ammonites are encamped against Jabesh, he is not found in any capital, but " coming after the herd out of the field " (1 Sam. 11⁵). And it is not in the framework of a kingly routine that he proves—*de facto*—who he is, the king of Israel. It is when he heard the news and " the Spirit of God came upon him " and " his anger was kindled greatly " (v. 6). It is when, with a most abrupt warning, he called out the host. It is when " the fear of the Lord fell on the people, and they came out with one consent " (v. 7). And now there takes place that which has been long awaited and is politically quite unambiguous : " And all the people went to Gilgal ; and there they made Saul king before the Lord in Gilgal ; and there they sacrificed sacrifices of peace offerings before the Lord ; and there Saul and all the men of Israel rejoiced greatly " (v. 15).

What is the meaning of all this ? The matter is quite unequivocal. The man Saul is a charismatic leader freely elected and called and appointed by God and endued by Him in strict immediacy with authority and power and commissioned for its supremely concrete exercise in exactly the same sense as Moses and Joshua and all the Judges before him. The only difference is that he bears the title " king of Israel," and enjoys and exercises the appropriate powers, and discharges the appropriate duties, and last and above all can hope to hand on his office to his son and therefore to found a royal house. Or, to see and express it the other way round, the king of Israel is in every respect a king like the kings of other nations, except that he is also a charismatic leader, owing his elevation and distinction (and the founding and maintenance of his house) directly and exclusively to Yahweh. He is, in fact, numbered among the prophets, and therefore he is impelled and enlightened and directed by the Spirit of Yahweh. In all that he resolves and does he is thrown back wholly upon the Spirit of Yahweh, and therefore he stands or falls by the fact that he does His will, that as a king and lord among men he is His servant.

The monarchy in Israel is a new form, but a new form of the old covenant, the one and unalterable covenant of God with His people and of the tribes one with another. In face of the sin of Israel the old form, a purely charismatic leadership, was no longer adequate. Note the last verse of the Book of Judges : " In those days there was no king in Israel : every man did that which was right in his own eyes " (Jud. 21²⁵). Again, it was the sin of Israel not to be satisfied with the old form. This is the shadow which lies from the very first on the new form of the covenant, the Israelitish monarchy. It did not need to be darkness. It could mean even higher and deeper grace, like the covenant, which, although it had become something stern and hard because of the sin of the first man, had not been destroyed, but had become all the higher and deeper grace in antithesis to the sin of man. In connexion with the constancy and the new glory of the grace of God in the form of the covenant which had become necessary by reason of Israel's transgression and which was desired in that transgression, we ought to note the end of the story of the retirement of Samuel which began when Saul actually assumed his kingship in the battle against the Ammonites. There we read that the people were very conscious and actually confessed that " we have added unto all our sins this evil, to ask us a king." But Samuel replies : " Fear not : ye have done all this wickedness : yet turn not aside from following the Lord, but serve the Lord with all your heart ; and turn ye not aside : for then should ye go after vain things, which cannot profit nor deliver ; for they are vain. For the Lord will not forsake his people for his great name's sake : because it hath pleased the Lord to make you his people. Moreover as for me, God forbid that I should sin against the Lord in ceasing to pray for you : but I will teach you the good and the right way : Only fear the Lord, and serve him in truth with all your heart : for consider how great things he hath done for you " (1 Sam. 12¹⁹ᶠ·). We are reminded of the intercession of Moses after the setting up and worshipping of the image of the bull in the wilderness, for here again we have the positive sign under which the altered situation and the charismatic leader, who is a king like the kings of other nations, is placed from the very first.

The final word of Samuel is, of course : " But if ye shall still do wickedly, ye shall be consumed, both ye and your king " (12^{25}). Because Yahweh has not abandoned His people, and Samuel has not ceased to pray for them, it cannot be otherwise than that the new form of the grace of God which corresponds to its sin should carry with it a new and not a lighter but a heavier and more detailed form of responsibility. The fact that He reigns in Israel—the whole non-political determination of the existence of this people—has acquired in the person of Israel's *melek* a terrifyingly visible exponent, so that paradoxically it has become in this figure a very concrete political factor. Has the people realised that by the existence of this figure it is committed more stringently than ever before to Yahweh ? Has it realised the solidarity with which it will stand or fall with the obedience or disobedience of this one man, its representative ? Above all, will the one who has to represent the figure of this one man be equal to the burden which is laid upon him by the fact that he has obviously to live and decide in a twofold function : as a king and as a charismatic, in a worldly role, and in a sacral ministry, the institutional helper and saviour of his people and himself thrown back wholly upon the free grace of God—and all this in a very definite but highly a-symmetrical relationship of the two elements ? M. Noth (p. 152) has described the relationship and therefore the situation of this *melek* as " indistinct," and as a historian he is no doubt right. But the texts seem to have regarded the relationship as quite distinct. Everything depended upon the relationship of the two elements being one of irreversible superiority and subordination. The one appointed king in Israel was to be and act as the first subject of Yahweh, the one elevated to be lord as His servant, and not otherwise. The evil against which Samuel warned, the evil which would inevitably mean the destruction of the king and of the people represented by him, obviously consisted in the reversing of the two elements, or even in the temptation to treat them as alternatives, thus balancing the one against the other. If the one elevated to be lord no longer understands that he is a servant and acts as such, if the *melek* no longer understands that he is a charismatic and acts as such, then it is all up with him, and also with his people. He cannot be the lord, the *melek*, the helper and saviour of his people that he ought to be as the bearer of his office. He no longer corresponds to the analogy of the lordship, the kingship of Yahweh, the God of the covenant. It is impossible to be an absolute lord and king in the sphere which belongs to this God. And it is here that Saul stumbles, and in him and with him the whole of Israel.

Of course the story of the sin of Saul is not anything like so drastic as that of the fall at Sinai. What we have called the " concealment " of human pride is now far more effective, and because of the union of the two elements in the one person of Saul the situation is much more difficult to estimate. Saul is not a worthless man, let alone a scoundrel like Abimelech in the Book of Judges. In his own way he is a figure of light. At any rate he is a genuine charismatic. That is why his transgression is so inconceivable. It is—*ceteris imparibus*—as if the prophet Moses also exercised the function of Aaron the priest and offended in that function, first talking with God and then listening to the people and making the image of the bull. That God is with Saul is seen in his successful campaigns against the Ammonites and the Amalekites and at first against the Philistines. And he for his part is ready—only too ready—to honour God by sacrifices (11^{15}, 13^9, 15^{21}). Even to the point of an outrage on his own son, he is prepared to keep vows of abstinence which he has proclaimed and sworn ($14^{24, \, 38f.}$). He cuts off them that have familiar spirits and wizards out of the land (28^9). Even at the fatal turning point in his career, he is just as ready as David honestly to confess his sin and to ask humbly enough for forgiveness ($15^{24f.}$). And one of the accounts of his fall closes with the striking words : " And Saul worshipped the Lord " (15^{31}). It is also true to his character as a charismatic that he knows the appointed mission of David (23^{17}), and even declares it (26^{25}). When God tells Samuel of the rejection of Saul he is very sorry : " He cried unto the Lord all night " (15^{11}), and we read in 15^{35} that " he mourned for Saul all the days of his life." In the same way David regarded Saul as sacrosanct during his life and even in his death. He was always the Lord's anointed and justice was done to his supposed killer (2 Sam. 1^{2-16}). He is lamented with Jonathan in the lamentation of 2 Sam. $1^{19f.}$: " Ye daughters of Israel, weep over Saul, who clothed you in scarlet, with other delights, who put on ornaments of gold upon your apparel " (v. 24). In his greatness and also in the fall which is the consequence of his transgression, yes, even in the rejection which comes upon him, he is the one who is elected and called and consecrated and sanctified by Yahweh, as is also true of Israel as a whole according to the witness of the Old Testament.

The mistake of Saul by which he destroys his kingship is outwardly a very trivial one in both the traditions which make up the present narrative. It is a very " venial " sin, easily explained and excused by the circumstances, and one that even arouses our sympathy, so that we are not a little inclined to side with Saul against his accuser, the ageing Samuel, and against the Yahweh of Samuel. According to one tradition ($13^{7f.}$) it was at the beginning of the war with the Philistines. Samuel delayed in coming to the host. The enemy was already advancing. For fear lest the people should leave him and disperse, Saul himself offered the burnt offerings. But as soon as this was done Samuel appeared and called the act of Saul that of a fool who had transgressed the commandment of God and whose kingship would not stand—God knew already to whom he would give it. What had happened ? It had merely happened that instead of waiting courageously for God to direct and lead, and thus remaining strong in face of the people, as Moses was, Saul had taken it upon himself to lead the people in their relationship with God, trying himself to create the decisive presupposition of adherence, and therefore of the success of the campaign, by the offering of this sacrifice. It had merely happened that on the religious side he did not want to act altogether as a servant but to some small extent as lord, setting the *melek* Saul above Saul the Lord's anointed. It had merely happened that instead of overcoming in his own person the wrong that Israel had done with its demand for an autocratic king, he granted it a new lease of life, setting before the people the false image upon which the people had fed in that perverted demand. It was not intended that Saul should act as king in this way. This attempt to grasp a cæsaro-papistical sovereignty was not permitted. Saul knew that it was not permitted, but he was guilty of it all the same. And for this reason he made himself impossible as Israel's king and in his own person he made Israel itself impossible. According to the other tradition ($15^{8f.}$) his offence consisted in his incomplete fulfilment of the total destruction of the Amalekites which Yahweh had commanded by the mouth of Samuel. He spared the life of king Agag, and he and his people spared the more valuable part of the cattle which they had taken from this hereditary enemy. Again Samuel confronted him : " For rebellion is as the sin of witchcraft, and stubbornness is as iniquity and idolatry. Because thou hast rejected the word of the Lord, he hath also rejected thee from being king " (v. 23). The explanation is not accepted that the best of the living booty has been spared to sacrifice to the Lord in Gilgal. The admission is not accepted that Saul feared the people and wished to please them. The request for forgiveness is not accepted. The demand that Samuel should yet go with him is not accepted, not even when " he laid hold upon the skirt of his mantle, and it rent." On the contrary, this is a sign : " The Lord hath rent the kingdom of Israel from thee this day, and hath given it to a neighbour of thine, that is better than thou" (v. 28). What had happened ? It had merely happened that Saul had allowed himself to make one small and neither unreasonable nor irreligious compromise with other kings and nations and gods, that he had thought it right to make this in effect almost insignificant agreement and accommodation, and that in so doing he gave the lord a slight precedence over the servant, the *melek* Saul over the charismatic. It had merely happened—not this time by commission but by omission—that he had been again what the people wanted and desired, what they demanded of a king in Israel. It is remarkable that the common element in both texts is Saul's fear of the people, his submission to them, and therefore his participation in their wrongdoing. The one who fears Israel cannot help Israel, cannot be its king by the grace of God. That is all that had happened. Saul had simply been afraid. He had become an autocrat out of fear. And in so doing he had passed sentence on himself and in his own person on Israel. In paradise, too, it was a matter of something which was theoretically almost without significance, but it was enough to make man impossible for paradise. For in the question : Who is lord and who is servant ? there is no more or less, only an either-or. If Saul failed in the smallest thing he failed in everything, and the Spirit of the Lord had to leave him to make way for an evil spirit. All the dark things which are then told concerning him are only the manifestation and consequence of the decision which he himself had made in his perversion and which was so terribly made concerning him : his hatred of David, so that he would have murdered him if he could; his massacre of the priests of Nob (22[6f.]) ; his descent from a puritanical strictness and flight to the witch of Endor ; his final suicide like Judas Iscariot. He was not rejected because of these sins; but in consequence of the one sin for which he was rejected he was involved in an irresistible process of disintegration and committed these sins too. And because he was guilty of this one sin as Israel's representative, he brought down not only his own sons but the people he had formerly saved to defeat and new subjection to the triumphant power of the Philistines. He was not content to be an obedient servant and therefore the true king of Israel. He wanted to be like the kings of other nations : a king as Israel meant it and not by the grace of God ; the autocrat which he showed himself in the frightfully arrogant transgression brought before us in both traditions. And the result was that all this affliction was determined and sealed. It had to come. And his career, and that of Israel, which had begun with such greatness and promise, could end only with this disaster, could have only this " tragic " result. His election could only be the prelude to the election of another and quite different king who in the first instance was to be called David.

3. We now return to the being and activity of Jesus Christ, and in the light of the work which He has done as the Son of God become man, the Lord become a servant, we maintain that He is the One who has accused us by turning and taking to Himself the accusation which is laid properly against us, against all men, against every man. He pronounced sentence on us by taking our place, by unreservedly allowing that God is in the right against Himself—Himself as the bearer of our guilt. He was the divine Judge and fulfilled the divine judgment in such a way that He caused Himself to be judged, so that we should not suffer what we deserved, so that we should be those who are judged in His person. This is the humility of the act of God which has taken place for us in Jesus Christ. But the man whom God meets in this way in Jesus Christ, the man to whom God becomes a brother in order to do this for him, is the very opposite of all this, the man who sets himself in the wrong by wanting to be his own judge instead of allowing that God is in the right against him.

Here, too, we must first say that this is a futile and impotent and useless undertaking which is foredoomed to failure. The real Judge not only wills to accuse and sentence and judge, but does so. According to the merciful election of God He was and is and will be the One who gave Himself and was crucified and died for us. He freely bowed Himself under the judgment which comes upon us. He lives and will live as the One who bowed Himself under this judgment. And this means that judgment has passed on the world. A sharp distinction has been made between good and evil in all their spheres both high and low. All men in both their public and their private being and activity are set in the light of this distinction. All created time, all human history and every individual history, is seen by God in its right and wrong, and moves forward to the manifestation of the judgment fulfilled in Him. As against that, man only wants to judge. He thinks he sits on a high throne, but in reality he sits only on a child's stool, blowing his little trumpet, cracking his little whip, pointing with frightful seriousness his little finger, while all the time nothing happens that really matters. He can only play the judge. He is only a dilettante, a blunderer, in his attempt to distinguish between good and evil, right and wrong, acting as though he really had the capacity to do it. He can only pretend to himself and others that he has this capacity and that there is any real significance in his judging. There is no necessity for all this. He can unquestioningly and unreservedly allow that God is in the right and accept and acquiesce in his decisions concerning him. He can then be at peace with God, knowing his own case, doing right in freedom and avoiding wrong in the same freedom. But instead he moves against God and sets up and defends and maintains his own right. In so doing he puts himself in the wrong. His own judging and deciding lead him into a constant fog and error. Neither in his own cause nor in that of others can he be a wise and righteous judge. He wants that which is therefore impossible, and he cannot attain it.

But he does want it, and in so doing he creates facts, as he does by his desire to be God and lord instead of man and servant. The history of every man is, in fact, the history of a specific view of what is right. And the history of all men is the history of their many and constantly arising and mutually contradictory and intersecting views. To live as a man means in effect to be at some point on the long road from the passionate search for a standard by which to judge our own human affairs and those of others, to the discovery of such a standard, its affirmation in the conviction that it is right, the first attempt to apply it to ourselves and to those around, the first successes and failures of this attempt, the hardening of the certainty that this and this alone is the real standard, the more or less happy or bitter experience of the unavoidable conflicts with others and the standards that they have discovered and applied, perhaps the partial triumph of our own law, perhaps partial or total defeat in the attempt to put into it effect, perhaps a final tolerable satisfaction with what has been achieved, perhaps a more or less noble resignation or a more or less conscious scepticism, but always the question whether it has really been worth while, whether we can really and seriously be satisfied with ourselves as the judge of ourselves and others that we willed to be and have been. Again, human life in society, whether on a small scale or a large, means the emergence and conflict, the more or less tolerable harmony and conjunction, of the different judges with their different rights, the battle of the ideas formed and the principles affirmed and the standpoints adopted and the various universal or individual systems, in which at bottom no one understands the language of the others because he is too much convinced of the soundness of his own seriously to want to understand the others, in which, therefore, what will be right as thought and spoken by one will be wrong as received by the others. The battle is between what is supposed to be good and what is supposed to be evil, but in this battle all parties—how can it be otherwise?—think that they are the friends of what is good and the enemies of what is evil. Therefore, quite contrary to the purpose and intention of those who take part in it, the more seriously this battle is waged, the more certainly it will lead to pain and tears and crying, so that at the end we have to ask seriously whether the upshot of it all is not a fresh triumph, not for a supposed evil, but for one which is very real. From this final result the theory and practice of what we call tolerance seem to be the final refuge and one which we have to discover again and again—a general lassitude to which men surrender for a time, only to break out again sooner or later in new dogmatisms and acts of judgment and conflicts and mutually caused troubles and well-intentioned wrongs. When man sets out to exercise his own power to judge, is not the essential thing which he achieves something which for all its insubstantiality is palpably and painfully real—the formation both microcosmically and macrocosmically of a world which is darkened and disrupted and bedevilled by its own self-righteousness? On the little stool which he thinks is a throne, man does create facts. He dreams, but even when he dreams, he himself is not a dream, but in all his corruption he is the real man who, even though we cannot explain how and why, has in fact broken peace with God and himself and other men, who thinks he knows about good and evil, whose being defies explanation, who in his factuality can only be described.

We see the concealment of human pride in this form, too, and especially in this form. What is seen does not appear even remotely to be bad. On the contrary, what seems to be more necessary to man and more praiseworthy than that he should know how to distinguish good and evil and therefore to judge himself? Where and what would he be, we might ask, if he did not want to know this, to learn about it and to make use of his learning ? If he had not been caught up either alone or with others in one of those outbreaks of self-righteousness, would he ever have thought it necessary to set himself any excellent or at any rate good motives and aims, and not only to set them, but seriously and in good faith to affirm them ? In this undertaking and the conduct which it involves for ourselves and others there is always more of integrity and virtue and idealism than there is of the error and vice and wickedness which we also encounter in it. Can we not say finally that it is an honest acceptance of the human situation as it is and therefore an act of true humility for man not to evade this knowing and distinguishing and the corresponding separating and sentencing and judging, but rather to see and practise in it his human maturity and his human task ? In this respect, too, and especially in this respect, is it not a matter of man's true human development, without which he would only vegetate, which he cannot therefore avoid ? What is the evil in it, when it is a matter of the theoretical and practical distinguishing of evil from good, and therefore of the presupposition of all doing of good and not doing of evil ? In fact, without the Word of God evil certainly cannot be brought to the light in this its most noble form.

We are again confronted by the wisdom of the serpent on Gen. 3, whose most powerful argument we have not so far considered. There is a definite content to the promise : *Eritis sicut Deus*, and to the concealed invitation to man to become the master of his own destiny. What the serpent has in mind is the establishment of ethics. Its teaching is that, far from there being any real menace in the warning in respect of the tree in the midst of the garden, the eating of the tree will mean that men's eyes are opened, that they will be as God, and that they will therefore be given to know good and evil (v. 5). God knows good and evil, and it is His glory as God and Lord and Creator that He does so. Is it not by this knowledge that He has done His creative work, and therefore distinguished and chosen and judged between cosmos and chaos, light and darkness, order and disorder ? Has He not placed on the right hand and the left, affirming and accepting here, denying and rejecting there ? Do not heaven and earth, the very existence of man—and in another way even that of the serpent—rest on this knowledge and activity ? Is man, therefore, to be prevented from doing the same, from taking his place at the side of God, from himself recognising the first and basic thing, and then doing it, from judging, therefore ? Does this really mean a fall into immorality ? On the contrary, is it not a rise to genuine morality, to the freedom of a knowledge which distinguishes and an activity which elects, and therefore to the freedom of genuine commitment, of a final and true unity with God ? From this point of view there seems to be nothing base or evil in the analysis of the prohibition laid upon man. From this point of view everything in this analysis seems to be concerned with things which are right, the most right of all. The only trouble is that it is an analysis, i.e., a dissolving or unravelling, of the divine commandment, and that it is the serpent, the beast of chaos that God has rejected and judged and originally and definitively set at His left hand, who conducts the analysis and leaves man to draw the practical consequences of it. And who, then, is to guard against all the possible misinterpretations ? In the last resort why should not this beast be the true illuminator and liberator of man, and his wisdom the beginning of all wisdom ? Why not ?

The concealment is particularly strong at this point. It is surprising that in the Christian Church more offence is not taken at the fact—or have we simply read it away?—that in Gen. 3 the desire of man for a knowledge of good and evil is represented as an evil desire, indeed the one evil desire which is so characteristic and fatal for the whole race. The consequences for the theory and practice of Christian ethics—and not only that—would be incalculable if only we were to see this and accept it instead of regarding this very questionable knowledge—whether sought in the Bible or the rational nature of man or conscience—as the most basic of all the gifts of God. The armour behind which the real evil of the pride of man conceals itself is obviously thicker and more impenetrable at this point than at any other.

But this should not prevent us from seeing that in his very desire for this knowledge, and therefore in the fact that he wants to be judge, man (1) completely misunderstands himself and can only confuse and confound himself in this desire. Of course, a distinction and choice, a judgment, necessarily has to be made between good and evil, right and wrong, order and disorder, that which is and that which is not. The existence of all creation and especially of man stands or falls with the fact that a definite choice has to be made between these alternatives, that there can be no peace or compact between them but only decision. In this crisis, unless there is a victorious defence of good and right and order and that which is, and a victorious repelling of evil and wrong and disorder and that which is not, nothing can either become or subsist, but annihilation will break at once and directly on the whole reality which is distinct from God. The relationship of God to this reality, and therefore its existence—for it exists only on the basis of God's relationship to it, by Him and with Him—rests on His decision, is realised in His judgment, and therefore rests on His knowledge of this alternative. But on *His* knowledge, *His* judgment and *His* decision. This is all the work of God and not of man. Man can only stand as God's witness on the basis of the work which He Himself has done. He can only hold by His decision and judgment and therefore by His knowledge revealed there. He lives in virtue of the fact that God knows and does what is necessary, that God is the great crisis without which heaven and earth cannot be even for a single second. He is a free man—free in his thinking and deciding and acting—only as he is willing to accept this. He does that which is good and right, he acts in order, as one who really is, when he regards that which God has chosen for him as self-evident and indeed the only thing which is possible, when he accepts and is perfectly satisfied with this divine choice without questioning the reasons for it, without trying to manipulate or verify or correct it, or to ratify it by his own choice. He is a free man when he thinks and decides and acts at peace with God, when his decision is simply and exclusively a repetition of the divine decision. If this is not

15

enough for him, if he wants to make a primary decision where the decision of God and therefore the divine knowledge of good and evil has already preceded him, this involves a foolish over-estimation of himself, as though he is one who can stand over that alternative and exercise the function of an Atlas bearing and holding together the great building of the universe. He does not know what he is asking when he wants to stand there and affirm and accept the cosmos and deny and reject chaos. He forgets that there is only One who can do that, and that he is not that One. And this desire means that man renounces the obedience in which he cannot even toy with the idea that there may be another choice than that which God has made or decision which is not a repetition of His decision, in which he cannot even want to know the opposite of the good which God has set before him, in which he can only wish to adjust himself to what God has already chosen and decided in His knowledge of the one good and its opposite, as the only possible Judge in this matter. And this desire means finally that at once and irrevocably man loses his freedom. He has already left the protective home of peace with God. He has already renounced his confidence in the righteousness of God's judgment. He has already lost the hold in the will of God which alone can give to his being as a creature any real possibility or dignity or rest or movement. He cannot abase himself worse than by desiring this knowledge and wanting to make himself judge.

But it also means (2) that man wills that which is objectively evil. Of course he does not believe that he is doing that which is evil but that which is good, that which is commanded and necessary, and therefore the best of all. In this form of sin there can be no question of any indolence or frivolity or negligence. On the contrary, there is a pathetic earnestness, an outward air of the most serious responsibility, the most stringent sense of duty, the most militant virtue. As judge of good and evil, man wants to stand at God's side in defence of the cosmos great and small against the invasion of chaos and disorder and wrong—himself a cherub with drawn sword at the gate of paradise, or at the very least a watchman on the walls of Jerusalem. He wants to spring into the breach, safeguarding the right with his own affirmation and negation, with his own building up and tearing down, successfully maintaining the *causa Dei* and the cause of man. And it is a really shattering fact that he is mistaken in all this, that he ought not to do it at any cost, because he lets hell loose by doing it. Why and how? Because he is not the man to cut this figure, and if he thinks that he is, then he is well on the way to creating the very opposite of all that he intends to create in his godless goodness—unleashing chaos and disorder and wrong. Because he already gives place to them by this very fact. It is an unleashing of evil when the man to whom it does not belong to distinguish evil from good and good from evil, who is not asked to do so, who cannot, who is prevented and forbidden, still wants to be the man who can and pretends that he is this strong man. The truth is that when man thinks that he can hold the front against the devil in his own strength and by his own invention and intention, the devil has already gained his point. And he looks triumphantly over his shoulder from behind, for man has now become a great fighter in his cause. I am already choosing wrong when I think that I know and ought to decide what is right, and I am doing wrong when I try to accomplish that which I have chosen as right. I am already putting myself in the wrong with others, and doing them wrong, when—it makes no odds how gently or vigorously I do it—I confront them as the öne who is right, wanting to break over them as the great crisis. For when I do this I divide myself and I break the fellowship between myself and others. I can only live at unity with myself, and we can only live in fellowship with one another, when I and we subject ourselves to the right which does not dwell in us and is not manifested by us, but which is over me and us as the right of God above, and manifested to me and us only from God, the right of His Word and commandment alone, the sentence and judgment of His Spirit. To use the words of the serpent in Gen. 3, when our eyes are opened to the possibility of our own exaltation in judgment, we become truly blind to what is right and wrong. There then begins the long misery of my moral existence, in which I pardon myself to-day in respect of that for which I am incontrovertibly judged by my true Judge, only to judge myself to-morrow for that in respect of which I am incontrovertibly pardoned, in which I am most confident where everything has gone astray, and tremble and hesitate and doubt and despair where I might have a sure hold and advance with the greatest certainty. And there begins the whole misery of the moral battle of everyone against everyone else, in which, whatever position we take up or line we adopt or banner we follow, we are always deceived about our friends as well as our enemies, wronging the former just as much by our affirmation as the latter by our negation, sowing and reaping discord as the children of discord. This being the case, the dreadful pagan saying is true that war is the father of all things—the war which is always holy and righteous and necessary, war under the sign of the promising crescent or the natural sickle or the useful hammer or the sacred cross, the war of blood or the (in God's sight probably no less infamous and terrible) cold war. When man thinks that his eyes are opened, and therefore that he knows what is good and evil, when man sets himself on the seat of judgment, or even imagines that he can do so, war cannot be prevented but comes irresistibly. When the Law and its commandments and prohibitions and promises and threatenings is taken out of the hands of God and put in those of man, when it is enforced and expounded and applied by man, then it can only bring wrath (Rom. 4[15]). The Law is binding and obligatory, it directs and protects, it is to salvation and comfort, the guarantee of order and peace, only when God Himself enforces and expounds and applies it, only when He Himself is the Law of man. Otherwise, as the Law of man its being and effect is the very opposite. The evangelical warning (in Mt. 7[1]) not to judge may be intended and kept only occasionally, but it goes right home to the kingdom of demons which is opposed to the kingdom of God and devastates the earth.

And at the bottom of all this, there is, above all (3) a serious error in the view and understanding of God. We have to consider this in three dimensions. It is decisive here, too, (*a*) that in the exercise of His office as Judge God does not sit on the pseudo-divine throne of a pure sovereignty in which man in his folly thinks that he must see Him and then envies Him and thinks that he can only be a real man as he tries to be like Him. God is indeed on the throne, knowing good and evil, deciding between the two, the true friend and helper of every-thing which owes its being to His election and affirmation and creation, and which is for that reason true being, and as such the true antagonist and enemy of everything that is alien to His will and is therefore rejected and denied and without being before Him. But God is not egotistic in this revelation and defence of His own honour and glory, nor is He concerned about the satisfaction of His own needs. As God He does not need to choose to be the Creator, to determine Himself as such, to enter into this antithesis, to set Himself on this frontier, to elect and affirm that which is, to reject and negate that which is not, to bind Himself to the one, to allow Himself to be attacked and summoned to overcome the other. What compulsion is there for Him to become and to be the world's Judge ? It is not He but creation which requires that He should be and lives by the fact that He is. We are the ones whom He takes to Himself in inconceivable mercy. We cannot maintain ourselves in being and in the good. We would be lost if He did not place Himself between us and nothingness, and therefore on this frontier. He did this. He maintains His own honour by delivering us from evil. And we are such fools that we dispute this honour on the maintenance of which not His but our own exist-ence depends. But, again, (*b*) He does actually maintain it. He knows good and evil. He affirms and helps on the one hand, to deny and destroy on the other. But He does not do it as the victor that man obviously imagines Him to be when he wants to act like Him. That He stands on guard on this frontier means that He gives up Himself to be with the creature in this antithesis, allowing Himself to be called in question and injured and shaken and assaulted by that which is not, taking to heart the weakness of the creature, and more than that its transgression and guilt and need, its deflection into nothingness, taking to Himself the judgment into which we fell by this deflection. He has no pleasure in His being and activity as Judge. It is only the most bitter sorrow that He takes to Himself. And the world lives by the fact that He does give Himself to bear this sorrow for it and with it and in its place—a sorrow compared with which all our sorrows both great and small are only shadows, the great and fearful sorrow which, because He bears it for us, gives to our shadowy sorrowing its place and meaning and hope, because in it as the sorrow of the Judge right is really done and the wrong done away. And we are such fools—we know not what we do—that we go and try to usurp His office as Judge, as though it were something to be desired. Finally, (c) He, God, who approaches and understands His office in this way, is not the kind of Judge whose verdict needs to be proved or its execution assisted. It belongs to us to attest it by our obedience : that is our human freedom and dignity and glory. We do not need to worry about the righteousness of it. And its execution does not need the assistance of what we do. His knowledge is the fulness of the truth concerning good and evil. And His knowledge as such is His will, and therefore the fulness of the necessary and redemptive decision between the two. And His will is also His act, and therefore the fulness of what has to be done for the actual maintaining and exalting of the one and the actual overthrowing and destroying of the other. In face of it all, human wisdom and resolve and power to act can consist only in a following out in thought and will and deed of His wisdom and resolve and power to act, not in going our own way, but in keeping strictly to His way. But our ignorance of God means that we conceive and hold and constantly return to the stupid and ridiculous notion that we can take our place at His side—as though He were a God who needed to be completed by us and helped by our counsel and assistance. We are deceived in this, as we have seen, and in this self-deception, in the delusion that we are doing good and avoiding evil, we actually eschew the good and do evil.

From this third standpoint, this is the man whom God has reconciled and converted to Himself in Jesus Christ. He is this incompetent and therefore unjust judge. He is arrogant, and sinful in His arrogance. And God has stooped down to Him in His reconciling grace. It is with reference to his mad undertaking that God has done for him what He has done in His Son : " The chastisement of our peace was upon him."

What happens when man establishes his own right and tries to enforce it as judge may be seen from the example of Ahab's aggression against Naboth in 1 K. 21, in which we have a fitting continuation of the self-idolisation of Israel in the wilderness and the overweening arrogance of Saul.

We start with the fact that Ahab (the son of Omri, king of northern Israel from 876 to 855) is represented by the biblical tradition as not in any way a more abnormal or despicable individual than Saul was. Nor is he a figure outside but within the sphere of the covenant and Word of Yahweh. Certainly the notice of his reign in 1 K. 16[38f.] (cf. [30]) is particularly unfavourable : that " he did more to provoke the Lord God of Israel to anger than all the kings of Israel that were before him," but the same had been said in v. 25 of his father Omri.

And the tradition has not concealed the fact that in many ways Ahab seems to have been an outstanding ruler. He was the first to bring to an end the tension in the relationships between the divided kingdoms. He was on friendly terms with Jehoshaphat, king of Judah, who was confessed to be a good ruler. In the Syrian invasion described in chap. 20, he showed himself to be a clever and resolute leader, and he was supported by a prophet of Yahweh. According to the word of this prophet Yahweh Himself had taken up his cause and given him the victory : " Because the Syrians have said, the Lord is God of the hills, but he is not God of the valleys, therefore will I deliver all this great multitude into thine hand, and ye shall know that I am the Lord " (20²⁸). And after this victory Ahab was for a time obviously the leader of Israel as a whole against the Syrian menace. The decisive charge against him is that (following out this policy) he concluded a marriage with Jezebel, daughter of the king of Zidon, and that in consequence of this union he introduced a strange cult into Samaria. The tradition calls this the cult of Baal, and it says of Ahab that he served Baal and worshipped him (16³¹ᶠ·). " But there was none like unto Ahab, which did sell himself to work wickedness in the sight of the Lord, whom Jezebel his wife stirred up. And he did very abominably in following idols, according to all things as did the Amorites, whom the Lord cast out before the children of Israel " (21²⁵ᶠ·). From what we learn concerning Ahab elsewhere, this has to be understood *cum grano salis*, at any rate to the extent that he did not introduce a new official religion of state or go over in person to an alien faith (cf. M. Noth, p. 210), but " only " made a concession to a foreign princess (presumably on political grounds), giving hospitality to the worship of her native god Melkart, just as the great Solomon had done to that of the gods of his foreign wives, according to 1 K. 11⁴ᶠ·—a concession of which Jezebel did, of course, make not only a defensive but an offensive use in her conflict with the prophets of Yahweh. It cannot be denied, however, that Ahab himself did take an active part in this conflict, in the persecution described in chap. 19, in which only 7000 were ultimately faithful to Yahweh. In addition to the prophets of Yahweh he consults the prophets of Baal who stand in the service of the queen and therefore speak to him as well (22⁶ᶠ·), although he knows that the prophets of Yahweh speak the truth (22¹⁶). He does not like to hear the prophets of Yahweh or the truth from their mouth, but all the same he does not dare to arrest the Micaiah who tells it to him so very plainly (22²⁶ᶠ·). And in his various encounters with Elijah this strong man obviously has for him a respect which borders on fear, and which prevents him, for example, from even lifting a finger to save the prophets of Baal when the judgment of God comes upon them so violently on Mount Carmel (18⁴⁰, 19¹). It has even been taken as a sign that in spite of everything Ahab did accept Yahweh as the God of Israel that his son and successor bore the name Ahaziah which is a compound of the divine name. In the texts which now concern us, in 1 K. 21, it is noticeable that Ahab is let off lightly and even protected. The idea of the act of aggression perpetrated on Naboth—we are not unnaturally reminded of the role of the woman in the story of the fall—derives not from Ahab but from Jezebel, and it is she who sees to its execution. Ahab simply allows her to do it and enjoys the fruit of her action. He had given or " sold himself " (1 K. 21²⁰, ²⁵) to the matter, and although he greeted his accuser Elijah with the words : " Has thou found me, O mine enemy ? " (v. 20), he not only accepted the sentence without opposition, but—we are reminded of the confession of Saul in 1 Sam. 15²⁴ᶠ·—when " Ahab heard those words, he rent his clothes, and put sackcloth upon his flesh, and fasted, and lay in sackcloth, and went softly " (v. 27). And Elijah received the word from God : " Seest thou how Ahab humbleth himself before me ? because he humbleth himself before me, I will not bring the evil in his days : but in his son's days will I bring the evil upon his house " (v. 28 f.). Compared with the story of Saul we see more, not less, of the light of the divine forgiveness.

It is obvious, however, that the objective transgression and sin of Ahab stands out all the more sharply against this background which subjectively was not altogether unfavourable and in some respects even favourable. The fact that he obviously did not rule without a divine mission, the fact that he was not altogether incompetent to fulfil it, the fact that he did not lack divine assistance—even in the form of the prophetic word—the fact that he was not ignorant of the truth of that word, and could submit to it: all this makes him responsible and guilty in a very definite sense, as stated in the charge against him which is formulated so very sharply in the tradition. In the story of Ahab we are much more clearly in the context of the covenant of grace, which, according to the Old Testament, is still valid even in the darkness of the northern kingdom, than we are in the stories of the first Jeroboam and his father Omri, not to speak of the immediate successors of Jeroboam. This makes his fall all the more heavy. And the presence and action of the foreign queen does not excuse him in the slightest. On the contrary, it is this which is against him, for it is his responsibility that she is there at all with her Baal and all the personnel of her cult. He himself is responsible for all her actions. In her person he has given or sold himself to the world and the spirit and power of the world outside the covenant. From the point of view of the Word and covenant of Yahweh the Melkart of this Jezebel can only be regarded as one of the many personifications of what natural theology with its appeal to a supposed natural revelation and its proclamation of a supposed natural law has in all times and places maintained as God and summoned men to worship. " Baal " is the common term used in the Old Testament to describe gods of this nature. And " Baal " is " lord " in the sense of owner—the owner of the light and power of nature in and under and over the earth, and especially of the light and power of the nature of man himself. Man outside the covenant and Word of God is necessarily man fallen and pledged and committed to some such Baal. Yahweh has called His people Israel from amongst the nations of such men. It is obvious, therefore, that the Baal or lord or owner of such a man—whether he is called Melkart or any other name—has no right of hospitality in the sphere of the covenant and Word of Yahweh. Like all the creations of natural theology, he is just as different from Yahweh as is the earth from heaven or water from fire. But Ahab gave him hospitality in Israel in honour of Jezebel. And Jezebel, honoured in this way, differs from other men fallen and pledged and committed to such Baals only in the intensity with which she is what she is. She is it more deeply and consistently and with greater religious genius than others. In her, natural theology, which is usually so mild and easy-going and tolerant, unsheathes its claws and becomes intolerant and militant and vicious. Jezebel has seen that her Baal can never be a guest but must always be lord, that if we give him a finger we cannot deny him the hand, and then the arm, and then the whole self. Hence the 450 prophets of Baal, as well as the 400 prophets of the groves " which eat at Jezebel's table " (18[19]), who, according to 22[6], seem to be quickly enough replaced by another 400 after the disaster at Carmel—the weed is not easily uprooted. Hence the determined offensive against Elijah and all the prophets of Yahweh. Hence also—" For whom such teachings do not serve, The name of man doth not deserve "—the general recognition and extension of this guest-religion which Elijah bewailed at Horeb. Hence Jezebel's action in the case of Naboth, which was only the application of her belief in Baal, of the natural law inherent in her natural theology. In all this she was completely self-consistent. She followed her law. She was not without her own greatness even in the terrible end which came upon her in 2 K. 9[30f.]. Of course her invasion of the sphere of the covenant and Word of Yahweh was a frightful undertaking which was bound to come to a terrible end. All the same, in the long run the role of Jezebel is theologically irrelevant. The really guilty party is the king of Israel, who is fully responsible for her and her actions, who gave her a place in the land and amongst the people of Yahweh, who gave her the opportunity to act according to her law, who was not faithful to his own law. It is neither to his credit nor does it justify him that when he chose the way of evil he had neither the insight nor perhaps the courage to tread it with resolution and consistency, but, in the words of Elijah on Carmel, he and his people with him halted between two opinions (18²¹). In substance the tradition is right—he did serve and worship Baal even though he may never have done so in a technical sense. There can be no neutrality or freedom to choose between Yahweh and Baal. We cannot draw from the two sources of revelation and and law. If we try to do so it means, as Elijah showed on Carmel—and the same is still true to-day—that we are taking sides with Baal against Yahweh.

The unjust judge in the story of 1 K. 21 is therefore Ahab himself, although it is Jezebel and those seduced by her who act, and he merely permits the actions and enjoys the result, and while it is done remains passively in the background—in bed. The point at issue is the possession of a vineyard in the vicinity of the royal palace of Jezreel. Its lawful owner is a certain Naboth. Ahab wants to acquire it in order to extend and round off his own territories. He wants to acquire it legally, either by purchase or by exchange for another and better vineyard. But Naboth is in the right when he refuses the offer. And his reason is quite understandable within the framework of Old Testament thinking. He will not surrender the portion of the Holy Land which he has inherited from his fathers. He cannot do so, as his answer tells us : " The Lord forbid it me, that I should give the inheritance of my fathers unto thee " (v. 3). It was by such a portion of the land—guaranteed by certain provisions of the Law—that the individual Israelite could participate with his forefathers and successors in the promise to the people. Ahab gives way at first, although he is " heavy and displeased." He still seems to bow to that Law and commandment and judgment of God which is sovereign over his own desires. But the continuation does not hold out too good a promise : " He laid him down upon his bed, and turned away his face, and would not eat " (v. 4). Why ? Is he sorry that the Law of God still has sway over him ? Does he regret his own very obvious and real hesitation to evade or to break it ? It is at this most favourable moment that Jezebel comes into action. " Dost thou now govern the kingdom of Israel ? arise, and eat bread, and let thine heart be merry : I will give thee the vineyard of Naboth the Jezreelite " (v. 7). I—in the function of the helpmate given by God to man according to Gen. 2¹⁸ᶠ·—the representative of the foreign spirit and the foreign power and the foreign god—taking the place of the man, thinking and speaking and acting for him, alienating him from his own Law. And this man is the king of Israel and, as such, the chosen guardian of the Law of God as the basis of all the rights of His people and all the members of His people. The I of this woman is the I of her Baal as diametrically and irreconcilably opposed to the commandment of Yahweh and the rights of His people which are based upon it ; the I of the lord and owner whose law is the law of nature and therefore the law of might, a law which is established without reference to the judgment of God and therefore without grace or promise, a law in face of which there can be no divine or human appeal, which simply posits and asserts itself, the law of the one who actually rules as the stronger. As though he did actually rule in Israel ! As though the king of Israel could play this part in relation to his people ! But the I of Jezebel and her Baal has taken to itself the law of action, and at the very point where the king of Israel with his people and even the lowliest of his subjects is ready to bow to the binding and protecting Law of God and to decide in accordance with it. He himself would not decide at all. Instead he went sulkily to bed and turned his face to the wall. And this is his decision. In this way he evaded the Law of God which called for decision. In this way he gave access to the foreign I and its law. And now this law fills his mind. It takes his place. In his place it becomes the judge of good and evil inclining in favour of his desire. As this judge in the place which does not belong to it, it secures for him the vineyard of Naboth. It is still a matter of a process of law enacted in all its forms. That it is an illegal process can be seen only from the fact that it is stage-managed as a legal process by the foreign I of Jezebel and her god acting in place of Ahab. The process is an act of aggression, as it must be as the act of this judging. But this is not evident. If it was impossible to acquire the vineyard by two legal methods, it must come to Ahab by a third method which was also the legal, as the forfeited property of a malefactor. But Naboth was not a malefactor. He had to be made a malefactor if he was to be treated in this way. And this involved lying and deceit. It is worth noting that here again we have delegation, or an exchange of the acting subject. It is Jezebel's plan which is executed. But those who execute it are the elders and leading men of Jezreel acting at her instigation. Jezebel herself remains in the background, awaiting news of the result, which she then communicates to the king. In the person of these elders the whole people of Israel has a very concrete part in the sin of its king. These men are well enough aware what they are doing—that they are judging unjust judgment. It is as if that foreign I had invaded them and taken possession. They do as they are told without any opposition. The guilt of the king, his judgment in his own case, palpably becomes their guilt. A fast is ordered and kept—a gathering for public repentance, perhaps in view of the great famine which had come in the reign of Ahab, or the Syrian menace. Naboth is called upon to lead it. And now comes the master-stroke of Jezebel and Baal. At the very height of the feast and in the presence of all the people, two men who have been hired come in and denounce Naboth in his place of prominence as a hypocrite, a man who is guilty of the worst possible offence against religion (Lev. 24[10f.]) and the state, who has cursed God and the king, who is therefore responsible for the evil for which they are fasting and repenting and praying. The accusation at the mouth of two witnesses is enough. The scandal is a public one. Sentence is passed on Naboth. He is hustled out of the city and stoned to death according to commandment and custom. The deed is done. Jezebel can give to Ahab the news he wanted : " Arise, take possession of the vineyard of Naboth, the Jezreelite, which he refused to give thee for money : for Naboth is not alive, but dead " (v. 15). And this is what Ahab does. Previously he has done nothing. He has become and been the unjust judge who breaks the Law of God and men only in his sleep, deciding and acting as an unjust judge must decide and act only in the person of this foreign I. As such, he has attained the objective which he had to set himself as such—the establishment and assertion of his right. But his right is as such wrong ; an act of aggression cloaked as right ; lying, deceit, robbery and murder.

It is worth pondering that when Elijah proclaims the judgment of Ahab and his house, the reference is not to his marriage with Jezebel, nor to the foreign religion which he had introduced, nor to the persecution of the prophets initiated in consequence, nor to the halting of the king and his people between two opinions, but to this act of aggression committed under the cloak of Law. The report of this final encounter between Ahab and Elijah is followed only (22[1-40]) by the story of the campaign to recapture Ramoth-Gilead which is undertaken with Jehoshaphat on the advice of the false prophets and against the warning of Micaiah the prophet of Yahweh. In this campaign Ahab is killed. We are reminded of Saul's last campaign against the Philistines (1 Sam. 28 and 31) which begins and ends in a similar gloom. In the one case, as in the other, we have the inevitable consequence of an earlier decision. In the story of Ahab this decision was made with the travesty of justice in the matter of Naboth's vineyard. The view of the tradition is not that this matter was, as it were, only the accidental drop which filled the cup to overflowing. It has its own importance, although it is indissolubly connected with all that precedes it. When

Jezebel and Baal take the place of the king and exercise " government in Israel " with the co-operation of the people, the king—and with the king his people—ceases to bow to the Law of God, and therefore to keep that of man, but makes himself the judge and *eo ipso* an unjust judge, in whose hands right is made wrong. The writing prophets of the Old Testament from Amos to the last of these witnesses are full of indications of the connexion and indeed the unity of Israel's apostasy from Yahweh to the gods of the nations and the unrighteousness which ineluctably flourishes in Israel in the name and under the cloak of righteousness.

A marginal note in conclusion. There is a remarkable affinity between Baal, the lord and owner, the god of all natural theology, who helped Ahab, as it were, in his sleep—but responsibly as an unjust judge and a murderer and a thief—to possess the vineyard of Naboth, and what the New Testament calls " Mammon," the " Mammon of unrighteousness." Therefore W. Vischer is probably right (*op. cit.*, II, p. 395) when at the end of his discussion of 1 K. 21 he recalls Mt. 6[24] : " No man can serve two masters : for either he will hate the one, and love the other ; or else he will hold to the one, and despise the other. Ye cannot serve God and mammon." Ahab tried to do this, and his act of aggression against Naboth was the proof that he could not do so. Neither can any of us.

4. To know human sin in the form of human pride we look for the last time to the being and activity of Jesus Christ and we now think of the final depth of His humiliation, of the Son of God who cried on the cross : " My God, my God, why hast thou forsaken me ? " (Mk. 15[34]), of the One who, although He was the Son of God, died as very man, was dead and buried and lay in the tomb—and all apparently in the most marvellous contradiction, but really in the most wonderful unity, the eternal and living and almighty God thrown back in the person of this man upon the free grace of God the Father, upon His unmerited justification, upon His undeserved mercy, upon the gift of His creative power believed in hope against hope (Rom. 4[18]). Taking our place, bearing the judgment of our sin, undertaking our case, He gave Himself to the depth of the most utter helplessness in which He could not and would not dispose even of the help of God, the depth in which He had nothing but nothingness under and behind and beside Him, and nothing but God before and above Him—nothingness in all its unsearchableness and power, and God as the One into whose Hands He was delivered up without reservation and without claim—He the man who was Himself also the Son of God. He did this for us. This is—in its sharpest form—the humility of the act of God which took place for us in Jesus Christ. But the man whose place and kind God made His own in Jesus Christ is, in clear antithesis to the One who in this way humbled Himself for him, the man who has always thought and still thinks that he can help himself and that in this self-help he has a claim to the help of God.

This opinion is untenable for the very reason that it is only an opinion. The One who was really and finally humbled, who was thrust into the deepest darkness, who went for us to the cross and death and the grave, was not of this opinion. And in the purpose of God, which was concealed from Him as from all men, He was already helped even when He went this way without this opinion, indeed even when He entered on this way. He was visibly and palpably helped when this purpose of God was manifested in His resurrection from the dead. In His resurrection He was justified. The free mercy of God accepted Him. By the creative power of God He was called with Him to incorruptible life—He, the One who would not help Himself or raise any claim to the help of God. This helpless man was the almighty God. But the man who does not want to be helpless, who thinks that he can be his own helper, holds a view which is empty and futile and without substance. He merely imagines of himself, and repeats to himself, that he can and will know how to help and save and liberate himself, giving himself a position and being, asserting and maintaining himself. He does not quite see how. He has not yet discovered ways and means to do it. But he will do so in some near or distant future. And when he does so, then he will find the help of God, which in its best and most instructive and attractive form will be a powerful confirmation and augmentation of his own self-help. All this is pure delusion. It is true, of course, that man can and should help himself in many things, both outwardly and inwardly. It is true that the means and capacities to do so are given to him, and constantly given again, by the goodness of God the Creator. But there is a limit to this. And beyond that limit man cannot help himself. And if it is one thing to help oneself to this thing or that thing, it is another to help and preserve and liberate oneself, to give onself a position and a being, to maintain and accompany and rule oneself in one's creaturely being as leader and guardian and saviour, to give life and freedom and joy to one's soul. This is what man thinks he can do. But this is what, in fact, no man has ever been able to do. He would need some place, an archimedian point, from which to do it. He does not have such a point. He stands over many things and has power over many things. But he does not stand over himself or have power over himself. Therefore he cannot help himself, either alone or with others. The point from which he could do this is not his point but God's. And he has no control over what can take place for him from this point, either in theory or in practice. He can live by the fact that God is his living helper, by the providence and election and calling of God. He can be helped altogether and perfectly, in heart and soul, by God. But if he moves away from God and tries to be his own helper he is simply moving into the void, as when he wants to be his own god and lord and judge. He is deceived by confusing himself with the many necessary and beautiful and useful and noble things to which, by the goodness of God, he can and should help himself. But he himself is not one of these things. He is completely helpless in relation to himself. And therefore the opinion that he can and must be his own helper is one which is quite untenable.

But, in fact, he does live in this opinion, which is a delusion. The history of every man is the history of his great and fantastic attempt to help himself. Throughout his life he rushes and grasps at this thing and that thing, striving and fighting in a dissatisfaction and longing which cannot be explained by the fact that this thing or that thing is useful and necessary and noble and satisfying, which does not stand in any relation to the extrinsic or intrinsic value of the things to which he can help himself if all goes well. In this longing and dissatisfaction he can never be satisfied with the attainable once he has attained it, but he must immediately demand and reach out after something more and different. Everything that he attains and can possess and enjoy is only a symbol of the real thing which he lacks, and for which he hungers and thirsts, to the possession and enjoyment of which he can never cease to look. And why not? Because he is not helped by all the things to which he can and does help himself. But he thinks—and he lives his real life in this opinion—that if only he can at last attain this or that goal, in this or that outward or inward enjoyment which hovers before him, he will help himself to that by which he himself will be helped, and there will be given to him not merely this or that good but rest to his heart and soul, and freedom and joy, salvation to himself. All human life is either the quiet and anxious striving or the noisy hunt for this thing, developing into a bitter conflict for it, and finally ending in sad or cynical but always weary resignation when the earth has been ransacked for it in vain and it has not been found. It cannot be found, because the help in which man can be his own helper, the salvation which he can prepare and make for himself, is an illusion. But what difference does this make to the fact that human life is spent in a search for this help and salvation and that the search goes on in one form or another to the very day of death? Similarly the history of the race as a whole is a history of the Titan who in different ways tries to be his own helper, the subject of his own redemptive history. What a misunderstanding when we think it is all a matter of what we value and seek as the " progress " necessary and possible to us, of our inventions and discoveries, of the establishment of our pious and impious philosophies and ethical or unethical principles, of our wars and treaties and new wars, of the movements in which we think we are caught up, of the reactions which they provoke to the things and ideas and persons which are from time to time in the foreground : the extension of our knowledge ; the improvement of our techniques ; the deepening of our understanding and the corresponding dissemination of instruction ; love and hate ; power and possession and desire ; the sway of this or that individual or people or position in itself and as such. Why do we never learn better from all the well-meant and clever and penetrating sermons which are preached about the very obvious futility and insecurity of striving for goods of this kind ? Why are we quite unable to do so ? Why is all that we can do, our effective progress, only an ascent or descent from one Titanism to another ? Why are we so strikingly the same in spite of all the changes in costume and scenery throughout the centuries ? Obviously because the fault lies much deeper. Because the goal of all these strivings is the thing which is an illusion. Because the compelling force behind all these strivings is the false idea that—if only we can acquire this or that—we will succeed in being our own helper and redeemer and saviour. Because man himself is the false being who wants to be this and cannot, but who will always want to be (because he is this false being, because he has the corrupted nature of the Titan). And it is part of the actual state of affairs that there is a function which man wants to ascribe to God in this undertaking. He wants to make God a partner in his deception. He does not break free from God even as the sinner who wants to help himself and therefore take the place of God. He does not do so even when he tries to do so with a conscious assertion and proclamation of his godlessness. It will only be one of the many possible self-deceptions, and usually he is not committed to it very deeply or for very long. Atheism is only a rather convulsive and primitive form of the faith in God which even the man who wants to help himself cannot escape, but which he tries to impress into the service of his undertaking. By some detour he usually finds a secret or open way back from avowed atheism. He needs a " higher being " to imagine that he is and can be his own helper, a being who will confirm and strengthen him in this idea, a god who will help him as he thinks to help himself. The whole process is impossible, either in detail or as a whole, without religion, or, at any rate, without " concealed religion "—and usually an explicit religious teaching and the corresponding cultus ; often enough a conscious and very serious and zealous attachment to one or other form of Christianity. The only trouble is that it will be the teaching and cult of a god—even a supposedly Christian god—who will not only prevent man from engaging in this undertaking, but by whom man will feel that he is stirred up and supported and strengthened and encouraged in this striving or hunt for the help which he can give himself, a god to whose help he will have a legitimate claim in his own desires because he is only a kind of supernatural complement of his own will. In this sense the life history of every man has at any rate the thin and perhaps alien covering of an (in its own way) sincere and necessarily habitual piety, and a by no means small or insignificant slab of religious and ecclesiastical history is an indispensable part of world-history as a whole. And it is not in the least surprising, but only too natural, that in the different spheres in which man the Titan moves this has always been one of the most conspicuous and interesting. The god who has been transformed into the helper of man belongs unalterably to the picture we have before us. In all this we are dealing with something inexplicable but factual. It is a pure fact that man is this Titan and that he has no option but to fashion his cosmos great and small into a titanic world—encouraged rather than halted by the recollection of God. This is how human life always presents itself, with innumerable variations in detail and as a whole. If man will not be helped by the fact that he is helped by God, the only alternative is to be his own helper and to try to have in God the One who helps him to help himself. We cannot explain why he does not will the one and therefore has to will the other. We can only describe this aspect of the being of man.

But here, too, we have also to remember the concealment of human pride. Wanting to be his own helper, man can appeal to the obvious rational consideration, the simplest reflex of human instinct : Who will think of me, or take an interest in me, or take up my case and help me—if I do not do it myself ? And again : Who knows what I need, my particular wants, if I do not do so myself ? And again : Who is responsible for helping me, who is my neighbour, if not myself ? It seems absurd and exaggerated to find anything evil in this, and especially the evil that I do it. Nothing is easier than to twist the question of the relation of our self-help to the help that we expect from God and to ask whether it is not true that the man who lets himself be helped by God will definitely be a man who draws from this his strength and is therefore bold to help himself ; whether we cannot therefore reverse this indisputable truth and take it to mean that God helps the bold, that man will be helped by God when he vigorously sets out to help himself. But, above all, it is the facts and experiences and results themselves which conceal it—that which in our own lives and in the narrower and wider circle of humanity we have accepted as the product of courageous self-help. How well it has been done in innumerable cases and over considerable tracts ! We thought it out cleverly and decided with a definite consciousness of aim. We dared and seized—or perhaps agreed—and what we desired was attained, and with it we felt that we were strangely taken and compelled and uplifted and borne, so that we were quite another man, and could always look back to it with pleasure and take courage for the future. Does not that mean that we have not merely helped ourselves to this or that, but really helped ourselves ? And do we not think we can see the same phenomenon in plenty of others ? Who, then, is to distinguish between that which we have successfully attained in this or that sphere when we have dared to help ourselves to it, and ourselves who seem to have been inspired and illuminated by that which by all indications has been outwardly well done, ourselves who have obviously not merely won this or that, but by means of it, in, with and under it, have gained or helped ourselves? Where is the evil under the cover of what is so obviously a good ? Are we not dealing again simply with man's true development ? We have to allow that unless we see it from the Word of God we shall never be able to recognise evil in this form.

For the last time we will consult the wisdom of the serpent in Gen. 3. The poor men in paradise are not as God. They are not lords of paradise. They are not even their own lords. They do not know good and evil, and they are forbidden to judge between them. There are so many conditions and limitations in paradise. Of course, there are also so many reminders of the covenant which God has made with them, so many reminders that He is for them the Judge who knows and is responsible, that He is the Lord of paradise and their Lord, that in His grace He is theirs, their God and helper, that He cares for them in the best and most sufficient and perfect way, that they are in His house where they do not need to help themselves. But also, of course, so many reminders of their own helplessness in face of these limitations, the helplessness in which they are only and can only be helped by God. What has the clever serpent to say to all this ? The central point is obviously as follows : that this helplessness (1) is not happy or sensible or necessary but painful and irrational and restrictive and imposed only by an obscure divine caprice ; and (2) that it is not obligatory or definitive but can be overcome and removed by a bold act ; they have only to cross the boundaries set, and in so doing they will experience that man is in a position to help himself and is not, therefore, thrown back upon the help of God. We have to remember that the subtle serpent is speaking only in theory. It is left for man to draw the conclusion and to will and do that which corresponds to it. The serpent does not sin. It is only the serpent. In its animal person it is only the impossible possibility of human sin. If man listens to the theory, and moves on to the corresponding practice, if by his listening and action he affirms the impossible possibility and therefore sins, the act is exclusively his own. And the character of his act as the self-help which is forbidden is disguised by all kinds of fine or useful results, or best of all it is hidden behind a possible appearance of necessity, of a justifiable desire for knowledge, of a proper pride, a joyfully grasped autonomy. The only trouble is that it is not analogous to the act of God the Creator and the life of creation, but to the dark movement of the beast of chaos and therefore of that which is not. The result is that—by the action of the good creatures of God—chaos in all its nothingness is brought into creation, and creation itself is given the character of the chaotic and that which is not. But who is to see and decide that this is the case : whether the supposed evil of this first act of self-help is not the first good, the prototype of everything that we have to call good and not evil in the sphere of humanity, as man's self-help. Why should not that which happened be the prototype of all true human development, and therefore not chaos but cosmos ? Why not ?

This is the concealment in face of which we have to state the truth, although we cannot claim to be able to set it aside by arguments. Here, too, the concealment is an element of sin itself. And sin itself cannot be argued away in any of its forms. It can only be seen and recognised as such. Three points have to be considered as we try to do this.

The attempt at self-help rests (1) on an error of man concerning himself. That we have a right and necessity to affirm ourselves, to be the active subject of our existence, and as such to be and think and act in autonomous responsibility to God and our neighbour, in fulfilment of the determinations of our creaturely nature—all this is open neither to question nor attack, but is simply the normal presupposition of our obedience. It would be to misunderstand and oppose man not to recognise that this self-affirmation, this active subjectivity, this autonomous responsibility, is the framework within which he has to

fill out his being in covenant with God and fellowship with his neighbour, and therefore his life as the soul of the body in the span of time
allotted to him. But what call is there for man to doubt that his
freedom is grounded in the free grace of God ? How does he come to
feel that he is threatened and attacked and harmed and wronged by
the limit set to him ? What is it that impels him, not to be thankful
within this limit, but to cross the limit, not to be free by the grace of
God, but to try to find his freedom in the dream and fiction that he
is gracious to himself, behaving as this dream-figure, the product of
his phantasy ? Why does he think that to be a true man he has to
be one who hates and despises the grace of God and finds a better
grace, that is to say his own ? We are confronted at this point by a
self-contradiction which is quite incomprehensible because there is
no reason for it. And obviously it cannot be resolved. Once he is
involved in it, man cannot overcome it. It will be constantly repeated.
All that we can say is that the self-help in which man tries to take or
give himself that which he can receive only as a gift of God is above
everything else a self-contradiction. There is no necessity, or only a
fictitious necessity, for man to see in his dependence on the grace of
God and therefore his own helplessness, a derangement if not worse,
or in the character of thankfulness which his self-affirmation, his being
as subject, his responsibility has therefore to assume, a kind of humiliation. And he has no positive gain to expect, he will not alter the
human situation in the very slightest, if he refuses this helplessness
and renounces the law of thankfulness by calling himself his own
helper. On the contrary, it is by doing this that he really brings about
his own humiliation and need. He loses himself, his soul, his life, by
undertaking his own cause, by trying to defend and maintain and save
himself. He lives by the fact that God is gracious to him. He lives
to the degree and extent that he sees in this the basis of his true and
most intimate being, of himself, that he does not try to find any other
basis, that all idea of himself being or becoming this basis is quite
alien to him. He is free to the extent that he knows himself to be
free by the grace of God, and continually allows himself to be made
free by it, and therefore does not make any attempt to free himself.
The degree to which he finds this difficult is the degree to which he
finds it difficult to be free, to affirm himself, to realise his subjectivity,
to accept his responsibility. And if he cannot do it, this means
necessarily that he cannot be free, that he shuts himself off from the
very thing which he madly seeks. If he despises and hates the grace
of God, and therefore his total reference to the grace of God, and
therefore his own helplessness, then—without knowing it—he despises
and hates himself most of all, as the one who can undertake and
achieve that which is proper to him only within the limit set to him.
There is no more terrible error than that which man can commit in
this direction. And he commits this error when he tries to help himself.

But in committing it, he does (2) the wrong from which nothing but ill can come. The good is obedience. And where grace is law, this is not a hard duty or unwilling subjection to an alien authority, but the free and joyful act of a thankful life. But titanic man can only do wrong. Salvation is the preservation which is guaranteed to man unconditionally and in all circumstances in his helplessness before God. But titanic man chooses evil as well as wrong. As such he can only bring destruction and himself to destruction. In his flight from an imaginary need he brings himself into real need. And the result of his refusing a supposed humiliation is real humiliation. He cannot escape it. He has already committed himself hopelessly to the first step on this way. If we will not be helpless before God, we can only be helpless abstractly and absolutely—the Golgotha, the dereliction of disobedience beyond which there is no Easter morning. Man sets out to be his own helper and that is what he has to be. He is left to himself, to his phantasy, his self-will, his projects and constructions and crafts, his natural capacities and powers in the service of the hopeless task of helping himself. And this is pure helplessness : to be without grace is to be without help. For it is to be put in a labyrinth from which there is no exit. It is to be condemned to the hopeless toil of a Sisyphus. It is to be forced to hunt and be hunted in a circle, like greyhound racing in which the dogs chase a mechanical hare which they can never catch. But in this case we are not dealing with a dog and a game, but with man as the creature whom God has set in covenant with Himself. What is at issue is the one life of this man. And he himself is both the hunted and the hunter, the one who is fooled and who regards himself as a fool. Man may think that he can and should be gracious to himself, but this is impossible. He thinks and acts as his own helper, but believing that he is his own best friend he is all the time his own worst enemy. Looking after his own interests, he does not advance but damage them. He is an active subject who at bottom cannot make anything of himself. He is responsible, but he does not know what he is talking about when he asserts his responsibility because he is no longer confronted by God. And he is not really a man who thinks and speaks and acts independently, but simply a marionette pulled by wires in a group of men who all share the same illusion of independence. When he is no longer confronted by God— who can be to him only the gracious God in all His freedom, who can confront him only as helpless man—he is no longer confronted by his fellowman, who can properly confront him only in God. Wanting to help himself, he has forgotten that he can be helped only with his neighbour and as he is ready to help his neighbour. He is set in a splendid isolation over against his neighbour, almost as it were behind the wall of a refrigerator, which is also a stronghold through whose tiny slits he shoots at him from all sides. But even in face of his neighbour he cannot help himself. He may try to be consistent, but it is impossible. He cannot acquire a single character or be a single personality. Without being aware of it, he is the sport of all kinds of winds and influences, the traditions and movements of the world around him. He is simply a chessman. He is a swaying reed, a blown leaf, not a living man, but one whose life is passing. The individual who wants to help himself forfeits his individuality. And the society which is made up of such individuals will always be a society which is a prey to dissolution.

When Adam and Eve made that move to self-help in paradise, and ate the fruit of the tree, what did they do to themselves and one another ? They had been incited to do this. They had allowed their peace with God to be broken. They had allowed the serpent successfully to approach them when he ought not to have approached them. And was not the only result that they ceased to be independent ? and that deceiving and deceived they were strangely separated from one another ? They had helped themselves so well that they suddenly became aware of their nakedness (v. 7) and were ashamed of it. And then, confirming the isolation and separation from one another which had come with their alienation from God, they made their second and this time open attempt at self-help and brought in the first fashion, that of the fig leaf. And this was followed (v. 8) by the lamentable necessity of being ashamed before God and trying to hide from Him, as though He had not created them good in their nakedness. *Naturalia* have become *turpia*. And then the pitiable excuse of the man : " The woman whom thou gavest to be with me, she gave me of the tree, and I did eat " (v. 12). Just like Aaron on Sinai : " There came out this calf." And then the pitiable excuse of the woman : " The serpent beguiled me, and I did eat " (v. 13). These texts are well worth pondering. They make it plain that man's attempt to help himself is a complete failure. He has tried to help himself and he has become catastrophically helpless. Such is the human subject when he tries to live out his subjectivity otherwise than in the framework of the free grace of God and therefore in the obedience of thankfulness.

We conclude by stating (3) what is in this matter the decisive misunderstanding, the misunderstanding of God. God is not the One in relation to whom there is any point or purpose in trying to help oneself. The undertaking would be legitimate and necessary if we could not trust God, or if we had to fear something at His hand— perhaps an inscrutable purpose which ignores man and aims at something beyond him, the purpose of a despot who is accidentally the power which controls the world and is therefore the destiny of man in the world. That is how Prometheus regarded Zeus, and he was right to try to help himself when chained to that Caucasian cliff. But God is not a despot like this. He has not a single feature in common with the Zeus of Prometheus. From all eternity He is the God of man, the God who is well-disposed to man. His power is that of the grace which He directs to man. Or is it that man fears the incapacity of a supreme being remote from the world and therefore remote from man—an incapacity to understand man in his humanity and needs, an incapacity, perhaps, really to draw near to him and to help him ? Deists old and new have thought of God in this way, and therefore we can quite understand that they have called upon man to help himself for the sake of his own safety. But God is not at all this high and remote incompetent. To Him belongs all power in heaven and in earth—as the power of His grace. He is not remote, but near, the nearest of all to man. He does not slumber or sleep, but is awake. He does not rest, but is constantly at work, operating without exception over and in and through everything that is. Or, conversely, does man fear the over-ruling of a divine principle of life at work in all things great and small, a principle which has no respect for the freedom of man and does despite and harm to his dignity? That is how the Idealists look at God, and again we can understand that in face of this god they ascribed this one effective divine activity to man himself, so that God merged into the figure of this one true helper, the spirit of man thrown back upon self-help. They ought to have seen that the one effective principle which can so easily change in this way has nothing whatever to do with God. The almighty power of grace does not do despite to the freedom of man. On the contrary, it is the basis of it. The God who is almighty in grace distinguishes Himself as the Creator from the creature, and therefore the being of the creature from His own being. He does not deny but gives to man his proper place in relation to Himself. He elects and calls him to be His partner, to an obedience which is not forced but free. The view of God which gives rise to the idea that man has necessarily to help himself is always a false one. When this idea is present we can presuppose that the ears of man which ought to hear the voice of the living God are already closed to Him, that this God is unknown, that under His name the form of a stranger, an idea of God (and all ideas of God are false) has taken His place, an idol who, it is thought, has to be met and resisted in this way. What else can man do but misunderstand himself and rush to his destruction when he is overshadowed by the dark cloud of this error concerning God? And is it not plain that nothing but the Word of the living God Himself will suffice to bring healing at this source of all corruption, to bring man back to a true knowledge of what God is in truth, and then to bring him to a knowledge of his true help, and to a knowledge of the utter folly of his own self-help?

But we are now speaking of man as alienated from the Word of God, the man of sin, who does not have either that first knowledge or the others which proceed from it. This is man from the fourth and final standpoint. His pride also means that he wants to be his own helper. He lives in this meaningless idea. This proud man God has reconciled and converted to Himself in Jesus Christ. The action of the divine physician corresponds to his mortal sickness. On his behalf Jesus Christ cried on the cross, the helpless One taking the place of all those who gaily help themselves: " My God, my God, why hast thou forsaken me ? "

Here, again, we can learn from the Old Testament. I am selecting the story of the conduct of the king and people in Jerusalem immediately before and after the final fall of the city in 587. We will consider it as reflected in the prophecy of Jeremiah. Of course, to get a comprehensive view of what Holy Scripture means by proud and arrogant and godless and destructive and forbidden human self-help we should have to look at the whole of the later history of the two Israelitish states as it developed from about the middle of the 8th century, i.e., when it was drawn into the power politics of the then Great Powers, and as it was regarded by the " classical " prophecy which emerged round about this period (cf. B. Duhm, *Israels Propheten*, 1916, p. 1 f., 89–318 ; W. Vischer, *op. cit.*, II, p. 479 f. ; M. Noth, *op. cit.*, p. 218 f.). The *terminus a quo* for the period was the emergence of the Assyrians to found their shortlived empire. According to Duhm, it was they who brought into being what we now call universal history as compared with the history of individual nations. However that may be, one of the consequences of the development which began with that emergence was that Israel lost the relative isolation which, with its immediate neighbours, it had hitherto enjoyed by the Mediterranean sea, and that ultimately its independent existence was destroyed altogether. Prophecy—a factor which we find and which operates only in Israel—accompanied both the initial stages and then the course and completion of this process with a message which was alien and indeed diametrically opposed to all the natural and even the religious tendencies and desires and expectations of Israel and its kings : that in it there is taking place the judgment of the God of Israel who is the Lord both of Israel and of all history. It is His plan and will that the disloyalty which they have shown again and again, their opposition as the partner of His covenant, the people of His election, should be answered by this development, that their status and existence as independent peoples and kingdoms should be brought to an end and completely destroyed. Prophecy described the Assyrian king Tiglath-Pileser as the rod of God's anger and the staff of His indignation against Israel (Is. 10[5f.]). Later the Babylonian king Nebuchadnezzar was called the servant of Yahweh into whose hand He the covenant God of Israel, who had " made the earth, the man and the beast that are upon the ground," had delivered up His own and surrounding territories (Jer. 27[5]). The prophets proclaimed that there could be no escape for Israel, no salvation, no successful resistance to the event which would take place in this century. Certainly they did not cease to magnify the grace of God to His people and to renew the promise which He had given in glowing colours. But they proclaimed His grace in a judgment which had now become inevitable and which went to the very root of the existence of Israel as a people. It was the promise of a fulfilment which would be like the resurrection of a field of dry bones (Ezek. 37), beyond any claims which Israel might make, or any ends which it might set, or any efforts which it might make for itself. With a warning to repent, they proclaimed the rapidly approaching end of both kingdoms, the impotence of kings and peoples alike to arrest this end, the need to acknowledge their impotence, and to accept this end. With increasing definiteness they characterised all attempts at self-help in face of this whole development as a repetition of the very sin which was coming under judgment. They connected the hope of Israel in a way which could not be mistaken with the renunciation of all such attempts. And now the startling thing : generally speaking their preaching did not meet with any response or obedience. They wrestled strongly, but in vain, against the flood of opposing tendencies. They thought and spoke in a way which was supremely true theologically and supremely realistic politically. But they and their word were a foreign body in their environment. Apart from the fact that they spoke the Word of God, the only point in their favour was that events actually proved them right : that history passed devastatingly over Israel ; that first the state of Israel and then that of Judah was completely eliminated ; that nothing was left to the men of Israel but the

God against whom they had sinned to the last in resisting His judgment, but whose hard hand they could not finally withstand—the covenant God, the Lord of the world, their Judge even as their strength, but as the strength which they had despised. In this context we cannot follow the whole drama from the beginning to the climax and in all the individual details. We must be content simply to look at the final act, with particular reference to the resistance of the Israelites to the grace of the divine judgment, their repudiation of their helplessness in face of God, their stubbornness against the only One who could help them, as revealed typically and with a supreme intensity in these closing stages.

Now that Samaria had fallen, and the Assyrian empire had been overthrown and replaced by the Babylonian, the time had long since passed when with any prospect of success the Davidic kings in Jerusalem could attempt, either in alliance with or opposition to the southern power of Egypt, to save what could apparently be saved. The time of the attempt of the ill-fated Jehoiakim to escape Babylonian suzerainty had also passed. In consequence of this rebellion Jerusalem was carried away captive for the first time under his son and successor Jehoiachin, the young king and his courtiers and all the social and economic and military leaders of Judah being deported to Babylon, where the king himself—an unforgettable figure in the later Old Testament tradition—lived out his days in a comparatively honourable captivity (Jer. 52³¹⁻³⁴). Judah was reduced and became a vassal state, a kingdom under a puppet ruler appointed by Nebuchadnezzar, the twenty-one-year-old descendant of David named Mattaniah (Jer. 52¹), to whom he surprisingly gave the new name Zedekiah (Yahweh my salvation, 2 K. 24¹⁷). Was it really the intention of the Babylonian ruler (W. Vischer, p. 535) in this way to " show that he was fulfilling the will of the native God of Jerusalem and Judah, both in salvation and judgment " ? This is what he actually did. And Jer. 23⁵ᶠ· (cf. 33¹⁵ᶠ·) can be taken to mean that in this situation the prophet saw that another opportunity had been given by God to the people : " Behold, the days come, saith the Lord, that I will raise unto David a righteous branch, and a King shall reign and prosper, and shall execute judgment and justice in the earth. In his days Judah shall be saved, and Israel shall dwell safely : and this is the name whereby he shall be called, The Lord our Salvation." But Zedekiah did not live up to his name. He was more obsequious and clever in accordance with the changed situation, but he was no more wise than his predecessors. Therefore in his days, too, Israel is not helped, or is helped only in the dark form of continuing and completed judgment.

Passing difficulties which occupy Nebuchadnezzar in his own territories raise in the captives and influential circles in Jerusalem and Judah the new hope that everything will perhaps turn out for the best, that there will be a liberation from Babylon and a restoration of the earlier monarchy. Judah's neighbours, Edom, Moab and Ammon, etc., are restive (Jer. 27³ᶠ·) and incite Zedekiah to common action. In Jer. 28 there is brought before us the scene when a false prophet called Hananiah comes to Jeremiah and dares to proclaim to him as the Word of the Lord that He, Yahweh, has already broken the yoke of the king of Babylon and that He will bring back the treasures of the temple and king Jehoiakin and the exiles to Jerusalem. Within two full years all this will take place. But Jeremiah withstands him " in the presence of the priests, and in the presence of all the people that stood in the⸲ house of the Lord." His answer is mildly ironical : " Amen : the Lord so do : the Lord perform the words which thou hast prophesied " (v. 6). But he cannot withhold the caveat : " The prophet which prophesieth of peace, when the word of the prophet shall come to pass, then shall the prophet be known, that the Lord hath truly sent him " (v. 9). Is Hananiah a prophet of this kind ? Jeremiah does not say so in words, but he answers all the more unmistakably by his action in putting yokes round his neck (27²ᶠ·), and carrying them mourning about the streets of Jerusalem, and sending them to the representatives of the other revolting powers.

The message of the yoke is : " The nation and kingdom which will not serve the same Nebuchadnezzar the king of Babylon, and that will not put their neck under the yoke of the king of Babylon, that nation will I punish, saith the Lord, with the sword, and with the famine, and with the pestilence, until I have consumed them out of the land " (27⁸). And conversely : " But the nations that bring their neck under the yoke of the king of Babylon, and serve him, those will I let remain still in their own land, saith the Lord, and they shall till it, and dwell therein " (27¹¹). Note that the judgment is not a fate. Judah can live even now if only it will live under the judgment which has already come upon it, if only it will bring itself under that judgment instead of resisting it. But Hananiah thinks differently, and he dares to oppose to the sign a countersign : " He took the yoke from off the prophet Jeremiah's neck, and brake it " (28¹⁰). To which Jeremiah replied : " Thou hast broken the yokes of wood ; but I shall make for them yokes of iron " (28¹³). And again : " Hear now, Hananiah : the Lord hath not sent thee ; but thou makest this people to trust in a lie Therefore thus saith the Lord ; Behold, I will cast thee from off the face of the earth : this year thou shalt die, because thou hast taught rebellion against the Lord " (28¹⁵f·). This is how things are. Rebellion against Nebuchadnezzar is rebellion against God, for it is God who has brought all peoples, and especially Israel, under the power of Nebuchadnezzar, a power which will prove to be unbreakable, which the king and people of Israel will certainly not be able to break.

Did Zedekiah hear and understand this ? We might conclude as much from the fact that in 29³ he sent an embassy to Nebuchadnezzar, perhaps to assure him once again of his loyalty. But this does not mean that he ceased to look anxiously to other possibilities or to dislike the unpatriotic and unpopular message of Jeremiah. We gain the impression that Jeremiah himself worked incessantly and in every possible way to make his message heard. Amongst the exiles in Babylon Ezekiel was active along the same lines and with the same lack of success. Perhaps to help him, perhaps in view to their influence on the situation in Jerusalem, Jeremiah wrote to the exiles (29¹f·) advising them to prepare for a longer (and perhaps originally a permanent) stay in Babylon, to build houses and plant gardens and found families, telling them to " seek the peace of the city whither I have caused you to be carried away captive, and pray unto the Lord for it : for in the peace thereof ye shall have peace," warning them against the false prophets who seem to have appeared there too, and giving them the promise : " For I know the thoughts that I think toward you, saith the Lord, thoughts of peace, and not of evil, to give you an expected end. Then shall ye call upon me, and ye shall go and pray unto me, and I will hearken unto you. And ye shall seek me, and find me, when ye shall search for me with all your heart. And I will be found of you, saith the Lord " (v. 11 f.). But in reply to this letter, or one like it, one of the exiles, a certain Shemaiah, sent a complaint to Zephaniah the high-priest in Jerusalem : " The Lord hath made thee priest . . . that ye should be officers in the house of the Lord, for every man that is mad, and maketh himself a prophet, that thou shouldest put him in prison, and in the stocks. Now therefore why hast thou not reproved Jeremiah of Anathoth, which makest himself a prophet to you ? For therefore he sent unto us in Babylon, saying, This captivity is long : build ye houses and dwell in them ; and plant gardens, and eat the fruit of them " (v. 26 f.). And if this complaint did not have any immediate consequences, it is clear from the comprehensive statement in 37² that the word of Jeremiah in Jerusalem did not have any effect on Zedekiah or his counsellors or the people at large. The attitude of Zedekiah himself was not too certain. He protected him as far as he could, and on more than one occasion (21¹f·, 37¹⁷, 38¹⁴) he asked for his advice and requested his prayers (37³). But in company with those around him, and the majority of the exiles in Babylon —once again we have a king sharing the guilt of his people and a people sharing the guilt of its king—he did not really listen to him. All the prophet's activity was in vain. Perhaps B. Duhm is right (p. 273) in his suggestion that the terrible passage, Jer. 20[7-18], belongs to this period, when the prophet brings against God the express complaint : " O Lord, thou hast deceived me, and I was deceived : thou art stronger than I, and hast prevailed : I am in derision daily, every one mocketh me. . . . The word of the Lord was made a reproach unto me, and a derision, daily. Then I said, I will not make mention of him, nor speak any more in his name. But his word was in mine heart as a burning fire shut up in my bones, and I was weary with forbearing, and I could not stay " (vv. 7–9). And then the description of his situation : " For I heard the defaming of many, fear on every side. Report, say they, and we will report it. All my familiars watched for my halting, saying, Peradventure he will be enticed, and we shall prevail against him, and we shall take our revenge on him " (v. 10). And then the complaint (and Duhm notes that even Job never dared to speak like this) : " Cursed be the day wherein I was born : let not the day wherein my mother bare me be blessed. Cursed be the man who brought tidings to my father, saying, a man child is born unto thee, making him very glad. And let that man be as the cities which the Lord overthrew, and repented not . . ." (v. 14 f.). But at the heart of it all there is, of course, the saying which shows us and explains why the prophet—however willingly or unwillingly he may be placed as he is—is not a man who can yield : " But the Lord is with me as a mighty terrible one " (v. 14).

In another sense than for the prophet the Lord is this for His chosen people, which also in its own way cannot leave the place where He has put it. Both king and people aim at greatness, and their fall is therefore inevitable. The laconic statement of 2 K. 24[20] is that " Zedekiah rebelled against the king of Babylon." The help which was expected and demanded and which in part materialised from Egypt may have played some role in all this. But it was certainly " a foolhardy step " (M. Noth, p. 245). Read the highly coloured parable in which Ezekiel (17[1-10]) describes and judges the institution and then the fall of Zedekiah and the exposition which he himself gives : " Behold, the king of Babylon is come to Jerusalem, and hath taken away the king thereof, and the princes thereof, and led them with him to Babylon ; and hath taken of the king's seed, and made a covenant with him, and hath taken an oath of him : he hath also taken the mighty of the land : that the kingdom might be base, that it might not lift itself up, but that by keeping of the covenant it might stand. But he rebelled against him in sending his ambassadors into Egypt, that they might give him horses and much people. Shall he prosper ? shall he escape that doeth such things ? or shall he break the covenant, and be delivered ? . . . Therefore thus saith the Lord God, As I live, surely mine oath that he hath despised, and my covenant that he hath broken, even it will I recompense upon his own head " (17[12-19]). If we accept the usual modern translation of the *berith* with Babylon as a treaty, to get the full weight of the passage we have to remember the association of the word for the original readers. The breaking of the " covenant " with the king of Babylon was the last and most flagrant breach of the covenant with Yahweh. And this breach of the covenant is actually and definitively visited on the head of Zedekiah and all those associated with him.

Nebuchadnezzar takes the field. The suppressing of a minor rebel in Jerusalem seems to be only a side-action in his enterprise, which is directed primarily against the threatened attack from Egypt. But while Nebuchadnezzar has his headquarters in the north, at Riblah in Syria, one part of his army invades Judah, and (according to Ezek. 24[1], in the ninth year of the reign of Zedekiah, 589) there commences a siege of Jerusalem and of the fortresses Lachish and Asekah south-west of the city. At first the siege was loose and intermittent, but later it was pressed in full earnest. This was the final battle, for Jeremiah, too, who would not be silenced. It was also his passion. How he opposed the despairing optimism of the besieged, we read in Jer. 21$^{1-10}$: " Thus saith the Lord, behold, I set before you the way of life, and the way of death. He that abideth in this city shall die by the sword, and by the famine, and by the pestilence : but he that goeth out, and falleth to the Chaldeans that besiege you, he shall live, and his life shall be unto him for a prey " (vv. 8–9). The mixture of anxiety and arrogance with which he was surrounded is seen in the strange events described in 34$^{8-22}$. Due to the obvious pressure of the situation, Zedekiah and the men of Jerusalem had the idea of proclaiming a general release of all Jewish slaves as ought to have been done every six years according to Ex. 21^2. But at this very moment the siege is temporarily raised. An Egyptian army is on the march (37^5). In jubilation at the liberation which has apparently come, the covenant solemnly accepted and published in the temple is regretted, and those who had been released were forced to come back and be slaves again. Jeremiah has to denounce this with great severity : " Behold, I proclaim a liberty for you, saith the Lord, to the sword, to the pestilence, and to the famine ; and I will make you to be removed into all the kingdoms of the earth " (34^{17}). And against the hope of relief at the hands of the Egyptians and the withdrawal of the besiegers : " Thus saith the Lord, Deceive not yourselves, saying, The Chaldeans shall surely depart from us : for they shall not depart. For though ye had smitten the whole army of the Chaldeans that fight against you, and there remained but wounded men among them, yet should they rise up every man in his tent, and burn this city with fire " (37$^{9f.}$). It is not they who will depart but the Egyptians : " Behold, Pharaoh's army, which is come forth to help you, shall return to Egypt into their own land. And the Chaldeans shall come again, and fight against this city, and take it, and burn it with fire " (37$^{7f.}$). The consequences of speeches like could not be evaded. Obviously the ruling war-party could only regard and treat them as a most serious sabotaging of the defence (an undermining of the will to resist). That this was the case is shown in the ostraka found at Lachish in 1935, reports written on potsherds by outposts of the besieged fortress to the commander shortly before it fell. They can still see his signals, although they cannot see those of Asekah (which has already fallen). They then say that there are in Jerusalem those " who weaken the hands of the land and the city " (cf. M. Noth, p. 246). This is almost word for word what the leaders in Jerusalem said of Jeremiah in 38^4 : " Let this man be put to death ; for thus he weakeneth the hands of the men of war that remain in this city, and the hands of the whole people, in speaking such words unto them : for this man seeketh not the welfare of this people, but its hurt." Indeed, during this interruption of the siege he was arrested when he tried to leave the city to see to the settlement of an inheritance in the land of Benjamin, the accusation being that he wanted to go over to the Chaldeans, an act of individual escape of which he had never even thought. And after several alarming crises (37$^{11-15}$, 38$^{1-13}$) in which the king tried to shelter him from the worst, but a foreigner Ebed-melech the Ethiopian finally saved him from certain death, he was finally kept a prisoner in the court of the prison. Meantime the city was starved out (39$^{1-10}$), and when one and a half years had passed it was captured in August 587. The king—who was now in his thirty-second year—made a last attempt to escape, but he was captured in the plains of Jericho by the pursuing Babylonians. He was then brought to Riblah, his young sons and the leaders of the people were executed before his eyes, and he himself was then blinded and brought in chains to Babylon, with a considerable part of the population. Jerusalem and the royal palace and the temple were destroyed by fire and the walls pulled down. It may be assumed that this was when the ark, the sacred thing of the tribes laid up in the inner court of the temple, was also destroyed (M. Noth, p. 248).

In this terrible disaster there ended the last of the many attempts at self-help made by Israel and finally by Judah throughout this period in direct opposition to the clear enough warnings of the prophets. The thought which undoubtedly underlies the accounts in Jer. 21–39 and 52, 2 K. 25$^{1-21}$ and 2 Chron. 36$^{11-20}$, is that the sin of the people was its destruction (the sin of pride, and pride in the form of the self-help which is forbidden to man). And we cannot consider this thought without being reduced to silence in fear and pity at the greatness of the folly which brought them to ruin, and in amazement at the vital and death-despising determination with which they went to the ruin of sword and famine and pestilence with which Jeremiah had so often threatened them, until no more signals could be seen in Jerusalem but the flames and smoke of the destruction, the dead on the walls and in the streets, and the pitiful processions of those who were being driven away to a northern exile. In the last resort these people did not do anything less great or more nonsensical than what the Spartans are honoured for doing at Thermopylae or the declining Nibelungs or the Swiss at St. Jacob. There is no self-evident reason why the Old Testament tradition, instead of accepting the accusations of his contemporaries, should take the side of Jeremiah, not glorifying the activity of king and people as a tragic but heroic resistance, but characterising it negatively as an act of disloyalty and disobedience which deservedly ends in gloom and death. But the Spartans and Germans and the old-time Swiss were not the elect people of God. Israel was. And as this people it was put to the test and called in question and brought into judgment. And by the prophetic word it was set in the light of this judgment in a way which cannot be said of other peoples. Therefore if the reminiscences and traditions of this people are to be true, they have to judge by quite different standards from those of other peoples. And if we are not to miss the distinctive thing within this history, then, however difficult it may be, we have to note this difference and not to reverse it, holding fast by the judgment which is implicitly pronounced on all man's self-help which evades the grace and Word of God. It is undoubtedly the case that the Bible does not find anything to praise in this man, but rather brings him into judgment.

We will now consider briefly the immediate consequence of the event of 587. This is important because the function and role of the great opponent Jeremiah is again set in the same light—the harsh light of the divine judgment—in which we see the king and people removed from the earth according to the threat addressed to the false prophet Hananiah (28^{16}). And this time Jeremiah, too, is " cast from off the face of the earth." He, too, disappears into the darkness. This takes place in the sequel in which, apart from God whom he had not seen, he saw nothing but the utter futility of his work. Because it does take place, he, if anyone after Moses, is a witness to Jesus Christ at the very heart of the Old Testament.

Judah had become a Babylonian province. A certain Gedaliah was appointed governor by Nebuchadnezzar. He did not live in Jerusalem but in Mizpah, on the northern frontier (40$^{7f.}$). He was joined by Jeremiah, who had been found in the court of the prison when the city was taken, bound in chains among the captives, but unconditionally released (Jer. 40$^{1-6}$) on the command of Nebuchadnezzar (39$^{11-12}$). " So he dwelt among the people " (39^{14}). Once again the situation was for a short time full of promise as he saw it. For Gedaliah accepted the policy which Jeremiah had always recommended and gave this charge to those who, after the catastrophe, came to him at Mizpah : " Fear not to serve the Chaldeans : dwell in the land, and serve the king of Babylon, and it shall be well with you. As for me, Behold, I will dwell at Mizpah to serve the Chaldeans which will come unto us : but ye, gather ye wine, and summer fruits, and oil, and put them in vessels, and dwell in your cities that ye have taken " (40$^{9-10}$). And for the moment it seemed as though the assembled remnant would maintain themselves as the people of God in this new obedience of a humility which they had hitherto scorned. But then among this remnant there is a reaction under the leadership of Ishmael a descendant of David, apparently in co-operation with

Baalis, king of the Ammonites (40^{14}). Gedaliah is assassinated, as are also the majority of the strange group of penitents found at Mizpah. The rest of the people are to take refuge in Ammon (41^{1-10}). But this never happens, for the violent reaction is overthrown with equal violence (41^{11-15}). Those responsible, however, do not have the wisdom and courage to resume the work and way of Gedaliah. They are afraid that what Ishmael has done to the governor appointed by the Babylonians will be avenged on them. They therefore decide to emigrate to Egypt (41^{16-18}). And now Jeremiah is again the centre of the old and fatal game. His intercession is requested (42^2). The will of God is sought at his hand (42^3). God is solemnly called to witness that they will follow the decision which He makes known to them (42^{5-6}). The divine decision communicated to this remnant by Jeremiah is as follows : " If ye will still abide in this land, then will I build you, and not pull you down, and I will plant you, and not pluck you up : for I repent me of the evil that I have done unto you. Be not afraid of the king of Babylon, of whom ye are afraid, be not afraid of him, saith the Lord : for I am with you to save you, and to deliver you from his hand. And I will shew mercies unto you, that he may have mercy upon you, and cause you to return to your own land " ($42^{10f.}$). But " if ye wholly set your faces to enter into Egypt, and go to sojourn there ; then it shall come to pass, that the sword, which ye feared, shall overtake you there in the land of Egypt, and the famine, whereof ye were afraid, shall follow close after you there in Egypt ; and there ye shall die " (42^{15-16}). " As mine anger and my fury hath been poured forth upon the inhabitants of Jerusalem ; so shall my fury be poured forth upon you, when ye shall enter into Egypt : and ye shall be an execration, and an astonishment, and a curse, and a reproach ; and ye shall see this place no more " (42^{18}). But the remnant was just as little able and willing to listen to this prophecy as the king and people in Jerusalem had been to what he said earlier. As though they had never given their solemn promise to hear and obey, their answer was : " Thou speakest falsely : the Lord God hath not sent thee to say, Go not into Egypt to sojourn there " (43^2). The end of this end is, therefore, that these unfortunates do indeed take the way back. They return to the place from which Yahweh had once called and led their fathers by the word of Moses. The difference is that this time the prophet does not lead. He is taken with the rest of the people, both the willing and the unwilling (43^{1-7}). Only one thing is lacking and this quickly takes place. The remnant of the people formally renounces Yahweh in favour of the cult of the queen of heaven which had already been practised both secretly and openly in Jerusalem. And to the futile protest of the prophet they return the defiant answer : " As for the word that thou hast spoken unto us in the name of the Lord, we will not hearken unto thee " (44^{16}). The basic intention and meaning of their self-help and that of all Israel and Judah are now laid bare. And so they disappear and Jeremiah with them. They for their part are given the lie by events. And he is silenced by them as he had been all his life.

Remarkably enough, the redaction of the main historical part of the Book of Jeremiah closes with the reproduction of a word of comfort addressed by Jeremiah to his friend and helper Baruch, who, as we read in 43^3, was entangled with him in the dispute about the flight into Egypt, and, as we see from 43^6, was actually carried into Egypt with the prophet. The oracle reproduced in the short chapter 45 does not belong to this final period but, as v. 1 plainly tells us, it dates back to the conflict between Jeremiah and king Jehoiakim almost twenty years before. But chronological exactness does not seem to have been the main aim of the man or men who compiled this historical part of the book. And the simplest explanation of the literary problem of chapter 45 (the one approved by B. Duhm) is probably this. Someone (perhaps Baruch himself) put the chapter here, without concealing the fact that the prophetic word contained in it belonged to an earlier situation, because the reader is anxious to know the fate of the prophet and of an unfaithful people in Egypt, and this is the final word. At any rate this little passage takes the place of any further information concerning the disappearance of prophet and people. And it is a concise epilogue on the deepest problem of the relationship between the sin and consequent destruction of the people on the one side and the role of the prophet on the other—a presentation which is the more paradoxical but all the more eloquent because it is not Jeremiah himself but Baruch who complains on behalf of Jeremiah, and Jeremiah is the one who, in the name of Yahweh, answers Baruch and therefore himself in respect of this complaint.

The complaint of Baruch in v. 3 is as follows : " Woe is me now ! for the Lord hath added grief to my sorrow ; I· fainted in my sighing, and I find no rest." It is the whole oppression of Jeremiah himself which is expressed in this outcry, the burden of the mission which he has undertaken and executed alone, the unpopularity and severity of his word, the futility of it, the terrible nature of the happenings which have proved it true, his own helpless participation in these happenings. An endless circle—grief, and sorrow, and fainting in sighing, and no rest ; and it is all caused by Yahweh. This was the situation of the prophet. This was his part in the sin of Israel. Was it not heavier than that of any of the others, even of Zedekiah, who was blinded and led in chains to Babylon ? He and the rest had always been blind, having only a confused and fragmentary awareness of what was happening, hardly realising let alone understanding either themselves or the context in which they acted and suffered. For if they had realised and understood, they would not have been the people they were and everything might have been different. But Jeremiah with his over-sensitive awareness had realised and understood it all from the beginning to the end. He had brought before them his own uncompromising and unhelpful knowledge without being able to alter in the very least either what they were and wanted or its consequences. Even at the end of all his years of conflict, he could not alter the fact that those who had been saved in the catastrophe only appeared to have been saved in order to return—and he himself had to go with them—to the house of bondage and to fall a prey to the darkness of the idolatry of the nations from which they had once been delivered with power by the hand of Yahweh. A circle again—back to the zero point which had once been the bleak point of departure at which the election and calling of God had found his people, or rather made it a people. That this was the case, that he was the witness of it, that he had to make his witness alone and in vain against the movement of this circle, with warnings and threatenings and sorrow and lamentation, this explains the " Woe is me now " into which Baruch broke, as it were, from the very heart of Jeremiah himself. But Baruch speaking for Jeremiah, and even Jeremiah himself with his cry of sorrow, do they not represent the others, all that remarkable people which, amongst other peoples, has a role analogous to that of the prophet, this prophet and all the prophets ? This people had been taken from all the peoples in order that in its particular humanity, which is human like that of all other peoples, it should be the witness of the Word and will and work of God, in order that it should refuse this task and be destroyed in refusing it. The fact that its way is the secret meaning of all that happens to the nations and the world cannot have any other practical meaning than that it was appointed to bring to light in its action the corruption of all men and nations as though it were exclusively its own, to reveal in its despairing self-help that by which they all have lived and live and will live, and the judgment which sooner or later has come and comes and will come on all of them in consequence. Israel-Judah had to bear in some sense typically in its historical existence the sin of man and the ensuing destruction of man. It had to reveal as its fruit the flaming sign of the divine judgment within history as it unfolds in all·the blindness and ignorance and lack of awareness of all other peoples. Do we understand Jeremiah unless we understand that he does not sigh for his own person and in his own name, but in the person and name of his people, representing the human partner elected and called by God ? He does not suffer in the least privately, but under that which is allotted to this people with its election and calling, under the refusal and destruction which is the price of this election and calling. We have to think of him, therefore, not merely as the one who stands magnificently alone in opposition and resistance to this people, but the one who is together with this isolated people, the representative of its election and calling, in solidarity with its being and status as a sinful people, sharing with it—and with a greater severity of suffering than that of any other member—the destruction which has come upon it in consequence of its sin. Jeremiah is the man who with this people suffers all that is threatened, the sword and famine and pestilence, and finally disappears with it into the unknown, because he himself can and will be only one of this people, a man of this people in the truest and fullest sense, because his election and calling as a prophet is nothing other than the election and calling of this people *in nuce*. Hence the impossibility of avoiding it, of escaping his mission. Hence the burning fire in his bones that he cannot bear but must bear. Hence the relentless necessity of his prophetic existence, which is not grounded in his own personal determination, but in the inflexibility of the divine purpose for and with this people. Hence, of course, the distress of his prophetic existence, his futile resistance to it, his sorrow, his continual unrest as the bearer of it. Hence the failure of his work, in which, for all their unlikeness, he is so intimately bound up with and ultimately so like the unfortunate Zedekiah. For how could the man who had to proclaim to the people the failure of their own self-help be himself a man who succeeded in helping himself ?

Yet the answer given by Jeremiah in vv. 4–5—to Baruch, and in Baruch to himself—is as follows : " The Lord saith thus ; Behold, that which I have built will I break down, and that which I have planted I will pluck up, even this whole land. And seekest thou great things for thyself ? seek them not : for, behold, I will bring evil upon all flesh, saith the Lord : but thy life will I give unto thee for a prey in all places whither thou goest." Is this really a word of comfort ? B. Duhm describes it as " a touching funeral oration on all the hopes which the prophet had cherished." As he sees it (p. 382 f.) the life-experience of Jeremiah and the result of his thinking was to see the necessity of a withdrawal of religion from history to inwardness, from the life of the people to the heart of the individual, from the visible to the invisible. This is an explanation which hardly seems to be tenable, because it uses categories in which, from all that we know, neither Jeremiah himself nor the tradition ever thought, and because it quite definitely cannot be read out of this answer to Baruch. But Duhm is perhaps right when he points out that the comfort of this saying is of a peculiar nature, having nothing whatever to do with the raising of what we usually call " hope." The fact which gives rise to the lamentation is not ignored. On the contrary, and this is why it is put here, the full depth and severity of the wound from which the prophet suffers is only now revealed. His grief and sorrow, his " Woe is me now," is expressly set in the great context of the suffering which the people of God as such has to suffer. What had been built is broken down again, what has been planted is torn up again, a work which has been done is undone, and that which is alive and flourishing is given up to death. The saying has reference to the temple built by Solomon at the command of God, which is now destroyed ; to the exaltation of David, which is reversed with the fate of the last of his successors ; to the bringing of the tribes into their land, which is now reversed with their scattering among the nations ; to the exodus from Egypt, which is made as though it had never been with the anxious exodus of the remnant to Egypt. And what the prophet bewails as the unhappy circle of his own existence belongs to the same category. " Seekest thou great things for thyself ? seek them not." The pulling down of what was built and the pulling up of what was planted was the necessary consequence of the self-help in which

Israel-Judah had failed to understand the meaning of that building and planting. Was Jeremiah anything other than the mouth elected by God of the people elected by God, the mouth through which the people pronounced against itself the divine sentence ? Could he separate himself from the people when the sentence was executed ? If he had wanted great things for himself, perhaps a reward for his faithfulness, would he not have taken the first step on the way of sin which had led the people to destruction ? Could he desire for himself anything but participation in the righteousness of God which really exalted this people, and therefore in the divine judgment, a participation which meant the destruction of his own prophetic existence ? " Seek them not " : Jeremiah did not seek them. The saying of Yahweh set him where his people stood, or rather where his people was beaten down, under the judgment of that necessary pulling down and rooting up. It taught him—and this was what made him a prophet of this people—to bow to the judgment to which the people itself would not bow until the very last, and therefore to vindicate in his existence the righteousness of God and the meaning of the election and calling of His people. But this direction has another dimension. And B. Duhm draws attention to it with his paraphrase : " Yahweh Himself suffers. Why then should man complain that he suffers ? " It is not simply a fate working itself out in the ordinary course of events that Israel-Judah and its representative Jeremiah has to lament, and that Yahweh, who has no part in it, has to alleviate with help and comfort. It is the fact that God Himself pulls down what He Himself has built; that He Himself pulls up what He Himself has planted. This is the secret of the evil which overtakes Israel-Judah and the prophet who is so inextricably bound up with it. God Himself has bound Himself to this people. His own truth and glory and power are, in a sense, invested in its existence. His love and grace and faithfulness were the element by which it lived. His cause was at stake in that of this tiny confederation. His covenant with them was the basis of their covenant with one another. Against Him and His goodness the people of this covenant had transgressed. They had offended Him. They had brought to Him dishonour and trouble. They had renounced His service. And if no other answer could be given than this great reversal of all that had been done previously, who was the first and real sufferer, who was the first to be disturbed and distressed and to suffer ? Not the men of this people, not their king, blinded and in chains, not Jerusalem burned and destroyed, not the dead and the bereaved, not the captives led away to Babylon, but the God of this people heaping to Himself sorrow on sorrow, the God who had always been gracious and was still gracious and could be gracious only in this way, only in judgment. Not even Jeremiah. " Seekest thou great things for thyself ? seek them not." What made him the prophet of God, who all his life had to proclaim this pulling down and rooting up in his prophetic word, who had therefore to stand in isolation from the rest of his people, seeking evil for it and not good, was simply the fact that he did not seek anything for himself, that he could not and would not demand anything other or better for himself than that he should share the sorrow of his people and God's people. To be in isolation once again ? No—and this is what makes the word a word of comfort—to share the sorrow of God and therefore truly to share the sorrow of his people. And to do so in such a way—as the conclusion of the saying has it—that when the evil which has been deserved comes upon all flesh—the horizon is now extended on the human plane—and when this evil not only comes upon him, but comes especially upon him as the elect prophet of the elect people, " his life will be given him for a prey in all places whither he goes." He cannot take it to himself That would be the self-help which as the one he is he cannot seek. The Israel-Judah which tried to take it to itself has perished. The prophets who induced it to do so and tried to hold out the prospect of divine help were false prophets. But God gives his life as a prey to the true prophet, and in his person to the people which He has elected and called and which can now know His grace only as judgment, and in virtue of the witness of this people and its prophets to all flesh, whom He can only withstand and on whom He can only bring evil—Himself the first to suffer—as it goes on its ways of self-help and therefore of pride and therefore of sin. But when in the final words of the saying we see the comfort of it as a positive promise, we have already left the sphere of man's sin, which is our present concern, and peeped into that of God's justification, on that other page of the great book of God which we have not yet turned.

3. THE FALL OF MAN

The second section was an answer to the question what the sin of man is. We must now answer the question who and what the man is who commits sin—man in his properties as a sinner, man under the definition under which he brings himself as such, man in the character which is proper to him as such, the man of sin.

Here, too, our answer must derive from the christological insight which is normative for the whole context. It must be with reference to Jesus Christ in whom it came to pass, and in whom by virtue of His resurrection from the dead it is plain and clear and true, that God the Lord became a servant for us, humbling Himself for the reconciliation of the world with Himself. In this light the comprehensive answer is necessarily that the man of sin is fallen man, fallen to the place where God who does not and cannot fall has humbled Himself for him in Jesus Christ. He is the man who exists in the depths where God visits him in Jesus Christ and takes His place with him. He is that which God became in Jesus Christ to be his Saviour—a servant, a slave, not in the freedom of God but as a miserable captive, not in the glory in which God became and was a servant, but in absolute need and unlimited shame.

The fall of man. The term corresponds exactly to what we have learned to know as the essence of sin—the pride of man. " Pride goes before a fall." The proverb is true. But we have to be more precise than that. The fall of man comes in and with the pride of man. He falls in exalting himself where he ought not to try to exalt himself, where, according to the grace of God, he might in humility be freely and truly man. He dies because he tries to take to himself a life which if he would thankfully receive it he might enjoy in peace. This was brought drastically to our notice, in the last section by our Old Testament illustrations of the different forms of human pride, and by the passage in Gen. 3, to which we made constant reference, and the content of which has always been regarded as the story of the fall of man, his entry into the *status corruptionis*.

We will begin by stating that in all that we have to say at this point we cannot and must not deviate at any cost from the revelation or Word of God. Just as we cannot see and understand and recognise and confess for ourselves that we have sinned and continue to sin in pride, so we cannot see and understand for ourselves that in so doing we have fallen and that we have to exist incontrovertibly and irrevocably in the depths as servants and slaves and captives. None of the depths of our being which we can accept and experience and measure for ourselves is the depth of the fall of man. What' we have to say of man in relation to the fall will always appear to be a dismal and depressing exaggeration when compared with the self-knowledge which man can attain for himself. If we start' with ourselves we can never say the things which have to be said. We will necessarily reject them.

The theology of the Enlightenment did not begin, as it is often shown to begin, with a criticism of trinitarian and christological teaching, or of the miracles of the Bible, or of the biblical picture of the world, or of the supranaturalism of the redeeming event attested in the Bible. Its starting-point in the " rational orthodoxy " which was conservative in all these matters was a readoption of the humanistic, Arminian, Socinian and finally the acknowledged Roman Catholic rejection of what were supposed to be the too stringent assertions of the Reformers concerning the fall of man—the indissolubility of human guilt, the radical enslavement of man to sin, the *servum arbitrium*. Originally and properly enlightenment means the enlightenment that things are not quite so bad with man himself. But if we cannot, and will not, see and understand in this respect, we will necessarily be blind in other respects. And there was an inability and refusal to see and understand in this respect because—without any real sense of what was being done or to what it would necessarily lead—a natural self-understanding of man was adopted as the norm of Christian thinking. In the sphere of this understanding the assertions could not, and never can, be made.

The self-understanding in which the man of sin knows himself as such and therefore as fallen man can only be the understanding of the man who hears and believes the Word of God, of the man who learns and accepts God's judgment concerning him and is ready to see and understand himself in the light of this judgment. No prior understanding attained in any other way can serve as a gateway or bridge to this understanding. And by the Word and judgment of God we do not mean a revealed theory of supernatural origin and content about man, but the address and claim of God concretely attested to him, the *viva vox evangelii* which comes to him, the Gospel of the Lord who in his place became a servant, who humbled Himself for him. The one who hears the *viva vox* of the Gospel is the only man who sees and understands this matter. He is the one who is instructed concerning himself. As far as concerns himself, he is the one who knows what instruction we have to give here. What we say here is to be measured by whether or not it corresponds to the instruction given to this man. And to all objections to what we have to say here we must address the counter-question whether the one who raises them is thinking and speaking from the knowledge of the man who hears and receives the Word of God, or on some other ground. In so far as he does think and speak on any other ground his competence to think and speak on this matter will be open to question.

At this point we may refer to some sentences of Calvin (*Inst.* II, 1, 3) in which he formulates this basic rule and makes a provisional survey of what has to be said when we observe this rule. According to the judgment of the flesh, writes Calvin, a man may well think that he knows himself to be upright (*probe*) when, with confidence in his own judgment and virtue, he reaches the point where he can take courage and stir himself up to the fulfilment of his duties, and declaring war upon his failings seek with all his power to strive after that which is beautiful and proper (*pulchrum et honestum*). *Qui autem se ad amussim divini iudicii inspicit et examinat, nihil reperit, quod animum ad bonam fiduciam erigat; ac quo penitius se excussit, eo magis deiicitur, donec omni fiducia prorsus abdicatus, nihil sibi ad vitam recte instituendam relinquit.* The essence of the fall, the situation of man in the *status corruptionis*, is simply this, that man's *fiducia* in himself is quite futile. But man can say this to himself only when it is first said concerning him as the judgment of God.

But there is a second preliminary observation which we have to make on the term fall, and it is one which not only makes it more precise but also restricts it. It restricts it, for, however we may describe the fallen being of man, we cannot say that man is fallen completely away from God, in the sense that he is lost to Him or that he has perished. It is true that the fall of man means that in his being there has opened up the gulf or vacuum of nothingness in the world which God created good. This is to the sorrow and dishonour of God, for with this nothingness He Himself has nothing to do·according to His positive will. It is also true that the being of fallen man has become, as it were, the edge of this gulf, indicating clearly and painfully enough the dreadful reality of chaos. It is clear that on this account, as itself the edge of this gulf, it is a being which is most seriously and severely threatened and burdened and disturbed and destroyed, a corrupt being. We shall have to say something about this—if not all that has to be said—in our present context. But it is not true that man has fallen right into the gulf and therefore out of the sphere of the positive will of God, that he has become nothing, and therefore does not exist before God. In the absurd way which is all that is possible in this connexion, man is able to be the edge of this gulf, and therefore relatively, although not absolutely and ontologically, godless. But he cannot really escape God. His godlessness may be very strong, but it cannot make God a " manless " God. Man in his fall cannot cease to be the creature and covenant-partner of God. He could not create himself and he cannot alter or undo his creation, either for good or fortunately for evil. He cannot make himself another being or destroy the being that he is. Again, he has not ordained and established the covenant, and it is not for him to dissolve it. We should be abandoning our starting-point, the knowledge in the light of which we have to think of man, if we were to try to ascribe to man an absolute and ontological godlessness. Man has not fallen lower than the depth to which God humbled Himself for him in Jesus Christ. But God in Jesus Christ did not become a devil or nothingness. His Word became flesh, participating in our corrupted being. But corruption does not mean the changing of man into another being, like the transformation of the fairy-tale prince into an evil and horrible beast. Let alone does it mean the annihilation of his existence. If this were the case the atonement would be pointless. Even the lost sheep remains in the sphere of the shepherd who seeks, even the lost coin in that of the woman who seeks, even the lost son feeding with the swine in the same world as the distant house of his father. Fallen man is dead. But for the miracle of his awakening from the dead, which he needs, and in which his reconciliation with God consists, it is necessary that he should still be there as a corpse, a human corpse. With the *Formula of Concord* we can call him *truncus et lapis* in order to describe his whole incapacity to help and save himself, but this does not mean that he has actually become wood and stone, and that he is no longer a man or present as a man. And although the covenant of God with man has been totally, and as far as man is concerned irremediably, broken by the fall of man, yet it has not been reversed or removed or destroyed as the omnipotent work of the grace of God. As eternally ordained and unalterably established by God, it is faithfully kept and restored and renewed by Him with reference to fallen man as God turns to him. God does not allow Himself to be diverted by the sin of man from addressing His Yes to him. He carries through His original Yes by reconciling him to Himself. It is a Yes which contains a strong and penetrating rejection of his sin and of his being as it has fallen through sin. It is the Yes of His grace judging man, the Yes of His sentence of death and its execution. But it is still His Yes, His covenant will which has not been overthrown and reversed by the fall and sin of man. It is the Yes which He carries through by Himself suffering through man and with man and for man, by taking to Himself the death of man. But He takes it to Himself in order to overcome it, in order to demonstrate His life as God by dying as man. To speak of an ontological godlessness of fallen man, of a sinfulness which has become the substance of man, of fallen man as an image of the devil, as Flacius Illyricus did, necessarily involves the belief that the living God who is in covenant with man and has become one with him has not merely suffered death but fallen a prey to it. But He has not fallen a prey to it. In taking it to Himself, in suffering it with and for us men in the person of His Son, He has conquered and destroyed it.

In this matter particularly we do want to take seriously the stringent insights of the Reformation, but if we are going to do so in a meaningful way we must not press them too far. Otherwise in an over-anxiety to say too much we shall in fact be saying too little, not merely abandoning the point from which we have to think and speak, but making it

16

impossible for us to think and say the serious things which have to be thought and said. The restriction that we have to establish does not really weaken but gives a supreme precision and point to the insight which we are developing. The terrible thing about the situation in which man finds himself as the one who commits sin, that which distinguishes the need and shame of his fallen being from a fate which has overtaken him, a fate which may be most severe, but which in all its severity has to be and can be borne, is simply the fact that as a sinner man has not in any way escaped from the sphere of the living God, of His Yes, of His gracious will, that he has not escaped from the relationship of Creator and creature and therefore from the covenant which God has instituted between Himself and man. He can fall ; he can fall away from God. But he cannot escape God, as Ps. 139$^{1-12}$ tells us in a startling way. For the man whom God has created and with whom He covenants, there is no corner in which he does not exist for God, in which he is not enclosed by the hand of God behind and before. There is no heaven or hell in which he is out of the reach of God's Spirit or away from His countenance. There is no change or destruction in which his being before God and co-existence with Him are brought to an end and he escapes that which they always mean for him. It would be an escape if in consequence of change or destruction he could no longer hear God or be known and reached by Him, having nothing further to do with Him. His fallen being would then be terrible, but it would be supportable. It would even have the character of a certain relief or redemption, as when a schoolboy is expelled for invincible ignorance or misconduct. But in the relation between God and man there is no question of an expulsion which is supportable in this way and even brings relief and redemption. It is in God's sphere that man sins and in God's sphere therefore he must be the one who sins, presupposing the full authority of the Word of God. The Word of God is always the judgment of man, and the truth of it is the truth of his being even in the *status corruptionis*. It is the Word of God which decides what he is and what he is not, what he can do and what he cannot do, what he will be and what he will not be. Nothing is subtracted from what according to this Word is the will of God and therefore the determination of man, the obedience demanded from man. And man himself is none other than the one he always was in relation to God, sharing the same creaturely being and capacity. The only difference is that under the authority of the Word of God and in possession of his human capacity he is condemned to exist before God as the one who resists, in an overthrowal of the covenant-relationship and therefore in an overthrowal of his relationship as a creature to the Creator. God still says Yes to him, but this now means that because he does not hear it he will not thankfully rejoice in it but can only hear the Yes as a destructive No. God can indeed cause His Yes to be heard in this way, and if man will not hear it as Yes He makes it to be heard as a No. Man still belongs to God, but this now means that in resisting God he is hurt as only God can hurt him, the God to whom man will not belong, whom man thinks that he can defy. The grace of God is still turned to man, but this now means that it is non-grace, wrath and judgment to the one who despises and hates it and will not live by it. God is his friend, but this means that He must be the enemy of the one who acts as though He were an enemy. He can still be a human creature before God with all the capacities and powers which belong to a man, but this means that he has continually to live in the disobedience and turning from God in which he has willed to exercise his capacities, in the service of the revolt against God in which he has willed to engage, so that in his relationship with God he is thrown back wholly upon himself and delivered up to his own impotence. God still claims him, but this means that in so far as God does this, in the being claimed which could be his true glory, his insufficiency towards God and therefore his shame are now manifested, with no possibility of excuse for his resistance or satisfaction at his insufficiency. God is still the Lord of his being and of that of the whole world, so that although man may wish to throw Him off he cannot do so ; but in the *status corruptionis* this means that in place of the faith and obedience in which man might live at peace with God there has entered the exciting but unprofitable dialectic of what we call " religion " as the supposed exaltation of the soul to God, the setting up and worshipping of images of His supposed being and essence ; religion as the action of sinful man which will inevitably involve flagrant continuations and confirmations and repetitions of his unfaithfulness and therefore sheer self-contradictions, with the continual rise and influence of the alternatives of doubt and scepticism and atheism ; religion as a matter on which men separate and fight more perhaps than any other. The religious relationship of man to God which is the inevitable consequence of his sin is a degenerate form of the covenant-relationship, the relationship between the Creator and the creature. It is the empty and deeply problematical shell of that relationship. But as such it is a confirmation that that relationship has not been destroyed by God, that God will not be mocked, that even forgetful man will not be able to forget Him. Man may escape faith and obedience, but he cannot escape—and this is what reveals the judgment under which he stands—this their surrogate. He has to bear witness to the Word of God and seal the fact that he cannot be without God in this way, in the form of religion, and therefore without any basis or confirmation in the divine subject, in conflict with that subject and therefore in every possible aberration (this is the place for a really meaningful exegesis of Rom. $1^{19f.}$). The situation of fallen man is, therefore, that in his fall there can be no question of a falling out of the sphere of the will and work of God. He can neither live with God nor can he die before Him. He is continually bound to

Him, but doomed to pass away and perish as the one who is bound to Him. This is what makes his situation so serious, and it is only in this light that we can see how very serious it is. For this reason we must not try to press too far this aspect of the description of the fall.

We now come to the point, and looking into the mirror of the obedience of the Son of God we ask plainly what is the appearance of the man to whom God stooped in Jesus Christ as to man fallen in sin, the man at whose side He ranged Himself, accepting solidarity with him, making Himself like him? What is the situation in which He placed Himself? What is the burden which He did not have to bear but which He has freely taken to Himself and borne and victoriously borne away? What is the *status corruptionis* which is set aside by His intervention but cannot be set aside except by His intervention? Our corruption cannot be any different, it cannot be greater and it cannot be less than that on account of which, and to overcome which, He suffered and died for us on the cross. What is this corruption of ours which is shown to us by Him as the Saviour who is as such the living Word of God to us?

Our first proposition in answer to this question is that in so far as this Word is the word of divine forgiveness addressed to man, the corruption from which it calls and takes him consists in the fact that man is God's debtor. He is a debtor who cannot pay. God has to excuse him. He does not expect from him any restitution or payment. He sees that he is not in any position to offer it. Indeed, when we consider what the debt is, we see that no other reaction to it is adequate but the divine forgiveness. Or, to put it positively, only the divine forgiveness is an adequate payment and restitution of the debt of man. But for all the divine sovereignty in which God forgives, He does not do so without any ground or basis, accidentally or arbitrarily. Nor does He forgive man in a good nature which treats the sin of man lightly. Nor does He forgive man simply because he is not in a position to make payment or restitution. God forgives man—and here we have to anticipate because it is a matter of the righteousness of God and the justification of man—primarily and decisively because His forgiveness alone is the restitution of the right which has been broken by the sin of man and the order which has been disrupted by His guilt. It is in this light that we have to measure the debt or guilt of sinful man.

Debt or guilt (ὀφείλημα, *debitum*) is the repudiation of an obligation, the failure to keep a promise, in which the offending party does an injury to the one to whom he is pledged, disturbing the relationship between them. The debtor is responsible both for his failure and repudiation, and also for the injury which is done to the other and the consequent disturbance in their mutual relationship. The sin of human pride in the relationship of man with God is a failure and repudiation of this kind, and as such it is the guilt or debt of man. He is not forced to commit this sin. As we have seen, there is no reason for it.

All that we can say is that he does commit it. It is his work, and he is responsible for it, and for the failure involved. For it is primarily a failure—a non-fulfilment of the obligation or commitment laid upon man in his relationship with God. The humility of faith and obedience demanded of man as the creature and covenant-partner of God is completely crowded out by its disorderly opposite. The freedom for which God has ordained man is not used. That for which God has made man capable and which He might expect of him is not forthcoming. There opens up that gulf, that vacuum, in the creation of God, not in heaven, not in the sphere of the stars and plants and beasts, but in the being of man, which God created good, perfectly good, like everything else. In his pride man thought that he could add something, and all that he has done is to take away. This is his repudiation, his failure. And it is in relation to God that he is in arrears with his non-fulfilment of that to which he was obliged and committed. It is the purpose and plan of God which he crosses, the will of God which he withstands, the glory of God which he diminishes. It is God who suffers through the failure which comes with human pride. God is too intimately bound up with man for Him not to be affected by man's repudiation and failure, for Him not to be genuinely disturbed and hurt and wounded by it. And man and man alone is responsible. It is he who does despite to God, who offends and disturbs Him. And it is he who is responsible for the involved marring and disturbing, indeed the obscuring and confusing of the relationship between God and himself, for the fact that God can no longer be to him the One He could be as his Creator and Lord, that the divine Yes to him must now be concealed in a No, that His love must have the character of a consuming fire. It is he who is responsible for the further change in his thinking about God and his attitude to Him and his whole life in the divine sphere which is the necessary consequence of this first change. It is he who is responsible for the fact that instead of being at peace with God the very best or worst that he can now hope for is the very problematical thing which he calls the religious life. It is he who is responsible for the general disturbance in the relationship between God and creation, the opening up of that gulf or vacuum, the presence of chaos within the good creation of God. By his repudiation and failure he has in a sense opened up the sluices to all this. This is the guilt or debt of man described in the most general terms.

The way in which it is put by Anselm of Canterbury (*Cur Deus homo*, I, 11, 13, 14) is very accurate and complete. I will refer to it here only in very summary form. Man as man is bound *Deo reddere quod debet*. This *debitum* consists in *rectitudo voluntatis*, the subjection of his will to the will of God. This subjection is the one great honour which he can render to God and which he is indeed committed to render to Him as man. Why this? Because it is the source and basis of all the works which are pleasing to God, and therefore it is in itself the attitude which is pleasing to God. If man does not give it, he robs God of that *quod suum est.* In so doing he withholds from God the one and total thing which he owes to Him, and that is *peccare.* He fails in relation to God, and as long as he is unable to make restitution he is *in culpa.* He has dishonoured God. The situation to which this gives rise is one which is quite untenable. It is objectively intolerable : *nihil minus tolerandum in rerum ordine, quam ut creatura creatori debitum honorem auferat et non solvat, quod aufert.* A reaction of some kind is necessary to overcome it. For *Deum impossibile est, honorem suum perdere.*

But we must inquire into this rather more closely. We have seen that the reaction by which God overcomes the situation is that of forgiveness, that He acts and reveals Himself as the God who forgives us our sins by giving up His Son in our place. This decides the fact, not only that we are His debtors, but also that we are incapable of making the reaction ourselves, that we are debtors who cannot pay, that His forgiveness is the only adequate and relevant and effective work in which this reaction can be and is, in fact, made. His forgiveness makes good our repudiation and failure and thus overcomes the hurt that we do to God, and the disturbance of the relationship between Himself and us, and the disturbance of the general relationship between the Creator and creation. His forgiveness repels chaos, and closes the gulf, and ensures that the will of God will be done on earth as it is in heaven. What, then, is the guilt of man in the light of the fact that God encounters him in this way, as the One who pardons his sin ? in the light of the fact that the God to whom man is indebted is the One whose wisdom corresponds to this pardon and who acts in righteousness in this way ?

The very fact that we put these questions means that our way has diverged from that of Anselm. Anselm rightly concluded the account quoted with the statement that the disturbance cannot be allowed to continue, that it has to be followed by some action which radically reverses it. For : *non decet Deum aliquid inordinatum in suo regno dimittere* (I, 12). On this ground he makes the remarkable assertion that it is not worthy of God to forgive man his sin *sola misericordia,* and therefore purely and absolutely and unconditionally. The divine forgiveness has to be thought of as conditioned by a prior satisfaction for the hurt done to the divine glory, by the restitution of that which man has stolen from God. Anselm himself raised the objection that there seems to be a contradiction in saying that a free forgiveness is unworthy of God when He demands that we should forgive those who sin against us *omnino,* purely, absolutely and unconditionally. But he thinks he can answer this difficulty by saying that God demands this from us because it is not for us but for God Himself to exact retribution. He raises a second objection, whether the way in which God wills to be merciful can be measured by any other standard than that of His own free will which because it is His is righteous of itself. But he thinks he can overcome this by saying that the freedom of God is inwardly conditioned by that *quod expedit aut quod decet, nec benignitas dicenda est, quae aliquid Deo indecens operatur.* A god who willed to lie would not be God. Nor would a god who willed to forgive without the prior fulfilment of this condition. From this necessity of the fulfilment of the condition of the divine forgiveness—a task for which man is not equal—Anselm deduced the necessity of the incarnation of God.

To this view—in addition to the objections which Anselm himself raised and gave a not very adequate answer—we have to address the following questions

Is the incarnation of God, which is the goal of the whole sequence of Anselm's thought, really no more than the fulfilment of a prior condition which enables God to forgive in a manner worthy of Himself ? Is it not itself the real accomplishment of His pure, absolute and unconditional forgiveness, His forgiveness *sola misericordia* ? Is Jesus Christ only the possibility and not rather the full actuality of the grace of God ? Is His intervention for us sinners anything other or less than the divine forgiveness itself ? And what does this forgiveness lack in order to be effective if it has taken place in Him ?

Again : Why should not this pure and free forgiveness which God has accomplished in His incarnation itself be His saving reaction to the sin and guilt of man, the restitution of that which has been stolen from Him, the satisfaction for the hurt done to His honour, the forceful overcoming of the consequent disturbance of the relationship between Himself and man ? Why should there not take place in this forgiveness the one and entire doing of the will of God on earth as it is done in heaven ? Why should not this forgiveness be the action of His perfect righteousness as well as that of His pure mercy, and therefore supremely worthy of God ? What right have we to construe the term forgiveness so weakly that it has the sense only of a kind of divine overlooking and excusing, having to be conditioned before it can be accepted as a serious divine action ? Is there any event more serious or incisive or effective than that in which God forgives man all his sins ? And does not the recognition of the divine decision in this event depend upon the fact that it is understood as pure and free forgiveness ?

Finally : Where is the recognition of the greatness of the guilt of man, and the incapacity of man to liberate himself from it, if the pure and free mercy of the unconditional divine forgiveness is not the act of his real liberation ? What is it that constitutes the greatness of the guilt of man, and his incapacity to rid himself of it, more than a mere assertion ? All that Anselm could say of this in the well-known chap. 20 of his treatise is that the obligation of man to God is so great that even the smallest sin is a dreadful thing which he cannot allow himself even to win the whole world or countless worlds. *Tanti ponderis* is sin. That is well and truly said. But Anselm could not get any further than this estimation of an immeasurable *quantitas peccati* along the chosen path of a formal balancing of the demand of God against the obligation of man. The infinite quantity of the guilt of man and man's incapacity to set it aside derive from the quality of it. The dreadful nature of the transgression committed by sinful man derives from the character of the obligation which he has broken. But how are we to see the quality of human guilt and the character of human obligation except in the light of the fact that God's answer and reaction is simply and unequivocally His forgiveness in sheer mercy ?

It is clear that the God who in sheer mercy encounters the man who has become His debtor, as the God who forgives him his sin, is the God who, without being untrue to Himself but supremely true, is gracious to man, because first He is gracious in Himself, in His own inward being, and that as such He is almighty and holy and righteous, the Creator of heaven and earth, the Lord of His covenant with man. This God, and not another ! And this God who is the same in every part of His being is the God attested in Holy Scripture, and decisively with the witness of His appearance and action in the manifestation and revelation of His own Son amongst fallen men, with the witness, therefore, that where sin took the upper hand His grace did not cease or retire, but overflowed in the form of avenging righteousness, showing itself to be super-abounding (Rom. 5[20]), so that in face of this opposition His forgiveness was His iron sceptre, His weapon, His sword of justice. This God, the God who judges in this way, is God alone, in His unchanging being and essence. The character of man's obligation and commitment to Him corresponds to this being and essence. Man is not merely subject to Him formally as the less to the greater, the finite to the infinite, the limited to the free. That is all true, but as the relationship of man to the living God it is true only with a very definite content—that the freedom and infinitude and greatness of the God who binds man to Himself is that of the grace which He addresses to him, and that the limitation and finitude and littleness of man and therefore His subjection is that of the one who can rejoice in the fact that without any co-operation of his own, in a way which is unmerited and incomprehensible, he is the object of this divine address. Why is it that man is under this obligation and commitment? Obviously only in order that he may accept this address, and exist in the freedom and joy and contentment which correspond to it, and be thankful. " My yoke is easy, and my burden light " (Mt. 11[30]). It does not involve any exorbitant demand. The demand has the character of a permission. God does not ask of man that he should be something different, but simply that he should be what he is, the man who is loved by Him, that he should freely confess himself the one to whom God has already freely addressed Himself. There is no need for terror at the greatness and remoteness and majesty of God. There is no sense in man trying to evade Him on the ground that his being is too unlike the divine being. For he does not have to seek and create a relationship to this being who is, in fact, very unlike him. The relationship is there already, open and self-evident, because it has been created by this One who is unlike him. It is the ground on which he can at once stand, the air which he can at once breathe without any effort or skill of his own. There is not even the shadow of a reason or excuse for pride. He does not need pride. It does not belong to his nature. Far from humility involving discouragement or shame or humiliation, it is in humility that he can and must be of good courage, as a king among all God's creatures. How can he ever attain anything higher than that God should be gracious to him and he should accept it?

But he becomes and is guilty to the extent that he transgresses this relationship and resists this God, diminishing His glory and disrupting His order. It is this which makes his pride so absurd and unpardonable, giving to it its character as nothingness. In the light of this it is clear that when the man of sin sees himself as such he can only be filled with terror, fearing the worst for himself, like someone who has entered on a slope which falls away too steeply for him. In the light of this we can and must say that even for the whole world we ought not to take the slightest step in this direction, that even on ·

the most relevant or weighty pretext we ought not to think a first thought in this direction, and that every step or thought made in this direction is a transgression that we cannot make good. And the Word of God does not accuse man merely of the individual thought or word or act, but convicts him because he lives his whole life on the basis of this pride, finding all his strength in it from first to last, in great things and in small. It convicts him that in his existence as man he lives and moves and has his being in this corruption of his nature which is good, in this breach of the covenant which God has made with him. Always and everywhere he is guilty of responding to the grace of God, not with a corresponding thankfulness, but in one or many forms of his wretched pride. He is the one who expresses himself in the act or acts of pride, and therefore he will always express and reveal himself in this way. We will come to this in our second proposition. But to show that man is inexcusably guilty of any one of his individual acts of pride is enough. The order in which he stands and exists is the order of the grace of God. This means that there is no reason or cause for any such act. When he commits it, he disrupts this order and places himself in the void, in nothingness, where he would inevitably perish were it not that the order still avails for him in spite of his transgression, were it not that God still restores and maintains it in his favour even as the order which he has disrupted.

We must now consider especially the reach of human guilt. When man is too proud to be the one who is loved by God, not confessing in humility the God who elects him and is gracious to him, then the guilt which he contracts means that he has placed himself under the divine judgment, under the burden of the No of God which corresponds to His Yes. He has contradicted the good will of God for him, and therefore he has to bear the fact that the same good will of God now contradicts him. This contradiction of arrogantly contradicting man by the good will of God is the wrath of God. To put it in fundamental and general terms, it is the unwillingness of God for everything that He did not and does not and will not will—the world of chaos, that which is not. It is the lordship of God on the left hand. And in particular it is the form of His love for man which that love must assume when it is ignored and disparaged and despised by man. It is the threat of divine rejection into the shadow of which man moves when he sins and becomes guilty, which he evokes when in his misery and pride he sets himself in contradiction to the good will of God. Man cannot alter by anything that he does what God is and wills in Himself. But it is inevitable that to the man who has become guilty before God, but who has not fallen from Him and cannot escape Him, God should appear as an enemy when He encounters him, that everything that God is for him should now be directed against him, that his whole being, the order of life which God has established and appointed, the good things which God has done and still does for him, should all openly or secretly become to him a burden and grief and embarrassment. It belongs to the freedom in which God is gracious to man that He cannot appear to man and encounter him as the One He is, when on the side of man the freedom to confess Him as the One He is has been senselessly abandoned and lost. In these circumstances God necessarily appears to him and encounters him in the alien form of a wrathful God.

The critics of the term "wrath of God" and especially A. Ritschl (*Rechtf. u. Vers.*, Vol. II, § 16 f.) were quite wrong when they said that "wrath" is not a quality or activity or attitude which can be explained in the light of God's being, or brought into harmony with His love and grace. In reply to this criticism we have to say plainly that the grace of God would not be grace if it were separated from the holiness in which God causes only His own and therefore His good will to prevail and be done, holding aloof from and opposing everything that is contrary to it, judging and excluding and destroying everything that resists it. And grace would not be free grace if it were bound to any single form of its appearance and manifestation, if God always had to show Himself monotonously as "love," or what we think of as love, if He were not permitted to negate that which has to be negated, if He could not conceal Himself when He is resisted, revealing His grace only in the alien form of unwillingness and wrath. Above all, grace would not be grace, the serious and effective address of God to man, the effective establishment of fellowship with him, if God did not oppose man's opposition to Himself, if He left man to go his own way unaccused and uncondemned and unpunished, if He ignored the miserable pride of man, if the man of sin had nothing to fear from Him, if it were not a fearful thing to fall into His hands (Heb. 12[29]). That His grace would not be grace without His judgment is just as true as the supposed opposite with which it is indissolubly connected, that there is no holiness of God which can be separated from His grace, and therefore no wrath of God—this is something which, unfortunately, A. Ritschl did not even remotely understand—that can be anything other than the redemptive fire of His love, which has its final and proper work in the fact that for our sake, for the sake of man fallen in sin and guilt, He did not spare His only Son.

And now—from the same point of departure—we can see why man himself is not in any position to make payment or restitution for his debt, that he cannot therefore escape the wrath of God, moving from this place in the shadow of the threatened rejection, or bringing about his reconciliation with God by any enterprise that he can conceive or execute. He has transgressed the grace of God. And the grace of God has become judgment. And he has no control over the grace of God—how else would it be grace ? To try to control it, to look beyond the form of it which judges him, to see it and have it again in its proper form, is simply a repetition of the sin of pride and a magnifying of the arrears in which man finds himself in relation to God. It is the sinister aspect of all religious history that in it men are caught in the act of committing again the very sin from which they are trying to free themselves. God is gracious to man in His freedom ; not because He has to be, not because man has some right or claim, not in a way in which man can control the manner in which He wills to be gracious. If God wills to be gracious in the form of His wrath and judgment—

and He has every reason to be gracious and to reveal the holiness of His grace only in this way—then it is not for man to try to turn the page. He can and must read only that which is set before him, only that which he has to read. There is for him only the one possibility and hope—that of faith in the grace of God in the alien form of judgment. In it—and in this faith the hope and possibility of the petition : " Forgive us our debts " as a pure petition—man will recognise and admit that he cannot turn the page, that he cannot forgive his own debts, that he cannot try to be gracious to himself, not even and least of all with the interest and help of God, because this is simply to renew the offence of which he has made himself guilty.

The conclusion of our discussion brings us back again to the beginning, to the way and work of God by which there is, in fact, brought about that which we ourselves cannot will or execute, the purification of our guilt, the restoration of the order which we have broken, the renewed brightness of the glory that we have obscured : the divine forgiveness. The fact that this is the way and work of God in face of human guilt makes it plain what human guilt is, how severe and great it is. It is plain from the fact that the fulfilment of the divine wrath and judgment, the righteousness of God, consists properly in the fact that in the giving up of His Son He freely and simply and unconditionally forgives us our guilt. For the moment we must simply recognise that any other means of remedying the disorder caused by human sin would be quite inadequate—not merely our own efforts to save ourselves, but even the severest punishment which might come upon us, even the destruction of ourselves and of the whole world. All thoughts of this kind in relation to our guilt and the wrath of God are only too human thoughts which, for all the fearfulness with which they may be invested, will not do justice to the true seriousness of the situation. Even if he were eternally cast into hell, would not man still be the sinner that he is ? What help would this punishment be ? And could the destruction of man and the world reverse the disorder introduced by his existence as the man of sin ? Would it not mean that in this way which is not perhaps so very unacceptable the transgressor would finally escape God ? As is known, there is one religion in which entry into Nirvana is prized as the very essence of redemption. Real order is and can be created only by the grace of God held out even to the man of sin, and in face of the man of sin, in Jesus Christ. It is and can be created only by the forgiveness of God. This reaction is adequate to the seriousness of the situation. The matter is as serious as this, and the situation as impossible as this, when we are found to be sinners against a gracious God. To sin is to do that which only God can put right, only God as He acts and reveals Himself as the gracious God. *Tanti ponderis est peccatum.*

We might say the same thing in some sentences of K. Olevian (*Expos. symb.*, 1576, p. 7, quoted in Heppe, *E.T.*, p. 312) which are very epigrammatic but can hardly be disputed : *Tantum tamque ingens malum est peccatum, ut mereatur aeternam hominis destructionem : immo vero tam ingens malum, ut ne aeterna quidem hominis destructione expietur ; unde sequitur, peccatum esse maius malum aeterna hominis damnatione, cum damnati ne aeternis quidem poenis tantum malum expiare aut superare possint ; denique tantum malum est vel uno peccato maiestatem Dei offendisse, ut minus malum sit omnis omnium creaturarum destructio. Nam ne omnium quidem creaturarum destructio aut redactio in nihilum aequivalens pretium esset expiando unico peccato, quod nonnisi morte Filii Dei expiari possit.*

We now make a second proposition in answer to the question of man's corruption. The fact that Jesus Christ died totally for the reconciliation of every man as such, for the man who exists in this way, means decisively that this corruption is both radical and total. That is to say, it means that the sinful reversal takes place at the basis and centre of the being of man, in his heart ; and that the consequent sinful perversion then extends to the whole of his being without exception.

The living Word of God does not offer man a partial instruction and direction. It either claims him altogether, the man himself, or it is not the living Word of God. For the content of it, the atonement made in Jesus Christ, does not consist in a partial alteration and amelioration of his knowledge and conduct, but in an absolutely comprehensive transforming of his situation, in his total conversion to the God from whom he had turned away in his pride. It is, therefore, the man himself, his heart, and from this centre again the man himself, the whole man, who, apart from what Jesus Christ has done and is for him, is caught in this turning away from God and has to exist as turned away from Him. This is the corruption—in the unity of his activity and being—in which God finds and sees him and takes up his cause and speaks to him. Man is what he does. And he does what he is. And in the circle of his being and activity he lives in this turning away—backwards and forwards from sin to sin.

This does not mean, as we have seen, that he has ceased to be a man. He has not lost—even in part—the good nature which was created by God, to acquire instead another and evil nature. In the many conflicts on this point it has often been stated how far this loss or alteration can go and cannot go—the loss or alteration being made as great as possible on the Augustinian-Reformed side and as little as possible on the Roman Catholic-Neo-Protestant side. But the whole idea is quite untenable. The Bible accuses man as a sinner from head to foot, but it does not dispute to man his full and unchanged humanity, his nature as God created it good, the possession and use of all the faculties which God has given him. He still has his determination for God, his being as the soul of a body, his being in his time. And if it is true (cf. *C.D.*, III, 1, § 41, 2.) that the divine likeness referred to in Gen. 1[27] consists in his fellow-humanity, we cannot even speak of the loss of his divine likeness ; for even as a sinner he has not ceased to be the husband with the wife and the wife with the husband, man as the fellow of all other men and with all other men as fellows. Nor can he step out of the covenant which God has made with him, however much he may want to do so and however much he has deserved to be expelled from it *cum infamia.* The seriousness of his situation is much greater than can be expressed by the idea of a setting aside or damaging of his nature which is good. It consists in the crying contradiction that he sets himself—his being in the integrity of his human nature and his being in covenant with God—in the service of evil, and that he now has to exist in that service. It consists in the fact that even in good things and as a good man he is godless, that in his proper nature he has fallen a victim to nothingness in his pride, that as the elect covenant-partner of God he is threatened with the divine rejection, and therefore with death and destruction. It is a matter of the *corruptio boni* or even *optimi*, and therefore of the *corruptio pessima.* In relation to what man is, and what he does not cease to be even as a sinner, everything is quite different with him. His existence as the man of sin is not a problem which is settled *in peiorem partem*, but one which is constantly raised and answered again *in peiorem partem.* The contradiction with what he is and continues to be even in the service of evil does not cease to cry out or become less strong and penetrating. Nor does his responsibility for what he does and is cease or decline. He is a miserable sinner, it is true, but that does not mean that he is the victim of an overhanging fate. And this being the case, he never has the right either to pity himself or to accept pity from others. He is never excusable in the sight of God. What makes him quite without excuse is that the contradiction in which he lives is not only that of his pride and fall against his being in the integrity of his human nature and his being in the covenant, but also that of the latter against the former ; and it is a contradiction which cannot be silenced. The only thing is that he cannot at one and the same time sell himself and then repent and redeem himself. He cannot resolve the contradiction which he makes and establishes. When he enters into this contradiction he has to be what he does and to do what he is.

We certainly cannot speak of any relic or core of goodness which persists in man in spite of his sin, as those who oppose and weaken the Augustinian-Reformed conception have so often tried to maintain and prove. Man himself in his nature and determination and attitude and capacity as they are still good is not a quantum which is confronted by his sinfulness as a greater or lesser quantum, more or less counterbalancing it according to the optimistic view of Roman Catholic and humanistic theologians, or failing to do so according to the pessimistic view of Augustine and the older Protestantism. What makes the situation so serious is that the one whole man whom God created good, whom He maintains and accompanies and rules in his creatureliness, who is to Him as he was at the very first, whom He does not

cease in the very least to recognise and honour and claim as His
covenant-partner, that this man elected and willed and ordained and
equipped for the service of God has turned away from Him and is
now what he inevitably must be in this turning away—corrupt and
guilty, the enemy of God, since he regards and treats God as his
enemy, the object of His wrath, since he is not willing to be the object
of His grace.

That he is " by nature " a " child of wrath " (Eph. 2³), inclined " by nature "
to hate God and his neighbour (*Heid. Cat. Qu.* 5) means that as the man he was
and is and will be as he derives from God and stands before Him he makes this
turning away from God and brings about his own perversion, in his pride becoming
guilty of this hatred of God and man, and having to exist in this inclination and
bent and perversion, contrary to God and also to himself and his nature, as a
living corpse. We must not try to explain away the dreadful paradox that he
lives out his own death. It is perhaps permissible to speak of the " poisoned "
nature of fallen man as in the *Heid. Cat. Qu.* 7, for as a sinner the man who was
created " good and in the image of God " (*Qu.* 6) is, in fact, a good being who
has been perverted by evil and can to that extent be described as " poisoned."
But in order to put the matter exactly, avoiding that idea of the fatefulness of
man's being in sin—to which even the term " poisoned nature " might give rise
—I would prefer, if we are going to use the word " poison," to describe man as
one who poisons himself in his pride. This is what we do, and in so doing we
are poisoned. It is not a matter of evil, but of the evil man, and of the fact
that man himself is evil.

But how can we derive any idea of a relic from this definition ?
The only relic that we can speak of is that of God's good and gracious
will operative to man and over him—the being of man before God,
as the object of His grace even in the form of judgment. But in so
far as man is always this with reference to God even in and under
His judgment, in so far as we have to do with his being before God,
the term " relic " is far too weak. What he is before God as the object
of His electing grace, he is, not merely partially, but decisively and
properly and altogether. Conversely we have to say of his being before
God, his being as the object of His grace, that as far as man is concerned, in his actions and as his work, it is completely perverted, so that
we cannot think of it as a constant pole in the flux of appearance,
or as a quiet island on which man is finally good and not merely good
in the midst of evil. We are confronted by a contradiction in which
there are no " relics " on either side, because it is a contradiction
which does not consist merely in that of two quantities, but of two
qualitative determinations of the one undivided being of man. We
certainly cannot speak in any sense of a core in man which is not
touched in any way by his badness.

The Word of God—and the atoning work of Jesus Christ as the
Representative of man, of the whole man—brings against man the
accusation that at the very core of his being—the heart, as the Bible
puts it—he is not good but evil, not upright but corrupt, not humble
but proud in one or other of the forms known to us, wanting to be

God and Lord and the judge of good and evil, and his own helper, and therefore hating God and his neighbour.

The " heart " means the centre or basis of his being, the root of " his thoughts and imaginations " (Gen. 6⁵). It means the man himself as an existing subject. If the thoughts and imaginations of his heart are evil, this means that the human subject as such transgresses, ἁμαρτάνει, *peccat*, that he is where he has no business to be but has still gone, that he has trespassed and can only continue to trespass, falling from one form of pride into another.

To use the remarkable expression of Gen. 8²¹, it means that man is evil from his youth. This is explained and sharpened in Ps. 51⁷ : " Behold, I was shapen in iniquity ; and in sin did my mother conceive me." In Jn. 3³ the seeing of the kingdom of God, and in Jn. 3⁵ the entry into that kingdom, is described as something which requires a new birth which comes to man " from above." As against this we are told expressly in v. 6 : " That which is born of the flesh is flesh." The history of the chosen people Israel, especially in the Deuteronomic sections, is presented as an unbroken series of divine acts of grace, in the prophetic interpretation of which the people is constantly called to decide between the way of good and the way of evil, between obedience and disobedience, and therefore between salvation and perdition. But throughout the long course of that history we never see an obedient Israel choosing the way of good and laying hold of salvation. We do not see it even at the dark climax of that history, where we might have expected it as the final goal. Least of all do we see it at the beginning. God was always faithful and His free election was the beginning and origin of this people. In confirmation of His election His hand and help were always over this people even in judgment. It was constantly preserved and redeemed. But from first to last, when was this people ever faithful ? when was it anything but unfaithful and obstinate and rebellious, deviating from His way ?

What does this mean ? It obviously means that in relation to the transgression and therefore the corruption of man there is no time in which man is not a transgressor and therefore guiltless before God. To use the phrase of Kant, he lives by an " evil principle," with a " bias towards evil," in the power of a " radical evil " which shows itself virulent and active in his life, with which in some incomprehensible but actual way he accepts solidarity, with which he is not identical, but to which he commits himself and is committed. He transgresses because he continually derives from the transgression which—against his nature, in a way which is foreign to himself, in flagrant contradiction with himself—he commits in and with the fact that he is. The very fact that he is means that he transgresses : against himself, but by and of himself, denying and forfeiting his freedom, which is a freedom for God and his neighbour and no other ; but as his own act and being, the way to captivity which he himself has gone. There never was a time when he was not proud. He is proud to the very depth of his being. He always was. He was always on that way and at that goal. He was always the one who sold himself. The accusation against him might appear to be disputable in this or that particular —it is not really—but it is quite indisputable in relation to man himself. And it is directed and aimed against man himself. It refers to man himself. He sins, but more than that, he is a sinner. That is why Jesus Christ died for him, not merely to put away this or that sin and offence, but to convert man himself to God. That is why Jesus Christ took his place, to set aside this false beginning and origin in order that he may be born again from above by the Spirit, in order that by that new beginning and origin he may be a new man If this is true, then it is also true that without it, as unreconciled man, he is by his beginning and origin flesh—the old man who always hated God and his neighbour and who was therefore a child of wrath.

This being the case, in the whole sphere of human activities there are no exceptions to the sin and corruption of man. There is no territory which has been spared and where he does not sin, where he is not perverted, where he still maintains the divine order and is therefore guiltless. At every point man is in the wrong and in arrears in relation to God. Because he himself as the subject of these activities is not a good tree, he cannot bring forth good fruit. Because his pride is radical and in principle, it is also total and universal and all-embracing, determining all his thoughts and words and works, his whole inner and hidden life, and his visible external movements and relationships. He is not just partly but altogether " flesh." He does not act in a fleshly way only in certain actions and passions and things done and things not done, but in all of them.

There is, therefore, no " nature-reserve," for among his actions there are none which are neutral or indeterminate in character ; there are no adiaphora in which he can act apart from the question of good and evil, of obedience and disobedience. In a sense, of course, he is always apart, for formally considered, his whole life consists in a series of activations of his human nature which is good as such. But in another sense he is never apart, for in all these activations he continually stands and thinks and speaks and acts in the presence of God and his neighbour. There is no sphere however narrow and insignificant, no time however short, when the grace of God is not over him and with him, and the commandment of God does not confront him in all its clarity and concretion, and demand that he hear and recognise and obey. He is always responsible to it. Neither in great things nor in small are there any matters where he can choose or judge for himself, giving his own answer and not having to select or refuse the answer for which he is elected and ordained and appointed by God, not having to give the answer which corresponds to a sharply defined divine expectation concerning him, that is, a divine demand and commandment concretely addressed to him here and now. There are, in fact, no spheres which are neutral, only spheres of decision ; no hours which are neutral, only hours of decision. Without exception they are all ordained by God and the good nature of man to be spheres and hours of obedience, but, in fact, seeing that the heart of man, the human subject, is evil and not good, they are all spheres and hours of disobedience.

Certainly the forms vary everywhere and every time and with every man, just as the form of the divine commandment which calls man to decision, i.e., summons him to a very definite decision, also varies for the individual and in the life of the individual. The corresponding form of the perversion of human decision and therefore of the sin and guilt of man will not be uniform. With every man, and in the different spheres and periods of the activities of every man, it will be highly individual, so that by human norms and standards and moulds it can be judged only approximately and with great caution. The accuser and judge is not the man himself or his fellowmen, but God who knows the heart. But since the Word of God accuses the heart of every man, that it is an evil and fleshly heart, for all the differentiations and reservations that we have to make in detail, there can be no doubt that in virtue of the centre which is the man himself as corrupter and corrupted, all the decisions of every man in all the spheres and periods of his activities are mistaken decisions, false answers to the questions continually addressed to him, wrong responses to the commandment which challenges him and calls him to freedom. There can be no doubt that he never has any reason to be proud, but only to be ashamed of his achievements and even of his will and thought and imagination. This is true even in relation to what seem to be the activations of his nature as it was created good. It is true even where he himself and others can ascribe to these activations a certain and perhaps a very high perfection. In such circumstances there will be every reason, and basic reason, to give glory to God the Creator. But at every point—and there is no reason why we should not constantly take note of it in detail—we are dealing not merely with any *corruptio*, but with the *corruptio optimi*. And that is what it is—the *corruptio optimi*, the selling and enslavement of the good man and his nature and all the activations of his nature to the service of evil and the work of his own pride.

It is a serious error to regard this as a pessimistic exaggeration. At every moment and in every situation we have to ask soberly and honestly : Who am I, and where do I stand, and what am I doing, and by what am I compelled ? How is it with me ? " Brother, how is it with thine heart ? ", as the ageing Tholuck privately used to ask his students, rather penetratingly, but, rightly understood. very relevantly. And again : At any given moment and in any given situation in my life, how is it with my response to the grace and commandment of God ? How is it with the clarity of my consciousness of my responsibility ? with my continuance in it, with the seriousness of my seeking the will of God, of my asking after that good and well-pleasing and perfect thing which is ascribed and applied to me here and now ? (Rom. 12^2). How is it with my determination to hold to that which I know to be right ? let alone with the adequacy of my knowledge and the corresponding action ? If there is any possibility of regarding as exaggerated the judgment that the whole man in all his actions is a sinner, sinful flesh, and therefore of disputing it, then it can consist only in the fact that we do not see these questions (and who can miss them ?), or that we do not recognise them to be relevant (but who can escape the relevance of any one of them ?), or that we give to them a moralistic turn in order to be able to return an optimistic answer (but there is not one of them which will not constantly evade this interpretation). We have to pay attention to these questions, which all proceed from and return to a single question—that of ourselves before God. But if we give due weight to these questions (or to this one question), then there can be no disputing the assertion of the totality of human sin and guilt. It is not decided in the antithesis between an all too human optimism and and all too human pessimism in our judgment of ourselves. It is decided in the hearing of what God has to say to us concerning ourselves in the Word of His grace.

But if it is decided there, then it is an equally serious error to regard this assertion as calculated to damage the necessary concreteness of the human knowledge of sin, the consciousness of our concrete responsibility, the mind for any further concrete opposition to the evil in us and around us, or even to replace it altogether by a general and sterile resignation in relation to the hope of an existence free from sin and guilt. This is quite impossible, because the assertion itself can be legitimately conceived and spoken only in the very concrete knowledge and responsibility and confrontation of a man who hears the Word of the grace of God and the question it poses ; only as the recognition of the divine sentence and judgment as concretely applied in this Word. But as an expression of this recognition it cannot be resigned, but will always be of itself the very concrete cry : " Deliver us from evil," in which the one who cries does not acquiesce in his corruption but looks for its radical and total removal. Moreover, as a concrete recognition of the divine sentence and judgment the assertion itself is a very concrete confession of the One whose activity is not in vain even where our activity is in vain in the very best of human lives, of the One who helps even where our human self-help can only confirm and increase the evil. Is it not this confession of Him as the rock of our confidence which alone makes necessary this assertion as the confession of our own total and radical sin and guilt ? But if the latter confession has its basis and truth in the former, it cannot be a resigned confession involving hopelessness and passivity. The one who is able and ready to make this confession is, in fact, clinging to the divine mercy. He concedes that he is in the wrong because he concedes that that mercy is in the right. He regards himself as impotent in the face of its omnipotence. He cannot and must not magnify himself because he is confronted with its over-powering glory. He expects nothing from himself, because from it he expects everything. Far from giving way to the weak lassitude of resignation, for the very reason that he waits only and altogether upon the Lord, he will mount up with wings like an eagle—with a power of which the critics of our proposition, both mild and wild, usually do not have even the slightest inkling.

The substance of this second proposition is co-extensive with what the earlier confessions of the Church all called the original sin of every living man consequent upon the fall of the first man. For the moment we will lay aside the question of the fall of the first man and our connexion with it. What is beyond question is that against this background the Early Church did say that the accusation against man in the Word of God is directed against man himself, and himself in the totality of his existence, so that, although it does relate specifically to individual acts, it relates primarily to his life as a whole, to the character which his activity has in his time in the light of its beginning and over the whole extent of it.

The accents can, of course, be differently placed : so differently that even when two sides want to confess the same truth, and there is a willingness to construe the opposite presentation *in meliorem partem*, it is almost impossible for either of them to recognise that truth in the statement of the other ; so differently that this is one of the points where division is inevitable in the Church, both the open division between the Evangelical and " Catholic " Churches and the latent division under which we have to suffer within the Evangelical Church.

On the one hand (1) we can take strictly the actual perversion, the pride of man and of the human heart, regarding the radicalness of his self-contradiction (the denial of his good nature as created and maintained by God) and therefore the radicalness of his corruption as limited only by the reconciling grace of God. This was the view of Augustine and the Reformers, including Melanchthon : *Peccatum originale est nativa propensio et quidam genialis impetus et energia, qua ad peccandum trahimur. . . . Sicut in igni est genuina vis, qua sursum fertur, sicut in magnete est genuina vis, qua ad se ferrum trahit, ita est in homine nativa vis ad peccandum (Loci,* 1521, Kolde, p. 81). Or it may be held that the corruption is much more limited by a relic of the capacity for good, a *potentia oboedentialis* which still remains to man and is seated in his understanding and heart and conscience. This is the popular Catholic and humanistic softening of the doctrine of the radicalness of sin.

Again, (2) the relationship between the evil life of man, *peccatum originale,* and individual acts of evil, *peccata actualia,* may be regarded as one of practical identity. We can quote Melanchthon again to the effect that there is no distinction between them in Scripture. *Est enim et originale peccatum plane actualis quaedam prava cupiditas.* And the sin in *peccata actualia* consists in the *pravus affectus,* the *pravus cordis motus contra legem Dei,* the *curvitas* or *iniquitas* which we call *peccatum originale* (p. 81). This *pravus affectus* determines all man's thoughts and words and works. In some way or other *omnia hominum opera, omnes hominum conatus* are *peccata actualia* (p. 85). There are no good works without the justifying grace of God and faith in it. The whole man is a transgressor, flesh, without the renewing of the Holy Spirit (p. 91 f.). On the other hand, on the popular Catholic and humanistic view, a certain separation may be made between original and actual sin, so that the evil tree may bring forth some fruits which are good or at any rate indifferent, and the totality of the sin and guilt of man is circumscribed.

Our decision in face of this antithesis is not for a moment in doubt. It is not that we are forced into the Reformation view by even the most serious heart-searching that we can and should undertake. For it is not upon any anthropology in itself and as such, but upon the knowledge of the grace of God, upon the understanding of the reconciliation of man with God which has taken place in Jesus Christ, that everything depends. If reconciliation, and therefore the justification of sinful man, consists in the fact that man himself in his totality is unreservedly converted to God, then there can be no reservations with regard to his corruption. In the knowledge of the grace of God which comes to him we have to see and confess that he is radically and totally evil, without qualification. The contrast is one of bitter seriousness. We are not at one with the Catholics and humanists—even those in our own ranks—in the knowledge of Christ, and therefore we cannot be at one with them in this as in so many other matters.

In the Early Church the *peccatum originale* which particularly concerns us here, the sinfulness of the life of man as such, was regarded as *peccatum hereditarium*, hereditary sin. The view was that the sin of the first man was a radical and total determination of all his successors, so that it came to them by propagation (*propagatio*), being passed on to them like a kind of spiritual disease and becoming the presupposition of their own existence. In our third proposition we will return to the connexion between each individual and the first man. But, however we may conceive and express this, there can be no doubt that the idea of a hereditary sin which has come to man by propagation is an extremely unfortunate and mistaken one. It probably arose through an early combination of what Paul says in Rom. 5¹² : that " by one man sin entered into the world, and death by sin, . . . for that (ἐφ' ᾧ)all have sinned," with the verse in Ps. 51⁵ which we have already quoted : " Behold, I was shapen in iniquity ; and in sin did my mother conceive me." Now exegetically there can be no question that the verse in the Psalm is not describing something which actually takes place in the world, forcing man to confess that he is from the very first a transgressor and in a state of sin and guilt ; rather we have here a precise form of the confession itself, an even more radical statement of the " from his youth " of Gen. 8²¹. The verse tells us that there is no time prior to man's transgression : the life of man is transgression from the very first. And the Pauline statement, although it certainly points to the connexion between Adam and all other men, is not referring to an actualisation of that connexion within the world, the propagating and inheriting of the sin of Adam. What place is there here for any idea of the propagation of the human race ? Is it supposed to be sinful in itself, or because of its connexion with sexual sin, the one sin perhaps which is the basis of all others ? Very few thinkers have ever dared to say this. But how can propagation be simply a vehicle by which the sin of an earlier man becomes that of a later ? Can there be any question at all of a vehicle of this kind ?

We cannot avoid a serious critical study of this question. There can be no objection to the Latin expression *peccatum originale* if it is not given this more exact definition. It is indeed quite adequate, telling us that we are dealing with the original and radical and therefore the comprehensive and total act of man, with the imprisonment of his existence in that circle of evil being and evil activity. In this imprisonment God speaks to him and makes Himself his liberator in Jesus Christ. But it is still his *peccatum*, the act in which he makes himself a prisoner and therefore has to be a prisoner. This is the point which is obscured by the term hereditary sin.[1] What I do as the one who receives an inheritance is something that I cannot refuse to do, since I am not asked concerning my willingness to accept it. It is only in a very loose sense that it can be regarded as my own act. It is my fate which I may acknowledge but for which I cannot acknowledge or regard myself responsible. And yet it is supposed to be my determination for evil, the corrupt disposition and inclination of my heart, the radical and total *curvitas* and *iniquitas* of my life, and I myself am supposed to be an evil tree merely because I am the heir of Adam. It is not surprising that when an effort is made to take the word " heir " seriously, as has

---

[1] Barth is here criticising the German term for original sin (*Erbsünde*), which conveys the idea of hereditary or inherited sin.—Trans.

occasionally happened, the term " sin " is necessarily dissolved. Conversely, when the term " sin " is taken seriously, the term " heir " is necessarily explained in a way which makes it quite unrecognisable, being openly or surreptitiously dissolved and replaced by other and more serious concepts. " Hereditary sin " has a hopelessly naturalistic, deterministic and even fatalistic ring. If both parts of the term are taken seriously, it is a *contradictio in adiecto* in face of which there is no help for it but to juggle away either the one part or the other.

It is perhaps better to abandon altogether the idea of hereditary sin and to speak only of original sin [1] (the strict translation of *peccatum originale*). What is meant is the voluntary and responsible life of every man—in a connexion with Adam that we have yet to show—which by virtue of the judicial sentence passed on it in and with his reconciliation with God is the sin of every man, the corruption which he brings on himself so that as the one who does so—and again in that connexion—he is necessarily and inevitably corrupt.

We can now continue our answer to the question of the corruption of man in a third proposition which we take from the comprehensive saying of Paul in Rom. 11^{32}. The fact that God willed to have mercy and did have mercy on all men in the sacrifice of Jesus Christ, means that " He hath concluded them all in disobedience." " Concluded " means that He has placed them under an authoritative verdict and sentence which cannot be questioned or disputed, let alone resisted, with all the consequences which that involves. This presupposition corresponds to the mercy of God. This concluding is co-extensive with it (like the reverse side of a coin). Those on whom He willed to have mercy and did have mercy are the very ones that He had concluded or placed under this verdict. In both cases the reference is to all men. If it is true that God has mercy on all, it is equally true that He has concluded all in disobedience.

We will first attempt a cautious paraphrase. We are dealing with two great contexts, or unities, in which all men stand according to the order and will of God. The one embraces them prospectively, in their future being. This is the unity of the divine mercy which is shown to them as the Son of God has come to them in the far country. The other embraces them retrospectively, in their past being. This is the unity of the divine concluding, the unity into which God has fused them and as which He sees and addresses and treats them, because in pride they have all willed to go their own ways in which they can only fall, the unity in which they are all in the state and being of disobedience according to the Word and sentence of God. It is the unity of their being in the far country in which God has sought them in His Son to call and to bring them home. These two unities meet and intersect in the present of all men, and a decision is made for all of them in the Gospel of Jesus Christ revealed and proclaimed to them and heard by them and either believed and confessed or not believed and not confessed by them. The apostolic word, and the confession of the community spoken provisionally for all men and indeed all creation,

---

[1] Barth suggests the term *Ursünde* as a new German equivalent.—Trans.

is this—that He, the Father, " hath delivered us out of the power of darkness, and translated us into the kingdom of his dear Son " (Col. 1[13]). The kingdom of darkness is the conclusion in disobedience, the unity into which the divine verdict had previously fused all men. Those who are translated by Him into the kingdom of His dear Son come out of this kingdom and leave it behind them—being delivered by " the Father of mercies and the God of all comfort " (2 Cor. 1[3]). Those who have their future in the one kingdom have their past in the other. It is of the latter that we must now speak.

Now that we are drawing to the close of our treatise on the pride and fall of man, let us emphasise once again that in all that we have to say in this connexion—from the standpoint of the present of the apostolic word and the faith and confession of the community—we are dealing with man's past, with the being which lies behind him. The first sentence at the head of this whole section was as follows : " The verdict of God pronounced in the resurrection of Jesus Christ crucified for us discloses who it was that was set aside in His death." The one who was set aside in Jesus Christ and who is defined and claimed and described as such in the divine verdict is the man of sin. We have tried to see the man of disobedience at the very point where he is set aside ; in the mirror of the obedience of the Son of God. The comprehensive and decisive thing which we have to say concerning him is that he is set aside ; he belongs to the past and he has no future. He can be known only as the one who died in Jesus Christ, only as the one who is disclosed in the resurrection of Jesus Christ and therefore in the divine verdict, so that we cannot know him at all except in this verdict which discloses him, except by the Word of God's grace to which we have had continually to return. The very sharpness in which we have seen him is only that of the light which shines backwards from this present, characterising him as one who has been replaced and is now past. To be exact, what we have had to say concerning him can only be put in the perfect or even the pluperfect tense. In the light of this present he is the one that we were, or had been, not the one that we can be or will be again. It was no chance or whim which made the Old Testament witness so rich in this connexion. The Old Testament is the indispensable lens by which we can read in the mirror of the obedience of the Son of God who and what we were before Him and without Him—men of sin and disobedience and pride, and therefore fallen men, guilty before God and radically and totally corrupt. If we are this, and continue to be so, the comprehensive and decisive thing which has to be said of us is that we can and will be so only as those who have already been set aside, in a nonsensical presentation of our own past, as our own shadows. To the contradiction of the being of the man of sin as such—and here we see the real paradox and absurdity of his being—there is added the contradiction of his being as one who is still alive, although he was put to death once and for all and actually died on the cross of Golgotha. We remember Paul's grounding and description of the impossibility of a persistence or continuance in sin on this fact : " Knowing that Christ being raised from the dead dieth no more ; death hath no more dominion over him. For in that he died, he died unto sin (our sin) once " (Rom. 6$^{9f.}$). There is no more freedom to commit it. Even the chaotic and unfree freedom to do so has passed. In the present—which is the present of the apostolic word and the faith and confession of the community —we are debarred from it in a twofold and definitive form. There is no future for it—or for us as those who commit it. As such we can only have been. That is how it is with our being in the kingdom of darkness, in the concluding in disobedience. God has had mercy on us and all men. Therefore this kingdom is behind us and all men. We and all men are released from this concluding and this prison.

What is before us and all men is only what Paul finally says concerning the crucified and risen Christ in Rom. 6^{10} : " In that he liveth, he liveth unto God." What this means for man he tells us in Gal. 2$^{19f.}$: " I am crucified with Christ : nevertheless I live ; yet not I, but Christ liveth in me : and the life which I now live I live by the faith of the Son of God, who loved me, and gave himself for me." And therefore : " Forgetting those things which are behind, and reaching forth unto those things which are before, I press toward the mark . . ." (Phil. 3^{13}).

It is, therefore, only subsequently, as we look back, that we can ask how it was with the concluding under which we all stood according to the will and order of God—beyond the threshold which Jesus Christ crossed for us and which we have crossed with Him and in Him. The kingdom of darkness is like the empires of the Egyptians and Assyrians and Babylonians and Medes and Persians into whose hand the witness of the Old Testament tells us that the people of God was given by the divine will and order because of their transgression. It is an empire which is no longer there, which belongs only to history. It did exist once. This is the first thing that we say and have to say when we ask concerning it.

" Wherein in time past ye walked (as those who are dead in trespasses and sins) according to the æon of this world " (Eph. 2$^{1f.}$). " At that time ye were without Christ . . . having no hope, and without God in the world " (2^{12}). Therefore we *were* that man of sin and pride and the fall. We *were* under that concluding, and in that kingdom.

The seriousness of this perception depends upon our taking seriously and without qualification the fact that it belongs to the past. But we still have to ask what this concluding and kingdom was under and in which we found ourselves in times past. The thankful determination to look and move forwards is hardly possible unless we see clearly what is behind us.

We again recall Rom. 11^{32} : that in this concluding and kingdom the reference was—or, in view of the close proximity of that which

is past, ought we perhaps for prudence' sake to continue to say is ?—
to all men. To the radicalness and totality of human sin laid down in
our second proposition there corresponds its universality.

The Bible does not use the word mankind. But it would be very
much to the point to introduce it as a substitute for " all." It is not
merely that we have individual or even many " fleshly " men. But
using the word to describe all men of all times and places, all mankind
is " flesh." Mankind as such sinned and came short of the glory of God
(Rom. 3²³)—and in the context of mankind as such, in conjunction
with it, the individual and the many, each with his own responsibility,
each with his own particular form of pride, each in his own fall, each
in his own specific and distinctive way. There is a solidarity between
the individual and all others, and therefore a unity of the whole of
mankind in pride and the fall. The sentence and judgment of God are
always and everywhere directed against both the individual and individuals, this king and this people as we have it in the Old Testament ;
but in their person they are directed against all men, in the person of
the king and people of Israel against all kings and all peoples, as we are
often enough told in the prophets, sometimes expressly and sometimes
by unmistakable implication. Just as the main side of the coin speaks
of the all-embracing mercy of God, the reverse side speaks of the
sentence of God which concludes all in disobedience, accusing them
all of disobedience and condemning and threatening them with rejection because of their disobedience. When, therefore, we see our sin and
guilt in the light of the Word of God's grace, we do not merely see it
as our own, but in our own we see the sin and guilt of man, of every man
and all men. In our own person we see all mankind sinful and guilty
before God. What took place on Golgotha took place *pro me*, not
exclusively but inclusively. It is *pro me* only because—first of all—it
is *pro nobis*, for the whole world. I cannot think of it as having taken
place *pro me* except as I address God as " Our Father which art in
heaven " and make the requests " Give us this day our daily bread,
And forgive us our trespasses, Lead us not into temptation, But deliver
us from evil." And now that Israel and the Gentiles have become one
people in the death of Jesus Christ no limit can be set to this " us."
Of myself I cannot be an object of the mercy of God except as I am
one of the " us " to whom God has shown it without restriction.
Therefore my conclusion in disobedience may be my own affair, but
as such it is also a common affair in which I was bound in solidarity
with all others—which of them did not sigh to find himself in one
form or other under the same conclusion ?—and as the object of the
mercy which is shown to us all I am still bound in the common past of
that conclusion. The term " mankind " is one which we have to call
a Christian term because it is only in the light of the Gospel that we
can make serious use of it—to describe the sum of all the men to whom
the mercy of God is shown because they are all sinful and guilty before

Him, being threatened by His rejection, concluded in disobedience, set under that accusing verdict.

Again, the Bible does not use the word history. It is, of course, a history book, *the* history book without parallel, the attestation of the presence and action and revelation of God as the attestation of a purely earthly and human history. In it we have to do with the occurrence of the will and Word and works of God among men. Not with the origins and relationships and complications and conjunctions and divisions and ends and new beginnings of human plans and enterprises as such, their motivation and accomplishment and teleology as constituting a single whole in all their obvious details. We find all this in biblical history only as it is revealed under the spotlight of this other occurrence.

That is why it seems to be so difficult, if not impossible, to derive a history of Israel from the Old Testament, or a history of early Christianity or a life of Jesus from the New. The sources always have to be wrested to yield a result of this kind. And what they have yielded under compulsion has never been of a kind to rejoice the heart of a historian. Of course, with many other things they do give us something which is recognisable as history, human history in itself and as such, but always incidentally, and with all kinds of strange abbreviations and extensions and twists which derive from the fact that they are really trying to tell us about happenings of quite a different nature, so that in face of them the historian is always confronted with a painful dilemma : either to let them say what they are trying to say, and not to have any history at all in our sense of the term, or to extract such a history from them at the cost of ignoring and losing what they are really trying to say.

When the word " all " is used (in Rom. 11^{32}, also 3^{23}, and also 5^{12}) it is very much to the point to think of what we mean by the word " history." The verdict that all have sinned certainly implies a verdict on that which is human history apart from the will and Word and work of God, in the abstraction which characterises the concept—the phenomena of that history, its continuous and differentiated progress from an unknown beginning to an unknown end. It is to be noted that this abstraction itself, the concept of a history of man and men and mankind apart from the will and Word and work of God, is itself the product of the perverted and sinful thinking of man, one of the manifestations of human pride. But the concept is no mere illusion, for it expresses the self-understanding of mankind existing in this abstraction or in the will for this abstraction, and constantly willing this abstraction afresh.

There is, in fact, a history of the world which is grounded on the ignoring and rejection of the will and Word and work of God and determined throughout by this ignoring and rejection. And a knowledge of the sin and guilt of man in the light of the Word of the grace of God implies a knowledge that this history is, in fact, grounded and determined in this way, by the pride of man ; a knowledge that its course and aims and movements and beginnings and ends and new beginnings have one thing in common in spite of all the differing and indeed opposing trends : that they all come under the judgment of God. History is concluded in disobedience. This does not mean that it is outside the divine control, that it is abandoned to chance or fate (the doctrine of Epicureans and Stoics both old and new), or, like an organic process, to the outworking of an indwelling law (the solemnly atheistic doctrine of Marxism), or indeed that it stands under the dominion of the devil (the opinion of fanatical Pietism). Again, the divine control of history does not cease to be the control of One who was and is and will be good to man—even to the man who in his pride has fallen away from Him. The history of the world which God made in Jesus Christ, and with a view to Him, cannot cease to have its centre and goal in Him. But in the light of this goal and centre God cannot say Yes but only No to its corruption. And those who hear the Word of the grace of God in the light of this goal and centre, cannot overlook or weaken or explain away or forget this No. It is the No of God which deep down conceals His Yes, His Yes to the poor corrupted men who act and suffer as the subject of history. But it is God's No to their corruption, to the history which is grounded and determined and characterised by that corruption, to the totality of that history as to the totality of every individual man.

What we call historical scholarship says the same thing from its own standpoint so far as it can understand and express it. Its aim is to seek and find in history only man himself, his enterprises and achievements. It may make the proviso that in the last resort we cannot prevent anyone from believing in a providence which directs history, but it definitely refuses to see or say anything of the manifestations or appearances of God in that history. In so doing it unconsciously recognises the divine No, the shadow which stretches right across it. For what this No says is that men as the subjects of this history, men in their pride, trying to be gods and lords and to justify and help themselves, are necessarily, as far as the eye can see (their own arrogant eye), completely on their own, ἄθεοι ἐν τῷ κόσμῳ (Eph. 2[12]), and that their history will necessarily be what it can only be when they are completely on their own. " God gave them up " is what we are told three times in Rom. 1[24f.] That is the conclusion of history in disobedience.

We do not forget that man has not forfeited his good nature and its dispositions and capacities by reason of his corruption and under the judgment of God which has come upon him. Even within this conclusion there may be and undoubtedly are the most surprising projects and commendable efforts and astonishing achievements, masterpieces both great and small of human skill and probity, which in this sense inspire us. The only thing is that they are not excluded from this conclusion, because they are bracketed together under the divine sentence with those human actions and achievements which are obviously less favourable and attractive, or even dangerous and reprehensible, all of them being classed as disobedience, pride and sin. That there are no genuine exceptions is shown in many ways. It is shown by the fact that they are all limited and relative. It is shown by the fact that sooner or later they are revealed as transitory and passing. It is shown in the fact that they are all exposed to abuse and to some extent fall victim to it. It is shown by the fact that there is a strange human vacillation in the assessment of what is supposed to be great and positive and valuable and helpful in history. And even if, allowing for the fact that there is this problematical side, we still maintain that in history as in nature the side of shadow has to be distinguished from that of light, there still remains the dreadful fact that, although we cannot deny all kinds of progress in detail, the many attempts which have been made to establish a teleology or progress in world-history as a whole have always proved to be unsuccessful. It is only fools—and at some point and in some way we are all fools—who will confuse the details with the whole, looking at technical development (in the widest sense of the word) and dreaming of a general progress of man and mankind in history as a whole. In spite of all the movement in his historical forms and activities, man himself is not progressive. In respect of his capacity, or incapacity, to live as *homo sapiens*, to make his being and his being together tolerable and stable, he is remarkably stationary, his actions and reactions being unfortunately only too similar to those of an unreasoning bullock plodding around a capstan. His pride is his hindrance, and it is one of the imaginations of his pride that one day he will achieve this modest control of his life. What is the obviously outstanding feature of world-history? Is it the occasional symphonies and euphonies? We must not ignore these. Is it the constant cacophonies? We certainly cannot ignore these. But the really outstanding thing beyond and in the antitheses is the all-conquering monotony—the monotony of the pride in which man has obviously always lived to his own detriment and to that of his neighbour, from hoary antiquity and through the ebb and flow of his later progress and recession both as a whole and in detail, the pride in which he still lives to his own and his neighbour's detriment and will most certainly continue to do so till the end of time. The man of pride can only live to his own and his neighbour's detriment. If it were otherwise he would not be this subject. That is the conclusion of world history in disobedience.

The Bible gives to this history and to all men in this sense the general title of Adam. Adam is mentioned relatively seldom both in the Old Testament and the New. There are only two passages which treat of him explicitly : Gen. 2-3 and Rom. 5[12-21] (to which we might add 1 Cor. 15[22] and [45]). The meaning of Adam is simply man, and as the bearer of this name which denotes the being and essence of all other men, Adam appears in the Genesis story as the man who owes his existence directly to the creative will and Word and act of God without any human intervention, the man who is to that extent the first man.

Who could see and attest the coming into being of heaven and earth and especially the coming into being of Adam and his corresponding individual existence ? It is not history but only saga which can tell us that he came into being in this way and existed as the one who came into being in this way—the first man. We miss the unprecedented and incomparable thing which the Genesis passages tell us of the coming into being and existence of Adam if we try to read and understand it as history, relating it either favourably or unfavourably to scientific palæontology, or to what we now know with some historical certainty concerning the oldest and most primitive forms of human life. The saga as a form of historical narration is a *genre* apart. And within this *genre* biblical saga is a special instance which cannot be compared with others but has to be seen and understood in and for itself. Saga in general is the form which, using intuition and imagination, has to take up historical narration at the point where events are no longer susceptible as such of historical proof. And the special instance of biblical saga is that in which intuition and imagination are used but in order to give prophetic witness to what has taken place by virtue of the Word of God in the (historical or pre-historical) sphere where there can be no historical proof. It is in this sphere of biblical saga that Adam came into being and existed. And it was in this sphere—again by virtue of the prophetically attested Word and judgment of God—that there took place the fall, the fall of the first man. The biblical saga tells us that world-history began with the pride and fall of man.

We shall not be returning at this point to a detailed account of the sin of Adam (which we dealt with *passim* in the second part of this section). But it is the name of Adam the transgressor which God gives to world-history as a whole. The name of Adam sums up this history as the history of the mankind which God has given up, given up to its pride on account of its pride. It sums up the meaning or meaninglessness of this history. It is Adamic history, the history of Adam. It began in and with his history, and—this is the Word and judgment of God on it, this is the explanation of its staggering monotony, this is the reason why there can never be any progress—it continually corresponds to his history. It is continually like it. With innumerable variations it constantly repeats it. It constantly re-enacts the little scene in the garden of Eden. There never was a golden age. There is no point in looking back to one. The first man was immediately the first sinner.

In the strict exegetical sense we ought not perhaps to combine the Yahwistic text of Gen. 3 with the passage Gen. 2^{2-3} which belongs to the Priestly text. Otherwise we might observe that the seventh day of creation, the first day in the life of man, in which he had nothing to do but to keep the sabbath with God Himself in peace and joy and freedom, was followed at once by the day of his pride and fall as the first day of his own will and work and activity and achievement. It is, however, not merely legitimate but necessary to combine Gen. 3 with Gen. 2^{5-25}, and therefore to say that man had hardly been formed of the dust of the earth and become a living soul by the breath of God, that he had hardly been put in the garden of Eden and charged to dress it and to keep it, that his creation had hardly been completed by that of the woman as an indispensable and suitable helpmeet, before he followed up and directly opposed all the good things that God had done for him by becoming disobedient to God.

The Old Testament tells us that world-history began in this way. It does so by placing this history at the head of all its histories so far as they deal with the will and work and activity and achievement of man. It will later tell us how everything else began in the same way, experiences of the goodness of God being immediately followed by the thoughts and words and works of the folly and wickedness of man. This is the structure of the whole history of Yahweh and Israel. And that history is a type of the history of God and all nations. God knows the historical existence of all nations and the will and achievements of all men and all groups of men only in this way, in correspondence and similarity with that of Adam on the first of his days of work and fellowship with his neighbour and fulfilment of his responsibility in relation to God, in that first act of world-history. " The Lord looked down from heaven upon the children of men, to see if there were any that did understand, and seek God. They are all gone aside, they are altogether become filthy : there is none that doeth good, no, not one. . . . They eat the bread of the Lord, and call not upon him " (Ps. 14²¹·). In the knowledge of God which embraces and sees to the heart of the men of every time and place, and according to the Word which is directed to all and appointed for the ears and hearts of all according to this knowledge, and in the judgment of this Word which is passed upon all, all men are continually as the first man Adam, for what God continually sees them do is what Adam first did.

Who is Adam ? The great unknown who is the first parent of the race ? There can be no doubt that this is how the biblical tradition intended that he should be seen and understood. But it is interested in him as such only for what he did. A sinner specially burdened with his act ? But compared with what the Old Testament tells us of others, and even of holy men, his offence was obviously so slight and trivial that in view of his particular fault we should hesitate to describe him even as the *primus inter pares*. Certainly there is no reason why a special accusation should be brought against him and his act. He simply did in the insignificant form of the beginner that which all men have done after him, that which is in a more or less serious and flagrant form our own transgression. He was in a trivial form what we all are, a man of sin. But he was so as the beginner, and therefore as *primus inter pares*. This does not mean that he has bequeathed it to us as his heirs so that we have to be as he was. He has not poisoned us or passed on a disease. What we do after him is not done according to an example which irresistibly overthrows us, or in an imitation of his act which is ordained for all his successors. No one has to be Adam. We are so freely and on our own responsibility. Although the guilt of Adam is like ours, it is just as little our excuse as our guilt is his. We and he are reached by the same Word and judgment of God in the same direct way. The only difference is that what we all are and do he was and did at the very gateway of history, and therefore he was reached first by the Word and judgment of God in a way which is typical for all his successors. That is Adam as seen and understood in the biblical tradition, the man who sinned at once, the man who was at once proud man, the man who stands at that gateway as the representative of all who follow, the one whom all his successors do in fact resemble (in the fact that they all sin at once as well).

The idea of representation is taken from the treatment in H. Heidegger (*Med. Theol. chr.*, 1696, X, 19). As he sees it, Adam acted as *persona publica*, as the representative head for the time being of the whole race, and therefore *in munere*, although not, of course, *ex munere*, seeing he acted sinfully (IX, 8). *Unde peccando non sibi duntaxat, sed posteris etiam, quos repraesentavit, peccavit; imo in et cum eodem ii, quos repraesentavit, peccarunt. Nam qui faciendo vel patiendo repraesentatur, is ipse quoque facere vel pati censetur.* Quenstedt (*Theol. did. pol.*, 1685, P. II, *cap. 2, sect. 2 qu. 7, ekth.* 6) said of the will of Adam that it was the *interpres omnium omnino qui in lumbis vel femore eius erant*. It expressed both his own and their *animus* against the Law of God. But some of the representatives of the older orthodoxy, e.g., W. Bucan (*Instit. theol.*, 1605, XV, 17), went too far when they tried to make out that the sin of Adam was not his own personal sin but that of the "nature" of the whole race pre-existent in him. Against this we have to consider that if he did not act personally, how could he act representatively for his successors who are bound with him in the same nature, and in such a way that their action is also personal? The later Protestant orthodoxy of both confessions did at any rate try to think out this matter rather more clearly.

But who are Adam's successors, and what is their relationship to this first man? The biblical tradition undoubtedly means that they were the physical descendants of Adam, the race which derived from him. But while they are connected with him in a creaturely order, how do they come to be like him in the act of transgression, sharing his guilt and his radical and total corruption? How do they come to be his children in the qualified biblical sense of the term—the bearers and representatives of the manner, or perversity, of his will and achievement? If by the word sin, whether it is Adam's sin or our own, we have always to think of a human decision and act, if the idea of a sinfulness which propagates itself through the generations and is inherited will no longer serve, then the answer to this question can only be that the successors of Adam are, in the language of the older theologians already quoted, those who are represented in his person and deed. They are those whose will is already in his will correctly interpreted and expressed as a corrupted will. To put it in another way, they are those whose free will and commission and omission, whose actualisations of their good human nature, always follow the rule and perverted order which, according to the prophetic witness, is manifested at once at the very beginning of world-history, in the person and act of Adam, which are typical for the persons and acts of all his successors. We are known by God in Adam, i.e., as those who are subject to the law revealed in him. In him, therefore, we have simply to recognise ourselves and mankind and the whole history of man. Adam is not a fate which God has suspended over us. Adam is the truth concerning us as it is known to God and told to us. The relationship between him and us, and us and him, is not, therefore, one which is pragmatically grounded and demonstrable, nor is it one which can be explained in terms of a transmission between him and us. It is God who establishes it. It is the Word of God which gives this name and title to mankind and the history of man. It is God's Word which fuses all men into unity with this man as *primus inter pares*. It is the Word of God which condemns at once his disobedience and therefore condemns our disobedience. It is the Word of God which forbids us to dream of any golden age in the past or any real progress within Adamic mankind and history or any future state of historical perfection, or indeed to put our hope in anything other than the atonement which has taken place in Jesus Christ.

It was along these lines that Calvin viewed the matter. He says (*Comm. on Jn.* 3⁶) : *Quod in persona unius Adae totum genus humanum corruptum fuit, non tam ex genitura provenit, quam ex Dei ordinatione.* . . . *Quare non tam unus quisque nostrum a parentibus suis vitium et corruptionem contrahit quam omnes pariter in uno Adam corrupti sumus.* In later orthodoxy, which commendably tried to avoid the idea of an *implantatio* or *insitio* and therefore of hereditary sin, the basic term used to describe this *ordinatio* of God was *imputatio*. Other terms used were *aestimatio*, *attributio* and *adiudicatio*, and, following Rom. 5¹⁸⁻¹⁹, it was expressly compared with the *imputatio iustitiae Christi* in the justification of the sinner : *Sicut Christi iustitia perfecta per gratiam Dei imputatur ad iustificationem vitae, ita Adami peccatum per iudicium Dei imputari posteris eius ad condemnationem necesse est* (H. Heidegger, *l.c.*, X, 19). When we examine the matter more closely, of course, we find that orthodoxy lacked the courage to draw all the necessary deductions. Was it really a matter of a *mera imputatio* and not of some kind of an infection ? Certain concessions were made in this respect to the traditional view. But the stronger the thinking in terms of *imputatio*, the more serious was the answer to the question of the relationship between Adam and us, for the closer was the approximation to the perception that it is based in the mystery of the judgment revealed in the Word of God under which Adam is placed with us and we with him.

The question still remains what is meant by this *imputatio* and what basis there is for the idea. Why is it that the strange and bitter truth concerning ourselves and mankind and the history of man is told us in Adam ? Polanus (*Synt. Theol. chr.*, 1609, col. 2069) comments on this point : *Quod Adami voluntas fuit nostra et nos in illo voluimus, verum est, sed ratio huius veritatis nulla est praeterquam voluntas creatoris.* This obviously means that it is the truth which God himself tells us, which is therefore indisputable, which we have to accept, however strange and bitter it may be. That is quite true. But we may still ask how far it really is the truth which is told to us, the Word of God concerning us which as such we can only hear and respect. And seeing the older dogmatics attained to this thought of the divine *ordinatio* or *imputatio*, and was well aware of the formal correspondence between the *condemnatio* of man and his *iustificatio*, it is surprising that it did not find in this correspondence the answer to this final question and to this whole group of problems.

Why and to what extent have we to hear and respect it as God's Word that the sin of Adam is written across the existence of all men, that in the person and act of Adam God has sentenced and condemned all mankind and human history, concluding it in disobedience ? A brief consideration of Rom. 5[12-21] will give us the answer. In this respect, too, the Word of divine judgment has its origin and proper place in the Word of divine grace, and derives its truth from this Word. Its power and authority will therefore be instructive to those who hear it in and with this Word. That is how Paul heard it.

Who is Adam to Paul ? What is to him the relevant thing in this primitive representative of a humanity which moves in circles in abstraction from the divine will and Word and work ? The fact that, according to v. 12, he is the one man by whom " sin entered into the world, and death by sin ; and so death passed upon all men, for that all have sinned " ? Yes, that is Adam as written across all human existence, the exponent of the rule under which all men stand. Paul hears this and respects it. God has written it across the whole history of man. It tells us the truth. But how does he know it ? Where and how has it impressed upon him its truth and validity, the necessary sequence of the one and the many, of all men in disobedience ? Where has he found this ? Where has it found him ? In Gen. 3 of course. But how could Gen. 3 become to him, as it obviously is, the divine Word which is decisive and normative and authoritative for his whole understanding of mankind and the history of man ?

According to the text of Rom. 5[12-21] there is only one answer to this question. In that first and isolated figure, in that one who is created and exists by the will and Word and work of God, in that great and typical sinner and debtor at the head of the whole race, in that dark representative of all his successors who bear his name, he recognised quite a different figure. This other, too, came directly from God, not as a creature only, but as the Son of God and Himself God by nature. He, too, was a sinner and debtor, but as the sinless and guiltless bearer of the sins of others, the sins of all other men. He, too, was the Representative of all others. The only difference is that He was not like them. He was not the *primus inter pares* in a sequence. He represented them as a genuine leader, making atonement by His obedience, covering their disobedience, justifying them before God. " Therefore as by the offence of one judgment came upon all to condemnation ; even so by the righteousness of one the free gift came upon all men unto justification of life. For as by one man's disobedience many were made sinners, so by the obedience of one shall many be made righteous " (vv. 18–19).

This Pauline argument is usually called the parallel between Adam and Christ. But at the very least we ought to speak of the parallel between Christ and Adam. For there can be no doubt that for Paul Jesus Christ takes the first place as the original, and Adam the second place as " the figure of him that was to come " (v. 14), the prophetic type of Jesus Christ. He knew Jesus Christ first and then Adam. But that means that in Adam, in his existence and act and function, in his relationship to the race which derived from him, he saw again, as it were, the negative side of Jesus Christ. In the unrighteous man at the head of the old race he saw again the righteous man at the head of the new. And even the term parallel calls for some explanation. It is not autonomously that the line of Adam and the many who are concluded with him in disobedience runs close to that of Jesus Christ in whose obedience God has willed to..have and has had mercy on many and indeed on all. We have only to note how the two are contrasted in vv. 15–17 to see that although they can be compared in form they cannot be compared in substance. The former is like the rainbow in relation to the sun. It is only a reflection of it. It has no independent existence. It cannot stand against it. It does not balance it. When weighed in the scales it is only like a feather. That is the relationship between the offence of men in the person and act of one and the free gift of righteousness and life which comes with the judgment of God in the person and act of this other. That is the relationship between the determination of all men and mankind and the history of man on the one hand and their determination on the other. We are reminded of Is. 54⁷ᶠ·: " For a small moment have I forsaken thee ; but with great mercies will I gather thee. In a little wrath I hid my face from thee for a moment ; but with everlasting kindness will I have mercy on thee, saith the Lord thy Redeemer ; " and of Ps. 30⁴ᶠ·: " Sing unto the Lord, O ye saints of his, and give thanks at the remembrance of his holiness. For his anger endureth but a moment ; in his favour is life ; weeping may endure for a night ; but joy cometh in the morning ; " and v. 11 f.: " Thou hast turned for me my mourning into dancing : thou hast put off my sackcloth, and girded me with gladness ; to the end that my glory may sing praise to thee, and not be silent. O Lord my God, I will give thanks unto thee for ever." Is it not clear who and what is the *prius* and who and what the *posterius* ? Even when we are told in 1 Cor. 15⁴⁵ that Jesus Christ is the ἔσχατος Ἀδάμ, this does not mean that in relation to the first Adam of Gen. 3 He is the second, but rather that He is the first and true Adam of which the other is only a type. It is in relation to the last Adam that this first Adam, the unknown of the Genesis story, has for Paul existence and consistence, and that in what is said of him he hears what is true and necessarily true of himself and all men. It is beyond the threshold which Jesus Christ has crossed, and every man in Him, that he hears in Him the sentence on himself and all men as a Word of God and not of man—a sentence against which there can be no appeal passed on the man of sin, who was every man, but who no longer exists now that God has had mercy on all with the same universality with which He once concluded all in disobedience.

61

THE JUSTIFICATION OF MAN

The right of God established in the death of Jesus Christ, and proclaimed in His resurrection in defiance of the wrong of man, is as such the basis of the new and corresponding right of man. Promised to man in Jesus Christ, hidden in Him and only to be revealed in Him, it cannot be attained by any thought or effort or achievement on the part of man. But the reality of it calls for faith in every man as a suitable acknowledgment and appropriation and application.

1. THE PROBLEM OF THE DOCTRINE OF JUSTIFICATION

The event of the death of Jesus Christ is the execution of the judgment of God, of the gracious God who in the giving of His Son in our place, and the lowly obedience of the Son in our place, reconciled the world with Himself, genuinely and definitely affirmed man as His creature in spite of his sin which cried to heaven, confirmed His faithfulness towards him and carried through His covenant with him. And the event of the resurrection is the revelation of the sentence of God which is executed in this judgment ; of the free resolve of His love, and therefore of the righteousness of this judgment, the righteousness of the Father in the giving of His Son, the righteousness of the Son in His lowly obedience, the righteousness which has come to man too, and especially to man, in this judgment.

But the judgment of God executed in the death of Jesus Christ, and the sentence of God revealed in His resurrection and executed in that judgment, have both of them a twofold sense. They have a negative sense in so far as they are the judgment and sentence of the God who is gracious to man, the burning, the consuming fire, the blinding light of His wrath on the corrupt and sinful man who is unfaithful to Him and therefore to himself. They have a positive sense in so far as they are the judgment and sentence of the God who has turned to man in goodness, mercy and grace ; His decision and pronouncement in man's favour, for man ; the work of His redemption ; His Word of power : " Rise up and walk." We can also say that they have a negative sense in so far as in that judgment and sentence God remains, and therefore confesses Himself to be, true to Himself (to the salvation of man) ; and a positive sense in so far as in the same judgment and sentence (to His own glory) He remains, and pronounces Himself to be, true to man. Or we can say that they have a negative sense in so far as His judgment and sentence are related to the being and activity and attitude of man, in so far as they have to do with the man of sin and his pride and fall; and a positive sense in so far as God looks back to the fact that as His creature and elect covenant-partner man is from all eternity and therefore unchangeably His own possession : looking back to His own will and plan and purpose, and looking forward to the goal which, in spite of man's being and activity and attitude as the man of sin, is still unchangeably set for him, since God Himself has set it. We can and must say these two things concerning the judgment of God executed in the death of Jesus Christ and the sentence of God revealed in His resurrection, because in both events we are dealing with the execution and revelation of the divine rejection of elected man and the divine election of rejected man. It was in the indissoluble unity and irreversible sequence of these happenings that the reconciliation of the world with God took place in Jesus Christ.

We have already spoken of the execution of the divine judgment in the humiliation and obedience of the Son of God to death, and of the Easter revelation of the sentence carried out in Him, in the first and—in the narrower sense of the term—christological part of our exposition (§ 59). And we have just completed (§ 60) our development of the negative sense of the divine sentence carried out in the death of Jesus Christ. In the mirror of Jesus Christ who was offered up for us and who was obedient in this offering it is made clear who we ourselves are, the ones for whom He was offered up, for whom He obediently offered Himself up. In the light of the humility in demonstration of which He acted as very God for us, suffering and dying for us, we are exposed and made known and have to acknowledge ourselves as the proud creatures who ourselves want to be god and lord and redeemer and helper, who have as such turned aside from God, who are therefore sinners : the enemies of God, because our disposition to Him is hostile ; those who choose and have fallen a prey to nothingness ; debtors who cannot clear themselves ; rejected therefore, and because rejected perishing. The sentence which was executed as the divine judgment in the death of Jesus Christ is that we are these proud creatures, that I am the man of sin, and that this man of sin and therefore I myself am nailed to the cross and crucified (in the power of the sacrifice and obedience of Jesus Christ in my place), that I am therefore destroyed and replaced, that as the one who has turned to nothingness I am done away in the death of Jesus Christ. This is —to put it rather more precisely—the negative side of the divine sentence executed in that judgment.

We must not lose sight of this negative side even when it is our task to develop the positive. In virtue of the resurrection of Jesus Christ from the dead it is just as much a valid truth of revelation as the positive. Jesus Christ rose again from the dead and lives and reigns to all eternity as the One who was crucified and died for us. The fact that this being destroyed and done away and replaced came on Him in our place—and in Him as our Substitute on us—is something which because it happened once and for all never ceases to be true for Him and therefore for us. By suffering death—our death—for us, He did for us that which is the basis of our life from the dead. Therefore we cannot be the ones for whom He has done this without being the ones for whom He has suffered. In God's eternal counsel the election of rejected man did not take place without the rejection of elected man : the election of Jesus Christ as our Head and Representative, and therefore our election as those who are represented by Him. Therefore the positive sense of the sentence executed in that judgment belongs together with the negative. It is the consequence of it and is related to it. If Jesus the Crucified lives, and we live in Him and with Him, the sentence of God revealed in His resurrection is valid in Him and therefore for us in that negative sense. Therefore the knowledge of the grace of God and the comfort which flows from it in this sentence, the knowledge, therefore, of its positive sense, is bound up with the fact that in it we do not cease to see ourselves as those who are condemned.

In turning now to the positive sense, we enter the particular sphere of the doctrine of justification. What we have to say here is that in the same judgment in which God accuses and condemns us as sinners and gives us up to death, He pardons us and places us in a new life before Him and with Him. And what we have to show is that this is possible, that the two belong together : our real sin and our real freedom from sin ; our real death and our real life beyond death ; the real wrath of God against us and His real grace and mercy towards us ; the fulfilment of our real rejection and also of our real election. We are dealing with the history in which man is both rejected and elected, both under the wrath of God and accepted by Him in grace, both put to death and alive : existing in a state of transition, not here only, but from here to *there* ; not there only, but from *here* to there ; the No of God behind and the Yes of God before, but the Yes of God only before as the No of God is behind. This history, the existence of man in this transition, and therefore in this twofold form, is the judgment of God in its positive character as the justification of man.

The doctrine of justification not only narrates but explains this history. It is the attempt to see and understand in its positive sense the sentence of God which is executed in His judgment and revealed in the resurrection of Jesus Christ.

The concept of right is the formal principle for the explanation given. It cannot be more than a formal principle. And what it means can be deduced only from the matter in question, from the history which has to be explained. The matter in question is the divine sentence as executed in the divine judgment and revealed by God. It is from this that we learn what " right " means. But the fact that we are dealing with God's sentence and judgment means that we have to use the concept. The Bible itself gives it to us in this connexion, and the Church has always accepted it in its proclamation and theology concerning this matter, sometimes with more and sometimes with less caution in respect of meanings foreign to the matter itself, sometimes with more and sometimes with less attachment to the meaning which it necessarily acquires and has as applied to this matter.

It is a question of explaining the fact and the extent to which in this history, or in the divine sentence on man which underlies this history, we are dealing with that which is just and right. It is a question of showing the right of God which gives right to man, and of the right which is given by God to man. The highly problematical point in the history is obviously the notorious wrong of man. In relation to God he is in the wrong, and therefore he is accused and condemned and judged by God. He is *homo peccator*, and in this history he never ceases to be *homo peccator*. How, then, in the same sentence of God, and therefore in the same history, can he be *homo iustus*? How can he be seriously in the wrong before God and in the divine sentence and judgment, and yet also before the same God and in the same sentence and judgment come to be and be seriously in the right? How can he be *simul peccator et iustus*? And how can God for His part (the omniscient and righteous Judge of good and evil) give right to man when man is obviously in the wrong before Him, and God Himself has put him in the wrong? To what extent does God act and speak and prove and show Himself in the justification of man—this man—as God the Father, Son and Holy Spirit, in whom there is no contradiction or caprice or disorder, no paradox or obscurity, but only light? To what extent does He demonstrate and maintain in this remarkable justification His righteousness as the Creator confronting the creature and as the Lord of His covenant with man? To what extent is the opposition which man has taken up in relation to God taken seriously and seriously overcome in this justification which is given to Him by God? To what extent is this justification not a mere overlooking or hiding of the pride and fall of man, a nominalistic " as if "—which is quite incompatible with the truthfulness of God and cannot be of any real help to man—but God's serious opposition and mighty resistance to the pride of man and therefore the real redemption of fallen man? How in this justification can God be effectively true to Himself and therefore to man—to man and therefore primarily to Himself? How can He judge man in truth and even in that judgment be gracious to Him? How can He be truly gracious to him even in the fact that He judges him? This is the problem of the doctrine of justification which we now have to develop.

Even an outline of the question which we have to answer is enough to show the particular importance of it. It is a matter of the genuineness of the presupposition, the inner possibility, of the reconciliation of the world with God, in so far as this consists of a complete alteration of the human situation, a conversion of sinful man to Himself as willed and accomplished by God. The Christian community as the community which proclaims this alteration to the world, because it knows and believes in it, derives from this presupposition, as does also the faith of every individual Christian. Therefore the Christian community and Christian faith stand or fall with the reality of the fact that in confirmation and restoration of the covenant broken by man the holy God has set up a new fellowship between Himself and sinful man, instituting a new covenant which cannot be destroyed or even disturbed by any transgression on the part of man. The community rests and acts on this basis. Faith lives by the certainty and actuality of the reconciliation of the world with God accomplished in Jesus Christ. There can be a basis for the community and certainty for faith only if this actuality is true, and true with a divine and unconditional clarity. What is not divinely true cannot be actual, and therefore cannot be basic and certain. But whether we are dealing with a divinely true actuality depends upon whether in this alteration of the human situation in the atonement—as the work of the grace and mercy of God—we are dealing with that which is just and right. It depends upon whether—however strange it may seem to us—there is a genuine justification : that is, whether the right of God which gives right to man and the right of man which is given by God to man is a true and indisputable right. If we do not have an indisputable divine right, and (for all its difference) an indisputable human right, how can the conversion of man to God be true, and how then can it be actual ? The Christian community would then be based merely on the hypothesis that this new conversion and therefore peace between God and man might be true and actual, and the certainty of faith on the suspicion that the hypothesis might be more than a hypothesis. And if there is no knowledge of the overruling righteousness of God, or knowledge only in the form of a mistaken apprehension distorted by partial or total misunderstandings, how can the community escape error and decay, how can faith be kept from doubt and dissolution into all kinds of unbeliefs and superstitions ? The task of the doctrine of justification is to demonstrate the righteousness of God which over-rules in the reconciling grace of God, and the grace of God which truly and actually overrules in the righteousness of God. It is the task of finding a reliable answer to the question : What is God for sinful man ? and what is sinful man before the God who is for him ? The basis of the community and the certainty of faith stands or falls with the answer to this question. The doctrine of justification undertakes to answer the question of this presupposition. Hence its importance and theological necessity.

But even a cursory glance at the problem reveals the particular difficulty of the doctrine. The sweet fruit is here found in a shell which is unusually hard and bitter. In whichever direction the theologian tries to move he is unusually hampered. Where is he to begin to think and where to cease? Can we take both the basic concepts, grace and right, in all their strictness? Can we relate them with sufficient strictness to one another, seeking the explanation of the one strictly in the other? Which aspects have to be brought to the forefront, and which necessarily pushed into the background? How can we prevent the whole falling apart like a heap of skittles stood up on end? Yet in a sense these are only technical matters which we might overcome were it not that they represent the much more pressing question: How are we going to think and say not merely anything at all, but the right thing, that which corresponds to the matter itself? Do we really know this presupposition, and therefore that which we have in some way to define and formulate? Do we really know what is the basis of the community and the certainty of faith, the grace and righteousness of God in their unity, and therefore that which we have to demonstrate? Do we really know God in the one and twofold mystery of His activity as we have to narrate and explain it? Where are we going to find the light which is necessary for this knowledge? And do we really know ourselves as the men who stand over against God in the mystery of this activity? What heavy responsibilities we undertake when we make this statement, what temptations we have to recognise and guard against on the right hand and the left, what misunderstandings we have to avoid, what obligation and freedom is necessary, what attention to the binding counsel of those who have preceded us in the consideration of this matter, what attention to the even more binding Word of God in the witness of the prophets and apostles, what determination to stick to that which is actually told us concerning the justification of man and to repeat it undisturbed by all the obvious doubts and objections! Which of us has any real knowledge of this matter? And if we have not, what is the value of all our repetition of ecclesiastical or even biblical theology, or our ever so original theorising? In the first and final instance the problem of justification is, for those whom it occupies, the problem of the fact of their own justification. Even when we have done our best, which of us can think that we have even approximately mastered the subject, or spoken even a penultimate word in explanation of it?

Certainly Martin Luther did not think so, and he was perhaps the man who worked and suffered and prayed more in relation to this matter than any man before or after him in the post-apostolic period. Even Paul himself did not think so. We remember the pregnant and almost too bold saying in Rom. 11[32] in which he stated the mystery of sin and the mystery of grace in their connexion and sequence in the sentence and judgment of God : " For God hath concluded them all in disobedience, that he might have mercy upon all." And he adds at once in v. 33 f. : " O the depth of the riches both of the wisdom and knowledge of God! How unsearchable are his judgments, and his ways past finding out! For who hath known the mind of the Lord? or who hath been his counsellor?"

Obviously this is not rejoicing in his own knowledge which has taken him so far, but adoration in face of the incommensurable height of the matter, and therefore modesty in respect of even the best of his own knowledge, as in 1 Cor. 13⁹ᶠ·, when he expressly spoke of it as a knowing in part, as the speaking and understanding and thinking of a child, as seeing through a mirror. But let us listen to what Luther has to say. *Non est jocandum cum articulo iustificationis*, he warns us: the example of Peter at Antioch shows us what dreadful havoc (*ingentes ruinas*) can be caused by a single slip or mistake in this matter (on *Gal.* 2¹², 1535, *W.A.* 40¹, 201, 26). The *causa iustificationis* is *lubrica* (i.e., there is something slippery and therefore unsafe and dangerous about it), not in and for itself, *per se enim est firmissima et certissima, sed quoad nos*, for us who try to grasp it and have to speak of it. Luther knows very well the hours of darkness when it seems as though the rays of the Gospel and grace are about to disappear behind thick clouds, and he knows other proved and hardy warriors who have the same experience. It is a good sign if we know this doctrine and can state it. But it is another thing to be able to use it *in praesenti agone*, when the Law as a word of wrath and sorrow and death, or perhaps only a single passage threatening us with perdition, strikes us and shakes us to the very core and takes away all our comfort, when even reason speaks against the Gospel and the flesh cannot and will not lay hold of the truth of it. It is then necessary to fight with all our power for a right understanding, *et ad hoc utatur humili oratione coram Deo et assiduo studio ac meditatione verbi. Et quanquam vehementissime decertaverimus, adhuc satis tamen sudabimus*, for we are not dealing with contemptible foes but with the strongest and most tenacious of all, which may include amongst others even the rest of the Church (on *Gal.* 1¹², *loc. cit.*, 128 f.). And in another word of warning : *Haec dictu sunt facilia, sed beatus, qui ista probe nosset in certamine conscientiae* (on *Gal.* 2¹⁹, *l.c.*, 271, 21). And again right at the beginning of the *praefatio* to the commentary on Galatians : *nec tamen comprehendisse me experior de tantae altitudinis, latitudinis, profunditatis sapientia, nisi infirmas et pauperes quasdam primitias et veluti fragmenta* (*l.c.*, 33, 11).

There is no doubt that the unusual difficulty of the doctrine of justification is an indication of its special function. In it we have to do with the turning, the movement, the transition of the existence of man without God and dead into the existence of man living for God, and therefore before Him and with Him and for Him. We will have to speak explicitly of this transition more than once in the whole doctrine of reconciliation. We will be dealing with it in the doctrines of sanctification and calling which we shall have to discuss in the second and third main parts of the doctrine of reconciliation. And where do we not have to do indirectly with this transition in the whole of the doctrine of reconciliation and indeed in dogmatics generally ? Where do we not in some measure stand before this same difficulty and have to listen to the impressive warning of Luther ? There is no part of dogmatics, no *locus*, where we can treat it lightly. At every point we are dealing with the one high Gospel. What we can and must say is that in the doctrine of justification we are dealing with the most pronounced and puzzling form of this transition because we are dealing specifically with the question of its final possibility. As we have seen already, how can it be that peace is concluded between a holy God and sinful man—by grace, but in a way which is completely and adequately right ? Later on, in the doctrines of sanctification and calling we shall have to speak of the crisis of this relationship and of the decision which is made in it. And the crisis of this relationship and the decision which is made in it are, as it were, the red thread which we can follow through all the *loci* of the doctrine of reconciliation and dogmatics generally, the thread which makes all our knowledge in some sense dramatic and exciting and dangerous, which makes it the kind of knowledge which, as Luther rightly perceived, cannot either arise or continue without humble prayer and constant attention to the Word of God. But in the doctrine of justification we have to do with the original centre of this crisis, and to that extent with its sharpest form, with what we can describe provisionally as the crisis which underlies the whole. If we find it running through the whole with all kinds of repetitions and variations, at this point where we grapple with the peculiar difficulty of it, it has to be seen and handled as the main theme—the question : How am I to lay hold of a gracious God ? And it is from here, and along the line which runs from here, that in different ways it works out everywhere.

It is, therefore, understandable that in at any rate some forms of Christian theology the doctrine of justification has had the function of a basic and central dogma in relation to which everything else will be either presupposition or consequence, either prologue or epilogue ; that its significance has been that of *the* Word of Gospel.

The discussion of this point brings us into implicit controversy with Ernst Wolf, "Die Rechtfertigungslehre als Mitte und Grenze reformatorischer Theologie" (*Evang. Theol.*, 1949–1950, p. 298 f.).

It was again Luther, above all others, who obviously regarded and described the doctrine of justification as *the* Word of the Gospel. To him it was not merely the decisive point, the hub, as it were, of the whole of Evangelical theology in controversy with the Romanists. It was this, in the sense of the *Schmalkaldic Articles* of 1537 (*Bek.-Schr. der ev.-luth. Kirche*, p. 415 f.)—in which it is called the *primus et principalis articulus* in this special sense : " In relation to this article we cannot doubt or yield an inch, though heaven and earth or all things passing may fall. . . . On this article stands all that we teach and live against the Papacy, the devil and the world. Therefore we must be sure and not doubt. Otherwise all is lost, and the Papacy and the devil and all will prevail against us." The fact that Luther linked together the Papacy, the devil and the world shows us, however, that Luther was not thinking merely in terms of the polemic against Rome. In the *praefatio* to the 1535 Galatians we are told immediately before the passage quoted earlier : *In corde meo iste unus regnat articulus, sc. fides Christi, ex quo, per quem et in quem omnes meae diu noctuque fluunt et refluunt theologicae cogitationes. Ea (doctrina) florente florent omnia bona, religio, verus cultus, gloria Dei, certa cognitio omnium statuum et rerum (l.c., 39).* Then in the *argumentum* of the same commentary we read (*l.c.*, 48, 28) : *Amisso articulo iustificationis amissa est simul tota doctrina christiana.* And on Gal. 1[3] (*l.c.*, 72, 20) : *Iacente articulo iustificationis iacent omnia. Necesse igitur est, ut quotidie acuamus (quemadmodum Moses de sua lege dicit) et inculcemus eum. Nam satis vel nimium non potest concipi et teneri.* According to Luther's exposition of Gal. 2[20] (*l.c.*, 296, 23) this article and this article alone has the power to refute all sects, anabaptists and sacramentarians, etc., seeing they are all at error in relation to it. Moreover it is by the *sententia de iustificatione* that Christianity is distinguished from all other religions : *soli enim christiani hinc locum credunt et sunt iusti non quia ipsi operantur, sed quia alterius opera apprehendunt, nempe passionem Christi* (*Schol. on Is.* 53²ᵗ·, 1534, *W.A.* 25, 329, 15 ; 330, 8). And in the same context (*l.c.*, 332) : this *Locus* is the *fundamentum Novi Testamenti, ex quo tanquam ex patenti fonte omnes thesauri divinae sapientiae profluunt.* Similarly in 1537 Luther could open a disputation (*W.A.* 39¹, 205, 2) with the words : *Articulus iustificationis est magister et princeps, dominus, rector et iudex super omnia genera doctrinarum, qui conservat et gubernat omnem doctrinam ecclesiasticam.* If it does not know and consider this article, the human reason is defenceless against the vainest errors. But a mind which is strengthened by it will stand against all their assaults. The dominating role which Luther assigned to the matter in his own sermons and other works corresponds to these declarations of principle. The well-known description of the doctrine as the *articulus stantis et cadentis ecclesiae* does not seem to derive from Luther himself, but it is an exact statement of his view. He found in it the one point which involved the whole.

Orthodox Lutheranism in the 16th and 17th centuries handed down his doctrine of justification from generation to generation—it is not our present business to inquire whether they understood it or not—and with a respectful loyalty tried to reproduce it exactly. Neither Melanchthon nor those who followed him tried to draw out the logical consequences, as, for example, in the order of dogmatics, of what Luther said concerning its primacy. They can hardly have understood that for Luther it was more than an indispensable point of controversy, that in it Luther saw that everything was at stake and not merely the opposition to Rome. We must not overlook the fact that there have been men (not confessional Lutherans) like Zinzendorf and the Bernese Samuel Lucius and John Wesley who followed Luther in this matter, but whose activity and expression did not lie in the narrower theological field. But it certainly betrays a lessening of interest in the subject, and would undoubtedly have earned the censure of Luther himself, when in the dogmatic works of later Lutheran orthodoxy, as in the much read *Comp. Theol. pos.* of W. Baier (1686, *Prol.* 1, 33), and also in the corresponding passages in Hollaz and·Buddeus, the doctrine was reckoned among the *articuli fundamentales secundarii*, on the ground that a Christian can believe and therefore attain forgiveness by faith without ever having reflected on *iustificatio per solam fidem et non per opera.* And when the tide of the moralistic Enlightenment of the 18th century had run its course, was it really a re-discovery of the meaning and intention of Luther, or was it a questionable discovery of the modern spirit, that in German theology in the 19th century the doctrine was again appealed to as the material principle of Protestantism ? At any rate, an influential contribution was made on the one side by a romantic historicism which was less concerned with theology than morphology, and on the other by a desire for speculative systematics kindled by idealistic philosophy. We cannot deny an actual parallelism between this neo-Lutheran emphasis and the statements of Luther himself. The only thing is that with the possible exception of M. Kähler, no one dared actually to plan and organise Evangelical dogmatics around the doctrine of justification as a centre. It is a matter for reflection that neither in the older or more recent Lutheranism has this ever been done.

There can be no question of disputing the particular function of the doctrine of justification. And it is also in order that at certain periods and in certain situations, in face of definite opposition and obscuration, this particular function has been brought out in a particular way, that it has been asserted as *the* Word of the Gospel, that both offensively and defensively it has been adopted as *the* theological truth. There have been times when this has been not merely legitimate but necessary, when attention has had to be focused on the theology of Galatians and Romans (or, more accurately, Rom. 1–8).

One such time was when Augustine had to take up arms because the, in a sense, innocent righteousness of works of the first centuries had obviously ceased to be innocent in the teaching of Pelagius and his followers and now threatened actually to obscure the Gospel as the message of the free grace of God. Another such time was that of the Reformation when Luther recognised that the sacramentalistic and moralistic misunderstanding of the much cited " grace " was the abuse which underlay all the other abuses of the mediæval Church, and he set out to overcome it. Another such time was the awakening at the beginning of the 19th century, with its very necessary reaction against the secularisation of the understanding of salvation in the Enlightenment, in. face of which post-Reformation orthodoxy—which had gone a good way along the same road—had shown itself to be powerless. Another such time may well be our own day, when in face of the notable humanistic religiosity which is our heritage from the 19th century, and in face of all ecclesiasticism, sacramentalism, liturgism and even existentialism, we have been glad enough, and still are, to find in the doctrine of justification a fully developed weapon with which to meet all these things.

But in theology it is good to look beyond the needs and necessities of the moment, to exercise restraint in a reaction however justified, to be constantly aware of the limits of the ruling trend (however true and well-founded it may be). And since our present business is with Church dogmatics, which is ecumenical at least in prospect, this must be our attitude in relation to the doctrine of justification, not because we deny but because we maintain our Évangelical position.

In the Church of Jesus Christ this doctrine has not always been *the* Word of the Gospel, and it would be an act of narrowing and unjust exclusiveness to proclaim and treat it as such. We have to express and assert it with its particular importance and difficulty and function. But we have also to remember that it relates only to one aspect of the Christian message of reconciliation. We have to understand this aspect with others. Neither explicitly nor implicitly have we to overlook this aspect. There never was and there never can be any true Christian Church without the doctrine of justification. In this sense it is indeed the *articulus stantis et cadentis ecclesiae.* There is no Christian Church without the truth of what God has done and does for man in virtue of its witness, without the manifestation of this truth in some form in its life and doctrine. But in the true Church of Jesus Christ the formulated recognition and attestation of this truth may withdraw, it may indeed be more or less hidden behind other aspects of the Christian message, without it being right and necessary to draw attention to its absence, to believe that its truth is denied and the unity of the Church is broken. When we come across actual cases of this we have to remind ourselves and others of something which has perhaps been forgotten or mistaken. But we for our part have to remain open to aspects of the Christian message which are perhaps new to us. It is the justification of man itself, and our very

confidence in the objective truth of the doctrine of justification, which
forbids us to postulate that in the true Church its theological outworking must *semper, ubique et ab omnibus* be regarded and treated as the
unum necessarium, the centre or culminating point of the Christian
message or Christian doctrine.

The view of A. Schweitzer and W. Wrede is probably exaggerated that in
Paul's doctrine of the δικαιοσύνη θεοῦ, or πίστεως, we have to do only with a "subsidiary crater," i.e., a controversial doctrine in his conflict with the Judaisers.
But so, too, was the doctrine of Luther and the younger Melanchthon that Paul
is only the great apostolic teacher of justification. The Christology of Paul is
more than simply an argument for his doctrine of justification. And his view of
the corporate and individual fellowship of Christians with Christ, his view of
the relationship between the Church and Israel as developed in Rom. 9–11, his
ethics too, all have their own roots and heads, although they cannot, of course,
be separated from this doctrine. In 1 Cor. 1[30] we read that Christ Jesus is made
unto us wisdom, righteousness, sanctification and redemption, and this obviously
means that we are pointed in at least three other directions. And the epistles of
Paul are not the whole of the New Testament. If caution is necessary in relation
to the view that the Pauline doctrine of justification is disputed in the Epistle
of James, there can be no doubt that the message of James and the Synoptics
and the Johannine writings and the other parts of the New Testament witness
cannot be simply equated with this doctrine, even though it is not excluded by
but included in them.

As already mentioned, the Church of the first centuries lived in a naive
Pelagianism (as also in a naive Adoptionism or Sabellianism). It did not know
any explicit doctrine of justification—*per nefas* and to its shame, we might say.
But if we are tempted to blame or accuse the Early Church for it, we must never
forget that we are dealing with the Church and theology of the Christendom of
the martyr-centuries, which obviously knew without the doctrine of justification
what their faith was all about, and for which the truth of the doctrine was not in
question, although they did not clearly understand it. The same can be said
of the later Greek Church and of the Eastern Church generally. The development of the doctrine of justification which began with Augustine was something
which belonged specifically to the Western Church. The East was much less
interested in the contrast between sin and grace than in that between death and
life, between mortality and immortality. It had no great concern for the problem
of law—the question of the possibility and basis of a positive relationship between
God and man. Therefore in this matter of justification (and this was no doubt
a limitation) it contented itself with the bare minimum.

In the West it was only at the time of the Reformation that the doctrine of
justification became a burning issue, or, to put it more exactly, it was only in
the questing German spirit of Luther. But then this doctrine—although not
only this doctrine—impressed itself upon the face of Protestantism in its relation
to the ancient Church. Not only this doctrine : note the place and function of
the doctrine in Calvin's *Institutio*. He saw its basic, critical importance. He
developed it (III, 11–18) broadly and carefully, marking off both the Romanist
errors on the one hand and the Protestant, like those of A. Osiander, on the
other. But in the obvious modern dispute amongst Calvin scholars concerning
his central doctrine no one would ever dream of maintaining that it is to be
found in his doctrine of justification. In many passages of his masterpiece, and
in other writings as well, he asserts that there are two main gifts which the
Christian owes to Christ or the Holy Spirit, *iustificatio* (or *remissio peccatorum*)
on the one hand, and indissolubly connected with it *sanctificatio* (or *renovatio*
or *regeneratio*) on the other. And if we consider as a whole his doctrine *De modo*

percipiendae gratiae in the third book of the *Institutes*, it seems more obvious to see in the second of these, the question of the development and formation of the Christian life and therefore of sanctification, the problem which controls and organises his thinking. This is in accordance with the tendency already found in Zwingli and in the reconstruction of the Church in Switzerland and other non-German territories which derives from him. In Calvin the doctrine of justification offered the necessary basis and critical certainty for the answering of this question, although not without being itself caught up in and rather overshadowed by the doctrine of predestination, which was raised later (*c*. 21–24) and which plumbed the matter even further. Or is the starting point the *insitio* of the Christian into Christ which is described at the very beginning of the third book (*c*. 1) and which is accomplished by the Holy Spirit ? Or do we have to seek the basic teaching in the doctrine of faith as such which we find developed in *c*. 2 ? One thing at least is certain—that if the theology of Calvin has a centre at all, it does not lie in the doctrine of justification. The doctrine of the older Reformed Church which followed him usually kept to the *schema* justification and sanctification so often laid down by him. By separating the two and pursuing them along different paths, it was more able to give the proper emphasis and therefore to take seriously the second question (that of sanctification, of the Christian's obedience of faith, of good works) than were the Lutherans. It was also less susceptible to the temptation which threatened from the very first to weaken and obscure the answer to the question of justification by mixing it with the question of sanctification (which could not be avoided). That this actually happened in Neo-Lutheran theology (including Ritschl and his followers) is the charge levelled against them rather violently but not unjustly by a Reformed teacher in Vienna, Edward Böhl (*Dogmatik* 1887, *Von der Rechtfertigung durch den Glauben* 1890). The only trouble is that the first and positive concern of the Calvinistic distinction seems to be concealed from Böhl himself. We might almost describe him as a Reformed hyper-Lutheran like his teacher and father-in-law, Hermann Kohlbrügge, for he thought that he could appeal to the doctrine of justification as the cardinal dogma of Protestantism (something which no Lutheran either old or new had ever dared to do).

But it is worth noting that in Luther himself—although we might easily miss it under the overpowering impression of his doctrine of justification and what he has to say concerning it—we can trace a pervasive and not by any means a thin line in which he did not speak with the onesidedness that we should expect from his talk of the *unicus articulus*, but with an obvious two-sidedness, with the same kind of two-sidedness as later characterises the thought of Calvin. He could speak (*Enarr. on Is.* 53⁸, 1544, *W.A.* 40ᴵᴵᴵ, 726, 24) of a twofold *sanatio* of man proceeding from the exalted Christ : the one the forgiveness of sins by virtue of His substitutionary death ; the other the gracious gift of a holy life purifying itself from sins. Or, again (*Pred. üb. Act.* 2¹ᶠ·, *W.A.* 52, 317, 22), of a twofold sanctification, the first perfect, the other imperfect but, in its own way, no less real. Or, again (*Pred. üb. Kor.* 1 5⁶ᶠ·, *W.A.* 21, 16), of a twofold purification, the first having taken place once and for all in Christ, the second to be accomplished day by day in us. Or, again (*Pred. üb. Luk.* 16¹ᶠ·, *E.A.* 13, 238), of a twofold justification, inwardly in the spirit and before God only by faith, outwardly and publicly, before men and according to the judgment of men by works. Or, again (*Pred. üb. Matth.* 22³⁴ᶠᶠ·, 1537, *W.A.* 45, 34), of a twofold help of Christ, the first consisting in the fact that He represented us before God, spreading out His wings over us against the devil like a hen over her chickens, the second that He feeds and nourishes us with the Holy Spirit as a hen does her chickens, so that we begin to love God and keep His commandments. Or, again (*zu Gal.* 3¹⁸, *W.A.* 40ᴵ, 408, 24), of a twofold fulfilling of the Law, the first by the imputation of the righteousness of Jesus Christ, the second by the gift of the Holy Spirit which begets a new life. In substance the distinction is one and the same. Luther connected the two elements of the atoning activity of God in Christ with the relationship between eternity and time, between the present and the future life of man, between heaven and earth, or (*zu Gal.* 2¹², *W.A.* 40¹, 427, 11) between the divine and the human nature of Jesus Christ. Many things have to be noted. As the parallels show, and in accordance with his basic view, (1) he never hesitates to assert the priority of the first of the two elements over the other : the one is the main part (*Pred. üb.* 1 *Petr.* 2²⁰ᶠ·, *W.A.* 21, 313, 22), the other is secondary. Again (2) on every available opportunity he shows the great difference between them. He describes them separately (with particular emphasis on the first) and therefore refrains from doing the very thing which was so often attempted under his name, the merging of the first into the second, or the second into the first, the interpretation of justification in terms of sanctification or of sanctification in terms of justification. But (3) he insists that both these parts have always to be properly maintained. If either of them is forgotten or neglected in favour of the other, this will inevitably involve the corruption either of faith or of its power and fruit. And (4) he perceives and confesses that the origin and unity of the two elements, the source and object of a necessarily complete Christian faith and the measure of a necessarily incomplete Christian obedience, is in Jesus Christ acting for us as very God and very man. It is clear—and this is our present concern—that side by side with the doctrine of justification and distinct from it, directly confronting and connected with it, but seen and asserted with the same clarity, he also knew and taught this second article, which Calvin was everywhere to present as that of *sanctificatio.* All these statements are, of course, drawn from the theology of the older Luther. More recent research (cf. Axel Gyllenkrok, *Rechtfertigung und Heiligung in der frühen ev. Theologie Luthers,* 1952) has shown that at first Luther did not dialectically equate justification and sanctification merely with one another, but also with Christology, and the three together with the Word of God, and the Word of God understood in this way and man's faith in the promised grace of God with the grace itself, and this again with the humble acknowledgment of sin. In this original and termendously profound enterprise of Luther there is no end to the parallels and coincidences of subject and object, of God and man, of giving and receiving, of passion and action. It was a *theologia crucis* which had strangely enough all the marks of a *theologia gloriae* : a theology which saw everything together from the standpoint of God (which will also be that of the believer). In his own lifetime Luther himself did not deny that this was his original enterprise, and we are always coming upon traces of it, blinding flashes and confusing uncertainties which we can explain only in the light of it. We do not have to decide here whether we prefer the younger Luther to the older. What is certain is that in that first stage of his thinking and teaching he did not manage to say plainly what he meant by the one thing or what he meant by the other, so that he could not establish with any theological clarity either a certainty of salvation or a Christian ethics. If we prefer the more violent dialectic of the younger Luther we must see to it that we are more successful than Luther himself in these two respects. It is also certain that, at the very latest in the early twenties—Gyllenkrok traces the beginning of the movement—Luther himself turned from this theology of parallels to a less interesting but more articulated theology of dissimilarities and distinctions—it was still exciting enough. If in his earlier period he had spoken almost suspiciously much of *humilitas,* he now began to practise it. His theology now became—I am almost bold to say for the first time—a *theologia viatorum.* It was reforming from the very first. In this new form it was effectively so for the edification of the Church. And the change is perhaps explicable from within if we can accept that it went hand in hand with a developing isolation of his Christology from the Christian anthropology which almost completely dominated his early thinking. At any rate we are forced to say that in the last resort Lutheranism old and new followed the direction of Luther—or at least the older Luther—when, like Calvin and Calvinism, it refused to centre its theology upon the one article of justification.

We have already drawn attention to the independent importance and function of the problem of sanctification side by side with that of justification not only in the older Protestantism but also in Calvin, and even Luther himself. But we have to remember that in this problem, from the historical standpoint, we have to do with the particular problem of Pietism and Methodism. Whatever reservations we may have with regard to this movement, an attempt to do justice to it is something which no Church dogmatics can evade.

But in conclusion we have also to remember that there is a third element in the reconciling work of God in Jesus Christ which, like sanctification, cannot be subsumed under the concept of justification, or can be so only very artificially and to the great detriment of the matter'. The office of Jesus Christ is that of the priest who sacrifices himself and the king who rules, but it is also that of the prophet. And the reconciling grace of God has a dimension and form which cannot simply be equated with justification or sanctification, the form and dimension of the calling of man, his teleological setting in the kingdom of God which comes and is present in Jesus Christ, the form of mission in relation to the community and in relation to the individual Christian the form of hope. There are many things that we can say against the theology of the last few centuries but they were not *saecula obscura* in this respect, that they brought out this aspect of the Christian message with a much greater clarity than it had for the great Christians of the 16th century. This was the time when the world-wide mission of the Church was taken up in earnest, the time of a new vision and expectation of the kingdom of God as coming and already come, the time of a new awakening of Christianity to its responsibility to state and society, the time of a new consciousness of its ecumenical existence and mission. These are actualities of Church history which a Church dogmatics cannot overlook. And here, as in the doctrine of sanctification, we shall have to adopt as far as we can the concern of the Eastern Church, which is so very remote from the tradition of the West, but is still genuinely grounded in the New Testament. One good reason for doing so is that in it we have to do with at least one of the roots of the secularised political and social Chiliasm of the Eastern world which, for all the horror and repugnance which it feels at its perversion, the Christian West has not so long outgrown that it can try to close its eyes to the *particula veri* perverted in this way. Now without justification there is certainly no calling, no mission, no hope, no responsibility to the world. We still have every reason to go very carefully into the great question of the Reformation and of Luther in particular. The modern movements and enterprises of which we have to think in this connexion have neglected this to their own hurt. It would not really harm the Eastern Church to try to understand seriously the doctrine of the justification of the sinner by faith alone—and certainly not the contemporary Eastern world. But, again, if we are going to consider properly what we have to consider in connexion with the prophetic office of Christ, we need a rather greater freedom than that which is allowed us if we move only within the framework of the Reformation doctrine of justification. All honour to the question : How can I find a gracious God ? But for too long it has been for Protestantism—at any rate European and especially German Protestantism—the occasion and temptation to a certain narcissism, and a consequent delay in moving in the direction we have just indicated.

The *articulus stantis et cadentis ecclesiae* is not the doctrine of justification as such, but its basis and culmination : the confession of Jesus Christ, in whom are hid all the treasures of wisdom and knowledge (Col. 2³) ; the knowledge of His being and activity for us and to us and with us. It could probably be shown that this was also the opinion of Luther. If here, as everywhere, we allow Christ to be the centre, the starting-point and the finishing point, we have no reason to fear that there will be any lack of unity and cohesion, and therefore of systematics in the best sense of the word.

The problem of justification does not need artificially to be absolutised and given a monopoly. It has its own dignity and necessity to which we do more and not less justice if we do not ascribe to it a totalitarian claim which is not proper to it, or allow all other questions to culminate or merge into it, or reject them altogether with an appeal to it, but if we accept it with all its limitations as this problem and try to answer it as such. Its very confusion and fusion with the problem of sanctification has only been to the detriment of its proper treatment. The general significance and reach of the doctrine of justification will themselves be better brought out if we accept it with all its limitations as this problem. And although other questions are all connected with it, and the answering of this question has for them the decisive significance of a leaven, they will then have their own particular place side by side with it. The doctrine of justification will then further the free development of the riches of Christian knowledge instead of hindering it. It can then be recalled with a good conscience as a warning where the importance of its particular truth is not recognised or where in the preoccupation with other interests it is far too rashly and unthinkingly assumed that it can be ignored. With a good conscience—for the inculcation of it will not be a compulsion, a Caudine yoke, a disqualification or artificial transmutation of that which at other times and places has rightly been important for others in the same knowledge of the one Jesus Christ. With a good conscience—for we can be open to the viewpoints of these others, and communication (and not simply tolerance) is then rightly possible in the Church. In its own place—in the context in which it has to be put and answered—the problem of justification does arise with a pitiless seriousness, and it has to be answered with the same seriousness : the problem of the presupposition and the possibility and the truth of the positive relationship of God with man, of the peace of man with God.

2. THE JUDGMENT OF GOD

By sin man puts himself in the wrong in relation to God. He makes himself impossible as the creature and covenant-partner of God. He desecrates the good nature which has been given and forfeits the grace which is addressed to him. He compromises his existence. For he has no right as sinner. He is only in the wrong.

The presupposition, the possibility and the truth of a positive relationship between God and man and the peace of man with God

consists (1) in there being a right which is superior, absolutely superior
to the wrong of which man is guilty and in which he now finds himself,
(2) in this right not merely being transcendent but worked out in
man and (3) in the wrong of man being set aside and a new human
right being established and set up in the working out of this higher
right. This higher right is the right of God, and its outworking, the
setting aside of the wrong of man and the restoration of his right, is
the judgment of God. The justification of man takes place in the
eventuation of this judgment.

We must first speak of the right of God which is absolutely superior
to the wrong of man. What kind of a right is this? We cannot see
it except in the judgment of God. But to understand this and the
justification of man, we must first lay down that it is right, the right
of God, which is worked out and executed in it. Where do we see the
freedom of God more clearly than in the justification of sinful man?
But nowhere do we see more clearly that it is true freedom and not
the false freedom of an arbitrary whim. The fact that God acts as
He does in the justification of man proves conclusively that He could
not act in this way just as well as any other but that what we have
here is not whim and caprice but right, the supreme right of all. Not,
of course, that God is determined and bound and limited by some
law which is different from Himself and therefore is forced to act in
this way. God does not stand under any alien law, any general truth
and possibility and presupposition embracing and conditioning and
limiting both Himself and the world and man. It would be a futile
undertaking to try to measure Him by any such law when answering
the question of His right. What we know or think we know as law,
truth, possibility and presupposition are hypotheses which (consciously
or unconsciously) we venture to hold because the world and man
actually derive from and are ruled by the One who is not merely the
supreme but the true and primary Law-giver, not *exlex* but Himself
lex, and therefore the source and norm and limit of all *leges*. There
can be no point in equating the essence of our laws and hypotheses
of right with the maxim on the basis of which God is our Creator and
Lord, and therefore trying to measure Him by one such principle of
order and to understand His activity in accordance with it. In the
justification of man God is in the right. Therefore any such path will
be a hopeless failure. The exposition of the doctrine of justification
has always suffered from the fact that attempts have been made to
determine the right of God in the activity which has to be explained
here by a hypothesis which is rashly held to be the same as His own
maxim, by a natural or moral law which is thought to be recognisable
as such. God—who is not a God " of confusion, but of peace " (1 Cor.
14³³)—is Himself (with supreme and inflexible strictness) law, maxim
and order: in perfect and unshakable harmony with Himself, in complete
loyalty to Himself, and, in distinction to the stars of the firmament

and all the phenomena of the nature and history of the created cosmos (although not at the expense of the richness of His inward being and outward activity), " without variableness or shadow of turning " (Jas. 1¹⁷). It is in this harmony with Himself that He very clearly acts in the justification of sinful man. This harmony with Himself is the right of God—the reliable anchor which is the basis of the community and the assurance of its faith. Nothing else could happen than that which does happen when God causes righteousness, His righteousness, to come to sinful man. If anything else could happen, if there were even the shadow of a well-founded doubt in relation to the presupposition and possibility and truth of justification, that would mean that God Himself is not law, that His harmony with Himself is discord, His freedom is whim and caprice, He Himself is *exlex*, in short, He is not God. Or, to put it the other way round, to doubt the truth of justification is to doubt God Himself. To reckon with any other possibility than that which is actualised in it is to reckon with the non-existence of God. To deny its actuality is to deny God. Or, again, to know God is to know the right of God in this matter. And, conversely, to know the right of God in this matter is to know God.

Hence the peculiar urgency of the problem of justification. It has its root in this problem of the right of God in His grace as addressed again and this time truly to sinful man. Therefore it brings us face to face with the whole, that is to say, the knowledge of God Himself. Of all the superficial catchwords of our age, surely one of the most superficial is that, whereas 16th century man was occupied with the grace of God, modern man is much more radically concerned about God Himself and as such. As though there were such a thing as God Himself and as such, or any point in seeking Him! As though grace were a quality of God which we could set aside while we leisurely ask concerning His existence! As though the Christian community and Christian faith had any interest in the existence or non-existence of this God Himself and as such! As though 16th century man with His concern for the grace of God and the right of His grace were not asking about God Himself and His existence with a radicalness compared with which the questioning of modern man is empty frivolity! As though that which seems to be lacking to modern man—and all the Christian Churches are very much to blame—were not that he has not learned to ask concerning God with this reality compared with which there is no other; that he asks concerning the existence of God without knowing for what he asks; that he maintains it perhaps without knowing what he is maintaining, or denies it without knowing what he is denying; that his asking and answering is necessarily frivolous because it is irrelevant! Obviously we cannot even begin to discuss with him until the discussion is lifted on to quite other ground by the proclamation of the Church, i.e., until the subject is put before him which alone gives any sense to the question about God—the one and only God who is gracious to man and who in His grace is in the right, faithful to Himself and in harmony with Himself.

The God who is present and active in the justification of man, and therefore as the gracious God, has right and is in the right. Not subject to any alien law, but Himself the origin and basis and revealer of all true law, He is just in Himself. This is the backbone of the event of justification.

It is the backbone of the relationship with God even in the Old Testament. Why does the Old Testament saint rest on the election of his people and the covenant which God made with it when its history is a continuous series of transgressions and consequent divine judgments? Why does he rest on the faithfulness and forbearance and mercy and grace of God when it is not concealed from him that he has not shown himself to be worthy of it and when it is revealed constantly by the triumph of his enemies that he has forfeited his right to appeal to that faithfulness? He plainly rests on God because he does not see in the election of Israel and God's covenant with it a happy chance or in the free loving-kindness of God a fortuitous favouritism, but the supreme and inflexible right of God; because His God is to Him One who is just in Himself, and not a being who one time can will and act in one way and another time in quite a different way. No, " thy right hand is full of righteousness " (Ps. 48¹⁰), " thy righteousness is like the great mountains " (Ps. 36⁶), it is " an everlasting righteousness " (Ps. 119¹⁴²). " For the righteous Lord loveth righteousness " (Ps. 11⁷): this is to him an ontological statement and therefore one which is indisputable and unchangeably valid. God is just in Himself. Because this is true for the Old Testament saint he does not merely think or believe but knows that God will be faithful to His election, that He will keep his covenant, that He will fulfil His promise. He therefore rests on his God, finding in Him his place of defence, his stronghold, his rock, in spite of everything which might cause him not to rest on Him. It is therefore in the election and covenant and loving-kindness of God that he sees this inward and therefore authentic and trustworthy justice of God.

But the same is true of the New Testament, and especially of the New Testament. How can Paul dare to pronounce himself and Christians both Jews and Gentiles free from the observance of the Law in view of the end of the Law as reached in Jesus Christ (Rom. 10⁴), referring them only and altogether to the Gospel of this One, to the ἀπολύτρωσις which has already taken place in Him (Rom. 3²⁴), to the love of God shed abroad in their hearts by the Holy Spirit (Rom. 5⁵), to the free obedience of the children of God impelled by the Spirit of God (Rom. 8¹⁴)? And all this in spite of the fact that the flesh and sin and death are still present realities both for him and for them. It was hardly *disputationis causa* that in his answer to this question he seized on the term δικαιοσύνη, nor was it by accident that in the first instance he always called it the δικαιοσύνη θεοῦ (and then as such the δικαιοσύνη πίστεως). This is the backbone of his Gospel, of his own faith and of the faith to which he summons men as an apostle. This is what makes possible and necessary the astonishing boldness of his message, and in practice of his way from the Synagogue to the ἐκκλησία, and out into the world as an ambassador of Jesus Christ. It is a matter of God and the righteousness of God. The grace of Jesus Christ deserves and demands faith and obedience and all confidence and all sacrifice and its relentless proclamation on the right hand and the left, both to Jews and Gentiles; its revelation and promulgation is the irruption of the last day, and the free word of its proclamation can anticipate the end of the last day and be pronounced as the final word even in a present which is still characterised by the flesh and sin and death, just because the grace of God as such is the outworking and fulfilment of the right of God, His righteous judgment. Why does Paul deny and reject the δικαιοσύνη διὰ νόμου (Gal. 2²¹), or ἐκ νόμου (Gal. 3²¹, Rom. 10⁵)? Why does he deny and reject all ἰδία δικαιοσύνη (Rom. 10³, Phil. 3⁹)? Because they do not work out in practice? Yes. Because they are opposed to the grace of Jesus Christ? Yes. But first and finally because being in opposition to grace they are opposed to the δικαιοσύνη θεοῦ, because in spite of their claims and appearance they do not rest on right but wrong, because they are not δικαιοσύνη but ἀδικία. In the revelation and efficacy (ἔνδειξις) of the grace of Jesus Christ proclaimed in the Gospel what comes first is not the justification of the believer in Jesus Christ but the basis of it—that God shows Himself to be just: εἰς τὸ εἶναι αὐτὸν δίκαιον, and only then and for that reason : καὶ δικαιοῦντα τὸν ἐκ πίστεως Ἰησοῦ (Rom. 3²⁶). In it God Himself is right. He is at one with Himself. He is faithful to Himself. That is its basic ⸢ontological content.⸥ And the corresponding content of the knowledge of God's own right in this matter—and therefore of the inflexibility of its goodness and necessity—is the mystery which marks off Paul's advocacy of this matter from an insubstantial and therefore equivocal assumption. He knows the point of departure in this matter, his own point of departure as an apostle of Jesus Christ. His feet are set on a rock. The faithfulness of God Himself, the πίστις τοῦ θεοῦ, which cannot be destroyed by any unfaithfulness of man (Rom. 3³), is the foundation of the πίστις in which he himself lives and which he proclaims. And the recognition of the πιστὸς ὁ θεός (" But God is true " : 2 Cor. 1¹⁸, cf. also 1 Cor. 1⁹) is the pledge and guarantee that His Word to the communities and the world is not an unreliable Yes and No. But how does he know that God is true to Himself ? The continuation (2 Cor. 1¹⁹) tells us that it is by the fact that in the Jesus Christ, the Son of God, proclaimed by Him what is revealed and active is not a Yes and No but the plain Yes of God.

This is the right of God which is maintained in the justification of sinful man, which marks it off even as a free act of grace from the caprice and arbitrariness of a destiny that apportions blindfold its favour and disfavour, which clothes it with majesty and dignity, which gives to the knowledge of faith an infallible certainty—that in the first instance God affirms Himself in this action, that in it He lives His own divine life in His unity as Father, Son and Holy Spirit. But in it He also maintains Himself as the God of man, as the One who has bound Himself to man from all eternity, as the One who has elected Himself for man and man for Himself. In the action of His grace He executes that which He willed and determined when to man as this creature He gave actuality and his human nature. In executing it He does not surrender anything. And in His relationship to man He does not transgress but fulfils His own law, beside which there is no other and above which there is no higher, the law which is Himself. In this respect, too, the grace which He exercises in justification is not one which is foreign to Him. It is not an act in the performance of which He has to alter or correct Himself, in which He has in part at least to cease to be God and therefore true to Himself. If it were otherwise, how could there be a confidence in His grace which corresponds to the deity of God ? How could the revelation of it be the solid basis of the community, the durable certainty of faith ? How could the confession of it be distinguished from a mere value-judgment of religion, dependent for its truth upon the power of the human religiosity expressed in it ? And beyond that, how could God have given up His own Son to execute it and His own Holy Spirit to reveal it ? In that He has done and does do this, He shows Himself to be the One who as the gracious God is righteous and as the righteous God gracious. It is not at the expense but in the exercise of His

Godhead that for the sake of all flesh His Word becomes flesh (Jn. 1^{14}). It is not a denial but a confirmation of His Godhead that He causes His Holy Spirit to dwell and work as the witness of His grace in those who are still threatened by sin and the flesh and death.

As the God who in all this was true to Himself, in the power of this His right, He encountered man in justification, the man who is in the wrong before Him. What is this wrong of man? We know it as the outrage of his pride in which in direct contrast to the nature and way of the God who is righteous in His grace he strives for a dignity which is not his. We know it as the movement in which man undoubtedly alienates himself from God, making God his enemy and bringing upon himself the wrath of God. We know it as the movement in which man can only wither, in which he can only corrupt and destroy himself and therefore the work of God. We know it as man's impossible and senseless alliance with the darkness which God the Creator has marked off from light and rejected, as the great and inconceivable, but for all its inconceivability very real, invasion of that which is, because God has willed and created it, by that which in itself is not. We know it as the fate which man deserves, which comes upon man, which man has to suffer, but which is an offence to God because it is contrary to His will, the greatness of which can be measured only by the fact that in His Son God has Himself risen up to meet it, and destroy it, becoming the Saviour of man in His encounter with it, and restoring His own offended honour. We have every reason to be horrified at the actuality of it. In nature and form and operation it belongs to a dimension which does not in any sense allow us even theoretically to ignore or overlook it, to understand it in terms of category, and to that extent to relativise and control it. We are at once forced to relinquish any attempts in this direction when we consider that we are no more able to control it in practice than we are to jump over our own shadow. And the decisive ground of this impossibility is that God Himself has risen up to control it, taking the matter once and for all into His own hands.

But whatever may be the wrong of man, there can be no doubt that it does not belong to the same dimension as the right of God and cannot stand against it. It does not alter in the slightest the seriousness with which we have to consider it, but we still have to remember that it is absolutely subordinate to the right of God, that for all its greatness it is infinitely small in relation to it. It is a matter of man's rebellion against God, of the invasion of God's good creation by chaos. God Himself—and first of all—takes it in all seriousness. He takes it so seriously that He encounters it in His own person. It grieves Him for our sake, His creatures and covenant-partners. It offends His glory that in committing it we turn against Him and therefore have to be without Him. But there can be no question whatever of its being His equal. If it is great before Him because it is wrong against *Him*, it is also small before Him because it is wrong, and therefore cannot either be or posit another right to compete with His right. It can say only No and not a corresponding Yes. It does not found any new being or new man or new world. It would like to do so. We cannot deny to it the reality of a desire for this. But no more. It is only its aim to found a kingdom. From the very first it has no power to do so. It is not in any way comparable with God the Creator, nor is its work in any way comparable with the creation of God. The wrong of man cannot in any way alter the right of God.

It cannot alter it especially to the extent that as the right of the Creator and the Lord of the covenant it is His right over man and to man. If man puts Himself in the wrong that means that as the creature and covenant-partner of God, man is unworthy of the right held out to him, that he forfeits that right, that he corrupts and destroys his existence. His concurrence with the right of God, to which he is determined by his election and calling and for which he is prepared by the good nature with which he is endowed, is the presupposition of his very existence. In conflict with God he can only wither and fade and perish and die and be lost. By the fact that he sets himself in the wrong he cannot take away the right which God has over Him and to Him. He cannot even break it or limit it. In face of his wrong, God is still God, and He is unchanged in His right, the right of the One who has elected and made Himself the Creator and the Lord of the covenant. Whatever man may do in the folly of his pride, he cannot disrupt this self-determination of God, nor can he make for himself a place or status or being in which to have what he obviously aims to have, an independent existence, a genuine freedom in face of God. Not even in hell can he have and enjoy this freedom. Every kind of demon possession is possible, but it is not possible to make the nature and existence of man devilish. Man may fall. Indeed he necessarily falls, and into the abyss, when he sets himself in the wrong against God. But in this fall into the abyss he cannot fall out of the sphere of God and therefore out of the right which God has over him and to him. Even in his most shameful thoughts and words and deeds, even in the most terrible denial and perversion of his good nature, even in the complete forfeiture of his rights and dignity as a man, even in the lowest depths of hell, whatever that may mean for him, he is still the man whom God has elected and created, and as such he is in the hand of God. He has not escaped the right of God over him and to him, but is still subjected to it, utterly and completely. He is still in the sphere of God's jurisdiction.

But God does exercise this jurisdiction. There can be no question, therefore, of His acquiescing in the fact that man puts himself in the wrong, of His consenting to man's wrong. He would not be God, the living God, if He could do that, let alone if He willed to do it and did it, if He were content to be in the right and true to Himself in face of man's wrong, to continue—although only, as it were, theoretically —to maintain His right over man and to man without exercising it, in such a way, therefore, that the hand is inactive in which He irresistibly holds man and by which man is inescapably held. His right is the right of the judgment which is executed by Him. It is not merely a valid right but one which is exercised. It is the right which God exercises for His own sake (because He is not a dead but the living God) and for the sake of the creature and covenant-partner man who even as a transgressor is still subject to His right, and therefore again, in this sense, for His own sake, because in these two ways man is His and belongs to Him.

Man's wrong cannot be merely his own affair. It takes place in his relationship with God. In essence it is directed against God. It contradicts and opposes His right. Because of this it demands the judgment which is the application of His right and the exercise of His righteousness. It has fallen victim to its execution. Because God is in the right against it in these two ways, the wrong of man cannot be maintained or tolerated. Man cannot be allowed to put himself in the wrong, to renounce the right which is set up for him by God, to execute in the sphere of the divine jurisdiction the movement in which he acts as though he were not subject to it and could in some way escape it. This movement is quite futile. It cannot attain its end. For with the man who executes it, it stands under the non-willing of God, under His superior contradiction and opposition, under the wrath of God. The fact that God applies and reveals His right means that between Him and the wrong of man, which is to say at once between Him and the man who puts himself in the wrong, there arises a conflict and crisis in which the man who puts himself in the wrong is not the judge of God, but in virtue of the unconditional superiority of His right God is the judge of man. Man's wrong, i.e., man himself as a wrongdoer cannot stand in the judgment of God. The righteousness of God means God's negating and overcoming and taking away and destroying wrong and man as the doer of it.

" The mighty God, even the Lord, hath spoken, and called the earth from the rising of the sun unto the going down thereof. Out of Zion, the perfection of beauty, God hath shined. Our God shall come, and shall not keep silence : a fire shall devour before him, and it shall be very tempestuous round about him. He shall call to the heavens from above, and to the earth, that he may judge his people. Gather my saints together unto me, those that have made a covenant with me by sacrifice. And the heavens shall declare his righteousness : for God is judge himself " (Ps. 50[1-6]). " For thou art not a God that hath pleasure in wickedness : neither shall evil dwell with thee " (Ps. 5[4]). " Therefore the ungodly shall not stand in the judgment, nor sinners in the congregation of the righteous. For the Lord knoweth the way of the righteous ; but the way of the ungodly shall perish " (Ps. 1[5f.]). " The face of the Lord is against them that do evil, to cut off the remembrance of them from the earth " (Ps. 34[16]). " The enemies of the Lord shall be as the fat of lambs : they shall consume ; into smoke shall they consume away " (Ps. 37[20]). " For thine arrows stick fast in me, and thy hand presseth me sore. There is no soundness in my flesh because of thine anger ; neither is there any rest in my bones because of my sin. For mine iniquities are gone over my head : as an heavy burden they are too heavy for me " (Ps. 38²ᶠ·). " For we are consumed by thine anger, and by thy wrath we are troubled. Thou hast set our iniquities before thee, our secret sins in the light of thy countenance. For all our days are passed away in thy wrath : we spend our years as a tale that is told " (Ps. 90⁷ᶠ·). These are only a few voices singled out from the great Old Testament chorus of witnesses to the crisis in which God is the Judge of sinful man. And the New Testament confirms this witness—on the basis of a quite different outlook from that which was possible for the Israelites in consequence of the visitations which came upon them : " For what fellowship hath righteousness with unrighteousness ? and what communion hath light with darkness ? " (2 Cor. 6¹⁴). And in the decisive passage : " The wrath of God is revealed from heaven against all ungodliness and unrighteousness of men, who hold the truth in unrighteousness " (Rom. 1¹⁸).

Note that this also means, and primarily, that it is not too small a thing for God to defend and maintain His right, His lordship and His claim as Creator and Lord of the covenant against the wrong of man, and man as the doer of that wrong, even to the point of bringing about this crisis. His stake in man is so great. His right over man and to man is so much on His heart. He carries it through with such consistency. He will so little tolerate man's refusal to accept His divine right. He is so much a living God, and the rule of His righteousness is so necessary and complete.

But in saying this have we not indirectly and implicitly said something else, something which is apparently the very opposite of His non-willing and contradicting and opposing and wrath ? Have we not said that the rule of His grace is so necessary and complete and that He is so much a gracious God ? Yes, indirectly we have said this, too. For what kind of a will is it in which God willed from all eternity to co-exist with man ? Seeing He is free, and it was not too small a thing for Him to will this, to will Himself in this co-existence in His eternal Son and Word, it is obviously His free and gracious will. And what kind of an eternal decree of God is it in which, conversely— and again in His eternal Son and Word—He elected man to this co-existence with Himself ? Seeing He did not owe this to man, yet man was not too small to Him that He should make this decree concerning him, it is obviously the decree of His free election of grace. What kind of a divine act is the creation of man, his endowment and equipment with his human nature as appointed to serve God, the setting up of his existence with its reality which is different from His own reality and yet absolutely related to His own existence ? Seeing that in it the planning and willing and capacity of man is nothing and the wisdom of the decision and act of God is everything, it is obviously the inconceivable work of the divine grace. If, then, the right of God over and to man is grounded in the inward right of His Godhead, if it is right in the strict and supreme sense, what other right can it be than that of His grace, and what else can the exercise and application of it be in His righteousness but in its very essence and at its very heart the realisation of His grace ? Or as a work of the righteousness of God—whatever may happen in it, whatever we may have to think and say concerning it—is it not at the same time a work of His grace that it is not too small a thing for Him to enter into this conflict with the wrong of man and therefore with the man who does it ? Do we not have to say that even in the non-willing, the wrath of God expressed in this conflict, even in the terrible " Away with thee " which is pronounced upon the wrong of man and therefore upon man as the doer of it, what rules finally and properly is grace, the divine Yes deeply buried under the divine No, in so far as God's free address to man is operative even in the No ? At any rate God has not turned away His face from him. He has not withdrawn His hand. He does not cease to speak with him and act towards him. He continues to do so, even if it is in this way. He still regards him as His elect. In a way which is painful but intensive He still encounters him as his God, and He treats him as His man. Even in the hiddenness of this crisis He still holds fellow-ship with him, and because in all its forms, and therefore in this form, this fellowship rests on His divine right, because it is a work of right-eousness, but because as the fellowship into which He has freely entered with man it cannot be otherwise understood than as grace, we cannot refuse to see that even in the judgment which comes upon man and his wrong God is gracious to man.

The crisis which comes upon man when he encounters the righteousness of God, but in which the grace of God is secretly present and operative, is frequently described in the Bible as chastisement. " Behold, happy is the man whom God correcteth : therefore despise not thou the chastening of the Almighty " (Job 5[17]). For : " as many as I love, I rebuke and chasten " (Rev. 3[19]). In an apparent paradox, Ps. 62[12] grounds and recognises the mercy of God in the fact that He renders " to every man according to his work." The normative con-ception is that of the father who shows his fatherly love to the son by the strict exercise of his fatherly right. This is the thought in Prov. 3[11f.]. " My son, despise not thou the chastening of the Lord ; neither be weary of his correction : For whom the Lord loveth he correcteth ; even as a father the son in whom he delighteth." And again in Heb. 12[7f.] : " If ye endure chastening, God dealeth with you as with sons ; for what son is he whom the father chasteneth not ? But if ye be without chastisement . . . then are ye bastards, and not sons." The original form of this conception, which plainly reveals its relation to the redemptive history, is perhaps in the promise given to David in 2 Sam. 7[14f.] with respect to his son : " I will be his father, and he shall be my son. If he commit iniquity, I will chasten him . . . but my grace shall not depart away from him." The wrath of God is purposeful, not purposeless and meaningless and unlimited. So little is it the latter than in contrast to the livelong and indeed eternal goodness of God its duration can be rather boldly described as only for a moment (Ps. 30[5], Is. 54[8]). The men of the Bible do not fail to recognise its seriousness. But they boldly count upon its formal limitation : " Thou shalt arise, and have mercy upon Zion : for the time to favour her, yea, the set time, is come " (Ps. 102[13]). And they always look back to its dominion : " The Lord hath chastened me sore : but he hath not given me over unto death " (Ps.

118¹⁸)—this was the passage which Paul had in mind in 2 Cor. 6⁹ : " As dying, and behold, we live ; as chastened, and not killed." " For thou, O God, hast proved us ; thou hast tried us, as silver is tried. Thou broughtest us into the net ; thou laidst affliction upon our loins. Thou hast caused men to ride over our heads ; we went through fire and through water ; but thou broughtest us out into a wealthy place " (Ps. 66¹⁰ᶠ·). " Now no chastening for the present seemeth to be joyous, but grievous : nevertheless afterward it yieldeth the peaceable fruit of righteousness unto them that are exercised thereby (τοῖς δι' αὐτῆς γεγυμνασμένοις) " (Heb. 12¹¹). Where there is this fruit, there has obviously been the corresponding seed.

We must give the precedence over everything else to this statement concerning the grace of God in the rule of His righteousness. Its basis is plain in the goal of this event, where the grace of God is evident in the destruction of the wrong of man and the restoration of the right which he has squandered and lost. But the right perception of everything else depends upon the perception that the goal of this rule of the divine righteousness does not contradict but corresponds to its beginning, that from the very first it moves towards this goal. What God does in the gracious act of justifying the ungodly is not a sidestep or an act of juggling. He Himself in this act is not a *deus ex machina*, an unjust judge. He is the righteous Judge. From the very first His action in righteousness is the rule of His grace, and the action of His grace is the rule of His righteousness. How else could it be trustworthy and therefore credible and therefore the genuine redemption of sinful man ? How else could the knowledge of it be the true consolation of sinful man which he can maintain in triumphant defiance of every temptation and doubt ? How else could it be both legitimate and possible to confess : " Therefore being justified by faith, we have peace with God " (Rom. 5¹) ? The subjective knowledge expressed in this Christian confession and rising far beyond any mere opinion or suspicion rests in the objective knowledge that the gracious justification of man is the work of God's eternal righteousness.

But this anticipation must not prevent us from facing without reservation the full seriousness of the ⟨crisis⟩ which comes on man in his encounter with the righteousness of God. We have been speaking of the grace of God which is hidden deep under the righteousness of God, which can disclose itself to us men who are wrongdoers only by the act of God, which is not simply disclosed and cannot be disclosed by us : as though we had only, as it were, to reverse the righteousness of God to find that its other side is grace ; or as though we could see through the righteousness of God as through a veil, thus coming to the consoling conclusion that the true meaning and purpose of the judgment of God is His grace. For how do we know this ? In itself, the grace of God is His free grace. And the knowledge of it (both ontic and noetic) is also free. It cannot be controlled by us. It cannot be comprehended even theoretically. God is indeed true to Himself and it is grounded in His divine right that He should be gracious in

Crisis

the rule of His righteousness. But that does not mean that of ourselves we can count on His grace, regarding it as our own, boasting of it, applying it to ourselves, claiming it. This has to happen. This is what faith does, as we often find it rather astonishingly in the Psalms. But faith does not do it in any impertinent way, with any arrogance, but in a freedom which can only be given to man, which has nothing whatever to do with his own capacity, which rests only on the fact that by the revelation of His grace, by the word of His promise, God has put it in a position to do it, to postulate grace. The believer is well aware that of himself he is not in a position and cannot put himself in a position to do this. He confesses that he is the man who is in the wrong before God and has therefore no right to do this. The man who is in the wrong before God has no insight into the grace hidden in the righteousness of God, let alone any claim to it, let alone any hold upon it. It is secretly present and at work for him, but that is nothing to him. In the act of his wrongdoing he protests against it; he exists (in flagrant contradiction to his being as the creature and covenant-partner of God) as one whom it does concern, who will not live by it, who will not be obedient to it, who rather flees and hates it. The pride of man which is his sin is that he will not know anything of the grace of God. And his fall is that he does not actually know anything of it, that having turned away from it he cannot take refuge in it or return to it. For how else can he have a gracious God?

He does not have a gracious God but a wrathful God. That is how he wants Him and that is how he has Him. The consequent crisis which comes upon him, that God will not accept his wrong, but exerts His right over him and to him, confronting him, therefore, in righteousness, is both total and inevitable. Setting himself in the wrong before God, he cannot and will not stand before Him. As this man he is completely impossible before God, without any hope of salvation. For wrong is an outrage and abomination to God. It has to perish. The right of God confronts it with such majesty. It cannot exist before it. It is taken and burnt up and destroyed by the life of God like dry wood by the fire. This is the event of His righteousness. What takes place in it is the breaking of a catastrophe. And wrong does not exist merely *in abstracto* but in the act and therefore in the heart of man. Man gives to it the nature and form which it could not have of itself, since it is not the creation of God. He gives to it a place and actuality in the created world to which it does not belong, in which there is no category of its possibility. Man is the dark corner where wrong can settle and spread and flourish in all its nothingness as though by right. It is therefore man who evokes the wrath of God, who comes into conflict with the righteousness of God, upon whom it breaks as crisis, as catastrophe, as mortal sickness. He is the one who is impossible and intolerable before God, who cannot remain in His presence but can only disappear. It is his existence

sinful man has to die

which is untenable. It is he who is confronted by the majestic right of God. It is he who must perish. " There is no peace, saith the Lord, unto the wicked " (Is. 48²², 57²¹). This applies to him. There is no escaping this judgment of God, this sentence and the execution of it, least of all by the consideration which is theologically quite true that at bottom the righteousness of God is that of the gracious God. This is true enough. But it means nothing to man as a wrongdoer. It has no significance for him. This man has to be repaid, and repaid according to his works. This man has to die. And it is, of course, the hidden grace of the righteousness of God which demands this retribution in virtue of which he cannot live but only die. God would not be gracious to him, and it would not be good for him—what would be the point ?—if he could live and not die, if the judgment of God were not to fall upon him, and in all its inescapable fulness and strictness.

We are speaking of this man, man the wrongdoer, the man who has identified himself with wrong, and who in so doing has fallen victim to the divine negating and overcoming and setting aside and destruction. But is there any other man ? Can the man who is this man also be quite a different man ? Certainly even as this man he has not ceased to be the good creature and the elect of God. Even as a wrongdoer he cannot fall from the hand of God ; he cannot, as it were, snatch himself out of the divine grasp. And that means that, even as he identifies himself with wrong, he cannot cease to be the man who is the divine work and possession. As God is still the same, so man is still the same even when that catastrophe breaks upon him, even in the consuming fire of the wrath of God, even in his mortal sickness, even when he has to perish, even in his dying and destruction. If he has no power to prevent this, this does not mean that he has the power to put an end to his existence as the good creature and the elect of God, which would mean that he has the power to escape the kingdom of God and effectively to oppose the will of God.

That is what Jonah tried to do : " But Jonah rose up to flee unto Tarshish from the presence of the Lord, and went down to Joppa ; and he found a ship going to Tarshish : so he paid the fare thereof, and went down unto it, to go with them unto Tarshish from the presence of the Lord " (Jon. 1³). But, of course, he failed. As God was still the same in relation to him, he was still the same before God, His commissioned prophet. He was this even when the terrible storm broke upon him and when he tried to sleep it out in the sides of the ship, as man so often likes to do when the judgment of God comes upon him. He was this even when he was to be cast into the sea, and actually was cast into the sea. He was this in the belly of the great fish and therefore in the final extremity of the divine judgment which overtook him. And his salvation was not a new thing, but the realisation of the inflexible divine purpose against which he had striven in vain.

If it is the case, then, that as a wrongdoer man has fallen victim to the strict and radical and definitive judgment of God but still continues to belong to Him as the good creature and elect of God, this means that the righteousness of God comes upon him as a crisis in the sense that its realisation involves a separation which cuts his existence at the very root, severing it right across, dividing him into a right and a left. For who and what is he? On the left hand he determines himself as a doer of the wrong with which he has identified himself and in which he is caught up in the divine judgment. On the right hand he does not cease to be a wrongdoer and therefore under the divine judgment, but he determines himself as man, as the possession of God, in the kingdom of God, the object of His positive will and purpose, on the way to the goal which God has marked out for him. On the left hand, therefore, he is the man who can only perish, who is overtaken by the wrath of God, who can only die, who has already been put to death and done away, and on the right hand he is the same man who even in this dying and perishing, even as the one who has been put away, is still the one who stands over against God, object of His purposes, surrounded and maintained by His life. To put it in another way, on the left hand man is the one who because of His wrong is condemned and rejected and abandoned by God, and on the right hand he is the same man as the one who even in his condemnation and rejection and abandonment is still pardoned and maintained by God, being kept for the fulfilment of His will and plan. We have to say at once that on both sides God acts righteously, because He acts in consequence of His right, of His faithfulness to Himself, and in execution of His right over and to man. On the left hand He acts righteously in His wrath which consumes the sinner, and on the right hand He acts righteously in the limitation, or more exactly in the interpretation of His wrath, in His holding fast to the man who even as a sinner that He can only chide is still His man. And God is righteous in this distinction as such: for satisfaction would not be done to His right if He could only chide on the left hand or only pardon on the right, if He accepted the identification of man with wrong, and was content simply to banish from the world both wrong and the wrongdoer, or if in spite of the wrong which man has done and his identification with it He allowed him to live at the price of not destroying the wrong which man has committed, of recognising *de facto* its right to exist. The righteousness of God would not be God's righteousness and therefore it would not be true righteousness if it did not proceed on both sides, i.e., if its fulfilment did not involve this division which cuts right across the whole of man's existence.

We take up an earlier point when we interject at once that this righteousness would not be the righteousness of God if the distinction as such—and that which happens to man on the left hand as well as the right—were not the work of His grace. We have seen that even that which God does on the left hand is grace. It is not too small a thing for God actually to continue His fellowship with man in the form of the wrath which consumes man because of his wrong. And we have seen that it would not in fact be good for man to continue to be as a wrongdoer, that it is therefore grace if he has to perish and die as such. But how much more the work of God on the right hand, in which He does not abandon man even in his fall into the abyss, in which He does not cast him out of His hand, in which He does not annul and extinguish his being as His creature and covenant-partner, in which He remains to him a home even in the far country into which he has wandered, in which even in death He surrounds and maintains him with His own life! If on both sides it is true that the final mystery of the righteousness of God is His grace, then it must be the case that man experiences both and therefore the totality of grace, wrath and destruction and death to the man of sin, pardon and preservation to the man who even as a sinner is the creature of God and elect. Necessarily, therefore, there is this separation in the execution of the right of God.

But now—at the risk of making the puzzle seem even harder—we must go on to add that the righteousness (and therefore the grace) of God would not be the righteousness (and grace) of God if its work were not carried right through on both sides, if as the work of God it were not a genuine and a perfect work. On the left hand, therefore, it is not at all the case that God condemns man only nominally and that only in appearance He destroys him with his wrong. And it is also not the case that He causes him only nearly or half to die and to perish. Again, on the right hand, it is not at all the case that He will only partly spare and preserve him, that He will allow or promise or grant him as His creature and elect only a partial right—a bare right to exist. On the contrary, on the left hand it is the case that God judges man and his wrong in all seriousness, that He destroys him genuinely and truly and altogether, that this man has actually to die, that the wrong with which he is identified has actually to be purged and consumed—a whole burnt offering in the flame of which both he and his sin are burnt up, disappearing in the smoke and savour, and ceasing to be. And on the right hand it is the case that God accepts His creature and elect genuinely and truly and altogether, that the faithfulness which He displays to him does not flicker like an exhausted lamp but shines out brightly like the sun. The words pardoning and preserving and maintaining which we have so far used to describe the activity of God on this side are far too weak, because here on this positive side we are dealing with the positive replacement of the wrong which has been set aside, with its crowding out by the new right of man, with the fact that to seal the passing of the dead and unrighteous man God introduces a new and righteous man in his place. In the one case as in the other therefore, in His No and also in His Yes, God does for man an honest and perfect work. In the one case, as in the other, He does not fashion a mere *quid pro quo*, a mere " as if," but actualities. He does not do a little pulling down here and a little building up there, but in both the pulling down and the building up He does a perfect work. The corresponding separation which comes to man in His judgment is also real and total. How can it be otherwise if it is the righteousness (and therefore the grace) of God which is at work in this judgment ?

And now a final definition. Will it solve the puzzle, or will it make plain to us that it cannot be solved—and point us to the divine solution ? Either way, we must add that the righteousness (and therefore the grace) of God would not be the righteousness (and therefore the grace) of God, if its dividing of man on the left hand and the right —man under the No of God on the one hand, and man under the Yes of God on the other—involved a state of dualism, that is to say, if the visible result of it was the static co-existence of two men, into whose divided being the one man is, as it were, torn apart and apportioned, in which he has either simultaneously or alternately to see himself, and in whose form and aspect he must understand himself : now coming partly or altogether under the one aspect, now under the other ; now in a relative or absolute freedom choosing the one aspect, now the other. What has this division to do with either righteousness or grace if the result of it is this dual existence of man ? if it involves this necessary or capricious vacillation between the two—mutually exclusive—forms of his being : the vacillation between extreme light and extreme darkness ? For how then can both be real : the fact that God is against him and the fact that God is for him ; the being of man on the left hand and his being on the right ; his death and his life ; the destroying of his wrong and the maintaining and establishing of his right ? And what kind of a picture of God does this give us, indeed what kind of a God does this involve ? What a hybrid being is the Almighty who—obviously in accordance with His own inward contradiction—has nothing better to offer to man than this dual existence ! And what a self-understanding it is, and the human life grounded upon it, which can consist only in this see-saw or criss-cross movement ! This state of dualism, this static co-existence of two quite different men, can only be the result of a misunderstanding, a caricature, of what we really have to see at this point. But if this is the case, then the only alternative is to understand the work of the dividing of man on the left hand and the right as the putting into effect of a history in which the man on the left hand is the Whence and the man on the right hand the Whither of the one man, the former being this man as he was and still is, the latter being this man as he will be and to that extent already is. The truth of human life under the control of the righteousness of God and therefore of His grace is not a being divided into two, but something which it is impossible to consider, which can only be lived by the passive and active participant, the drama of the one human life in its dynamic sequence and co-relation. I was and still am the former man : man as a wrongdoer, whose wrong and whose being in identification with his wrong can only perish and has in fact perished when confronted with the righteousness of God, with the life of the One who is majestically and unconditionally in the right, falling a victim to death, and actually dying and being removed and erased and destroyed under the wrath of God. But I am already and will be the latter man : the man whom God has elected and created for himself, whose right he himself has squandered and spoiled, but God has protected and maintained and re-established in defiance of his wrong, in defiance of the catastrophe which necessarily overtook him as the doer of that wrong ; the man who is not unrighteous but righteous before God, righteous, because he is in an accord which has been maintained and restored with the right of God Himself. It is in this way that God is in the right both against man and for him. It is in this way that He activates and lives out His righteousness in the encounter with man. And it is in this way that man lives before Him his true and genuine life as a man : one and the same man in spite of this division on the left hand and the right, in spite of the sequence, and the being in sequence, which is his life in this division ; his being in the present of this yesterday and to-day, in the simultaneity of this past and this future. In this way, in this history, there is fulfilled the co-existence of the two, of God and of man. " This thy brother was dead, and is alive again ; and was lost, and is found " (Lk. 15³²). That is man. No, that is the mystery of God's dealings with man, the mystery of His overruling of human existence. For here we find both the strict righteousness of God and in that righteousness His free grace. This history is God's justification of the godless, the *iustificatio impii.*

But when we look at it in this way we come upon the real puzzle of it all.

For all the difficulty in carrying through the construction, it is at least conceivable, or at a pinch it can be made conceivable, and therefore it is no genuine puzzle, that I recognise and understand myself in this dualism, in this static co-existence of two diametrically opposed aspects. Here I am, on the one hand, in my empirical reality—unconsciously in error and consciously at fault. Here I am, supremely compromised in a way that I cannot overcome. Here I am, perishing, moving forward to a destruction which I can already foresee and which is to that extent already present. But here I am, on the other hand, in my ideal reality ; my human nature which is quite unaffected by all this, my proper self in which I am in the right and therefore finally secure against myself and everything that speaks against me and the fall which I cannot deny. Why not ? At some point, not on the surface perhaps, but in the depth of my being, I can appear to myself both as this empirical man and also as this ideal man. I can obviously learn to handle this antithesis between the empirical and the ideal. And in this way I can make the dualism conceivable. Many of us do, in fact, conceive of it in this way, and in this alternation, this ebb and flow of the two pictures, which is so restless and and yet at bottom so peaceful, so disturbing and yet in the last resort so consoling, we can attain to a view of ourselves in which we actually live or think we live. We are speaking of the schema which underlies every natural religion and philosophy. If this schema is not known instinctively to every man, it can easily be known and its application learned. And if the understanding of self in this schema does involve a certain riddle, its solution can be described as attainable in theory and to some extent at least applicable in practice. The only trouble is that this schema, this picture, this riddle and the approximate solutions of this riddle have nothing whatever to do with the righteousness and grace of God, with what man is before God both on the left hand and on the right, with his justification by God. And conversely the divine justification of man has nothing whatever to do with the distinction and relationship of an empirical and an ideal picture of man.

The justification of man by God belongs neither to the empirical nor to the ideal world, for God who is at work in it is one God and the Creator of all the visible and invisible reality distinct from Himself which is beyond this contrast.

Nor is it possible to see how the man on the left hand is to be empirical man or the man on the right hand ideal man. To be sure, this corresponds to the well-known Platonic distinction, but this is not in any sense identical with the division which comes to man in the judgment of God. Is not the so-called ideal man the reflection of the pride of the man who is set on the left hand of God, and does not the poor empirical man have a certain similarity to the man to whom God says Yes, because even as he is he has not ceased to be the creature of God and His elect ?

Again, the justification of man by God is an event between God and man, not the static relationship of their being, but the being of God and man in a definite movement which cannot be reproduced in two pictures which can be placed alongside and studied together. It takes place as the history of God with man. That which is twofold but one in it is the righteousness and grace of the one God above, condemning and pardoning, killing and making alive ; and corresponding to this divine activity the dark Whence and the bright Whither of the one man below, experiencing His judgment—his transition and progress from that yesterday to this to-morrow, his coming out of the wrong which is removed and destroyed, his coming, therefore, out of his own death, and in that coming—this is his present—his going forward to his new right and therefore to his new life.

As this history the justification of man is a genuine puzzle, unlike that of the dualism which can be caught in that picture. The justification of man cannot be caught in any picture, not even in moving pictures. The reason for this is that the man who lives in this history of God with him is not in any sense perceptible to himself. We have described this history as a drama which cannot be seen by any spectators but can only be lived by those who participate in it. But obviously—and we cannot put this too strongly—there can be no self-experience of this drama. The fact that it is our history which is in train, that we participate in this drama, is something which must be true and actual quite otherwise than in some depth of our own self, and recognisable as the truth quite otherwise than in the contemplation of one of the phenomena which meet us in these depths. Where and when do we find ourselves in that present, in the transition and progress from that yesterday to this to-morrow ? In what past of this our time do we see our wrong actually removed and erased and extirpated, and ourselves actually put to death and buried and destroyed with it ? And in what future of this our time do we see our right established and ourselves righteous and acquitted ? When and where do we find ourselves in the distinction and unity of this past and coming to be ? When and where can we think of ourselves as those who are justified by God ?

If justification is a happening which we experience in ourselves, if we can find ourselves in it, so that there is no puzzle, but it can all be readily conceived, then we must have made a mistake and we must retrace our steps at a most important point in our previous deliberations, for the judgment of God cannot be so total and comprehensive as we have supposed. Let us suppose for a moment that the wrong of man is not so great, that it is not the radical evil that we have assumed, that the conflict between it and the righteousness of God is not so bitter, the wrath of God not so consuming, the catastrophe which breaks on man not so serious, the perishing and dying not a real but a partial or perhaps only a symbolical perishing and dying. And let us suppose, on the other hand, that God's Yes to man is not so strong and unequivocal, that the new right of man is not so sure, that the obliteration of his wrong is not so clear and definitive and certain, that the activity of God on the right hand is not a perfect and complete activity. Let us suppose that on the left hand as on the right everything is relative and not absolute, that the antithesis is only quantitative and not qualitative, that the transition from the one to the other, from yesterday to to-morrow, is also relative and quantitative. It is true that in *this* transition, *this* coming out and going in, we shall be able at bottom to experience ourselves, we shall be perceptible and comprehensible to ourselves, however great may be the step involved. We know this kind of judgment in this kind of history, which may be very serious and meaningful both in its backward and also in its forward reach, but which is not entirely serious, and not entirely meaningful. Histories and crises and revolutions of this kind do exist. And in them it is not impossible to experience ourselves, to be perceptible and comprehensible to ourselves. But if this is the case, we are not dealing with the righteousness and grace of God, which does an honest and total work both on the left hand and on the right. We are not dealing with the revolution of God. And it is this revolution which is our present concern. We cannot, therefore, retrace our steps or make the matter easier than it is.

If we stand in His judgment, in the history which He has set in train, then this means that the antithesis between our yesterday and to-morrow is absolute and qualitative, that there are no half-measures, no possible mitigations either on the left hand or on the right, that our situation is entirely serious both in its backward and also in its forward reach, the situation of absolute decision. And in this entirely serious and decisive situation—" as dying, and, behold, we live "— we do not know ourselves, we never have and we never shall. That this history is my history, that I am the one who is so forcefully divided by the righteousness and grace of God, that I am caught up in this transition, that I am the man who participates in this drama, that that which is said of the prodigal is said of me—this is something which I do not see and therefore do not understand. There is no man who can try to maintain that he experiences and understands himself as the prodigal son, for it is said of the prodigal that he was dead and is alive again, and was lost, and is found. No one can try to maintain that this is an expression of his self-understanding. That man is, in fact, the prodigal son is the genuine riddle before which we stand at this point.

Of course, it is not a meaningless riddle. It is a genuine one to the extent that it is to us insoluble, that it cannot be solved on the basis of any subjective experience or with the development of any self-understanding. But it is a riddle which has been solved in quite a different way—and one which is not actually hidden from the knowledge of man (i.e., his knowledge of the revelation of God). It is all exactly as we have described it. It cannot be found in us or conceived by us. It is an absolute riddle. The dividing of the righteousness and grace of God as we have described it is an event : a dividing which is forcefully prefigured by the Creator's dividing of light and darkness, of the waters above the firmament and the waters below the firmament, of the sea and the land ; a dividing to left and right which is comprehensive, total and definitive. And the absolutely serious situation created by this event is our situation. It is our wrong and death which is behind us, our right and life which is before us. The transition from that past to this future is our present. We are the participants in this great drama. That history is, in fact, our history. We have to say indeed that it is our true history, in an incomparably more direct and intimate way than anything which might present itself as our history in our own subjective experience, than anything which we might try to represent as our history in explanation of our own self-understanding. It is indeed a riddle. But in spite of the riddle of it, it is not a fairy-tale or a myth. Compared with it, measured by the reality of it all, the things which we think we know of ourselves—in the unriddling of riddles which are not genuine riddles —are a fairy-tale and a myth : our life-histories, and the sum of all life-histories ; that which we usually call universal history ; the way in which all this presents itself to us ; the way in which we usually explain and construct our own existence and the existence of the race; the way in which we experience and perceive and then conceive ourselves in the obvious relative and quantitative divisions and transitions of our life—not to speak of the picture in which we think we possess and recognise ourselves now in an empirical and now in an ideal form. Here in the sphere of our supposed or actual competence—we think and postulate and speculate. Here we brag. Here we spin and ramble and dream to our heart's content. Here our reason takes to phantasy and our modest poetic powers attempt to reason. Here we produce images of events and forms in face of which it may well be asked how they apply to us or what concern they are of ours. Here we are never truly alone, but we " exist " enthusiastically in some higher or lower " transcendence." But what is demanded at this point is caution, reserve, scepticism. The one history in which we are all undoubtedly and absolutely and directly alone as in our own true history is the history of man's justification by God in the unmitigated antithesis of our transition from the yesterday which stands under the No of God to the to-morrow which stands under His Yes. For all that it is a riddle, it is our true and actual to-day, and very different from any fairy tale or myth.

What is it that makes it so puzzling to us ? It is necessarily puzzling. The reason is that we cannot experience and perceive and comprehend ourselves in this our real to-day. Our real to-day, the to-day of our true and actual transition from wrong to right, from death to life, and therefore the to-day of the judgment which falls upon us by the righteousness and grace of God, is always a strange to-day. We must now give it its name and utter the decisive word which we have so far withheld. It is the to-day of Jesus Christ. The day of the judgment of God which overtakes us, of the clash of the righteousness of God with our wrong, and therefore with ourselves, the day on which our wrong and death becomes to us the past and our right and life the future—that day is His day. It is as His day that it is our day. His history is as such our history. It is our true history (incomparably more direct and intimate than anything we think we know as our history). Jesus Christ comes to us. In Him we are quite alone, torn away originally and finally from the whole world of fairy tale and myth, taken right beyond all our empirical and ideal pictures of ourselves, genuinely alone, and therefore the men who stand in that judgment and transition. In all our previous consideration we were looking tacitly at Him, not with the intention of looking past us men, but with the intention, as we look at this man, of looking at all us other men in a first and final reality and truth—with the intention of finding ourselves in Him, of finding in Him God's mighty and righteous and gracious contesting of our wrong, of finding in Him our justification. We could not have entertained our previous considerations at all except with reference to Him. What other source could there be for the statements we have made ? How else could we know of that high right of God which is superior to our wrong, which is grounded in itself and the ground of all other right ? How else of the nature and extent, the curse of human wrong ? How else of the clash of the two, of the wrath of God which consumes man as the doer of wrong with the wrong itself ? How else of the steadfast faithfulness of God to man as His creature and elect, the faithfulness which is the ultimate ground of his justification ? How else of the dividing of man on the left hand and the right, of the condemnation and pardon in both of which God is both righteous and gracious ? How else of the fact that on both sides the work of God is a complete and perfect work ? How else that both apply to the one man, and that they are not the basis of any dualism, but the transition of the one man from his dark yesterday to his bright to-morrow, the history of man, his redemptive history ? We have not invented all this. We have found it at the place where it is reality and truth, the reality and truth which applies to us and comprehends us, our own reality and truth. We have found it where we ourselves are and not merely appear to be. We have found it where we do not merely seek ourselves in opinions but find ourselves in knowledge. We have found it where we are not called upon to think and express things which are rambling and vacillating, but firm and definite. We speak of the proclamation of Jesus Christ, of the happening of His death on the cross, of the revelation of it in His resurrection from the dead, or, better and more exactly, of Jesus Christ Himself, who lives, who is present and active, who gives Himself to be known as the Crucified and Risen, not merely in the proclamation of Him, but by virtue of the proclamation of Him. It is all true and actual in Him and therefore in us. It cannot, therefore, be known to be valid and effective in us first, but in Him first, and because in Him in us. We are in Him and comprehended in Him, but we are still not He Himself. Therefore it is all true and actual in this Other first and not in us. That is why our justification is not a matter of subjective experience and understanding. That is why we cannot perceive and comprehend it. That is why it is so puzzling to us.

It is a matter of the knowledge of this Other, of His transition from the curse of death to the glory of life, of His to-day, which will always be to us a strange to-day, although it is ours. It is a matter of the knowledge of His history, which will always be to us a strange history although it is our history. It is a matter of the knowledge of this Other Himself, who will always be to us a stranger although He comprehends us and we are in Him. It is a matter of the rule of the righteousness of God in Him, which, although it rules over us and applies to us, is always a strange righteousness : *iustitia aliena*, because first and essentially it is *iustitia Christi*, and only as such *nostra*, *mea iustitia*.

In the final part of this section we must take up and explain the fact that as the righteousness of Jesus Christ, and therefore a strange righteousness, this righteousness is ours, mine. We shall be developing what has been our tacit presupposition from the very first—the righteousness of the divine judgment in its original and proper and typical character as the righteousness of Jesus Christ and therefore a righteousness which is strange to us.

By the righteousness of God we have meant the realisation of His right in its relation to the wrong of man, to man as a wrongdoer. It is, therefore, identical with the judgment of God. And in respect of the men concerned in that judgment it is identical with their justification. We have thought of it as the divine inauguration of the history in which one and the same man was in the wrong, and as a wrongdoer had to be negated by God and die, and has in fact died, only to be affirmed and maintained by God in that death, being carried through it to become the man who is in the right before Him and can live as such. But this righteousness, this judgment of God, this justification by God which comes to man, is something which has taken place concretely in Jesus Christ. It had to take place in Him because in His person as the Son of the Father He is Himself both very God electing and creating man and very man elected by God and as such ordained from all eternity to fulfil all the righteousness of God. It could take place in Him, because as very God and very man He was competent and qualified to accomplish and suffer the contest between God and man, to be both the Judge and the judged in this conflict. It could take place only in Him because only He as this one person could be both subject and object in this history, uniting the antithesis of it in Himself: Himself the full end which is made in it; and Himself also the new beginning which is made in it; and both in the place and therefore in the name of all other men, for them and in their favour. It took place in Him in that He as the true Son of God became true man, and in this unity of His person became the Judge of all other men: their Judge as the One who was judged in their place—delivered up in His death, and reinstated in His resurrection from the dead. As it has taken place in Jesus Christ this is the justification of sinful man. We will now try to understand it in detail.

What has in fact taken place in Jesus Christ? We will first give the general answer that there has taken place in Him the effective self-substitution of God for us sinful men. The contest of God with the man of sin and of this man with God is inevitable. The right of God holds sway, and it has to be executed in righteousness. The judgment of God is inevitable. This is true in respect of man. If there is salvation for him, it is only as judgment is passed. But this judgment involves the destruction of wrong and of the man who does wrong. It also involves the defence and restoration and reinstatement of the right of the man elected and created by God, the life of man in this right before Him. But man is not at all adapted for this twofold way of dealing with wrong, either actively or passively, either as subject or object, either as a creature or as sinful man. As the man who has put himself in the wrong both before God and against Him, he is not suitable for participation in this happening. As a creature, where can he find the capacity, and, as the sinner that he is, where can he find the will, actively to co-operate in this process (perhaps with the help of divine grace), or even to suffer and experience and receive that which must come upon him in the course of it ? Seeing that it is a matter of the replacement of his absolute wrong by his absolute right, of his death by his life from this death, it belongs to the very nature of the case that he cannot be considered, but falls short, as the divine partner in this happening. But it has to concern him. The righteousness of God has to overtake him, the judgment of God to fall on him. It must be his justification. Obviously both God and man belong to this happening. But if man is disqualified, if he is not present, and has no place, how can it be inaugurated and take place and attain its end ? It does take place and it attains its end in the fact that God takes the matter out of the hands of man and conducts it as His own—even though it is the affair of sinful man. God does not merely confront him as God and Lord and Judge, but as such He effectively takes His place at the side of sinful man, indeed, He takes the place of sinful man, representing him against Himself. His eternal Word becomes flesh. He Himself in His Word becomes man. Why ? In order that He may not only conduct His own case against all men, but take up and conduct the case of all men, which they themselves cannot conduct, in that process between Him and them. In order that He may be for them what they cannot be for themselves—an active subject and a passive object in that conflict. In order that He may take over on their behalf the suffering and activity for which they are not adapted, which is completely beyond their capacity and will. In order to carry through as their Representative the justification which cannot take place or be carried through if they fall short. Not from His own side. Not as God, Lord and Judge. But from their side. As the God, Lord and Judge who is man, servant and judged. In general terms, what has taken place in Jesus Christ is the divine participation in the situation of the man confronted by His right, encountering His righteousness and in need of His justification ; the divine intervention for Him in virtue of which man can do all this and suffer all this, in virtue of which man can and will be the partner of God, at which the righteousness and judgment of God aims and does not aim in vain. It is as God identifies Himself with man—His participation and intervention is as direct and complete as that—it is as He becomes a man and as this man the Representative of all men, it is as He makes His own the cause of all men that justification can and does take place. To make it possible, God became man. This is the meaning of the existence of Jesus Christ. If there is a justification of sinful and proud man, the man who has fallen into the abyss in his pride, but from whom God has not withheld His hand, who cannot therefore fall from the hand of God, then it is to be sought in Jesus Christ. It has actually taken place in Him, as there has taken place in Him God's participation in man, His identification with Him, His intervention for all men. We do not postulate this event. We derive its significance and necessity and scope from the simple fact that it has taken place. Jesus Christ lives, very God and very man. If we look at Him and see Him, then we find in Him the justification of man which has taken place in Him, and we know that we do not need to seek it elsewhere, that we shall seek it elsewhere in vain. We will now turn to two more detailed explanations.

On the one side the justification of man in Jesus Christ is the destruction of his wrong and his own setting aside as the doer of that wrong. The man of sin, proud man who has fallen in his pride, is destroyed in this justification. He becomes the man of yesterday. This is the first thing which we cannot find in any event in our own life, which we cannot, therefore, picture as a determination of our own existence. And for the good reason that it has not actually happened in our existence as such. Looking at ourselves we can only say that this fatal man of yesterday is still the man of to-day, and we have no prospect other than that he will also be the man of to-morrow. But in Jesus Christ, the very man in whom the very God has intervened for us, and acted in our place, it is all quite different. That man has been set aside. He has perished. He is only to the extent that he was ; that he is the same as the one who died as that man.

On this side we have to do with a definite action of the Son of God. It has been carried through by Him in His unity with the man Jesus of Nazareth, in our midst and as one of us, but it has been carried through also in the power of God and therefore effectively. And (because in this power it applies to all men) it is in force and effective for all men. This action of the Son of God and the man Jesus Christ is the act of obedience in which, very God in His willingness and capacity for this obedience, He chose and willed and did that which is humble, making Himself like the man who had fallen so deeply into the abyss in his pride, unreservedly placing Himself at his side, and indeed taking his place. Why ? In order to accept his responsibility, in order in his place to enter and tread to the end the way which as the way of sinful man, in fulfilment of the right of God, could only be the way to death. He did not shrink from this intervention for man and its consequence. As the Brother and Representative of all men He was ready to give Himself as very God and very man to do away with that which is impossible and intolerable to God, the wrong of man and unrighteous man, to make a full end of it, to banish from the world both the offence and the one who had caused offence.

He has therefore suffered for all men what they had to suffer : their end as evil-doers ; their overthrow as the enemies of God ; their extirpation in virtue of the superiority of the divine right over their wrong. They had to suffer this, but they could not suffer it, not one of them.

For even if it had been, or were to be, laid upon one of them really to taste and experience in his suffering and death the judgment of God on himself and his wrong, how could he experience it for others, for all others ? And even if it were laid on all men really to taste and experience the judgment of God, even if they were willing and able to do so, how could they who have given offence, suffering merely what they have deserved, banish the offence from the world by their death, even their eternal death ? For the offence would still be there. It would not be as though it had never happened. It would not be made good. As something which had been it would remain as an unerased blot on the world of God's creation, an element in its history. And even if by their suffering of the divine judgment they were able to erase the blot, even if their suffering and death were costly enough for that, would not the will of God for elect and created man be given the lie by their destruction ? To satisfy His righteousness they would have to perish genuinely and finally, to fall from His hand. But then God would not be the God who has sworn to be faithful to them. Or He for His part would not have kept His oath and covenant with them.

What we men must suffer—if it is to be suffered in accordance with the righteousness of God—can be suffered for us only by God Himself as man : if, that is to say, it is to take place validly and effectively for us all ; if it is to be the one and total destruction of wrong and all wrongdoers ; if it is to be the erasure of that blot from the world of God's creation ; if at the same time it is to be the keeping of His faith, the carrying out of His covenant with man, not to man's destruction but to his salvation, to the justification of the unjust. And Jesus Christ was ready and gave Himself up to suffer and perish and die in that way—in accordance with the perfect righteousness of God. God judged the world in Him—and judged it in righteousness—by delivering Himself up in Him to be judged. To suffer validly and effectively for us His own judgment upon us, He condescended to us, He humbled Himself so profoundly, He was willing to be so lowly, and in our flesh the eternal Son, the man Jesus of Nazareth, rendered the obedience of humility to the eternal Father, thus fully satisfying the righteousness of God on its negative side, the side of wrath. God identified Himself with man in Jesus Christ. In the person of this one man He set a term, an end, He was Himself the end which must come upon us all. And because of that our wrong has in fact become a thing of the past. It is no longer there. It is extinguished. It is present only as something which has been eternally removed and destroyed. And we men as the doers of it, as those who willingly identified ourselves with it, are dead and buried. We, too, are in fact a thing of the past. We are present only to the extent that our existence as such has this past. In Him our sin and we ourselves have perished. In Him we all start at the divine No which has been spoken with such power and carried through with such effect ; at the liberation which is an accomplished fact in this No because it is spoken and carried through in Jesus Christ. This liberation which has taken place in Him is the presupposition of our future. And the freedom given to us by this No is our present. In Him our wrong and we ourselves as the doers of it are behind us. He has taken it away from us. He has taken us away from it. He has set aside and cancelled our existence as the doers of it. In this respect it is of decisive importance to see that He has done this in the act of His humble obedience. He has done this deed by suffering. He was, of course, the subject of this happening. Taking our place and suffering for us, He did not do what we as wrongdoers are always doing, and He did what we do not do. He was lowly where we are proud. He condescended to us where we arrogantly try to rise up. He the Lord became a servant. He the Judge became the judged. He accepted what was laid upon Him by the Father. He let the will of the Father be His will. He drank the bitter cup instead of putting it from Him. He suffered the shame of the cross. And all this in freedom, in free obedience, in the obedience of humility. In this humility He expressed and revealed His deity, and in it, in the power of His deity, He made an end of sin and the old man of sin in His own person, speaking that liberating No. We do not therefore leave behind us a vacuum when we start at this No, when we have behind us sin and the sinner. That they are behind us, that it is all up with sin and the sinner, rests on the fact that that liberating No has been spoken in this way, in the lowly obedience of Jesus Christ. Our arrogant disobedience has been set aside once and for all in Him. He has not merely suffered for us, but suffering for us He has done the right for us, and therefore suffered effectively and redemptively for us. Judged in Him we cannot be to-morrow the proud men we were yesterday. Those men are no longer there, for yesterday we were delivered up to the divine judgment. As those who are freed from our past in Him, we no longer have the freedom (the false freedom) to return to our old pride. Between us and our past there stands positively and divisively the act of right which is His death. That is the final and decisive thing that we have to see in order to realise that our wrong and we ourselves as the doers of it are really and truly at an end. That, then, is the righteousness of God in its concrete form as the righteousness of Jesus Christ, as our justification accomplished in Him, on its first and negative side ; the gracious and redemptive work of God on the left hand.

On the other side, the justification of man in Jesus Christ is the establishment of his right, the introduction of the life of a new man who is righteous before God. This man, his life, is the future of man in Jesus Christ—the same in whom that first man is put to death and is therefore past. Man will live as this righteous man when he has died and therefore only *was* as that unrighteous man. But this second thing, too, we shall not find in any event of our life. That we live as righteous men is not an immanent determination of our existence

and cannot therefore be conceived. It is not in our existence that
man has acquired this future. Looking at ourselves we should have
to regard this future as that of the man of to-morrow as just as unreal
and impossible as the fact that that man of yesterday is our past.
In Jesus Christ, the very man who as such is the eternal Son of the
eternal Father, this future man, the new and righteous man, lives in
an unassailable reality. In Him I am already the one who will be
this righteous man and live as such, just as in Him I am still only the
unrighteous man, to the extent that I once was this man. In this
positive sense Jesus Christ lives in our place, for us, in our name.
As our wrong and death are our past in His name, in Him, so our
righteousness and life are our future.

On this second and positive side of our justification as it has taken
place in Jesus Christ, we are dealing with something specific which
has happened to Him, the Son of God, in His unity with our fellow-man
Jesus of Nazareth. As the true Son of God and Son of Man, as our
Lord and our Brother, He is not merely the subject but the object of
the righteousness in which God vindicates and establishes His right
amongst us. He received something which in what He did—it was
the act of His lowly obedience and He carried it through to death—
He neither would nor could take to Himself. He received to what He
did the answer of the free omnipotent grace of God His Father. The
hidden good will of God, to which He subjected Himself without
reserve and was obedient even to death, was proclaimed to Him.
God acknowledged the right of the One who gave Himself to judge
the world by letting Himself be judged in its place. God confirmed
the innocence of the One who allowed Himself to be accused and condemned and put to death for the guilty. God revealed the meaning
and purpose of His wrath, His consuming love, to the One who had
exposed Himself to it and borne it to the very end. The righteousness
of God did not merely take place by Him, in the obedience of His
Son acting in His passion for us, but when it had taken place by Him
in the act of His death, it was also revealed in Him as the righteousness of the eternal faithfulness and grace of God, as the righteousness
of His positive will, which was present from the very first, although
only latent in His non-willing, His will to introduce the new and
righteous man, His will that this man should live. This is something
which Jesus Christ has not done, which has come to Him as the answer
to what He has done, but just as real, just as concrete, just as visible,
audible, perceptible, just as historical as the death which He took
upon Himself and in which He acted passively. We speak of His
resurrection from the dead by the glory of the Father (Rom. 6⁴).

As He was delivered up, as He delivered up Himself, for our offences,
so this took place for our sake, for our justification (Rom. 4²⁵). It
was for us that He received what He did receive in it. As He did what
He has done in our place, for us, so the answer which God the Father

gave Him in respect of His act of obedience applies to us. The good will of the Father, which was hidden in His dying for us and revealed to Him in His resurrection, was and is the good will of God with us. His right, which was acknowledged by God in His resurrection, the right of the Judge judged on our behalf, was and is our right. His innocence, the innocence in which He bore and bore away our sin, the innocence which was manifested in His resurrection, was and is our innocence. The consuming love which revealed itself in His resurrection as the meaning and goal of the divine wrath which He bore for us was and is the love in which God willed to seek us and to find us, to carry us and to embrace us. The righteousness revealed to Him, the Representative of the unrighteous, as the righteousness of the faithfulness and grace of God, was and is therefore the revelation of the promise made to us, that we should live before Him as the righteous. As He in His act of humility has carried through for all men the end to which we had all fallen victim, so for all men He has actually opened the gate of righteousness and life. His resurrection is the beginning from which we all come when we leave the past which He has concluded, going forward in Him to the future which is already present.

We ourselves could not open this door. We could not make this beginning. We could not make this future our future. We could not do so even if we were in a position (which we are not) to make our wrong as though it had never been, to obliterate ourselves as the enemies of God that we are, and thus to suffer for ourselves what Jesus Christ has suffered for us ; with our death to satisfy the righteousness of God on its negative side. Even if we had the power to do this, where should we find the power to raise ourselves from our wrong before God to our right, to move from the death to which we have fallen a prey to life ? If the putting to death cannot be our own work, how much less our resurrection ! Even Jesus Christ did not secure for Himself His resurrection from the dead. On this side He was a pure recipient. He was crowned, He did not crown Himself. How, then, can we act in this matter ? We cannot even receive that which Jesus Christ has received from God for ourselves, on our own initiative, or otherwise than in Him. What He received was God's answer to the act of His lowly obedience, the confirmation of His innocence, the reward and revelation of the righteousness which He maintained in bearing our wrong. That He received this answer, this confirmation, this reward for us, does not alter the fact but shows plainly that anything we could receive and only receive for ourselves, apart from Him, would be very different from the future and hope of our right and life. Left to ourselves, the only thing that we can expect after our destruction as evil-doers is to have no future.

Negatively, the justification of sinful man before God means a basic turning away from his wrong and from himself as the doer of it. Positively, it means his basic turning to God. Neither as the one nor as the other can it be his own affair—neither as our work nor as our experience. It is our affair, of course, but on the negative side and more particularly on the positive it is our affair as it has been conducted and carried through by the one Jesus Christ—in His work and in that which happened to Him. By virtue of His resurrection from the dead, by virtue of the righteousness revealed in His life, in Him and from Him we have a future and hope, the door has been opened, and we cross the threshold from wrong to right, and therefore from death to life. Risen with Him from the dead, we do this, or rather it takes place for us. What God has applied to Him, He has applied to us. We are the righteous and living men that we shall be. In Him our justification is a complete justification, fulfilled on the right hand as on the left.

We note that it takes place in Jesus Christ and in Him first with this clear and inextinguishable differentiation and unity. In relation to Him, to His death and resurrection, we are forced to speak of the twofold character of the divine judgment. But again in relation to Him we affirm that the divine judgment is a single act and therefore one which cannot be divided or separated, a strictly coherent history. In Him there takes place that transition of man from his wrong to his right, from death to life. It would not be the act of judgment of the one God if it were not this one complete act, beginning here and completed there, beginning in the death and completed in the resurrection of Jesus Christ, beginning with the destruction of human wrong, completed in the establishment of human right, beginning with the doing away of unrighteous man, completed in the life of the righteous— but a single act with this differentiation. And both have taken place on behalf of all men in the one Jesus Christ; in this indissoluble relationship, in this irreversible sequence.

We must take note of the indissoluble relationship. The life of the new and righteous man acquires a place only with the passing and death of the old man of unrighteousness. The one has to perish in order that the other may begin. There is no place for the new man alongside the old. He can only crowd him out and replace him. He can only have him behind him. His day can break only when the day of this other is over. This is what took place in the death of Jesus Christ. Jesus Christ lives as the One in whom this has taken place; as the Crucified, as the One who was delivered up for our transgressions, as the One who has taken the place of the man of unrighteousness, who has put him to death and destroyed him. He lives as the One in whose self-sacrifice the justification of man begins. The fact that there is no more place for the old man, that he has been put to death and has perished, shows itself to be true and actual in the fact that he is replaced by the new, that the day of the new has broken, that Jesus Christ has been made the Victor in His resurrection from the dead. Jesus Christ lives as the risen One, as the bearer of the right which God has given to man, as the recipient of His grace, completing the justification of man by His receiving of it.

A *theologia gloriae*, the magnifying of what Jesus Christ has received for us in His resurrection, of what He is for us as the risen One, can have no meaning unless it includes within itself a *theologia crucis*, the magnifying of what He has done for us in His death, of what He is for us as the Crucified. But an abstract *theologia crucis* cannot have any meaning either. We cannot properly magnify the passion and death of Jesus Christ unless this magnifying includes within itself the *theologia gloriae*—the magnifying of the One who in His resurrection is the recipient of our right and life, the One who has risen again from the dead for us. The magnifying in its unity of the transition which has taken place in Jesus Christ is the true confession of our justification. It can be a true confession only in this totality, in its application to the transition of the strictly coherent history which has taken place in Him.

But we must also take note of the irreversible sequence in this unity. How can it be the unity of this history, this transition, if it is reversible, if it can be thought of as a cycle? It is not for nothing that Jesus Christ called Himself " the Way " (Jn. 14⁶). A garden path may be circular. But a garden path is not a true way. A true way has a beginning and an end which is different from it, which lies somewhere else. The same applies to a true history—and to a true transition. That which has been in Jesus Christ is still present in Him as that which has been—the wrong which is blotted out, and the wrong-doer with it. This cannot and must not happen again. It must never again become the future. Rather the future will always be the past of human wrong and the human wrong-doer. This is something upon which in all our future we can only look back. Israel cannot again return to the depths of the Red Sea, where it was kept by the mighty hand of God, and the enemy was destroyed. What Jesus Christ has done to put our sin and death behind Him and, therefore, behind us, He has done once and for all. He cannot and must not do it again. It cannot become for us a fresh problem of our future, as though it had not been done. And what He has received as right-eousness and life He has again received once and for all in our place and for us. In Him it is our future which cannot become the past. It is our hope which cannot be changed into care and uncertainty and doubt and sorrow. What He has done for us as the eternal Son of God He has done rightly, and what He has received for us from the eternal Father He has received rightly. In Him, therefore, there is set both a *terminus a quo* and a *terminus ad quem*, between which we are now on the way, but which cannot for that reason be confounded or confused with one another. If we do confound or confuse them, if we try to return along the way upon which He has set us, we shall again be looking past Him, we shall again be holding to ourselves instead of to Him. Our justification, as it has taken place in Him, has given to God's history with us—notwithstanding its coherence and totality—a very definite direction. If we look at Him, we can look and go only in this direction, from here to there, but not in the reverse direction.

The Western seriousness with which we emphasise the beginning of justifica-tion is a good and necessary thing. In it we insist on the fact that in relation to Jesus Christ we can look only from *here* to there, only from the death on the cross to the resurrection, only from the yesterday of our death as it was suffered by Him for us to the to-morrow of our life as He has received it for us. But we must see to it that this seriousness—there are examples of this both in Roman Catholic and also in Protestant circles—does not, at a certain point which is hard to define, become a pagan instead of a purely Christian seriousness, changing suddenly into a Nordic morbidity, losing the direction in which alone it can have any Christian meaning, suddenly beginning to look backwards instead of forwards, transforming itself into the tragedy of an abstract *theologia crucis* which can have little and finally nothing whatever to do with the Christian knowledge of Jesus Christ. Certainly the self-sacrifice of Jesus Christ in death, and the death to which we are delivered up in His death, can never occupy us too much. But we miss what He has done for us in it if we understand it in isolation from what He has received for us in His resurrection, if we do not try to see it in its movement to what He has received for us. We will not inquire at this point whether there may not be the corresponding danger of the obscuring of the direction of the justification which has taken place for us in Jesus Christ by a far too ready forgetfulness of its *terminus a quo*, of the lowly obedience in which Jesus Christ undertook to withstand the wrath of God in our place on the cross. On the whole, the danger in the West is not in this direction. One of the things we have to learn from the Eastern Church is an unwearied looking forward from the *terminus a quo* to the *terminus ad quem* of our justification, the joy which is commanded us in relation to Jesus Christ who is the " Way," boundless joy in what He has received in our place, what we have received in Him. The knowledge of our justification as it has taken place in Him cannot possibly be genuinely serious except in this joy, the Easter joy, which looks in this direction.

Our conclusion brings us back to our starting-point with the question : What is the meaning of the judgment of God, and therefore of the justification of man (as it has taken place in Jesus Christ), for God Himself ? The question is not an idle one. Let us suppose that it is an activity which is purely external, which is accomplished merely with reference to man, but which does not affect Himself and mean anything for Him. There are many views of God for which this possibility might seem to be worthy of consideration. The justification of man is perhaps worked out and presented to man in one of the many spheres within this world, perhaps one of the most important, perhaps the most central of all, but only as a process within the world which follows the law of a dialectic within the world ; in such a way, therefore, that God has nothing more to do with it than that He is the final mystery which embraces it, as it does everything that takes place in the world. It is evident that if this is the case there can be no question of any true or final certainty concerning its occurrence. It takes place with all the ambiguity of all world events, about the meaning of which, both in detail and as a whole, man may have his well-founded suspicions, but in face of which he must always accept—even in the light of his most notable hypotheses—a continuing doubt whether after all everything might not be quite otherwise. Nor can the justification of man have any true or final importance or urgency. There may be many important relations between God and the world, and also between God and man, and they may be ordered approximately according to the statement of the Christian doctrine of justification. But why should this doctrine be of any urgent concern to man—who does not always have religious, let alone specifically Christian, interests —if this relationship is only external for God, and does not mean anything to Him, or anything more than any other relationship? If this is the case, do I have to have an answer at all, an absolutely reliable answer, to the question how I am to find a gracious God? The urgency of the question, as a request for an absolutely reliable answer, obviously stands or falls with the fact that the justification of man has a meaning for God Himself, that it has for Him at least as much meaning as it has for us. Then, and only then, does the question touch us closely. Then, and only then, is there the prospect of an answer which is not merely pious but true, not merely notable but certain. Only if God Himself is involved can we be seriously and totally involved and count on it that we are not involved in vain. For that reason our final question is not by any means an idle one.

Now we have left far behind us the possibility that God Himself is not involved, that the justification of man before Him does not mean anything for Him, or anything more than any other event. That is has supreme significance for God is already decided by the fact that He allowed its fulfilment to cost Him no less than His own interposition, the incarnation of His eternal Word. The One who made Himself ours in Jesus Christ, in order that justified in this One we might be His, is obviously involved in this matter not merely externally and indirectly but with a supreme directness. For obviously it also and in the first instance (how could it be otherwise?) concerns Himself. Our question cannot, therefore, be whether it has a meaning for God. This is a fact which is already decided. But it is a fact which we cannot leave without clarification. In this respect, too, we must be able to proceed with a purer knowledge. We have to ask, therefore, what meaning it has for God.

Our starting-point is again the fact that what is executed in God's righteousness and therefore in His judgment and therefore in the justification of unrighteous man, in the *mortificatio* and *vivificatio* which have come to man in Jesus Christ, is the right of God Himself which is, as such, the supreme and only true right. The right of God, the law which is Himself, rules and illuminates and is glorified in this His work. As we have seen, in the totality of it, in both its great dimensions, it is the work of the grace in which He has addressed man from all eternity, of the faithfulness which He has sworn to Him from all eternity. But fulfilled on this eternal basis, in its character as the work of His free mercy, it is from first to last the application of His supreme and only true right. In other words, it is the expression and therefore the self-affirmation of the One who is the essence and basis and source and guarantee and norm of all right. That this is the case we have already described as the backbone of the doctrine of justification.

What the justification which has this basis means for unrighteous man we have already seen in outline and we shall come to see in detail. That it means for God Himself, not merely something, but the supreme thing of all, rests on the fact that for its accomplishment His only Son and therefore He Himself in the person of His Son is not too big a price to pay. But what does this work mean for Him? We have already answered this question in the words of Rom. 3^{26}. It means for Him that He Himself is just (in this work), that in it He affirms His right and therefore Himself. We do not take too great a liberty if we paraphrase : In this work of the justification of unrighteous man God also and in the first instance justifies Himself. If this is true in a general and comprehensive way, then we are in a better position to see the hinge on which justification as the justification of man turns, the source from which it flows as man's justification, the original movement in which God sets this work in train as a work for man and to man. Its basic necessity is then quite clear, and with it the basic necessity of our knowledge of it and again the supreme degree of certainty of the true knowledge of it. If it is the case that in our justification God also and in the first instance justifies Himself, then in the knowledge of it we have to do with the knowledge of God Himself, who in the fact that He affirms His right proves that He is the One who neither can nor will deceive. But to what extent is it true that in our justification God does also and in the first instance justify Himself?

One thing is certain. It can be true only on the presupposition that God as God is in Himself the living God, that His eternal being of and by Himself has not to be understood as a being which is inactive because of its pure deity, but as a being which is supremely active in a positing of itself which is eternally new. His immutability is not a holy immobility and rigidity, a divine death, but the constancy of His faithfulness to Himself continually reaffirming itself in freedom. His unity and uniqueness are not the poverty of an exalted divine isolation, but the richness of the one eternal origin and basis and essence of all fellowship. The fact that according to His revelation God is the triune God means that He is in Himself the living God. In the light of God's revelation the idea of a God who is dead because of His pure deity is anthropomorphic. As against this, the statement that in and with the justification of man God also and in the first instance justifies Himself does not at any rate contain any anthropomorphism. It is not, therefore, a presumptuous statement, the kind of statement which encroaches on the divine glory. Quite the contrary. With its particular application it tells us that God is the living God. It tells us this with reference to the eternal right in which God Himself is law, in which He is faithful to Himself in His wholly sovereign freedom, in which He is in agreement with Himself. The activity of God in His righteousness, in His judgment, in the justification of unrighteous man, is the activity of the One who is God in this eternal right—its application and outworking. In this activity He affirms Himself in this His right. This is the meaning of justification for God Himself. In this sense it is true that in it God also and in the first instance justifies Himself.

We say " in the first instance " in order to bring out the precedence —the unconditional precedence—of the dignity and importance of this direction and reach of the divine activity. But it does not take place only within the framework of an external relation of God to man. It is not a contingent action which might never have taken place or might have had a quite different theme and content. Its basis is in the life of God Himself. In it we have to do with the living being of God as God. There can be no question of belittling it for that reason, as His action in relation to man. On the contrary, it is for that reason that it has its significance even in that relation ; that it is the act of His true and concrete participation in man. And the fact that in the justification of man God in the first instance justifies Himself gives to the justification of man, to the judgment that kills and makes alive in which this is executed, its holiness, the true and divine seriousness which in contrast to all the immanent judgments and crises and catastrophes and revolutions and their relative and limited killing and making alive, with their relative and limited certainty, distinguishes it as His judgment, the revolution of God. But what does it mean and to what extent does it actually happen that in this occurrence God in the first instance justifies Himself ?

We are simply pointing to the most obvious aspect when we say that in the justification of man we have to do with the expression of God's right as Creator ; His right to man as His creature, a creature which does not belong to itself or to anyone else but to God, which as His exclusive handiwork is also His exclusive possession. This right of God is compromised by sin, by the existence of man as the man of sin, by the fact of his pride and fall. We have described this fact as the invasion by chaos of the cosmos of God's creating, as the blot on His creation. Is God the Creator and Lord in relation to this blot on the cosmos and man, or is He not ? Is He the Creator and Lord if this invasion is possible or tolerable, if evil can sustain and make good its claim to actuality ? The justification of man is plainly God's decision that this claim is empty, that this invasion and blot is impossible and intolerable, that it cannot be suffered. It is God's contradiction of the contradiction raised against Himself. For this reason it is an act of judgment, an act of judgment which aims to destroy the wrong of man and positively to re-establish the right of God. As that history, that transition, that *mortificatio* and *vivificatio*, it proves that God takes sin seriously as the compromising of His right as Creator, that He is not willing by one hair's breadth to forego His right in face of it. He said : " Let there be light," not : " Let there be darkness." Therefore He intervenes against darkness. He marks off light from darkness and darkness from light. He beats back and beats down the assault upon His right to man, the attempt upon His right and creation. He does so with all the radicalness and totality with which this is done in the justification of man. In so doing, He justifies in the first instance Himself as the Creator of man, the Creator of the heavens and the earth.

But His right goes deeper than that. It is the right of the Creator, but it is also the right of His grace extended to man. Man is not merely His handiwork and possession. Beyond that—in answer to the call of God—he is His covenant-partner, who has not merely been given existence, but who is appointed for salvation, to whose existence He has given the end of eternal life, i.e., of fellowship with Himself in the form of service to Him. Man is the elect creature of God. God's right to him is therefore the right of His gracious election. The transgression of man compromises this right. It is man's attempt to break loose from His election, from the covenant with God. Has God stretched out His hand to him in vain ? Is He going to accept the defection of His covenant-partner ? Will He have to abandon the idea of attaining with him the appointed goal ? Will the salvation promised to man, being lost by man, remain in the hand which God has stretched out in vain, or elsewhere in the clouds ? Will it not be the salvation of the one for whom it is meant, who is elected to attain it ? The justification of unrighteous man shows that God does not accept this rejecting and despising of His grace. It is the intervention of God against it in judgment, His intervention for the right of His grace. The man who sets Himself in the wrong against it must die as a wrong-doer, but He must rise again as the recipient of the right of the elect, of the covenant-partner of God, which is granted to Him. The one man must go, the other come. The right of God, with which man's wrong cannot compete, demands this. And this is what takes place in the justification of man, to man's own redemption and salvation, but obviously in the first instance to the glory and justification of the gracious God Himself, to the demonstration that He cannot be mocked as the gracious God. Hence His consuming wrath, whose consuming is that of His love, which will not in any sense accept that rejection. Hence the inconceivable crowning of unrighteous man with grace and mercy. If we are to understand this event, everything depends upon the exclusion of any idea of a weak overlooking and pardoning of human wrong. Such an idea has nothing whatever to do with the truth of the grace and mercy of God. What we have to see here is rather that God does not weakly submit. He does not renounce the grace of election and the covenant. He does not yield in His will to save. He does not surrender the right in which He is in this will towards man. This will has to be done, and it is done in the justification of sinful man. In this way God in the first instance justifies Himself.

But we must look higher still, to the fulfilment of justification in

Jesus Christ. As it has taken place in Him as our justification, the justification of man, it is the work of God, the divine action in the death of Jesus Christ, the divine receiving in His resurrection from the dead. It is the work of God in its unity with what the man Jesus of Nazareth, our fellow-man and brother, has done and received. But in its unity with His human doing and receiving it is the work of God. And as the work of God in Jesus Christ it is both our justification and also—here in a sense at its inward centre—the justification in which God justifies Himself.

Here in Jesus Christ it begins with the action of the Son of God, with the humble obedience in which He abases Himself, giving Himself, undertaking to become man, in order that in His holy person He may take the place of all men, making an end of their wrong and of themselves as wrongdoers in His own death, casting them out in His holy person into outer darkness. But in speaking this No and accomplishing this liberation in our place and for us, He has also—and in the first instance—proved Himself to be the Son of God, very God from all eternity. In this act which is fully free, fully humble, without any claims, an act of pure obedience, He has claimed and exercised and put into effect and revealed His divine right, the right of the Son of God. The obligation of this Son, the Son of God, is not one which is originally alien to Him. It is not one which is laid upon Him from without. It is not one which is accepted by Him merely as a necessary duty. On the contrary, it is His divine glory and right to act with this obligation, to be perfectly obedient to the Father in freedom and humility and without any claim. Yet the speaking of this No, the accomplishing of this liberation, is from first to last a divine work. In rendering obedience in this work, He acts in His own way as the Son in exactly the same conformity with the divine nature, with exactly the same divine glory and right, as the One who lays this obligation upon Him and demands this obedience from Him. And He does what He does in execution of the divine will and purpose which is His own. Recognising and executing the right of the Father, He exercises His own right which is specifically that of the Son. Therefore the specific obligation in which He acts in the justification of man is not a new or alien one, let alone one which is unworthy of Him, which He has undertaken only unwillingly. He is the One in whom God elected man as His man and Himself as the God of man from all eternity. Again, He is the One in whom, in relation to whom, according to whose image, God created the heavens and the earth and man. Again, He is the One in whose person God made the eternal covenant of grace with man. In undertaking to become man and to act as the Representative of all men in His death and passion, what He does is simply the fulfilling of the office which, according to the counsel of God (His own as well as that of the Father), is His own office, the office of the Son from the very beginning, from all eternity. In His substitutionary death and passion, in this act of humble obedience, on what other ground has He acted than on the ground and in expression and confirmation of His own divine right as Son? In willing to do this and doing it, He did what as the Son He ought to do, what He could do in virtue of His right as Son. And He did it concretely as the legitimate bearer and representative and executor of the divine right of creation and the covenant to man and over man. All this obviously means that in the act of His obedience, and therefore of His substitutionary death and passion, in the first instance He justified Himself. Before God the Father, before the angels, and men and all other creatures He conducted and represented Himself as the One who was in the beginning with God and was Himself God, as the One by whom all things came to be, as the Lord who is over all things and everything. As the Lamb which bears and bears away the sin of the world He has exercised and put into effect His divine right of rule, setting it on a candlestick. And the fact that He has done this makes what He has done for us as the same One, the justification of man, indisputably valid and irresistibly effective. To deny or doubt that the sin of the world has been borne by Him and borne away in Him is to deny or doubt His right as the Son and therefore the eternal right of God. We must not be guilty of any such doubt or denial.

Again, here in Jesus Christ our justification is accomplished in the receiving of the Son of God, in that which comes to Him, crucified, dead and buried—and all in His unity with the man Jesus of Nazareth —as the act of grace and power of the Father in His resurrection from the dead. This is His divine confirmation as our Representative and therefore our divine confirmation in the right which is restored and the new life which is given to us in Him. This is the revelation of the love in which God has sought and found us in His death and converted us to Himself. This is—primarily and above all—the glory of the divine right which is revealed in Jesus Christ, which shines upon us from Him, in the application and outworking of which we are loved and justified by God, being set on the way to our right and to eternal life. The one divine right is indeed the right of the Father who delivered up His Son for us, sending Him into the world and interposing Him as our Representative, the right of the obligation which was laid upon Him and accepted by Him, the right of the high command which He obeyed in that free and humble act in which He made no claim. The demand which He met was not meaningless or arbitrary. It was not the formal and therefore the empty demand of a categorical imperative. It rested on the supremely concrete right of God. And this right was the right of the Father, of the God who as the Father of Jesus Christ, and in Him, is the Father of us all, the Father *par excellence*, the one true Father. The demand which Jesus Christ obeyed was therefore the demand of the fatherly right of God. And this fatherly right is the right of the grace, the mecry of God, the right of the One who has loved and elected man from all eternity, appointing him to His covenant with Him, making Himself his covenant-partner. We can and must add that it is the right of God who in His wisdom sees and perceives and measures what is the dimension of the wrong of man, how deep is the plight in which he has plunged himself as a wrong-doer, how great is the damage which he has done in creation in so doing, and beyond that, who and what alone can ward off disaster, and beyond that again, in what true and effective help and salvation consist. We have to say further that it is the right of the omnipotence of God, who lets evil do its evil work, as it has done in the death of Jesus Christ, to the very limit of its capacity, in order to reduce it *ad absurdum* and bring it to shame by its own action, its attack upon Himself in the person of His Son. All this, His grace and wisdom and omnipotence, was the fatherly right of God in which He demanded the obedience which the Son—in execution of His own right as the Son—rendered even to death, even the death of the cross. And His resurrection from the dead by the glory of the Father is the demonstration of the fatherly, because gracious and wise and omnipotent, right of that demand. On the basis of the free and sovereign, not the blind or tyrannical but the fatherly, will and decree of God it all had to happen as it did happen in the suffering and death and burial of Jesus Christ. This necessity, this fatherly will and decree, could not be something alien to the Son. He did not have to make it His own. He could not refuse it the completely free obedience in which—as the acting subject of what took place—He put it into effect and accomplished it to the very end. But His resurrection from the dead is the expression and confirmation of the right of this necessity, of the right of the demand to which He was obedient, as a fatherly right. In it it is revealed as the right of the One who in His grace does not will the death of a sinner, but that he should be converted and live; as the right of the One who in His wisdom knows the sickness of man but also the means to heal him; as the right of the One who in His omnipotence can give power to death, but in order to give it a meaning, in order to set for it a positive goal, in order to limit and overcome it and to take away its power from it. What comes to Jesus Christ in His resurrection, what He receives in it, as the Representative of all men and therefore on their, on our behalf, is that the fatherly right of the divine demand fulfilled in Him is made manifest, visible, audible and perceptible in Him, just as He has made it manifest, visible, audible and perceptible as the divine demand in the act of obedience of His death (in execution of His right as the Son), even to the point of His cry and question : " My God, my God, why hast thou forsaken me ? " (Mk. 15³⁴). " So let all thine enemies perish, O Lord : but let them that love thee be as the sun when he goeth forth in his might " (Jud. 5³¹). For it happened to Him in His resurrection that by His necessary death God achieved His end with man. The man of sin was put to death in Him, so that in Him this man, freed from the burden of His past, which was that of His wrong and pride and fall, became free for His future as a righteous man, free to live as this righteous man, and more than that, free for His salvation, for the eternal life accorded to him, that he should be God's, " and live under Him in His kingdom, and serve Him in eternal righteousness and innocence and felicity, as He has risen from the dead and lives and reigns to all eternity." He has indeed risen from the dead as the One who in His person receives this future for us. The demand to which He was obedient in His death and passion had this right of ours as its goal, because the right which underlay it was the fatherly right of God. This is what came to Him (and in Him to all of us) in His resurrection from the dead, the demonstration of the right of God chastising the Son because He loved Him, and loving Him even as He chastised Him. It was the self-demonstration of God as His and our gracious and wise and omnipotent and righteous Father. It was the fulfilment of our justification as the self-justification of God.

But did God need to justify Himself ? we may ask as we survey in retrospect this whole discussion. It is clear that He did not need to do so. He does not need anything. God is completely free. God does not owe anyone anything—least of all an account of the righteousness of what He does or does not do. But as the living God—as distinct from all the godheads of philosophies and religions—is He not free and able to justify Himself ? May it not be that of His own good pleasure He did in fact (and in the first instance) will to justify Himself, and actually do so, in our justification (and supremely in the fact that it took place in Jesus Christ) ? What, then, can we bring against it, especially if we appeal to His freedom or argue that He does not need anything of this nature ? A quite unnecessary concern for His majesty? Certainly God is—and was and will be—righteous without having to prove Himself righteous. But seeing He willed to and did prove Himself righteous, it is only right to count on it that He did not do so in vain. That the knowledge of our own justification by Him may be clear and certain, is it not right that He should first will to be known by us as the God who is right and just and righteous in Himself ? Is it not right that for our sake He should have willed to avail Himself, and actually did avail Himself, of His freedom to justify Himself ? Is it not right that in practice He should have loved man supremely and drawn him to Himself most intimately by not allowing him, when He justifies him, to stand and wonder and gape in astonishment at His own right as at a closed door, but by demonstrating His own right— His right as Creator and covenant Lord, His divine right as Father and Son—causing it to shine forth and to be proclaimed, and therefore to be known to man ? " The sun of righteousness with healing in his wings " (Mal. 4²). Supposing we cannot truly and actually and firmly know our own justification, without any problems or doubts, apart from this—if the door is in fact closed ? Supposing that in our own righteousness we have a complete and utter need to know Him and His righteousness on the basis of His self-demonstration, so that knowing Him we may participate in His own inner life ? Well, the door is not in fact closed to us. In justifying us, God in the first instance shows Himself to be righteous. He is revealed and may be known by us as such. Therefore we are well advised to let drop this anxious questioning of Him and instead to ask ourselves what use we are going to make of the freedom which He obviously willed to give to us in that He willed to make, and actually did make, use of this freedom of His ; what use we are going to make of the freedom to know in our own justification the One who is eternally righteous, and in so doing to know the light and the power and the indisputable validity and the irresistible efficacy of our own justification.

3. THE PARDON OF MAN

Pardon—by God and therefore unconditionally pronounced and unconditionally valid—that is man's justification. In the judgment of God, according to His election and rejection, there is made in the midst of time, and as the central event of all human history, referring to all the men who live both before and after, a decision, a divisive sentence. Its result—expressed in the death and resurrection of Jesus Christ—is the pardon of man. And this as such is man's justification, this alone, but with unconditional truth and efficacy, so that apart from it there is no justification, but in it there is the total justification of man. Whether man hears it, whether he accepts it and lives as one who is pardoned is another question. Where men do hear it and accept it and dare to live as those who are pardoned, it is realised that its power is total and not partial, and there will be no refusal to give to it a total and not a partial honour.

The sentence of God passed in His judgment is a divisive sentence. And it is in virtue of the division that its result is man's pardon. It divides between his wrong, himself as a wrongdoer, as the object of the divine rejection on the one hand, and himself as the elect of God, His creature and covenant-partner on the other. It tears away the latter man from the former, and the former from the latter. It opens up between the one and the other an unbridgeable gulf. It makes the one an old man whose time has run its course, who belongs to the past, in order to introduce a new man who can move forward into the future in which there is no place for a return of the first man. It makes the one a shadow, a ghost, in order to give breath and flesh and blood, a real existence, to the other. It locks up the one in order to free the other : to free him from his identification with the first man and his wrong; to free him for the right (his own right as a man) which is freely granted to him when he is parted from that first man and his wrong—his existence in identification with wrong—is renounced. When he is free for this right, he is free for life on the basis and under the protection of this right, as a righteous man. This is the divisive and pardoning sentence of God passed in God's judgment.

Three things are clear. This pardon (1) can only be God's sentence on man. The division between the man of sin and man himself, the opening up of a gulf between them, the separation of the past and the future, the locking up of the old man and free emergence of a new man, cannot be a human but only a divine work. It is creation—a new creation, but still like the first creation, which also involved at bottom a great division. Man would have to be able to put himself to death in order to make himself alive as a new man, to remove himself and then to rise up again, if it were his own affair to carry through and to put into effect this judgment and in this judgment this divisive sentence, to pardon himself. If he does in fact stand in this judgment and under this divisive sentence, it is because it is the sentence and judgment of God. If he is pardoned, then it is God who has done it—God who has made him a righteous instead of an unrighteous man. This is what God has done in Jesus Christ.

But this pardon (2) can be received and taken to heart and put into effect by him only as the sentence of God on him and therefore as the Word of God's revelation addressed to him. The fact that he is pardoned by God is not his truth but God's truth. He cannot, therefore, reveal and tell it to himself. He can only let himself be told it as it is revealed to him by God. His transition from his existence as the old man to his existence as the new, his coming out of his past and his going forward into his new and different future, can never be by virtue of his own capacity. He cannot accomplish it himself. He can only find it accomplished. In the same way, the knowledge of himself as the one who is caught up in this transition can take place only in the sphere of a human self-knowledge in which he repeats the knowledge with which God knows him in that sentence. How else could he come to it except on the presupposition that it has already been made known to him by God—which is what God does in His Word? Except on this presupposition he can never know himself as a sinner against God and before Him. In the same way, and more so, he can never know himself as one whose sin and sinful being are pardoned. To receive and take to heart and put into effect means in both respects to accept what is told us concerning ourselves by God Himself. Anything that we may try to tell ourselves in both respects can neither have the genuine content that we are sinners and that we are justified nor be seriously received and taken to heart and put into effect by us. The pardon effected in Jesus Christ is not our word but God's Word.

But if our pardon is God's sentence and the content of His Word to us, then (3) it has an authority and force and validity which are not partial but total, not relative but absolute. When this sentence was passed concerning us, something took place which cannot be reversed. This pardon does not mean only that something is said concerning us, or, as it were, pasted on us, but that a fact is created, a human situation which is basically altered. We are, in fact, those who are pardoned by God. We have peace with God. And our corresponding self-knowledge—if it is really a self-knowledge in which we repeat what is told us by His Word concerning us—cannot possibly be exposed to any legitimate doubt or genuine problems. The only legitimate and genuine answer to the unconditional Yes in which God pardons man is an equally unconditional human Yes, a confession in which there are no ifs or buts. Any question marks which we may try to put—and reasons enough can be found for them—can only be a rejection of God's judgment and sentence and Word, a basically impudent and a correspondingly dangerous presumption, for all the subjectively well-founded and sincere humility with which we may put them. The divine pardon which has taken place in Jesus Christ has a binding force. It speaks of a being and possession of the man to whom it applies.

We cannot overlook the fact that in the Old Testament Psalter, side by side with the pure worship of God, His acts and glory and faithfulness, and side by side with all the complaint and sorrow and longing and above all the penitence —indeed together with these—we not infrequently hear a voice of extraordinary confidence, in which other writers, and sometimes the same, boast of their own righteousness before God and man, appealing to their innocence and the purity of their heart and purposes and ways, and formally undertaking to plead their case with God on that ground. I will give a few examples : " I was also upright before him, and I kept myself from mine iniquity. Therefore hath the Lord recompensed me according to my righteousness, according to the cleanness of my hands in his eyesight. With the merciful thou wilt shew thyself merciful ; with an upright man thou wilt shew thyself upright ; with the pure thou wilt shew thyself pure " (Ps. 18[23f.]). " For thou, Lord, wilt bless the righteous ; with favour wilt thou compass him as with a shield " (Ps. 5[12]). " For thou hast maintained my right and my cause ; thou satest in the throne judging right " (Ps. 9[4]). " The righteous shall flourish like the palm-tree ; he shall grow like a cedar in Lebanon. Those that be planted in the house of the Lord shall flourish in the courts of our God. They shall still bring forth fruit in old age ; they shall be fat and flourishing ; to show that the Lord is upright ; he is my rock, and there is no unrighteousness in Him " (Ps. 92[12f.]). " The righteous shall be glad in the Lord, and shall trust in him ; and all the upright in heart shall glory " (Ps. 64[10]). The man whose delight is in the Law of the Lord, and who meditates in it day and night, is " like a tree planted by the rivers of water, that bringeth forth his fruit in his season : his leaf also shall not wither ; and whatsoever he doeth shall prosper " (Ps. 1[3]). For that reason, when he is in need and oppression, he demands : " Judge me, O Lord, according to my righteousness, and according to mine integrity that is in me. Oh let the wickedness of the wicked come to an end ; but establish the just : for the righteous God trieth the hearts and reins " (Ps. 7[8f.]). " Judge me, O Lord ; for I have walked in mine integrity : I have trusted also in the Lord ; therefore I shall not slide. Examine me, O

Lord, and prove me ; try my reins and my heart. For thy loving-kindness is before mine eyes : and I have walked in thy truth " (Ps. 26¹ᶠ·). And on occasion the positive complaint : " Verily I have cleansed my heart in vain, and washed my hands in innocency. For all the day long have I been plagued, and chastened every morning " (Ps. 73¹³ᶠ·). And against this background, what considerations concerning the ungodly, the proud, the " enemies," their threatenings, their unmerited fortune, their power, what prayers not merely for deliverance from them—but also—much bewailed by inoffensive Christians—for their overthrow and destruction ! What are we to say to all this ? And to Job's persistent protesting of his good conscience in face of all the clever and strong entreaties of his friends ; not only to them, but even to God Himself—a position which he surrenders only when God speaks to him " from the storm " : " I have heard of thee by the hearing of the ear : but now mine eye seeth thee " (Job 42⁵) ? And what does it mean that twice (42⁷ᶠ·) it was expressly granted in distinction to his prudent friends that he was right in his impetuous insistence upon his right ? To a smaller degree, but with the same distinctive assertiveness, we find the same insistence in Paul : " Let a man so account of us, as of the ministers of Christ, and stewards of the mysteries of God. Moreover, it is required in stewards, that a man be found faithful. But with me it is a very small thing that I should be judged of you, or of man's judgment : yea, I judge not mine own self. For I know nothing by myself ; yet am I not hereby justified : but he that judgeth me is the Lord " (1 Cor. 4²ᶠ·), concerning whom we are then told that when He comes and brings to light the hidden things of darkness and counsels of the hearts everyone will receive—Paul does not say recognition or condemnation but quite simply—praise of God. With a view to this he warned the Corinthians not to judge before the time. This is the apostle's opinion of a righteousness by faith only. And what of the famous passage in Rom. 8³⁰ᶠ·, in which—this time to the highest possible degree—a straight line is drawn from the election of those who love God to their calling and justifying and glorifying, with the conclusion : " If God be for us, who can be against us ? He that spared not his own Son, but delivered him up for us all, how shall he not with him also freely give us all things ? Who shall lay anything to the charge of God's elect ? It is God that justifieth. Who is he that condemneth ? It is Christ that died, yea rather, that is risen again, who is even at the right hand of God, who also maketh intercession for us." We do not need to force upon the confident words of the Psalms and Job any other sense than that which they obviously have according to their exact wording and context. But we must not read them outside the context of the rest of the Old Testament. We must hear them together with the other voices which sound in the Psalms. And if we do we shall see that for all their strangeness they did not really say anything other than what Paul said. On the contrary, what we have to ask is whether what Paul said—and much less brokenly at any rate in Rom. 8—is not a direct each of the Old Testament voice. The fact that the " innocence-motif " is also found in Babylonian Psalms does not alter in the slightest the fact that in the Psalms of Israel it has its meaning and right and necessity only from Israel's gracious election, on the basis of which God willed to set up and maintain His covenant with Israel. Israel was a notorious failure as a partner in the covenant (cf. Pss. 78 and 106). Behind the words of the Psalms there stand the catastrophic judgments which were God's answer to the unfaithfulness of His people. Their sequence, Israel's pitiable condition amongst the nations, exposed to external pressure and internal influence, the painful continuance within it of the unfaithfulness which has brought it to this pass : all these are the present, the negative presupposition of the words. But their positive presupposition is the recollection which these things have not extinguished of the faithfulness of God which has not been shaken by these things, which is quite unmerited, but absolutely certain in itself, which cannot be denied by those who see it, but now for the first time—and not in half-tones but *fortissime*—attested. It is the pious, the pure, the innocent, the blameless, the upright, who are confident of their righteousness in face of their enemies, and with a consciousness of their righteousness cry out for the righteousness of God; those who do not forget His covenant and faithfulness but have it before their eyes, and with it the light which in spite of all these things lies upon their lives, who cannot, therefore, cease to boast of their right. If all the other things which have to be said are said in the Psalms—and often in the same Psalms—then this has to be said too, and preferably more strongly and clearly than anything else : " Truly God is good to Israel, even to such as are of a clean heart " (Ps. 73¹). The man who is of a clean heart not only can but must appeal to God's goodness to Israel, and therefore to his own knowledge of that goodness, notwithstanding all that can be said against Israel and against himself as a member of this people. He does not now have to do with this, but with what God is for Israel and therefore for him. The man who clings to this is bound to find comfort. He is this man. He would be falling at once into impurity of heart and unrighteousness—he would, strangely enough, be making himself guilty of an impropriety against God—if he let go this calling, if he did not appeal or did not appeal unconditionally from this righteousness of his to the righteousness of God, if he did not regard God with a final seriousness as his rock, his fortress, and his shield, on which ultimately all his " enemies " could only dash themselves to pieces. If Job is found wanting (42¹ᶠ·) in that he doubted or rather murmured against the righteousness of God, repudiating it, insisting on his own right against God, as though he could deal with Him like an advocate who is sure of his case, if in this respect he has to withdraw and repent in sack-cloth and ashes, yet the wrath of God (42⁷ᶠ·) is not kindled against him but against his friends, who tried to make him err in that in which even in his wrong he was, in fact, right, in the fact that with doubt and murmuring and revolt—with a badly croaking voice, as it were—he still could and would and indeed had to hold fast to God, and as one who was righteous in this seek for himself righteousness with Him. In this very fact he was the servant of God, and in saying this concerning Him even in his protest, he spoke rightly. But what became of the three very excellent theologians with their very exact and accurate knowledge of the righteousness of God and the humility which is demanded of man ? They were directed to bring a burnt-offering of seven bullocks and seven rams—not for Job but for themselves. For God was willing to accept the intercession of Job—the more audacious but more perspicacious Job—on their behalf, and to spare them the evil that they had deserved, which He did. But Job's fate is " turned " when he makes intercession for them. His brothers and sisters and former acquaintances come to him and eat with him in his house and give him excellent comfort : " every one also gave him a piece of money, and an earring of gold." Job himself—the sun of righteousness rises visibly and tangibly upon him—is blessed more than he had been before, acquiring 14,000 sheep, 6,000 camels, 1,000 yoke of oxen, 1,000 she asses, and 7 sons and 3 daughters into the bargain (the latter being called " little dove," " sweet savour " and " little rouge-pot "), " and in all the land were no women found so fair as the daughters of Job : and their father gave them inheritance among their brethren. After this lived Job 140 years, and saw his sons, and his sons' sons, even four generations, and died, being old and full of days." Whether or not this conclusion is the work of a later redactor of the Book of Job does not make the slightest difference. Whoever may be the author, it is as it should be. For (with or without this ending) the meaning of the Book of Job is that God acknowledges with a supreme reality the one who, even though he may do it all too humanly, dares indefatigably to acknowledge Him. He affirms the human self-affirmation without which this acknowledgment is not possible, which, if there is to be this acknowledgment, is not merely legitimate but required. If we accept that in the light of the covenant fulfilled in Jesus Christ the self-affirmation hazarded by Paul ("If God be for us, who can be against us?") is quite in order, being embraced and supported by the divine Yes to this most audacious enterprise, then we can and must reckon with the fact that in Job and the Psalmists too, in their time of the expectation and promise and prophecy of the fulfilment of the covenant, we are dealing with something quite other than a form of the righteousness of Law and works (in spite of appearances and all the justifiable arguments to the contrary). And this other with which we are dealing is the Yes of man to the divine sentence and pardon which is pronounced in the judgment of the faithful God. Where this pardon is accepted, there could and can be, both *ante* and *post Christum*, only an unconditional Yes—without any question marks.

But when we have said this, and said it once and for all, we have to add that the justification of man is something which takes place. The pardon of man is spoken. It is the living Word of the living God in the present of every man. When we speak of what this term describes, we are never speaking of a state but of a history, of the transition which does, of course, move in one direction and therefore not in another, but which has a *terminus a quo* and a *terminus ad quem*, and therefore moves from here to there, in which there is a beginning and a completing, a coming and a going, in which man stands under a twofold determination to the extent that he goes forward from the "before" of his wrong and therefore his death to the "after" of his right and therefore his life. The work of the divine sentence—of the pardon which is unconditional because it is spoken by God and revealed to man in the Word of God—is that man is placed on this way, that he is in fact permitted to go forward in this impossible and incomprehensible way from here to there, that by the act of God he becomes the man of this history—the history of Jesus Christ. He becomes the man who in every present has both this past and this future; the one as past and the other as future; the one set aside behind him, the other as a promise before him; irreversible in the same sequence as the death and resurrection of Jesus Christ—but in this sequence not merely the one and the other but both at once, and in their specific and highly distinctive ways equally actual and equally serious; not intermingled in any present (as though at bottom they were not twofold) but both distinct in every present; not separated in any present, but—in that sequence, as moments in that history—indissolubly bound together in every present.

Looking backwards—this is the necessary statement with which we must begin—justification is therefore the divine pardon of sinful man. It is the sentence of God in virtue of which man is separated from that past and therefore the sentence of God on the man who can go forward from that past to quite a different future. In every present he is still the man he was, the man of sin, the man of pride, and as such fallen man. He is not this man to remain such, but to be so no longer, to become another man. But he still is this man. How can he be the man of this history, caught up in this transition, how can God's pardon be spoken to him as such, how can it apply to him, if he is not this man, if he is already free and therefore does not need this pardon? The man who is justified and therefore pardoned by God is the man in whom it comes to pass that he is separated from that past. This happens in every present in such a way that he is found by God in that past. God meets him as the doctor coming to the sick and not the whole, as the shepherd who leaves the ninety-nine sheep to seek the lost, as the father who stretches out his arms to the son who has gone into the far country and orders for him the fatted calf, as the Saviour who sits down to meat with publicans and sinners. Justification begins as man's acquittal from sin, from his being as a sinner. Only as it begins there can it and will it be completed in the re-establishment of his right, the renewal of his life. If man is without sin and therefore not a sinner, how can it apply to him? It does apply to him, it is God's righteous sentence on him, because he is still not righteous but unrighteous, because he is still the old man and not yet the new. It is *iustificatio impii*. That is the secret of it. That is what makes it the work which can only be the creative work of God, a *creatio ex nihilo*, or rather *ex contrario*. That is what characterises it as a work of grace, as the basis of the work of reconciliation. It is needed by the man who has fallen away from God, who resists Him in his pride. It is this man that God has in mind, that God loves, because it is this man that He has elected and created. It is this man that God justifies. It is to this man that He maintains and demonstrates His faithfulness to this unfaithful man—beginning with the fact that He is in the right against him, that He asserts His right, and therefore that He is angry with this unfaithful man, that He condemns and kills and causes him to perish as such, but in so doing beginning his justification, aiming thereby to separate him completely from this unfaithful man, to lead him into freedom. This separation has to take place in him. Sinful man is the man in whom it must and will happen, but has not yet happened, whose self-identification with his wrong has not yet been reversed. It is this man to whom God's sentence applies. It is he who is pronounced free—free from himself—by this sentence.

No one has ever known his justification—or what justification is at all, and therefore what really takes place in this divine pardon, no one has ever found himself acquitted in this divine judgment, no one has ever tasted the surpassing glory of this event, no one has ever known how to make use of the freedom of the man acquitted by God, without having had to recognise himself as a sinner before God even as all this took place. The man who knows his own and man's justification in truth and clarity is the man who knows himself as the one who has this past and comes from it, who in the present must still confess that he is this man even in his transition to the future. If he is now found and knows it, he has still to recognise that he is lost apart from this being found. If grace comes to him and he knows it, he must lay hold of the fact that he does not deserve it, that he has forfeited it and will always forfeit it. If he is now the work of a new divine creation and knows it, he cannot hide the fact that he had fallen a victim to nothingness, and that apart from this work he would necessarily do so again and again. If the divine pardon avails for him and he hears the Word of God in which it is pronounced, he will still see that he would be imprisoned to all eternity, and that every moment he would be imprisoned afresh, if it were not that every moment as the hearer of this pardon he can be the one who is acquitted by God. The pardon of God directed to him is valid and effective for him, but not grounded in him. It has no basis at all in him. It is only heard and accepted and received by him, as the present and gift of God. As it comes to him, he finds himself set on this way. He has his past as an unrighteous man behind him and his future as a righteous man before him. But where would he be even for a single moment without it ? What is he even now as the one to whom this comes in sovereign power, who is intended and addressed and forcefully set on this way by God in actualisation of His divine right but for that very reason in free grace ? he to whom God is so incomprehensibly and incontestably and irresistibly good according to this pardon ? he who now has to thank God and can never thank him enough for the fact that He willed to turn to him in this way, in this sentence ? he to whom there is now given this *terminus a quo* which he could not make or procure for himself ? Where, and breaking out from where, does he find himself in this *terminus a quo* and therefore at the beginning of this way ? As who and what, even when sought and found by God, can he offer himself to God or place himself at His disposal ? As what material for anything that God might do with him and make of him ? Certainly not as the one he will become when he enters this way. Certainly not as the righteous man he will be at the end of this way. Only as the one who is not yet this man, who is still unrighteous. Only, in fact, as the one who, to his own amazement, can now break out and go this way, living in the apprehension of the promise of this end. Only, in fact, as the one who—not yet having attained to this end—is still the old man, sinful and proud, who can only be accused and deplored as such, who has every reason to confess himself to be such with serious penitence, to concede that God is in the right against him, who can live provisionally only in the apprehension of the promise of this end, of his right and therefore of his justified life. That he can be as such, on the way from that beginning to that goal, that he can apprehend God's promise, that he can cling to it, and that in so doing he can live provisionally—that is the beginning of his justification.

There is no present in which the justification of man is not still this beginning of justification, and where if it is recognised it does not have to be continually recognised as such. There is no man justified by God who does not have to recognise and confess that he is still unrighteous, still the proud rebel before Him, who does not have to grant that God is always in the right against him and therefore that he is always in the wrong against God. If he is not willing to be this, that means necessarily that he does not wish to be pardoned, justified. If he wants to deny that he is this, that means that he denies the promise, that he does not know it, that he is not caught up in this breaking out of acquitted man. Where there is this breaking out, where the justification of man takes place, it is the justification of the unrighteous, and the one to whom it comes will not refuse to admit that he is still this one, that as such he finds himself in this breaking out, and that only as such can he do so. He can do so only as the one who can go forward from the midst of an evil past—not good, but bad—to a good future, who dares to go forward not because he himself but God has acquitted and authorised and empowered him. Daring to go forward, in accordance with the truth of the situation, he will give all the glory to God and to himself none at all, but only the corresponding dishonour and unworthiness and incapacity and unwillingness. The divine pardon does not burst into man's willingness but his unwillingness. Man will always be a miracle and a puzzle to himself as he breaks out in this way. He will never find in himself any reason for doing so. He will not be of the opinion that he has made even the slightest contribution to it. He will rather confess freely and frankly that his own contribution is only his own great corruption, in which without any co-operation or merit of his own he is found by the divine pardon—not in his self-judgment but in the judgment of God—reached and converted to God and set on the way to his right and life. The man who is pardoned by God, the righteous man, is always as such this man. To be sure, he is also another man, but even as this other he is still this man; even as he goes forward he is still the one who comes from this place. And let us say expressly, he is always this man totally and altogether, from top to toe, just as in the same present of the divine pardon he is always that other man totally and altogether, from top to toe, the man who goes forward to the goal of his righteousness, who has indeed already arrived, who is alive there as a righteous man. Neither in the one case nor in the other are we dealing with a quantum, rising here and dropping there like a fluid in two communicating tubes, but in both cases we are dealing with a single and a total human existence. He himself, as he is, in soul and body, in his person with all his thoughts and words and works, is already at the goal as the man who is pardoned by God, and he himself is also only at the beginning; already righteous before God and yet still only a sinner; called to a complete and unreserved and unconditional certainty and comfort and joy, but also to a complete and unreserved and unconditional humility and penitence, directed to pray with all possible seriousness : " Forgive us our trespasses,"

" God be merciful to me, a sinner." How can it be otherwise when his justification is this transition, when the man justified by God is the man of this history, when man's pardon is the living Word of the living God to living man, when the fact created by it is man transposed into this conversion to God and caught up in this conversion ?

To illustrate what we have called the beginning of justification—*N.B.* in its simultaneity with its completion—we will select from the seven so-called Penitential Psalms of the Old Testament the two which can be described as such with relatively the greatest clarity, Pss. 32 and 51.

First of all, Ps. 32. We see from its opening, heart and conclusion that it has to do with justification in its unity and totality. " Blessed is he whose transgression is forgiven, whose sin is covered. Blessed is the man unto whom the Lord imputeth not iniquity, and in whose spirit there is no guile " (vv. 1–2). That is the opening. And the conclusion is the triumphant : " Many sorrows shall be to the wicked : but he that trusteth in the Lord, mercy shall compass him about. Be glad in the Lord, and rejoice, ye righteous ; and shout for joy, all ye that are upright in heart " (vv. 10–11). But the central portion is as follows : " For this shall every one that is godly pray unto thee in a time when thou mayest be found : surely in the floods of great waters they shall not come nigh unto him. Thou art my hiding place ; thou shalt preserve me from trouble ; thou shalt compass me about with songs of deliverance " (vv. 6–7). The man who speaks in these three parts of the Psalm is obviously a man who has known the covenant faithfulness of the God of Israel, and in it the faithfulness of his God and therefore of His justifying sentence, and therefore himself as the one who is acquitted by this sentence, who in face of every threat is thus in a position to appeal to God as his helper, to live in that appeal with absolute comfort and cheerfulness and indeed joy, and to bear testimony to that joy. Note that within the framework of this presentation of justification as completed this Psalm is a penitential Psalm. But is this really only the framework and not the picture which the Psalm envisaged ? the substance of its message ? Does it not hang in the balance whether it would not be better described as a Psalm of thanksgiving ?

Now in v. 2 we read of the guileless spirit and in v. 11 of the upright heart of those who are certain in this way and can and must confess as much. It obviously all depends on the condition of their heart—which in the Old Testament means themselves at the centre of their being and out to the periphery of their whole existence—whether their transgression is forgiven, their sin covered, and therefore out of sight, their iniquity not imputed and therefore past (vv. 1–2) ; whether they appeal to God and in so doing can have an absolute certainty that they will be kept in every emergency and need (vv. 6, 7, 10) ; whether they can and must rejoice and be glad and shout for joy because of it (v. 11). What is needed is a spirit without guile, an upright heart, if all this—and therefore a completed justification—is not to be empty presumption and imagination.

But what kind of a heart is this ? To see what is meant our best plan is to look at the instructional passage strangely interposed between the middle of the Psalm and the end, a passage which reproduces the voice of God, which the Psalmist declares at a decisive point that he has already heard and is ready to hear again : " I will instruct thee and teach thee in the way which thou shalt go : I will direct mine eye upon thee. Be ye not as the horse, or as the mule, which have no understanding : whose mouth must be held in with bit and bridle, lest they come near unto thee " (vv. 8–9). The Psalmist has let God tell him that he was like a horse or mule, that his heart was an unruly heart, that he would not let himself be led where he ought to come and go.

In what did this opposition consist in which he was reached by the divine pardon and from which he was delivered by it ? According to v. 3 it consisted

D.R.—19

decisively in the fact that he kept silence concerning " it," concerning his transgression, sin and guilt, that he would not accept it, that he would not admit it to God or man or even to himself, that he tried to live it down in a self-confident blustering. It is strange that the man who is justified, the sinner who can live strong and joyful before God as a righteous man, recognises in this silence the really sinful thing about his past. This silence was the seed of death in his existence in this past. In this silence he would not be what he was, a transgressor, a sinner, a debtor. And by this silence he was not doing himself any good as he thought and purposed, but only harm. He was making himself insufferable. In this silence he withstood God, and God withstood him. In it he could only be broken on God : " When I kept silence, my bones waxed old through my roaring all the day long. For day and night thy hand was heavy upon me : my moisture is turned into the drought of summer " (vv. 3–4). All obviously without any awareness that he was suffering in this way and on the point of perishing because of the falseness and insincerity of his heart, because of this conflict with God.

In this darkness he found the eye of God (v. 8), the eye of the Lord, directed upon him, as was the case with Peter (Lk. 22^{61}) in the court of the high-priest, and he was shown the way which he must go (v. 8), and bound with bit and bridle (v. 9). In this darkness there took place the beginning of his justification. What did this mean for him ? In what did it consist ? " I acknowledged my sin unto thee, and mine iniquity have I not hid. I said, I will confess my transgressions unto the Lord " (v. 5a). The really sinful thing about the past, that silence, now falls away, according to the instruction, the direction of the Lord (v. 8). The horse or mule finds that it is bound. It has acquired understanding. Its unruliness is curbed. Man can and will let himself be led where he should come and go. With the fact that this had happened, that he could no longer conceal himself but had to confess, he did not in any sense conclude : " It is already forgiven " (G. Keller), but he could say and indeed had to say : " *Thou* forgavest the iniquity of my sin " (v. 5). Thou ! Being bound in such a way that he had to confess himself a sinner, he encountered the God who established against his wrong His own right, who therefore made an end of his past, who was the justifying, pardoning God. He became the man of that history. Confessing his sin, giving God the right against him, he could seize with joyful certainty his own right, raising that song of praise—" Blessed is he "—to the life which had been given to him in the very midst of that consuming drought, moving forward directly to the completion of his justification, with a guileless spirit and an upright heart.

And then Ps. 51. It is easier to understand than Ps. 32 because it does not contain any of the confusing interchange of speaker and hearer which is so frequent in the Psalms, but is a simple prayer in I-Thou form. And it is predominantly and almost exclusively a prayer of confession (in the two different forms of a prayer for the forgiveness of sin and a confession of sin). To this there is, of course, added once again the forward looking request for renewal. The only thing is—and this makes Ps. 51 outwardly much harder to survey than Ps. 32—that of these three complexes only that of the confession of sin (vv. 5–7) is expressed in any unified sequence. The two others inter-cross with one another and with a fourth, which is the most important of all (vv. 8 and 18–19), and which expresses to some extent the principle of the beginning of justification in penitence. The final verses 20–21 may have been added by a later writer, since they obviously cannot be reconciled with what is said about sacrifice in vv. 18–19.

It is important and instructive that the Psalm does not begin, as we might logically have supposed, with a confession of sin, but with a request for the forgiveness of sin : " Have mercy upon me, O God, according to thy loving-kindness : according unto the multitude of thy tender mercies blot out my transgressions. Wash me throughly from mine iniquity, and cleanse me from my sin " (vv. 1–2).

We have the same line of thought in v. 7 : " Purge me with hyssop, and I shall be clean : wash me, and I shall be whiter than snow," and again in v. 9 : " Hide thy face from my sins, and blot out all mine iniquities." These words express a fourfold knowledge. The speaker knows (1) that there is something intolerable in his life—his transgression, guilt, sin, impurity, misdeeds. He knows (2) that if he is to be helped this intolerable thing must not be merely alleviated or weakened but taken right away, blotted out, cleansed, washed away, removed from the presence of God, and that he himself must be purged. He knows (3) that the removal of this intolerable thing cannot be his work but only God's : a divine blotting out, cleansing, and washing away ; not man's hiding of his sin but God's hiding of His face from his sin, and therefore its radical putting away. He knows finally (4) that he can turn to God with the request to do this because there is grace and great mercy with God. This last is decisive : he knows that he can ask God for it, that he is free to do so. And he makes use of this freedom. He does what he can do in this freedom. The Israelite has only to think seriously of the covenant and its Lord to know this freedom. And clearly this Israelite does think of the covenant and its Lord. He knows His grace and mercy. He therefore knows that even as the sinner he is he can approach Him with the request that his sin should be put away. And how is it that he knows the other things : the intolerable nature of his sin, the necessity of its radical putting away, God as the One who alone can do this ? How else but in the knowledge of this freedom ! Naturally not with a theoretical and dead knowledge, but with a knowledge which is alive because it is put into effect, in the use of this freedom, by doing what he can do in this freedom. As he does this he knows God and himself and what he needs. And what is this but the knowledge of his justification as it has certainly not been completed but has very definitely begun ? How could he know all this if it were not that as a beginner, but in very truth, he is already the man of this history ?

Now obviously the confession of sin is not, as it were, a precondition of this history, and especially of the prayer for forgiveness which initiates it and for which the Israelite has this freedom. On the contrary, it is as he dares to make this request, and actually does make it, that he has the freedom to confess that he himself is a sinner and to confess his sin : " For I acknowledge my transgressions, and my sin is ever before me. Against thee, thee only have I sinned, and done this evil in thy sight : that thou mightest be justified when thou speakest, and be clear when thou judgest. Behold, I was shapen in iniquity ; and in sin did my mother conceive me " (vv. 3–5). This obviously means that the request for forgiveness corresponds exactly to the situation of the one who makes it. He is the man who has sinned, who has sinned against God, who has done that which is displeasing to Him, against whom God is absolutely in the right, who is himself absolutely in the wrong against God and therefore guilty, not merely in individual thoughts and words and works, but, as expressed in these, in the very root of his existence (in what will later be called his heart). And, conversely, his situation corresponds exactly to his request for forgiveness. The request is not addressed to God incidentally. It does not simply express one disposition of man. It is not dispensable. For man himself, the whole man, just as he is, is expressed in it. This is what he is, the one who is with God and before Him, who has transgressed against Him, who can only displease Him, who is entirely in the wrong against Him, not merely on the surface but to the very core, not partially, but in the unity of his existence. What is the confession of sin other than the discovery of the true situation, not of man alone, but of man in relation to God, to the God of grace and tender mercy, to whom he can and does draw near with his request, and over against Him man who has no other possibility, who cannot utter anything else in the face of God but this request : " Be merciful to me, a sinner " ? But what else is this situation except once again the justification which has certainly not been completed but has very definitely begun ?

What the Psalmist has in mind as the subject-matter of his prayer—and obviously not only as the subject-matter but also as the presupposition—is, as the continuation shows, his justification as the history which moves irresistibly from its beginning to its completion, that transition in its inconceivable but absolutely irresistible totality. How else, having made that confession of sin, could he go on to say with such confidence—apparently as a supreme and final request : " Make me to hear joy and gladness ; that the bones which thou hast broken may rejoice " (v. 8) ? Joy, gladness, rejoicing ? Can we already demand that ? None of the *gradus ad Parnassum* in which we first emerge from the depths and painfully make our way upwards ? No process of sanctification which has to come between our aversion from ourselves and our conversion to God ? No : " whom he justified, them he also glorified " (Rom. 8^{30}). The man who asks for the forgiveness of his sins, and confesses his sins and enters into the light of the situation between God and man as it really is, can and should as such and at once (as this beginner) expect to be satisfied with joy and gladness, and he can and should therefore pray for it, for his new right before God, the new possibility of living before Him. How can he really be crying from the depths for the grace and tender mercy of God if he is not reaching for this supreme gift ? Reaching ! This is what is meant when he says : " Create in me a clean heart, O God ; and renew a right spirit within me. Cast me not away from thy presence ; and take not thy holy spirit from me. Restore unto me the joy of thy salvation ; and uphold me with thy free spirit " (vv. 10–12). " Deliver me from blood-guiltiness, O God, thou God of my salvation " (v. 14a). Note that instead of any intervening and preparatory operations to make it possible we have at once the new creation of a clean heart, i.e., of the man who has already turned to God from himself and his sin ; at once the gift of a new and right or constant spirit, the spirit with which man can only look forward and not backward, the willing spirit, by which man is protected and kept as set up in this way, in and by which the joy of God's salvation is created and continually renewed ; at once man's redemption from death ; at once life and salvation ; at once the creation and gift of a human existence which is not hidden from the face of God, which can stand before it, because it is righteous before it and is therefore commended to its care, before that same face of God from which the sin of man is hidden (v. 9) and has perished. What is it that man has apprehended if not this promise when he has the freedom and makes use of the freedom to pray for the forgiveness of his sin ? As the one who does this, how can he fail to reach out for the fulfilment of this promise ? and therefore to pray for the continuance, the progress, the completion of this transition, that the Holy Spirit who has given him this freedom will not be taken from him, but continue His work within him, that the justification which He has begun will be completed by Him —for in its totality it can be only the work of God ?

How bold and certain is this forward reach we can see from vv. 13 and 14b–15. They go beyond the problem which occupies us here, but for that very reason they show the breadth of the Psalmist's vision : " Then will I teach transgressors thy ways ; and sinners shall be converted unto thee. . . . And my tongue shall sing aloud of thy righteousness. O Lord, open thou my lips ; and my mouth shall shew forth thy praise." Compare this with the confession of sin in vv. 3–5. The same man expects already that he will not merely participate in that completion in his own person, but that in that completion he will be an instrument to glorify God, a witness, a teacher, a prophet to others, his fellow sinners. Yes, the very same man. The completion of justification cannot and will not be a private matter, but as such his commissioning for the service for God among men. It will attain its end in his calling. In the calling of the same man. The man and only the man who starts there, the man who prays for the forgiveness of his sin—with the knowledge of his sin, will be the right man for this, for the service of God, for prophecy. And he will be that man.

There still remain vv. 6 and 16–17, in which we have in a sense the key to the whole : " Behold, thou desirest truth in the inward parts, and in the hidden part thou shalt make me to know wisdom " (v. 6). The truth in the inward parts which is pleasing to God is obviously what we have called the true situation between God and man as revealed in the request for forgiveness and the confession of sin. When man is placed in this situation, when he realises it, God makes him to know wisdom. He instructs him concerning Himself as the God and man as the man of this history, of its beginning and its completion. The Psalmist prays for this divine instruction. He prays that this wisdom may be revealed to him. He would not pray for it if it were not already being revealed to him. We are told the same in vv. 16–17, the only verses in the Psalm which are not direct petition : " For thou desirest not sacrifice ; else would I give it ; thou delightest not in burnt offering. The sacrifices of God are a broken spirit : a broken and a contrite heart, O God, thou wilt not despise." What is it that He will not despise ? What is it that is pleasing to Him ? What is it that He demands ? What is it that He also creates and accomplishes ? Simply this, that the situation between Himself and God should be made clear, that man should stand before him as he is and deal with Him as He Himself is. But that means the broken spirit and contrite heart of man, for whom there is no other possibility but to ask for forgiveness and confess his sin. He despises the proud who will not do this. But the man who will He not only does not despise but has pleasure in him, desiring and exalting and glorifying him. He receives him, He gives him His promise, He is already on the way to its fulfilment for him. He will keep it to him. He can and will use him in His service. He sacrifices to Him the sacrifice to which all other sacrifices can only point and without which they are empty, the sacrifice which He has demanded and which is well-pleasing to Him, the sacrifice of himself, that God may accomplish in him and with him that which is His purpose for him.

The beginning of justification—its beginning in the midst of human sin— is described much more strongly in a New Testament passage than in these or the other Penitential Psalms or anywhere else in the Old. This passage is the seventh chapter of Romans, a chapter which continually demands our attention and has always caused difficulty in interpretation. It is described· much more strongly here because after all that has gone before in chapters 3–6 the reader is not prepared to be brought back so suddenly and violently to this situation from which the man who is justified by God starts. He is not prepared to be reminded of the character of justification as *creatio ex opposito*. It is also described much more strongly here because the astonishing and quite improbable nature of the fact that man's justification begins in the midst of his sin is brought out in this passage with such a complex and minute description of what sin means for man, and therefore in a much more penetrating way. Finally, it is described much more strongly here because this presentation is so terribly closed, almost reminding us of a prison cell in which there seems to be only a small and barred and inaccessible window to allow any light to enter. A situation from which to start ? But where can we start ? How is it possible in these circumstances to find ourselves in that transition ? Certainly there can be no question of this New Testament passage making the mystery of the whole affair any the less difficult, although in contrast to the Old Testament texts it is written with a direct knowledge of the crucified and risen Jesus Christ. On the contrary, it is only as we look back from this passage that we can see how great the mystery really is in those two Psalms.

If we are to understand Rom. 7 we must not forget even for a single moment that we are in the sphere of the problem and proclamation of justification. The chapter does not interrupt the great sequence of Rom. 3–8, but with its apparently backward movement it brings it to its climax. The man who comes out into the light in Rom. 8—still sighing heavily enough, still conscious of his supreme daring and peril—is the same man as the one who in Rom. 7 looks in this direction from afar, still surrounded by darkness. And the man of Rom. 7 is concerned with the darkness which engulfs, or rather fills him, not for its own sake, but for the magnifying of the light which greets him from afar. There is, therefore, no more forceful presentation of justification as transition than the turning of Rom. 7^{24-25} with the cry : " O wretched man that I am ! who shall deliver me from the body of this death ? " followed by what is hazarded only as a cry : " Thanks be to God through Jesus Christ our Lord." But then the bolt is drawn again and Rom. 7 is briefly and mercilessly—we might almost think definitively—summed up : " So then with the mind I myself serve the law of God ; but with the flesh the law of sin." Yet at once and without any link we move on to Rom. 8^{1-2} : " There is therefore now no condemnation to them which are in Christ Jesus, who walk not after the flesh, but after the Spirit. For the law of the Spirit of life in Christ Jesus hath made me free from the law of sin and death." The man who can know this without presumption or self-deception, and who can and must say it with such definiteness, is the same man who has before him and knows and says that which precedes it, the man who comes from the one to go forward to the other. Obviously he is the only one who can do this. But he can. The justified man speaks of his sin as in Rom. 7. And we must not overlook the fact that even the opening section of chapter 7 (vv. 1–6 : a good third of the chapter) establishes this message of freedom in all its forms. The parable of the woman who is made legally free by the death of her husband, indisputably free for re-marriage, is developed and expounded in these verses. Her husband, or rather ours, has been put to death. That is to say, we ourselves in the lusts of our sins, our being in the flesh, the end of which can only be death (v. 5). It is all up with him. How did this come about ? We read : διὰ τοῦ σώματος τοῦ Χριστοῦ, by virtue of our being in the unity of our existence with that of Jesus Christ. Our putting to death has taken place in His existence, in His putting to death (as we are shown in·Rom. $6^{6, 8, 11}$). Our being in the flesh is destroyed in Him. But if we are dead to that in which we were held (ἐν ᾧ κατειχόμεθα, v. 6), that is to say, our being in the flesh, if we are dead to the Law which controlled and bound and committed us as long as we lived as this man, as long as we were in the flesh, then we are free from this man (v. 6), free for another man, that is, free to bring forth fruit to God instead of to death (v. 4), free for service in the completely new possibility not of the letter but of the Spirit (v. 6). The continuation must not make us forget that this is how Rom. 7 opens. And there can be no doubt that we are in the middle of a description of justification. Already in Rom. 6—from the standpoint of the sanctification to be realised in obedience—we have had a comprehensive and penetrating and express study of the new thing which necessarily and at once follows the destruction of the old as it has taken place in Jesus Christ. The beginning of Rom. 7 has established the fact that we have to reckon with this new thing as a possibility created by God and the reason why we have to do so. Rom. 8 will introduce it as an actuality. We might think that there was nothing to prevent Paul from going straight on from Rom. 7^6 to Rom. 8^1.

But he knew well enough what he was about when he did not do so. In Rom. 6^{14}—at the very heart of his insistence upon the necessity of the new life in obedience—he had given as the reason for his bold statement : " Sin shall not have dominion over you," the even bolder one : " For ye are not under the law, but under grace." And then in Rom. 7^{1-6} he proclaimed explicitly, with man's liberation from the flesh, his liberation from the Law which controlled and engaged and committed man in and with his being in the flesh. If the ensuing description of the freedom created by it was to have a genuine ring, this could not be stated as a truth which is lightly uttered and easily accepted.

A first reason for this is that there is for Paul a Law, the continuance and validity of which he never thought to question. The Law is not against the promises (Gal. 3²¹). " Do we then make void the law through faith ? God forbid : yea, we establish the law " (Rom. 3³¹). In the message of the δικαιοσύνη θεοῦ (Rom. 3²¹) apprehended in faith in Jesus Christ we have to do with the righteousness attested by the Law and the prophets (Rom. 3²¹). The demand of the Law (its δικαίωμα) will be fulfilled in those who walk after the Spirit and not after the flesh (Rom. 8⁴). According to Gal. 5¹⁴ and Rom. 13⁸, ¹⁰ love, the love of the neighbour, is the fulfilling of the Law. As distinct from the Jew who boasts of the Law but actually breaks it, the heathen who are called to be the people of God by faith have the work of the Law written upon their heart, so that they are doers of it, and as such will show themselvës to be justified (Rom. 2¹³⁻¹⁵). In 1 Cor. 9²¹, rejecting the claim or blame that he was ἄνομος, Paul called himself an ἔννομος Χριστοῦ. In Gal. 6² he spoke expressly of a " law of Christ," and in the present context in Rom. 8² he referred to a " law of the Spirit of life," remarkably enough describing it as the subject of man's liberation. There can be no question of any liberation from this Law or abrogation of it. This Law is itself the ἕτερος ἀνήρ for whom, according to Rom. 7³, man has become free with the death of the first man. It has nothing whatever to do with sin (v. 7) and with death (v. 13). We ourselves in our relation to it have much to do with these but not the Law. According to v. 22 and v. 25 it is the Law of God. Its aim, according to v. 10, is the life of man. According to v. 12 it is holy, and " its commandment is holy, and just and good." According to v. 14 it is spiritual. As a spiritual man Paul can only confess that it is καλός (v. 16). " After the inward man " he can only delight in it (v. 22). In the νοῦς enlightened by it, rightly perceiving what is revealed to him, he can only serve it (vv. 23 and 25). This must not be forgotten in relation to the statement that we are not under the Law but under grace, and that we are dead to the Law and freed from it. The Law of God is not affected by this statement. On the contrary, this statement is the most positive indication of the fulfilment of the Law. Rom. 7² is, at any rate, an assurance on this side. He could not proceed without introducing it.

But obviously something else lay more closely on his heart in the apparent digression of Rom. 7⁷⁻²⁵. The transition from the transgression to the fulfilment of this Law is not immediately self-evident. In the illustration at the beginning of the chapter Paul showed that the liberation of the wife for union with another would be adultery as long as the first husband was alive, and therefore an illegitimate and false liberation (v. 3). The problem of vv. 7–25 is the question of the actual death of the first husband and therefore of the legitimacy and truth of our liberation. Where will we have to look if we are going to find that things are as they are described in Rom. 7¹⁻⁶ and later in 8¹ᶠ· ? We can at once rule out the negative answer of Rom. 7²ᶠ· Yet with bitter words Paul explains that when he looks at himself and takes stock of himself he finds that that first man is very much alive, that his being in the flesh which (in v. 5 according to the whole tenor of chapter 6) he has put into the past is still the present. Note that in the decisive statements of vv. 14–25 he uses the present tense. We need not exclude from these statements some recollection of what Paul was before his conversion to Christ and calling as an apostle. But we cannot possibly limit them to this recollection of his earlier life. Even as a Christian and apostle Paul sees and judges the whole of his life as expressed in these statements. So seriously does he understand man's justification as God's new and concealed miraculous act that he not only saw it begin once in his earlier life at the very heart of the life of the first man, his own being and flesh, but he continually sees it begin again in this way. Every morning and every evening his situation is one of departure in the very midst of sin. And only as he sees this, only as he acknowledges that this is his situation even as a Christian and an apostle, only as he looks away from himself, dare he take the leap forward : " There is therefore now no condemnation to them which are in Christ Jesus " (Rom. 8¹). From this point the leap can and must be hazarded, in this most realistic and therefore genuinely spiritual self-knowledge. But it can be hazarded only from this point. The function of vv. 7–25 is therefore to retard. They show clearly the point of departure from which the way leads forward. In this way they safeguard the mystery of justification as the transition from wrong to right, from death to life. They prevent us from representing this transition as anything but an event and this event as anything but a miraculous act of God. They prevent us from trying to attain any knowledge of it except as the knowledge of God and therefore as the knowledge of faith in the strictest sense.

And the instrument used by Paul for this purpose is again the concept of law, but this time with a meaning and usage quite the opposite from that of the Law of God. In v. 23 he speaks expressly of a ἕτερος νόμος, and in the same verse (and again in v. 25) he calls it the νόμος τῆς ἁμαρτίας. In Rom. 8² it is more widely described as the νόμος τῆς ἁμαρτίας καὶ τοῦ θανάτου. It is obviously the νόμος τοῦ ἀνδρός (v. 3), the law of the husband which binds the wife so that apart from the death of the husband she can be free for another only in adultery and therefore illegitimately and falsely. It is the νόμος from which we are freed on the presupposition of the death of this husband, the destruction of our being in the flesh (v. 4 and v. 6). Διὰ τοῦ σώματος τοῦ Χριστοῦ that first man, our being in the flesh, has died and been destroyed, and our liberation from that law has been achieved. But when Paul, the Christian and apostle, looks at himself and takes stock of himself, he finds that he is still one who is in the flesh (ἐν σαρκί v. 25), that that first man is still alive, that his past is still his present, that that ἕτερος νόμος is still in force. He is, he has his seat, and Paul is aware of him, ἐν τοῖς μέλεσίν μου (twice in v. 23), obviously his whole physico-psychical existence so far as he can see and view and conceive this as his own. He reigns there in contrast to the νόμος τοῦ θεοῦ in which as a Christian and apostle Paul delights after the inward man (v. 22), but in which he only delights " also," only in the knowledge of his νοῦς (vv. 23 and 25) in which he does not see himself. In so far as he does not see himself he has to confess that another rules in his members, this law, the law of sin and death. The use of this concept to describe the matter, the same concept originally used to describe the holy and just and good order and expression of the will of God, is perhaps rather bold. But it is very illuminating in relation to what Paul wishes to say. His aim is to magnify sin as the situation in which justification begins, in order that justification itself may be shown to be truly great, because far greater. He therefore shows both to himself and to the Christians in Rome that sin is the determination of human existence from which he and they are liberated only by justification as the miraculous act of God, from which apart from that act they are not liberated. He calls upon faith in justification to be faith alone : not man's secret understanding and control of himself. He therefore speaks not only of a Law of God but also of a law of sin, and even as a Christian and apostle every morning and evening he can only see and confess that he is a doer of this law. Naturally this law of sin is only a reflection distorted out of all recognition. It is only a poor caricature, an aping of the Law of God. Naturally it is comparable with it only in the fact that it is a law. It is the law of anomaly, but of the anomaly of its peculiar finality and consistency once man has fallen a victim to it, of the authority, the power to command and control, which sinful man cannot outgrow or escape but only God. Sin is not something accidental which the man who engages in it can brush off again like a speck of dust from his clothes. Being directed against God, it has in it something of the nature of God to the extent that it acquires, and with it the life of the man who engages in it, a negative logic and necessity which neither it nor the man who engages in it can evade. Both it and sinful man exist with and under and by virtue of an evil, we might almost say a demonic, right of wrong, according to which sin can bring forth only further sin and the sinful man can move only in a circle. Justification is the breaking of this right of wrong, the liberation of man from it and therefore from this *circulus vitiosus.* He does not imagine that he can accomplish it himself, even in the form of a grateful welcoming and acceptance of the restoring grace of God, which is, of course, within his capacity. He exists under the law of sin. And his transition from sin to righteousness presupposes the breaking of this law and man's liberation from it. But he will never find this liberation actualised in himself, in his members. In himself, in his members, he will always come up against this law, against the power and force of this law, against himself as the one who does not fail to do sin but does it, and does not do 'good but fails to do it. Where and how will he see this liberation as something which has happened to him, and himself as the man who is freed from this law, free for the fulfilment of the Law of God ?

Certainly not—the answer is tempting—in the Law of God in so far as he knows this and works it out in the life which he sees, in so far as he sees himself as one who knows the Law, and its outworking in his life. He does, of course, know and respect and value the Law of God. How could Paul say anything else as a Christian and an apostle ? He would be denying himself if he did. Moreover, he can and must sincerely confess (v. 25) that in the knowledge of his νοῦς he serves it and therefore that he does at least will to be obedient. Why should he question this ? On the contrary, he is in a position to ascribe to himself as something positive this knowledge and the good which rests upon it. Can he not find his liberation in this element of his self-knowledge—notwithstanding that other element in which, like all other men, he finds himself subject to the law of sin ? Can he not at least find himself in this knowledge, his transcendental ego, beyond the power of that other law and therefore liberated from it ? That is how Kant viewed the justification of man. But Paul cut off this solution both for himself and for his readers. What agitated him especially in Rom. 7⁷⁻¹³ was the really frightful discovery that it is in his knowledge of the Law of God and his attempt to keep it that the sinful man experiences the fact that as a sinful man he does not have the freedom either to sin or not to sin, but rather that he will only sin and sin again, that as a sinner he stands under the law of sin, that he is irresistibly subject to it and that he does in fact obey it. That is the outworking of the Law of God which he sees in his own life. " I had not known sin (sin not only as aberration but as an aberration which controls me), but by the law (of God) " (v. 7a). I had not previously known myself to be incapable of amendment, to be under the compulsion of sin, but in the light of the Law of God I have found this to be so. How ? " I had not known lust, except the law had said, Thou shalt not covet. But sin, taking occasion by the commandment, wrought in me all manner of concupiscence " (vv. 7b–8a). Because the Law called me to humility, it was revealed who I am and what I think in contrast to the Law of God ; it was shown at every point what is in me, the pride in which I myself will to be Lord and God, to help myself, to justify myself. As the hearer of the commandment of God I awaken as the man of sin. The authority, the power of the law of sin, the aim of that law is this evil awakening of the sinner, the opening of this bud, the ripening of this fruit of sin, as it takes place only—but surely—in its confrontation with the Law of God, in the light of His revelation.

Is there, therefore, such a thing as latent sin ? That is undoubtedly the meaning of Paul. But he puts it more strongly : " For without the law sin was dead. For I was alive without the law once " (vv. 8b–9a). I was therefore alive as a sinner, although I was dead in trespasses and sins, as is said of the Christians who once lived as heathens in Eph. 2¹. We have the same in Rom. 4¹⁵ : " For where no law is, there is no transgression," and in Rom. 5¹³, which s most illuminating for the present passage : " But until the law sin was in the world : but sin is not imputed when there is no law," i.e., it is not alive, it is not manifest as such. It is committed, but without a knowledge of its character as sin. It has terrible consequences, but they have no obvious connexion with it. It reigns, but it does not stand out in concrete form in the being and activity of man. Sin emerges from its anonymous existence when man encounters the self-revealing God and therefore His Law. This process is described in Rom. 5²⁰ in the words : " Moreover the law entered, that the offence might abound," πλεονάσῃ (like water in a pot placed over the fire). Rom. 7⁹ᵇ⁻¹⁰, following on from what is said in v. 8, speaks of it even more pregnantly as a formal resurrection of sin : " When the commandment came, sin revived," with terrible consequences for man : " and I died. And the commandment, which was ordained to life, I found to be unto death." As the sin of the man who receives the Law of God it acquires an aspect, and character, and form. It rejoices and triumphs—a regular Easter festival at the celebration of which the man who has received the commandment of God can only die and perish as the one who has committed it.

What Paul has before him in these verses (as in Rom. 5¹³⁻¹⁴, ²⁰) can only be the experience of Israel as distinct from other peoples. In contrast to others it is the people of the election, the calling, the covenant, and therefore of the gracious will and commandment of God revealed to it, the people confronted with the Law of God. There is no doubt that it knows the Law. It does not reject it at root. It knows that its existence depends upon the covenant with God and therefore upon the Law of God. It continually returns to it. It is continually summoned to try to serve it, as Paul says of himself in v. 25. Its boast is to be the people of the divine Law. Not in spite but because of this, it takes place in its history that Israel shows itself to be—and obviously has to show itself to be—what (in that anonymity) all other peoples also are, but what is only revealed in Israel, a people of proud and covetous transgressors, flagrantly and drastically contradicting and resisting God as His partner in the covenant which He has concluded with it, a people which in the very light of His special turning to it walks in the darkness like no other people and for that reason suffers under the heavy hand of God like no other people. All men are sinners (Rom. 5¹²), but the only notorious sinners (with all that that involves) are those to whom the will of God is revealed and proclaimed and known.

Does it lie in the nature of the Law that this should be the case ? That would mean the exculpation of these notorious sinners. And it might suit the men of whom Paul is speaking, by whom he means not only his fellow-Israelites but the Christians of Rome, who, whether they were Jews or Gentiles, were just as much confronted by the Law of God as he was. If only they could thrust back upon God the responsibility for the terrible conjunction of their knowledge of the commandment of God and their living and rejoicing and triumphant sin unambiguously declared as such ! If only they could make God responsible for it and then enjoy themselves as notorious sinners ! Paul is at great pains to guard against this in these verses. The commandment of God has nothing whatever to do with sin (v. 7). It is holy (v. 12). It has nothing whatever to do with the corruption and death which strike the sinner (v. 13a). In itself it is the ἀγαθόν (v. 16). The Law of God has no character or office or function in which it has made man a sinner qualified in this way, or delivered him up as such to death. No, sin takes occasion (ἀφορμὴν λαβοῦσα, vv. 8 and 11) by the encounter of man with the commandment of God in order that by its misuse it might make him the sinner qualified in this way. It deceives man when it does this (v. 11), when it causes him to sin with a high hand against God even in His presence. Sin shows itself in its true colours by deliberately delivering him up to death διὰ τοῦ ἀγαθοῦ, διὰ τῆς ἐντολῆς. In this perversion it shows itself to be καθ' ὑπερβολὴν ἁμαρτωλός. But it is quite capable of this taking occasion, this misuse, this perversion, this self-revelation of its sinister majesty. This is the working out of its law, the consequence of its opposition to God and His will. Only where this will is revealed can sin be revealed. But where this will is revealed—it is brought to light by the sun—is it, too, revealed, revealed as the power which is not superior to God but superior to man, as the lord to whom

3. The Pardon of Man 587

he has sold himself (v. 14) by committing it, as his law-giver and commander, whom he cannot escape as sinful man, subjected to whom he is a debtor to the grace of God, grasping at life and running headlong to death. If he looks at himself with an eye and νοῦς enlightened by the Law of God, that is the state of affairs which he sees. He comes up against the law of sin as the law which he obeys, the copy of the Law of God which he actually lives to please. He comes up against the outworkings of his obligation to this Law in all his impulses and thoughts and words and works. It is not the heathen, secular, godless man who lives in this self-knowledge and is constantly forced back to it, but the man who is elected and called : Paul the Christian and the apostle interpreting the experience of Israel. It cannot, therefore, be the case that looking at his own perhaps very real relationship with God and His Law (as in the case of Paul) a man will find his freedom from the law of sin and regard himself as justified. On the contrary, when he looks at this relationship, and himself as he exists in this relationship, he will be forced to recognise his obligation to this quite different law—and he cannot possibly regard himself as justified.

Vv. 14-25—this is the decisive part of the chapter—describe the position of man in relation to the Law of God as one who is subject to the law of sin. V. 14 is a brief summary of the whole, as later gathered together in other words in v. 25b: " We know that the law (of God) is spiritual." Later, in Rom. 8², it is described as the Law of the Spirit. This means that as such it has the authority and power to overcome and destroy the law of sin and death, to free man at a stroke and altogether from its usurped authority and power. As such it comes to him with this promise. But the fulfilment of the promise is the completion of justification, not the beginning of which Paul is now speaking. The situation from which it starts is characterised by the fact that to the knowledge that the Law is spiritual there corresponds the confession : " But I am carnal, sold under sin." As I see and know myself in my confrontation by the Law of God, as the promise comes to me but only comes, I am not spiritual but σαρκινός, fleshly, which means (this is the definition of the term " carnal ") : not free in relation to sin, but bound, just as much bound as a slave who is sold. Sin is my owner and lord. This is brought out in two short sequences, vv. 15-17 and 18-20.

Vv. 15-17 begin with the statement that I cannot recognise myself in what I accomplish, in my own actual achievements (κατεργάζεσθαι), in the details and the totality of my life's work, more especially from that point where, enlightened by the Law of God, I am supposed to be able to understand and recognise myself and my achievement and to be at unity with myself. I cannot do this because I have to say : " For what I would, that do I not ; but what I hate, that do I " (v. 15). My non-doing is in contradiction with my will, my doing with my non-will. I contradict myself in my achievements, in the results of my doing and non-doing. Certainly (v. 16) in this contradiction, to the extent that I myself and my will are opposed to my doing, I agree with the Law of God and call it good. But what is the value of this contradiction and agreement (v. 17) when my doing and non-doing, my achievements, do not have a share in it ? To my shame, I have to admit that in the event of my achievements it is not I myself who am revealed at work, but the sin which dwells within me and lays its law upon me. How then can I recognise myself in this event—except as the house in which sin dwells and is master ?

Vv. 18-20 belong—in the reverse sense—to the same picture : What does not dwell in me, in my flesh, is, unfortunately (v. 18), the ἀγαθόν, or (v. 22) the Law of God. If I am flesh, as admitted in v. 14, how can I be the house of the Law of God ? And if this Law is spiritual, as again in v. 14, how can it dwell in this house ? I and the ἀγαθόν can only exclude each other like fire and water. What is present in me—this is possible in the flesh—is the good will, not the doing of good—for which I should have to be spiritual and not carnal. Is the latter really wanting ? Yes (v. 19) : " the good that I would I do not, but the evil which I would not, that I do." Is it really I ? Have I really to admit to my shame that I am the doer of what I would not (v. 20) ? It is not I who am at work, but—unfortunately I am not the master of my own house—the sin which dwelleth in me. In the completed action I have to admit to myself that I am only a kind of agent and not the subject, that I am only a functioning object.

The chapter closes with vv. 21–25, which towards the end are interrupted by a short but remarkable conversation which the apostle has with himself (vv. 24–25a) and which calls for a separate appraisal. The subject of the verses was the self-contradiction of sinful man : his will or non-will on the one hand, his doing or non-doing and therefore his achievements on the other, this man here and that man there. There can be no question how Paul views and describes himself. He identifies himself with the first I, the willing or non-willing I. And the whole difficulty, the contradiction expanded in vv. 15–20 is simply this, that he cannot recognise himself in his actual doing or non-doing, in his achievements, that he cannot identify himself as the one who wills with the one who achieves, that he is a stranger to himself in what he attains and accomplishes. Twice he says that it is not I who am at work, but the sin which dwells in me (vv. 17 and 20). Here we have a direct proof that in this whole chapter Paul is speaking of himself as a Christian and an apostle and not placing himself in the situation either of an unbelieving Jew—perhaps his own before his conversion— or of an unbelieving Gentile. How could an unbeliever see himself from a distance in this way, confessing that he is a stranger to himself ? No Jewish or Gentile unbeliever would be able or willing to see and confess that he is in this contradiction with himself. What would distinguish him from the Christian and the apostle Paul would be this, that in the last resort he would, in spite of everything, declare himself to be at unity and satisfied with himself. It is another matter that existence in this contradiction is his situation, too, although he does not know it. But the Christian and the apostle Paul does know this human situation. He sees the contradiction. He is involved in it himself in that distance from himself. He knows that he has to bear it, to live in it. He also knows— and this is what he goes on to speak about in v. 21 f.—that he cannot bear it or live in it. In this respect he is radically different from the unbeliever. The latter may be conscious of a certain inner unrest, tension or opposition. It is not for nothing that his situation is in truth the same as that of the Christian and apostle Paul. In what the latter knows concerning himself that situation is brought to light instead of remaining hidden. But is it not to be expected that even in its hiddenness it will from time to time be noticeable ? Yet not in such a way that the unbeliever is not in a position, as he thinks, to come to terms with himself, and at least to bear the conflict, and to live in spite of it. What he knows as inner unrest is always within his own unity and satisfaction with himself. It can actually be borne and he can live. But Paul knows that this is impossible. He knows that the conflict in which he finds himself, which he has to bear and in which he has to live, is the conflict between Law and law, the conflict between the Law of God which he knows with his *νοῦς*, which he is ready to serve in his willing and non-willing, by which he sees and judges himself, between this Law and (discovered by it) the law of sin, to which he finds himself obedient and subject in his doing and non-doing, his actual achievement. To be master in this conflict would mean to be obedient to the Law of God (which is what he wills), to overthrow and break the law of sin, to destroy it as a law which binds him, to bring his doing and non-doing, his achievement, into line with his willing and non-willing. But this is the very thing which he finds he cannot do.

Rather (v. 21)—behind and in his achievement, which unfortunately contradicts his willing and non-willing according to the Law of God—he finds the power of another law which is superior to him. By reason of this law it comes to pass that, although he not only wills the good but wills to do the good, yet when he translates his will into action evil is just as present (παράκειται) in him as the willing (but unfortunately only the willing) of the good (v. 18). He finds (vv. 22–23) that all his sincere and earnest agreement with the Law of God, his best will to be righteous before it, the correspondingly determined attitude of the " inner man," does not alter in the slightest the fact that in his members, in the physico-psychical existence which he sees, this other law is in control. At the very point where he ought to accomplish what the Law of God demands and he himself wills in accordance with that Law, this other law is in victorious conflict (ἀντιστρατευόμενος) with what he himself recognises to be right and binding (the νόμος τοῦ θεοῦ), treating him as though he was already its prisoner (αἰχμαλωτίζων). In his achievement he does not obey the Law of God but this other law. It is not at all the case that in his doing and non-doing he overcomes it as he would like, breaking it and destroying it as the law which binds him. It is rather the case that in his doing and non-doing he confirms the authority and power of this other law. The fault is not with the Law of God. He has to acknowledge that the fault is with himself. It is no consolation to him to consider his better will and knowledge, just as this better will and knowledge cannot actually free him from his guilt.

V. 25b gathers together once more what has been said about his prison cell. It is obvious that he does not try to deduce any exculpation of himself or improvement of his situation from the fact that he sees himself at this distance. No : " So then I myself, the same man (αὐτὸς ἐγώ), the one who knows it (νοΐ) and wills it, serve the law of God ; but with the flesh the law of sin." This is the meaning of the contradiction discovered in vv. 15–20, and this is the hopelessness of it. " No man can serve two masters " (Mt. 6²⁴). But the speaker here has to confess that he does in fact serve two masters. This is the plight of man, of Paul the Christian and apostle. He must exert himself to shake off this yoke, to escape.

His exposition is outstanding for the sober factuality of the presentation, but towards the end it is interrupted by a strange cry, or rather by two cries, the one answering the other (vv. 24–25a). Here we have to do with the little window which does let at least a glimmer of light into the prison cell. And here again we have a direct proof that in this context Paul is not speaking in recollection—or only in recollection—of an earlier period in his life, or in the assumed role of a Jewish or Gentile unbeliever. " O wretched man that I am ! who shall deliver me (tear me out) from the body of this death ? " We make Paul extremely rhetorical if we take it that his complaint is only in recollection. And he drops the assumed role of a Jewish or Gentile unbeliever when—we might almost say from the outside—he answers his own complaint : " I thank God through Jesus Christ our Lord." The two sayings are very abrupt. And they come together very abruptly. But they are only meaningful together, the one pointing backwards, the other forwards. And together they fix the mathematical point at which the justification of man takes place as his transition from wrong to right, from death to life.

We will take the second of the two sayings first (v. 25a). It is simply an expression of thanks : " God be thanked for that which is true and actual and valid and effective by our Lord Jesus Christ as the decision which He has made, the act which He has accomplished." It is not stated what this is. In the preceding verses from 7 on we cannot see anything at all for which thanks might be given—not even for the fact that Paul can and must know the revelation and Law of God and think and will in the light of it. For, as we have seen, it is as one who knows and loves the Law of God that he is plunged into that contradiction, that he finds himself powerless in face of the law of sin in his members. The way from this point to the thankful praise of God as we have it, for instance, in Ps. 119, is a necessary way but a far one. There can be little question that here Paul has in a sense placed himself at the end of that way. Hence in striking contrast to the baffled question : " Who shall deliver me ? " thanks are actually ascribed to God, and to God in the light of His being and activity in Jesus Christ. The question itself is left unanswered, like the question of Jesus Christ on the cross : " My God, my God, why hast thou forsaken me ? " (Mk. 15³⁴), or like the whole question of Job. In the boldest possible anticipation, but one which is obviously self-evident to Paul the Christian and apostle, he looks back upon the question and all that it implies from the far distance. The question and all that it implies have ceased to be. What was once true is true no longer. What was not true is now true. All at once there is cause simply to be thankful. Therefore he is thankful. Is not this the forward leap of the man who is justified by God, the attestation of Jesus Christ raised again from the dead ? But note that he tells us explicitly only that he is thankful and to whom he is thankful, not for what. Or are we to conclude for what he is thankful from the fact that, after all that has gone before, he is thankful, and from the One to whom he is thankful ? At any rate, the half-verse is enough to make it possible for us to say that in the second and third parts of Rom. 7 we have an exposition of the beginning of justification, as suggested by vv. 1–6 and the wider context.

But we must not forget that in the conclusion which follows this radiant half-verse—we now seem to hear the prison door closing to genuinely and finally —Paul takes up again the contrast of v. 14, confessing that he is the one man serving two lords, and therefore doing that which it is not possible to do, that he is therefore the " wretched " man of v. 24. Nor must we forget the baffled and unanswered question of this wretched man—this wretched Christian and apostle Paul : " Who shall deliver me from the body of this death ? " (It does not seem possible to translate it in any other way, because τούτου cannot well refer to σώματος but only to θανάτου.) Paul is speaking of this, of a particular " body of death," or nexus of death, or kingdom of death. And his concern is for the redemption of man from the body of this death. In v. 4 he had spoken of another σῶμα, the σῶμα τοῦ Χριστοῦ, which can also be called a σῶμα τοῦ θανάτου to the extent that in it and by it there is a putting to death (a θανατοῦσθαι) of man, but a redemptive putting to death, a freeing of man from the law of sin and for life under the Law of God by the death of that " first man." To belong to that body, to the fellowship of that death, obviously means redemption, future, hope. Not so to belong to the body of death which is shown in vv. 7–23 to be the nexus or fellowship of all men under the law of sin. It is the body of the death which is absolutely without a future, hopeless and non-redemptive. It is the body from whose context and association man must be torn and delivered if he is to be able to live. The whole situation depicted in vv. 14–23 obviously has this character of death—the whole self-contradiction in which Paul sees himself entangled as one who knows and loves the Law of God on the one hand and is a slave of the law of sin on the other. But since this self-contradiction is a fact and cannot be resolved, since it cannot be resolved and is a fact, it can bring man only to corruption and death, to this utterly non-redemptive death. But, according to v. 4, this situation—man's incorporation in " the body of this death "—is already his past, thanks to the " body of Christ," in and with which he has been put to death as one who " is in the flesh," freed from this law of sin, taken out of this contradiction, torn out from " the body of this death." But, according to v. 24, it is still his present, in so far as all this has not taken place in his own person, but validly and effectively for him in the person of Jesus Christ ; for him, who in his own person, in so far as even as a Christian and apostle he is still this man Paul, he is still in the flesh and therefore is still subject to the law of sin and therefore still exists in this contradiction and therefore still belongs to " the body of this death." From this " still " even as a Christian and an apostle he can only cry daily as we hear him cry in the baffled question : " Who shall deliver me ? " as though we had never read what is stated in v. 4 and he himself had never written it. Living already and altogether by the answer, living already and altogether in the deliverance which has already come to him, he still has to live in and with this question. He could not do the one if he tried to refuse the other, to be only the man of the answer, not to be wholly and utterly the wretched man of the question. He can only be both at once. But not in that unhappy contradiction (in which he lives only "also," which is only his past reaching into his present), but rather in the transition, the history of justification, in that transition as it is really both at once, as indicated in the relationship of the two sayings in v. 24 and v. 25a. If we read carefully the exposition in Rom. 8 we shall soon realise that even there the "also," and therefore the "both together," has not completely disappeared, nor has the " wretched man " of Rom. 7 : the beginning of justification in the very midst of man's sin.

If on this side, the left side, with reference to the *terminus a quo*, there is no place for human arrogance or frivolity, for the expunging or interpreting or adorning or explaining away of the past from which the justified man comes at every present, much less on the other side, the right side, with reference to the *terminus ad quem* of his way, is there any place for human uncertainty and half-heartedness, for the belittling and weakening and qualifying and questioning of the goal to which the justified man moves in every present. How much less ! For if the knowledge that as a man justified by God he is a sinner is serious, the knowledge that as a sinner he is justified by God is even more serious. Simply because it is on this side and not the other that we have to do with the positive will of God to man, with his affirmation of man. As His affirmation of sinful man it includes his negation. The Yes cannot be heard unless the No is also heard. Hence the necessary recollection of the place from which we come, of the being which is still the being of man in all his forward movement—the being of the sinner who lives only by the grace of God. But although it includes the negation, it is still God's affirmation of man. This is what makes what we have to consider on the right hand so much more serious than that which on the left hand we can never consider too much with the seriousness appropriate to this sphere. What we have to say concerning the irreversible direction of the transition, the history in which the justification of man takes place, is relevant in this connexion. The new thing which comes from God has as such precedence over the old of man. The right which is ascribed to him by God has as such precedence over his own wrong. His life has precedence over his death. The goal, the *terminus ad quem* of his way, has precedence over its *terminus a quo* and beginning. That which he already is in virtue of God's explicit pardon has precedence over what he still is in virtue of what is implicit in it. The completion of his justification has precedence over its commencement. If—without confusion or separation—we have to consider and emphasise both moments of this event, giving its due weight to the first as well, we have to do so in this order and sequence, in such a way that the direction of the whole stands steadily before us, in such a way therefore that the precedence finally rests with the second about which we must now speak. It is not at all the case that the two moments are related like the two ends of a scales or see-saw, both of which may rise or fall according to the accidental or arbitrary weighting of the one or the other. It is not at all the case that the justified sinner can alternately or with a turn of the wheel be wholly and utterly the sinner and wholly and utterly justified, so that alternately or with a turn of the wheel he has to see himself as the one and then as the other. The dialectic of justification is not that of a to and fro, or an up and down, but at every present it is that of a history in which the wrong of the justified man is (in all its reality) behind him and his right before him, in which, therefore, he can have his future only in the movement to his right and his past only in his wrong (in all its reality), in which he can be only on the way from there to here, because that and that alone corresponds to the positive will of God.

We will now proceed at once to the proposition which emphasises the positive will of God, that on its forward aspect justification is the divine pardon of sinful man. It is the sentence of God in virtue of which man has that past behind him and is turned to a new future which is no longer burdened with that past and determined by the good will of God with him. Who is man ? According to the divine sentence which justifies him he is the man of the history in which there takes place both this turning away and this turning to. The one divine sentence which justifies man is wholly negation as we look backwards and wholly affirmation, promise, *promissio*, as we look forwards. In the same sentence in which the justifying divine sentence strikes him and confirms that he both was and still is a sinner standing under the divine No, he is already addressed and characterised as the one who will be under His Yes. As the object of His negation he is already the object of His affirmation and promise. And in virtue of this affirmation and promise he is already placed in His right, he is already made free for life. The sentence which justifies him is pardon, divine pardon, and as such valid and effective, as such God's mighty disposing concerning him, in virtue of which, even as the man he was and is, he is set on the way and in the movement from there to here, he already is the man he will be. He is still sick, but when this doctor comes he is already healed. The sheep is still lost, but when it is sought by this shepherd it is already found. The son is still lost, but this father looks for him and he is already at home. Those who are still publicans and sinners, when the Saviour sits down to meat with them, are already the holy people of God. The man in the temple does not know what else to plead but that God should be merciful to him, a sinner, and he is already justified, and returns to his house as such. The justification of man as determined and accomplished and pronounced in the divine sentence is both at once in this order and sequence : it is *creatio ex contrario*, but *creatio* ; *iustificatio impii*, but *iustificatio*. The grace of God, as it is addressed and comes to the sinful man who has fallen away from Him and resists Him in his pride, is free grace, sovereign, unmerited, miraculous, but valid and effective. In the sentence of God as His repudiation and promise the old man is already the new man, the unfaithful covenant-partner the faithful, the one who has set himself in the wrong the one who is set in the right, the dead raised again and alive. This is the divine pardon as God's affirmation and promise. And as directed to man it is His powerful summons. As the man he was, and still is, man can and should look forward and go forward to what he will be, to what, now that he is free for it, he already is. It is of this "already" that we must now speak.

First, we can and must regard it as a test of the genuineness of the knowledge and confession of sin whether the man who is willing and ready to accuse himself of corruption and transgression, and therefore to bewail the fact that he is lost, can with the same or an even greater willingness and readiness accept and affirm the sentence of God on this other side, so that as the sinner he has seen and confessed himself to be, as the man who must give himself up for lost, he can grasp the promise of God and look and go forward and not backward ; whether he really can do this ; whether he can accept and affirm the fact that God is gracious to him the sinner, that He is his redeemer, the redeemer of the lost ; whether he will hold to the right which God ascribes to him ; whether he is confident to live the life which God grants to him. The question is a very serious one. For by the same judgment of God he is a sinner and yet a justified sinner, lost and yet saved, a victim to death and yet raised again from death to life. God's sentence on him pronounces all this as an indivisible whole. God's sentence sets him irresistibly in the movement from that past to this future. But if he is not able to grasp this promise and enter this way, how does it stand with the genuineness of his knowledge of sin and confession of sin, of his accusation of himself and bewailing of his estate ? What is the basis of it, however deep and powerful it may be, however violent and fierce, perhaps far surpassing in its vehemence that of the Psalmists and Paul ? It is quite possible to have a very human defeatism and pessimism whose agitations and convulsions, accusations and bewailings, have nothing whatever to do with the sentence of God and submission to it. It is quite possible that—in this way—man is only trying to escape the sentence of God. It is quite possible that all his expressions of despair are only the symptoms of the old unbroken pride in which he now withdraws to the last and perhaps the surest citadel, that of a violent self-abnegation. Has this man really given God the right against himself, has he really accepted His sentence, if he has to accept the fact—and he declares that he has to accept it—that he knows himself to be negated and rejected by God, but cannot make anything of the Yes of God, and does not see anything of the future which is opened up to him, of the right to live which is granted to him ? If anyone tries to resist this, if he can and must resist it, then he simply shows that it is not the No of God which he maintains that he accepts and to which he maintains that he submits. His vanity still peeps out through the very rents in his garment. The No of God is never without the Yes which follows it. It is not an autonomous Word. It is only an indispensable foreword. It is the repudiation, the meaning and goal of which is the promise. The man who can hold aloof from the promise has not heard the repudiation. His knowledge and confession of sin cannot therefore be genuine, no matter how serious they may be.

In the modern novel there are not lacking portrayals which give us the impression that the author originally had in mind something like God's pardon of sinful man. But in fact they do not go beyond what is often a strikingly honest depiction of his vileness. Such portrayals cannot be totally sincere any more than those of earlier periods, the vileness of which consisted in the fact that they would not accept the vileness of man, but ascribed to him qualities which in the circumstances could not be real qualities but only an illusion of real qualities.

The knowledge and confession of sin are serious only where in and with them there is the only true penitence in which man gives up all his proud boasting, even the humbly proud boasting of his corruption and lost estate, and grants that God is wholly in the right, accepting His Yes no less than His No, and in fact more so, because in it we have to do with His positive will. True penitence will show itself as such in the fact that man will not rest in what he was and still is and has to accept and confess, but will resolutely turn to what he will be and already is. In true penitence man makes in simple obedience the turning for which he is pronounced free in the justifying sentence of God, which is therefore both legitimate and possible. He bows to the one total and indivisible disposing of God. He does not leave out the first step. But in and with the first he makes the second ; in and with the confession of sin he lays hold of God's promise of grace. God's pardon demands this total obedience. And where it is accepted by man, he finds it. The man who will not recognise that he is a justified sinner is just as disobedient, and more so, than the man who tries to deny that only as a sinner is he justified.

The justification of man begins in his past and it is completed in his future. But as his past as a sinner is still his present, so his future as a righteous man is already his present. The fact that although he is still a sinner he is already righteous, that in the same present in which he comes out of his past as a sinner he goes forward to the future as a righteous man—this fact is the promise addressed to him in the judgment and sentence of God. There is no doubt that it speaks of his future. This other man, the righteous, the one he was not and still is not, is the man he will be. This future is promised to him as the past is repudiated. But the promise that he will be this man is addressed to him here and now, to-day, in the midst of the present. It is not an uncertain promise like the hopes which he might create for himself or which might be created for him by circumstances and relationships and even other men. It is the promise the power of which is the irrevocable decision of God in which he is already this other man, the righteous. It is not a general promise like the great ideas of humanity, to hear of which may be a very different thing from relating them to oneself, but the promise of· his God, which applies to him with a supreme immediacy and directness. It is not an empty promise like the fine expectations which may gladden and comfort but of which we cannot for the moment make anything in practice, but the promise of the eternal God, which as it is given and received can be used at once as such, to which we can hold and with which we can at once begin to live. The future which it promises to man is not just any future. It is the *futurum exactum* of God. As man accepts it, as he reaches out for it, as he apprehends it as the promise of God, its fulfilment is no longer distant only, but already near even in its distance. He does not live and think and act any longer simply as the man he was and still is, but in the leap which he can now make forward, in anticipation of the man he will be, as already that other man, the righteous, which he was not and which in the light of the past he is not yet. In the receiving and presence of the promise and his relationship to it he is already the man he will be. That is the completion of man's justification.

Naturally there can be no question of a simple equality or identity between future and present, between the fulfilment as such and the promise, between what man will be and what he is. Even on this side the being of the justified sinner is a differentiated being, and as such it is stretched like a bow. But, again, there cannot be any question of a mutual exclusion, of a future which is distant and not near, and therefore of a present which is apart from the future, of a fulfilment which has still to come, and therefore of an empty promise, of the righteous man who will be as now absent, and therefore of the exclusive presence of the one who was not and still is not righteous.

And the distinction which we have to consider is one which cannot properly be described in quantitative terms, as though that which is ascribed to the justified man with the promise and therefore in the present is only a little thing, whereas that which we expect in the future is a greater, as though the one is only a part and the other the whole. When an inheritance reverts to a man, and it is quite certain, it is not smaller because he has not yet entered into it (except in the form of a first instalment or a pledge). The moment it becomes his it becomes his altogether. The wrong which according to the divine sentence is behind man is all his wrong. The death from which he

comes is his whole death. So, too, the right and life which are before
him according to the same sentence are his whole right and life. In
his past, as it reaches into the present, he is wholly in the wrong and
dead. So, too, in his future as with the promise it reaches into the
present he is wholly in the right and alive. The only thing is that as
long as he lives in time and considers his own person, he is both together : *simul peccator et iustus*, yet not half *peccator* and half *iustus*,
but both altogether. And the pardon of man, declared in the promise
concerning him, the reality of his future already in the present, is no
less than this : *totus iustus*. That this is the case will be clear if we
try briefly to unfold the content of the promise in the receiving of
which the justification of man is completed.

We can gather together the whole of the promise, as the Creed
does, (1) under the term, the forgiveness of sins. From the point of
view of every human present this is undoubtedly something which is
altogether future—the completed justification to which the justified
man looks and moves. There is no moment in his life in which he does
not have to look for and await and with outstretched hands request
both forgiveness and therefore freedom from his sins. No one can
evade the fifth petition of the Lord's Prayer. Its force can never grow
less in the Christian life. A second test of the genuineness of a man's
justification as his being in transition is whether the actuality of this
petition forces itself increasingly upon him or whether that actuality
is lost, whether in this case it has ever been actual, whether, therefore,
he does live in this transition which is his justification. If he does live
in this transition, he can understand the forgiveness of sins only as
the work in which God comes to him as he has absolute need of forgiveness in the light of his past and his present, not as the state in which
he for his part goes forward to God. He can have forgiveness of sins
only as he receives it from God, as God gives it to him. There can be
no question of any other receiving, or having, or possessing of forgiveness, of any other certainty concerning it. This is all true as the act
of God takes place for him, as the gift of God is recognised and taken
by him. The content of the promise is that God wills to do and will
do this act for him, that he can recognise and take this gift. To
receive the forgiveness of sins means, therefore, to receive the promise
of the forgiveness of sins. To have the forgiveness of sins means to
hold to the promise, to look forward with confidence in it, to go forward obediently to its direction. To be certain of the forgiveness of
sins means finally not to doubt the promise of it as such for its own
sake. If he looks behind him, or into the depth of his present as
determined by his past, man can never receive or enjoy the comfort
of the forgiveness of sins ; he cannot have it. He has it only as it
comes to him in the promise, not otherwise.

But what does the forgiveness of sins mean ? It is only in appearance that its reference is merely to the past. It has this reference.

But only in the sense that it denotes the line which is put under his past, making it the past and marking it off as such. But at what point in my past do I see this line clearly put under it? Even if I thought I knew some such place, what about all that has become the past since? And with what justification and certainty can I affirm that it is put under it as I come from my past? When do we not have to look continually for it to be put under it? It is only in this way that this cancellation can be the content of the promise addressed to man. We ask: What is meant by this cancellation? Forgiveness obviously does not mean to make what has happened not to have happened. Nothing that has happened can ever not have happened. The man in whose life what had happened came not to have happened would not be the same man. He is this man in the totality of his history. He stands before God and is known to Him as this man. The man who receives forgiveness does not cease to be the man whose past (and his present as it derives from his past) bears the stain of his sins. The act of the divine forgiveness is that God sees and knows this stain infinitely better than the man himself, and abhors it infinitely more than he does even in his deepest penitence— yet He does not take it into consideration, He overlooks it, He covers it, He passes it by, He puts it behind Him, He does not charge it to man, He does not " impute " it (2 Cor. 5¹⁹), He does not sustain the accusation to which man has exposed himself, He does not press the debt with which he has burdened himself, He does not allow to take place the destruction to which he has inevitably fallen victim. That God forgives means that He pardons. But the divine pardoning is not a weak remission. As pardoning it is the great—we might almost say the wrathful—act of divine power and defiance. God proves His superiority to all the contradiction and opposition arrayed against Him. He proves His unshakable lordship over man. He does so by despising the sin of man, by ignoring it although it has happened, by not allowing His relationship to man to be determined by it. Again, the divine pardoning is not an unlawful remission. As pardoning, it is the exercise of His supreme right, and at the same time the restoration of a state of right between Himself and man, the effective assertion of His glory in relation to man. Again, it is not merely a verbal remission. As pardoning, it is the effectual and righteous alteration of the human situation from its very foundation. If God's sentence concerning man is that He will know nothing of this stain, then the stain is washed away and removed, and although man still bears it, in spite of it he is without stain, in spite of his wrong he is in the right. The divine pardoning is not a remission " as if " man were not a sinner. As pardoning, it is the creative work of God, in the power of which man, even as the old man that he was and still is, is no longer that man, but is already another man, the man he will be, the new man. That is the forgiveness of sins as the final stroke under man's past.

future

But obviously we cannot understand it as such without seeing that not only has an old page been closed but a new one opened. And it is by this that it is truly characterised as the future to which man is continually summoned to look and move. If it is God's powerful and righteous and effective and indeed creative covering and overlooking and despising and disparaging of his pride, then obviously it does not merely create a *tabula rasa*, a clear field into which any new thing may come. By the divine pardon man is placed in a very definite new situation from which to start. For one thing it is only in this way, but in this way seriously, that he definitely becomes one who knows the grace and therefore the love and therefore the kingly freedom of God and of His right and will. Again, it is in this way, and radically in this way, that he becomes one who knows himself as the creature to whom God in pardoning him can only be gracious, about whom He can only be concerned. And finally, however great and powerful his sin may be, however accusingly and temptingly it may stand before him, he can think of it now only as the stain which is covered and overlooked and despised and disparaged by God and not worthy of further consideration. These are the three moments of the new freedom of the man whose sin God has forgiven : He can hold to the grace and will and right of God ; he can learn humility ; and he can confidently and definitively turn his back on his sin. His ability to do this is the new page which is opened with the forgiveness of sins. But where and when did we ever find this new situation in our own past, so that we have only to recall it to live in the power of this recollection ? Where and when do we find it as an assured state in our present ? If we ever could or can find it, then it is surely only as the promise which is given us by God and which we had and have to recognise and take as such. It is only as the future to which we could go forward and have in fact gone forward with more or less certain steps, only to be instructed again and again that it would be newly disclosed to us as our future, that it will be disclosed to us as such even in our present.

But we do not forget that the promise is the promise of God, and that forgiveness as its content is the total forgiveness of God. As pardoning, as that concluding stroke, as freedom for a new being, it is His complete forgiveness of all our sins. The fact that it is for us something future, that enclosed in the promise of God it can only be hoped and awaited and prayed for, does not in any way limit it or lessen its power. It does not mean that as man lays hold of the promise he cannot receive it here and now with unconditional certainty and unlimited fulness. No, he can and should receive it and have it in the same present in which he knows that he is always utterly in need of it. Where and when the promise is given to him, it is true and reliable ; it cannot fail in anything of its content. As eschatology it is "realised eschatology." In and with it, its whole content enters the present of man. Where and when man trusts the promise, where and when he dares to treat it as directed to himself, to apply it to himself, to accept it as true of himself, there the forgiveness of sins takes place, that line is drawn, the new situation from which he can set out is created. There absolution is not simply pronounced to him. It takes place. There he receives forgiveness, the divine pardon, and the freedom of a new and the only true capacity. There he already has it, and he can and should dare to live as one who is forgiven.

The phrase " the forgiveness of sins " is well adapted to sum up all that has to be said in this connexion. But it is better not to try to sum it all up in this phrase. The content of the promise in the receiving of which the justification of man is completed is (2) his institution into a specific right which replaces the wrong which he has committed and which God has ignored. His justification is completed in this positive work of God, in virtue of which he becomes one who can lift up his head and hold it high because he can stand before Him, because he is pleasing to Him, because he is God's righteous man. He will be this righteous man. How can we ever put this in any but the future tense ? The man who in the light of his past sets himself before the God who encounters him can never do anything but spread out before Him his wrong, with the petition : *quod vixi, tege.* But there is a right which even as the one who is in the wrong with God he can receive, with which God wills to and will clothe him even though he is stripped of every right in His presence—and in such a way that he can boldly claim and assert it as his right, boasting of it, being confident of his case under its protection. It is not merely the restored right of the creature and the covenant-partner ; according to the New Testament witness, it is the right of the child of God. In spite of his sin man is justified by God and before God not merely in the sense that God confirms and maintains him as His creature and covenant-partner, but in the sense that He receives him into His house, that He accepts and addresses and treats him as essentially His. Beyond the very real and intimate co-existence of God and man, as the final goal of their reconciliation, as the final meaning of the peace re-established between them, the term " child of God " signifies the unprecedented fact of a kinship of being which God has promised and guaranteed to man. It therefore signifies something which is more than reconciliation and peace, which rather seals the reconciliation and peace of man with God, which makes it so sure that it cannot be abrogated or lost, an ontological relationship in which the event of reconciliation, the restoration of peace between man and God, is crowned, and its result is anchored. It does not signify merely that man is bound to God, but also and primarily that God is bound to man. For if God calls man His child, if therefore man *is* His child, then God acknowledges that He is his Father, and therefore He *is* his Father. God has bound Himself to man and therefore He is bound to man in the same way that He has bound man to Himself and man is therefore bound to Him. The divine sonship of man is not his divinity. It is only ascribed to him, imparted to him, given to him. He is only received and adopted by God as His child. He is only instituted as such. But in it he belongs to God by a kinship of being. He does so on the basis and in the power of the fact that God declares that He Himself belongs to him, and makes it so. If God is his Father, and he is the child of this Father, God is as little God without him as he is man without God, and he has the right of a son in relation to God as God has the right of a Father in relation to him—the right to a being with Him, the right to immediate access to Him, the right to call upon Him, the right to rely upon Him, the right to expect and to ask of Him everything that he needs. This right of sonship is the essence of every right of man. And the promise of this right is the completion of the justification of sinful man. It is with the promise of this right that God encounters and defies and withstands sin and wrong, the chaos which has invaded His creation. The existence of such children of God is the Yes with which He overcomes the No of man. It is also the meaning of His own No in face of the fall of man. It is what God wills with man, and what He wills victoriously in justifying him as a sinner. With it—with the fact that He calls man His child, and causes him to be His child—He definitively draws that line under his past and places him in the new situation from which to start, a situation behind which he cannot 'go. With it He gives him a future, a future which with a final and supreme clarity and certainty is new and different.

Do we need to emphasise particularly that the right of divine sonship ascribed to him is really his future, the given promise, to the fulfilment of which he can only look and move in every present? Who amongst us looking backward to his past has ever found that he is a child of God and therefore in a kinship of being with Him, just as indispensable to God as God is to him, in possession of this whole and truly princely right in relation to Him? We know this, if at all, only as that which God promises and ascribes, and as we trust and receive and accept God's promise. We are "begotten again unto a lively hope" (1 Pet. 1³) in this being. But in this connexion we must also emphasise that in and with the promise of God, included in it, and only to be apprehended in and with it, in this "lively hope," the divine sonship of man comes right into his present, so that it has not only to be considered and admired and awaited and longed for as a distant goal, but lived out already here and now. "We are the children of God" (Rom. 8¹⁶, 1 Jn. 3²). It may be covered over and concealed by that which overshadows and burdens and harasses us from our past, and basically so, so that there can be no question of any perception. "It doth not appear what we shall be" (1 Jn. 3²). But this cannot alter the fact. This cannot either remove it or diminish even a fraction of its relevance. What we are according to God's promise, those to whom God has bound Himself, calling them His children, what we have, the right to hold to this and to appeal to it, the right to cry " Abba, Father " (Gal. 4[6], Rom. 8[15]), is the immutable thing which, although it may now be concealed from us, cannot be even touched, let alone shaken or overthrown, by any questioning of circumstances and relationships, of the judgment of other man, or of our own uncertainties and doubts, however superficial or profound. It is the irrevocable right of man. In the light of the promise which comes to us from God, we stand here on the rock of our justification which never moves and which will always bear us. Even in the most powerful assaults from behind, even in the severest conflict with all that we are " still " or " not yet," we are not merely permitted but commanded without fear or awe, without what would here be a false shame and reserve, to boast of the fact and continually to proclaim : " We are the children of God." In so doing we do not usurp anything that is not ours. Rather we would again be encroaching on the honour of God if we were not willing to boast of it and continually to return to it—so long as it is the bold and humble boasting of and returning to His promise and therefore to our justification by His gracious and miraculous act.

But the totality of completed justification must be considered from a further standpoint which is related to the one just mentioned and yet different from it. It is (3) man's placing in a state of hope. We can, of course, describe hope simply as the supreme form of the right of the children of God. We can also describe the whole state of the justified sinner as his state in hope, in so far as in the forgiveness of sins proclaimed to him, in the divine sonship ascribed to him, he has to do with the promise of God and therefore with that which he has to hope and expect from God.

But, again, it is not at all self-evident that man should live in this hope and expectation, that he should not refrain but should actually dare to look and to move forward to the goal which is set before him, that he should be aware of and accept the fact that the promise reaches into his present, that he should rouse himself and continue to hold to it and to find true and radical comfort in it, that he should not grow tired of doing this. Who amongst us has ever found in his past this inflexible hope corresponding to the inflexibility of the promise? where and when in his past? and how far even now in his present? The fact that he hopes, and therefore that he lives in and with the promise, the fact that here and now he allows himself to be told the future thing : " Thy sins be forgiven thee," the fact that here and now he confidently repeats what he is told in the promise : " We are the children of God," the fact that he is the man who not only represents himself as doing this but actually does it : this is obviously a thing apart, and yet again it is the content of the promise in which his justification is completed. In this context it tells us : Thou mayest hope and thou canst hope ; indeed, thou art the man who actually will hope ; thou art the man on whose heart this lively hope is already written ; as the man who has this lively hope thou art already on the other side of that line, born again as the child which thou art as addressed by God. This address or promise obviously has to be apprehended, for the very reason that in it it is a matter of its apprehension as such, of confidence in it, of hazarding it and keeping to it. Just as we can and must pray for the ability to pray and for actual prayer, so with all seriousness we can and must hope for the ability to hope and for actual hope, for this is itself the content of the promise to whose fulfilment we continually look and move.

But there is more to it than that. In the hope in which man's justification is fulfilled it is not merely a matter of the looking and reaching out for the promised forgiveness of sins and divine sonship which has to be new every day and every hour. It is a matter of that. But it is clear that hoping for it as such implies a looking and reaching out for a goal at which the state of the justified man as indicated by the forgiveness of sins and divine sonship, although not different, will be revealed and shown and will work itself out in a different way from anything that can or will ever take place on his pilgrimage from an ever new past through an ever new present to an ever new future, in his movement, his history, in time. His justification takes place in the temporal course of this history, and everything that he is and does as justified by God is only in this transition. It is genuine and complete, but contradictory, concealed under this contradiction. It is only in the being together of that which is antithetical, in the form of a riddle, in the mystery of the *simul peccator et iustus*. The justified man exists —this is the completion of his justification—as he hopes from day to day and hour to hour, in the hope—which we now have to write with big letters—for a final goal of his hope, for the solution of the riddle, the removal of the contradiction, the revelation of the mystery of his history in all those transitions which he continually has to make. He does not grope in the dark. He knows the way on which he finds himself—not only its direction but its goal. He knows that he is not caught up in a futile vacillation or movement in a circle. He lives in the constant differentiation of his future from his past, his right from his wrong, his life from his death. He lives by the constant projection of his future, the constant prevailing of the promised forgiveness of sins and divine sonship against the accusation and menace from which he comes, by the superiority, the forward-pointing thrust of the divine sentence : *totus iustus*, in face of the backward-pointing *totus peccator*. But it is still the case that in every present the past is still present, that the forgiveness of sins and the divine sonship enclosed in the promise has to be sought and apprehended afresh every moment out of the deepest need, that he cannot hear the *totus iustus* without being willing continually to hear the *totus peccator*. It is still the case that he can hold to that which is promised, to the unshakable and indestructible thing which cannot be lost, because it cannot be revoked, only in the assured but continually renewed striding, only in the joyful and confident but hazardous and laborious movement which is described by Paul in Phil. 3[12] : " Not as though I had already attained, either were already made perfect : but I follow after, if that I may apprehend that for which also I am apprehended . . ." This is neither vacillation nor movement in a circle. But neither is it a *progressus in infinitum*. In it all he obviously looks to a decision in which the relativity and contradiction and provisional nature of the decisions in consequence of which he now exists are taken away, in which the movement in which he now goes through these decisions, from the one to the other, comes to rest because it has attained its goal, in which the forgiveness of sins and the divine sonship, the fulfilment of the promise given to him, do not need to be sought and apprehended any more, in which the *totus iustus* will be the final word, the only, uncontradicted word. On the way itself he knows about this goal, about the end of this form of his righteousness before God, about the beginning of its new and definitive form. And as he treads the way he moves forward to this goal. Essentially the goal is not different but just the same as that towards which he now moves every day and every hour—his right before God, his life under the protection of this right—but it will be the goal beyond which there is no need of any further movement. According to the strong expression of 2 Cor. 5[21], he will have become the righteousness of God. He will no longer be merely expecting and seeking his right to be with God beyond that concluding stroke, his right to an existence in the glory of the service of God, his right to eternal salvation. He will no longer have to pray that he may have it. He will simply have it and exercise it. He will simply be in the possession and under the protection of this right, because he will live in the immediate fellowship of his being with the being of God who is the source and essence of all right and life, of all being and salvation. He will be unconditionally free to serve Him. He will be at the point to which he is now on the way. And this arriving will simply be the revelation of his journeying, of his history in time. His eternal life will consist in the disclosing of the justification of his life in this world. It will be this temporal life itself in the newness which is already ascribed to it in the judgment and sentence of God, in the righteous form which is already given to it by the divine pardon, when the old and sinful form has finally been left behind and cannot again reach into the present. It will be pure present, a present which is wholly and exclusively determined and filled by the future ascribed in the divine promise, without any togetherness with the past, a present in which nothing at all can be said of him but *totus iustus*, in which he can know himself only as such. But in this way it will be the full present of life and service and salvation and glory which is now the hidden thing in every present, which now in this temporal present he has to traverse step by step, which he can traverse confidently and joyfully just because that which is hidden in it is this future thing, the pure present of eternal life.

"And if children, then heirs" is what we are told in Rom. 8[17], and again in 1 Pet. 1[3] : " Begotten again to a lively hope." " Inheritance " is the decision, the hidden thing in all the decisions in which here and now the justified man can have the full forgiveness of all his sins and be a full child of God. " Inheritance " is the being which is the hidden thing in the righteous being which here and now is promised to him without reserve in the divine promise. " Inheritance " is the present of eternal life which is the hidden thing in every temporal present in which he finds himself in this transition. The entry into and taking possession of the inheritance will be the revelation of this hidden thing, the drawing aside of the veil by which it is now concealed, the removing of the contradiction, the solving of the riddle, the dispersing of the mystery of his temporal being. To have the forgiveness of sins and to be a child of God means to be one who awaits this inheritance and moves towards it. To be justified (Col. 1[12]) is to be " made meet to partake of the inheritance of the saints in light." This making meet to partake of the inheritance is the completion of man's justification. The righteous man is the one who is waiting in this way, the one who is made a partaker, the one who irrevocably and with all that it implies is appointed an heir, the one who already lives as this heir, who moves towards the revelation of justification and in it eternal life. He will live in and by this great hope as it is given to him as such. As such he will never lose sight of the promise, he will never be hesitant to lay hold of it, nor will he ever fail or fall away in obedience to its direction. He will know the hidden thing in every time as the eternal thing, the depth of every present in which he moves already to the future of the pure present. He will wait patiently for the revelation of it, and in so doing he will constantly rise up with wings like an eagle—a pilgrim who is hard pressed but not pressed down, often weary but not exhausted, often distressed but not in despair, often astray but not lost, seeking but also finding, asking but also receiving, and in the last analysis—in the light of his ultimate goal—merry and joyful. The pardon of man, the completion of his justification, is his appointment as this pilgrim, his institution into the state of the great hope. His sins are forgiven him in order that he may be this pilgrim. In this consists his supreme right as a son. It is clear that the promise, too, is a future which he has continually to seize and apprehend, that it stands continually before him and wills to be continually lived. But it is clear again that in this form too, as a concrete possibility, the promise reaches into every present of the justified man. It is to-day, to-day, that it stands before him as the future. Therefore it is to-day, to-day, that it can and should be affirmed and seized and apprehended and put into effect as such. It is to-day, to-day that its content, the great hope, can and should be lived—the power of the world to come as the power of this world. The righteous sentence of God opens wide to sinful man even in this world the gate of the world to come. If he subjects himself to this sentence, if he abandons the self-sufficiency of his pusillanimity, if he gives God the right against himself—the God who in this way enters the lists so powerfully on his behalf—what else is there for him to do but to go through this gate, to be the one who hopes with a great hope, which he is permitted and indeed commanded to be by God, which he is already by the divine sentence ?

To close our discussion we will consider something of the witness of the Old Testament Psalter. Paul undoubtedly had the Psalter in mind when in Rom. 7 he spoke of the beginning of justification in the midst of the sin and lost estate of man, and then in Gal. 2 or Rom. 8 or Phil. 3 of its completion in the pardon of man. And with the words of the Psalter the first community responded to the evangelical record of the obedience, the humility, the humiliation and the crucifixion of the Lord, to the history of the beginning and completion of their —and not only their—justification proclaimed in and with this record. It is also worthy of note that it was by studying and meditating on the Book of the Psalms that Luther was impelled to his remarkable rediscovery of justification : his movement was from the Psalms to Romans, Galatians and Hebrews, not *vice versa*. Nor must we overlook the fact that as the self-attestation of the Old Testament people of God which lives by the promise and therefore the pardoning of sinful man by the gracious God, the Psalter both as a whole and in detail has the irreversible direction of that history, that its emphasis and controlling note are therefore on the revealing of what the Israelite knows as his future and therefore as his present when God is the righteous Judge and is at work as such. For all its variety the Psalter is, as it were, a single voice : the attestation of that to which the individual Israelite believes he holds and does in fact hold, both as a member of his people and for his own person, in reliance on the divine sentence and promise ; the attestation of his right as not only maintained and confirmed but triumphantly renewed by God in spite of his sin and the loss which it involved ; the attestation of his hope, in which he dares to live already in the present, to find comfort and even to rejoice in his holy and angry God in the midst of all his trials. It is no accident that whether its statements are directly addressed to God or speak of God in the third person, the Psalter is always a prayer-book. The background from which the man who speaks in it comes is not forgotten. For the most part the Psalmists bring it out explicitly. Where they do not do so, it has to be read in in order to understand them : the oppression and need and lost estate of this people and its individual members in the world around them which are the result of their sin ; the past of their unfaithfulness and therefore of their perdition which reaches into their present and completely obscures it. It is from this darkness, and completely enveloped in this darkness, that the Psalmists come before God in prayer. And in this we see the transition, justification as history. (Has the Psalter ever been consistently examined and appraised as a reflection of the history of Israel ?) Side by side with Psalms 78 and 106, in which the guilt and punishment of Israel are in great measure recalled, we have to set a Psalm like 136, where this same past which elsewhere is judged so negatively is already set unconditionally against the eternally enduring goodness of God. And in Psalms 32 and 51, with their painful and shocking recollection of the origin of the individual Israelite, we have already seen the tendency which makes it difficult for the reader to understand them altogether as Penitential Psalms and not rather as a peculiar type of Psalms of thanksgiving and praise. The Psalter as a whole ends on this note—it must have been a tremendous Nevertheless in the time of its redaction—not looking backward but forward. But we will allow some of the individual witnesses to speak for themselves.

And first of all, corresponding to the great hope of the justified man of which we have just been speaking, the hope which already fills and determines the present, Ps. 116[5f.] : " Gracious is the Lord, and righteous ; yea, our God is merciful. . . . Return unto thy rest, O my soul ; for the Lord hath dealt bountifully with thee. For thou hast delivered my soul from death, mine eyes from tears, and my feet from falling. I will walk before the Lord in the land of the living. I believed, therefore have I spoken : I was greatly afflicted. . . . What shall I render unto the Lord, for all his benefits toward me ? I will take the cup of salvation, and call upon the name of the Lord. . . . Precious in the sight of the Lord is the death of his saints. O Lord, truly I am thy servant ; I am thy servant, and the son of thine handmaid : thou hast loosed my bonds. I will offer to thee the sacrifice of thanksgiving, and will call upon the name of the Lord . . . in the courts of the Lord's house, in the midst of thee, O Jerusalem. Praise ye the Lord." And then Ps. 118[14f.] : " The Lord is my strength and song, and is become my salvation. The voice of rejoicing and salvation is in the tabernacles of the righteous : the right hand of the Lord doeth valiantly. The right hand of the Lord is exalted : the right hand of the Lord doeth valiantly. I shall not die, but live, and declare the works of the Lord. The Lord hath chastened me sore : but he hath not given me over unto death. Open to me the gates of righteousness : I will go into them, and I will praise the Lord. This is the gate of the Lord, into which the righteous shall enter. I will praise thee ; for thou hast heard me, and art become my salvation. The stone which the builders refused is become the head stone of the corner. This is the Lord's doing ; it is marvellous in our eyes. This is the day which the Lord hath made ; we will rejoice and be glad in it." And on the same level Ps. 16[5f.] : " The Lord is the portion of mine inheritance and of my cup : thou maintainest my lot. The lines are fallen unto me in pleasant places ; yea, I have a goodly heritage. . . . Therefore my heart is glad, and my glory rejoiceth : my flesh also shall rest in hope. For thou wilt not leave my soul in hell ; neither wilt thou suffer thine holy one to see corruption. Thou wilt shew me the path of life : in thy presence is fulness of joy ; at thy right hand there are pleasures for evermore." These are, of course, statements on the very highest level, like the song of praise in Is. 26[2f.] : " Open ye the gates, that the righteous nation which keepeth truth may enter in. Thou wilt keep him in perfect peace, whose mind is stayed on thee : because he trusteth in thee. Trust ye in the Lord for ever : for the Lord Jehovah is the rock of ages."

To assess these statements we must first take a few steps backward, entering into the shadow of the present in which man can only grasp the promise as such, but enlightened and strengthened by it can already look to the height, the future, whose light can, on the other hand, make his present so bright. It is at this distance that Ps. 130 speaks (in the familiar Prayer Book version) : " Out of the deep have I called unto thee, O Lord : Lord, hear my voice. O let thine ears consider well : the voice of my complaint. If thou, Lord, wilt be extreme to mark what is done amiss : O Lord, who may abide it ? For there is mercy with thee : therefore shalt thou be feared. I look for the Lord ; my soul doth wait for him : in his word is my trust. My soul fleeth unto the Lord : before the morning watch, I say, before the morning watch. O Israel, trust in the Lord, for with the Lord there is mercy : and with him is plenteous redemption. And he shall redeem Israel : from all his sins." There is to some extent a backward reference in Ps. 25[10f.], but not at the price of its forward direction : " All the paths of the Lord are mercy and truth unto such as keep his covenant and his testimonies. For thy name's sake, O Lord, pardon mine iniquity : for it is great. What man is he that feareth the Lord ? him shall he teach in the way that he shall choose. . . . The secret of the Lord is with them that fear him ; and he will shew them his covenant. Mine eyes are ever toward the Lord ; for he shall pluck my feet out of the net. Turn thee unto me,.and have mercy upon me ; for I am desolate and afflicted. The troubles of my heart are enlarged : O bring thou me out of my distresses. Look upon mine affliction and my pain ; and forgive all my sins. . . . O keep my soul, and deliver me : let me not be ashamed ; for I put my trust in thee. . . . Redeem Israel, O God, out of all his troubles." Ps. 143$^{1f.}$ goes further back, but always with the same direction : " Hear my prayer, O Lord, give ear to my supplications : in thy faithfulness answer me, and in thy righteousness. And enter not into judgment with thy servant, O Lord : for in thy sight shall no man living be justified." And v. 5 f. : " I remember the days of old ; I meditate on all thy works ; I muse on the work of thy hands. I stretch forth my hands unto thee : my soul thirsteth after thee, as a thirsty land. Hear me speedily, O Lord : my spirit faileth ; hide not thy face from me, lest I be like them that go down into the pit. Cause me to hear thy loving-kindness in the morning ; for in thee do I trust ; cause me to know the way wherein I should walk ; for I lift up my soul unto thee." And v. 10 f. : " Teach me to do thy will ; for thou art my God : thy spirit is good ; lead me into the land of uprightness. Quicken me, O Lord, for thy name's sake : for thy righteousness' sake bring my soul out of trouble."

But then, and from that very point, we have the new advance of those whose back is to the wall and yet who do not fear, the new hold and leap into the future (Ps. 142^5) : " I cried unto thee, O Lord : I said, Thou art my refuge and my portion in the land of the living." And (in v. 7) : " Bring my soul out of prison, that I may praise thy name : the righteous shall compass me about ; for thou shalt deal bountifully with me." Ps. 18$^{1f.}$ puts it even more dramatically : " I will love thee, O Lord, my strength. The Lord is my rock, and my fortress, and my deliverer : my God, my strength, in whom I will trust ; my buckler, and the horn of my salvation, and my high tower." Then in v. 6 : " In my distress I called upon the Lord, and cried unto my God : he heard my voice out of his temple, and my cry came before him, even into his ears." But then everything becomes different and the one who was anxious and oppressed seems to rise up with an almost superabundant vitality in v. 28 f. : " For thou wilt light my candle : the Lord my God will enlighten my darkness. For by thee I have run through a troop ; and by my God have I leaped over a wall. As for God, his way is perfect : the word of the Lord is tried : he is a buckler to all those that trust in him. For who is God save the Lord ? or who is a rock save our God ? It is God that girdeth me with strength, and maketh my way perfect. He maketh my feet like hinds' feet, and setteth me upon my high places. He teacheth my hands to war, so that a bow of steel is broken by mine arms. Thou hast also given me the shield of thy salvation : and thy right hand hath holden me up, and thy gentleness hath made me great. Thou hast enlarged my steps under me, that my feet did not slip." We find the same movement in Ps. 17$^{6f.}$: " I have called upon thee, for thou wilt hear me, O God : incline thine ear unto me, and hear my speech. Shew thy marvellous loving-kindness, O thou that savest by thy right hand them which put their trust in thee from those that rise up against them. Keep me as the apple of the eye, hide me under the shadow of thy wings." And then the voice of the redeemed in v. 15 : " As for me, I will behold thy face in righteousness : I shall be satisfied, when I awake, with thy likeness." Similarly in Ps. 73$^{21f.}$: " Thus my heart was grieved, and I was pricked in my reins. So foolish was I, and ignorant : I was as a beast before thee. Nevertheless I am continually with thee ; thou hast holden me by my right hand. Thou shalt guide me with thy counsel, and afterward receive me to glory. Whom have I in heaven but thee ? and there is none upon earth that I desire beside thee. My flesh and my heart faileth : but God is the strength of my heart, and my portion for ever. For, lo, they that are far from thee shall perish : thou hast destroyed all them that go a whoring from thee. But it is good for me to draw near to God : I have put my trust in the Lord God, that I may declare all thy works." And then Ps. 103 plainly looks back from the goal upon the whole way and its starting-point in the unforgettable praise of the Lord to which the Psalmist calls his soul, his very self, because he finds himself called to it : the Lord (v. 3 f.) "who forgiveth all thine iniquities ; who healeth all thy diseases ; who redeemeth thy life from destruction ; who crowneth thee with loving-kindness and tender mercies ; who satisfieth thy mouth with good things ; so that thy youth is renewed like the eagle's." For (v. 8) "the Lord is merciful and gracious, slow to anger, and plenteous in mercy. He hath not dealt with us after our sins ; nor rewarded us according to our iniquities. For as the heaven is high above the earth, so great is his mercy toward them that fear him. As far as the east is from the west, so far hath he removed our transgressions from us. Like as a father pitieth his children, so the Lord pitieth them that fear him." With this we may compare Ps. 85, which is bold to say the same expressly of the people of Israel as such : "Lord, thou hast been favourable unto thy land : thou hast brought back the captivity of Jacob. Thou hast forgiven the iniquity of thy people, thou hast covered all their sin. Thou hast turned away all thy wrath : thou hast turned thyself from the fierceness of thine anger " (v. 1 f.). "Surely his salvation is nigh them that fear him ; that glory may dwell in our land. Mercy and truth are met together ; righteousness and peace have kissed each other. Truth shall spring out of the earth ; and righteousness shall look down from heaven " (v. 9 f.). Finally, we must follow word for word the best-known and most inexhaustible of all the Psalms, Ps. 23 : the confession of the man whose shepherd is the Lord, who therefore will lack nothing, who will be led on the right path, who need fear no evil but is comforted as he goes through the valley of the shadow, for whom a table is prepared and fully provided in the presence of his enemies, whose head is anointed with oil, who expects to be followed by goodness and mercy all the days of his life, and to dwell in the house of the Lord for ever—that, and so far only that. Every sentence speaks of the completion of the justification of the sinful man, of his pardon. Therefore every sentence is in the strict sense "eschatological," looking into the furthest and final future, and from there back again into the present. Every sentence is like the call of those who wait for the morning in Ps. 130⁶ᶠ·, but for that reason every sentence is the word of thanksgiving and praise of a man who to-day, to-day, can rejoice in the coming morning. Ps. 23 is a summary of the whole Psalter, and therefore the explanation of the clear songs of triumph with which the book closes from Ps. 145 onwards. It is the self-documentation *in nuce* of the existence of the sinner justified by the gracious God.

4. JUSTIFICATION BY FAITH ALONE

When we speak of the man who is pardoned in this judgment of God and therefore justified, the man of this history, of this transition, who moves from wrong to right, from death to life, whom do we really mean ? Who is he ? What man is this ?

The man of some century, perhaps the 16th or the 1st of our era, which was particularly affected by religious revolution and renewal ? Or the man of the European Middle Ages who was so near to the earth and the sea and the forest and the beast of prey, who was preoccupied with the struggle for existence, who was still so familiar with death, who still continued to live cheerfully in the paganism of his fathers, who was therefore self-evidently open to every kind of mysticism and magic and mythology ? Or the painfully civilised man in the framework of the firm traditions which were refashioned in the 17th century and since then have determined the 19th century and the beginning of our own— the conservative Liberal for whom Christianity, like the political and social order, was a much discussed but obviously effective factor, who if he was not a libertine or an extreme rationalist did not want to live altogether apart from the Church (" From time to time I view the old with favour, and take care not to break with it "), for whom missions and evangelisation and life in community, and also the reform of manners and jurisprudence, pacifism, the emancipation of women, the race-question, the social question, even socialism—and right into the 19th century the emancipation of slaves—were still novelties in which he had to be interested only by special prophets and " movements," and in which he was interested only unwillingly and in the teeth of every kind of reaction ? Or the modern spiritual man, who not only was not prevented but was actually impelled by his exposure to rapid scientific and technical progress to form for himself, as an idealist or a romantic (with or without Christian influences, and perhaps applying the newly discovered ancient Asiatic wisdom), a more or less solid counterpoise to it, or an " island of the blessed " in the form of æsthetic culture or a corresponding stoical or enthusiastic *ethos* ? Or the deeply discontented man of the Nihilists at the beginning of our century, who had learned from Schopenhauer and Nietzsche, Ibsen, Björnson and Strindberg (the remarkable Northern disciples of Kierkegaard), Tolstoy and Dostoievski, that more or less everything worth while had perished, that it was better—if only we knew where to go—to contract out of the world as out of a club whose achievements we could no longer view with favour, and who sometimes turned to the New Testament at any rate for confirmation of this frame of mind ? Or, finally, ourselves, the fathers and sons of the generation of threatened over-population and the working out of the soil by obvious exploitation, of the awakening of Asia and Africa—the man of the first and second and the dreaded third world war ? The man who after all the individualism, criticism and scepticism from which he has come can find nothing more sensible than life in the avowed friend-foe relationship of nations and classes and races and economic claims and interests ? The man who has no better way of correcting this unhappy relationship than by the ideology and establishment of totalitarian states, and who seems to have learned from the recent collapse of a first form of this totalitarianism nothing more than what we see before us in the rise and development of two new totalitarianisms which are rivals and very dissimilar, but which at heart belong very closely together ? The man who momentarily believes and imagines that he sees himself in existentialism, although it is open to dispute whether what he sees is supposed to be his vileness or his divinity, or finally his wise and benignant humanity after the pattern of a reviving classical humanism ? Or the man who tries to keep himself healthy, or to stave off destruction, or at a pinch to arrest himself on the very verge of madness, with the help of a refined psychology and pedagogy ? Or simply the man who is uprooted both inwardly and outwardly, the displaced man, the man who has been led into every kind of error, the man who is our fellow-man to-day in so many known and so many more unknown forms ? in which we must not overlook the remarkable but undeniable fact that this modern man is confronted by the phenomenon—if not of the Gospel, at least of the Church which ostensibly or actually proclaims the Gospel, of its factual power (however it may be interpreted), and that in disillusionment, agitation, protest or repudiation he has to reckon with it in a way which certainly could not have been foreseen even forty years ago. In all the phases and developments of the past there did exist, and at the present day there still exists with a greater or lesser definiteness and authenticity, the consciously and actively Christian man, it may be in the great Churches, it may be in all kinds of separate societies, it may be as an individual in the most diverse positive and negative relationships to the spirit and tendency of the age. Of this man we shall have to speak particularly in the two final sections, of the community existing in the world, and of the individual Christian as such living within it.

Our question here concerns the man justified by God, the man to whom there refers, and of whom there has to be said, everything that we have heard concerning the judgment of God passed upon him and the pardon of God applying to him and valid for him. Is there such a man ? Does he even exist ? Has he ever existed ? Will he ever exist ? The Christian does not really need to look at the heathen and unbelieving and indifferent to be forced to ask this question. Is he himself, the Christian, the man justified by God ? Does he know himself as a man who is really on the way from Rom. 7 to Rom. 8, who can take Ps. 23 sincerely on his heart and therefore legitimately on his lips in this movement and as the subject of this history ?

Nor is there any sense in thinking that the question : Where and who is this man ? is one which has become a burning question only in relation to our own environment, to the man and the men of our own age—we probably take ourselves much too seriously as such. We would seek this man with just the same uncertainty and difficulty if we could transport ourselves into 16th century Wittenberg or Geneva, or into the streets and cathedrals and cloisters of the German Middle Ages, or into the Italy of Francis of Assisi, or into the empire of Constantine which had so suddenly found itself Christian, or into the gatherings of the earliest Christian communities, or even into the catacombs—not to speak of the world outside, in which the light of Christianity has shone for so long, and still shines.

The history of theoretical atheism in the West, which Fritz Mauthner (1920 f.) was at pains to write in four big volumes, shows us at any rate (together with H. Reuter's older work, *Geschichte der religiösen Aufklärung im Mittelalter*, 1875) that what has been propagated as theoretical godlessness in our own age (and much less energetically to-day than half a century ago) was only an irruption of the same thinking which had lived on strongly enough in a more hidden stratum of the European spirit through all the preceding and ostensibly Christian centuries —and very deeply indeed in the full flower of what was supposed to be a Christian mysticism. What would be revealed if ever a history of practical atheism were written, e.g., concerning the real relationship between the general hostility to religion of the present-day East and the Christianity of the modern West on both sides of the Atlantic ? It is with particular reference to practical atheism both old and new that the question : Where and who is the man justified by God ? forces itself to our notice.

What is he then, measured by the actuality not only of modern man, but of humanity as a whole as we have so far seen it, of which we can hardly expect that it will be essentially different in the future from what it has been in the past and still is to-day ? Is it that all the time we have simply been speaking of an idea, constructing an ideal picture, recounting a fairy story, a myth : the myth of a turning and pilgrimage which can at least be thought and conceived by man.

of the history whose subject he would like to imagine himself; a myth which lacks nothing in meaning and beauty, but only in reality, as something " which never was on land or sea ; " a myth which may like any other illusion alternately interest or bore us, give us pleasure or annoy us. We ourselves do not accept the view that the man justified by God is an idea, an ideal construction, a myth, an illusion. We believe that we have to recognise and confess his reality. But if this is not to be a mere opinion, as against which we might equally well be of a different opinion, we must consider closely the grounds on which we have to adopt it.

The difficulty in relation to the existence or non-existence of the man justified by God is by no means small. Indeed, if it is not noted, it will at once gain in strength and be fatal. In its more harmless form, which is always well to the forefront, it consists in the universal and very serious questioning of the existence of this man throughout the whole range of history both secular and ecclesiastical. Whether we look at the past or at the present there is unfortunately not a little but very much to be said for the nagging suspicion that when we maintain it we have to do perhaps only with an ideal or mythical construction and therefore with an illusion.

If we try to dispute this, we must be careful that our argumentation does not unconsciously and all the more weightily serve to confirm it. This is necessarily the case if we set the existence of this man in some kind of transcendent sphere, proclaiming and describing him only as a kind of guiding intellectual concept, and thus secretly giving up all attempt to maintain and prove his actual being. What can this mean except that the questioning is affirmed and indeed that it is laid down as self-evident that the only possible answer is a simple negation of that which is questioned ? And what else does this involve than that the whole doctrine of justification—the whole answer, re-member, to the question concerning the God who is gracious to man— is made the theme of a hypothesis airily constructed with the aid of religion and thought and poetry ? We must be clear that if in the doctrine of justification we are not dealing with a hypothesis of this kind, but with a well-founded answer to this question, then we cannot accept the calling in question of this man. It is necessarily destroyed and swept right away, and with it both that simple negation and that nagging suspicion.

But the real difficulty, the great difficulty, does not arise from the questioning. It results rather from the nature of the self-demonstration of the man justified by God, by which the questioning is in fact de-stroyed and the suspicion swept away. It is in fact a matter of his self-demonstration. He has actually the power to do it, and he exer-cises it. But this means that the one who accepts it, who rests upon it, who in face of all history both secular and ecclesiastical, including the present and his own life's history, counts on the existence of this man and dares calmly and publicly to count on it in the presence of others, has from the very first and radically to give up all attempts to be sure of himself, to prove himself to himself, to proclaim and represent himself as the man who destroys this questioning and sweeps away this suspicion. He must be clear and he must accept the fact that it is not he who controls the reality and existence and the revelation of this man, that he is not in a position to introduce him or to point to him even with his little finger, that he is not in a position to come forward as an advocate to argue and fight for him. He must know that he will betray and corrupt the matter, which is the whole doctrine of justification, just as much and perhaps even worse than the one who puts the existence of this man in some transcendent sphere, if he sets out even in the slightest degree to declare and conduct himself as owner, lord and master. He must abandon every claim to be able to do anything himself in this matter. He cannot expect any effect or success of himself. Why not ? Not because the historical question, the problem of experience with which he is confronted, is so terribly difficult, the calling in question of justified man by everything else that we know of man so serious, the nagging suspicion that it is all a myth or something of that kind so hard to dispel. These are all child's play compared with the fact that the thing or person that we here have to recognise and confess will and can be recognised and confessed of himself and as such, according to his sovereign nature, only in the response to and on the basis of his self-demonstration, of the fact that he does not accept any advocate, that he strikes all arguments out of the hands of those who come forward as such. This is the great inherent difficulty of the matter which we have to face because we are definitely caught in it if we do not see and recognise it, although there is the risk that we will not be able to escape it even if we do. It consists in this. The existence of the justified man proves and maintains and establishes itself as real to itself with sovereign power. It is more real than all human conceptions of history both secular and ecclesiastical. But while this is true, we can never master it, we can never control it, we can never avail ourselves of it, we can never use it, we can never make anything of it. All that we can do (a riddle and a miracle even to ourselves) is simply to know about it, without any claim and in the most profound thankfulness. All that we can do, again without any claim and in the most profound thankfulness, is to be its witness, and again without any attempt to advocate it. Of course, when we do that it will be with an absolutely unconditional and joyful certainty. But then and only then. Not otherwise. If we are not ready to conceal—submerge—ourselves, if it is too small a thing for us to be those who humbly know and witness, if we are of the opinion that there must be some better way which by-passes the simple self-demonstration of what has to be demonstrated, if we will not cease to look for such a way, then we will merely show that we ourselves have not yet caught sight of what has to be demonstrated, that we are not qualified to speak on this matter. More than that, we will compromise the only possible and effective demonstration—the self-demonstration of the man justified by God—because we will regard it as incredible and ineffective in our own person. But who is ready to accept this? to agree that this is our situation in the question concerning this man? not to try in some way to evade and escape this situation? It is such a temptation to regard it as impossible and to act accordingly. The great difficulty is that the recognition and confession of justified man is not possible except at this price, on the surrender of every claim to our own human assertion of it, or is possible only in the form of an empty and hollow and ineffective substitute. But the payment of this price is not self-evident. Why not? Because it is not self-evident that anyone has the price to pay, that anyone can conceal himself as he should in order to be qualified to speak in this matter, as a witness of the man justified by God. No one is by nature. No one is on the basis of a religious disposition. No one is because he lives in and by a definite cultural or ecclesiastical tradition and the stimuli and forces of that tradition. No one is because he receives the sacraments, or is a genius, or a brave man, or baptised—even as a believer—or converted, or a passably good Christian. No one. And naturally the great temptation in this great difficulty is to agree that we are unable, and thus to fold our hands, to refrain from doing what we have to do—as though it were not possible for all of us every moment to do what has to be done. For the ability required is a genuinely and concretely human ability, but the possession of it can be shown only by the use made of it, and when a man does make use of it it is shown not to be an ability which he himself has contributed and exchanged as a presupposition, in the form of a capacity of his own. He is just the man who does actually do this and can do it. He stands at a new beginning which he has not made himself but which is made with him. And if he ever does this again, and therefore can do it, it will be without any presupposition ; it will again be a new beginning. And the essence of every such new beginning will be the demonstration in which the man justified by God shows himself to be real and existent to himself. The man who knows about him in this way, and is made his witness in this way, will of himself find himself placed where he belongs as such : summoned to, and made able and ready for, the action of humility which corresponds to this recognition and confession. No one can create for himself or take to himself or maintain as his own possession this direction into humility and therefore the adaptation for this action. Again, no one who follows after it, in the self-revelation and demonstration of the justified man, the holding fast to his reality and existence, will not at once have it and put it into effect, in the discovery and the gift of this encounter, in the readiness of the thanks to which he will definitely find himself summoned in this encounter.

We are speaking of what takes place in the genuinely and concretely human situation of faith. It is faith which can do what has to be done and what cannot be done by anyone naturally. It is in faith that a man surmounts the great difficulty which consists in the fact that he is not adapted of himself to do justice to the sovereign self-demonstration of the justified man—not to speak of the lesser difficulty caused by the historical questioning of this man, the anxiety whether he is not after all a myth or an illusion. Having passed through the first door which was closed, he will not be halted for a single moment by this second door. In faith he has the price of humility which has to be paid, and he pays it. Faith is itself the absolutely humble but absolutely positive answer to the question of the reality and existence of the man justified by God, to the question who and where this man is. The one who can and does believe knows this man well. He will confess him, and therefore he will confess the judgment and pardon of God, the reality of that history, of that transition of man from his Yesterday to his To-day. In his own person? Yes, but in his own person in its solidarity with all other men, and therefore virtually and prospectively in their persons too. Because he recognises and confesses him in his own person, he also recognises and confesses him in the riddle of the man of every age and clime ; he recognises and confesses his infinitely greater reality as compared with every opposing human picture. He will regard his own being in contrast to his reality, and therefore the riddle of his own person, as not less but much more dubious than all the dubieties which he might encounter in past and present history both secular and ecclesiastical. If his faith is the taking away of that which separates himself from the man justified by God, how can it hold back in relation to others, how can it not be virtually and prospectively a faith for others ?—however much he may see the reality and existence of the man justified by God called in question by them, however tempted he may be to that nagging suspicion in relation to them. Faith breaks through the calling in question, the suspicion, radically and therefore all along the line.

We have now reached the point where we can and must consider the great catchword, the concept which became so well-known in theology, but which so far we have prudently avoided and kept in the background : that the justification of sinful man is his justification by faith alone.

The combination of the words δικαιοσύνη and πίστις is obviously a special element in the theology of Paul. He spoke of δικαιοσύνη πίστεως (Rom. 4[13]), or τῆς πίστεως (Rom. 4[11]), of δικ. ἐκ πίστεως (Rom. 9[30], 10[6]), and in Phil. 3[9] of δικ. διὰ πίστεως and ἐπὶ τῇ πίστει. In Paul all these combinations indicate the place where and the manner in which man's relationship to the redemptive activity accomplished in the judgment and sentence of God, His δικαιοῦν, the δικαιοσύνη θεοῦ in its actuality, is known and accepted and apprehended, is in fact " realised " on the part of man. There is no instance of the combination δικ. διὰ τὴν πίστιν. This means that from the standpoint of biblical theology the root is cut of all the later conceptions which tried to attribute to the faith of man a merit for the attainment of justification or co-operation in its fulfilment, or to identify faith, its rise and continuance and inward and outward work with justification. The pardon of sinful man in the judgment is God's work, His δικαιοῦν, His δικαιοσύνη. Paul has not marked this off so sharply from any supposed or ostensible δικ. ἐκ νόμου or ἐν νόμῳ or ἐξ ἔργων, from any ἰδία δικ. (Rom. 10³) or ἐμὴ δικ. (Phil. 3⁹), from any justification of man by his own attitude and action, merely in order to accept this other human attitude and action, the work of faith, as the true means to create the right of man. As a human attitude and action faith stands over against the divine attitude and action described as δικαιοῦν, without competing with it, or preparing it, or anticipating it, or co-operating with it, let alone being identical with it. As far as I can see—the passage in 1 Cor. 12⁹ where πίστις is called one of the gifts of the Holy Spirit is not relevant—Paul nowhere says explicitly that there can be faith only on the basis of a divine work and gift. But if this is so, it is merely because it was for him the most self-evident presupposition. Yet even as grounded in the work and gift of God the work of faith is still a human work. And its part in the justification of man is that it alone is the human work—we can say this quite definitely in the sense of Paul—which is adapted, which corresponds on the human side, to his divine justification. Not because of its intrinsic value. Not because of its particular virtue, or any particular power of its own. But because God accepts it as the human work which corresponds to His work. Because, according to the phrase adapted from Gen. 15⁶ (Gal. 3⁶, Rom. 4³ᶠ·) it is " reckoned " (ἐλογίσθη) to man by God as δικαιοσύνη, as a righteous human work, i.e., a work which corresponds to His righteousness. God recognises, not that by this action man fulfils a condition or attains something which makes him worthy of the divine pardon, but that in this action of man, and this action alone, His pardon actually comes fully into its own. God recognises that in this way, and only in this way, but in this way seriously and fully, His work and Word will be accepted, " realised " by man, that in this action of man to which He awakens and calls him, His own action has its counterpart and analogy—in Rom. 3³ the one word πίστις can denote both the action of God and the analogous human action. God recognises that in the man who is caught up in this action He meets the man who makes a faithful and authentic and adequate response to His own faithfulness ; that He finds the man who does this, who believes, adapted to be the hearer and witness of His pardon. It is the good pleasure of God which singles out from all others this particular human action. But by that good pleasure it is, of course, radically singled out from all others. The election and calling of Abraham are manifested in the fact that he believes, and that his faith is imputed to him for righteousness. Thus far Paul.

As the doctrine of " justification by faith " (alone) this conception of Paul was rediscovered in the century of the Reformation, and as such it was both attacked and defended. It was understood and misunderstood on both sides and in the centre in the most diverse ways. And it finally became one of the most important (the most important of all in Lutheranism) of the basic doctrines of Evangelical Christendom. In our discussions up to this point we have concentrated all our attention upon the " objective " content of the doctrine of justification. The time has now come when we must turn to what has become this very important " subjective " side.

" Justification by faith " cannot mean that instead of his customary evil works and in place of all kinds of supposed good works man chooses and accomplishes the work of faith, in this way pardoning and therefore justifying himself. As his action, the action of sinful man, faith cannot do this. Nor does it make any odds whether a man means by faith a mere knowledge and intellectual understanding of the divine work and judgment and revelation and pardon (*notitia*), or an assent of the mind and will to it, the acceptance as true of that which is proclaimed as the truth of this work of God (*assensus*), or finally a heart's trust in the significance of this work for him (*fiducia*). It is not in and with all this that a man justifies himself, that he pardons himself, that he sets himself in that transition from wrong to right, from death to life, that he makes himself the subject of that history, the history of redemption. There is always something wrong and misleading when the faith of a man is referred to as his way of salvation in contrast to his way in wicked works, or his true way of salvation in contrast to his way in the supposed good works of false faith and superstition. Faith is not an alternative to these other ways. It is not the way which—another Hercules at the crossroads—man can equally well choose and enter, which he can choose and enter by the same capacity by which he might go any other way. Even in the action of faith he is the sinful man who as such is not in a position to justify himself, who with every attempt to justify himself can only become the more deeply entangled in his sin. He is awakened and called to will and achieve this by the work of God (otherwise he certainly will not do it). But in so far as it is his own—as it must be—even in his faith he confirms and repeats himself. Even as a believer he can represent himself to God only as the one he is in virtue of his past, only with the request : " God be merciful to me, a sinner." If his faith is his justification, his pardon, if in faith he can recognise the man justified by God in his own person, if, because in his own person, he can see in the man justified by God the divine mystery of grace of the existence of all his fellow-men, he does not owe this in the very least to what he is and feels and thinks and says and does as a believing man. He is as little justified in faith as in his other good or evil works. He needs justification just as much in faith as anywhere else, as in the totality of his being. In relation to it, considering himself as a believer, he cannot see himself as justified, he cannot be certain of his own justification or of the justification of man in general and as such. In faith he will be no less aware of his transgression and need and shame than in his other states and achievements. The image of himself as a believer—in so far as he has time and the desire to concern himself with it—can only incite and impel him to that other request : " Lord, I believe ; help thou mine unbelief " (Mk. 9²⁴). There is as little praise of man on the basis of his faith as on that of his works. For there is as little justification of man " by "—that is to say, by means of—the faith produced by him, by his treading the way of faith, by his achievement of the emotions and thoughts and acts of faith, by his whole consciousness of faith and life of faith, as there is a justification " by " any other works. Faith is not at all the supreme and true and finally successful form of self-justification. If it tried to be this, if man tried to believe with this purpose and intention and claim, then even if his faith was not a " dead " faith, even if it was a most " hearty " faith, even if it was a fiduciary faith most active in love, it would be the supreme and most proper form of his sin as the sin of pride. To play off a faith in which man thinks that he can and should pardon and justify himself against other attempts at self-justification in the form of fidelity to the Law and good works is not merely nonsensical. It is the enterprise and conduct of a Pharisaism which is the most evil Pharisaism of all : the Pharisaism of the publican. It may well happen that the most audacious man of works, the Christian or secular pietist or activist, will go back to his house justified rather than this man : not by his little works but because—who can tell ?—there is perhaps behind his works in some hidden form a real faith which is completely lacking in the one who simply justifies himself in all his righteousness of faith. If it is in his real righteousness of faith that a Christian can and should boast, then he above all men must know better than this ; he must not on any account regard it as his own ; he must not on any account tread the way of self-righteousness as one who is justified by faith, but only the way of the real publican.

Of the Reformers Calvin made this distinction with particular sharpness. Faith as such cannot contribute anything to our justification : *nihil afferens nostrum ad conciliandum Dei gratiam (Inst.* III, 13, 5). It is not a *habitus.* It is not a quality of grace which is infused into man (on *Gal.* 3⁶ ; *C.R.* 50, 205). *La foi ne justifie pas entant que c'est une oeuvre que nous faisons.* If we believe, we come to God quite empty *(vuides), non pas en apportant aucune dignité ni mérite à Dieu.* God has to close His eyes to the feebleness of our faith, as indeed He does. He does not justify us *pour quelque excellence qu'elle ait en soy,* but *tellement que d'autant qu'elle défaut ;* only in virtue of what it lacks as a human work does He justify man (Serm. on *Gen.* 15 ; *C.R.* 23, 722 f.). For that reason there is no point in inquiring as to the completeness of our faith. Exegetes who understand the ἐλογίσθη of Gen. 15⁶ as follows : *Abram a esté reputé preud'homme et que c'a esté une vertu à luy de croire à Dieu* are condemned by Calvin quite freely and frankly : *ces chiens-là nous doivent bien estre abominables. Car voilà les blasphèmes les plus énormes que Satan puisse dégorger (ib.* 688). As if there were nothing worse than this confusion ! And, indeed, according to the fresh Reformation understanding of the Pauline justification by faith there could not be anything worse than this confusion. It is clear that if faith was to be a virtue, a power and an achievement of man, and if as such it was to be called a way of salvation, then the way was opened up for the antinomian and libertarian misunderstanding, the belief that a dispensation from all other works was both permitted and commanded. And the objection of Roman critics was only too easy, that in the Reformation *sola fide* this one human virtue, power and achievement was wildly overestimated at the expense of all others. Even at the present day there is still cause most definitely to repudiate this misinterpretation, for which the Pauline text is not in any sense responsible.

But what is faith ? What is the meaning of it as the human action which makes a faithful and authentic and adequate response to the faithfulness of God, which does justice to the reality and existence of the justified man created by God's pardon, which meets with the divine approval in its suitability to this object, which is recognised and judged and accepted by Him as right, in which therefore the knowledge of justification is a genuinely and concretely human event ? Let us say at once that there is more to be said of faith than that in it and by it man comes to his justification, to justification in general and as such, i.e., that he is aware and certain of it and of the happening of it as the work of God, of its application to his person, *pro me*, but to his person in solidarity with all men, and therefore for all men, *pro nobis*. On this specific aspect faith is indeed the life of the Christian community and individual Christian life within the world and the human race in its totality. But the justification of sinful man, the restoration of his peace with God, is only one of the problems of the Christian life. And so faith has other dimensions than that of its relation to man's justification. It has other forms than that in which it is the knowledge, the apprehension, the realisation of the right addressed to man in the judgment and sentence of God. This is its centre. This is faith in the truest sense. But the centre has a circumference. We will return to this in the final section of this first part of the doctrine of reconciliation. For the moment our inquiry concerns its relation to the justification of man, or, to put it briefly and in a rather misleading way, justifying faith.

Now if we are going to answer this question we cannot avoid taking a few further steps along the way of criticism which we intimated at the very outset. If demythologising is anywhere necessary and demanded, it is at this point. Our very first task was to set aside *a limine* a basic misunderstanding, to reject the idea that, in virtue of an inner quality of what the believing man does, faith is the real means which man can use to justify himself and himself to declare the divine pardon. In order to grasp the essential nature of the faith in which man comes to justification we must at once develop the principle underlying this rejection.

Faith, we have said, is wholly and utterly humility. To put it negatively, it takes place in faith that man's affirmation and approval of his pride, his satisfaction with it, is completely destroyed. Not that he will finally amend himself in faith. It is the sinful man, the proud man, who believes. But in believing he has nothing more to do with his pride, with himself as the proud man he is. He has no further use for himself as such. And therefore he has no use—primarily and finally—for any kind of pride of faith. Faith is the abdication of vain-glorious man from his vain-glory. We do not say, his liberation from it, its defeat and destruction. It would be the supreme triumph of vain-glorious man if he could just control his vain-glory, exercising it one minute and then suddenly or gradually shaking it off like the snow on his hat. That would be the new pride in which man would only show that he has not yet begun to believe. No, even in the believer we have to do with very vain-glorious man. The only thing is that—although he still exercises vain-glory—he has acquired a distaste, a radical and total distaste for it. The only thing is that he cannot find any more pleasure in what he does as vain-glorious man, that he despairs of himself as this man. He no longer expects anything of what he does as such. He sees the corruption of his utterly proud action. He sees that he will not attain what he continually hopes from it. He sees into what trouble it is bringing him, that at the end of all his vain-glorious ways—the vain-glorious ways of all men—disillusionment awaits him, ridicule, defeat, meaninglessness, indeed nonsense and contradiction, destruction, nothingness and death. He is under no misapprehension as to the fact that he still goes these ways, with their ever new and concealed turnings. The only thing is that now he cannot affirm and approve them, he cannot affirm and approve himself as he goes them. The fact that he believes means for him—this is how we must put it—that he has become a bankrupt sinner, a proud man humbled, a proud man who with a terrible certainty has become aware of the limitations of his pride, and therefore of the limitations of all his being and activity, his own limitations, who is forced to say No to his pride, and therefore to all his being and activity, and therefore to himself. It is a No which he cannot and will not fulfil, i.e., put into effect, of himself—otherwise he would not be despairing of self, but would again be regarding himself as unlimited. Yet it is a No which he cannot avoid saying, with which he simply has to live in self-negation as the man he is within these limits. This is a general and rather formal description of the critical work of faith. It is obvious that the man who does it cannot be uncritical of himself in relation to this work too, and therefore that as a believer—in face of his pride—he can only think humbly of this work of his in itself and as such.

Faith is not a self-chosen humility, like the Colossian error (Col. 2²³). It is not the humility of pessimism, scepticism, defeatism, misanthropy, a weariness with the world and oneself and life. These are possibilities which a man can choose for himself, and in fact often does choose. They cannot be substituted for the humility of faith. They differ from the humility of faith in this, that we need not surrender to them, that we can take courage and be persuaded against them, that with or without the help of clever psychology we can liberate ourselves from them or let them take their course. They differ from the humility of faith in the fact that there is nothing at all of humility in the man who lays hold of them, that they are simply particular forms of the same pride in which he might equally well choose the very opposite possibilities. As against that, choosing the humility of faith is not something which a man can either do or not do. And when he does choose it, it is not a form of his pride, but he admits that he is proud, and is ashamed of the fact.

But faith is not an enforced humility, an acquiescence, a withdrawal, a surrender which is imposed upon him by fate and circumstances. Such compulsion is not in any sense a guarantee that that to which man is compelled is true humility and not a pride which is for the time being somewhat intimidated and suppressed. And such compulsion has only the character of a negation, a deprivation and limitation which comes upon man, so that the apparent humility to which it gives rise is a passive and unwilling and therefore a joyless humility. The humility of faith, on the other hand, while it is a necessity for man, and not something which he can control, is still a matter of his free and, at bottom, joyful decision, even though it does consist in the fact that a man is dissatisfied with his own action, deeply mistrustful of his vain-glory and openly discontented with all his ways. But faith does not mean unhappiness—on the contrary. Humility has nothing to do with discouragement—on the contrary. And if others pity a man because he is humbled, they only show that they have completely misunderstood him. Their pity ought to be for themselves if they for their part know nothing of this humbling. The humility of faith is a genuine but a comforted despair. And it is better to despair in the comfort of this humility than to be comforted without its despair.

Faith is the humility of obedience. It is no accident that at this point we have to turn to the thought which is decisive for the christological view which we have followed throughout : the humble obedience of the Lord who for our sake became a servant. But for the moment we will keep this connexion in reserve. Let us conclude our provisional description. Faith differs from any mere thinking and believing and knowing, or indeed from any other trusting, in the fact that it is an obeying. For that reason its humility is neither a matter of our own choice nor of an outward compulsion. It is a free decision, but made with the genuine necessity of obedience. To put it the other way round, it is a necessary decision, but made with the necessity of a genuine and therefore a free obedience. For that reason the despair without which faith would not be faith is a comforted despair. On the one hand it is the believer's own self-affirmed self-despair : he cannot and does not want to be rid of it. He declines every suggestion for ridding himself of it. He refuses every mitigation of it. He believes in his own freedom when he accepts it, when he dares to live in and with it. But, on the other hand, it is not his own choice and invention. It is laid upon him. He is not responsible for it. He cannot on account of it justify himself either to himself or others. It is not his guilt. It does not belong to it. It is despair at his guilt, a despair in which he is lifted above his guilt—not by his own effort and contriving, but as it is laid upon him. He cannot let it be talked or taken away from him. He gives himself to it and he persists in it in obedience—and neither he himself nor anyone else can absolve him from this obedience. From both these sides—the humility of faith is the humility of obedience—it is not a wild and desperate despair but a comforted despair, *desperatio fiducialis* (Luther).

We must bear all this in mind if we are to understand the great negation in the Pauline and Reformation doctrine of justification by faith, and especially Luther's *sola fide* : the opposition of faith to all and every work; the two statements (1) that no human work as such either is or includes man's justification (not even the work of faith as such), but (2) that the believer is actually the man justified by God. This second and positive statement obviously needs to be worked out and established, and we must now address ourselves to this task. But clearly it can be meaningful only when the way is cleared for it by the first and negative statement, i.e., when the faith of the man justified by God is opposed to all his works (even the work which he does when he believes), and opposed in such a way that there can be no returning to the view that his works might either be or include his justification. The one who is righteous by faith can only live in an atmosphere which is purified completely from the noxious fumes of the dream of other justifications. That is what Paul and the Reformers said in their negative statement.

The works to which they referred in this context are the thoughts and words and achievements of sinful man, including the works which he is able and willing and ready to do and produce as such in relation to the revelation of God and in obedience to His Law. The negative statement of Paul and the Reformers is that no human works, not even those which are demanded by the Law, which can be seriously expected of man and regarded as good, either are or include his justification. As works to advance his justification they are not expected of him and they are not good.

In this context Paul obviously meant by ἔργα the works which the Old Testament demanded of the members of God's chosen people Israel to mark their distinction from other peoples or positively to attest the fact that they belonged to the covenant which He had made with them. He did not reject or underestimate these works of the Law as such. According to accounts in the Acts of the Apostles, which it is better not to reject, he did himself, as a Christian and an apostle, occasionally perform such works. But—as he saw it, not in contradiction to, but in agreement with this Law, as a legitimate interpretation of it— he unconditionally rejected the idea that the doing of any of the works demanded by the Law either is or includes the justification of any sinner. And if, as the Galatian errorists taught, the fulfilment of the works of the Law is placed side by side with faith, as something which will justify a man, if it is commanded as a necessary completion of the work of faith, if it is to be laid and enforced upon Gentile believers as necessary, then this is judged to be an apostasy from faith and its radical denial. Faith is relentlessly opposed to the works of this Law, and Gentile believers are in practice forbidden to allow themselves to be won over to the doing of this Law, the introduction of circumcision, the keeping of the Sabbath, purifications, etc. This was an antithesis which could not come easily to a man who was not a stranger to the world of these works but quite at home in it if not bound by it. It is a complete misunderstanding to think that in Galatians and Romans and Philippians, and Colossians too, he is involved in a wilful movement of emancipation and liberation, as do the Jews who hate him for it and the Liberals of all times who cannot sufficiently praise him. But, as contained in these Epistles, the message of this conservative and not at all revolutionary Jew of the dispersion was bound to have that ring once faith as the place at which man comes to justification was exposed to the rivalry of works, the works of that Law which to him was still and indeed only now genuinely holy. As he saw it, the Law was not at all given for this purpose. The justification of man cannot be accomplished or revealed by the fulfilment of its works. When this question arose, Paul could see only an Either-Or between faith and the works of the Law. And faced with this alternative he could see only one outcome—the rejection of all its works in favour of faith, and for Gentile Christians only faith and the works of faith, which cannot as such be considered as justifying works. The *sola fide* does not actually occur in the Pauline texts. Yet it was not an importation into the texts, but a genuine interpretation of what Paul himself said without using the word *sola*, when Luther translated Rom. 3²⁸ : " Therefore we conclude that a man is justified by faith alone without the deeds of the law." Say what we will about the possibility and the freedom and the right and the compulsion and the practical necessity of the doing of works—the works of the Law or the works of faith—according to Paul a man is not justified by the fact that he does these works, and therefore to that extent he is justified χωρὶς ἔργων νόμου, without them. And the faith by which a man is justified stands alone against this " without," even though it is not without works, even though it is a faith which " worketh by love " (Gal. 5⁶). But if he is not justified by the works of the holy Law of God, but by faith, then obviously he is justified only by faith, by faith alone, *sola fide*. The Reformers dared to see the situation in their own time in the light of the situation of Galatians, and therefore indirectly (and often very directly) to equate the Law of Israel with the cultic and general order of the late mediæval Roman Church, the doing of its works with the achievements of the ostensible or actual piety of their contemporaries in correspondence with that order, the Galatian errorists with the exponents of the ecclesiastical doctrine of justification current in their day, and finally the apostle as the preacher of the faith which alone justifies—with themselves. We have only to read Luther's exposition of the Romans in 1516, and especially his commentary on Galatians in the definitive form of 1535, to see to what extent exposition and application—this exposition—intermingle with one another almost from the very first verses of the New Testament text to the very last. And fundamentally the same is true of the commentaries of Calvin, who was a much more careful exegete, and who occasionally at least did bring out the difference between the two ages. The risk involved in this kind of *explicatio* and *applicatio* was a very big one. The strength of Reformation theology is the directness with which it tried to place itself under Scripture and listen to it and allow it to speak, the power with which it dug out its buried centre, allowing it to illuminate the tangle of corruptions and new beginnings, the dissolution of old and the development of new ties in its own day, the courage in that light to decide with God and to call for decisions in the name of God. But this very strength was perhaps its weakness—a too hasty identification of the biblical situation with its own, and therefore as a result of its own impetuous understanding of the present a failure to see many of the nuances, and the other aspects and parts of the biblical texts, or conversely, because of its impetuous exposition of the texts, a lack of many of the necessary nuances and differentiations in its judgment of the present. Only those who have tried to understand and expound the Bible, and especially Paul as a man of his own day, only those who have happily escaped the dangers which threaten us on these two sides (exposition and application), are entitled to cast the first stone. Certainly in Galatians (not to speak of other parts of Paul's writings and of Scripture

generally) there were and are many more things to be discovered than what
Luther discovered then. Certainly there was and is much more to be said of
the Roman Church and Roman theology both then and since than what the
Reformers said then within the *schema* of Galatians. We do not need to consider
ourselves bound either in the one respect or in the other by their attitude.

But in the relationship between the original and Reformation Paulinism
there is one very important thing which is unaffected by any doubts we may
have about Reformation exegesis. For it cannot well be denied that it was
only at the time of the 16th century Reformation that, if not the whole of the
New Testament or the whole of Paul, at least Paul in his conflict with Judaism
in the Church, was again understood at all adequately and sympathetically.
From its very beginnings in the 2nd century the Catholic Church did not understand this Paul (with the exception of Marcion who misunderstood him). At a
later date even Augustine, the only name we can consider, did not understand
him as the Reformers did. He did not understand the principle underlying the
Pauline distinction of faith and works. He did not understand the passion of
the antithesis, of the mutual exclusiveness with which he viewed the two. He
did not understand the bearing of the antithesis on the exposition either of faith
or works or especially of justification itself. How could Augustine—and in his
wake all Catholic exegesis and dogmatics—possibly have understood justification
as a process which is fulfilled in the human subject, allowing it simply to begin
with faith and to be completed with the infused grace of love, if he had had
before him the contrast of Galatians as it revealed itself afresh to Luther ? The
most primitive post-apostolic Church had moved too far away from the world
of the Old Testament, and conversely it had too quickly become a doublet of
the community and order of the Old Testament, to be able to adopt the Pauline
view of the Law as the order of life which is revealed and holy but of no value
at all for the justification of man. A detour was necessary to rediscover what
the Law did and did not mean for Paul. The Reformers—and in the first instance
Luther—had to be confronted by the problem of another order of life, the order
of life and the redemptive system of the Roman Church, which was there and
was administered and imposed on mediæval man with a claim to justifying power,
which introduced man to the outworking of that process. These are exegetical
points—I am mentioning only the most important in our narrower context—
the illumination of which by Reformation theology we cannot very well deny,
no matter how arbitrary that theology may have been in matters of detail.

Even in its application of the Pauline insights to the contemporary scene,
we have to note that it cost Luther in particular no less than it did Paul to win
through to his understanding of the " Law " as we find it in his writings—to
the most radical departure from the view that man can and must attain his
justification as a sinner by the fulfilment of the works prescribed by the Law.
The Law was for him primarily and concretely the demand of the monkish
regulations which had become obligatory by reason of his oath. He had expected his justification by the observance of these regulations no less seriously
than Paul had once expected his by the observance of the Law of Moses. And
by Law in its wider sense he meant the whole structure of duties with which
the Church had surrounded the way to the sacraments and their reception
and therefore access to the grace of God, the life which is well-pleasing to God
within the framework of the *corpus christianum*. With Luther, too, it was
not a repudiation of this Law as such, nor was it a demand for freedom in
opposition to it, which led him to his doctrine of justification by faith alone.
By nature Luther was even more conservative than Paul. And the situation
was even more complicated for him than it was for Paul to the extent that what
the Law meant for him was normative as the Law of the Church of Christ and
therefore as the Law of faith, e.g., the monkish oaths were an exposition of the
evangelical sayings, the system of indulgences, which brought about an open

breach was an exposition of the evangelical summons to repentance, and the ecclesiastical and especially the papal authority which guaranteed the whole was the authority of the Lord and His apostles which it was never his intention to repudiate. It is common knowledge with what hesitancy he won through to the perception that all this was not the Law of Christ and the Gospel, that it was not the holy and just and good Law of God as Paul had seen it in the Law of Israel. It is common knowledge with what reluctance he first stood out against this supposed Law of God except in so far as it was a matter of remedying palpable abuses, and with what anxious and, to those near and rather more distant from him, almost painful reserve he time and again confessed that he had no interest in, indeed that he was opposed to, the contesting of this Law as such. To the Law and its works he did not really oppose freedom but (even in his proclamation of the *libertas christiana*) faith. It is wrong to censure him, and a grotesque misunderstanding to applaud him, as a Liberal. And in this respect Zwingli and Calvin, too, were fundamentally in agreement. They did not come as he did from the cloister, but from a pious humanism. By nature they were much less conservatively inclined. They were never so attached as Luther to the whole idea of the *corpus christianum*. But in attitude, doctrine and action they were the very reverse of arbitrary innovators. It was not by a boldly snatched inspiration, or a sudden insight, or, as it were, a flick of the wrist that any of the Reformers—Melanchthon seems to come relatively the nearest—made the step from the exposition of Paul to the contemporary application, thus adopting his position and making his doctrine the lever for their own reforming enterprise.

And above all, in relation to this aspect of the matter, we can only maintain that the reaction of the Roman Church and theology to the doctrine of justification as presented by the Reformers in succession to Paul did allow that the Reformers were in the right at least to this extent, that in the opposition to them there is no sign of any understanding of the Paul of Galatians and Romans, or of the antithesis and exclusiveness of faith and works which he there develops in the question of justification.

Among the more notable Romanist theologians of the 16th century there were a few of whom it can be said that they did at least hear and understand the thesis of the Reformers and tried to treat it seriously. I will cite as an example Cardinal Caspar Contarini, who at the time of the colloquy of Ratisbon around 1541 wrote a treatise, *De iustificatione*, in which he tried to consider and present the matter, as it were, on two different levels : a first, on which to the great offence of his own party he described it in propositions which Luther himself might almost have written ; and a second on which his expositions moved along the usual lines of contemporary Romanist theology. As he saw it, the righteousness of the justified man is at one and the same time one which is imputed to him, the righteousness of Christ which can be apprehended only in faith, and an inherent righteousness which has to be put into effect in works of charity. His intention was that precedence should be expressly given to the first aspect over the second. It is not surprising that both parties accused him of temporising. And although he ought to be mentioned here, he did not found any school, and it was only perhaps his early death which saved him from ecclesiastical censure. The Church was not willing to learn anything in this matter but only to continue unaltered, and that is what it did.

The Roman Church adopted an official attitude to the Reformation teaching in the decree of the Council of Trent on justification (*Sess.* VI, 1547). And, unfortunately, we have to admit that in this decree it laid down its attitude for all time. The decree itself is theologically a clever and in many respects a not unsympathetic document which has caused superficial Protestant readers to ask whether there might not be something to say for it. But if we study it more closely it is impossible to conceal the fact that not even the remotest impression seems to have been made upon its exponents by what agitated the Reformers or, for that matter, Paul himself in this whole question of faith and works. Even more depressing is the reason for this lack of understanding : that what was not only to the Reformers but to Paul the climax of justification in its character as a divine work for man was to them a completely unknown quantity. Otherwise how could they possibly have described the death of Christ as the mere *causa meritoria* of justification (c. 7), transferring justification itself into the sphere of the Church which controls sacramental grace on the one hand, and of the believer who makes use of the Church's means of grace on the other ? How could they possibly have described it as a process in the man who enjoys the blessings of the Church's redemptive system and fulfils its demands ? What was this but the very idea which Paul had contested so vehemently, that there is a justification which can be attained in the sphere of the institution of the Law by the accomplishment of its provisions ? Does it sufficiently mark off the happening envisaged in the Tridentinum from that to which Paul so sharply opposed justification by faith that in the former it is set under the sign of the *meritum Christi* and the stipulation of infused grace ? Where in Paul—not only the Paul of Galatians but Paul generally—do we find anything like the *gratia praeveniens* in virtue of which even before a man believes and is baptised he is set in motion *ad convertendum se ad suam iustificationem*, that is, to the " disposing " (c. 5 and can. 4–5) of himself for grace as his own *liberum arbitrium*, which has only been weakened (c. 1), assenting to it and co-operating with it (*assentiendo et cooperando*) ? Does Paul know anything of a natural man who, by reason of this *gratia praeveniens*, is in a position to accept the revelations and promises of God, out of fear of Him to turn to His mercy, to trust in the goodness addressed to him *propter Christum*, to begin to love Him, to hate and despise his sins and to repent, and finally to ask for baptism and a new life and obedience (c. 6) ? And could Paul possibly have described baptism as the *causa instrumentalis* of what he called δικαιοσύνη, as the Council of Trent does (c. 7) ? Is there in Paul anything like a sacramentally infused and therefore inherent righteousness (c. 16) ? Could he have described true Christian faith as a mere *initium salutis* (c. 8) and therefore as something which needs to be filled out in relation to justification ? Could he have forbidden it to a Christian as a *vana et omni pietati remota fiducia*, the very words of the Tridentinum (c. 9), to cling in faith and to find comfort in the fact that his sins are forgiven ? Could he have regarded it as a " heretical and schismatic " opinion that Christian faith has an unconditional and not a conditional assurance of this, and that so far as it does not have this unconditional assurance it is not the true Christian faith which justifies a man ? Where did he ever say, and how could he possibly have said, that (c. 9) although the Christian ought not to doubt the mercy of God, the merits of Christ and the power of the sacraments, yet in view of his own *infirmitas* and *indispositio* even in faith there can be no absolute assurance *de sua gratia*, in the question whether there is grace for him ? Above all, where did he ever bring the sanctification of a Christian and his justification into the relationship which forms the substance of the positive teaching of the Tridentinum : that justification is only completed in sanctification, in the doing of the good and meritorious works provoked and made possible and accomplished by the grace of justification (c. 16)—a grace which only begins with the forgiveness of sins (c. 7) ? Where did he ever say, and how could he possibly say, that faith justifies a man in so far as it works by love ? How could he possibly speak of an *incrementum* or *augmentum* of the grace of justification by the exercise of love, by the accomplishment of certain works, which carries with it an augmentation of the glory to be expected in eternity (c. 10 and can. 24 and 32) ? Or finally 'of a repetition of justification—the actual phrase is *rursus iustificari*—in view of the situation of a fall from grace which constantly arises in practice in the life of every Christian, a repetition which has to take place in the sacrament of penance by means of priestly absolution and the annexed satisfactions on the part of the one who is restored to grace (*c.* 14) ? Is not all this in effect a very exact parallel to the whole institution and enterprise in face of which, in the matter of man's justification, Paul gave to faith that isolated and exclusive position ? Does it not mean that in spite of Gal. 2[16] there is " flesh " which is justified by " the works of the law " ? The decisive polemical sentence of the Tridentinum is as follows : *Anathema sit*, whoever maintains, *fidem iustificantem nihil aliud esse quam fiduciam divinae misericordiae peccata remittentis propter Christum, vel eam fidem solam esse, qua iustificamur* (*can.* 12). Now Paul certainly spoke of love and hope as well as faith, and if our thinking is to be Pauline we must follow him in this. But in the matter of man's justification he spoke only of faith. And if faith undoubtedly has for him other dimensions than that in which in relation to man's justification it is *fiducia divinae misericordiae peccata remittentis propter Christum*, yet there can also be no doubt that in the contexts in which he connects δικαιοσύνη and πίστις faith is just this and nothing but this : the confidence of sinful man in the demonstration of the undeserved faithfulness of God as given in Jesus Christ, a demonstration in which he finds that his sins are forgiven. If there is any corresponding faithfulness of sinful man to the faithful God, it consists only in this confidence. As he gives God this confidence, he finds himself justified, but not otherwise. That was what the Reformers maintained.

They did not have the unequivocal backing of Paul for all their statements. But they undoubtedly had it for this statement. If the Roman Church of the time had been circumspect but open, it could have pointed to certain undeniable gaps in the Reformers' understanding of Paul and the Bible generally ; but for its own part it would have been ready to learn from this statement of Reformation theology, thus taking the initiative in the comprehensive reformation of the whole Church (and its better unification). But by placing this statement under anathema it placed itself under the ἀνάθεμα ἔστω with which Paul was ready to defend himself in Gal. 1[8f.] even against an angel from heaven, if he chanced to preach any other gospel than that which he himself championed against the Galatian errorists in this letter. It is difficult to see in the Tridentine doctrine of justification anything better than what Paul meant by another gospel. It has no light from above. It is admirably adapted to serve as a touchstone to show where we all stand in the matter. There are Protestant doctrines of justification—we will not enter into them now—which do not pass this test because they themselves are far too Tridentine.—The aim of that Council was to be a reforming Council, and in many of its practical decisions this is what it actually was. But with its doctrine of justification the Roman Church closed the door to self-reformation and deprived itself of all possibility of seizing the initiative in uniting the divided Church. It was impossible for the Evangelical Churches to return to fellowship with Rome when the decisive point of dispute was handled in this way. They could not surrender truth to unity. This reaction of the Roman Church was convincing proof that the Reformation application of the Pauline (and not only the Pauline) texts to the contemporary situation was both meaningful and necessary here at the very heart of the tragic controversy, and that it will remain so—seeing that the Roman Church cannot very well go back on that decree. A Church which maintains that its official decisions are infallible can commit errors which are irreformable. It has more than once done so.

We have said that justifying faith, the faith which recognises and apprehends man's justification, is the obedience of humility. We have also said that in relation to man's justification it excludes all works. When it is a matter of the recognising and apprehending of justifica-tion, it denies the competence, the relevance, the power and the value of all human action. The two propositions mutually condition and determine each other. We can and must interpret them in the light of each other.

Because faith is obedient humility, abnegation, it will and must exclude any co-operation of human action in the matter of man's justification. It will and must be alone in this matter. It will and must be only faith. If it hesitated to be this, if in the recognising and apprehending of justification it tried to base itself on any human action which takes place either before faith or in faith or as a result of faith, it would cease to be obedience; it would cease to be the humility of obedience. It would be trying to be something more and better than man's comforted despair, comforted because as the decision of obedience it is both free and necessary. There would be no real renunciation and No to pride, no real distaste for it, seeing that in addition to the fact that he believes man would still be leaning and relying on himself. If all works are not excluded and do not continue to be excluded in this matter, he cannot and will not attain to the recognising and apprehending of his justification in his faith.

But, again, this proud isolation of faith, the *sola fide* and therefore the exclusion of all competing works can have meaning and truth only in the fact that it is based upon the humility of faith. There can be no question of any arbitrary defiance, of any titanic self-assertion of man even in this form. And therefore human works as such cannot be regarded with contempt or indifference, and rejected. They are the (in itself) inevitable and good actualisation of the (in itself) good creaturely nature of man. They can and must be done. And faith itself would not be faith if it did not work by love, if it were not as Luther put it "a living, active, busy thing." The resignation, distaste, negation and despair of humility do not relate to man's activity as such but to the pride which is at work in all his activity. We recall that the humility of faith can have nothing to do with pessimism, scepticism, defeatism and the like. Nor can the exclusion of works on the basis of this humility have anything to do with indifferentism, quietism or libertinism. We have to see to it that we are not led astray by suspicions and objections at this point, so that we fall back again into the error of works. As Rom. 6 shows, such suspicions and objections were raised already against Paul's own preaching of faith and justification. We also have to see to it, of course, that we do not think and speak and live in ways which give substance to these objections and suspicions. Where there is justification, there is also sanctification. Where there is faith, there are also love and works. The man who, justified by faith, has peace with God has also peace with his neighbour and himself: That he lives as one who is righteous by faith to the exclusion of all works is something that he will establish and attest in his works—the particular doctrine of justification that we find in the Epistle of James. If in relation to justification no work is important and every work indifferent, in relation to this confirmation every work is important and none indifferent.   It cannot be otherwise if it is really in the humility of faith (not in something arbitrary) that he has the certainty and joy of faith, and in faith of justification.

But we must now go deeper.   We have described faith as the humility which involves necessarily the exclusion of works.   In so doing we have obviously described it in its negative form.   We must now face up to the question of its positive form.   But this is a question which we cannot answer until we see why it must first of all and above all have this negative form.

How is it that many writers could describe it, and had to describe it, as an empty outstretched hand ?   How is it that Calvin described it as an empty vessel, as man's *exinanitio* before God (*Inst.* III, 11, 7), as a *res mere passiva, nihil afferens nostrum* (*ibid.* 13, 5) ?   How is it that we find such trenchant statements as : *Dieu besogne en telle sorte qu'il n'y a rien de nostre costé* (*C.R.* 23, 706) ?   Or : over against the *misericordia* of God to which man must cling in faith there stands nothing but the *miseria* of man, who can meet God only as *prorsus nudus et vacuus* (*Inst.* III, 11, 16) ?   Luther put it in much the same way : " I must go out naked from all service, works and merit" (*Pred. üb. Ex.* 19[14t.], *W.A.* 16, 420, 12).   We may also recall a verse which Zinzendorf wrote as the prolegomenon to his famous song, " Go forth . . ."   It runs as follows :

> " Rise up, rise up, O Zion, rise in thy misery
> And poverty and dust, and thine will be the day.
> Have nothing, but believe,
> That the Lord, the soul's true husband, can be thy stay."

Was it really such a new and strange and shocking thing when in my exposition of the Epistle to the Romans in 1921 I described faith as a " vacuum " ?   Do we not have to describe it in this way too ?   Yet why do we have to describe it in this way—negatively ?

One thing is certain, that as an abstract admission of human weakness and nothingness such statements cannot have any meaning as a self-confession of the faith which according to 1 Jn. 5[4] is the victory which overcometh the world.   That we are good for nothing is true, but it is not so relevant that the confession of this truth has independent significance.   Nor can the negative form of faith, faith as a vacuum, be asserted as a singular magnifying of the glory of God, as though that glory were the greater the less man is before it, and greatest of all when man is absolutely nothing.   It is significant even for the negative form of faith that it is faith in God.   Before God man is not nothing but something, someone.   God is far from finding pleasure in the nothingness of man as such.   Above all, we do not have here a directive to mystical self-emptying, to entrance into the night of quiescence, of silence, of an artificial anticipation of death : not even (and more especially not) when such experiments appeal expressly to the example of the death and passion of Christ and are portrayed as the mystic's imitation of this event.   Certainly there is an imitation of this event in faith.   But it is a return to the conception of a faith which justifies man *per se* if the imitation of the work of Christ is described as a work which man can do to attain his own justification, as a task which is laid upon him in this sense; if therefore the basis of the humility of faith, and of its exclusiveness in face of every work, is sought in the necessity of this self-emptying, in a theology of the *imitatio Christi* which understands itself in this way. There is nothing, nothing at all, to justify the belief that God has created us for the practice of this self-emptying, or that it has to be recognised and adopted as the way to reconciliation with God. When a man ventures to make this experiment, where does he find himself but in the enclosed circle of his proud being and activity? If faith in its negative form is indeed an emptying, then it is certainly an emptying of all the results of such practices of self-emptying. It begins at the point where all the works of man are at an end, including his quiescence and silence and anticipatory dying. Christian faith is the day whose dawning means the end of the mystical night.

Christian faith has this negative form of renunciation because positively it is the appropriate response to what at the beginning of this section we described as the self-demonstration of the man justified by God. It is this self-demonstration of his justification which in faith a man recognises and accepts as true and certain, to which in faith he clings as he has to cling to it, as he can alone cling to it. The appropriate response to this self-demonstration of his righteousness can only be the humility which regards it as adequate and indeed perfect and therefore exclusively adequate, in which all the weapons and instruments and keys with which he might try to demonstrate to himself his justification fall away of themselves, in which all the gadgets and engines which he might have invented and constructed for this purpose come to a halt of themselves, in which he of himself renounces the invention and construction of any further devices of this nature, in which he is ready to let this self-demonstration of his righteousness speak for itself, and simply to be the hearer of it and obedient to it. And because it is a matter of the triumphing of this self-demonstration over him, faith has to have this negative form; it has to be humble obedience to the exclusion of all his own works.

But the self-demonstration of the justified man to which faith clings is the crucified and risen Jesus Christ who lives as the author and recipient and revealer of the justification of all men. It is in Him that the judgment of God is fulfilled and the pardon of God pronounced on all men. In the second and third sections of this part, and therefore in our whole description of the term justification, we have been speaking of Him and therefore of justified man, of His history and therefore of our own, of His transition from the past to the future, from sin to right, from death to life, and therefore of ours, of His present and therefore of ours. It happened that in the humble obedience of the Son He took our place, He took to Himself our sins and death in order to make an end of them in His death, and that in so doing He did the right, He became the new and righteous man. It also happened that in His resurrection from the dead He was confirmed and recognised and revealed by God the Father as the One who has done and been that for us and all men. As the One who has done that, in whom God Himself has done that, who lives as the doer of that deed, He is our man, we are in Him, our present is His, the history of man is His history, He is the concrete event of the existence and reality of justified man in whom every man can recognise himself and every other man—recognise himself as truly justified. There is not one for whose sin and death He did not die, whose sin and death He did not remove and obliterate on the cross, for whom He did not positively do the right, whose right He has not established. There is not one to whom this was not addressed as his justification in His resurrection from the dead. There is not one whose man He is not, who is not justified in Him. There is not one who is justified in any other way than in Him—because it is in Him and only in Him that an end, a bonfire, is made of man's sin and death, because it is in Him and only in Him that man's sin and death are the old thing which has passed away, because it is in Him and only in Him that the right has been done which is demanded of man, that the right has been established to which man can move forward. Again, there is not one who is not adequately and perfectly and finally justified in Him. There is not one whose sin is not forgiven sin in Him, whose death is not a death which has been put to death in Him. There is not one whose right has not been established and confirmed validly and once and for all in Him. There is not one, therefore, who has first to win and appropriate this right for himself. There is not one who has first to go or still to go in his own virtue and strength this way from there to here, from yesterday to to-morrow, from darkness to light, who has first to accomplish or still to accomplish his own justification, repeating it when it has already taken place in Him. There is not one whose past and future and therefore whose present He does not undertake and guarantee, having long since accepted full responsibility and liability for it, bearing it every hour and into eternity. There is not one whose peace with God has not been made and does not continue in Him. There is not one of whom it is demanded that he should make and maintain this peace for himself, or who is permitted to act as though he himself were the author of it, having to make it himself and to maintain it in his own strength. There is not one for whom He has not done everything in His death and received everything in His resurrection from the dead.

Not one. That is what faith believes. And in believing that it is justifying faith, i.e., a faith which knows and grasps and realises the justification of man as the decision and act and word of God. It is faith in Jesus Christ, who was crucified and raised again for us—faith in Him as the One in whom our judgment has taken place, our pardon has been pronounced. Faith comes about where Jesus Christ prevails on man, and in Jesus Christ the self-demonstration of the justified man. Faith knows Him and apprehends Him. It lets itself be told and accepts the fact and trusts in it that Jesus Christ is man's justification. It affirms and receives the fact that He is for us, that our redemptive history—that of all men and every man—has taken place in Him. The believer looks to Him and in Him to himself and his fellow-man of every age and clime, both near and distant, to find in Him their righteousness before God, their yesterday and to-morrow, their end, their beginning, their pardon, their peace with God, the whole reality which is the subject of the 23rd Psalm, and therefore man's justification.

It is this positive aspect which makes the negative form of faith so necessary. For because it is faith in Jesus Christ, it can be true and living faith only as the humility of obedience; it has to be an empty hand, an empty vessel, a vacuum. It can be said of the believer at all times and in all circumstances : " What hast thou that thou didst not receive ? " (1 Cor. 4[7]), and : " By the grace of God I am what I am " (1 Cor. 15[10]). What is he in relation to Jesus Christ, to his own justification as it is an event in Him, except the recipient of it living by the grace of God ? He believes that Jesus Christ, and in Him God, is for him. But if Jesus Christ, and in Him God, is for him, of what importance are all the thoughts and words and attitudes and enterprises and achievements in which he tries to be for himself ? He cannot expect anything from them, from his works, as far as the attainment of his justification is concerned. If he looks to Jesus Christ, to the event of his own redemptive history as it has taken place in Him, how can he also look to himself and his works ? what interest can he have in them ? how can he expect and claim that in them and therefore in himself there is, as it were, a little redemptive history, the completion, the continuation, the real fulfilment of the great history which has taken place in Jesus Christ ? If he believes in Him, he knows and grasps his own righteousness as one which is alien to him, as the righteousness of this other, who is justified man in his place, for him. He will miss his own righteousness, he will fall from it, if he thinks he can and should know and grasp and realise it in his own acts and achievements, or in his faith and the result of it. He will be jeopardising, indeed he will already have lost, the forgiveness of his sins, his life as a child of God, his hope of eternal life, if he ever thinks he can and should seek and find these things anywhere but at the place where as the act and work of God they are real as the forgiveness of his sins, as his divine sonship, as his hope, anywhere but in the one Jesus Christ. To the extent that he tries to rely on himself and man and the will and achievement of man, he will be forced to despair of himself and man. For he himself, the man on whom he can rely, is not here but there, in that One. He lives in His history. He must be sought and found in Him. Faith ceases to be faith, it becomes its opposite, unbelief, hating and despising God, rejection, the crucifying afresh of the One in whom He gave Himself for us, if it looks anywhere but to Him, if the believer tries to look at himself and to rely and trust on his own activity and accomplishment. We have already eliminated the false bases of the *sola fide*, the exclusiveness of faith. We will not return to this. But the true basis is the exclusiveness of the One in whom faith believes. What is the *sola fide* but a faint yet necessary echo of the *solus Christus* ? He alone is the One in whom man is justified and revealed to be justified. He alone has fulfilled the penitence in which the conversion of man to God is actually and definitively accomplished. He alone has prayed in Gethsemane : " Thy will be done." He alone has judged the world by letting Himself be judged by it and for it. He alone has shown Himself the One who in our place has destroyed the old and brought in the new. He alone was the One who was able to do this, who was sent into the world to do it, who was ordained to do it from all eternity as the Son of the Father. He alone as such is raised again from the dead and lives and rules as the man who exists for all others and justifies them all in His own person, at every moment of time, and then to all eternity. He alone : no creature either in heaven or on earth beside Him ; no man who is justified in and of himself or otherwise than in Him ; no man in whom the justified man can give that self-demonstration of his existence and reality. He gives it, but He alone. And because faith is faith in Him, for that reason it is justifying faith only in that isolation. For that reason it spurns and rejects the rivalry and co-operation of any attempts of man to bring about his own conversion to God, to try to accomplish of himself the destruction of the old and the introduction of the new, of right and life, the evening of the past and the dawning of the future. This is forbidden and prevented by the object of faith, by that to which it looks, and clings, by which it lives, in which it rejoices, by which it is continually renewed, in which it has its basis as faith. In His own isolation Jesus Christ directs faith in Him into the same isolation ; He gives to it the defiance in which it wills to be alone as the reception of the divine pardon, as the assurance of the forgiveness of sins, the divine sonship and the hope of eternal life, in which it wills to be nothing but pure trust in the effective and manifest mercy and gracious act of God, and therefore trust in the good right of man. It is impossible to see how the *solus Christus*, the *sola iustitia Christi* can have any other correlative than the *fides Christi* as the *sola fides*, which absolutely excludes any other helpers or helps, the faith which will constantly renew itself in this exclusion, the faith which will always have the character of humble obedience and which in this humble obedience will defy all competition. If we have even the remotest idea of what is meant by positive faith, we cannot try to have or state it otherwise. We will always think of faith and works as strict alternatives in this particular context.

In this light, what else is there to say concerning the positive form of justifying faith? It has this positive form. Or, rather, its form as humble obedience, in which it is renunciation, openness to its object and therefore faith in Jesus Christ, is in the last resort negative only in appearance. As openness to this object, as the knowing and grasping of the alien righteousness of Jesus Christ, it can be only a maintaining of that humble obedience, a comforted despair, in so far as it is a human form of being, a human act and experience. But what does " only " mean when the object with which the believer has to do, the object which encounters him and is encountered by him, is Jesus Christ and his own justification in Him? when it is from this point that he is plunged into this comforted despair? Certainly all vain-glory is excluded in this encounter. But a quite different glory is promised. This encounter obviously means the end of all reliance on man, of all dependence on his own resources, of all anxiety concerning himself, of all worry about making the decision which means his conversion to God, of all responsibility for this decision. Faith means that man can be, in virtue of the object of faith and therefore of Jesus Christ, because he really is in Him, because his true history has taken place in Him. Faith means that at every moment and in every situation man can rely on the fact that the movement between God and man which has taken place in Jesus Christ has taken place in supreme reality for him and therefore is his movement. Faith means that man can have confidence in relation to this alien righteousness fulfilled there in Jesus Christ with a twofold reference, to yesterday and to-morrow. It is his righteousness fulfilled with this same twofold reference. The Now of Jesus Christ is his Now. Everything depends on the fact that faith is not empty in so far as it does not look into the void, in so far as it is not directed at the formless mystery of something supernatural, but has this concrete object. Everything depends on the fact that it is being in encounter with the living Jesus Christ, a being from and to this object. That is what is meant by Christian faith. That is the meaning of the form of being, the act and experience in which man can believe in response to the Christian message. He knows and affirms and understands himself in Christian faith, not in the abstraction of his being for himself—he is not for himself but Jesus Christ is for him—but from and to what he is in Jesus Christ. He is what he is in so far as this One is for him. He knows and affirms and understands himself in the light and power of the promise which is given thereby. He accepts this promise, and in such a way that he refers it to himself and therefore to all his fellows. He looks away from everyone and everything else to this promise. He bows to the judgment accomplished in virtue of it. He accepts the pardon pronounced in it on himself and all men. He dares to live as one on whom this judgment has passed, to whom this pardon applies. He dares to consider all other men in the light of the fact that this judgment has been passed on them, this pardon applies to them. He makes a legitimate use of this pardon which is plain to understand as it applies to himself and all men, as it is heard by himself and all men. He knows that he is free *realiter* : free from the old which has passed, free for the new which is coming. Faith is the liberation which comes to man in encounter with Jesus Christ in whom God is for him. The man who believes knows that he has not come to God but God has come to him, that he has done nothing for God but God has done for him not only that which is necessary but far more, that He has come to his side and indeed taken his place as a brother, that He has set him right, that He has drawn him irrevocably to Himself. Faith is life in the freedom which is given thereby, on the basis of the right order which is created thereby. Faith can never be anything else but a venture. Faith can never be lived except in a Notwithstanding : notwithstanding all that man finds himself and his fellowmen to be, notwithstanding all that he and his fellow-men may try to do. But it is lived in the Notwithstanding which has its basis in the divine Therefore of its object, in the existence and reality of the justified man in the one Jesus Christ. It is simply the venture of obedience and therefore of the deepest humility, which is the only thing possible in face of the self-demonstration of justified man. But ventured in this relationship, and therefore in this humility, it is the being of sinful man in which he finds that he is really and truly justified, that his sins are forgiven, that he is a child of God, and an heir of the hope of eternal life, but in which there also opens up a view of his fellow-men, for whom all this is true and actual in Jesus Christ however it may be with their individual faith.

And now as our final word along the christological line to which we finally had to submit in explanation of justification by faith alone, we have to say expressly that in faith in its character as justifying faith we do have to do with an *imitatio Christi*. We have more than once touched on the fact that as a human attitude, as emerges from the twofold use of the word πίστις, it does represent an imitation of God, an analogy to His attitude and action. It is the confidence of man which gives a corresponding and appropriate answer to the faithfulness of God as effective and revealed in His judgment and sentence. But in particular and concretely, it is an imitation of Jesus Christ, an analogy to His attitude and action.

It is expressly demanded of Christians in Eph. 5¹ that they should be " imitators of God." In this connexion may I recall what I wrote in *C.D.* I, 1, p. 272 f. concerning the " divine conformity " of faith. And in relation to the imitation of Christ in particular, the important idea of discipleship is obviously relevant, although we can only refer to it here without developing it. The term πίστις is brought into direct combination with ἀναλογία in Rom. 12⁶ : the ἀναλογία τῆς πίστεως is the norm which true prophecy must observe and which distinguishes between the true and the false. To whom faith and prophecy are analogous—not identical, but corresponding, similar in all their dissimilarity—there can, of course, be no question as far as Paul himself is concerned. The μορφή which is to be shown in Christians—and in Galatians this definitely means in the justifying faith of Christians as opposed to all righteousness of works—is the μορφή Χριστοῦ (Gal. 4¹⁹). Phil. 2⁵ speaks of a definite φρονεῖν, which primarily, originally and properly is in Jesus Christ, is His own φρονεῖν, but which is to be repeated in those who are "in Christ Jesus," in those who know and apprehend themselves as being in Him. And, according to Phil. 2³ᶠ·, this Christ-like φρονεῖν of Christians is the ταπεινοφροσύνη in which each esteems others better than himself. In so far as Jesus Christ has practised and demonstrated it, it must necessarily be reflected *ceteribus imparibus* in those who belong to Him—that is, in those who believe in Him.

We return for the last time to the form of faith as the obedience of humility. In the first instance we called this the negative form of faith, and we understood it in its character as pure receptivity in relation to its object. But in view of the fact that faith is receptivity in relation to this object, we then had to amend as follows : that it is negative only in appearance, in its human and external aspect, and that it is the fulness of faith, its object, which gives to it this character. Now we must advance a further step and say that when we call faith humility, the obedience of humility, we say the most positive possible thing that we can say of it as a human form of being, a human act and experience. For in this way it imitates Jesus Christ in whom it believes, it corresponds to Him, it has a similarity with the One who " for your sakes became poor, that ye through his poverty might be rich " (2 Cor. 8⁹). Similarity with Him in the high mystery of the condescension in which as the Lord He became a servant, in which as a child He lay in a crib in the stall at Bethlehem, in which in Jordan He entered the way of penitence, in which He was hungry and thirsty and had nowhere to lay His head, in which He washed the feet of His disciples, in which He prayed alone in Gethsemane, in which He was rejected by Israel and judged and condemned by the Gentiles, in which He hung in opprobrium on the cross of Golgotha. Faith is a weak and distant but definite echo or reflection of all this. It cannot be otherwise. For it is the mystery of the true Godhead of Jesus Christ that He was able and willing to do what He did do in obedience according-ing to Phil. 2⁷⁻⁸ : that He emptied Himself, humbled Himself. And a man finds his justification as he believes in this One who became poor. Faith itself, therefore, becomes a poverty, a repetition of this divine downward movement, a human reflection of the existence of the One who, according to Is. 53², was like " a root out of a dry ground," who had " no form nor comeliness ; and when we shall see him, there is no beauty that we should desire him," a human imitation of what God has done for man in this One. Not that faith for its part either wills or does anything for him. Not that it justifies him because there is in it this repetition, reflection and imitation, because it is so poor, because it is an analogy to Jesus Christ in the form of that humility, in its form as an empty hand, an empty vessel, and therefore a comforted despair. As a human form of being, a human act and experience, it will always be a profoundly imperfect correspondence, it will always be similar only in the greatest dissimilarity, it will not therefore give to man any glory or merit. It is not faith if it does not renounce all such glory and merit and even the brightness of its poverty, if it looks even momentarily to itself as the copy instead of to the original, if it places any of its confidence in the former and not all its confidence in the latter. For if it does this, even if it is a supremely perfect analogy of humble obedience, seeing it can never be more than an analogy, it can have as little substance as a shadow on the wall in relation to the figure which it reflects. Yet it cannot be denied that justifying faith is in fact a concrete correspondence to the One in whom it believes, and that if it is not, it is not justifying faith. It is not a mere figure of speech to say that in faith man finds that the history of Jesus Christ is his history, that his sin is judged in Him, that his right is established in Him, that his death is put to death and his life is born in Him, that he can regard himself as justified in His righteousness because it is his own righteousness, because his faith is a real apprehension of his real being in Christ. It is, therefore, quite unavoidable that there should be a correspondence to his being in Christ in the sphere of his own being as differentiated from it, his being in the flesh and therefore his walking in faith. The great humility of the Son of God must and will make its impress on the lesser humility of the man who believes in Him. The faith of that man will be characterised by it. If he believes in Him, if he trusts and relies on Him as the One who has taken his place and lives for him, then that means that that One has prevailed over him and that he has become obedient to Him. To believe and to realise that He lives for us means (without any claim but quite unquestioningly) to live with Him. If we have not become obedient to Him, how can we trust and rely on Him, how can we believe in Him? But if we have become obedient to Him, it is inevitable that the divine humility in which Jesus Christ is the righteous man should be the pattern which we who believe in Him should follow.

This will be the starting-point for at least one section of theological ethics as presented from the particular standpoint of the atonement. But it has brought us already to a consideration of the second sphere of the doctrine of reconciliaton itself, in which we have to set the doctrine of sanctification over against that of justification. We will not therefore pursue it in the present context. But in so far as in Christology we have reached the climax of the doctrine of justification, what we can say is that, even in its emptiness and passivity, justifying faith has this character of supreme fulness and activity, and that without it it would not be justifying faith: the character which is proper to it because Jesus Christ who is the object of it is, in the words of Heb. 12², its author and finisher, and therefore the One who forms it.

Christology in the sense of a reference to Jesus Christ as the object and content and therefore the formative norm of justifying faith may very well be described as the climax of the doctrine of justification. In their interrelatedness and correspondence the terms " justification " and " faith " are like the two sides of the foundation of a Gothic building, from which the two pillars or arches rise up, first parallel and then converging until they finally come to rest in a vertex and keystone, thus acquiring meaning as the bearers of the vault which, in a perfect structure of this kind, seems rather to float above them than to be borne up by them. The comparison is quite a good one for the doctrine of justification by faith, which, like all doctrines, necessarily has something of the character of a building. And in it we cannot overemphasise as *tertium comparationis* the floating of the vault (i.e., the ultimate truth of God) above the pillars and the keystone. As regards the thing represented in this construction, we must be clear that in this matter Jesus Christ is not the last word but the first, not the climax but the foundation (in 1 Cor. 3¹¹ the θεμέλιον) of the whole. Everything that has to be regarded as the reality and truth of justification and faith and their mutual relationship begins in Him and derives from Him. In Him on the one hand there takes place the demonstration of the justified man, and He Himself on the other hand is the One who prevails on man in faith as the knowing and apprehending of justification. At one and the same time he is both the ontic and the noetic principle, the reality and also the truth of both justification and faith.

This is the witness of the writing which has a particular importance in this connexion as a source and a criterion, the Epistle to the Galatians. The didactic and polemical strength of this Epistle, its whole secret, lies in the strictness with which Paul thought and spoke of justification and faith not only with reference to Jesus Christ but in the light of Jesus Christ. We will bring to a close our presentation not only of the relationship of the two concepts but of the whole doctrine of justification with some references to the central substance of this Epistle. It is our belief that any doctrine of the inexhaustible truth and reality of justification—if it is to present the only Gospel and not another—will not only close with a reference to this centre but will have to be continually renewed from it.

First of all some answers to the question : Who is Paul himself, that he dares to represent himself and obviously has to represent himself as the preacher of the only Gospel beside which there is no other ? At the very outset (1¹) we are confronted by the abrupt contrast : He is an apostle, the human doer of this human work, the human preacher of this human word—not of man or by man, not of himself, but " by Jesus Christ, and God the Father, who raised him from the dead." If he had been called and commissioned and authorised by men he might have preached, he would have had to preach, another Gospel. Because Jesus Christ lives, because he is sent by Him, he can only preach the justification which has taken place in Him and therefore justification by faith alone. For who is Jesus Christ ? He is (1⁴) the One " who gave himself for our sins, that he might deliver us from this present evil world, according to the will of God and our Father." Paul is committed to Him, to this One who was delivered up for the sins of all, for the taking away of those sins, and therefore for the redemption of all. He is instructed by His revelation and by that alone (1¹²). For the event of his calling, in which he recognises his eternal election, from which he can therefore as little separate himself as he can cease to be himself, is (1¹⁵ᶠ·) that it pleased God to reveal His Son in him, and to make him a witness of this living One in whose self-sacrifice men are liberated from their sins and therefore redeemed, awakening him to faith, to faith in this living One, to the πίστις Χριστοῦ Ἰησοῦ and therefore to the knowledge of the true and actual justification of man, and therefore to a knowledge of the impossibility of a justification ἐξ ἔργων νόμου (2¹⁶). By His Law, the Law of this living One, he has died to the " Law "—the error of a justification of man by the fulfilment of another law than this—in order that he may now live for God. In His crucifixion he himself is crucified and therefore destroyed and done away, the man who willed to justify himself in this impossible way. It has become impossible for him to try to go further along this impossible way (2¹⁹). But this means that the life of Jesus Christ has become his true and actual life, that his life in itself and as such his ζῆν ἐν σαρκί has become only his sphere and opportunity for faith, that it can be lived only as his life in the faith in Him, " the Son of God, who loved me and gave himself for me " (2²⁰). The bridge behind him has been broken. The boats on which he might have set out on the way back have been burned. He has no ground or air or light for any other life. Any such life, any further seeking of a justification by the Law, would only mean that he rejects the grace of God, that he thinks Christ might have died in vain, that he transgresses the true and actual Law under which he stands. He cannot do this. He is prevented by this living One, by His revelation, by the identity of His present with his own. He cannot escape His law. Therefore it only remains to live in faith in Him. That is why he does not know anything else in which to glory (6¹⁴) but " the cross of our Lord Jesus Christ, by whom the world is crucified unto me, and I unto the world." This means that in and with the crucifixion of Christ a humanity which is directed to self-justification and which undertakes such self-justification has become non-existent for him, and he for it. What he has given up, what it has cost him to leave this world behind—that it needed a crucifixion, the crucifixion of Jesus Christ, to cause him to pay this price, or rather to pay it for him—we can infer from the passage 1¹³⁻¹⁴, in which he recalls the past in all its splendour : his conversation amongst the Jews, his persecuting and wasting the Church of God, the distinction which he won by it above many of his own contemporaries and fellow-countrymen, his existence as one who was particularly zealous (ζηλωτής) for the traditions of the fathers. He was at home in this world. It was his own. Any other than Jesus Christ—the One he persecuted—could not have uprooted him from it. But He brought about what is described in 1¹⁵ᶠ·. And even the moment of *imitatio Christi* is not concealed : " I bear in my body the marks (στίγματα) of Jesus " (6¹⁷). He is marked off for Him. He cannot seek to please men. If he did he would not be the servant of Christ (1¹⁰). This is Paul according to his own picture of himself. This is the necessity in which as an apostle he has to say what he does say in this Epistle. He does not say it because it suits him, or because the logic of his theology demands it, but because he finds himself in the power of Jesus Christ.

He is confronted by the Galatian Churches. The seriousness of the situation is revealed by the fact that in 1² he refrains from addressing them directly as the Churches of God or of Christ. The continuation of the letter shows indisputably that he did not dream of denying them this character. God has called them " by the grace of Jesus Christ " (1⁶) no less than himself. Jesus Christ the Crucified has been " evidently set forth " before them (3¹) so that everything Paul says about His power over himself has to be recognised by them as His power over them. He tells them quite without reservation in 3²⁶ : " For ye are all the children of God by faith in Jesus Christ." They have been baptised into Him. They have put Him on (3²⁷). They belong to Him (3²⁹, 5²⁴). Paul is the witness of all this. They had once received him not only as an angel of God—Paul has no great good to say of angels in this letter, as we see from 1⁸ and 3¹⁹—but as Jesus Christ Himself (4¹⁴) : an expression which, as he uses it, can hardly indicate simply a supreme degree of human warmth and respect, but beyond that the seriousness with which they received him in accordance with his mission, in accordance with the " I live, yet not I, but Christ liveth in me." " Ye did run well," he can testify elsewhere (5⁷). He does not think of this as something which has not happened. He does not wipe it out. He does not treat the Galatians as renegades. In face of the situation which has arisen in Galatia he certainly believes that something like a regeneration is necessary. He compares himself to a woman (4¹⁹) who must travail again for a child which has already been born. But it is only that Christ may again win a form (μορφή) among them and in them ; that their faith may again acquire the form in which alone it can be faith in Jesus Christ and therefore justifying faith. The danger in which he sees them is a terrible one. In the light of Christ all these positive things can be said of them, yet he sees that they have fallen under a spell (3¹) by which not merely some things but all things are compromised. He is afraid that he has bestowed his labour upon them in vain (4¹¹). Yet there is no passage in the whole letter from which it may be deduced that he has given them up, that he has ceased to see and address them in the light of Christ. There is no passage in which his faith in the divine act which justifies man does not enter in in relation to them. He holds them fast in this faith : " I have confidence in you through the Lord, that ye will be none otherwise minded " (5¹⁰). In this we have to see a consequence of his institution as an apostle, which was not of man but of Jesus Christ, of his firm foundation in his election and calling. If his office were in his own power, he would think and speak like the member or leader of a party, and he could simply abandon and anathematise the Galatian Churches. He cannot do this because they are not " his " Churches, in which he can rejoice or be mistaken, which he can recognise or reject as such, but in spite of everything they are the Churches of Jesus Christ. For that reason it is not they but their seducers that he places under the anathema of 1⁸⁻⁹. He calls them " foolish " Galatians, but he does not cease to call them ἀδελφοί (3¹⁵, 4¹², ³¹, 5¹³, 6¹). We may well ask whether this faithfulness of the apostle, in which he follows the faithfulness of God, does not speak just as eloquently for the cause he represents in this Epistle as anything that he says expressly in its favour.

But the faith in which and on which he addresses them—this is said no less than three times in the one verse, 2¹⁶—is the πίστις Χριστοῦ, and as such—we have this combination three times in the same verse—it is the faith in which man knows and apprehends his justification, the justification which can be known and apprehended and realised only in this work—this again is maintained three times in 2¹⁶—and not in doing the works of the Law. Why not ? Not because faith as such is better than these works. In all Galatians there is not a single word of praise for faith as such, nor is there a single word in which works as such are disparaged. Of the three factors—justification, faith and Christ—the basic and controlling one is obviously the last. The next verse (2¹⁷) goes on at once to speak of ζητοῦν δικαιωθῆναι ἐν Χριστῷ. In Jesus Christ the blessing of Abraham has come on the Gentiles (3¹⁴). As those who belong to him, they are the direct seed of Abraham and heirs according to the promise (given to him) (3²⁹). God has sent His Son in the fulness of time, born of a woman, subject to the Law, in order to redeem them that were under the Law, that they might receive the υἱοθεσία (4⁴ᶠ·). It is He who has done this, redeeming us from the curse of the Law by Himself being made a curse, as it is written : " Cursed is every one that hangeth on a tree " (3¹³). And by doing it He has made us free for liberty (5¹). We are called unto liberty (5¹³). We have our liberty already (2⁴). Because He has made it for us, because He has called us to it, because it is our freedom in Him, the general proposition is true : " By the works of the law shall no flesh be justified " (2¹⁶) ; not because of the weakness of the flesh which cannot do these works, but because of the perfection with which Christ has done them. For the same reason the great imperative of Galatians is : " Stand fast in the liberty wherewith Christ hath made us free, and be not entangled again with the yoke of bondage " (5¹) ; not because freedom is a fine and a good thing in itself and as such (in itself and as such it can also be the freedom of the flesh, 5[18]), but because it is a freedom which has been won for us by Him. And in what can it actually consist but in freedom to believe in Him, in the renunciation of all efforts aimed at self-justification, in the one decision of trust in Him, and therefore in the blessing of Abraham, in life in the divine sonship, in entry into the status of heirs, and therefore in participation in the divine justification? It is the freedom of those in whose hearts there dwells the Spirit of His Son, who for that reason are no longer slaves but sons, and can call God their Father (4[6f.]). There is one way out from the conclusion that all men are under sin, but only one : the promise of the πίστις 'Ιησοῦ Χριστοῦ (3[22]). As one who has received this promise and therefore who simply believes, Paul speaks to the Galatians as those who have also received it and who ought also simply to believe. " And as many as walk according to this rule (τῷ κάνονι τούτῳ), peace be on them, and mercy, and upon the Israel of God " (6[16]).

To turn aside from this rule, to give up this freedom which has been won by Christ and is found in Him, to give up justifying faith, is the temptation into which the Galatians have been led by the false teachers who have entered in and won some success amongst them. As appears from the letter, and as Paul expressly says, it is only a question of a " little leaven " (5[9]), of a slight modification of the Christian position and teaching, which might easily be represented as a mere externality, but which in fact—" a little leaven leaveneth the whole lump "—is bound to put everything on a different basis, to give a different meaning and direction to the existence of these communities and the whole faith of the Galatian Christians. Concretely we learn two things : Circumcision (5[3, 6, 11], 6[13, 15]) and the observance of the Jewish feasts (4[10]) are to be made obligatory. In other words, they are to be made to give to their Christian faith and life the form of a variation of the Jewish religion of Law. It is by the doing of these works that they are to stand on the foundation of the divine covenant and therefore in the sphere of the divine justification of man. Their faith in Jesus Christ is to become a particular form within the redemptive system appointed by the Old Testament Law. It can be developed only within this system, on the presupposition of the fulfilment of its demands. There is no question of setting aside faith or the Gospel, but rather of domesticating it, of integrating it into the well-known and natural view of man that his relationship with God is something in which he can and must help himself, that the grace of God is something which he can and must create and assure to himself by definite observances. The point at issue is the attachment of the Christian community to the great continuity of religious history, in which not without reason Judaism was conscious of having the last word in face of all kinds of local and historical peculiarities of a different origin by virtue of its appeal to the revelation entrusted to it by God. And from the point of view of faith in the Gospel, the point at issue was its necessary completion, consolidation and rounding off—which need not be taken too tragically as a matter of external form—by a *conditio sine qua non* within which it was still possible to speak about grace quite comfortably and seriously and profoundly. This proposal was most illuminating to the Galatian communities. They did not notice—this is why Paul calls them " foolish " in 3[1f.]—the basic difference between the reformation to which they gave themselves and their foundation as Christian communities, the apostolic preaching which they had received. They believed that this change of position was both necessary and possible. They probably thought (like the Israelites when Aaron made for them the golden calf) that in making it they would set themselves on the way to healthy ecclesiastical development ; that it was the natural transition from the heavenly revelation to its earthly development, from the event to the institution, from the Spirit to its tenable and necessary form in the world.

The remarkable surprise which Paul had for them in his letter was the uncovering of the basic contradiction in which they had entangled themselves ;

not only their contradiction to him, but to themselves, to their foundation and existence as Christian communities, above all to Jesus Christ, whom they did not wish to deny but in their own way to confess, although, in fact, they did not confess but deny Him. They have been led astray (5¹⁰), they have been hindered so that they do not obey the truth (5⁷), he tells them. What they have begun in the Spirit they are trying to complete in the flesh (3³). Not, therefore, as they imagined, to complete in the necessary and salutary giving of form to the Spirit, but in alienation from the Spirit, in a relapse into non-spiritual humanity. Not in an appropriate and demanded development of the heavenly, but in its transmutation into something earthly. Not (as though this were necessary) in the insertion of the Gospel into the context of the covenant which God made with Abraham, but—this was the hardest thing of all that Paul said to them, 4³ᶠ·— in apostasy from this covenant, in a relapse into heathenism, into bondage to natural forces, the στοιχεῖα τοῦ κόσμου, from the service of which they had been snatched by the preaching of the Gospel when they believed, in betrayal of the καινὴ κτίσις which had been promised to Abraham, which had been offered to them as his children, which had already dawned for them, and in the light of which there could be no question of circumcision or uncircumcision or any other ordinances (6¹⁵). They want to make themselves the Israel of God by the way on which they have entered, but if they go that way they deny themselves as the Israel of God. So much for your ecclesiastical progress, is the message which they have to hear from Paul.

But what is he contending against and what is he contending for with his complaint, with his earnest appeal, with his unconditional demand that they should return at once and completely renounce this way? Against a worse and in favour of a better order of salvation and life and religion and theology and Church government? This is how the matter appears on the outside, and we shall obviously have to consider and estimate it from this standpoint. But, in fact, what Paul does is simply this. Speaking both on behalf of and in opposition to the Galatian communities, he sets against the supposed reformation in Galatia Jesus Christ Himself, Jesus Christ, the One who has called both him and them, Jesus Christ as his and their true and only righteousness, to which we can do justice and in which we can participate only in faith in Him, and not in any circumstances or in any sense in a form of faith discovered and stylised and systematised by man as obedience to the Law of God. The only thing which counts is the " new creation." But the new creation is real in Christ and nowhere else. Therefore the only thing which counts can be known and apprehended and realised by man only in faith in Him and not in any other way : not because faith as such is better than circumcision and the other works of the Law ; but because Jesus Christ and therefore the true justification of man can be known and apprehended and realised by man only in faith. Therefore the decisive argument of Paul against the Church-reformation in Galatia is this—that the persuasion (πεισμονή) to which the Galatians have fallen victim does not come from the One who has called them (5⁸). If they obeyed His voice, they could not go this way. " In Christ Jesus neither circumcision availeth (ἰσχύει) anything, nor uncircumcision, neither Judaism nor heathenism—nor any other ' -ism '—but faith which worketh by love " (5⁶). Strong in faith and therefore believing in Christ, they could not even enter into this discussion of an improvement of the Gospel and of faith. They could only break it off. They could only retrace at once any steps they had gone in this direction. Such steps could and can only lead them out of the freedom won for them by Jesus Christ and into bondage, making their life in righteousness of no effect. If they were right, then Jesus Christ had died in vain (2²¹). More than that, they ought logically to accuse and condemn as a servant of sin the One who in His death won that freedom for them (2¹⁷), taking their place at the side of those who crucified Him. If they persist in that way, it will not help them (5²). They can tread it only in separation from Him, only as they destroy their being in Him and His being in them (5[4]). Note that the moment of *imitatio* can be seen on this side, too : those who go this way will be spared the offence of the cross, the threat of persecution under which those who believe in the Crucified continually stand (5[11], 6[12]). For at bottom (and it can easily be seen in practice) this way is simply a fresh accommodation to the world, the evil world from which they are delivered by Jesus Christ (1[4]). A Christianity which has been fitted into the system of human self-justification, which has become a religion, which has been domesticated, has never brought down persecution upon itself. Paul knows and counts on it that all these things are far from the mind and intention of the Galatian communities. But for that very reason he shows them that no less is at stake. It is not a matter merely of the Gospel or the Law, faith or works, himself or the false teachers, but Christ or no Christ—or, as Luther boldly but not unjustly put it—Christ or Belial. And this being the case, everything is at stake—the Gospel and faith and righteousness. As a righteousness which is hid with Christ in God, it is only in faith that it can be the hope of the Christian and that it can be awaited as such (5[5]).

The strength of the Reformation exposition of righteousness by faith alone consisted in a word in this, that it saw and made plain that the living Jesus Christ—and His righteousness as man's righteousness—is the scarlet thread which runs through Galatians and therefore through the rest of Holy Scripture. This is something that we cannot say of so many expositions of this matter both old and new. That is why in the substance of our understanding of this matter we definitely have to take our stand with them.

We will conclude by quoting without comment a section of the *Heidelberg Catechism*, of which it may well be said that it represents the insight and confession of all the Reformation Churches of the 16th century.

Question 60 : How art thou righteous before God ?

Answer : Only by true faith on Jesus Christ. In such a way therefore that although my conscience accuses me that I have grievously sinned against the commandments of God, and have failed to keep them, and am always inclined to every form of evil, yet without any merit of my own God of His mere mercy gives me the perfect satisfaction and holiness of Christ, and accounts that I have never committed or had any sin, but have myself fulfilled the obedience which Christ has achieved for me, if only I receive this benefit with a believing heart.

Question 61 : Why dost thou say that thou art righteous only by faith ?

Answer : Not because I please God by reason of the worthiness of my faith, but because only the satisfaction, righteousness and holiness of Christ is my righteousness before God, and I cannot receive and appropriate it in any way except only by faith.

Question 64 : But doth not this doctrine make wild and careless folk ?

Answer : No, for it is impossible that those who are implanted into Christ by true faith should not bring forth the fruit of thanksgiving.

§ 62

THE HOLY SPIRIT AND THE GATHERING OF THE
CHRISTIAN COMMUNITY

The Holy Spirit is the awakening power in which Jesus Christ
has formed and continually renews His body, i.e., His own earthly-
historical form of existence, the one holy catholic and apostolic
Church. This is Christendom, i.e., the gathering of the community
of those whom already before all others He has made willing and
ready for life under the divine verdict executed in His death and
revealed in His resurrection from the dead. It is therefore the
provisional representation of the whole world of humanity justified
in Him.

1. THE WORK OF THE HOLY SPIRIT

A simple picture will help to make clear the previous course of
our presentation of the doctrine of reconciliation and the meaning of
the final turn in which we must now give to its development (within
the framework of this first part). The Christology is like a vertical
line meeting a horizontal. The doctrine of the sin of man is the horizontal line as such. The doctrine of justification is the intersection
of the horizontal line by the vertical. The remaining doctrine, that
of the Church and of faith, is again the horizontal line, but this time
seen as intersected by the vertical. The vertical line is the atoning
work of God in Jesus Christ. The horizontal is the object of that
work ; man and humanity. We now come to the final aspect (within
the event of reconciliation) of this whole encounter. The particular
problem involved might be described as the subjective realisation of
the atonement. The one reality of the atonement has both an objective and a subjective side in so far as—we cannot separate but we
must not confuse the two—it is both a divine act and offer and also
an active human participation in it : the unique history of Jesus
Christ ; but enclosed and exemplified in this the history of many other
men of many other ages. We could develop the Christology only with
a constant recollection of this other side. The doctrine of sin has shown
us who and what the man is whose active participation in the act of
God is in question. In the doctrine of justification we made the
transition from the one to the other. It only remains to show what is
involved in this other as determined by it, in this active participation
of man in the divine act of reconciliation. We will describe it in this

section in terms of the Christian community and then in a final section in terms of Christian faith. The adding of the adjective " Christian " to a human action—the action of the Christian community and the Christian individual—indicates that we are now dealing with man as he stands in a particular relationship to Jesus Christ, and to that extent with the subjective realisation of the atonement. (In this context we can only mention these presuppositions, but for a more explicit treatment, cf. *CD* I, 1, §§ 6 and 12 ; I, 2, §§ 16–18, and II, 2, § 25.)

There is no μετάβασις εἰς ἄλλο γένος. There is no abandonment of the sphere of the creed. It is significant that at this point, the transition from the second to the third article, the word *credo* is specifically mentioned. It tells us that we can know the man who belongs to Jesus Christ only in faith. Nor is there any abandonment of the christological subject-matter of the doctrine of reconciliation. The history which we consider when we speak of the Christian community and Christian faith is enclosed and exemplified in the history of Jesus Christ. In a way which is still hidden, the history of Jesus Christ is the history of the reconciliation of the world with God. It is not exhausted in the history of the Christian community and Christian faith. But in this history—as the proclamation of the meaning of world history which has yet to be revealed—we do have to do with the history of Jesus Christ. And it is not as though now, from the standpoint of human history, existence and activity which is now maintained, we are really coming to grips—as so much mythology would say—with the real heart, the " existential " relevance, the substance of the Christian message, to which the Christology and the doctrine of justification are related as the husk to the kernel. Here, too, of course, we do have to do with the substance of it, but not separated from the substance which we had to present in the Christology and the doctrine of justification. We are not now in a different sphere ; we are simply looking at it from a different angle. The Christian community and Christian faith belong to the substance of the one confession which has its centre in Jesus Christ. In the Christian Church we have to do with man, his history, existence and activity in this peculiar but provisional form. If the Christology and the doctrine of justification are a myth, so, too, is what we now have to say of man, for it is no less strange, no less amazing, no less inaccessible from the point of view of man's self-knowledge, no less a mystery. And if it is a mystery but not a myth, so, too, it is with the Christology and the doctrine of justification, in which we have to do with the basis and object of everything that we must now see and say concerning man. The fact that according to the third article there is a man who actively participates in the divine act and offer in the form of the Christian community and Christian faith, the fact that this part belongs as such to the creed, is not at all self-evident. Indeed, to be precise, it is far less self-evident than creation, or than the incarnation of the

Son of God. It is far less self-evident because in it the mystery of
creation and of the incarnation is now in a sense brought home to us,
because in the Christian community and its faith man is directly strange
and amazing and inaccessible to himself. All this takes place only in
his concrete adherence to Jesus Christ, only on the basis of the reality
of the justification as it has taken place in Him, only in virtue of the
truth of the divine verdict as it has been pronounced in Him. The
fact that there is the Christian community and Christian faith and
therefore this man is, of course—we are reminded of the remarkable
pause indicated in the New Testament between the ascension and
Pentecost—a new thing, another dimension of the one mystery, a
further step in the way and progress of the one God in His address to
man, and yet not a new thing in the way and progress of the one God
in the context of His own work, but only its provisional end as it had
been in view from the very first. It is not identical with creation and
the incarnation. Conceptually it has to be kept apart. Yet it had
been in view, it had been envisaged in the incarnation and even in
creation. It is actual and comprehensible only as it derives from and
is related to them. It cannot, therefore, be separated from them.

In this concluding phase of our presentation, the concept and
reality of the Holy Spirit must be the centre of our attention. He
is the controlling theme of everything that Christianity believes and
must confess in the third article : *credo in Spiritum Sanctum.* We
speak of human experience and action when we speak of the community
and faith, and therefore of the subjective realisation of the atonement.
Yet it is that human experience and action which is not of man's
" own reason and power " or in virtue of his own capacity, resolve
or effort, but (Luther) " the Holy Spirit has called me by the Gospel,
enlightened me with His gifts, sanctified and maintained me in a right
faith, as He calls and gathers and enlightens the whole of Christendom,
keeping it to Jesus Christ in the true and only faith." The Holy
Spirit is the " *doctor veritatis* " (Tertullian), the *digitus Dei* (Augustine),
by whom this takes place. Man is sinful, proud and fallen man who
has neither arm, nor hand, nor even a finger to do it for himself, who
as such is neither willing nor able to participate actively in the divine
act of reconciliation. If this is to take place in the Christian community and Christian faith, if man is to will what of himself he cannot
will and do what of himself he cannot do, then it must be on the basis
of a particular address and gift, in virtue of a particular awakening
power of God, by which he is born again to this will and ability, to
the freedom of .this action, and under the lordship and impulse of
which he is another man, in defiance of his being and status as a
sinner. God in this particular address and gift, God in this awakening
power, God as the Creator of this other man, is the Holy Spirit. It
is still God Himself in this work, in the strict sense in which the same
must be said of the work of creation and the objective realisation of

the work of atonement in Jesus Christ. Man, however, is not of himself open or ready or willing for a profitable, a living knowledge of this objective realisation and therefore for its subjective realisation. He can only be amazed at himself when he finds himself caught up in it, when he can count on the fact that the verdict pronounced in Jesus Christ applies to himself with everyone else, that the justification of sinful man accomplished in Him is his justification and that of all men. He can never understand this in any way but that God has opened his eyes to this knowledge, that God has made him free and ready for it, that a miracle has taken place in him. He will not claim it as his own conversion, but maintain it only as God's own converting of him to Himself. In all the experiences in which it takes place, in all the insights which he gains by it, in all the decisions which he makes and executes in it, He will give God the glory. They are undoubtedly his experiences and insights and decisions and actions, but in relation to all of them he will simply be thankful. In any other attitude he would merely betray the fact that he does not know what he is doing when he confesses the Christian community and Christian faith, no matter how sincerely and earnestly he may do it. The Holy Spirit, for whose work the community, and in and with the community the believing Christian, is thankful, is not the spirit of the world, nor is He the spirit of the community, nor is He the spirit of any individual Christian, but He is the Spirit of God, God Himself, as He eternally proceeds from the Father and the Son, as He unites the Father and the Son in eternal love, as He must be worshipped and glorified together with the Father and the Son, because He is of one substance with them. He is not man's own spirit and He never will be. He is God, attesting Himself to the spirit of man as his God, as the God who acts for him and to him. He is God, coming to man, and coming to him in such a way that He is revealed to him as the God who reconciles the world and man to Himself, in such a way therefore that what He is and does for him as such becomes the Word which man can hear and actually does hear, in such a way, therefore, that man allows himself to be reconciled with Him (2 Cor. 5[20]). God's self-attestation makes what He does the Word which is spoken to this man and received and accepted by him. The Holy Spirit is God in this His self-attestation—God in the power which quickens man to this profitable and living knowledge of His action. He is God intervening and acting for man, addressing Himself to him, in such a way that He says Yes to Himself and this makes possible and necessary man's human Yes to Him.

From all this it is self-evident that neither the Christian community nor the individual Christian can subjugate or possess or control Him, directing and overruling His work. He makes man free, but He Himself remains free in relation to him : the Spirit of the Lord. He awakens man to faith, but it is still necessary to believe in Him, *in Spiritum*

Sanctum, in the very same fellowship with Him and the very same distance from Him with which we believe *in unum Deum Patrem* and *in Jesum Christum, Filium eius unicum*. The relationship of the Christian community and the individual Christian to Him is not created by them but by Him—with a supreme reality and certainty. But this means that it can only be one of obedience and of prayer for His new coming and witness and quickening : *Veni creator Spiritus*. In everything that we have to say concerning the Christian community and Christian faith we can move only within the circle that they are founded by the Holy Spirit and therefore that they must be continually refounded by Him, but that the necessary refounding by the Holy Spirit can consist only in a renewal of the founding which He has already accomplished. To put it in another way, the receiving of the Holy Spirit which makes the community a Christian community and a man a Christian will work itself out and show itself in the fact that only now will they really expect Him, only now will they want to receive Him ; and where He is really expected, where there is a desire to receive Him, that is the work which He has already begun, the infallible sign of His presence.

But the Spirit and therefore the awakening power which is the presupposition of the community and faith is the Holy Spirit. The word " holy " does not merely repeat and emphasise the fact that He is divine, that He is Himself God. According to 1 Cor. 8⁵ there are many gods, and to attest them there are many spirits. The real operation of these spirits is not, of course, a secret, but they can be understood as the many forms of the spirit of the world and man as they correspond to the nature of those gods. Man can possess the spirits no less than they possess him. At bottom he has as much control over them as they have over him. But the Holy Spirit is clearly marked off from these spirits by the fact that He is the Spirit of the God who acts in Jesus Christ, reconciling the world to Himself and revealing Himself in the world as the doer of this work. He does not attest to man something quasi-divine (not even if it claims to be transcendence itself). He does not mediate to him the knowledge of a supposed higher wisdom. He does not subject him to the yoke of a supposed power. He attests to him the Son, who in obedience to the will of the Father took up and trod to the very end the way into the far country—his Judge who gave Himself to be judged in his place. He attests his transition from wrong to right, from death to life, as it was fulfilled in this judgment. He attests that which was accomplished thereby as his justification. He attests the verdict of the Father on the world and himself as spoken in His death and revealed in His resurrection. He attests the grace of God as the righteousness of God and the righteousness of God as the grace of God. And all this, not as the impartation of an abstract historical truth, not as abstract doctrine, but in attestation of the living Jesus Christ Himself :

nothing, therefore, but what is His history, nothing but what is true and actual in Him, nothing but what is Himself. He actually spends Himself in His attestation in so far as He is the Spirit of the Father and of the Son who accomplishes and reveals the will of the Father. He is the Spirit of Jesus Christ, His power awakening man to a knowledge of the God acting in Him. In this way He is the Spirit of God. In this way He is holy, and He makes man holy.

And this involves the final point, that He is sent by Jesus Christ and comes to man. According to Jn. 20^{22}, He blows as His breath in the freedom described in Jn. 3^8. He is the form of His action, in which His action is not excluded and does not cease because it has taken place, in which it cannot become the object of historical impartation or abstract doctrine. It is the form of His action in which this action continues, in which it is made present to the man to whom He gives Himself and who receives Him as the action which in its singularity takes place to-day, in which as he is free to know and grasp it in faith, as he participates in it, it makes him its contemporary. It is the form of His action in which this action hastens from His resurrection as its first revelation to a few to its final and general revelation to all. It is the expression and confirmation of His life as the theme of that action.

It is strange but true that fundamentally and in general practice we cannot say more of the Holy Spirit and His work than that He is the power in which Jesus Christ attests Himself, attests Himself effectively, creating in man response and obedience. We describe Him as His awakening power. Later we will have to describe Him as His quickening and enlightening power. To that extent we have not yet said of Him everything that there is to say. But fundamentally and generally there is no more to say of Him than that He is the power of Jesus Christ in which it takes place that there are men who can and must find and see that He is theirs and they are His, that their history is genuinely enclosed in His and His history is equally genuinely enclosed in theirs. Anything beyond this description of fact is either a report of His history as such : His way, His act and experience, His life as the subject of the action in which God reconciled the world to Himself, or it is an account of its significance and relevance and effect in the life of the community which recognises and confesses Him as the Lord, in the life of the faith and—as we shall see later—of the love and hope of the Christian. The confession : *credo in Spiritum Sanctum*, in which we are concerned with the relationship, the fellowship, indeed the unity between Him and the community, between Him and the individual Christian, occupies in the creed a strangely isolated position—almost, we might say, as though it were naked and empty. But if the decision is made in Him, it is in Him that the whole is both questioned and answered.

How gladly we would hear and know and say something more,

something more precise, something more palpable concerning the way in which the work of the Holy Spirit is done ! How does it really happen that the history of Jesus Christ, in which the history of all men is virtually enclosed and accomplished, is actualised, in the first instance only in the history of a few, of a small minority within the many of whom this cannot so far be said, but even in the history of the few typically for the history of the many ? How can it really be—the question of the Virgin in Lk. 1³⁴—that there is an actualising of this history in other human histories ? By what ways does God bring it about that in the perverted hearts, in the darkened knowledge and understanding, in the rebellious desires and strivings of sinful men —for that is what even the few are—there takes place this awakening, in which they can know Jesus Christ as theirs and themselves as His ? How is there really born in them the new man who knows and recognises and confesses Jesus Christ ? How can there be in history such a thing as Christianity, and men who seriously want to be Christians ?

The confession *credo in Spiritum Sanctum* does not tell us anything concerning this How. It merely indicates the fact that all this does take place, did take place and will continually take place again. It merely tells us that the God who created man on the earth and under heaven, who has reconciled him to Himself in His Son, has done and does and will do this as well, the opening of blind eyes and deaf ears, the raising up of lame feet, the training of useless hands, the awakening of dead hearts to the hearing and obedience of His Word. Even the New Testament, although time and again it places the Holy Spirit between the event of Christ on the one hand and the Christian community and Christian faith on the other, does not really tell us anything about the How, the mode of His working.

And the saying about the wind which blows and is heard, but we do not know whence it comes or whither it goes (Jn. 3⁸), seems to repel any question as to the explanation of the fact that it does blow and is heard. All that is said of it is an attestation and confirmation of the fact that the Holy Spirit is the Spirit of Jesus Christ, that His power is on certain men, that He comes to them as such, that He is " poured out " on them, that He " sits " on them and " fills " them (Ac. 2¹ᶠ·), that He is effective and manifest in the rise of the community and the existence of Christian men to the extent that they receive Him or begin to receive Him. Beyond the description and assertion of this fact there did not emerge any doctrine of the Holy Spirit and His work even in the secondary and later theology of the Church. All that could be done was to refer forward to this special work of God from Christology and the doctrine of justification (or sanctification or calling), and to refer backward to it from the doctrine of the Church and of faith (or love or hope).

It is obviously futile to try to go beyond this twofold reference. God Himself—concretely, the work and Word of the living Jesus Christ

—stands between the two, His free gift and creation, so that here, if anywhere, apart from this twofold reference, we can only say : " Let everything in us keep silence." This is what makes the preaching of Pentecost so difficult and so easy. This is what is expressed in the preaching of Pentecost with such crystal clarity and yet with such mystery—*N.B.* not only or primarily in the preaching of Whitsunday, but as the clarity and mystery of all preaching, all proclamation of the relationship, the fellowship, the unity which exists, which has to be continued and renewed, which has constantly to be founded anew, between Jesus Christ on the one hand and the Christian community, the Christian and man in general on the other.

The " demonstration of the Spirit and (therefore) of power " to which Paul referred in 1 Cor. 2⁴ is shown unmistakably by the context not to be a demonstration which Paul thought he had given or could give in Corinth, but the demonstration which God had given and would continue to give there in Jesus Christ. Not without the apostolic preaching of Him, or the apostolic direction and instruction and guidance for the building up and maintaining of the community, but as the apostle pointed forward from the one and backward from the other to this centre as the point where his teaching reached its limit and therefore could only be silent, because there, and from there, the decision was reached whether his teaching of Jesus Christ and of justification as it took place in Him was the proclamation of a myth or God's own Word, whether his teaching of the Church and of faith was again the proclamation of a myth or God's own Word. Paul simply attested the ἀπόδειξις πνεύματος καὶ δυνάμεως.

For this reason (in view of what we have said earlier) this introductory section can be very brief. It will be enough if we simply write below all that we have said so far and above all that we have still to say the confession which is the confession of this sovereign goal and presupposition of all Christian teaching : *credo in Spiritum Sanctum.*

2. THE BEING OF THE COMMUNITY

As the work of the Holy Spirit the Christian community, Christendom, the Church is a work which takes place among men in the form of a human activity. Therefore it not only has a history, but—like man (*CD* III, 2 § 44)—it exists only as a definite history takes place, that is to say, only as it is gathered and lets itself be gathered and gathers itself by the living Jesus Christ through the Holy Spirit. To describe its being we must abandon the usual distinctions between being and act, status and dynamic, essence and existence. Its act is its being, its status its dynamic, its essence its existence. The Church *is* when it takes place that God lets certain men live as His servants, His friends, His children, the witnesses of the reconciliation of the world with Himself as it has taken place in Jesus Christ, the preachers of the victory which has been won in Him over sin and suffering and death, the heralds of His future revelation in which the glory of the Creator will be declared to all creation as that of His love and faithfulness and mercy. The Church *is* when it happens to these men in common that they may receive the verdict on the whole world of men which has been pronounced in the resurrection of Jesus Christ from the dead. By the pronunciation of this verdict, which they can receive and have received by the awakening power of the Holy Spirit, they are gathered and they allow themselves to be gathered, they gather themselves, as they have received it and do receive it. The Church *is* when these men subject themselves to the law of the Gospel, " the law of the Spirit of life " (Rom. 8²), when they become obedient to it, when they keep to the fact, as to an imperative which is true of all of them in common, that God was and is and will be faithful to man in His great wrath against man's unfaithfulness to Him, that He has given Himself up for him in His Son, that in this One He has reestablished His own damaged right and the lost right of man, that in Him He has maintained and fulfilled His covenant and concluded eternal peace. The Church *is* when these men as the first-fruits of all creation can know and have to acknowledge the Lord of the world in His faithfulness as the Lord of the covenant which He has maintained and fulfilled, and therefore as their Lord. The Church *is* in the particular relationship of these men, when this is possible and actual under the sovereignty of Jesus Christ in their common hearing and obeying, when they can make a common response with their existence to the work of Jesus Christ received by them as Word.

In all this we are simply paraphrasing the basic meaning of the word ἐκκλησία. The Latin rendering in *Cat. Rom.* (I, 10, 2) is correct : *Significat ecclesia evocationem.* The Church is a community which hastens towards and comes together in a public convocation. In the same text, and also in *C.A.* VII and VIII, it is a *congregatio* : a *coetus*, to use a favourite (if rather static and institutional) phrase of the days of orthodoxy ; or even further removed from the original sense, a *societas*, a *corpus*.

The English equivalent " church " or " kirk," and the German " Kirche," is usually explained to be a mutilated rendering of the adjective κυριακή. But it may go back to the same root to which the Latin words *circare*, *circa*, *circum*, *circulus*, etc., belong, indicating the circumscribed sphere in which this gathering, this hastening and coming together of the community, takes place, or even more concretely the half-circular apse with the altar and the bishop's throne on which the assembled congregation was focused in its worship in churches built after the older Roman style. A third guess is that the word " church " comes from the term κηρυγεία (the office of a herald). None of these explanations is completely satisfying. What is certain is that Luther preferred not to use the word at all, but to speak of the " community," the " congregation," the " company " or " little company," or even " Christendom." There is no doubt that we do have to fill it out and interpret it in this sense in accordance with its New Testament use and the Old Testament original *qahal*. The Church as ἐκκλησία, as *evocatio* or *congregatio*, is a description of an event. The same is true of the explanatory formula added to the description of the *ecclesia* in the creed, the *communio sanctorum*, no matter whether by the word *sanctorum* we mean the *sancti* (the *fideles*, *vocati*), those who enter into fellowship with one another in the Church, or the *sancta*, the redemptive occurrence attested in the Church's *kerygma*, in which its members have their specific and conscious part. It is unquestionable that the *communio*, too, is not the being of a state or institution, but the being of an event, in which the assembled and self-assembling community is actively at work : the living community of the living Lord Jesus Christ in the fulfilment of its existence.

The Church *is* when it takes place, and it takes place in the form of a sequence and nexus of definite human activities. In these human activities as such it can be studied from the very beginning of our era by all those who have the opportunity and give to it the necessary attention. It is a phenomenon of world history which can be grasped in historical and psychological and sociological terms like any other. There is, there takes place, a gathering and separation of certain men to this fellowship. This involves—in varying degrees of strictness or looseness—an ecclesiastical organisation and constitution and order. In this gathering and separation there takes place its cultus, teaching, preaching, instruction, theology, confession, and all in definite relationships to the political and economic and social conditions and movements, to the scholarship and art and morality, of the surrounding world. It all develops in and with this world, but according to its own laws, with a tradition which is in many ways related and in many ways differentiated, with its distinctive purpose and stamp, but with obvious connexions and similarities and reciprocal actions in relation to other human phenomena and their history. It is a specific and yet also an integrated, a distinctive and yet not a unique element in the whole of human culture, its achievements and its destinies. In all this—to use the term which has become classical—the Church is visible, *ecclesia visibilis*. It is one historical factor with others, asserting itself and immediately noticeable as such. Nor is it, as it were, accidental or *per nefas* that it is visible in this way. It is essential to it to be so ; just as essential as that in another sense it should be invisible : *ecclesia invisibilis*. The work of the Holy Spirit to which it owes its existence is something which is produced concretely and historically in this world. It is the awakening power of the Word made flesh, of the Son of God, who Himself entered the lowliness of an historical existence in this world, who as very God became and is very man. Like begets like. The Christian faith awakened by Him is a definite human activity and therefore a definite human phenomenon. For all the peculiarity of his activity the Christian is an ordinary man with other men. Similarly the Christendom in which there are Christians is a human work and as such a human phenomenon which can be generally observed. Where there is this awakening, where the Church is born of the Word of God (Zwingli), itself " the mother which conceives and bears every Christian by the Word of God which it reveals and produces, enlightening and kindling the hearts so that they grasp and receive and cling and hold fast to it " (Luther), there there arises in some form a historical quantity which can be observed, which is at work and which can be calculated in historical terms.

According to the Gospels, the Church came into being quite visibly with the calling of the twelve apostles who were all named and who correspond in number to the twelve tribes of Israel. It developed visibly with the addition of the thousands on the day of Pentecost, and among the Gentiles in the form of the ἐκκλησίαι of Asia Minor, Greece and Rome, and later the whole Mediterranean littoral, and then the far North and East and South—a very visible counterpart to the visible temporal Empire. In the world of Constantine the Great and of Charlemagne and later of the Houses of Saxony and Hohenstauffen, it assumed visible forms which can only be described as terrifying. It again took historical form in consequence of the denial of Evangelical renewal in the 16th century, and the necessity to re-establish itself in relation to this renewal. And the Reformers guarded themselves very carefully against the idea that by the Church they meant only a *civitas platonica*, the pure idea of a Christian community and therefore only an invisible Church. They at once gave themselves to the task of building on the ruins of the past a new and visible Church based on the newly perceived Word of God and in new obedience to that Word. And they succeeded well enough in a form which is also to some extent terrifying. And since then, whenever it has been thought that such reconstruction is necessary and possible, it has always been—and no sect, however spiritual, can completely escape it—with a certain visibility, with a separation which every eye can see, with the establishment of certain cultic and intellectual and legal and social and æsthetic forms which mark it off more or less distinctively from other temporal or religious societies or from other forms of the Christian community. The Church never has been and never is absolutely invisible.

There is an ecclesiastical Docetism which will not accept this, which paradoxically tries to overlook the visibility of the Church, explaining away its earthly and historical form as something indifferent, or angrily negating it, or treating it only as a necessary evil, in order to magnify an invisible fellowship of the Spirit and of spirits. This view is just as impossible as christological Docetism, not only in point of history, but also in point of substance. For the work of the Holy Spirit as the awakening power of Jesus Christ would not take place at all if the invisible did not become visible, if the Christian community did not take on and have an earthly-historical form. The individual Christian can exist only in time and space as a doer of the Word (Jas. 1[22]) and therefore in a concrete human form and basically visible to everyone. Similarly the Christian community as such cannot exist as an ideal commune or universum, but—also in time and space— only in the relationship of its individual members as they are fused together by the common action of the Word which they have heard into a definite human fellowship; in concrete form, therefore, and visible to everyone. If we say with the creed *credo ecclesiam*, we do not proudly overlook its concrete form; just as when we confess *credo resurrectionem carnis* we cannot overlook the real and whole man who is a soul and yet also a body, we cannot overlook his hope as though the resurrection was not also promised to him. Nor do we look penetratingly through this form, as though it was only something transparent and the real Church had to be sought behind it ; just as we cannot overlook or look through the pleasing or less pleasing face of the neighbour whom we are commanded to love. We look at the visible aspect of the Church—this is the state of it. And as we look at what is seen—not beside it or behind but in it—we see what is not seen. Hence we cannot rid ourselves in this way of the generally visible side of the Church. We cannot take refuge from it in a kind of wonderland. The *credo ecclesiam* can and necessarily will involve much distinguishing and questioning, much concern and shame. It can and necessarily will be a very critical *credo*. In relation to the side of the Church which is generally visible it can and necessarily will express what does not amount to much more than a hope and a yearning. But it does take the Church quite seriously in its common visibility—which is its earthly and historical existence. It confesses faith in the invisible aspect which is the secret of the visible. Believing in the *ecclesia invisibilis* we will enter the sphere of labour and conflict of the *ecclesia visibilis*. Without doing this, without a discriminate but serious participation in the historical life of the community, its activity, its upbuilding, its mission, in a kind of purely theoretical and abstract churchliness, no one has ever seriously repeated the *credo ecclesiam*. Those who try to repeat it in a way which looks above the Church, only dreaming of its existence in time and space, must see to it that they are not secretly pandering to a christological Docetism as well, or, at any rate, that they are really taking seriously the true humanity of Jesus Christ. Faith in His community has this in common with faith in Him, that it, too, relates to a reality in time and space, and therefore to something which is at bottom generally visible. If, then, we believe in Him, we cannot refuse—however hesitantly or anxiously or contentiously—to believe in His community in its spatio-temporal existence, and therefore to be a member of it and personally a Christian. We will return to the implications of this in the second part of the doctrine of reconciliation under the title of the true humanity of Jesus Christ. For the moment it is enough to point to it by way of demarcation.

When we have done this, the emphasis in the present context must be upon the fact that the community called into being by the Holy Spirit, although it does not exist and must not be sought abstractly in the invisible, also does not exist and must not be sought abstractly in the visible. It does exist openly in a very concrete form, a historical phenomenon like any other. But what it is, the character, the truth of its existence in time and space, is not a matter of a general but a very special visibility. Without this it is invisible. What is visible to all is the event of the *congregatio* and *communio* of certain men, its characteristic activities and achievements, its peculiarities by which it is distinguished from other historical structures, its deficiencies which it has with them in common, its relative advantages. But what actually takes place, what this is in truth, is not visible to all; it is visible to Christians only in this particular way or not at all. Without this special visibility all that can be seen is the men united in it and their common activity, and this will be explained in terms of the categories which are regarded as the most appropriate for the understanding and appraisal of common human activities, with an attempt to subordinate it to some picture of the world and of history. On this view it can be understood as a religious society within human society generally and side by side with other organisations. The attention paid to it will be with reference to its past and present in this connexion and on this level. Its structure and message and claims and activity as this particular society within or side by side with others, its greater or lesser, welcome or unwelcome significance and co-operation and power in the spheres of culture and the state, will be registered and either lauded or tolerated, supported or contested, with varying degrees of attention. It will be taken seriously, but within the limits of the two-dimensional view in which it can be generally known, as one earthly-historical factor with others. And when we say that we are already saying too much, because on this view there cannot be any other but earthly-historical factors.

In this connexion we may recall the level on which and the manner in which the Church is usually spoken of by the average statesman or politician, by the journalist who pontificates concerning the Church and the Churches and things ecclesiastical and by the pure historicist, psychologist and sociologist. All these very obviously and obstinately keep to the external picture which is visible to them, and with a mixture of ignorance, irony and nervousness they steer clear of anything wider.

It is plain that fundamentally the Church is forced to acknowledge the picture which it offers on this view. Indeed it is essential to it to be external, to exist in the dimensions of this level, and therefore to offer this external picture. It is equally plain that for its own part it cannot agree to be seen and understood for what it is in this external picture as such. It has to know the third dimension of its existence. Yet it also has to know that it is defenceless against the interpretations to which it is subject on this two-dimensional view. For where there is not this special visibility, where there cannot be an insight into its earthly and historical form, even what it can confess and ever so impressively explain concerning its true being as visible in this external picture will, of course, have its greater or lesser interest as its particular ideology and may even be noted with a nod of the head, but it will at once be translated onto the historical and psychological and sociological level and irresistibly absorbed into the external picture as such. No matter what attitude it takes up, what it is will still be invisible, and for the first time genuinely invisible. And then it will always be tempted to give way, to see and understand itself only in this external picture, to acquiesce in it, to be a kind of religious society, to build itself up and to develop as such, to be active, setting itself aims and achieving results as such, to live peaceably with the rest of society on this basis and in this sphere, even to assert itself—perhaps with a certain measure of triumph but certainly with assurance, because, like everything else on this level, religion can always present itself as a necessary human need, and because it is unquestionably in a position to meet that need. But this is a temptation which comes to the Church from without, from its own humanity. From within it will never find itself tempted to try to exist only in two dimensions and therefore in an abstract visibility. From within, in the light of its awakening by the Holy Spirit, it will always have to see and understand and confess itself in three dimensions, whether this is understood from without or not.

If in the great Schleiermacher's *Glaubenslehre* we have, as it were, a fall of Christianity, or the canonisation of it, this is to be found in the wonderfully logical introduction in which on the basis of ethics (what Schleiermacher calls the general philosophy of history) it is defined and described as a " pious society "—naturally of a particular kind—that is to say, " a monotheistic form of faith related to the teleological direction of piety," and essentially distinguished from all others by the fact " that everything in it is connected with the redemption accomplished by Jesus of Nazareth " (§ 11). In this definition everything has been more or less correctly perceived. The only thing is that the third dimension, in which the Church is what it is, is completely absent.

To be sure, the confession *credo ecclesiam* does refer necessarily to a human society which exists concretely in history and which may at a pinch be defined as a pious society or something similar. But its true reference is to what this society *is* in its concrete historical form, and therefore to a character which is proper to it not in its general but its particular visibility, a character in which it is invisible without this particular visibility. In this character, notwithstanding its concrete historical form, indeed in this form as in everything declared by the Christian confession, the Church has to be believed. No one really needs to believe the Christianity defined and described by Schleiermacher : in its own way it is a historical phenomenon like all others, and as such it can at bottom be perceived generally. What Christianity really is, the being of the community as " the living community of the living Lord Jesus Christ," calls for the perception of faith, and is accessible only to this perception and not to any other. It has this character in virtue of the reconciling and self-revealing grace of God, in virtue of the mission and work of the Holy Spirit, and therefore in the power of Jesus Christ Himself. Only in this power is it recognisable in this character. The glory of Jesus Christ was hidden when He humbled Himself, when He took our flesh, when in our flesh He was obedient to God, when He destroyed our wrong, when He established our right. So, too, the glory of the humanity justified in Him is concealed. And this means that the glory of the community gathered together by Him within humanity is only a glory which is hidden from the eyes of the world until His final revelation, so that it can be only an object of faith. What it is, its mystery, its spiritual character, is not without manifestations and analogies in its generally visible form. But it is not unequivocally represented in any such generally visible manifestations and analogies. The men united in it and their action are in every respect generally visible. They are so as the elect and called of God, and their works as good works. But the being of the community in its temporal character is hidden under considerable and very powerful appearances to the contrary. There is no direct identity between what the community is and any confession, theology or cultus ; any party, trend, group or movement in the being of the community as it may be generally perceived ; anything within it which can be demonstrated or delimited or counted or formulated in a purely human way ; or, of course, any of the individuals assembled and active within it. There is nothing within it which does not prompt, which may not itself be, the question whether and how far it has a part in what the community is. There is nothing within it which does not continually have to receive again this part, which does not have to be believed in its participation. The gathering and maintaining and completing of the community, as the mystery of what its visible form is on this level, is in the hand of God, and as His own work, a spiritual reality, its third dimension, it is invisible, it cannot be perceived but only believed. For in what its generally visible history is on that level it does not belong only to the creaturely world but actually to the world of flesh, of fallen man. It is always sinful history—just as the individual believer is not only a creature but a sinful man. Woe to it if what it is is directly identical with what it is as generally visible, or if it accepts as its being its concrete historical form, equating itself with it and trying to exist in it abstractly! For we should then have to say of it that it is not Israel but Edom or Moab, that it is not the Church of Jesus Christ but the synagogue of Antichrist. This is the sword which always and everywhere hangs over the *ecclesia visibilis.* According to the will and in the power of the act of God, even in its visibility it can and should attest its invisible glory, i.e., the glory of the Lord justifying man and of man justified by the Lord. But it loses the ability to do this, it becomes unserviceable to the will and act of God, to the extent that in its visible being it wants to be something more and better than the witness of its invisible being, if it is content or indeed insists on representing and maintaining and asserting and communicating itself as a historical factor, taking itself and its doctrine and sacraments and sacramental observances and ordinances and spiritual authority and power in the more usual sense of the word to be the meaning of its existence, its greatness, its true and final word, in place of the underlying and overruling power of Jesus Christ and His Spirit. The question whether it does this has to be directed not only to the Papal Church and the other great world Churches, but no less seriously to even the smallest of Church groups, the modesty of whose external existence often seems to stand in strange relationship to the notorious arrogance of their claims. It is always and everywhere a living question, wherever the Church is and is therefore visible, in face of every cultus or law or confession or theology. Where the Holy Ghost is at work the step to visibility is unavoidable, but it is always and everywhere surrounded by this temptation. The third dimension from which this step is made must remain open. It can be made legitimately only when we remember that the men gathered into the community and acting as such still stand in need of the grace of God, i.e., of their invisible Lord and His invisible Spirit ; that it is He who controls the Church without in any sense being controlled by it.

Where and when does it not hang by a knife's edge whether or not there is this remembrance in the community ? If there is not, the Church not only becomes like the world, but denying its true secret it becomes especially worldly. Luther knew what he was talking about when he dared to say (*Pred. üb. Matth.* 28¹, 1531, *W.A.* 34¹, 276, 7) : *Non est tam magna peccatrix ut christiana ecclesia.* It is the Church which prays, "Forgive us our trespasses," which therefore knows and confesses that it needs the forgiveness of sins. It is always God's redemption of a sinful Church when it is aware of that denial of its secret and therefore of its extreme worldliness. We have to do with this redemption, or rather with this Redeemer, who alone can guarantee its hidden character, when we confess : *credo ecclesiam.*

No concrete form of the community can in itself and as such be the object of faith. Even the man Jesus as such, the *caro Christi*, cannot be this, just as the individual Christian cannot believe in his faith as a work. The community can believe in itself only when it believes in its Lord and therefore in what it is, in what it really is in its concrete form. The work magnifies the master. The visible attests the invisible. The glory of the community consists in the fact that it can give God the glory, and does not cease to do so. Its glory can appear only where there appears the glory of Jesus Christ and the sinner justified by Him. But as long as time endures, until the final manifestation of God and man in the future of Jesus Christ, the place where this takes place is hidden in its concrete form, with which it is only indirectly and not directly identical. For that reason this occurrence must be believed in the concrete form of the history which is visible to all.

It is worth noting that even in the *Cat. Rom.* (I, 10, 17–18) we find this expressly recognised : *Cum igitur hic articulus (sc. de ecclesia) intelligentiae nostrae facultatem et vires superet, iure optimo confitemur, nos ecclesiae ortum, munera et dignitatem non humana ratione cognoscere, sed fidei oculis cernere. . . . Neque enim homines huius ecclesiae auctores fuerunt, sed Deus ipse immortalis. . . . Nec potestas, quam accedit, humana est, sed divino munere tributa. Quare, quemadmodum naturae viribus comparari non potest, ita etiam fide solum intelligimus, in ecclesia claves caelorum esse eique potestatem peccata remittendi, excommunicandi verumque Christi corpus consecrandi traditam.* For the moment we may leave it open whether excommunication is one of the most important functions of the Church, or whether the consecration of the true body of Christ is one of its functions at all. What matters is that *in thesi* it is maintained : *fide solum intelligimus.*

If only there were something corresponding to this in the encyclical of Pius XII, " *Mystici Corporis* " (1943), which is normative for the modern Romanist view ! But instead of that it does not even speak of the necessity of faith in the Church, and in the decisive explanation of the term *Mysticum corpus* (Herder edit., 1947, p. 60 f.), although we do not find a conceptual equation, we have what amounts to the same thing, an unconditional identification of the mystery of the Church as created and maintained and ruled by Christ through the Holy Spirit with its historical action and judicial organisation. It is the Holy Spirit who exalts the Christian above all other communities and every natural order. Its external structure is a very secondary matter (*aliquid inferioris omnino ordinis*) (p. 64). But since it derives directly from Jesus Christ, even the visible and organised Church is a *societas perfecta* (p. 66). Between it and the invisible Church of the Spirit and love there is no antithesis worth mentioning : *nulla veri nominis oppositio vel repugnantia.* What is visible in the Church as human weakness is not the fault of its constitution but of the deplorable evil disposition of individuals (the *lamentabilis singulorum ad malum proclivitas*)—a weakness which its divine author knows how to handle for the best and with supreme wisdom even though it may be found in higher placed members of the body. Of the Church as such it can be finally confessed with triumph : " Without any fault at all (*utique absque ulla labe*) the pious mother shines forth in the sacraments by which her children are borne and nourished, in the faith which she has always kept inviolate, in the most holy laws to which she engages all, and in the evangelical counsels which she gives, finally in the heavenly gifts and graces by which she produces with inexhaustible fertility whole hosts of martyrs, virgins and confessors. We cannot make it a matter of reproach to her if some of her members are sick or wounded. In their name she makes her daily prayer to God : ' Forgive us our trespasses,' and with the strong heart of a mother she makes their spiritual nurture her unceasing concern " (p. 68 f.). Note that it is in the name of individual offenders among its members that it makes the petition mentioned by Luther. When it does this there is no question of praying in its own name and therefore of acknowledging itself *ecclesia peccatrix*. It itself is always right in everything. What the Church is is not hidden. It does not need to be believed. It can be directly deduced from what the Church is and does as the visible Church, from the excellence of its existence as it may be seen by all. But why call it " mystical " if it can be perceived directly without any difficulty ? We must not overlook the fact that within modern Roman Catholicism there are those who think and speak of the Church in a way which is very different and which seems to give fresh life to the *fide solum intelligimus*, cf. the stimulating writings of H. U. v. Balthasar (*Geschleifte Bastionen*) and F. Heer (*Das Experiment Europa*). But for the moment it is hard to see how there can be any further discussion with the official Roman Catholic doctrine of the Church when it so obviously continues to harden in this way.

Looking forward once more to the second part of the doctrine of reconciliation, we emphasise the fact that if the *credo ecclesiam* contains within it a critical caveat in face of its whole earthly and historical form, if it sets it in question, it does not negate it so that there can be no question of an escape into invisibility. On the contrary, if this reservation is taken seriously as such, then we are both challenged and permitted not to burk but resolutely to take the unavoidable step into visibility. *Credo ecclesiam* then means that the Church can take itself seriously in the world of the earthly and visible, with all humility but also with all comfort, at once directed and established by its third dimension. According to its best knowledge and conscience, it can and should create the forms which are indispensable to it as the human society which it essentially is, the forms which are best adapted to its edification and the discharge of its mission. It can and should think and discuss and decide with the necessary prudence and boldness concerning such things as canon, dogma, constitution, order and cultus. In its great hours it has always rightly done this and will continue to do so. It must do it in faith and obedience. It has to remember that it is not itself God but is responsible to God, that it does not have the last word. But with this reservation in relation to itself, with a con-sciousness of the relativity of its decisions, their provisional nature, their need of constant reform, standing under and not over the Word it can go to work with quiet determination, accepting the risk, but with the courage and authority of faith and obedience, and therefore without the false affectation which in order not to do anything ques-tionable will never do anything at all, which in every conditional assertion scents an attempt at the unconditional, which out of a simple fear of hardening, orthodoxy, authoritarianism and hierarchy can never get past the stage of questioning and protesting (as though in the last resort formlessness and therefore chaos is the condition which is best pleasing to God). If the Church has a good conscience in its relation to the " Jerusalem which is above, which is the mother of us all " (Gal. 4²⁶), and therefore to its basis in God, and therefore to itself, it will find it all the more humble and appropriate to give itself to the task of earthly and historical ordering in every form, instead of trying to imitate the unconditioned nature of God by refusing the conditions which are indispensable to its community and its service in earth. If it lives also and primarily in its third dimension, it can and should act confidently on the level of its phenomenal being. If the Church continues in the humility of its Lord and therefore in respect for His and its own secret, then the sword of rejection which hangs over all Church life is the protective sword of its election and calling. It lives by the awakening power of the Holy Spirit. In the world it can never be anything other than an *église du désert*, anything better than a " moving tent " like the biblical tabernacle. But it does live by the awakening power of the Holy Spirit. It is called to tarry for Him and to obey Him. The Church which does this seriously will in the long run prove to be the best Church even in the visibility of history.

But what is this being of the community, this spiritual character, this secret, which is hidden in its earthly and historical form and therefore invisible, or visible only to the special perception of faith ? The answer—which does indeed point to a third dimension—can only be this : The community is the earthly-historical form of existence of Jesus Christ Himself. The time has now come to adopt the New Testament term used to describe this matter. The Church is His body, created and continually renewed by the awakening power of the Holy Spirit. Jesus Christ also lives as the Crucified and Risen in a heavenly-historical form of existence ; at the right hand of the Father, before whom He is the advocate and intercessor for all men as the Judge who was judged in their place, the One who was obedient for them all, their justification. But He does not live only and exclusively in this form, enclosed within it. He does not live only above human history on earth, addressing Himself to it only from above and from afar and from without. He Himself lives in a special element of this history created and controlled by Him. He therefore lives in an earthly-historical form of existence within it. This particular element of human history, this earthly-historical form of existence of Jesus Christ, is the Christian community. He is the Head of this body, the community. And it is the body which has its Head in Him. It belongs to Him, and He belongs to it. We can put it even more strongly : Because He is, it is ; it is, because He is. That is its secret, its being in the third dimension, which is visible only to faith.

But because He is its Head, the Christian community which is His body is the gathering of those men whom already before all others He has made willing and ready for life under the divine verdict executed in His death and revealed in His resurrection from the dead. This is the creation of the body by its Head, of the body with which He coexists as the Head and which co-exists with Him as its Head, which as the body is the earthly-historical form of existence of the Head. What distinguishes the men united in the community and therefore the community itself is that they acknowledge what has been done from God by Him, the Lord who became a servant, not only for them but for all men ; that they recognise as such the One who is not only their Lord but the Lord of the whole world ; and that they confess Him with their life. The verdict of God pronounced in Him not only on them but on the whole world is accepted by them and in force. It has found in them open ears and a ready heart. Ultimately the community will not be alone in this. Rather, " at the name of Jesus every knee shall bow, of things in heaven and things in earth, and things under the earth ; and that every tongue should confess that Jesus Christ is Lord, to the glory of God the Father " (Phil. 2[10f.]). But this will not take place in the continuity of earthly history, but in its breaking off, in the end and goal of all time as brought about by God the Father (again in the—general—revelation of Jesus Christ). That will be the irruption of the other side of all human history. What distinguishes the community is that there is already revealed to it in faith that which as it concerns all will then be revealed to all. It realises, it sees and acknowledges and confesses " already before all others " what has been done for all in Jesus Christ, and what, as it has been done for all, will be seen and acknowledged and confessed by all when He appears as the Judge of the quick and the dead. It exists already before all others in the light of Easter Day as the dawning of the Last Day—already, i.e., within the as yet unbroken continuity of earthly history. It exists eschatologically, i.e., in correspondence with the " already " of Easter Day, which was the dawning of the Last Day within earthly history. In this existence which looks back to Easter Day and forward to the Last Day the community belongs together with the living Lord Jesus Christ Himself because He belongs together with it, because this its existence is the earthly-historical form of His existence. As it subjects itself to the divine sentence pronounced in Him, it lives with Him as His people, His fellowship, His community, in this choice and decision and work. The only thing is that of all other human choices and decisions and works this particular choice and decision and work does not arise spontaneously from the spirit of the men united in it, but from their awakening by the Holy Spirit. Its basis and truth and continuance are therefore in the choice and decision, the work and the living Word of Jesus Christ Himself. Thus in the particular activity which distinguishes it as His community in the world it does not belong to itself, but to Him; it does not live of itself, but can only follow the movement of His life; it has not to present and maintain and carry through to success its own cause, but (notwithstanding all the humanity, all the corruption and lostness which characterise the men united in it) can reflect and illustrate and in that way attest in its own activity His activity. The people which has not assumed and cannot assume or continue, but to which it is given and of which it is and will be demanded, to do this, is the Christian community. It believes that it is this people when it confesses : *credo ecclesiam*. And that it undeniably is and will be and continually becomes this in its concrete form—for its faith is not empty, but faith in Jesus Christ—is the secret of Church history, which cannot be destroyed by the " medley of error and force " which it may also appear to be, but which shines out in world history only by its own power, and can therefore be perceived only by the faith which sees it shine in this power and is itself awakened by it.

We must now explain briefly the remarkable New Testament expression σῶμα Χριστοῦ. And first it will be as well to try to survey together the different meanings within which the word σῶμα oscillates. To understand the New Testament usage we must not forget that in the first instance it means a dead body, a corpse. But in relation to the human body it also means the living body, either as contrasted with the soul, or with its individual parts, the members, or even with the blood in which it has its life (as in the texts relating to the

Lord's Supper). From this we may conclude that σῶμα is the seat of the earthly-historical life, so that being in it can indicate the time of man's being on earth, and the σῶμα in which he lives the limitation of that time. But σῶμα is also the medium of man's experience and suffering, the organ or instrument of his activity. We must also not forget that (in Rev. 18¹³) it can indicate the bodily possession, or slave, and (in Col. 2¹⁷) the body which throws a shadow in distinction from the shadow. In the sequence Χριστός-σῶμα-ἐκκλησία the word σῶμα can have all these different meanings with greater or lesser pregnancy.

We will start with the main passage, 1 Cor. 12¹². Here primarily we have to note that in the first instance it is not the community which is called a body, or compared to it, but Christ Himself. He is a body. By nature He is not simply one (for a body is the unity of many members), but one in many. It is not that σῶμα is a good image for the community as such, but that Jesus Christ is by nature σῶμα. Hence the force of Paul's argument in 1 Cor. 12⁴⁻³¹ for the necessity of the unity and plurality of gifts in the community (which, although they differ from another, are all gifts of the one Spirit). It is in the " bodily nature," in the simplicity and plurality of Jesus Christ Himself, that the Corinthians are able to recognise the necessary order, the relatedness and the freedom of their life as His community. From Him they are one as ἐκκλησία, that is to say, they are His body, and members of this body in the reception of the different gifts of the one Spirit granted to them : ὑμεῖς δέ ἐστε σῶμα Χριστοῦ καὶ μέλη ἐκ μέρους (1 Cor. 12²⁷). The community is not σῶμα because it is a social grouping which as such has something of the nature of an organism, which reminds us of an organism, which, *ceteris imparibus*, can therefore quite suitably be compared with it, which can be called a σῶμα. It is σῶμα because it actually derives from Jesus Christ, because of Him it exists as His body. The relationship to Him, or rather from Him, is everywhere evident : οἱ πολλοὶ ἐν σῶμά ἐσμεν ἐν Χριστῷ (Rom. 12⁵). He is the " Head " of this body, the centre which constitutes its unity, organises its plurality, and guarantees both (Col. 1¹⁸, Eph. 5²³). " From Him (ἐξ οὗ) all the body by joints and bands supported, and knit together, increaseth with the increase of God " (αὔξει τὴν αὔξησιν τοῦ θεοῦ, Col. 2¹⁹, Eph. 4¹⁶). The work of the ministry of the saints is for the edification of His body (Eph. 4¹²). " We are members of his body " (Eph. 5³⁰), and He is its Saviour (Eph. 5²³). Apart from Jesus Christ there is no other principle or *telos* to constitute and organise and guarantee this body. Even the *kerygma*, baptism, the Lord's Supper, the faith and love and hope of Christians, the work and word of the apostle, cannot have this function. It is the function of Jesus Christ alone. As the Head He is Himself and primarily the body, and He constitutes and organises and guarantees the community as His body.

He does this as the One who was crucified on Golgotha. Of course as the One crucified there He was raised again on the third day and is therefore able to act. All the same, to understand who it is that acts, we must first think of the meaning of σῶμα as a dead body or corpse, as in Rom. 7⁴ : " Ye also are become dead to the law by the body of Christ," or, again, Col. 3¹⁵ : " Ye are called to peace in one body " (His), or Col. 1²² : " He hath reconciled us in the body of his flesh through death," " by the cross " (Eph. 2¹⁶), or 1 Pet. 2²⁴ : " He bare our sins in his own body on the tree," or Heb. 10¹⁰ : "We are sanctified through the offering of the body of Jesus Christ once for all." He lives and acts as the One who was put to death in the body, who offered up His earthly-historical existence, who was deprived of it, who in His body delivered up to death, bore and bore away " the body of sin " (Rom. 6⁶), the " body of the flesh " (Col. 2¹¹), the " body of this death " (Rom. 7²⁴). In Him it was all humanity in its corruption and lostness, its earthly-historical existence under the determination of the fall, which was judged and executed and destroyed, and in that way liberated for a new determination, for its being as a new humanity. It was the body of everyman which became a corpse in Him and was buried as a corpse with Him. All men, " Jew and Greek, bond and free, male and female," as they are now representatively gathered in the community, were one in God's election (Eph. 1⁴), were and are one in the fulfilment of it on Golgotha, are one in the power of His resurrection, one in Jesus Christ (εἶς, Gal. 3²⁸), His body together in their unity and totality.

This is revealed in His resurrection from the dead, in the light of which it can and must be said to the community : " Ye are the body of Christ " (1 Cor. 12²⁷). In His risen body the sinful, fleshly humanity which had fallen a prey to death and had been destroyed in Him is awakened to being in a new right and life. " The body without the spirit is dead " (Jas. 2²⁶). Without the Holy Spirit the body of Jesus Christ and in it all humanity can only be dead. But the body of Jesus Christ was not a body abandoned by the Holy Spirit. The Holy Spirit has shown Himself to it as the life-giving Spirit. The body of this One who was slain has become a body which is alive by the Spirit : σῶμα πνευματικόν, 1 Cor. 15⁴⁴). During the forty days He appeared to His disciples in this body. He, the one man Jesus of Nazareth, who had been raised from the dead—that is the concrete history of the forty days. But not He alone, abstractly as this one man, just as He had not died alone, abstractly as this one man. But the one man who as their Representative and the Representative of all men, the bearer of their sin and flesh and death, had delivered all this up to the past in His death, dying on the cross—this one man now appeared to His disciples (in their own person first and then of all humanity) as the bearer of their new right and life, and as such the Revealer of their future, Himself in His person, in His body, the promised πνεῦμα ζωοποιοῦν, which is His remarkable title as the " last Adam " (1 Cor. 15⁴⁵). The content of Easter Day and the Easter season consisted in this, not in an " attesting miracle," not merely in a parthenogenesis of the Christian faith, but in the appearance of the body of Jesus Christ, which embraced their death in its death, their life in its life, their past and their future in itself, thus including them all in itself. As He encountered them in this corporeity, the disciples heard addressed to themselves as such, to the ἐκκλησία which arose in virtue of it, the call which is the disclosure of the secret of His earthly-historical existence : " Ye are the body of Christ."

Therefore the mystery of the community is not in the first instance its own. In the first instance it is His mystery : the mystery of His death in which He was this Victor ; the mystery of His resurrection in which He was this Revealer. In His body He is elected, called and instituted from all eternity as this Victor and Revealer. It is His body which includes them all to their salvation and the salvation of the world. Because it includes them, it is their body and they are His body. In Him they themselves have turned away from sin and flesh and death as their past and have turned to the right and life as their future. His mystery is theirs. Having been given life by the Spirit, and Himself a life-giving Spirit, He has made it known to them—His election and birth and calling and institution as their Head and the Head of all men, His earthly-historical existence as that of their Representative and Substitute and Advocate, and there-fore as the truth of their own earthly-historical existence. He is always the Head of this body. He is the giver and they are the recipients. He is the Master and they are the brethren (Mt. 23⁸). He is the vine and they are the branches (Jn. 15⁵). " Without me ye can do nothing "—you cannot be my body, you cannot be a body at all. For only He, Jesus Christ, the " last Adam," is the unity in plurality of humanity which the first Adam could only prefigure. He alone can be the Head of a body which includes them all—so that if they are to be a body, they can only be His body.

The mystery of the community is not in the first instance its own mystery in the further sense that its Head Jesus Christ was elected the Head of all human-ity (as the last and true Adam, 1 Cor. 15⁴⁵f.), that He was made the one Mediator between God and all men (1 Tim. 2⁵), that He died for the sins of the whole

2. The Being of the Community 665

world (1 Jn. 2²), and that He rose again as the Revealer of the right and life of all men (1 Cor. 15²¹ᶠ·). The New Testament never expressly uses the term body of humanity as a whole, of the totality of Jews and Greeks, slaves and free men, males and females. It uses it only of the Christian community. For only in this community is there a dispensing and eating of the bread which is broken in common. Only in it is there the visible fellowship (κοινωνία) of this body, the perceiving and attesting of His real presence, the recognisable and recognised union of a concrete human fellowship with Him (1 Cor. 10¹⁶). ὅτι εἷς ἄρτος : " Because it is the one bread which the many break and eat (together) " —ἕν σῶμα οἱ πολλοί ἐσμεν : " we, the many, are one body "—οἱ γὰρ πάντες ἐκ τοῦ ἑνὸς ἄρτου μετέχομεν : " for we are all partakers of the one bread " (1 Cor. 10¹⁷). Their communion with one another, their common action in remembrance of Him, their common proclamation of the death of the Lord until He comes (1 Cor. 11²⁶), as it takes place in this action, does not create and put into effect their union with Jesus Christ—which is unnecessary ; it reveals and publishes and documents that union, it is that union in concreto, as the earthly-historical activity and experience of these particular men. Where there is not this communion, we cannot speak with the New Testament of a union of men with Jesus Christ and therefore of a real presence of His body. To that extent the expression σῶμα Χριστοῦ is in the New Testament an esoteric expression. The reality indicated by it is to be seen only in the concrete life of the community. A saying like 1 Cor. 12²⁷ (" Ye are the body of Christ, and members in particular ") is obviously not a part of missionary preaching. It is clearly a kind of repetition of the call which in the forty days was not directly addressed to humanity as a whole but to the few whom the risen One encountered. But it is open to question whether the same can be true of the saying in 1 Cor. 12¹² in which Jesus Christ Himself is called a body. For how can we proclaim His death and resurrection to Jews and Gentiles as their own death and the promise of their right and life without proclaiming Him as the Head and Representative and Mediator of all men, the " last Adam " ? And how can we do that without approximating very closely to the concept of the body of Christ including and uniting all men ? That logic drives us in this direction is something we have to remember for an understanding of the being and mission of the community. As σῶμα Χριστοῦ it is not an end in itself. In the first instance and originally Jesus Christ as the Head is the one body visible in the bread, and the community only because He is this one body and calls it to be and makes it a unity. Similarly, the community itself, participating in the bread, is only the arrow which points to that unity of the many which is grounded and—although hidden—actual in the fact that He is the Mediator and Substitute and Representative of all men. How can it be the body of this Head if it tries to be a house with closed doors and windows, if it tries to exist like a ghetto, if as the body of Christ it wants to be defined by its own limits ? If it has a right understanding of itself in its common breaking and eating of the one bread and therefore in its concrete life as a community, then as the body of Christ it has to understand itself as a promise of the emergence of the unity in which not only Christians but all men are already comprehended in Jesus Christ. The great truth of Eph. 1²³ can never be forgotten but must always shine out in it. As His body it is " the fulness of him that filleth all in all." And the same is true of Eph. 1⁹ᶠ· : God has " made known unto us the mystery of his will, according to his free resolve purposed in himself and to be accomplished in the fulness of times ἀνακεφαλαιώσασθαι τὰ πάντα : to give to all things their head in Christ—to all things, both which are in heaven, and which are on earth, in him, in whom also we have obtained an inheritance, being predestinated according to the purpose of him who worketh all things after the counsel of his own will, that we should be to the praise of his glory, who already have our hope in him " (προηλπικότες, lit. those who have hoped before in Him).

This is the Magna Carta of the being of the community in Him. We do not decrease but bring out its true glory if we understand the exclusiveness in which it is called and is His body in the world as an exclusiveness which is relative, provisional and teleological. Sayings like Col. 1^{18}, ^{24}: "The church is his body," or, conversely, Eph. 1^{23}: "His body is the church," or Rom. 12^5, in which the many are one body in Him, or the direct statement in Eph. 5^{30} that "we are members of his body," speak of the glory of the being of the community in so far as they speak properly of the glory of Jesus Christ Himself and therefore of the σωτὴρ τοῦ κόσμου (Jn. 4^{42}; 1 Jn. 4^{14}), of His being and work for the whole of humanity which is both one and many. In the first instance they are christological and therefore teleological statements, and only as such ecclesiological.

For that reason they do not provide any basis for the idea of a Church which exists *ipsa quasi altera Christi persona*, as fully proclaimed in the encyclical "*Mystici corporis*" (p. 54). There are not two or possibly three bodies of Christ : the historical, in which He died and rose again ; the mystical which is His community ; and that in which He is really present in the Lord's Supper. For there are not three Christs. There is only one Christ, and therefore there is only one body of Christ.

For the same reason there is no need to take the statements symbolically or metaphorically. As His earthly-historical form of existence, the community is His body, His body is the community. Why, and to what extent ? Because the community and those who belong to it have received the " manifestation of the Spirit" (1 Cor. 12^7) in the unity and diversity of His gifts (Rom. 12^6), because they have " drunk " with Him (1 Cor. 12^{13}) and therefore are free to confess Jesus as *Kyrios* (1 Cor. 12^3). To put the same thing in another way, because the Gospel once and still proclaimed to them has shown itself powerful and effective and fruitful to and in and among them, as described in the thanksgivings with which Paul opens a whole series of his letters. The equating of the body of Christ and the community is valid only with reference to this divine action, but it is unconditionally and actually valid with this reference. With this reference these sayings can be uttered with no less definiteness than the great christological statements concerning the death of Jesus Christ implying our death as it has already taken place in Him, and the resurrection of Jesus Christ implying our future resurrection. Here we have the invisible being of the community, the being which is visible only to faith. This is what permits and enjoins us to celebrate " thanksgiving " (εὐχαριστία) within it, to give thanks as Paul does for its existence. For in the community the truth of these christological statements, the justification of man as it has taken place in Jesus Christ, is known, in as much as Jesus Christ has shown His power and revealed and asserted Himself within it. For in Him " ye heard the word of truth, the gospel of your salvation ; in whom also after that ye believed, ye were sealed with that holy Spirit of promise, which is the earnest of our inheritance, until the redemption of the purchased possession, unto the praise of his glory " (Eph. $1^{13f.}$). With the foundation and preservation of the community this event actually takes place in the space and time of these men, in the sphere of their experience and activity, although it is an event which, according to 1 Cor. $2^{9, 14}$, cannot be brought about by any human experience or activity. In the light of this event, as the Spirit who raised up Jesus from the dead dwells within them (Rom. 8^{11}), the community can be referred to as the body of Christ, and its members as members of this body. In the light of this event its earthly-historical existence can be known as the earthly historical existence of Jesus Christ Himself (who, as its Head, is in heaven at the right hand of the Father), so that He can concretely ask the persecutor of the community (Ac. 9^4) : " Saul, Saul, why persecutest thou me ? ", and He can say no less definitely of that which is done (or not done) to the least of His brethren (Mt. 25^{40}, ^{45}) : " Ye have done it (or not done it) unto me." With reference to this event the equation of the body of

Christ and the community has itself to be described as a very secondary christological statement, but one which is of decisive practical importance for the time of the community in the world.

We must be clear that the community is not made the body of Christ or its members members of this body by this event, by the Spirit of Pentecost, by the fulness of His gifts, by the faith awakened by Him, by the visible, audible and tangible results of the preaching and receiving of the Gospel, let alone by baptism and the Lord's Supper (as so-called " sacraments "). It is the body, and its members are members of this body, in Jesus Christ, in His election from all eternity (Rom. 8[29], Eph. 1[4]). And it became His body, they became its members, in the fulfilment of their eternal election in His death on the cross of Golgotha, proclaimed in His resurrection from the dead. In this respect the insight of patristic tradition cited in " *Mystici Corporis* " (and combining Jn. 19[40] and Gen. 3[20]) is not only ingenious but substantially correct : *in cruce ecclesiam e latere salvatoris esse natam instar novae Evae matris omnium viventium* (p. 28). The only thing is that we at once have the usual encroachment when this " new " Eve is equated with the infallible teaching and ruling ecclesiastical institution (p. 32) which is focused on the papacy as the visible head of this Church in place of the invisible Christ (p. 40). There can be no doubt that the work of the Holy Spirit is merely to " realise subjectively " the election of Jesus Christ and His work as done and proclaimed in time, to reveal and bring it to men and women. By the work of the Holy Spirit the body of Christ, as it is by God's decree from all eternity and as it has become in virtue of His act in time, acquires in all its hiddenness historical dimensions. The Holy Spirit awakens the " poor praise on earth " appropriate to that eternal-temporal occurrence, the answer to the Easter message in the hearts and on the lips of individual men, faith and the one and varied recognition of obedience to the Son of God as the Head of all men. " Thou worthy Light, shine here below / Teach us our Saviour Christ to know / That we in Him alone may stand / Who brought us to our fatherland. *Kyrie eleis.*" It is the work of the Holy Spirit that the Lord does do this in His mercy, that He shines on men to give them this knowledge of Jesus Christ and themselves. And in this knowledge, in and with Jesus Christ, His body is known as His community, His community as His body. It is known because this union has already been created in that eternal and temporal happening. It is known in such a way that its being precedes the knowledge of it, and the knowledge of it can only follow its being.

Where the knowledge of it does follow its being, there the men who share this knowledge are necessarily called to it and claimed by it. The mystery of Jesus Christ is then in fact the mystery of their own existence. The Corinthians are necessarily summoned (1 Cor. 12[4-31]) not only to the preservation of their unity but also to the freedom of varied movements in the sphere of the one and manifold Spirit and His gift and gifts given to them : " God hath tempered the body together " (v. 24) ; " But now hath God set members every one of them in the body, as it hath pleased him " (v. 18) ; " But it is the same God which worketh all in all." If they confess Jesus Christ as Lord, which can only be by the Holy Spirit (v. 3), they confess themselves as His body, and therefore the necessity not to deny either the unity of the community or the diversity of its membership, not to suppress either but to maintain both. How they would misunderstand themselves as the community and its members, how they would misunderstand the one Spirit and His many gifts, if they were ever in danger of doing this, if they were ever tempted to it, if it became to them a source of self-will and arrogance and division! God does not tempt anyone (Jas. 1[13]) and neither does His Holy Spirit. Such dangers cannot derive from their being as the community of Jesus Christ. When they are awakened by the Holy Spirit, when they know Jesus Christ and in this knowledge are really in Him as He is in them, " in the midst " (Mt. 18[20]), then they are in the one bread which they break and eat together and in that way represent and attest both Him and themselves—His body as it was crucified on Good Friday and raised on Easter Day; then they are representatives and precursors of all the Jews and Greeks, the slaves and the free men, the males and the females who are many in Him and who are also one in Him. Their unity cannot jeopardise their plurality, nor their plurality their unity.

We are again reminded of the temporary, provisional and teleological character of this special being of the community as the body of Christ when we think of Jas. 1^{18} : " Of his own will begat he us with the word of truth, that we should be a kind of first-fruits ($\dot{a}\pi a \rho \chi \acute{\eta}$ $\tau\iota s$) of his creatures ; " or of 1 Pet. 2^9 : " Ye are a chosen generation, a royal priesthood, an holy nation, a people of possession ; that ye should proclaim the manifestations of power ($\dot{a}\rho\epsilon\tau a\acute{\iota}$) of him who hath called you out of darkness into his marvellous light ; " or finally of Mt. 5^{14} : " Ye are the light of the world," which stands in a similar relationship of apparent contradiction and real agreement to Jn. 8^{12} : " I am the light of the world," as does Paul's reference to the body which is the body of Christ and as such His community.

The concept the body of Christ necessarily comprehends the perception of the being of the community as visible in faith. It will now be our task to expound this perception in the form of an analysis of the four predicates given to the *ecclesia* in the Nic.-Const. creed (381) : *Una, sancta, catholica, apostolica*.

Credo unam ecclesiam. The Christian believes—and there is—only one Church. This means that it belongs to the being of the community to be a unity in the plurality of its members, i.e., of the individual believers assembled in it, and to be a simple unity, not having a second or third unity of the same kind side by side with it. The statement follows necessarily from all that we have seen concerning it. In all the riches of His divine being the God who reconciled the world with Himself in Jesus Christ is One. Jesus Christ, elected the Head of all men and as such their Representative who includes them all in Himself in His risen and crucified body is One. The Holy Spirit in the fulness and diversity of His gifts is One. In the same way His community as the gathering of the men who know and confess Him can only be one.

At this point we must quote word for word the passage in Eph. 4^{1-7}, because it says *in nuce* all that has to be said : " I therefore, the prisoner of the Lord, beseech you that ye walk worthy of the vocation wherewith ye are called, with all lowliness and meekness, with longsuffering, forbearing one another in love ; endeavouring to keep the unity of the Spirit in the bond of peace. There is one body, and one Spirit, even as ye are called in one hope of your calling ; one Lord, one faith, one baptism, one God and Father of all, who is above all, and through all, and in you all. But unto every one of us is given grace according to the measure of the gift of Christ." The limit within which there can be a real plurality among those who are addressed in this way is plain. It is the plurality of these individuals within the community, corresponding to the plurality in which they are elected and reconciled in Jesus Christ and called and endowed by His Spirit. In the event their calling and endowment follows their gathering to the equally real unity of His body. They are therefore included in it once and for all—with the absolute uniqueness of the Lord whom they all know and confess. That is how the matter is stated in 1 Cor. 12⁴⁻³¹ and Rom. 12³⁻⁸. In the New Testament there can be no question of a plurality of unities. The unity is a single unity. Otherwise it is not what the New Testament knows as the ἐκκλησία.

For this reason (1) the visible and the invisible Church are not two Churches—an earthly-historical fellowship and above and behind this a supra-naturally spiritual fellowship. As we have already seen, the one is the form and the other the mystery of one and the self-same Church. The mystery is hidden in the form, but represented and to be sought out in it. The visible lives wholly by the invisible. The invisible is only represented and to be sought out in the visible. But neither can be separated from the other. Both in their unity are the body, the earthly-historical form of existence of the one living Lord Jesus Christ.

For the same reason (2) the *ecclesia militans* and the *ecclesia triumphans* are not two Churches but one Church. In the one case, it is still gathered, and builds up itself and lives by its mission, both as a whole and in its members, to-day. In the other, it did so in past days or centuries, so that it already belongs to-day to the sphere of completion. But the dead no less than the living have a part in the " communion of saints." It is not only the living who speak and act, but their predecessors, their words and works, their history, which does not end on their departure, but on their departure often only enters its decisive stage among their successors, standing in an indissoluble relationship with the history of the present. Always and everywhere the Church exists in these two dimensions. We to-day, therefore, exist only as confronted not only with the persons and problems of to-day, but (whether we are aware of it or not) with the persons and problems of all Church history. The *ecclesia triumphans* is " with Christ " (Phil. 1²³). With Him, the Head of the body, it takes part in the glory which is still hidden from the *ecclesia militans*. But for this very reason it can never be far from it. Christ Himself is not far from it. As the heavenly Head of His whole body on earth He is in the midst of it. And with Him the *ecclesia triumphans* is also with it and in the midst of it. Actively and not merely passively engaged with it, it waits for the completion of the whole as the presupposition of every present. It impels it towards its completion. Conversely, in the *ecclesia triumphans* the *ecclesia militans* has, as it were, its spearhead in the sphere of completion, in which it already exists eschatologically. Therefore the Church which was and the Church which is are very concretely one Church. And the Church which will be will still be the one Church. " All live unto him " (Lk. 20³⁸) : not only on that side, but on this ; not only on this side, but on that. And because they live to Him, they are one community.

For the same reason (3) the people of Israel in its whole history *ante et post Christum* and the Christian Church as it came into being on the day of Pentecost are two forms and aspects (*CD* II, 2, § 34, 1) of the one inseparable community in which Jesus Christ has His earthly-historical form of existence, by which He is attested to the whole world, by which the whole world is summoned to faith in Him. For what the Christian Church is, Israel was and is before it—His possession (Jn. 1[11]), His body. He Himself in the one person is the crucified Messiah of Israel who as such is the secret Lord of the Church, the risen Lord of the Church who as such is the manifested Messiah of Israel. In its Old Testament form the community attests Him as the man elected and called by God who as such was invested with the sins of the whole world, and bore the judgment of God, and in this form of a servant was truly the Lord. In its New Testament form the community attests Him as the God electing and calling man, who has not given Himself in vain, but to have mercy on His own, to set him right, for him. In its form as Israel it attests the justification which begins strangely and terribly in the midst of a world of sin and death, its *terminus a quo*. In its form as the Church it attests its *terminus ad quem*, its strange and glorious consummation in a new world of right and life. On the one hand there is the promise, on the other its fulfilment. On the one hand there is the man who hears, on the other the man who believes. On the one hand there is the perishing form, on the other the form which comes. In its form as Israel the community is still identical with a nation. In the Church its mission as a community for the world is actualised in the fact that it gathers into itself not only Jews awakened to faith in their Messiah but Gentiles, i.e., men from all nations who believe in Him as the Saviour of the world. But how can we distinguish or separate except *a parte potiori* ? The man who suffers the judgment of God, the secret of the Old Testament history, is revealed as the faithful servant of God in the New. The God attested by the New Testament witnesses, the God who in His mercy creates right and life, is the God who was not concealed from the Old Testament witnesses. Does the Church no longer know the beginning of justification ? Did Israel not know of its consummation ? Was the promise empty for Israel because it was not fulfilled ? Now that it has been fulfilled, does the Church not need to hold with Abraham to the promise as such ? Has Israel heard without in any sense believing ? Is not the faith of the Church based on simple hearing ? As this chosen people, was not Israel potentially the Church for the world ? Is not the Christian world of Jews and Gentiles a little Israel within the nations which border it ? There are differences which we cannot overlook. We are dealing with two forms, two aspects, two " economies " of grace. But it is the one history, beginning there, having its centre in Jesus Christ, and here hastening to its culmination. It is the bow of the one covenant which stretches over the whole. It was therefore essential to the Church from the very beginning, and it always will be, to represent this unity in itself and to exist in it. That is why it has always read the Old Testament with the New, and the Old before the New, as the attestation of the one work and the one revelation of the one God. That is why, from the very first, it has thought of itself as the Church of Jews and Gentiles, and to that extent as the " Israel of God " (Gal. 6¹⁶), as " all Israel " (Rom. 11²⁶). To try to deny this unity would be to deny Jesus Christ Himself.

Where the Church has taken Rom. 9–11 seriously, it has not been able to escape or explain away the fact that its unity in this sense is compromised by the existence of a Judaism which does not believe in Jesus Christ. More than anything else, this makes its own existence problematical. For it belongs to its nature and situation as the community in the world to be separated from all kinds of religions and religious communities. Its very aim as a missionary community is to call men out of these, to call them from false gods to the true God. But this being the case, the existence of the Synagogue side by side with the Church is an ontological impossibility, a wound, a gaping hole in the body of Christ, something which is quite intolerable. For what does the Church have which the Synagogue does not also have, and long before it (Rom. 9⁴⁻⁵)—especially Jesus Christ Himself, who is of the Jews, who is the Jewish Messiah, and only as such the Lord of the Church ? The decisive question is not what the Jewish Synagogue can be without Him, but what the Church is as long as it confronts an alien and hostile Israel ? " Jewish Missions " is not the right word for the call to remove this breach, a call which must go out unceasingly from the Church to these brethren who do not yet know their unity with it—a unity which does not have to be established but is already there ontologically, who will not accept what they already are, and what they were long before us poor Gentiles. And what a dreadful thing when the Church itself has so little understood its own nature that it has not only withheld this knowledge from its brethren but made it difficult if not impossible for them ! *Credo unam ecclesiam ?* This confession gives rise to other and very difficult questions. But here in the so-called Jewish question we face the deepest obscurity which surrounds it. The Jewish question ? If Paul is right, then in the light and context of that confession it is really the Christian question.

Because the community is a single unity we have to say finally (4) that we can legitimately speak of historically existent Christian " Churches " in the plural only with reference to the geographically separated and therefore different congregations. We must not forget that it is in the concrete event of its gathering that the community has its invisible and also its visible being, that it is the earthly-historical *communio sanctorum*, that the Lord Himself is in the midst of it by His Spirit, that it is His own earthly-historical form of existence, that it lives as the body of which He is the Head. If this gathering takes place there as well as here, if in essential accordance with its commission it has to take place in many localities, it is also essential to it that in its unity it should exist in this geographical separation and difference : a difference which corresponds to its environment and history and language and customs and ways of life and thought as conditioned by the different localities, and also to its personal composition. In this respect the same thing does not suit every Church or every place and time. This has never been taken seriously enough in our missionary thinking. But it can, of course, be taken too seriously, as has often happened. The local presuppositions and conditions of a Christian community cannot have the significance and function of factors which underlie and therefore actually separate the Churches, nor should they be thought of in this way. The local community, with its local characteristics, cannot be basically and essentially another community in relation to others. Each in its own place can only be the one community beside which there are no others. Each in and for itself and with its local characteristics can only be the whole, as others are in their own locality.

The New Testament plural ἐκκλησίαι does not speak of a plurality of Churches genuinely and radically different from each other. It is one and the same community, separated only by geographical distance and what it involves. This one community is grounded in the same Gospel, and awakened and maintained and ruled by the same Spirit, although as the community of the same Lord it exists at one and the same time in Thessalonica, Galatia, Corinth and Rome. Whatever we may understand by the seven Churches of Asia Minor with their seven angels (Rev. 2–3), none of them has its own Lord or Spirit or Gospel. Each of these individual communities in relation to the concrete event of its gathering is called and trusted and expected by the One who is over them all to be the community of the Lord in its own locality, immediately and directly in the fulness of the gifts and the corresponding responsibility given to it. It was on this presupposition that Paul addressed the communities founded or otherwise commissioned by him. It was in this sense—and only in this sense—that the Reformers could occasionally speak of the " Churches " (as in the first words of the *Confession of Augsburg* : *ecclesiae magno consensu apud nos docent.*)

Each community has its own locality, its own environment, tradition, language, etc. But in that locality, as established and appointed by the Lord of all the communities, it should be the one complete community. It should take itself seriously as such, and know that it is responsible as such. When this is the case, then geographical distance and difference cannot give rise to any genuine or essential difference or distance, but the community in one place can and must and will recognise itself in the community of another, and *vice versa*. The unity of the community will then be mutually attested and affirmed in spite of the differences. Everywhere the edification and ministry and mission and confession will be unanimous. But this unity, and mutual recognition in this unity, the *magnus consensus* of the *ecclesiae*, can be basically and necessarily and infallibly and unconditionally guaranteed only by the fact that each community is individually founded by the one Lord of all the communities, and that, founded in Him in obedience to His Spirit, it is continually ruled by Him. All human mediation of this unity, all the mutual understanding and agreement and co-ordination between the individual members, can only be a free human service. It cannot supply, let alone create, the guarantee of unity, the mutual recognition of the individual communities. This does not mean that the existence of a particular organ of mediation, an institution which demands and maintains the oneness of the locally separated communities, is completely impossible. What it does mean is that such an organ or institution is not an integral constituent of the essence of the Church. The one Church does not exist either in an ideal or in an organised or organising totality to which the individual communities stand in the relationship of participating Churches (like the digits in a figure or the notes in a chord). The one Church exists in its totality in each of the individual communities.

It is evident that even in New Testament days there were some helpful and serious human links between the Churches. The mutual ἀσπάζεσθαι which there was according to the letters of Paul was hardly a mere formality. Individuals seem often to have been on the way between them. Above all, of course, we have to think of the ministry of the apostles which had precedence over them all and was more or less respected by them all. What we do not find in the New Testament is the existence of what might truly be called a Church government which is superior to the individual communities and the external guarantee of their unity as the community of Jesus Christ.

The discussion in Ac. 15 between Paul and Barnabas as the delegates of the community in Syrian Antioch and the "apostles and elders" in Jerusalem has often been described as an Apostolic Council. Was this, then, the beginning of the synodal direction of the Church ? But the result of it was not a decree or dogma conjointly accepted by this assembly, but the consolation which, according to v. 31, was sent by the believers of Jerusalem to their brethren at Antioch. And the incident as a whole did not involve the appearance of an institution, but the *ad hoc* introduction and execution of an act, the practical result of which was accorded only a partial and occasional respect. What can be gathered from this passage (as from 2 Cor. 8–9) is that in relation to the other and later communities that at Jerusalem occupied a position of peculiar dignity at any rate up to A.D. 70. But there can be no question of the others being ruled through it or by it.

As far as the apostolate of Paul is concerned, it is plain from his Epistles that his relationship to the communities was definitely not that of a universal bishop. If he had adopted towards them an attitude veering in this direction, this would have appeared, e.g., in 1 Cor. 1 and 3 in his reaction to the parties at Corinth. He would not have put his own group on the same level as that of Apollos and the others, but singled out their views as normal because those of the whole Church. And from the fact that he had " planted " in Corinth, whereas Apollos had only " watered " (1 Cor. 3⁶), he would have deduced the clear precedence of his own work over that of the other teacher. But in vv. 7–8 he calmly says : " So then neither is he that planteth anything, neither he that watereth ; but God that giveth the increase. Now he that planteth and he that watereth are one : and every man shall receive his own reward according to his own labour. For we are labourers together with God : ye are God's husbandry, ye are God's building." None of this smacks of the hierarchical guaranteeing of the unity of the Church. Naturally Paul came to the communities with a higher authority—but with that of the servant and, as a called apostle, of the unique and not the institutional servant of Jesus Christ. With this unique apostolic authority he speaks like the other first and direct witnesses to the Church of every age. But as, according to Gal. 1¹, he had received it " not of men, neither by man, but by Jesus Christ," so he exercises it simply in the fact that he makes the authority of Jesus Christ visible and audible in the Churches. He teaches and warns and beseeches " in Christ's stead " (2 Cor. 5²⁰). He does not rule in His place. He is not His vicar. His place is in the διακονία τῆς καταλλαγῆς (2 Cor. 5¹⁸). We are again reminded of the way in which the unity of the Church is proclaimed in the great passage in Eph. 4¹ᶠ· If this is the word of a Deutero-Paul, he has understood the apostle in a remarkable way. And the saying in 2 Cor. 1[24] is unquestionably Pauline : " Nor for that we have dominion over your faith, but are helpers of your joy "—and this to the community at Corinth, which—we might think—had such bitter need of an earthly lord over their faith to represent the heavenly Lord and the whole Church. Neither here nor anywhere else does Paul place himself over his community. Even where he speaks most definitely he places himself alongside it, questioning, arguing, beseeching, even pleading and imploring. Or rather, he places himself within it. We never find him playing the role of a superior even in relation to the heads of the individual communities, who in any case are not very often mentioned (cf. Rom. 12[8], Phil. 1[1]).

Strangely enough, it is even more difficult to show that Peter (cf. O. Cullmann, *Petrus*, 1952, p. 251 f.) exercised any total rule over the individual communities. From the very first he assumed a position of leadership among the disciples. He had had a special part in the resurrection appearances. In the first days he was the leader of the Church in Jerusalem. But then he gave up this position to James, the Lord's brother, at the time (why ?) when Jerusalem ceased to be the only Christian community. In subordination to James he then seems to have headed the mission to the Jews. On the basis of later sources it seems tenable that he finally came to Rome (why ?) and that he died there as a martyr. But if we are not to put too much credence in later reports, it cannot be proved that he was ever the Bishop of Rome, and even if he was, it cannot be proved that as such he had a function in relation to the whole Church.

It certainly cannot be maintained that the existence of a synodal or episcopal organ to guarantee the unity of the communities is essential to the New Testament idea of the Church, even if the texts do not record all the actual and perhaps very strong connexions which did exist in New Testament days. If these connexions did exist in any form, and if their organs (if there were any) were of great practical value for mutual correlation and co-ordination, it is still obviously the case that no one thought of them as basically indispensable for founding and maintaining the unity of the communities, that no one, therefore, thought of them as necessary to salvation, that no one ascribed to them either infallible authority or unconditional efficacy. Rather, those who proclaimed the authority of Jesus Christ pointed to Him and His Spirit as the creator and guarantee of their unity (even of their unity one with another)—confident that fundamentally He was a sufficient guarantee in the matter, and presupposing that there could not be any other beside Him. Our own decision will have to be the same in relation to it.

As far as the correlation and co-ordination of individual communities is concerned, love and prudence may prove many things to be necessary by way of service in this matter of unity. But that is another matter, as is also the question what possible forms of Church government must be considered and which is relatively the best. We will return to these items in the second and third parts of the doctrine of reconciliation, when we have to consider the building up and the mission of the community. But our present question is the gathering of the community by the Holy Spirit, the one single being of the one single community. And we can name only one authority which is fundamentally indispensable, necessary to salvation, infallible and unconditionally effective to guarantee its existence as such in the geographically separate communities : the Lord who attests Himself in the prophetic and apostolic word, who is active by His Spirit, who as the Spirit has promised to be in the midst of every community gathered by Him and in His name. He rules the Church and therefore the Churches. He is the basis and guarantee of their unity.

We cannot name any other legitimate plurality of Churches, one which does not destroy but affirms their unity, other than those which we have mentioned already, the visible and the invisible, the militant and the triumphant Church, Israel and the Christian community, and the local congregations. Any other plurality means the co-existence of Churches which are genuinely divided. That is, in the event of their gathering, and therefore by their basis and invisible being, in their faith, although they all regard it as the Christian faith, they are so different from one another and confront one another as such strangers that they cannot recognise and acknowledge one another, at any rate seriously, as the community of Jesus Christ. At best they will be able kindly to tolerate one another as believing differently, and at worst they will fight against one another, mutually excluding each other with some definiteness and force. The existence of this kind of plurality of " Churches " is in conflict with both Eph. 4 and the *credo unam ecclesiam*. Under no head and in no sense can it be regarded as legitimate. Certainly it is possible to understand and explain historically the separation and opposition of such Churches. Certainly in the sphere of state and society their co-existence and opposition can be made tolerable for participants and non-participants alike with the assistance or under the supremacy of the doctrine of toleration. Certainly it can be stabilised and canalised in terms of practical law. Certainly among the more enlightened on both sides, or perhaps with some depth even among a majority of those who believe differently, there may arise a tacit or to some extent perhaps even an explicit agreement as to the relative and temporary nature of the opposition, with more or less radical glimpses of a unity which is already present in some point of convergence. It may also be that for good reasons or bad the consciousness of existing differences becomes blunted in whole groups of Churches, so that they become an external factor without internal necessity. There is no justification theological, spiritual or biblical for the existence of a plurality of Churches genuinely separated in this way and mutually excluding one another internally and therefore externally. A plurality of Churches in this sense means a plurality of lords, a plurality of spirits, a plurality of gods. There is no doubt that to the extent that Christendom does consist of actually different and opposing Churches, to that extent it denies practically what it confesses theoretically—the unity and the singularity of God, of Jesus Christ, of the Holy Spirit. There may be good grounds for the rise of these divisions. There may be serious obstacles to their removal. There may be many things which can be said by way of interpretation and mitigation. But this does not alter the fact that every division as such is a deep riddle, a scandal. And in face of this scandal the whole of Christendom should be united in being able to think of it only with penitence, not with the penitence which each expects of the other, but with the penitence in which—whatever may be the cost—each is willing to precede the other. If a man can acquiesce in divisions, if he can even take pleasure in them, if he can be complacent in relation to the obvious faults and errors of others and therefore his own responsibility for them, then that man may be a good and loyal confessor in the sense of his own particular denomination, he may be a good Roman Catholic or Reformed or Orthodox or Baptist, but he must not imagine that he is a good Christian. He has not honestly and seriously believed and known and confessed the *una ecclesia*. For the *una ecclesia* cannot exist if there is a second or third side by side with or opposed to it. It cannot exist in opposition to another Church. It cannot be one among many.

It is an impossible situation that whole groups of Christian communities should exhibit a certain external and internal unity among themselves and yet stand in relation to other groups of equally Christian communities in an attitude more or less of exclusion. It is an impossible situation that such groups should confront each other in such a way that their confession and preaching and theology are mutually contradictory, that what is revelation here is called error there, that what is heresy here is taught and reverenced as dogma there, that the order and cultus and perhaps the ethics of the one should be found and called strange and alien and unacceptable and perhaps even reprehensible by the other, that the adherents of the one should be able to work together with those of the other in every possible secular cause, but not to pray together, not to preach and hear the Word of God together, not to keep the Lord's Supper together. It is an impossible situation that either tacitly or expressly, with an open severity or a gentler friendliness, the one should say to the other, or, in fact, give it to be understood, or at any rate think of the other : You have another Spirit ; You are not within but without ; You are not what you presumptuously call yourselves, the community of Jesus Christ.

We have to recall the effects of this disunity on the mission fields of Asia and Africa, in the face of Islam and Buddhism. But we have also to recall its effects on the so-called home fields of the Christian Church which were evangelised a thousand years ago and more, where with the dispelling of the mediæval illusion of a Christian West the Church is mercilessly confronted—in all its disunity— with the tremendous alienation of the baptised masses from the Gospel. We have to think of the Church's difficulty in being impressively and credibly and convincingly, even to its own more or less living members, "the church of the living God, the pillar and ground of the truth " (1 Tim. 3^{15}), when it is constituted in this way ; when it exists as the Church only in co-existence with separate Churches, of which each one involves for every other criticism, competition, disruption and hostility. Where it ought to be a matter of true faith, does not the constant possibility of a comparison between faith and faith constitute a threat to the very question of the true faith and the answering of that question ? What is the Church if it can only express itself as a repetition of the plurality and contradictions of the world of heathen religions and the conflicts of secular totalitarianism ? What is the objective truth of its message if it has to contradict itself so evidently in its subjective realisations ? Is there not a good deal to be said for the thesis of E. Hirsch, who rather disconcertingly begins his *Geschichte der neueren evangelischen Theologie*, 1949 f., with the Peace of Westphalia of 1648, because then the general consciousness of Europe learned to acquiesce in the fact that Europe was divided religiously into two and even three great confessions, and it began to wonder at these conflicting absolutes, these bearers of revelation, each of which claimed for itself alone the truth and God ? " Lutheran, Papist, Calvinist, All three faiths are present, But where, we ask, is Christianity ? " Other powerful factors may have contributed at the same time or later, but the Peace of Westphalia was, as it were, the original manifestation of the historicals force which conceived and bore and produced modern Evangelical theology, the historicist, psychologist and relativist theology of Neo-Protestantism. Is there not something in this ? In the great process of the modern alienation between the Church and countless numbers of its members—which as a process of disillusionment in relation to the mediæval idea may not be altogether bad—the co-existence and opposition of the Churches in place of the one Church has, at any rate, been a very potent factor for evil, constituting a serious difficulty even for serious Christians, although not one which is inherent in the nature of the matter itself.

For the disunity of the Church is not grounded in the nature of the matter— in the existence of the Church, for example, in the temporary and imperfect conditions of the time between the ascension and the coming again of Jesus Christ. It was not created or sent out into this time in this plurality when the risen Jesus Christ breathed on His disciples. Exegetically it was not perhaps so strained as appears at first sight when the Early Church found an exhortation to unity in the seamless robe of Christ which was woven of a piece and which the soldiers did not wish to rend at the cross, but for which they cast lots (Jn. 19²³). Certainly there is no trace of this plurality in the New Testament, and in view of the being of the community as the body of Christ it is—ontologically, we can say—quite impossible ; it is possible only as sin is possible.

We must not try to explain and justify it as a development of the riches of the grace given to man in Jesus Christ, a development which derives from the Holy Spirit and which is therefore normal and acceptable. We must not try to explain and justify it by the image of the different elements and forces and functions in the one organism. or of the different branches and twigs of the one tree, or of the different families of a human clan. We must not deduce this plurality of Churches from some principle, as though the contradictions were necessities of the *una ecclesia*, as though this Church had to be divided into the Churches of the East and the West, as though the Church of the West had to be divided into the Romanist and Evangelical, as though the Evangelical Church had to be divided into the Lutheran and Reformed and Anglican, as though the wider divisions all proceeded necessarily from the nature of the case, as though in all this there was no trouble, no disorder, only the outworking of a law immanent in the Christian community. All this is simply the arbitrary view of a philosophy of history. It is not in accordance with the law of the matter itself. It is not permitted even by the thought of God's providence which certainly does overrule in all this and traces of which can clearly be seen. For the matter itself (we should read Jn. 17²¹⁻²³ word by word) demands always, and in all circumstances, *unam ecclesiam*. And if history contradicts this, then it speaks only of the actuality and not the truth. Even under the fatherly and effective providence of God which can cause it to work for good, a scandal is still a scandal. The disunity of the Church is a scandal. And there are some cases where the scandal is not even serious, but has only the character of a foolish embroilment.

The question is : What is the meaning of the confession : *credo unam ecclesiam*, in face of this scandal ? We shall have to return to this in detail when we speak of the upbuilding of the community. For the moment we will simply give the main outline.

One thing is certain—this *credo* cannot consist in a movement of escape up or on from the visibility of the divided Church to the unity of an invisible Church. It is such a movement when the individual

believer withdraws in disgust or superiority from his own and therefore from all other Churches, when he shuts himself off with his God
and Christ and Holy Spirit in some hermit's retreat or ivory tower,
enjoying his own private faith, being happy after his own fashion,
and possibly with the contemplation of the *una sancta* which for the
moment has its only representative in his own person. This is to
abandon not only the distress but the hope of the community and
indeed oneself. For there are no retreats and towers of this kind.
We are either in the *communio sanctorum* or we are not *sancti*. A
private monadic faith is not the Christian faith. Again, it is a movement of flight when one of the divided Churches or a number of them
try to bring unity nearer by ceasing to take themselves seriously, by
letting slip the special responsibility which they have, by denying and
renouncing their special character for the sake of internal or external
peace, by trying to exist in a kind of nondescript Christianity. The
way to a self-chosen supra-confessionalism is not by a long chalk the
way to the unity of the Church, but the way to a new separation, the
particular feature of which will be its featurelessness as a Church.
Where the Church is divided in the way which now concerns us, the
division reaches right down to its invisible being, its relationship to
God and Jesus Christ and the Holy Spirit, and it develops from
this, the external division being the result of an internal disruption, so
that neither individuals nor the whole Church can overcome it by a
flight to the invisible, but only by a healing of both its visible and
its invisible hurt.

For the same reason we cannot try to realise the *credo unam
ecclesiam* externally *in abstracto*. Self-evidently this cannot be done
by a *cogite intrare*, by any political or social pressure exercised by one
Church or group of Churches on another. But again, it cannot be
done by any form of understanding or agreement concerning the relative and reconcilable nature of the differences, or by any form of
unconditional mutual recognition or practical co-operation which leaves
open the questions which have to be mutually posed, or by any form
of artificial suppression of the mutual difficulties which are the basis
of disunity. What is demanded is the unity of the Church of Jesus
Christ, not the externally satisfying co-existence and co-operation of
different religious societies. To establish the latter is not too difficult
on the basis and under the dominion of the idea of toleration, provided
there is sufficient good will. Alliances and pacts and unions are often
possible on this basis and have been attempted often enough and even
seem to have been successful. Supposing, however, that on both sides
the necessity and freedom of faith are not considered, but faith has to
suffer shipwreck in favour of the attainment of political and social and
moral and practical tactical ends to which it is subordinated, and
before which it is reduced to silence, together with the confession of
it ? Supposing that at bottom this, too, is a movement of escape ?

Supposing that a conscious or unconscious spirit of indifference is the father of the thought and the corresponding acts and enterprises ? To believe in the unity of the Church of Jesus Christ in its disunity can never be the work of a feeble or uncertain or uncritical faith, or of a Church which takes itself less seriously, but only of a Church which takes itself more seriously, and of a faith which is strong and certain and genuinely critical.

From this we can go on to say that the distress and scandal consists in the fact that in its visible and also in its invisible being, in its form and also in its essence, the one community of Jesus Christ is not one, and that neither the community itself in its divided and opposing communions nor the individual Christians united in them can simply evade this disunity or overcome it by any kind of passivity or activity, notwithstanding the fact that to overcome it is undoubtedly envisaged and demanded by the *credo unam ecclesiam.* The individual communions and all of us in and with them find ourselves at some point and with some distinctness in this disunity of the one Church, and therefore on the one side or the other—not in the Eastern Church, shall we say ? but the Western, not Roman Catholics but Evangelicals, and Evangelicals, it may be with conviction or with reservations, but preponderately in the form of Lutherans or Reformed or Anglicans or Baptists or Mennonites. Why not ? Each of these Churches is still the Church even in the disunity. In each communion it confesses : *credo unam ecclesiam.* And every Christian stands more or less resolutely on the ground of his own communion, it may be by baptism, environment and upbringing, it may be by his own choice and decision. The division is a shame and a scandal, but this does not alter the fact that concretely the gathering to the community means for each of us the gathering to one of these divided communions. And it is not an acceptance of the scandal or an acquiescence in the shame if we say that we are not only permitted but commanded to start from this fact in our confession of the *una ecclesia.* All Churches and all the Christians united in them are called upon primarily to take themselves seriously even in their distinctness and therefore in their separate existence and confession—not necessarily to remain in them, and certainly not to harden in them, but to reach out from them to the one Church. If they do not do this here, they will not do it at all. If they jettison and abandon what they are as the Church in the disunity of the Church, how can they know its unity or be zealous and active in relation to it ? Just as the knowledge of justification cannot begin anywhere else or in any other way than with the recognition of the sin of the man justified by God, so the knowledge of the one community of Jesus Christ can begin only with its recognition in one of the forms of its unfortunate disunity, and not without a humble loyalty to one, to this specific confession which is, without doubt, highly contestable in its separation and isolation. The one depends on the other. The man who knows the justification of himself and all men in Jesus Christ, and who therefore acknowledges himself a sinner with all men and as such looks and moves forward to his right and life, will look and move forward to the one Church only from the place where he is ecclesiastically a Roman Catholic or Lutheran or Methodist or some other, a place which in its isolation and exclusiveness is a sinful place. And it is here, too, in its very doubtful particular existence that each Christian community or group of communities has to come to grips with its summons to the one Church. But what does it mean, to begin here, to go on from here, and therefore, and above all, to be loyal here in humility?

It will certainly mean attentively to pursue the intentions of this particular Church to their origins and actual meaning, to try to follow them out, to work out and to put into effect the various possibilities within this sphere, to pay attention and to give a voice to this particular witness. The promise of the Lord that where two or three are gathered together in His name He is there in the midst (Mt. 18[20]) will be true of this Church in spite of the doubtful nature of its separate existence. At some time, in some antithesis, when its fathers came forward with its particular confession and order, it was born of a choice and decision of faith, having its relative necessity and right as the complement to some omission or error on the other side. But a relative necessity and right may still give at least a relative justification for its continuance. It may be, therefore, that it and the Christians who belong to it have, for the time being, no cause to renounce their particular existence and doctrine and form of life, but, on the contrary, they find that they are called upon to cherish and renew and develop it.

But that is a possibility which naturally all Churches are only too ready to regard as applicable to their own case. Therefore we have to be more precise. A Church can appeal with a good conscience to this possibility of its own relative justification only when and to the extent that it is honestly and seriously committed to it for the sake of Jesus Christ; only when and to the extent that it not merely thinks but believes it can serve Him in accordance with the intentions which distinguish it from others; only when and to the extent that its particular existence and teaching and form as distinct from others are necessary to its faith and salvation; only when and to the extent that it has to recognise and confess that it is bound, not by its own confession, but by the Word of God. If this is the case, then it not only can, but ought to, maintain its cause. It ought not to be confused in it by any appeals for love and peace. Where the question of truth is sacrificed to that of love and peace, we are not on the way to the one Church. But it is no light thing when an individual Church maintains that for the sake of the truth and faith and eternal salvation and Jesus Christ it can do no other, it can only persist in its individual existence. Is it really sure? Can it be sure? There are other grounds for this persistence, just as there were other grounds for the emergence of the separation in question : national peculiarities, particular historical and social groupings, the existence of leading personalities, with whose spirits the Holy Spirit seems at the time to have been strangely united ; and to-day, the understandable attachment of the sons to the fathers, the natural weight of all and especially religious traditions, perhaps laid down in the most respected texts and established by written law and even property and endowment, the usage and custom of the land, the instinct of self-preservation, the requirements of prestige natural to every human society and especially to one which looks back to so great an antiquity. Is the difference and opposition of this or that Church something which really cannot be surrendered in relation to others ? Do we really believe, or do we only think, that we have to cling to it ? Can we really do no other, in response to the question of truth, or does it only seem that we can do no other, in consideration of certain actualities ? Must we really accept the continuance of the bastions which separate us or can they be in part or totally broken ? Have we perhaps overlooked the fact that they have been broken long since, or exist only as an external factor and in the interpretative historical phantasy of a relative minority ? These are questions which no individual Church—however large or small— should basically exclude or allow to rest, let alone deliberately suppress.

Why not ? Because each individual Church lives by the certainty and the claim, not only that it is the Church as well as others, but that it especially is the Church, that it is the Church in a peculiar way, that in a sense it alone among the Churches is the Church, the authentic, true, living and faithful Church of Jesus Christ. It may be in relation to its particularly ancient and assured tradition, if possible reaching right back to the apostles by the succession of its ministers. It may be in relation to its particularly zealous reformation in accordance with Holy Scripture, or the particular zeal and conscientiousness with which it exercises itself to follow Jesus in practice. Now there is good reason why every Christian fellowship—even to the many more or less influential liberal and unitarian movements, and often these most seriously—should in some way claim Jesus Christ especially for itself. Each individual Church should let itself be burdened with this certainty and claim. For it is in this that the unity of the Church is proclaimed in all its perverse plurality. If only we would pay attention to it as proclaimed in this way ! If only we would everywhere allow Jesus Christ genuinely to speak and to rule, genuinely and continuously subjecting ourselves to His guidance and instruction and direction, genuinely allowing Him to be the Lord of the Church ! Naturally not in the theory, the historical or speculative philosophy, the dogma, the particular Christology, in which He has been imprisoned and, as it were, encysted, but Himself, the living Lord, speaking by the Holy Spirit to the Church to-day in the witness of the prophets and apostles. He is appealed to as such on every hand. The older and also the more recent traditions all remember Him as such. His real presence as such is held to become an event in the world in the Roman mass, the Lutheran Lord's Supper, the Reformed exposition of Holy Scripture, the Methodist preaching of conversion, the eloquent or silent testimony of fraternal spiritual fellowship, or practical turning to one's fellows in accordance with His will. What would be the result if His real presence as the living and speaking Lord was genuinely accepted, if it was not merely maintained but allowed to become an event in the form in which it is earnestly believed ? What would take place in and with it in every Church—great or small, old or new—would definitely be the question directed to it, not from without, not by those who believe otherwise, but from its own heart, by the Lord whom it believes and knows and confesses, the question of truth which is put to it from above : whether and to what extent in its particular tradition and teaching and form it really serves Him, it really proclaims Him, it is really faithful to Him, and therefore— since it honestly and sincerely believes that it is His Church—to itself ?

And where would He not have to ask this question, where would He not actually ask it, if there were an unconditional openness to His work and an unconditional committal to His Spirit ? If His real presence were really allowed to become event instead of simply being cherished, then everywhere there would be a crisis in ecclesiastical self-consciousness, rather like the proving by fire described in 1 Cor. 3[12f.], in which every man's work is made manifest, that which he has so far built on the one foundation beside which there is no other : gold, silver, precious stones or wood, hay, stubble. The problem of the individual existence of Churches, which had been regarded as settled and set aside, would then be reopened, and radically reopened, in such a way as it had never been opened by external protests on the part of more or less friendly or hostile " sister-Churches," in such a way that the reopening of it could not be resisted with a good conscience or with any basic reservation. All would then find themselves drawn up in their own place, and doubt, scepticism, indifference and the like would be everywhere impossible. From their own place all would orientate themselves to the centre which in loyalty to their own cause they regard as their own peculiar centre. But from that place—presupposing that they are really willing to be controlled from it—they would themselves be orientated. The unity of the Church— which is not under the power of any man because the living Lord Jesus Christ in His own power is Himself this unity—would then begin not only to be a reality but to be realised as such in the many Churches. In face of the scandal of the divided Church *credo unam ecclesiam* would obviously mean in the first instance not merely the ascription, but—in the very place where every man is, in his own separate Church —the actual granting to Jesus Christ of the power to open this problem of the one Church and therefore the calling in question of the contrary plurality. In and with Him, the One, the unity of His body and therefore of the Church cannot for very long remain completely hidden from the faith which will ascribe and actually grant to Him the power to do this.

If appearances are not deceptive, it was the prophetic intention of Count Zinzendorf in the founding of his remarkable " brotherhoods ", not to split the confessional Churches, not to replace them by a super-Church, but as they came together freely as loyal members of the particular Churches to confront them typically with the unity which they had not lost and actually could not lose in Jesus Christ Himself, who remarkably enough was elected their common Elder Brother. It is no accident that the very man who in his preaching and poetry and dogmatics (so far as he had any) was perhaps the only genuine Christocentric of the modern age (fools would say : Christomonist), must also perhaps be called the first genuine ecumenicist, i.e., the first really to speak and think wholly in terms of the matter itself.

We cannot begin by contesting or waiving aside the confessions and orders of the separated Churches, by an over-hasty and arbitrary and self-confident breaking of the bastions, by a dissolution of the law. It is a matter of its fulfilment. It is a question of everywhere taking seriously faith in the real presence of Jesus Christ, or rather the real presence as it is believed, in obedience to His Word and Spirit. In spite of every current error and misunderstanding, He will have kept His promise to be in the midst even in the disunited Church. If we really grant Him His Word and the exercise of His power, He will not say from the very outset a general and exclusive No to the various particular traditions and doctrines and forms. Even in the proving by fire in 1 Cor. 3 it is not everything which is burned up. And when it is a matter of the unity of the divided Churches from and in Jesus Christ, the burning up of that which is individual is not the first and most important consequence. Certainly when He is allowed to speak and rule the inevitable crisis of the individual, the radical re-opening of the problem of the existence of particular Churches, will ineluctably involve the fact that—in his own place—every man will be committed to what is on the human level, the level of Church history, a humble loyalty to his own cause, which means, of course, that he will be open to the particular traditions and doctrines and forms of other Churches, very practically and concretely open to the question whether and to what extent they, too, might not stand under a particular Yes of the living Lord Jesus Christ which has not yet been heard or is no longer heard on this side ; whether and to what extent there ought not to be on this side a willingness to learn from them instead of simply opposing them. Who knows : Is it really possible to be glad and confident in our own faith so long as we regard ourselves as sheltered and secure in that faith against the faith of those who believe otherwise, so long as we think that we can simply shutter up ourselves against it ?

It is at this point that what we said earlier about penitence really enters in. No one, none of the separated Churches, can expect the others to hold or even to consider its case against them. They stand and fall to their own Lord. If we are seriously to hear Jesus Christ, then we must hear them even if they for their part give no sign that they are willing and able to hear us. They are perhaps harder of hearing than we are. But all the same, it may be that they can say something to us which we have to hear for our own sake. And perhaps the only way to call them out of their isolation, to cause them to hear us, is first of all to hear them. But this is not the place for tactical considerations. A prudent guest at the Lord's table (Lk. 14[10]) will seat himself with the other guests whatever proud looks he may have to face.

In the realisation of faith in the one Church in face of its disunity, the decisive step is that the divided Churches should honestly and seriously try to hear and perhaps hear the voice of the Lord by them and for them, and then try to hear, and perhaps actually hear, the voice of the others. Where a Church does this, in its own place, and without leaving it, it is on the way to the one Church. It is clear that in so doing it has already abandoned its claim to be identical with the one Church in contrast to the others, and in this sense to be the only Church. The claim has been dashed out of its hand by the One who is the unity of the Church. If it will not accept this, it cannot be on the way to the one Church, and with its exclusive *credo unam ecclesiam* it can only confirm the disunity of the one Church. But if it really hears the Lord afresh, it has already abandoned its claim and this *credo*. And if it lets Him open the question of its individual existence, then it will automatically be open to the other Churches in the sense that it will be willing and ready to let them say something to it, thus renouncing, in fact, its isolation as the only Church, its exclusion of all other Churches.

But then there seriously arises the practical question what is to become of its individual existence, its particular confessions and ordinances ? It is quite clear that this question does confront it. It may be that it will be necessary to scrap, or at least to revise or modify, its particular constitution. It may be that at many points it will need to be liberated or renewed in its separate existence. Note that it is not true to itself if at bottom it tries to resist this. Or it may be that much that is proper to it will now prove for the first time to be right, that it will be committed to the cherishing and continuance of it with a genuine joy and stringency. No Church will emerge from this fiery trial unscathed, unaltered, unrenewed, authorised merely to persist : something of wood, hay and stubble will necessarily have to be sacrificed. But—with constant reference to the promise of the Lord—it is not merely probable but certain that everywhere there will be preserved and established something of gold, silver and precious stones. And even if the form is not exactly one and the same, will not that which remains in the one place be so near and similar to that which remains in the other that on both sides we will actually find that we are positively on the way to unity and we must and will mutually perceive that we find ourselves on this way? But we must not close our eyes to this. And, above all, we must not cease to move further along this way—which means, that we must not be afraid to enter the way of the *credo unam ecclesiam* at its very beginning, at the acknowledged centre of every Christian community, and therefore at the lordship of the One to whom the Church belongs, whose body it is, who is Himself its true unity. As we look from Him, the actual unity of the Church will certainly be visible at a greater or lesser distance.

Credo sanctam ecclesiam. Holy means set apart, marked off, and therefore differentiated, singled out, taken (and set) on one side as a being which has its own origin and nature and meaning and direction —and all this with a final definitiveness, decisively, inviolably and unalterably, because it is God who does it. The term indicates the contradistinction of the Christian community to the surrounding world, and in particular to the other gatherings and societies which exist in the world. It is not a natural society after the manner of the nations, nor is it based on social contracts, or agreements, or temporary or permanent understandings and arrangements. It is not a society of necessity and compulsion like the state, nor is it a free society for a particular purpose like an order or a club or an economic or cultural union. It has its own basis and its own goal. It cannot, therefore, understand itself in the light of the basis of other societies or follow their goals. In what it does it goes its own way and makes use of its own method, which it cannot exchange for those used by other societies, but which, again, it cannot try to force on those societies. In assessing the greatness or the littleness, the value or the shame, the success or the lack of success of what it does, it has its own standard, so that it cannot judge itself by the standards which apply to other societies. It has quite different conditions even in the question of its membership; or, strictly speaking, it has only one, and from its own point of view, a very definite condition, although one which in the last resort is incomprehensible to every other human society, the condition of faith. It cannot possibly waive this condition, just as it necessarily has to waive all those which may apply elsewhere. In short, it has its own law, and in its life it is pledged to that law and that law alone.

But it is still undoubtedly a human society in and like others, with its own sphere of power and interests and influence. Its members are still men like others, and they may also belong to some, or even many, human societies. It is still in a sense the neighbour of these societies. For all its distinctiveness, what it does is not beyond comparison with what they do. It can be compared with it at many points. In many respects it runs parallel with it. It is bound to it in practice by all kinds of relationships. We obviously have to underline the *credo ecclesiam* in this respect too. That is to say, the invisible being of the Church in its visibility is in this respect too the matter of a special knowledge which is not accessible and cannot be attributed to every man, which is not amenable to the control of man at all. As long as the community lives in the world its holiness, like its unity, is covered by its actual likeness and relationships to other societies, by the twofold citizenship of its members, of Christians, in itself, but also in more than one of these other *civitates*. If the confession is true, *credo sanctam ecclesiam*, then it is a matter of revelation and of the knowledge of revelation. The confession does not describe a matter which is open to all, but a discovery which no one can make without the Holy Spirit and to which no one can hold without a continuance of His revealing work. But on this presupposition, which cannot be omitted or forgotten, this means that the community is (in the sense which we have sketched) holy, and holy with a final and categorical definitiveness, inviolably and unalterably.

To understand this matter it is very much to the point to remember that the creed says : *credo ecclesiam*, not *credo in ecclesiam*. We cannot believe in the Church—the holy Church—as we believe in God the Father, Son and Holy Spirit. According to the third article we can believe only in God the Holy Spirit, and as we know and confess His work we can also believe the existence of the holy Church, just as later we can believe the forgiveness of sins as He declarēs it to man, or in the first article the heaven and earth as created by God the Father. If it is seriously true and can be known in faith, the holiness of the Church is not that of the Holy Spirit but that which is created by Him and ascribed to the Church. It is He who marks it off and separates it. It is He who differentiates it and singles it out. It is He who gives it its peculiar being and law of life. It is holy as it receives it from Him to be holy. But though it is holy it is still a part of the creaturely world in which there can be no question of believing as we believe in God.

Calvin laid great stress on this : *Ideo enim credere in Deum nos testamur, quod et in ipsum ut veracem animus noster se reclinat et fiducia nostra in ipso acquiescit ; quod in ecclesiam non ita conveniret (Instit. IV, 1, 2).* But the *Cat. Rom.* also explains (I, 10, 19) that in relation to the Church we must be content with the *credo* without the *in, ut hac etiam diversa loquendi ratione Deus omnium effector in creatis rebus distinguatur, praeclaraque omnia quae in ecclesiam collata sunt, beneficia divinae bonitati accepta referamus.*

What else can the holiness of the Church be but the reflection of the holiness of Jesus Christ as its heavenly Head, falling upon it as He enters into and remains in fellowship with it by His Holy Spirit ? He is the One who is originally differentiated and singled out as the eternal Son of God appointed the Reconciler of the world with God, and then as the executor of the divine counsel in His incarnation and the work of obedience on the cross, and as the recipient of the divine verdict in His resurrection. In the existence of the community we have to do with the earthly-historical form of His existence. As it is gathered and built up and commissioned by the Holy Spirit it becomes and is this particular part of the creaturely world, acquiring a part in His holiness, although of and in itself it is not holy, it is nothing out of the ordinary, indeed as His community within Adamic humanity it is just as unholy as that humanity, sharing its sin and guilt and standing absolutely in need of its justification. " And for their sakes I sanctify myself, that they also might be sanctified through the truth " (Jn. 17¹⁹).

Hence Calvin says (*Serm. on Mt.* 2²³, *C.R.* 46, 455 f.) that there is no *plénitude de saincteté sinon au Chef.* Just as Joseph among his brethren and Samson among his people were both set apart (Nazirites) for their sake and as their liberators, so in fulfilment of these Old Testament types the " Nazarene " Jesus was *separé d'avec tous les autres fidèles* in order to make common cause with them. *Pourquoi donc ceste discrétion a elle este mise ? C'est afin qu'il ait luy seul toute prééminence, afin que chacun s'addresse à luy, que nous puisions de ceste fontaine, qui ne tarit jamais : et que cependant nous ne laissions pas toutefois d'estre conjoints à luy.* And again in astonishing agreement with Calvin the *Cat. Rom.* (I, 10, 12) : the Church is holy *inter tot peccatores . . . quod veluti corpus cum sancto capite, Christo Domino, coniungitur.* There is a fine voice from modern Evangelical theology to the same effect, that of M. Kähler (*Wiss. d. chr. Lehre,* 1893, p. 389) : As the assurance of the justified rests on the holiness of the self-sufficient God and His electing grace, so, too, does the holiness of the Church. " In its claim to this quality which it cannot lose there lies the confession of the power of the Reconciler which overcomes the world." The measure of agreement seems to be particularly great in this important insight.

But the insight has far-reaching consequences of a positive as well as a critical nature. We will begin with two positive affirmations.

The community as the body of Jesus Christ is holy because and in the fact that He, the Head, is holy : in its connexion with Him, in its unity with Him, in the light which falls necessarily upon it from Him when it belongs to Him in the work of the Holy Spirit. But if this is true then obviously the converse is true, (1) that all the corresponding holiness of individual members on the basis of His relationship with them and theirs with Him, all the differentiation and separation of individual men by the gift of the Holy Spirit, by their awakening to faith and the knowledge of Him, is equivalent to the fact that they are members of His body and therefore that they are in the community. Where and when He calls these men—and not others, addressing and setting aside this man or that woman as His own, it does not mean, as the matter has often been put, and is still put, in a very doubtful way, that there arises between Him and them a private relationship. The fact that these individuals can as such partake of His grace and live with Him and for Him has no autonomous or ultimate significance. It has significance only as in so doing they become members of His body, or, rather, are revealed to be such to themselves and others. To be awakened to faith and to be added to the community are one and the same thing. Therefore there are not two separations or differentiations : an individual one for its own sake, and therefore the creation of certain *homines sancti* whose existence can be an end in itself, satisfying both the One who calls them to it and those who are called ; and then a collective one which is necessary and meaningful in some quite different way, the gathering and separation of these individual Christians into a community. There is only one separation, that of the *communio sanctorum* : the awakening of the faith of individuals, the purpose of which is their gathering into the community—the gathering of the community in the form of the awakening of the faith of individuals.

In the Old Testament the partner of Yahweh was the people Israel as it existed, of course, in the totality of those who belonged to it. In and with Israel the individual Israelite was also the partner of Yahweh, but only as the representative of his people. So, too, the partner of Jesus Christ attested in the New Testament is the community which, of course, exists and is seen in the faith of its individual members, the ἡμεῖς of the Lord's Prayer, the ὑμεῖς of the Epistles ; not a Christian individual who is not as such, or is merely subsequently and incidentally and not primarily and essentially, within the community. It is not a matter of the higher value of the collective as compared with the individual, but if we like of a definite order and sequence. We can put it this way : the collective is the purpose and the individual the form of the subjective admission of reconciliation by the work of the Holy Spirit. The two terms can be used only when we relate them to a single point. If we take them to indicate two competing realities then they can only prevent us from understanding the point at issue. The community lives in Christians, Christians live in the community, and in this way Jesus Christ lives in the world. In this way they are holy in Him and with Him.

Note that in the first proposition we have said something which is very like but not exactly the same as the well-known dictum : *extra ecclesiam nulla salus.* We find the substance, if not the actual words, of this dictum in many of the fathers (*C.D.* I, 2, p. 212). In the strict sense it claims that without participation as a member in the being and life of the Church there can be no participation in the reconciling act of divine redemption. But this is what we must be careful not to say. In this sense it would be true to say : *extra Christum nulla salus.* But the Church as His body is only the form of existence in which He encounters the world historically, the community of those who know and confess their salvation and that of the world in Him. It serves Him in the world reconciled by Him. It proclaims the redemptive act of God as it took place in Him. Yet it is not outside adherence to the Church, but outside the adherence of all men to Him as known and confessed and proclaimed by the Church, that there is no salvation. We must also be careful not to maintain that participation in the salvation of the world grounded in Jesus Christ is bound absolutely to the mediation of the Church and therefore to its proclamation. We have to reckon with the hidden ways of God in which He may put into effect the power of the atonement made in Jesus Christ (Jn. 10[16]) even *extra ecclesiam*, i.e., other than through its ministry in the world. He may have provided and may still provide in some other way for those who are never reached, let alone called to Him, by the Church. It does not detract from the glory of the community or weaken its commission if we keep at least an open mind in this respect. What we can say of the community is only this, though we can say it in all seriousness : *extra ecclesiam nulla revelatio, nulla fides, nulla cognitio salutis*—and in so far as the knowledge and revelation of Jesus Christ and faith in Him and the ministry of the proclamation of His name constitutes the holiness of the Church : *extra ecclesiam nulla sanctitas.* What is true is that the typical and ministerial separation of an individual, in virtue of which he is distinguished and marked off from other men as one who believes and knows, is as such his separation to life and ministry in and with the community. If he does not have it as such, he does not have it at all. And if he withdraws from the fellowship of the Church, in so doing he denies himself as *sanctus*, as one who believes and knows. What is true is that there is no legitimate private Christianity. The question which in this light we have to address not only to all forms of mysticism and pietism but also to Kierkegaard is plain to see. As Calvin puts it (*Instit.* IV, 1, 10), to try to be a Christian in and for oneself is to be a *transfuga et desertor religionis* and therefore not a Christian. *Discessio ab ecclesia* is a *Dei et Christi abnegatio* and therefore worse than the position of the one who, never having come to faith and knowledge, is *extra ecclesiam*, has no part in its differentiation and separation, is not a *sanctus* and perhaps never will be. Such a *transfuga et desertor religionis* may even risk and forfeit his salvation, i.e., his participation in the reconciliation of the world with God. It may be something akin to the sin against the Holy Ghost of which he is guilty. For the Holy Ghost leads him directly into the community and not into a private relationship with Christ. *Nec ullum atrocius fingi crimen potest, quam sacrilega perfidia : violare coniugium, quod nobiscum (nobiscum* not *mecum) unigenitus Dei Filius contrahere dignatus est* (Calvin *l.c.*).

The community is holy because and as Jesus Christ is holy. But if this is true, then we can say of it (2) that, as what it is as differentiated in essence from the world and all its *civitates*, it is indestructible. In this respect the older dogmatics called it infallible. What was meant by this expression in Evangelical dogmatics was that the separation in which it exists cannot be reversed, that it cannot lose its distinctness and separateness within the world. Because it is from Jesus Christ, because it is His body, it cannot cease to be this, it cannot become something else, it cannot be subjected to another law than that which is laid upon it. It has not taken it upon itself to be holy, and it cannot set aside its calling. It has it from God and no man can take it from it—just as Israel never could or can in any crisis of its history in the covenant of God with it cease to be the people elected and called and commissioned by God. The Church exists in unity with this people of the old covenant. The perennial nature of Israel as the people of Jesus Christ is that of the Church.

The community may sometimes be pushed to the wall, persecuted, suppressed and outwardly destroyed, as has actually happened to Israel in many of its historical forms both past and present. What is worse, it may, like Israel, be guilty of failure and error. It may deny its Lord and fall from Him. It may degenerate. Indeed it has never existed anywhere except as a Church which has degenerated to a greater or lesser, a more serious or a less serious degree : not even in the New Testament period and certainly not according to the records of Church history, and, worst of all, where it has been most conscious and boasted most loudly of its purity—just as, according to the Old

Testament, Israel does not seem at any time to have been—and, least of all, in the times of supreme self-consciousness—what it was ordained to be in faithfulness to its faithful God. The Church stands in the fire of the criticism of its Lord. It is also exposed to the criticism of the world and this criticism has never been altogether false and unjust. It has always needed, and it always will need, self-examination and self-correction. It cannot exist except as *ecclesia semper reformanda*—if only it had always understood itself in this light and acted accordingly! Its acts and achievements, its confessions and orders, its theology and the ethics advocated by it and lived out by its members, never were and never are infallible at any point; and, again, they are most fallible where there is the arbitrary attempt to deck them out with infallibility—not least the ethics lived out by Christians. When has Christian ethics not wavered between a pharisaical legalism and an antinomian libertinism, between a " spiritual " sectarianism and a complacent respectability, between a weary pietism and a feverish activism, between the attractions of conservatism and those of revolution (or perhaps only of Bohemianism)? When has it been the case that men could simply see the good works of Christians and had to glorify their Father which is in heaven (Mt. 5[16])? Taking it all in all, the community of Jesus Christ in the world may at times be clothed with every kind of pomp and glory; but what a frail vessel it is, exposed to every kind of assault, and actually assaulted both outwardly and above all inwardly!

It was most apposite and ought not to have been discontinued that in 17th and 18th century Basel (after the daily sermon) the prayer was used in all Churches : " Have mercy, O Lord, upon the most pitiful and parlous state of thy dear Church in Germany, France, Piedmont, England, Hungary, etc., and most of all in an honourable Confederacy and surrounding territories." Yes, indeed, to this very day : *Kyrie eleison.* And as Luther used to emphasise : " Forgive us our trespasses "—to be prayed not merely in the name of individuals but by the Church as such in its own name.

But in face of all that has come and still comes upon the Church, in face of all that can be said concerning it and against it, *credo sanctam ecclesiam.* The *credo* is obviously indispensable. We cannot say this except as a confession of faith. But it belongs to the confession of faith to say it.

What Jesus said in Mt. 16[18] is still true : " The gates of hell shall not prevail against it." And what He said in Lk. 22[31f.] to Peter (who three times denied Him) : " Simon, Simon, behold, Satan hath desired to have you, that he may sift you as wheat ; But I have prayed for thee, that thy faith fail not." And again in Jn. 17[15] : " I pray not that thou shouldest take them out of the world, but that thou shouldest keep them from the evil." The perennial nature of the community rests only on this promise and prayer. But it does rest on it. To deny the perennial nature of the community is to deny the power of this prayer and promise. *Item docent, quod una sancta ecclesia perpetuo mansura sit (Confession of Augsburg VII).*

The body of Jesus Christ may well be sick or wounded. When has it not been ? But as the body of this Head it cannot die. The faith of the community may waver, its love may grow cold, its hope may become dreadfully tenuous, but the foundations of its faith and love and hope, and with it itself, are unaffected. The reflection of what the Holy Spirit was in eternity and will be in eternity does not cease to fall on it. It finds itself on a way which is not of its own seeking. It has not set itself on this way, and it cannot leave it. No one can arrest it on this way, nor can it halt of itself. It may limp on it and stumble and fall. It may lie on it apparently dead, like the man who fell among thieves on the way from Jerusalem to Jericho. But death is behind it. " Being born again, not of corruptible seed, but of incorruptible, by the word of God, which liveth and abideth for ever " (1 Pet. 1²³), it cannot again fall victim to it. It has always risen again, and it always will rise again, beaten down justly by God or justly or unjustly by man, but not cut off from the world, perishing in the one form to begin again with new power in another, almost or altogether extinguished in one place to build itself up the more joyfully as a young Church in another. Its authority and effects and influence and successes may be small, very small. They may threaten to disappear almost or altogether. But the authority and power of God are behind it and it will never fail. It may become a beggar, it may act like a shopkeeper, it may make itself a harlot, as has happened and still does happen, yet it is always the bride of Jesus Christ. Its existence may be a travesty of His, but as His earthly-historical form of existence it can never perish. It can as little lose its being as He can lose His. What saves it and makes it indestructible is not that it does not basically forsake Him—who can say how deeply and basically it has often enough forsaken Him and still does ?—nor is it this or that good that it may be or do, but the fact that He does not forsake it, any more than Yahweh would forsake His people Israel in all His judgments.

From this it is clear that it is always a responsible and dangerous matter to criticise the Church. Again and again there may be the possibility of doing this with justice, and therefore the necessity to do it. But when we feel impelled to do it we must see to it that it really is necessary, that is to say, that it is demanded. A tacit criticism of the Church may be more relevant and effective than a violent one. But the danger is always that not only the Christians who direct and represent the cause of the Church, but in these weak brethren and their action Jesus Christ Himself will be criticised, attacked, condemned and perhaps rejected. To the fact that the Church can serve Him only according to His attestation in Holy Scripture, and can therefore speak and act only with a relative and provisional and therefore at bottom contestable authority, there corresponds the further fact that any criticism can only be relative and itself limited by the attestation of Jesus Christ in Holy Scripture. Spiritual things must be spiritually discerned, on the basis of a serious hearing, in the form of a conscientious distinguishing between that in which in any given case the Church does err, giving place to alien voices and powers and denying its Lord, and that in which in all its weakness and corruption it does perhaps contend for the truth.

attesting the voice and power of the good Shepherd, being faithful to Him in all its unfaithfulness. If we can never hear the Church without some scruple, if we always have some cause to object to its word and attitude, in the strict sense we can confront it only with more or less searching questions, not with apodictic repudiations and condemnations and rejections ; and whether the utterance of them be loud or quiet, it must proceed always from the recognition : I myself am in the *ecclesia semper reformanda*, and responsible for it. The first question must therefore be addressed to myself : What is the basis of my scruple and objection ? to what extent am I really authorised to make it ? The legitimate, prophetic, reformation attack upon the Church and its doctrine and order and life and attitudes can be conducted only on its own ground, in the name of Jesus Christ, and with the intention of re-establishing it more firmly on this ground which it is perhaps on the point of denying, and with a new and better awareness of this ground. Do I myself stand on this ground when I criticise the Church ? Am I concerned to serve its cause ? Have I the ability to hold out something new and better ? Legitimate scruples and objections can have nothing to do with the cheap anti-clerical clamour of the gutter. They can derive only from the solidarity in which we subject ourselves first—and then the Church —to the criticism to which it is subjected by its living Lord. For that reason, even though they may go very deep and have to be expressed sharply, they can never be made legitimately and therefore effectively except with a final brotherly mildness, restraint and consideration, except with a final respect for the Church's holiness. How much justifiable and necessary criticism of the Church has at bottom failed simply because it has not derived from this solidarity and has not, therefore, been made with this mildness and respect !

All this is relevant to the mutual relationship of the Churches as distinct from one another in spite of the unity of the Church, to their unavoidable criticism of one another within this relationship. Their division rests on the doubtful light in which they appear to one another, on the scruples and objections which they have to raise against each other. But, however doubtful may be the light in which one Church appears to the other, this other must not forget that it, too, is holy only from its living Lord, and that the other may also be holy from the one living Lord. Therefore no matter how well-grounded and necessary and sharp may be the criticism which it brings against it, it can never harden into an absolute condemnation and rejection. Ultimately it can have only the character of a penetrating question addressed to it. As the rejection and condemnation of another Church it might well be directed against Jesus Christ Himself. It can succeed only in the humility in which we on this side—perhaps better than the other—know that the holiness of the community on both sides is His work, the gift of His Holy Spirit, so that it cannot either be claimed as a possession on the one side or called in question as the work and gift of the Lord on the other : as though our own Church were the mistress of the Lord and the other were not under His lordship. In the last resort it was Luther himself who in answer to the question (*W.A.* 40¹, 69 f.) how Paul, in spite of everything, could still address the Galatian communities as ἐκκλησίαι stated quite plainly : *Sic et nos hodie vocamus Ecclesiam Romanam Sanctam et omnes episcopatus sanctos, etiamsi sint subversi et ministri eorum impii. Deus enim regnat in medio inimicorum, (item) Antichristus sedet in templo Dei et Satan adest in medio filiorum Dei. Ideo ecclesia etiamsi sit in medio nationis pravae et perversae . . . luporum et latronum, hoc est tyrranorum spiritualium, nihilominus Ecclesia est.* Even in the city of Rome (although it is worse than Sodom and Gomorrah) baptism and the Lord's Supper and the voice and word of the Gospel and Holy Scripture and the ministry and the name of Christ and the name of God still remain. Where these are found in a people, that people is holy. *Ideo Romana Ecclesia est sancta.* Luther could expressly say the same (71, 19) of the communities of the *phanatici*, but only on the same basis, and it was on this basis alone that he claimed the character of holiness for his own Church in Wittenberg (69, 29). *Ego, tu, sancti sumus : ecclesia, civitas, populus sanctus est non sua sed aliena, non activa sed passiva sanctitate* (70, 19). It is another matter whether and to what extent Luther did justice to this insight in his polemics against Rome and the *phanatici*. It is certainly no light or simple task actually to do it justice in a given case. What is certain is that even in the most extreme cases the mutual judgment in the relationship between the divided Churches cannot go further than the affirmation that in its character as a community of Jesus Christ the one is more or less and perhaps completely hidden from the other so that it can neither see it nor understand it. It cannot therefore go beyond a very serious question concerning this quality of holiness. But is it hidden from itself as a community of Jesus Christ ? Does it not have to believe that it is such without seeing it ? On this basis its judgment cannot become a judgment which rejects the other Church altogether as a Church of Jesus Christ. For only Jesus Christ Himself can pronounce this judgment on it. Pronounced by another Church which itself lives by His holiness, it is not merely presumptuous but worse, for it means that the rejecting Church runs the most serious danger, and has perhaps already fallen victim to it, of rejecting in the rejected Church Jesus Christ Himself and the holiness in which He allows it to participate, thus making itself definitely unholy and ceasing to be His community.

We turn from the positive to some critical conclusions from the fact that the holiness of the community has to be understood wholly as the reflection of the holiness of Jesus Christ and therefore only as the gift of His Holy Spirit.

If this is the case then (1) we have to consider that its separation in the world does not, as it were, automatically, necessarily and consistently coincide with the peculiarity of its common being and activity in which it often distinguishes and marks itself off from the activity of the world and that of other neighbouring human societies. To quote Luther again : *christiana sanctitas non est activa, sed passiva sanctitas*. We have seen that the Church does exist in activity, and indeed in a specific and special activity, the human activity directed in accordance with its own law. But it is not the Church which makes its special activity holy. It is not itself which by its special activity in the world marks itself off from that of other societies. But this means that it does not lie in its power or under its control to give to its own activity the predicate " Christian." It would do well always to apply this adjective to its own activities only with the greatest reserve and therefore relatively seldom. In all seriousness there are what we may call " Christian " activities, which are as such different from all others and as such holy, a holy activity of the community within the world. There is in fact a coincidence of its divine separation and its own separations in and with its activity (in its preaching, in its worship, in its constitution, in its ordinances, in its theology, in its attitude in questions and decisions which affect the world). There are human acts and attitudes which are holy as such, i.e., which have the character of real witness to the One whose earthly historical existence the Church is allowed to be. But that they have this character is always dependent upon the answering witness of the One whom they aim and profess to attest. It is a matter of His special care, of His free grace which He has promised to address to His community without committing it into the hands of His community. In respect of its holiness the community is bound to Him—and He to it—only to the extent that He constantly wills to bind Himself and does in fact bind Himself to it. He is always the Subject, the Lord, the Giver of the holiness of its action. Its action as such can only be a seeking, an asking after holiness, a prayer for it. And not the community but He Himself decides the rightness of its seeking, asking and prayer, and therefore whether and to what extent He will hear it, confirming and blessing its action as a true witness to Him. Neither in great things nor in small can it be holy of itself and therefore without His Holy Spirit. And in great things and in small the presence and gift of His Holy Spirit are directly His own work. It can be in the right in its activity, therefore, only to the extent that it acquires this right from Him. If He does not give it, then even its ostensibly most holy work is profane : its preaching is simply a kind of explanation and instruction, or enthusiastic protestation ; its baptism and Lord's Supper are religious rites like others ; its theology is a kind of philosophy, its mission a species of propaganda, etc. They may all have their interest and importance and practical value from other standpoints—intellectual, moral, psychological, sociological—but they cannot be holy without the work of the living Lord of the community. No institutions within which its activity is done, no good will on the part of the men who act, no old or new technique which is used, can make them holy or prevent them from again becoming secular. The community is wholly in the hands of its Lord, and that means that it is thrown back on His having mercy upon it and making its unholy activity holy and acknowledging it as such.

This does not contradict its indestructibility. Its indestructibility consists in this open relationship to Him, in the fact that it is entirely in His hand and thrown back on hope in Him, in the sovereignty in which He turns to it and the acknowledgment in which it, for its part, turns to Him. It cannot attain it in any other way. It is holy and indestructible in the fact that it *abdicata omni sua sapientia a Spiritu Sancto doceri se per verbum Dei patitur* (Calvin, *Instit.* IV, 8, 3).

If it is the case that the holiness of the community is the reflection of the holiness of the Lord and therefore the free gift of His Holy Spirit, then (2) we have also to consider critically that its separation and holiness will not automatically, necessarily and consistently take place in the mere fact that certain men unite together in it, or enter its existing unity, thus becoming and being members of it. This does, of course, take place as well wherever the community arises or is present. It belongs to the aspect which is visible to everyone that such and such men come to it with their profession of faith and desire to receive baptism and are received by it and actually become members and, as such, are Christians, or, at any rate, appear to be. But to be Christians, and therefore holy members of the holy community means —for " if any man hath not the Spirit of Christ, he is none of his " (Rom. 8[9])—that they have actually been awakened to faith in Him, that they have found themselves members of the community in this fact, that in fulfilment of their faith and election and calling they have asked for baptism and received it as a confirmation, that with a lively faith they are Christians and therefore in the community. Is this really true of all those of whom the community is composed as visible to every man ? Of how many of them is it true ? Of which of them ? This was the question which, in the 16th century, deeply disturbed not only the Anabaptist communities and other so-called sectarians but the great Churches of the Reformation. They all wrestled with this question in their confessional writings or in other ways. It is a question which is deeply disturbing even to-day. The Church which is not deeply disturbed by it is not a Christian Church. It is the question which runs parallel to that of the holiness of its common action and is indissolubly connected with it—the question of the holiness of its members. If it is in its members, if its common action is their action, then the holiness of its action and its own holiness obviously stands or falls with that of the Christians assembled in it. But which are the holy members ? Who are the true Christians ?

Est autem ecclesia congregatio sanctorum (*Confession of Augsburg* VII). What is meant emerges unmistakably from the German text : " the congregation of all believers." And it is affirmed by Art. VIII even in the Latin that the Church is *proprie* (properly) the *congregatio sanctorum et vere credentium.* But is there a community which is holy only *improprie* ? The continuation of Art. VII is well-known : *in qua evangelium pure docetur et sacramenta recta administrantur.* This is correct—although not exhaustive—as an answer to the question of the holiness of its activity. But can we separate this question from that of the holiness of its members who are the subjects of its activity ? Is there no relationship at all between that *pure* and *recta* and the *vere credere* of those who are gathered into the community and are active as such ? Can we simply ignore this second question, as Art. VIII seems to come near to doing, merely so as not to provide an opening to the Donatist heresy ? Can we be content simply to make the true enough statement that the truth of the Gospel is not tied to the worthiness or unworthiness of the Church's ministers ? Is not the question inescapable if the Church is not only a sphere *in qua* this action takes place but, as the obvious subject of this action, the " congregation of all believers " ? It could not actually lie dormant even in the great Churches of the Reformation but always demanded some kind of answer.

But when it is posed, there were and are attempts to answer it which are far too facile. On the surface they are opposed to each other, but in fact they are complementary. They are both illegitimate and, for that reason, they can both be set aside at a stroke.

The first points to baptism as the factor by which a man is placed in the *communio sanctorum* and on the basis of which he is a true member of it. It is in and by the fact that he is baptised that he receives the Holy Spirit and comes to a true faith, thus becoming a member of the body of Christ and a holy member of His holy community. The number of true Christians is therefore the number of the baptised. How can it be otherwise when baptism has this power *ex opere operato* ? We are not concerned for the moment whether this is good baptismal teaching. Nor are we considering the absurd result that in this way (*via* infant baptism) whole populations of whole countries have automatically been made and can automatically be made the holy community. Even if we did not have to face this practice, the decisive objection to this view is that in it the question of the gathering of the community by the Lord Himself is mischievously evaded, the spiritual mystery of the community being replaced and crowded out by an arrogantly invented sacramental mystery. What kind of a conception of the Holy Spirit is it, of His presence and operation, of the awakening to faith, and of membership of the body of Christ, when all this can be imparted to a man simply by the correct fulfilment of an action initiated by men ? What kind of a conception of the community is it when the community has the power to constitute and augment itself as a holy community simply by this action ?

But it was no better when the attempt was made to recognise the holiness of Christians (and therefore the holiness of the community) by certain attitudes and actions which distinguish Christians from other men : perhaps by their regular attendance at service and Holy Communion, or more seriously by their conversion to the faith under certain conditions, or by what they do or do not do, by a certain style or habit of Christian life, by ways of life which are usual or even unusual, and all presupposing the existence of some law or standard by which the presence of these distinguishing marks of Christianity can be established. But where is the law which can serve as a measure to distinguish who has or has not the Holy Spirit, who believes or does not believe, who belongs to the community of the saints or does not belong ? What decides and distinguishes in this case is not a sacramental *opus operatum* but a religious and moral *opus operantis*—as though the Lord, the Holy Spirit and His gift could be enclosed in the sphere of certain human works thought out by men. Again it is obvious that the question of the Holy Spirit and His gathering of the community has been—we can only say mischievously—evaded. Again the real mystery of the community has been replaced and crowded out by one which has been arrogantly invented (this time a religious and moral). What kind of a conception of the holiness of its members and therefore of its own holiness is this ? What kind of a conception of the Holy Spirit ?

There can only be vacillation in face of these two attempts to answer our question. There can never be either a valid and clear-cut decision or any kind of compromise between them. As a rule, the result will be either the reaction of a powerful moralism against the recognised danger of sacramentalism, or that of a powerful sacramentalism against the recognised danger of moralism. It is to be hoped that on neither side the reaction will be too powerful because the *aporia* into which we are betrayed when we try to choose either one or the other is quite hopeless. But if we try to combine the two, will not the combination simply aggravate the evil which attaches to both ? In both cases the answering of the question is made too facile. In both cases we have to do with imitations, substitutes. Both rest on illusions. Both miss the one point on which everything turns. Therefore both have to be abandoned.

We will try to answer the question from our presupposition, and we will begin by stating that at all times and in all situations holy members of the holy Church, and therefore true Christians, were and are the men assembled in it who are thereto elected by the Lord, called by His Word, and constituted by His Spirit : just so many, no more and no less, these men and no others. It is He who knew them and willed them and created them as such. It is He who knows and preserves them as His saints.

But are there "others" in His community, who have not come
to it by Him, who have not been baptised and are not members on
the basis of His affirmation, who take their confession on their lips
and in some way participate in the life of the community—but only
in appearance, who are not therefore saints, true Christians? It
would be an obvious exaggeration to try to maintain that this is
not possible. There is no doubt—and this is what the eyes of the
world see—that the Church is also a human *civitas* or *societas*, a
union of men. Hidden in this it lives as the body of Jesus Christ.
But it does exist and recruit as this union on the basis of human
insights and judgments and decisions. We cannot expect that these
human insights and judgments and decisions (conditioned and limited
as such) will be plainly and automatically and directly identical with
those of its Lord, or that they can prejudice or even anticipate His,
His knowledge of men and resolve concerning them, His activity
by which He makes them members of His body. It may well be
that they are blessed and ratified by Him, and to that extent are
made in His name, not merely in claim but in truth. But the community constitutes and recruits itself knowing the fact, and knowing
it as its limit, that in this, too, it is in His hand and is thrown back
on the hope of His ratification and blessing, on the free grace of His
Holy Spirit. It can constitute and recruit itself only in faith in Him.
In this respect, too, it must acknowledge His sovereignty. But this
involves an acknowledgment that it may make mistakes, that even
amongst those who belong to it in the eyes of men there may be some
who are not members of His body, who are not at all elected and
called by Him, who are not awakened by His Holy Spirit to faith in
Him.

As we see from the parable in Mt. 13²⁴ᶠ·, there may be tares among the wheat,
or from that in Mt. 13⁴⁷ᶠ there may be bad fish amongst those which come into
the net. Who knows how many tares ? Who knows how many bad fish ?
There was a Judas even among the twelve apostles. And so *C.A.* VIII reckons
with the fact that " in this life there remain many false Christians and hypocrites
and even notorious sinners among the faithful." It may well be, therefore, that
the fellowship of the Church as such can only be called a *societas mixta*, and in
that case only *improprie*, improperly, the body of Jesus Christ.

We have to take this possibility into account, not on the obvious
but very doubtful ground that when we look at supposed fellow-
Christians we have every reason to think of the tares rather than the
wheat, but because the final and authoritative decision whether such
and such baptised and professing members of the community whom
we regard as genuine believers are really such is not our affair but His,
while we can only go by what we see.

But in the strict sense it would also be an exaggeration if we thought
we knew and tried to maintain that it is not only possible but actually
the case that in the community there are, in fact, both believing

Christians and unbelieving, both true Christians and false, so that we can regard what we see as the Church only improperly as the community of Jesus Christ, treating it as such only with a limited seriousness. For how can we know this if it is really the Lord who decides the emergence and development of His body and therefore who is or is not a true member of it and therefore a true member of His community? Why should it not be His pleasure actually to think much better and make much more of all those who as baptised and professing Christians are visibly members of His community like ourselves than we can ever imagine in our general or particular mistrust of supposed fellow-Christians? And how can we possibly know how many and which He has placed on His right hand as His own people, and how many and which He has placed on His left hand as those who are not called or as Judases? According to the standard of human knowledge and judgment the community can and must decide whom it must and will accept and recognise as visible adherents, or whom it must and will refuse to recognise or expel. There are serious grounds for both, and in this connexion we shall have to consider at a later stage the problem of Church discipline. But there is no Church discipline—and it is a misunderstanding and misapplication of the saying about the keys of the kingdom of heaven in Mt. 16[19] to expound it in this way—in which it is given to men to decide what men are or are not members of the body of Christ and therefore true Christians and therefore saints. As we can only believe the Christian community as such in its identity with the holy community of Jesus Christ, so we can only believe ourselves and others as its holy members.

We are obviously thrown back entirely on faith even if in a supposed awareness of the mixed character of the Church union we try to seek out an " inner circle " of true believers or to make common cause with certain others as *sancta ecclesiola in ecclesia*. It is evident that Luther did occasionally toy with this idea. But fortunately he neither developed it systematically nor attempted to apply it in practice. For who is to decide and who is able to decide who belongs or does not belong to this *ecclesiola*?

But if it is a matter of the perception of faith, then we all do well to begin with the question how it is with ourselves. According to *Qu.* 54 of the *Heidelberg Catechism*, when I look at the community elected to eternal life from the whole of the human race by the Son of God, gathered and protected and preserved by His Spirit and Word in the unity of the true faith from the beginning of the world to its end, I may and can and should believe with supreme confidence and joy " that I am and will eternally remain a living member of the same." I am not asked or allowed, indeed I am forbidden, to doubt this. But—since I cannot see myself as this living member—I can cease to doubt it only in faith. And faith means that I look to Jesus Christ, that I subject myself to His verdict and cling to it, that in Him and in virtue of His verdict, in spite of everything which is against me, I am not condemned but justified, not rejected but accepted, not outside but inside, although I cannot know anything for myself but the consciousness of my faith ("Lord, I believe; help thou mine unbelief"), my baptism and my profession. If I believe this for myself, it obviously means that I give myself into His hand with all that is against me and with all that I think I know positively of myself: trusting, but genuinely into His hand. When I do this I do not need to doubt my election and calling, my true Christianity, my holiness; indeed I cannot and must not do so. But if this is the case with me, why should it be otherwise with my supposed fellow-Christians? In relation to them I can obviously only believe that they are not merely supposed Christians, Christians in appearance only, or even Judases. In relation to them I am obviously not summoned to doubt but to believe, and to this end, in relation to them, too, to look to Jesus Christ to whose verdict they are ready to subject themselves in virtue of their baptism and their profession: notwithstanding all that speaks against them and as I see it seems to speak against them. In relation to myself and to them, and therefore to them as well as myself, what can I do but commend both myself and them, them and myself, to His hand and His decision? To them as to me, to me as to them, it is the hidden decision of His free grace which I cannot forestall either positively or negatively. But I can— and obviously should—accept it in advance as right, both for them and for me, for me and for them. He is the Holy One, and as such the Lord and the Head, the Creator and Preserver of His holy community and its holy members. Can I really show my holiness in any other way than by trusting Him as Paul did in the salutations of his Epistles (as in 1 Cor. 1²), trusting that my fellow-Christians are not Christians only in appearance or Judases, but on the basis of His decision and act living members of His body and holy, although their holiness can be just as little perceived and established as my own? Am I not myself acting as a Christian only in appearance, and as a Judas, if I refuse to do this, if I will not allow to be in their favour that which is in my favour? Certainly we do not have any knowledge of that which is invisible in this respect, and we ought to maintain that we do not have it. But when we believe in Jesus Christ, presupposing that we are in the community which is before us and that we live with it, we are required to accept as a working hypothesis that other members as well as ourselves can be holy and not unholy; not on the basis of their own thought and will and action, but in spite of the doubtful nature of all human thought and will and action, as those who are separated by the Lord of the community and therefore genuinely, as real Christians. It is only on this presupposition that the admittedly serious problem of Church discipline can be meaningfully faced. It can never be exercised seriously except among those who are mutually ready to accept each other as Christians.

From the knowledge of the origin of the holiness of the community in that of Jesus Christ there follows (3) the critical question of its obedience. We cannot develop this in the present context. The second part of the doctrine of reconciliation will be the right place to do this. For the moment, in order to prevent a threatened misunderstanding, we have simply to remember that the question is posed, and posed acutely. The statement of Luther that the Church's holiness is not active but passive must not be taken to mean that the Church, with its activity and members, is only as it were covered by a holiness which Jesus Christ places over it from without, so that although its human and visible existence is certainly protected by its invisible holiness it is also blurred by it as by a shade, so that it is not affected or disturbed by it, but is left to go its own way in independence of it. It does not mean that on this great presupposition, for good or evil, according to the best conscience of the men united in it, the community can and must develop and shape and order and control itself and its movements, and always with the comfortable assurance that though this may be more for evil than for good, it cannot itself create and maintain its holiness, but can live only by the holiness of its Lord. It does not mean that its holiness has only—in the deepest sense of the word—a theoretical and not a practical and concrete significance for its human and visible existence. If our previous understanding of the holiness of the community is right, that it is the working in it and to it of the free act of grace of Jesus Christ and the gift of His Holy Spirit, then a deduction of this kind is quite impossible. It is true enough that in this holiness it remains invisible to the world and even to itself apart from faith. It is imparted to it only in so far as there is this working in it and to it. It cannot and will not be visible to every man. It cannot and will not become a predicate of its historical existence which can be maintained in neutrality. It will never be visible even to itself except with reference to its Lord, with the prayer for His Holy Spirit, and for His working within it. It will be visible only in faith. It is not a hypostasis which hovers statically over it and in the knowledge and confession of which it can rejoice in a this-sidedness which for its part both rests and moves in itself. Jesus Christ is not the Holy One for Himself, but for the world and in the first instance for His community in the world. He is not the Holy One in some height or distance above its earthly and historical existence but in it and to it (as His own earthly-historical form of existence). It is not for nothing, therefore, that it is in His hand and even in its this-sidedness, but in its very this-sidedness, in its human doing and non-doing, in its common action and the life of all its members it is continually confronted with His presence as the Holy One, it is continually exposed to His activity, it is continually jolted by Him, it is continually asked whether and to what extent it corresponds in its visible existence to the fact that it is His body, His earthly-historical form of existence. How can it believe and know and confess itself as His holy community, how can its adherents believe and know and confess themselves as its holy members, without looking to Him ? But how can they look to Him without being continually asked how they are really conducting themselves in their relation to Him in their existence here ? And how can they find themselves questioned in this way without hearing His instruction, without being called to obedience to Him, without being asked concerning their obedience ? It would be a singular faith which refused to be asked concerning its character as obedience—as love to the One in whom it is reposed. No, it cannot create and assure its own holiness. It can only trust His holiness and therefore its own. But there is another No, which is this : No, it cannot legitimately trust His holiness and therefore its own without recognising and confessing and respecting it as the imperative and standard of its own human activity, without finding that indolence and self-will are both forbidden and distasteful, without being very definitely stirred into action by His holiness, the holiness of the living Lord, without being summoned to a very definite expectation and movement. His holiness is not given to it as a kind of umbrella under which it can rest or walk up and down at will, but as a pillar of cloud and fire like that which determined the way of the Israelites in the wilderness, as the mystery by which it has to direct itself in its human Church work—although it always remains a mystery. Whether it does this or not, whether it does it in part or altogether, is the question of obedience which is put to it. It cannot answer this question of its holiness by any answer of its own. It can never make itself holy by its human Church work—not even when it has nothing with which to reproach itself in the doing of it. For when it has done all that it has to do, because it is commanded, it will have good reason to know and confess with Lk. 17^{10} that we are unprofitable servants. The question of its holiness—and that of its activity and members—can be answered only with reference to the holiness of its Head. The basis of its holiness is its living Head, present to it as His body and acting in it and to it. This being the case, it is the *conditio sine qua non* of the only possible answer to this question of its holiness that it accepts the question of obedience which is raised by it, and takes it into account in every aspect of its human Church work.

Credo catholicam ecclesiam. The adjective " catholic " means general, comprehensive. It speaks of an identity, a continuity, a universality, which is maintained in all the differences. Applied to the Church it means that it has a character in virtue of which it is always and everywhere the same and always and everywhere recognisable in this sameness, to the preservation of which it is committed. In the character of this sameness it exists and shows itself to be the true Church, the Church of Jesus Christ. Where it does not exist and is not recognisable in this sameness, where it is not concerned to preserve it, where it is not " catholic," it is not the true Church, the Church of Jesus Christ. The term " catholic " speaks explicitly of the true Church activating and confirming its identical being in all its forms. Implicitly it speaks of the contrast between the true Church and the false. It is the false Church in every form in which it does not activate or confirm its identical being but has and reveals and maintains an alien being. It is then a " heretical " Church, i.e., a Church which chooses for itself such an alien being. At the very worst it may even become an " apostate " Church, i.e. one which falls away, which turns its back on the being of the true Church and denies it. Either way it is *eo ipso* a schismatic Church, i.e., one which breaks away from the fellowship of the true Church, a sect which has cut itself off from it. The word " catholic " signifies, therefore, that element in the concept Church which both unites and divides, which is both irenical and polemical. It speaks of what rivets the Church together as a Church. But by this riveting it means something definite, something which cannot be exchanged for anything else. To that extent it speaks of what separates the Church from that which is only ostensibly or supposedly the Church, but which is not the Church.

The Reformation and the Evangelical theology of the 17th century did not allow their claim to the catholicity of their cause to be spoiled by the fact that it was so violently disputed by the Romanist Church under this very name. And in England the refusal to give up this word has persisted not merely in Anglicanism but right up to our own days in Congregationalism. The surrender is, in fact, quite impossible. A Church is catholic or it is not the Church. It was a sign of the greatest thoughtlessness and weakness on our part when in common usage we allowed the word to be taken from us, so that as a title it is now for the most part abandoned to the Romanists and we ourselves are—wherever possible with great emphasis and pleasure—described as a-catholics, heretics, schismatics and sectarians, and it is to us a most derogatory matter if we think we can establish or even report of someone that he is guilty of " catholicising " or " catholic " tendencies. As though a genuine Church and theology could have any other tendency at all than one which is not merely " catholicising " but seriously " catholic ! "

Credo catholicam ecclesiam simply means that—although I do not have faith in it but in the Holy Spirit and through Him in the Father and the Son—I believe in the existence of a community which in the essence which makes it a Christian community is unalterable in spite of all its changes of form, which in this essence never has altered and never can or will alter. And negatively, I do not believe that a community which is different in essence is the Christian community. To bring the two together, I believe in the existence of a true Church and not in that of a false Church.

The plurality or variety which is embraced by the Church in virtue of its unalterable essence or against which it maintains and is pledged to maintain its unalterable essence was at first understood primarily in a geographical sense. The Church is the same in all countries and in all parts of the earth, and in essence it has to present itself as the same in all of them. " Catholic " had, therefore, and in the first instance still has, the narrower sense of " ecumenical ", i.e. identical in the whole inhabited world, in all parts of the globe where men live and where it can exist as the Church.

" Because " ecumenical " only brings out one dimension of the term " catholic " we may deplore the fact that it has been chosen to describe the modern attempts at reunion and unity. Some part of the responsibility must be attributed to the meaningless but passionate opposing of the terms " Catholic " and " Protestant." But there are signs that as progress is made in these attempts the wider term " catholic " will fill out or burst through the narrower term " ecumenical."

From the geographical meaning of the word there has derived and still derives the wider sense in which the reference is to the relationship of the Christian community to the other natural and historical human societies. In essence the Church is the same in all races, languages, cultures and classes, in all forms of state and society. If it is to remain the true Church, it cannot be essentially determined by any of these societies. It cannot allow its conception of itself to be dictated by them. It cannot adjust itself to them. In all the apparently unavoidable accommodations of a practical and technical kind, it must see to it that it does not become guilty of deviation from the way which can only be the same in all spheres, or of disloyalty to the commission which it has to discharge in them all. With greater ease or difficulty it can enter into symbiosis with all societies, but it cannot accept any kind of essential dependence on them. Christians will always be Christians first, and only then members of a specific culture or state or class or the like. Similarly in all these different spheres the Church must always be the Church first, and only then, in the first instance in the advocacy of its own cause, and to that extent always with a certain alienation, can it enter into positive relationships with these other spheres.

Christianity exists in Germany and Switzerland and Africa, but there is no such thing as a German or Swiss or African Christianity. There is a Church in England, but in the strict sense there is no Church of England. It was quite intolerable when some twenty years ago the rise of Hitler was seriously claimed as a kind of divine revelation, or when to satisfy the racial laws of National Socialism it was proposed to found special congregations of Jewish Christians. How much longer will it be possible in the United States and South Africa to ratify the social distinctions between whites and blacks by a corresponding division in the Church, instead of calling it in question in the social sphere by the contrary practice of the Church ? And in the tension of this present age will it be given not merely to the Churches of the Eastern bloc but above all to those of the supposedly free West to escape in time, and effectively, the influence of the world around them upon their message and function ? Every Church in every age has good reason to ask concering its catholicity in this sense. Does it exist only as a kind of respectable local, regional or national tradition valued and cherished by certain circles and sections ? Or as one of the instruments of the power of society or the ruling class in society ? Or—as happens again and again—as a union which is cleverly tolerated or even encouraged by statesmanship to satisfy certain religious needs or to buttress the morality and outlook which is desired for the well-being of the state ? By its very antithesis (e.g., the combating of a materialistic philosophy) may it not be guilty of self-betrayal as a secularised Church ? Does it exist of its essence and in faithfulness to its essence ? We must never think that we can arrive at a position where we will not be disturbed by this question.

But the term catholic then has an even wider temporal dimension. It tells us that the Church has maintained itself and has to maintain itself in the identity of its essence even in the historical sequence of its forms. It exists in history. It is history. It makes history. But this being the case, it is clear that in this respect it exists only in change. It is on a way which is surrounded by a continually changing landscape and in which it is itself continually subject to change—but in which it can never become anything other than itself, in which it is obliged and summoned always to be the same and continually to maintain itself as the same in forms which are always new.

At this point we must resist with equal firmness two imminent errors.

The " catholic " and therefore the true Church is not the oldest Church as such. It is not, therefore, that Church which at a later time and even to-day can appeal with the greatest certainty to the continuity and conformity of its structure with that of the most primitive Church. In this respect the *Scots Confession* of 1560 remarked dryly but correctly (Art. 18) that in point of age and the dignity which it confers Cain ultimately has precedence over both Abel and Seth. It is not because it was the oldest community, but because it was that of the direct witnesses to Jesus Christ that the community of the New Testament is for every age the typical, " catholic " community. Even in the form which immediately followed the Church was at once questioned concerning its catholicity, so that in an answering of the question of the catholicity of the Church in its later forms this form is not without interest and importance but cannot claim to be in any basic sense normative. All honour to the apostolic fathers and the rest of the 2nd century. All honour, too, to the churchmanship and theology of the early days of the Reformation and their confessional statements. But the question of the true Church cannot possibly resolve itself simply into that of conformity with any forms which are earlier in point of time. Reaction in the form of a return to any fathers is ecclesiastical romanticism ; it has never been the way to maintain or restore the catholicity of the Church. For the same reason the character of the Church as a true Church can never be deduced from or established by the proof of a legal succession (we will return to this question) of its ministry linking it with the ancient or most ancient Church. The Church of any age, ancient or modern, most ancient or most modern, is the true and therefore the catholic, the general and comprehensive Church, only to the extent that in its own age it participates in the essence of the one Church, being faithful to it and knowing how to do it justice in its visible expression.

Conversely, it is not the newness, the modernity, the up-to-dateness of a Church which as such proves and commends it as the true and catholic Church. There was a proud *theologia moderna* even in the 15th century. At the time of Protestant orthodoxy the introduction of Aristotelianism was the last word in modernity about 1600, as was that of Cartesianism a little later. After 1700 the modern theology was one which knew how to be orthodox, pietistic and enlightened at one and the same time. Naturally all the different forms of theological and ecclesiastical Liberalism boasted of their modernity as a sign of truth. According to Troeltsch and his contemporaries in age and controversy,

" Neo-Protestantism " was definitely the most important of all the keys to the kingdom of heaven. And we must not forget that at that time there was in the Church and in theology a trend and school of " modern positivism." But modernity, up-to-dateness, has nothing whatever to do with the question of the truth of the Church. For that reason the idea of progress is a highly doubtful one as applied to the Church. What counts in the Church is not progress but reformation—its existence as *ecclesia semper reformanda*. *Semper reformari*, however, does not mean always to go with the time, to let the current spirit of the age be the judge of what is true and false, but in every age, and in controversy with the spirit of the age, to ask concerning the form and doctrine and order and ministry which is in accordance with the unalterable essence of the Church. It means to carry out to-day better than yesterday the Christian community's one task which needs no revision, and in this way to " sing unto the Lord a new song." It means never to grow tired of returning not to the origin in time but to the origin in substance of the community. The Church is catholic when it is engaged in this *semper reformari*, so that catholicism has nothing to do with conservatism either, but very much to do with the sound common sense of the prayer of the robust Nicholas Selnecker (which is still to be found even in the new Swiss hymnbook) : " Against proud spirits stand and, fight,/Who lift themselves in lofty might,/And always bring in something new,/ To falsify thy teaching true." Therefore neither flirtation with the old nor flirtation with the new makes the Church the true Church, but a calm consideration of that which as its abiding possession is superior to every yesterday and to-day and is therefore the criterion of its catholicity.

But the Church is also the catholic, the general and comprehensive and therefore true community of Jesus Christ in its relationship to its individual members, to Christians. The Christian is first a member of the Christian community and only then, and as such, this individual Christian in his particular Christian being and nature and presence. And this means that the Christian faith is first the faith of the Christian community and only then and as such, affirmed and shared by them, the faith of the men united in it. It does not have in them, as it were, its original and normative form. It is not the sum, as it were, of the different individual acts of Christian faith, which would necessarily mean the cross-cut, agreement and compromise between them. In and with their individual faith Christians participate in and with the faith of the community. In this their faith has its basis, norm and limit. It derives from it and is built up on it. And the same is true of all the personal knowledge and confession of faith. It is, as such, basically co-ordinated with and subordinated to the knowledge and confession of the community. It is true in so far as it is " catholic " and therefore has a part in the knowledge and confession of the community. As personal knowledge and confession it has its own place and right and freedom within the knowledge and confession of the community, not outside it, not elsewhere, not *in abstracto*. It is true that the community for its own part has no external power to prevent its members going beyond and therefore leaving the place and right and freedom of their own within the comprehensive unity of the common faith, knowledge and confession. But it is responsible for their not being able to do this without a serious attestation of that which makes them the community or its members. And above all it is responsible for their maintaining in a pure and living form their being as the Christian community in face of all the caprices of individuals and whatever may be the individual ways of its members. As the body of Jesus Christ conjoined with its Head it has priority over its members and it has to maintain this priority not only for the sake of the Head but also for that of the members. That is what " catholic " means in this dimension.

It hardly needs to be said that we are dealing here with a point of view which has been most flagrantly neglected in modern Protestantism since the 18th century. From the visible standpoint our Protestant national Churches are little more than great unions, or communities of interest, of individuals who are Christian or are called Christian, individualists, each of whom—like the people of Israel in the time of the Judges—does that which is right in his own eyes, so that although some may act together in particular *ecclesiolae* called movements, we cannot inquire too closely what it really is that unites them. Even less can we inquire what these Churches are as a whole, a question which would yield the most gratuitous and to a large extent unconvincing answers. If we will and can and must maintain the form revealed in them, then we can only sigh : *Kyrie eleison.* Destroying as they do the relationship between the community and its members, they are hopelessly a-catholic Churches, hardly distinguishable, if at all, from heretical sects, or sects which verge on heresy, in the matter which now concerns us.

The most obvious example is the 1911 *Constitution of the Evangelical Reformed Church of the City of Basel.* It begins with a kind of hymnal introit to which a conscientious exegete could hardly give any but an Arian sense : " In the name and to the glory of God our Creator and Father, who has given us Jesus Christ as our Saviour and Redeemer and through Him called us out of darkness into His marvellous light. Amen." Then it is explained that the Church of Basel is a " member of the universal Christian Church," the heir and successor in law of the Church which in 1529 " was renewed by the decree of the people and congregations on the basis of Holy Scripture," and one of the Churches " which resulted from the Reformation." The remarkable interpretation of this " resulted from " is that the basis of its teaching is " Jesus Christ and His Gospel, which it has sought out from the Bible under the guidance (not of the Holy Spirit but) of Christian conscience, experience and scholarship, and which it proclaims and endeavours to put into practice." Further : " In loyalty to the basic principles of Protestantism it expects its members to come to a personal conviction in the great Evangelical truths on the basis of reflection and experience." But who are these members ? " All Protestants residing in the canton of the city of Basel," or (according to the official commentary) " all Christians of Evangelical profession who have not expressly declared their withdrawal." In spite of this, or by this means, it is their aim " to contribute to the furtherance of the kingdom of God on earth by the Gospel as the unfailing source of eternal life and personal and social progress."

The faith which dares to maintain the *credo unam sanctam ecclesiam* in face of a Church which expresses and manifests itself in this way will have to be strong enough to remove a few by no means negligible mountains. We may certainly ask whether—if this is the state of affairs, as it is not merely in Basel and Switzerland—it is not, after all, better that it should be stated in the solemn and shameless way which is customary in Switzerland. But, however that may be, it makes no odds : *rebus sic stantibus* the community of Jesus Christ obviously has to be and wills to be believed even as expressed and manifested in this or some similar form. Just as a zealous Roman Catholic will not hesitate to confess the *Una Sancta* even when he thinks of Alexander VI and its representation in him, so we will not be ashamed to do the same even in relation to the constitution of the Church of Basel and similar depressing phenomena. But as long as the voice of theology is not entirely stilled even in the sphere of Churches of this kind, we cannot refrain from addressing to them the following question : What is really at the back of their minds ? On the one hand they expressly call themselves a member of the universal (catholic) Church, resulting from the Reformation and referred back to Jesus Christ and His Gospel. On the other, they deduce this reformation on the basis of Holy Scripture historico-politically from a decision of the people and congregations made in the year 1529 ; they hand over the exposition and proclamation of the Gospel unreservedly to the Christian conscience, experience and not very closely defined scholarship of its members—those who have not expressly declared their withdrawal ; and apparently they do not expect from these members anything more necessary than that they should " come to a personal conviction " in the Christian " truths on the basis of reflection and experience." And all this as a contribution to the furtherance of the kingdom of God on earth. Fortunately this only stands on paper, or is accepted only in the hearts and minds of unruly " Protestants," while all the time *Dei providentia hominum confusione* the unalterable essence of the community of Jesus Christ persists even in Churches of this kind and therefore in Basel, continually pointing us in quite a different direction. But we cannot conceal the fact that a Church is in error, that it is not loyal but disloyal to its unalterable essence, if it thinks that it can and should manifest and express itself in this way, with this reversal of its true priorities.

A contrary example which ought to put us to shame is that of the decisive statements on the Church in the confession of the Protestant Batak-Church of Sumatra (which was drawn up without any Western participation at a synod held at Sipoholon in November 1951) :

" We believe and confess : The Church is the congregation of those who believe in Jesus Christ and are called, gathered, sanctified and maintained by God through the Holy Spirit.

" We believe and confess : The Church is holy. The Church is not holy because of the holiness of its members themselves, but because Christ the Head is holy. Therefore the Church is holy because Christ has sanctified them and God sees them to be holy. Because the Church is holy, it is called the ' holy people,' ' the temple of the Holy Ghost ' and the ' dwelling-place of God.'

" We believe and confess : The Church is a universal Church. The universal Church is the gathering of all the saints who already participate in the Lord Jesus Christ and His gifts, in the Gospel, in the Holy Spirit, in faith and love and hope. (The Church comes . . .) from all lands and peoples and races and tribes and tongues, although their customs and laws are different.

" We believe and confess : There is one Church. It is based on what we are told in Eph. 4^4, 1 Cor. 12^{20}. For there is one body which is the Church. Although the members are many, the body is one. The unity of the Church mentioned here differs from what is usually meant by worldly unity. For it is a spiritual unity."

Lk. 13$^{29-30}$!

What does it mean : *credo catholicam ecclesiam* ? Gathering together what we have worked out in these four dimensions we can say : I believe that the Christian community is one and the same in essence in all places, in all ages, within all societies, and in relation to all its members. I believe that it can be the Christian community only in this identity, and therefore that it is its task to maintain itself in this identity, and therefore in this identity to will to be, and continually to become and to remain, the Christian community, and nothing else, and therefore the true Church in all these dimensions. This has to be believed because, in fact, it is continually threatened in this identity at every point and in all these dimensions. It has to be believed because in all its visible existence it is a focal point of conflict between the true Church and the false. It is, in fact, always in danger. And the most serious danger which threatens it is always to become a community of a different essence and therefore a-catholic— it may be by reason of differences of locality, it may be by reason of unavoidable temporal change, it may be by reason of the influence of other human societies, it may be by reason of the variety of its individual members, and often enough and perhaps always in a concurrence of all these moments, which are the necessary elements of its earthly-historical existence. There is no Church which is not in fact open to attack in respect of its catholicity, its true character, and therefore its Christianity. There is hardly a Church which in this respect has not been seriously, perhaps very seriously, damaged and even destroyed on the one side or the other (and possibly on all of them together). For this reason it never has been, and never is, visible in practice as the true Church " the temple of God " (1 Cor. 3^{16}), the " habitation of God in the Spirit " (Eph. 2^{22}), the " bride without spot or wrinkle " (Eph. 5^{27}), the " pillar and ground of truth " (1 Tim. 3^{15}). It has never been visible as such to outsiders who could and can be amused or irritated with it in terms of Lessing's parable of the three rings, nor has it ever been visible as such to itself and its members in relation to what they see. Because this is the case with its catholicity, we have to say at every point : *credo catholicam ecclesiam.* Just as without faith we cannot see its unity or holiness, so without faith we cannot see its catholicity. Conversely, it can be asserted as a negative criterion of catholicity—measured by which the Churches which most emphasise that they are " catholic " will not stand—that where a Church thinks it cannot and should not merely believe its catholicity but should be able—in its own form—to see and maintain it, then in its arrogance and unreadiness to repent this Church shows itself to be a-catholic. A real Church cannot possibly fail to see that it is only a theatre of conflict between the true Church and the false, and that in the battle which has to be fought out in this respect it is no less threatened than any others. A true Church is humbly content to be thrown back entirely upon faith in respect of its truth, and confidently to exist in this faith as the true community of Jesus Christ.

Is it superfluous at this point to refer particularly to a specific form of the supposed perception of the catholicity of the Church—superfluous because at first sight the error responsible seems so banal as almost to be unworthy of serious consideration ?

The view is simply this : that if a Church or communion has a big, even a very big membership, then that is a pointer or prejudice in favour of the truth being on its side, whereas a tiny Church or group in a corner comes at once under the suspicion that it is a sect simply because it seems that in it we have to do only with a very few people. This sounds dreadfully banal, because so obviously it does not look beyond the surface. It is comforting to think that the good God likes to be on the side of the big battalions, so that we have only to look to these to find traces of the true Church. Certainly great membership rolls and good attendance and full churches and halls (and even lecture rooms) are facts which naturally impress us—who can fail to be impressed by them ?—but what do they really have to do with the truth ? It was again the *Scots Confession* of 1560 which rightly pointed out that the Scribes and Pharisees were certainly in a majority against Jesus and His disciples, and ·yet they were wrong. And even Romanist dogmatics (B. Bartmann, vol. 2, p. 199) explains that the predicate *catholica* must not be understood mechanically and quantitatively, but spiritually and qualitatively—as a divine claim of the Church which cannot be based on numbers but only on the actual superiority of the truth. This is prettily illustrated by the fact (*op. cit.* p. 161) that in his necessary ratification of the decree of a council the Pope is not bound by the decision of the majority, but if he believes it to be right he can take up and definitively justify the *pars minor et sanior*. To elect and vote in the Church is always a doubtful matter. It may decide what seems most opportune in the community in any given situation. But it certainly cannot decide what is the truth whether it is opportune or not. In the primitive Church an attempt was usually made to avoid it. Voting was replaced by decisions *per acclamationem*. But it may be asked whether this is any better or more free from problems. The *veritas catholica* may undoubtedly lie with the minority. It may occasionally lie with the tiniest of minorities, in a veritable corner. It may lie only with the two or three gathered together (as in Mt. 18²⁰) in the name of Jesus Christ. That they number several millions is of no avail to those who are not gathered in His name. The whole legitimacy of the Reformation rests upon this possibility. There are some who go further and boldly affirm that the *veritas catholica* will very likely, indeed will fairly (or most) certainly, be found within the minority. An empty Church is regarded as a comforting indication and prejudice in favour of the fact that the pure Gospel is proclaimed in it. Is there not something strangely and in its way impressively pathetic about the existence of a small Church or group ? In certain circumstances does it not involve a genuine pleasure and exaltation to be in a minority—perhaps the tiniest of minorities : the little flock to which it is the Father's good pleasure to give the kingdom, which is therefore a kind of advance guard of God ? In Schiller's words : " What is majority ? Majority is folly." Good sense is never found but with the few.

But here again we must be careful. There have been minorities whose resistance to the majority has not been legitimate because their cause has had nothing whatever to do with the *veritas catholica*, because in them we are dealing only with manifestations of an utterly a-catholic individualism—in the garb of particularism and sectarianism. In the history of the Church both before and after the 16th century there have been far too many little movements of reform instigated by men who appealed readily to the fact that a majority proves nothing, that truth and the good God are more likely to be on the side of the small and even the smallest battalions, and yet in the long run they proved to be no more lasting than a kind of carnival procession. Conversely, the evangelical record itself tells us, not morosely but with joy (Mk. 3⁷ᶦ·), that a great multitude (πολὺ πλῆθος) followed Jesus of Nazareth and that when they heard what He did a great multitude came to Him from Judæa and Jerusalem and Transjordania and even the districts around Tyre and Sidon. This is not noted as a proof of the Messiahship of Jesus or the coming of God's kingdom amongst men, but as a fact which is in its own way significant. Again the 3,000 and later the 5,000 who, according to Ac. 2⁴¹ and 4⁴, received the Word and were baptised after the events of the day of Pentecost were not by any means negligible and did not appear so either to Luke or to Theophilus. We have also to consider that in the long run every minority, however content it may be as such, however proud of itself, has all the same a concealed or open tendency to become the majority, and that this has, in fact, often been the case. The transition is undoubtedly a dangerous one and sometimes fatal. There was something very far wrong when barely 300 years later the little flock of Lk. 12 became the imperial world-Church of Constantine, and many a minority in the Church has lost more than it has gained by becoming a majority, or a big Church instead of a small. But it is not fundamentally the case that when the few become many the truth also becomes error. Many a victory for catholic truth may be won by such transitions. Again, the truth may in the first instance have been with the majority. Why not ? If the greater number is not always a guarantee of the truth, it does not need always to be against the truth. It can be a witness which those who find themselves in the minority may do well to hear. They may well have gone too far forward or lagged too far behind. The *pars maior* may be to them the *pars sanior*, representing genuine continuity and therefore the genuine *semper reformari*. In any case it is a very serious and responsible thing for a minority to oppose the majority in the community—a risk which no one ought to undertake too easily. For if a smaller number does not mean that catholic truth is not on this side, it certainly does not mean that it is.

The matter may seem banal, but it can be very misleading in practice, both on the one side and on the other. For that reason it is as well to state expressly that in this sense, too, there can be no perception of the catholicity of a Church, whether by small numbers or by great. As a spiritual and qualitative predicate, as the promise given to it, in its visible and historical expression either in the many or in the few, catholicity can only be believed.

But that means that objectively it is exactly the same with the catholicity and therefore the truth of the Christianity of a Church as it is with its unity and holiness : the Church has no control over it. Its being as *ecclesia catholica*, the fact that everywhere and at all times and in relation to all other societies and to all its individual members it is one and the same, is actual in the fact that it is the body, the earthly-historical form of the existence of Jesus Christ. Therefore catholicity as its own actuality is grounded in Him as its Head. It falls upon it as the reflection of the light which gives light in Him. It comes to it in the event of His living Word and work by the Holy Spirit, in its visitation by and encounter with Him. He is the man who maintains His sovereign identity both here and there, yesterday and to-day, within and on behalf of all historical forms, in face of all individual Christians. The community is catholic as He lives and speaks and acts in His community. But this means that in this respect, too, it is made responsible and called to obedience and questioned concerning its obedience by Him. Of Him it lacks nothing to enable it to rejoice in this identity of its being even in its concrete historical form in all these dimensions. But in this concrete form it lives as His body in this world. It is spiritual by nature, but it exists in terms of this world. Therefore there is always something lacking in its expression of itself. It may be one thing here, another there. Indeed, in the strict sense it is everything everywhere. Its expression in terms of this world is always a compromising, and obscuring and denying of its spiritual nature. It acts like the sleeping disciples in the Garden of Gethsemane. It is like Peter who at first was so self-confident, and then struck so recklessly and finally denied so blatantly. It is even like Judas Iscariot. As the true Church it would always die and perish if He did not speak to it, if it did not hear His voice, summoning it to watch and pray : to watch over its being in all its dimensions, in its preaching and doctrine and theology, but also in its constitution and order and various ministries, and even in its actions and attitudes in face of the problems of the world around it ; and to pray that in all these things it may remain with Him and in love to Him, " that we may seek no other Lord, but Jesus in a true faith, trusting in Him with all our might." For what is the good of all its watching if it does not pray that this may take place, that it may, therefore, be or be again a Christian community ? What is the good of it if this does not take place with the hearing of its prayer ? It is to pray that it should watch—or, rather, all its watching, and its related action and activity, should be a prayerful watching. As long as it is in the world and therefore itself worldly, even in all its watching and its watchful activity, it can never of itself secure that it should remain with its Head as His living body. This time in the words of Zwingli : " O Lord, raise up thine own chariot, Or all our ways will perish." Zwingli did not allow either his heart or his hand to sink when he thought and prayed in this way. Those who are slack in obedience are the ones who will not think and pray in this way. But the community will think and pray in this way when it is brisk and ready to obey, when it does not throw over the reins, when it is in practical earnest to protect itself against all the threatened invasions. It will not avoid the care and effort and labour and inward and outward conflict which it costs sincerely to build only on the Son of God who gathers and protects and maintains it as His community. It will be energetic to know as an event a deeper perception, a purer confession, a fuller uniting of its members in love to Him, a more confident and yet more humble, an objectively more relevant and subjectively more practical attestation to the world around of His lordship as the obedient servant of God. And when it does not spare any efforts, when it does not shun any inward or outward tension, when, in the words of 1 Cor. 16[13], it stands fast in the faith and is manly and strong, when, in the words of Heb. 12[4], it resists unto blood, then it will see clearly that it is not itself or anything resulting from its labour and conflict which makes it the true Christian community, but He alone, the Son of God who gathers and protects and maintains it, His work and His Spirit.

In unity with Him it will persist in its contradistinction to Him. It will therefore know that its work and the results of that work are one thing, but quite another is the attaining and achieving and possessing ($\kappa\alpha\tau\alpha\nu\tau\hat{\alpha}\nu$) of the unity of its faith in the Son of God (Eph. 4[13f.]), that being of the full-grown man in the fulness in which Christ Himself is a full-grown man. It can only be summoned and warned and directed, to leave the state of νήπιοι, not to be tossed to and fro and carried about with every wind of doctrine by the sleight of men, not to be deceived by cunning craftiness, but ἀληθεύοντες ἐν ἀγάπῃ to grow up in its whole being (τὰ πάντα) to Him which is the Head. To this summons, warning and direction alone can it give its attention and obedience.

And if in anything at all, then in this clear knowledge of its limit it will be catholic—in its satisfaction with Jesus Christ Himself, in the fact that it will not give to its activity any other character than that of a diaconate or witness in His service, that it will be zealous and loyal in this character, that it will not invest it with any kind of mysterious importance or magic or thaumaturgy or supernatural legality or authoritative claim, that, in the words of 1 Thess. 5¹⁷, it will simply prove it by praying without ceasing. He, the living Son of God, is Himself its identical and continuing and universal essence, maintaining and asserting itself in all dimensions. He is the source and norm of its identity : the *veritas catholica.* He constitutes the community the true Church and as such marks it off from the false. He is the man by whose irenics and polemics it lives, without whose judgment executed in His Word and by His Spirit, without whose uniting and excluding, it can only be an obscure sect even in its supposedly most perfect forms. As He makes it one and holy, so He makes it universal. And therefore faith in Him, which can never cease to be a busy faith, is the only effective and not really passive but supremely active realisation of the *credo catholicam ecclesiam.*

Credo apostolicam ecclesiam. It is excellent that in the creed of 381 after *una, sancta, catholica* there appeared for the first time a fourth predicate which has since become a firm constituent of the liturgy of at least the Roman and Eastern Catholic Churches : *apostolica.* All four predicates describe the one being of the Christian community. But we can and should read and understand them as mounting to a climax. *Una* describes its singularity. *Sancta* describes the particularity which underlies this singularity. *Catholica* describes the essence in which it manifests and maintains itself in this particularity and singularity. And finally, *apostolica* does not say anything new, in relation to these three definitions, but describes with remarkable precision the concrete spiritual criterion which enables us to answer the question whether and to what extent in this or that case we have or have not to do with the one holy catholic Church. The criterion is not sociological or juridical or psychological, but spiritual. The word *credo* is still in front, and must not be forgotten. Even the criterion that the Church is apostolic, with all that that involves, can be known only in faith, and cannot be seen except in faith.

There is no doubt that, according to the ecclesiology of the Roman Catholic Church, the predicate *apostolica*, and with it the other three predicates, all need the decisive interpretation given by the term *Romana*. It is the Roman Church, i.e., the Church which stands in unity with the bishop of Rome and under his teaching authority and jurisdiction, which is the apostolic and therefore the one holy universal Church. More recent Roman Catholic theology certainly reckons with the possibility that there might be a kind of *una, sancta, catholica et apostolica ecclesia* even outside the visible bastions of the Roman Church. It can even consider the question whether the better part of it, or the best elements of truth, which it has itself neglected, may not be found to-day outside rather than inside that Church. But it cannot do this without the proviso that this Church outside, so far as it may be *una, sancta, catholica et apostolica*, is even in spite of its own ignorance and contrary will objectively, invisibly and actually the Roman Church, united with the bishop of Rome, pledged to him as its overlord and destined to return to him as the *vicarius Christi*. Beyond this line even the most magnanimous interpretation of the Church cannot go. All the same—and this is one of the merits of the inviolability of an ancient liturgy—the word *Romana* has not succeeded in penetrating into it. " Roman " would, of course, be a sociological and juridical criterion of what is apostolic. When we equate it with Roman, apostolic gives us a moment in the idea of the Church which can be seen and established neutrally by every man. And from this standpoint the unity and holiness and catholicity of the Church become qualities which can be seen and established neutrally, thus escaping the *fide solum intelligimus* of the *Cat. Rom.* There were inner reasons why the creed could not be expanded in this way. We can be clear that on the basis of the ecumenical creed when we speak of the Church as apostolic—even though on the other side a powerful " Roman" stands behind it—we have to do with a criterion which is spiritual.

It is, however, a concrete criterion. In this it differs from the moments in the idea of the Church which we have considered hitherto. In attempting to fill out the first three terms we could point only to Jesus Christ as the Head of the community which is His body, and therefore to the work of the Holy Spirit. Even in relation to the last term " catholic " Jesus Christ alone is the *veritas catholica*, and it is He who makes the Church the catholic Church, His Church, the true, Christian Church, and therefore, as we have seen, the one holy Church. The question may rightly be asked whether in saying this we have not said too much because we have said too little for faith, for the faith which asks after knowledge, *fides quaerens intellectum*. In respect of catholic can we not make some concrete statement, not a sociological and juridical but a spiritual statement and therefore one which can be made and grasped only in faith, yet a concrete statement in relation to that controlling relationship of Jesus Christ as the Head to the community as His body which underlies the truth and therefore the unity and holiness of the Church ?

It was Cyril of Jerusalem who in his *Catechetical Lectures* (18, 26) gave to Christians travelling abroad this advice : " When you come into a city, do not simply ask : Where is the house of the Lord ? for the godless heretics are bold to call their dens the house of the Lord. Do not simply ask : Where is the Church? but : Where is the catholic Church ? " But supposing modern heretics dare to call their " den " the catholic Church ? Supposing the Christian stranger hears them speak as heretics always love to do—not going outside the tradition—with particular emphasis and warmth of Jesus Christ ? Supposing he hears them appeal to the Holy Spirit—perhaps with the saying in 2 Cor. 3^{17} : " Where the Spirit of the Lord is, there is liberty "—and is conscious of a very highly spiritual being ? It is not at all a matter of distinguishing absolutely between the true and the false, the catholic and the heretical. For the most part the distinction will be between the greater or lesser clarity and distinctness of the catholic, or the greater or lesser proximity of the heretical. To some extent, therefore, it will be made in the half-light of a middle sphere. What is the position when an Evangelical Christian attends a Roman Catholic mass or an assembly of Protestant individualists which has more or less the character of a sect, or when he reads the dogmatics of a Tersteegen or a Biedermann, or in short whenever he encounters any kind of Christianity and he cannot withhold a certain Yes, a certain understanding which unites him, but at bottom he cannot either understand or approve or accept it, but for the most part and therefore for himself is forced to say a very exclusive No ? What is really the position in one of the ecumenical conferences when one day we have to take part in, or to be ready to accept, the morning worship of Swedish-Lutherans, the next that of American Baptists, and the day after perhaps that of Eastern Catholics which seems to us incredibly antiquated and probably almost pagan in its demands : singing *Cantate Domino* in all kinds of tongues, some of which we trust, some of which are definitely outlandish and suspicious ? In such situations we cannot escape some kind of distinction, even though it may be more comforting to let ourselves be reminded by the constantly recurring name of Jesus Christ that it all seems to have to do with the one centre. But the question is with what clarity and distinctness, and this question cannot be settled by the " We all believe in one God" of our male-voice choirs. What is the real ground of our predominant No—or sometimes of our participating and to some extent understanding Yes—if both are not simply to be the expression of an emotional attraction or aversion but are based on real perception ? Above all, what is the standard by which we can be certain of our own cause, our own standing in the true Church, our preference for this or that place in the true Church ? What is the standard by which, with equal decision on the left hand and on the right, and with a good conscience, we can publicly take our stand in this place and not in that ?

It is here that the predicate " apostolic " comes in. It gives us a concrete criterion, the one and only *nota ecclesiae*, not in competition with the decisive determination of the Church by the existence and work of its living Lord, but as the true and authentic interpretation of this basic determination. It is truly helpful, of course, only when we do not try to deprive it of its character as a spiritual criterion.

Apostolic means in the discipleship, in the school, under the normative authority, instruction and direction of the apostles, in agreement with them, because listening to them and accepting their message. The Church is the true Church and therefore the one holy Church in the fact and to the extent that it is apostolic in this sense, and by this fact it can and should be known as such and distinguished from the false Church. Even the predicate apostolic, and especially this predicate, describes the being of the community as an event. This mutual relationship to the apostles is obviously something which can take place only in a history between them. And for good or evil the man who wants to see and recognise it as the apostolic community must himself take part in this history. He cannot be a neutral and decide its apostolicity from outside. He must be a living member, and as such must know its basis in the apostles, himself standing in their discipleship, in their school, under their authority and direction, himself hearing their witness, himself being taught and questioned by them. He must be put by them in a definite movement, in the movement in which they found themselves, in which they still find themselves to-day—for in the New Testament they are still before us in living speech and action. To be in the community of Jesus Christ means to take part in this movement. And it is and is known as the true Church by the fact that where it exists as such it finds itself in this movement. This movement is a very concrete but a spiritual process. It is definitely distinguished from other such movements. It is the work of the Holy Spirit, and as such it can be known in its concrete distinction only by the Holy Spirit and therefore in faith.

Thus the apostolicity of the Church cannot and must not be sought on historical and juridical grounds. The particular temptation in this respect is the equivocal notion of the " apostolic succession." It is a temptation when it is understood on the presupposition of a supernatural jurisprudence which can be supported by historical proof—that by the rite of laying on of hands there is a technical inheritance or transmission of the apostolic authority and teaching office and ministry, in which in some sense it flows over from a supreme officebearer in the Church, e.g., from a bishop, to his successor, and from this successor to the inferior ministers who will be ordained by him. This is found where the list of the predecessors of the bishop who ordains to-day can demonstrably be traced back without a break through the centuries to a first bishop of the place in question who was one of the twelve apostles ordained by Christ Himself. To stand in the apostolic succession in this sense is to be in a Church which is proved to be a true Church by the fact that its ministers are attached to this line and therefore to the stream guaranteed by it, that they have a part in the apostolic grace of office which, through the centuries, has passed from one hand to another. Thus, on the one hand, apostolicity and the true Church are a matter which we can know by reference to a transmitted list of bishops, which we can prove by the historico-critical investigation of this list, and which in favourable circumstances we can establish beyond doubt by digging up some apostolic remains. It is obvious that neither the Holy Spirit nor faith is necessary for this purpose, but only an uncritical or critical archæological knowledge of the lists. And, on the other hand, apostolicity and therefore the true Church are an understanding and acceptance of the system in consequence of which apostolicity is like the sovereignty of a hereditary ruler or even a farm handed down from father to son. By means of the laying on of hands it passes from one bishop to a second, who is then empowered to ordain and will transmit it to a third as the successor of the first. At every stage it has a desired result for the lower clergy who take part in it, and through them for the rest of the community, the laity. Once again, it is clear that to accept this system does not need either the Holy Spirit or faith but only a definite idea of law.

We may or may not be convinced of the rightness of this without either acceptance or rejection of the *credo ecclesiam*. All that is needed is to recognise and assess the fact that—whatever else may be said— this is the law and practice of the Church.

For our part we can only note that there are whole Churches, especially the Roman Catholic, but also the Eastern Orthodox, and the Anglican not far behind, who not only regard the apostolicity grounded in this kind of apostolic succession as a particular adorn- ment of their particular estate, but, insisting more or less emphatically upon it, deduce and claim from it their character as the catholic and therefore the true Church.

In this respect the Lutheran Church of Sweden is an exception. It seems to have particularly good evidence that the apostolic succession of its archbishops and bishops was maintained without a break at the time of the Reformation. But it expressly refrains from ascribing to this fact any dogmatic significance, treating it only as a welcome adornment of its constitution as a Church. In this respect it does not meet with the approval of the stricter Anglicans, who cannot have the same historical certainty in view of what took place under Henry VIII, but who attach to the matter a supreme doctrinal importance. There is no doubt that the bishops who suddenly appeared in Lutheran Germany some twenty or thirty years ago cannot have the "succession" in view of the great disruption of it in the 16th century. It may well be suspected of them that they would like to have it. The idea seems to have been considered of acquiring it by way of the Swedes who are more fortunate and so indifferent in the matter. The latest development is that even in the Reformed sphere (è.g., Holland) there are individual ministers who feel most unhappy that they do not stand in the legiti- mate line of succession in their administration of preaching, baptism and the Lord's Supper, and they are casting uncertain glances here, there and every- where to try to secure it in some concealed way from someone who already has it. Who knows what wonderful things we may not see in relation to this question !

All that we can do, perhaps, is just to—wonder. It is only one difficulty that when we understand the apostolic succession in this way, then as a historical and juridical hypothesis it ceases to be part of the *credo ecclesiam*. The question also arises what is this " apostol- icity " which a man who is a bishop can transfer institutionally and ritually to another man so that he becomes a bishop, and can then pass it on institutionally and ritually to the inferior clergy ? Is it actually the Holy Spirit, whom the apostles received from the Lord, and in whose power they preached ? If this is the doctrine of the succession, then it means that the grace of office legitimately passed from one man to another by means of a fixed rite is nothing more or less than the Holy Spirit Himself in the form of a particular gift which is decisively important for the being of the community. But in that case, who and what is the Holy Spirit ? Is He the sovereign God, who as Spirit moves where He will, awakening the hearts of men to the unity of the faith and their lips to attest it ?—or is He something quite different ? When we speak of Him, and of the existence and continuance of the Christian community in the world as founded by

Him, are we speaking of the result of the free act of grace in which
God the Father continually attests Himself through the Son, and the
Son to the glory of the Father even in this time between the resurrection and the return, manifesting Himself as present and active, as
the Lord of the world ?—or are we speaking of a peculiar supra-natural
substance which once came into human history and has now passed—
like a newly discovered force of nature—into the hands and control
of certain men who are competent in this matter and who can use
and apply it ? It is at this point that the decision is made. If He is
the Spirit who moves as He will, if the history of the community in
the world is the result of His free acts of grace, then this does not
exclude His ability to give Himself from a higher minister of the Church
to a lower. But why only or preferably from a higher ? On what
ground do we know or hold that His work and gift are preferably—
and for the rest of the Church decisively—a matter for bishops and
other clergy ? We will leave that point for the moment, however,
and grant that it is certainly not excluded that He Himself and,
therefore, apostolic authority and power and mission may be imparted
by the witness of a bishop to another man—remembering always,
of course, that He moves where He will, *ubi et quando Deo visum est.*
And why should it not be by the laying on of hands, as in the case of
Saul in Ac. 9[17] at the hands of Ananias (who was not, of course, a
bishop but simply a disciple who dwelt in Damascus), and as attested
in 1 Tim. 4[14], 2 Tim. 1[6] and Heb. 6[2] ? It is the very essence of the
foundation and continuance of the apostolic community that what
took place between the apostles and the first three and five thousand
in Jerusalem can take place again and has, in fact, taken place again.
But the question is whether there is an institution, and in the sphere
of that institution a rite of ordination, in fulfilment of which the Holy
Spirit has to pass from one man to another, so that He can be controlled
and His presence and action confined ? Of course, the practical powers
and legal authority of a bishop can be transferred institutionally and
ritually from one man to another, like the staff and mitre and ring
which symbolise them. But how can apostolic authority and power
and mission, how can the Holy Spirit be transferred, when obviously
apostolicity is His work and gift ?—as though the Holy Spirit were a
legal or technical or symbolical It, a property in the hands of one or
many exalted members of the community which, without further ado,
can be transferred by them into the power of others—simply because
it has been institutionally arranged in this way, and simply because
it takes place with due legality and ritual.

Is it possible to think of the canalisation of the transference from one member
of the community to another (if there is any such transference) of the *charisma*
described in 1 Cor. 12 and Rom. 12 ? Certainly we must calmly consider and
accept the fact that Mt. 16[18f.] does speak of an absolutely extraordinary authority,
power and mission of the apostles, and of its ultimate concentration specifically

on Peter. But in this passage there is no mention at all of any institutionally guaranteed continuance of the authority, power and mission even of Peter, in another person appointed by him, of a *successor Petri* in that sense. And if in the Pastoral Epistles and Acts we can discover or suspect traces of an incipient or developed " primitive catholicism," there is no doubt that apostolic succession in this sense, as an institutional and ritual mediation and transference of the Holy Spirit and therefore of apostolicity, is not a constituent part of these texts.

No, just as Jesus Christ is a free subject when it takes place that the apostles become apostles, it is again an event in which Jesus Christ is a free subject and His Spirit moves where He wills when the apostolic community comes into being and exists as such, when there is an apostolic succession in the true sense in which this overburdened expression can be understood.

In what, then, does the apostolicity of the Church consist as a criterion of its catholicity, holiness and unity ? One thing is clear, that it belongs together with its character as the body, the earthly-historical form of the existence of Jesus Christ in this interim period. If, apart from His hidden being at the right hand of the Father, in which He is the Head of His body, He also exists in this interim period in earthly-historical form in His community in the world, then it belongs to this that He gives Himself to be known in this earthly-historical form to it and to the world through it.

But the earthly-historical medium of His self-manifestation is those in whose midst He has lived on earth, in history, as the Word of God made flesh, those who have seen and heard and handled Him in the servant-form of His flesh, but also in His glory. These are the apostles. It is He Himself who has chosen and called and ordained and sent them out for this purpose and as such. Now since they—and they alone—are His direct witnesses, they belong together with Him in a unique and special way, with Peter at their head in all his weakness. They are shown in Him to have both positively and negatively an exemplary significance. They share in His peculiar earthly-historical position. In this position they are the rock on which He willed to build His Church, on which He has built it and still builds it : with the witness to Him which is peculiarly their own, which can only be heard and independently accepted and reproduced, but not augmented or in any way replaced, by the community which receives it, which in all the being and upbuilding and life and work of the community must always be maintained and confirmed as their apostolic witness. For in it it receives His own witness to Himself. Accepting the word of the apostles, it allows Him to speak. Being led by them, it is led by Him. His Holy Spirit acts and works in the concrete form of the power and truth of their word.

They are not in any sense the lords of the community, nor do they play any autonomous role in relation to it. Jesus Christ makes use of them. Their authority, power and mission consists in the fact that He does this. In this they are the rock on which He builds His Church. They are this only in this relationship of His to them, only as He Himself qualifies them. Without Him they would only be a pile of sand. And it is not they who build His community but He who builds it as He makes use of them. They are only His servants. Only in this way is there any correspondence to His own being in which He has manifested Himself to them, and therefore to the content of their preaching. For what is He Himself but the servant of God and man, and as such the Lord ? How could they try to be lords in His name ? The warning against this possibility sounds out unmistakably in the Gospels. Obviously witnesses of the One who Himself only served can only be those who for their part will only serve the Lord who Himself served and therefore their fellow-men. For this they are chosen and called and ordained by Him.

And it is this serving which in relation to the community gives them their exemplary, their normative significance, their greatness. In this they are the holy apostles. It is actually the case that He speaks through them. The man who hears them hears Him. The man who does not hear them does not hear Him. The " keys of the kingdom of heaven " are actually in their hands (Mt. 16^{19}). If they open it to a man, it is open. If they close it, it is closed. He uses them as His servants beside whom He has no other servants of the same kind. To that extent there devolves on them the whole responsibility in relation to the community and the world. There is no way to Him which does not lead past them. The hidden glory at the right hand of the Father in which He is manifest to the Father and to Himself has no other earthly-historical complement than that of their witness. The awakening power of His Holy Spirit has no other earthly-historical form than that of the power of their witness. The community is present and present only when their witness is sounded out and received and accepted and reproduced.

Thus the existence of His community is always its history in its encounter with this witness—the history in which it is faithful or unfaithful to it in its exposition and application. There is, therefore, a legitimate apostolic succession, the existence of a Church in the following of the apostles, only when it takes place in this history that the apostolic witness finds in a community discipleship, hearing, obedience, respect and observance. But it is in the fact that they serve that the apostles follow the Lord Himself and precede the community. It would, therefore, be very strange if the community for its part tried to follow them in any other authority, power and mission than that of their service, if, for example, it tried to follow them in an institutional possession of and control over the high mystery of the free Holy Spirit, in the power to overrule His work and gift, as though it were a matter of money or property or of the legal regulation of certain human demands and interests. In this attitude of glad possession and control, how alien it would be not only to the apostles but to the servant of God who is the Lord of the apostles and its Lord! How alien it would be if it tried to be great by ruling in the name of the apostles and in His name, which would be to rule over Him and them! In this matter there is only one true succession, and even on the part of the Church it is the succession of service. If the community is really to find itself and to act in line with Jesus Christ and His apostles, there is only one attitude, and that is the attitude of subjection and obedience.

It is a matter of the *ministerium Verbi*, of the *Verbum incarnatum*, Jesus Christ Himself. But this would necessarily be abused and corrupted and changed into a *dominium* even by those who wish to be serious Christians if the relationship of the Church to its Lord were unformed because immediate, if it had control of His earthly-historical form. The relationship is not unformed, however, but formed. It is not immediate but mediate. And its mediacy or form is the relationship of the Church to the apostles, or, more exactly, the relationship of the apostles to the Church, the loud or quiet declaration of their witness. It has not to subject itself, nor does it owe obedience, to their witness, but to Jesus Christ, who is the Lord over all things, whom even they can only serve with their witness. But through their witness He speaks to His community. And if in the community it is a matter of His service, the *ministerium Verbi incarnati*, this means that the Church finds itself in the school of the apostles, that in this school it learns the meaning of obedience and practises obedience, making after them the movement of service which it sees them make—after them because they know immediately what it is all about, what is the meaning of service in this particular case. If the Church learns and exercises its *ministerium* in this school, then it will certainly be kept from corrupting and transforming it into a *dominium*. There can be no supposed human control over the Holy Spirit. But in the measure that it does learn and practise it in this school the Church acquires and has the true power which in exemplary form is effective and visible in the apostles as the servants of Jesus Christ, and therefore something of the power of the one great servant of God the attesting of whom has taught them obedience, who Himself is the man who instructs and guides and corrects and qualifies them in this school. It will never regret it if it enters this apostolic succession, if it remains in it, if it does not desire anything better, if it takes part in it with a modesty and humility and yet also an attention and zeal which continually increase, if it becomes an apostolic community in this sense.

Potestas ecclesiastica means *ministerium ecclesiasticum*. Assuming that this is grasped and taken to heart, we can then reverse the statement : *ministerium ecclesiasticum* means *potestas ecclesiastica*. But it is advisable simply to accept and not to state it as reversed in this way. For when it is reversed it is only too easily the case that it is not grasped and taken to heart in its original form.

It will be seen that in this matter we really have to do with a history which—beginning in Jesus Christ Himself, continuing in His apostles and completing itself in His community—has already taken place and constantly has to take place again. Of what avail are institutions if this history does not take place ? But it takes place where Jesus Christ lives as the Lord of His body, and therefore in conformity with the earthly-historical form of His existence, in the witness of the apostles. The Church is in this school and it is the *ecclesia apostolica* as by the ministry of the apostles He speaks in it and to it and it accepts Him as the One who speaks in it and to it. If we want to know where is the true Church, the one holy catholic Church, and how it can be distinguished from the false or doubtful Church, then we must try to see where it exists as the apostolic community in this sense. Where and to the extent that we meet it in this character, there and to that extent we can know it with certainty to be the true Church. But the blind cannot pronounce on colours or the deaf on music. To be competent for this knowledge, we have ourselves to take part in this history, to learn and practise in this school as living members of the community. The process by which the Church becomes and is apostolic and therefore the true Church is a spiritual process. In the same way the knowledge of it can only be a spiritual knowledge.

All the same, as we have seen, it is a concrete knowledge. For all the care that is needed, it is actually possible on one side to make even more concrete the line which we have drawn in the preceding paragraphs.

What we have learned to know as apostolicity and therefore as the mark of the true Church is quite naturally identical in substance with the term which in a very different dogmatic context has been used to describe the authority of the Bible as the source and norm of the existence and doctrine and order of the Church—the " Scripture-principle."

In the first instance the apostles are the original disciples of the evangelical records. They were selected and brought together as the twelve in correspondence with the traditional twelve tribes of Israel. As such they represent primarily the inseparable connexion of the new people of God with the old, the sprouting of the new from the old as from a root. In the first instance, therefore, they are a remarkable confirmation of the authority of the Old Testament. In their person the community—even the Gentile community—is from the very first and definitively confronted with the Law and the prophets and the writings of the book of Yahweh as the attestation of the One who was already the meaning and hope of the existence and history of Israel, and who in the fulness of time was revealed as the Head of His body as it already existed in that form, in which it is given to the Christian Church of every age to see itself as in a glass.

It is worth noting that the creed of 381 did not adopt this relationship with the Old Testament in its definition of the Church but in its description of the Holy Spirit who is the basis of the Church : *qui locutus est per sanctos prophetas.*

At the same time, however, the twelve were in exemplary fashion the authentic eye-witnesses of that revelation of the Head, the Messiah of Israel who, as such, was the Saviour of the world.   They were chosen by Him to carry the recollection of Him, and, as such, they were representative of the authority of the New Testament.   From this point of view the importance of the number recedes.   It is significantly breached, indeed we can and must say that it is burst wide open, by the apostasy of Judas.   Among the authors of the New Testament Matthew, Peter, John, James and the other Judas are those who still count to tradition as apostles in the original sense, but there is no news of the other members of that first circle.   There has now been forcefully added to them, or rather there stands over against them as the great apostle, Paul—the apostle to the Gentiles, a Benjaminite and a Pharisee.   According to the picture given in the Acts, it is he who *de facto* if not *de iure* has replaced Iscariot.   " Apostolic " now has the comprehensive sense of the witness of those who had direct personal knowledge of Jesus Christ as the Crucified and Risen—and in the special case of Paul only as the Crucified who was risen, only as the One who was alive from the dead.   And what showed and declared itself to be apostolic in this sense has been plainly recognised with the Old Testament as the canonical Scripture of the New Testament.

Thus the apostolic community means concretely the community which hears the apostolic witness of the New Testament, which implies that of the Old, and recognises and puts this witness into effect as the source and norm of its existence.   The apostolic Church is the Church which accepts and reads the Scriptures in their specific character as the direct attestation of Jesus Christ alive yesterday and to-day, respecting them as the canon and following their direction. It was in the Reformation of the 16th century that the Scriptures were rediscovered and given their proper place, and together with them the being of the Church as described in this fourth predicate— apostolicity as the criterion of its being as the one true universal Church.   The Evangelical Church recognises and confesses something that was hidden and forgotten and even denied for centuries : that the truth of the Christian community in its apostolic verification consists in its history in the concrete encounter with the concrete biblical witness ; that in this witness its truth is given to it, but also given over to it, once and for all; that it is present, but has to be continually sought and found and considered, in this encounter with the witness of Scripture, in its exposition and application.   The Church is apostolic and therefore catholic when it exists on the basis of Scripture and in conformity with it, i.e., in the orientation which it accepts when it looks only in the direction indicated by the witness which speaks to it in Scripture, with no glances aside in any other direction. The Bible itself cannot do this merely as a sacred but closed book. As such it belongs to the very constitution of all supposed or actual, more or less Christian Churches. But this does not of itself make them true Churches. What counts is that the Bible speaks and is heard. Again, the Bible cannot do it merely as the book of the law of the Church's faith and order. To the degree that it is treated as such, it is, in fact, controlled. Like the apostles, it does not will to rule but to serve. And it is where it is allowed to serve that it really rules ; that it is not betrayed to any human control. It is not a prescript either for doctrine or for life. It is a witness, and as such it demands attention, respect and obedience —the obedience of the heart, the free and only genuine obedience. What it wants from the Church, what it impels the Church towards— and it is the Holy Spirit moving in it who does this—is agreement with the direction in which it looks itself. And the direction in which it looks is to the living Jesus Christ. As Scripture stirs up and invites and summons and impels the Church to look in this same direction there takes place the work of the Spirit of Scripture who is the Holy Spirit. Scripture then works in the service of its Lord, and the Church becomes and is apostolic and therefore the true Church.

We cannot go into details, but I will indicate certain lines of approach which need to be considered. The Church is apostolic and therefore the true Church where its external order—what is called Church government—is made so loose by respect for the direction of Scripture that all encroachment on the lordship of the One who is alone the Lord is either avoided or so suppressed and eliminated in practice that there is place for His rule. Whether this will be better done by a monarchical or an aristocratic or a democratic form of constitution is a question which has to be considered, but it is only secondary. All these forms have their own dangers. The lordship of Jesus Christ can be attacked equally by individuals, by a group and by the totality of Christians in the Church. And it is difficult to claim that any one of these forms has absolutely and in all circumstances to be set up and put into effect as that which is based on the Bible and in loyalty to the One whom it attests. In the obedience to Him which Scripture attests to be necessary, His community may prefer this or that form, but as it does so it will always be aware that it is only He who has the right and the power to govern the Church, not any man or men, even as His representatives. According to the witness of Scripture, He is not absent but present in the midst. He may be represented, i.e., attested, by one or many, but He does not need any vicar, either in the form of individuals, or in that of a group, or in that of the totality or the majority of the community. He needs Christians who will be only His servants. The order of the true apostolic Church and its administration can always be recognised by the fact that this is taken into account.

Again, the Church is apostolic and therefore the true Church where its regard for the direction of Scripture always gives to its preaching, doctrine, instruction and theology a strict concentration on the recognition of Jesus Christ alone, of Jesus Christ as God revealed and speaking and acting, of His death and resurrection, of the salvation which appeared in Him as the only salvation of men and the world, of the kingdom which has drawn near in Him, of the hope of His coming, of faith in Him—all under this sign, all with reference to this reality, all thinking from and thinking back to this point. This has nothing whatever to do with any kind of orthodoxy. Orthodoxy has usually done far too little than too much in this direction. There are many forms in which this can be recognised and many tongues in which it can be confessed. But it will always be the business of a Church orientated by Scripture to recognise and confess it. It will always have to clarify and purify its word in respect of the possible admixture of alien elements from all kinds of neighbouring centres and truths and priorities and directions. It will always focus its thinking and word on the one thing which it has been charged to speak by the one person. As a teaching Church it will always be, and will always have to be, a listening Church—listening to that one person. We can recognise it as the Church of the true Gospel by the fact that it is caught up in this endeavour and does not grow weary of it.

Again, it is apostolic and therefore true where the faith and, we may say at once, the piety of its members, as they all take notice of the direction of Scripture, is not centred in itself, in the human experience, insight and will without which it cannot, of course, subsist, but is a piety which is held from above, from without, being maintained in that peace of God which is higher than reason, not in any depth of Christian feeling or power of thought or activity, but in the peace which is enclosed and which consists in Jesus Christ. Of course, it will then be a living and visible piety in the sphere of reason in all its dimensions, in every kind of experience and insight and will. But in the true Church what makes a man a true Christian is that he does not put any part of his confidence in any respect upon himself, his own vitality, but that his heart is elsewhere, above, in blessedness, with the Lord, and that he is held and guided by Him. Where the members of the community are Christians with this direction, because they are guided and brought up in it, we shall have no difficulty in recognising them as the true community.

And now, finally, we can put the question and answer it from a very different standpoint. The direction which was peculiar to the apostles and which we find in Scripture involved for them a particular and highly individual human attitude and way of existence which we can only describe as one of supreme realism. For them their discipleship, apostolate, authority, power and mission was not an end in itself. From first to last—at this point we are forced back to our key thought—it was absolutely a matter of their service, their ministry as heralds. As their distinctive title " apostle " shows us, they were sent out to preach the Gospel in the world, a light which had been kindled to give light to all that are in the house (Mt. 5^{15})—nothing more. The character given to them is not great or significant in itself. Not even in the highest conceivable sense is it a matter of their own good or ill, of their own honour, or even of the self-reposing structural importance and dignity of the work which they have to accomplish in this character. Their being and their work both point beyond themselves. Their field is the world, and they are only sowers who pass over it. They renounce any self-grounded or self-reposing rightness or importance of their distinctive being and activity. It is the special direction in which they look, to the One who has made them His and whom they have recognised as theirs, which forces them to make this renunciation. It cannot be otherwise than that even in this renunciation they should be a normative pattern to the community gathered by their ministry. As an apostolic Church the Church can never in any respect be an end in itself, but, following the existence of the apostles, it exists only as it exercises the ministry of a herald. It builds up itself and its members in the common hearing of the Word of God which is always new, in common prayer, in baptism and the Lord's Supper, in the practice of its inner fellowship, in theology. But it cannot forget that it cannot do these things simply for its own sake, but only in the course of its commission—only in an implicit and explicit outward movement to the world with which Jesus Christ and in His person God accepted solidarity, for which He died, and in which He rose again in indication of the great revelation of the inversion accomplished in Him. For this reason the Church can never be satisfied with what it can be and do as such. As His community it points beyond itself. At bottom it can never consider its own security, let alone its appearance. As His community it is always free from itself. In its deepest and most proper tendency it is not churchly, but worldly—the Church with open doors and great windows, behind which it does better not to close itself in upon itself again by putting in pious stained-glass windows. It is holy in its openness to the street and even the alley, in its turning to the profanity of all human life—the holiness which, according to Rom. 12⁵, does not scorn to rejoice with them that do rejoice and to weep with them that weep. Its mission is not additional to its being. It is, as it is sent and active in its mission. It builds up itself for the sake of its mission and in relation to it. It does it seriously and actively as it is aware of its mission and in the freedom from itself which this gives. If it is the apostolic Church determined by Scripture and therefore by the direction of the apostles, it cannot fail to exist in this freedom and therefore in a strict realism more especially in relation to itself. And when it does this it cannot fail to be recognisable and recognised as apostolic and therefore as the true Church.

3. THE TIME OF THE COMMUNITY

The time of the community is the time between the first *parousia* of Jesus Christ and the second. " *Parousia* " means the immediate visible presence and action of the living Jesus Christ Himself. His first immediate visible presence and action was that in which He encountered the disciples in the forty days after Easter as the Judge who was judged for the unjust. His second presence and action will be His final coming in His revelation as the Judge of the quick and the dead. The community exists between His coming then as the risen One and this final coming. Its time is, therefore, this time between. Its movement is from direct vision to direct vision ; and in this movement by His Holy Spirit He Himself is invisibly present as the living Head in the midst of it as His body.

That it lives in this time and movement is both the weakness of the community and its strength. We will first speak of its strength, then of its weakness.

Its strength consists in the fact that it comes from Easter. It has in its ears the message of those who then saw Him face to face. By the awakening power of the Holy Spirit it is gathered in the unity of the faith to this message, i.e., to the One who, according to this message, is the living Lord. For in faith in this message it can recognise the One of whom it speaks, the Judge who was judged for the unjust, as its Lord who is also the Lord of the world. In faith in this message it can hear the verdict of God executed in His death and proclaimed in His resurrection—the justification of sinful man. In faith in this message it can receive and accept this verdict, beginning to live in recognition of it. Above all, it can itself proclaim this message, representing the truth of it to the world by its word and by its existence. It can itself attest the One of whom this message speaks : not in its own strength, on its own responsibility, or at its own risk ; not from a standpoint or in an enterprise which it has itself selected and made its own, and for which it must, therefore, bear the responsibility, which it must excuse and justify; but in the power of its secured and promised being as the one holy universal apostolic Church, in which it is wholly dependent upon its Lord and is wholly sustained by Him. This is its strength. From this standpoint, from behind, from its origin in the resurrection of Jesus Christ, in all the groupings of history there is none which is so strong and durable, none which has such impetus, which can be so sure of its cause and its future, as the Christian community, even in its most modest and questionable forms. It exists in the light of Easter Day. Its day is one of the days of work which follow this first day, this Sunday.

But at the same time it looks forwards. It has the message of the resurrection of Jesus Christ in its ears. It lives with it and by it. It reproduces it. But this message as such is only of a First, a beginning. Of course, it is a beginning—this is what makes it so powerful—which includes in itself and indicates the end and the whole. The First is the first-fruits, who, risen again from the dead, is the Judge of the quick and the dead (the Judge who was judged for them as their Substitute). It is as the One who had become this in the power of His death that He appeared to that first group, the twelve and those around them, and to Saul who became Paul. He is proclaimed as such by the message from which the community comes and with and by which it lives. And yet as the message of the revelation of the One He is it is only a beginning—the message of His first *parousia* which, as such, is aimed and pointed at His second, His relation to all those whom it concerns, to all those whom He judged in His death by allowing Himself to be judged in their place. In this revelation even the community which first believes in Him will see Him as the disciples saw Him on Easter Day, but they will see Him definitively, whereas the disciples then saw Him only transitorily. The community which has this beginning behind it, which comes from Easter, has this end and goal, this consummation before it. This is what constitutes the particular dynamic of its existence and situation. This is what constitutes the direction which it receives from the Lord living and ruling invisibly in the midst. It comes from Him as the First, to look and move towards Him as the Last. It waits for Him. It hastens towards Him. And that means towards His revelation as the One He is for all in His visibility for all. It waits for the seeing of that which, receiving the message, it can now believe, for the definitive seeing by itself and all men of Him who has changed and turned the whole human situation, turning it back to God. As it is awakened to faith in the Easter message it hears and knows and understands it already as the verdict of God on all sinful humanity which has been executed and declared and is therefore valid and effective. It knows already that which others do not know. It knows it in faith. It does not yet see it—any more than others—but it knows it. It lives in this knowing of faith. In this knowing of its faith and in its life by it, it is the one holy universal apostolic Church, the community of Jesus Christ. In this knowing of faith it is stronger than the world and overcomes it—not in scorn and enmity, but in confidence and hope, looking to the end and goal to which it moves, and to which, without knowing it, the world moves with it. The community knows that it is the world which God has already reconciled to Himself in Jesus Christ. It knows that the judgment upon it has already been executed. It knows its justification accomplished on the cross of Golgotha. By and in this faith in it it lives. In the oneness of this faith it is gathered as the Christian community. In this faith it is in the world, itself worldly. In this faith it is led and carried as on eagles' wings to the glory of the second and final *parousia* of Jesus Christ ; that is, to the universal direct and definitive revelation and vision of the Judge who justifies sinful humanity and of the sinful humanity justified by Him.

This teleological direction of its existence which is the consequence of its origin constitutes its strength. There are, of course, other societies which have a teleological direction, which look forward to the future with all kinds of promises and expectations. But the Christian community has the advantage that in its beginning it already has behind it the end which it awaits. To that extent it proceeds from the fulfilment of its hope. Its hope is not the expression of a longing and striving. It is the expression of the impetus by which it exists. It also has the advantage that the end which it awaits is universal and not particular, uniting and not dividing, a goal of peace and not a party goal. It has again the advantage that as it waits for it and looks and hastens towards it, it is engaged in a conflict, but in a conflict in which it is not against any one but for everyone, in the one conflict that the eyes of all—in the first instance the eyes of faith—may be opened to what has already taken place for them, for their justification as already accomplished and proclaimed by God. Its strength consists in the fact that in the unity of the faith it is gathered in every age, from many peoples and tribes, to be a provisional representation of all humanity as justified in Jesus Christ. This is what gives to its existence in the world its incomparable meaning and significance and power, at all times and in all circumstances, and again even in its most modest and questionable forms.

In short, it is strong because it knows what time is—time which begins and ends, but for that reason the filled-out present of every time, between every yesterday and to-morrow. It is strong because for it Easter stands behind every yesterday, the first *parousia* of the One who is its Lord, but who as the great Servant of God is also the Lord of the whole world, of all men. It is strong because for it His coming in glory is proclaimed and present beyond every morning— His second and final *parousia*. It knows what time is because it knows that it is this time between, and because in this knowledge it is held and impelled and directed both behind and before. But we must also perceive and state that its weakness, too, consists in that in which it is strong. All that we have to say of its weakness in its time, this time between, can be summarised in a statement based on 2 Cor. 5^7 : that it is only in faith—in a faith which does not have its possibility or basis or support in any form of sight—that it can be strong and therefore " walk," pursuing its way in this time. If it is not awakened to faith and made strong in it by the Holy Spirit, this weakness will be fatal. But even in the strength of its faith it is weak in the fact that its faith is not sight, that it must be content to move in faith and without any kind of sight from the first to the second and last *parousia* of Jesus Christ. It will be seen that its weakness, too, is to some extent ontologically grounded in the nature of its time, the time between. For it is the time between His first and second presence and action in immediate visibility. It is no longer the time of Easter, and it is not yet the time, i.e., the moment of His return. The community moves from the one point to the other like a ship—a constantly recurring picture—sailing over an ocean a thousand fathoms deep. The Lord Himself is in the midst, but He is also at the one point and the other, as the One who has come and the One who comes, concealed as the author and finisher of its faith (Heb. 12^2) both in its beginning, in the event of which the Easter message speaks, and also in its end, to which this event and its own beginning refers it. .

This event of the beginning, the resurrection of Jesus Christ from the dead, is not a factor of " history " which it can see as such and to which it can cling in another way than faith. The living Lord did not encounter at all the men of the Sanhedrin, or Pilate and his people, or the folk of Jerusalem and Galilee, let alone the wider circles of the then population of the world, but only His disciples, and even His disciples in such a way that, although they could see Him directly, they were placed in the decision of faith or lack of faith, so that they first had to make the decision of faith, or, at any rate, they all did make that decision without exception. Again He encountered His disciples only transitorily at that time, in the forty days which found their definitive conclusion in the final event described as His ascension, so that even they—although with the recollection of those days—were thrown back wholly and utterly upon the Holy Spirit of the living Lord, and therefore wholly and utterly upon faith in Him. The message which is the basis of the community spoke of this event which did not have an open but an esoteric and more than that a transitory character. And if it could not be accepted by those who were the witnesses of it except by the Holy Spirit and therefore in faith, if even for them it could not retain its impressiveness in any other way, how much more is this the case for the community which is thrown back on their message, which is founded by them and in effect only by them! How much more is it the case for the many of later ages to which we also belong, who have not seen Him and have not been able to see Him in that event! They, we, have only been able to hear of the event of His revelation as the living Lord and therefore of His existence as such. We have only been able to hear of it as mediated through the message of these first witnesses, to be awakened to faith as the hearers of this message. That is how it is with the beginning of the community in its time, the time between. In relation to the character of the Easter event itself, and in relation to the slender thread by which the news of it is mediated to the community, this beginning is wrapped in a concealment which can be penetrated only by the living Lord Himself in the work of His Holy Spirit, or from the point of view of the community only by faith in Him.

But there is more to be said in relation to this beginning. Supposing the event of Easter had quite a different character from that which it actually has according to the New Testament accounts. Supposing it had the open character of an act of human " history." Supposing the news of it had the nature of a report which is basically plausible to every man. We have still to explain how it could have for those who received the report and even for its direct witnesses the meaning and character in which it is the basis of the Christian community, the meaning and character of the revelation of that which took place in the death of Jesus Christ ; how that event came and comes to be a declaration concerning the end of the history of sinful humanity, the alteration, the turning of its situation, its conversion to God. The Christian community believes that this has taken place in the death of Jesus Christ because it has been proclaimed by God Himself in His resurrection from the dead—the reconciliation of the world with God. But in face of the event of His resurrection, or because it hears of this event, it can only believe as it is revealed to it by the Holy Spirit in this event and in its hearing of the account of it. That which is the real point of this event and the account of it would in any case be wrapped in the concealment of revelation and faith : the proclamation of the justification of sinful man which has taken place in it. In this sense it was hidden even from the direct witnesses of this event, to the extent that in the forty days the life of the crucified and risen Jesus Christ could be seen by them only as His life, but was concealed from them as their own life and that of all men, and therefore as the justification of themselves and all men in His life from death, a life which they confront as mortal men, as those who die (every day according to 1 Cor. 15[31]), because they are still sinners, a life which they can only hope and expect to receive from Him as their own life and therefore as their own justification. " Hid with Christ in God " (Col. 3[3]), this life and therefore their reconciliation, the reconciliation of the world with God, could not be seen but only believed by them even in the forty days (and more particularly afterwards)

Even in these days their corruptible had not put on incorruption, their mortal immortality. Even in these days and in the light of these days, in the hearing of the divine verdict pronounced in this event, if they were not wrapped in complete obscurity in relation to their altered situation and that of the world, they could not do more than see in a glass darkly (1 Cor. 13^{12}), they were thrown back on the knowledge of faith. They had not yet reached the stage of being " like " Him (1 Jn. 3^2). Nor has this stage been reached by any means in the community founded by their message. The event of reconciliation proclaimed in the resurrection of Jesus Christ, the justification of sinful man, can and will always be found and known in Him, in the person of its Head, but for the time being it will be found and known only in Him—in Him as it has taken place for it and for all men, yet not with reference to its common life and that of its members (even the best of them), but only as it looks to Him and holds to Him and in its proclamation of the good news of this event points to Him, in faith in Him, therefore, and in the call to faith in Him. This is the other aspect of the great hiddenness of the beginning from which the community comes. If He who lives invisibly in the midst did not disclose to it what it means for it and for the whole world that He has risen again from the dead, what this tells us of the power of His death to renew both it and the world, if His Holy Spirit did not utter in the midst the verdict proclaimed in His resurrection, of what avail would it be to come from this beginning, however great and wonderful it may be ? It would be quite dumb. It would not be the word by which it can feed and live. Even on this basis it can be made strong only by Jesus Christ Himself. Therefore it cannot recognise and confess too strictly that even on this basis it will stumble, indeed it will lie quite helpless, without Him. It has of itself no kind of power over this beginning—either over the Easter event in itself and as such, or over that which is proclaimed in it and with it. It has no hold over it. It can only be the case that this event as such, and in it the proclamation of the atonement made in the death of Jesus Christ, has taken place, that the community has actually come under the grip and is in the power of this event, and that it actually realises in faith that this is so. On the basis of this beginning it can be strong in faith. It can be strong to overcome all difficulties and obstacles. But without faith, if it were a matter of some kind of seeing, it can only be weak, and mortally so.

This is even more true in relation to the goal of its way. If we accept that on the basis of this beginning it is strong in faith, this means that from that point, from the resurrection of Jesus Christ, we are referred to an end in which He will be just as visible to it and the world as the One He is, the One in whom God has reconciled it and the world to Himself, as He was to the disciples in the forty days, an end in which the world will therefore be visible to the community and itself as the world reconciled to God in Him, the world in which (Phil. 2^{11}) " every tongue shall confess that He is Lord, to the glory of God the Father." But how does the community know this goal and end of its way? It knows it only in the form of its beginning. It knows the returning Lord only in the form in which He came then according to the record. That the goal and end of its way is enclosed in this beginning, that the future form of its Lord, in which He comes to it and it can expect Him, is enclosed in this form, is something which it cannot see but can only believe as it looks back to Easter. It can believe it because He Himself says it who is alive in the midst by His Holy Spirit, because He Himself discloses Himself to it as the One who has not only come but will come again, and come again in a way which is quite different. What at very best (as disclosed in faith) it sees in the light of this beginning is only an individual event in the midst of the times. And with this event what does it see and know of the final event which proclaims itself in this one event, which terminates time and includes all times, in which before its very eyes and the eyes of the whole world all past time will in a single moment, the moment of eternity, become present? If in faith in that account of the beginning Jesus Christ is before it as the first-fruits of the dead, it does not in any sense see the host of the dead, as the first-fruits of which He has risen, and which will then be gathered around Him as a host of the living. If in faith in Him it hears the proclamation, made then in His resurrection from the dead, of the justification of all sinful humanity which took place in His death, it does not know anything at all of the method or extent of its actual accomplishment, or what kind of a reality is the justified humanity which is finally to be revealed as such. Even assuming that it (or its members) knows this reality in its own life in faith in Him, what does it know not merely of the individual but of the universal character of the atonement made in Him, of the justification of all men as it took place in Him, even of those with whom it does not find itself united in the unity of faith in Him? And, above all, if it knows, if Christians know in faith that they are reconciled to God, justified, in His person, in Him as their Head, what do they really know of themselves, i.e., of their being with Him, of the form of their being in which there will be no more contradiction between their being from above in faith and their being from below as poor lost sinners, in which they will be no longer on the march from their wrong to their right, from their death to their life, but already at the goal, absolutely in the right and in life? In virtue of their beginning their faith includes all this as faith in Jesus Christ as risen again from the dead. Christians, the Christian community is summoned from this beginning to hope for all this, to expect it, to hasten towards it. But obviously in such a way that from this beginning its faith must take a sharp turn and become hope, continually renewing and revealing itself as faith directed to this goal and end, as faith in the Lord who comes again in this glory. What in virtue of this beginning it knows in faith is not at all self-evidently the knowledge of what faith has to know to be living and strong as faith directed to this goal and end. Even from this standpoint it has to be the gift and event of faith. There can be no question of seeing, even with a forward reference to the second *parousia* of Jesus Christ. What would the community be, and in what mortal weakness would it lie, if it were not awakened to faith by its Lord through His Holy Spirit, if it were not led " from faith to faith " (Rom. 1^{17}), and thus made strong forwards as well as backwards, if it did not receive of His fulness " grace for grace " (Jn. 1^{16}) ? It is indeed voyaging over a sea a thousand fathoms deep.

And we must not neglect to consider its actual condition at every moment and in every momentary situation between the beginning and the end, between the resurrection of Jesus Christ and His return. In the present context we are leaving aside all the complaints and accusations which arise from the fact that Church history is from first to last a history of continual human failure and defeat, that what is called Christianity is a very doubtful concern, that what are called Christians are a type of men who have always been exposed to many criticisms. In the last resort, it is not this which concerns us, but what we may call the ontological weakness of the Christian community as such, the weakness by which it is oppressed even in its best times and forms and achievements, because its time is this time, the time between.

There is this point to consider on the one hand. It is the community of the God who wills (1 Tim. 2^4) that all men should be saved and come to a knowledge of the truth. It has its faith, and, knowing in faith for all others, it knows what it has to say to all others. But it is so alone in the world. It has gained whole masses of adherents both in the past and to-day, but in spite of that it has no illusions. It is such a small minority side by side with and in the midst of all other human societies. In relation to them and to the world it can only be a very small and modest light in this world. How this contradicts its beginning in the resurrection of Jesus Christ, its commission : " Go and make disciples of all nations " (Mt. 28^{19}), and its end, that " at the name of Jesus every knee should bow, of things in heaven, and things in earth, and things under the earth " (Phil. 2^{11}) ! What is the Christian faith in the midst of so much unbelief and error and superstition, and, above all, such a sea of ignorance that a decision has to be made between it and its different negations ? What is Church history in the human history which flows round it and over it ? The Christian community can answer these questions, but not with a knowledge which is divorced from faith and grounded and supported from without, not with an anthropology and philosophy of history, not with a knowledge of the ways of God both behind and before, only with its very being, only with the faithfulness in which both outwardly and inwardly it actually is what it is. But this means again, only as it believes, and, because it can have faith only as it receives it, only as He who is its Lord awakens it to faith and keeps it watchful in faith. " If it had not been the Lord who was on our side, now may Israel say, if it had not been the Lord who was on our side, when men rose up against us, then they had swallowed us up quick " (Ps. 124$^{1f.}$). " Our help is in the name of the Lord, who made heaven and earth " (Ps. 124^8). It is because this is so that it is strong, stronger than all others. If it were not so, it would be weaker than all others, fatally weak. It is called upon to believe that it is so.

The second point to consider is that it can be sure of itself only in faith, and therefore it is made sure only in the awakening and sustaining of its faith by One who is able to do this. We have seen that it is the community of Jesus Christ, the one holy catholic apostolic Church. This is its being concealed in its visible form. This can be seen and confessed only under the *credo* or not at all. For " the spirit truly is ready, but the flesh is weak " (Mk. 14^{38}). The Christian community exists at every point in an unbroken concealment, in the weakness of the flesh. Where is it palpable even to itself, let alone to the world, that it comes from the resurrection of Jesus Christ and moves to His return, and that He Himself is present in its midst as its Head ? It is only the Spirit who is truly " ready." He comes to our aid. He intercedes for the saints according to the will of God (Rom. 8$^{26f.}$). But He is the Spirit of faith, who bears witness to us that we are the children of God by the fact that we may cry, " Abba, Father," and that at bottom we cannot cry anything else (Rom. 8$^{15f.}$). He is the Spirit in obedience to whom the community (Rom. 8$^{19f.}$) and all creation can only groan for its redemption from the bondage of corruption and therefore for liberty in the glory of the children of God. As it obeys Him and does this it is strong ; it can and must say this *credo* with confidence and joy even in relation to its own existence. And as it does that it can be absolutely certain of itself and its cause. But only as it does this. Only as it does not deny the weakness in which it is what it is. Only as it knows the thousand fathom depth on which it sails, but is not afraid. In the time which is its time, the time between, from the very beginning of the way to the end, and especially in the midst, there is no point without this Nevertheless.

But this time, which in its delimitation both behind and before is the basis of the peculiar strength and weakness of the Christian community, is in a supremely qualified sense *its* time, the time which is spared and appointed for the sake of the gathering and existence and mission of the community, the time which is given to it, the time which it has to recognise according to its true meaning, the time which it has to buy up (Col. 4^5, Eph. 5^{16}), turning it to profitable account. The community is and has the answer which has to be given to the question of the good and gracious purpose of God in the puzzling distance between the first *parousia* of Jesus Christ and the second, the question of the time between, in which with the world it is held, as it were, suspended between the provisional and transitory and particular revelation of its reconciliation with God in Jesus Christ and the perfect and definitive and universal revelation of it in His final coming. The life of the community shows us with what we have to do in this time between. It is the true fulness of it. To that extent it is its time.

It might have been quite different. The time which is our time might not have been at all, because there was no time at all, because all time had long since come to its end. The first *parousia* of Jesus Christ might immediately have been His last. In a moment, in the twinkling of an eye, the event of Easter morning might have been the sounding of the last trumpet (1 Cor. 15⁵²), the event of the final revelation, presence and action of the Judge who was judged for sinful men, and therefore the event of the last day, the final judgment. In a certain sense it is this. Its content is unquestionably one and the same—the proclamation of the One who was judged on Golgotha as the Judge of the quick and the dead, and with Him the irruption of redemption, of the consummation. The only thing is that on Easter Day it all had only this provisional and transitory and particular form, a penultimate character. It really was the end—in this penultimate character. The Lord who will come again in glory is the One who with the empty tomb behind Him already encountered the disciples in the forty days and Saul on the outskirts of Damascus. God had already pronounced His decision on sinful man, the Word of grace and judgment, the final " Let there be light." Human history was actually terminated at this point. The resurrection of all the dead had already been indicated. Enclosed in the life of this One, their eternal life had already become an event. This is the point of the well-known sayings of Jesus concerning His imminent coming, the imminent redemption and consummation. Even in this form it did not lack anything in intensive power and scope. It might have had the intensive and extensive power and scope and therefore the form which it will have in the second and last *parousia* of Jesus Christ. All time might have terminated then.

But this did not happen. It is better not to say that time continued, but rather than a further time, a new time commenced. This is already proclaimed by the fact that according to the tradition there was not simply one Easter event, but an Easter history in an Easter time. All that the tradition reports is a sequence of days and happenings in which the coming again of the Lord in glory was constantly reaffirmed. And the end and climax of this Easter time, described as the ascension, points forward unmistakably to a future of this new and further time which is limited, but the end of which cannot for the moment be seen. His first *parousia* is over. There has begun an interval of time of uncertain duration. A distance in time separates the first *parousia* from the second and the second from the first as though it were arrested by an invisible hand. What might have been a single happening, what we might almost have thought would have to be a single happening, divides into two. Not that the connexion is lost. In both cases it is one and the same. And in the person of the One who acts it not only hangs together, but both on the one side and on the other, in its Whence and alsö in its Whither, it is actually the same event. " Lo, I am with you alway, even unto the end of the world " (Mt. 28²⁰). Yet it cannot be seen in this connexion, in this unity. Its " then " and its " one day," its whence and its whither, are distinct from one another. The two characters of the event are distinct from one another. In the one case it appears in its provisional and transitory and particular form, in the other in its perfect and final and universal. Between the two there opens up the new and further space of time, that of all the days to the end of the world : the time between, which is more properly called the end-time, because in both those forms it is the end—the end of all the ways of God—which it has before it and yet already behind it. This end-time is our time.

Let us imagine for a moment that there were no such end-time. In that case God would not have caused any new and further time to begin. Without interposing this interval He would have wound up all time and the existence of heaven and earth and everything within them in the way that as their Creator He caused them all to begin and as one day He will in fact bring them to an end. He would have reconciled the world to Himself in Jesus Christ, and the resurrection of Jesus Christ, like the seventh day of the story of creation, but far surpassing it, or rather fulfilling its prophetic meaning, would have been the beginning of His rest from all His works, and therefore the beginning of the eternal Sabbath. In this case God would have renounced any further activity in and with the world beyond what He accomplished and revealed in Jesus Christ. He would simply have contemplated the totality of what He had done to it and in it (as He did His work of creation), and He would have found it well done, and therefore not in need of any continuation. But this means that He would have been satisfied with the existence of the generations *ante Christum natum* and with their history, i.e., with what He had done for them as Creator and Reconciler. He would not have needed any further generations and their history. He would not have expected any further human response to what He accomplished and revealed in Jesus Christ, to the execution of His judgment and to the proclamation of the verdict operative in His judgment.

Note that in this case the fulfilment of the covenant, the reconciliation of the world with Him, would have been a kind of unilateral decision and exercise of force, the revelation of it a dictatorial declaration of will, and the whole a sovereign overpowering of humanity to His own glory and its own continuance, but still an overpowering, a sovereign act of grace in which He wanted no thanks and did not expect to receive any. Why should this not have been His resolve and will and act? When He sacrificed Himself in the death of His Son for man, when He declared His severity and mercy to him in His resurrection from the dead, did He not do something supreme and final which renders quite superfluous any correspondence on the part of man, or the continuance of humanity, and therefore further generations and their history, and therefore all further time (e.g., ourselves and the fact that we still have time)? And when we again consider the two thousand years of history and culture *post Christum*, and even that which appears within it as the history of the Church, we may well be tempted to ask whether there was any real value in postponing the second *parousia* of Jesus Christ, and therefore allowing a new and further time to commence and to continue even to this present, this puzzling time of ours, the time between. Would it not have better served both the glory of God and the salvation of man if all that has happened since had not happened, if that eternal Sabbath had in fact begun? For after all there was no real need of this afterwards. Indeed this afterwards can only obscure and compromise the turning which was made in Jesus Christ. Often enough it has, in fact, obscured and compromised it.

What does it mean, then, that God—whose thoughts in this matter, too, are higher than our thoughts—quite obviously did not will and think in this way, that this interval did begin and does continue, that we have behind us as a promise and an admonition and a warning the temporal sabbath of the resurrection of Jesus Christ, the penultimate end, but that the dawning of the eternal Sabbath of His second *parousia* is still before us? What does it mean that God still has a time for humanity, for us? In the first instance, of course, it means that even after He has done and spoken that supreme and final thing, even after He has set and revealed—in that penultimate form—its goal and end, His activity in and with the world and humanity created by Him has not in fact ended. That the world is still there and that this new and further time has begun carries with it as a final presupposition the fact that God is still at work as its Lord. Strangely enough, for what more can God will and work when everything has already been accomplished? But that is how it is. And if that is how it is, it is obvious that He still has a goal and goals, that He still expects something in the world and humanity created and preserved by Him. He has spoken His final Word, but He has not yet finished speaking it. The last hour has struck, but it is still striking. And this means that there is still space for humanity, and in that space it can still exist— surplus space, and a surplus existence, but still a possibility of being, and actual being. It can still develop. There is still a history. A history which is a postscript, but a real history, and therefore more generations, more opportunities for human existence from God and before God and to God, more opportunities of fellowship, of psycho-physical life, more spans of life—and all within the great and astonishing span which has still been allotted to the world as a whole. It has to have this great span, this end-time.

Negatively, this results from the fact that—however final was that which was done in the death of Jesus Christ and revealed in His resurrection—it was not a unilateral decision of force or a dictatorial declaration of will or a sovereign overpowering. God did not will to act and He did not act in this way in Jesus Christ. This is not the aspect of what He did for His own glory and our good, of the act of grace in which He confirmed Himself as the Creator of man and the Lord of the covenant for which He elected him, of His conflict with the pride and fall of man, and the conversion of man to Himself—although this is indeed His last and supreme achievement. And note that it is not He, the God of Abraham, Isaac and Jacob, the Father of Jesus Christ, the God of all mercy and comfort, who would have thought and acted in this way. We may think that this would have contributed to His glory or been of great benefit for the world, but it would have been the act of an abstract and godless grace, not His own grace, not the divine grace addressed to man in Jesus Christ, but a faithfulness full of unfaithfulness, just because it is a unilateral decision which overrides man, eliminating and ignoring him. Grace which does not want any response, any thanks? Grace which does not yearn for any correspondence on the part of man? No eternal glory of the world consummated in this way could alter the fact that an act of this kind is unfriendly to man, that it is at bottom an ungracious act. No sovereignty of which man might boast in the exercise of such grace can alter the fact that it is brutal grace—grace as brutal man might conceive it, but not the grace of the true and living God, who is Father, Son and Holy Spirit. The fact that between the first end which has already come and the future final end there is interposed our time, the end-time, shows us first of all that we have to rid our minds completely of all thought of a god or a grace of this kind.

What is the purpose of the space which is still given to man, of his actual existence in this new and further time after the reconciliation of the world with God as already seen and proclaimed in Jesus Christ? We can now give the positive answer. Its purpose is obviously this—that God will not allow His last Word to be fully spoken or the consummation determined and accomplished and proclaimed by Him to take place in its final form until He has first heard a human response to it, a human Yes; until His grace has found its correspondence in a voice of human thanks from the depths of the world reconciled with Himself; until here and now, before the dawning of His eternal Sabbath, He has received praise from the heart of His human creation. That is the greatness of His grace. That is the reach of His condescension. That is the seriousness of the solidarity to which He has committed Himself with us men in the person of His Son. He does not will to be without man, to have become his Reconciler and to become his Redeemer over the head of man. He does not will the isolation of His Son, the blindness, the deafness, the exclusion of the others for whom He died. He wills a body, an earthly-historical form of the existence of this Head. He wills open eyes and ears for what took place in His death, and therefore for the turning from wrong to right, from death to life, which came about in the human situation. He wills human hearts which see this turning, and human tongues which confess it. He wills not only that the justification which has taken place in Jesus Christ should have taken place, but that the news of it should be sounded out and should meet with faith. In order that this may happen, He still gives to the world space, time and existence, He allows the end-time to commence and continue. It is the sphere in which there can be this correspondence.

He did not need it. He might have done without it. But it is a further dimension of His friendliness to man (Tit. 3⁴) that He willed not to do without it, not to forego man's Yes to His action, his praise and thanks, not to have reconciled him, not to redeem and perfect him, without summoning him to this response and giving him the opportunity for it. Of course it is always deficient. Even as a response to the grace of God it stands always in need of grace. Not all will believe and know and confess. Those who do so will be a minority in all the generation even of this end-time. They will, of course, not only be unable to neglect but they will be irresistibly constrained to call others to their faith, to participate in what they know and confess. But they will not be surprised if they always find themselves in a minority, if with their faith and knowledge and confession they have to go their way representatively for the others. Thus the response which God expects will always in fact be a modest one even externally. And more particularly internally, from the point of view of the quality of the faith and knowledge and confession even of this minority. It is provided that they always have this treasure in very earthen vessels (2 Cor. 4⁷), that their thanks are always very equivocal, that their faith is smaller than a grain of mustard seed, that their knowledge is wrapped in obscurity, that their confession is an impotent stammering. It is provided that their praise of God will always be that " poor praise on earth " in which ultimately they can only pray that it will be received in grace, in the hope that " it will be better in heaven when I am in the choirs of the blessed." There is no perfection in it, only the deep and radical imperfection of the cry, " Abba, Father." Even the voice of this minority is only the voice of the sinful humanity justified only in Jesus Christ, which can only believe in its right as established in Him. It certainly cannot escape a wonderful similarity with its Lord who became a servant. When we consider its situation, it is not in any sense arbitrary to think of the night and day and other night of His burial.

Nevertheless, and for this very reason, for the sake of what takes place in the world in and through this people of those who believe and know and confess, the second *parousia* of Jesus Christ is postponed. That this may take place there is still time even though the last hour has struck : time for the work of the Holy Spirit and for the prayer for Him ; time for faith and repentance ; time for preaching the Gospel throughout the world ; time for the Christian community, and in this sense the time of grace. God does expect its " poor praise on earth." He is divinely good and gracious in the fact that He will actually receive it. And in this sense the end-time is the time of the community. It does not have it and its existence in it merely for its own sake. As we have seen, it cannot be an end in itself. It has it for God, who is so very much for us men that He will not have it otherwise than that before He has finished speaking His last Word some, and even many, should already be for Him. And it has it for the world in order that as a provisional representation of the justification which has taken place in Jesus Christ it may be the sign which is set up in it, which is given to it, which summons it, in order that it may be to it a shining light—a feeble and defective but still a shining light—until the dawning of the great light which will be the end of all time and therefore of this end-time, the coming Jerusalem in which Rev. 21[22] tells us there will be no more temple because the Almighty God will Himself be its temple. The Christian community will then have rendered its service. Its time will end with all time. But there is still time. And the time which is now is its time, and the time of its service. It renders it in the strength and weakness which both have their basis in the nature of this time. But in strength or in weakness it can render it gladly because it knows why we still have time, and it can do the decisive thing which gives meaning, real meaning, to the time which is given us.

§ 63

THE HOLY SPIRIT AND CHRISTIAN FAITH

The Holy Spirit is the awakening power in which Jesus Christ summons a sinful man to His community and therefore as a Christian to believe in Him : to acknowledge and know and confess Him as the Lord who for him became a servant; to be sorry both on his own behalf and on that of the world in face of the victory over his pride and fall which has taken place in Him; and again on his own behalf and therefore on that of the world to be confident in face of the establishment of his new right and life which has taken place in Him.

1. FAITH AND ITS OBJECT

We must now speak of that which makes a man a Christian, of the basis of the Christian existence of the individual, and therefore of faith. It is a matter of the faith of the Christian community which, as such, is that of its individual human members, those who are called Christians and who may perhaps be serious Christians.

In the modern period there have been massive theological structures which have begun at the very point where we now end. They started with the presupposition that, whatever may be the attitude to it, Christian faith as such is a fact and phenomenon which is generally known and which can, as such, be explained to everybody ; or rather more cautiously, that a generally plausible account can be given of it because the possibility of it can be demonstrated and explained in the light of general anthropology. According to this type of structure the task of dogmatics is the description of Christian faith as such (the *fides qua creditur*) and the enumeration, exposition and explanation of its characteristic expressions (the *fides quae creditur*). And all on the further underlying presupposition that the really interesting and vital problem of the Christian is the one which is nearest to hand, that is to say, himself, his existence as a Christian, and therefore the fact and phenomenon of his faith. Dogmatics, therefore, is the " doctrine of faith."

The following comments may be made on this view. It is certainly true that at every point Church dogmatics has to bring out and describe the content of the knowledge and confession of Christian faith. To that extent it is not absolutely impossible that it should be understood and called the doctrine of faith. If it does not do this it is because its leading concept is that of the right knowledge and confession of Christian faith, and as the essence of this that of dogma—not the dogma laid down by the Church, but the dogma which is authoritative and normative for the Church. Christian faith itself and as such belongs to the content of the right knowledge and confession of Christian faith implied in the doctrine of the Holy Spirit and therefore in the third article of the creed. It belongs to that of which the right knowledge and confession has to be sought in dogmatics. But for that very reason the basic presupposition of these modern structures is called in question. Christian faith is not in any sense a fact and phenomenon which is generally known and which can as such be explained to everybody. The Christian religion is a fact and phenomenon of this kind. As such it can be considered and estimated historically, psychologically, sociologically and perhaps even philosophically. But the Christian religion is not as such Christian faith. Christian faith is something concealed in the Christian religion (like the true Church in its visibility). As such it can only be believed. It can be known and confessed only in faith. For the same reason we must question the other version of the presupposition, that the possibility of it can be demonstrated and explained in the light of general anthropology. A human self-understanding which includes the possibility of faith can itself be only that of an anthropology which for its part derives from the actuality of faith, which is a specific form of that knowledge and confession, whereas the possibilities which can be demonstrated and explained in the light of anthropology may perhaps be religious, but they are not those of Christian faith. If faith itself belongs to the content of the knowledge and confession of Christian faith, we have to note that although it knows and confesses itself it cannot in any sense think of itself as grounded in itself. As *fides qua creditur* it cannot regard itself as a primary datum (δός μοι ποῦ στῶ) and therefore as the author of its so-called "expressions," the *fides quae creditur*. It can think of itself only as a last thing which follows, and can only follow, a fourth, a third, a second—and, above all, and supremely a first, so that it needs a whole series of bases and finally, or first of all, its new basis in which all the intermediate bases are themselves grounded. Christian faith knows and confesses that it is this last thing. In no case can its knowledge and confession begin with itself. It knows and confesses first its one basis which includes all the others. It knows and confesses itself only as referred wholly and utterly to this first thing, only as the consequence of it. That is why in this first part of the doctrine of reconciliation we had to speak first of all (implying all that follows and therefore this last thing) of Jesus Christ Himself, the Lord who became a servant, the Judge who was Himself judged for us. Then, of course, we had to speak at once of man, but of man in his antagonism to Jesus Christ—the man of sin. Then in the doctrine of justification we had to expound the divine Nevertheless pronounced to man in Jesus Christ. Then at last, in the first form of ecclesiology, we had to come to the underlying form of the subjective realisation of this whole being and occurrence as fulfilled by man too. The other form of it, Christian faith, or concretely, the Christian who knows this whole being and occurrence in faith, has accompanied us as a presupposition all along our way. But it is only now that he can properly become for a short time an independent theme.

The objection against the underlying but all the more powerful presupposition of those modern doctrines of faith is in moral categories an objection against their arrogance. They rest on the fact that in the last centuries (on the broad way which leads from the older Pietism to the present-day theological existentialism inspired by Kierkegaard) the Christian has begun to take himself seriously in a way which is not at all commensurate with the seriousness of Christianity. They represent Christian truth as though its supreme glory is to rotate around the individual Christian with his puny faith, so that there is cause for gratification if they do not regard him as its lord and creator. From the bottom up we can neither approve nor make common cause with this procedure of modern doctrines of faith. We shall give to the individual Christian and his faith the attention which he demands, but it must be at this point—not at the beginning of our way, but very briefly at the end.

We will begin by considering the relationship of Christian faith to its object. Faith is a human activity which cannot be compared with any other in spontaneity and native freedom. But it is in a relationship. It is in relationship to its object, to something which confronts the believer, which is distinct from him, which cannot be exhausted in his faith, which cannot be absorbed by his believing existence, let alone only consist in it and proceed from it and stand or fall with it. The very opposite is true, that faith stands or falls with its object. It is a subjective realisation. That is, as a human activity it consists in the subjectivisation of an objective *res* which in its existence and essence and dignity and significance and scope takes precedence of this subjectivisation and therefore of the human subject active in it, being independent of and superior to this subject and what he does or does not do. It does not owe anything at all to this human subject and his activity, his faith. What takes place in faith is simply that in a specific activity, which in this sense it to some extent expects, this objective *res* finds existence and essence and dignity and significance and scope, creating respect for itself and actually being respected in the presence of this activity—but only as it was already the object of this subject, only as it had all these things, existence, essence, dignity, significance and scope even for this subject, and without his activity and faith and respect. Faith is simply following, following its object. Faith is going a way which is marked out and prepared. Faith does not realise anything new. It does not invent anything. It simply finds that which is already there for the believer and also for the unbeliever. It is simply man's active decision for it, his acceptance of it, his active participation in it. This constitutes the Christian. In believing, the Christian owes everything to the object of his faith : the incomprehensible fact that he may not only be in relation to this object, but may be active in this being. The great advantage which he has over all others, and which he can never prize too highly, is that this object is not only there for him but that he for his part can be there for this object. It does not remain only a matter of its relationship with him. He himself enters into a relationship with it. This distinguishes the Christian from the non-Christian. The object is like a circle enclosing all men and every individual man. In the case of the Christian this circle closes with the fact that he believes. In the case of non-Christians it is still open at the point where he ought to believe but does not yet believe, or no longer believes. The unbeliever has not accepted the relationship to that which is in relationship to him. He is abnormal in this respect. Faith is the normalising of the relationship between man and this object. It is the act in which man does that which this object demands, that which is proper to him in face of this object—the fulfilment of the correspondence to what this object is and means of itself for every man.

But enough of this formal description of the problem. The " object " of faith, the objective *res* subjectivised in faith, is Jesus Christ, in whom God has accomplished the reconciliation of the world, of all men with Himself—the living Jesus Christ Himself, in whom this occurrence, this fulfilment, this restoration of the broken covenant between God and man, is not an event of the past, not a theoretical truth and doctrine, but for all humanity and all men (irrespective of their attitude to Him) a personal present, no, a present person. He, the living Jesus Christ, is the circle enclosing all men and every man and closed in Christian faith—the circle of divine judgment and divine grace. The great abnormality of unbelief consists in the perversion of the relationship to Him. The normalisation of the human relationship to him is the concern of faith as the human activity in which not all men but Christians are engaged. In the second section we will describe it as this activity. In the present section—because this is what determines it as activity—we will describe it as activity in this relationship of the Christian to Christ.

A first thing which characterises the Christian in this respect is the fact that it consists in the orientation of man on Jesus Christ. It is faith in Him. The man who believes looks to Him, holds to Him and depends on Him. He renounces all self-determination in His favour. To the fact that the circle objectively drawn around man closes in faith there corresponds the further fact that the closed circle of man's being is opened in faith whereas it remains closed in unbelief. In faith man ceases to be in control. He can be this only when he is not orientated on Jesus Christ, at any rate decisively, at the very centre of his being, with what the Bible calls his " heart." To describe this relationship we have already thought in terms of the " eccentric." In faith man is no longer in control at his centre. Or rather, at his centre, he is outside himself and therefore in control. The orientation on Jesus Christ which takes place in faith is not external and occasional. It is not one of the orientations in which he may find himself in his relationship with other things and persons. If he believes, this means that he can no longer fix his " heart " on other things (even the most important) or on other persons (even the dearest and most indispensable). At the centre of his being he is no longer here or there, but at this very definite place outside himself which cannot be exchanged for any other. His mind is then set (Col. 3^2) on " things above, not on things on the earth." " Things above " are not simply the other world generally. They are defined in Col. 3^1 : " where Christ sitteth on the right hand of God." All other seeking or orientation is subordinate to this, in which it has its measure and law. All human striving for the beyond is exhausted in this. Man sees that it is an illusion that he can himself be in control at this centre, or that outside himself he can be in any other place, in other things or persons, or even in some other beyond. He is lifted above himself, but in the only direction in which this can take place. If a man believes, this means that he has found in Jesus Christ an object which does not merely concern him and concern him urgently, which does not merely call him to itself and therefore out of himself, which does not merely claim him, but which is the one true object, which concerns him necessarily and not incidentally, centrally and not casually. It means that he has found in Him the true centre of himself which is outside himself. It means that he must now cling to Him, and depend on Him, that he finds that he belongs to Him.

We can say the same thing in another way. Faith is the human activity which is present and future, which is there, in the presence of the living Jesus Christ and of what has taken place in Him, with a profound spontaneity and a native freedom, but also with an inevitability in face of His actuality. The reverse is equally true : with an inevitability, but with a native freedom. " In the face of "means with eyes open for His actuality as it is before the eyes of all men. " We all with open face mirror the glory of the Lord " (2 Cor. 3¹⁸). How can the mirror be a mirror if it does not reflect that which faces it ? Again, how can it reflect it if it is covered ? Again, what is there of its own in that which is reflected by it ? If it is not covered, what can it reflect but that which faces it ? This reflecting of the glory of the Lord is made possible by the uncovering of the human face, by the seeing which is the result of this uncovering, by the fact that in this seeing man becomes the mirror of that which faces him, the " glory of the Lord," and, above all, by the " glory of the Lord " itself. It is the free but necessary work of faith which is completely bound to its object, which stands or falls with it and with its existence, essence, dignity, significance and scope. In this work man himself is nothing. He is not in control. He simply finds himself in that orientation. He accepts it. In it he sees and reaches out and grows beyond himself. In it he is for the first time faithful to himself. For as the doer of this work he loses his own life to find it again as he loses it (Mk. 8³⁵). This work can hardly be described as anything but renunciation in favour of the living Lord Jesus Christ. But as he does it, he does a genuine and free work, his own proper work. That is the first thing. Faith is in Jesus Christ. It is the action of the Christian in the face of this His Lord, in direct responsibility to Him, in renunciation in His favour.

The second thing that we have to say of faith in its relationship to Jesus Christ as its object is that, as it is related to, it is also based upon it.

We do not compromise its character as a free human act if we say that as a free human act—more genuinely free than any other—it has its origin in the very point on which it is also orientated. It is also the work of Jesus Christ who is its object. It is the will and decision and achievement of Jesus Christ the Son of God that it takes place as a free human act, that man is of himself ready and willing and actually begins to believe in Him. The two things are not a contradiction but belong together. If the Son makes us free, we are

free indeed (Jn. 8^{36}). The Son makes a man free to believe in Him.
Therefore faith in Him is the act of a right freedom, not although but
just because it is the work of the Son.
A man does not have this freedom unless the Son makes him free.
The Christian is a sinful man like all others. In his proud heart, in
consequence of the proud thoughts and words and acts which proceed
from that heart, he is not ready and willing to accept that orientation
on Jesus Christ. He is not free for the faith in which everything depends
on renouncing. He is not prepared to lose his life in order to gain it.
There is a great gulf between him and faith. It did not need to be
so. It belongs basically and decisively to the good nature of man as
God created it that he should be able to believe. Believing might have
been more natural to him than breathing. He was created to be the
covenant-partner of God and therefore for God. The gulf between
him and faith is something contrary to nature. It is created only
by his being in the act of pride. But it is there. And seeing that we
are all radically involved in this act of pride, no one has ever surmounted it. Even the believing Christian has not done so. He knows
that he ought not even to try. He knows that with all other men he
is concluded in disobedience (Rom. 11^{32}), that it is the supreme pride
and therefore the supreme fall of man if he undertakes to believe of
himself, as though he could do so, as though he could make himself
do it and move to do it. He may make the laborious and profoundly
dishonest attempt to regard as true something which he cannot regard
as true because it is too high for him. He may even make the further
and still more painful effort to persuade himself that this convulsive
acceptance is redemptive. But a self-fabricated faith is the climax
of unbelief. Whatever a man may do in this way he never comes
any nearer to faith. Indeed, he moves away from it. For in faith
it is not a matter of this or that truth or this or that redemption, but
of the person who is Himself truth and redemption. And in relation
to this person it is not a matter of proposing and doing something for
ourselves, but of following Him, of repeating His decision. But how
can any man do that ? The Christian knows—and the non-Christian
experiences it in practice—that he can make nothing of this person
in his own strength, that He remains always as inaccessible to him
as sinful man as He is inimitable, that " in his own reason and strength
he can neither believe in Him nor come to Him," that in his own
reason and strength he will move instead in the very opposite direction. Whenever faith takes place in a man, it will always mean a
swimming against this current—a counter-movement which is not
undertaken in his own reason and strength. We do not forget that
it is the counter-movement of a free human act. But the freedom of
it is not the evil freedom which man in his pride has made for himself
and which he thinks he can possess for himself and use for himself.
As a genuine freedom for this counter-movement it is completely alien

to the personal reason and power of proud man entangled in his pride. It is a new freedom and therefore his true freedom. How can he procure it for himself when in his proud heart and the proud being determined by it he is not the one who can have it or win it or even know about it? How can he jump over his own shadow, which is to break free from himself as the one who casts this shadow? In other words, how can sinful man—there is an obvious *contradictio in adiecto*—believe?

If we tried to give an answer to the question as put, to posit some supreme possibility of faith, our answer would be mistaken from the very outset. Seeing we have to do with sinful man, the mere " possibility " of faith would obviously be confronted by the other possibility which is the only true possibility, that of the man who in his own reason and strength simply goes with the current in the opposite direction. Who is to choose between them? Who is the man who will choose aright and therefore choose the possibility of faith? The only man who enters into the picture at all is the man who not only can go in the opposite direction, but actually does go in that direction, who not only has the possibility of choosing the sin of pride, but is a proud sinner from the crown of his head to the sole of his foot. The possibility of faith may be very wonderful and it may be held out in a very attractive way, but what does it mean to him? In the rivalry between a possible faith and actual sin, faith will always come off second best. The rivalry will have ended in favour of sin even before it has begun. The whole idea of a possibility of faith confronted by that of unbelief, the whole conception of man as a Hercules at the crossroads able to choose between faith and sin (and therefore unbelief), is a pure illusion. Whatever may be the possibility of faith, this Hercules has always already chosen unbelief.

But there is a necessity of faith, and it is as we point to this that we shall give a sound answer to our question. Faith does not stand or hover somewhere in face of the possibility of unbelief (which is not a possibility but the solid actuality of sinful man). It is not itself a mere possibility, grand and attractive but impotent and useless like all mere possibilities. It has itself the character of an actuality, an actuality which is absolutely superior to that other actuality. In this superiority it is not a mere alternative to unbelief. It is not a mere chance, or proposition. It is not for man to choose first whether he himself will decide (what an illusion!) for faith or for unbelief. Faith makes the solid actuality of unbelief an impossibility. It sweeps it away. It replaces it by itself. It does not build a bridge over the gulf. It closes it. It has already closed it. This takes place in the necessity of faith in the strength of which the only act which remains for a man is the genuinely free act of faith. This is its foundation. It is because this is its foundation that it is both negatively and positively so vigorous as the human act as which we still have to describe it. And it is because it is grounded in this necessity that when it takes place as a human act it has the adamantine, unquestioning and joyful certainty which characterises it and in which it cannot be compared even remotely with the certainty of any other human action. But this necessity of faith does not lie in man. It does not lie even in the good nature of man as created for God, let alone in his being as the sinner who in denial and perversion of his good nature has turned away from God and in so doing deprived himself already of the possibility of faith. It does not even lie in faith in itself and as such. It is to be found rather in the object of faith. It is this object which forces itself necessarily on man and is in that way the basis of his faith. This object is the living Lord Jesus Christ, in whom it took place, in whom it has taken place for every man, in whom it confronts man as an absolutely superior actuality, that his sin, and he himself as the actual sinner he is, and with his sin the possibility of his unbelief, is rejected, destroyed and set aside, that he is born again as a new man of obedience, who now has the freedom for faith, and only in that faith his future. In this destroying and renewing of man as it took place in Jesus Christ there consists the necessity of faith, because beyond this destroying and renewing there remains for sinful man only faith in the One in whom it has taken place. In the death of Jesus Christ both the destroying and the renewing have taken place for all men, and the fact that they have taken place has been revealed as valid for all men in His resurrection from the dead. Therefore objectively, really, ontologically, there is a necessity of faith for them all. This object of faith is, in fact, the circle which encloses them all, and which has to be closed by every man in the act of his faith. Jesus Christ is not simply one alternative or chance which is offered to man, one proposition which is made to him. He is not put there for man's choice, *à prendre ou à laisser*. The other alternative is, in fact, swept away in Him.

With Max v. Schenkendorf: "Arise, thou morning light,/Gone is the ancient night,/Which daily comes again." For, "The devil's claim of old,/On all our human fold,/Is forfeited and lost." And with Ambrosius Lobwasser: "For God's salvation everywhere,/From Heaven is sprinkled down,/That is, He has His own dear Son,/Sent down from heaven's highest throne,/That everything on earth,/In Him may have new birth."

With the divine No and Yes spoken in Jesus Christ the root of human unbelief, the man of sin, is pulled out. In its place there is put the root of faith, the new man of obedience. For this reason unbelief has become an objective, real and ontological impossibility and faith an objective, real and ontological necessity for all men and for every man. In the justification of the sinner which has taken place in Jesus Christ these have both become an event which comprehends all men.

And it is the awakening power of the Holy Spirit that this impossibility as such and this necessity as such so confront a man and illuminate him that he does the only objective, real and ontological thing which he can do, not omitting or suppressing or withholding but necessarily speaking the Yes of the free act which corresponds to it, choosing that for which he is already chosen by the divine decision, and beside which he has no other choice, that is to say, faith. How can he have faith if not in this way? The divine decision is not made and cannot be made in him, in his spirit. It can only be repeated. For how can he destroy himself as the old man, posit himself as the new, and therefore free himself for the true freedom in which he can believe? But, again, how can he have anything else in that way but the freedom to believe? Of himself he may have many other things, very many : " Lord, I believe ; help thou mine unbelief." But not in that way. In that way he can have only the freedom to believe. And how can the fact that he believes be anything meaner or weaker or more doubtful than an absolute necessity, his most proper and inward necessity, to obey which is not something strange but self-evident? No other human action is self-evident. But the action of faith is the doing of the self-evident—just because it takes place in the free choice beside which man has no other choice, so that it is his genuinely free choice. The Holy Spirit is the power in which Jesus Christ the Son of God makes a man free, makes him genuinely free for this choice and therefore for faith. He is the power in which the object of faith is also its origin and basis, so that faith can know and confess itself only as His work and gift, as the human decision for this object, the human participation in it which he makes in his own free act but which he can only receive, which he can understand only as something which is received, which he can continually look for as something which is received again and which has to be confirmed in a new act. It is not that he is strong when he believes. But the One in whom he believes shows Himself to be strong over him when he believes—strong as the One who is raised again from the dead to awaken him first from the death of unbelief to the life of faith. Faith means to be awake on the basis of this awakening : to be awake to the strong One who awakens him and who alone can awaken him ; to be awake to the necessity with which He does this, a necessity which excludes all pseudo-freedoms ; to be awake to the self-evident nature of the arising which, on the part of man, will directly follow his awakening. Faith is at once the most wonderful and the simplest of things. In it a man opens his eyes and sees and accepts everything as it—objectively, really and ontologically—is. Faith is the simple discovery of the child which finds itself in the father's house and on the mother's lap. But this simple thing is also the mystery of faith because only in Jesus Christ is it true and actual that things are as man discovers them, and because man's own discovery can itself be an event only in the fact that man is again awakened by Him to see and accept everything as it is : that the night has passed and the day dawned ; that there is peace between God and sinful man, revealed truth, full and present salvation. This simple thing, and this mystery, constitute the being of the Christian, his being by the One in whom he believes.

We now come to a third and decisive thing. Indeed, in the narrower context in which we are now speaking, it can also be the final thing. This is that in the twofold relationship of faith to Jesus Christ, as faith is orientated and based on Him as its object, there takes place in it the constitution of the Christian subject. At a later stage we shall have to understand faith as the particular human action of this subject. And we do not forget that it becomes and is this subject only in this action : not on the basis of a creaturely character of this action as such, but in virtue of the fact that as it is orientated so it is also based on Jesus Christ. Yet it is also true, and we must say it expressly, that in this action there begins and takes place a new and particular being of man.

" But of him are ye in Christ Jesus " (1 Cor. 1³⁰). " For we are his workman-ship (ποίημα), created (κτισθέντες) in Christ Jesus unto good works " (Eph. 2¹⁰). " Blessed be the God and Father of our Lord Jesus Christ, which according to his abundant mercy hath begotten us again " (ἀναγεννήσας ἡμᾶς, 1 Pet. 1³)—an expression which is expounded in 1²³ : " not of corruptible seed, but of incorruptible, by the word of God, which liveth and abideth for ever." New being, new creation (Gal. 6¹⁵, 2 Cor. 5¹⁷), new birth—they are all predicates which are ascribed only to the Christian, and they are all too strong to be taken only as figurative expressions to describe the changed feelings and self-under-standing of Christians. Christians do not lose their character as members of the race which God created good and which fell from Him. But in these predi-cates they are addressed as something other than those with whom in other respects they are still bound in the twofold solidarity of creatureliness and sin. We read in Ac. 11²⁶ that they were first called Χριστιανοί in Syrian Antioch, a name of which we read in 1 Pet. 4¹⁶ that it pledged them to glorify God. That to be a bearer of this name involves a real change of the form of human existence seems to come out in Agrippa's ironical words to Paul as reported in Ac. 26²⁸ : " Almost thou persuadest me to be made (ποιῆσαι) a Christian." It is not without theological significance that this name—that the fact that these folk are adherents of Christ—should have prevailed. And it is not only in Acts and the Pastoral Epistles that what distinguishes them as adherents is described by the term πιστοί. We find the same in 2 Cor. 6¹⁵, where they are contrasted with the ἄπιστοι of their heathen environment, under whose yoke they are not to submit, with whom they can have no μετοχή, no κοινωνία, no συμφώνησις, no μερίς. Being themselves ἐκ πίστεως, they have a part in the blessing of πιστὸς Ἀβραάμ (Gal. 3⁹). πιστός can be used either as a substantive or as an adjective. In 2 Cor. 6¹⁵ it is absolute. In Col. 1¹, Eph. 1¹, 1 Pet. 1²¹ and Ac. 16¹⁵ it is related to Christ or to the God who raised Him from the dead. In Col. 1¹ and Eph. 1¹ it is set in juxtaposition with the term ἅγιοι, clearly emphasising that which marks off sub-jectively those who are described in this way. That it is an abbreviation for πιστεύοντες or ὄντες ἐκ πίστεως is evident from Jn. 20²⁷ : μὴ γίνου ἄπιστος, ἀλλὰ πιστός. The translation " faithful " seems unavoidable. If only it did not carry the suggestion of a psychological consistency which is not conveyed in the very least by πιστός ! This does, of course, speak of a being of those who are described in this way, of the being of which they are participants as they are πιστεύοντες, but of the being of which they are real and objective participants in the fulfilment of this act and as the subjects of it. Just as the sinful man is what he does as such, so he is what he does when as a sinful man he is awakened to faith and can live by it.

We recall that the creaturely subject constituted in the being and work of Jesus Christ is seriously and definitively the new man himself as he is brought into peace with God from his struggle against Him, and is therefore a partaker of the salvation allotted to him. It is the world as it is loved by God and reconciled by Him to Himself in Jesus Christ. The faith which has Jesus Christ for its object is therefore faith in this being and action of His for the world, for all men and for every man. And those who can believe in Him—in Paul's phrase, those who are of faith (of faith in Him)—are the first-fruits and representatives of the humanity and the world to which God has addressed Himself in Jesus Christ. It is their business to give to the God who has done this, to " the living God who is the Saviour of all men " (1 Tim. 4^{10}), the glory which the others do not give Him, and in so doing to attest to them that which they do not know although it avails for them. What Christians have in and for themselves in the sharply differentiated particularity of their being they have as the bearers and representatives of a specially qualified and emphasised solidarity with all other men.

That the living God of 1 Tim. 4^{10} is " specially " (μάλιστα) the Saviour of those that believe means that in the first instance—in His activity to and with them as the spearhead of the whole cosmos, concretely revealed to them and concretely known by them, demanding their concrete service—He is a Saviour for them.

We recollect further that the creaturely subject awakened in this special sense by God through the power of the Holy Spirit is the Christian community in the world : the " We " who pray the Lord's Prayer or simply cry " Abba, Father," the " You " who are reminded in the apostolic message of their origin and nature, the people drawn from both Jews and Gentiles which is, as such, the body whose Head is Jesus Christ, the people in which His truth is known in obedience, and acknowledged in humility and confessed in thankfulness, the people which lives and builds up itself to be a light shining in the world (Phil. 2^{15}) in reflection of His glory. This people as such is the provisional representation of the justification which has taken place in Jesus Christ. The faith which has Him as its object is as such faith in Him as the Creator and Lord of the fellowship of the saints. It is faith as it lives by and for and in and with this fellowship—the faith of this fellowship and as such the faith of individual Christians. Just as a man would not be a man in and for himself, in isolation from his fellow-men, so a Christian would not be a Christian in and for himself, separated from the fellowship of the saints. With his personal faith he is a member of this body of Christ. In the New Testament sense of the term this does not involve any deficiency in his own being and having in relation to that of the whole. It does not involve any limitation of his responsibility by that of the whole or of the others who are in this whole with him. It does not involve, therefore, any diminution of the freedom of his faith. As a member of this body he is in direct touch with its Head. As he believes in and with the community—he does it as a whole, for it is only as a whole that he is a member—the whole with its gift and commission is his whole, and he believes with a royal freedom. What it does involve is that he can believe only in and with the community, only in the sphere and context of it, only in the limitation and determination set by its basis and goal. The royal freedom of his faith is the freedom to stand in it as a brother or a sister, to stand with other brothers and sisters in the possession granted to it and the service laid upon it. If faith is outside the Church it is outside the world, and therefore a-Christian. It does not have as its object " the Saviour of all men, and specially of them that believe."

But when all that is said and considered, we have to add at once that the creaturely subject constituted in the being and work of Jesus Christ and awakened as such by the power of the Holy Spirit is in the last resort the individual Christian in the act of his personal faith. The humanity and world loved by God, fallen from Him and reconciled by Him to Himself, lives in individual men and their particular creatureliness and sin. And the community founded and preserved and ruled by Jesus Christ in the world lives in individual Christians and the multifarious but unitary activity of their faith. There are no saints without the fellowship, but there is no fellowship without the saints. If there is no Christian I and Thou and He outside the twofold, Christ-centred circle of the We and You and They of the race and the community, then the general no less than the particular is an abstraction, not to say an illusion, since it does not become event in the Christian I and Thou and He, in the personal faith of the members of the body of Christ. It is of this event that we must now speak.

As a human act it consists in a definite acknowledgment, recognition and confession. As this human act it has no creative but only a cognitive character. It does not alter anything. As a human act it is simply the confirmation of a change which has already taken place, the change in the whole human situation which took place in the death of Jesus Christ and was revealed in His resurrection and attested by the Christian community. But it obviously belongs to the alteration of the human situation which Christian faith can only confirm, that it does find this confirmation, that there are men who do recognise and acknowledge and confess it, who can be the witnesses of it—

in other words, that there are individual Christian subjects. It is not
their faithfulness which makes them this (not even when it is understood as the act of their believing). That would simply mean that
they could do it and have done it of themselves. By their faithfulness
(as the doers of this act of believing) they simply confirm without
knowing it—and it is to be hoped without boasting about it—that
they are the subjects who in some astonishing way are capable of
and willing and ready for this act and therefore for this acknowledgment, recognition and confession. How has this happened? How
do they come to be qualified to do this? They obviously cannot be,
and will not be, as the sinful men they are like all other men. If they
are all the same, since the faith and therefore the acknowledgment,
recognition and confession are their act, it is evident that the event
of their faith (while it has no creative aspect as their act) is more than
cognitive in character. From the point of view of the presupposition
at work in their act, from the point of view of the men as its doers,
it is clearly the positing of a new being, the occurrence of a new creation,
a new birth of these men. In their act these sinful men confirm that
they are the witnesses of the alteration of the human situation which
has taken place in Jesus Christ : not the men who are altered in it—
for as such they cannot so far be seen—but certainly, and this is the
astonishing thing—as those for whom it has happened and not not happened, as the witnesses of it. It belongs to the alteration of the human
situation as it has taken place in Jesus Christ that it now has at least
the confirmation of its witness in certain human subjects. Not because
they believe, not in the power in which they do believe, but as they
do actually believe (in strength or weakness), as they do it and are
in a position to do it, they become and are Christians in the midst of
all other men—men with this particular characteristic as men. To
this extent we cannot deny to the event of their faith a certain creative
character.

But how does it acquire this character, which it can have only
on the presupposition of what man himself does in it, but which on
this presupposition it cannot derive from sinful man ? It is here that
we must obviously try to think seriously of the object of faith and
therefore of Jesus Christ as its starting-point. Christian faith is both
orientated and based on Him. The believer is enclosed by Him both
before and behind : he is encircled by Him. He owes it to Him that
he can believe at all, and that he does believe. He believes as one
who is confronted and apprehended by Him (Phil. 3^{12}), as the one in
face of whom He is the stronger and has proved Himself to be the
stronger. In face of him He is the stronger in virtue of what He has
done for all men and therefore for him in His death, and of the fact
that God has manifested Him for all men and therefore for him as
the One who has done this in His resurrection from the dead. And
in face of him He proves Himself to be the stronger by the irresistible

awakening power of His Holy Spirit. In this strength and in this proof He calls him to faith. And in so doing He creates the presupposition on the basis of which the sinful man can and actually does believe. He introduces him as a new subject which is capable of and willing and ready for this act, as a witness of His act and revelation, as a Christian. Because the faith of this sinful man is directed on Him and effected by Him, the event of his faith is not merely cognitive as a human act but it is also creative in character. The new being effective and revealed in it, the new creation, the new birth —they are all the mystery of the One in whom he believes and whom he can acknowledge and recognise and confess in faith. When it is this One who closes the circle around him, a man can and must do that which he does in faith.

It remains to ask how we have to think of this closing of the circle and therefore of the creative mystery of the Christian existence. On the one hand we are dealing with the being and action of Jesus Christ, on the other with the particular, the most particular, fact of the existence of the individual man. For this reason we have to seek our answer in the form of the being and action of Jesus Christ in which it encloses within itself His being and action in a special relationship between Him and this particular man. His being and action has this form. He confronts all men. He confronts His community. But in so doing He also confronts the individual as such. He confronts thee and me, this one and that one. His act and revelation took place for the world and the fellowship of the saints, but they also took place for thee and for me, for this one and that one. As the Mediator, the Saviour and the Lord, He lives not only in the outer but also in this inner circle, and therefore as thy Mediator, Saviour and Lord, and mine. " Jesus lives "—and I with Him—which means that from all eternity God has thought of me, elected me, acted for me in Him, called me to Himself in Him as His Word. This is—in general terms— the form of His being and activity in which He Himself is the mystery in the event of faith, in which He gives to this event a creative as well as a cognitive character. For when I, as the sinful man I still am, recognise and acknowledge and confess Him in this way, taking my place in the Christian community, this means that I also am reached and found and seized by Him—by His being and activity, and therefore that I discover and confirm myself as the subject also intended and envisaged in His being and activity, as a man whom His existence as the Saviour of the world and the Head of His community also concerns, who is also bound and committed to Him as the Saviour and Head. If I discover myself as this subject, what can I do but confirm myself as such ? What can I do, therefore, but that which is proper to this subject as a member of the world reconciled and the community founded by Him, that is to say, believe ?

But in saying " also " we have said too little and not been

sufficiently clear. When a man can and must believe, it is not merely a matter of an " also," of his attachment as an individual to the general being and activity of the race and the community as determined by Jesus Christ. In all the common life of that outer and inner circle he is still himself. He is uniquely this man and no other. He cannot be repeated or represented. He is incomparable. He is this in his relationship with God and also in his relationship with his fellows. He is this soul of this body, existing in the span of this time of his. He is this sinful man with his own particular pride and in his own special case. For all his common life he is alone in this particularity. It is not simply that he also can and must believe, but that just he can and must believe. And if the being and activity of Jesus Christ Himself is the mystery of the event in which he actually does so, then we must put it even more strongly and precisely : that in this event it takes place that Jesus Christ lives not only " also " but " just " as his Mediator and Saviour and Lord, and that He shows Himself just to him as this living One. He became a servant just for him. It was just his place that He took, the place which is not the place of any other. In this place He died just for him, for his sin. And, again, in his place He was raised again from the dead. Therefore the Yes which God the Father spoke to Him as His Son in the resurrection is spoken not only also but just to him, this man. In Him it was just his pride, his fall which was overcome. In Him it is just his new right which has been set up, his new life which has appeared. And in Him it is just he who is called to new responsibility, who is newly claimed. It is just he who is not forgotten by Him, not passed over, not allowed to fall, not set aside or abandoned. It is just he—and this is the work of the Holy Spirit—who has been sought out, and reached, and found by Him, just he whom He has associated with Himself and Himself with him. God did not will to be God without being just his God. Jesus did not will to be Jesus without being just his Jesus. The world was not to be reconciled with God without just this man as an isolated individual being a man—this man—reconciled with God. The community was not to be the living body of Christ without just this man being a living member of it. The whole occurrence of salvation was not to take place but just for him, as the judgment executed just on him, the grace addressed in this judgment just to him, just his justification, just his conversion to God. The gift and commission of the community of Jesus Christ is personally just his gift and commission. And all this not merely incidentally, among other things, or only in part for him, but altogether, in its whole length and breadth and height and depth just for him, because Jesus Christ, in whom all this is given to the world and the community, in whom God Himself has sacrificed Himself for it, is Jesus, the Christ, just for him. That this shines out in a sinful man is the mystery, the creative fact, in the event of faith in which he becomes and is a Christian, so that he can and must acknowledge and recognise and confess as such what is proper to him as this subject.

What do I acknowledge and recognise and confess as this subject? That Jesus Christ Himself is *pro me*, just for me. But it is not the first thing to acknowledge and recognise and confess this. The first thing is that Jesus Christ is, in fact, just for me, that I myself am just the subject for whom He is. That is the point. That is the newness of being, the new creation, the new birth of the Christian. Everything else follows from this, especially the fact that, whatever may be the force of the basis and validity of the *pro me*, it can never be a *pro me* in the abstract, but includes in itself and is enclosed by the communal *pro nobis* and the even wider *propter nos homines*. We can and should give it all its own weight as *pro me*. It carries the *pro nobis* and the *propter nos homines*, just as it is carried by them. There is no *pro nobis* or *propter nos homines* which does not include in itself and is not enclosed by the *pro me*. In its connexion, its unity with this, it has its own dignity and truth and actuality, which, if it is not greater, is certainly not less—the dignity, truth and actuality which is proper to the individual Christian subject, just to me and to thee, to this one and that one, who are believers in Jesus Christ.

In saying this we have made the statement or statements which bring us to the high-water mark of our serious agreement with one line of Luther's thinking, with that of Pietism old and new, with that of Kierkegaard, with that of a theology like W. Herrmann's, and with that of the theological existentialism of our own day (so far as it can be seriously regarded as theological). In this respect they all were and are right : that the question of the individual Christian subject has to be put, and that it has to be answered with the *pro me* of faith. Without the *pro me* of the individual Christian there is no legitimate *pro nobis* of the faith of the Christian community and no legitimate *propter nos homines* of its representative faith for the non-believing world. The being and activity of Jesus Christ has essentially and necessarily the form in which He addresses Himself, not only also, but just to the individual man, to thee and to me, to this man and that man, in which He makes common cause with the individual in his very isolation, in which His Holy Spirit speaks just to his spirit.

It has been an unfortunate necessity in recent years to criticise the I-hymns which came into our hymn-books with the transition from the 16th to the 17th century (cf. *C.D.* I, 2, p. 252 f.), and the I-piety which underlies them. Such criticism is a counterblast to the general subjectivist trend of modern Protestantism, and in face of this aberration it will constantly have to be made. But as is obvious from the presence of the I-Psalms in the Bible, it can only be a relative and not an absolute criticism. It cannot try to eliminate or suppress altogether either the I-hymns or I-piety. It must be content with a limited objective. Not only is it impossible to reject as such the glance at the *pro me*, but this glance is actually necessary and commanded in connexion and unity with what the Christian faith is beyond this. It acts as a kind of catalysator in which every *pro nobis* and beyond that every *propter pro homines* has to show whether those who confess it are competent subjects, or whether what they seem to confess is only an abstract theory which cannot have in their mouth the power of witness but only the nature of myth. But there is more to it than that. *Credo* as a baptismal confession is said in the first person singular, and it is not accidental that in this form it is the confession of the Christian Church and is made representatively for the unbelieving world and as proclamation to it. When the community says *credo*, then in its members on the one hand and proleptically with men of the world on the other, it gathers itself into a single person, just as Jesus Christ its Head is an individual who represents many individuals and unites them with Himself, and according to the biblical view Adam was also a representative individual and the prototype of Jesus Christ (Rom. 5^{14}). In the light of this we cannot deny, but are forced to maintain, that each individual as such—not in identity with Adam or even with Jesus Christ, but in analogy with Adam by virtue of his creatureliness, and with Jesus Christ by virtue of his justification—stands in the place of many, of all, uniting and representing in himself as this man the whole race, and in himself as this Christian the community. In his existence as an individual he is not a particle or a sample or a specimen. He is the one who is and has and does and signifies the whole and everything. He is the one who is responsible for all and everything. His life in all the narrowness of its limits is the theatre of the whole action of loss and salvation. In all its pettiness it is the object of the whole judgment and grace of God. From and to all eternity the eye of God is wholly directed upon it and His almighty hand wholly occupied with it. In all the work of God, in what God does and says as Creator, Reconciler and Redeemer, he is not merely envisaged in general, or together with others. He is not only also but just the object of God's love and wrath and mercy. He is not only also but just the temple of His Holy Spirit. What God does is all of it done just for him, just for thee and me. What God wills is all expected just of him, just of thee and me. Is there any I-hymn which can express this strongly enough ? Is not the confession of faith itself necessarily the strongest I-hymn of all ? For what would faith be if it were not the event in which it suddenly flashes on a man that everything that God does and wills is with reference to him, that it is therefore *pro me* ?

But having said that, we must take to point out at once what must never happen in this respect. The *pro me* must never be systematised and itself made a systematic principle and applied as such. Its nerve and meaning is in the fact that Jesus Christ is *pro me*. Therefore the I-hymn can be composed and sung and sounded forth legitimately only as a hymn to Christ. This is what Zinzendorf perceived in contrast to the Pietism of his day, and this is what he taught and practised in his own baroque but not incorrect fashion. What has to be seen and understood and said—this is the canon of the criticism we have to make— is what Jesus Christ is just for thee and me, for the individual as such, and what Jesus Christ expects just of him.

When this is observed, the *pro nobis* and the even more comprehensive *propter nos homines* will not be submerged and disappear in the *pro me*, but in and with the *pro me* they will necessarily be given the same degree of honour. The existence of the community and its gift and mission, the existence of the world and the salvation of God allotted and addressed to it, cannot then be mere (if possible facultative) consequences of the Christian existence of the individual, mere peripheral phenomena and incidental determinations of his personal salvation. In and with the *pro me*, Jesus Christ the Lord of the community and the Saviour of the world will assert Himself as the subject of the *pro me*. Only in the light of its object can the faith in which the individual becomes aware and certain of his own justification be the faith of the community and a faith which is open and addressed to the world. It will therefore be prevented from becoming a morose or humdrum or sentimental or Bohemian private enterprise. In this light, in the light of its object, it will always be enclosed by, as it encloses, that twofold We-faith. In it it will have its catalysator, as it is itself its catalysator. It will necessarily be preserved from the subtle egoism which would be proper to it as an abstract I-faith. But only in the light of its object ! In the words of M. Gerhardt : " In me and in my living,/Is nothing on this earth,/What Christ to me hath given,/Of love alone is worth."

Again, it cannot happen that the *pro me*, the relationship of the activity and will of God to the individual, is made as such the basis and measure of all things, as though at bottom we were dealing with the relationship of the individual to the activity and will of God, as though the value, truth and actuality of God were to be found only in what thou and I, the individual sees to be of value, truth and actuality for him, only in what he acknowledges and confesses to be " existentially " relevant to him. In respect of what can be *pro me*, of what can be " existentially " relevant, we have to refrain from interpreting it in the light of any kind of anthropology or ontology or pre-understanding, into the framework of which the God who is *pro me* in Jesus Christ can be fitted and to the measure of which He can be cut as in a bed of Procrustes. Jesus Christ will be to the man who believes in Him something more, something other, than an obscure point of contact, or a mere exponent or cipher of his I-faith. He will be allowed to proclaim Himself as the One He is as the object and origin of his I-faith. And it will be left to Him to decide the fact and extent that He is *pro me*, that He is existentially relevant to thee and to me. Every anthropology and ontology will have its norm and law in Him, not *vice versa*. The usurping invasion of theology by a subjectivist philosophy—and it was no accident that this coincided with the rise of Pietism—will then be checked, although, of course, there will be a true appraisal of the problem of the individual Christian subject. It will be acknowledged that Christian faith is an " existential " happening, that it is from first to last I-faith, which can and should be sung in I-hymns. But there will take place the necessary " de-mythologisation " of the " I " which Paul carried through in Gal. 2²⁰ : " I live, yet not I, but Christ liveth in me."

We remember all this only in passing. The genuine " interests " of Christian individualism will be asserted when we learn to jerk ourselves free—and do, in fact, jerk ourselves free—from the abstractions which have been so kindly received in modern Protestantism.

2. THE ACT OF FAITH

We have now said and considered what we had to say concerning the object of faith, its origin, and finally and above all the basis of the Christian subject, and therefore the coming into being and the being of the Christian. In what follows we must always keep this in mind as the presupposition, but we must turn no less resolutely to the other aspect of the problem. Christian faith is a free human act.

From this particular standpoint it is *the* act of the Christian life. Of course, the same may be said of love and hope as well as faith. But in line with our first main consideration and attempted understanding of reconciliation, the being and work of Jesus Christ as the Lord who became a servant for us (§ 59), its counterpart in human sin in the form of pride (§ 60), the justification of sinful man in Him (§ 61), and the gathering and foundation of the Christian community by Him (§ 62), this act of the Christian life has the form of faith. Like love and hope from other aspects, faith is *the* act of the Christian life to the extent that in all the activity and individual acts of a man it is the most inward and central and decisive act of his heart, the one which—if it takes place—characterises them all as Christian, as expressions and confirmations of his Christian freedom, his Christian responsibility, his Christian obedience. On whether or not this act takes place depends whether these acts are rightly done from the Christian standpoint. If a man does them in faith, if in doing them he first performs the basic act of faith, then he does them as a Christian, he does them rightly from the Christian standpoint. As against that (Rom. 14[23]), whatsoever is not of faith, is not done of and in this basic act of faith, is sin. By what we have called in the title the act of faith we mean the basic Christian act which, when it takes place, is *the* act of the Christian life, the Christian act which embraces and controls all individual acts and activities, permeating and determining them like the leaven of Mt. 13[33]. We must now describe faith as this act.

We will try to do this by developing it under three mutually related terms. It is an acknowledgment, a recognition and a confession. As all these terms indicate, it is a knowledge.[1] And as the object and basis is the same in every case, so in every case it is an active knowledge. Why a knowledge? As we have seen, underlying it there is the presupposition of a creative event—the being and activity of Jesus Christ in the power of His Holy Spirit awakening man to faith. As the event of a human act on this basis, faith is a cognitive event, the simple taking cognisance of the preceding being and work of Jesus Christ. But we are not dealing with an automatic reflection, with a stone lit up by the sun, or wood kindled by a fire, or a leaf blown by the wind. We are dealing with man. It is, therefore, a spontaneous, a free, an active event. This active aspect is expressed in the three terms : acknowledgment, recognition and confession.

Christian faith is an acknowledgment. In our description of that taking cognisance this must come first. It might be objected that acknowledgment includes and presupposes recognition, so that the latter ought to be treated first. This may be true enough in other cases, but when it is the taking cognisance of Christian faith the reverse is true. The recognition is certainly included in the acknowledgment, but it can only follow it. Acknowledging is a taking cognisance which is obedient and compliant, which yields and subordinates itself. This obedience and compliance is not an incidental and subsequent characteristic of the act of faith, but primary, basic and decisive. It is not preceded by any other kind of knowledge, either recognition or confession. The recognition and confession of faith are included in and follow from the fact that they are originally and properly an acknowledgment, the free act of obedience.

In the older dogmatics the classical definition of faith was that it takes place in the three acts of *notitia, assensus* and *fiducia*. This seems evident enough, for cognisance of a thing implies a prior acquaintance. But what does *notitia* mean

---

[1] In the German the three terms are *Anerkennen, Erkennen* and *Bekennen* : three different forms of *Kennen*.—Trans.

in this case ? Calvin makes this his starting point and he fills it out at once and quite correctly in this way: faith is the *notitia divinae erga nos voluntatis ex eius verbo percepta* (*Instit.* III, 2, 6). But how can there be an acquaintance with the will of God for us taken from His word except in that act of acknowledgment and therefore of obedience and compliance ? Calvin's more precise definition of faith (*l.c.* 2, 7) is that it is the *divinae erga nos benevolentiae firma certaque cognitio*. But concerning the term *cognitio* or *intelligentia* Calvin had already remarked at the beginning of His work (I, 6, 2) that it is basically present only *ubi reverenter amplectimur, quod de se testari Deus voluit. Neque enim perfecta solum, vel numeris suis completa fides, sed omnis recta Dei cognitio ab oboedientia nascitur.* For this reason Paul described it as the task of his apostolate to call to the ὑπακοή (Rom. 1⁵) or the λειτουργία τῆς πίστεως (Phil. 2¹⁷). If we were to use the terminology of the older dogmatics, we should have to speak first of *assensus* and only then of *notitia*—although this would have sounded very strange to its authors with their concern for formal logic. The only thing is that acknowledgment is much more than *assensus* and recognition than *notitia*.

In our exposition of this basic acknowledgment, we will start with the fact that the calling of sinful man to faith in Jesus Christ is identical with his calling to the community of Jesus Christ built on the foundation of the apostles and prophets, the community which is His body, the earthly-historical form of His existence. On the level of an earthly-historical event—of which we are now speaking—his encounter with this object of his faith will therefore be in some form his encounter with the Christian community, a direct or indirect encounter with its ministry or proclamation or one of its activities. And what he will experience in this encounter if he comes to faith will be this, that the relative authority and freedom in which the Christian community exists in the world and in which he experiences its existence will confront him, not in some kind of non-obligatory way, but with such compulsion that he must not only accept and respect it but submit to its law and desire to associate himself with it and join it. Why ? Not because of what the community is and represents and does in the world and as a worldly phenomenon. It always was and is the more than doubtful Christians who are impressed by the phenomenon of the Church as such and won by it to submit to it and join it. And woe to the Church which loves and is out to try to impress men as such ! For what has this kind of impressing to do with Christian faith and its acknowledging, or even with an introduction to it ? If a man comes to Christian faith, this means that in the encounter with the community of Jesus Christ he encounters Jesus Christ Himself, that in its relative authority and freedom he encounters His absolute authority and freedom, the law to which the community itself is subject, and therefore a law which is superior to him and binds him. If he comes to faith, then this means that through its ministry and proclamation he does not submit to it but to its law and therefore to the Lord Jesus Christ Himself, and that in so doing he will necessarily desire to associate with it and join it. It is not the Church which has won him for itself, but—by the ministry and proclamation of the Church—Jesus Christ has won him for Himself, bringing him to the point where he can freely acknowledge Him (and with Him the community which represents Him), where he can show himself obedient and compliant to Him (and therefore to it), where he can put to Him (and therefore to himself and the community) the question of Ac. 8³⁶ : " What doth hinder me to be baptised ? "

Acknowledgment as the basic moment in the act of Christian faith has reference to Jesus Christ Himself—presupposing, of course, the mediatorial ministry of the Christian community which is His body and the consequence of an active acknowledgment of its existence and the desire to be a member of it. It has reference to the fact which the community represents in the world, to the person by whom it is constituted and who is its living law.

At this point we must clear away certain misunderstandings. The active acknowledgment of Christian faith, in which recognition and confession are included and from which they result, does not have reference to any doctrine, theory or theology represented by or in the community. It does not have reference to any creed or dogma formulated and championed by the community, not even the most ancient and universal. Even less does it have reference to the dogmatics which gathers together and expounds that dogma, not even the most churchly of dogmatics. Nor does it have reference—as the Reformers so sharply emphasised—to the histories of the Old and the New Testaments, to the prophetic and apostolic theology as such on whose witness the proclamation of the community is founded. At its root as this acknowledgment Christian faith is not the subservient acceptance of any reports or propositions, irrespective of whether they are biblical or churchly or modern. At this root it is indeed an obedient acceptance. But the object of it is the One whom the Bible attests and the Church as taught by the Bible proclaims, the living Jesus Christ Himself, none other. He is the Lord. He is sovereign. He is the Master, who cannot be replaced by the prophets and apostles with their word about Him, whom they only desire to serve with their word, who cannot be replaced by the Church with its word of proclamation, whom it, too, can only desire to serve. It is Jesus Christ who is acknowledged by Christian faith. Of course—we will return to this in a moment—not Jesus Christ as portrayed according to the measure and capacity of imagination, metaphysics or history, but as attested by Holy Scripture and proclaimed by the community. Yet Jesus Christ Himself, not a biblical text which attests Him or a biblical or churchly thesis which proclaims Him. That " Jesus Christ is my Lord " (Luther) is what Christian faith maintains when in this acknowledgment it begins to accept " this " as true. It does so in obedience to the Bible's witness to it and in indebtedness to the Church's proclamation of it. But in so far as this act is a basic acknowledging it accepts only " this " as true. And " this " is more than a " this." It is superior to every

" this." It is the basis and fulfilment of every " this." It is He Himself, the living Jesus Christ, the Head of the Church, the Lord of Scripture. It is most important to maintain this expressly and in face of all false orthodoxy because this is the point which decides whether we will understand faith rightly : that it is the work of human insight, resolve and action ; but that as this human work it is real Christian faith only directly in the encounter with its object, only as the gift of the Holy Spirit of Jesus Christ Himself, only as the work of the obedience which is pledged to Him and the freedom which is given by Him. This truth is either denied or hopelessly obscured in a conception of faith which involves as its basic act the acceptance of certain statements which attest and proclaim Him, which does not, therefore, consist in simple obedience to Himself.

Are we in agreement at this point with W. Herrmann and our contemporary R. Bultmann ? In the result it might appear so, but perhaps only in relation to the negative element in this result, our opposition to a false orthodoxy, our refusal to ground the act of faith in the acceptance of the texts of the Bible or the propositions of the Church. If only there were an obvious unity on the positive element, that the living Lord Jesus Christ attested by the Bible and proclaimed by the Church is the One who must be accepted and acknowledged at the basis of the act of faith, and therefore that the negation must be made only on this ground (and not on the ground merely of certain ethico-anthropological propositions) ! To the extent that this is not clear, and so long as it is not clear, it is better to leave open the question of this agreement. For it is much to be feared that in what we are now going to say we shall have the support neither of Herrmann nor of Bultmann.

Christian faith is a recognition. That is how we have to continue. This statement can only be secondary. Recognition is not of itself and as such the basic act of faith, which consists in that obedient and compliant taking cognisance. Faith is a recognition only to the extent that a recognition is included in that obedient and compliant taking cognisance. When we say this, we say that it is only the statement which is secondary. For that which proceeds from the acknowledgment as a second thing is already included in it as the first. If we may, and must, understand and formulate positively the definition given by Calvin—" All true knowledge of God (*omnis recta Dei cognitio*) is born of obedience "—then as the basic act of faith this obedience is not an obedience without knowledge, a blind obedience without insight or understanding, an obedience which is rendered only as an emotion or an act of will. How could a recognition proceed from it or in any way follow it if it were not already contained in this first thing as a second ?

It was Calvin again who, at the beginning of his great tractate on faith (*Instit.* III, 2, 2) hastened to rebut as sharply as he could the scholastic conception of a *fides implicita*, a readiness to subject reason to the teaching of the Church. This was a *commentum* which would not merely bury true faith but completely destroy it. *Non in ignorantia, sed in cognitione sita est fides :* and not in a bare knowledge of God, but in the knowledge of His concrete and revealed will with us. How can we lay hold of our salvation in faith if it is not an *explicita divinae bonitatis agnitio, in qua consistit nostra iustitia :* the knowledge that God is our gracious Father in the atonement made by Christ ?

But there is a recognition in the basic act of that obedience, of that acknowledgment (we must now continue) because the living Jesus Christ who is the object of that acknowledgment, to whom man subjects himself in the obedience of faith, is Himself not without form, but is the Jesus Christ attested in Holy Scripture and proclaimed by the community. In faith we have to do with Him and only with Him, but with Him as attested by Scripture and proclaimed by the community. But when as the One who is attested by Scripture and proclaimed by the community He encounters man and calls him to faith, and presents Himself to him as his Lord, He does not do so in a featureless way which is at the mercy of every possible conception and interpretation, but He does so as a genuine object with a very definite form which cannot be exchanged or mistaken for any other form, which is determined by His own being and His own revelation of His being, which is His authentic form. It is in this authentic form that from the very first, with the very first step, He becomes to everyone who comes to faith, and is obedient to Him, the object of his recognition. By what particular features of this form, to what extent, and with what distinctness or indistinctness, He is first recognised is a secondary question—that of the subjective fulfilment of the knowledge of Jesus Christ proffered to him. What is decisive is the objective truth that in and with the fact that he is called by Him to the obedience of faith he is given ground and cause to recognise Him in His authentic form, and therefore rightly. He would not obey Him if at the same time he did not begin in some way to see and understand Him, if of his obedience there were not born in outline a *recta cognitio.* Not any *cognitio*, but in outline, in what is at first a very primitive and rudimentary and even at best a very imperfect form, a *recta cognitio.* It is a right recognition in so far as it is in the form determined by His own being and His own revelation of His being that He encounters man in the witness of Scripture and the proclamation of the community ; in so far, therefore, as the subjective fulfilment of the knowledge objectively proffered to man is limited and controlled by the fact that it always takes place in the sphere of Holy Scripture which attests Him and the community which proclaims Him in obedience to Scripture.

This sphere is a wide one, which leaves open to the believer many and different possibilities of seeing and understanding Jesus Christ and therefore of the subjective fulfilment of the right knowledge proffered to him.

We have considered the general definition of Calvin, that it is a matter of the recognition : *Deum nobis esse propitium patrem, reconciliatione per Christum facta.* This is the very compressed insight of Calvin. It is not indefinite but very definite because it has obviously arisen and been formed in this sphere. Against it we may set the rather more express statement which Luther offered as his knowledge of Jesus Christ in the passage of the Catechism already mentioned. The decisive (and of itself very explicit) declaration is : " I believe, that Jesus Christ . . . is my Lord." But obviously he could not and would not make this in the void, so he added to the name of Jesus Christ : " very God, eternally begotten of the Father, and very man, born of the Virgin Mary," and to the words " my Lord " : " who has redeemed and purchased and loosed me, lost and sinful man, from all sin, from death and from the power of the devil, not with gold or silver, but with His own sacred and precious blood, with His innocent death and passion, that I may be His, and live under Him in His kingdom, and serve Him in eternal righteousness, innocence and felicity, as He is raised from the dead, and lives and reigns to all eternity." This is a more developed, but again a particular and selective, description of the knowledge of the One who is acknowledged as Lord. It is Luther's own description, but it is not for that reason arbitrary or strange or indefinite. It is obviously made in the sphere of Scripture and the community and to that extent it is most definite. The description in the well-known answer to the first question of the *Heidelberg Catechism* takes a different turn, but again it has this in common with those of Luther and Calvin, that it is made in that sphere, and with the responsibility which that involves, so that for all its peculiarity it is both definite and in order—as *recta cognitio*.

The recognition of Christian faith can and should be varied. The reason for this is as follows. Although its object, the Jesus Christ attested in Scripture and proclaimed by the community, is single, unitary, consistent and free from contradiction, yet for all His singularity and unity His form is inexhaustibly rich, so that it is not merely legitimate but obligatory that believers should continually see and understand it in new lights and aspects. For He Himself does not present Himself to them in one form but in many—indeed, He is not in Himself uniform but multiform. How can it be otherwise when He is the true Son of the God who is eternally rich ? Of course, all knowledge of Jesus Christ will have not merely its basis but its limit and standard in the witness of Scripture and the proclamation of the Church. It is possible only within this definite sphere. It is only in this sphere that Jesus Christ has a form for us men, that He can therefore be an object of our knowledge and known by us. Again, it is a wide sphere with many possibilities. But in correspondence with the uniqueness and unity of Jesus Christ Himself it is a sphere with limits, and these limits are always the criterion in the question whether what we regard as the knowledge of faith in Jesus Christ is true knowledge, whether indeed it can be seriously called knowledge or not. Outside this sphere, Jesus Christ has no form for us ; He is not an object of our knowledge and He cannot be known by us. The believer whom He has definitely encountered in this sphere and not elsewhere will not even try to seek Him outside this sphere. If he did, both Jesus Christ and his faith would dissolve into nothingness. The problem of the knowledge of faith in Jesus Christ is, therefore, absolutely tied up with the existence of this sphere, as is the answering of the problem with respect for this sphere. This knowledge is nourished by the witness of Scripture and its exposition and application in the proclamation of the community. It cannot refuse to accept this as its norm, and to be criticised and corrected by it as it listens to the exposition and application of it in the fellowship of the saints.

Here in the question of the knowledge of faith is the place where the biblical texts, and in their subordinate place the propositions and and confession and dogma of the Church, and in their proper degree and dignity the teaching and theory and theology advocated by and in the community, all have their own functions. If to believe means *eo ipso* to associate and attach oneself to the community, then the knowledge of faith necessarily consists in the fact that a man enrols and continues in the school in which the community has always found and from which it can never remove itself, that of the witness of Scripture, in which he cannot help but learn with the community and therefore listen as well to the voice and word of the community. In the measure that it takes place in this context, the knowledge of faith is genuine knowledge—and the question of its range and form and particular direction, although it is serious, is only secondary. What matters is that it is a knowledge which is qualified by the context in which alone it can take place. And since we all have to have this qualification, it may well be that those who are first in respect of the range and form and particular direction of their knowledge of faith are really the last, and that those who seem to be insignificant and uninteresting are really the first. It is a matter of recognising in this context the Lord whom we acknowledge. We must all see to it that in our recognition we accept our particular responsibility to Him. As He is the object and origin of faith in general, He is also of the recognition of faith. And He is the ultimate Judge who they are that truly recognise Him when they acknowledge Him.

But we have not yet explained what we really mean by recognition. We must not allow ourselves to be persuaded by any anti-intellectualism that there is not a definite element of knowing—of which the existence of this sphere of Scripture and the Church is the basis and limit and norm. If we believe, then (whatever may be the range and form and particular direction) we know in whom we believe. There may be many things which as believers in Him we should and could know (and perhaps need to know), but we are never complete ignoramuses, who cannot distinguish and think and speak. If we do not know, we do not recognise, and if we do not recognise, it will be a poor look-out for the basis of our faith, the primary acknowledgment and obedience in which faith in Jesus Christ has its root. At bottom, we shall not believe at all. Of course, faith and its knowing will always be an initial faith and knowing. But without an initial knowing there can be no initial faith, for faith takes place only in that sphere of Scripture and the community in which Jesus Christ has a form and is an object of knowledge and can be known, in which, therefore, everyone in his own measure can know something concerning Him. Not outside this sphere, not outside faith and recognition, but in this sphere, in faith and its recognition, everyone can know something, everyone can know what he needs to know. We can even dare to say that every Christian —in however primitive and rudimentary a way—can and must be a theologian, and that no matter how primitive and rudimentary he can and must be a good theologian, having a true vision of the One in whom he believes, having true thoughts concerning Him and finding the right words to express those thoughts. Of course, if what he feels and wants is something without form, then he is not a theologian, but he is also not a Christian. For Jesus Christ is not without form, but in the sphere in which he encounters Him He is both form and object —and in the same sphere in which he listens to the word of Scripture and to that of the community (and therefore to Himself) he can know Him. Theological scholarship in the narrower sense can only develop with a particular responsibility, and according to a method which has to be continually sought out and clarified, enduring with coherent form, that which in this sphere can be known and is actually known by every real Christian.

Of course, the knowing of faith and its recognition can never be an abstract knowing.

It is to be feared that when our older dogmaticians found the beginning of faith in *notitia* they were thinking of an abstract knowledge of all kinds of truths of faith as formulated in the Bible or dogmatics, the sort of knowledge which a man may amass and enjoy without its having any further relevance to him. They then thought it necessary to proceed to the *assensus* in which a man decides to accept these truths for himself, to make them his own, until finally he attains to *fiducia* in them and penetrates to their true meaning and flavour. We have seen why this is impossible from the very outset. In all the so-called truths of faith we have to do with the being and activity of the living God towards us, with Jesus Christ Himself, whom faith cannot encounter with a basic neutrality, but only in the decision of obedience. The idea of an abstract knowledge of this object—we might almost say the idea of a theologian abstracted from the fact that he is a Christian—is one which has no substance.

But positively the knowing of faith cannot be an abstract knowledge because it is only one element in the active recognition of faith. It is an indispensable element. It is an integral element. It decides its meaning and direction. It shows us what must be the object and origin of the recognition of faith. But it is only one element. Taken alone, as an abstract knowledge of God and the world and even of Jesus Christ, it can only be described as unimportant and even, as Jas. 2[19] tells us, negative, a possibility or impossibility of demonic being. The knowing of faith is, of course, a true and genuine knowing. It is related to its object. It is an objective and, as such, a theoretical knowing. We can say this quite calmly, and it must not be denied. But, as such, it is at once a practical knowing. It both knows and recognises. It is this to the extent that as a knowing about Jesus Christ it includes in itself from the very first a knowing about the believer himself. It is already included in the root of faith as the acknowledgment of Jesus Christ, it is born of that obedience as cognition, that the One in whom I believe and about whom I can know when I believe in Him, that this One—we now come to the final proposition of our second section—is what He is and does what He does for me, *pro me*; that He is "my Lord," as Luther so rightly emphasised in a formula which unfolded so much objective knowledge ; that He is my Lord and therefore my Saviour and Mediator, my Redeemer from sin and death and the devil, my hope of service in righteousness, innocence and felicity, because He died for me and rose again for me. This is just what He is in the form which is determined and limited by the witness of Scripture and the proclamation of the community. This is just what He is as He has always been understood by every normative confession and dogma, by every healthy teaching and theology. This is just what He is as alone He can be perceived and understood in the sphere in which He may be known and is known. This is what Christian faith knows concerning Him. And in knowing this, the believer knows of himself that he himself is the man for whom Jesus Christ is, for whom, in whose place, He acts and rules, in short, with whom He deals as an all-powerful and all-loving human lord—if there were such a thing—would have to deal with a man who is utterly attached and subject to him. He knows that he himself is the man who is the possession of this Lord. But if this is what he knows concerning Jesus Christ and therefore himself, it is not an abstract or dead or neutral, but a concrete and living and— do we need to say it ?—a supremely and profoundly implicated knowledge. Let us say it for once, it is his existential knowledge, his knowledge in the active recognition of his faith.

But we have still to take a further step. We have not yet done sufficient justice to the active character of the recognition of Christian faith. The fact that it is active is based on what we have just described as the believer's knowledge concerning Jesus Christ and therefore himself. But if it is an active recognition—a recognition in the full sense of this important word—then necessarily it reaches out from that knowledge to the awareness, the self-understanding and self-apprehension, of the whole man, thus becoming an action and decision of the whole man. What does it mean when I know that it is true, that it is actually the case, that Jesus Christ is for me, that He takes my place, that I am the possession which He controls, which He has controlled from all eternity, that He has died and risen again for me ? What follows from this ? Does nothing follow ? Can I simply know that this is so, although with a concrete and living and implicated knowledge ? From this knowledge, from the recognition characterised by this knowledge, does there not necessarily follow a total disturbance of my being, a radical decision in relation to my situation *vis à vis* myself and the world ? Does not this recognition—without ceasing to be recognition, but becoming recognition in the deepest sense—necessarily take on the form of a free act which is characterised as a basic act by the fact that it is—we must not say only, but just—the act of my heart ?

Here we must halt for a moment. We have come to a point in our discussion which is not entirely free from danger. We have referred to a total but not an absolute disturbance, a radical but not an eschatological decision, a free act of man, of the human heart, grounded in the act of God, but not the act of God itself and as such. Therefore even at this climax of our exposition of the recognition of faith we are speaking of most important penultimate things, but not of ultimate things.

One description of what is involved in the believer's knowledge concerning Jesus Christ and himself is as follows. The real event of faith in Jesus Christ consists in the fact that the event of salvation as it took place in Jesus Christ is made present or re-enacted in it. Ths history of Jesus Christ, His death and resurrection, becomes the history of the believer. The whole significance of what has taken place in Jesus Christ ἐφ' ἅπαξ consists in the offer that it be repeated in the existence of those who receive the *kerygma* concerning it. The truth and power of faith consist in the fact that man avails himself of this offer, takes up his cross, and dies with Christ to himself and the world, that he may be open for the future of his life. If this is a true description, we have been speaking already not merely of the penultimate but of the ultimate things, of the absolute disturbance, of the eschatological decision, of the act of God in itself and as such, as these take place in faith.

There have been many attempts to make the history of Jesus Christ coincident with that of the believer, and *vice versa*. The theology of the younger Luther (up to 1519) was nothing but a powerful move in this direction. But we cañ approve and make common cause with it neither in its earlier forms nor in that authoritatively represented to-day by R. Bultmann. The real presentation (*repraesentatio*) of the history of Jesus Christ is that which He Himself accomplishes in the work of His Holy Spirit when He makes Himself the object and origin of faith. Christian faith takes note of this, and clings to it and responds to it, without itself being the thing which accomplishes it, without any identity between the redemptive act of God and faith as the free act of man. Jesus Christ and His death and resurrection do not cease to be its object and origin. It is always grounded in the fact that Jesus Christ becomes and is and remains its object and origin. What takes place in the recognition of the *pro me* of Christian faith is not the redemptive act of God itself, not the death and resurrection of Jesus Christ, not the presentation and repetition of His obedience and sacrifice and victory. What is Bultmann's conception but an existentialist translation of the sacramentalist teaching of the Roman Church, according to which, at the climax of the mass, with the transubstantiation of the elements—in metaphysical identity with what took place then and there—there is a " bloodless repetition " of the sacrifice of Christ on Golgotha ? Those who regard this doctrine of the mass as basically untenable will find it impossible to make what took place ἐφ' ἅπαξ in Jesus Christ coincident with what takes place in faith. With the later Luther they will understand faith as a recognition and apprehension (*comprehendere*) of Jesus Christ as the One who died and rose again for us men and in our place, but they will not confuse it with the dying and rising again of Jesus Christ, nor will they confuse the dying and rising again of Jesus Christ with what takes place in faith. Therefore when they speak of what takes place in faith, they will not speak of an absolute disturbance or an eschatological decision or the redemptive act of God.

When I say this I am not looking only at Bultmann. I am also looking in quite a different direction (of which I am reminded by the closeness of his thesis to the Roman theory of the sacrifice of the mass). In modern Roman Catholic theology there is a promising but, of course, unofficial movement which is apparently aiming in the direction of what we might call a christological renaissance. I am not thinking only of the well-known book which Hans Urs von Balthasar addressed to me, in which I find an understanding of the concentration on Jesus Christ attempted in *C.D.*, and the implied Christian concept of reality, which is incomparably more powerful than that of most of the books which have clustered around me. For H. U. v. Balthasar has with him and under him quite a chorus of German and especially French friends who in different ways and with varying emphases all seem to wish to look again to the centre, to the " author and finisher of our faith " (Heb. 12²), who alone can make possible either theology itself or any attempt at ecumenical agreement. And more recently H. U. v. Balthasar himself has written a small series of other notable books, on Theresa of Lisieux, Elisabeth of Dijon and Reinhold Schneider. And if I understand aright their theological content, it seems plain to me that he too (like Bultmann, but with infinitely richer material) sees from that centre which he has grasped so clearly and finely a whole field of possible and actual representations of the history of Jesus Christ, the repetitions or re-enactments of His being and activity by the saints or by those who achieve some measure of sanctity. And as the author sees and represents them these have taken place and do take place in history *post Christum* and in our own time with such significance, such positive and stimulating force, that the One whose being and activity is supposedly reproduced obviously fades into the background as compared with His saints. I now have an inkling of something which at first I could not understand : what is meant by the " christological constriction " which my expositor and critic urged against me in terms of mild rebuke. But we must bring against him the counter-question, whether in all the spiritual splendour of the saints who are supposed to represent and repeat Him Jesus Christ has not ceased—not in theory but in practice—to be the object and origin of Christian faith. I do not know sufficiently whether the " christological renaissance " in the sphere of Roman Catholicism is developing in the same way in the case of its other representatives. If so, it unfortunately means that this promising new beginning in Roman Catholic theology is in danger of returning to, or it may be has never left, the well-worn track on which the doctrine of justification is absorbed into that of sanctification—understood as the pious work of self-sanctification which man can undertake and accomplish in his own strength. My concern is whether this is perhaps the case. For the doctrine of the sacrifice of the mass, the archetype of the whole idea of representation, is still unshaken. If I were a Roman Catholic theologian, I would begin my attempt at reconsideration and cautious amendment at the point where the Roman Catholic Church has in practice its christological centre, perhaps reaching out from there to an appraisal of the saints which would be more subdued—and probably less impressive, but all the more truthful because it gives more honour to the Holy One. If only we were agreed—and this applies to my neighbour on the left as well as on the right—that the ultimate and the penultimate things, the redemptive act of God and that which passes for our response to it, are not the same. Everything is jeopardised if there is confusion in this respect.

That is the danger which threatens at this point and which we must here avoid. And we must see to it that we do not fall into it again by way of certain theories of baptism which are current even in Protestantism. Faith is the free act of man, and is wonderful enough in relationship to Jesus Christ as its object and origin. It is a recognition and apprehension of His being and activity for man. But it is not the repetition of it. The being and activity of Jesus Christ needs no repetition. It is present and active in its own truth and power.

Faith is the free act of man. If this is secure, we cannot speak too strongly of what takes place in it as the recognition and apprehension of Jesus Christ, as the subjective realisation of the *pro me*. There is no doubt that in it as this recognition there is a comprehensive disturbance and decision, an act of the human heart which carries with it, and after it, a total change in man's whole situation. There can also be no doubt that this act and this disturbance and decision do stand in a very direct and intimate relationship to the object and origin of that apprehension, to Jesus Christ and therefore to His death and resurrection. The concept which forces itself upon us is that which says neither too much nor too little, the concept of analogy. What follows from the fact that the recognition of faith is a knowing of the believer—an active knowledge about Jesus Christ which is personal and moves him—is obviously this, that he has to shape his existence, or, more exactly, his understanding and apprehension of his existence, his attitude to himself and the world, in a way which is in some sense parallel to the One who as his Lord took his place, that he has to model himself in conformity with the One in whom he believes, that he can and will be man only in the likeness of Jesus Christ as the One who died and rose again for him. If there are those to whom this seems to be saying too little, let them be careful that in attempting to do better they do not do worse. Is not this the greatest thing we can say of man, of what he can will and do and be in faith ? Not the final thing, certainly. Here and now, short of the end of the ways of God, the final thing can be said only with reference to the man Jesus. But it is the greatest penultimate thing, the greatest thing concerning the man who with God is on the way to this end, the greatest and most wonderful thing concerning the man who, as the sinful man of the world that he is, can still believe and be a Christian. He expresses himself as a Christian in the fact that he is able and willing to be only in the likeness of Jesus Christ and His death and resurrection, in both an inward *mortificatio* and an inward *vivificatio*. We must now develop this in relation to the active recognition of faith.

If it is the case that I can clearly recognise in faith that what took place in the death of Jesus Christ and was revealed in His resurrection took place for me and was revealed as efficacious for me, then that immediately carries with it a very definite practical self-recognition: Not, of course, a fantastic notion that I am a kind of second Christ. That would lead me out of faith and its knowledge, in which He has for me the form of another, in which He is object, and there would be no solid ground under my feet. And the notion could only be an illusion. I am not the Lord who became a servant. I am not the Son

who in obedience to the Father allowed Himself to be judged as my
Judge and the Judge of all men. The glory of God has not been
revealed in me as in His resurrection. Far from being a Saviour, I
am only a proud man like all other men, and as such I have fallen a
prey to eternal death and perdition. I can only believe in Him as the
One who is also, who is just, my Saviour. And I cannot do this in
my own reason and strength, but only as He encounters me in the
witness of Scripture and the proclamation of His community, only
as He awakens me to it by the power of His Holy Spirit. But this
faith in Him, this recognition of Jesus Christ, carries with it ineluctably
a recognition of myself—and in this recognition a real estimate, an
understanding and apprehension of myself—in which, without even
remotely being or becoming like Him, I see myself as the man I am
irresistibly determined by Him, unmistakably stamped by Him, clearly
set in His light from the depth, the lowest depth, in which I find
myself in relation to Him. Faith in Him necessarily calls me to the
recognition of myself in the power of which—and this is the real act
of the heart in faith—I can only wish to be the man determined and
stamped by Him and set in His light.

But what is this determining and stamping and enlightening of
the believer in Jesus Christ, the Christian ? In accordance with what
we have tried to make clear concerning faith within the context of
the doctrine of justification, we must distinguish two great aspects
and try briefly to indicate the peculiar characteristics of each. They
correspond to the positive and negative character of the substitutionary
being and activity of Jesus Christ Himself (as the *analogans*), and they
mark the beginning and end of the way on which the life of the Christian
—the one who recognises Jesus Christ in faith—will become and be
the *analogatum*, the parallel, the likeness—no more but no less—of
His justifying being and activity. What is this *analogans* ? What
do I know in faith as that which has taken place and been revealed
in Jesus Christ for me ?

We recall the first thing—the overcoming, we do not say now of
the pride and fall of man in general but of my pride and my fall in
particular. It is the overcoming of that which I myself had not overcome and could not overcome. I myself, the man of sin, who has not
and will not overcome himself, am the one who finds that he is overcome in Him. My proud heart is vanquished. My proud thoughts
and words and works as they flow from that heart are vanquished.
The plight of my imprisonment, to which I had betrayed myself in
my pride, and in which I could only languish in my pride, is vanquished.
The man of sin is vanquished. Vanquished means removed, destroyed,
put to death. That is the substitutionary being and activity of Jesus
Christ on its negative side. That is what He has done for me in His
death, and what, again for me, is shown to be done in His resurrection.
If I recognise Him in faith, that means that I find that I am the one

to whom this has happened in Him. What follows from this? It cannot be denied that something very necessary and direct must follow for my self-understanding and self-apprehension, for my whole attitude to myself. But what?

Caution is demanded. We say too much if we try to deduce from the overcoming which has come to me in Jesus Christ that it has taken place in me, that I have to understand and conceive of myself as the man who has it behind him. For although that removing and destruction and putting to death has come to me it has not taken place in me. When I believe in Jesus Christ and see what has come to me in Him, I still find in myself my pride and fall. In this respect there is no sense in trying to imagine that my history coincides with that of Jesus Christ and that therefore sin and death in me have no further power over me. In relation to my being in Jesus Christ, I can and must maintain this, but better not in relation to myself. I have overcome in Him, but not in myself, not even remotely. It is a poor theology that grasps at equality with Jesus Christ—a perfectionism which will not accept any distinction between me and Him.

But we say too little if we allow and accept the overcoming of my pride and fall which has taken place in Him, but are then acquiescent and content that it should not take place in me, that the old Adam, as more than one example shows, should be cheerfully alive with all his qualities and impossible possibilities, that he should be permitted to carry on just as before, my consolation being that he is overcome in Jesus Christ, and the reflection that I still cannot overcome him being the excuse for granting him this permission. It is a poor theology that persists in the inequality between me and Jesus Christ—a pious cushion which is content to maintain the distinction from Him.

What, then, is the alternative? What is it that really follows from the recognition that my pride and fall are vanquished in the death of Jesus Christ and that this is manifest in His resurrection? It follows that I am seriously alarmed at myself, that I am radically and heartily sorry for my condition, that I can no longer boast of myself and my thoughts and words and works and especially my heart, but can only be ashamed of them, that I can think of myself and my acts only with remorse and penitence. Of myself—and we must add at once, of the world, the world of men to which I belong, which in the strict sense, although in my own individual way, I resemble in all these things, which is my mirror and of which I myself am the mirror. What is to become of this world which is my world, and of myself who belong to it from the crown of my head to the sole of my foot? To what must I see both it, and myself with it, roll and fall and plunge to destruction?—not, of course, because it is my own (perhaps rather too pessimistic) view that both it and myself are not in the best of ways, but because I recognise that both it and myself are vanquished, i.e., removed and destroyed and put to death, in Jesus Christ, because

I have to see that in Him an end has been made of both it and myself. That is the total disturbance which I have to accept, which I cannot spare myself, when I know Jesus Christ and myself in Him.

This is what the older theologians called *mortificatio*, the *mortificatio* which does not come to a Christian and which he does not have to effect once only, but continually, which does not determine his attitude only occasionally, but is everywhere present as a muffled undertone. It is the Christian attitude on its negative side. The knowledge of faith involves no less than this. This heartfelt act of penitence cannot be avoided by anyone who knows Jesus Christ as his Saviour and is determined and stamped and enlightened by Him. It is not more than this. We are not dealing with the ultimate things, with the absolute disturbance. No one must imagine that in what may take place as his heartfelt act of penitence or sorrow or remorse, of *mortificatio*, it is all up with himself and the world, the world and himself are really brought to an end. " Putting off the world " ? There is no such thing. Certainly, we are not dealing with anything less than penitence : a break, a tear, the sharp piercing of the two-edged sword of the Word of God (Heb. 4¹²), which will necessarily cut through the old Adam in so far as he is as a believer, a new subject in the knowledge of faith (different from when he did not believe) ; a wound, a pain from which he can never again be free, which from the heart, the affected centre of his existence, will continually accompany and penetrate all his thoughts and words and works, which will constantly thwart and disturb him in his pride, which will not allow him to give himself up to his evil cause and to himself and the world. Not a loud, but at any rate a small : " I dismiss you," will be his response to what has come to him—not in himself but in Jesus Christ—as this overcoming, to what in faith in Him he can and must recognise to be his overcoming. And to this extent he will exist in analogy with Him. For all the unlikeness there will be a likeness. For all the similarity there will be a parallelism, a correspondence. In his own modest way he offers a likeness of His being and activity. The publican in the temple in Lk. 18⁹ᶠ· and the prodigal son of Lk. 15¹¹ᶠ· are a likeness of the One who as the Lamb of God took away the sin of the world : no more, but no less. And the man who believes in this One and knows himself in Him can and must and will unreservedly place himself at least alongside the publican and the prodigal—we have in them the minimum —and with them be the likeness, the *analogatum*, of what Jesus Christ has been and done, and is and does, for him.

But the second thing which I recognise as having taken place and been revealed for me in Jesus Christ is the restoration, we do not say now of the right and life of man in general, but of my right and life. This is the positive side which I as little create or can create as the negative. I myself have denied and forfeited my right. I have hazarded my life and lost it. But this right and life have been restored in the act of obedience in which Jesus Christ sacrificed Himself for me, and manifested in His resurrection from the dead. He stands in my place as my righteousness and life. If I know Him and myself in Him— and that is the knowledge of faith—this means that I see myself as the one to whom that right and life are given, as the one to whom He has given Himself as righteous and alive for me. But, again, and from this positive standpoint, what follows from this?

Caution is again demanded. We say too much if we try to deduce from my restoration as it has taken place in Jesus Christ that it has taken place in me, that before God and man and myself I can boast of a right which is under my own name, which has come into my own possession, and of a life which I can live and enjoy as my own life. On this side, too, there is no sense in imagining that my history coincides with that of Jesus Christ. That triumphant restoration has not really taken place in my heart, in my activities and attitudes. Nothing has taken place or can be perceived in me of the glory of that right and life. To what can I cling in myself? What can I show to God and man, and in my own conscience to myself? In relation to Jesus Christ I can know and boast that my right stands like the mountains, and that I shall not die but live, and proclaim the works of the Lord. But what am I in myself? What can I know in relation to myself? Where and how can I find in myself anything but imaginary assurances in and with which I shall then have to live? It is a bad theology that maintains an exact similarity with Jesus Christ, a false because arbitrary assurance of salvation, in which man wants everything to be different and thinks that he can have everything different.

But, again, we say too little if we conceive the idea that, although ultimately Jesus Christ has ordered everything positively in my favour, yet I myself am so far removed from Him that for the moment I do not have anything of it at all, that I am still accused of my old and recurrent wrong, that I can only accuse myself in respect of it, that I must still fear death as the wages of my sin—just as though nothing had happened. And the certain result is, of course, that although my right and life as restored in Jesus Christ are my consolation as a profound and supreme truth, yet they are, as it were, in cold storage, they are for the moment of no practical value, and therefore a dangerous consolation. For the moment it is the case in practice that as concerns my restoration I am thrown back on myself; I must provide and answer for my own right, or make myself worthy of it; I must earn and attain my own life. For the moment it is my own affair in practice to set myself at rights with God and man and my own conscience, and it is my own affair to live in the peace which is attained in this way. It is a bad theology which has no assurance of salvation, which persists in dissimilarity with Jesus Christ, which looks away from Him to a situation of man which He has not altered, which falls back on some pride or subtle form of the righteousness of works, thus evading the one thing which is necessary even on this side. This, too, is obviously quite incompatible with the knowledge of faith.

What, then, is the alternative ? What is it that really follows from the recognition that my right and life have been restored once and for all in the death of Jesus Christ and manifested once and for all in His resurrection ? It follows that although there is no escape from the accusation of my wrong and the threat of judgment and death which it involves, I can still have a complete and assured, and because assured, a comforted and strong and joyful confidence. I can rely on that which has taken place for me. I can regard myself as secure in my heart. I can think my few thoughts in peace, say my few words in peace, do my few works in peace. I can look forward from myself as I am, and from the things of myself as they are and as they are done. To what ? Certainly not to the void of a better future, but to the fulfilment of the promise given to me in Jesus Christ, to the revelation of the verdict pronounced in Him which ascribes to me right and life. I can trust. On this positive side faith is simply trust—that is why the older theologians talked of *fiducia*. Not an arbitrary trust, but a trust which responds to the Word of God spoken to me. Not an indefinite trust, but a trust which is grounded in the knowledge of faith as the knowledge of Jesus Christ. And we must add that in this responsive and well-grounded trust we have to do not only with myself but with the community and the world. That which took place and was manifested positively in Jesus Christ took place and was manifested for the world—and therefore also and just for me. When, as a member of the community, I confidently recognise that it took place and was manifested for me, I must at once relate it as well to the community and the world. In it, in the world reconciled with God in Jesus Christ, I recognise as in a mirror myself as a reconciled man. And I, for my part, have to recognise and understand and conduct myself as the mirror of its reconciliation. It would be a strange Christian confidence if I were to have a sure trust for myself but to give up for lost the Church and the surrounding world to which I belong both in evil and in good ; if I were to succeed in despairing not of myself but of the Church and the world. If I know my right and my life in Jesus Christ, then I must hold to the fact, and act by it, that in Him my right and life are promised to them, not, of course, in any optimistic misjudgment of their nature and ways, but in view of the salvation which has come and the hope which is given both to them and to me. That I have confidence is the radical decision which I cannot avoid but have to make when I know Jesus Christ and myself in Him.

This is what the older theologians called *vivificatio*, the *vivificatio* which does not come to a Christian once only but continually, which does not determine his attitude only occasionally, but is everywhere present—this time as a clear overtone. Again we must say that the knowledge of faith involves no less than this. When a man knows in Jesus Christ his Saviour and that of the world, when, therefore, he is determined and stamped and enlightened by Him, this heartfelt act cannot be omitted. On this side, too, there is nothing more : no ultimate things, no eschatological decision. No one must imagine that in and with what he experiences and practises as his *vivificatio* the new heaven and the new earth has dawned even for himself, let alone for the Church and the world. But there can be nothing less than this confidence—a confidence on the old earth and under the old heaven but resolutely grasped. And in the light of it little renovations and provisional sanctifications and reassurances and elucidations will necessarily penetrate the whole man, who in the knowledge of faith has undoubtedly become a new subject. At this point we are already peeping into the sphere of the second part of the doctrine of reconciliation, which, as far as the anthropological material is concerned, will be discussed under the titles sanctification and love. In the present context a few very brief indications must suffice. It cannot be otherwise than that, when a man believes, then, in spite of all the limitations in which he still exists, in the knowledge of the restoration of his right and life as it has taken place in Jesus Christ, he will become a free man, i.e., a man who is no longer a simple servant and victim of his pride, but who is called away from it to the obedience of humility, for which he is also both ready and willing. As he bears that deep wound and accepts that bitter pain of penitence, he will hope for the grace of God and in that hope he will be at bottom a cheerful man. And although on his journey from the beginning of his way to the end he will often enough be assaulted and he will have to fight and he will often be thrown down, but will always rise up again and continue, yet in his relationship with God and man and himself he will be seriously and finally a peaceful man, peaceful because held by the One in whom he is already restored, in whom he is already the righteous and protected covenant-partner of God. He is, of course, exposed to all kinds of questions, and for that reason he has no claim. But he is such a man. He is the response to that which has taken place and been revealed, not in him, but in Jesus Christ for him. And in this attitude he is a copy, a parallel, a likeness of His being and activity for him. In all his imperfection He is a reflection of His perfection, a little light in His great light. He exists, then, in his petty thankfulness for the demonstration of His almighty grace.

To sum up : In the power of faith in Jesus Christ there can take place no more and no less, and it must and will take place with a supreme reality (in the sphere of the penultimate things), that as the Christian knows the overcoming of his pride and fall and the restoration of his right and life in Christ, in the light of this happening he can be with Christ in penitence but also in confidence. This takes place in the power of faith as it is an active recognition of Jesus

Christ. And it is this that makes faith an event in its character as recognition. It is not the event of the redemptive act of God. It can only follow this. It is subsequent and at the deepest possible level subordinate to it. But it has this in common with it, that it, too, is an event—in the sphere and context of the awakening of the Christian who can be and remain for ever a living member of it.

Christian faith is a confession. At the very first we called it generally an act of taking cognisance. We described this as basically an act of acknowledgment in which we then saw an act of recognition from which this proceeded. In this limited and definite sense Christian faith is man's taking cognisance of Jesus Christ. Now that we have seen how it is filled out we must return to the general concept as such.

Is it just a taking cognisance ? As we are using the concept, most definitely not. The taking is accompanied by giving, the acknowledgment and recognition by confession. A Christian who simply acknowledges and recognises without confessing is not a Christian. Even in his supposed acknowledgment and recognition of Jesus Christ he is deceiving himself and others. But he cannot deceive Jesus Christ, who as Himself the truth knows that he neither acknowledges nor recognises Him. The goal of the freedom in which He makes a man genuinely free—free to believe in Him—is the freedom to be His witness. And so the goal of faith as the free act of man is the act of his witness and therefore of his confession. What is acknowledged and recognised by man in faith is the radiance of God, His *qabod*, δόξα, *gloria*, glory, honour, self-manifestation in the being and activity of Jesus Christ. But this radiance cannot be stopped in and by the one who acknowledges and recognises it. It breaks through and lights up the man himself. The man on whom it falls cannot help but be lit up by it. " A city that is set on a hill cannot be hid " (Mt. 5¹⁴ᶠ·). To light a candle and put it under a bushel is nonsense : it belongs to the candlestick. The man who believes in Jesus Christ is, as such, the lighted candle which belongs *per se* to the candlestick. His taking cognisance is also a giving. There is nothing concealed which shall not be revealed, nothing hid which shall not be made known. What is told to the disciple by his Lord in darkness, he speaks out in light ; what he hears from Him in the ear, he preaches upon the house-tops (Mt. 10²⁶ᶠ·). The consequence is irresistible that where anyone believes as a Christian a history is enacted : a history of the heart, which, as such, is audible and visible in world-history ; an individual history which, as such, calls for impartation and communication ; a secret history which, as such, has a public character and claim ; a history which is not apparent—for what does it matter that a man finds himself summoned to that obedience and compliance in relation to Jesus Christ, and resolved upon it in his own freedom, and what is the little penitence and confidence in which this is revealed in his attitude ?—but a history of immeasurable dynamic because it takes place in the light of the great history of God. The fire and the sword which Jesus came to bring on earth (Lk. 12⁴⁹, Mt. 10³⁴) are shown to be effective in it. It may be that the Christian does not desire at all but is opposed to the idea of putting himself at the disposal of this dynamic, of being a witness and confessor. But he is not asked concerning his own wishes or aversions. When he believes in Jesus Christ he is at the disposal of this dynamic. Whether he wills it or not—and if he does not will it, perhaps only the less so—the free act of his faith is as such the free act of his confession. He cannot be a Christian without bearing this fire and sword.

What does confessing mean ? This is not the place to develop the concept in its full reach and especially in relation to the substantive " confession." We will simply sketch some of the main outlines which are indispensable to an understanding of it as an integral moment in the concept—the act—of faith.

In general terms, confessing is the moment in the act of faith in which the believer stands to his faith, or, rather, to the One in whom he believes, the One whom he acknowledges and recognises, the living Jesus Christ ; and does so outwardly, again in general terms, in face of men. Confessing as the act of faith in Jesus Christ means " to confess him before men " (Mt. 10³²), not to conceal the fact that we belong to Him, and the involved alteration of our attitude, which would be to deny Him, but, since both negatively and positively it is a matter of the attitude of the whole man, to be that altered man who belongs to Him in our whole being and therefore outwardly as well. To that extent confessing is not a special action of the Christian. All that is demanded is that he should be what he is. And what he is, or what he does as the free act of his faith, is not, as we have seen, something absolutely different and new in relation to what others do or can do. It is not action in the *eschaton*. When he is penitent and confident, he is only relatively different from others. He is absolutely different only in the mystery of his existence as grounded in Jesus Christ, not in what he himself is and does on this basis. His confessing is striking and extraordinary and surprising and spectacular and aggressive, both in itself and in its effects, only in the eyes and ears of those who lack categories to understand what he is and does on this basis. But—without concealing this from their eyes and ears—he simply stands to what he is. If he stands out in this respect, if his action acquires the character of a venture, if he does something which is perhaps annoying to others and dangerous to himself, if he accepts the risk of a collision with their action, if he provokes unfriendly or even hostile reactions on their part, if, as a confessor, he has to suffer in some way, it is not because he intends all this. It proceeds from his action, but he himself does not impart to it the quality to provoke it. It has this from the object and origin of his faith. It has it from the mystery of his existence which he himself cannot control. Because he is little light reflecting the great light, his action stands out from that of others, he becomes a witness of the great light, without especially willing to do so, and without in any way helping to do so. His task is that he should not cease to be that little light reflecting the great light. His task is that he should not place that little light under a bushel. If he sees to this, he does the act of confessing which is required of him, the confession of faith.

It is required of him by the very fact that in accordance with creation and by nature humanity means fellowship. This is equally true, indeed it is genuinely true, only of the humanity of the Christian. Since faith is his free human act, he cannot perform it without his neighbours, without communication with them. He cannot try to keep it concealed from them. Whatever may be their attitude to him, he owes this to them. To exist privately is to be a robber. And things would have come to a pretty pass if in faith in Jesus Christ anyone tried to be a robber. This is all the less possible in so far as what is required is not an act of particular heroism, but simply that in the sight and audience of his fellows he should stand to his faith, i.e., to the One in whom he believes and to what his attachment to Him involves for himself, that he should not be unbelieving, but believing.

Above all, the necessary summons to confession is concretely given by the existence of others who, according to their confession in the world, are likewise caught up in the act of faith by the existence of the Christian community. It is not on the basis of his own discovery and private revelation, but by the mediatorial ministry of the community which is itself in the school of the prophets and apostles, that a man comes under the awakening power of the Holy Spirit and therefore to faith. This is his starting-point in the act of faith, and to what other goal will he return ? He can as little deny it as a child its mother. He needs it, just as he needs the awakening power of the Holy Spirit and that school if he is to stand and continue in that faith to which he has come, to live by his faith. And it needs him, for its ministry is not concluded but must go on, and it is not an easy ministry, but calls for the assistance of the witness of every believer, and in a given situation a great deal, indeed everything, may depend upon the assistance of his witness. He can never escape the communion of the saints ; he can never leave it in the lurch. If he did he would be denying himself and his own faith which is the faith of the community. For good or evil, he has to confess it, he has to be with Jesus Christ and to repent and to have confidence together with it. He has to confess his attachment to it and to its Head publicly to the world. He will therefore desire baptism. And by the fact that he is baptised, and is known as one who is baptised, he has to make it plain that he is one for whom Jesus Christ has overcome, and whose right and life Jesus Christ has restored. As a living member of His body he will concretely show himself to be thankful in this basic act of all confession. But finally the world around him is itself and as such no less concrete —the world which does not confess Jesus Christ because it obviously does not acknowledge and recognise Him. He is surrounded by men who seem to know nothing of what has taken place and been revealed for them too in Him, of the judgment which has been executed on them and the verdict which has been proclaimed over·them in Him, who seem to be very far removed from anything that could seriously be called either repentance or confidence, who seem to know nothing of what faith is, because they do not know the One in whom to believe, let alone do what it is open for them to do. What is the significance of the existence of this world for the one to whom it is given to believe within this world? For in everything else he belongs to it. He finds the fashion of it in himself. He has a full part in its sin and death. He can understand better than it can itself its opposition or indifference to faith. He knows more radically than it does both the fact, and the reason for it, that no man of himself can either come to faith or live by his faith. He knows who and what is needed for this to come about in the life of a man. Above all, in the midst of other men he is the one who knows the decisive fact—who knows it in this active knowledge of himself—that Jesus Christ died and rose again not only for him but for them, that it is the world which God has reconciled to Himself in Him. And this being the case, can he keep this knowledge to himself, can he refrain from confessing his faith, when even the very stones would cry out to impart the knowledge which he has received, when it is actually the case that not the stones only but all the creatures of God proclaim : " God was in Christ reconciling the world to himself " ? It is his task to make this known in human language for human ears, and with the act of his human life before human eyes—yet again, not in great deeds, but in the mere fact that he is who he is, and that as such he says what he has to say and does what he has to do and makes open use of the freedom which is given him to do this. If it is not possible for a man of the world who has come to faith and can live by faith to deny himself, then in face of the world—his world—he can only be, very humbly but very courageously, a confessing Christian in the confessing community.

INDEXES

I. SCRIPTURE REFERENCES

ROMANS (continued)

CHAP.	PAGE
8^{17}	330, 604
8^{18}	330
$8^{19f.}$	331, 733
8^{23}	330
8^{24}	331
8^{26}	308
$8^{26f.}$	733
8^{29}	667
$8^{30f.}$	571, 580
8^{32}	166, 237, 250, 252, 393
8^{34}	230, 235, 314
$8^{34f.}$	327
$9-11$	524, 671
9^{3}	425
$9^{4f.}$	394, 671
9^{30}	614
9^{33}	392
10^{3}	531, 615
10^{4}	531
10^{5}	531
10^{6}	614
10^{9}	299
10^{12}	160
11^{15}	74
11^{26}	671
11^{32}	396, 501 ff., 519, 745
$11^{33f.}$	519
12	717
12^{1}	295
12^{2}	497
$12^{3f.}$	669
12^{5}	663, 666, 725
12^{6}	634, 666
12^{8}	674
12^{10}	189
12^{15}	724
12^{16}	189
12^{17}	243
$12^{19f.}$	243
$13^{1f.}$	189
13^{8}	583
13^{10}	107, 583
$14^{2f.}$	295
14^{4}	235
$14^{8f.}$	321
$14^{11f.}$	235
14^{15}	250
14^{23}	392, 758
15^{14}	33

1 CORINTHIANS

CHAP.	PAGE
1	673
1^{2}	160, 699
1^{9}	532
1^{18}	250
1^{23}	191, 250, 289, 299
$1^{26f.}$	189
1^{30}	101, 524, 749

CHAP.	PAGE
2^{2}	191
2^{4}	650
2^{9}	666
2^{10}	308
2^{14}	666
3	673
$3^{6f.}$	673
3^{11}	637
$3^{12f.}$	682 f.
3^{16}	708
$4^{2f.}$	571
$4^{3f.}$	235
4^{7}	631
$5^{6f.}$	525
5^{7}	277
6^{11}	321
6^{14}	329
8^{6}	646
9^{21}	583
$10^{16f.}$	665
11^{24}	231
11^{25}	252
11^{26}	250, 299, 665
12	717
$12^{3f.}$	666 f.
$12^{4f.}$	663, 667, 669
12^{7}	666
12^{9}	615
12^{12}	663, 665
12^{13}	312, 666
12^{16}	189
12^{18}	667
12^{20}	707
12^{24}	667
12^{27}	663 f.
13^{8}	33, 331
$13^{9f.}$	520
13^{12}	331, 730
14^{33}	186, 529
15	329
15^{3}	255, 295, 299
15^{4}	304
$15^{4f.}$	335
15^{8}	335
15^{10}	631
15^{14}	299, 334, 352
$15^{17f.}$	299
15^{19}	324, 329
15^{20}	299
$15^{21f.}$	665
15^{22}	329, 507
15^{28}	349
15^{31}	189, 729
$15^{42f.}$	330
15^{44}	50, 664
15^{45}	308, 507, 513, 664
15^{52}	734
15^{53}	330
$15^{54f.}$	307, 330, 344
15^{56}	253
16^{13}	711

II. NAMES

III. SUBJECTS

800 *Indexes*